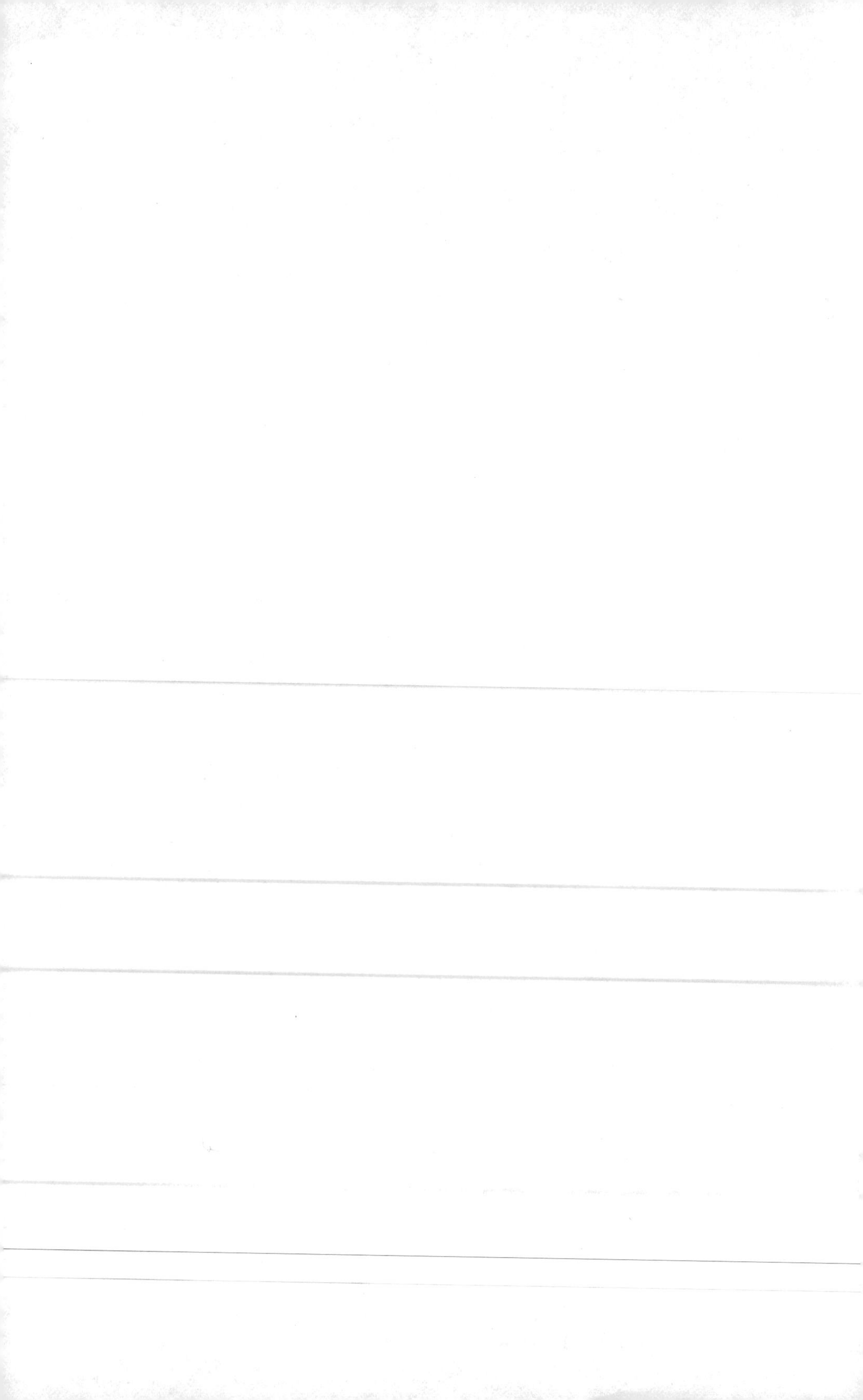

The Companion to
The Catechism of the Catholic Church

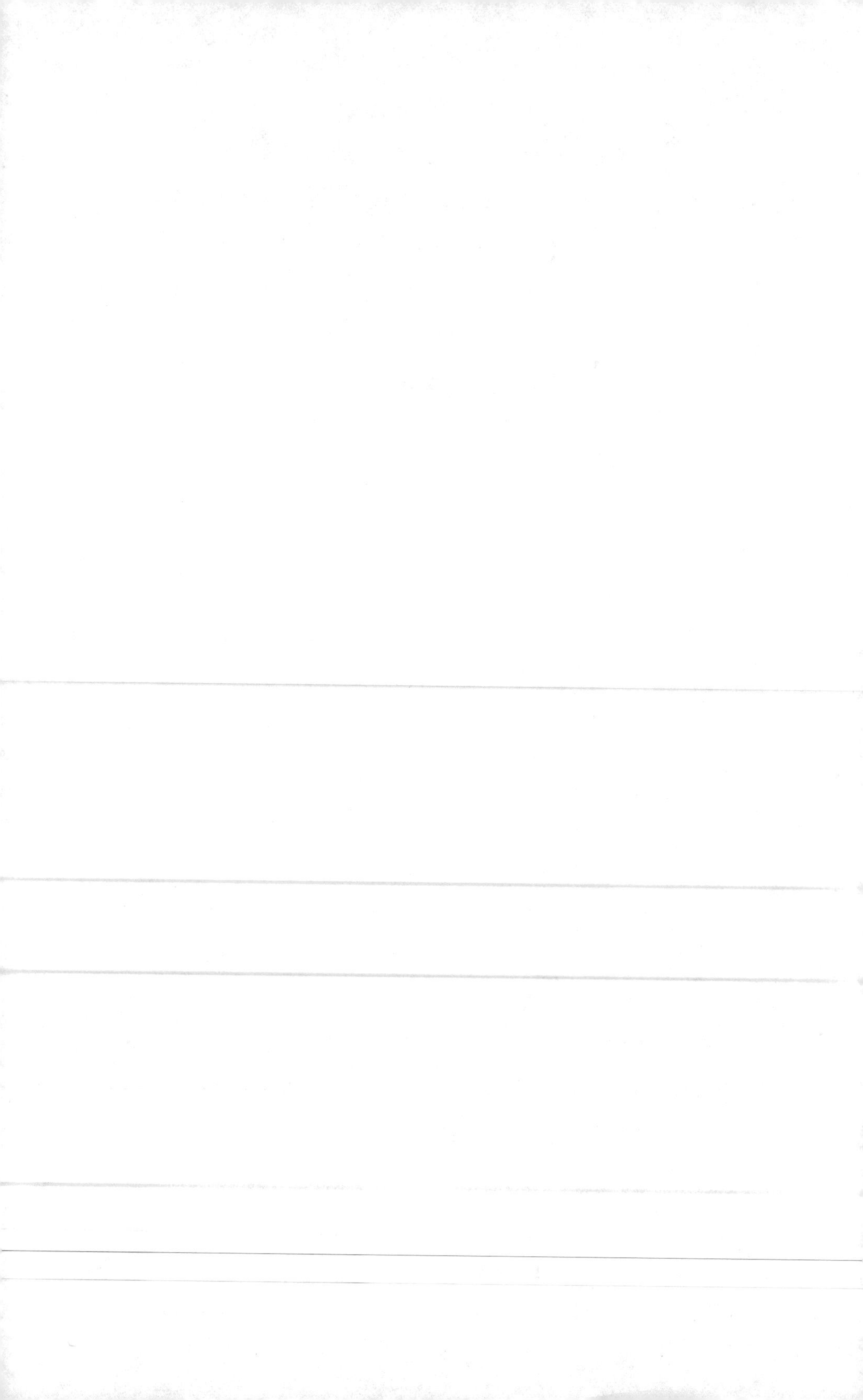

The Companion
to
The Catechism of the Catholic Church

~

A Compendium of Texts
Referred to in
The Catechism of the Catholic Church

IGNATIUS PRESS SAN FRANCISCO

Cover art by David Clark
Cover design by Roxanne Mei Lum

ISBN 0-89870-481-2 (HB)
ISBN 0-89870-482-0 (PB)
Library of Congress catalogue number 94-75256
Printed in the United States of America

CONTENTS

PREFACE

In summarizing the fundamental content of the Catholic faith, the *Catechism of the Catholic Church*, as John Paul II states, "presents the '*newness of the Council*' and at the same time situates it *in the whole of Tradition*. The Catechism", he goes on to say in his letter to priests for Holy Thursday 1993, "is so filled with the treasures found in Sacred Scripture and in the Fathers and Doctors of the Church in the course of two thousand years that it will enable each of us to become like the man in the Gospel parable 'who brings out of his treasure what is new and what is old' (Mt 13:52), the ancient and ever-new riches of the divine deposit."

These many "treasures" are displayed at different levels within the Catechism—from the simplest and most concise summary form given in the "In Brief" sections to the more extensive treatment provided by supplementary explanations and quotations in smaller print. An opportunity for still further enrichment is afforded by indirect references, given in the footnotes, to a wide variety of patristic, liturgical, magisterial and hagiographic sources. The texts to which these references refer are intended, as the Prologue indicates, to give an in-depth understanding of the relevant passages of the Catechism and to be a working tool for catechesis. In addition, they heighten our awareness of the continuity of doctrine, as it unfolds in Scripture, is discussed in texts drawn from the Fathers and Doctors of the Church, and receives its most recent treatment in conciliar texts and papal documents. At times the references are to a single verse of Scripture or to a single paragraph from a conciliar text. At others, they are to entire documents.

The purpose of the present volume is to gather together in a single source this wealth of reference texts and documents for the convenience of the English-speaking reader of the Catechism. To facilitate use, the arrangement here follows the paragraph numbering of the Catechism. All texts are provided in English translation, either reprinted from existing publications or newly translated here. It is hoped that this companion volume to the Catechism will prove a rich source of enlightenment, inspiration and reflection for all who seek to know and understand the Catholic faith.

Editor's Note

Several small points are to be noted. There are minor discrepancies between the references in the original French edition of the Catechism and those in the approved English translation. In general this volume follows the 1994 English edition of the *Catechism of the Catholic Church*. However, some of the interesting documents cited in the French edition, but omitted in the English edition, have been included. Conversely, some of the references which have been added in the English edition refer to citations within the texts referred to in the French edition. These have been omitted.

Sometimes the reference for a direct quotation in the French has become an indirect (i.e., "cf.") reference in the English. These also have been omitted.

PROLOGUE

Acts 2:42 And they devoted themselves to the apostles' teaching and fellowship, to the breaking of bread and the prayers. 3

***Catechesi tradendae* 1–2** The Church has always considered catechesis one of her primary tasks, for, before Christ ascended to His Father after His resurrection, He gave the apostles a final command—to make disciples of all nations and to teach them to observe all that He had commanded. He thus entrusted them with the mission and power to proclaim to humanity what they had heard, what they had seen with their eyes, what they had looked upon and touched with their hands, concerning the Word of Life. He also entrusted them with the mission and power to explain with authority what He had taught them, His words and actions, His signs and commandments. And He gave them the Spirit to fulfill this mission. 4

Very soon the name of catechesis was given to the whole of the efforts within the Church to make disciples, to help people to believe that Jesus is the Son of God, so that believing they might have life in His name, and to educate and instruct them in this life and thus build up the Body of Christ. The Church has not ceased to devote her energy to this task.

The most recent Popes gave catechesis a place of eminence in their pastoral solicitude. Through his gestures, his preaching, his authoritative interpretation of the Second Vatican Council (considered by him the great catechism of modern times), and through the whole of his life, my venerated predecessor Paul VI served the Church's catechesis in a particularly exemplary fashion. On March 18, 1971, he approved the General Catechetical Directory prepared by the Sacred Congregation for the Clergy, a directory that is still the basic document for encouraging and guiding catechetical renewal throughout the Church. He set up the International Council for Catechesis in 1975. He defined in masterly fashion the role and significance of catechesis in the life and mission of the Church when he addressed the participants in the first International Catechetical Congress on September 25, 1971, and he returned explicitly to the subject in his Apostolic Exhortation *Evangelii nuntiandi*. He decided that catechesis, especially that meant for children and young people, should be the theme of the fourth general assembly of the synod of Bishops, which was held in October 1977 and which I myself had the joy of taking part in.

***Catechesi tradendae* 18** Catechesis cannot be dissociated from the Church's pastoral and missionary activity as a whole. Nevertheless it has a specific character which was repeatedly the object of inquiry during the preparatory work and throughout the course of the fourth general assembly of the synod of Bishops. The question also interests the public both within and outside the Church. 6

This is not the place for giving a rigorous formal definition of catechesis, which has been sufficiently explained in the General Catechetical Directory. It is for specialists to clarify more and more its concept and divisions.

In view of uncertainties in practice, let us simply recall the essential landmarks—they are already solidly established in Church documents—that are essential for an exact understanding of catechesis and without which there is a risk of failing to grasp its full meaning and import.

All in all, it can be taken here that catechesis is an education of children, young people and adults in the faith, which includes especially the teaching of Christian doctrine imparted, generally speaking, in an organic and systematic way, with a view to initiating the hearers into the fullness of Christian life. Accordingly, while not being formally identified with them, catechesis is built on a certain number of elements of the Church's pastoral mission that have a catechetical aspect, that prepare for catechesis, or that spring from it. These elements are: the initial proclamation of the Gospel or missionary preaching through the *kerygma* to arouse faith, apologetics or examination of the reasons for belief, experience of Christian living, celebration of the sacraments, integration into the ecclesial community, and apostolic and missionary witness.

Let us first of all recall that there is no separation or opposition between catechesis and evangelization. Nor can the two be simply identified with each other. Instead, they have close links whereby they integrate and complement each other.

The Apostolic Exhortation *Evangelii nuntiandi* of December 8, 1975, on evangelization in the modern world, rightly stressed that evangelization—which has the aim of bringing the Good News to the whole of humanity, so that all may live by it—is a rich, complex and dynamic reality, made up of elements, or one could say moments, that are essential and different from each other, and that must all be kept in view simultaneously. Catechesis is one of these moments—a very remarkable one—in the whole process of evangelization.

14 (1) **Matthew 10:32** So every one who acknowledges me before men, I also will acknowledge before my Father who is in heaven. . . .

14 (2) **Romans 10:9** . . . because, if you confess with your lips that Jesus is Lord and believe in your heart that God raised him from the dead, you will be saved.

23 (1) ***Catechesi tradendae* 20–22** Nevertheless, the specific aim of catechesis is to develop, with God's help, an as yet initial faith, and to advance in fullness and to nourish day by day the Christian life of the faithful, young and old. It is in fact a matter of giving growth, at the level of knowledge and in life, to the seed of faith sown by the Holy Spirit with the initial proclamation and effectively transmitted by Baptism.

Catechesis aims therefore at developing understanding of the mystery of Christ in the light of God's word, so that the whole of a person's humanity is impregnated by that word. Changed by the working of grace into a new creature, the Christian thus sets himself to follow Christ and learns more and more within the Church to think like Him, to judge like Him, to act in conformity with His commandments, and to hope as He invites us to.

To put it more precisely: within the whole process of evangelization, the aim of catechesis is to be the teaching and maturation stage, that is to say, the period in which the Christian, having accepted by faith the person of Jesus Christ as the one Lord and having given Him complete adherence by sincere conversion of heart, endeavors to know better this Jesus to whom he has entrusted himself: to know His "mystery," the kingdom of God proclaimed by Him, the requirements and promises contained in His Gospel message, and the paths that He has laid down for anyone who wishes to follow Him.

It is true that being a Christian means saying "yes" to Jesus Christ, but let us remember that this "yes" has two levels: It consists in surrendering to the word of God and relying on it, but it also means, at a later stage, endeavoring to know better and better the profound meaning of this word.

In his closing speech at the fourth general assembly of the synod, Pope Paul VI rejoiced "to see how everyone drew attention to the absolute need for systematic catechesis, precisely because it is this reflective study of the Christian mystery that fundamentally distinguishes catechesis from all other ways of presenting the word of God."

In view of practical difficulties, attention must be drawn to some of the characteristics of this instruction:

—It must be systematic, not improvised but programmed to reach a precise goal;

—It must deal with essentials, without any claim to tackle all disputed questions or to transform itself into theological research or scientific exegesis;

—It must nevertheless be sufficiently complete, not stopping short at the initial proclamation of the Christian mystery such as we have in the *kerygma*;

—It must be an integral Christian initiation, open to all the other factors of Christian life.

I am not forgetting the interest of the many different occasions for catechesis connected with personal, family, social and ecclesial life—these occasions must be utilized and I shall return to them in Chapter VI—but I am stressing the need for organic and systematic Christian instruction, because of the tendency in various quarters to minimize its importance.

It is useless to play off orthopraxis against orthodoxy: Christianity is inseparably both. Firm and well-thought-out convictions lead to courageous and upright action; the endeavor to educate the faithful to live as disciples of Christ today calls for and facilitates a discovery in depth of the mystery of Christ in the history of salvation.

It is also quite useless to campaign for the abandonment of serious and orderly study of the message of Christ in the name of a method concentrating on life experience. "No one can arrive at the whole truth on the basis solely of some simple private experience, that is to say, without an adequate explanation of the message of Christ, who is 'the way, and the truth, and the life' (Jn. 14:6)."

Nor is any opposition to be set up between a catechesis taking life as its point of departure and a traditional doctrinal and systematic catechesis. Authentic catechesis is always an orderly and systematic initiation into the revelation that God has given of Himself to humanity in Christ Jesus, a revelation stored in the depths of the Church's memory and in Sacred Scripture, and constantly communicated from one generation to the next by a living, active *traditio*. This revelation is not however isolated from life or artificially juxtaposed to it. It is concerned with the ultimate meaning of life and it illumines the whole of life with the light of the Gospel, to inspire it or to question it.

That is why we can apply to catechists an expression used by the Second Vatican Council with special reference to priests: "Instructors (of the human being and his life) in the faith."

(2) ***Catechesi tradendae* 25** Thus through catechesis the Gospel *kerygma* (the initial 23
ardent proclamation by which a person is one day overwhelmed and brought to the decision to entrust himself to Jesus Christ by faith) is gradually deepened, developed in its implicit consequences, explained in language that includes an appeal to reason, and channelled towards Christian practice in the Church and the world. All this is no less evangelical than the *kerygma*, in spite of what is said by certain people who consider that catechesis necessarily rationalizes, dries up and eventually kills all that is living, spontaneous and vibrant in the *kerygma*. The truths studied in catechesis are the same truths that touched the person's heart when he heard them for the first time. Far from blunting or exhausting them, the fact of knowing them better should make them even more challenging and decisive for one's life.

In the understanding expounded here, catechesis keeps the entirely pastoral perspective with which the synod viewed it. The broad meaning of catechesis in no way contradicts but rather includes and goes beyond a narrow meaning which was once commonly given to catechesis in didactic expositions, namely, the simple teaching of the formulas that express faith.

In the final analysis, catechesis is necessary both for the maturation of the faith of Christians and for their witness in the world: It is aimed at bringing Christians to "attain to the unity of the faith and of the knowledge of the Son of God, to mature manhood, to the measure of the stature of the fullness of Christ"; it is also aimed at making them prepared to make a defense to anyone who calls them to account for the hope that is in them.

24 1 **Peter** 2:2 Like newborn babes, long for the pure spiritual milk, that by it you may grow up to salvation. . . .

25 1 **Corinthians** 13:8 Love never ends; as for prophecies, they will pass away; as for tongues, they will cease; as for knowledge, it will pass away.

I

THE PROFESSION OF FAITH

(1) ***Gaudium et spes* 19–21** The dignity of man rests above all on the fact that he is called to communion with God. The invitation to converse with God is addressed to man as soon as he comes into being. For if man exists it is because God has created him through love, and through love continues to hold him in existence. He cannot live fully according to truth unless he freely acknowledges that love and entrusts himself to his creator. Many however of our contemporaries either do not at all perceive, or else explicitly reject, this intimate and vital bond of man to God. Atheism must therefore be regarded as one of the most serious problems of our time, and one that deserves more thorough treatment. 29

The word atheism is used to signify things that differ considerably from one another. Some people expressly deny the existence of God. Others maintain that man cannot make any assertion whatsoever about him. Still others admit only such methods of investigation as would make it seem quite meaningless to ask questions about God. Many, trespassing beyond the boundaries of the positive sciences, either contend that everything can be explained by the reasoning process used in such sciences, or, on the contrary, hold that there is no such thing as absolute truth. With others it is their exaggerated idea of man that causes their faith to languish; they are more prone, it would seem, to affirm man than to deny God. Yet others have such a faulty notion of God that when they disown this product of the imagination their denial has no reference to the God of the Gospels. There are also those who never enquire about God; religion never seems to trouble or interest them at all, nor do they see why they should bother about it. Not infrequently atheism is born from a violent protest against the evil in the world, or from the fact that certain human ideals are wrongfully invested with such an absolute character as to be taken for God. Modern civilization itself, though not of its very nature but because it is too engrossed in the concerns of this world, can often make it harder to approach God.

Without doubt those who wilfully try to drive God from their heart and to avoid all questions about religion, not following the biddings of their conscience, are not free from blame. But believers themselves often share some responsibility for this situation. For atheism, taken as a whole, is not present in the mind of man from the start (*Atheismus, integre consideratus, non est quid originarium*). It springs from various causes, among which must be included a critical reaction against religions and, in some places, against the Christian religion in particular. Believers can thus have more than a little to do with the rise of atheism. To the extent that they are careless about their instruction in the faith, or present its teaching falsely, or even fail in their religious, moral, or social life, they must be said to conceal rather than to reveal the true nature of God and of religion.

Modern atheism often takes on a systematic form also which, in addition to other causes, so insists on man's desire for autonomy as to object to any dependence on God at all. Those who profess this kind of atheism maintain that freedom consists in this, that man is an end to himself, and the sole maker, with supreme control, of his own history (*propriae suae historiae solus artifex et demiurgus*). They claim that this outlook cannot be reconciled with the assertion of a Lord who is author and end of all things, or that at least it makes such an affirmation altogether unnecessary. The sense of power which modern technical progress begets in man may encourage this outlook.

Among the various kinds of present-day atheism, that one should not go unnoticed which looks for man's autonomy through his economic and social emancipation. It holds that religion, of its very nature, thwarts such emancipation by raising man's hopes in a future life, thus both deceiving him and discouraging him from working for a better form of life on earth. That is why those who hold such views, wherever they gain control of the state, violently attack religion, and in order to spread atheism, especially in the education of young people, make use of all the means by which the civil authority can bring pressure to bear on its subjects.

The Church, as given over to the service of both God and man, cannot cease from reproving, with sorrow yet with the utmost firmness, as she has done in the past, those harmful teachings and ways of acting which are in conflict with reason and with common human experience, and which cast man down from the noble state to which he is born.

She tries nevertheless to seek out the secret motives which lead the atheistic mind to deny God. Well knowing how important are the problems raised by atheism, and urged by her love for all men, she considers that these motives deserve an earnest and more thorough scrutiny.

The Church holds that to acknowledge God is in no way to oppose the dignity of man, since such dignity is grounded and brought to perfection in God. Man has in fact been placed in society by God, who created him as an intelligent and free being; but over and above this he is called as a son to intimacy with God and to share in his happiness. She further teaches that hope in a life to come does not take away from the importance of the duties of this life on earth but rather adds to it by giving new motives for fulfilling those duties. When, on the other hand, man is left without this divine support and without hope of eternal life his dignity is deeply wounded, as may so often be seen today. The problems of life and death, of guilt and of suffering, remain unsolved, so that men are not rarely cast into despair.

Meanwhile, every man remains a question to himself, one that is dimly perceived and left unanswered. For there are times, especially in the major events of life, when no man can altogether escape from such self-questioning. God alone, who calls man to deeper thought and to more humble probing, can fully and with complete certainty supply an answer to this questioning.

Atheism must be countered both by presenting true teaching in a fitting manner and by the full and complete life of the Church and of her members. For it is the function of the Church to render God the Father and his incarnate Son present and as it were visible, while ceaselessly renewing and purifying herself under the guidance of the Holy Spirit. This is brought about chiefly by the witness of a living and mature faith, one namely that is so well formed that it can see difficulties clearly and overcome them. Many martyrs have borne, and continue to bear, a splendid witness to this faith. This faith should show its fruitfulness by penetrating the whole life, even the worldly activities, of those who believe, and by urging them to be loving and just especially towards those in need. Lastly, what does most to show God's presence clearly is the brotherly love of the faithful who, being all of one mind and spirit, work together for the faith of the Gospel and present themselves as a sign of unity.

Although the Church altogether rejects atheism, she nevertheless sincerely proclaims that all men, those who believe as well as those who do not, should help to establish right order in this world where all live together. This certainly cannot be done without a dialogue that is sincere and prudent. The Church therefore deplores the discrimination between believers and unbelievers which some civil authorities unjustly practice in defiance of the fundamental rights of the human person. She demands effective freedom for the faithful to be allowed to build up God's temple in this world also. She courteously invites atheists to weigh the merits of the Gospel of Christ with an open mind.

For the Church knows full well that her message is in harmony with the most secret desires of the human heart, since it champions the dignity of man's calling, giving hope once more to those who already despair of their higher destiny. Her message, far from impairing man, helps him to develop himself by bestowing light, life, and freedom. Apart from this message nothing is able to satisfy the heart of man: "Thou hast made us for thyself, O Lord, and our heart is restless until it rest in thee."

(2) **Matthew 13:22** As for what was sown among thorns, this is he who hears the 29
word, but the cares of the world and the delight in riches choke the word, and it proves unfruitful.

(3) **Genesis 3:8–10** And they heard the sound of the Lord God walking in the 29
garden in the cool of the day, and the man and his wife hid themselves from the presence of the Lord God among the trees of the garden. But the Lord God called to the man, and said to him, "Where are you?" And he said, "I heard the sound of thee in the garden, and I was afraid, because I was naked; and I hid myself."

(4) **Jonah 1:3** But Jonah rose to flee to Tarshish from the presence of the Lord. 29
He went down to Joppa and found a ship going to Tarshish; so he paid the fare, and went on board, to go with them to Tarshish, away from the presence of the Lord.

(1) **Acts 14:15** "Men, why are you doing this? We also are men, of like nature with 32
you, and bring you good news, that you should turn from these vain things to a living God who made the heaven and the earth and the sea and all that is in them. . . ."

(2) **Acts 14:17** ". . . yet he did not leave himself without witness, for he did good 32
and gave you from heaven rains and fruitful seasons, satisfying your hearts with food and gladness."

(3) **Acts 17:27–28** ". . . that they should seek God, in the hope that they might 32
feel after him and find him. Yet he is not far from each one of us, for

'In him we live and move and have our being';

as even some of your poets have said,

'For we are indeed his offspring.' . . ."

(4) **Wisdom 13:1–9** 32

For all men who were ignorant of God were foolish by nature;
and they were unable from the good things that are seen to know
him who exists,
nor did they recognize the craftsman while paying heed to his works;
but they supposed that either fire or wind or swift air,
or the circle of the stars, or turbulent water,
or the luminaries of heaven were the gods that rule the world.
If through delight in the beauty of these things men assumed them
to be gods,
let them know how much better than these is their Lord,
for the author of beauty created them.

And if men were amazed at their power and working,
let them perceive from them
how much more powerful is he who formed them.
For from the greatness and beauty of created things
comes a corresponding perception of their Creator.
Yet these men are little to be blamed,
for perhaps they go astray
while seeking God and desiring to find him.
For as they live among his works they keep searching,
and they trust in what they see, because the things that are seen
are beautiful.
Yet again, not even they are to be excused;
for if they had the power to know so much
that they could investigate the world,
how did they fail to find sooner the Lord of these things?

33 ***Gaudium et spes* 14, 2** Man is not deceived when he regards himself as superior to bodily things and as more than just a speck of nature or a nameless unit in the city of man. For by his power to know himself in the depths of his being he rises above the whole universe of mere objects. When he is drawn to think about his real self he turns to those deep recesses of his being where God who probes the heart awaits him, and where he himself decides his own destiny in the sight of God. So when he recognizes in himself a spiritual and immortal soul, he is not being led astray by false imaginings that are due to merely physical or social causes. On the contrary, he grasps what is profoundly true in this matter.

36 (1) **Vatican Council I (1870): DS 3026** [*Against those denying natural theology*]. If anyone shall have said that the one true God, our Creator and our Lord, cannot be known with certitude by those things which have been made, by the natural light of human reason: let him be anathema.

36 (2) ***Dei Verbum* 6** By divine Revelation God wished to manifest and communicate both himself and the eternal decrees of his will concerning the salvation of mankind. He wished, in other words, "to share with us divine benefits which entirely surpass the powers of the human mind to understand."

The sacred Synod professes that "God, the first principle and last end of all things, can be known with certainty from the created world, by the natural light of human reason" (cf. Rom. 1:20). It teaches that it is to his Revelation that we must attribute the fact "that those things, which in themselves are not beyond the grasp of human reason, can, in the present condition of the human race, be known by all men with ease, with firm certainty, and without the contamination of error."

36 (3) **Genesis 1:26–27** Then God said, "Let us make man in our image, after our likeness; and let them have dominion over the fish of the sea, and over the birds of the air, and over the cattle, and over all the earth, and over every creeping thing that creeps upon the earth." So God created man in his own image, in the image of God he created him; male and female he created them.

38 (1) **Vatican Council I (1870): DS 3005** [*The necessity of revelation*]. Indeed, it must be attributed to this divine revelation that those things, which in divine things are impenetrable to human reason by itself, can, even in this present condition of the human race, be known readily by all with firm certitude and with no admixture of

error. Nevertheless, it is not for this reason that revelation is said to be absolutely necessary, but because God in His infinite goodness has ordained man for a supernatural end, to participation, namely, in the divine goods which altogether surpass the understanding of the human mind, since "eye hath not seen, nor ear heard, neither hath it entered into the heart of man, what things God hath prepared for them that love Him" [1 Cor. 2:9; can. 2 and 3].

(2) ***Dei Verbum* 6:** see 36 (2). 38

(3) **St. Thomas Aquinas, *Summa theologiae* I, 1, 1** 38

Question 1. on what sort of teaching Christian theology is and what it covers

In order to keep our efforts within definite bounds we must first investigate this holy teaching and find out what it is like and how far it goes. Here there are ten points of inquiry:

1. about the need for this teaching;
2. whether it be science;
3. whether it be single or several;
4. whether it be theoretical or practical;
5. how it compares with other sciences;
6. whether it be wisdom;
7. what is its subject;
8. whether it sets out to prove anything;
9. whether it should employ metaphorical or symbolical language;
10. whether its sacred writings are to be interpreted in several senses.

article 1. is another teaching required apart from philosophical studies?

THE FIRST POINT: 1. Any other teaching beyond that of science and philosophy seems needless. For man ought not to venture into realms beyond his reason; according to *Ecclesiasticus, Be not curious about things far above thee.* Now the things lying within range of reason yield well enough to scientific and philosophical treatment. Additional teaching, therefore, seems superfluous.

2. Besides, we can be educated only about what is real; for nothing can be known for certain save what is true, and what is true is identical with what really is. Yet the philosophical sciences deal with all parts of reality, even with God; hence Aristotle refers to one department of philosophy as theology or the divine science. That being the case, no need arises for another kind of education to be admitted or entertained.

ON THE OTHER HAND the second epistle to Timothy says, All Scripture inspired of God is profitable to teach, to reprove, to correct, to instruct in righteousness. Divinely inspired Scripture, however, is no part of the branches of philosophy traced by reasoning. Accordingly it is expedient to have another body of sure knowledge inspired by God.

REPLY: It should be urged that human well-being called for schooling in what God has revealed, in addition to the philosophical researches pursued by human reasoning.

Above all because God destines us for an end beyond the grasp of reason; according to Isaiah, Eye hath not seen, O God, without thee what thou hast prepared for them that love thee. Now we have to recognize an end before we can stretch out and exert ourselves for it. Hence the necessity for our welfare that divine truths surpassing reason should be signified to us through divine revelation.

We also stood in need of being instructed by divine revelation even in religious matters the human reason is able to investigate. For the rational truth about God would have appeared only to few, and even so after a long time and mixed with many mistakes; whereas on knowing this depends our whole welfare, which is in God. In these circumstances, then, it was to prosper the salvation of human beings and the more widely and less anxiously, that they were provided for by divine revelation about divine things.

These then are the grounds of holding a holy teaching which has come to us through revelation beyond the discoveries of the rational sciences.

Hence: 1. Admittedly the reason should not pry into things too high for human knowledge, nevertheless when they are revealed by God they should be welcomed by faith: indeed the passage in *Ecclesiasticus* goes on, *Many things are shown thee above the understanding of men.* And on them Christian teaching rests.

2. The diversification of the sciences is brought about by the diversity of aspects under which things can be known. Both an astronomer and a physical scientist may demonstrate the same conclusion, for instance that the earth is spherical; the first, however, works in a mathematical medium prescinding from material qualities, while for the second his medium is the observation of material bodies through the senses. Accordingly there is nothing to stop the same things from being treated by the philosophical sciences when they can be looked at in the light of natural reason and by another science when they are looked at in the light of divine revelation. Consequently the theology of holy teaching differs in kind from that theology which is ranked as a part of philosophy.

47 **Vatican Council I (1870): DS 3026** [*Against those denying natural theology*]. If anyone shall have said that the one true God, our Creator and our Lord, cannot be known with certitude by those things which have been made, by the natural light of human reason: let him be anathema.

50 **Vatican Council I (1870): DS 3015** [*The twofold order of knowledge*]. By enduring agreement the Catholic Church has held and holds that there is a twofold order of knowledge, distinct not only in principle but also in object: (1) in principle, indeed, because we know in one way by natural reason, in another by divine faith; (2) in object, however, because, in addition to things to which natural reason can attain, mysteries hidden in God are proposed to us for belief which, had they not been divinely revealed, could not become known [can. 1]. Wherefore, the Apostle, who testifies that God was known to the Gentiles "by the things that are made" [Rom. 1:20], nevertheless, when discoursing about grace and truth which "was made through Jesus Christ" [cf. John 1:17] proclaims: "We speak the wisdom of God in a mystery, a wisdom which is hidden, which God ordained before the world, unto our glory, which none of the princes of this world knows. . . . But to us God hath revealed them by His Spirit. For the Spirit searcheth all things, yea the deep things of God" [I Cor. 2:7, 8, 10]. And the Only-begotten Himself "confesses to the Father, because He hath hid these things from the wise and prudent, and hath revealed them to little ones" [cf. Matt. 11:25].

52 **Ephesians 1:4–5** . . . even as he chose us in him before the foundation of the world, that we should be holy and blameless before him. He destined us in love to be his sons through Jesus Christ, according to the purpose of his will. . . .

53 (1) **St. Irenaeus, *Adversus haereses* III, 17, 1** It certainly was in the power of the apostles to declare that Christ descended upon Jesus, or that the so-called superior Savior [came down] upon the dispensational one, or he who is from the invisible places upon him from the Demiurge; but they neither knew nor said anything of the kind: for, had they known it, they would have also certainly stated it. But what really was the case, that did they record, [namely,] that the Spirit of God as a dove descended upon Him; this Spirit, of whom it was declared by Isaiah, "And the Spirit of God

shall rest upon Him," as I have already said. And again: "The Spirit of the Lord is upon Me, because He hath anointed Me." That is the Spirit of whom the Lord declares, "For it is not ye that speak, but the Spirit of your Father which speaketh in you." And again, giving to the disciples the power of regeneration into God, He said to them, "Go and teach all nations, baptizing them in the name of the Father, and of the Son, and of the Holy Ghost." For [God] promised, that in the last times He would pour Him [the Spirit] upon [His] servants and handmaids, that they might prophesy; wherefore He did also descend upon the Son of God, made the Son of man, becoming accustomed in fellowship with Him to dwell in the human race, to rest with human beings, and to dwell in the workmanship of God, working the will of the Father in them, and renewing them from their old habits into the newness of Christ.

(2) **St. Irenaeus, *Adversus haereses* IV, 12, 4** The Lord, too, does not do away 53
with this [God], when He shows that the law was not derived from another God, expressing Himself as follows to those who were being instructed by Him, to the multitude and to His disciples: "The scribes and Pharisees sit in Moses' seat. All, therefore, whatsoever they bid you observe, that observe and do; but do not ye after their works: for they say, and do not. For they bind heavy burdens, and lay them upon men's shoulders; but they themselves will not so much as move them with a finger." He therefore did not throw blame upon that law which was given by Moses, when He exhorted it to be observed, Jerusalem being as yet in safety; but He *did* throw blame upon those persons, because they repeated indeed the words of the law, yet were without love. And for this reason were they held as being unrighteous as respects God, and as respects their neighbors. As also Isaiah says: "This people honoreth Me with their lips, but their heart is far from Me: howbeit in vain do they worship Me, teaching the doctrines and the commandments of men." He does not call the law given by Moses commandments of men, but the traditions of the elders themselves which they had invented, and in upholding which they made the law of God of none effect, and were on this account also not subject to His Word. For this is what Paul says concerning these men: "For they, being ignorant of God's righteousness, and going about to establish their own righteousness, have not submitted themselves to the righteousness of God. For Christ is the end of the law for righteousness to every one that believeth." And how is Christ the end of the law, if He be not also the final cause of it? For He who has brought in the end but Himself also wrought the beginning; and it is He who does Himself say to Moses, "I have surely seen the affliction of my people which is in Egypt, and I have come down to deliver them;" it being customary from the beginning with the Word of God to ascend and descend for the purpose of saving those who were in affliction.

(3) **St. Irenaeus, *Adversus haereses* IV, 21, 3** If any one, again, will look into Jacob's 53
actions, he shall find them not destitute of meaning, but full of import with regard to the dispensations. Thus, in the first place, at his birth, since he laid hold on his brother's heel, he was called Jacob, that is, *the supplanter*—one who holds, but is not held; binding the feet, but not being bound; striving and conquering; grasping in his hand his adversary's heel, that is, victory. For to this end was the Lord born, the type of whose birth he set forth beforehand, of whom also John says in the Apocalypse: "He went forth conquering, that He should conquer." In the next place, [Jacob] received the rights of the first-born, when his brother looked on them with contempt; even as also the younger nation received Him, Christ, the first-begotten, when the elder nation rejected Him, saying, "We have no king but Caesar." But in Christ every blessing [is summed up], and therefore the latter people has snatched away the blessings of the

former from the Father, just as Jacob took away the blessing of this Esau. For which cause his brother suffered the plots and persecutions of a brother, just as the Church suffers this self-same thing from the Jews. In a foreign country were the twelve tribes born, the race of Israel, in as much as Christ was also, in a strange country, to generate the twelve-pillared foundation of the Church. Various colored sheep were allotted to this Jacob as his wages; and the wages of Christ are human beings, who from various and diverse nations come together into one cohort of faith, as the Father promised Him, saying, "Ask of Me, and I will give Thee the heathen for Thine inheritance, the uttermost parts of the earth for Thy possession." And as from the multitude of his sons the prophets of the Lord [afterwards] arose, there was every necessity that Jacob should beget sons from the two sisters, even as Christ did from the two laws of one and the same Father; and in like manner also from the handmaids, indicating that Christ should raise up sons of God, both from freemen and from slaves after the flesh, bestowing upon all, in the same manner, the gift of the Spirit, who vivifies us. But he (Jacob) did all things for the sake of the younger, she who had the handsome eyes, Rachel, who prefigured the Church, for which Christ endured patiently; who at that time, indeed, by means of His patriarchs and prophets, was prefiguring and declaring beforehand future things, fulfilling His part by anticipation in the dispensations of God, and accustoming His inheritance to obey God, and to pass through the world as in a state of pilgrimage, to follow His word, and to indicate beforehand things to come. For with God there is nothing without purpose or due signification.

56 (1) **Genesis 9:9–10** "Behold, I establish my covenant with you and your descendants after you, and with every living creature that is with you, the birds, the cattle, and every beast of the earth with you, as many as came out of the ark."

56 (2) **Genesis 9:16** "When the bow is in the clouds, I will look upon it and remember the everlasting covenant between God and every living creature of all flesh that is upon the earth."

56 (3) **Genesis 10:20–31** These are the sons of Ham, by their families, their languages, their lands and their nations.

To Shem also, the father of all the children of Eber, the elder brother of Japheth, children were born. The sons of Shem: Elam, Asshur, Arpachshad, Lud, and Aram. The sons of Aram: Uz, Hul, Gether, and Mash. Arpachshad became the father of Shelah; and Shelah became the father of Eber. To Eber were born two sons: the name of the one was Peleg, for in his days the earth was divided, and his brother's name was Joktan. Joktan became the father of Almodad, Sheleph, Hazarmaveth, Jerah, Hadoram, Uzal, Diklah, Obal, Abimael, Sheba, Ophir, Havilah, and Jobab; all these were the sons of Joktan. The territory in which they lived extended from Mesha in the direction of Sephar to the hill country of the east. These are the sons of Shem, by their families, their languages, their lands, and their nations.

57 (1) **Acts 17:26–27** And he made from one every nation of men to live on all the face of the earth, having determined allotted periods and the boundaries of their habitation, that they should seek God, in the hope that they might feel after him and find him. Yet he is not far from each one of us. . . .

57 (2) **Deuteronomy 4:19** And beware lest you lift up your eyes to heaven, and when you see the sun and the moon and the stars, all the host of heaven, you be drawn away and worship them and serve them, things which the Lord your God has allotted to all the peoples under the whole heaven.

(3) **Deuteronomy 32:8** 57

When the Most High gave to the nations their inheritance,
when he separated the sons of men,
he fixed the bounds of the peoples
according to the number of the sons of God.

(4) **Wisdom 10:5** 57

Wisdom also, when the nations in wicked agreement had been confounded,
recognized the righteous man and preserved him blameless before God,
and kept him strong in the face of his compassion for his child.

(5) **Genesis 11:4–6** Then they said, “Come, let us build ourselves a city, and a 57
tower with its top in the heavens, and let us make a name for ourselves, lest we be scattered abroad upon the face of the whole earth.” And the Lord came down to see the city and the tower, which the sons of men had built. And the Lord said, “Behold, they are one people, and they have all one language; and this is only the beginning of what they will do; and nothing that they propose to do will now be impossible for them. . . .”

(6) **Romans 1:18–25** For the wrath of God is revealed from heaven against all 57
ungodliness and wickedness of men who by their wickedness suppress the truth. For what can be known about God is plain to them, because God has shown it to them. Ever since the creation of the world his invisible nature, namely, his eternal power and deity, has been clearly perceived in the things that have been made. So they are without excuse; for although they knew God they did not honor him as God or give thanks to him, but they became futile in their thinking and their senseless minds were darkened. Claiming to be wise, they became fools, and exchanged the glory of the immortal God for images resembling mortal man or birds or animals or reptiles. Therefore God gave them up in the lusts of their hearts to impurity, to the dishonoring of their bodies among themselves, because they exchanged the truth about God for a lie and worshiped and served the creature rather than the Creator, who is blessed for ever! Amen.

(1) **Genesis 9:16:** see 56 (2). 58

(2) **Luke 21:24** . . . they will fall by the edge of the sword, and be led captive among 58
all nations; and Jerusalem will be trodden down by the Gentiles, until the times of the Gentiles are fulfilled.

(3) ***Dei Verbum* 3** God, who creates and conserves all things by his Word, (cf. Jn. 58
1:3), provides men with constant evidence of himself in created realities (cf. Rom. 1:19–20). And furthermore, wishing to open up the way to heavenly salvation, he manifested himself to our first parents from the very beginning. After the fall, he buoyed them up with the hope of salvation by promising redemption (cf. Gen. 3:15); and he has never ceased to take care of the human race. For he wishes to give eternal life to all those who seek salvation by patience in well-doing (cf. Rom. 2:6–7). In his own time God called Abraham, and made him into a great nation (cf. Gen. 12:2). After the era of the patriarchs, he taught this nation, by Moses and the prophets, to recognize him as the only living and true God, as a provident Father and just judge. He taught them, too, to look for the promised Savior. And so, throughout the ages, he prepared the way for the Gospel.

58 (4) **Genesis 14:18** And Melchizedek king of Salem brought out bread and wine; he was priest of God Most High.

58 (5) **Hebrews 7:3** He is without father or mother or genealogy, and has neither beginning of days nor end of life, but resembling the Son of God he continues a priest for ever.

58 (6) **Ezekiel 14:14** ". . . even if these three men, Noah, Daniel, and Job, were in it, they would deliver but their own lives by their righteousness, says the Lord God."

59 **Galatians 3:8** And the scripture, foreseeing that God would justify the Gentiles by faith, preached the gospel beforehand to Abraham, saying, "In you shall all the nations be blessed."

60 (1) **Romans 11:28** As regards the gospel they are enemies of God, for your sake; but as regards election they are beloved for the sake of their forefathers.

60 (2) **John 11:52** . . . and not for the nation only, but to gather into one the children of God who are scattered abroad.

60 (3) **John 10:16** And I have other sheep, that are not of this fold; I must bring them also, and they will heed my voice. So there shall be one flock, one shepherd.

60 (4) **Romans 11:17–18** But if some of the branches were broken off, and you, a wild olive shoot, were grafted in their place to share the richness of the olive tree, do not boast over the branches. If you do boast, remember it is not you that support the root, but the root that supports you.

60 (5) **Romans 11:24** For if you have been cut from what is by nature a wild olive tree, and grafted, contrary to nature, into a cultivated olive tree, how much more will these natural branches be grafted back into their own olive tree.

62 ***Dei Verbum* 3:** see 58 (3).

63 **Exodus 19:6** ". . . and you shall be to me a kingdom of priests and a holy nation. These are the words which you shall speak to the children of Israel."

64 (1) **Isaiah 2:2–4**

It shall come to pass in the latter days
    that the mountain of the house of the Lord
shall be established as the highest of the mountains,
    and shall be raised above the hills;
and all the nations shall flow to it,
    and many peoples shall come, and say:
"Come, let us go up to the mountain of the Lord,
    to the house of the God of Jacob;
that he may teach us his ways
    and that we may walk in his paths."
For out of Zion shall go forth the law,
    and the word of the Lord from Jerusalem.
He shall judge between the nations,
    and shall decide for many peoples;

and they shall beat their swords into plowshares,
and their spears into pruning hooks;
nation shall not lift up sword against nation,
neither shall they learn war any more.

(2) **Jeremiah 31:31–34** "Behold, the days are coming, says the Lord, when I will 64
make a new covenant with the house of Israel and the house of Judah, not like the covenant which I made with their fathers when I took them by the hand to bring them out of the land of Egypt, my covenant which they broke, though I was their husband, says the Lord. But this is the covenant which I will make with the house of Israel after those days, says the Lord: I will put my law within them, and I will write it upon their hearts; and I will be their God, and they shall be my people. And no longer shall each man teach his neighbor and each his brother, saying, 'Know the Lord,' for they shall all know me, from the least of them to the greatest, says the Lord; for I will forgive their iniquity, and I will remember their sin no more."

(3) **Hebrews 10:16** "This is the covenant that I will make with them after those 64
days, says the Lord: I will put my laws on their hearts, and write them on their minds. . . ."

(4) **Ezekiel 36** "And you, son of man, prophesy to the mountains of Israel, and 64
say, O mountains of Israel, hear the word of the Lord. Thus says the Lord God: Because the enemy said of you, 'Aha!' and, 'The ancient heights have become our possession,' therefore prophesy, and say, Thus says the Lord God: Because, yea, because they made you desolate, and crushed you from all sides, so that you became the possession of the rest of the nations, and you became the talk and evil gossip of the people; therefore, O mountains of Israel, hear the word of the Lord God: Thus says the Lord God to the mountains and the hills, the ravines and the valleys, the desolate wastes and the deserted cities, which have become a prey and derision to the rest of the nations round about; therefore thus says the Lord God: I speak in my hot jealousy against the rest of the nations, and against all Edom, who gave my land to themselves as a possession with wholehearted joy and utter contempt, that they might possess it and plunder it. Therefore prophesy concerning the land of Israel, and say to the mountains and hills, to the ravines and valleys, Thus says the Lord God: Behold, I speak in my jealous wrath, because you have suffered the reproach of the nations; therefore thus says the Lord God: I swear that the nations that are round about you shall themselves suffer reproach.

"But you, O mountains of Israel, shall shoot forth your branches, and yield your fruit to my people Israel; for they will soon come home. For, behold, I am for you, and I will turn to you, and you shall be tilled and sown; and I will multiply men upon you, the whole house of Israel, all of it; the cities shall be inhabited and the waste places rebuilt; and I will multiply upon you man and beast; and they shall increase and be fruitful; and I will cause you to be inhabited as in your former times, and will do more good to you than ever before. Then you will know that I am the Lord. Yea, I will let men walk upon you, even my people Israel; and they shall possess you, and you shall be their inheritance, and you shall no longer bereave them of children. Thus says the Lord God: Because men say to you, 'You devour men, and you bereave your nation of children,' therefore you shall no longer devour men and no longer bereave your nation of children, says the Lord God; and I will not let you hear any more the reproach of the nations, and you shall no longer bear the disgrace of the peoples and no longer cause your nation to stumble, says the Lord God."

The word of the Lord came to me: "Son of man, when the house of Israel dwelt in their own land, they defiled it by their ways and their doings; their conduct before me was like the uncleanness of a woman in her impurity. So I poured out my wrath upon them for the blood which they had shed in the land, for the idols with which they had defiled it. I scattered them among the nations, and they were dispersed through the countries; in accordance with their conduct and their deeds I judged them. But when they came to the nations, wherever they came, they profaned my holy name, in that men said of them, 'These are the people of the Lord, and yet they had to go out of his land.' But I had concern for my holy name, which the house of Israel caused to be profaned among the nations to which they came.

"Therefore say to the house of Israel, Thus says the Lord God: It is not for your sake, O house of Israel, that I am about to act, but for the sake of my holy name, which you have profaned among the nations to which you came. And I will vindicate the holiness of my great name, which has been profaned among the nations, and which you have profaned among them; and the nations will know that I am the Lord, says the Lord God, when through you I vindicate my holiness before their eyes. For I will take you from the nations, and gather you from all the countries, and bring you into your own land. I will sprinkle clean water upon you, and you shall be clean from all your uncleannesses, and from all your idols I will cleanse you. A new heart I will give you, and a new spirit I will put within you; and I will take out of your flesh the heart of stone and give you a heart of flesh. And I will put my spirit within you, and cause you to walk in my statutes and be careful to observe my ordinances. You shall dwell in the land which I gave to your fathers; and you shall be my people, and I will be your God. And I will deliver you from all your uncleannesses; and I will summon the grain and make it abundant and lay no famine upon you. I will make the fruit of the tree and the increase of the field abundant, that you may never again suffer the disgrace of famine among the nations. Then you will remember your evil ways, and your deeds that were not good; and you will loathe yourselves for your iniquities and your abominable deeds. It is not for your sake that I will act, says the Lord God; let that be known to you. Be ashamed and confounded for your ways, O house of Israel.

"Thus says the Lord God: On the day that I cleanse you from all your iniquities, I will cause the cities to be inhabited, and the waste places shall be rebuilt. And the land that was desolate shall be tilled, instead of being the desolation that it was in the sight of all who passed by. And they will say, 'This land that was desolate has become like the garden of Eden; and the waste and desolate and ruined cities are now inhabited and fortified.' Then the nations that are left round about you shall know that I, the Lord, have rebuilt the ruined places, and replanted that which was desolate; I, the Lord, have spoken, and I will do it.

"Thus says the Lord God: This also I will let the house of Israel ask me to do for them: to increase their men like a flock. Like the flock for sacrifices, like the flock at Jerusalem during her appointed feasts, so shall the waste cities be filled with flocks of men. Then they will know that I am the Lord."

64 (5) **Isaiah 49:5–6**

And now the Lord says,
who formed me from the womb to be his servant,
to bring Jacob back to him,
and that Israel might be gathered to him,
for I am honored in the eyes of the Lord,
and my God has become my strength—
he says:
"It is too light a thing that you should be my servant
to raise up the tribes of Jacob
and to restore the preserved of Israel;

I will give you as a light to the nations,
that my salvation may reach to the end of the earth."

(6) **Isaiah 53:11** 64
. . . he shall see the fruit of the travail of his soul and
be satisfied;
by his knowledge shall the righteous one, my servant,
make many to be accounted righteous;
and he shall bear their iniquities.

(7) **Zephaniah 2:3** 64
Seek the Lord, all you humble of the land,
who do his commands;
seek righteousness, seek humility;
perhaps you may be hidden
on the day of the wrath of the Lord.

(8) **Luke 1:38** And Mary said, "Behold, I am the handmaid of the Lord; let it be 64
to me according to your word." And the angel departed from her.

Genesis 3:15 70
". . . I will put enmity between you and the woman,
and between your seed and her seed;
he shall bruise your head,
and you shall bruise his heel."

Genesis 9:16 ". . . When the bow is in the clouds, I will look upon it and remember 71
the everlasting covenant between God and every living creature of all flesh that is upon the earth."

John 14:6 Jesus said to him, "I am the way, and the truth, and the life; no one comes 74
to the Father, but by me. . . ."

(1) **1 Timothy 6:20** O Timothy, guard what has been entrusted to you. Avoid the 84
godless chatter and contradictions of what is falsely called knowledge. . . .

(2) **2 Timothy 1:12–14** . . . and therefore I suffer as I do. But I am not ashamed, 84
for I know whom I have believed, and I am sure that he is able to guard until that Day what has been entrusted to me. Follow the pattern of the sound words which you have heard from me, in the faith and love which are in Christ Jesus; guard the truth [*bonum depositum*] that has been entrusted to you by the Holy Spirit who dwells within us.

***Lumen gentium* 20** That divine mission, which was committed by Christ to the apos- 87
tles, is destined to last until the end of the world (cf. Mt. 28:20), since the Gospel, which they were charged to hand on, is, for the Church, the principle of all its life for all time. For that very reason the apostles were careful to appoint successors in this hierarchically constituted society.

In fact, not only had they various helpers in their ministry, but, in order that the mission entrusted to them might be continued after their death, they consigned, by will and testament, as it were, to their immediate collaborators the duty of completing and consolidating the work they had begun, urging them to tend to the whole flock, in which the Holy Spirit had appointed them to shepherd the Church of God (cf. Acts 20:28). They accordingly designated such men and then made the ruling that likewise on their death other proven men should take over their ministry. Amongst those various offices which have been exercised in the Church from the earliest times the chief place, according to the witness of tradition, is held by the function of those who, through their appointment to the dignity and responsibility of bishop, and in virtue consequently of the unbroken succession, going back to the beginning, are regarded as transmitters of the apostolic line. Thus, according to the testimony of St. Irenaeus, the apostolic tradition is manifested and preserved in the whole world by those who were made bishops by the apostles and by their successors down to our own time.

In that way, then, with priests and deacons as helpers, the bishops received the charge of the community, presiding in God's stead over the flock of which they are the shepherds in that they are teachers of doctrine, ministers of sacred worship and holders of office in government. Moreover, just as the office which the Lord confided to Peter alone, as first of the apostles, destined to be transmitted to his successors, is a permanent one, so also endures the office, which the apostles received, of shepherding the Church, a charge destined to be exercised without interruption by the sacred order of bishops. The sacred synod consequently teaches that the bishops have by divine institution taken the place of the apostles as pastors of the Church, in such wise that whoever listens to them is listening to Christ and whoever despises them despises Christ and him who sent Christ (cf. Lk. 10:16).

89 **John 8:31–32** Jesus then said to the Jews who had believed in him, "If you continue in my word, you are truly my disciples, and you will know the truth, and the truth will make you free."

90 (1) **Vatican Council I (1870): DS 3016: *nexus mysteriorum*** [*The role of reason in teaching supernatural truth*]. And, indeed, reason illustrated by faith, when it zealously, piously, and soberly seeks, attains with the help of God some understanding of the mysteries, and that a most profitable one, not only from the analogy of those things which it knows naturally, but also from the connection of the mysteries among themselves and with the last end of man; nevertheless, it is never capable of perceiving those mysteries in the way it does the truths which constitute its own proper object. For, divine mysteries by their nature exceed the created intellect so much that, even when handed down by revelation and accepted by faith, they nevertheless remain covered by the veil of faith itself, and wrapped in a certain mist, as it were, as long as in this mortal life, "we are absent from the Lord: for we walk by faith and not by sight" [II Cor. 5:6 f.].

90 (2) ***Lumen gentium* 25** Among the more important duties of bishops that of preaching the Gospel has pride of place. For the bishops are heralds of the faith, who draw new disciples to Christ; they are authentic teachers, that is, teachers endowed with the authority of Christ, who preach the faith to the people assigned to them, the faith which is destined to inform their thinking and direct their conduct; and under the light of the Holy Spirit they make that faith shine forth, drawing from the storehouse of revelation new things and old (cf. Mt. 13:52); they make it bear fruit and with watchfulness they ward off whatever errors threaten their flock (cf. 2 Tim. 4:14). Bishops who teach in communion with the Roman Pontiff are to be revered by all as witnesses of divine and Catholic truth; the faithful, for their part, are obliged to submit to their bishops' decision, made in the name of Christ, in matters of faith and

morals, and to adhere to it with a ready and respectful allegiance of mind. This loyal submission of the will and intellect must be given, in a special way, to the authentic teaching authority of the Roman Pontiff, even when he does not speak *ex cathedra* in such wise, indeed, that his supreme teaching authority be acknowledged with respect, and that one sincerely adhere to decisions made by him, conformably with his manifest mind and intention, which is made known principally either by the character of the documents in question, or by the frequency with which a certain doctrine is proposed, or by the manner in which the doctrine is formulated.

Although the bishops, taken individually, do not enjoy the privilege of infallibility, they do, however, proclaim infallibly the doctrine of Christ on the following conditions: namely, when, even though dispersed throughout the world but preserving for all that amongst themselves and with Peter's successor the bond of communion, in their authoritative teaching concerning matters of faith and morals, they are in agreement that a particular teaching is to be held definitively and absolutely. This is still more clearly the case when, assembled in an ecumenical council, they are, for the universal Church, teachers of and judges in matters of faith and morals, whose decisions must be adhered to with the loyal and obedient assent of faith.

This infallibility, however, with which the divine redeemer wished to endow his Church in defining doctrine pertaining to faith and morals, is co-extensive with the deposit of revelation, which must be religiously guarded and loyally and courageously expounded. The Roman Pontiff, head of the college of bishops, enjoys this infallibility in virtue of his office, when, as supreme pastor and teacher of all the faithful—who confirms his brethren in the faith (cf. Lk. 22:32)—he proclaims in an absolute decision a doctrine pertaining to faith or morals. For that reason his definitions are rightly said to be irreformable by their very nature and not by reason of the assent of the Church, in as much as they were made with the assistance of the Holy Spirit promised to him in the person of blessed Peter himself; and as a consequence they are in no way in need of the approval of others, and do not admit of appeal to any other tribunal. For in such a case the Roman Pontiff does not utter a pronouncement as a private person, but rather does he expound and defend the teaching of the Catholic faith as the supreme teacher of the universal Church, in whom the Church's charism of infallibility is present in a singular way. The infallibility promised to the Church is also present in the body of bishops when, together with Peter's successor, they exercise the supreme teaching office. Now, the assent of the Church can never be lacking to such definitions on account of the same Holy Spirit's influence, through which Christ's whole flock is maintained in the unity of the faith and makes progress in it.

Furthermore, when the Roman Pontiff, or the body of bishops together with him, define a doctrine, they make the definition in conformity with revelation itself, to which all are bound to adhere and to which they are obliged to submit; and this revelation is transmitted integrally either in written form or in oral tradition through the legitimate succession of bishops and above all through the watchful concern of the Roman Pontiff himself; and through the light of the Spirit of truth it is scrupulously preserved in the Church and unerringly explained. The Roman Pontiff and the bishops, by reason of their office and the seriousness of the matter, apply themselves with zeal to the work of enquiring by every suitable means into this revelation and of giving apt expression to its contents; they do not, however, admit any new public revelation as pertaining to the divine deposit of faith.

(1) **1 John 2:20** But you have been anointed by the Holy One, and you all know. **91**

91 (2) **1 John 2:27** . . . but the anointing which you received from him abides in you, and you have no need that any one should teach you; as his anointing teaches you about everything, and is true, and is no lie, just as it has taught you, abide in him.

91 (3) **John 16:13** When the Spirit of truth comes, he will guide you into all the truth; for he will not speak on his own authority, but whatever he hears he will speak, and he will declare to you the things that are to come.

94 (1) ***Gaudium et spes*** **44, 2** The Church has a visible social structure, which is a sign of its unity in Christ: as such it can be enriched, and it is being enriched, by the evolution of social life—not as if something were missing in the constitution which Christ gave the Church, but in order to understand this constitution more deeply, express it better, and adapt it more successfully to our times. The Church is happy to feel that, with regard to the community it forms and each of its members, it is assisted in various ways by men of all classes and conditions. Whoever contributes to the development of the community of mankind on the level of family, culture, economic and social life, and national and international politics, according to the plan of God, is also contributing in no small way to the community of the Church insofar as it depends on things outside itself. The Church itself also recognizes that it has benefited and is still benefiting from the opposition of its enemies and persecutors.

94 (2) ***Dei Verbum*** **23–24** The spouse of the incarnate Word, which is the Church, is taught by the Holy Spirit. She strives to reach day by day a more profound understanding of the sacred Scriptures, in order to provide her children with food from the divine words. For this reason also she duly fosters the study of the Fathers, both Eastern and Western, and of the sacred liturgies. Catholic exegetes and other workers in the field of sacred theology should zealously combine their efforts. Under the watchful eye of the sacred Magisterium, and using appropriate techniques they should together set about examining and explaining the sacred texts in such a way that as many as possible of those who are ministers of the divine Word may be able to distribute fruitfully the nourishment of the Scriptures of the People of God. This nourishment enlightens the mind, strengthens the will and fires the hearts of men with the love of God. The sacred Synod encourages those sons of the Church who are engaged in biblical studies constantly to renew their efforts, in order to carry on the work they have so happily begun, with complete dedication and in accordance with the mind of the Church.

Sacred theology relies on the written Word of God, taken together with sacred Tradition, as on a permanent foundation. By this Word it is most firmly strengthened and constantly rejuvenated, as it searches out, under the light of faith, the full truth stored up in the mystery of Christ. Therefore, the "study of the sacred page" should be the very soul of sacred theology. The ministry of the Word, too—pastoral preaching, catechetics and all forms of Christian instruction, among which the liturgical homily should hold pride of place—is healthily nourished and thrives in holiness through the Word of Scripture.

94 (3) ***Unitatis redintegratio*** **4** Today, in many parts of the world, under the influence of the grace of the Holy Spirit, many efforts are being made in prayer, word and action to attain that fullness of unity which Jesus Christ desires. The sacred Council exhorts, therefore, all the Catholic faithful to recognize the signs of the times and to take an active and intelligent part in the work of ecumenism.

The term "ecumenical movement" indicates the initiatives and activities encouraged and organized, according to the various needs of the Church and as opportunities offer, to promote Christian unity. These are: first, every effort to avoid expressions, judgments and actions which do not represent the condition of our separated brethren with truth and fairness and so make mutual relations with them more difficult. Then, "dialogue" between competent experts from different Churches and communities; in their meetings, which are organized in a religious spirit, each explains the teaching of his communion in greater depth and brings out clearly its distinctive features. Through such dialogue everyone gains a truer knowledge and more just appreciation of the teaching and religious life of both communions. In addition, these communions engage in that more intensive cooperation in carrying out any duties for the common good of humanity which are demanded by every Christian conscience. They also come together for common prayer, where this is permitted. Finally, all are led to examine their own faithfulness to Christ's will for the Church and, wherever necessary, undertake with vigor the task of renewal and reform.

Such actions, when they are carried out by the Catholic faithful with prudent patience and under the attentive guidance of their bishops, promote justice and truth, concord and collaboration, as well as the spirit of brotherly love and unity. The results will be that, little by little, as the obstacles to perfect ecclesiastical communion are overcome, all Christians will be gathered, in a common celebration of the Eucharist, into the unity of the one and only Church, which Christ bestowed on his Church from the beginning. This unity, we believe, subsists in the Catholic Church as something she can never lose, and we hope that it will continue to increase until the end of time.

However, it is evident that the work of preparing and reconciling those individuals who wish for full Catholic communion is of its nature distinct from ecumenical action. But there is no opposition between the two, since both proceed from the marvellous ways of God.

In ecumenical work, Catholics must assuredly be concerned for their separated brethren, praying for them, keeping them informed about the Church, making the first approaches toward them. But their primary duty is to make a careful and honest appraisal of whatever needs to be renewed and done in the Catholic household itself, in order that its life may bear witness more clearly and faithfully to the teachings and institutions which have been handed down from Christ through the apostles.

For although the Catholic Church has been endowed with all divinely revealed truth and with all means of grace, yet its members fail to live by them with all the fervor that they should. As a result the radiance of the Church's face shines less brightly in the eyes of our separated brethren and of the world at large, and the growth of God's kingdom is retarded. Every Catholic must therefore aim at Christian perfection and, each according to his station, play his part, that the Church, which bears in her own body the humility and dying of Jesus, may daily be more purified and renewed, against the day when Christ will present her to himself in all her glory without spot or wrinkle.

While preserving unity in essentials, let everyone in the Church, according to the office entrusted to him, preserve a proper freedom in the various forms of spiritual life and discipline, in the variety of liturgical rites, and even in the theological elaborations of revealed truth. In all things let charity prevail. If they are true to this course of action, they will be giving ever richer expression to the authentic catholicity and apostolicity of the Church.

On the other hand, Catholics must gladly acknowledge and esteem the truly Christian endowments for our common heritage which are to be found among our separated brethren. It is right and salutary to recognize the riches of Christ and virtuous works in the lives of others who are bearing witness to Christ, sometimes even to the shedding of their blood. For God is always wonderful in his works and worthy of all praise.

Nor should we forget that anything wrought by the grace of the Holy Spirit in the hearts of our separated brethren can contribute to our own edification. Whatever is truly Christian is never contrary to what genuinely belongs to the faith; indeed, it can always bring a more perfect realization of the very mystery of Christ and the Church.

Nevertheless, the divisions among Christians prevent the Church from realizing the fullness of catholicity proper to her in those of her sons who, though joined to her by baptism, are yet separated from full communion with her. Furthermore, the Church herself finds it more difficult to express in actual life her full catholicity in all its aspects.

This sacred Council is gratified to note that the participation by the Catholic faithful in ecumenical work is growing daily. It commends this work to the bishops everywhere in the world for their diligent promotion and prudent guidance.

102 (1) **Hebrews 1:1–3** In many and various ways God spoke of old to our fathers by the prophets; but in these last days he has spoken to us by a Son, whom he appointed the heir of all things, through whom also he created the world. He reflects the glory of God and bears the very stamp of his nature, upholding the universe by his word of power. When he had made purification for sins, he sat down at the right hand of the Majesty on high. . . .

102 (2) **Psalm 104**

Bless the Lord, O my soul!
O Lord my God, thou art very great!
Thou art clothed with honor and majesty,
who coverest thyself with light as with a garment,
who hast stretched out the heavens like a tent,
who hast laid the beams of thy chambers on the waters,
who makest the clouds thy chariot,
who ridest on the wings of the wind,
who makest the winds thy messengers,
fire and flame thy ministers.

Thou didst set the earth on its foundations,
so that it should never be shaken.
Thou didst cover it with the deep as with a garment;
the waters stood above the mountains.
At thy rebuke they fled;
at the sound of thy thunder they took to flight.
The mountains rose, the valleys sank down
to the place which thou didst appoint for them.
Thou didst set a bound which they should not pass,
so that they might not again cover the earth.

Thou makest springs gush forth in the valleys;
they flow between the hills,
they give drink to every beast of the field;
the wild asses quench their thirst.
By them the birds of the air have their habitation;
they sing among the branches.

From thy lofty abode thou waterest the mountains;
the earth is satisfied with the fruit of thy work.

Thou dost cause the grass to grow for the cattle,
and plants for man to cultivate,
that he may bring forth food from the earth,
and wine to gladden the heart of man,
oil to make his face shine,
and bread to strengthen man's heart.
The trees of the Lord are watered abundantly,
the cedars of Lebanon which he planted.
In them the birds build their nests;
the stork has her home in the fir trees.
The high mountains are for the wild goats;
the rocks are a refuge for the badgers.
Thou hast made the moon to mark the seasons;
the sun knows its time for setting.
Thou makest darkness, and it is night,
when all the beasts of the forest creep forth.
The young lions roar for their prey,
seeking their food from God.
When the sun rises, they get them away
and lie down in their dens.
Man goes forth to his work
and to his labor until the evening.

O Lord, how manifold are thy works!
In wisdom hast thou made them all;
the earth is full of thy creatures.
Yonder is the sea, great and wide,
which teems with things innumerable,
living things both small and great.
There go the ships,
and Leviathan which thou didst form to sport in it.

These all look to thee,
to give them their food in due season.
When thou givest to them, they gather it up;
when thou openest thy hand, they are filled with good things.
When thou hidest thy face, they are dismayed;
when thou takest away their breath, they die
and return to their dust.
When thou sendest forth thy Spirit, they are created;
and thou renewest the face of the ground.

May the glory of the Lord endure for ever,
may the Lord rejoice in his works,
who looks on the earth and it trembles,
who touches the mountains and they smoke!
I will sing to the Lord as long as I live;
I will sing praise to my God while I have being.
May my meditation be pleasing to him,
for I rejoice in the Lord.
Let sinners be consumed from the earth,
and let the wicked be no more!

Bless the Lord, O my soul!
Praise the Lord!

102 (3) **John 1:1** In the beginning was the Word, and the Word was with God, and the Word was God.

103 ***Dei Verbum* 21** The Church has always venerated the divine Scriptures as she venerated the Body of the Lord, in so far as she never ceases, particularly in the sacred liturgy, to partake of the bread of life and to offer it to the faithful from the one table of the Word of God and the Body of Christ. She has always regarded, and continues to regard the Scriptures, taken together with sacred Tradition, as the supreme rule of her faith. For, since they are inspired by God and committed to writing once and for all time, they present God's own Word in an unalterable form, and they make the voice of the Holy Spirit sound again and again in the words of the prophets and apostles. It follows that all the preaching of the Church, as indeed the entire Christian religion, should be nourished and ruled by sacred Scripture. In the sacred books the Father who is in heaven comes lovingly to meet his children, and talks with them. And such is the force and power of the Word of God that it can serve the Church as her support and vigor, and the children of the Church as strength for their faith, food for the soul, and a pure and lasting fount of spiritual life. Scripture verifies in the most perfect way the words: "The Word of God is living and active" (Heb. 4:12), and "is able to build you up and give you the inheritance among all those who are sanctified" (Acts 20:32; cf. 1 Th. 2:13).

104 ***Dei Verbum* 24** Sacred theology relies on the written Word of God, taken together with sacred Tradition, as on a permanent foundation. By this Word it is most firmly strengthened and constantly rejuvenated, as it searches out, under the light of faith, the full truth stored up in the mystery of Christ. Therefore, the "study of the sacred page" should be the very soul of sacred theology. The ministry of the Word, too—pastoral preaching, catechetics and all forms of Christian instruction, among which the liturgical homily should hold pride of place—is healthily nourished and thrives in holiness through the Word of Scripture.

108 **Luke 24:45** Then he opened their minds to understand the scriptures. . . .

109 ***Dei Verbum* 12, 1** Seeing that, in sacred Scripture, God speaks through men in human fashion, it follows that the interpreter of sacred Scriptures, if he is to ascertain what God has wished to communicate to us, should carefully search out the meaning which the sacred writers really had in mind, that meaning which God had thought well to manifest through the medium of their words.

111 ***Dei Verbum* 12, 3** But since sacred Scripture must be read and interpreted with its divine authorship in mind, no less attention must be devoted to the content and unity of the whole of Scripture, taking into account the Tradition of the entire Church and the analogy of faith, if we are to derive their true meaning from the sacred texts. It is the task of exegetes to work, according to these rules, towards a better understanding and explanation of the meaning of sacred Scripture in order that their research may help the Church to form a firmer judgment. For, of course, all that has been said about the manner of interpreting Scripture is ultimately subject to the judgment of the Church which exercises the divinely conferred commission and ministry of watching over and interpreting the Word of God.

(1) **Luke 24:25–27** And he said to them, "O foolish men, and slow of heart to 112
believe all that the prophets have spoken! Was it not necessary that the Christ should suffer these things and enter into his glory?" And beginning with Moses and all the prophets, he interpreted to them in all the scriptures the things concerning himself.

(2) **Luke 24:44–46** Then he said to them, "These are my words which I spoke to 112
you, while I was still with you, that everything written about me in the law of Moses and the prophets and the psalms must be fulfilled." Then he opened their minds to understand the scriptures, and said to them, "Thus it is written, that the Christ should suffer and on the third day rise from the dead. . . ."

(3) **Psalm 22:15 (22:14: RSV)** 112

I am poured out like water,
  and all my bones are out of joint;
my heart is like wax,
  it is melted within my breast. . . .

Romans 12:6 Having gifts that differ according to the grace given to us, let us use 114
them: if prophecy, in proportion to our faith. . . .

(1) **1 Corinthians 10:2** . . . and all were baptized into Moses in the cloud and in 117
the sea. . . .

(2) **Hebrews 3–4:11** Therefore, holy brethren, who share in a heavenly call, con- 117
sider Jesus, the apostle and high priest of our confession. He was faithful to him who appointed him, just as Moses also was faithful in God's house. Yet Jesus has been counted worthy of as much more glory than Moses as the builder of a house has more honor than the house. (For every house is built by some one, but the builder of all things is God.) Now Moses was faithful in all God's house as a servant, to testify to the things that were to be spoken later, but Christ was faithful over God's house as a son. And we are his house if we hold fast our confidence and pride in our hope.

Therefore, as the Holy Spirit says,

"Today, when you hear his voice,
do not harden your hearts as in the rebellion,
on the day of testing in the wilderness,
where your fathers put me to the test
and saw my works for forty years.
Therefore I was provoked with that generation,
and said, 'They always go astray in their hearts;
they have not known my ways.'
As I swore in my wrath,
'They shall never enter my rest.'"

Take care, brethren, lest there be in any of you an evil, unbelieving heart, leading you to fall away from the living God. But exhort one another every day, as long as it is called "today," that none of you may be hardened by the deceitfulness of sin. For we share in Christ, if only we hold our first confidence firm to the end, while it is said,

"Today, when you hear his voice,
do not harden your hearts as in the rebellion."

Who were they that heard and yet were rebellious? Was it not all those who left Egypt under the leadership of Moses? And with whom was he provoked forty years? Was it not with those who sinned, whose bodies fell in the wilderness? And to whom did he swear that they should never enter his rest, but to those who were disobedient? So we see that they were unable to enter because of unbelief.

Therefore, while the promise of entering his rest remains, let us fear lest any of you be judged to have failed to reach it. For good news came to us just as to them; but the message which they heard did not benefit them, because it did not meet with faith in the hearers. For we who have believed enter that rest, as he has said,

> "As I swore in my wrath,
> 'They shall never enter my rest,'"

although his works were finished from the foundation of the world. For he has somewhere spoken of the seventh day in this way, "And God rested on the seventh day from all his works." And again in this place he said,

> "They shall never enter my rest."

Since therefore it remains for some to enter it, and those who formerly received the good news failed to enter because of disobedience, again he sets a certain day, "Today," saying through David so long afterward, in the words already quoted,

> "Today, when you hear his voice,
> do not harden your hearts."

For if Joshua had given them rest, God would not speak later of another day. So then, there remains a sabbath rest for the people of God; for whoever enters God's rest also ceases from his labors as God did from his.

Let us therefore strive to enter that rest, that no one fall by the same sort of disobedience.

117 (3) **Revelation 21:1–22:5** Then I saw a new heaven and a new earth; for the first heaven and the first earth had passed away, and the sea was no more. And I saw the holy city, new Jerusalem, coming down out of heaven from God, prepared as a bride adorned for her husband; and I heard a loud voice from the throne saying, "Behold, the dwelling of God is with men. He will dwell with them, and they shall be his people, and God himself will be with them; he will wipe away every tear from their eyes, and death shall be no more, neither shall there be mourning nor crying nor pain any more, for the former things have passed away."

And he who sat upon the throne said, "Behold, I make all things new." Also he said, "Write this, for these words are trustworthy and true." And he said to me, "It is done! I am the Alpha and the Omega, the beginning and the end. To the thirsty I will give from the fountain of the water of life without payment. He who conquers shall have this heritage, and I will be his God and he shall be my son. But as for the cowardly, the faithless, the polluted, as for murderers, fornicators, sorcerers, idolaters, and all liars, their lot shall be in the lake that burns with fire and sulfur, which is the second death."

Then came one of the seven angels who had the seven bowls full of the seven last plagues, and spoke to me, saying, "Come, I will show you the Bride, the wife of the Lamb." And in the Spirit he carried me away to a great, high mountain, and showed me the holy city Jerusalem coming down out of heaven from God, having the glory of God, its radiance like a most rare jewel, like a jasper, clear as crystal. It had a great, high wall, with twelve gates, and at the gates twelve angels, and on the gates the names of the twelve tribes of the sons of Israel were inscribed; on the east three gates, on the north three gates, on the south three gates, and on the west three gates. And the wall of the city had twelve foundations, and on them the twelve names of the twelve apostles of the Lamb.

And he who talked to me had a measuring rod of gold to measure the city and its gates and walls. The city lies foursquare, its length the same as its breadth; and he measured the city with his rod, twelve thousand stadia; its length and breadth and height are equal. He also measured its wall, a hundred and forty-four cubits by a man's measure, that is, an angel's. The wall was built of jasper, while the city was pure gold, clear as glass. The foundations of the wall of the city were adorned with every jewel; the first was jasper, the second sapphire, the third agate, the fourth emerald, the fifth onyx, the sixth carnelian, the seventh chrysolite, the eighth beryl, the ninth topaz, the tenth chrysoprase, the eleventh jacinth, the twelfth amethyst. And the twelve gates were twelve pearls, each of the gates made of a single pearl, and the street of the city was pure gold, transparent as glass.

And I saw no temple in the city, for its temple is the Lord God the Almighty and the Lamb. And the city has no need of sun or moon to shine upon it, for the glory of God is its light, and its lamp is the Lamb. By its light shall the nations walk; and the kings of the earth shall bring their glory into it, and its gates shall never be shut by day—and there shall be no night there; they shall bring into it the glory and the honor of the nations. But nothing unclean shall enter it, nor any one who practices abomination or falsehood, but only those who are written in the Lamb's book of life.

Then he showed me the river of the water of life, bright as crystal, flowing from the throne of God and of the Lamb, through the middle of the street of the city; also, on either side of the river, the tree of life with its twelve kinds of fruit, yielding its fruit each month; and the leaves of the tree were for the healing of the nations. There shall no more be anything accursed, but the throne of God and of the Lamb shall be in it, and his servants shall worship him; they shall see his face, and his name shall be on their foreheads. And night shall be no more; they need no light of lamp or sun, for the Lord God will be their light, and they shall reign for ever and ever.

(1) ***Dei Verbum* 8, 3** The sayings of the Holy Fathers are a witness to the life-giving presence of this Tradition, showing how its riches are poured out in the practice and life of the Church, in her belief and her prayer. By means of the same Tradition the full canon of the sacred books is known to the Church and the holy Scriptures themselves are more thoroughly understood and constantly actualized in the Church. Thus God, who spoke in the past, continues to converse with the spouse of his beloved Son. And the Holy Spirit, through whom the living voice of the Gospel rings out in the Church—and through her in the world—leads believers to the full truth, and makes the Word of Christ dwell in them in all its richness (cf. Col. 3:16). 120

(2) **Council of Rome (382): DS 179** Likewise it has been said: Now indeed we must treat of the divine Scriptures, what the universal Catholic Church accepts and what she ought to shun. 120

The order of the Old Testament begins here: Genesis one book, Exodus one book, Leviticus one book, Numbers one book, Deuteronomy one book, Josue Nave one book, Judges one book, Ruth one book, Kings four books, Paralipomenon two books, Psalms one book, Solomon three books, Proverbs one book, Ecclesiastes one book, Canticle of Canticles one book, likewise Wisdom one book, Ecclesiasticus one book.

Likewise the order of the Prophets. Isaias one book, Jeremias one book, with Ginoth, that is, with his lamentations, Ezechiel one book, Daniel one book, Osee one book, Micheas one book, Joel one book, Abdias one book, Jonas one book, Nahum one book, Habacuc one book, Sophonias one book, Aggeus one book, Zacharias one book, Malachias one book.

Likewise the order of the histories. Job one book, Tobias one book, Esdras two books, Esther one book, Judith one book, Machabees two books.

(3) **Council of Florence (1442): DS 1334–36** It professes one and the same God as the author of the Old and New Testament, that is, of the Law and the Prophets 120

and the Gospel, since the saints of both Testaments have spoken with the inspiration of the same Holy Spirit, whose books, which are contained under the following titles it accepts and venerates. [The books of the canon follow].

Besides it anathematizes the madness of the Manichaeans, who have established two first principles, one of the visible, and another of the invisible; and they have said that there is one God of the New Testament, another God of the Old Testament.

120 (4) **Council of Trent (1546): DS 1501–4** The sacred and holy ecumenical and general Synod of Trent, lawfully assembled in the Holy Spirit, with the same three Legates of the Apostolic See presiding over it, keeping this constantly in view, that with the abolishing of errors, the purity itself of the Gospel is preserved in the Church, which promised before through the Prophets in the Holy Scriptures our Lord Jesus Christ the Son of God first promulgated with His own mouth, and then commanded "to be preached" by His apostles "to every creature" as the source of every saving truth and of instruction in morals [Matt. 28:19 ff., Mark 16:15], and [the Synod] clearly perceiving that this truth and instruction are contained in the written books and in the unwritten traditions, which have been received by the apostles from the mouth of Christ Himself, or from the apostles themselves, at the dictation of the Holy Spirit, have come down even to us, transmitted as it were from hand to hand, [the Synod] following the examples of the orthodox Fathers, receives and holds in veneration with an equal affection of piety and reverence all the books both of the Old and of the New Testament, since one God is the author of both, and also the traditions themselves, those that appertain both to faith and to morals, as having been dictated either by Christ's own word of mouth, or by the Holy Spirit, and preserved in the Catholic Church by a continuous succession. And so that no doubt may arise in anyone's mind as to which are the books that are accepted by this Synod, it has decreed that a list of the Sacred books be added to this decree.

They are written here below:

Books of the Old Testament: The five books of Moses, namely, Genesis, Exodus, Leviticus, Numbers, Deuteronomy; Josue, Judges, Ruth, four books of Kings, two of Paralipomenon, the first book of Esdras, and the second which is called Nehemias, Tobias, Judith, Esther, Job, the Psalter of David consisting of 150 psalms, the Proverbs, Ecclesiastes, the Canticle of Canticles, Wisdom, Ecclesiasticus, Isaias, Jeremias with Baruch, Ezechiel, Daniel, the twelve minor Prophets, that is Osee, Joel, Amos, Abdias, Jonas, Michaeas, Nahum, Habacuc, Sophonias, Aggaeus, Zacharias, Malachias; two books of the Machabees, the first and the second.

Books of the New Testament: the four Gospels, according to Matthew, Mark, Luke, and John; the Acts of the Apostles, written by Luke the Evangelist, fourteen epistles of Paul the Apostle, to the Romans, to the Corinthians two, to the Galatians, to the Ephesians, to the Philippians, to the Colossians, two to the Thessalonians, two to Timothy, to Titus, to Philemon, to the Hebrews; two of Peter the Apostle, three of John the Apostle, one of the Apostle James, one of the Apostle Jude, and the Apocalypse of John the Apostle. If anyone, however, should not accept the said books as sacred and canonical, entire with all their parts, as they were wont to be read in the Catholic Church, and as they are contained in the old Latin Vulgate edition, and if both knowingly and deliberately he should condemn the aforesaid traditions let him be anathema.

121 ***Dei Verbum* 14** God, with loving concern contemplating, and making preparation for, the salvation of the whole human race, in a singular undertaking chose for himself a people to whom he would entrust his promises. By his covenant with Abraham (cf. Gen. 15:18) and, through Moses, with the race of Israel (cf. Ex. 24:8), he did acquire

a people for himself, and to them he revealed himself in words and deeds as the one, true, living God, so that Israel might experience the ways of God with men. Moreover, by listening to the voice of God speaking to them through the prophets, they had daily to understand his ways more fully and more clearly, and make them more widely known among the nations (cf. Ps. 21:28–29; 95:1–3; Is. 2:1–4; Jer. 3:17). Now the economy of salvation, foretold, recounted and explained by the sacred authors, appears as the true Word of God in the books of the Old Testament, that is why these books, divinely inspired, preserve a lasting value: "For whatever was written in former days was written for our instruction, that by steadfastness and the encouragement of the Scriptures we might have hope" (Rom. 15:4).

***Dei Verbum* 20** Besides the four Gospels, the New Testament also contains the Epistles of St. Paul and other apostolic writings composed under the inspiration of the Holy Spirit. In accordance with the wise design of God these writings firmly establish those matters which concern Christ the Lord, formulate more and more precisely his authentic teaching, preach the saving power of Christ's divine work and foretell its glorious consummation. **124**

For the Lord Jesus was with his apostles as he had promised (cf. Mt. 28:20) and he had sent to them the Spirit, the Counsellor, who would guide them into all the truth (cf. Jn. 16:13).

(1) **1 Corinthians 10:6** Now these things are warnings for us, not to desire evil as they did. **128**

(2) **1 Corinthians 10:11** Now these things happened to them as a warning, but they were written down for our instruction, upon whom the end of the ages has come. **128**

(3) **Hebrews 10:1** For since the law has but a shadow of the good things to come instead of the true form of these realities, it can never, by the same sacrifices which are continually offered year after year, make perfect those who draw near. **128**

(4) **1 Peter 3:21** Baptism, which corresponds to this, now saves you, not as a removal of dirt from the body but as an appeal to God for a clear conscience, through the resurrection of Jesus Christ. . . . **128**

(1) **Mark 12:29–31** Jesus answered, "The first is, 'Hear, O Israel: The Lord our God, the Lord is one; and you shall love the Lord your God with all your heart, and with all your soul, and with all your mind, and with all your strength.' The second is this, 'You shall love your neighbor as yourself.' There is no other commandment greater than these." **129**

(2) **1 Corinthians 5:6–8** Your boasting is not good. Do you not know that a little leaven leavens the whole lump? Cleanse out the old leaven that you may be a new lump, as you really are unleavened. For Christ, our paschal lamb, has been sacrificed. Let us, therefore, celebrate the festival, not with the old leaven, the leaven of malice and evil, but with the unleavened bread of sincerity and truth. **129**

(3) **1 Corinthians 10:1–11** I want you to know, brethren, that our fathers were all under the cloud, and all passed through the sea, and all were baptized into Moses in the cloud and in the sea, and all ate the same supernatural food and all drank the same supernatural drink. For they drank from the supernatural Rock which followed them, and the Rock was Christ. Nevertheless with most of them God was not pleased; for they were overthrown in the wilderness. **129**

Now these things are warnings for us, not to desire evil as they did. Do not be idolaters as some of them were; as it is written, "The people sat down to eat and drink and rose up to dance." We must not indulge in immorality as some of them did, and twenty-three thousand fell in a single day. We must not put the Lord to the test, as some of them did and were destroyed by serpents; nor grumble, as some of them did and were destroyed by the Destroyer. Now these things happened to them as a warning, but they were written down for our instruction, upon whom the end of the ages has come.

129 (4) ***Dei Verbum* 16** God, the inspirer and author of the books of both Testaments, in his wisdom has so brought it about that the New should be hidden in the Old and that the Old should be made manifest in the New (cf. St. Augustine, *Quaest. in Hept.* 2, 73: PL 34, 623). For, although Christ founded the New Covenant in his blood (cf. Lk. 22:20; 1 Cor. 11:25), still the books of the Old Testament, all of them caught up into the Gospel message, attain and show forth their full meaning in the New Testament (cf. Mt. 5:17; Lk. 24:27; Rom. 16:25–26; 2 Cor. 3:14–16) and, in their turn, shed light on it and explain it.

136 ***Dei Verbum* 11** The divinely revealed realities, which are contained and presented in the text of sacred Scripture, have been written down under the inspiration of the Holy Spirit. For Holy Mother Church, relying on the faith of the apostolic age, accepts as sacred and canonical the books of the Old and the New Testaments, whole and entire, with all their parts, on the grounds that, written under the inspiration of the Holy Spirit (cf. Jn. 20:31; 2 Tim. 3:16; 2 Pet. 1:19–21; 3:15–16), they have God as their author, and have been handed on as such to the Church herself. To compose the sacred books, God chose certain men who, all the while he employed them in this task, made full use of their powers and faculties so that, though he acted in them and by them, it was as true authors that they consigned to writing whatever he wanted written, and no more.

Since, therefore, all that the inspired authors, or sacred writers, affirm should be regarded as affirmed by the Holy Spirit, we must acknowledge that the books of Scripture, firmly, faithfully and without error, teach that truth which God, for the sake of our salvation, wished to see confided to the sacred Scriptures. Thus "all Scripture is inspired by God, and profitable for teaching, for reproof, for correction and for training in righteousness, so that the man of God may be complete, equipped for every good work" (2 Tim. 3:16–17; Gk. text).

137 **Origen, *Homily on Exodus* 4, 5** Who is that man whom God fills with that spirit with which he filled Moses and Aaron when they performed these prodigies and signs, that, illuminated by the same spirit, he may be able to discuss what they did? For I do not think these various and diverse remarkable things are otherwise explained unless they are discussed in that same spirit by which they were done, for the apostle Paul also says, "Let the spirit of the prophets be subject to the prophets." The words of the prophets, therefore, are not said to be "subject" to just anyone to be explained, but "to the prophets." But since the same blessed Apostle orders us to become imitators of this grace, that is of the prophetic gift, although it is "imperfect" and in our power, saying: "But be zealous for the better gifts, but rather that you may prophesy," let us also attempt to assume a zeal for the good gifts and, if we have any, to prove it, but to await the fullness of the gift from the Lord. For this reason the Lord says through the prophet: "Open your mouth, and I will fill it." For that reason another Scripture says, "Prick the eye and it produces a tear; prick the heart and it produces understanding." Lest therefore, from despair, we deliver ourselves to silence which by no means edifies the Church of God, let us resume briefly to speak about what things we are able and in what measure we are able.

Isaiah 50:4 141
The Lord God has given me
the tongue of those who are taught,
that I may know how to sustain with a word
him that is weary.
Morning by morning he wakens,
he wakens my ear
to hear as those who are taught.

(1) ***Dei Verbum* 5** "The obedience of faith" (Rom. 16:26; cf. Rom. 1:5; 2 Cor. 10:5– 143
6) must be given to God as he reveals himself. By faith man freely commits his entire self to God, making "the full submission of his intellect and will to God who reveals," and willingly assenting to the Revelation given by him. Before this faith can be exercised, man must have the grace of God to move and assist him; he must have the interior helps of the Holy Spirit, who moves the heart and converts it to God, who opens the eyes of the mind and "makes it easy for all to accept and believe the truth." The same Holy Spirit constantly perfects faith by his gifts, so that Revelation may be more and more profoundly understood.

(2) **Romans 1:5** . . . through whom we have received grace and apostleship to bring 143
about the obedience of faith for the sake of his name among all the nations. . . .

(3) **Romans 16:26** . . . but is now disclosed and through the prophetic writings is 143
made known to all nations, according to the command of the eternal God, to bring about the obedience of faith. . . .

(1) **Genesis 12:1–4** Now the Lord said to Abram, "Go from your country and your 145
kindred and your father's house to the land that I will show you. And I will make of you a great nation, and I will bless you, and make your name great, so that you will be a blessing. I will bless those who bless you, and him who curses you I will curse; and by you all the families of the earth shall bless themselves."

So Abram went, as the Lord had told him; and Lot went with him. Abram was seventy-five years old when he departed from Haran.

(2) **Genesis 23:4** "I am a stranger and a sojourner among you; give me property 145
among you for a burying place, that I may bury my dead out of my sight."

(3) **Hebrews 11:17** By faith Abraham, when he was tested, offered up Isaac, and he 145
who had received the promises was ready to offer up his only son. . . .

(1) **Genesis 15:6** And he believed the Lord; and he reckoned it to him as righteous- 146
ness.

(2) **Genesis 15:5** And he brought him outside and said, "Look toward heaven, and 146
number the stars, if you are able to number them." Then he said to him, "So shall your descendants be."

(1) **Genesis 18:14** ". . . Is anything too hard for the Lord? At the appointed time I 148
will return to you, in the spring, and Sarah shall have a son."

148 (2) **Luke 1:48**

. . . for he has regarded the low estate of his handmaiden.
For behold, henceforth all generations will call me blessed. . . .

149 **Luke 2:35**

". . . (and a sword will pierce through your own soul also),
that thoughts out of many hearts may be revealed."

150 (1) **Jeremiah 17:5–6**

Thus says the Lord:
"Cursed is the man who trusts in man
  and makes flesh his arm,
  whose heart turns away from the Lord.
He is like a shrub in the desert,
  and shall not see any good come.
He shall dwell in the parched places of the wilderness,
  in an uninhabited salt land. . . ."

150 (2) **Psalm 40:5 (40:4: RSV)**

Blessed is the man who makes
  the Lord his trust,
who does not turn to the proud,
  to those who go astray after false gods!

150 (3) **Psalm 146:3–4**

Put not your trust in princes,
  in a son of man, in whom there is no help.
When his breath departs he returns to his earth;
  on that very day his plans perish.

151 (1) **Mark 9:7** And a cloud overshadowed them, and a voice came out of the cloud, "This is my beloved Son; listen to him."

151 (2) **Matthew 11:27** All things have been delivered to me by my Father; and no one knows the Son except the Father, and no one knows the Father except the Son and any one to whom the Son chooses to reveal him.

153 (1) **Galatians 1:15** But when he who had set me apart before I was born, and had called me through his grace. . . .

153 (2) **Matthew 11:25** At that time Jesus declared, "I thank thee, Father, Lord of heaven and earth, that thou hast hidden these things from the wise and understanding and revealed them to babes. . . ."

155 **Vatican Council I (1870): DS 3010** [*That faith in itself is a gift of God*]. Moreover, although the assent of faith is by no means a blind movement of the intellect, nevertheless, no one can "assent to the preaching of the Gospel," as he must to attain salvation, "without the illumination and inspiration of the Holy Spirit, who gives to all a sweetness in consenting to and believing in truth" (Council of Orange). Wherefore, "faith" itself in itself, even if it "worketh not by charity" [cf. Gal. 5:6], is a gift of God, and its act is a work pertaining to salvation, by which man offers a free obedience to God Himself by agreeing to, and cooperating with His grace, which he could resist.

(1) **Mark 16:20** And they went forth and preached everywhere, while the Lord worked with them and confirmed the message by the signs that attended it. Amen. 156

(2) **Hebrews 2:4** . . . while God also bore witness by signs and wonders and various miracles and by gifts of the Holy Spirit distributed according to his own will. 156

(1) **CIC Canon 748, §2** Persons cannot ever be forced by anyone to embrace the Catholic faith against their conscience. 160

(2) **John 18:37** Pilate said to him, "So you are a king?" Jesus answered, "You say that I am a king. For this I was born, and for this I have come into the world, to bear witness to the truth. Every one who is of the truth hears my voice." 160

(3) **John 12:32** ". . . and I, when I am lifted up from the earth, will draw all men to myself." 160

(1) **Mark 16:16** He who believes and is baptized will be saved; but he who does not believe will be condemned. 161

(2) **John 3:36** He who believes in the Son has eternal life; he who does not obey the Son shall not see life, but the wrath of God rests upon him. 161

(3) **John 6:40** ". . . For this is the will of my Father, that every one who sees the Son and believes in him should have eternal life; and I will raise him up at the last day." 161

(4) **Council of Trent (1547): DS 1532** But when the Apostle says that man is justified "by faith" [can. 9] and "freely" [Rom. 3:22, 24], these words must be understood in that sense in which the uninterrupted consent of the Catholic Church has held and expressed, namely, that we are therefore said to be justified by faith, because "faith is the beginning of human salvation," the foundation and root of all justification, "without which it is impossible to please God" [Heb. 11:6] and to come to the fellowship of His sons; and are, therefore, said to be justified gratuitously, because none of those things which precede justification, whether faith, or works merit the grace itself of justification; for, "if it is a grace, it is not now by reason of works; otherwise (as the same Apostle says) grace is no more grace" [Rom. 11:6]. 161

(1) **Mark 9:24** Immediately the father of the child cried out and said, "I believe; help my unbelief!" 162

(2) **Luke 17:5** The apostles said to the Lord, "Increase our faith!" 162

(3) **Luke 22:32** ". . . but I have prayed for you that your faith may not fail; and when you have turned again, strengthen your brethren." 162

(4) **Romans 15:13** May the God of hope fill you with all joy and peace in believing, so that by the power of the Holy Spirit you may abound in hope. 162

162 (5) **James 2:14–26** What does it profit, my brethren, if a man says he has faith but has not works? Can his faith save him? If a brother or sister is ill-clad and in lack of daily food, and one of you says to them, "Go in peace, be warmed and filled," without giving them the things needed for the body, what does it profit? So faith by itself, if it has no works, is dead.

But some one will say, "You have faith and I have works." Show me your faith apart from your works, and I by my works will show you my faith. You believe that God is one; you do well. Even the demons believe—and shudder. Do you want to be shown, you shallow man, that faith apart from works is barren? Was not Abraham our father justified by works, when he offered his son Isaac upon the altar? You see that faith was active along with his works, and faith was completed by works, and the scripture was fulfilled which says, "Abraham believed God, and it was reckoned to him as righteousness"; and he was called the friend of God. You see that a man is justified by works and not by faith alone. And in the same way was not also Rahab the harlot justified by works when she received the messengers and sent them out another way? For as the body apart from the spirit is dead, so faith apart from works is dead.

163 **St. Thomas Aquinas, *Summa theologiae* II–II, 4, 1**

Question 4. the virtue of faith

On the virtue of faith there are eight points of inquiry:

1. what faith is;
2. what power of the soul is its subject;
3. whether charity is the form of faith;
4. whether formed faith is the same numerically as unformed faith;
5. whether faith is a virtue;
6. and one virtue;
7. its relationship to other virtues;
8. a comparison of faith's certitude with the certitude peculiar to the intellectual virtues.

article 1. whether the definition of faith in Hebrews is accurate

THE FIRST POINT: 1. The definition of faith in *Heb.* 11, *Faith is the substance of things to be hoped for, the evidence of things that appear not*, seems inexact. Since faith, as established earlier, is a theological virtue, it is a quality and therefore not a substance.

2. Further, the objects of diverse virtues are themselves diverse. Since things to be hoped for are the object of hope, they should not be included as object in a definition of faith.

3. Further, since, as we will show, charity is the form of faith, faith is completed more by charity than by hope. Things to be loved rather than things to be hoped for should, then, enter into a definition of faith.

4. Further, the one thing ought not to be classified under several genera. Now substance and evidence are diverse genera; the one is not subsumed under the other. Therefore it is illogical to define faith as substance and as evidence. Thus the definition given is illogical.

5. Further, evidence clarifies the truth of a point for which the evidence is adduced; things that appear are matters whose truth has been made clear. A contradiction of both these points seems implicit, therefore, in the phrase *the evidence of things that appear not*, since evidence makes something apparent that first was not. Thus the phrase, *of things that appear not*, is incorrect, and faith is wrongly defined.

ON THE OTHER HAND, this text is of Apostolic authority.

REPLY: Some theologians, it is true, maintain that the words of this text are not a definition of faith, because, as Aristotle states, *a definition points to the quiddity and*

essence of something. Careful reflection, however, shows that this verse touches on all the elements whereby faith is definable, although it does not cast the words in definitional form, even as philosophers treat of the rules of the syllogism without observing the syllogistic form.

For proof bear in mind that since habits are known through their acts and acts through their objects, the habit of faith should be defined through its proper act in relationship to the proper object. As noted, the act of faith is belief, an act of mind fixed on one alternative by reason of the will's command. This implies that the act of faith has a reference both to the will's object, i.e. the good or end, and to the mind's object, i.e. the true. And because faith is a theological virtue, having the one reality as its object and its end, it follows necessarily that the object of faith and its end stand in a mutual relationship. As has been shown, the object of faith is the unseen first truth and those matters that we hold because of the first truth. Accordingly, the first truth necessarily stands to the act of faith as its end under the aspect of its being unseen. This in turn involves the characteristic of being something to be hoped for; *We hope for that which we see not*, because to see the truth is to have it and as shown earlier, no one hopes for what he has already, but for what he does not have yet.

The words, *faith is the substance of things to be hoped for*, then, refer to the relationship of the act of faith to the end, the object of the will. We use the word 'substance' for the very beginning of any reality, especially when all that follows is contained virtually in this fundamental beginning. For example, we may say that first indemonstrable principles are the substance of a science, since the rudiments of a science existing in us are its first principles, in which the whole science is virtually contained. So understood faith is the substance of things to be hoped for, since the very beginning of things hoped for exists in us through the assent of faith, which virtually contains all that we hope for. For we hope to receive blessedness by seeing in clear vision the truth we now cling to by faith. This is clear from what has been shown concerning beatitude.

The words, *the evidence of things that appear not*, describe the relationship of the act of faith to the kind of thought object which the object of faith is. Evidence is understood here as the effect of evidence, since it is evidence that brings about the mind's adherence to any truth; thus in this text the mind's firm hold on the truths of faith that appear not is called *evidence*. In another version the term conviction is used as well, since the believer's mind is convinced by divine authority to assent to the unseen.

Anyone interested in reducing the text to definitional form can say that faith is that habit of mind whereby eternal life begins in us and which brings the mind to assent to things that appear not. Thus this text sets faith off from all other attitudes of mind. *Evidence* separates faith from opinion, suspicion and doubt, in none of which does the mind adhere firmly to anything. *Of things that appear not* marks faith off from science and intuition, in both of which a truth does become apparent. *The substance of things to be hoped for* draws the line between the virtue of faith and faith taken in its commonplace meaning, which does not have reference to our hope for blessedness.

All other definitions of faith that we have are explanations of this one. Augustine's, *Faith is a virtue by which things not seen are believed*; Damascene's, *Faith is an unquestioning consent*; the definition of some that faith is a form of mental certitude that is greater than opinion, less than science—all these are equivalents of the words, *Faith is the evidence of things that appear not*. Dionysius's definition, *Faith is the abiding foundation of those who believe, putting them in the truth and showing forth the truth in them*, is equivalent to, *Faith is the substance of things to be hoped for*.

Hence: 1. 'Substance' is not used here in the sense in which it is the most general genus, distinguished against the other genera, but in the sense that a likeness to

substance exists in every genus, for example, in any genus we call that first member which virtually contains all other members their substance.

2. Because faith is present in the mind in so far as the mind is motivated by the will, it follows that faith is related as to its end to the objects of virtues perfective of the will. Among these, as will be shown, is hope, the object of which is accordingly mentioned in the definition of faith.

3. There can be love for both the seen and the unseen, the near and the distant. This is why things to be loved do not have such a close affinity to faith as do things to be hoped for, hope always being bent upon the distant and the unseen.

4. *Substance* and *evidence* as they are employed in defining faith do not imply different kinds of faith, nor different acts, but, as is clear from what we have said, different relationships of the one act to its several objects.

5. Evidence based on the proper principles of any being make it clearly manifest. Evidence based on divine authority, however, does not make a reality manifest in its own being. This is the kind of evidence touched on in the definition of faith.

172 **Ephesians 4:4–6** There is one body and one Spirit, just as you were called to the one hope that belongs to your call, one Lord, one faith, one baptism, one God and Father of us all, who is above all and through all and in all.

186 (1) **Romans 10:9** . . . because, if you confess with your lips that Jesus is Lord and believe in your heart that God raised him from the dead, you will be saved.

186 (2) **1 Corinthians 15:3–5** For I delivered to you as of first importance what I also received, that Christ died for our sins in accordance with the scriptures, that he was buried, that he was raised on the third day in accordance with the scriptures, and that he appeared to Cephas, then to the twelve.

191 **St. Ambrose, *Explanatio symboli ad initiandos* 11** As then there are twelve Apostles, so are there twelve pronouncements. Sign yourselves. *Which done*: I BELIEVE [in God the Father almighty, and in Jesus Christ his only Son our Lord, conceived by the Holy Ghost, born of Mary] THE VIRGIN. You have the Godhead of the Father, the Godhead of the Son; you have the incarnation of the Son, as I have said. [Suffered] UNDER [Pontius Pilate, dead and] BURIED. You have the passion and burial. Behold here four pronouncements: let us see others. THE THIRD DAY [he rose again, ascended into the heavens, sat at the right hand of God the Father, thence about to come to judge the living] AND THE DEAD. Behold four further pronouncements, that is now eight pronouncements. Let us see four others. [I believe] ALSO IN THE HOLY GHOST, [holy church, the communion of saints, the remission of sins,] THE RESURRECTION [of the flesh, the life everlasting. Amen]. Behold, answering to the twelve Apostles, twelve pronouncements comprised.

192 (1) **DS 1–64** [Editor's note: DS 1–64 contains texts of the Creed from a variety of ancient sources. In most cases there is no or only very minor variation. Only a selection is reproduced here.]

Most Ancient Forms of the Apostolic Creed: DS 1–2

The creed which is called Apostolic is composed essentially of (1) a Trinitarian part, three articles professing faith in three divine persons; (2) a Christological part which was added to the first section.

There are extant, however, certain formulae composed in the manner of creeds, but lacking the Christological part. These formulae seem to be more ancient than

the Apostolic Creed. An achristological formula of this kind—which seems to be the most ancient of all—exists in a work infected with Gnosticism written between the years 150 and 180, *Testamentum in Galilaea D.N.J. Christi* (or in an almost identical work *Gespräche Jesu mit seinem Jüngern nach der Auferstehung*) where the short Creed (reads):

"[I believe] in the Father almighty,—and in Jesus Christ, our Savior;—and in the Holy Spirit, the Paraclete, in the holy Church, and in the remission of sins."

Another achristological formula, perhaps already used in the liturgy of Egypt probably in the third century, is shown by a papyrus discovered in *Dêr-Balyzeh*, written in the seventh or eighth century (cf. *Dict. d'Archéol. chrét. et de Lit.* s.v. Canon, II, 2, 1882 ff.):

"I believe in God almighty;—and in his only-begotten Son, our Lord Jesus Christ; —and in the Holy Spirit and in the resurrection of the body <in> the holy Catholic Church."

The More Ancient Western Form of the Apostolic Creed [Called Roman (R)]: DS 11

[According to the Psalter of Rufinus (The Roman form)]

1. I believe in God, the Father almighty;
2. and in Christ Jesus, His only-begotten Son, our Lord,
3. who was born of the Holy Spirit and the Virgin Mary,
4a. was crucified by Pontius Pilate, and was buried;
b.
5. the third day He arose again from the dead;
6a. He ascended into heaven,
b. sits at the right hand of the Father,
7. whence He is coming to judge the living and the dead;
8. and in the Holy Spirit,
9a. the holy [Church,]
b.
10a.
b. the forgiveness of sins,
11. the resurrection of the body. Amen.

[According to the Psalter of Aethelstane]

1. I believe in God the Father almighty
2. and in Christ Jesus, His only begotten Son, our Lord
3. born of the Holy Spirit and Mary the virgin
4a. was crucified by Pontius Pilate and was buried
b.
5. the third day He arose again from the dead
6a. He ascended into heaven
b. sits at the right hand of the Father
7. whence He is coming to judge the living and the dead
8. and in the Holy Spirit
9a. the holy [Church]
10a.
b. the forgiveness of sins
11. the resurrection of the body. Amen.
12.

The More Recent Western Form of the Apostolic Creed: DS 30

[According to the Roman Order]

1a. I believe in God the Father almighty
b. creator of heaven and earth
2. and in Jesus Christ, His only son, our Lord
3. who was conceived of the Holy Spirit, born of the Virgin Mary
4a. suffered under Pontius Pilate, crucified, died, and was buried
b. descended into hell
5. on the third day He arose from the dead
6a. He ascended to heaven
b. sits at the right hand of God the Father Almighty
7. thence He shall come to judge the living and the dead
8. I believe in the Holy Spirit
9a. the holy Catholic Church
b. the communion of saints
10. the remission of sins
11. the resurrection of the body
12. and life everlasting.

The Eastern Form of the Apostolic Creed
[of Saint Cyril of Jerusalem]: DS 41

1a. We believe in one God the Father Almighty
b. The creator of heaven and earth
c. and of all things visible and invisible
2a. and in one Lord Jesus Christ the only begotten Son of God
b. who was begotten of the Father
c. true God
d. before all ages
e. by whom all things were made
3a. (who for our salvation)
b. was made flesh (of the Holy Spirit and Mary the virgin) and was made man
4a. was crucified (under Pontius Pilate) and was buried
b.
5a. arose on the third day
b. (according to the Scriptures)
6a. and ascended into heaven
b. and sits at the right hand of the Father
7a. and comes in glory to judge the living and the dead
b. of whose kingdom there will be no end
8a. and in one Holy Spirit the Paraclete
b.
c.
d.
e. who spoke among the prophets
9. and one holy [Catholic] church
10a. and in one baptism of repentance
b. in the dismissal of sins
11. and in the resurrection of the flesh
12. and in life everlasting

The Creed of Epiphanius
(Longer Form: Exposition of Nicene Creed proposed to certain catechumens in the Orient): DS 44–45

We believe in one God, the Father almighty, the creator of all things invisible and visible; and in one Lord Jesus Christ, the son of God, the only begotten born of God the Father, that is of the substance of the Father, God of God, light of light, true God of true God, begotten not made, consubstantial to the Father, by whom all things were made, both those in heaven and those on earth, both visible and invisible, who for us men and for our salvation came down and became man, that is, was completely born of holy Mary ever-virgin by the Holy Spirit, was made man, that is, assumed perfect human nature, soul and body and mind, and all whatever is man except sin, not from the seed of man nor by means of man, but having fashioned unto himself a body into one holy unity; not as he lived in the prophets and talked and worked in them, but became man completely ("for the word was made flesh," he did not submit to an alteration, nor did he change his own divine nature into human nature); he combined both the divine nature and the human into the only holy perfection of himself; (for there is one Lord Jesus Christ, and not two; the same God, the same Lord, the same King); but the same suffered in the flesh and arose again and ascended into heaven with the very body and sits in glory at the right hand of the Father, in that very body he is coming in glory to judge the living and the dead; of whose kingdom there shall be no end:—and we believe in the Holy Spirit who spoke in the law, and taught by the prophets, and descended to the Jordan, spoke by the Apostles, and lives in the saints; thus we believe in him: that he is the Holy Spirit, the Spirit of God, the perfect Spirit, the Spirit Paraclete, uncreated, proceeding from the Father and receiving of the Son, in whom we believe.

We believe in one catholic and apostolic Church, and in one baptism of repentance, and in the resurrection of the dead, and the just judgment of souls and bodies, and in the kingdom of heaven, and in life eternal.

But those who say that there was a time when the Son or the Holy Spirit was not, that he was made from nothing or is of another substance or essence, alleging that the Son of God or the Holy Spirit was changed or altered, these the catholic and apostolic Church, your mother and our mother, anathematizes. We also anathematize those who do not confess the resurrection of the dead, and besides all the heresies which are not consistent with this true faith.

(2) **DS 75–76** 192

The Creed "Quicumque"
[Which is called "Athanasian"]

Whoever wishes to be saved, needs above all to hold the Catholic faith; unless each one preserves this whole and inviolate, he will without a doubt perish in eternity.—But the Catholic faith is this, that we venerate one God in the Trinity, and the Trinity in oneness; neither confounding the persons, nor dividing the substance; for there is one person of the Father, another of the Son, (and) another of the Holy Spirit; but the divine nature of the Father and of the Son and of the Holy Spirit is one, their glory is equal, their majesty is coeternal. Of such a nature as the Father is, so is the Son, so (also) is the Holy Spirit; the Father is uncreated, the Son is uncreated, (and) the Holy Spirit is uncreated; the Father is immense, the Son is immense, (and) the Holy Spirit is immense; the Father is eternal, the Son is eternal, (and) the Holy Spirit is eternal: and nevertheless there are not three eternals, but one eternal; just as there are not three uncreated beings, nor three infinite beings, but one uncreated, and one infinite; similarly the Father is omnipotent, the Son is omnipotent, (and) the Holy

Spirit is omnipotent: and yet there are not three omnipotents, but one omnipotent; thus the Father is God, the Son is God, (and) the Holy Spirit is God; and nevertheless there are not three gods, but there is one God; so the Father is Lord, the Son is Lord, (and) the Holy Spirit is Lord: and yet there are not three lords, but there is one Lord; because just as we are compelled by Christian truth to confess singly each one person as God and [and also] Lord, so we are forbidden by the Catholic religion to say there are three gods or lords. The Father was not made nor created nor begotten by anyone. The Son is from the Father alone, not made nor created, but begotten. The Holy Spirit is from the Father and the Son, not made nor created nor begotten, but proceeding. There is therefore one Father, not three Fathers; one Son, not three Sons; one Holy Spirit, not three Holy Spirits; and in this Trinity there is nothing first or later, nothing greater or less, but all three persons are coeternal and coequal with one another, so that in every respect, as has already been said above, both unity in Trinity, and Trinity in unity must be venerated. Therefore let him who wishes to be saved, think thus concerning the Trinity.

But it is necessary for eternal salvation that he faithfully believe also the incarnation of our Lord Jesus Christ. Accordingly it is the right faith, that we believe and confess, that our Lord Jesus Christ, the Son of God is God and man. He is God begotten of the substance of the Father before time, and he is man born of the substance of his mother in time: perfect God, perfect man, consisting of a rational soul and a human body, equal to the Father according to his Godhead, less than the Father according to humanity. Although he is God and man, yet he is not two, but he is one Christ; one, however, not by the conversion of the Divinity into a human body, but by the assumption of humanity in the Godhead; one absolutely not by confusion of substance, but by unity of person. For just as the rational soul and body are one man, so God and man are one Christ. He suffered for our salvation, descended into hell, on the third day arose again from the dead, ascended to heaven, sits at the right hand of God the Father almighty; thence he shall come to judge the living and the dead; at his coming all men have to arise again with their bodies and will render an account of their own deeds: and those who have done good, will go into life everlasting, but those who have done evil, into eternal fire.—This is the Catholic faith; unless every one believes this faithfully and firmly, he cannot be saved.

192 (3) **Council of Toledo XI (675): DS 525–41** [*The Trinity*] We confess and believe the holy and ineffable Trinity, the Father, and the Son, and the Holy Spirit, one God naturally, to be of one substance, one nature, and also of one majesty and power. And we profess that the Father, indeed, is not begotten, not created but unbegotten. For He from whom both the Son received His nativity and the Holy Spirit His procession takes His origin from no one. Therefore, He is the source and origin of all Godhead; also is the Father Himself of His own essence, He who ineffably begot the Son [Another version: Father, essence indeed ineffable, Son of His own substance] from an ineffable substance; nor did He, however, beget other than what He Himself is: God God, light light, from Him, therefore, is *all paternity in heaven and on earth* [Eph. 3:15].—We confess also that the Son was born, but not made, from the substance of the Father without beginning before all ages, because neither the Father without the Son, nor the Son without the Father ever at any time existed. And yet not as the Son from the Father, so the Father from the Son, because the Father did not receive generation from the Son, but the Son from the Father. The Son, therefore, is God from the Father; the Father, however, is God, but not from the Son; Father indeed of the Son, not God from the Son. He, however, is Son of the Father and God from the Father. However, the Son is equal in all things to God the Father, because at no time did He either begin or cease to be born. We believe

that He is of one substance with the Father, and because of this we say that He is ὁμοούσιος to the Father, that is, of the same substance with the Father, for ὅμος in Greek means one, οὐσία means substance, and the two joined together mean "one substance." For, neither from nothing, nor from any other substance, but from the womb of the Father, that is, from His substance, we must believe that the Son was begotten or born. Therefore, the Father is eternal, and the Son is eternal. But if He always was Father, He always had a Son to whom He was Father; and by reason of this we confess that the Son was born of the Father without beginning. Neither do we call the same Son of God a part of a divided nature because of the fact that He is begotten of the Father; but we assert that the perfect Father begot the perfect Son without diminution or division, because it is a characteristic of Divinity alone not to have an unequal Son. Also, this Son is Son of God by nature, not by adoption, whom we must believe God the Father begot neither by will nor by necessity; for, neither does any necessity happen [*al. capit*, 'take hold'] in God, nor does will precede wisdom.—We believe also that the Holy Spirit, who is the third person in the Trinity, is God, one and equal with God the Father and the Son, of one substance, also of one nature; that He is the Spirit of both, not, however, begotten nor created but proceeding from both. We believe also that this Holy Spirit is neither unbegotten nor begotten, lest if we say unbegotten, we should affirm two Fathers, or if begotten, we should be proven to declare two Sons; He is said to be the Spirit, however, not only of the Father but at the same time of the Father and the Son. For, neither does He proceed from the Father into the Son, nor does He proceed from the Son to sanctify the creature, but He is shown to have proceeded at the same time from both, because He is acknowledged to be the love or holiness of both. Therefore, we believe that this Holy Spirit was sent by both, as the Son was sent by the Father; but He is not considered less than the Father and the Son, as the Son, on account of the body He assumed, testifies that He Himself is less than the Father and the Holy Spirit.

This is the account of the Holy Trinity that has been handed down. We must call and believe it to be not triple but triune. Neither can we rightly say that in one God is the Trinity, but that one God is the Trinity. In the relative names of persons, however, the Father refers to the Son, the Son to the Father, and the Holy Spirit to both, in that while relatively three persons are asserted, we yet believe they are one nature or substance. Neither as three persons, so do we predicate three substances, but one substance, however three persons. For, as He is Father, not to Himself, but to the Son; and as He is Son not to Himself but to the Father, similarly also the Holy Spirit refers in a relative sense not to Himself, but to the Father and to the Son, in that He is proclaimed the Spirit of the Father and the Son.—Likewise when we say "God," no relationship is expressed, as the Father to the Son, or the Son to the Father, or the Holy Ghost to the Father and the Son, but God applies especially to Himself. For, if we are asked concerning the individual persons, we must confess that each is God. Therefore, we say that the Father is God, the Son is God, and the Holy Spirit is God each singly; yet there are not three Gods, but there is one God. Likewise also we say that the Father is omnipotent, the Son is omnipotent, and the Holy Spirit is omnipotent, each singly; not, however, three omnipotent Gods, but one omnipotent God, as also we predicate one light and one principle. We confess and believe, therefore, that singly each person is wholly God and that all three persons are one God; they have one indivisible and equal Godhead, majesty or power, neither is it lessened in the single person, nor increased in the three persons, because it does not have anything less when each person of God is spoken of singly, nor more when all three persons are called one God.—Therefore, this Holy Trinity, which is the one and true God, neither excludes number nor is it contained in number.—For in the relation of persons number appears, but in the substance of divinity, what might be enumerated is not understood. Therefore, in this alone they imply number, that they are related to each other; and in this, that they are to themselves, they lack number. For natural unity is so suitable to this Holy Trinity that there cannot be a plurality in the three persons. For this reason, then, we believe that saying in Sacred Scripture: "Great is our Lord and great is his power; and of his Wisdom there is no number" [Ps. 146:5]. Neither because we have said that these three persons are one God, are we able to say that the same one is the Father who is the Son, or that He is the Son who is the Father, or that He who is the Holy Spirit is either the Father or the Son. For He is not the Father who is the Son, nor is He the Son who is the Father, nor is the Holy Spirit He who is either the Father or the Son, even though the Father is the same as the Son, the Son the same as the Father, the Father and the Son the same as the Holy Spirit; that is, in nature one God. For, when we say that the same one is not the Father as the Son, we refer to the distinction of persons. When, however, we say that the Father is the same as the Son, the Son the same as the Father, the Holy Spirit the same as the Father and the Son, it is plain that the reference is to the nature or substance by which He is God, because in substance they are one; for we are distinguishing persons, we are not dividing the Deity.—We acknowledge, therefore, the Trinity in a distinction of persons; we profess unity on account of the nature or substance. Therefore, the three are one, that is, in nature, not in person. We must not, however, consider these three persons separable, since we believe that no one before the other, no one after the other, no one without the other ever existed or did anything. For, they are found inseparable both in that which they are, and in that which they do, because between the generating Father and the generated Son and the proceeding Holy Spirit we believe that there was no interval of time in which either the begetter at any time preceded the begotten, or the begotten was lacking to the begetter, or the proceeding Holy Spirit appeared after the Father or the Son. Therefore, for this reason we proclaim and believe that this Trinity is inseparable and unconfused. These three, therefore, are called persons, as our ancestors define, that they may be recognized, not that they may be separated. For, if we give attention to that which Holy Scripture says of Wisdom: "She is the brightness of eternal light" [Wisd. 7:26], as we see the splendor inhering inseparably in light, so we confess that the Son cannot be separated from the Father. Therefore, just as we do not confuse these three persons of one and inseparable nature, so do we in nowise declare them separable. Since, indeed, the Trinity itself has so deigned to show this clearly to us that even in these names by which it wished the persons to be recognized singly, it does not permit one to be understood without the other; for neither is the Father recognized without the Son, nor is the Son found without the Father. Indeed, the very relation of personal designation forbids the persons to be separated, whom, even when it does not name them together, it implies together. Moreover, no one can hear anyone of those names without being constrained to think also of another. Since, then, these three are one and the one three, there is yet remaining to each person His own property. For the Father has eternity without nativity, the Son eternity with nativity, and the Holy Spirit procession without nativity with eternity.

[*The Incarnation*] Of these three persons we believe that for the liberation of the human race only the person of the Son became true man without sin from the holy and immaculate Virgin Mary, from whom He is begotten in a new manner and by a new birth; in a new manner, because invisible in divinity, He became visible in flesh; by a new birth, however, is He begotten, because inviolate virginity without the experience of sexual intercourse supplied the material of human flesh made fruitful by the Holy Spirit. This Virgin birth is neither grasped by reason nor illustrated by example, because if grasped by reason, it is not miraculous; if illustrated by example, it will not be unique. Yet we must not believe that the Holy Spirit is Father of the

Son, because of the fact that Mary conceived by the overshadowing of the same Holy Spirit, lest we seem to assert that there are two Fathers of the Son, which is certainly impious to say.—In this marvelous conception, with Wisdom building a house for herself, *the Word was made flesh and dwelt among us* [John 1:14]. The Word itself, however, was not so converted and changed that He who willed to become man ceased to be God; but the *Word was made flesh* in such a way that not only are the Word of God and the flesh of man present, but also the soul of a rational man, and this whole is called God on account of God, and man on account of man. In this Son of God we believe there are two natures, one of divinity, the other of humanity, which the one person of Christ so united in Himself that the divinity can never be separated from the humanity, nor the humanity from the divinity. Christ, therefore, is perfect God and perfect man in the unity of one person; but it does not follow, because we have asserted two natures in the Son, that there are two persons in Him, lest—which God forbid—a quaternity be predicated of the Trinity. For God the Word has not received the person of man, but the nature, and to the eternal person of divinity He has united the temporal substance of flesh.—Likewise we believe that the Father, the Son, and the Holy Spirit are of one substance, but we do not say that the Virgin Mary gave birth to the unity of the Trinity, but only to the Son, who alone assumed our nature in the unity of His person. Also, we must believe that the entire Trinity accomplished the Incarnation of the Son of God, because the works of the Trinity are inseparable. However, only the Son *took the form of a servant* [cf. Phil. 2:7] in the singleness of His person, not in the unity of His divine nature; in what is proper to the Son, not in what is common to the Trinity; and this form was adapted to Him for unity of person so that the Son of God and the Son of man is one Christ, that is, Christ in these two natures exists in three substances; of the Word, which must refer to the essence of God alone, of the body, and of the soul, which pertain to true man.

He has, therefore, in Himself the twofold substance of His divinity and our humanity. We understand, however, that by the fact that He proceeded from God the Father without beginning, He was born only, for He was neither made nor predestined; by the fact, however, that He was born of the Virgin Mary, we must believe that He was born, made, and predestined. Yet both births in Him are marvelous, because He was both begotten by the Father without a mother before all ages and in the end of the ages He was born of a mother without a father; He who, however, according as He is God created Mary, according as He is man was created from Mary; He is both father and son of His mother Mary. Likewise by the fact that He is God, He is equal to the Father; by the fact that He is man, He is less than the Father. Likewise we must believe that He is both greater and less than Himself; for in the form of God even the Son Himself is greater than Himself on account of the humanity He assumed, than which the divinity is greater; in the form, however, of a servant He is less than Himself, that is, in His humanity, which is recognized as less than His divinity. For, as by reason of the body which He assumed He is believed to be not only less than the Father but also less than Himself, so according to His divinity He is coequal with the Father, and both He and the Father are greater than man, which the person of the Son alone assumed. Likewise to the question whether the Son could so be equal to and less than the Holy Spirit, as we believe that He is now equal to, now less than the Father, we reply: According to the form of God He is equal to the Father and to the Holy Spirit, according to the form of a servant, He is less than both the Father and the Holy Spirit; because neither the Holy Spirit nor the Father, but only the person of the Son assumed a body, by which He is believed to be less than those two persons. Likewise we believe that this Son, inseparable from God the Father and the Holy Spirit, is distinguished from them by His person, and distinguished from other men by the nature He assumed [another version, from the manhood assumed]. Likewise with reference to man it is His person that is preeminent; but with reference to the Father and the Holy Spirit it is the divine nature or substance. Yet we must believe that the Son was sent not only by the Father but also by the Holy Spirit; because He himself said through the prophet *And now the Lord has sent me and His Holy Spirit* [Isa. 48:16]. We believe also that He was sent by Himself, because we acknowledge that not only the will but also the works of the whole Trinity are inseparable. For, He who before all ages was called the only begotten, in time became the first born; the only begotten on account of the substance of the Godhead, the first born on account of the nature of the body which He assumed.

[*The Redemption*] In this form of assumed human nature we believe according to the truth of the Gospels that He was conceived without sin, born without sin, and died without sin, who alone *for us became sin* [II Cor. 5:21], that is, a sacrifice for our sin. And yet He endured His passion without detriment to His divinity, for our sins, and condemned to death and to the cross, He accepted the true death of the body; also on the third day, restored by His own power, He arose from the grave.

In this example, therefore, of our Head we confess is accomplished [another version: with true faith] the true resurrection of the body of all the dead. Neither do we believe that we shall rise in an ethereal or any other body (as some madly say) but in that in which we live and exist and move. When this example of His holy resurrection was finished, our same Lord and Savior returned by ascending to His paternal home, which in His divinity He had never left. There sitting at the right hand of the Father, He awaits the end of time to be the judge of all the living and the dead. Thence with the holy angels and men He will come to judge, and to render to everyone the due of his own reward, according *as each one* living in the body *has done good or evil* [II Cor. 5:10]. We believe that the holy Catholic Church, purchased by the price of His blood, will reign with Him for eternity. Established in her bosom we believe in and confess one baptism for the remission of all sins. In this faith we both truly believe in the resurrection of the dead and we await the joys of the future life. We must pray and beg for this only, that when, the judgment finished and over, the Son *will hand over the kingdom to God the Father* [I Cor. 15:24], that He may render us participators of His kingdom, so that through this faith in which we cling to Him, we may reign with Him without end.—This exposition is the pledge of our confession through which the teaching of all heretics is destroyed, through which the hearts of the faithful are cleansed, through which also we ascend gloriously to God for all eternity. Amen.

192 (4) **Lateran Council IV (1215): DS 800–802** Firmly we believe and we confess simply that the true God is one alone, eternal, immense, and unchangeable, incomprehensible, omnipotent and ineffable, *Father and Son and Holy Spirit*: indeed three Persons but one essence, substance, or nature entirely simple. The Father from no one, the Son from the Father only, and the Holy Spirit equally from both; without beginning, always, and without end; the Father generating, the Son being born, and the Holy Spirit proceeding; consubstantial and coequal and omnipotent and coeternal; one beginning of all, creator of all visible and invisible things, of the spiritual and of the corporal; who by His own omnipotent power at once from the beginning of time created each creature from nothing, spiritual, and corporal, namely, angelic and mundane, and finally the human, constituted as it were, alike of the spirit and the body. For the devil and other demons were created by God good in nature, but they themselves through themselves have become wicked. But man sinned at the suggestion of the devil. This Holy Trinity according to common essence undivided, and according to personal properties distinct, granted the doctrine of salvation to the human race, first through Moses and the holy prophets and his other servants according to the most methodical disposition of the time.

And finally the only begotten Son of God, Jesus Christ, incarnate by the whole Trinity in common, conceived of Mary ever Virgin with the Holy Spirit cooperating, made true man, formed of a rational soul and human flesh, one Person in two natures, clearly pointed out the way of life. And although He according to divinity is immortal and impassible, the very same according to humanity was made passible and mortal, who, for the salvation of the human race, having suffered on the wood of the Cross and died, descended into hell, arose from the dead and ascended into heaven. But He descended in soul, and He arose in the flesh, and He ascended equally in both, to come at the end of time, to judge the living and the dead, and to render to each according to his works, to the wicked as well as to the elect, all of whom will rise with their bodies which they now bear, that they may receive according to their works, whether these works have been good or evil, the latter everlasting punishment with the devil, and the former everlasting glory with Christ.

One indeed is the universal Church of the faithful, outside which no one at all is saved, in which the priest himself is the sacrifice, Jesus Christ, whose body and blood are truly contained in the sacrament of the altar under the species of bread and wine; the bread (changed) into His body by the divine power of transubstantiation, and the wine into the blood, so that to accomplish the mystery of unity we ourselves receive from His (nature) what He Himself received from ours. And surely no one can accomplish this sacrament except a priest who has been rightly ordained according to the keys of the Church which Jesus Christ Himself conceded to the Apostles and to their successors. But the sacrament of baptism (which at the invocation of God and the indivisible Trinity, namely, of the Father and of the Son and of the Holy Spirit, is solemnized in water) rightly conferred by anyone in the form of the Church is useful unto salvation for little ones and for adults. And if, after the reception of baptism, anyone shall have lapsed into sin, through true penance he can always be restored. Moreover, not only virgins and the continent but also married persons pleasing to God through right faith and good work merit to arrive at a blessed eternity.

(5) **Council of Lyons II (1274): DS 851–61** 192

Profession of Faith of Michael Palaeologus

We believe that the Holy Trinity, the Father, and the Son, and the Holy Spirit, is one God omnipotent and entire Deity in the Trinity, coessential and consubstantial, coeternal and co-omnipotent, of one will, power, and majesty, the creator of all creatures, from whom are all things, in whom are all things, through whom all things which are in the heavens and on the earth, visible, invisible, corporal, and spiritual. We believe that each individual Person in the Trinity is one true God, complete and perfect.

We believe that the same Son of God, the Word of God, is eternally born from the Father, consubstantial, co-omnipotent, and equal through all things to the Father in divinity, temporally born from the Holy Spirit and Mary ever Virgin with a rational soul; having two births, one eternal birth from the Father, the other temporal from the mother; true God and true man, proper and perfect in each nature, not adopted nor phantastic, but the one and only Son of God, in two and from two natures, that is divine and human, in the singleness of one person impassible and immortal in divinity, but in humanity for us and for our salvation having suffered in the true passion of the flesh, died, and was buried, descended to hell, and on the third day arose again from the dead in the true resurrection of the flesh, on the fortieth day after the resurrection with the flesh in which He arose and with His soul ascended into heaven and sits at the right hand of God the Father, whence He will come to judge the living and the dead, and will return to each one according to his works whether they were good or evil.

We believe also that the Holy Spirit is complete and perfect and true God, proceeding from the Father and the Son, coequal and consubstantial, co-omnipotent, and coeternal through all things with the Father and the Son. We believe that this holy Trinity is not three Gods but one God, omnipotent, eternal, invisible, and unchangeable.

Variant Readings

We believe that the true Church is holy, Catholic, apostolic, and one, in which is given one holy baptism and true remission of all sins. We believe also in the true resurrection of this flesh, which now we bear, and in eternal life. We believe also that the one author of the New and the Old Testament, of the Law, and of the Prophets and the Apostles is the omnipotent God and Lord. This is the true Catholic Faith, and this in the above mentioned articles the most holy Roman Church holds and teaches. But because of diverse errors introduced by some through ignorance and by others from evil, it (the Church) says and teaches that those who after baptism slip into sin must not be rebaptized, but by true penance attain forgiveness of their sins. Because if they die truly repentant in charity before they have made satisfaction by worthy fruits of penance for (sins) committed and omitted, their souls are cleansed after death by purgatorical or purifying punishments, as Brother John [Parastron] has explained to us. And to relieve punishments of this kind, the offerings of the living faithful are of advantage to these, namely, the sacrifices of Masses, prayers, alms, and other duties of piety, which have customarily been performed by the faithful for the other faithful according to the regulations of the Church. However, the souls of those who after having received holy baptism have incurred no stain of sin whatever, also those souls who, after contracting the stain of sin, either while remaining in their bodies or being divested of them, have been cleansed, as we have said above, are received immediately into heaven. The souls of those who die in mortal sin or with original sin only, however, immediately descend to hell, yet to be punished with different punishments. The same most holy Roman Church firmly believes and firmly declares that nevertheless on the day of judgment "all" men will be brought together with their bodies "before the tribunal of Christ" "to render an account" of their own deeds [Rom. 14:10].

The same holy Roman Church also holds and teaches that the ecclesiastical sacraments are seven: namely, one is baptism, concerning which we have spoken above; another is the sacrament of confirmation which the bishops confer through the imposition of hands when anointing the reborn; another is penance; another the Eucharist; another the sacrament of orders; another is matrimony; another extreme unction, which according to the doctrine of St. James is given to the sick. The same Roman Church prepares the sacrament of the Eucharist from unleavened bread, holding and teaching that in the same sacrament the bread is changed into the body, and the wine into the blood of Jesus Christ. But concerning matrimony it holds that neither one man is permitted to have many wives nor one woman many husbands at the same time. But she (the Church) says that second and third marriages successively are permissible for one freed from a legitimate marriage through the death of the other party, if another canonical impediment for some reason is not an obstacle.

Also this same holy Roman Church holds the highest and complete primacy and spiritual power over the universal Catholic Church which she truly and humbly recognizes herself to have received with fullness of power from the Lord Himself in Blessed Peter, the chief or head of the Apostles whose successor is the Roman Pontiff. And just as to defend the truth of Faith she is held before all other things, so if any questions shall arise regarding faith they ought to be defined by her judgment. And to her anyone burdened with affairs pertaining to the ecclesiastical world can appeal; and in all cases looking forward to an ecclesiastical examination, recourse can be had to her judgment, and all churches are subject to her; their prelates give obedience and reverence to her. In her, moreover, such a plentitude of power rests that she receives the other churches to a share of her solicitude, of which many patriarchal churches the same Roman Church has honored in a special way by different privileges—its own prerogative always being observed and preserved both in general Councils and in other places.

(6) **Council of Trent (1565): DS 1862–70** 192

Profession of Faith
[from the Bull of Pius IV, *Iniunctum nobis*]

I, N., with firm faith believe and profess all and everything which is contained in the creed of faith, which the holy Roman Church uses, namely: I believe in one God the Father Almighty, creator of heaven and earth, of all things visible and invisible; and in one Lord Jesus Christ, the only-begotten Son of God, and born of the Father before all ages, God of God, light of light, true God of true God, begotten not made, consubstantial with the Father, by whom all things were made; who for us men and for our salvation descended from heaven, and became incarnate by the Holy Spirit of the Virgin Mary, and was made man; he was also crucified for us under Pontius Pilate, suffered and was buried; and he rose on the third day according to the Scriptures, and ascended into heaven; he sitteth at the right hand of the Father, and will come again with glory to judge the living and the dead, of whose kingdom there shall be no end; and in the Holy Spirit, the Lord and giver of life, who proceeds from the Father and the Son; who together with the Father and the Son is adored and glorified; who spoke through the prophets; and in one holy Catholic and apostolic Church. I confess one baptism for the remission of sins, and I await the resurrection of the dead, and the life of the world to come. Amen.

The apostolic and ecclesiastical traditions and all other observances and constitutions of that same Church I most firmly admit and embrace. I likewise accept Holy Scripture according to that sense which our holy Mother Church has held and does hold, whose [office] it is to judge of the true meaning and interpretation of the Sacred Scriptures; I shall never accept nor interpret it otherwise than in accordance with the unanimous consent of the Fathers.

I also profess that there are truly and properly seven sacraments of the New Law instituted by Jesus Christ our Lord, and necessary for the salvation of mankind, although not all are necessary for each individual; these sacraments are baptism, confirmation, the Eucharist, penance, extreme unction, order, and matrimony; and [I profess] that they confer grace, and that of these baptism, confirmation, and order cannot be repeated without sacrilege. I also receive and admit the accepted and approved rites of the Catholic Church in the solemn administration of all the aforesaid sacraments. I embrace and accept each and everything that has been defined and declared by the holy Synod of Trent concerning original sin and justification.

I also profess that in the Mass there is offered to God a true, proper sacrifice of propitiation for the living and the dead, and that in the most holy sacrament of the Eucharist there is truly, really, and substantially present the body and blood together with the soul and the divinity of our Lord Jesus Christ, and that there takes place a conversion of the whole substance of bread into the body, and of the whole substance of the wine into the blood; and this conversion the Catholic Church calls transubstantiation. I also acknowledge that under one species alone the whole and entire Christ and the true sacrament are taken.

I steadfastly hold that a purgatory exists, and that the souls there detained are aided by the prayers of the faithful; likewise that the saints reigning together with Christ should be venerated and invoked, and that they offer prayers to God for us, and that their relics should be venerated. I firmly assert that the images of Christ and of the Mother of God ever Virgin, and also of the other saints should be kept and retained, and that due honor and veneration should be paid to them; I also affirm that the power of indulgences has been left in the Church by Christ, and that the use of them is especially salutary for the Christian people.

I acknowledge the holy Catholic and apostolic Roman Church as the mother and teacher of all churches; and to the Roman Pontiff, the successor of the blessed Peter, chief of the Apostles and vicar of Jesus Christ, I promise and swear true obedience.

Also all other things taught, defined, and declared by the sacred canons and ecumenical Councils, and especially by the sacred and holy Synod of Trent, (and by the ecumenical Council of the Vatican, particularly concerning the primacy of the Roman Pontiff and his infallible teaching), I without hesitation accept and profess; and at the same time all things contrary thereto, and whatever heresies have been condemned, and rejected, and anathematized by the Church, I likewise condemn, reject, and anathematize. This true Catholic faith, outside of which no one can be saved, (and) which of my own accord I now profess and truly hold, I, N., do promise, vow, and swear that I will, with the help of God, most faithfully retain and profess the same to the last breath of life as pure and inviolable, and that I will take care as far as lies in my power that it be held, taught, and preached by my subjects or by those over whom by virtue of my office I have charge, so help me God, and these holy Gospels of God.

192 (7) ***Fides Damasi*: DS 71–72** We believe in one God the Father almighty and in our one Lord Jesus Christ the Son of God and in (one) Holy Spirit God. Not three Gods, but Father and Son and Holy Spirit one God do we worship and confess: not one God in such a way as to be solitary, nor the same in such wise that he himself is Father to himself and he himself is Son to himself; but the Father is he who begot, and the Son is he who is begotten; the Holy Spirit in truth is neither begotten nor unbegotten, neither created nor made, but proceeding from the Father and the Son, coeternal and coequal and the cooperator with the Father and the Son, because it is written: "*By the word of the Lord the heavens were established*" (that is, by the Son of God), "*and all the power of them by the spirit of his mouth*" [Ps. 32:6], and elsewhere: "*Send forth thy spirit and they shall be created and thou shalt renew the face of the earth*" [Ps. 103:30]. And therefore we confess one God in the name of the Father and of the Son and of the Holy Spirit, because god is the name of power, not of peculiarity. The proper name for the Father is Father, and the proper name for the Son is Son, and the proper name for the Holy Spirit is Holy Spirit. And in this Trinity we believe in one God, because what is of one nature and of one substance and of one power with the Father is from one Father. The Father begot the Son, not by will, nor by necessity, but by nature.

The Son in the fullness of time came down from the Father to save us and to fulfill the Scriptures, though he never ceased to be with the Father, and was conceived by the Holy Spirit and born of the Virgin Mary; he took a body, soul, and sense, that is, he assumed perfect human nature; nor did he lose, what he was, but he began to be, what he was not; in such a way, however, that he is perfect in his own nature and true in our nature.

For he who was God, was born a man, and he who was born a man, operates as

God; and he who operates as God, dies as a man; and he who dies as a man, arises as God. He having conquered the power of death with that body, with which he was born, and suffered, and had died, arose on the third day, ascended to the Father, and sits at his right hand in glory, which he always has had and always has. We believe that cleansed in his death and in his blood we are to be raised up by him on the last day in this body with which we now live; and we have hope that we shall obtain from him either life eternal, the reward of good merit or the penalty of eternal punishment for sins. Read these words, keep them, subject your soul to this faith. From Christ the Lord you will receive both life and reward.

Isaiah 44:6 198
Thus says the Lord, the King of Israel
and his Redeemer, the Lord of hosts:
"I am the first and I am the last;
besides me there is no god. . . ."

Philippians 2:10–11 . . . that at the name of Jesus every knee should bow, in heaven 201
and on earth and under the earth, and every tongue confess that Jesus Christ is Lord,
to the glory of God the Father.

Mark 12:35–37 And as Jesus taught in the temple, he said, "How can the scribes 202
say that the Christ is the son of David? David himself, inspired by the Holy Spirit,
declared,
'The Lord said to my Lord,
Sit at my right hand,
till I put thy enemies under thy feet.'
David himself calls him Lord; so how is he his son?" And the great throng heard him gladly.

(1) **Isaiah 45:15** 206
Truly, thou art a God who hidest thyself,
O God of Israel, the Savior.

(2) **Judges 13:18** And the angel of the Lord said to him, "Why do you ask my name, 206
seeing it is wonderful?"

Exodus 3:5–6 Then he said, "Do not come near; put off your shoes from your feet, 208
for the place on which you are standing is holy ground." And he said, "I am the God of your father, the God of Abraham, the God of Isaac, and the God of Jacob." And Moses hid his face, for he was afraid to look at God.

(1) **Exodus 32** When the people saw that Moses delayed to come down from the 210
mountain, the people gathered themselves together to Aaron, and said to him, "Up, make us gods, who shall go before us; as for this Moses, the man who brought us up out of the land of Egypt, we do not know what has become of him." And Aaron said to them, "Take off the rings of gold which are in the ears of your wives, your sons, and your daughters, and bring them to me." So all the people took off the rings of gold which were in their ears, and brought them to Aaron. And he received the gold at their hand, and fashioned it with a graving tool, and made a molten calf; and they said, "These are your gods, O Israel, who brought you up out of the land of Egypt!" When Aaron saw this, he built an altar before it; and Aaron made proclamation and said, "Tomorrow shall be a feast to the Lord." And they rose up early on the morrow,

and offered burnt offerings and brought peace offerings; and the people sat down to eat and drink, and rose up to play.

And the Lord said to Moses, "Go down; for your people, whom you brought up out of the land of Egypt, have corrupted themselves; they have turned aside quickly out of the way which I commanded them; they have made for themselves a molten calf, and have worshiped it and sacrificed to it, and said, 'These are your gods, O Israel, who brought you up out of the land of Egypt!'" And the Lord said to Moses, "I have seen this people, and behold, it is a stiff-necked people; now therefore let me alone, that my wrath may burn hot against them and I may consume them; but of you I will make a great nation."

But Moses besought the Lord his God, and said, "O Lord, why does thy wrath burn hot against thy people, whom thou hast brought forth out of the land of Egypt with great power and with a mighty hand? Why should the Egyptians say, 'With evil intent did he bring them forth, to slay them in the mountains, and to consume them from the face of the earth'? Turn from thy fierce wrath, and repent of this evil against thy people. Remember Abraham, Isaac, and Israel, thy servants, to whom thou didst swear by thine own self, and didst say to them, 'I will multiply your descendants as the stars of heaven, and all this land that I have promised I will give to your descendants, and they shall inherit it for ever.'" And the Lord repented of the evil which he thought to do to his people.

And Moses turned, and went down from the mountain with the two tables of the testimony in his hands, tables that were written on both sides; on the one side and on the other were they written. And the tables were the work of God, and the writing was the writing of God, graven upon the tables. When Joshua heard the noise of the people as they shouted, he said to Moses, "There is a noise of war in the camp." But he said, "It is not the sound of shouting for victory, or the sound of the cry of defeat, but the sound of singing that I hear." And as soon as he came near the camp and saw the calf and the dancing, Moses' anger burned hot, and he threw the tables out of his hands and broke them at the foot of the mountain. And he took the calf which they had made, and burnt it with fire, and ground it to powder, and scattered it upon the water, and made the people of Israel drink it.

And Moses said to Aaron, "What did this people do to you that you have brought a great sin upon them?" And Aaron said, "Let not the anger of my lord burn hot; you know the people, that they are set on evil. For they said to me, 'Make us gods, who shall go before us; as for this Moses, the man who brought us up out of the land of Egypt, we do not know what has become of him.' And I said to them, 'Let any who have gold take it off'; so they gave it to me, and I threw it into the fire, and there came out this calf."

And when Moses saw that the people had broken loose (for Aaron had let them break loose, to their shame among their enemies), then Moses stood in the gate of the camp, and said, "Who is on the Lord's side? Come to me." And all the sons of Levi gathered themselves together to him. And he said to them, "Thus says the Lord God of Israel, 'Put every man his sword on his side, and go to and fro from gate to gate throughout the camp, and slay every man his brother, and every man his companion, and every man his neighbor.'" And the sons of Levi did according to the word of Moses; and there fell of the people that day about three thousand men. And Moses said, "Today you have ordained yourselves for the service of the Lord, each one at the cost of his son and of his brother, that he may bestow a blessing upon you this day."

On the morrow Moses said to the people, "You have sinned a great sin. And now I will go up to the Lord; perhaps I can make atonement for your sin." So Moses returned to the Lord and said, "Alas, this people have sinned a great sin; they have made for themselves gods of gold. But now, if thou wilt forgive their sin—and if not, blot me, I pray thee, out of thy book which thou hast written." But the Lord said to Moses, "Whoever has sinned against me, him will I blot out of my book. But now go, lead the people to the place of which I have spoken to you; behold, my angel shall go before you. Nevertheless, in the day when I visit, I will visit their sin upon them."

And the Lord sent a plague upon the people, because they made the calf which Aaron made.

(2) **Exodus 33:12–17** Moses said to the Lord, "See, thou sayest to me, 'Bring up **210**
this people'; but thou hast not let me know whom thou wilt send with me. Yet thou hast said, 'I know you by name, and you have also found favor in my sight.' Now therefore, I pray thee, if I have found favor in thy sight, show me now thy ways, that I may know thee and find favor in thy sight. Consider too that this nation is thy people." And he said, "My presence will go with you, and I will give you rest." And he said to him, "If thy presence will not go with me, do not carry us up from here. For how shall it be known that I have found favor in thy sight, I and thy people? Is it not in thy going with us, so that we are distinct, I and thy people, from all other people that are upon the face of the earth?"

And the Lord said to Moses, "This very thing that you have spoken I will do; for you have found favor in my sight, and I know you by name."

(3) **Exodus 34:9** And he said, "If now I have found favor in thy sight, O Lord, let **210**
the Lord, I pray thee, go in the midst of us, although it is a stiff-necked people; and pardon our iniquity and our sin, and take us for thy inheritance."

Isaiah 44:6 **212**

Thus says the Lord, the King of Israel
    and his Redeemer, the Lord of hosts:
"I am the first and I am the last;
    besides me there is no god. . . ."

Psalm 85:11 (85:10: RSV) **214**

Steadfast love and faithfulness will meet;
    righteousness and peace will kiss each other.

Deuteronomy 7:9 Know therefore that the Lord your God is God, the faithful **215**
God who keeps covenant and steadfast love with those who love him and keep his commandments, to a thousand generations. . . .

(1) **Wisdom 13:1–9** **216**

For all men who were ignorant of God were foolish by nature;
and they were unable from the good things that are seen to
    know him who exists,
nor did they recognize the craftsman while paying heed to his
    works;
but they supposed that either fire or wind or swift air,
or the circle of the stars, or turbulent water,
or the luminaries of heaven were the gods that rule the world.
If through delight in the beauty of these things men assumed
    them to be gods,
let them know how much better than these is their Lord,

for the author of beauty created them.
And if men were amazed at their power and working,
let them perceive from them
how much more powerful is he who formed them.
For from the greatness and beauty of created things
comes a corresponding perception of their Creator.
Yet these men are little to be blamed,
for perhaps they go astray
while seeking God and desiring to find him.
For as they live among his works they keep searching,
and they trust in what they see, because the things that are seen
  are beautiful.
Yet again, not even they are to be excused;
for if they had the power to know so much
that they could investigate the world,
how did they fail to find sooner the Lord of these things?

216 (2) **Psalm 115:15**
May you be blessed by the Lord,
  who made heaven and earth!

216 (3) **Wisdom 7:17–21**
For it is he who gave me unerring knowledge of what exists,
to know the structure of the world and the activity of the elements;
the beginning and end and middle of times,
the alternations of the solstices and the changes of the seasons,
the cycles of the year and the constellations of the stars,
the natures of animals and the tempers of wild beasts,
the powers of spirits and the reasonings of men,
the varieties of plants and the virtues of roots;
I learned both what is secret and what is manifest. . . .

217 **John 17:3** And this is eternal life, that they know thee the only true God, and Jesus Christ whom thou hast sent.

218 (1) **Deuteronomy 4:37** And because he loved your fathers and chose their descendants after them, and brought you out of Egypt with his own presence, by his great power. . . .

218 (2) **Deuteronomy 7:8** . . . but it is because the Lord loves you, and is keeping the oath which he swore to your fathers, that the Lord has brought you out with a mighty hand, and redeemed you from the house of bondage, from the hand of Pharaoh king of Egypt.

218 (3) **Deuteronomy 10:15** . . . yet the Lord set his heart in love upon your fathers and chose their descendants after them, you above all peoples, as at this day.

218 (4) **Isaiah 43:1–7**
But now thus says the Lord, he who created you, O Jacob,
  he who formed you, O Israel:
"Fear not, for I have redeemed you;
  I have called you by name, you are mine.

When you pass through the waters I will be with you;
and through the rivers, they shall not overwhelm you;
when you walk through fire you shall not be burned,
and the flame shall not consume you.
For I am the Lord your God,
the Holy One of Israel, your Savior.
I give Egypt as your ransom,
Ethiopia and Seba in exchange for you.
Because you are precious in my eyes,
and honored, and I love you,
I give men in return for you,
peoples in exchange for your life.
Fear not, for I am with you;
I will bring your offspring from the east,
and from the west I will gather you;
I will say to the north, Give up,
and to the south, Do not withhold;
bring my sons from afar
and my daughters from the end of the earth,
every one who is called by my name,
whom I created for my glory,
whom I formed and made."

(5) **Hosea 2** Say to your brother, "My people," and to your sister, "She has obtained **218**
pity."

"Plead with your mother, plead—
for she is not my wife,
and I am not her husband—
that she put away her harlotry from her face,
and her adultery from between her breasts;
lest I strip her naked
and make her as in the day she was born,
and make her like a wilderness,
and set her like a parched land,
and slay her with thirst.
Upon her children also I will have no pity,
because they are children of harlotry.
For their mother has played the harlot;
she that conceived them has acted shamefully.
For she said, 'I will go after my lovers,
who give me my bread and my water,
my wool and my flax, my oil and my drink.'
Therefore I will hedge up her way with thorns;
and I will build a wall against her,
so that she cannot find her paths.
She shall pursue her lovers,
but not overtake them;
and she shall seek them,
but shall not find them.
Then she shall say, 'I will go
and return to my first husband,
for it was better with me then than now.'

And she did not know
    that it was I who gave her
    the grain, the wine, and the oil,
and who lavished upon her silver
    and gold which they used for Baal.
Therefore I will take back
    my grain in its time,
    and my wine in its season;
and I will take away my wool and my flax,
    which were to cover her nakedness.
Now I will uncover her lewdness
    in the sight of her lovers,
    and no one shall rescue her out of my hand.
And I will put an end to all her mirth,
    her feasts, her new moons, her sabbaths,
    and all her appointed feasts.
And I will lay waste her vines and her fig trees,
    of which she said,
'These are my hire,
    which my lovers have given me.'
I will make them a forest,
    and the beasts of the field shall devour them.
And I will punish her for the feast days of the Baals
    when she burned incense to them
and decked herself with her ring and jewelry,
    and went after her lovers,
    and forgot me, says the Lord.

"Therefore, behold, I will allure her,
    and bring her into the wilderness,
    and speak tenderly to her.
And there I will give her her vineyards,
    and make the Valley of Achor a door of hope.
And there she shall answer as in the days of her youth,
    as at the time when she came out of the land of Egypt.

"And in that day, says the Lord, you will call me, 'My husband,' and no longer will you call me, 'My Baal.' For I will remove the names of the Baals from her mouth, and they shall be mentioned by name no more. And I will make for you a covenant on that day with the beasts of the field, the birds of the air, and the creeping things of the ground; and I will abolish the bow, the sword, and war from the land; and I will make you lie down in safety. And I will betroth you to me for ever; I will betroth you to me in righteousness and in justice, in steadfast love, and in mercy. I will betroth you to me in faithfulness; and you shall know the Lord.

"And in that day, says the Lord,
    I will answer the heavens
    and they shall answer the earth;
and the earth shall answer the grain, the wine, and the oil,
    and they shall answer Jezreel;
    and I will sow him for myself in the land.
And I will have pity on Not pitied,
    and I will say to Not my people, 'You are my people';
    and he shall say, 'Thou art my God.'"

(1) **Isaiah 49:14–15** **219**

But Zion said, "The Lord has forsaken me,
my Lord has forgotten me."
"Can a woman forget her sucking child,
that she should have no compassion on the son of her womb?
Even these may forget,
yet I will not forget you. . . ."

(2) **Isaiah 62:4–5** **219**

You shall no more be termed Forsaken,
and your land shall no more be termed Desolate;
but you shall be called My delight is in her,
and your land Married;
for the Lord delights in you,
and your land shall be married.
For as a young man marries a virgin,
so shall your sons marry you,
and as the bridegroom rejoices over the bride,
so shall your God rejoice over you.

(3) **Ezekiel 16** Again the word of the Lord came to me: "Son of man, make known **219**
to Jerusalem her abominations, and say, Thus says the Lord God to Jerusalem: Your origin and your birth are of the land of the Canaanites; your father was an Amorite, and your mother a Hittite. And as for your birth, on the day you were born your navel string was not cut, nor were you washed with water to cleanse you, nor rubbed with salt, nor swathed with bands. No eye pitied you, to do any of these things to you out of compassion for you; but you were cast out on the open field, for you were abhorred, on the day that you were born.

"And when I passed by you, and saw you weltering in your blood, I said to you in your blood, 'Live, and grow up like a plant of the field.' And you grew up and became tall and arrived at full maidenhood; your breasts were formed, and your hair had grown; yet you were naked and bare.

"When I passed by you again and looked upon you, behold, you were at the age for love; and I spread my skirt over you, and covered your nakedness: yea, I plighted my troth to you and entered into a covenant with you, says the Lord God, and you became mine. Then I bathed you with water and washed off your blood from you, and anointed you with oil. I clothed you also with embroidered cloth and shod you with leather, I swathed you in fine linen and covered you with silk. And I decked you with ornaments, and put bracelets on your arms, and a chain on your neck. And I put a ring on your nose, and earrings in your ears, and a beautiful crown upon your head. Thus you were decked with gold and silver; and your raiment was of fine linen, and silk, and embroidered cloth; you ate fine flour and honey and oil. You grew exceedingly beautiful, and came to regal estate. And your renown went forth among the nations because of your beauty, for it was perfect through the splendor which I had bestowed upon you, says the Lord God.

"But you trusted in your beauty, and played the harlot because of your renown, and lavished your harlotries on any passer-by. You took some of your garments, and made for yourself gaily decked shrines, and on them played the harlot; the like has never been, nor ever shall be. You also took your fair jewels of my gold and of my silver, which I had given you, and made for yourself images of men, and with them played the harlot; and you took your embroidered garments to cover them, and set my oil and my incense before them. Also my bread which I gave you—I fed you with fine flour and oil and honey—you set before them for a pleasing odor, says the Lord God. And you took your sons and your daughters, whom you had borne to me, and these you sacrificed to them to be devoured. Were your harlotries so small a matter that you slaughtered my children and delivered them up as an offering by fire to them? And in all your abominations and your harlotries you did not remember the days of your youth, when you were naked and bare, weltering in your blood.

"And after all your wickedness (woe, woe to you! says the Lord God), you built yourself a vaulted chamber, and made yourself a lofty place in every square; at the head of every street you built your lofty place and prostituted your beauty, offering yourself to any passer-by, and multiplying your harlotry. You also played the harlot with the Egyptians, your lustful neighbors, multiplying your harlotry, to provoke me to anger. Behold, therefore, I stretched out my hand against you, and diminished your allotted portion, and delivered you to the greed of your enemies, the daughters of the Philistines, who were ashamed of your lewd behavior. You played the harlot also with the Assyrians, because you were insatiable; yea, you played the harlot with them, and still you were not satisfied. You multiplied your harlotry also with the trading land of Chaldea; and even with this you were not satisfied.

"How lovesick is your heart, says the Lord God, seeing you did all these things, the deeds of a brazen harlot; building your vaulted chamber at the head of every street, and making your lofty place in every square. Yet you were not like a harlot, because you scorned hire. Adulterous wife, who receives strangers instead of her husband! Men give gifts to all harlots; but you gave your gifts to all your lovers, bribing them to come to you from every side for your harlotries. So you were different from other women in your harlotries: none solicited you to play the harlot; and you gave hire, while no hire was given to you; therefore you were different.

"Wherefore, O harlot, hear the word of the Lord: Thus says the Lord God, Because your shame was laid bare and your nakedness uncovered in your harlotries with your lovers, and because of all your idols, and because of the blood of your children that you gave to them, therefore, behold, I will gather all your lovers, with whom you took pleasure, all those you loved and all those you loathed; I will gather them against you from every side, and will uncover your nakedness to them, that they may see all your nakedness. And I will judge you as women who break wedlock and shed blood are judged, and bring upon you the blood of wrath and jealousy. And I will give you into the hand of your lovers, and they shall throw down your vaulted chamber and break down your lofty places; they shall strip you of your clothes and take your fair jewels, and leave you naked and bare. They shall bring up a host against you, and they shall stone you and cut you to pieces with their swords. And they shall burn your houses and execute judgments upon you in the sight of many women; I will make you stop playing the harlot, and you shall also give hire no more. So will I satisfy my fury on you, and my jealousy shall depart from you; I will be calm, and will no more be angry. Because you have not remembered the days of your youth, but have enraged me with all these things; therefore, behold, I will requite your deeds upon your head, says the Lord God.

"Have you not committed lewdness in addition to all your abominations? Behold, every one who uses proverbs will use this proverb about you, 'Like mother, like daughter.' You are the daughter of your mother, who loathed her husband and her children; and you are the sister of your sisters, who loathed their husbands and their children. Your mother was a Hittite and your father an Amorite. And your elder sister is Samaria, who lived with her daughters to the north of you; and your younger sister, who lived to the south of you, is Sodom with her daughters. Yet you were not content to walk in their ways, or do according to their abominations; within a very little time you were more corrupt than they in all your ways. As I live, says the Lord

God, your sister Sodom and her daughters have not done as you and your daughters have done. Behold, this was the guilt of your sister Sodom: she and her daughters had pride, surfeit of food, and prosperous ease, but did not aid the poor and needy. They were haughty, and did abominable things before me; therefore I removed them, when I saw it. Samaria has not committed half your sins; you have committed more abominations than they, and have made your sisters appear righteous by all the abominations which you have committed. Bear your disgrace, you also, for you have made judgment favorable to your sisters; because of your sins in which you acted more abominably than they, they are more in the right than you. So be ashamed, you also, and bear your disgrace, for you have made your sisters appear righteous.

"I will restore their fortunes, both the fortunes of Sodom and her daughters, and the fortunes of Samaria and her daughters, and I will restore your own fortunes in the midst of them, that you may bear your disgrace and be ashamed of all that you have done, becoming a consolation to them. As for your sisters, Sodom and her daughters shall return to their former estate, and Samaria and her daughters shall return to their former estate; and you and your daughters shall return to your former estate. Was not your sister Sodom a byword in your mouth in the day of your pride, before your wickedness was uncovered? Now you have become like her an object of reproach for the daughters of Edom and all her neighbors, and for the daughters of the Philistines, those round about who despise you. You bear the penalty of your lewdness and your abominations, says the Lord.

"Yea, thus says the Lord God: I will deal with you as you have done, who have despised the oath in breaking the covenant, yet I will remember my covenant with you in the days of your youth, and I will establish with you an everlasting covenant. Then you will remember your ways, and be ashamed when I take your sisters, both your elder and your younger, and give them to you as daughters, but not on account of the covenant with you. I will establish my covenant with you, and you shall know that I am the Lord, that you may remember and be confounded, and never open your mouth again because of your shame, when I forgive you all that you have done, says the Lord God."

(4) **Hosea 11** **21**

When Israel was a child, I loved him,
    and out of Egypt I called my son.
The more I called them,
    the more they went from me;
they kept sacrificing to the Baals,
    and burning incense to idols.
Yet it was I who taught Ephraim to walk,
    I took them up in my arms;
    but they did not know that I healed them.
I led them with cords of compassion,
    with the bands of love,
and I became to them as one
    who eases the yoke on their jaws,
    and I bent down to them and fed them.
They shall return to the land of Egypt,
    and Assyria shall be their king,
    because they have refused to return to me.
The sword shall rage against their cities,
    consume the bars of their gates,
    and devour them in their fortresses.

My people are bent on turning away from me;
so they are appointed to the yoke,
and none shall remove it.

How can I give you up, O Ephraim!
How can I hand you over, O Israel!
How can I make you like Admah!
How can I treat you like Zeboiim!
My heart recoils within me,
my compassion grows warm and tender.
I will not execute my fierce anger,
I will not again destroy Ephraim;
for I am God and not man,
the Holy One in your midst,
and I will not come to destroy.
They shall go after the Lord,
he will roar like a lion;
yea, he will roar,
and his sons shall come trembling from the west;
they shall come trembling like birds from Egypt,
and like doves from the land of Assyria;
and I will return them to their homes, says the Lord.
Ephraim has encompassed me with lies,
and the house of Israel with deceit;
but Judah is still known by God,
and is faithful to the Holy One.

220 **Isaiah 54:8**

In overflowing wrath for a moment
I hid my face from you,
but with everlasting love I will have compassion on you,
says the Lord, your Redeemer.

221 (1) **1 Corinthians 2:7–16** But we impart a secret and hidden wisdom of God, which God decreed before the ages for our glorification. None of the rulers of this age understood this; for if they had, they would not have crucified the Lord of glory. But, as it is written,

"What no eye has seen, nor ear heard,
nor the heart of man conceived,
what God has prepared for those who love him,"

God has revealed to us through the Spirit. For the Spirit searches everything, even the depths of God. For what person knows a man's thoughts except the spirit of the man which is in him? So also no one comprehends the thoughts of God except the Spirit of God. Now we have received not the spirit of the world, but the Spirit which is from God, that we might understand the gifts bestowed on us by God. And we impart this in words not taught by human wisdom but taught by the Spirit, interpreting spiritual truths to those who possess the Spirit.

The unspiritual man does not receive the gifts of the Spirit of God, for they are folly to him, and he is not able to understand them because they are spiritually discerned. The spiritual man judges all things, but is himself to be judged by no one. "For who has known the mind of the Lord so as to instruct him?" But we have the mind of Christ.

(2) **Ephesians 3:9–12** . . . and to make all men see what is the plan of the mystery hidden for ages in God who created all things; that through the church the manifold wisdom of God might now be made known to the principalities and powers in the heavenly places. This was according to the eternal purpose which he has realized in Christ Jesus our Lord, in whom we have boldness and confidence of access through our faith in him. **221**

(1) **Matthew 5:29–30** If your right eye causes you to sin, pluck it out and throw it away; it is better that you lose one of your members than that your whole body be thrown into hell. And if your right hand causes you to sin, cut it off and throw it away; it is better that you lose one of your members than that your whole body go into hell. **226**

(2) **Matthew 16:24–26** Then Jesus told his disciples, "If any man would come after me, let him deny himself and take up his cross and follow me. For whoever would save his life will lose it, and whoever loses his life for my sake will find it. For what will it profit a man, if he gains the whole world and forfeits his life? Or what shall a man give in return for his life?" **226**

Pope Vigilius, Letter to all the People of God (5 February 552): DS 415 The Father, however, with the same only-begotten Son and the Holy Spirit is one in deity and of an equal and undivided nature. Our Lord entrusted the fulness of this faith to the Apostles, saying: "Go, and teach all nations, baptizing them in the name of the Father, and of the Son, and of the Holy Spirit". "In the name", he said, not in the names, so that in those in whom there is one strength, one power, one deity, one eternity, one glory, one omnipotence, one blessedness, one operation, and one nature, there would also be the integrity of one name. Indeed, nothing in the deity is divided, when only what is proper to the persons is designated by a clear distinction. All, therefore, that is the Trinity remains consubstantial and undivided divinity. **233**

(1) **Deuteronomy 32:6** **238**

Do you thus requite the Lord,
 you foolish and senseless people?
Is not he your father, who created you,
 who made you and established you?

(2) **Malachi 2:10** Have we not all one father? Has not one God created us? Why then are we faithless to one another, profaning the covenant of our fathers? **238**

(3) **2 Samuel 7:14** I will be his father, and he shall be my son. When he commits iniquity, I will chasten him with the rod of men, with the stripes of the sons of men. . . . **238**

(4) **Psalm 68:6 (68:5: RSV)** **238**

Father of the fatherless and protector of widows
 is God in his holy habitation.

(1) **Isaiah 66:13** **239**

As one whom his mother comforts,
 so I will comfort you;
you shall be comforted in Jerusalem.

239 (2) **Psalm 131:2**
But I have calmed and quieted my soul,
like a child quieted at its mother's breast;
like a child that is quieted is my soul.

239 (3) **Psalm 27:10**
For my father and my mother have forsaken me,
but the Lord will take me up.

239 (4) **Ephesians 3:14** For this reason I bow my knees before the Father. . . .

239 (5) **Isaiah 49:15**
"Can a woman forget her sucking child,
that she should have no compassion on the son of her womb?
Even these may forget,
yet I will not forget you. . . ."

242 **DS 150:** DS 150 is the Niceno-Constantinopolitan (Nicene) Creed, which follows paragraph 184 in the *Catechism of the Catholic Church* (CCC).

243 (1) **Genesis 1:2** The earth was without form and void, and darkness was upon the face of the deep; and the Spirit of God was moving over the face of the waters.

243 (2) **DS 150:** DS 150 is the Nicene Creed, which follows paragraph 184 in the CCC.

243 (3) **John 14:17** . . . even the Spirit of truth, whom the world cannot receive, because it neither sees him nor knows him; you know him, for he dwells with you, and will be in you.

243 (4) **John 14:26** But the Counselor, the Holy Spirit, whom the Father will send in my name, he will teach you all things, and bring to your remembrance all that I have said to you.

243 (5) **John 16:13** When the Spirit of truth comes, he will guide you into all the truth; for he will not speak on his own authority, but whatever he hears he will speak, and he will declare to you the things that are to come.

244 (1) **John 14:26:** see 243 (4).

244 (2) **John 15:26** But when the Counselor comes, whom I shall send to you from the Father, even the Spirit of truth, who proceeds from the Father, he will bear witness to me. . . .

244 (3) **John 16:14** He will glorify me, for he will take what is mine and declare it to you.

244 (4) **John 7:39** Now this he said about the Spirit, which those who believed in him were to receive; for as yet the Spirit had not been given, because Jesus was not yet glorified.

245 **DS 150:** DS 150 is the Nicene Creed, which follows paragraph 184 in the CCC.

St. Leo the Great, letter "*Quam laudabiliter*" to Turibius, Bishop of Astorga (21 July 447): DS 284 Thus in the first chapter it is shown how impiously they think about the divine Trinity when they assert that the persons of the Father and the Son and the Spirit are one and the same, so that the same God is now called Father, now Son, now Holy Spirit; and that there is not one who begets, another who is begotten, and another who proceeds from the two; but that there is a single unity in three words but not in three persons. They took this kind of blasphemy from the opinion of Sabellius, whose disciples are rightly called patripassionists; because if the Son himself is also the Father, the Cross of the Son is the suffering of the Father; and all that the Son in obedience to the Father endured in the form of a slave, the Father suffered in himself. Which is unequivocally contrary to the Catholic faith which confesses the Trinity of the deity to be consubstantial [*homousion*], so that the Father and the Son and the Spirit are undivided without confusion, eternal without time, equal without difference: because it is not one same person who fills the unity in the Trinity, but the same essence. . . . 247

(1) ***Ad gentes divinitus* 2** The Church on earth is by its very nature missionary since, according to the plan of the Father, it has its origin in the mission of the Son and the Holy Spirit. This plan flows from "fountain-like love," the love of God the Father. As the principle without principle from whom the Son is generated and from whom the Holy Spirit proceeds through the Son, God in his great and merciful kindness freely creates us and, moreover, graciously calls us to share in his life and glory. He generously pours out, and never ceases to pour out, his divine goodness, so that he who is creator of all things might at last become "all in all" (1 Cor. 15:28), thus simultaneously assuring his own glory and our happiness. It pleased God to call men to share in his life and not merely singly, without any bond between them, but he formed them into a people, in which his children who had been scattered were gathered together (cf. Jn. 11:52). 248

(2) **Council of Lyons II (1274): DS 850** In faithful and devout profession we declare that the Holy Spirit proceeds eternally from the Father and the Son, not as from two beginnings, but from one beginning, not from two breathings but from one breathing. The most holy Roman Church, the mother and teacher of all the faithful, has up to this time professed, preached, and taught this; this she firmly holds, preaches, declares, and teaches; the unchangeable and true opinion of the orthodox Fathers and Doctors, Latin as well as Greek, holds this. But because some through ignorance of the irresistible aforesaid truth have slipped into various errors, we in our desire to close the way to errors of this kind, with the approval of the sacred Council, condemn and reject (those) who presume to deny that the Holy Spirit proceeds eternally from the Father and the Son; as well as (those) who with rash boldness presume to declare that the Holy Spirit proceeds from the Father and the Son as from two beginnings, and not as from one. 248

(1) **1 Corinthians 12:4–6** Now there are varieties of gifts, but the same Spirit; and there are varieties of service, but the same Lord; and there are varieties of working, but it is the same God who inspires them all in every one. 249

(2) **Ephesians 4:4–6** There is one body and one Spirit, just as you were called to the one hope that belongs to your call, one Lord, one faith, one baptism, one God and Father of us all, who is above all and through all and in all. 249

257 *Ad gentes divinitus* **2–9** The Church on earth is by its very nature missionary since, according to the plan of the Father, it has its origin in the mission of the Son and the Holy Spirit. This plan flows from "fountain-like love," the love of God the Father. As the principle without principle from whom the Son is generated and from whom the Holy Spirit proceeds through the Son, God in his great and merciful kindness freely creates us and, moreover, graciously calls us to share in his life and glory. He generously pours out, and never ceases to pour out, his divine goodness, so that he who is creator of all things might at last become "all in all" (1 Cor. 15:28), thus simultaneously assuring his own glory and our happiness. It pleased God to call men to share in his life and not merely singly, without any bond between them, but he formed them into a people, in which his children who had been scattered were gathered together (cf. Jn. 11:52).

This universal plan of God for the salvation of mankind is not carried out solely in a secret manner, as it were, in the minds of men, nor by the efforts, even religious, through which they in many ways seek God in an attempt to touch him and find him, although God is not far from any of us (cf. Acts 17:27); their efforts need to be enlightened and corrected, although in the loving providence of God they may lead one to the true God and be a preparation for the Gospel. However, in order to establish a relationship of peace and communion with himself, and in order to bring about brotherly union among men, and they sinners, God decided to enter into the history of mankind in a new and definitive manner, by sending his own Son in human flesh, so that through him he might snatch men from the power of darkness and of Satan (cf. Col. 1:13; Acts 10:38) and in him reconcile the world to himself. He appointed him, through whom he made the world, to be heir of all things, that he might restore all things in him (cf. Eph. 1:10).

Jesus Christ was sent into the world as the true Mediator between God and men. Since he is God, all the fullness of the divine nature dwells in him bodily (Col. 2:9); as man he is the new Adam, full of grace and truth (Jn. 1:14), who has been constituted head of a restored humanity. So the Son of God entered the world by means of a true incarnation that he might make men sharers in the divine nature; though rich, he was made poor for our sake, that by his poverty we might become rich (2 Cor. 8:9). The Son of man did not come to be served, but to serve and to give his life as a ransom for many, that is for all (cf. Mk. 10:45). The fathers of the Church constantly proclaim that what was not assumed by Christ was not healed. Now Christ took a complete human nature just as it is found in us poor unfortunates, but one that was without sin (cf. Heb. 4:15; 9:28). Christ, whom the Father sanctified and sent into the world (cf. Jn. 10:36), said of himself: "The Spirit of the Lord is upon me, because he anointed me; to bring good news to the poor he sent me, to heal the broken-hearted, to proclaim to the captive release, and sight to the blind" (Lk. 4:8); and on another occasion: "The Son of man has come to seek and to save what was lost" (Lk. 9:10).

Now, what was once preached by the Lord, or fulfilled in him for the salvation of mankind, must be proclaimed and spread to the ends of the earth (Acts 1:8), starting from Jerusalem (cf. Lk. 24:27), so that what was accomplished for the salvation of all men may, in the course of time, achieve its universal effect.

To do this, Christ sent the Holy Spirit from the Father to exercise inwardly his saving influence, and to promote the spread of the Church. Without doubt, the Holy Spirit was at work in the world before Christ was glorified. On the day of Pentecost, however, he came down on the disciples that he might remain with them forever (cf. Jn. 14:16); on that day the Church was openly displayed to the crowds and the spread of the Gospel among the nations, through preaching, was begun. Finally, on that day was foreshadowed the union of all peoples in the catholicity of the faith by means of the Church of the New Alliance, a Church which speaks every language, understands and embraces all tongues in charity, and thus overcomes the dispersion of Babel. The "acts of the apostles" began with Pentecost, just as Christ was conceived in the Virgin Mary with the coming of the Holy Spirit and was moved to begin his ministry by the descent of the same Holy Spirit, who came down upon him while he was praying. Before freely laying down his life for the world, the Lord Jesus organized the apostolic ministry and promised to send the Holy Spirit, in such a way that both would be always and everywhere associated in the fulfillment of the work of salvation. Throughout the ages the Holy Spirit makes the entire Church "one in communion and ministry; and provides her with different hierarchical and charismatic gifts," giving life to ecclesiastical structures, being as it were their soul, and inspiring in the hearts of the faithful that same spirit of mission which impelled Christ himself. He even at times visibly anticipates apostolic action, just as in various ways he unceasingly accompanies and directs it.

From the beginning of his ministry the Lord Jesus "called to himself" those whom he wished and he caused twelve of them to be with him and to be sent out preaching" (Mk. 3:14; cf. Mt. 10:1–42). Thus the apostles were both the seeds of the new Israel and the beginning of the sacred hierarchy. Later, before he was assumed into heaven (cf. Acts 1:11), after he had fulfilled in himself the mysteries of our salvation and the renewal of all things by his death and resurrection, the Lord, who had received all power in heaven and on earth (cf. Mt. 28:18), founded his Church as the sacrament of salvation; and just as he had been sent by the Father (cf. Jn. 10:21), so he sent the apostles into the whole world, commanding them: "Go, therefore, and make disciples of all nations, baptizing them in the name of the Father and of the Son and of the Holy Spirit; teaching them to observe all that I have commanded you" (Mt. 28:19 ff.); "Go into the whole world, preach the Gospel to every creature. He who believes and is baptized shall be saved; but he who does not believe, shall be condemned" (Mt. 16:15 ff.). Hence the Church has an obligation to proclaim the faith and salvation which comes from Christ, both by reason of the express command which the order of bishops inherited from the apostles, an obligation in the discharge of which they are assisted by priests, and one which they share with the successor of St. Peter, the supreme pastor of the Church, and also by reason of the life which Christ infuses into his members: "From him the whole body, being closely joined and knit together through every joint of the system, according to the functioning in due measure of each single part, derives its increase to the building up of itself in love." (Eph. 4:16). The mission of the Church is carried out by means of that activity through which, in obedience to Christ's command and moved by the grace and love of the Holy Spirit, the Church makes itself fully present to all men and peoples in order to lead them to the faith, freedom and peace of Christ by the example of its life and teaching, by the sacraments and other means of grace. Its aim is to open up for all men a free and sure path to full participation in the mystery of Christ.

Since this mission continues and, in the course of history, unfolds the mission of Christ, who was sent to evangelize the poor, then the Church, urged on by the Spirit of Christ, must walk the road Christ himself walked, a way of poverty and obedience, of service and self-sacrifice even to death, a death from which he emerged victorious by his resurrection. So it was that the apostles walked in hope and by much trouble and suffering filled up what was lacking in the sufferings of Christ for his body, which is the Church. Often, too, the seed was the blood of Christians.

This task which must be carried out by the order of bishops, under the leadership of Peter's successor and with the prayers and cooperation of the whole Church, is one and the same everywhere and in all situations, although, because of circumstances, it may not always be exercised in the same way. The differences which must be recognized in this activity of the Church, do not flow from the inner nature of the mission itself, but from the circumstances in which it is exercised.

These circumstances depend either on the Church itself or on the peoples, classes or men to whom its mission is directed. Although the Church possesses in itself the totality and fullness of the means of salvation, it does not always, in fact cannot, use every one of them immediately, but it has to make beginnings and work by slow stages to give effect to God's plan. Sometimes after a successful start it has cause to mourn a setback, or it may linger in a state of semi-fulfilment and insufficiency. With regard to peoples, classes and men it is only by degrees that it touches and penetrates them and so raises them to a catholic perfection. In each situation and circumstance a proper line of action and effective means should be adopted.

The special undertakings in which preachers of the Gospel, sent by the Church, and going into the whole world, carry out the work of preaching the Gospel and implanting the Church among people who do not yet believe in Christ, are generally called "missions." Such undertakings are accomplished by missionary activity and are, for the most part, carried out in defined territories recognized by the Holy See. The special end of this missionary activity is the evangelization and the implanting of the Church among peoples or groups in which it has not yet taken root. All over the world indigenous particular churches ought to grow from the seed of the word of God, churches which would be adequately organized and would possess their own proper strength and maturity. With their own hierarchy and faithful, and sufficiently endowed with means adapted to the living of a full Christian life, they should contribute to the good of the whole Church. The principal instrument in this work of implanting the Church is the preaching of the Gospel of Jesus Christ. It was to announce this Gospel that the Lord sent his disciples into the whole world, that men, having been reborn by the word of God (cf. 1 Pet. 1:23), might through baptism, be joined to the Church which, as the Body of the Word Incarnate, lives and is nourished by the word of God and the Eucharist (cf. Acts 4:23).

Various stages, which are sometimes intermingled, are to be found in this missionary activity of the Church; first there is the beginning or planting and then a time of freshness and youthfulness. Nor does the Church's missionary activity cease once this point has been passed; the obligation to carry on the work devolves on the particular churches already constituted, an obligation to preach the Gospel to all who are still outside.

Moreover, it often happens that, owing to various cases, the groups among whom the Church operates are utterly changed so that an entirely new situation arises. Then the Church must consider whether these new circumstances require that she should once again exercise her missionary activity. The situation, however, is often of such a nature that for the time being there is no possibility of directly and immediately preaching the Gospel. In that case missionaries, patiently, prudently, and with great faith, can and ought at least bear witness to the love and kindness of Christ and thus prepare a way for the Lord, and in some way make him present.

It is clear, therefore, that missionary activity flows immediately from the very nature of the Church. Missionary activity extends the saving faith of the Church, it expands and perfects its catholic unity, it is sustained by its apostolicity, it activates the collegiate sense of its hierarchy, and bears witness to its sanctity which it both extends and promotes. Missionary work among the nations differs from the pastoral care of the faithful and likewise from efforts aimed at restoring Christian unity. Nevertheless, these two latter are very closely connected with the Church's missionary endeavor because the division of Christians is injurious to the holy work of preaching the Gospel to every creature, and deprives many people of access to the faith. Because of the Church's mission, all baptized people are called upon to come together in one flock that they might bear unanimous witness to Christ their Lord before the nations. And if they cannot yet fully bear witness to one faith, they should at least be imbued with mutual respect and love.

The reason for missionary activity lies in the will of God, "who wishes all men to be saved and to come to the knowledge of the truth. For there is one God and one Mediator between God and men, himself a man, Jesus Christ, who gave himself as a ransom for all" (1 Tim. 2:4–5), "neither is their salvation in any other" (Acts 4:12). Everyone, therefore, ought to be converted to Christ, who is known through the preaching of the Church, and they ought, by baptism, to become incorporated into him, and into the Church which is his body. Christ himself explicitly asserted the necessity of faith and baptism (cf. Mk. 16:16; Jn. 3:5), and thereby affirmed at the same time the necessity of the Church, which men enter through baptism as through a door. Hence, those cannot be saved, who, knowing that the Catholic Church was founded through Jesus Christ, by God, as something necessary, still refuse to enter it, or to remain in it. So, although in ways known to himself God can lead those who, through no fault of their own, are ignorant of the Gospel to that faith without which it is impossible to please him (Heb. 11:6), the Church, nevertheless, still has the obligation and also the sacred right to evangelize. And so, today as always, missionary activity retains its full force and necessity.

By means of this activity the mystical Body of Christ unceasingly gathers and directs its energies towards its own increase (Eph. 4:11–16). The members of the Church are impelled to engage in this activity because of the charity with which they love God and by which they desire to share with all men in the spiritual goods of this life and the life to come.

Finally, by this missionary activity God is fully glorified, when men fully and consciously accept the work of salvation which he accomplished in Christ. By means of it God's plan is realized, a plan to which Christ lovingly and obediently submitted for the glory of the Father who sent him in order that the whole human race might become one people of God, form one body of Christ, and be built up into one temple of the Holy Spirit; all of which, as an expression of brotherly concord, answers to a profound longing in all men. And thus, finally, the intention of the creator in creating man in his own image and likeness will be truly realized, when all who possess human nature, and have been regenerated in Christ through the Holy Spirit, gazing together on the glory of God, will be able to say "Our Father."

Missionary activity is intimately bound up with human nature and its aspirations. In manifesting Christ, the Church reveals to men their true situation and calling, since Christ is the head and exemplar of that renewed humanity, imbued with that brotherly love, sincerity and spirit of peace, to which all men aspire. Both Christ and the Church which bears witness to him transcend the distinctions of race and nationality, and so cannot be considered as strangers to anyone or in any place. Christ is the Truth and the Way which the preaching of the Gospel lays open to all men when it speaks those words of Christ in their ear: "Repent, and believe the Gospel" (Mk. 1:15). Since he who does not believe is already judged (cf. Jn. 3:18), the words of Christ are at once words of judgment and grace, of life and death. For it is only by putting to death that which is old that we can come to newness of life. Now although this refers primarily to people, it is also true of various worldly goods which bear the mark both of man's sin and the blessing of God: "For all have sinned and have need of the glory of God" (Rom. 3:23). No one is freed from sin by himself or by his own efforts, no one is raised above himself or completely delivered from his own weakness, solitude or slavery; all have need of Christ who is the model, master, liberator, savior, and giver of life. Even in the secular history of mankind the Gospel has acted as a leaven in the interests of liberty and progress, and it always offers itself as a leaven with regard to brotherhood, unity and peace. So it is not without reason that Christ is hailed by the faithful as "the hope of the nations and their savior."

The period, therefore, between the first and second coming of the Lord is the time of missionary activity, when, like the harvest, the Church will be gathered from the four winds into the kingdom of God. For the Gospel must be preached to all peoples before the Lord comes (cf. Mk. 13:10).

Missionary activity is nothing else, and nothing less, than the manifestation of God's plan, its epiphany and realization in the world and in history; that by which God, through mission, clearly brings to its conclusion the history of salvation. Through preaching and the celebration of the sacraments, of which the holy Eucharist is the center and summit, missionary activity makes Christ present, he who is the author of salvation. It purges of evil associations those elements of truth and grace which are found among peoples, and which are, as it were, a secret presence of God; and it restores them to Christ their source who overthrows the rule of the devil and limits the manifold malice of evil. So whatever goodness is found in the minds and hearts of men, or in the particular customs and cultures of peoples, far from being lost is purified, raised to a higher level and reaches its perfection, for the glory of God, the confusion of the demon, and the happiness of men. Thus missionary activity tends towards eschatological fullness; by it the people of God is expanded to the degree and until the time that the Father has fixed by his own authority (cf. Acts 1:7); of it was it said in prophecy: "Enlarge the space for your tent and spread out your tent clothes unsparingly" (Is. 54:2). By missionary activity the mystical Body is enlarged until it reaches the mature fullness of Christ (cf. Eph. 4:13); the spiritual temple where God is adored in spirit and truth (cf. Jn. 4:23) grows and is built up on the foundation of the apostles and prophets, Jesus Christ himself being the chief cornerstone (Eph. 2:20).

258 **Council of Constantinople II (553): DS 421** If anyone does not confess that (there is) one nature or substance of the Father and of the Son and of the Holy Spirit, and one power and one might, and that the Trinity is consubstantial, one Godhead being worshipped in three subsistences, or persons, let such a one be anathema. For there is one God and Father, from whom are all things, and one Lord Jesus Christ, through whom are all things, and one Holy Spirit, in whom are all things.

259 (1) **John 6:44** No one can come to me unless the Father who sent me draws him; and I will raise him up at the last day.

259 (2) **Romans 8:14** For all who are led by the Spirit of God are sons of God.

260 **John 17:21–23** . . . that they may all be one; even as thou, Father, art in me, and I in thee, that they also may be in us, so that the world may believe that thou hast sent me. The glory which thou hast given me I have given to them, that they may be one even as we are one, I in them and thou in me, that they may become perfectly one, so that the world may know that thou hast sent me and hast loved them even as thou hast loved me.

263 **John 14:26** But the Counselor, the Holy Spirit, whom the Father will send in my name, he will teach you all things, and bring to your remembrance all that I have said to you.

265 **Paul VI, *The* Credo *of the People of God* 9** We believe in this one God, who is as completely one in his most holy essence as in the rest of his perfections; in his

omnipotence, in his infinite knowledge, in his providence, in his will and his love. He is who is, as he himself revealed to Moses. He is love, as John the Apostle taught us. These two names, therefore, Being and Love, express the same unattainable truth concerning him who manifested himself to us and who, inhabiting light inaccessible, is in himself above every name, above every thing and every created intelligence. God only can grant us a true and perfect knowledge of himself, revealing himself as Father, Son and Holy Spirit in whose eternal life we are called by grace to share here on earth in the obscurity of faith and after death in everlasting light. The mutual bonds which eternally constitute the three Persons, each one of whom is one and the same divine Being, are themselves the inmost and blessed life of the Most Holy God, which is infinitely beyond our possibilities of understanding. Wherefore, we give thanks to the divine Goodness that so many believers can testify with us before men to the unity of God, even though they do not know the mystery of the Most Holy Trinity.

(1) **Genesis 1:1** In the beginning God created the heavens and the earth. **268**

(2) **John 1:3** . . . all things were made through him, and without him was not any- **268**
thing made that was made.

(3) **Matthew 6:9** Pray then like this: **268**
Our Father who art in heaven,
Hallowed be thy name.

(4) **2 Corinthians 12:9** . . . but he said to me, "My grace is sufficient for you, for my **268**
power is made perfect in weakness." I will all the more gladly boast of my weaknesses, that the power of Christ may rest upon me.

(5) **1 Corinthians 1:18** For the word of the cross is folly to those who are perishing, **268**
but to us who are being saved it is the power of God.

(1) **Jeremiah 27:5** "It is I who by my great power and my outstretched arm have **269**
made the earth, with the men and animals that are on the earth, and I give it to whomever it seems right to me. . . ."

(2) **Jeremiah 32:17** ". . . 'Ah Lord God! It is thou who hast made the heavens and **269**
the earth by thy great power and by thy outstretched arm! Nothing is too hard for thee. . . .'"

(3) **Luke 1:37** ". . . For with God nothing will be impossible." **269**

(4) **Esther 4:17b (13:9: RSV)** "O Lord, Lord, King who rulest over all things, for **269**
the universe is in thy power and there is no one who can oppose thee if it is thy will to save Israel. . . ."

(5) **Proverbs 21:1** **269**
The king's heart is a stream of water in the hand of the Lord;
he turns it wherever he will.

(6) **Tobit 13:2** **269**
For he afflicts, and he shows mercy;
he leads down to Hades, and brings up again,
and there is no one who can escape his hand.

270 **Matthew 6:32** For the Gentiles seek all these things; and your heavenly Father knows that you need them all.

273 (1) **2 Corinthians 12:9** . . . but he said to me, "My grace is sufficient for you, for my power is made perfect in weakness." I will all the more gladly boast of my weaknesses, that the power of Christ may rest upon me.

273 (2) **Philippians 4:13** I can do all things in him who strengthens me.

280 **Romans 8:18–23** I consider that the sufferings of this present time are not worth comparing with the glory that is to be revealed to us. For the creation waits with eager longing for the revealing of the sons of God; for the creation was subjected to futility, not of its own will but by the will of him who subjected it in hope; because the creation itself will be set free from its bondage to decay and obtain the glorious liberty of the children of God. We know that the whole creation has been groaning in travail together until now; and not only the creation, but we ourselves, who have the first fruits of the Spirit, groan inwardly as we wait for adoption as sons, the redemption of our bodies.

281 (1) **Egeria, *Peregrinatio ad loca sancta* 46** Ladies, my sisters, I must describe this, lest you think that it is done without explanation. It is the custom here, throughout the forty days on which there is fasting, for those who are preparing for baptism to be exorcised by the clergy early in the morning, as soon as the dismissal from the morning service has been given at the Anastasis. Immediately a throne is placed for the bishop in the major church, the Martyrium. All those who are to be baptized, both men and women, sit closely around the bishop, while the godmothers and godfathers stand there; and indeed all of the people who wish to listen may enter and sit down, provided they are of the faithful. A catechumen, however, may not enter at the time when the bishop is teaching them the law. He does so in this way: beginning with Genesis he goes through the whole of Scripture during these forty days, expounding first its literal meaning and then explaining the spiritual meaning. In the course of these days everything is taught not only about the Resurrection but concerning the body of faith. This is called catechetics.

When five weeks of instruction have been completed, they then receive the Creed. He explains the meaning of each of the phrases of the Creed in the same way he explained Holy Scripture, expounding first the literal and then the spiritual sense. In this fashion the Creed is taught.

And thus it is that in these places all the faithful are able to follow the Scriptures when they are read in the churches, because all are taught through those forty days, that is, from the first to the third hours, for during the three hours instruction is given. God knows, ladies, my sisters, that the voices of the faithful who have come to catechetics to hear instruction on those things being said or explained by the bishop are louder than when the bishop sits down in church to preach about each of those matters which are explained in this fashion. The dismissal from catechetics is given at the third hour, and immediately, singing hymns, they lead the bishop to the Anastasis, and the office of the third hour takes place. And thus they are taught for three hours a day for seven weeks. During the eighth week, the one which is called the Great Week, there remains no more time for them to be taught, because what has been mentioned above must be carried out.

Now when seven weeks have gone by and there remains only Holy Week, which is here called the Great Week, then the bishop comes in the morning to the major church, the Martyrium. To the rear, at the apse behind the altar, a throne is placed for the bishop, and one by one they come forth, the men with their godfathers, the women with their godmothers. And each one recites the Creed back to the bishop. After the Creed has been recited back to the bishop, he delivers a homily to them all, and says: "During these seven weeks you have been instructed in the whole law of the Scriptures, and you have heard about the faith. You have also heard of the resurrection of the flesh. But as for the whole explanation of the Creed, you have heard only that which you are able to know while you are still catechumens. Because you are still catechumens, you are not able to know those things which belong to a still higher mystery, that of baptism. But that you may not think that anything would be done without explanation, once you have been baptized in the name of God, you will hear of them during the eight days of Easter in the Anastasis following the dismissal from church. Because you are still catechumens, the most secret of the divine mysteries cannot be told to you."

(2) **St. Augustine, *De catechizandis rudibus* 3, 5** The narration is complete when 281
the beginner is first instructed from the text: *In the beginning God created heaven and earth*, down to the present period of Church history. That does not mean, however, that we ought to repeat verbatim the whole of the Pentateuch, and all the books of Judges and Kingdoms and Esdras, and the entire Gospel and the Acts of the Apostles (if we have learned them by heart), or relate in our own words all that is contained in these books, and thus develop and explain them; for which neither time serves nor any need calls. But we ought to present all the matter in a general and comprehensive summary, choosing certain of the more remarkable facts that are heard with greater pleasure and constitute the cardinal points in history; these we ought not to present as a parchment rolled up and at once snatch them out of sight, but we ought by dwelling somewhat upon them to untie, so to speak, and spread them out to view, and offer them to the minds of our hearers to examine and admire. But the remaining details we should weave into our narrative in a rapid survey. In this way not only are the points which we desire most to emphasize brought into greater prominence by keeping the others in the background, but also he whose interest we are anxious to stimulate by the narration does not reach them with a mind already exhausted, and we avoid confusing the memory of him whom we ought to instruct by our teaching.

***Nostra aetate* 2** Throughout history even to the present day, there is found among 282
different peoples a certain awareness of a hidden power, which lies behind the course of nature and the events of human life. At times there is present even a recognition of a supreme being, or still more of a Father. This awareness and recognition results in a way of life that is imbued with a deep religious sense. The religions which are found in more advanced civilizations endeavor by way of well-defined concepts and exact language to answer these questions. Thus, in Hinduism men explore the divine mystery and express it both in the limitless riches of myth and the accurately defined insights of philosophy. They seek release from the trials of the present life by ascetical practices, profound meditation and recourse to God in confidence and love. Buddhism in its various forms testifies to the essential inadequacy of this changing world. It proposes a way of life by which men can, with confidence and trust, attain a state of perfect liberation and reach supreme illumination either through their own efforts or by the aid of divine help. So, too, other religions which are found throughout the world attempt in their own ways to calm the hearts of men by outlining a program of life covering doctrine, moral precepts and sacred rites.

The Catholic Church rejects nothing of what is true and holy in these religions. She has a high regard for the manner of life and conduct, the precepts and doctrines which, although differing in many ways from her own teaching, nevertheless often reflect a ray of that truth which enlightens all men. Yet she proclaims and is in duty bound to proclaim without fail, Christ who is the way, the truth and the life (Jn. 1:6). In him, in whom God reconciled all things to himself (2 Cor. 5:18–19), men find the fulness of their religious life.

The Church, therefore, urges her sons to enter with prudence and charity into discussion and collaboration with members of other religions. Let Christians, while witnessing to their own faith and way of life, acknowledge, preserve and encourage the spiritual and moral truths found among non-Christians, also their social life and culture.

286 **Vatican Council I (1870): DS 3026** [*Against those denying natural theology*]. If anyone shall have said that the one true God, our Creator and our Lord, cannot be known with certitude by those things which have been made, by the natural light of human reason: let him be anathema.

287 (1) **Acts 17:24–29** ". . . The God who made the world and everything in it, being Lord of heaven and earth, does not live in shrines made by man, nor is he served by human hands, as though he needed anything, since he himself gives to all men life and breath and everything. And he made from one every nation of men to live on all the face of the earth, having determined allotted periods and the boundaries of their habitation, that they should seek God, in the hope that they might feel after him and find him. Yet he is not far from each one of us, for

'In him we live and move and have our being';

as even some of your poets have said,

'For we are indeed his offspring.'

Being then God's offspring, we ought not to think that the Deity is like gold, or silver, or stone, a representation by the art and imagination of man. . . ."

287 (2) **Romans 1:19–20** For what can be known about God is plain to them, because God has shown it to them. Ever since the creation of the world his invisible nature, namely, his eternal power and deity, has been clearly perceived in the things that have been made. So they are without excuse. . . .

287 (3) **Isaiah 43:1**

But now thus says the Lord, he who created you, O Jacob,
he who formed you, O Israel:
"Fear not, for I have redeemed you;
I have called you by name, you are mine. . . ."

287 (4) **Psalm 115:15**

May you be blessed by the Lord,
who made heaven and earth!

287 (5) **Psalm 124:8**

Our help is in the name of the Lord,
who made heaven and earth.

287 (6) **Psalm 134:3**

May the Lord bless you from Zion,
he who made heaven and earth!

288 (1) **Genesis 15:5** And he brought him outside and said, "Look toward heaven, and number the stars, if you are able to number them." Then he said to him, "So shall your descendants be."

(2) **Jeremiah 33:19–26** The word of the Lord came to Jeremiah: "Thus says the Lord: If you can break my covenant with the day and my covenant with the night, so that day and night will not come at their appointed time, then also my covenant with David my servant may be broken, so that he shall not have a son to reign on his throne, and my covenant with the Levitical priests my ministers. As the host of heaven cannot be numbered and the sands of the sea cannot be measured, so I will multiply the descendants of David my servant, and the Levitical priests who minister to me." **288**

The word of the Lord came to Jeremiah: "Have you not observed what these people are saying, 'The Lord has rejected the two families which he chose'? Thus they have despised my people so that they are no longer a nation in their sight. Thus says the Lord: If I have not established my covenant with day and night and the ordinances of heaven and earth, then I will reject the descendants of Jacob and David my servant and will not choose one of his descendants to rule over the seed of Abraham, Isaac, and Jacob. For I will restore their fortunes, and will have mercy upon them."

(3) **Isaiah 44:24** **288**

Thus says the Lord, your Redeemer,
 who formed you from the womb:
"I am the Lord, who made all things,
 who stretched out the heavens alone,
 who spread out the earth—Who was with me? . . ."

(4) **Psalm 104:** see 102 (2). **288**

(5) **Proverbs 8:22–31** **288**

The Lord created me at the beginning of his work,
 the first of his acts of old.
Ages ago I was set up,
 at the first, before the beginning of the earth.
When there were no depths I was brought forth,
 when there were no springs abounding with water.
Before the mountains had been shaped,
 before the hills, I was brought forth;
before he had made the earth with its fields,
 or the first of the dust of the world.
When he established the heavens, I was there,
 when he drew a circle on the face of the deep,
when he made firm the skies above,
 when he established the fountains of the deep,
when he assigned to the sea its limit,
 so that the waters might not transgress his command,
when he marked out the foundations of the earth,
 then I was beside him, like a master workman;
and I was daily his delight,
 rejoicing before him always,
rejoicing in his inhabited world
 and delighting in the sons of men.

(1) **DS 150:** DS 150 is the Nicene Creed, which follows paragraph 184 in the CCC. **291**

291 (2) Hymn, "Veni Creator Spiritus"

Come, O Creator, Spirit blest,
And in our souls take up thy rest;
Come with thy grace and heavenly aid;
To fill the hearts which thou hast made.

Great Paraclete, to thee we cry,
O highest gift of God most high,
O Fount of Life, O Fire of Love,
And sweet anointing from above!

Thou in thy sevenfold gifts art known;
The finger of God's hand we own;
The promise of the Father thou,
Who dost the tongue with pow'r endow.

Our senses kindle from above,
And make our hearts o'erflow with love;
With patience firm and virtue high
The weakness of our flesh supply.

Drive far from us the foe we dread
And grant us thy true peace instead;
So shall we not, with thee for Guide,
Turn from the path of life aside.

Oh, may thy grace on us bestow
The Father and the Son to know,
And thee, through endless times confess'd,
Of both th' eternal Spirit blest.

All glory while the ages run
Be to the Father and the Son,
Who rose from death; the same to thee,
O Holy Ghost, eternally! Amen.

291 (3) Byzantine Troparion of Pentecost, Vespers

O Heavenly King, Consoler,
the Spirit of Truth,
present in all places and filling all things,
the Treasury of Blessing and the Giver of Life,
come and dwell in us,
cleanse us of all stain and save our souls,
O Good One!

292 (1) Psalm 33:6

By the word of the Lord the heavens were made,
and all their host by the breath of his mouth.

292 (2) Psalm 104:30

When thou sendest forth thy Spirit, they are created;
and thou renewest the face of the ground.

(3) **Genesis 1:2–3** The earth was without form and void, and darkness was upon 292
the face of the deep; and the Spirit of God was moving over the face of the waters.
And God said, "Let there be light"; and there was light.

Wisdom 9:9 295
With thee is wisdom, who knows thy works
and was present when thou didst make the world,
and who understands what is pleasing in thy sight
and what is right according to thy commandments.

(1) **Vatican Council I (1870): DS 3022–24** [*Against materialism*]. If anyone shall 296
not be ashamed to affirm that nothing exists except matter: let him be anathema.

[*Against pantheism*]. If anyone shall say that one and the same thing is the substance or essence of God and of all things: let him be anathema.

[*Against special forms of pantheism*]. If anyone shall say that finite things, both corporeal and spiritual, or at least the spiritual, have emanated from the divine substance,

or, that the divine essence by a manifestation or evolution of itself becomes all things,

or, finally, that God is universal or indefinite being, because by determining Himself, He created all things distinct in genera, in species, and in individuals: let him be anathema.

(2) **Vatican Council I (1870): DS 3025** [*Against pantheists and materialists*]. If any- 296
one does not confess that the world and all things which are contained in it, both spiritual and material, as regards their whole substance, have been produced by God from nothing [cf. n. 1783],

[*Against the Guentherians*], or, shall have said that God created not by a volition free of all necessity, but as necessarily as He necessarily loves Himself [cf. n. 1783],

[*Against the Guentherians and the Hermesians*], or, shall have denied that the world was created to the glory of God: let him be anathema.

(1) **Psalm 51:12 (51:10: RSV)** 298
Create in me a clean heart, O God,
and put a new and right spirit within me.

(2) **Genesis 1:3** And God said, "Let there be light"; and there was light. 298

(3) **2 Corinthians 4:6** For it is the God who said, "Let light shine out of darkness," 298
who has shone in our hearts to give the light of the knowledge of the glory of God in the face of Christ.

(1) **Psalm 19:2–5a (19:1–4a: RSV)** 299
The heavens are telling the glory of God;
and the firmament proclaims his handiwork.
Day to day pours forth speech,
and night to night declares knowledge.
There is no speech, nor are there words;
their voice is not heard;
yet their voice goes out through all the earth,
and their words to the end of the world.

(2) **Job 42:3** ". . . 'Who is this that hides counsel without knowledge?'. . ." 299

299 (3) **St. Leo the Great, letter "*Quam laudabiliter*" to Turibius, Bishop of Astorga (21 July 447): DS 286** The sixth annotation shows that they said that the devil was never good, nor that his nature was a work of God, but that he emerged from chaos and darkness: because, they say, he had no author but is himself the origin and substance of all evil. But the true faith confesses that . . . the substance of all creatures, spiritual and corporal, is good and no nature is bad. Hence the devil would have been good if he had remained as he had been created. But because he made bad use of his natural excellence "and did not remain in the truth", he did not change into a contrary substance, but fell from the supreme good to which he should have adhered, just as those who assert such things rush forth from the truth to falsehood and betray their nature in freely abusing it and by their own willful perversity are condemned. For certainly there will be evil in them and this evil will not be their substance but the punishment of their substance.

299 (4) **Council of Braga II (561): DS 455–63** If anyone believes, as Manichaeus and Priscillian have said, that human souls or angels have arisen from the substance of God, let him be anathema.

If anyone says that human souls first sinned in the heavenly habitation and in view of this were hurled down into human bodies on earth, as Priscillian has affirmed, let him be anathema.

If anyone says that the devil was not first a good angel made by God, and that his nature was not a work of God, but says that he came forth from darkness, and does not have any author of himself, but is himself the origin and substance of evil, as Manichaeus and Priscillian have said, let him be anathema.

If anyone believes that the devil made some creatures in the world and by his own authority the devil causes thunder and lightning, and storms and spells of dryness, just as Priscillian has asserted, let him be anathema.

If anyone believes that human souls [*al.* souls and human bodies] are bound by a fatal sign [*al.* by fatal stars], just as the pagans and Priscillian have affirmed, let him be anathema.

If anyone believes that the twelve signs or stars, which the astrologers are accustomed to observe, have been scattered through single members of the soul or body, and say that they have been attributed to the names of the Patriarchs, just as Priscillian has asserted, let him be anathema.

If anyone condemns human marriage and has a horror of the procreation of living bodies, as Manichaeus and Priscillian have said, let him be anathema.

If anyone says that the formation of the human body is a creation of the devil, and says that conceptions in the wombs of mothers are formed by the works of demons, and for this reason does not believe in the resurrection of the body, just as Manichaeus and Priscillian have said, let him be anathema.

If anyone says that the creation of all flesh is not the work of God, but belongs to the wicked angels, just as Priscillian has said, let him be anathema.

299 (5) **Lateran Council IV (1215): DS 800** Firmly we believe and we confess simply that the true God is one alone, eternal, immense, and unchangeable, incomprehensible, omnipotent and ineffable, *Father and Son and Holy Spirit*: indeed three Persons but one essence, substance, or nature entirely simple. The Father from no one, the Son from the Father only, and the Holy Spirit equally from both; without beginning, always, and without end; the Father generating, the Son being born, and the Holy Spirit proceeding; consubstantial and coequal and omnipotent and coeternal; one beginning of all, creator of all visible and invisible things, of the spiritual and of the corporal; who by His own omnipotent power at once from the beginning of time created

each creature from nothing, spiritual, and corporal, namely, angelic and mundane, and finally the human, constituted as it were, alike of the spirit and the body. For the devil and other demons were created by God good in nature, but they themselves through themselves have become wicked. But man sinned at the suggestion of the devil. This Holy Trinity according to common essence undivided, and according to personal properties distinct, granted the doctrine of salvation to the human race, first through Moses and the holy prophets and his other servants according to the most methodical disposition of the time.

(6) **Council of Florence (1442): DS 1333** Most strongly it believes, professes, and declares that the one true God, Father and Son and Holy Spirit, is the creator of all things visible and invisible, who, when He wished, out of His goodness created all creatures, spiritual as well as corporal; good indeed, since they were made by the highest good, but changeable, since they were made from nothing, and it asserts that nature is not evil, since all nature, in so far as it is nature, is good. 299

(7) **Vatican Council I (1870): DS 3002** [*The act of creation in itself, and in opposition to modern errors, and the effect of creation*]. This sole true God by His goodness and "omnipotent power," not to increase His own beatitude, and not to add to, but to manifest His perfection by the blessings which He bestows on creatures, with most free volition, "immediately from the beginning of time fashioned each creature out of nothing, spiritual and corporeal, namely angelic and mundane; and then the human creation, common as it were, composed of both spirit and body" [Lateran Council IV]. 299

Sirach 43:28 300

Where shall we find strength to praise him?
For he is greater than all his works.

(1) **Isaiah 10:5–15** 304

Ah, Assyria, the rod of my anger,
the staff of my fury!
Against a godless nation I send him,
and against the people of my wrath I command him,
to take spoil and seize plunder,
and to tread them down like the mire of the streets.
But he does not so intend,
and his mind does not so think;
but it is in his mind to destroy,
and to cut off nations not a few;
for he says:
"Are not my commanders all kings?
Is not Calno like Carchemish?
Is not Hamath like Arpad?
Is not Samaria like Damascus?
As my hand has reached to the kingdoms of the idols
whose graven images were greater than those of
Jerusalem and Samaria,
shall I not do to Jerusalem and her idols
as I have done to Samaria and her images?"

When the Lord has finished all his work on Mount Zion and on Jerusalem he will punish the arrogant boasting of the king of Assyria and his haughty pride. For he says:

"By the strength of my hand I have done it,
  and by my wisdom, for I have understanding;
I have removed the boundaries of peoples,
  and have plundered their treasures;
  like a bull I have brought down those who sat on thrones.
My hand has found like a nest
  the wealth of the peoples;
and as men gather eggs that have been forsaken
  so I have gathered all the earth;
and there was none that moved a wing,
  or opened the mouth, or chirped."

Shall the axe vaunt itself over him who hews with it,
  or the saw magnify itself against him who wields it?
As if a rod should wield him who lifts it,
  or as if a staff should lift him who is not wood!

304 (2) **Isaiah 45:5–7**

I am the Lord, and there is no other,
  besides me there is no God;
  I gird you, though you do not know me,
that men may know, from the rising of the sun
  and from the west, that there is none besides me;
  I am the Lord, and there is no other.
I form light and create darkness,
  I make weal and create woe,
  I am the Lord, who do all these things.

304 (3) **Deuteronomy 32:39**

"'See now that I, even I, am he,
  and there is no god beside me;
I kill and I make alive;
  I wound and I heal;
  and there is none that can deliver out of my hand. . . .'"

304 (4) **Sirach 11:14**

Good things and bad, life and death,
  poverty and wealth, come from the Lord.

304 (5) **Psalm 22**

My God, my God, why hast thou forsaken me?
Why art thou so far from helping me, from the words of
  my groaning?
O my God, I cry by day, but thou dost not answer;
  and by night, but find no rest.

Yet thou art holy,
  enthroned on the praises of Israel.
In thee our fathers trusted;
  they trusted, and thou didst deliver them.
To thee they cried, and were saved;
  in thee they trusted, and were not disappointed.

But I am a worm, and no man;
 scorned by men, and despised by the people.
All who see me mock at me,
 they make mouths at me, they wag their heads;
"He committed his cause to the Lord; let him deliver him,
 let him rescue him, for he delights in him!"

Yet thou art he who took me from the womb;
 thou didst keep me safe upon my mother's breasts.
Upon thee was I cast from my birth,
 and since my mother bore me thou hast been my God.
Be not far from me,
 for trouble is near
 and there is none to help.

Many bulls encompass me,
 strong bulls of Bashan surround me;
 they open wide their mouths at me,
 like a ravening and roaring lion.

I am poured out like water,
 and all my bones are out of joint;
my heart is like wax,
 it is melted within my breast;
my strength is dried up like a potsherd,
 and my tongue cleaves to my jaws;
 thou dost lay me in the dust of death.

Yea, dogs are round about me;
 a company of evildoers encircle me;
 they have pierced my hands and feet—
I can count all my bones—
 they stare and gloat over me;
they divide my garments among them,
 and for my raiment they cast lots.

But thou, O Lord, be not far off!
 O thou my help, hasten to my aid!
Deliver my soul from the sword,
 my life from the power of the dog!
Save me from the mouth of the lion,
 my afflicted soul from the horns of the wild oxen!

I will tell of thy name to my brethren;
 in the midst of the congregation I will praise thee:
You who fear the Lord, praise him!
 all you sons of Jacob, glorify him,
 and stand in awe of him, all you sons of Israel!

For he has not despised or abhorred
 the affliction of the afflicted;
and he has not hid his face from him,
 but has heard, when he cried to him.

From thee comes my praise in the great congregation;
 my vows I will pay before those who fear him.

The afflicted shall eat and be satisfied;
those who seek him shall praise the Lord!
May your hearts live for ever!

All the ends of the earth shall remember
and turn to the Lord;
and all the families of the nations
shall worship before him.
For dominion belongs to the Lord,
and he rules over the nations.

Yea, to him shall all the proud of the earth bow down;
before him shall bow all who go down to the dust,
and he who cannot keep himself alive.
Posterity shall serve him;
men shall tell of the Lord to the coming generation,
and proclaim his deliverance to a people yet unborn,
that he has wrought it.

304 (6) **Psalm 32**

Blessed is he whose transgression is forgiven,
whose sin is covered.
Blessed is the man to whom the Lord imputes no iniquity,
and in whose spirit there is no deceit. *Selah*

When I declared not my sin, my body wasted away
through my groaning all day long.
For day and night thy hand was heavy upon me;
my strength was dried up as by the heat of summer. *Selah*

I acknowledged my sin to thee,
and I did not hide my iniquity;
I said, "I will confess my transgressions to the Lord";
then thou didst forgive the guilt of my sin. *Selah*

Therefore let every one who is godly
offer prayer to thee;
at a time of distress, in the rush of great waters,
they shall not reach him.
Thou art a hiding place for me,
thou preservest me from trouble;
thou dost encompass me with deliverance. *Selah*

I will instruct you and teach you
the way you should go;
I will counsel you with my eye upon you.
Be not like a horse or a mule, without understanding,
which must be curbed with bit and bridle,
else it will not keep with you.

Many are the pangs of the wicked;
but steadfast love surrounds him who trusts in the Lord.
Be glad in the Lord, and rejoice, O righteous,
and shout for joy, all you upright in heart!

(7) **Psalm 35** 304

Contend, O Lord, with those who contend with me;
fight against those who fight against me!
Take hold of shield and buckler,
and rise for my help!
Draw the spear and javelin
against my pursuers!
Say to my soul,
"I am your deliverance!"

Let them be put to shame and dishonor
who seek after my life!
Let them be turned back and confounded
who devise evil against me!
Let them be like chaff before the wind,
with the angel of the Lord driving them on!
Let their way be dark and slippery,
with the angel of the Lord pursuing them!

For without cause they hid their net for me;
without cause they dug a pit for my life.
Let ruin come upon them unawares!
And let the net which they hid ensnare them;
let them fall therein to ruin!

Then my soul shall rejoice in the Lord,
exulting in his deliverance.
All my bones shall say,
"O Lord, who is like thee,
thou who deliverest the weak
from him who is too strong for him,
the weak and needy from him who despoils him?"

Malicious witnesses rise up;
they ask me of things that I know not.
They requite me evil for good;
my soul is forlorn.
But I, when they were sick—
I wore sackcloth,
I afflicted myself with fasting.
I prayed with head bowed on my bosom,
as though I grieved for my friend or my brother;
I went about as one who laments his mother,
bowed down and in mourning.

But at my stumbling they gathered in glee,
they gathered together against me;
cripples whom I knew not
slandered me without ceasing;
they impiously mocked more and more,
gnashing at me with their teeth.
How long, O Lord, wilt thou look on?
Rescue me from their ravages,
my life from the lions!

Then I will thank thee in the great congregation;
 in the mighty throng I will praise thee.

Let not those rejoice over me
 who are wrongfully my foes,
and let not those wink the eye
 who hate me without cause.
For they do not speak peace,
 but against those who are quiet in the land
 they conceive words of deceit.
They open wide their mouths against me;
 they say, "Aha, Aha!
 our eyes have seen it!"

Thou hast seen, O Lord; be not silent!
 O Lord, be not far from me!
Bestir thyself, and awake for my right,
 for my cause, my God and my Lord!
Vindicate me, O Lord, my God, according to thy righteousness;
 and let them not rejoice over me!
Let them not say to themselves,
 "Aha, we have our heart's desire!"
Let them not say, "We have swallowed him up."

Let them be put to shame and confusion altogether
 who rejoice at my calamity!
Let them be clothed with shame and dishonor
 who magnify themselves against me!

Let those who desire my vindication
 shout for joy and be glad,
 and say evermore,
"Great is the Lord,
 who delights in the welfare of his servant!"
Then my tongue shall tell of thy righteousness
 and of thy praise all the day long.

304 (8) **Psalm 103**

Bless the Lord, O my soul;
 and all that is within me, bless his holy name!
Bless the Lord, O my soul,
 and forget not all his benefits,
who forgives all your iniquity,
 who heals all your diseases,
who redeems your life from the Pit,
 who crowns you with steadfast love and mercy,
who satisfies you with good as long as you live
 so that your youth is renewed like the eagle's.

The Lord works vindication
 and justice for all who are oppressed.
He made known his ways to Moses,
 his acts to the people of Israel.
The Lord is merciful and gracious,
 slow to anger and abounding in steadfast love.

He will not always chide,
nor will he keep his anger for ever.
He does not deal with us according to our sins,
nor requite us according to our iniquities.
For as the heavens are high above the earth,
so great is his steadfast love toward those who fear him;
as far as the east is from the west,
so far does he remove our transgressions from us.
As a father pities his children,
so the Lord pities those who fear him.
For he knows our frame;
he remembers that we are dust.

As for man, his days are like grass;
he flourishes like a flower of the field;
for the wind passes over it, and it is gone,
and its place knows it no more.
But the steadfast love of the Lord is from everlasting to everlasting
upon those who fear him,
and his righteousness to children's children,
to those who keep his covenant
and remember to do his commandments.

The Lord has established his throne in the heavens,
and his kingdom rules over all.
Bless the Lord, O you his angels,
you mighty ones who do his word,
hearkening to the voice of his word!
Bless the Lord, all his hosts,
his ministers that do his will!
Bless the Lord, all his works,
in all places of his dominion.
Bless the Lord, O my soul!

(9) **Psalm 138** 304

I give thee thanks, O Lord, with my whole heart;
before the gods I sing thy praise;
I bow down toward thy holy temple
and give thanks to thy name for thy steadfast love and thy faithfulness;
for thou hast exalted above everything
thy name and thy word.
On the day I called, thou didst answer me,
my strength of soul thou didst increase.

All the kings of the earth shall praise thee, O Lord,
for they have heard the words of thy mouth;
and they shall sing of the ways of the Lord,
for great is the glory of the Lord.
For though the Lord is high, he regards the lowly;
but the haughty he knows from afar.

Though I walk in the midst of trouble,
thou dost preserve my life;

thou dost stretch out thy hand against the wrath of my enemies,
and thy right hand delivers me.
The Lord will fulfil his purpose for me;
thy steadfast love, O Lord, endures for ever.
Do not forsake the work of thy hands.

305 **Matthew 10:29–31** Are not two sparrows sold for a penny? And not one of them will fall to the ground without your Father's will. But even the hairs of your head are all numbered. Fear not, therefore; you are of more value than many sparrows.

307 (1) **Genesis 1:26–28** Then God said, "Let us make man in our image, after our likeness; and let them have dominion over the fish of the sea, and over the birds of the air, and over the cattle, and over all the earth, and over every creeping thing that creeps upon the earth." So God created man in his own image, in the image of God he created him; male and female he created them. And God blessed them, and God said to them, "Be fruitful and multiply, and fill the earth and subdue it; and have dominion over the fish of the sea and over the birds of the air and over every living thing that moves upon the earth."

307 (2) **Colossians 1:24** Now I rejoice in my sufferings for your sake, and in my flesh I complete what is lacking in Christ's afflictions for the sake of his body, that is, the church. . . .

308 (1) **1 Corinthians 12:6** . . . and there are varieties of working, but it is the same God who inspires them all in every one.

308 (2) **Matthew 19:26** But Jesus looked at them and said to them, "With men this is impossible, but with God all things are possible."

308 (3) **John 15:5** I am the vine, you are the branches. He who abides in me, and I in him, he it is that bears much fruit, for apart from me you can do nothing.

308 (4) **Philippians 4:13** I can do all things in him who strengthens me.

310 (1) **St. Thomas Aquinas, *Summa theologiae* I, 25, 6**
article 6. could God make better things than he does?

THE SIXTH POINT: 1. How could he? For whatever he does is with the utmost wisdom and power. The better a thing is done so much the more is this the case. So God cannot do better than he does.

2. Again, Augustine argues, *If God could but would not beget a Son equal to himself he would be jealous*. Likewise he would be the same if he could but would not make better things. But God is a complete stranger to jealousy. Therefore God makes things that are the best, and cannot be bettered.

3. Moreover, what is far and away the best cannot be bettered; nothing is more than the most. Now Augustine says, *Each thing made by God is good, and when all are taken together very good indeed, for in them all consists the wondrous beauty of the universe.* Therefore God cannot improve on the good of the universe.

4. Besides, the man Christ is full of grace and truth, and possesses the Spirit without stint, and so cannot be better. Again, heaven is said to be the supreme good, and so cannot be better. Again the blessed virgin Mary is raised above all the choirs of angels, and so cannot be better than she is. Therefore God cannot improve on what he has done.

ON THE OTHER HAND there is the text in *Ephesians*, *God is powerful and able to do all things more abundantly than we understand or desire.*

REPLY: A thing has a double goodness. One of its nature, thus to be rational is of the nature of man. In this regard, God cannot make a thing to be better than it is, though he can make something else that is better. For instance he cannot make 4 to be more than 4, for then it would not be 4 but another number; the *Metaphysics* note that the addition of an essential difference in the definition of a species is like the addition of a unit to a number. The second goodness is other than the nature or essence of a thing, thus for a human being to be virtuous and wise. In this sense God can improve on things as they are.

Yet to speak without reservation, God can make a better thing than anything he has made.

Hence: 1. When we speak about God making anything better, the 'better' can be taken substantively, and then the statement is true: he can make another to be a better thing than the one he does make, and, as we have explained, he can make the same thing better in one way though not in another. If, however, 'better' be taken adverbially to refer to the manner of the making, then God cannot work better than he does, or from greater wisdom and goodness. If, however, it refers to the mode of the making with respect to the thing made, then he can make better, for he could give things a better manner of existing as to their qualities, though not their substance.

2. To be his father's equal is in the nature of a son when he grows up. But to be better than as made by God is not in any creature's nature. Hence the comparison fails.

3. Supposing the things that are, the universe cannot be better than it is; its good consists in the world-order, most handsome it is and bestowed by God. For one part to be improved out of recognition would spoil the proportions of the whole design; overstretch one lute-string and the melody is lost. All the same God could make other things, or add them to those he has made, and there would be another and better universe.

4. Christ's humanity, from being united with God, heaven, from being the enjoyment of God, and the blessed Virgin, from being the mother of God, have a certain infinite dignity deriving from the infinite good, which is God; in this respect there can be nothing better, just as there can be nothing better than God.

(2) **St. Thomas Aquinas, *Summa contra gentiles* III, 71** Now, from these conclu- 310
sions it becomes evident that divine providence, whereby He governs things, does not prevent corruption, deficiency, and evil from being found in things.

Indeed, divine governance, whereby God works in things, does not exclude the working of secondary causes, as we have already shown. Now, it is possible for a defect to happen in an effect, because of a defect in the secondary agent cause, without there being a defect in the primary agent. For example, in the case of the product of a perfectly skilled artisan, some defect may occur because of a defect in his instrument. And again, in the case of a man whose motive power is strong, he may limp as a result of no defect in his bodily power to move, but because of a twist in his leg bone. So, it is possible, in the case of things made and governed by God, for some defect and evil to be found, because of a defect of the secondary agents, even though there be no defect in God Himself.

Moreover, perfect goodness would not be found in created things unless there were an order of goodness in them, in the sense that some of them are better than others. Otherwise, all possible grades of goodness would not be realized, nor would any creature be like God by virtue of holding a higher place than another. The highest beauty would be taken away from things, too, if the order of distinct and unequal things were removed. And what is more, multiplicity would be taken away from things if inequality of goodness were removed, since through the differences by which things are distinguished from each other one thing stands out as better than another; for instance, the animate in relation to the inanimate, and the rational in regard to the irrational. And so, if complete equality were present in things, there would be but one created good, which clearly disparages the perfection of the creature. Now, it is a higher grade of goodness for a thing to be good because it cannot fall from goodness; lower than that is the thing which can fall from goodness. So, the perfection of the universe requires both grades of goodness. But it pertains to the providence of the governor to preserve perfection in the things governed, and not to decrease it. Therefore, it does not pertain to divine goodness, entirely to exclude from things the power of falling from the good. But evil is the consequence of this power, because what is able to fall does fall at times. And this defection of the good is evil, as we showed above. Therefore, it does not pertain to divine providence to prohibit evil entirely from things.

Again, the best thing in any government is to provide for the things governed according to their own mode, for the justice of a regime consists in this. Therefore, as it would be contrary to the rational character of a human regime for men to be prevented by the governor from acting in accord with their own duties—except, perhaps, on occasion, due to the need of the moment—so, too, would it be contrary to the rational character of the divine regime to refuse permission for created things to act according to the mode of their nature. Now, as a result of this fact, that creatures do act in this way, corruption and evil result in things, because, due to the contrariety and incompatibility present in things, one may be a source of corruption for another. Therefore, it does not pertain to divine providence to exclude evil entirely from the things that are governed.

Besides, it is impossible for an agent to do something evil, unless by virtue of the fact that the agent intends something good, as is evident from the foregoing. But, to prohibit universally the intending of the good for the individual on the part of created things is not the function of the providence of Him Who is the cause of every good thing. For, in that way, many goods would be taken away from the whole of things. For example, if the inclination to generate its like were taken away from fire (from which inclination there results this particular evil which is the burning up of combustible things), there would also be taken away this particular good which is the generation of fire and the preservation of the same according to its species. Therefore, it is not the function of divine providence totally to exclude evil from things.

Furthermore, many goods are present in things which would not occur unless there were evils. For instance, there would not be the patience of the just if there were not the malice of their persecutors; there would not be a place for the justice of vindication if there were no offenses; and in the order of nature, there would not be the generation of one thing unless there were the corruption of another. So, if evil were totally excluded from the whole of things by divine providence, a multitude of good things would have to be sacrificed. And this is as it should be, for the good is stronger in its goodness than evil is in its malice, as is clear from earlier sections. Therefore, evil should not be totally excluded from things by divine providence.

Moreover, the good of the whole takes precedence over the good of a part. It is proper for a governor with foresight to neglect some lack of goodness in a part, so that there may be an increase of goodness in the whole. Thus, an artisan hides the foundations beneath earth, so that the whole house may have stability. But, if evil were removed from some parts of the universe, much perfection would perish from the universe, whose beauty arises from an ordered unification of evil and good things. In fact, while evil things originate from good things that are defective, still, certain good things also result from them, as a consequence of the providence of the governor. Thus, even a silent pause makes a hymn appealing. Therefore, evil should not have been excluded from things by divine providence.

Again, other things, particularly lower ones, are ordered to man's good as an end. Now, if no evils were present in things, much of man's good would be diminished, both in regard to knowledge and in regard to the desire or love of the good. In fact, the good is better known from its comparison with evil, and while we continue to suffer certain evils our desire for goods grows more ardent. For instance, how great a good health is, is best known by the sick; and they also crave it more than do the healthy. Therefore, it is not the function of divine providence totally to exclude evils from things.

For this reason, it is said: "I make peace and create evil" (Isa. 45:7; Douay modified); and again: "There is no evil in a city which God will not do" (Amos 3:6).

Now, with these considerations we dispose of the error of those who, because they noticed that evils occur in the world, said that there is no God. Thus, Boethius introduces a certain philosopher who asks: "If God exists, whence comes evil?" But it could be argued to the contrary: "If evil exists, God exists." For, there would be no evil if the order of good were taken away, since its privation is evil. But this order would not exist if there were no God.

Moreover, by the foregoing arguments, even the occasion of error is removed from those who denied that divine providence is extended to these corruptible things, because they saw that many evils occur in them; they said, moreover, that only incorruptible things are subject to divine providence, things in which no defect or evil part is found.

By these considerations, the occasion of erring is also taken away from the Manicheans who maintained two first agent principles, good and evil, as though evil could have no place under the providence of a good God.

So, too, the difficulty of some people is solved; namely, whether evil actions are from God. Indeed, since it has been shown that every agent produces its action by acting through the divine power, and, consequently that God is the cause both of all effects and all actions, and since it was also shown that evil and defects occur in things ruled by divine providence as a result of the establishment of secondary causes in which there can be deficiency, it is evident that bad actions, according as they defective, are not from God but from defective proximate causes; but, in so far as they possess something of action and entity, they must be from God. Thus limping arises from the motive power, in so far as it possesses something of motion, but in regard to what it has by way of defect it is due to the crookedness of the leg.

(1) **St. Augustine, *De libero arbitrio* I, 1, 1** 311

Evodius. Tell me, I ask, whether God is the author of evil?

Augustine. If you make it clear about what evil you are inquiring I will tell you. For we speak of evil with a twofold meaning—one when we say that someone has done badly, the other when one suffers some evil.

E. I want to know about both [kinds of evil].

A. But, if you know, or if you believe that God is good (and it is not right to believe otherwise), then God does no evil. Again, if we acknowledge that God is just (for to deny that is wrong too), then [by consequence] He rewards the good, as He punishes the wicked. These punishments surely are bad for those who suffer them. Wherefore, if no one endures penalties unjustly, which we must believe, because we believe that this universe is ruled by divine providence, it follows that God is in no way the author of that former kind of evil. Of this second kind He is the author.

E. Is there then another, the author of this evil, of which God is found not to be the author?

A. There is assuredly. For without an author evil could not exist. But if you ask who that one is; it can not be stated. Because it is not some one individual. For anyone who is bad is the author of his own evildoing. If you are not sure on this point, then mark what was said above—that evil deeds are punished by God's justice. Indeed they would not be punished justly unless there were the will to do them.

E. I know not whether any one can sin who has not learned to sin. But if this be true, then who is that from whom we have learned to sin, I ask?

A. Do you esteem learning to be something good?

E. Who can dare to say that learning is something bad?

A. What if it is neither good nor bad?

E. To me it seems good.

A. Well, indeed. That is, if knowledge is given by learning, or if knowledge is awakened: and truly no one learns anything but by learning, or think you not so?

E. I think that by learning, good things only are learned.

A. See, therefore, whether evil things are not learned: for learning has its origin from [the verb] to learn.

E. Whence, therefore, are evil things done by men, if they are not learned?

A. Perhaps it is from this, that man turns himself away from learning, that is, estranges himself from the fact of learning. But whether this or something else be true, this surely is evident—that learning is good, and because it is derived from [the verb] to learn, evil things can not be learned. For, if they are learned, they are contained in learning, and consequently learning will be not good: but learning, as you grant, is good, therefore evil things are not learned; and it is to no purpose that you ask who that is from whom we learn to do badly. Or, if evil things are learned, then they are learned to be avoided, not to be done. Whence it follows that to do evil is nothing other than to wander away from learning.

E. I think strongly that teachings are two; one by which we learn to do right, another, but which we learn to do wrong. But when you were asking whether learning is a good thing, the love of good itself took my attention, so that I looked at that learning which is of well doing, whence I answered that it is good. But now I am reminded that there is another [learning], which beyond doubt I affirm to be evil, and it is for the author of that that I inquire.

A. Do you think, at any rate, that intelligence is a good thing?

E. So surely do I think intelligence to be good, that I can not see what in man is more excellent: and I would not say in any way that any understanding can be bad.

A. How then, if one does not understand when he is taught, can he seem to you to have learned?

E. No, not at all.

A. If, therefore, all understanding is good, and no one learns who understands not, [it follows] that everyone who learns does well: for everyone who learns understands; and everyone who understands does well. Therefore whosoever inquires for the author by whom we learn anything, inquires surely for the author by whom we do well. Wherefore, make an end now to your wanting to investigate some unknown evil teacher. For, if he is evil, he is not a teacher: if he is a teacher, he is not evil.

311 (2) **St. Thomas Aquinas *Summa theologiae* I–II, 79, 1**

Question 79. the intellectual powers

THE NEXT INQUIRY concerns the powers of understanding, with thirteen topics:

1. whether the understanding is a power of the soul or its essence;
2. whether, granted that it is a power, it is a receptive power;

3. granted that it is a receptive power, whether there is an abstractive intellectual power;
4. whether this belongs to the soul;
5. whether there is one abstractive intellect for all men;
6. whether memory belongs to the understanding;
7. whether it is a power distinct from the understanding;
8. whether reason is a power distinct from the understanding;
9. whether the lower and the higher reason differ as powers;
10. whether intelligence is a power distinct from the understanding;
11. whether the speculative and practical intellect differ as powers;
12. whether synderesis is a power belonging to the intellectual order;
13. whether conscience is a power belonging to the intellectual order.

article 1. whether the understanding is a power of the soul

THE FIRST POINT: 1. There are reasons for thinking that the understanding is not a power of the soul but its essence. For the understanding seems to be the same as the mind. But mind is the soul's essence, not a power, for Augustine says, *Mind and spirit do not merely have a relationship to something, they indicate an essence.* It follows that the understanding is the soul's very essence.

2. Besides, the various kinds of power the soul has are not unified in one particular power but only in the soul's essence. Now appetitive and intellective powers differ in kind among the soul's powers, as is said in the *De Anima.* They unite in the mind, which is where Augustine places intelligence and will. Hence mind and understanding are the very essence of the soul, not a power of it.

3. Again, according to Gregory, *man understands as the angels do.* But angels are described as minds and intelligences. So the mind and intellect of man is not some power of the soul but the soul itself.

4. And again, it is immateriality that makes a substance intellectual. But the soul is essentially immaterial. So it seems that the soul is capable of understanding by its essence.

ON THE OTHER HAND Aristotle speaks of an intellective power of the soul, as is clear in the *De Anima.*

REPLY: It follows necessarily from what was said earlier that the understanding is a power of the soul and not the very essence of the soul. A thing's essence can be the immediate source of its activity only when its activity is its being. For as any power is related to its activity as to its actuation, so essence has itself in relation to existence. Now in God alone is understanding the same as being. In creatures with intelligence, the understanding is a power of the one that understands.

Hence: 1. Sense sometimes means a power, sometimes the sense-soul itself, the sense-soul being named from its principal power, sense. And likewise the intellectual soul sometimes gets named from the intellect as its principal power, in the way, as the *De Anima* remarks, that *the intellect is a substance.* And in this way Augustine says that mind is spirit or essence.

2. Appetitive and intellective constitute different kinds of power in the soul because of the different aspects under which they bear on their object. But appetite shares something with intellect and something with sense so far as acting with or without a bodily organ is concerned, for appetite depends on knowledge. Accordingly Augustine places will in the mind and Aristotle places it in the reason.

3. In angels there is no power except the understanding and the will that issues from it. For this reason an angel is called a mind or an intellect, for this is the entire scope of its power. But a soul has numerous other powers such as the nutritive and sensitive and so the comparison breaks down.

4. It is not true that the non-materiality of a created intellectual substance is his understanding, but rather that through non-materiality he has the power of understanding. Hence the understanding does not have to be the soul's substance, but rather its power and ability.

312 (1) **Tobit 2:12–18, vulg.** Now this trial the Lord therefore permitted to happen to him, that an example might be given to posterity of his patience, as also of holy Job. For whereas he had always feared God from his infancy, and kept his commandments, he repined not against God because the evil of blindness had befallen him, but continued immovable in the fear of God, giving thanks to God all the days of his life. For as the kings insulted over holy Job: so his relations and kinsmen mocked at his life, saying: Where is your hope, for which you gave alms, and buried the dead? But Tobit rebuked them, saying: Speak not so: For we are the children of saints, and look for that life which God will give to those that never change their faith from him.

312 (2) **Romans 5:20** Law came in, to increase the trespass; but where sin increased, grace abounded all the more. . . .

314 **Genesis 2:2** And on the seventh day God finished his work which he had done, and he rested on the seventh day from all his work which he had done.

318 **Decree of the Sacred Congregation of Studies, 27 July 1914: DS 3624** Therefore by the very purity of his being, God is distinct from all finite things. The first inference from this is that the world could only have proceeded from creation by God; then that the creative power which per se reaches to being qua being cannot be communicated, even miraculously, to any finite nature; and finally that no created agent can have an influence on the being of any effect without itself being moved by the First Cause.

322 (1) **Matthew 6:26–34** "Look at the birds of the air: they neither sow nor reap nor gather into barns, and yet your heavenly Father feeds them. Are you not of more value than they? And which of you by being anxious can add one cubit to his span of life? And why are you anxious about clothing? Consider the lilies of the field, how they grow; they neither toil nor spin; yet I tell you, even Solomon in all his glory was not arrayed like one of these. But if God so clothes the grass of the field, which today is alive and tomorrow is thrown into the oven, will he not much more clothe you, O men of little faith? Therefore do not be anxious, saying, 'What shall we eat?' or 'What shall we drink?' or 'What shall we wear?' For the Gentiles seek all these things; and your heavenly Father knows that you need them all. But seek first his kingdom and his righteousness, and all these things shall be yours as well.

"Therefore do not be anxious about tomorrow, for tomorrow will be anxious for itself. Let the day's own trouble be sufficient for the day. . . ."

322 (2) **Psalm 55:23 (55:22: RSV)**

Cast your burden on the Lord,
and he will sustain you;
he will never permit
the righteous to be moved.

326 (1) **Psalm 115:16**

The heavens are the Lord's heavens,
but the earth he has given to the sons of men.

(2) **Psalm 19:2 (19:1: RSV)** 326

The heavens are telling the glory of God;
and the firmament proclaims his handiwork.

(1) **Vatican Council I (1870): DS 3002** [*The act of creation in itself, and in opposition to modern errors, and the effect of creation*]. This sole true God by His goodness and "omnipotent power," not to increase His own beatitude, and not to add to, but to manifest His perfection by the blessings which He bestows on creatures, with most free volition, "immediately from the beginning of time fashioned each creature out of nothing, spiritual and corporeal, namely angelic and mundane; and then the human creation, common as it were, composed of both spirit and body" [Lateran Council IV]. 327

(2) **Paul VI, *The* Credo *of the People of God* 8** We believe in one God, the Father, the Son and the Holy Spirit, Creator of what is visible—such as this world where we live out our lives—and of the invisible—such as the pure spirits which are also called angels—and Creator in each man of his spiritual and immortal soul. 327

(1) **Pius XII, encyclical *Humani generis* (1950): DS 3891** The question is also raised by some whether angels are personal creatures; and whether matter differs essentially from spirit. Others destroy the true "gratuity" of the supernatural order, since they think that God cannot produce beings endowed with intellect without ordering and calling them to the beatific vision. This is not all: the notion of original sin, without consideration of the definitions of the Council of Trent, is perverted, and at the same time the notion of sin in general as an offense against God, and likewise the concept of the satisfaction made by Christ for us. And there are those who contend that the doctrine of transubstantiation, inasmuch as it is founded on an antiquated philosophical presence of Christ in the Most Holy Eucharist, is reduced to a kind of symbolism, so that the consecrated species are no more than efficacious signs of the spiritual presence of Christ, and of His intimate union with the faithful members in the mystical body. 330

(2) **Luke 20:36** . . . for they cannot die any more, because they are equal to angels and are sons of God, being sons of the resurrection. 330

(3) **Daniel 10:9–12** Then I heard the sound of his words; and when I heard the sound of his words, I fell on my face in a deep sleep with my face to the ground. 330

And behold, a hand touched me and set me trembling on my hands and knees. And he said to me, "O Daniel, man greatly beloved, give heed to the words that I speak to you, and stand upright, for now I have been sent to you." While he was speaking this word to me, I stood up trembling. Then he said to me, "Fear not, Daniel, for from the first day that you set your mind to understand and humbled yourself before your God, your words have been heard, and I have come because of your words. . . ."

(1) **Job 38:7** 332

. . . when the morning stars sang together,
and all the sons of God shouted for joy?

(2) **Genesis 3:24** He drove out the man; and at the east of the garden of Eden he placed the cherubim, and a flaming sword which turned every way, to guard the way to the tree of life. 332

332 (3) **Genesis 19** The two angels came to Sodom in the evening; and Lot was sitting in the gate of Sodom. When Lot saw them, he rose to meet them, and bowed himself with his face to the earth, and said, "My lords, turn aside, I pray you, to your servant's house and spend the night, and wash your feet; then you may rise up early and go on your way." They said, "No; we will spend the night in the street." But he urged them strongly; so they turned aside to him and entered his house; and he made them a feast, and baked unleavened bread, and they ate. But before they lay down, the men of the city, the men of Sodom, both young and old, all the people to the last man, surrounded the house; and they called to Lot, "Where are the men who came to you tonight? Bring them out to us, that we may know them." Lot went out of the door to the men, shut the door after him, and said, "I beg you, my brothers, do not act so wickedly. Behold, I have two daughters who have not known man; let me bring them out to you, and do to them as you please; only do nothing to these men, for they have come under the shelter of my roof." But they said, "Stand back!" And they said, "This fellow came to sojourn, and he would play the judge! Now we will deal worse with you than with them." Then they pressed hard against the man Lot, and drew near to break the door. But the men put forth their hands and brought Lot into the house to them, and shut the door. And they struck with blindness the men who were at the door of the house, both small and great, so that they wearied themselves groping for the door.

Then the men said to Lot, "Have you any one else here? Sons-in-law, sons, daughters, or any one you have in the city, bring them out of the place; for we are about to destroy this place, because the outcry against its people has become great before the Lord, and the Lord has sent us to destroy it." So Lot went out and said to his sons-in-law, who were to marry his daughters, "Up, get out of this place; for the Lord is about to destroy the city." But he seemed to his sons-in-law to be jesting.

When morning dawned, the angels urged Lot, saying, "Arise, take your wife and your two daughters who are here, lest you be consumed in the punishment of the city." But he lingered; so the men seized him and his wife and his two daughters by the hand, the Lord being merciful to him, and they brought him forth and set him outside the city. And when they had brought them forth, they said, "Flee for your life; do not look back or stop anywhere in the valley; flee to the hills, lest you be consumed." And Lot said to them, "Oh, no, my lords; behold, your servant has found favor in your sight, and you have shown me great kindness in saving my life; but I cannot flee to the hills, lest the disaster overtake me, and I die. Behold, yonder city is near enough to flee to, and it is a little one. Let me escape there—is it not a little one?—and my life will be saved!" He said to him, "Behold, I grant you this favor also, that I will not overthrow the city of which you have spoken. Make haste, escape there; for I can do nothing till you arrive there." Therefore the name of the city was called Zoar. The sun had risen on the earth when Lot came to Zoar.

Then the Lord rained on Sodom and Gomorrah brimstone and fire from the Lord out of heaven; and he overthrew those cities, and all the valley, and all the inhabitants of the cities and what grew on the ground. But Lot's wife behind him looked back, and she became a pillar of salt. And Abraham went early in the morning to the place where he had stood before the Lord; and he looked down toward Sodom and Gomorrah and toward all the land of the valley, and beheld, and lo, the smoke of the land went up like the smoke of a furnace.

So it was that, when God destroyed the cities of the valley, God remembered Abraham, and sent Lot out of the midst of the overthrow, when he overthrew the cities in which Lot dwelt.

Now Lot went up out of Zoar, and dwelt in the hills with his two daughters, for he was afraid to dwell in Zoar; so he dwelt in a cave with his two daughters. And the first-born said to the younger, "Our father is old, and there is not a man on earth to come in to us after the manner of all the earth. Come, let us make our father drink wine, and we will lie with him, that we may preserve offspring through our father." So they made their father drink wine that night; and the first-born went in, and lay with her father; he did not know when she lay down or when she arose. And on the next day, the first-born said to the younger, "Behold, I lay last night with my father; let us make him drink wine tonight also; then you go in and lie with him, that we may preserve offspring through our father." So they made their father drink wine that night also; and the younger arose, and lay with him; and he did not know when she lay down or when she arose. Thus both the daughters of Lot were with child by their father. The first-born bore a son, and called his name Moab; he is the father of the Moabites to this day. The younger also bore a son, and called his name Ben-ammi; he is the father of the Ammonites to this day.

(4) **Genesis 21:17** And God heard the voice of the lad; and the angel of God called 332
to Hagar from heaven, and said to her, "What troubles you, Hagar? Fear not; for God has heard the voice of the lad where he is. . . ."

(5) **Genesis 22:11** But the angel of the Lord called to him from heaven, and said, 332
"Abraham, Abraham!" And he said, "Here am I."

(6) **Acts 7:53** ". . . you who received the law as delivered by angels and did not keep 332
it."

(7) **Exodus 23:20–23** "Behold, I send an angel before you, to guard you on the way 332
and to bring you to the place which I have prepared. Give heed to him and hearken to his voice, do not rebel against him, for he will not pardon your transgression; for my name is in him.

"But if you hearken attentively to his voice and do all that I say, then I will be an enemy to your enemies and an adversary to your adversaries.

"When my angel goes before you, and brings you in to the Amorites, and the Hittites, and the Perizzites, and the Canaanites, the Hivites, and the Jebusites, and I blot them out. . . ."

(8) **Judges 13** And the people of Israel again did what was evil in the sight of the 332
Lord; and the Lord gave them into the hand of the Philistines for forty years.

And there was a certain man of Zorah, of the tribe of the Danites, whose name was Manoah; and his wife was barren and had no children. And the angel of the Lord appeared to the woman and said to her, "Behold, you are barren and have no children; but you shall conceive and bear a son. Therefore beware, and drink no wine or strong drink, and eat nothing unclean, for lo, you shall conceive and bear a son. No razor shall come upon his head, for the boy shall be a Nazirite to God from birth; and he shall begin to deliver Israel from the hand of the Philistines." Then the woman came and told her husband, "A man of God came to me, and his countenance was like the countenance of the angel of God, very terrible; I did not ask him whence he was, and he did not tell me his name; but he said to me, 'Behold, you shall conceive and bear a son; so then drink no wine or strong drink, and eat nothing unclean, for the boy shall be a Nazirite to God from birth to the day of his death.'"

Then Manoah entreated the Lord, and said, "O, Lord, I pray thee, let the man of God whom thou didst send come again to us, and teach us what we are to do with the boy that will be born." And God listened to the voice of Manoah, and the angel of God came again to the woman as she sat in the field; but Manoah her husband was not with her. And the woman ran in haste and told her husband, "Behold, the man who came to me the other day has appeared to me." And Manoah arose and went after his wife, and came to the man and said to him, "Are you the man who spoke to this woman?" And he said, "I am." And Manoah said, "Now when your words come true, what is to be the boy's manner of life, and what is he to do?" And the angel of the Lord said to Manoah, "Of all that I said to the woman let her beware. She may not eat of anything that comes from the vine, neither let her drink wine or strong drink, or eat any unclean thing; all that I commanded her let her observe."

Manoah said to the angel of the Lord, "Pray, let us detain you, and prepare a kid for you." And the angel of the Lord said to Manoah, "If you detain me, I will not eat of your food; but if you make ready a burnt offering, then offer it to the Lord." (For Manoah did not know that he was the angel of the Lord.) And Manoah said to the angel of the Lord, "What is your name, so that, when your words come true, we may honor you?" And the angel of the Lord said to him, "Why do you ask my name, seeing it is wonderful?" So Manoah took the kid with the cereal offering, and offered it upon the rock to the Lord, to him who works wonders. And when the flame went up toward heaven from the altar, the angel of the Lord ascended in the flame of the altar while Manoah and his wife looked on; and they fell on their faces to the ground.

The angel of the Lord appeared no more to Manoah and to his wife. Then Manoah knew that he was the angel of the Lord. And Manoah said to his wife, "We shall surely die, for we have seen God." But his wife said to him, "If the Lord had meant to kill us, he would not have accepted a burnt offering and a cereal offering at our hands, or shown us all these things, or now announced to us such things as these." And the woman bore a son, and called his name Samson; and the boy grew, and the Lord blessed him. And the Spirit of the Lord began to stir him in Mahanehdan, between Zorah and Eshtaol.

332 (9) **Judges 6:11–24** Now the angel of the Lord came and sat under the oak at Ophrah, which belonged to Joash the Abiezrite, as his son Gideon was beating out wheat in the wine press, to hide it from the Midianites. And the angel of the Lord appeared to him and said to him, "The Lord is with you, you mighty man of valor." And Gideon said to him, "Pray, sir, if the Lord is with us, why then has all this befallen us? And where are all his wonderful deeds which our fathers recounted to us, saying, 'Did not the Lord bring us up from Egypt?' But now the Lord has cast us off, and given us into the hand of Midian." And the Lord turned to him and said, "Go in this might of yours and deliver Israel from the hand of Midian; do not I send you?" And he said to him, "Pray, Lord, how can I deliver Israel? Behold, my clan is the weakest in Manasseh, and I am the least in my family." And the Lord said to him, "But I will be with you, and you shall smite the Midianites as one man." And he said to him, "If now I have found favor with thee, then show me a sign that it is thou who speakest with me. Do not depart from here, I pray thee, until I come to thee, and bring out my present, and set it before thee." And he said, "I will stay till you return."

So Gideon went into his house and prepared a kid, and unleavened cakes from an ephah of flour; the meat he put in a basket, and the broth he put in a pot, and brought them to him under the oak and presented them. And the angel of God said to him, "Take the meat and the unleavened cakes, and put them on this rock, and pour the broth over them." And he did so. Then the angel of the Lord reached out the tip of the staff that was in his hand, and touched the meat and the unleavened cakes; and there sprang up fire from the rock and consumed the flesh and the unleavened cakes; and the angel of the Lord vanished from his sight. Then Gideon perceived that he was the angel of the Lord; and Gideon said, "Alas, O Lord God! For now I have seen the angel of the Lord face to face." But the Lord said to him, "Peace be to you; do not fear, you shall not die." Then Gideon built an altar there to the Lord, and called it, The Lord is peace. To this day it still stands at Ophrah, which belongs to the Abiezrites.

(10) **Isaiah 6:6** Then flew one of the seraphim to me, having in his hand a burning coal which he had taken with tongs from the altar. 332

(11) **1 Kings 19:5** And he lay down and slept under a broom tree; and behold, an angel touched him, and said to him, "Arise and eat." 332

(12) **Luke 1:11** And there appeared to him an angel of the Lord standing on the right side of the altar of incense. 332

(13) **Luke 1:26** In the sixth month the angel Gabriel was sent from God to a city of Galilee named Nazareth. . . . 332

(1) **Matthew 1:20** But as he considered this, behold, an angel of the Lord appeared to him in a dream, saying, "Joseph, son of David, do not fear to take Mary your wife, for that which is conceived in her is of the Holy Spirit. . . ." 333

(2) **Matthew 2:13** Now when they had departed, behold, an angel of the Lord appeared to Joseph in a dream and said, "Rise, take the child and his mother, and flee to Egypt, and remain there till I tell you; for Herod is about to search for the child, to destroy him." 333

(3) **Matthew 2:19** But when Herod died, behold, an angel of the Lord appeared in a dream to Joseph in Egypt, saying. . . . 333

(4) **Matthew 4:11** Then the devil left him, and behold, angels came and ministered to him. 333

(5) **Matthew 26:53** Do you think that I cannot appeal to my Father, and he will at once send me more than twelve legions of angels? 333

(6) **Mark 1:13** And he was in the wilderness forty days, tempted by Satan; and he was with the wild beasts; and the angels ministered to him. 333

(7) **Luke 22:43** And there appeared to him an angel from heaven, strengthening him. 333

(8) **2 Maccabees 10:29–30** When the battle became fierce, there appeared to the enemy from heaven five resplendent men on horses with golden bridles, and they were leading the Jews. Surrounding Maccabeus and protecting him with their own armor and weapons, they kept him from being wounded. And they showered arrows and thunderbolts upon the enemy, so that, confused and blinded, they were thrown into disorder and cut to pieces. 333

(9) **2 Maccabees 11:8** And there, while they were still near Jerusalem, a horseman appeared at their head, clothed in white and brandishing weapons of gold. 333

333 (10) **Luke 2:8–14** And in that region there were shepherds out in the field, keeping watch over their flock by night. And an angel of the Lord appeared to them, and the glory of the Lord shone around them, and they were filled with fear. And the angel said to them, "Be not afraid; for behold, I bring you good news of a great joy which will come to all the people; for to you is born this day in the city of David a Savior, who is Christ the Lord. And this will be a sign for you: you will find a babe wrapped in swaddling cloths and lying in a manger." And suddenly there was with the angel a multitude of the heavenly host praising God and saying,

"Glory to God in the highest,
and on earth peace among men with whom he is pleased!"

333 (11) **Mark 16:5–7** And entering the tomb, they saw a young man sitting on the right side, dressed in a white robe; and they were amazed. And he said to them, "Do not be amazed; you seek Jesus of Nazareth, who was crucified. He has risen, he is not here; see the place where they laid him. But go, tell his disciples and Peter that he is going before you to Galilee; there you will see him, as he told you."

333 (12) **Acts 1:10–11** And while they were gazing into heaven as he went, behold, two men stood by them in white robes, and said, "Men of Galilee, why do you stand looking into heaven? This Jesus, who was taken up from you into heaven, will come in the same way as you saw him go into heaven."

333 (13) **Matthew 13:41** The Son of man will send his angels, and they will gather out of his kingdom all causes of sin and all evildoers. . . .

333 (14) **Matthew 24:31** . . . and he will send out his angels with a loud trumpet call, and they will gather his elect from the four winds, from one end of heaven to the other.

333 (15) **Luke 12:8–9** "And I tell you, every one who acknowledges me before men, the Son of man also will acknowledge before the angels of God; but he who denies me before men will be denied before the angels of God. . . ."

334 (1) **Acts 5:18–20** . . . they arrested the apostles and put them in the common prison. But at night an angel of the Lord opened the prison doors and brought them out and said, "Go and stand in the temple and speak to the people all the words of this Life."

334 (2) **Acts 8:26–29** But an angel of the Lord said to Philip, "Rise and go toward the south to the road that goes down from Jerusalem to Gaza." This is a desert road. And he rose and went. And behold, an Ethiopian, a eunuch, a minister of the Candace, queen of the Ethiopians, in charge of all her treasure, had come to Jerusalem to worship and was returning; seated in his chariot, he was reading the prophet Isaiah. And the Spirit said to Philip, "Go up and join this chariot."

334 (3) **Acts 10:3–8** About the ninth hour of the day he saw clearly in a vision an angel of God coming in and saying to him, "Cornelius." And he stared at him in terror, and said, "What is it, Lord?" And he said to him, "Your prayers and your alms have ascended as a memorial before God. And now send men to Joppa, and bring one Simon who is called Peter; he is lodging with Simon, a tanner, whose house is by the seaside." When the angel who spoke to him had departed, he called two of his servants and a devout soldier from among those that waited on him, and having related everything to them, he sent them to Joppa.

(4) **Acts 12:6–11** The very night when Herod was about to bring him out, Peter 334
was sleeping between two soldiers, bound with two chains, and sentries before the door were guarding the prison; and behold, an angel of the Lord appeared, and a light shone in the cell; and he struck Peter on the side and woke him, saying, "Get up quickly." And the chains fell off his hands. And the angel said to him, "Dress yourself and put on your sandals." And he did so. And he said to him, "Wrap your mantle around you and follow me." And he went out and followed him; he did not know that what was done by the angel was real, but thought he was seeing a vision. When they had passed the first and the second guard, they came to the iron gate leading into the city. It opened to them of its own accord, and they went out and passed on through one street; and immediately the angel left him. And Peter came to himself, and said, "Now I am sure that the Lord has sent his angel and rescued me from the hand of Herod and from all that the Jewish people were expecting."

(5) **Acts 27:23–25** ". . . For this very night there stood by me an angel of the God 334
to whom I belong and whom I worship, and he said, 'Do not be afraid, Paul; you must stand before Caesar; and lo, God has granted you all those who sail with you.' So take heart, men, for I have faith in God that it will be exactly as I have been told. . . ."

(1) **Matthew 18:10** "See that you do not despise one of these little ones; for I 336
tell you that in heaven their angels always behold the face of my Father who is in heaven. . . ."

(2) **Luke 16:22** The poor man died and was carried by the angels to Abraham's 336
bosom. The rich man also died and was buried. . . .

(3) **Psalm 34:7** 336

The angel of the Lord encamps
around those who fear him, and delivers them.

(4) **Psalm 91:10–13** 336

. . . no evil shall befall you,
no scourge come near your tent.

For he will give his angels charge of you
to guard you in all your ways.
On their hands they will bear you up,
lest you dash your foot against a stone.
You will tread on the lion and the adder,
the young lion and the serpent you will trample under foot.

(5) **Job 33:23–24** 336

". . . If there be for him an angel,
a mediator, one of the thousand,
to declare to man what is right for him;
and he is gracious to him, and says,
'Deliver him from going down into the Pit,
I have found a ransom. . . .' "

(6) **Zechariah 1:12** ". . . Then the angel of the Lord said, 'O Lord of hosts, how 336
long wilt thou have no mercy on Jerusalem and the cities of Judah, against which thou hast had indignation these seventy years?'. . ."

336 (7) **Tobit 12:12** ". . . And so, when you and your daughter-in-law Sarah prayed, I brought a reminder of your prayer before the Holy One; and when you buried the dead, I was likewise present with you. . . ."

337 ***Dei Verbum* 11:** see 136.

338 **St. Augustine, *De Genesi contra Manichaeos* 1, 2, 4** Suppose, however, that they do not say, "Why did God suddenly decide to make heaven and earth?" but remove the word "suddenly" and only say, "What did God decide to make heaven and earth?" For we do not say that this world has the same duration as God, for this world does not have the same eternity as the eternity that God has. God certainly made the world, as thus time began to be along with the creation that God made, and in this sense time is called eternal. Nonetheless, time is not eternal in the same way that God is eternal, because God who is the maker of time is before time. So too, all the things that God has made are very good, but they are not good in the same way that God is good, because he is their maker, while they are made. Nor did he give birth to them out of himself so that they are what he is; rather he made them out of nothing so that they are equal neither to him by whom they have been made nor to his Son through whom they have been made. For this is just. But if they say, "Why did God decide to make heaven and earth?" we should answer them that those who desire to know the will of God should first learn the power of the human will. They seek to know the causes of the will of God though the will of God is itself the cause of all that exists. For if the will of God has a cause, there is something that surpasses the will of God—and this we may not believe. Hence, one who asks, "Why did God make heaven and earth?" should be told, "Because he willed to." For the will of God is the cause of heaven and earth, and the will of God, therefore, is greater than heaven and earth. One who asks, "Why did God will to create heaven and earth?" is looking for something greater than the will of God, though nothing greater can be found. Hence, let human temerity hold itself in check, and let it not seek what is not lest it not find what is. If anyone desires to know the will of God, let him become a friend of God. For, if anyone wanted to know the will of a man of whom he was not a friend, everyone would laugh at his impudence and folly. But one becomes a friend of God only by the highest purity of morals and by that goal of the command, of which the Apostle speaks, "The goal of the command is charity from a pure heart and a good conscience and faith unfeigned," and if they had this, they would not be heretics.

342 **Psalm 145:9**

The Lord is good to all,
and his compassion is over all that he has made.

343 **Genesis 1:26** Then God said, "Let us make man in our image, after our likeness; and let them have dominion over the fish of the sea, and over the birds of the air, and over the cattle, and over all the earth, and over every creeping thing that creeps upon the earth."

346 (1) **Hebrews 4:3–4** For we who have believed enter that rest, as he has said,

"As I swore in my wrath,
'They shall never enter my rest,'"

although his works were finished from the foundation of the world. For he has somewhere spoken of the seventh day in this way, "And God rested on the seventh day from all his works."

(2) **Jeremiah 31:35–37** 346
Thus says the Lord,
who gives the sun for light by day
and the fixed order of the moon and the stars for light by night,
who stirs up the sea so that its waves roar—
the Lord of hosts is his name:
"If this fixed order departs
from before me, says the Lord,
then shall the descendants of Israel cease
from being a nation before me for ever."
Thus says the Lord:
"If the heavens above can be measured,
and the foundations of the earth below can be explored,
then I will cast off all the descendants of Israel
for all that they have done, says the Lord."

(3) **Jeremiah 33:19–26** The word of the Lord came to Jeremiah: "Thus says the Lord: If you can break my covenant with the day and my covenant with the night, so that day and night will not come at their appointed time, then also my covenant with David my servant may be broken, so that he shall not have a son to reign on his throne, and my covenant with the Levitical priests my ministers. As the host of heaven cannot be numbered and the sands of the sea cannot be measured, so I will multiply the descendants of David my servant, and the Levitical priests who minister to me." 346

The word of the Lord came to Jeremiah: "Have you not observed what these people are saying, 'The Lord has rejected the two families which he chose'? Thus they have despised my people so that they are no longer a nation in their sight. Thus says the Lord: If I have not established my covenant with day and night and the ordinances of heaven and earth, then I will reject the descendants of Jacob and David my servant and will not choose one of his descendants to rule over the seed of Abraham, Isaac, and Jacob. For I will restore their fortunes, and will have mercy upon them."

Genesis 1:14 And God said, "Let there be lights in the firmament of the heavens to separate the day from the night; and let them be for signs and for seasons and for days and years. . . ." 347

***Roman Missal*, Easter Vigil, 24, prayer after the first reading** Lord God, the creation of man was a wonderful work, his redemption still more wonderful. May we persevere in right reason against all that entices to sin and so attain to everlasting joy. 349

We ask this through Christ our Lord.
Amen.

(1) ***Gaudium et spes* 12, 1** Believers and unbelievers agree almost unanimously that all things on earth should be ordained to man as to their center and summit. 358

(2) ***Gaudium et spes* 24, 3** Furthermore, the Lord Jesus, when praying to the Father "that they may all be one . . . even as we are one" (Jn. 17:21–22), has opened up new horizons closed to human reason by implying that there is a certain parallel between the union existing among the divine persons and the union of the sons of God in truth and love. It follows, then, that if man is the only creature on earth that God has wanted for its own sake, man can fully discover his true self only in a sincere giving of himself. 358

358 (3) ***Gaudium et spes* 39, 1** We know neither the moment of the consummation of the earth and of man nor the way the universe will be transformed. The form of this world, distorted by sin, is passing away and we are taught that God is preparing a new dwelling and a new earth in which righteousness dwells, whose happiness will fill and surpass all the desires of peace arising in the hearts of men. Then with death conquered the sons of God will be raised in Christ and what was sown in weakness and dishonor will put on the imperishable: charity and its works will remain and all of creation, which God made for man, will be set free from its bondage to decay.

360 (1) **Tobit 8:6**

"... Thou madest Adam and gavest him Eve his wife
as a helper and support.
From them the race of mankind has sprung.
Thou didst say, 'It is not good that the man should be alone;
let us make a helper for him like himself.'..."

360 (2) ***Nostra aetate* 1** In this age of ours, when men are drawing more closely together and the bonds of friendship between different peoples are being strengthened, the Church examines with greater care the relation which she has to non-Christian religions. Ever aware of her duty to foster unity and charity among individuals, and even among nations, she reflects at the outset on what men have in common and what tends to promote fellowship among them.

All men form but one community. This is so because all stem from the one stock which God created to people the entire earth (cf. Acts 17:26), and also because all share a common destiny, namely God. His providence, evident goodness, and saving designs extend to all men (cf. Wis. 8:1; Acts 14:17; Rom. 2:6–7; 1 Tim. 2:4) against the day when the elect are gathered together in the holy city which is illumined by the glory of God, and in whose splendor all peoples will walk (cf. Apoc. 21:23 ff.).

Men look to their different religions for an answer to the unsolved riddles of human existence. The problems that weigh heavily on the hearts of men are the same today as in the ages past. What is man? What is the meaning and purpose of life? What is upright behavior, and what is sinful? Where does suffering originate, and what end does it serve? How can genuine happiness be found? What happens at death? What is judgment? What reward follows death? And finally, what is the ultimate mystery, beyond human explanation, which embraces our entire existence, from which we take our origin and towards which we tend?

363 (1) **Matthew 16:25–26** For whoever would save his life will lose it, and whoever loses his life for my sake will find it. For what will it profit a man, if he gains the whole world and forfeits his life? Or what shall a man give in return for his life?

363 (2) **John 15:13** Greater love has no man than this, that a man lay down his life for his friends.

363 (3) **Acts 2:41** So those who received his word were baptized, and there were added that day about three thousand souls.

363 (4) **Matthew 10:28** And do not fear those who kill the body but cannot kill the soul; rather fear him who can destroy both soul and body in hell.

363 (5) **Matthew 26:38** Then he said to them, "My soul is very sorrowful, even to death; remain here, and watch with me."

(6) **John 12:27** "Now my soul is troubled. And what shall I say? 'Father, save me from this hour'? No, for this purpose I have come to this hour. . . ." 363

(7) **2 Maccabees 6:30** When he was about to die under the blows, he groaned aloud and said: "It is clear to the Lord in his holy knowledge that, though I might have been saved from death, I am enduring terrible sufferings in my body under this beating, but in my soul I am glad to suffer these things because I fear him." 363

(1) **1 Corinthians 6:19–20** Do you not know that your body is a temple of the Holy Spirit within you, which you have from God? You are not your own; you were bought with a price. So glorify God in your body. 364

(2) **1 Corinthians 15:44–45** It is sown a physical body, it is raised a spiritual body. If there is a physical body, there is also a spiritual body. Thus it is written, "The first man Adam became a living being"; the last Adam became a life-giving spirit. 364

Council of Vienne (1312): DS 902 [*The soul as a form of the body*]. Furthermore, with the approval of the above mentioned sacred council we reprove as erroneous and inimical to the Catholic faith every doctrine or position rashly asserting or turning to doubt that the substance of the rational or intellective soul truly and in itself is not a form of the human body, defining, so that the truth of sincere faith may be known to all, and the approach to all errors may be cut off, lest they steal in upon us, that whoever shall obstinately presume in turn to assert, define, or hold that the rational or intellective soul is not the form of the human body in itself and essentially must be regarded as a heretic. 365

(1) **Pius XII, encyclical *Humani generis* (1950): DS 3896** Wherefore, the *magisterium* of the Church does not forbid that the teaching of "evolution" be treated in accord with the present status of human disciplines and of theology, by investigations and disputations by learned men in both fields; insofar, of course, as the inquiry is concerned with the origin of the human body arising from already existing and living matter; and in such a way that the reasoning of both theories, namely of those in favor and of those in opposition, are weighed and judged with due seriousness, moderation, and temperance; and provided that all are ready to yield to the judgment of the Church, to which Christ has entrusted the duty of interpreting Sacred Scriptures authentically, and of preserving the dogmas of faith. Yet some with daring boldness transgress this freedom of discussion, acting as if the origin of the human body from previously existing and living matter, were already certain and demonstrated from certain already discovered indications, and deduced by reasoning, and as if there were nothing in the sources of divine revelation which demands the greatest moderation and caution in this thinking. 366

(2) **Paul VI, *The* Credo *of the People of God* 8** We believe in one God, the Father, the Son and the Holy Spirit, Creator of what is visible—such as this world where we live out our lives—and of the invisible—such as the pure spirits which are also called angels—and Creator in each man of his spiritual and immortal soul. 366

(3) **Lateran Council V (1513): DS 1440** Since in our days (and we painfully bring this up) the sower of cockle, ancient enemy of the human race, has dared to disseminate and advance in the field of the Lord a number of pernicious errors, always rejected by the faithful, especially concerning the nature of the rational soul, namely, that it is mortal, or one in all men, and some rashly philosophizing affirmed that this 366

is true at least according to philosophy, in our desire to offer suitable remedies against a plague of this kind, with the approval of this holy Council, we condemn and reject all who assert that the intellectual soul is mortal, or is one in all men, and those who cast doubt on these truths, since it [the soul] is not only truly in itself and essentially the form of the human body, as was defined in the canon of Pope Clement V our predecessor of happy memory published in the (general) Council of Vienne but it is also multiple according to the multitude of bodies into which it is infused, multiplied, and to be multiplied. . . .

367 (1) **Council of Constantinople IV (870): DS 657** Can. 11. Although the Old and the New Testaments teach that man has one rational and intellectual soul, and all the Fathers speaking the word of God and all the teachers of the Church declare the same opinion, certain persons giving attention to the inventors of evil, have reached such a degree of impiety that they impudently declare that man has two souls, and by certain irrational attempts "through wisdom which has been made foolish" [1 Cor. 1:20], they try to strengthen their own heresy.

Although the Old and New Testaments teach that man has one rational and intellectual soul, and all the Fathers and teachers of the Church teach the same opinion, there are some who think that he has two souls, and by certain irrational attempts they strengthen their own heresy. Therefore, this holy and ecumenical synod loudly anathematizes the originators of such impiety and those who agree with them; and if anyone shall dare to speak contrary to the rest, let him be anathema.

367 (2) **Vatican Council I (1870): DS 3005:** see 38 (1).

367 (3) ***Gaudium et spes* 22, 5** All this holds true not for Christians only but also for all men of good will in whose hearts grace is active invisibly. For since Christ died for all, and since all men are in fact called to one and the same destiny, which is divine, we must hold that the Holy Spirit offers to all the possibility of being made partners, in a way known to God, in the paschal mystery.

367 (4) **Pius XII, encyclical *Humani generis* (1950): DS 3891:** see 330 (1).

368 (1) **Jeremiah 31:33** But this is the covenant which I will make with the house of Israel after those days, says the Lord: I will put my law within them, and I will write it upon their hearts; and I will be their God, and they shall be my people.

368 (2) **Deuteronomy 6:5** . . . and you shall love the Lord your God with all your heart, and with all your soul, and with all your might.

368 (3) **Deuteronomy 29:3 (29:4: RSV)** . . . but to this day the Lord has not given you a mind [heart] to understand, or eyes to see, or ears to hear.

368 (4) **Isaiah 29:13** And the Lord said:

"Because this people draw near with their mouth
    and honor me with their lips,
    while their hearts are far from me,
and their fear of me is a commandment of men learned by rote. . . ."

368 (5) **Ezekiel 36:26** A new heart I will give you, and a new spirit I will put within you; and I will take out of your flesh the heart of stone and give you a heart of flesh.

368 (6) **Matthew 6:21** For where your treasure is, there will your heart be also.

(7) **Luke 8:15** And as for that in the good soil, they are those who, hearing the word, hold it fast in an honest and good heart, and bring forth fruit with patience. 368

(8) **Romans 5:5** . . . and hope does not disappoint us, because God's love has been poured into our hearts through the Holy Spirit which has been given to us. 368

(1) **Genesis 2:7** . . . then the Lord God formed man of dust from the ground, and breathed into his nostrils the breath of life; and man became a living being. 369

(2) **Genesis 2:22** . . . and the rib which the Lord God had taken from the man he made into a woman and brought her to the man. 369

(1) **Isaiah 49:14–15** 370

But Zion said, "The Lord has forsaken me,
my Lord has forgotten me."
"Can a woman forget her sucking child,
that she should have no compassion on the son of her womb?
Even these may forget,
yet I will not forget you. . . ."

(2) **Isaiah 66:13** 370

As one whom his mother comforts,
so I will comfort you;
you shall be comforted in Jerusalem.

(3) **Psalm 131:2–3** 370

But I have calmed and quieted my soul,
like a child quieted at its mother's breast;
like a child that is quieted is my soul.
O Israel, hope in the Lord
from this time forth and for evermore.

(4) **Hosea 11:1–4** 370

When Israel was a child, I loved him,
and out of Egypt I called my son.
The more I called them,
the more they went from me;
they kept sacrificing to the Baals,
and burning incense to idols.
Yet it was I who taught Ephraim to walk,
I took them up in my arms;
but they did not know that I healed them.
I led them with cords of compassion,
with the bands of love,
and I became to them as one
who eases the yoke on their jaws,
and I bent down to them and fed them.

(5) **Jeremiah 3:4–19** 370

". . . Have you not just now called to me,
'My father, thou art the friend of my youth—
will he be angry for ever,
will he be indignant to the end?'

Behold, you have spoken,
but you have done all the evil that you could."

The Lord said to me in the days of King Josiah: "Have you seen what she did, that faithless one, Israel, how she went up on every high hill and under every green tree, and there played the harlot? And I thought, 'After she has done all this she will return to me'; but she did not return, and her false sister Judah saw it. She saw that for all the adulteries of that faithless one, Israel, I had sent her away with a decree of divorce; yet her false sister Judah did not fear, but she too went and played the harlot. Because harlotry was so light to her, she polluted the land, committing adultery with stone and tree. Yet for all this her false sister Judah did not return to me with her whole heart, but in pretense, says the Lord."

And the Lord said to me, "Faithless Israel has shown herself less guilty than false Judah. Go, and proclaim these words toward the north, and say,

'Return, faithless Israel,
says the Lord.
I will not look on you in anger,
for I am merciful,
says the Lord;
I will not be angry for ever.
Only acknowledge your guilt,
that you rebelled against the Lord your God
and scattered your favors among strangers under every green tree,
and that you have not obeyed my voice,
says the Lord.
Return, O faithless children,
says the Lord;
for I am your master;
I will take you, one from a city and two from a family,
and I will bring you to Zion.

" 'And I will give you shepherds after my own heart, who will feed you with knowledge and understanding. And when you have multiplied and increased in the land, in those days, says the Lord, they shall no more say, "The ark of the covenant of the Lord." It shall not come to mind, or be remembered, or missed; it shall not be made again. At that time Jerusalem shall be called the throne of the Lord, and all nations shall gather to it, to the presence of the Lord in Jerusalem, and they shall no more stubbornly follow their own evil heart. In those days the house of Judah shall join the house of Israel, and together they shall come from the land of the north to the land that I gave your fathers for a heritage.

" 'I thought
how I would set you among my sons,
and give you a pleasant land,
a heritage most beauteous of all nations.
And I thought you would call me, My Father,
and would not turn from following me.' "

372 ***Gaudium et spes* 50, 1** Marriage and married love are by nature ordered to the procreation and education of children. Indeed children are the supreme gift of marriage and greatly contribute to the good of the parents themselves. God himself said: "It is not good that man should be alone" (Gen. 2:18), and "from the beginning (he) made them male and female" (Mt. 19:4); wishing to associate them in a special way with his own creative work, God blessed man and woman with the words: "Be fruitful and multiply" (Gen. 1:28). Without intending to underestimate the other ends of

marriage, it must be said that true married love and the whole structure of family life which results from it is directed to disposing the spouses to cooperate valiantly with the love of the Creator and Savior, who through them will increase and enrich his family from day to day.

(1) **Council of Trent (1546): DS 1511** If anyone does not confess that the first 375
man Adam, when he had transgressed the commandment of God in Paradise, immediately lost his holiness and the justice in which he had been established, and that he incurred through the offense of that prevarication the wrath and indignation of God and hence the death with which God had previously threatened him, and with death captivity under his power, who thenceforth "had the empire of death" [Heb. 2:14], that is of the devil, and that through that offense of prevarication the entire Adam was transformed in body and soul for the worse, let him be anathema.

(2) ***Lumen gentium* 2** The eternal Father, in accordance with the utterly gratuitous 375
and mysterious design of his wisdom and goodness, created the whole universe, and chose to raise up men to share in his own divine life; and when they had fallen in Adam, he did not abandon them, but at all times held out to them the means of salvation, bestowed in consideration of Christ, the Redeemer, "who is the image of the invisible God, the firstborn of every creature" (Col. 1:15). All the elect, before time began, the Father "foreknew and also predestined to become conformed to the image of his Son, that he should be the firstborn among many brethren" (Rom. 8:29). He determined to call together in a holy Church those who should believe in Christ. Already present in figure at the beginning of the world, this Church was prepared in marvellous fashion in the history of the people of Israel and in the old Alliance. Established in this last age of the world, and made manifest in the outpouring of the Spirit, it will be brought to glorious completion at the end of time. At that moment, as the Fathers put it, all the just from the time of Adam, "from Abel, the just one, to the last of the elect" will be gathered together with the Father in the universal Church.

(1) **Genesis 2:17** ". . . but of the tree of the knowledge of good and evil you shall 376
not eat, for in the day that you eat of it you shall die."

(2) **Genesis 3:16** To the woman he said, 376
"I will greatly multiply your pain in childbearing;
in pain you shall bring forth children,
yet your desire shall be for your husband,
and he shall rule over you."

(3) **Genesis 3:19** 376
". . . In the sweat of your face
you shall eat bread
till you return to the ground,
for out of it you were taken;
you are dust,
and to dust you shall return."

(4) **Genesis 2:25** And the man and his wife were both naked, and were not ashamed. 376

1 John 2:16 For all that is in the world, the lust of the flesh and the lust of the 377
eyes and the pride of life, is not of the Father but is of the world.

378 (1) **Genesis 2:8** And the Lord God planted a garden in Eden, in the east; and there he put the man whom he had formed.

378 (2) **Genesis 3:17–19** And to Adam he said,
"Because you have listened to the voice of your wife,
and have eaten of the tree
of which I commanded you,
'You shall not eat of it,'
cursed is the ground because of you;
in toil you shall eat of it all the days of your life;
thorns and thistles it shall bring forth to you;
and you shall eat the plants of the field.
In the sweat of your face
you shall eat bread
till you return to the ground,
for out of it you were taken;
you are dust,
and to dust you shall return."

381 (1) **Ephesians 1:3–6** Blessed be the God and Father of our Lord Jesus Christ, who has blessed us in Christ with every spiritual blessing in the heavenly places, even as he chose us in him before the foundation of the world, that we should be holy and blameless before him. He destined us in love to be his sons through Jesus Christ, according to the purpose of his will, to the praise of his glorious grace which he freely bestowed on us in the Beloved.

381 (2) **Romans 8:29** For those whom he foreknew he also predestined to be conformed to the image of his Son, in order that he might be the first-born among many brethren.

385 (1) **Romans 5:20** Law came in, to increase the trespass; but where sin increased, grace abounded all the more. . . .

385 (2) **Luke 11:21–22** When a strong man, fully armed, guards his own palace, his goods are in peace; but when one stronger than he assails him and overcomes him, he takes away his armor in which he trusted, and divides his spoil.

385 (3) **John 16:11** . . . concerning judgment, because the ruler of this world is judged.

385 (4) **1 John 3:8** He who commits sin is of the devil; for the devil has sinned from the beginning. The reason the Son of God appeared was to destroy the works of the devil.

388 **Romans 5:12–21** Therefore as sin came into the world through one man and death through sin, and so death spread to all men because all men sinned—sin indeed was in the world before the law was given, but sin is not counted where there is no law. Yet death reigned from Adam to Moses, even over those whose sins were not like the transgression of Adam, who was a type of the one who was to come.

But the free gift is not like the trespass. For if many died through one man's trespass, much more have the grace of God and the free gift in the grace of that one man Jesus Christ abounded for many. And the free gift is not like the effect of that one man's sin. For the judgment following one trespass brought condemnation, but the free gift following many trespasses brings justification. If, because of one man's trespass, death reigned through that one man, much more will those who receive the abundance of grace and the free gift of righteousness reign in life through the one man Jesus Christ.

Then as one man's trespass led to condemnation for all men, so one man's act of righteousness leads to acquittal and life for all men. For as by one man's disobedience many were made sinners, so by one man's obedience many will be made righteous. Law came in, to increase the trespass; but where sin increased, grace abounded all the more, so that, as sin reigned in death, grace also might reign through righteousness to eternal life through Jesus Christ our Lord.

1 Corinthians 2:16 "For who has known the mind of the Lord so as to instruct him?" But we have the mind of Christ. 389

(1) ***Gaudium et spes* 13, 1** Although set by God in a state of rectitude, man, enticed by the evil one, abused his freedom at the very start of history. He lifted himself up against God, and sought to attain his goal apart from him. Although they had known God, they did not glorify him as God, but their senseless hearts were darkened, and they served the creature rather than the creator. What Revelation makes known to us is confirmed by our own experience. For when man looks into his own heart he finds that he is drawn towards what is wrong and sunk in many evils which cannot come from his good creator. Often refusing to acknowledge God as his source, man has also upset the relationship which should link him to his last end; and at the same time he has broken the right order that should reign within himself as well as between himself and other men and all creatures. 390

(2) **Council of Trent (1546): DS 1513** If anyone asserts that this sin of Adam, which is one in origin and transmitted to all is in each one as his own by propagation, not by imitation, is taken away either by the forces of human nature, or by any remedy other than the merit of the one mediator, our Lord Jesus Christ, who has reconciled us to God in his own blood, "made unto us justice, sanctification, and redemption" [I Cor. 1:30]; or if he denies that that merit of Jesus Christ is applied to adults as well as to infants by the sacrament of baptism, rightly administered in the form of the Church: let him be anathema. "For there is no other name under heaven given to men, whereby we must be saved. . ." [Acts 4:12]. Whence that word: "Behold the lamb of God, behold Him who taketh away the sins of the world" [John 1:29]. And that other: "As many of you as have been baptized, have put on Christ" [Gal. 3:27]. 390

(3) **Pius XII, encyclical *Humani generis* (1950): DS 3897** When there is a question of another conjectural opinion, namely, of polygenism so-called, then the sons of the Church in no way enjoy such freedom. For the faithful in Christ cannot accept this view, which holds that either after Adam there existed men on this earth, who did not receive their origin by natural generation from him, the first parent of all; or that Adam signifies some kind of multitude of first parents; for it is by no means apparent how such an opinion can be reconciled with what the sources of revealed truth and the acts of the *magisterium* of the Church teach about original sin, which proceeds from a sin truly committed by one Adam, and which is transmitted to all by generation, and exists in each one as his own. 390

390 (4) **Paul VI, allocution of 11 July 1966**

Beloved sons, We are particularly happy to greet you today as participants in the symposium on original sin. We want to express to you Our keen and profound gratitude for so promptly and generously accepting Our invitation to pool your intellectual abilities in order to shed greater light on one of the basic mysteries of our Catholic faith.

As a matter of fact—as dear Father Dhanis, the organizer and director of the symposium, rightly observed in the kind and devoted address which he made to Us in your name—the mystery of original sin has very close connections with the mystery of the Incarnate Word, and Savior of the human race, with His passion, death and glorious resurrection, and hence with the message of salvation that has been entrusted to the Catholic Church. For what is the real aim of the Church's pastoral activity if not the redemption of human nature which—wonderfully created by Almighty God in Adam and miserably fallen in him—has been even more wonderfully recreated and regenerated to divine life by the merciful God through the grace of the one Mediator, Jesus Christ?

You know very well, beloved sons, that the dogma of original sin was not extraneous to the drafts of the Second Vatican Council's Constitutions which were accepted by Our predecessor of venerable memory, John XXIII, nor was it extraneous to the Acts of the 21st Ecumenical Council.

In fact, a chapter, number 8, was inserted in the schema of the Dogmatic Constitution *De deposito Fidei pure custodiendo* that was to deal with *De peccato originali in filiis Adae*. For reasons known to you, this schema was not made a part of the final program of the Council's debates and deliberations. And yet Catholic doctrine on original sin was reaffirmed in the Second Vatican Council, even if in shorter formulations on the occasion of other Constitutions, particularly in connection with the Council's main theme, the mystery of the Church.

Thus you find a clear teaching in the Dogmatic Constitution *Lumen gentium*—in full agreement with Divine Revelation and with the teaching of the earlier Councils of Carthage, Orange and Trent—on the fact and universality of original sin, as well as on the intimate nature of the state from which mankind fell as a result of Adam's sin: "*Aeternus Pater, liberrimo et arcano sapientiae ac bonitatis suae consilio, mundum universum creavit, homines ad participandam vitam divinam elevare decrevit, eosque lapsos in Adamo non dereliquit, semper eis auxilia ad salutem praebens, intuitu Christi Redemptoris, qui est imago Dei invisibilis, primogenitus omnis creaturae.*"

It was only logical that a more extended reference to the dogma of original sin should be made in the Pastoral Constitution *Gaudium et spes*, in which the Council confronted and fully developed the eagerly-awaited and very important subject of the Church in the world of today. Consequently, it is not surprising that the document, referring in its introductory part to the conditions of man in the contemporary world, points up the sad consequences of original sin, which had already been denounced in vivid and effective terms by the Apostle in his Letter to the Romans—although the Council, following the example of St. Paul himself, doesn't present original sin as the only source of evil in mankind. In fact, you read these words in the Constitution: "*Revera inaequilibria quibus laborat mundus hodiernus, cum inaequilibrio illo fundamentaliori connectuntur, quod in hominis corde radicatur. In ipso enim homine plura elementa sibi invicem oppugnant. Unde in seipso divisionem patitur, ex qua etiam tot ac tantae discordiae in societate oriuntur.*"

Chapter 1 of the same Constitution (*De humanae personae diginitate*), tacitly recalling the third chapter of Genesis and the doctrine of the Council of Trent, uses explicit terms to describe the first man's sin as the main source of the moral disorder existing in mankind: "*In justitia a Deo constitutus, homo tamen, suadente Maligno, inde ab exordio historiae, libertate sua abusus est, seipsum contra Deum erigens et finem suum extra Deum attingere cupiens.*"

Finally, with the aim of lifting men's hearts and rekindling their hopes, the Council joins St. Paul in pointing out to them the figure of Christ the Savior, the founder of the Church, the new Adam, whose light confirms and illustrates all that happened in the first Adam and that continues to happen in his offspring. "*Reapse*," you read in this document of ours, "*nonnisi in mysterio Verbi incarnati mysterium hominis vere clarescit. Adam enim, primus homo, erat figura futuri (Rom 5, 14), scilicet Christi Domini. Christus, novissimus Adam, in ipsa revelatione mysterii Patris Ejusque amoris, hominem ipsum homini plene manifestat eique altissimam ejus vocationem patefacit. Nil igitur mirum in Eo praedictas veritates suum invenire fontem atque attingere fastigium. . . . Tale et tantum est hominis mysterium, quod per Revelationem christianam credentibus illucescit. Per Christum et in Christo igitur illuminatur aenigma doloris et mortis, quod extra Ejus Evangelium nos obruit.*"

As these texts—which We thought it fitting to recall to your attention—make clear, the Second Vatican Council did not aim at any deepening or any rounding out of the Catholic doctrine on original sin, which had already been sufficiently declared and defined, as We said, at the Councils of Carthage (418), Orange (529) and Trent (1546). It simply wanted to confirm this doctrine and to apply it as required by its own aims, which were mainly pastoral.

Your symposium of exegetes and theologians who are experts in this subject has a very different task set before it. With filial devotion you have offered Us for Our consideration a list of the papers that are to be presented, in the hope of receiving, in turn, a word of consent and direction from Us. That list makes it clear that you, beloved sons, intend to hit the nail on the head, as they say, on the current status of Catholic exegesis and theology regarding the dogma of original sin, with special reference to the findings of modern natural sciences, such as anthropology and paleontology. The fruit of your comparative study ought to be a more modern definition and presentation of original sin, in the sense of better satisfying the demands of faith and reason as manifested and felt by men today.

Now then, We want to praise highly this magnanimous resolve of yours. We hope that it will bear abundant fruits, first of all for the progress of ecclesiastical learning, and then chiefly for the greater effectiveness of the Church's pastoral activity. For We are fully convinced that bishops and priests cannot worthily carry out their mission of enlightening and saving the modern world if they are not in a position to present, defend and illustrate the truths of divine faith with ideas and words that are more understandable to minds trained in present-day philosophical and scientific learning.

This recalls automatically the warning that Our predecessor issued in the memorable allocution with which he opened the 21st Ecumenical Council. "*Oportet*," John XXIII very wisely observed, "*ut quemadmodum cuncti sinceri rei christianae, catholicae, apostolicae fautores vehementer exoptant, eadem doctrina amplius et altius cognoscatur eaque plenius animi imbuantur atque formentur; oportet ut haec doctrina certa et immutabilis, cui fidele obsequium est praestandum, ea ratione pervestigetur et exponatur, quam tempora postulant nostra. Est enim aliud ipsum depositum Fidei, seu veritates, quae veneranda doctrina nostra continentur, aliud modus quo eaedem enuntiantur, eodem tamen sensu eademque sententia.*"

Catholic exegetes and theologians are therefore granted all the freedom of research and of judgment required by the scientific nature of the studies they are carrying on and by the pastoral aim of the salvation of souls, to which every activity in the Church must be directed as its supreme goal. But there are limits which cannot and must not be imprudently exceeded by the exegete, the theologian, and the scientist who really want to safeguard and illuminate their own faith and that of other Catholics.

These limits are marked out by the living magisterium of the Church, which is the proximate norm of truth for all the faithful, as We Ourself recalled in the Encyclical *Mysterium Fidei*. In this encyclical, in the course of denouncing certain explanations of the dogma of transubstantiation which were upsetting the minds of the faithful, We expressed disapproval of excessive liberty in the interpretation of the dogmas of the Christian religion: "*Quasi cuique doctrinam semel ab Ecclesia definitam in oblivione adducere liceat aut eam ita interpretari ut genuina verborum significatio, seu probata conceptuum vis extenuetur.*"

And so, beloved sons, in the course of your discussions and in reaching your conclusions, always keep in mind the principles of sound Catholic exegesis that have been spelled out many times by Our immediate predecessors and that have recently been confirmed in the Dogmatic Constitution *Dei Verbum*, which deals with Divine Revelation. According to these principles, there is an intimate and indispensable connection between Sacred Tradition, Sacred Scripture and the magisterium of the Church, so that the Council was able to conclude chapter 2, dealing with the transmission of Revelation, with this affirmation: "*Patet igitur Sacram Traditionem, Sacram Scripturam et Ecclesiae Magisterium, juxta sapientissimum Dei consilium, ita inter se connecti et consociari, ut unum sine aliis non consistat, omniaque simul, singula suo modo sub actione unius Spiritus Sancti, ad animarum salutem efficaciter conferant.*"

With a conviction, therefore, that the doctrine of original sin—with regard to its existence and universality, and also its nature as a true sin, even in Adam's descendants, and its sad consequences for soul and body—is a truth revealed by God in various passages of the Old and the New Testament—and especially in Genesis 3, 1–20, and in the Letter to the Romans 5, 12–19, with which you are very familiar—you should take the greatest possible care, in delving into the meaning of the biblical texts and spelling it out more clearly, to stick to the indispensable norms which come from the *analogia fidei*, from the declarations and definitions of the above-mentioned Councils, and from the documents issued by the Apostolic See. In this way, you will be sure to respect "*id quod Ecclesia catholica ubique diffusa semper intellexit*," which means the sense of the universal teaching Church and learning Church, which the Fathers of the Second Council of Carthage—which dealt with original sin against the Pelagians—regarded as "*regulam fidei*."

Thus it is obvious that you will regard the explanations of original sin given by some modern authors as irreconcilable with genuine Catholic doctrine. Starting out from the undemonstrated hypothesis of polygenism, they deny, more or less clearly, that the sin from which this great trash heap of ills in mankind is derived, was first of all the disobedience of Adam, "the first man," a figure of the man to come—a sin that was committed at the beginning of history. As a consequence, such explanations do not agree with the teaching of Sacred Scripture, Sacred Tradition, and the Church's magisterium, according to which the sin of the first man is transmitted to all his descendants not through imitation but through propagation, *inest unicuique proprium*, and is *mors animae*, which means privation and not just an absence of holiness and justice, even in newborn infants.

The theory of evolution will not seem acceptable to you whenever it is not decisively in accord with the immediate creation of each and every human soul by God, and whenever it does not regard as decisively important for the fate of mankind the disobedience of Adam, the universal first parent. This disobedience must not be considered as not having made Adam lose the holiness and justice in which he had been constituted.

Beloved sons, these are the reflections and exhortations that We thought it appropriate to address to you at the beginning of your symposium. In the light of the universal Savior, who was promised for the hope and consolation of the first parents right after their fall, you will investigate the abyss of human malice that was dug by original sin, and which found its triumphal Redeemer in Jesus Christ, since: "*Ubi abundavit delictum, superabundavit gratia per Jesum Christum Dominum nostrum.*"

Regarding this subject to which you are about to apply your minds, let what the First Vatican Council affirmed be verified: "*Ratio, fide illustrata, cum sedulo, pie et sobrie quaerit, aliquam Deo dante mysteriorum intelligentiam eamque fructuosissimam assequitur.*"

In the confident expectation that your symposium's conclusions will be an effective help in carrying out Our ministry as supreme guardian and interpreter of the faith we share, We impart Our apostolic blessing to you as a pledge of heavenly enlightenment.

(1) **Genesis 3:1–5** Now the serpent was more subtle than any other wild creature 391
that the Lord God had made. He said to the woman, "Did God say, 'You shall not eat of any tree of the garden'?" And the woman said to the serpent, "We may eat of the fruit of the trees of the garden; but God said, 'You shall not eat of the fruit of the tree which is in the midst of the garden, neither shall you touch it, lest you die.'" But the serpent said to the woman, "You will not die. For God knows that when you eat of it your eyes will be opened, and you will be like God, knowing good and evil."

(2) **Wisdom 2:24** 391

. . . but through the devil's envy death entered the world,
and those who belong to his party experience it.

(3) **John 8:44** You are of your father the devil, and your will is to do your father's 391
desires. He was a murderer from the beginning, and has nothing to do with the truth, because there is no truth in him. When he lies, he speaks according to his own nature, for he is a liar and the father of lies.

(4) **Revelation 12:9** And the great dragon was thrown down, that ancient serpent, 391
who is called the Devil and Satan, the deceiver of the whole world—he was thrown down to the earth, and his angels were thrown down with him.

2 Peter 2:4 For if God did not spare the angels when they sinned, but cast them into 392
hell and committed them to pits of nether gloom to be kept until the judgment. . . .

Matthew 4:1–11 Then Jesus was led up by the Spirit into the wilderness to be 394
tempted by the devil. And he fasted forty days and forty nights, and afterward he was hungry. And the tempter came and said to him, "If you are the Son of God, command these stones to become loaves of bread." But he answered, "It is written,

'Man shall not live by bread alone,
but by every word that proceeds from the mouth of God.'"

Then the devil took him to the holy city, and set him on the pinnacle of the temple, and said to him, "If you are the Son of God, throw yourself down; for it is written,

'He will give his angels charge of you,'

and

'On their hands they will bear you up,
lest you strike your foot against a stone.'"

Jesus said to him, "Again it is written, 'You shall not tempt the Lord your God.'" Again, the devil took him to a very high mountain, and showed him all the kingdoms of the world and the glory of them; and he said to him, "All these I will give you, if you will fall down and worship me." Then Jesus said to him, "Begone, Satan! for it is written,

'You shall worship the Lord your God
and him only shall you serve.'"
Then the devil left him, and behold, angels came and ministered to him.

397 (1) **Genesis 3:1–11** Now the serpent was more subtle than any other wild creature that the Lord God had made. He said to the woman, "Did God say, 'You shall not eat of any tree of the garden'?" And the woman said to the serpent, "We may eat of the fruit of the trees of the garden; but God said, 'You shall not eat of the fruit of the tree which is in the midst of the garden, neither shall you touch it, lest you die.'" But the serpent said to the woman, "You will not die. For God knows that when you eat of it your eyes will be opened, and you will be like God, knowing good and evil." So when the woman saw that the tree was good for food, and that it was a delight to the eyes, and that the tree was to be desired to make one wise, she took of its fruit and ate; and she also gave some to her husband, and he ate. Then the eyes of both were opened, and they knew that they were naked; and they sewed fig leaves together and made themselves aprons.

And they heard the sound of the Lord God walking in the garden in the cool of the day, and the man and his wife hid themselves from the presence of the Lord God among the trees of the garden. But the Lord God called to the man, and said to him, "Where are you?" And he said, "I heard the sound of thee in the garden, and I was afraid, because I was naked; and I hid myself." He said, "Who told you that you were naked? Have you eaten of the tree of which I commanded you not to eat?"

397 (2) **Romans 5:19** For as by one man's disobedience many were made sinners, so by one man's obedience many will be made righteous.

398 **Genesis 3:5** ". . . For God knows that when you eat of it your eyes will be opened, and you will be like God, knowing good and evil."

399 (1) **Romans 3:23** . . . since all have sinned and fall short of the glory of God. . . .

399 (2) **Genesis 3:5–10** ". . . For God knows that when you eat of it your eyes will be opened, and you will be like God, knowing good and evil." So when the woman saw that the tree was good for food, and that it was a delight to the eyes, and that the tree was to be desired to make one wise, she took of its fruit and ate; and she also gave some to her husband, and he ate. Then the eyes of both were opened, and they knew that they were naked; and they sewed fig leaves together and made themselves aprons.

And they heard the sound of the Lord God walking in the garden in the cool of the day, and the man and his wife hid themselves from the presence of the Lord God among the trees of the garden.

But the Lord God called to the man, and said to him, "Where are you?" And he said, "I heard the sound of thee in the garden, and I was afraid, because I was naked; and I hid myself."

400 (1) **Genesis 3:7–16** Then the eyes of both were opened, and they knew that they were naked; and they sewed fig leaves together and made themselves aprons.

And they heard the sound of the Lord God walking in the garden in the cool of the day, and the man and his wife hid themselves from the presence of the Lord God among the trees of the garden. But the Lord God called to the man, and said to him, "Where are you?" And he said, "I heard the sound of thee in the garden, and I was afraid, because I was naked; and I hid myself." He said, "Who told you that you were naked? Have you eaten of the tree of which I commanded you not to eat?" The man said, "The woman whom thou gavest to be with me, she gave me fruit of the tree, and I ate." Then the Lord God said to the woman, "What is this that you have done?" The woman said, "The serpent beguiled me, and I ate."

The Lord God said to the serpent,
"Because you have done this,
cursed are you above all cattle,
and above all wild animals;
upon your belly you shall go,
and dust you shall eat
all the days of your life.
I will put enmity between you and the woman,
and between your seed and her seed;
he shall bruise your head
and you shall bruise his heel."

To the woman he said,
"I will greatly multiply your pain in childbearing;
in pain you shall bring forth children,
yet your desire shall be for your husband,
and he shall rule over you."

(2) **Genesis 3:17** And to Adam he said, 400
"Because you have listened to the voice of your wife,
and have eaten of the tree
of which I commanded you,
'You shall not eat of it,'
cursed is the ground because of you;
in toil you shall eat of it all the days of your life. . . ."

(3) **Genesis 3:19** 400
". . . In the sweat of your face
you shall eat bread
till you return to the ground,
for out of it you were taken;
you are dust,
and to dust you shall return."

(4) **Genesis 2:17** ". . . but of the tree of the knowledge of good and evil you shall 400
not eat, for in the day that you eat of it you shall die."

(5) **Romans 5:12** Therefore as sin came into the world through one man and death 400
through sin, and so death spread to all men because all men sinned. . . .

(1) **Genesis 4:3–15** In the course of time Cain brought to the Lord an offering of 401
the fruit of the ground, and Abel brought of the firstlings of his flock and of their fat portions. And the Lord had regard for Abel and his offering, but for Cain and his offering he had no regard. So Cain was very angry, and his countenance fell. The Lord said to Cain, "Why are you angry, and why has your countenance fallen? If you do well, will you not be accepted? And if you do not do well, sin is couching at the door; its desire is for you, but you must master it."

Cain said to Abel his brother, "Let us go out to the field." And when they were in the field, Cain rose up against his brother Abel, and killed him. Then the Lord said to Cain, "Where is Abel your brother?" He said, "I do not know; am I my brother's keeper?" And the Lord said, "What have you done? The voice of your brother's blood is crying to me from the ground. And now you are cursed from the ground, which has opened its mouth to receive your brother's blood from your hand. When you till the ground, it shall no longer yield to you its strength; you shall be a fugitive and a wanderer on the earth." Cain said to the Lord, "My punishment is greater than I can bear. Behold, thou hast driven me this day away from the ground; and from thy face I shall be hidden; and I shall be a fugitive and a wanderer on the earth, and whoever finds me will slay me." Then the Lord said to him, "Not so! If any one slays Cain, vengeance shall be taken on him sevenfold." And the Lord put a mark on Cain, lest any who came upon him should kill him.

401 (2) **Genesis 6:5** The Lord saw that the wickedness of man was great in the earth, and that every imagination of the thoughts of his heart was only evil continually.

401 (3) **Genesis 6:12** And God saw the earth, and behold, it was corrupt; for all flesh had corrupted their way upon the earth.

401 (4) **Romans 1:18–32** For the wrath of God is revealed from heaven against all ungodliness and wickedness of men who by their wickedness suppress the truth. For what can be known about God is plain to them, because God has shown it to them. Ever since the creation of the world his invisible nature, namely, his eternal power and deity, has been clearly perceived in the things that have been made. So they are without excuse; for although they knew God they did not honor him as God or give thanks to him, but they became futile in their thinking and their senseless minds were darkened. Claiming to be wise, they became fools, and exchanged the glory of the immortal God for images resembling mortal man or birds or animals or reptiles.

Therefore God gave them up in the lusts of their hearts to impurity, to the dishonoring of their bodies among themselves, because they exchanged the truth about God for a lie and worshiped and served the creature rather than the Creator, who is blessed for ever! Amen.

For this reason God gave them up to dishonorable passions. Their women exchanged natural relations for unnatural, and the men likewise gave up natural relations with women and were consumed with passion for one another, men committing shameless acts with men and receiving in their own persons the due penalty for their error.

And since they did not see fit to acknowledge God, God gave them up to a base mind and to improper conduct. They were filled with all manner of wickedness, evil, covetousness, malice. Full of envy, murder, strife, deceit, malignity, they are gossips, slanderers, haters of God, insolent, haughty, boastful, inventors of evil, disobedient to parents, foolish, faithless, heartless, ruthless. Though they know God's decree that those who do such things deserve to die, they not only do them but approve those who practice them.

401 (5) **1 Corinthians 1–6** Paul, called by the will of God to be an apostle of Christ Jesus, and our brother Sosthenes,

To the church of God which is at Corinth, to those sanctified in Christ Jesus, called to be saints together with all those who in every place call on the name of our Lord Jesus Christ, both their Lord and ours:

Grace to you and peace from God our Father and the Lord Jesus Christ.

I give thanks to God always for you because of the grace of God which was given you in Christ Jesus, that in every way you were enriched in him with all speech and all knowledge—even as the testimony to Christ was confirmed among you—so that you are not lacking in any spiritual gift, as you wait for the revealing of our Lord Jesus Christ; who will sustain you to the end, guiltless in the day of our Lord Jesus Christ. God is faithful, by whom you were called into the fellowship of his Son, Jesus Christ our Lord.

I appeal to you, brethren, by the name of our Lord Jesus Christ, that all of you agree and that there be no dissensions among you, but that you be united in the same mind and the same judgment. For it has been reported to me by Chloe's people that there is quarreling among you, my brethren. What I mean is that each one of you says, "I belong to Paul," or "I belong to Apollos," or "I belong to Cephas," or "I belong to Christ." Is Christ divided? Was Paul crucified for you? Or were you baptized in the name of Paul? I am thankful that I baptized none of you except Crispus and Gaius; lest any one should say that you were baptized in my name. (I did baptize also the household of Stephanas. Beyond that, I do not know whether I baptized any one else.) For Christ did not send me to baptize but to preach the gospel, and not with eloquent wisdom, lest the cross of Christ be emptied of its power.

For the word of the cross is folly to those who are perishing, but to us who are being saved it is the power of God. For it is written,

"I will destroy the wisdom of the wise,
and the cleverness of the clever I will thwart."

Where is the wise man? Where is the scribe? Where is the debater of this age? Has not God made foolish the wisdom of the world? For since, in the wisdom of God, the world did not know God through wisdom, it pleased God through the folly of what we preach to save those who believe. For Jews demand signs and Greeks seek wisdom, but we preach Christ crucified, a stumbling block to Jews and folly to Gentiles, but to those who are called, both Jews and Greeks, Christ the power of God and the wisdom of God. For the foolishness of God is wiser than men, and the weakness of God is stronger than men.

For consider your call, brethren; not many of you were wise according to worldly standards, not many were powerful, not many were of noble birth; but God chose what is foolish in the world to shame the wise, God chose what is weak in the world to shame the strong, God chose what is low and despised in the world, even things that are not, to bring to nothing things that are, so that no human being might boast in the presence of God. He is the source of your life in Christ Jesus, whom God made our wisdom, our righteousness and sanctification and redemption; therefore, as it is written, "Let him who boasts, boast of the Lord."

When I came to you, brethren, I did not come proclaiming to you the testimony of God in lofty words or wisdom. For I decided to know nothing among you except Jesus Christ and him crucified. And I was with you in weakness and in much fear and trembling; and my speech and my message were not in plausible words of wisdom, but in demonstration of the Spirit and of power, that your faith might not rest in the wisdom of men but in the power of God.

Yet among the mature we do impart wisdom, although it is not a wisdom of this age or of the rulers of this age, who are doomed to pass away. But we impart a secret and hidden wisdom of God, which God decreed before the ages for our glorification. None of the rulers of this age understood this; for if they had, they would not have crucified the Lord of glory. But, as it is written,

"What no eye has seen, nor ear heard,
nor the heart of man conceived,
what God has prepared for those who love him,"

God has revealed to us through the Spirit. For the Spirit searches everything, even the depths of God. For what person knows a man's thoughts except the spirit of the man which is in him? So also no one comprehends the thoughts of God except the Spirit of God. Now we have received not the spirit of the world, but the Spirit which is from God, that we might understand the gifts bestowed on us by God. And we impart this in words not taught by human wisdom but taught by the Spirit, interpreting spiritual truths to those who possess the Spirit.

The unspiritual man does not receive the gifts of the Spirit of God, for they are folly to him, and he is not able to understand them because they are spiritually discerned. The spiritual man judges all things, but is himself to be judged by no one. "For who has known the mind of the Lord so as to instruct him?" But we have the mind of Christ.

But I, brethren, could not address you as spiritual men, but as men of the flesh, as babes in Christ. I fed you with milk, not solid food; for you were not ready for it; and even yet you are not ready, for you are still of the flesh. For while there is jealousy and strife among you, are you not of the flesh, and behaving like ordinary men? For when one says, "I belong to Paul," and another, "I belong to Apollos," are you not merely men?

What then is Apollos? What is Paul? Servants through whom you believed, as the Lord assigned to each. I planted, Apollos watered, but God gave the growth. So neither he who plants nor he who waters is anything, but only God who gives the growth. He who plants and he who waters are equal, and each shall receive his wages according to his labor. For we are God's fellow workers; you are God's field, God's building.

According to the grace of God given to me, like a skilled master builder I laid a foundation, and another man is building upon it. Let each man take care how he builds upon it. For no other foundation can any one lay than that which is laid, which is Jesus Christ. Now if any one builds on the foundation with gold, silver, precious stones, wood, hay, straw—each man's work will become manifest; for the Day will disclose it, because it will be revealed with fire, and the fire will test what sort of work each one has done. If the work which any man has built on the foundation survives, he will receive a reward. If any man's work is burned up, he will suffer loss, though he himself will be saved, but only as through fire.

Do you not know that you are God's temple and that God's Spirit dwells in you? If any one destroys God's temple, God will destroy him. For God's temple is holy, and that temple you are.

Let no one deceive himself. If any one among you thinks that he is wise in this age, let him become a fool that he may become wise. For the wisdom of this world is folly with God. For it is written, "He catches the wise in their craftiness," and again, "The Lord knows that the thoughts of the wise are futile." So let no one boast of men. For all things are yours, whether Paul or Apollos or Cephas or the world or life or death or the present or the future, all are yours; and you are Christ's; and Christ is God's.

This is how one should regard us, as servants of Christ and stewards of the mysteries of God. Moreover it is required of stewards that they be found trustworthy. But with me it is a very small thing that I should be judged by you or by any human court. I do not even judge myself. I am not aware of anything against myself, but I am not thereby acquitted. It is the Lord who judges me. Therefore do not pronounce judgment before the time, before the Lord comes, who will bring to light the things now hidden in darkness and will disclose the purposes of the heart. Then every man will receive his commendation from God.

I have applied all this to myself and Apollos for your benefit, brethren, that you may learn by us not to go beyond what is written, that none of you may be puffed up in favor of one against another. For who sees anything different in you? What have you that you did not receive? If then you received it, why do you boast as if it were not a gift?

Already you are filled! Already you have become rich! Without us you have become kings! And would that you did reign, so that we might share the rule with you! For I think that God has exhibited us apostles as last of all, like men sentenced to death; because we have become a spectacle to the world, to angels and to men. We are fools for Christ's sake, but you are wise in Christ. We are weak, but you are strong. You are held in honor, but we in disrepute. To the present hour we hunger and thirst, we are ill-clad and buffeted and homeless, and we labor, working with our own hands. When reviled, we bless; when persecuted, we endure; when slandered, we try to conciliate; we have become, and are now, as the refuse of the world, the off-scouring of all things.

I do not write this to make you ashamed, but to admonish you as my beloved children. For though you have countless guides in Christ, you do not have many fathers. For I became your father in Christ Jesus through the gospel. I urge you, then, be imitators of me. Therefore I sent to you Timothy, my beloved and faithful child in the Lord, to remind you of my ways in Christ, as I teach them everywhere in every church. Some are arrogant, as though I were not coming to you. But I will come to you soon, if the Lord wills, and I will find out not the talk of these arrogant people but their power. For the kingdom of God does not consist in talk but in power. What do you wish? Shall I come to you with a rod, or with love in a spirit of gentleness?

It is actually reported that there is immorality among you, and of a kind that is not found even among pagans; for a man is living with his father's wife. And you are arrogant! Ought you not rather to mourn? Let him who has done this be removed from among you.

For though absent in body I am present in spirit, and as if present, I have already pronounced judgment in the name of the Lord Jesus on the man who has done such a thing. When you are assembled, and my spirit is present, with the power of our Lord Jesus, you are to deliver this man to Satan for the destruction of the flesh, that his spirit may be saved in the day of the Lord Jesus.

Your boasting is not good. Do you not know that a little leaven leavens the whole lump? Cleanse out the old leaven that you may be a new lump, as you really are unleavened. For Christ, our paschal lamb, has been sacrificed. Let us, therefore, celebrate the festival, not with the old leaven, the leaven of malice and evil, but with the unleavened bread of sincerity and truth.

I wrote to you in my letter not to associate with immoral men; not at all meaning the immoral of this world, or the greedy and robbers, or idolaters, since then you would need to go out of the world. But rather I wrote to you not to associate with any one who bears the name of brother if he is guilty of immorality or greed, or is an idolater, reviler, drunkard, or robber—not even to eat with such a one. For what have I to do with judging outsiders? Is it not those inside the church whom you are to judge? God judges those outside. "Drive out the wicked person from among you."

When one of you has a grievance against a brother, does he dare go to law before the unrighteous instead of the saints? Do you not know that the saints will judge the world? And if the world is to be judged by you, are you incompetent to try trivial cases? Do you not know that we are to judge angels? How much more, matters pertaining to this life! If then you have such cases, why do you lay them before those who are least esteemed by the church? I say this to your shame. Can it be that there is no man among you wise enough to decide between members of the brotherhood, but brother goes to law against brother, and that before unbelievers?

To have lawsuits at all with one another is defeat for you. Why not rather suffer wrong? Why not rather be defrauded? But you yourselves wrong and defraud, and that even your own brethren.

Do you not know that the unrighteous will not inherit the kingdom of God? Do not be deceived; neither the immoral, nor idolaters, nor adulterers, nor sexual perverts, nor thieves, nor the greedy, nor drunkards, nor revilers, nor robbers will inherit the kingdom of God. And such were some of you. But you were washed, you were sanctified, you were justified in the name of the Lord Jesus Christ and in the Spirit of our God.

"All things are lawful for me," but not all things are helpful. "All things are lawful for me," but I will not be enslaved by anything. "Food is meant for the stomach and the stomach for food"—and God will destroy both one and the other. The body is not meant for immorality, but for the Lord, and the Lord for the body. And God raised the Lord and will also raise us up by his power. Do you not know that your bodies are members of Christ? Shall I therefore take the members of Christ and make them members of a prostitute? Never! Do you not know that he who joins himself to a prostitute becomes one body with her? For, as it is written, "The two shall become one flesh." But he who is united to the Lord becomes one spirit with him. Shun immorality. Every other sin which a man commits is outside the body; but the immoral man sins against his own body. Do you not know that your body is a temple of the Holy Spirit within you, which you have from God? You are not your own; you were bought with a price. So glorify God in your body.

401 (6) **Revelation 2–3** "To the angel of the church in Ephesus write: 'The words of him who holds the seven stars in his right hand, who walks among the seven golden lampstands.

"'I know your works, your toil and your patient endurance, and how you cannot bear evil men but have tested those who call themselves apostles but are not, and found them to be false; I know you are enduring patiently and bearing up for my name's sake, and you have not grown weary. But I have this against you, that you have abandoned the love you had at first. Remember then from what you have fallen, repent and do the works you did at first. If not, I will come to you and remove your lampstand from its place, unless you repent. Yet this you have, you hate the works of the Nicolaitans, which I also hate. He who has an ear, let him hear what the Spirit says to the churches. To him who conquers I will grant to eat of the tree of life, which is in the paradise of God.'

"And to the angel of the church in Smyrna write: 'The words of the first and the last, who died and came to life.

"'I know your tribulation and your poverty (but you are rich) and the slander of those who say that they are Jews and are not, but are a synagogue of Satan. Do not fear what you are about to suffer. Behold, the devil is about to throw some of you into prison, that you may be tested, and for ten days you will have tribulation. Be faithful unto death, and I will give you the crown of life. He who has an ear, let him hear what the Spirit says to the churches. He who conquers shall not be hurt by the second death.'

"And to the angel of the church in Pergamum write: 'The words of him who has the sharp two-edged sword.

"'I know where you dwell, where Satan's throne is; you hold fast my name and you did not deny my faith even in the days of Antipas my witness, my faithful one, who was killed among you, where Satan dwells. But I have a few things against you: you have some there who hold the teaching of Balaam, who taught Balak to put a stumbling block before the sons of Israel, that they might eat food sacrificed to idols and practice immorality. So you also have some who hold the teaching of the Nicolaitans. Repent then. If not, I will come to you soon and war against them with the sword of my mouth. He who has an ear, let him hear what the Spirit says to the churches. To him who conquers I will give some of the hidden manna, and I will give him a white stone, with a new name written on the stone which no one knows except him who receives it.'

"And to the angel of the church in Thyatira write: 'The words of the Son of God, who has eyes like a flame of fire, and whose feet are like burnished bronze.

" 'I know your works, your love and faith and service and patient endurance, and that your latter works exceed the first. But I have this against you, that you tolerate the woman Jezebel, who calls herself a prophetess and is teaching and beguiling my servants to practice immorality and to eat food sacrificed to idols. I gave her time to repent, but she refuses to repent of her immorality. Behold, I will throw her on a sickbed, and those who commit adultery with her I will throw into great tribulation, unless they repent of her doings; and I will strike her children dead. And all the churches shall know that I am he who searches mind and heart, and I will give to each of you as your works deserve. But to the rest of you in Thyatira, who do not hold this teaching, who have not learned what some call the deep things of Satan, to you I say, I do not lay upon you any other burden; only hold fast what you have, until I come. He who conquers and who keeps my works until the end, I will give him power over the nations, and he shall rule them with a rod of iron, as when earthen pots are broken in pieces, even as I myself have received power from my Father; and I will give him the morning star. He who has an ear, let him hear what the Spirit says to the churches.'

"And to the angel of the church in Sardis write: 'The words of him who has the seven spirits of God and the seven stars.

" 'I know your works; you have the name of being alive, and you are dead. Awake, and strengthen what remains and is on the point of death, for I have not found your works perfect in the sight of my God. Remember then what you received and heard; keep that, and repent. If you will not awake, I will come like a thief, and you will not know at what hour I will come upon you. Yet you have still a few names in Sardis, people who have not soiled their garments; and they shall walk with me in white, for they are worthy. He who conquers shall be clad thus in white garments, and I will not blot his name out of the book of life; I will confess his name before my Father and before his angels. He who has an ear, let him hear what the Spirit says to the churches.'

"And to the angel of the church in Philadelphia write: 'The words of the holy one, the true one, who has the key of David, who opens and no one shall shut, who shuts and no one opens.

" 'I know your works. Behold, I have set before you an open door, which no one is able to shut; I know that you have but little power, and yet you have kept my word and have not denied my name. Behold, I will make those of the synagogue of Satan who say that they are Jews and are not, but lie—behold, I will make them come and bow down before your feet, and learn that I have loved you. Because you have kept my word of patient endurance, I will keep you from the hour of trial which is coming on the whole world, to try those who dwell upon the earth. I am coming soon; hold fast what you have, so that no one may seize your crown. He who conquers, I will make him a pillar in the temple of my God; never shall he go out of it, and I will write on him the name of my God, and the name of the city of my God, the new Jerusalem which comes down from my God out of heaven, and my own new name. He who has an ear, let him hear what the Spirit says to the churches.'

"And to the angel of the church in Laodicea write: 'The words of the Amen, the faithful and true witness, the beginning of God's creation.

" 'I know your works: you are neither cold nor hot. Would that you were cold or hot! So, because you are lukewarm, and neither cold nor hot, I will spew you out of my mouth. For you say, I am rich, I have prospered, and I need nothing; not knowing that you are wretched, pitiable, poor, blind, and naked. Therefore I counsel you to buy from me gold refined by fire, that you may be rich, and white garments to clothe you and to keep the shame of your nakedness from being seen, and salve to anoint your eyes, that you may see. Those whom I love, I reprove and chasten; so be zealous and repent. Behold, I stand at the door and knock; if any one hears my voice and opens the door, I will come in to him and eat with him, and he with me. He who conquers, I will grant him to sit with me on my throne, as I myself conquered and sat down with my Father on his throne. He who has an ear, let him hear what the Spirit says to the churches.'"

403 (1) **Council of Trent (1546): DS 1512** If anyone asserts that the transgression of Adam has harmed him alone and not his posterity, and that the sanctity and justice, received from God, which he lost, he has lost for himself alone and not for us also; or that he having been defiled by the sin of disobedience has transfused only death "and the punishments of the body into the whole human race, but not sin also, which is the death of the soul," let him be anathema, since he contradicts the Apostle who says: "By one man sin entered into the world, and by sin death, and so death passed upon all men, in whom all have sinned" [Rom. 5:12].

403 (2) **Council of Trent (1546): DS 1514** "If anyone denies that infants newly born from their mothers' wombs are to be baptized," even though they be born of baptized parents, "or says they are baptized indeed for the remission of sins, but that they derive nothing of original sin from Adam, which must be expiated by the laver of regeneration" for the attainment of life everlasting, whence it follows, that in them the form of baptism for the remission of sins is understood to be not true, but false: let him be anathema. For what the Apostle has said: "By one man sin entered into the world, and by sin death, and so death passed upon all men, in whom all have sinned" [Rom. 5:12], is not to be understood otherwise than as the Catholic Church spread everywhere has always understood it. For by reason of this rule of faith from a tradition of the apostles even infants, who could not as yet commit any sins of themselves, are for this reason truly baptized for the remission of sins, so that in them there may be washed away by regeneration, what they have contracted by generation. "For unless a man be born again of water and the Holy Ghost, he cannot enter into the kingdom of God" [John 3:5].

404 **Council of Trent (1546): DS 1511–12** If anyone does not confess that the first man Adam, when he had transgressed the commandment of God in Paradise, immediately lost his holiness and the justice in which he had been established, and that he incurred through the offense of that prevarication the wrath and indignation of God and hence the death with which God had previously threatened him, and with death captivity under his power, who thenceforth "had the empire of death" [Heb. 2:14], that is of the devil, and that through that offense of prevarication the entire Adam was transformed in body and soul for the worse, let him be anathema.

If anyone asserts that the transgression of Adam has harmed him alone and not his posterity, and that the sanctity and justice, received from God, which he lost, he has lost for himself alone and not for us also; or that he having been defiled by the sin of disobedience has transfused only death "and the punishments of the body into the whole human race, but not sin also, which is the death of the soul," let him be anathema, since he contradicts the Apostle who says: "By one man sin entered into the world, and by sin death, and so death passed upon all men, in whom all have sinned" [Rom. 5:12].

Council of Trent (1546): DS 1513: see 390 (2). 405

(1) **Council of Orange II (529): DS 371–72** If anyone says that by the offense 406
of Adam's transgression not the whole man, that is according to body and soul, was changed for the worse [St. Augustine], but believes that while the liberty of the soul endures without harm, the body only is exposed to corruption, he is deceived by the error of Pelagius and resists the Scripture which says: "*The soul, that has sinned, shall die*" [Ezech. 18:20]; and: "*Do you not know that to whom you show yourselves servants to obey, you are the servants of him whom you obey?*" [Rom. 6:16]; and: *Anyone is adjudged the slave of him by whom he is overcome* [II Pet. 2:19].

If anyone asserts that Adam's transgression injured him alone and not his descendants, or declares that certainly death of the body only, which is the punishment of sin, but not sin also, which is the death of the soul, passed through one man into the whole human race, he will do an injustice to God, contradicting the Apostle who says: *Through one man sin entered in the world, and through sin death, and thus death passed into all men, in whom all have sinned* [Rom. 5:12; cf. St. Augustine].

(2) **Council of Trent (1546): DS 1510–16** That our Catholic faith, "without 406
which it is impossible to please God" [Heb. 11:16] may after the purging of errors continue in its own perfect and spotless purity, and that the Christian people may not be "carried about with every wind of doctrine" [Eph. 4:14], since that old serpent, the perpetual enemy of the human race, among the very many evils with which the Church of God in these our times is troubled, has stirred up not only new, but even old dissensions concerning original sin and its remedy, the sacred ecumenical and general Synod of Trent lawfully assembled in the Holy Spirit with the same three legates of the Apostolic See presiding over it, wishing now to proceed to the recalling of the erring and to the confirming of the wavering, and following the testimonies of the Holy Scriptures and of the holy Fathers and of the most approved Councils, as well as the judgment and the unanimity of the Church itself, has established, confesses, and declares the following concerning original sin:

If anyone does not confess that the first man Adam, when he had transgressed the commandment of God in Paradise, immediately lost his holiness and the justice in which he had been established, and that he incurred through the offense of that prevarication the wrath and indignation of God and hence the death with which God had previously threatened him, and with death captivity under his power, who thenceforth "had the empire of death" [Heb. 2:14], that is of the devil, and that through that offense of prevarication the entire Adam was transformed in body and soul for the worse, let him be anathema.

If anyone asserts that the transgression of Adam has harmed him alone and not his posterity, and that the sanctity and justice, received from God, which he lost, he has lost for himself alone and not for us also; or that he having been defiled by the sin of disobedience has transfused only death "and the punishments of the body into the whole human race, but not sin also, which is the death of the soul," let him be anathema, since he contradicts the Apostle who says: "By one man sin entered into the world, and by sin death, and so death passed upon all men, in whom all have sinned" [Rom. 5:12].

If anyone asserts that this sin of Adam, which is one in origin and transmitted to all is in each one as his own by propagation, not by imitation, is taken away either by the forces of human nature, or by any remedy other than the merit of the one mediator, our Lord Jesus Christ, who has reconciled us to God in his own blood, "made unto us justice, sanctification, and redemption" [I Cor. 1:30]; or if he denies that that merit of Jesus Christ is applied to adults as well as to infants by the sacrament of baptism, rightly administered in the form of the Church: let him be anathema. "For there is no other name under heaven given to men, whereby we must be saved. . ." [Acts 4:12]. Whence that word: "Behold the lamb of God, behold Him who taketh away the sins of the world" [John 1:29]. And that other: "As many of you as have been baptized, have put on Christ" [Gal. 3:27].

"If anyone denies that infants newly born from their mothers' wombs are to be baptized," even though they be born of baptized parents, "or says they are baptized indeed for the remission of sins, but that they derive nothing of original sin from Adam, which must be expiated by the laver of regeneration" for the attainment of life everlasting, whence it follows, that in them the form of baptism for the remission of sins is understood to be not true, but false: let him be anathema. For what the Apostle has said: "By one man sin entered into the world, and by sin death, and so death passed upon all men, in whom all have sinned" [Rom. 5:12], is not to be understood otherwise than as the Catholic Church spread everywhere has always understood it. For by reason of this rule of faith from a tradition of the apostles even infants, who could not as yet commit any sins of themselves, are for this reason truly baptized for the remission of sins, so that in them there may be washed away by regeneration, what they have contracted by generation. "For unless a man be born again of water and the Holy Ghost, he cannot enter into the kingdom of God" [John 3:5].

If anyone denies that by the grace of our Lord Jesus Christ, which is conferred in baptism, the guilt of original sin is remitted, or even asserts that the whole of that which has the true and proper nature of sin is not taken away, but says that it is only touched in person or is not imputed, let him be anathema. For in those who are born again, God hates nothing, because "there is no condemnation, to those who are truly buried together with Christ by baptism unto death" [Rom. 6:4], who do not "walk according to the flesh" [Rom. 8:1], but putting off "the old man" and putting on the "new, who is created according to God" [Eph. 4:22 ff.; Col. 3:9 ff.], are made innocent, immaculate, pure, guiltless and beloved sons of God, "heirs indeed of God, but co-heirs with Christ" [Rom. 8:17], so that there is nothing whatever to retard their entrance into heaven. But this holy Synod confesses and perceives that there remains in the baptized concupiscence of an inclination, although this is left to be wrestled with, it cannot harm those who do not consent, but manfully resist by the grace of Jesus Christ. Nay, indeed, "he who shall have striven lawfully, shall be crowned" [II Tim. 2:5]. This concupiscence, which at times the Apostle calls *sin* [Rom. 6:12 ff.] the holy Synod declares that the Catholic Church has never understood to be called sin, as truly and properly sin in those born again, but because it is from sin and inclines to sin. But if anyone is of the contrary opinion, let him be anathema.

This holy Synod declares nevertheless that it is not its intention to include in this decree, where original sin is treated of, the blessed and immaculate Virgin Mary mother of God, but that the constitutions of Pope Sixtus IV of happy memory are to be observed, under the penalties contained in these constitutions, which it renews.

407 (1) **Hebrews 2:14** Since therefore the children share in flesh and blood, he himself likewise partook of the same nature, that through death he might destroy him who has the power of death, that is, the devil. . . .

407 (2) ***Centesimus annus* 25** The events of 1989 are an example of the success of willingness to negotiate and of the Gospel spirit in the face of an adversary determined not to be bound by moral principles. These events are a warning to those who, in the name of political realism, wish to banish law and morality from the political arena. Undoubtedly, the struggle which led to the changes of 1989 called for clarity, moderation, suffering and sacrifice. In a certain sense, it was a struggle born of prayer, and

it would have been unthinkable without immense trust in God, the Lord of history, who carries the human heart in his hands. It is by uniting his own sufferings for the sake of truth and freedom to the sufferings of Christ on the cross that man is able to accomplish the miracle of peace and is in a position to discern the often narrow path between the cowardice which gives in to evil and the violence which, under the illusion of fighting evil, only makes it worse.

Nevertheless, it cannot be forgotten that the manner in which the individual exercises freedom is conditioned in innumerable ways. While these certainly have an influence on freedom, they do not determine it; they make the exercise of freedom more difficult or less difficult, but they cannot destroy it. Not only is it wrong from the ethical point of view to disregard human nature, which is made for freedom, but in practice it is impossible to do so. Where society is so organized as to reduce arbitrarily or even suppress the sphere in which freedom is legitimately exercised, the result is that the life of society becomes progressively disorganized and goes into decline.

Moreover, man, who was created for freedom, bears within himself the wound of original sin, which constantly draws him towards evil and puts him in need of redemption. Not only is *this doctrine an integral part of Christian revelation*; it also has great hermeneutical value insofar as it helps one to understand human reality. Man tends towards good, but he is also capable of evil. He can transcend his immediate interest and still remain bound to it. The social order will be all the more stable, the more it takes this fact into account and does not place in opposition personal interest and the interests of society as a whole, but rather seeks ways to bring them into fruitful harmony. In fact, where self-interest is violently suppressed, it is replaced by a burdensome system of bureaucratic control which dries up the wellsprings of initiative and creativity. When people think they possess the secret of a perfect social organization which makes evil impossible, they also think that they can use any means, including violence and deceit, in order to bring that organization into being. Politics then becomes a "secular religion" which operates under the illusion of creating paradise in this world. But no political society—which possesses its own autonomy and laws—can ever be confused with the Kingdom of God. The Gospel parable of the weeds among the wheat (cf. Mt 13:24–30; 36–43) teaches that it is for God alone to separate the subjects of the Kingdom from the subjects of the Evil One, and that this judgment will take place at the end of time. By presuming to anticipate judgment here and now, man puts himself in the place of God and sets himself against the patience of God.

Through Christ's sacrifice on the cross, the victory of the Kingdom of God has been achieved once and for all. Nevertheless, the Christian life involves a struggle against temptation and the forces of evil. Only at the end of history will the Lord return in glory for the final judgment (cf. Mt 25:31) with the establishment of a new heaven and a new earth (cf. 2 Pt 3:13; Rev 21:1); but as long as time lasts the struggle between good and evil continues even in the human heart itself.

What Sacred Scripture teaches us about the prospects of the Kingdom of God is not without consequences for the life of temporal societies, which, as the adjective indicates, belong to the realm of time, with all that this implies of imperfection and impermanence. The Kingdom of God, being *in* the world without being *of* the world, throws light on the order of human society, while the power of grace penetrates that order and gives it life. In this way the requirements of a society worthy of man are better perceived, deviations are corrected, the courage to work for what is good is reinforced. In union with all people of good will, Christians, especially the laity, are called to this task of imbuing human realities with the Gospel.

408 ***Reconciliatio et paenitentia* 16** Sin, in the proper sense, is always a *personal* act, since it is an act of freedom on the part of an individual person, and not properly of a group or community. This individual may be conditioned, incited and influenced by numerous and powerful external factors. He may also be subjected to tendencies, defects and habits linked with his personal condition. In not a few cases such external and internal factors may attenuate, to a greater or lesser degree, the person's freedom and therefore his responsibility and guilt. But it is a truth of faith, also confirmed by our experience and reason, that the human person is free. This truth cannot be disregarded, in order to place the blame for individuals' sins on external factors such as structures, systems or other people. Above all, this would be to deny the person's dignity and freedom, which are manifested—even though in a negative and disastrous way—also in this responsibility for sin committed. Hence there is nothing so personal and untransferable in each individual as merit for virtue or responsibility for sin.

As a personal act, sin has its first and most important consequences in the *sinner himself*: that is, in his relationship with God, who is the very foundation of human life; and also in his spirit, weakening his will and clouding his intellect.

At this point we must ask what was being referred to by those who, during the preparation of the Synod and in the course of its actual work, frequently spoke of *social sin*.

The expression and the underlying concept in fact have various meanings.

To speak of *social sin* means in the first place to recognize that, by virtue of a human solidarity which is as mysterious and intangible as it is real and concrete, each individual's sin in some way affects others. This is the other aspect of that solidarity which on the religious level is developed in the profound and magnificent mystery of the *Communion of Saints*, thanks to which it has been possible to say that "every soul that rises above itself, raises up the world". To this *law of ascent* there unfortunately corresponds the *law of descent*. Consequently one can speak of a *communion of sin*, whereby a soul that lowers itself through sin drags down with itself the Church and, in some way, the whole world. In other words, there is no sin, not even the most intimate and secret one, the most strictly individual one, that exclusively concerns the person committing it. With greater or lesser violence, with greater or lesser harm, every sin has repercussions on the entire ecclesial body and the whole human family. According to this first meaning of the term, every sin can undoubtedly be considered as *social* sin.

Some sins however by their very matter constitute a direct attack on one's neighbor and, more exactly, in the language of the Gospel, against one's brother or sister. They are an offense against God because they are offenses against one's neighbor. These sins are usually called *social sins*, and this is the second meaning of the term. In this sense *social* sin is sin against love of neighbor, and in the law of Christ it is all the more serious in that it involves the second Commandment, which is "like unto the first". Likewise, the term *social* applies to every sin against justice in interpersonal relationships, committed either by the individual against the community or by the community against the individual. Also *social* is every sin against the rights of the human person, beginning with the right to life and including the life of the unborn, or against a person's physical integrity. Likewise *social* is every sin against others' freedom, especially against the supreme freedom to believe in God and adore him; *social* is every sin against the dignity and honor of one's neighbor. Also social is every sin against the common good and its exigencies in relation to the whole broad spectrum of the rights and duties of citizens. The term *social* can be applied to sins of commission or omission—on the part of political, economic or trade union leaders who though in a position to do so do not work diligently and wisely for the improvement and transformation of society according to the requirements and potential of the given historic moment; as also on the part of workers who through absenteeism or non-cooperation fail to ensure that their industries can continue to advance the well-being of the workers themselves, of their families, and of the whole of society.

The third meaning of *social sin* refers to the relationships between the various human communities. These relationships are not always in accordance with the plan of God, who intends that there be justice in the world, and freedom and peace between individuals, groups and peoples. Thus the class struggle, whoever the person who leads it or on occasion seeks to give it a theoretical justification, is a *social evil*. Likewise, obstinate confrontation between blocs of nations, between one nation and another, between different groups within the same nation—all this too is a *social evil*. In both cases one may ask whether moral responsibility for these evils, and therefore sin, can be attributed to any person in particular. Now it has to be admitted that realities and situations such as those described, when they become generalized and reach vast proportions as social phenomena, almost always become anonymous, just as their causes are complex and not always identifiable. Hence if one speaks of *social sin* here, the expression obviously has an analogical meaning. However, to speak even analogically of *social sins* must not cause us to underestimate the responsibility of the individuals involved. It is meant to be an appeal to the consciences of all, so that each may shoulder his or her responsibility seriously and courageously in order to change those disastrous conditions and intolerable situations.

Having said this in the clearest and most unequivocal way, one must add at once that there is one meaning sometimes given to *social sin* that is not legitimate or acceptable, even though it is very common in certain quarters today. This usage contrasts *social sin* and *personal sin*, not without ambiguity, in a way that leads more or less unconsciously to the watering down and almost the abolition of *personal* sin, with the recognition only of *social* guilt and responsibilities. According to this usage, which can readily be seen to derive from non-Christian ideologies and systems—which have possibly been discarded today by the very people who formerly officially upheld them—practically every sin is a social sin, in the sense that blame for it is to be placed not so much on the moral conscience of an individual but rather on some vague entity or anonymous collectivity, such as the situation, the system, society, structures, or institutions.

Whenever the Church speaks of *situations* of sin, or when she condemns as *social sins* certain situations or the collective behavior of certain social groups, big or small, or even of whole nations and blocs of nations, she knows and she proclaims that such cases of *social sin* are the result of the accumulation and concentration of many *personal sins*. It is a case of the very personal sins of those who cause or support evil or who exploit it; of those who are in a position to avoid, eliminate or at least limit certain social evils but who fail to do so out of laziness, fear or the conspiracy of silence, through secret complicity or indifference; of those who take refuge in the supposed impossibility of changing the world, and also of those who side-step the effort and sacrifice required, producing specious reasons of a higher order. The real responsibility, then, lies with individuals.

A situation—or likewise an institution, a structure, society itself—is not in itself the subject of moral acts. Hence a situation cannot in itself be good or bad.

At the heart of every *situation of sin* are always to be found sinful people. So true is this that even when such a situation can be changed in its structural and institutional aspects by the force of law, or—as unfortunately more often happens—by the law of force, the change in fact proves to be incomplete, of short duration, and ultimately vain and ineffective—not to say counterproductive—if the people directly or indirectly responsible for that situation are not converted.

409 **1 Peter 5:8** Be sober, be watchful. Your adversary the devil prowls around like a roaring lion, seeking some one to devour.

410 (1) **Genesis 3:9** But the Lord God called to the man, and said to him, "Where are you?"

410 (2) **Genesis 3:15**

"... I will put enmity between you and the woman,
and between your seed and her seed;
he shall bruise your head,
and you shall bruise his heel."

411 (1) **1 Corinthians 15:21–22** For as by a man came death, by a man has come also the resurrection of the dead. For as in Adam all die, so also in Christ shall all be made alive.

411 (2) **1 Corinthians 15:45** Thus it is written, "The first man Adam became a living being"; the last Adam became a life-giving spirit.

411 (3) **Philippians 2:8** And being found in human form he humbled himself and became obedient unto death, even death on a cross.

411 (4) **Romans 5:19–20** For as by one man's disobedience many were made sinners, so by one man's obedience many will be made righteous. Law came in, to increase the trespass; but where sin increased, grace abounded all the more. . . .

411 (5) **Pius XII, bull *Ineffabilis Deus* (1854): DS 2803** . . . To the honor of the Holy and Undivided Trinity, to the glory and adornment of the Virgin Mother of God, to the exaltation of the Catholic Faith and the increase of the Christian religion, by the authority of our Lord Jesus Christ, of the blessed Apostles, Peter and Paul, and by Our own, We declare, pronounce, and define that the doctrine, which holds that the most Blessed Virgin Mary at the first instant of her conception, by a singular grace and privilege of Almighty God, in virtue of the merits of Christ Jesus, the Savior of the human race, was preserved immaculate from all stain of original sin, has been revealed by God, and on this account must be firmly and constantly believed by all the faithful.

411 (6) **Council of Trent (1547): DS 1573** If anyone shall say that a man once justified can sin no more, nor lose grace, and that therefore he who falls and sins was never truly justified; or, on the contrary, that throughout his whole life he can avoid all sins even venial sins, except by a special privilege of God, as the Church holds in regard to the Blessed Virgin: let him be anathema.

412 **Romans 5:20** Law came in, to increase the trespass; but where sin increased, grace abounded all the more. . . .

422 (1) **Luke 1:55**

". . . as he spoke to our fathers,
to Abraham and to his posterity for ever."

422 (2) **Luke 1:68**

"Blessed be the Lord God of Israel,
for he has visited and redeemed his people. . . ."

(1) **Matthew 16:18** And I tell you, you are Peter, and on this rock I will build my church, and the powers of death shall not prevail against it. 424

(2) **St. Leo the Great, *Sermo* 4, 3** The gates of hell will not prevail over this [Peter's] confession, the chains of death will not bind it: for these words are words of life. And as they raise to heaven those who confess them, they plunge into hell those who deny them. For this reason it is said to blessed Peter: I will give to you the keys of the Kingdom of Heaven. And whatsoever you shall bind on earth shall be bound also in heaven; and whatsoever you shall loose on earth shall be loosed in heaven. The right to exercise this power passed also to the other apostles and the institution arising from this decision extended to all the leaders of the Church; but it is not in vain that what is intended for all is confided to one man. For this power is entrusted to Peter in this singular fashion because the form of Peter is intended for all those who rule the Church. Peter's privilege is therefore everywhere present where a judgment is rendered in virtue of his equity. Nor is either the severity or the leniency too great where nothing is bound, nothing loosed, but what blessed Peter would have bound or loosed. And when Jesus' passion approached, which would shake the constancy of all the disciples, he said Simon, Simon, behold Satan has asked for you, that he may sift you like wheat. But I have prayed for you, that your faith may not fail. And you, when you shall have turned back, strengthen your brothers, lest you enter into temptation. The danger of the temptation to fear was common to all the apostles, and they all had like need of the aid of divine protection, for the devil desired to frighten and bring about the fall of all of them. Nevertheless, the Lord has a special concern for Peter, and prays specifically for Peter's faith, as if the future condition of the others would be more secure if the soul of the leader was not vanquished. Therefore in Peter the strength of all is confirmed, and the aid of divine grace is so ordered that the steadfastness, which is given to Peter by Christ, is conferred on the apostles through Peter. 424

(3) **St. Leo the Great, *Sermo* 51, 1** 424

S. Peter's confession shown to lead up to the Transfiguration.

The Gospel lesson, dearly-beloved, which has reached the inner hearing of our minds through our bodily ears, calls us to the understanding of a great mystery, to which we shall by the help of God's grace the better attain, if we turn our attention to what is narrated just before.

The Savior of mankind, Jesus Christ, in founding that faith, which recalls the wicked to righteousness and the dead to life, used to instruct His disciples by admonitory teaching and by miraculous acts to the end that He, the Christ, might be believed to be at once the Only-begotten of God and the Son of Man. For the one without the other was of no avail to salvation, and it was equally dangerous to have believed the Lord Jesus Christ to be either only God without manhood, or only man without Godhead, since both had equally to be confessed, because just as true manhood existed in His Godhead, so true Godhead existed in His Manhood. To strengthen, therefore, their most wholesome knowledge of this belief, the Lord had asked His disciples, among the various opinions of others, what they themselves believed, or thought about Him: whereat the Apostle Peter, by the revelation of the most High Father passing beyond things corporeal and surmounting things human by the eyes of his mind, saw Him to be Son of the living God, and acknowledged the glory of the Godhead, because he looked not at the substance of His flesh and blood alone; and with this lofty faith Christ was so well pleased that he received the fulness of blessing, and was endued with the holy firmness of the inviolable Rock on which the Church should be built and conquer the gates of hell and the laws of death, so that, in loosing or binding the petitions of any whatsoever, only that should be ratified in heaven which had been settled by the judgment of Peter.

424 (4) **St. Leo the Great, *Sermo* 62, 2**

The Creed takes up S. Peter's confession as the fundamental doctrine of the Church.

In that rule of Faith, dearly-beloved, which we have received in the very beginning of the Creed, on the authority of apostolic teaching, we acknowledge our Lord Jesus Christ, whom we call the only Son of God the Father Almighty, to be also born of the Virgin Mary by the Holy Ghost. Nor do we reject His Majesty when we express our belief in His crucifixion, death, and resurrection on the third day. For all that is God's and all that is Man's are simultaneously fulfilled by His Manhood and His Godhead, so that in virtue of the union of the Passible with the Impassible, His power cannot be affected by His weakness, nor His weakness overcome by His power. And rightly was the blessed Apostle Peter praised for confessing this union, who when the Lord was inquiring what the disciples knew of Him, quickly anticipated the rest and said, "Thou art Christ, the Son of the living God." And this assuredly he saw, not by the revelation of flesh or blood, which might have hindered his inner sight, but by the very Spirit of the Father working in his believing heart, that in preparation for ruling the whole Church he might first learn what he would have to teach, and for the solidification of the Faith, which he was destined to preach, might receive the assurance, "Thou art Peter, and upon this rock I will build My Church, and the gates of hell shall not prevail against it." The strength, therefore, of the Christian Faith, which, built upon an impregnable rock, fears not the gates of death, acknowledges the one Lord Jesus Christ to be both true God and true Man, believing Him likewise to be the Virgin's Son, Who is His Mother's Creator; born also at the end of the ages, though He is the Creator of time: Lord of all power, and yet one of mortal stock: ignorant of sin, and yet sacrificed for sinners after the likeness of sinful flesh.

424 (5) **St. Leo the Great, *Sermo* 83, 3** When Jesus' passion approached, which would shake the constancy of all the disciples, he said Simon, Simon, behold Satan has asked for you, that he may sift you like wheat. But I have prayed for you, that your faith may not fail. And you, when you shall have turned back, strengthen your brothers, lest you enter into temptation. The danger of the temptation to fear was common to all the apostles, and they all had like need of the aid of divine protection, for the devil desired to frighten and bring about the fall of all of them. Nevertheless, the Lord has a special concern for Peter, and prays specifically for Peter's faith, as if the future condition of the others would be more secure if the soul of the leader was not vanquished. Therefore in Peter the strength of all is confirmed, and the aid of divine grace is so ordered that the steadfastness, which is given to Peter by Christ, is conferred on the apostles through Peter. For after his resurrection the Lord, who had conferred the keys of the Kingdom upon St. Peter, responds to the threefold confession of divine love by saying three times, with mystical intent: Feed my sheep. And now this holy pastor certainly does just this and obeys the Lord's command by strengthening us with his exhortations and praying for us unceasingly so that no temptation will overcome us. But if, as we must believe, he extends his merciful care to the whole people of God everywhere, how much more does he deign to offer his aid to us his children, among whom he reposes upon a sacred bower of a blessed sleep, in the very flesh with which he ruled us? And so, beloved, since we see such a great aid divinely instituted for us, it is right and just for us to rejoice in the merits and the dignity of our leader, giving thanks to the everlasting King and Redeemer, our Lord Jesus Christ, that he has given such power to him whom he set over the

Church, to the praise and glory of his name, to whom be honor and glory world without end. Amen.

John 7:16 So Jesus answered them, "My teaching is not mine, but his who sent 427
me. . . ."

(1) **Luke 1:31** And behold, you will conceive in your womb and bear a son, and 430
you shall call his name Jesus.

(2) **Matthew 2:7** Then Herod summoned the wise men secretly and ascertained 430
from them what time the star appeared. . . .

(1) **Psalm 51:4** 431

Against thee, thee only, have I sinned,
  and done that which is evil in thy sight,
so that thou art justified in thy sentence
  and blameless in thy judgment.

(2) **Psalm 51:9–12** 431

Hide thy face from my sins,
  and blot out all my iniquities.

Create in me a clean heart, O God,
  and put a new and right spirit within me.
Cast me not away from thy presence,
  and take not thy holy Spirit from me.
Restore to me the joy of thy salvation,
  and uphold me with a willing spirit.

(3) **Psalm 79:9** 431

Help us, O God of our salvation,
  for the glory of thy name;
deliver us, and forgive our sins,
  for thy name's sake!

(1) **John 3:18** He who believes in him is not condemned; he who does not believe 432
is condemned already, because he has not believed in the name of the only Son of God.

(2) **Acts 2:21** "'. . . And it shall be that whoever calls on the name of the Lord 432
shall be saved.'. . ."

(3) **Acts 5:41** Then they left the presence of the council, rejoicing that they were 432
counted worthy to suffer dishonor for the name.

(4) **3 John 7** For they have set out for his sake [name] and have accepted nothing 432
from the heathen.

(5) **Romans 10:6–13** But the righteousness based on faith says, Do not say in your 432
heart, "Who will ascend into heaven?" (that is, to bring Christ down) or "Who will descend into the abyss?" (that is, to bring Christ up from the dead). But what does it say? The word is near you, on your lips and in your heart (that is, the word of faith which we preach); because, if you confess with your lips that Jesus is Lord and believe

in your heart that God raised him from the dead, you will be saved. For man believes with his heart and so is justified, and he confesses with his lips and so is saved. The scripture says, "No one who believes in him will be put to shame." For there is no distinction between Jew and Greek; the same Lord is Lord of all and bestows his riches upon all who call upon him. For, "every one who calls upon the name of the Lord will be saved."

432 (6) **Acts 9:14** ". . . and here he has authority from the chief priests to bind all who call upon thy name."

432 (7) **James 2:7** Is it not they who blaspheme the honorable name which was invoked over you?

433 (1) **Exodus 25:22** There I will meet with you, and from above the mercy seat, from between the two cherubim that are upon the ark of the testimony, I will speak with you of all that I will give you in commandment for the people of Israel.

433 (2) **Leviticus 16:2** . . . and the Lord said to Moses, "Tell Aaron your brother not to come at all times into the holy place within the veil, before the mercy seat which is upon the ark, lest he die; for I will appear in the cloud upon the mercy seat. . . ."

433 (3) **Leviticus 16:15–16** "Then he shall kill the goat of the sin offering which is for the people, and bring its blood within the veil, and do with its blood as he did with the blood of the bull, sprinkling it upon the mercy seat and before the mercy seat; thus he shall make atonement for the holy place, because of the uncleannesses of the people of Israel, and because of their transgressions, all their sins; and so he shall do for the tent of meeting, which abides with them in the midst of their uncleannesses. . . ."

433 (4) **Numbers 7:89** And when Moses went into the tent of meeting to speak with the Lord, he heard the voice speaking to him from above the mercy seat that was upon the ark of the testimony, from between the two cherubim; and it spoke to him.

433 (5) **Sirach 50:20**

Then Simon came down, and lifted up his hands
  over the whole congregation of the sons of Israel,
to pronounce the blessing of the Lord with his lips,
  and to glory in his name. . . .

433 (6) **Hebrews 9:5** . . . above it were the cherubim of glory overshadowing the mercy seat. Of these things we cannot now speak in detail.

433 (7) **Hebrews 9:7** . . . but into the second only the high priest goes, and he but once a year, and not without taking blood which he offers for himself and for the errors of the people.

434 (1) **John 12:28** ". . . Father, glorify thy name." Then a voice came from heaven, "I have glorified it, and I will glorify it again."

434 (2) **Acts 16:16–18** As we were going to the place of prayer, we were met by a slave girl who had a spirit of divination and brought her owners much gain by soothsaying. She followed Paul and us, crying, "These men are servants of the Most High God, who proclaim to you the way of salvation." And this she did for many days. But Paul was annoyed, and turned and said to the spirit, "I charge you in the name of Jesus Christ to come out of her." And it came out that very hour.

(3) **Acts 19:13–16** Then some of the itinerant Jewish exorcists undertook to pronounce the name of the Lord Jesus over those who had evil spirits, saying, "I adjure you by the Jesus whom Paul preaches." Seven sons of a Jewish high priest named Sceva were doing this. But the evil spirit answered them, "Jesus I know, and Paul I know; but who are you?" And the man in whom the evil spirit was leaped on them, mastered all of them, and overpowered them, so that they fled out of that house naked and wounded. **434**

(4) **Mark 16:17** And these signs will accompany those who believe: in my name they will cast out demons; they will speak in new tongues. . . . **434**

(5) **John 15:16** You did not choose me, but I chose you and appointed you that you should go and bear fruit and that your fruit should abide; so that whatever you ask the Father in my name, he may give it to you. **434**

(1) **Exodus 29:7** And you shall take the anointing oil, and pour it on his head and anoint him. **436**

(2) **Leviticus 8:12** And he poured some of the anointing oil on Aaron's head, and anointed him, to consecrate him. **436**

(3) **1 Samuel 9:16** "Tomorrow about this time I will send to you a man from the land of Benjamin, and you shall anoint him to be prince over my people Israel. He shall save my people from the hand of the Philistines; for I have seen the affliction of my people, because their cry has come to me." **436**

(4) **1 Samuel 10:1** Then Samuel took a vial of oil and poured it on his head, and kissed him and said, "Has not the Lord anointed you to be prince over his people Israel? And you shall reign over the people of the Lord and you will save them from the hand of their enemies round about. And this shall be the sign to you that the Lord has anointed you to be prince over his heritage. . . ." **436**

(5) **1 Samuel 16:1** The Lord said to Samuel, "How long will you grieve over Saul, seeing I have rejected him from being king over Israel? Fill your horn with oil, and go; I will send you to Jesse the Bethlehemite, for I have provided for myself a king among his sons." **436**

(6) **1 Samuel 16:12–13** And he sent, and brought him in. Now he was ruddy, and had beautiful eyes, and was handsome. And the Lord said, "Arise, anoint him; for this is he." Then Samuel took the horn of oil, and anointed him in the midst of his brothers; and the Spirit of the Lord came mightily upon David from that day forward. And Samuel rose up, and went to Ramah. **436**

(7) **1 Kings 1:39** There Zadok the priest took the horn of oil from the tent, and anointed Solomon. Then they blew the trumpet; and all the people said, "Long live King Solomon!" **436**

(8) **1 Kings 19:16** . . . and Jehu the son of Nimshi you shall anoint to be king over Israel; and Elisha the son of Shaphat of Abelmeholah you shall anoint to be prophet in your place. **436**

436 (9) **Psalm 2:2**

The kings of the earth set themselves,
and the rulers take counsel together,
against the Lord and his anointed, saying. . . .

436 (10) **Acts 4:26–27**

"'. . . The kings of the earth set themselves in array,
and the rulers were gathered together,
against the Lord and against his Anointed'—

for truly in this city there were gathered together against thy holy servant Jesus, whom thou didst anoint, both Herod and Pontius Pilate, with the Gentiles and the peoples of Israel. . . ."

436 (11) **Isaiah 11:2**

And the Spirit of the Lord shall rest upon him,
the spirit of wisdom and understanding,
the spirit of counsel and might,
the spirit of knowledge and the fear of the Lord.

436 (12) **Isaiah 61:1**

The Spirit of the Lord God is upon me,
because the Lord has anointed me
to bring good tidings to the afflicted;
he has sent me to bind up the brokenhearted,
to proclaim liberty to the captives,
and the opening of the prison to those who are bound. . . .

436 (13) **Zechariah 4:14** Then he said, "These are the two anointed who stand by the Lord of the whole earth."

436 (14) **Zechariah 6:13** ". . . It is he who shall build the temple of the Lord, and shall bear royal honor, and shall sit and rule upon his throne. And there shall be a priest by his throne, and peaceful understanding shall be between them both."

436 (15) **Luke 4:16–21** And he came to Nazareth, where he had been brought up; and he went to the synagogue, as his custom was, on the sabbath day. And he stood up to read; and there was given to him the book of the prophet Isaiah. He opened the book and found the place where it was written,

"The Spirit of the Lord is upon me,
because he has anointed me to preach good news to the poor.
He has sent me to proclaim release to the captives
and recovering of sight to the blind,
to set at liberty those who are oppressed,
to proclaim the acceptable year of the Lord."

And he closed the book, and gave it back to the attendant, and sat down; and the eyes of all in the synagogue were fixed on him. And he began to say to them, "Today this scripture has been fulfilled in your hearing."

437 (1) **Luke 1:35** And the angel said to her,

"The Holy Spirit will come upon you,
and the power of the Most High will overshadow you;
therefore the child to be born will be called holy,
the Son of God. . . ."

(2) **Matthew 1:16** . . . and Jacob the father of Joseph the husband of Mary, of whom 437
Jesus was born, who is called Christ.

(3) **Romans 1:3** . . . the gospel concerning his Son, who was descended from David 437
according to the flesh. . . .

(4) **2 Timothy 2:8** Remember Jesus Christ, risen from the dead, descended from 437
David, as preached in my gospel. . . .

(5) **Revelation 22:16** "I Jesus have sent my angel to you with this testimony for 437
the churches. I am the root and the offspring of David, the bright morning star."

(1) **Matthew 2:2** "Where is he who has been born king of the Jews? For we have 439
seen his star in the East, and have come to worship him."

(2) **Matthew 9:27** And as Jesus passed on from there, two blind men followed him, 439
crying aloud, "Have mercy on us, Son of David."

(3) **Matthew 12:23** And all the people were amazed, and said, "Can this be the 439
Son of David?"

(4) **Matthew 15:22** And behold, a Canaanite woman from that region came out and 439
cried, "Have mercy on me, O Lord, Son of David; my daughter is severely possessed
by a demon."

(5) **Matthew 20:30** And behold, two blind men sitting by the roadside, when they 439
heard that Jesus was passing by, cried out, "Have mercy on us, Son of David!"

(6) **Matthew 21:9** And the crowds that went before him and that followed him 439
shouted, "Hosanna to the Son of David! Blessed is he who comes in the name of the
Lord! Hosanna in the highest!"

(7) **Matthew 21:15** But when the chief priests and the scribes saw the wonderful 439
things that he did, and the children crying out in the temple, "Hosanna to the Son
of David!" they were indignant. . . .

(8) **John 4:25–26** The woman said to him, "I know that Messiah is coming (he 439
who is called Christ); when he comes, he will show us all things." Jesus said to her,
"I who speak to you am he."

(9) **John 6:15** Perceiving then that they were about to come and take him by force 439
to make him king, Jesus withdrew again to the mountain by himself.

(10) **John 11:27** She said to him, "Yes, Lord; I believe that you are the Christ, the 439
Son of God, he who is coming into the world."

(11) **Matthew 22:41–46** Now while the Pharisees were gathered together, Jesus 439
asked them a question, saying, "What do you think of the Christ? Whose son is he?" They said to him, "The son of David." He said to them, "How is it then that David, inspired by the Spirit, calls him Lord, saying,

> 'The Lord said to my Lord,
> Sit at my right hand,
> till I put thy enemies under thy feet'?

If David thus calls him Lord, how is he his son?" And no one was able to answer him a word, nor from that day did any one dare to ask him any more questions.

439 (12) **Luke 24:21** But we had hoped that he was the one to redeem Israel. Yes, and besides all this, it is now the third day since this happened.

440 (1) **Matthew 16:16–23** Simon Peter replied, "You are the Christ, the Son of the living God." And Jesus answered him, "Blessed are you, Simon Bar-Jona! For flesh and blood has not revealed this to you, but my Father who is in heaven. And I tell you, you are Peter, and on this rock I will build my church, and the powers of death shall not prevail against it. I will give you the keys of the kingdom of heaven, and whatever you bind on earth shall be bound in heaven, and whatever you loose on earth shall be loosed in heaven." Then he strictly charged the disciples to tell no one that he was the Christ.

From that time Jesus began to show his disciples that he must go to Jerusalem and suffer many things from the elders and chief priests and scribes, and be killed, and on the third day be raised. And Peter took him and began to rebuke him, saying, "God forbid, Lord! This shall never happen to you." But he turned and said to Peter, "Get behind me, Satan! You are a hindrance to me; for you are not on the side of God, but of men."

440 (2) **John 6:62** Then what if you were to see the Son of man ascending where he was before?

440 (3) **Daniel 7:13**

I saw in the night visions,
and behold, with the clouds of heaven
    there came one like a son of man,
and he came to the Ancient of Days
    and was presented before him.

440 (4) **Isaiah 53:10–12**

Yet it was the will of the Lord to bruise him;
    he has put him to grief;
when he makes himself an offering for sin,
    he shall see his offspring, he shall prolong his days;
the will of the Lord shall prosper in his hand;
    he shall see the fruit of the travail of his soul and be satisfied;
by his knowledge shall the righteous one, my servant,
    make many to be accounted righteous;
    and he shall bear their iniquities.
Therefore I will divide him a portion with the great,
    and he shall divide the spoil with the strong;
because he poured out his soul to death,
    and was numbered with the transgressors;
yet he bore the sin of many,
    and made intercession for the transgressors.

440 (5) **John 19:19–22** Pilate also wrote a title and put it on the cross; it read, "Jesus of Nazareth, the King of the Jews." Many of the Jews read this title, for the place where Jesus was crucified was near the city; and it was written in Hebrew, in Latin, and in Greek. The chief priests of the Jews then said to Pilate, "Do not write, 'The King of the Jews,' but, 'This man said, I am King of the Jews.'" Pilate answered, "What I have written I have written."

(6) **Luke 23:39–43** One of the criminals who were hanged railed at him, saying, 440
"Are you not the Christ? Save yourself and us!" But the other rebuked him, saying, "Do you not fear God, since you are under the same sentence of condemnation? And we indeed justly; for we are receiving the due reward of our deeds; but this man has done nothing wrong." And he said, "Jesus, remember me when you come into your kingdom." And he said to him, "Truly, I say to you, today you will be with me in Paradise."

(1) **Deuteronomy 14:1** "You are the sons of the Lord your God; you shall not cut 441
yourselves or make any baldness on your foreheads for the dead. . . ."

(2) **Deuteronomy 32:8** 441

When the Most High gave to the nations their inheritance,
when he separated the sons of men,
he fixed the bounds of the peoples
according to the number of the sons of God.

(3) **Job 1:6** Now there was a day when the sons of God came to present themselves 441
before the Lord, and Satan also came among them.

(4) **Exodus 4:22** ". . . And you shall say to Pharaoh, 'Thus says the Lord, Israel is 441
my first-born son. . . .'"

(5) **Hosea 2:1** Say to your brother, "My people," and to your sister, "She has ob- 441
tained pity."

(6) **Hosea 11:1** 441

When Israel was a child, I loved him,
and out of Egypt I called my son.

(7) **Jeremiah 3:19** 441

"'I thought
how I would set you among my sons,
and give you a pleasant land,
a heritage most beauteous of all nations.
And I thought you would call me, My Father,
and would not turn from following me. . . .'"

(8) **Sirach 36:11 (36:12: RSV)** 441

Have mercy, O Lord, upon the people called by thy name,
upon Israel, whom thou hast likened to a first-born son.

(9) **Wisdom 18:13** 441

For though they had disbelieved everything because of their magic arts,
yet, when their first-born were destroyed, they acknowledged thy
people to be God's son.

(10) **2 Samuel 7:14** I will be his father, and he shall be my son. When he com- 441
mits iniquity, I will chasten him with the rod of men, with the stripes of the sons of men. . . .

(11) **Psalm 82:6** 441

I say, "You are gods,
sons of the Most High, all of you. . . ."

441 (12) **1 Chronicles 17:13** I will be his father, and he shall be my son; I will not take my steadfast love from him, as I took it from him who was before you. . . .

441 (13) **Psalm 2:7**

I will tell of the decree of the Lord:
He said to me, "You are my son,
today I have begotten you. . . ."

441 (14) **Matthew 27:54** When the centurion and those who were with him, keeping watch over Jesus, saw the earthquake and what took place, they were filled with awe, and said, "Truly this was the Son of God!"

441 (15) **Luke 23:47** Now when the centurion saw what had taken place, he praised God, and said, "Certainly this man was innocent!"

442 (1) **1 Thessalonians 1:10** . . . and to wait for his Son from heaven, whom he raised from the dead, Jesus who delivers us from the wrath to come.

442 (2) **John 20:31** . . . but these are written that you may believe that Jesus is the Christ, the Son of God, and that believing you may have life in his name.

442 (3) **Matthew 16:18** And I tell you, you are Peter, and on this rock I will build my church, and the powers of death shall not prevail against it.

443 (1) **Matthew 26:64** Jesus said to him, "You have said so. But I tell you, hereafter you will see the Son of man seated at the right hand of Power, and coming on the clouds of heaven."

443 (2) **Mark 14:61–62** But he was silent and made no answer. Again the high priest asked him, "Are you the Christ, the Son of the Blessed?" And Jesus said, "I am; and you will see the Son of man seated at the right hand of Power, and coming with the clouds of heaven."

443 (3) **Matthew 11:27** All things have been delivered to me by my Father; and no one knows the Son except the Father, and no one knows the Father except the Son and any one to whom the Son chooses to reveal him.

443 (4) **Matthew 21:34–38** ". . . When the season of fruit drew near, he sent his servants to the tenants, to get his fruit; and the tenants took his servants and beat one, killed another, and stoned another. Again he sent other servants, more than the first; and they did the same to them. Afterward he sent his son to them, saying, 'They will respect my son.' But when the tenants saw the son, they said to themselves, 'This is the heir; come, let us kill him and have his inheritance.' . . ."

443 (5) **Matthew 24:36** "But of that day and hour no one knows, not even the angels of heaven, nor the Son, but the Father only. . . ."

443 (6) **Matthew 5:48** You, therefore, must be perfect, as your heavenly Father is perfect.

443 (7) **Matthew 6:8–9** ". . . Do not be like them, for your Father knows what you need before you ask him. Pray then like this:

Our Father who art in heaven,
Hallowed be thy name. . . ."

(8) **Matthew 7:21** "Not every one who says to me, 'Lord, Lord,' shall enter the kingdom of heaven, but he who does the will of my Father who is in heaven. . . ." 443

(9) **Luke 11:13** ". . . If you then, who are evil, know how to give good gifts to your children, how much more will the heavenly Father give the Holy Spirit to those who ask him!" 443

(10) **John 20:17** Jesus said to her, "Do not hold me, for I have not yet ascended to the Father; but go to my brethren and say to them, I am ascending to my Father and your Father, to my God and your God." 443

(1) **Matthew 3:17** . . . and lo, a voice from heaven, saying, "This is my beloved Son, with whom I am well pleased." 444

(2) **Matthew 17:5** He was still speaking, when lo, a bright cloud overshadowed them, and a voice from the cloud said, "This is my beloved Son, with whom I am well pleased; listen to him." 444

(3) **John 10:36** ". . . do you say of him whom the Father consecrated and sent into the world, 'You are blaspheming,' because I said, 'I am the Son of God'? . . ." 444

Acts 13:33 ". . . this he has fulfilled to us their children by raising Jesus; as also it is written in the second psalm, 445

'Thou art my Son,
today I have begotten thee.' . . ."

(1) **Exodus 3:14** God said to Moses, "I AM WHO I AM." 446

(2) **1 Corinthians 2:8** None of the rulers of this age understood this; for if they had, they would not have crucified the Lord of glory. 446

(1) **Matthew 22:41–46** Now while the Pharisees were gathered together, Jesus asked them a question, saying, "What do you think of the Christ? Whose son is he?" They said to him, "The son of David." He said to them, "How is it then that David, inspired by the Spirit, calls him Lord, saying, 447

'The Lord said to my Lord,
Sit at my right hand,
till I put thy enemies under thy feet'?

If David thus calls him Lord, how is he his son?" And no one was able to answer him a word, nor from that day did any one dare to ask him any more questions.

(2) **Acts 2:34–36** 447

". . . For David did not ascend into the heavens; but he himself says,

'The Lord said to my Lord, Sit at my right hand,
till I make thy enemies a stool for thy feet.'

Let all the house of Israel therefore know assuredly that God has made him both Lord and Christ, this Jesus whom you crucified."

(3) **Hebrews 1:13** But to what angel has he ever said, 447

"Sit at my right hand,
till I make thy enemies
a stool for thy feet"?

447 (4) **John 13:13** You call me Teacher and Lord; and you are right, for so I am.

448 (1) **Matthew 8:2** . . . and behold, a leper came to him and knelt before him, saying, "Lord, if you will, you can make me clean."

448 (2) **Matthew 14:30** . . . but when he saw the wind, he was afraid, and beginning to sink he cried out, "Lord, save me."

448 (3) **Matthew 15:22** And behold, a Canaanite woman from that region came out and cried, "Have mercy on me, O Lord, Son of David; my daughter is severely possessed by a demon."

448 (4) **Luke 1:43** And why is this granted me, that the mother of my Lord should come to me?

448 (5) **Luke 2:11** . . . for to you is born this day in the city of David a Savior, who is Christ the Lord.

449 (1) **Acts 2:34–36**
". . . For David did not ascend into the heavens; but he himself says,
'The Lord said to my Lord, Sit at my right hand,
till I make thy enemies a stool for thy feet.'
Let all the house of Israel therefore know assuredly that God has made him both Lord and Christ, this Jesus whom you crucified."

449 (2) **Romans 9:5** . . . to them belong the patriarchs, and of their race, according to the flesh, is the Christ. God who is over all be blessed for ever. Amen.

449 (3) **Titus 2:13** . . . awaiting our blessed hope, the appearing of the glory of our great God and Savior Jesus Christ. . . .

449 (4) **Revelation 5:13** And I heard every creature in heaven and on earth and under the earth and in the sea, and all therein, saying, "To him who sits upon the throne and to the Lamb be blessing and honor and glory and might for ever and ever!"

449 (5) **Philippians 2:6** . . . who, though he was in the form of God, did not count equality with God a thing to be grasped. . . .

449 (6) **Romans 10:9** . . . because, if you confess with your lips that Jesus is Lord and believe in your heart that God raised him from the dead, you will be saved.

449 (7) **1 Corinthians 12:3** Therefore I want you to understand that no one speaking by the Spirit of God ever says "Jesus be cursed!" and no one can say "Jesus is Lord" except by the Holy Spirit.

449 (8) **Philippians 2:9–11** Therefore God has highly exalted him and bestowed on him the name which is above every name, that at the name of Jesus every knee should bow, in heaven and on earth and under the earth, and every tongue confess that Jesus Christ is Lord, to the glory of God the Father.

450 (1) **Revelation 11:15** Then the seventh angel blew his trumpet, and there were loud voices in heaven, saying, "The kingdom of the world has become the kingdom of our Lord and of his Christ, and he shall reign for ever and ever."

(2) **Mark 12:17** Jesus said to them, "Render to Caesar the things that are Caesar's, and to God the things that are God's." And they were amazed at him. 450

(3) **Acts 5:29** But Peter and the apostles answered, "We must obey God rather than men. . . ." 450

(4) ***Gaudium et spes* 45, 2** The Word of God, through whom all things were made, was made flesh, so that as a perfect man he could save all men and sum up all things in himself. The Lord is the goal of human history, the focal point of the desires of history and civilization, the center of mankind, the joy of all hearts, and the fulfilment of all aspirations. It is he whom the Father raised from the dead, exalted and placed at his right hand, constituting him judge of the living and the dead. Animated and drawn together in his Spirit we press onwards on our journey towards the consummation of history which fully corresponds to the plan of his love: "to unite all things in him, things in heaven and things on earth" (Eph. 1:10). 450

(1) **John 1:14** And the Word became flesh and dwelt among us, full of grace and truth; we have beheld his glory, glory as of the only Son from the Father. 454

(2) **John 1:18** No one has ever seen God; the only Son, who is in the bosom of the Father, he has made him known. 454

(3) **John 3:16** For God so loved the world that he gave his only Son, that whoever believes in him should not perish but have eternal life. 454

(4) **John 3:18** He who believes in him is not condemned; he who does not believe is condemned already, because he has not believed in the name of the only Son of God. 454

(5) **John 1:1** In the beginning was the Word, and the Word was with God, and the Word was God. 454

(6) **Acts 8:37** And Philip said, "If you believe with all your heart, you may." And he replied, "I believe that Jesus Christ is the Son of God." 454

(7) **1 John 2:23** No one who denies the Son has the Father. He who confesses the Son has the Father also. 454

(1) **Deuteronomy 6:4–5** "Hear, O Israel: The Lord our God is one Lord; and you shall love the Lord your God with all your heart, and with all your soul, and with all your might. . . ." 459

(2) **Mark 8:34** And he called to him the multitude with his disciples, and said to them, "If any man would come after me, let him deny himself and take up his cross and follow me. . . ." 459

Liturgy of the Hours, Saturday, 461
Canticle at Evening Prayer (Philippians 2:6–11)

Though he was in the form of God,
Jesus did not deem equality with God
something to be grasped at.
Rather, he emptied himself

and took the form of a slave,
being born in the likeness of men.

He was known to be of human estate,
and it was thus that he humbled himself,
obediently accepting even death,
death on a cross!

Because of this,
God highly exalted him
and bestowed on him the name
above every other name,

So that at Jesus' name
every knee must bend
in the heavens, on the earth,
and under the earth,
and every tongue proclaim
to the glory of God the Father:
JESUS CHRIST IS LORD!

465 (1) **1 John 4:2–3** By this you know the Spirit of God: every spirit which confesses that Jesus Christ has come in the flesh is of God, and every spirit which does not confess Jesus is not of God. This is the spirit of antichrist, of which you heard that it was coming, and now it is in the world already.

465 (2) **2 John 7** For many deceivers have gone out into the world, men who will not acknowledge the coming of Jesus Christ in the flesh; such a one is the deceiver and the antichrist.

468 (1) **Council of Constantinople II (553): DS 424** If anyone says that the union of the Word of God with man was made according to grace, or according to operation, or according to dignity, or according to equality of honor, or according to authority or relation, or temperament, or power, or according to good will—as if man was pleasing to God the Word because it seemed well to Him regarding Himself, as [mad] Theodore declares; or according to homonymy, by which the Nestorians who call God the Word Jesus and Christ, and name the man separately Christ and the Son, and, though plainly speaking of two persons, pretend to speak of one person and one Christ according to name only, and honor, and dignity, and worship, but does not confess that the union of the Word of God to a body animated with a rational and intellectual soul, took place according to composition or according to subsistence, as the Holy Fathers have taught, and on this account one subsistence of Him, who is the Lord Jesus Christ, one of the Holy Trinity, let such a one be anathema.

468 (2) **Council of Ephesus (431): DS 255** If anyone portions out to two persons, that is to say subsistences, the words in the Gospels and the apostolic writings, whether said about Christ by the saints, or by Him concerning Himself, and attributes some as if to a man specially understood beside the Word of God, others as befitting God alone, to the Word of God the Father, let him be anathema.

469 **St. Leo the Great, *Sermo I in Nativitate Domini* 21, 2–3** Therefore the Word of God, Himself God, the Son of God who "in the beginning was with God," through whom "all things were made" and "without" whom "was nothing made," with the

purpose of delivering man from eternal death, became man: so bending Himself to take on Him our humility without decrease in His own majesty, that remaining what He was and assuming what He was not, He might unite the true form of a slave to that form in which He is equal to God the Father, and join both natures together by such a compact that the lower should not be swallowed up in its exaltation nor the higher impaired by its new associate. Without detriment therefore to the properties of either substance which then came together in one person, majesty took on humility, strength weakness, eternity mortality: and for the paying off of the debt belonging to our condition, inviolable nature was united with passible nature, and true God and true man were combined to form one Lord, so that, as suited the needs of our case, one and the same Mediator between God and men, the Man Christ Jesus, could both die with the one and rise again with the other.

Rightly therefore did the birth of our Salvation impart no corruption to the Virgin's purity, because the bearing of the Truth was the keeping of honor. Such then beloved was the nativity which became the Power of God and the Wisdom of God even Christ, whereby He might be one with us in manhood and surpass us in Godhead. For unless He were true God, He would not bring us a remedy. Unless He were true Man, He would not give us an example. Therefore the exulting angel's song when the Lord was born is this, "Glory to God in the Highest," and their message, "peace on earth to men of good will." For they see that the heavenly Jerusalem is being built up out of all the nations of the world: and over that indescribable work of the Divine love how ought the humbleness of men to rejoice, when the joy of the lofty angels is so great?

Let us then, dearly beloved, give thanks to God the Father, through His Son, in the Holy Spirit, Who "for His great mercy, wherewith He has loved us," has had pity on us: and "when we were dead in sins, has quickened us together in Christ," that we might be in Him a new creation and a new production. Let us put off then the old man with his deeds: and having obtained a share in the birth of Christ let us renounce the works of the flesh. Christian, acknowledge thy dignity, and becoming a partner in the Divine nature, refuse to return to the old baseness by degenerate conduct. Remember the Head and the Body of which thou art a member. Recollect that thou wert rescued from the power of darkness and brought out into God's light and kingdom. By the mystery of Baptism thou wert made the temple of the Holy Ghost: do not put such a denizen to flight from thee by base acts, and subject thyself once more to the devil's thraldom: because thy purchase money is the blood of Christ, because He shall judge thee in truth Who ransomed thee in mercy, who with the Father and the Holy Spirit reigns for ever and ever. Amen.

John 14:9–10 Jesus said to him, "Have I been with you so long, and yet you do not know me, Philip? He who has seen me has seen the Father; how can you say, 'Show us the Father'? Do you not believe that I am in the Father and the Father in me? The words that I say to you I do not speak on my own authority; but the Father who dwells in me does his works. . . ." 470

Letter of Pope St. Damasus I to the Eastern bishops, condemning Apollinarianism (c. 378): DS 149 Know therefore that we have recently condemned the godless Timothy, the ill-instructed disciple of the heretic Apollinaris, with his impious teaching, nor do we concede that his relics have any value for any reason. . . . For Christ, the Son of God, our Lord, won the fullest salvation for the human race by his own passion, to set the whole man free from the crimes of the guilty. If anyone should say he lacks anything in his humanity or in his divinity, he is full of the spirit of the devil and has shown himself to be a son of Gehenna. So why do you ask me 471 again to condemn Timothy who has already here by the judgment of the Apostolic See. . . been condemned with Apollinaris his teacher?

472 (1) **Mark 6:38** And he said to them, "How many loaves have you? Go and see." And when they had found out, they said, "Five, and two fish."

472 (2) **Mark 8:27** And Jesus went on with his disciples, to the villages of Caesarea Philippi; and on the way he asked his disciples, "Who do men say that I am?"

472 (3) **John 11:34** . . . and he said, "Where have you laid him?" They said to him, "Lord, come and see."

473 (1) **St. Gregory the Great, letter "*Sicut aqua frigida*" to Eulogius, Patriarch of Alexandria (August 600), 10, 39: DS 475** Thus also the Father alone is said to know, because the Son (being) consubstantial with Him, on account of His nature, by which He is above the angels, has knowledge of that, of which the angels are unaware. Thus, also, this can be the more precisely understood because the Only-begotten having been incarnate, and made perfect man for us, in His human nature indeed did know the day and the hour of judgment, but nevertheless He did not know this from His human nature. Therefore, that which in (nature) itself He knew, He did not know from that very (nature), because God-made-man knew the day and hour of the judgment through the power of His Godhead. . . . Thus, the knowledge which He did not have on account of the nature of His humanity—by reason of which, like the angels, He was a creature—this He denied that He, like the angels, who are creatures, had. Therefore (as) God and man He knows the day and the hour of judgment; but on this account, because God is man.

473 (2) **Mark 14:36** And he said, "Abba, Father, all things are possible to thee; remove this cup from me; yet not what I will, but what thou wilt."

473 (3) **Matthew 11:27** All things have been delivered to me by my Father; and no one knows the Son except the Father, and no one knows the Father except the Son and any one to whom the Son chooses to reveal him.

473 (4) **John 1:18** No one has ever seen God; the only Son, who is in the bosom of the Father, he has made him known.

473 (5) **John 8:55** But you have not known him; I know him. If I said, I do not know him, I should be a liar like you; but I do know him and I keep his word.

473 (6) **Mark 2:8** And immediately Jesus, perceiving in his spirit that they thus questioned within themselves, said to them, "Why do you question thus in your hearts? . . ."

473 (7) **John 2:25** . . . because he knew all men and needed no one to bear witness of man; for he himself knew what was in man.

473 (8) **John 6:61** But Jesus, knowing in himself that his disciples murmured at it, said to them, "Do you take offense at this? . . ."

474 (1) **Mark 8:31** And he began to teach them that the Son of man must suffer many things, and be rejected by the elders and the chief priests and the scribes, and be killed, and after three days rise again.

(2) **Mark 9:31** . . . for he was teaching his disciples, saying to them, "The Son of man will be delivered into the hands of men, and they will kill him; and when he is killed, after three days he will rise." **474**

(3) **Mark 10:33–34** . . . saying, "Behold, we are going up to Jerusalem; and the Son of man will be delivered to the chief priests and the scribes, and they will condemn him to death, and deliver him to the Gentiles; and they will mock him, and spit upon him, and scourge him, and kill him; and after three days he will rise." **474**

(4) **Mark 14:18–20** And as they were at table eating, Jesus said, "Truly, I say to you, one of you will betray me, one who is eating with me." They began to be sorrowful, and to say to him one after another, "Is it I?" He said to them, "It is one of the twelve, one who is dipping bread into the dish with me. . . ." **474**

(5) **Mark 14:26–30** And when they had sung a hymn, they went out to the Mount of Olives. And Jesus said to them, "You will all fall away; for it is written, 'I will strike the shepherd, and the sheep will be scattered.' But after I am raised up, I will go before you to Galilee." Peter said to him, "Even though they all fall away, I will not." And Jesus said to him, "Truly, I say to you, this very night, before the cock crows twice, you will deny me three times." **474**

(6) **Mark 13:32** "But of that day or that hour no one knows, not even the angels in heaven, nor the Son, but only the Father. . . ." **474**

(7) **Acts 1:7** He said to them, "It is not for you to know times or seasons which the Father has fixed by his own authority. . . ." **474**

Council of Constantinople III: DS 556–59 And so we proclaim two natural wills in Him, and two natural operations indivisibly, inconvertibly, inseparably, unfusedly according to the doctrine of the holy Father, and two natural wills not contrary, God forbid, according as impious heretics have asserted, but the human will following and not resisting or hesitating, but rather even submitting to His divine and omnipotent will. For, it is necessary that the will of the flesh act, but that it be subject to the divine will according to the most wise Athanasius. For, as His flesh is called and is the flesh of the Word of God, so also the natural will of His flesh is called and is the proper will of the Word of God as He Himself says: "Because I came down from heaven, not to do my own will but the will of my Father who sent me" [cf. John 6:38], calling the will of the flesh His own. For the body became His own. For as His most holy and immaculate animated flesh deified has not been destroyed but in its own status and plan remained, so also His human will deified has not been destroyed, but on the contrary it has been saved according to the theologian Gregory who says: "For to wish of that one an entire deification, which is understood in the Savior, is not contrary to God." **475**

But we glorify two natural operations indivisibly, inconvertibly, unfusedly, inseparably in our Lord Jesus Christ Himself, our true God, that is, the divine operation and the human operation, according to Leo the divine preacher who very clearly asserts: "For each form does what is proper to itself with the mutual participation of the other, that is, the Word doing what is of the Word and the flesh accomplishing what is of the flesh". For at no time shall we grant one natural operation to God and to the creature, so that neither what was created, we raise into divine essence, nor what is especially of divine nature, we cast down to a place begetting creatures. For of one and the same we recognize the miracles and the sufferings according to the one and the other of these natures from which He is and in which He has to be as the admirable Cyril says. Therefore we, maintaining completely an unconfused and undivided (opinion), in a brief statement set forth all: that we, believing that He is one of the Holy Trinity, our Lord Jesus Christ our true God, and after the incarnation assert that His two natures radiate in His one substance, in which His miracles and His sufferings through all His ordained life, not through phantasy but truly He has shown, on account of the natural difference which is recognized in the same single substance, while with the mutual participation of the other, each nature indivisibly and without confusion willed and performed its own works; according to this plan we confess two natural wills and operations concurring mutually in Him for the salvation of the human race.

These things, therefore, having been determined by us with all caution and diligence, we declare that no one is permitted to introduce, or to describe, or to compare, or to study, or otherwise to teach another faith. But whoever presumes to compare or to introduce or to teach or to pass on another creed to those wishing to turn from the belief of the Gentiles or of the Jews or from any heresy whatsoever to the acknowledgement of truth, or who (presumes) to introduce a novel doctrine or an invention of discourse to the subversion of those things which now have been determined by us, (we declare) these, whether they are bishops or clerics, to be excommunicated, bishops indeed from the bishopric, but priests from the priesthood; but if they are monks or laymen, to be anathematized.

476 (1) **Lateran Council (649): DS 504** If anyone does not properly and truly confess according to the holy Fathers, two nativities of our one Lord and God Jesus Christ, as before the ages from God and the Father incorporally and eternally, and as from the holy ever Virgin, Mother of God Mary, corporally in the earliest of the ages, and also one and the same Lord of us and God, Jesus Christ, consubstantial with man and His Mother according to the human nature, and the same one passible in the flesh, and impassible in the Godhead, circumscribed in the body, uncircumscribed in Godhead, the same one uncreated and created, terrestrial and celestial, visible and intelligible, comprehensible and incomprehensible, that all mankind which fell under sin, might be restored through the same complete man and God, let him be condemned.

476 (2) **Galatians 3:1** O foolish Galatians! Who has bewitched you, before whose eyes Jesus Christ was publicly portrayed as crucified?

476 (3) **Council of Nicea II (787): DS 600–603**

Definition of the Sacred Images and Tradition

(I. Definition) . . . We, continuing in the regal path, and following the divinely inspired teaching of our Holy Fathers, and the tradition of the Catholic Church, for we know that this is of the Holy Spirit who certainly dwells in it, define in all certitude and diligence that as the figure of the honored and life-giving Cross, so the venerable and holy images, the ones from tinted materials and from marble as those from other material, must be suitably placed in the holy churches of God, both on sacred vessels and vestments, and on the walls and on the altars, at home and on the streets, namely such images of our Lord Jesus Christ, God and Savior, and of our undefiled lady, or holy Mother of God, and of the honorable angels, and, at the same time, of all the saints and of holy men. For, how much more frequently through the imaginal formation they are seen, so much more quickly are those who contemplate these, raised to the memory and desire of the originals of these, to kiss and to render honorable adoration to them, not however, to grant true *latria* according to our faith, which is proper to divine nature alone; but just as to the figure of the revered and life-giving Cross and to the holy gospels, and to the other sacred monuments, let an oblation of incense and lights be made to give honor to these as was the pious custom with the ancients. "For the honor of the image passes to the original"; and he who shows reverence to the image, shows reverence to the substance of Him depicted in it.

(II. Proof) For thus the doctrine of our Holy Fathers, that is, the tradition of the Catholic Church which has received the Gospel from and even to the end of the world is strengthened. Thus we follow Paul, who spoke in Christ [II Cor. 2:17], and all the divine apostolic group and the paternal sanctity *keeping the traditions* [II Thess. 2:14] which we have received. Thus prophetically we sing the triumphal hymns for the Church: *Rejoice exceedingly, O daughter of Sion, sing forth, O daughter of Jerusalem: be joyful and be happy with all your heart. The Lord has taken from you the injustices of those adverse to you: He has redeemed you from the power of your enemies. The Lord is king in your midst: You will not see more evils* [Wisd. 3:14 f.: LXX] *and peace to you unto time eternal.*

(III. Declaration) Those, therefore, who dare to think or to teach otherwise or to spurn according to wretched heretics the ecclesiastical traditions and to invent anything novel, or to reject anything from these things which have been consecrated by the Church: either the Gospel or the figure of the Cross, or the imaginal picture, or the sacred relics of the martyr; or to invent perversely and cunningly for the overthrow of anyone of the legitimate traditions of the Catholic Church; or even, as it were, to use the sacred vessels or the venerable monasteries as common things; if indeed they are bishops or clerics, we order (them) to be deposed; monks, however, or laymen, to be excommunicated.

(1) **John 19:34** But one of the soldiers pierced his side with a spear, and at once there came out blood and water. **478**

(2) **Pius XII, encyclical *Mystici Corporis* (1943): DS 3812** But such a most loving knowledge as the divine Redeemer from the first moment of His Incarnation bestowed upon us, surpasses any zealous power of the human mind; since through that beatific vision, which He began to enjoy when He had hardly been conceived in the womb of the Mother of God, He has the members of His mystical body always and constantly present to Him, and He embraces all with His redeeming love. **478**

John 16:14–15 He will glorify me, for he will take what is mine and declare it to you. All that the Father has is mine; therefore I said that he will take what is mine and declare it to you. **485**

(1) **Matthew 1:20** But as he considered this, behold, an angel of the Lord appeared to him in a dream, saying, "Joseph, son of David, do not fear to take Mary your wife, for that which is conceived in her is of the Holy Spirit. . . ." **486**

(2) **Matthew 2:1–12** Now when Jesus was born in Bethlehem of Judea in the days of Herod the king, behold, wise men from the East came to Jerusalem, saying, "Where is he who has been born king of the Jews? For we have seen his star in the East, and have come to worship him." When Herod the king heard this, he was troubled, and all Jerusalem with him; and assembling all the chief priests and scribes of the people, he inquired of them where the Christ was to be born. They told him, "In Bethlehem of Judea; for so it is written by the prophet: **486**

'And you, O Bethlehem, in the land of Judah,
are by no means least among the rulers of Judah;

for from you shall come a ruler
who will govern my people Israel.' "

Then Herod summoned the wise men secretly and ascertained from them what time the star appeared; and he sent them to Bethlehem, saying, "Go and search diligently for the child, and when you have found him bring me word, that I too may come and worship him." When they had heard the king they went their way; and lo, the star which they had seen in the East went before them, till it came to rest over the place where the child was. When they saw the star, they rejoiced exceedingly with great joy; and going into the house they saw the child with Mary his mother, and they fell down and worshiped him. Then, opening their treasures, they offered him gifts, gold and frankincense and myrrh. And being warned in a dream not to return to Herod, they departed to their own country by another way.

486 (3) **Luke 1:35** And the angel said to her,
"The Holy Spirit will come upon you,
and the power of the Most High will overshadow you;
therefore the child to be born will be called holy,
the Son of God. . . ."

486 (4) **Luke 2:8–20** And in that region there were shepherds out in the field, keeping watch over their flock by night. And an angel of the Lord appeared to them, and the glory of the Lord shone around them, and they were filled with fear. And the angel said to them, "Be not afraid; for behold, I bring you good news of a great joy which will come to all the people; for to you is born this day in the city of David a Savior, who is Christ the Lord. And this will be a sign for you: you will find a babe wrapped in swaddling cloths and lying in a manger." And suddenly there was with the angel a multitude of the heavenly host praising God and saying,
"Glory to God in the highest,
and on earth peace among men with whom he is pleased!"

When the angels went away from them into heaven, the shepherds said to one another, "Let us go over to Bethlehem and see this thing that has happened, which the Lord has made known to us." And they went with haste, and found Mary and Joseph, and the babe lying in a manger. And when they saw it they made known the saying which had been told them concerning this child; and all who heard it wondered at what the shepherds told them. But Mary kept all these things, pondering them in her heart. And the shepherds returned, glorifying and praising God for all they had heard and seen, as it had been told them.

486 (5) **John 1:31–34** ". . . I myself did not know him; but for this I came baptizing with water, that he might be revealed to Israel." And John bore witness, "I saw the Spirit descend as a dove from heaven, and it remained on him. I myself did not know him; but he who sent me to baptize with water said to me, 'He on whom you see the Spirit descend and remain, this is he who baptizes with the Holy Spirit.' And I have seen and have borne witness that this is the Son of God."

486 (6) **John 2:11** This, the first of his signs, Jesus did at Cana in Galilee, and manifested his glory; and his disciples believed in him.

488 ***Lumen gentium* 61** The predestination of the Blessed Virgin as Mother of God was associated with the incarnation of the divine word: in the designs of divine Providence she was the gracious mother of the divine Redeemer here on earth, and above all others and in a singular way the generous associate and humble handmaid of the

Lord. She conceived, brought forth, and nourished Christ, she presented him to the Father in the temple, shared her Son's sufferings as he died on the cross. Thus, in a wholly singular way she cooperated by her obedience, faith, hope and burning charity in the work of the Savior in restoring supernatural life to souls. For this reason she is a mother to us in the order of grace.

(1) **Genesis 3:15** 489

"... I will put enmity between you and the woman,
and between your seed and her seed;
he shall bruise your head,
and you shall bruise his heel."

(2) **Genesis 3:20** The man called his wife's name Eve, because she was the mother of all living. 489

(3) **Genesis 18:10–14** The Lord said, "I will surely return to you in the spring, and Sarah your wife shall have a son." And Sarah was listening at the tent door behind him. Now Abraham and Sarah were old, advanced in age; it had ceased to be with Sarah after the manner of women. So Sarah laughed to herself, saying, "After I have grown old, and my husband is old, shall I have pleasure?" The Lord said to Abraham, "Why did Sarah laugh, and say, 'Shall I indeed bear a child, now that I am old?' Is anything too hard for the Lord? At the appointed time I will return to you, in the spring, and Sarah shall have a son." 489

(4) **Genesis 21:1–2** The Lord visited Sarah as he had said, and the Lord did to Sarah as he had promised. And Sarah conceived, and bore Abraham a son in his old age at the time of which God had spoken to him. 489

(5) **1 Corinthians 1:27** ... but God chose what is foolish in the world to shame the wise, God chose what is weak in the world to shame the strong. ... 489

(6) **1 Samuel 1** There was a certain man of Ramathaimzophim of the hill country of Ephraim, whose name was Elkanah the son of Jeroham, son of Elihu, son of Tohu, son of Zuph, an Ephraimite. He had two wives; the name of the one was Hannah, and the name of the other Peninnah. And Peninnah had children, but Hannah had no children. 489

Now this man used to go up year by year from his city to worship and to sacrifice to the Lord of hosts at Shiloh, where the two sons of Eli, Hophni and Phinehas, were priests of the Lord. On the day when Elkanah sacrificed, he would give portions to Peninnah his wife and to all her sons and daughters; and, although he loved Hannah, he would give Hannah only one portion, because the Lord had closed her womb. And her rival used to provoke her sorely, to irritate her, because the Lord had closed her womb. So it went on year by year; as often as she went up to the house of the Lord, she used to provoke her. Therefore Hannah wept and would not eat. And Elkanah, her husband, said to her, "Hannah, why do you weep? And why do you not eat? And why is your heart sad? Am I not more to you than ten sons?"

After they had eaten and drunk in Shiloh, Hannah rose. Now Eli the priest was sitting on the seat beside the doorpost of the temple of the Lord. She was deeply distressed and prayed to the Lord, and wept bitterly. And she vowed a vow and said, "O Lord of hosts, if thou wilt indeed look on the affliction of thy maidservant, and remember me, and not forget thy maidservant, but wilt give to thy maidservant a son, then I will give him to the Lord all the days of his life, and no razor shall touch his head."

As she continued praying before the Lord, Eli observed her mouth. Hannah was speaking in her heart; only her lips moved, and her voice was not heard; therefore Eli took her to be a drunken woman. And Eli said to her, "How long will you be drunken? Put away your wine from you." But Hannah answered, "No, my lord, I am a woman sorely troubled; I have drunk neither wine nor strong drink, but I have been pouring out my soul before the Lord. Do not regard your maidservant as a base woman, for all along I have been speaking out of my great anxiety and vexation." Then Eli answered, "Go in peace, and the God of Israel grant your petition which you have made to him." And she said, "Let your maidservant find favor in your eyes." Then the woman went her way and ate, and her countenance was no longer sad.

They rose early in the morning and worshiped before the Lord; then they went back to their house at Ramah. And Elkanah knew Hannah his wife, and the Lord remembered her; and in due time Hannah conceived and bore a son, and she called his name Samuel, for she said, "I have asked him of the Lord."

And the man Elkanah and all his house went up to offer to the Lord the yearly sacrifice, and to pay his vow. But Hannah did not go up, for she said to her husband, "As soon as the child is weaned, I will bring him, that he may appear in the presence of the Lord, and abide there for ever." Elkanah her husband said to her, "Do what seems best to you, wait until you have weaned him; only, may the Lord establish his word." So the woman remained and nursed her son, until she weaned him. And when she had weaned him, she took him up with her, along with a three-year-old bull, an ephah of flour, and a skin of wine; and she brought him to the house of the Lord at Shiloh; and the child was young. Then they slew the bull, and they brought the child to Eli. And she said, "Oh, my lord! As you live, my lord, I am the woman who was standing here in your presence, praying to the Lord. For this child I prayed; and the Lord has granted me my petition which I made to him. Therefore I have lent him to the Lord; as long as he lives, he is lent to the Lord."

And they worshiped the Lord there.

492 **Ephesians 1:3–4** Blessed be the God and Father of our Lord Jesus Christ, who has blessed us in Christ with every spiritual blessing in the heavenly places, even as he chose us in him before the foundation of the world, that we should be holy and blameless before him.

494 (1) **Luke 1:28–38** And he came to her and said, "Hail, O favored one, the Lord is with you!" But she was greatly troubled at the saying, and considered in her mind what sort of greeting this might be. And the angel said to her, "Do not be afraid, Mary, for you have found favor with God. And behold, you will conceive in your womb and bear a son, and you shall call his name Jesus.

He will be great, and will be called the Son of the Most High;
and the Lord God will give to him the throne of his father David,
and he will reign over the house of Jacob for ever;
and of his kingdom there will be no end."

And Mary said to the angel, "How shall this be, since I have no husband?" And the angel said to her,

"The Holy Spirit will come upon you,
and the power of the Most High will overshadow you;
therefore the child to be born will be called holy,
the Son of God.

And behold, your kinswoman Elizabeth in her old age has also conceived a son; and this is the sixth month with her who was called barren. For with God nothing will be impossible." And Mary said, "Behold, I am the handmaid of the Lord; let it be to me according to your word." And the angel departed from her.

(2) **Romans 1:5** . . . through whom we have received grace and apostleship to bring about the obedience of faith for the sake of his name among all the nations. . . . **494**

(3) ***Lumen gentium* 56** The Father of mercies willed that the Incarnation should be preceded by assent on the part of the predestined mother, so that just as a woman had a share in bringing about death, so also a woman should contribute to life. This is pre-eminently true of the Mother of Jesus, who gave to the world the Life that renews all things, and who was enriched by God with gifts appropriate to such a role. It is no wonder then that it was customary for the Fathers to refer to the Mother of God as all holy and free from every stain of sin, as though fashioned by the Holy Spirit and formed as a new creature. Enriched from the first instant of her conception with the splendor of an entirely unique holiness, the virgin of Nazareth is hailed by the heralding angel, by divine command, as "full of grace" (cf. Lk. 1:28), and to the heavenly messenger she replies: "Behold the handmaid of the Lord, be it done unto me according to thy word" (Lk. 1:38). Thus the daughter of Adam, Mary, consenting to the word of God, became the Mother of Jesus. Committing herself whole-heartedly and impeded by no sin to God's saving will, she devoted herself totally, as a handmaid of the Lord, to the person and work of her Son, under and with him, serving the mystery of redemption, by the grace of Almighty God. Rightly, therefore, the Fathers see Mary not merely as passively engaged by God, but as freely cooperating in the work of man's salvation through faith and obedience. For, as St. Irenaeus says, she "being obedient, became the cause of salvation for herself and for the whole human race." Hence not a few of the early Fathers gladly assert with him in their preaching: "the knot of Eve's disobedience was untied by Mary's obedience: what the virgin Eve bound through her disbelief, Mary loosened by her faith." Comparing Mary with Eve, they call her "Mother of the living," and frequently claim: "death through Eve, life through Mary." **494**

(1) **Matthew 13:55** Is not this the carpenter's son? Is not his mother called Mary? And are not his brothers James and Joseph and Simon and Judas? **495**

(2) **Council of Ephesus (431): DS 251** For in the first place no common man was born of the holy Virgin; then the Word thus descended upon him; but being united from the womb itself he is said to have endured a generation in the flesh in order to appropriate the producing of His own body. Thus [the holy Fathers] did not hesitate to speak of the holy Virgin as the Mother of God. **495**

(1) **DS 10–64:** see 192 (1), beginning with DS 11. [Editor's note: DS 10–64 contains texts of the Creed from a variety of ancient sources. In most cases there is no or only very minor variation. Only a selection is reproduced here.] **496**

(2) **Romans 1:3** . . . the gospel concerning his Son, who was descended from David according to the flesh. . . . **496**

(3) **John 1:13** . . . who were born, not of blood nor of the will of the flesh nor of the will of man, but of God. **496**

497 (1) **Matthew 1:18–25** Now the birth of Jesus Christ took place in this way. When his mother Mary had been betrothed to Joseph, before they came together she was found to be with child of the Holy Spirit; and her husband Joseph, being a just man and unwilling to put her to shame, resolved to divorce her quietly. But as he considered this, behold, an angel of the Lord appeared to him in a dream, saying, "Joseph, son of David, do not fear to take Mary your wife, for that which is conceived in her is of the Holy Spirit; she will bear a son, and you shall call his name Jesus, for he will save his people from their sins." All this took place to fulfil what the Lord had spoken by the prophet:

"Behold, a virgin shall conceive and bear a son,
and his name shall be called Emmanuel"

(which means, God with us). When Joseph woke from sleep, he did as the angel of the Lord commanded him; he took his wife, but knew her not until she had borne a son; and he called his name Jesus.

497 (2) **Luke 1:26–38** In the sixth month the angel Gabriel was sent from God to a city of Galilee named Nazareth, to a virgin betrothed to a man whose name was Joseph, of the house of David; and the virgin's name was Mary. And he came to her and said, "Hail, O favored one, the Lord is with you!" But she was greatly troubled at the saying, and considered in her mind what sort of greeting this might be. And the angel said to her, "Do not be afraid, Mary, for you have found favor with God. And behold, you will conceive in your womb and bear a son, and you shall call his name Jesus.

He will be great, and will be called the Son of the Most High;
and the Lord God will give to him the throne of his father David,
and he will reign over the house of Jacob for ever;
and of his kingdom there will be no end."

And Mary said to the angel, "How shall this be, since I have no husband?" And the angel said to her,

"The Holy Spirit will come upon you,
and the power of the Most High will overshadow you;
therefore the child to be born will be called holy,
the Son of God.

And behold, your kinswoman Elizabeth in her old age has also conceived a son; and this is the sixth month with her who was called barren. For with God nothing will be impossible." And Mary said, "Behold, I am the handmaid of the Lord; let it be to me according to your word." And the angel departed from her.

498 (1) **St. Justin, *Dialogus cum Tryphone Judaeo* 99** Then I continued, 'I will now show you that the whole Psalm referred to Christ, by repeating and expounding it. The opening words of the Psalm, "O God, my God, look upon me, why hast Thou forsaken me," foretold in old times what would be said in Christ's time. For, while hanging on the cross, He exclaimed, "My God, My God, why hast Thou forsaken Me"? And the words, "Far from my salvation are the words of my sins. O my God, I shall cry by day, and Thou wilt not hear, and by night, and it is not for want of understanding in me," depicted the very things that He was about to do. For, on the day of His crucifixion He took three of His disciples to the Mount of Olives, opposite the Temple in Jerusalem, and prayed thus: "Father, if it be possible, let this cup pass away from Me;' but He ended His prayer by saying, 'Not My will, but Thine be done," thus making it clear that He had really become a man capable of suffering. To offset the calumny that He did not know then that He was to suffer, He immediately adds in the Psalm, "And it is not want of understanding in Me." Just as it was not

from lack of understanding that God asked Adam where he was, and Cain where Abel was, but to convince each what sort of man he was, and to provide us with knowledge of all things through the Holy Writ; so Christ signified that there was no lack of understanding on His part, but on the part of those who, refusing to believe that He was the Christ, thought that they put Him to death and that He would remain in Hades as any ordinary person.

(2) **Origen, *Contra Celsum* I, 32** Let us return, however, to the words put into the mouth of the Jew, where the *mother of Jesus* is described as having been *turned out by the carpenter who was betrothed to her, as she had been convicted of adultery and had a child by a certain soldier named Panthera.* Let us consider whether those who fabricated the myth that the virgin and Panthera committed adultery and that the carpenter turned her out, were not blind when they concocted all this to get rid of the miraculous conception by the Holy Spirit. For on account of its highly miraculous character they could have falsified the story in other ways without, as it were, unintentionally admitting that Jesus was not born of an ordinary marriage. It was inevitable that those who did not accept the miraculous birth of Jesus would have invented some lie. But the fact that they did not do this convincingly, but kept as part of the story that the virgin did not conceive Jesus by Joseph, makes the lie obvious to people who can see through fictitious stories and show them up. Is it reasonable that a man who ventured to do such great things for mankind in order that, so far as in him lay, all Greeks and barbarians in expectation of the divine judgment might turn from evil and act in every respect acceptably to the Creator of the universe, should have had, not a miraculous birth, but a birth more illegitimate and disgraceful than any? As addressing Greeks and Celsus in particular who, whether he holds Plato's doctrines or not, nevertheless quotes them, I would ask this question. Would He who sends souls down into human bodies compel a man to undergo a birth more shameful than any, and not even have brought him into human life by legitimate marriage, when he was to do such great deeds and to teach so many people and to convert many from the flood of evil? Or is it more reasonable (and I say this now following Pythagoras, Plato and Empedocles, whom Celsus often mentions) that there are certain secret principles by which each soul that enters a body does so in accordance with its merits and former character? It is therefore probable that this soul, which lived a more useful life on earth than many men (to avoid appearing to beg the question by saying 'all' men), needed a body which was not only distinguished among human bodies, but was also superior to all others. 498

(3) **Origen, *Contra Celsum* I, 69** After this he muddles Christianity with the view of some sect as though Christians shared their opinions and applies his objections to all people converted by the divine word, saying *a god would not have had a body such as yours.* But we say to this that at his advent into this life, as he was born of a woman, he assumed a body which was human and capable of dying a human death. For this reason, in addition to other things, we say that he was also a great wrestler, because his human body was tempted in all points like all other men, and yet was no longer like sinful men in that it was entirely without sin. For it appears clear to us that 'he did no sin neither was guile found in his mouth', and God delivered him up, who knew no sin, as a pure offering for all those who had sinned. Celsus then says: *The body of a god would not have been born as you, Jesus, were born.* Yet he perceived that if he had been born as the Bible says, his body could somehow have been more divine than that of the multitude and in some sense the body of God. Moreover, he disbelieves the stories recorded about his conception by the Holy Spirit, and believes that his father was a certain Panthera who corrupted the virgin. That is why he said that *the* 498

body of a god would not have been born as you were born. But on these matters we have spoken at length in the earlier part of the book.

498 (4) **1 Corinthians 2:8** None of the rulers of this age understood this; for if they had, they would not have crucified the Lord of glory.

499 (1) **St. Leo the Great, Letter "*Lectis dilectionis tuae*" to Flavian (13 June 449): DS 291** Likewise the only-begotten and eternal [Son] of the eternal Father "was born of the Holy Spirit and the Virgin Mary". This temporal birth in no way diminishes or adds to the eternal birth, but is entirely expended in restoring man who had been deceived so that he might conquer death and destroy by his own strength the devil who had dominion over death. For we cannot conquer the author of sin and death unless [the Son] takes up our nature and makes it his own, he whom neither sin can defile nor death restrain.

Indeed he was conceived by the Holy Spirit within the womb of the virgin mother, who bore him without losing her virginity just as she conceived without losing her virginity. . . .

499 (2) **St. Leo the Great, Letter "*Lectis dilectionis tuae*" to Flavian (13 June 449): DS 294** Consequently, the Son of God entered into these lowly conditions of the world, after descending from His celestial throne, and though He did not withdraw from the glory of the Father, He was generated in a new order and in a new nativity. In a new order, because invisible in His own, He was made visible in ours; incomprehensible [in His own], He wished to be comprehended; permanent before times, He began to be in time; the Lord of the universe assumed the form of a slave, concealing the immensity of His majesty; the impassible God did not disdain to be a passible man and the immortal [did not disdain] to be subject to the laws of death. Moreover, He was generated in a new nativity, because inviolate virginity [that] did not know concupiscence furnished the material of His body. From the mother of the Lord, nature, not guilt, was assumed; and in the Lord Jesus Christ born from the womb of the Virgin, because His birth was miraculous, nature was not for that reason different from ours. For He who is true God, is likewise true man, and there is no falsehood in this unity, as long as there are alternately the lowliness of man and the exaltedness of the Divinity. For, just as God is not changed by His compassion, so man is not destroyed by His dignity. For each nature does what is proper to it with the mutual participation of the other; the Word clearly effecting what belongs to the Word, and the flesh performing what belongs to the flesh. One of these gleams with miracles; the other sinks under injuries. And just as the Word does not withdraw from the equality of the paternal glory, so His body does not abandon the nature of our race.

499 (3) **Council of Constantinople II (553): DS 427** If anyone says that the holy glorious ever-virgin Mary is falsely but not truly the Mother of God; or (is the Mother of God) according to relation, as if a mere man were born, but as if the Word of God became incarnate [and of her] from her, but the birth of the man according to them being referred to the Word of God as being with the man when he was born, and falsely accuses the holy synod of Chalcedon of proclaiming the Virgin Mother of God according to this impious conception which was invented by Theodore; or, if anyone calls her the mother of the man or the mother of the Christ, as if the Christ were not God, but does not confess that she is exactly and truly the Mother of God, because God the Word, born of the Father before the ages, was made flesh from her in the last days, and that thus the holy Synod of Chalcedon confessed her (to be), let such a one be anathema.

(4) **Pope Pelagius I, Letter to King Childebert I (3 February 557): DS 442** 499
Of this holy and blessed and consubstantial Trinity I believe and I confess that one person, that is, the Son of God in these last days descended from heaven, without leaving the Fatherly seat nor the government of the world, and that the Holy Spirit came upon the Virgin Mary and the power of the Most High overshadowed her, that this Word and Son of God mercifully entered the womb of the same holy Virgin Mary and from her flesh united to herself flesh animated by a rational and intellectual soul; nor that the Son of God first created flesh and afterwards came into it, but, as it is written, "wisdom built herself a house" so that as soon as there was flesh in the womb of the Virgin, it was the flesh of the Word of God, whence, without any permutation or change of the Word or of nature's flesh, the Word and Son of God was made man, one in both natures, that is, the divine and human natures, and that Christ Jesus true God and the same true man proceeded, that is, was born, while his mother's virginity remained intact: for the Virgin remained such in bearing him just as she had in conceiving him. On account of this we confess that the same blessed virgin Mary is truly Mother of God: for she bore the incarnate Word of God. Therefore one and the same Jesus Christ is the true Son of God and also true son of man, perfect in divinity and likewise perfect in humanity, so that he exists totally in what is his and totally in what is ours; and by a second birth he took up from man, his mother, what he was not, in such a way that he did not cease being what by the first birth, from the Father, he was. For this reason we believe him to be from two natures and in two natures which remain undivided and unconfused: undivided certainly because even after the assumption of our nature the one Christ remained and remains Son of God: unconfused, however, because we believe the natures to be so united in one person and subsistence that each retains its properties and neither is converted into the other. And therefore, as we have often said, we confess one and the same Christ to be true Son of God, and the same to be true son of man, consubstantial with the Father according to divinity and consubstantial with us according to humanity, like us in all things except sin; able to suffer in the flesh, the very same unable to suffer in divinity. We confess that he freely suffered in the flesh under Pontius Pilate for our salvation, died in the flesh, rose the third day, in the same flesh glorified and incorruptible, and . . . ascended into heaven and sits at the right hand of the Father.

(5) **Lateran Council (649): DS 503** If anyone does not properly and truly confess 499
in accord with the holy Fathers, that the holy Mother of God and ever Virgin and immaculate Mary in the earliest of the ages conceived of the Holy Spirit without seed, namely, God the Word Himself specifically and truly, who was born of God the Father before all ages, and that she incorruptibly bore [Him?], her virginity remaining indestructible even after His birth, let him be condemned.

(6) **Creed of the Council of Toledo XVI (693): DS 571** Hence, although the 499
works of the Trinity are inseparable, still we faithfully profess . . . that it was not the whole Trinity that took up flesh, but only the Son of God, who is begotten before all ages from the substance of God the Father, was born of the Virgin Mary at the end of the ages as the Gospel testifies when it says "the Word was made flesh and dwelt among us". . . . The angel's greeting when he says that the Holy Spirit will come upon her and proclaims that the power of the Most High, which is the Son of God the Father, will overshadow her, shows that the entire Trinity cooperates in the flesh of that same Son. And as the Virgin acquired the modesty of virginity before conception, so also she experienced no loss of her integrity; for she conceived a virgin, gave birth a virgin, and after birth retained the uninterrupted modesty of an intact virgin. . . .

499 (7) **Council of Trent (1555): DS 1880** Since the depravity and iniquity of certain men have reached such a point in our time that, of those who wander and deviate from the Catholic faith, very many indeed not only presume to profess different heresies but also to deny the foundations of the faith itself, and by their example lead many away to the destruction of their souls, we, in accord with our pastoral office and charity, desiring, in so far as we are able with God, to call such men away from so grave and destructive an error, and with paternal severity to warn the rest, lest they fall into such impiety, all and each who have hitherto asserted, claimed or believed that Almighty God was not three in persons and of an entirely uncomposed and undivided unity of substance and one single simple essence of divinity; or that our Lord is not true God of the same substance in every way with the Father and the Holy Spirit, or that He was not conceived of the Holy Spirit according to the flesh in the womb of the most blessed and ever Virgin Mary, but from the seed of Joseph just as the rest of men; or that the same Lord and our God, Jesus Christ, did not submit to the most cruel death of the Cross to redeem us from sins and from eternal death, and to reunite us with the Father unto eternal life; or that the same most blessed Virgin Mary was not the true mother of God, and did not always persist in the integrity of virginity, namely, before bringing forth, at bringing forth, and always after bringing forth, on the part of the omnipotent God the Father, and the Son, and the Holy Spirit, with apostolic authority we demand and advise, etc.

499 (8) ***Lumen gentium* 52** Wishing in his supreme goodness and wisdom to effect the redemption of the world, "when the fullness of time came, God sent his Son, born of a woman . . . that we might receive the adoption of sons" (Gal. 4:4). "He for us men, and for our salvation, came down from heaven, and was incarnated by the Holy Spirit from the Virgin Mary." This divine mystery of salvation is revealed to us and continued in the Church, which the Lord established as his body. Joined to Christ the head and in communion with all his saints, the faithful must in the first place reverence the memory "of the glorious ever Virgin Mary, Mother of God and of our Lord Jesus Christ."

500 (1) **Mark 3:31–35** And his mother and his brothers came; and standing outside they sent to him and called him. And a crowd was sitting about him; and they said to him, "Your mother and your brothers are outside, asking for you." And he replied, "Who are my mother and my brothers?" And looking around on those who sat about him, he said, "Here are my mother and my brothers! Whoever does the will of God is my brother, and sister, and mother."

500 (2) **Mark 6:3** ". . . Is not this the carpenter, the son of Mary and brother of James and Joses and Judas and Simon, and are not his sisters here with us?" And they took offense at him.

500 (3) **1 Corinthians 9:5** Do we not have the right to be accompanied by a wife, as the other apostles and the brothers of the Lord and Cephas?

500 (4) **Galatians 1:19** But I saw none of the other apostles except James the Lord's brother.

500 (5) **Matthew 27:56** . . . among whom were Mary Magdalene, and Mary the mother of James and Joseph, and the mother of the sons of Zebedee.

500 (6) **Genesis 13:8** Then Abram said to Lot, "Let there be no strife between you and me, and between your herdsmen and my herdsmen; for we are kinsmen. . . ."

(7) **Genesis 14:16** Then he brought back all the goods, and also brought back his kinsman Lot with his goods, and the women and the people. 500

(8) **Genesis 29:15** Then Laban said to Jacob, "Because you are my kinsman, should you therefore serve me for nothing? Tell me, what shall your wages be?" 500

(1) **John 19:26–27** When Jesus saw his mother, and the disciple whom he loved standing near, he said to his mother, "Woman, behold, your son!" Then he said to the disciple, "Behold, your mother!" And from that hour the disciple took her to his own home. 501

(2) **Romans 8:29** For those whom he foreknew he also predestined to be conformed to the image of his Son, in order that he might be the first-born among many brethren. 501

(3) **Revelation 12:17** Then the dragon was angry with the woman, and went off to make war on the rest of her offspring, on those who keep the commandments of God and bear testimony to Jesus. And he stood on the sand of the sea. 501

Luke 2:48–49 And when they saw him they were astonished; and his mother said to him, "Son, why have you treated us so? Behold, your father and I have been looking for you anxiously." And he said to them, "How is it that you sought me? Did you not know that I must be in my Father's house?" 503

(1) **1 Corinthians 15:45** Thus it is written, "The first man Adam became a living being"; the last Adam became a life-giving spirit. 504

(2) **Colossians 1:18** He is the head of the body, the church; he is the beginning, the first-born from the dead, that in everything he might be pre-eminent. 504

(1) **John 3:9** Nicodemus said to him, "How can this be?" 505

(2) **2 Corinthians 11:2** I feel a divine jealousy for you, for I betrothed you to Christ to present you as a pure bride to her one husband. 505

1 Corinthians 7:34–35 . . . and his interests are divided. And the unmarried woman or girl is anxious about the affairs of the Lord, how to be holy in body and spirit; but the married woman is anxious about worldly affairs, how to please her husband. I say this for your own benefit, not to lay any restraint upon you, but to promote good order and to secure your undivided devotion to the Lord. 506

***Lumen gentium* 63** By reason of the gift and role of her divine motherhood, by which she is united with her Son, the Redeemer, and with her unique graces and functions, the Blessed Virgin is also intimately united to the Church. As St. Ambrose taught, the Mother of God is a type of the Church in the order of faith, charity, and perfect union with Christ. For in the mystery of the Church, which is itself rightly called mother and virgin, the Blessed Virgin stands out in eminent and singular fashion as exemplar both of virgin and mother. Through her faith and obedience she gave birth on earth to the very Son of the Father, not through the knowledge of man but by the overshadowing of the Holy Spirit, in the manner of a new Eve who placed her faith, not in the serpent of old but in God's messenger without wavering in doubt. The Son whom she brought forth is he whom God placed as the first-born among many brethren (Rom. 8:29), that is, the faithful, in whose generation and formation she cooperates with a mother's love. 507

514 **John 20:30** Now Jesus did many other signs in the presence of the disciples, which are not written in this book. . . .

515 (1) **Mark 1:1** The beginning of the gospel of Jesus Christ, the Son of God.

515 (2) **John 21:24** This is the disciple who is bearing witness to these things, and who has written these things; and we know that his testimony is true.

515 (3) **Luke 2:7** And she gave birth to her first-born son and wrapped him in swaddling cloths, and laid him in a manger, because there was no place for them in the inn.

515 (4) **Matthew 27:48** And one of them at once ran and took a sponge, filled it with vinegar, and put it on a reed, and gave it to him to drink.

515 (5) **John 20:7** . . . and the napkin, which had been on his head, not lying with the linen cloths but rolled up in a place by itself.

516 (1) **Matthew 17:5** He was still speaking, when lo, a bright cloud overshadowed them, and a voice from the cloud said, "This is my beloved Son, with whom I am well pleased; listen to him."

516 (2) **Mark 9:7** And a cloud overshadowed them, and a voice came out of the cloud, "This is my beloved Son; listen to him."

517 (1) **Ephesians 1:7** In him we have redemption through his blood, the forgiveness of our trespasses, according to the riches of his grace. . . .

517 (2) **Colossians 1:13–14** He has delivered us from the dominion of darkness and transferred us to the kingdom of his beloved Son, in whom we have redemption, the forgiveness of sins.

517 (3) **1 Peter 1:18–19** You know that you were ransomed from the futile ways inherited from your fathers, not with perishable things such as silver or gold, but with the precious blood of Christ, like that of a lamb without blemish or spot.

517 (4) **2 Corinthians 8:9** For you know the grace of our Lord Jesus Christ, that though he was rich, yet for your sake he became poor, so that by his poverty you might become rich.

517 (5) **Luke 2:51** And he went down with them and came to Nazareth, and was obedient to them; and his mother kept all these things in her heart.

517 (6) **John 15:3** You are already made clean by the word which I have spoken to you.

517 (7) **Isaiah 53:4**

Surely he has borne our griefs
and carried our sorrows;
yet we esteemed him stricken,
smitten by God, and afflicted.

517 (8) **Romans 4:25** . . . who was put to death for our trespasses and raised for our justification.

St. Irenaeus, *Adversus haereses* II, 22, 4 Being thirty years old when He came to be baptized, and then possessing the full age of a Master, He came to Jerusalem, so that He might be properly acknowledged by all as a Master. For He did not seem one thing while He was another, as those affirm who describe Him as being man only in appearance; but what He was, that He also appeared to be. Being a Master, therefore, He also possessed the age of a Master, not despising or evading any condition of humanity, nor setting aside in Himself that law which He had appointed for the human race, but sanctifying every age, by that period corresponding to it which belonged to Himself. For He came to save all through means of Himself—all, I say, who through Him are born again to God—infants, and children, and boys, and youths, and old men. He therefore passed through every age, becoming an infant for infants, thus sanctifying infants; a child for children, thus sanctifying those who are of this age, being at the same time made to them an example of piety, righteousness, and submission; a youth for youths, becoming an example to youths, and thus sanctifying them for the Lord. So likewise He was an old man for old men, that He might be a perfect Master for all, not merely as respects the setting forth of the truth, but also as regards age, sanctifying at the same time the aged also, and becoming an example to them likewise. Then, at last, He came on to death itself, that He might be "the first-born from the dead, that in all things He might have the pre-eminence," the Prince of life, existing before all, and going before all. 518

(1) **Romans 15:5** May the God of steadfastness and encouragement grant you to live in such harmony with one another, in accord with Christ Jesus. . . . 520

(2) **Philippians 2:5** Have this mind among yourselves, which is yours in Christ Jesus. . . . 520

(3) **John 13:15** For I have given you an example, that you also should do as I have done to you. 520

(4) **Luke 11:1** He was praying in a certain place, and when he ceased, one of his disciples said to him, "Lord, teach us to pray, as John taught his disciples." 520

(5) **Matthew 5:11–12** "Blessed are you when men revile you and persecute you and utter all kinds of evil against you falsely on my account. Rejoice and be glad, for your reward is great in heaven, for so men persecuted the prophets who were before you. . . ." 520

(1) **Acts 13:24** Before his coming John had preached a baptism of repentance to all the people of Israel. 523

(2) **Matthew 3:3** For this is he who was spoken of by the prophet Isaiah when he said, 523

> "The voice of one crying in the wilderness:
> Prepare the way of the Lord,
> make his paths straight."

(3) **Luke 7:26** What then did you go out to see? A prophet? Yes, I tell you, and more than a prophet. 523

(4) **Matthew 11:13** For all the prophets and the law prophesied until John. . . . 523

523 (5) **Acts 1:22** "... beginning from the baptism of John until the day when he was taken up from us—one of these men must become with us a witness to his resurrection."

523 (6) **Luke 1:41** And when Elizabeth heard the greeting of Mary, the babe leaped in her womb; and Elizabeth was filled with the Holy Spirit. . . .

523 (7) **Luke 16:16** "The law and the prophets were until John; since then the good news of the kingdom of God is preached, and every one enters it violently. . . ."

523 (8) **John 3:29** He who has the bride is the bridegroom; the friend of the bridegroom, who stands and hears him, rejoices greatly at the bridegroom's voice; therefore this joy of mine is now full.

523 (9) **Mark 6:17–29** For Herod had sent and seized John, and bound him in prison for the sake of Herodias, his brother Philip's wife; because he had married her. For John said to Herod, "It is not lawful for you to have your brother's wife." And Herodias had a grudge against him, and wanted to kill him. But she could not, for Herod feared John, knowing that he was a righteous and holy man, and kept him safe. When he heard him, he was much perplexed; and yet he heard him gladly. But an opportunity came when Herod on his birthday gave a banquet for his courtiers and officers and the leading men of Galilee. For when Herodias' daughter came in and danced, she pleased Herod and his guests; and the king said to the girl, "Ask me for whatever you wish, and I will grant it." And he vowed to her, "Whatever you ask me, I will give you, even half of my kingdom." And she went out, and said to her mother, "What shall I ask?" And she said, "The head of John the baptizer." And she came in immediately with haste to the king, and asked, saying, "I want you to give me at once the head of John the Baptist on a platter." And the king was exceedingly sorry; but because of his oaths and his guests he did not want to break his word to her. And immediately the king sent a soldier of the guard and gave orders to bring his head. He went and beheaded him in the prison, and brought his head on a platter, and gave it to the girl; and the girl gave it to her mother. When his disciples heard of it, they came and took his body, and laid it in a tomb.

524 **Revelation 22:17** The Spirit and the Bride say, "Come." And let him who hears say, "Come." And let him who is thirsty come, let him who desires take the water of life without price.

525 (1) **Luke 2:6–7** And while they were there, the time came for her to be delivered. And she gave birth to her first-born son and wrapped him in swaddling cloths, and laid him in a manger, because there was no place for them in the inn.

525 (2) **Luke 2:8–20** And in that region there were shepherds out in the field, keeping watch over their flock by night. And an angel of the Lord appeared to them, and the glory of the Lord shone around them, and they were filled with fear. And the angel said to them, "Be not afraid; for behold, I bring you good news of a great joy which will come to all the people; for to you is born this day in the city of David a Savior, who is Christ the Lord. And this will be a sign for you: you will find a babe wrapped in swaddling cloths and lying in a manger." And suddenly there was with the angel a multitude of the heavenly host praising God and saying,

"Glory to God in the highest,
and on earth peace among men with whom he is pleased!"

When the angels went away from them into heaven, the shepherds said to one another, "Let us go over to Bethlehem and see this thing that has happened, which the Lord has made known to us." And they went with haste, and found Mary and Joseph, and the babe lying in a manger. And when they saw it they made known the saying which had been told them concerning this child; and all who heard it wondered at what the shepherds told them. But Mary kept all these things, pondering them in her heart. And the shepherds returned, glorifying and praising God for all they had heard and seen, as it had been told them.

(1) **Matthew 18:3–4** . . . and said, "Truly, I say to you, unless you turn and become like children, you will never enter the kingdom of heaven. Whoever humbles himself like this child, he is the greatest in the kingdom of heaven. . . ." 526

(2) **Matthew 23:12** . . . whoever exalts himself will be humbled, and whoever humbles himself will be exalted. 526

(3) **Galatians 4:19** My little children, with whom I am again in travail until Christ be formed in you! 526

(1) **Luke 2:21** And at the end of eight days, when he was circumcised, he was called Jesus, the name given by the angel before he was conceived in the womb. 527

(2) **Galatians 4:4** But when the time had fully come, God sent forth his Son, born of woman, born under the law. . . . 527

(3) **Colossians 2:11–13** In him also you were circumcised with a circumcision made without hands, by putting off the body of flesh in the circumcision of Christ; and you were buried with him in baptism, in which you were also raised with him through faith in the working of God, who raised him from the dead. And you, who were dead in trespasses and the uncircumcision of your flesh, God made alive together with him, having forgiven us all our trespasses. . . . 527

(1) **Liturgy of the Hours, Magnificat antiphon of Evening Prayer II of the Epiphany** Three mysteries mark this holy day: today the star leads the Magi to the infant Christ; today water is changed into wine for the wedding feast; today Christ wills to be baptized by John in the river Jordan to bring us salvation. 528

(2) **Matthew 2:2** "Where is he who has been born king of the Jews? For we have seen his star in the East, and have come to worship him." 528

(3) **Numbers 24:17–19** 528

"... I see him, but not now;
I behold him, but not nigh:
a star shall come forth out of Jacob,
and a scepter shall rise out of Israel;
it shall crush the forehead of Moab,
and break down all the sons of Sheth.
Edom shall be dispossessed,
Seir also, his enemies, shall be dispossessed,
while Israel does valiantly.
By Jacob shall dominion be exercised,
and the survivors of cities be destroyed."

528 (4) **Revelation 22:16** "I Jesus have sent my angel to you with this testimony for the churches. I am the root and the offspring of David, the bright morning star."

528 (5) **John 4:22** You worship what you do not know; we worship what we know, for salvation is from the Jews.

528 (6) **Matthew 2:4–6** . . . and assembling all the chief priests and scribes of the people, he inquired of them where the Christ was to be born. They told him, "In Bethlehem of Judea; for so it is written by the prophet:

'And you, O Bethlehem, in the land of Judah,
are by no means least among the rulers of Judah;
for from you shall come a ruler
who will govern my people Israel.' "

529 (1) **Luke 2:22–39** And when the time came for their purification according to the law of Moses, they brought him up to Jerusalem to present him to the Lord (as it is written in the law of the Lord, "Every male that opens the womb shall be called holy to the Lord") and to offer a sacrifice according to what is said in the law of the Lord, "a pair of turtledoves, or two young pigeons." Now there was a man in Jerusalem, whose name was Simeon, and this man was righteous and devout, looking for the consolation of Israel, and the Holy Spirit was upon him. And it had been revealed to him by the Holy Spirit that he should not see death before he had seen the Lord's Christ. And inspired by the Spirit he came into the temple; and when the parents brought in the child Jesus, to do for him according to the custom of the law, he took him up in his arms and blessed God and said,

"Lord, now lettest thou thy servant depart in peace,
according to thy word;
for mine eyes have seen thy salvation
which thou hast prepared in the presence of all peoples,
a light for revelation to the Gentiles,
and for glory to thy people Israel."

And his father and his mother marveled at what was said about him; and Simeon blessed them and said to Mary his mother,

"Behold, this child is set for the fall and rising of many in Israel,
and for a sign that is spoken against
(and a sword will pierce through your own soul also),
that thoughts out of many hearts may be revealed."

And there was a prophetess, Anna, the daughter of Phanuel, of the tribe of Asher; she was of a great age, having lived with her husband seven years from her virginity, and as a widow till she was eighty-four. She did not depart from the temple, worshiping with fasting and prayer night and day. And coming up at that very hour she gave thanks to God, and spoke of him to all who were looking for the redemption of Jerusalem.

And when they had performed everything according to the law of the Lord, they returned into Galilee, to their own city, Nazareth.

529 (2) **Exodus 13:2** "Consecrate to me all the first-born; whatever is the first to open the womb among the people of Israel, both of man and of beast, is mine."

529 (3) **Exodus 13:12–13** . . . you shall set apart to the Lord all that first opens the womb. All the firstlings of your cattle that are males shall be the Lord's. Every firstling of an ass you shall redeem with a lamb, or if you will not redeem it you shall break its neck. Every first-born of man among your sons you shall redeem.

(1) **Matthew 2:13–18** Now when they had departed, behold, an angel of the Lord appeared to Joseph in a dream and said, "Rise, take the child and his mother, and flee to Egypt, and remain there till I tell you; for Herod is about to search for the child, to destroy him." And he rose and took the child and his mother by night, and departed to Egypt, and remained there until the death of Herod. This was to fulfil what the Lord had spoken by the prophet, "Out of Egypt have I called my son." 530

Then Herod, when he saw that he had been tricked by the wise men, was in a furious rage, and he sent and killed all the male children in Bethlehem and in all that region who were two years old or under, according to the time which he had ascertained from the wise men. Then was fulfilled what was spoken by the prophet Jeremiah:

"A voice was heard in Ramah,
wailing and loud lamentation,
Rachel weeping for her children;
she refused to be consoled,
because they were no more."

(2) **John 15:20** ". . . Remember the word that I said to you, 'A servant is not greater than his master.' If they persecuted me, they will persecute you; if they kept my word, they will keep yours also. . . ." 530

(3) **Matthew 2:15** . . . and remained there until the death of Herod. This was to fulfil what the Lord had spoken by the prophet, "Out of Egypt have I called my son." 530

(4) **Hosea 11:1** 530

When Israel was a child, I loved him,
and out of Egypt I called my son.

Galatians 4:4 But when the time had fully come, God sent forth his Son, born of woman, born under the law. . . . 531

Romans 5:19 For as by one man's disobedience many were made sinners, so by one man's obedience many will be made righteous. 532

Luke 2:41–52 Now his parents went to Jerusalem every year at the feast of the Passover. And when he was twelve years old, they went up according to custom; and when the feast was ended, as they were returning, the boy Jesus stayed behind in Jerusalem. His parents did not know it, but supposing him to be in the company they went a day's journey, and they sought him among their kinsfolk and acquaintances; and when they did not find him, they returned to Jerusalem, seeking him. After three days they found him in the temple, sitting among the teachers, listening to them and asking them questions; and all who heard him were amazed at his understanding and his answers. And when they saw him they were astonished; and his mother said to him, "Son, why have you treated us so? Behold, your father and I have been looking for you anxiously." And he said to them, "How is it that you sought me? Did you not know that I must be in my Father's house?" And they did not understand the saying which he spoke to them. And he went down with them and came to Nazareth, and was obedient to them; and his mother kept all these things in her heart. 534

And Jesus increased in wisdom and in stature, and in favor with God and man.

(1) **Luke 3:23** Jesus, when he began his ministry, was about thirty years of age, being the son (as was supposed) of Joseph, the son of Heli. . . . 535

535 (2) **Acts 1:22** "... beginning from the baptism of John until the day when he was taken up from us—one of these men must become with us a witness to his resurrection."

535 (3) **Luke 3:10–14** And the multitudes asked him, "What then shall we do?" And he answered them, "He who has two coats, let him share with him who has none; and he who has food, let him do likewise. Tax collectors also came to be baptized, and said to him, "Teacher, what shall we do?" And he said to them, "Collect no more than is appointed you." Soldiers also asked him, "And we, what shall we do?" And he said to them, "Rob no one by violence or by false accusation, and be content with your wages."

535 (4) **Matthew 3:7** But when he saw many of the Pharisees and Sadducees coming for baptism, he said to them, "You brood of vipers! Who warned you to flee from the wrath to come? . . ."

535 (5) **Matthew 21:32** For John came to you in the way of righteousness, and you did not believe him, but the tax collectors and the harlots believed him; and even when you saw it, you did not afterward repent and believe him.

536 (1) **Isaiah 53:12**

Therefore I will divide him a portion with the great,
and he shall divide the spoil with the strong;
because he poured out his soul to death,
and was numbered with the transgressors;
yet he bore the sin of many,
and made intercession for the transgressors.

536 (2) **Mark 10:38** But Jesus said to them, "You do not know what you are asking. Are you able to drink the cup that I drink, or to be baptized with the baptism with which I am baptized?"

536 (3) **Luke 12:50** I have a baptism to be baptized with; and how I am constrained until it is accomplished!

536 (4) **Matthew 26:39** And going a little farther he fell on his face and prayed, "My Father, if it be possible, let this cup pass from me; nevertheless, not as I will, but as thou wilt."

536 (5) **Luke 3:22** . . . and the Holy Spirit descended upon him in bodily form, as a dove, and a voice came from heaven, "Thou art my beloved Son; with thee I am well pleased."

536 (6) **Isaiah 42:1**

Behold my servant, whom I uphold,
my chosen, in whom my soul delights;
I have put my Spirit upon him,
he will bring forth justice to the nations.

536 (7) **Isaiah 11:2**

And the Spirit of the Lord shall rest upon him,
the spirit of wisdom and understanding,
the spirit of counsel and might,
the spirit of knowledge and the fear of the Lord.

Mark 1:12–13 The Spirit immediately drove him out into the wilderness. And he was in the wilderness forty days, tempted by Satan; and he was with the wild beasts; and the angels ministered to him. 538

(1) **Psalm 95:10** 539
For forty years I loathed that generation
and said, "They are a people who err in heart,
and they do not regard my ways."

(2) **Mark 3:27** But no one can enter a strong man's house and plunder his goods, unless he first binds the strong man; then indeed he may plunder his house. 539

Matthew 16:21–23 From that time Jesus began to show his disciples that he must go to Jerusalem and suffer many things from the elders and chief priests and scribes, and be killed, and on the third day be raised. And Peter took him and began to rebuke him, saying, "God forbid, Lord! This shall never happen to you." But he turned and said to Peter, "Get behind me, Satan! You are a hindrance to me; for you are not on the side of God, but of men." 540

***Lumen gentium* 3** The Son, accordingly, came, sent by the Father who, before the foundation of the world, chose us and predestined us in him for adoptive sonship. For it is in him that it pleased the Father to restore all things (cf. Eph. 1:4–5 and 10). To carry out the will of the Father Christ inaugurated the kingdom of heaven on earth and revealed to us his mystery; by his obedience he brought about our redemption. The Church—that is, the kingdom of Christ—already present in mystery, grows visibly through the power of God in the world. The origin and growth of the Church are symbolized by the blood and water which flowed from the open side of the crucified Jesus (cf. Jn. 19:34), and are foretold in the words of the Lord referring to his death on the cross: "And I, if I be lifted up from the earth, will draw all men to myself" (Jn. 12:32; Gk.). As often as the sacrifice of the cross by which "Christ our Pasch is sacrificed" (1 Cor. 5:7) is celebrated on the altar, the work of our redemption is carried out. Likewise, in the sacrament of the eucharistic bread, the unity of believers, who form one body in Christ (cf. 1 Cor. 10:17), is both expressed and brought about. All men are called to this union with Christ, who is the light of the world, from whom we go forth, through whom we live, and towards whom our whole life is directed. 542

(1) **Matthew 8:11** I tell you, many will come from east and west and sit at table with Abraham, Isaac, and Jacob in the kingdom of heaven. . . . 543

(2) **Matthew 10:5–7** These twelve Jesus sent out, charging them, "Go nowhere among the Gentiles, and enter no town of the Samaritans, but go rather to the lost sheep of the house of Israel. And preach as you go, saying, 'The kingdom of heaven is at hand.' . . ." 543

(3) **Matthew 28:19** Go therefore and make disciples of all nations, baptizing them in the name of the Father and of the Son and of the Holy Spirit. . . . 543

(4) **Mark 4:14** The sower sows the word. 543

(5) **Mark 4:26–29** And he said, "The kingdom of God is as if a man should scatter seed upon the ground, and should sleep and rise night and day, and the seed should sprout and grow, he knows not how. The earth produces of itself, first the blade, then the ear, then the full grain in the ear. But when the grain is ripe, at once he puts in the sickle, because the harvest has come." 543

543 (6) **Luke 12:32** "Fear not, little flock, for it is your Father's good pleasure to give you the kingdom. . . ."

544 (1) **Luke 7:22** And he answered them, "Go and tell John what you have seen and heard: the blind receive their sight, the lame walk, lepers are cleansed, and the deaf hear, the dead are raised up, the poor have good news preached to them. . . ."

544 (2) **Matthew 11:25** At that time Jesus declared, "I thank thee, Father, Lord of heaven and earth, that thou hast hidden these things from the wise and understanding and revealed them to babes. . . ."

544 (3) **Matthew 21:18** In the morning, as he was returning to the city, he was hungry.

544 (4) **Mark 2:23–26** One sabbath he was going through the grainfields; and as they made their way his disciples began to pluck heads of grain. And the Pharisees said to him, "Look, why are they doing what is not lawful on the sabbath?" And he said to them, "Have you never read what David did, when he was in need and was hungry, he and those who were with him: how he entered the house of God, when Abiathar was high priest, and ate the bread of the Presence, which it is not lawful for any but the priests to eat, and also gave it to those who were with him?"

544 (5) **John 4:6–7** Jacob's well was there, and so Jesus, wearied as he was with his journey, sat down beside the well. It was about the sixth hour.

There came a woman of Samaria to draw water. Jesus said to her, "Give me a drink."

544 (6) **John 19:28** After this Jesus, knowing that all was now finished, said (to fulfil the scripture), "I thirst."

544 (7) **Luke 9:58** And Jesus said to him, "Foxes have holes, and birds of the air have nests; but the Son of man has nowhere to lay his head."

544 (8) **Matthew 25:31–46** "When the Son of man comes in his glory, and all the angels with him, then he will sit on his glorious throne. Before him will be gathered all the nations, and he will separate them one from another as a shepherd separates the sheep from the goats, and he will place the sheep at his right hand, but the goats at the left. Then the King will say to those at his right hand, 'Come, O blessed of my Father, inherit the kingdom prepared for you from the foundation of the world; for I was hungry and you gave me food, I was thirsty and you gave me drink, I was a stranger and you welcomed me, I was naked and you clothed me, I was sick and you visited me, I was in prison and you came to me.' Then the righteous will answer him, 'Lord, when did we see thee hungry and feed thee, or thirsty and give thee drink? And when did we see thee a stranger and welcome thee, or naked and clothe thee? And when did we see thee sick or in prison and visit thee?' And the King will answer them, 'Truly, I say to you, as you did it to one of the least of these my brethren, you did it to me.' Then he will say to those at his left hand, 'Depart from me, you cursed, into the eternal fire prepared for the devil and his angels; for I was hungry and you gave me no food, I was thirsty and you gave me no drink, I was a stranger and you did not welcome me, naked and you did not clothe me, sick and in prison and you did not visit me.' Then they also will answer, 'Lord, when did we see thee hungry or thirsty or a stranger or naked or sick or in prison, and did not minister to thee?' Then he will answer them, 'Truly, I say to you, as you did it not to one of the least of these, you did it not to me.' And they will go away into eternal punishment, but the righteous into eternal life."

(1) **1 Timothy 1:15** The saying is sure and worthy of full acceptance, that Christ 545
Jesus came into the world to save sinners. And I am the foremost of sinners. . . .

(2) **Luke 15:11–32** And he said, "There was a man who had two sons; and the 545
younger of them said to his father, 'Father, give me the share of property that falls to me.' And he divided his living between them. Not many days later, the younger son gathered all he had and took his journey into a far country, and there he squandered his property in loose living. And when he had spent everything, a great famine arose in that country, and he began to be in want. So he went and joined himself to one of the citizens of that country, who sent him into his fields to feed swine. And he would gladly have fed on the pods that the swine ate; and no one gave him anything. But when he came to himself he said, 'How many of my father's hired servants have bread enough and to spare, but I perish here with hunger! I will arise and go to my father, and I will say to him, "Father, I have sinned against heaven and before you; I am no longer worthy to be called your son; treat me as one of your hired servants."' And he arose and came to his father. But while he was yet at a distance, his father saw him and had compassion, and ran and embraced him and kissed him. And the son said to him, 'Father, I have sinned against heaven and before you; I am no longer worthy to be called your son.' But the father said to his servants, 'Bring quickly the best robe, and put it on him; and put a ring on his hand, and shoes on his feet; and bring the fatted calf and kill it, and let us eat and make merry; for this my son was dead, and is alive again; he was lost, and is found.' And they began to make merry.

"Now his elder son was in the field; and as he came and drew near to the house, he heard music and dancing. And he called one of the servants and asked what this meant. And he said to him, 'Your brother has come, and your father has killed the fatted calf, because he has received him safe and sound.' But he was angry and refused to go in. His father came out and entreated him, but he answered his father, 'Lo, these many years I have served you, and I never disobeyed your command; yet you never gave me a kid, that I might make merry with my friends. But when this son of yours came, who has devoured your living with harlots, you killed for him the fatted calf!' And he said to him, 'Son, you are always with me, and all that is mine is yours. It was fitting to make merry and be glad, for this your brother was dead, and is alive; he was lost, and is found.'"

(1) **Mark 4:33–34** With many such parables he spoke the word to them, as they 546
were able to hear it; he did not speak to them without a parable, but privately to his own disciples he explained everything.

(2) **Matthew 13:44–45** "The kingdom of heaven is like treasure hidden in a field, 546
which a man found and covered up; then in his joy he goes and sells all that he has and buys that field.

"Again, the kingdom of heaven is like a merchant in search of fine pearls. . . ."

(3) **Matthew 22:1–14** And again Jesus spoke to them in parables, saying, "The 546
kingdom of heaven may be compared to a king who gave a marriage feast for his son, and sent his servants to call those who were invited to the marriage feast; but they would not come. Again he sent other servants, saying, 'Tell those who are invited, Behold, I have made ready my dinner, my oxen and my fat calves are killed, and everything is ready; come to the marriage feast.' But they made light of it and went off, one to his farm, another to his business, while the rest seized his servants, treated them shamefully, and killed them. The king was angry, and he sent his troops and

destroyed those murderers and burned their city. Then he said to his servants, 'The wedding is ready, but those invited were not worthy. Go therefore to the thoroughfares, and invite to the marriage feast as many as you find.' And those servants went out into the streets and gathered all whom they found, both bad and good; so the wedding hall was filled with guests.

"But when the king came in to look at the guests, he saw there a man who had no wedding garment; and he said to him, 'Friend, how did you get in here without a wedding garment?' And he was speechless. Then the king said to the attendants, 'Bind him hand and foot, and cast him into the outer darkness; there men will weep and gnash their teeth.' For many are called, but few are chosen."

546 (4) **Matthew 21:28–32** "What do you think? A man had two sons; and he went to the first and said, 'Son, go and work in the vineyard today.' And he answered, 'I will not'; but afterward he repented and went. And he went to the second and said the same; and he answered, 'I go, sir,' but did not go. Which of the two did the will of his father?" They said, "The first." Jesus said to them, "Truly, I say to you, the tax collectors and the harlots go into the kingdom of God before you. For John came to you in the way of righteousness, and you did not believe him, but the tax collectors and the harlots believed him; and even when you saw it, you did not afterward repent and believe him. . . ."

546 (5) **Matthew 13:3–9** And he told them many things in parables, saying: "A sower went out to sow. And as he sowed, some seeds fell along the path, and the birds came and devoured them. Other seeds fell on rocky ground, where they had not much soil, and immediately they sprang up, since they had no depth of soil, but when the sun rose they were scorched; and since they had no root they withered away. Other seeds fell upon thorns, and the thorns grew up and choked them. Other seeds fell on good soil and brought forth grain, some a hundredfold, some sixty, some thirty. He who has ears, let him hear."

546 (6) **Matthew 25:14–30** "For it will be as when a man going on a journey called his servants and entrusted to them his property; to one he gave five talents, to another two, to another one, to each according to his ability. Then he went away. He who had received the five talents went at once and traded with them; and he made five talents more. So also, he who had the two talents made two talents more. But he who had received the one talent went and dug in the ground and hid his master's money. Now after a long time the master of those servants came and settled accounts with them. And he who had received the five talents came forward, bringing five talents more, saying, 'Master, you delivered to me five talents; here I have made five talents more.' His master said to him, 'Well done, good and faithful servant; you have been faithful over a little, I will set you over much; enter into the joy of your master.' And he also who had the two talents came forward, saying, 'Master, you delivered to me two talents; here I have made two talents more.' His master said to him, 'Well done, good and faithful servant; you have been faithful over a little, I will set you over much; enter into the joy of your master.' He also who had received the one talent came forward, saying, 'Master, I knew you to be a hard man, reaping where you did not sow, and gathering where you did not winnow; so I was afraid, and I went and hid your talent in the ground. Here you have what is yours.' But his master answered him, 'You wicked and slothful servant! You knew that I reap where I have not sowed, and gather where I have not winnowed? Then you ought to have invested my money with the bankers, and at my coming I should have received what was my own with interest. So take the talent from him, and give it to him who has the ten talents. For

to every one who has will more be given, and he will have abundance; but from him who has not, even what he has will be taken away. And cast the worthless servant into the outer darkness; there men will weep and gnash their teeth.' . . ."

(7) **Matthew 13:10–15** Then the disciples came and said to him, "Why do you 546
speak to them in parables?" And he answered them, "To you it has been given to know the secrets of the kingdom of heaven, but to them it has not been given. For to him who has will more be given, and he will have abundance; but from him who has not, even what he has will be taken away. This is why I speak to them in parables, because seeing they do not see, and hearing they do not hear, nor do they understand. With them indeed is fulfilled the prophecy of Isaiah which says:

'You shall indeed hear but never understand,
  and you shall indeed see but never perceive.
For this people's heart has grown dull,
  and their ears are heavy of hearing,
  and their eyes they have closed,
lest they should perceive with their eyes,
  and hear with their ears,
and understand with their heart,
  and turn for me to heal them.' . . ."

Luke 7:18–23 The disciples of John told him of all these things. And John, calling 547
to him two of his disciples, sent them to the Lord, saying, "Are you he who is to come, or shall we look for another?" And when the men had come to him, they said, "John the Baptist has sent us to you, saying, 'Are you he who is to come, or shall we look for another?'" In that hour he cured many of diseases and plagues and evil spirits, and on many that were blind he bestowed sight. And he answered them, "Go and tell John what you have seen and heard: the blind receive their sight, the lame walk, lepers are cleansed, and the deaf hear, the dead are raised up, the poor have good news preached to them. And blessed is he who takes no offense at me."

(1) **John 5:36** But the testimony which I have is greater than that of John; for the 548
works which the Father has granted me to accomplish, these very works which I am doing, bear me witness that the Father has sent me.

(2) **John 10:25** Jesus answered them, "I told you, and you do not believe. The 548
works that I do in my Father's name, they bear witness to me. . . ."

(3) **John 10:38** ". . . but if I do them, even though you do not believe me, believe 548
the works, that you may know and understand that the Father is in me and I am in the Father."

(4) **Mark 5:25–34** And there was a woman who had had a flow of blood for twelve 548
years, and who had suffered much under many physicians, and had spent all that she had, and was no better but rather grew worse. She had heard the reports about Jesus, and came up behind him in the crowd and touched his garment. For she said, "If I touch even his garments, I shall be made well." And immediately the hemorrhage ceased; and she felt in her body that she was healed of her disease. And Jesus, perceiving in himself that power had gone forth from him, immediately turned about in the crowd, and said, "Who touched my garments?" And his disciples said to him, "You see the crowd pressing around you, and yet you say, 'Who touched me?'" And he looked around to see who had done it. But the woman, knowing what had been done

to her, came in fear and trembling and fell down before him, and told him the whole truth. And he said to her, "Daughter, your faith has made you well; go in peace, and be healed of your disease."

548 (5) **Mark 10:52** And Jesus said to him, "Go your way; your faith has made you well." And immediately he received his sight and followed him on the way.

548 (6) **John 10:31–38** The Jews took up stones again to stone him. Jesus answered them, "I have shown you many good works from the Father; for which of these do you stone me?" The Jews answered him, "It is not for a good work that we stone you but for blasphemy; because you, being a man, make yourself God." Jesus answered them, "Is it not written in your law, 'I said, you are gods'? If he called them gods to whom the word of God came (and scripture cannot be broken), do you say of him whom the Father consecrated and sent into the world, 'You are blaspheming,' because I said, 'I am the Son of God'? If I am not doing the works of my Father, then do not believe me; but if I do them, even though you do not believe me, believe the works, that you may know and understand that the Father is in me and I am in the Father."

548 (7) **John 11:47–48** So the chief priests and the Pharisees gathered the council, and said, "What are we to do? For this man performs many signs. If we let him go on thus, every one will believe in him, and the Romans will come and destroy both our holy place and our nation."

548 (8) **Mark 3:22** And the scribes who came down from Jerusalem said, "He is possessed by Beelzebul, and by the prince of demons he casts out the demons."

549 (1) **John 6:5–15** Lifting up his eyes, then, and seeing that a multitude was coming to him, Jesus said to Philip, "How are we to buy bread, so that these people may eat?" This he said to test him, for he himself knew what he would do. Philip answered him, "Two hundred denarii would not buy enough bread for each of them to get a little." One of his disciples, Andrew, Simon Peter's brother, said to him, "There is a lad here who has five barley loaves and two fish; but what are they among so many?" Jesus said, "Make the people sit down." Now there was much grass in the place; so the men sat down, in number about five thousand. Jesus then took the loaves, and when he had given thanks, he distributed them to those who were seated; so also the fish, as much as they wanted. And when they had eaten their fill, he told his disciples, "Gather up the fragments left over, that nothing may be lost." So they gathered them up and filled twelve baskets with fragments from the five barley loaves, left by those who had eaten. When the people saw the sign which he had done, they said, "This is indeed the prophet who is to come into the world!"

Perceiving then that they were about to come and take him by force to make him king, Jesus withdrew again to the mountain by himself.

549 (2) **Luke 19:8** And Zacchaeus stood and said to the Lord, "Behold, Lord, the half of my goods I give to the poor; and if I have defrauded any one of anything, I restore it fourfold."

549 (3) **Matthew 11:5** . . . the blind receive their sight and the lame walk, lepers are cleansed and the deaf hear, and the dead are raised up, and the poor have good news preached to them.

549 (4) **Luke 12:13–14** One of the multitude said to him, "Teacher, bid my brother divide the inheritance with me." But he said to him, "Man, who made me a judge or divider over you?"

(5) **John 18:36** Jesus answered, "My kingship is not of this world; if my kingship 549
were of this world, my servants would fight, that I might not be handed over to the Jews; but my kingship is not from the world."

(6) **John 8:34–36** Jesus answered them, "Truly, truly, I say to you, every one who 549
commits sin is a slave to sin. The slave does not continue in the house for ever; the son continues for ever. So if the Son makes you free, you will be free indeed. . . ."

Luke 8:26–39 Then they arrived at the country of the Gerasenes, which is opposite 550
Galilee. And as he stepped out on land, there met him a man from the city who had demons; for a long time he had worn no clothes, and he lived not in a house but among the tombs. When he saw Jesus, he cried out and fell down before him, and said with a loud voice, "What have you to do with me, Jesus, Son of the Most High God? I beseech you, do not torment me." For he had commanded the unclean spirit to come out of the man. (For many a time it had seized him; he was kept under guard, and bound with chains and fetters, but he broke the bonds and was driven by the demon into the desert.) Jesus then asked him, "What is your name?" And he said, "Legion"; for many demons had entered him. And they begged him not to command them to depart into the abyss. Now a large herd of swine was feeding there on the hillside; and they begged him to let them enter these. So he gave them leave. Then the demons came out of the man and entered the swine, and the herd rushed down the steep bank into the lake and were drowned.

When the herdsmen saw what had happened, they fled, and told it in the city and in the country. Then people went out to see what had happened, and they came to Jesus, and found the man from whom the demons had gone, sitting at the feet of Jesus, clothed and in his right mind; and they were afraid. And those who had seen it told them how he who had been possessed with demons was healed. Then all the people of the surrounding country of the Gerasenes asked him to depart from them; for they were seized with great fear; so he got into the boat and returned. The man from whom the demons had gone begged that he might be with him; but he sent him away, saying, "Return to your home, and declare how much God has done for you." And he went away, proclaiming throughout the whole city how much Jesus had done for him.

Mark 3:13–19 And he went up on the mountain, and called to him those whom 551
he desired; and they came to him. And he appointed twelve, to be with him, and to be sent out to preach and have authority to cast out demons: Simon whom he surnamed Peter; James the son of Zebedee and John the brother of James, whom he surnamed Boanerges, that is, sons of thunder; Andrew, and Philip, and Bartholomew, and Matthew, and Thomas, and James the son of Alphaeus, and Thaddaeus, and Simon the Cananaean, and Judas Iscariot, who betrayed him.

Then he went home. . . .

(1) **Mark 3:16** Simon whom he surnamed Peter. . . . 552

(2) **Mark 9:2** And after six days Jesus took with him Peter and James and John, and 552
led them up a high mountain apart by themselves; and he was transfigured before them. . . .

(3) **Luke 24:34** . . . who said, "The Lord has risen indeed, and has appeared to 552
Simon!"

(4) **1 Corinthians 15:5** . . . and that he appeared to Cephas, then to the twelve. 552

552 (5) **Luke 22:32** ". . . but I have prayed for you that your faith may not fail; and when you have turned again, strengthen your brethren."

553 (1) **John 10:11** I am the good shepherd. The good shepherd lays down his life for the sheep.

553 (2) **Matthew 18:18** Truly, I say to you, whatever you bind on earth shall be bound in heaven, and whatever you loose on earth shall be loosed in heaven.

554 (1) **Matthew 16:22–23** And Peter took him and began to rebuke him, saying, "God forbid, Lord! This shall never happen to you." But he turned and said to Peter, "Get behind me, Satan! You are a hindrance to me; for you are not on the side of God, but of men."

554 (2) **Matthew 17:23** ". . . and they will kill him, and he will be raised on the third day." And they were greatly distressed.

554 (3) **Luke 9:45** But they did not understand this saying, and it was concealed from them, that they should not perceive it; and they were afraid to ask him about this saying.

554 (4) **Matthew 17:1–8** And after six days Jesus took with him Peter and James and John his brother, and led them up a high mountain apart. And he was transfigured before them, and his face shone like the sun, and his garments became white as light. And behold, there appeared to them Moses and Elijah, talking with him. And Peter said to Jesus, "Lord, it is well that we are here; if you wish, I will make three booths here, one for you and one for Moses and one for Elijah." He was still speaking, when lo, a bright cloud overshadowed them, and a voice from the cloud said, "This is my beloved Son, with whom I am well pleased; listen to him." When the disciples heard this, they fell on their faces, and were filled with awe. But Jesus came and touched them, saying, "Rise, and have no fear." And when they lifted up their eyes, they saw no one but Jesus only.

554 (5) **2 Peter 1:16–18** For we did not follow cleverly devised myths when we made known to you the power and coming of our Lord Jesus Christ, but we were eyewitnesses of his majesty. For when he received honor and glory from God the Father and the voice was borne to him by the Majestic Glory, "This is my beloved Son, with whom I am well pleased," we heard this voice borne from heaven, for we were with him on the holy mountain.

555 (1) **Luke 24:27** And beginning with Moses and all the prophets, he interpreted to them in all the scriptures the things concerning himself.

555 (2) **Isaiah 42:1**

Behold my servant, whom I uphold,
my chosen, in whom my soul delights;
I have put my Spirit upon him,
he will bring forth justice to the nations.

556 **Luke 9:33** And as the men were parting from him, Peter said to Jesus, "Master, it is well that we are here; let us make three booths, one for you and one for Moses and one for Elijah"—not knowing what he said.

(1) **John 13:1** Now before the feast of the Passover, when Jesus knew that his hour 557
had come to depart out of this world to the Father, having loved his own who were
in the world, he loved them to the end.

(2) **Mark 8:31–33** And he began to teach them that the Son of man must suffer 557
many things, and be rejected by the elders and the chief priests and the scribes, and
be killed, and after three days rise again. And he said this plainly. And Peter took him,
and began to rebuke him. But turning and seeing his disciples, he rebuked Peter, and
said, "Get behind me, Satan! For you are not on the side of God, but of men."

(3) **Mark 9:31–32** . . . for he was teaching his disciples, saying to them, "The Son 557
of man will be delivered into the hands of men, and they will kill him; and when he
is killed, after three days he will rise." But they did not understand the saying, and
they were afraid to ask him.

(4) **Mark 10:32–34** And they were on the road, going up to Jerusalem, and Jesus 557
was walking ahead of them; and they were amazed, and those who followed were
afraid. And taking the twelve again, he began to tell them what was to happen to him,
saying, "Behold, we are going up to Jerusalem; and the Son of man will be delivered
to the chief priests and the scribes, and they will condemn him to death, and deliver
him to the Gentiles; and they will mock him, and spit upon him, and scourge him,
and kill him; and after three days he will rise."

(1) **Matthew 21:1–11** And when they drew near to Jerusalem and came to Beth- 559
phage, to the Mount of Olives, then Jesus sent two disciples, saying to them, "Go
into the village opposite you, and immediately you will find an ass tied, and a colt
with her; untie them and bring them to me. If any one says anything to you, you
shall say, 'The Lord has need of them,' and he will send them immediately." This
took place to fulfil what was spoken by the prophet, saying,

> "Tell the daughter of Zion,
> Behold, your king is coming to you,
> humble, and mounted on an ass,
> and on a colt, the foal of an ass."

The disciples went and did as Jesus had directed them; they brought the ass and the colt, and put their garments on them, and he sat thereon. Most of the crowd spread their garments on the road, and others cut branches from the trees and spread them on the road. And the crowds that went before him and that followed him shouted, "Hosanna to the Son of David! Blessed is he who comes in the name of the Lord! Hosanna in the highest!" And when he entered Jerusalem, all the city was stirred, saying, "Who is this?" And the crowds said, "This is the prophet Jesus from Nazareth of Galilee."

(2) **John 6:15** Perceiving then that they were about to come and take him by force 559
to make him king, Jesus withdrew again to the mountain by himself.

(3) **John 18:37** Pilate said to him, "So you are a king?" Jesus answered, "You say 559
that I am a king. For this I was born, and for this I have come into the world, to bear
witness to the truth. Every one who is of the truth hears my voice."

(4) **Matthew 21:15–16** But when the chief priests and the scribes saw the wonderful 559
things that he did, and the children crying out in the temple, "Hosanna to the Son
of David!" they were indignant; and they said to him, "Do you hear what these are
saying?" And Jesus said to them, "Yes; have you never read,

'Out of the mouth of babes and sucklings
thou hast brought perfect praise'?"

559 (5) **Psalm 8:3 (8:1b–2: RSV)**
Thou whose glory above the heavens is chanted
by the mouth of babes and infants,
thou hast founded a bulwark because of thy foes,
to still the enemy and the avenger.

559 (6) **Luke 19:38** . . . saying, "Blessed is the King who comes in the name of the Lord! Peace in heaven and glory in the highest!"

559 (7) **Luke 2:14**
"Glory to God in the highest,
and on earth peace among men with whom he is pleased!"

559 (8) **Psalm 118:26**
Blessed be he who enters in the name of the Lord!
We bless you from the house of the Lord.

562 **Galatians 4:19** My little children, with whom I am again in travail until Christ be formed in you!

568 **St. Leo the Great, *Sermo* 51, 3** And in this Transfiguration the foremost object was to remove the offense of the cross from the disciple's heart, and to prevent their faith being disturbed by the humiliation of His voluntary Passion by revealing to them the excellence of His hidden dignity. But with no less foresight, the foundation was laid of the Holy Church's hope, that the whole body of Christ might realize the character of the change which it would have to receive, and that the members might promise themselves a share in that honor which had already shone forth in their Head. About which the Lord had Himself said, when He spoke of the majesty of His coming, "Then shall the righteous shine as the sun in their Father's Kingdom," whilst the blessed Apostle Paul bears witness to the self-same thing, and says: "for I reckon that the sufferings of this time are not worthy to be compared with the future glory which shall be revealed in us:" and again, "for ye are dead, and your life is hid with Christ in God. For when Christ our life shall appear, then shall ye also appear with Him in glory." But to confirm the Apostles and assist them to all knowledge, still further instruction was conveyed by that miracle.

569 **Hebrews 12:3** Consider him who endured from sinners such hostility against himself, so that you may not grow weary or fainthearted.

573 ***Dei Verbum* 19** Holy Mother Church has firmly and with absolute constancy maintained and continues to maintain, that the four Gospels just named, whose historicity she unhesitatingly affirms, faithfully hand on what Jesus, the Son of God, while he lived among men, really did and taught for their eternal salvation, until the day when he was taken up (cf. Acts 1:1–2). For, after the ascension of the Lord, the apostles handed on to their hearers what he had said and done, but with that fuller understanding which they, instructed by the glorious events of Christ and enlightened by the Spirit of truth, now enjoyed. The sacred authors, in writing the four Gospels, selected certain of the many elements which had been handed on, either orally or already in written form, others they synthesized or explained with an eye to the situ-

ation of the churches, the while sustaining the form of preaching, but always in such a fashion that they have told us the honest truth about Jesus. Whether they relied on their own memory and recollections or on the testimony of those who "from the beginning were eyewitnesses and ministers of the Word," their purpose in writing was that we might know the "truth" concerning the things of which we have been informed (cf. Lk. 1:2–4).

(1) **Mark 3:6** The Pharisees went out, and immediately held counsel with the Hero- 574
dians against him, how to destroy him.

(2) **Mark 14:1** It was now two days before the Passover and the feast of Unleavened 574
Bread. And the chief priests and the scribes were seeking how to arrest him by stealth, and kill him. . . .

(3) **Matthew 12:24** But when the Pharisees heard it they said, "It is only by Beelze- 574
bul, the prince of demons, that this man casts out demons."

(4) **Mark 2:7** "Why does this man speak thus? It is blasphemy! Who can forgive 574
sins but God alone?"

(5) **Mark 2:14–17** And as he passed on, he saw Levi the son of Alphaeus sitting at 574
the tax office, and he said to him, "Follow me." And he rose and followed him.

And as he sat at table in his house, many tax collectors and sinners were sitting with Jesus and his disciples; for there were many who followed him. And the scribes of the Pharisees, when they saw that he was eating with sinners and tax collectors, said to his disciples, "Why does he eat with tax collectors and sinners?" And when Jesus heard it, he said to them, "Those who are well have no need of a physician, but those who are sick; I came not to call the righteous, but sinners."

(6) **Mark 3:1–6** Again he entered the synagogue, and a man was there who had 574
a withered hand. And they watched him, to see whether he would heal him on the sabbath, so that they might accuse him. And he said to the man who had the withered hand, "Come here." And he said to them, "Is it lawful on the sabbath to do good or to do harm, to save life or to kill?" But they were silent. And he looked around at them with anger, grieved at their hardness of heart, and said to the man, "Stretch out your hand." He stretched it out, and his hand was restored. The Pharisees went out, and immediately held counsel with the Herodians against him, how to destroy him.

(7) **Mark 7:14–23** And he called the people to him again, and said to them, "Hear 574
me, all of you, and understand: there is nothing outside a man which by going into him can defile him; but the things which come out of a man are what defile him." And when he had entered the house, and left the people, his disciples asked him about the parable. And he said to them, "Then are you also without understanding? Do you not see that whatever goes into a man from outside cannot defile him, since it enters, not his heart but his stomach, and so passes on?" (Thus he declared all foods clean.) And he said, "What comes out of a man is what defiles a man. For from within, out of the heart of man, come evil thoughts, fornication, theft, murder, adultery, coveting, wickedness, deceit, licentiousness, envy, slander, pride, foolishness. All these evil things come from within, and they defile a man."

(8) **Mark 3:22** And the scribes who came down from Jerusalem said, "He is pos- 574
sessed by Beelzebul, and by the prince of demons he casts out the demons."

574 (9) **John 8:48** The Jews answered him, "Are we not right in saying that you are a Samaritan and have a demon?"

574 (10) **John 10:20** Many of them said, "He has a demon, and he is mad; why listen to him?"

574 (11) **Mark 2:7:** see 574 (4).

574 (12) **John 5:18** This was why the Jews sought all the more to kill him, because he not only broke the sabbath but also called God his own Father, making himself equal with God.

574 (13) **John 7:12** And there was much muttering about him among the people. While some said, "He is a good man," others said, "No, he is leading the people astray."

574 (14) **John 7:52** They replied, "Are you from Galilee too? Search and you will see that no prophet is to rise from Galilee."

574 (15) **John 8:59** So they took up stones to throw at him; but Jesus hid himself, and went out of the temple.

574 (16) **John 10:31** The Jews took up stones again to stone him.

574 (17) **John 10:33** The Jews answered him, "It is not for a good work that we stone you but for blasphemy; because you, being a man, make yourself God."

575 (1) **John 1:19** And this is the testimony of John, when the Jews sent priests and Levites from Jerusalem to ask him, "Who are you?"

575 (2) **John 2:18** The Jews then said to him, "What sign have you to show us for doing this?"

575 (3) **John 5:10** So the Jews said to the man who was cured, "It is the sabbath, it is not lawful for you to carry your pallet."

575 (4) **John 7:13** Yet for fear of the Jews no one spoke openly of him.

575 (5) **John 9:22** His parents said this because they feared the Jews, for the Jews had already agreed that if any one should confess him to be Christ, he was to be put out of the synagogue.

575 (6) **John 18:12** So the band of soldiers and their captain and the officers of the Jews seized Jesus and bound him.

575 (7) **John 19:38** After this Joseph of Arimathea, who was a disciple of Jesus, but secretly, for fear of the Jews, asked Pilate that he might take away the body of Jesus, and Pilate gave him leave. So he came and took away his body.

575 (8) **John 20:19** On the evening of that day, the first day of the week, the doors being shut where the disciples were, for fear of the Jews, Jesus came and stood among them and said to them, "Peace be with you."

(9) **John 7:48–49** ". . . Have any of the authorities or of the Pharisees believed in 575
him? But this crowd, who do not know the law, are accursed."

(10) **Luke 13:31** At that very hour some Pharisees came, and said to him, "Get 575
away from here, for Herod wants to kill you."

(11) **Luke 7:36** One of the Pharisees asked him to eat with him, and he went into 575
the Pharisee's house, and took his place at table.

(12) **Luke 14:1** One sabbath when he went to dine at the house of a ruler who 575
belonged to the Pharisees, they were watching him.

(13) **Matthew 22:23–34** The same day Sadducees came to him, who say that there 575
is no resurrection; and they asked him a question, saying, "Teacher, Moses said, 'If a man dies, having no children, his brother must marry the widow, and raise up children for his brother.' Now there were seven brothers among us; the first married, and died, and having no children left his wife to his brother. So too the second and third, down to the seventh. After them all, the woman died. In the resurrection, therefore, to which of the seven will she be wife? For they all had her."

But Jesus answered them, "You are wrong, because you know neither the scriptures nor the power of God. For in the resurrection they neither marry nor are given in marriage, but are like angels in heaven. And as for the resurrection of the dead, have you not read what was said to you by God, 'I am the God of Abraham, and the God of Isaac, and the God of Jacob'? He is not God of the dead, but of the living." And when the crowd heard it, they were astonished at his teaching.

But when the Pharisees heard that he had silenced the Sadducees, they came together.

(14) **Luke 20:39** And some of the scribes answered, "Teacher, you have spoken 575
well."

(15) **Matthew 6:2–18** "Thus, when you give alms, sound no trumpet before you, 575
as the hypocrites do in the synagogues and in the streets, that they may be praised by men. Truly, I say to you, they have received their reward. But when you give alms, do not let your left hand know what your right hand is doing, so that your alms may be in secret; and your Father who sees in secret will reward you.

"And when you pray, you must not be like the hypocrites; for they love to stand and pray in the synagogues and at the street corners, that they may be seen by men. Truly, I say to you, they have received their reward. But when you pray, go into your room and shut the door and pray to your Father who is in secret; and your Father who sees in secret will reward you.

"And in praying do not heap up empty phrases as the Gentiles do; for they think that they will be heard for their many words. Do not be like them, for your Father knows what you need before you ask him. Pray then like this:

> Our Father who art in heaven,
> Hallowed be thy name.
> Thy kingdom come.
> Thy will be done,
>   On earth as it is in heaven.
> Give us this day our daily bread;
> And forgive us our debts,
>   As we also have forgiven our debtors;

And lead us not into temptation,
But deliver us from evil.

For if you forgive men their trespasses, your heavenly Father also will forgive you; but if you do not forgive men their trespasses, neither will your Father forgive your trespasses.

"And when you fast, do not look dismal, like the hypocrites, for they disfigure their faces that their fasting may be seen by men. Truly, I say to you, they have received their reward. But when you fast, anoint your head and wash your face, that your fasting may not be seen by men but by your Father who is in secret; and your Father who sees in secret will reward you. . . ."

575 (16) **Mark 12:28–34** And one of the scribes came up and heard them disputing with one another, and seeing that he answered them well, asked him, "Which commandment is the first of all?" Jesus answered, "The first is, 'Hear, O Israel: The Lord our God, the Lord is one; and you shall love the Lord your God with all your heart, and with all your soul, and with all your mind, and with all your strength.' The second is this, 'You shall love your neighbor as yourself.' There is no other commandment greater than these." And the scribe said to him, "You are right, Teacher; you have truly said that he is one, and there is no other but he; and to love him with all the heart, and with all the understanding, and with all the strength, and to love one's neighbor as oneself, is much more than all whole burnt offerings and sacrifices." And when Jesus saw that he answered wisely, he said to him, "You are not far from the kingdom of God." And after that no one dared to ask him any question.

578 (1) **John 8:46** Which of you convicts me of sin? If I tell the truth, why do you not believe me?

578 (2) **John 7:19** ". . . Did not Moses give you the law? Yet none of you keeps the law. Why do you seek to kill me?"

578 (3) **Acts 13:38–41** ". . . Let it be known to you therefore, brethren, that through this man forgiveness of sins is proclaimed to you, and by him every one that believes is freed from everything from which you could not be freed by the law of Moses. Beware, therefore, lest there come upon you what is said in the prophets:

'Behold, you scoffers, and wonder, and perish;
for I do a deed in your days,
a deed you will never believe, if one declares it to you.'"

578 (4) **Acts 15:10** Now therefore why do you make trial of God by putting a yoke upon the neck of the disciples which neither our fathers nor we have been able to bear?

578 (5) **Galatians 3:10** For all who rely on works of the law are under a curse; for it is written, "Cursed be every one who does not abide by all things written in the book of the law, and do them."

578 (6) **Galatians 5:3** I testify again to every man who receives circumcision that he is bound to keep the whole law.

579 (1) **Romans 10:2** I bear them witness that they have a zeal for God, but it is not enlightened.

(2) **Matthew 15:3–7** He answered them, "And why do you transgress the com- 579
mandment of God for the sake of your tradition? For God commanded, 'Honor your father and your mother,' and, 'He who speaks evil of father or mother, let him surely die.' But you say, 'If any one tells his father or his mother, What you would have gained from me is given to God, he need not honor his father.' So, for the sake of your tradition, you have made void the word of God. You hypocrites! Well did Isaiah prophesy of you, when he said. . . ."

(3) **Luke 11:39–54** And the Lord said to him, "Now you Pharisees cleanse the 579
outside of the cup and of the dish, but inside you are full of extortion and wickedness. You fools! Did not he who made the outside make the inside also? But give for alms those things which are within; and behold, everything is clean for you.

"But woe to you Pharisees! for you tithe mint and rue and every herb, and neglect justice and the love of God; these you ought to have done, without neglecting the others. Woe to you Pharisees! for you love the best seat in the synagogues and salutations in the market places. Woe to you! for you are like graves which are not seen, and men walk over them without knowing it."

One of the lawyers answered him, "Teacher, in saying this you reproach us also." And he said, "Woe to you lawyers also! for you load men with burdens hard to bear, and you yourselves do not touch the burdens with one of your fingers. Woe to you! for you build the tombs of the prophets whom your fathers killed. So you are witnesses and consent to the deeds of your fathers; for they killed them, and you build their tombs. Therefore also the Wisdom of God said, 'I will send them prophets and apostles, some of whom they will kill and persecute,' that the blood of all the prophets, shed from the foundation of the world, may be required of this generation, from the blood of Abel to the blood of Zechariah, who perished between the altar and the sanctuary. Yes, I tell you, it shall be required of this generation. Woe to you lawyers! for you have taken away the key of knowledge; you did not enter yourselves, and you hindered those who were entering."

As he went away from there, the scribes and the Pharisees began to press him hard, and to provoke him to speak of many things, lying in wait for him, to catch at something he might say.

(4) **Isaiah 53:11** 579

. . . he shall see the fruit of the travail
of his soul and be satisfied;
by his knowledge shall the righteous one, my servant,
make many to be accounted righteous;
and he shall bear their iniquities.

(5) **Hebrews 9:15** Therefore he is the mediator of a new covenant, so that those 579
who are called may receive the promised eternal inheritance, since a death has occurred which redeems them from the transgressions under the first covenant.

Galatians 4:4 But when the time had fully come, God sent forth his Son, born of 580
woman, born under the law. . . .

(1) **John 11:28** When she had said this, she went and called her sister Mary, saying 581
quietly, "The Teacher is here and is calling for you."

(2) **John 3:2** This man came to Jesus by night and said to him, "Rabbi, we know 581
that you are a teacher come from God; for no one can do these signs that you do, unless God is with him."

581 (3) **Matthew 22:23–24** The same day Sadducees came to him, who say that there is no resurrection; and they asked him a question, saying, "Teacher, Moses said, 'If a man dies, having no children, his brother must marry the widow, and raise up children for his brother.' . . ."

581 (4) **Matthew 22:34–36** But when the Pharisees heard that he had silenced the Sadducees, they came together. And one of them, a lawyer, asked him a question, to test him. "Teacher, which is the great commandment in the law?"

581 (5) **Matthew 12:5** Or have you not read in the law how on the sabbath the priests in the temple profane the sabbath, and are guiltless?

581 (6) **Matthew 9:12** But when he heard it, he said, "Those who are well have no need of a physician, but those who are sick. . . ."

581 (7) **Mark 2:23–27** One sabbath he was going through the grainfields; and as they made their way his disciples began to pluck heads of grain. And the Pharisees said to him, "Look, why are they doing what is not lawful on the sabbath?" And he said to them, "Have you never read what David did, when he was in need and was hungry, he and those who were with him: how he entered the house of God, when Abiathar was high priest, and ate the bread of the Presence, which it is not lawful for any but the priests to eat, and also gave it to those who were with him?" And he said to them, "The sabbath was made for man, not man for the sabbath. . . ."

581 (8) **Luke 6:6–9** On another sabbath, when he entered the synagogue and taught, a man was there whose right hand was withered. And the scribes and the Pharisees watched him, to see whether he would heal on the sabbath, so that they might find an accusation against him. But he knew their thoughts, and he said to the man who had the withered hand, "Come and stand here." And he rose and stood there. And Jesus said to them, "I ask you, is it lawful on the sabbath to do good or to do harm, to save life or to destroy it?"

581 (9) **John 7:22–23** Moses gave you circumcision (not that it is from Moses, but from the fathers), and you circumcise a man upon the sabbath. If on the sabbath a man receives circumcision, so that the law of Moses may not be broken, are you angry with me because on the sabbath I made a man's whole body well?

581 (10) **Matthew 5:1** Seeing the crowds, he went up on the mountain, and when he sat down his disciples came to him.

581 (11) **Mark 3:8** . . . and Jerusalem and Idumea and from beyond the Jordan and from about Tyre and Sidon a great multitude, hearing all that he did, came to him.

582 (1) **Galatians 3:24** So that the law was our custodian until Christ came, that we might be justified by faith.

582 (2) **John 5:36** But the testimony which I have is greater than that of John; for the works which the Father has granted me to accomplish, these very works which I am doing, bear me witness that the Father has sent me.

582 (3) **John 10:25** Jesus answered them, "I told you, and you do not believe. The works that I do in my Father's name, they bear witness to me. . . ."

(4) **John 10:37–38** ". . . If I am not doing the works of my Father, then do 582
not believe me; but if I do them, even though you do not believe me, believe the works, that you may know and understand that the Father is in me and I am in the Father."

(5) **John 12:37** Though he had done so many signs before them, yet they did not 582
believe in him. . . .

(6) **Numbers 28:9** "On the sabbath day two male lambs a year old without blemish, 582
and two tenths of an ephah of fine flour for a cereal offering, mixed with oil, and its drink offering. . . ."

(7) **Matthew 12:5** Or have you not read in the law how on the sabbath the priests 582
in the temple profane the sabbath, and are guiltless?

(8) **Mark 2:25–27** And he said to them, "Have you never read what David did, 582
when he was in need and was hungry, he and those who were with him: how he entered the house of God, when Abiathar was high priest, and ate the bread of the Presence, which it is not lawful for any but the priests to eat, and also gave it to those who were with him?" And he said to them, "The sabbath was made for man, not man for the sabbath. . . ."

(9) **Luke 13:15–16** Then the Lord answered him, "You hypocrites! Does not each 582
of you on the sabbath untie his ox or his ass from the manger, and lead it away to water it? And ought not this woman, a daughter of Abraham whom Satan bound for eighteen years, be loosed from this bond on the sabbath day?"

(10) **Luke 14:3–4** And Jesus spoke to the lawyers and Pharisees, saying, "Is it lawful 582
to heal on the sabbath, or not?" But they were silent. Then he took him and healed him, and let him go.

(11) **John 7:22–24** ". . . Moses gave you circumcision (not that it is from Moses, 582
but from the fathers), and you circumcise a man upon the sabbath. If on the sabbath a man receives circumcision, so that the law of Moses may not be broken, are you angry with me because on the sabbath I made a man's whole body well? Do not judge by appearances, but judge with right judgment."

(1) **Luke 2:22–39** And when the time came for their purification according to the 583
law of Moses, they brought him up to Jerusalem to present him to the Lord (as it is written in the law of the Lord, "Every male that opens the womb shall be called holy to the Lord") and to offer a sacrifice according to what is said in the law of the Lord, "a pair of turtledoves, or two young pigeons." Now there was a man in Jerusalem, whose name was Simeon, and this man was righteous and devout, looking for the consolation of Israel, and the Holy Spirit was upon him. And it had been revealed to him by the Holy Spirit that he should not see death before he had seen the Lord's Christ. And inspired by the Spirit he came into the temple; and when the parents brought in the child Jesus, to do for him according to the custom of the law, he took him up in his arms and blessed God and said,

"Lord, now lettest thou thy servant depart in peace,
according to thy word;
for mine eyes have seen thy salvation
which thou hast prepared in the presence of all peoples,

a light for revelation to the Gentiles,
and for glory to thy people Israel."

And his father and his mother marveled at what was said about him; and Simeon blessed them and said to Mary his mother,

"Behold, this child is set for the fall and rising of many in Israel,
and for a sign that is spoken against
(and a sword will pierce through your own soul also),
that thoughts out of many hearts may be revealed."

And there was a prophetess, Anna, the daughter of Phanuel, of the tribe of Asher; she was of a great age, having lived with her husband seven years from her virginity, and as a widow till she was eighty-four. She did not depart from the temple, worshiping with fasting and prayer night and day. And coming up at that very hour she gave thanks to God, and spoke of him to all who were looking for the redemption of Jerusalem.

And when they had performed everything according to the law of the Lord, they returned into Galilee, to their own city, Nazareth.

583 (2) **Luke 2:46–49** After three days they found him in the temple, sitting among the teachers, listening to them and asking them questions; and all who heard him were amazed at his understanding and his answers. And when they saw him they were astonished; and his mother said to him, "Son, why have you treated us so? Behold, your father and I have been looking for you anxiously." And he said to them, "How is it that you sought me? Did you not know that I must be in my Father's house?"

583 (3) **Luke 2:41** Now his parents went to Jerusalem every year at the feast of the Passover.

583 (4) **John 2:13–14** The Passover of the Jews was at hand, and Jesus went up to Jerusalem. In the temple he found those who were selling oxen and sheep and pigeons, and the money-changers at their business.

583 (5) **John 5:1** After this there was a feast of the Jews, and Jesus went up to Jerusalem.

583 (6) **John 5:14** Afterward, Jesus found him in the temple, and said to him, "See, you are well! Sin no more, that nothing worse befall you."

583 (7) **John 7:1** After this Jesus went about in Galilee; he would not go about in Judea, because the Jews sought to kill him.

583 (8) **John 7:10** But after his brothers had gone up to the feast, then he also went up, not publicly but in private.

583 (9) **John 7:14** About the middle of the feast Jesus went up into the temple and taught.

583 (10) **John 8:2** Early in the morning he came again to the temple; all the people came to him, and he sat down and taught them.

583 (11) **John 10:22–23** It was the feast of the Dedication at Jerusalem; it was winter, and Jesus was walking in the temple, in the portico of Solomon.

584 (1) **Matthew 21:13** He said to them, "It is written, 'My house shall be called a house of prayer'; but you make it a den of robbers."

(2) **Psalm 69:10** 584
When I humbled my soul with fasting,
it became my reproach.

(3) **Acts 2:46** And day by day, attending the temple together and breaking bread 584
in their homes, they partook of food with glad and generous hearts. . . .

(4) **Acts 3:1** Now Peter and John were going up to the temple at the hour of prayer, 584
the ninth hour.

(5) **Acts 5:20** "Go and stand in the temple and speak to the people all the words 584
of this Life."

(6) **Acts 5:21** And when they heard this, they entered the temple at daybreak and 584
taught.

Now the high priest came and those who were with him and called together the council and all the senate of Israel, and sent to the prison to have them brought.

(1) **Matthew 24:1–2** Jesus left the temple and was going away, when his disciples 585
came to point out to him the buildings of the temple. But he answered them, "You see all these, do you not? Truly, I say to you, there will not be left here one stone upon another, that will not be thrown down."

(2) **Matthew 24:3** As he sat on the Mount of Olives, the disciples came to him 585
privately, saying, "Tell us, when will this be, and what will be the sign of your coming and of the close of the age?"

(3) **Luke 13:35** ". . . Behold, your house is forsaken. And I tell you, you will not 585
see me until you say, 'Blessed is he who comes in the name of the Lord!' "

(4) **Mark 14:57–58** And some stood up and bore false witness against him, saying, 585
"We heard him say, 'I will destroy this temple that is made with hands, and in three days I will build another, not made with hands.' "

(5) **Matthew 27:39–40** And those who passed by derided him, wagging their heads 585
and saying, "You who would destroy the temple and build it in three days, save yourself! If you are the Son of God, come down from the cross."

(1) **Matthew 8:4** And Jesus said to him, "See that you say nothing to any one; but 586
go, show yourself to the priest, and offer the gift that Moses commanded, for a proof to the people."

(2) **Matthew 16:18** And I tell you, you are Peter, and on this rock I will build my 586
church, and the powers of death shall not prevail against it.

(3) **Matthew 17:24–27** When they came to Capernaum, the collectors of the half- 586
shekel tax went up to Peter and said, "Does not your teacher pay the tax?" He said, "Yes." And when he came home, Jesus spoke to him first, saying, "What do you think, Simon? From whom do kings of the earth take toll or tribute? From their sons or from others?" And when he said, "From others," Jesus said to him, "Then the sons are free. However, not to give offense to them, go to the sea and cast a hook, and take the first fish that comes up, and when you open its mouth you will find a shekel; take that and give it to them for me and for yourself."

586 (4) **Luke 17:14** When he saw them he said to them, "Go and show yourselves to the priests." And as they went they were cleansed.

586 (5) **John 4:22** You worship what you do not know; we worship what we know, for salvation is from the Jews.

586 (6) **John 18:20** Jesus answered him, "I have spoken openly to the world; I have always taught in synagogues and in the temple, where all Jews come together; I have said nothing secretly. . . ."

586 (7) **John 2:21** But he spoke of the temple of his body.

586 (8) **Matthew 12:6** I tell you, something greater than the temple is here.

586 (9) **John 2:18–22** The Jews then said to him, "What sign have you to show us for doing this?" Jesus answered them, "Destroy this temple, and in three days I will raise it up." The Jews then said, "It has taken forty-six years to build this temple, and will you raise it up in three days?" But he spoke of the temple of his body. When therefore he was raised from the dead, his disciples remembered that he had said this; and they believed the scripture and the word which Jesus had spoken.

586 (10) **John 4:23–24** ". . . But the hour is coming, and now is, when the true worshipers will worship the Father in spirit and truth, for such the Father seeks to worship him. God is spirit, and those who worship him must worship in spirit and truth."

586 (11) **Matthew 27:51** And behold, the curtain of the temple was torn in two, from top to bottom; and the earth shook, and the rocks were split. . . .

586 (12) **Hebrews 9:11** But when Christ appeared as a high priest of the good things that have come, then through the greater and more perfect tent (not made with hands, that is, not of this creation). . . .

586 (13) **Revelation 21:22** And I saw no temple in the city, for its temple is the Lord God the Almighty and the Lamb.

587 (1) **Luke 2:34** . . . and Simeon blessed them and said to Mary his mother,
"Behold, this child is set for the fall and rising of many in Israel,
and for a sign that is spoken against. . . ."

587 (2) **Luke 20:17–18** But he looked at them and said, "What then is this that is written:
'The very stone which the builders rejected
has become the head of the corner'?
Every one who falls on that stone will be broken to pieces; but when it falls on any one it will crush him."

587 (3) **Psalm 118:22**
The stone which the builders rejected
has become the head of the corner.

588 (1) **Luke 5:30** And the Pharisees and their scribes murmured against his disciples, saying, "Why do you eat and drink with tax collectors and sinners?"

(2) **Luke 7:36** One of the Pharisees asked him to eat with him, and he went into 588
the Pharisee's house, and took his place at table.

(3) **Luke 11:37** While he was speaking, a Pharisee asked him to dine with him; so 588
he went in and sat at table.

(4) **Luke 14:1** One sabbath when he went to dine at the house of a ruler who 588
belonged to the Pharisees, they were watching him.

(5) **John 7:49** ". . . But this crowd, who do not know the law, are accursed." 588

(6) **John 9:34** They answered him, "You were born in utter sin, and would you 588
teach us?" And they cast him out.

(7) **John 8:33–36** They answered him, "We are descendants of Abraham, and have 588
never been in bondage to any one. How is it that you say, 'You will be made free'?"
Jesus answered them, "Truly, truly, I say to you, every one who commits sin is a slave to sin. The slave does not continue in the house for ever; the son continues for ever. So if the Son makes you free, you will be free indeed. . . ."

(8) **John 9:40–41** Some of the Pharisees near him heard this, and they said to him, 588
"Are we also blind?" Jesus said to them, "If you were blind, you would have no guilt; but now that you say, 'We see,' your guilt remains. . . ."

(1) **Matthew 9:13** ". . . Go and learn what this means, 'I desire mercy, and not 589
sacrifice.' For I came not to call the righteous, but sinners."

(2) **Hosea 6:6** 589

For I desire steadfast love and not sacrifice,
the knowledge of God, rather than burnt offerings.

(3) **Luke 15:1–2** Now the tax collectors and sinners were all drawing near to hear 589
him. And the Pharisees and the scribes murmured, saying, "This man receives sinners and eats with them."

(4) **Luke 15:22–32** "But the father said to his servants, 'Bring quickly the best 589
robe, and put it on him; and put a ring on his hand, and shoes on his feet; and bring the fatted calf and kill it, and let us eat and make merry; for this my son was dead, and is alive again; he was lost, and is found.' And they began to make merry.

"Now his elder son was in the field; and as he came and drew near to the house, he heard music and dancing. And he called one of the servants and asked what this meant. And he said to him, 'Your brother has come, and your father has killed the fatted calf, because he has received him safe and sound.' But he was angry and refused to go in. His father came out and entreated him, but he answered his father, 'Lo, these many years I have served you, and I never disobeyed your command; yet you never gave me a kid, that I might make merry with my friends. But when this son of yours came, who has devoured your living with harlots, you killed for him the fatted calf!' And he said to him, 'Son, you are always with me, and all that is mine is yours. It was fitting to make merry and be glad, for this your brother was dead, and is alive; he was lost, and is found.'"

(5) **John 5:18** This was why the Jews sought all the more to kill him, because he 589
not only broke the sabbath but also called God his own Father, making himself equal with God.

589 (6) **John 10:33** The Jews answered him, "It is not for a good work that we stone you but for blasphemy; because you, being a man, make yourself God."

589 (7) **John 17:6** "I have manifested thy name to the men whom thou gavest me out of the world; thine they were, and thou gavest them to me, and they have kept thy word. . . ."

589 (8) **John 17:26** ". . . I made known to them thy name, and I will make it known, that the love with which thou hast loved me may be in them, and I in them."

590 (1) **Matthew 12:6** I tell you, something greater than the temple is here.

590 (2) **Matthew 12:30** He who is not with me is against me, and he who does not gather with me scatters.

590 (3) **Matthew 12:36–37** ". . . I tell you, on the day of judgment men will render account for every careless word they utter; for by your words you will be justified, and by your words you will be condemned."

590 (4) **Matthew 12:41–42** The men of Nineveh will arise at the judgment with this generation and condemn it; for they repented at the preaching of Jonah, and behold, something greater than Jonah is here. The queen of the South will arise at the judgment with this generation and condemn it; for she came from the ends of the earth to hear the wisdom of Solomon, and behold, something greater than Solomon is here.

591 (1) **John 10:36–38** ". . . do you say of him whom the Father consecrated and sent into the world, 'You are blaspheming,' because I said, 'I am the Son of God'? If I am not doing the works of my Father, then do not believe me; but if I do them, even though you do not believe me, believe the works, that you may know and understand that the Father is in me and I am in the Father."

591 (2) **John 3:7** ". . . Do not marvel that I said to you, 'You must be born anew.'. . ."

591 (3) **John 6:44** No one can come to me unless the Father who sent me draws him; and I will raise him up at the last day.

591 (4) **Isaiah 53:1**

Who has believed what we have heard?
And to whom has the arm of the Lord been revealed?

591 (5) **Mark 3:6** The Pharisees went out, and immediately held counsel with the Herodians against him, how to destroy him.

591 (6) **Matthew 26:64–66** Jesus said to him, "You have said so. But I tell you, hereafter you will see the Son of man seated at the right hand of Power, and coming on the clouds of heaven." Then the high priest tore his robes, and said, "He has uttered blasphemy. Why do we still need witnesses? You have now heard his blasphemy. What is your judgment?" They answered, "He deserves death."

591 (7) **Luke 23:34** And Jesus said, "Father, forgive them; for they know not what they do." And they cast lots to divide his garments.

(8) **Acts 3:17–18** "And now, brethren, I know that you acted in ignorance, as did also your rulers. But what God foretold by the mouth of all the prophets, that his Christ should suffer, he thus fulfilled. . . ." 591

(9) **Mark 3:5** And he looked around at them with anger, grieved at their hardness of heart, and said to the man, "Stretch out your hand." He stretched it out, and his hand was restored. 591

(10) **Romans 11:25** Lest you be wise in your own conceits, I want you to understand this mystery, brethren: a hardening has come upon part of Israel, until the full number of the Gentiles come in. . . . 591

(11) **Romans 11:20** That is true. They were broken off because of their unbelief, but you stand fast only through faith. So do not become proud, but stand in awe. 591

(1) **Matthew 5:17–19** "Think not that I have come to abolish the law and the prophets; I have come not to abolish them but to fulfil them. For truly, I say to you, till heaven and earth pass away, not an iota, not a dot, will pass from the law until all is accomplished. Whoever then relaxes one of the least of these commandments and teaches men so, shall be called least in the kingdom of heaven; but he who does them and teaches them shall be called great in the kingdom of heaven. . . ." 592

(2) **John 8:46** Which of you convicts me of sin? If I tell the truth, why do you not believe me? 592

(3) **Matthew 5:33** "Again you have heard that it was said to the men of old, 'You shall not swear falsely, but shall perform to the Lord what you have sworn.' . . ." 592

(4) **Hebrews 9:15** Therefore he is the mediator of a new covenant, so that those who are called may receive the promised eternal inheritance, since a death has occurred which redeems them from the transgressions under the first covenant. 592

(1) **John 5:16–18** And this was why the Jews persecuted Jesus, because he did this on the sabbath. But Jesus answered them, "My Father is working still, and I am working." This was why the Jews sought all the more to kill him, because he not only broke the sabbath but also called God his own Father, making himself equal with God. 594

(2) **John 1:14** And the Word became flesh and dwelt among us, full of grace and truth; we have beheld his glory, glory as of the only Son from the Father. 594

(1) **John 7:50** Nicodemus, who had gone to him before, and who was one of them, said to them. . . . 595

(2) **John 9:16–17** Some of the Pharisees said, "This man is not from God, for he does not keep the sabbath." But others said, "How can a man who is a sinner do such signs?" There was a division among them. So they again said to the blind man, "What do you say about him, since he has opened your eyes?" He said, "He is a prophet." 595

(3) **John 10:19–21** There was again a division among the Jews because of these words. Many of them said, "He has a demon, and he is mad; why listen to him?" Others said, "These are not the sayings of one who has a demon. Can a demon open the eyes of the blind?" 595

595 (4) **John 19:38–39** After this Joseph of Arimathea, who was a disciple of Jesus, but secretly, for fear of the Jews, asked Pilate that he might take away the body of Jesus, and Pilate gave him leave. So he came and took away his body. Nicodemus also, who had at first come to him by night, came bringing a mixture of myrrh and aloes, about a hundred pounds' weight.

596 (1) **John 9:16** Some of the Pharisees said, "This man is not from God, for he does not keep the sabbath." But others said, "How can a man who is a sinner do such signs?" There was a division among them.

596 (2) **John 10:19** There was again a division among the Jews because of these words.

596 (3) **John 9:22** His parents said this because they feared the Jews, for the Jews had already agreed that if any one should confess him to be Christ, he was to be put out of the synagogue.

596 (4) **Matthew 26:66** ". . . What is your judgment?" They answered, "He deserves death."

596 (5) **John 18:31** Pilate said to them, "Take him yourselves and judge him by your own law." The Jews said to him, "It is not lawful for us to put any man to death."

596 (6) **Luke 23:2** And they began to accuse him, saying, "We found this man perverting our nation, and forbidding us to give tribute to Caesar, and saying that he himself is Christ a king."

596 (7) **Lk 23:19** . . . a man who had been thrown into prison for an insurrection started in the city, and for murder.

596 (8) **John 19:12** Upon this Pilate sought to release him, but the Jews cried out, "If you release this man, you are not Caesar's friend; every one who makes himself a king sets himself against Caesar."

596 (9) **John 19:15** They cried out, "Away with him, away with him, crucify him!" Pilate said to them, "Shall I crucify your King?" The chief priests answered, "We have no king but Caesar."

596 (10) **John 19:21** The chief priests of the Jews then said to Pilate, "Do not write, 'The King of the Jews,' but, 'This man said, I am King of the Jews.' "

597 (1) **Mark 15:11** But the chief priests stirred up the crowd to have him release for them Barabbas instead.

597 (2) **Acts 2:23** . . . this Jesus, delivered up according to the definite plan and foreknowledge of God, you crucified and killed by the hands of lawless men.

597 (3) **Acts 2:36** ". . . Let all the house of Israel therefore know assuredly that God has made him both Lord and Christ, this Jesus whom you crucified."

597 (4) **Acts 3:13–14** The God of Abraham and of Isaac and of Jacob, the God of our fathers, glorified his servant Jesus, whom you delivered up and denied in the presence of Pilate, when he had decided to release him. But you denied the Holy and Righteous One, and asked for a murderer to be granted to you. . . .

(5) **Acts 4:10** . . . be it known to you all, and to all the people of Israel, that by 597
the name of Jesus Christ of Nazareth, whom you crucified, whom God raised from the dead, by him this man is standing before you well.

(6) **Acts 5:30** The God of our fathers raised Jesus whom you killed by hanging him 597
on a tree.

(7) **Acts 7:52** Which of the prophets did not your fathers persecute? And they killed 597
those who announced beforehand the coming of the Righteous One, whom you have now betrayed and murdered. . . .

(8) **Acts 10:39** And we are witnesses to all that he did both in the country of the 597
Jews and in Jerusalem. They put him to death by hanging him on a tree. . . .

(9) **Acts 13:27–28** For those who live in Jerusalem and their rulers, because they 597
did not recognize him nor understand the utterances of the prophets which are read every sabbath, fulfilled these by condemning him. Though they could charge him with nothing deserving death, yet they asked Pilate to have him killed.

(10) **1 Thessalonians 2:14–15** For you, brethren, became imitators of the churches 597
of God in Christ Jesus which are in Judea; for you suffered the same things from your own countrymen as they did from the Jews, who killed both the Lord Jesus and the prophets, and drove us out, and displease God and oppose all men. . . .

(11) **Luke 23:34** And Jesus said, "Father, forgive them; for they know not what 597
they do." And they cast lots to divide his garments.

(12) **Acts 3:17** "And now, brethren, I know that you acted in ignorance, as did also 597
your rulers. . . ."

(13) **Acts 5:28** . . . saying, "We strictly charged you not to teach in this name, yet 597
here you have filled Jerusalem with your teaching and you intend to bring this man's blood upon us."

(14) **Acts 18:6** And when they opposed and reviled him, he shook out his garments 597
and said to them, "Your blood be upon your heads! I am innocent. From now on I will go to the Gentiles."

(1) **Hebrews 12:3** Consider him who endured from sinners such hostility against 598
himself, so that you may not grow weary or fainthearted.

(2) **Matthew 25:45** ". . . Then he will answer them, 'Truly, I say to you, as you 598
did it not to one of the least of these, you did it not to me.' . . ."

(3) **Acts 9:4–5** And he fell to the ground and heard a voice saying to him, "Saul, 598
Saul, why do you persecute me?" And he said, "Who are you, Lord?" And he said, "I am Jesus, whom you are persecuting. . . ."

(4) **Hebrews 6:6** . . . if they then commit apostasy, since they crucify the Son of 598
God on their own account and hold him up to contempt.

(5) **1 Corinthians 2:8** None of the rulers of this age understood this; for if they 598
had, they would not have crucified the Lord of glory.

599 **Acts 3:13** The God of Abraham and of Isaac and of Jacob, the God of our fathers, glorified his servant Jesus, whom you delivered up and denied in the presence of Pilate, when he had decided to release him.

600 (1) **Psalm 2:1–2**

Why do the nations conspire,
  and the peoples plot in vain?
The kings of the earth set themselves,
  and the rulers take counsel together,
  against the Lord and his anointed, saying. . . .

600 (2) **Matthew 26:54** ". . . But how then should the scriptures be fulfilled, that it must be so?"

600 (3) **John 18:36** Jesus answered, "My kingship is not of this world; if my kingship were of this world, my servants would fight, that I might not be handed over to the Jews; but my kingship is not from the world."

600 (4) **John 19:11** Jesus answered him, "You would have no power over me unless it had been given you from above; therefore he who delivered me to you has the greater sin."

600 (5) **Acts 3:17–18** "And now, brethren, I know that you acted in ignorance, as did also your rulers. But what God foretold by the mouth of all the prophets, that his Christ should suffer, he thus fulfilled. . . ."

601 (1) **Isaiah 53:11–12**

. . . he shall see the fruit of the travail
  of his soul and be satisfied;
by his knowledge shall the righteous one, my servant,
  make many to be accounted righteous;
  and he shall bear their iniquities.
Therefore I will divide him a portion with the great,
  and he shall divide the spoil with the strong;
because he poured out his soul to death,
  and was numbered with the transgressors;
yet he bore the sin of many,
  and made intercession for the transgressors.

601 (2) **John 8:34–36** Jesus answered them, "Truly, truly, I say to you, every one who commits sin is a slave to sin. The slave does not continue in the house for ever; the son continues for ever. So if the Son makes you free, you will be free indeed. . . ."

601 (3) **Acts 3:14** But you denied the Holy and Righteous One, and asked for a murderer to be granted to you. . . .

601 (4) **Acts 3:18** But what God foretold by the mouth of all the prophets, that his Christ should suffer, he thus fulfilled.

601 (5) **Acts 7:52** Which of the prophets did not your fathers persecute? And they killed those who announced beforehand the coming of the Righteous One, whom you have now betrayed and murdered. . . .

(6) **Acts 13:29** And when they had fulfilled all that was written of him, they took him down from the tree, and laid him in a tomb. **601**

(7) **Acts 26:22–23** ". . . To this day I have had the help that comes from God, and so I stand here testifying both to small and great, saying nothing but what the prophets and Moses said would come to pass: that the Christ must suffer, and that, by being the first to rise from the dead, he would proclaim light both to the people and to the Gentiles." **601**

(8) **Isaiah 53:7–8** **601**

He was oppressed, and he was afflicted,
yet he opened not his mouth;
like a lamb that is led to the slaughter,
and like a sheep that before its shearers is dumb,
so he opened not his mouth.
By oppression and judgment he was taken away;
and as for his generation, who considered
that he was cut off out of the land of the living,
stricken for the transgression of my people?

(9) **Acts 8:32–35** Now the passage of the scripture which he was reading was this: **601**

"As a sheep led to the slaughter
or a lamb before its shearer is dumb,
so he opens not his mouth.
In his humiliation justice was denied him.
Who can describe his generation?
For his life is taken up from the earth."

And the eunuch said to Philip, "About whom, pray, does the prophet say this, about himself or about some one else?" Then Philip opened his mouth, and beginning with this scripture he told him the good news of Jesus.

(10) **Matthew 20:28** ". . . even as the Son of man came not to be served but to serve, and to give his life as a ransom for many." **601**

(11) **Luke 24:25–27** And he said to them, "O foolish men, and slow of heart to believe all that the prophets have spoken! Was it not necessary that the Christ should suffer these things and enter into his glory?" And beginning with Moses and all the prophets, he interpreted to them in all the scriptures the things concerning himself. **601**

(12) **Luke 24:44–45** Then he said to them, "These are my words which I spoke to you, while I was still with you, that everything written about me in the law of Moses and the prophets and the psalms must be fulfilled." Then he opened their minds to understand the scriptures. . . . **601**

(1) **Romans 5:12** Therefore as sin came into the world through one man and death through sin, and so death spread to all men because all men sinned. . . . **602**

(2) **1 Corinthians 15:56** The sting of death is sin, and the power of sin is the law. **602**

(3) **Philippians 2:7** . . . but emptied himself, taking the form of a servant, being born in the likeness of men. **602**

602 (4) **Romans 8:3** For God has done what the law, weakened by the flesh, could not do: sending his own Son in the likeness of sinful flesh and for sin, he condemned sin in the flesh. . . .

603 (1) **John 8:46** Which of you convicts me of sin? If I tell the truth, why do you not believe me?

603 (2) **John 8:29** ". . . And he who sent me is with me; he has not left me alone, for I always do what is pleasing to him."

604 **1 John 4:19** We love, because he first loved us.

605 (1) **Romans 5:18–19** Then as one man's trespass led to condemnation for all men, so one man's act of righteousness leads to acquittal and life for all men. For as by one man's disobedience many were made sinners, so by one man's obedience many will be made righteous.

605 (2) **2 Corinthians 5:15** And he died for all, that those who live might live no longer for themselves but for him who for their sake died and was raised.

605 (3) **1 John 2:2** . . . and he is the expiation for our sins, and not for ours only but also for the sins of the whole world.

607 (1) **Luke 12:50** I have a baptism to be baptized with; and how I am constrained until it is accomplished!

607 (2) **Luke 22:15** And he said to them, "I have earnestly desired to eat this passover with you before I suffer. . . ."

607 (3) **Matthew 16:21–23** From that time Jesus began to show his disciples that he must go to Jerusalem and suffer many things from the elders and chief priests and scribes, and be killed, and on the third day be raised. And Peter took him and began to rebuke him, saying, "God forbid, Lord! This shall never happen to you." But he turned and said to Peter, "Get behind me, Satan! You are a hindrance to me; for you are not on the side of God, but of men."

608 (1) **Luke 3:21** Now when all the people were baptized, and when Jesus also had been baptized and was praying, the heaven was opened. . . .

608 (2) **Matthew 3:14–15** John would have prevented him, saying, "I need to be baptized by you, and do you come to me?" But Jesus answered him, "Let it be so now; for thus it is fitting for us to fulfil all righteousness." Then he consented.

608 (3) **John 1:36** . . . and he looked at Jesus as he walked, and said, "Behold, the Lamb of God!"

608 (4) **Jeremiah 11:19**

But I was like a gentle lamb
led to the slaughter.
I did not know it was against me
they devised schemes, saying,
"Let us destroy the tree with its fruit,
let us cut him off from the land of the living,
that his name be remembered no more."

(5) **Exodus 12:3–14** ". . . Tell all the congregation of Israel that on the tenth day of this month they shall take every man a lamb according to their fathers' houses, a lamb for a household; and if the household is too small for a lamb, then a man and his neighbor next to his house shall take according to the number of persons; according to what each can eat you shall make your count for the lamb. Your lamb shall be without blemish, a male a year old; you shall take it from the sheep or from the goats; and you shall keep it until the fourteenth day of this month, when the whole assembly of the congregation of Israel shall kill their lambs in the evening. Then they shall take some of the blood, and put it on the two doorposts and the lintel of the houses in which they eat them. They shall eat the flesh that night, roasted; with unleavened bread and bitter herbs they shall eat it. Do not eat any of it raw or boiled with water, but roasted, its head with its legs and its inner parts. And you shall let none of it remain until the morning, anything that remains until the morning you shall burn. In this manner you shall eat it: your loins girded, your sandals on your feet, and your staff in your hand; and you shall eat it in haste. It is the Lord's passover. For I will pass through the land of Egypt that night, and I will smite all the first-born in the land of Egypt, both man and beast; and on all the gods of Egypt I will execute judgments: I am the Lord. The blood shall be a sign for you, upon the houses where you are; and when I see the blood, I will pass over you, and no plague shall fall upon you to destroy you, when I smite the land of Egypt. **608**

"This day shall be for you a memorial day, and you shall keep it as a feast to the Lord; throughout your generations you shall observe it as an ordinance for ever. . . ."

(6) **John 19:36** For these things took place that the scripture might be fulfilled, "Not a bone of him shall be broken." **608**

(7) **1 Corinthians 5:7** Cleanse out the old leaven that you may be a new lump, as you really are unleavened. For Christ, our paschal lamb, has been sacrificed. **608**

(1) **Hebrews 2:10** For it was fitting that he, for whom and by whom all things exist, in bringing many sons to glory, should make the pioneer of their salvation perfect through suffering. **609**

(2) **Hebrews 2:17–18** Therefore he had to be made like his brethren in every respect, so that he might become a merciful and faithful high priest in the service of God, to make expiation for the sins of the people. For because he himself has suffered and been tempted, he is able to help those who are tempted. **609**

(3) **Hebrews 4:15** For we have not a high priest who is unable to sympathize with our weaknesses, but one who in every respect has been tempted as we are, yet without sin. **609**

(4) **Hebrews 5:7–9** In the days of his flesh, Jesus offered up prayers and supplications, with loud cries and tears, to him who was able to save him from death, and he was heard for his godly fear. Although he was a Son, he learned obedience through what he suffered; and being made perfect he became the source of eternal salvation to all who obey him. . . . **609**

(5) **John 18:4–6** Then Jesus, knowing all that was to befall him, came forward and said to them, "Whom do you seek?" They answered him, "Jesus of Nazareth." Jesus said to them, "I am he." Judas, who betrayed him, was standing with them. When he said to them, "I am he," they drew back and fell to the ground. **609**

609 (6) **Matthew 26:53** Do you think that I cannot appeal to my Father, and he will at once send me more than twelve legions of angels?

610 (1) **Matthew 26:20** When it was evening, he sat at table with the twelve disciples. . . .

610 (2) **1 Corinthians 11:23** For I received from the Lord what I also delivered to you, that the Lord Jesus on the night when he was betrayed took bread. . . .

610 (3) **1 Corinthians 5:7** Cleanse out the old leaven that you may be a new lump, as you really are unleavened. For Christ, our paschal lamb, has been sacrificed.

611 (1) **Luke 22:19** And he took bread, and when he had given thanks he broke it and gave it to them, saying, "This is my body which is given for you. Do this in remembrance of me."

611 (2) **Council of Trent (1562): DS 1752** If anyone says that by these words: "Do this for a commemoration of me" [Luke 22:19; I Cor. 11:24], Christ did not make the apostles priests, or did not ordain that they and other priests might offer His own body and blood: let him be anathema.

611 (3) **Council of Trent (1563): DS 1764** Sacrifice and priesthood are so united by the ordinance of God that both have existed in every law. Since, therefore, in the New Testament the Catholic Church has received from the institution of the Lord the holy, visible sacrifice of the Eucharist, it must also be confessed that there is in this Church a new visible and external priesthood [can. 1], into which the old has been translated [Heb. 7:12]. Moreover, that this was instituted by that same Lord our Savior [can. 3], and that to the apostles and their successors in the priesthood was handed down the power of consecrating, of offering and administering His body and blood, and also of forgiving and retaining sins, the Sacred Scriptures show and the tradition of the Catholic Church has always taught [can. 1].

612 (1) **Matthew 26:42** Again, for the second time, he went away and prayed, "My Father, if this cannot pass unless I drink it, thy will be done."

612 (2) **Luke 22:20** And likewise the cup after supper, saying, "This cup which is poured out for you is the new covenant in my blood. . . ."

612 (3) **Hebrews 5:7–8** In the days of his flesh, Jesus offered up prayers and supplications, with loud cries and tears, to him who was able to save him from death, and he was heard for his godly fear. Although he was a Son, he learned obedience through what he suffered. . . .

612 (4) **Romans 5:12** Therefore as sin came into the world through one man and death through sin, and so death spread to all men because all men sinned. . . .

612 (5) **Hebrews 4:15** For we have not a high priest who is unable to sympathize with our weaknesses, but one who in every respect has been tempted as we are, yet without sin.

612 (6) **Acts 3:15** . . . and killed the Author of life, whom God raised from the dead. To this we are witnesses.

(7) **Revelation 1:17** When I saw him, I fell at his feet as though dead. But he laid his right hand upon me, saying, "Fear not, I am the first and the last. . . . 612

(8) **John 1:4** In him was life, and the life was the light of men. 612

(9) **John 5:26** For as the Father has life in himself, so he has granted the Son also to have life in himself. . . . 612

(10) **Matthew 26:42** Again, for the second time, he went away and prayed, "My Father, if this cannot pass unless I drink it, thy will be done." 612

(1) **John 8:34–36** Jesus answered them, "Truly, truly, I say to you, every one who commits sin is a slave to sin. The slave does not continue in the house for ever; the son continues for ever. So if the Son makes you free, you will be free indeed. . . ." 613

(2) **1 Corinthians 5:7** Cleanse out the old leaven that you may be a new lump, as you really are unleavened. For Christ, our paschal lamb, has been sacrificed. 613

(3) **1 Peter 1:19** . . . but with the precious blood of Christ, like that of a lamb without blemish or spot. 613

(4) **Exodus 24:8** And Moses took the blood and threw it upon the people, and said, "Behold the blood of the covenant which the Lord has made with you in accordance with all these words." 613

(5) **Leviticus 16:15–16** "Then he shall kill the goat of the sin offering which is for the people, and bring its blood within the veil, and do with its blood as he did with the blood of the bull, sprinkling it upon the mercy seat and before the mercy seat; thus he shall make atonement for the holy place, because of the uncleannesses of the people of Israel, and because of their transgressions, all their sins; and so he shall do for the tent of meeting, which abides with them in the midst of their uncleannesses. . . ." 613

(6) **1 Corinthians 11:25** In the same way also the cup, after supper, saying, "This cup is the new covenant in my blood. Do this, as often as you drink it, in remembrance of me." 613

(1) **Hebrews 10:10** And by that will we have been sanctified through the offering of the body of Jesus Christ once for all. 614

(2) **John 10:17–18** ". . . For this reason the Father loves me, because I lay down my life, that I may take it again. No one takes it from me, but I lay it down of my own accord. I have power to lay it down, and I have power to take it again; this charge I have received from my Father." 614

(3) **John 15:13** Greater love has no man than this, that a man lay down his life for his friends. 614

(4) **Hebrews 9:14** . . . how much more shall the blood of Christ, who through the eternal Spirit offered himself without blemish to God, purify your conscience from dead works to serve the living God. 614

(5) **1 John 4:10** In this is love, not that we loved God but that he loved us and sent his Son to be the expiation for our sins. 614

615 **Council of Trent (1547): DS 1529** The causes of this justification are: the final cause indeed is the glory of God and of Christ and life eternal; the efficient cause is truly a merciful God who gratuitously "washes and sanctifies" [I Cor. 6:11], "signing and anointing with the Holy Spirit of promise, who is the pledge of our inheritance" [Eph. 1:13 f.]; but the meritorious cause is His most beloved only-begotten Son, our Lord Jesus Christ, "who when we were enemies" [cf. Rom. 5:10], "for the exceeding charity wherewith he loved us" [Eph. 2:4], merited justification for us [can. 10] by His most holy passion on the wood of the Cross, and made satisfaction for us to God the Father; the instrumental cause is the sacrament of baptism, which is the "sacrament of faith," without which no one is ever justified. Finally the unique formal cause is the "justice of God, not that by which He Himself is just, but by which He makes us just" [can. 10 and 11], that, namely, by which, when we are endowed with it by him, we are renewed in the spirit of our mind, and not only are we reputed, but we are truly called and are just, receiving justice within us, each one according to his own measure, which the "Holy Spirit distributes to everyone as he wills" [I Cor. 12:11], and according to each one's own disposition and cooperation.

616 (1) **Galatians 2:20** I have been crucified with Christ; it is no longer I who live, but Christ who lives in me; and the life I now live in the flesh I live by faith in the Son of God, who loved me and gave himself for me.

616 (2) **Ephesians 5:2** And walk in love, as Christ loved us and gave himself up for us, a fragrant offering and sacrifice to God.

616 (3) **Ephesians 5:25** Husbands, love your wives, as Christ loved the church and gave himself up for her. . . .

618 (1) ***Gaudium et spes* 22, 2** He who is the "image of the invisible God" (Col. 1:15), is himself the perfect man who has restored in the children of Adam that likeness to God which had been disfigured ever since the first sin. Human nature, by the very fact that it was assumed, not absorbed, in him, has been raised in us also to a dignity beyond compare. For, by his incarnation, he, the son of God, has in a certain way united himself with each man. He worked with human hands, he thought with a human mind. He acted with a human will, and with a human heart he loved. Born of the Virgin Mary, he has truly been made one of us, like to us in all things except sin.

618 (2) **Mark 10:39** And they said to him, "We are able." And Jesus said to them, "The cup that I drink you will drink; and with the baptism with which I am baptized, you will be baptized. . . ."

618 (3) **John 21:18–19** ". . . Truly, truly, I say to you, when you were young, you girded yourself and walked where you would; but when you are old, you will stretch out your hands, and another will gird you and carry you where you do not wish to go." (This he said to show by what death he was to glorify God.) And after this he said to him, "Follow me."

618 (4) **Colossians 1:24** Now I rejoice in my sufferings for your sake, and in my flesh I complete what is lacking in Christ's afflictions for the sake of his body, that is, the church. . . .

618 (5) **Luke 2:35**

". . . (and a sword will pierce through your own soul also),
that thoughts out of many hearts may be revealed."

(1) **Isaiah 53:10** 623

Yet it was the will of the Lord to bruise him;
he has put him to grief;
when he makes himself an offering for sin,
he shall see his offspring, he shall prolong his days;
the will of the Lord shall prosper in his hand. . . .

(2) **Romans 5:19** For as by one man's disobedience many were made sinners, so 623
by one man's obedience many will be made righteous.

(1) **John 19:42** So because of the Jewish day of Preparation, as the tomb was close 624
at hand, they laid Jesus there.

(2) **Hebrews 4:4–9** For he has somewhere spoken of the seventh day in this way, 624
"And God rested on the seventh day from all his works." And again in this place he said, "They shall never enter my rest." Since therefore it remains for some to enter it, and those who formerly received the good news failed to enter because of disobedience, again he sets a certain day, "Today," saying through David so long afterward, in the words already quoted,

"Today, when you hear his voice, do not harden your hearts."

For if Joshua had given them rest, God would not speak later of another day. So then, there remains a sabbath rest for the people of God. . . .

(3) **John 19:30** When Jesus had received the vinegar, he said, "It is finished"; and 624
he bowed his head and gave up his spirit.

(4) **Colossians 1:18–20** He is the head of the body, the church; he is the beginning, 624
the first-born from the dead, that in everything he might be pre-eminent for in him all the fulness of God was pleased to dwell, and through him to reconcile to himself all things, whether on earth or in heaven, making peace by the blood of his cross.

(1) **Psalm 16:9–10** 627

Therefore my heart is glad, and my soul rejoices;
my body also dwells secure.
For thou dost not give me up to Sheol,
or let thy godly one see the Pit.

(2) **1 Corinthians 15:4** . . . that he was buried, that he was raised on the third day 627
in accordance with the scriptures. . . .

(3) **Luke 24:46** . . . and said to them, "Thus it is written, that the Christ should 627
suffer and on the third day rise from the dead. . . ."

(4) **Matthew 12:40** For as Jonah was three days and three nights in the belly of 627
the whale, so will the Son of man be three days and three nights in the heart of the earth.

(5) **Jonah 2:1 (1:17: RSV)** And the Lord appointed a great fish to swallow up 627
Jonah; and Jonah was in the belly of the fish three days and three nights.

(6) **Hosea 6:2** 627

After two days he will revive us;
on the third day he will raise us up,
that we may live before him.

627 (7) **John 11:39** Jesus said, "Take away the stone." Martha, the sister of the dead man, said to him, "Lord, by this time there will be an odor, for he has been dead four days."

628 (1) **Colossians 2:12** . . . and you were buried with him in baptism, in which you were also raised with him through faith in the working of God, who raised him from the dead.

628 (2) **Ephesians 5:26** . . . that he might sanctify her, having cleansed her by the washing of water with the word. . . .

629 **Hebrews 2:9** But we see Jesus, who for a little while was made lower than the angels, crowned with glory and honor because of the suffering of death, so that by the grace of God he might taste death for every one.

632 (1) **Hebrews 13:20** Now may the God of peace who brought again from the dead our Lord Jesus, the great shepherd of the sheep, by the blood of the eternal covenant. . . .

632 (2) **1 Peter 3:18–19** For Christ also died for sins once for all, the righteous for the unrighteous, that he might bring us to God, being put to death in the flesh but made alive in the spirit; in which he went and preached to the spirits in prison. . . .

633 (1) **Philippians 2:10** . . . that at the name of Jesus every knee should bow, in heaven and on earth and under the earth. . . .

633 (2) **Acts 2:24** But God raised him up, having loosed the pangs of death, because it was not possible for him to be held by it.

633 (3) **Revelation 1:18** . . . and the living one; I died, and behold I am alive for evermore, and I have the keys of Death and Hades.

633 (4) **Ephesians 4:9** (In saying, "He ascended," what does it mean but that he had also descended into the lower parts of the earth? . . .)

633 (5) **Psalm 6:6 (6:5: RSV)**

For in death there is no remembrance of thee;
in Sheol who can give thee praise?

633 (6) **Psalm 88:11–13 (88:10–12: RSV)**

Dost thou work wonders for the dead?
Do the shades rise up to praise thee? *Selah*
Is thy steadfast love declared in the grave,
or thy faithfulness in Abaddon?
Are thy wonders known in the darkness,
or thy saving help in the land of forgetfulness?

633 (7) **Psalm 89:49 (89:48: RSV)**

What man can live and never see death?
Who can deliver his soul from the power of Sheol? *Selah*

(8) **1 Samuel 28:19** "... Moreover the Lord will give Israel also with you into the 633
hand of the Philistines; and tomorrow you and your sons shall be with me; the Lord will give the army of Israel also into the hand of the Philistines."

(9) **Ezekiel 32:17–32** In the twelfth year, in the first month, on the fifteenth day of 633
the month, the word of the Lord came to me: "Son of man, wail over the multitude of Egypt, and send them down, her and the daughters of majestic nations, to the nether world, to those who have gone down to the Pit:

'Whom do you surpass in beauty?
Go down, and be laid with the uncircumcised.'

They shall fall amid those who are slain by the sword, and with her shall lie all her multitudes. The mighty chiefs shall speak of them, with their helpers, out of the midst of Sheol: 'They have come down, they lie still, the uncircumcised, slain by the sword.'

"Assyria is there, and all her company, their graves round about her, all of them slain, fallen by the sword; whose graves are set in the uttermost parts of the Pit, and her company is round about her grave; all of them slain, fallen by the sword, who spread terror in the land of the living.

"Elam is there, and all her multitude about her grave; all of them slain, fallen by the sword, who went down uncircumcised into the nether world, who spread terror in the land of the living, and they bear their shame with those who go down to the Pit. They have made her a bed among the slain with all her multitude, their graves round about her, all of them uncircumcised, slain by the sword; for terror of them was spread in the land of the living, and they bear their shame with those who go down to the Pit; they are placed among the slain.

"Meshech and Tubal are there, and all their multitude, their graves round about them, all of them uncircumcised, slain by the sword; for they spread terror in the land of the living. And they do not lie with the fallen mighty men of old who went down to Sheol with their weapons of war, whose swords were laid under their heads, and whose shields are upon their bones; for the terror of the mighty men was in the land of the living. So you shall be broken and lie among the uncircumcised, with those who are slain by the sword.

"Edom is there, her kings and all her princes, who for all their might are laid with those who are slain by the sword; they lie with the uncircumcised, with those who go down to the Pit.

"The princes of the north are there, all of them, and all the Sidonians, who have gone down in shame with the slain, for all the terror which they caused by their might; they lie uncircumcised with those who are slain by the sword, and bear their shame with those who go down to the Pit.

"When Pharaoh sees them, he will comfort himself for all his multitude, Pharaoh and all his army, slain by the sword, says the Lord God. For he spread terror in the land of the living; therefore he shall be laid among the uncircumcised, with those who are slain by the sword, Pharaoh and all his multitude, says the Lord God."

(10) **Luke 16:22–26** "... The poor man died and was carried by the angels to 633
Abraham's bosom. The rich man also died and was buried; and in Hades, being in torment, he lifted up his eyes, and saw Abraham far off and Lazarus in his bosom. And he called out, 'Father Abraham, have mercy upon me, and send Lazarus to dip the end of his finger in water and cool my tongue; for I am in anguish in this flame.' But Abraham said, 'Son, remember that you in your lifetime received your good things, and Lazarus in like manner evil things; but now he is comforted here, and you are in anguish. And besides all this, between us and you a great chasm has been fixed, in

order that those who would pass from here to you may not be able, and none may cross from there to us.'. . ."

633 (11) **Council of Rome (745): DS 587** Clement, who in his ignorance of the holy Fathers rejects their writings and synodal acts, imputes Judaism to Christians when he preaches that a man may marry the widow of his deceased brother, and then preaches that Christ, in his descent into hell, led out everyone, the just and the wicked, is to be deprived of all priestly faculties and placed under anathema.

633 (12) **Benedict XII, libellus *Cum dudum* (1341): DS 1011** Also that the Armenians believe and hold that Christ descended from heaven and became incarnate for the salvation of men, not on account of the fact that the sons propagated from Adam and Eve after their sin contracted from them original sin, from which through the incarnation and death of Christ they will be saved, since they say that no such sin exists in the sons of Adam; but they say that Christ for the salvation of man became incarnate and suffered, because through His passion the sons of Adam who preceded the aforesaid passion have been freed from hell in which they were, not because of original sin which was in them, but because of the gravity of the personal sin of our first parents. They also believe that Christ for the salvation of children who were born after His passion became incarnate and suffered, because by His passion He entirely destroyed hell. . . .

633 (13) **Clement VI, letter "*Super quibusdam*" (1351): DS 1077** Thirteenth, that Christ did not destroy a lower hell by descending into hell.

633 (14) **Council of Toledo IV (625): DS 485** According to the divine Scriptures and the doctrine we have received from the holy Fathers, we confess that the Father, Son, and Holy Spirit are of one divinity and substance; believing in the difference of persons, preaching oneness in divinity, we neither confuse the persons nor divide the substance. We say that the Father is neither made nor begotten by anyone, but we affirm that the Son is not made but begotten of the Father, and we profess that the Spirit is in truth neither created nor begotten but proceeds from the Father and the Son, but that the Son himself, our Lord Jesus Christ Son of God and creator of all, was begotten of the substance of the Father before all ages and came down in the final age for the world's redemption from the Father, but never ceased being with the Father; for he was incarnate from the Holy Spirit and the holy and glorious virgin Mary Mother of God and was alone born of her; likewise Christ the Lord Jesus, one of the Trinity, took up a man complete with soul and flesh, remaining what he was, taking up what he was not, equal to the Father according to his divinity, less than the Father according to his humanity, possessing in one person the properties of two natures; for there were in him two natures, God and man, but there were not two sons or two gods, but he himself was one person in two natures; suffering passion and death for our salvation, not in virtue of his divinity, but in the weakness of his humanity, he descended into hell to lead out the saints who were held there, and having overcome the dominion of death, he rose; then he was assumed into heaven and he will come again to judge the living and the dead; cleansed by his death and blood we have received the remission of sins; we will be raised by him on the last day in the flesh in which we now live and in the form in which the Lord himself arose, to receive from him eternal life for the merits of justice or the sentence of eternal punishment for sins. This is the faith of the Catholic Church; we maintain and hold this confession, and whoever preserves this most firmly will have everlasting salvation.

(15) **Matthew 27:52–53** . . . the tombs also were opened, and many bodies of 633
the saints who had fallen asleep were raised, and coming out of the tombs after his resurrection they went into the holy city and appeared to many.

(1) **Matthew 12:40** For as Jonah was three days and three nights in the belly of 635
the whale, so will the Son of man be three days and three nights in the heart of the earth.

(2) **Romans 10:7** . . . or "Who will descend into the abyss?" (that is, to bring 635
Christ up from the dead).

(3) **Ephesians 4:9** (In saying, "He ascended," what does it mean but that he had 635
also descended into the lower parts of the earth? . . .)

(4) **Acts 3:15** . . . and killed the Author of life, whom God raised from the dead. 635
To this we are witnesses.

Acts 9:3–18 Now as he journeyed he approached Damascus, and suddenly a light 639
from heaven flashed about him. And he fell to the ground and heard a voice saying to him, "Saul, Saul, why do you persecute me?" And he said, "Who are you, Lord?" And he said, "I am Jesus, whom you are persecuting; but rise and enter the city, and you will be told what you are to do." The men who were traveling with him stood speechless, hearing the voice but seeing no one. Saul arose from the ground; and when his eyes were opened, he could see nothing; so they led him by the hand and brought him into Damascus. And for three days he was without sight, and neither ate nor drank.

Now there was a disciple at Damascus named Ananias. The Lord said to him in a vision, "Ananias." And he said, "Here I am, Lord." And the Lord said to him, "Rise and go to the street called Straight, and inquire in the house of Judas for a man of Tarsus named Saul; for behold, he is praying, and he has seen a man named Ananias come in and lay his hands on him so that he might regain his sight." But Ananias answered, "Lord, I have heard from many about this man, how much evil he has done to thy saints at Jerusalem; and here he has authority from the chief priests to bind all who call upon thy name." But the Lord said to him, "Go, for he is a chosen instrument of mine to carry my name before the Gentiles and kings and the sons of Israel; for I will show him how much he must suffer for the sake of my name." So Ananias departed and entered the house. And laying his hands on him he said, "Brother Saul, the Lord Jesus who appeared to you on the road by which you came, has sent me that you may regain your sight and be filled with the Holy Spirit." And immediately something like scales fell from his eyes and he regained his sight. Then he rose and was baptized. . . .

(1) **John 20:13** They said to her, "Woman, why are you weeping?" She said to 640
them, "Because they have taken away my Lord, and I do not know where they have laid him."

(2) **Matthew 28:11–15** While they were going, behold, some of the guard went 640
into the city and told the chief priests all that had taken place. And when they had assembled with the elders and taken counsel, they gave a sum of money to the soldiers and said, "Tell people, 'His disciples came by night and stole him away while we were asleep.' And if this comes to the governor's ears, we will satisfy him and keep you out of trouble." So they took the money and did as they were directed; and this story has been spread among the Jews to this day.

640 (3) **Luke 24:3** . . . but when they went in they did not find the body.

640 (4) **Luke 24:12** But Peter rose and ran to the tomb; stooping and looking in, he saw the linen cloths by themselves; and he went home wondering at what had happened.

640 (5) **Luke 24:22–23** Moreover, some women of our company amazed us. They were at the tomb early in the morning and did not find his body; and they came back saying that they had even seen a vision of angels, who said that he was alive.

640 (6) **John 11:44** The dead man came out, his hands and feet bound with bandages, and his face wrapped with a cloth. Jesus said to them, "Unbind him, and let him go."

640 (7) **John 20:5–7** . . . and stooping to look in, he saw the linen cloths lying there, but he did not go in. Then Simon Peter came, following him, and went into the tomb; he saw the linen cloths lying, and the napkin, which had been on his head, not lying with the linen cloths but rolled up in a place by itself.

641 (1) **Luke 24:9–10** . . . and returning from the tomb they told all this to the eleven and to all the rest. Now it was Mary Magdalene and Joanna and Mary the mother of James and the other women with them who told this to the apostles. . . .

641 (2) **Matthew 28:9–10** And behold, Jesus met them and said, "Hail!" And they came up and took hold of his feet and worshiped him. Then Jesus said to them, "Do not be afraid; go and tell my brethren to go to Galilee, and there they will see me."

641 (3) **John 20:11–18** But Mary stood weeping outside the tomb, and as she wept she stooped to look into the tomb; and she saw two angels in white, sitting where the body of Jesus had lain, one at the head and one at the feet. They said to her, "Woman, why are you weeping?" She said to them, "Because they have taken away my Lord, and I do not know where they have laid him." Saying this, she turned round and saw Jesus standing, but she did not know that it was Jesus. Jesus said to her, "Woman, why are you weeping? Whom do you seek?" Supposing him to be the gardener, she said to him, "Sir, if you have carried him away, tell me where you have laid him, and I will take him away." Jesus said to her, "Mary." She turned and said to him in Hebrew, "Rabboni!" (which means Teacher). Jesus said to her, "Do not hold me, for I have not yet ascended to the Father; but go to my brethren and say to them, I am ascending to my Father and your Father, to my God and your God." Mary Magdalene went and said to the disciples, "I have seen the Lord"; and she told them that he had said these things to her.

641 (4) **1 Corinthians 15:5** . . . and that he appeared to Cephas, then to the twelve.

641 (5) **Luke 22:31–32** "Simon, Simon, behold, Satan demanded to have you, that he might sift you like wheat, but I have prayed for you that your faith may not fail; and when you have turned again, strengthen your brethren."

642 **Acts 1:22** ". . . beginning from the baptism of John until the day when he was taken up from us—one of these men must become with us a witness to his resurrection."

643 (1) **Luke 22:31–32** "Simon, Simon, behold, Satan demanded to have you, that he might sift you like wheat, but I have prayed for you that your faith may not fail; and when you have turned again, strengthen your brethren."

(2) **John 20:19** On the evening of that day, the first day of the week, the doors being shut where the disciples were, for fear of the Jews, Jesus came and stood among them and said to them, "Peace be with you." **643**

(3) **Mark 16:11** But when they heard that he was alive and had been seen by her, they would not believe it. **643**

(4) **Mark 16:13** And they went back and told the rest, but they did not believe them. **643**

(1) **John 20:24–27** Now Thomas, one of the twelve, called the Twin, was not with them when Jesus came. So the other disciples told him, "We have seen the Lord." But he said to them, "Unless I see in his hands the print of the nails, and place my finger in the mark of the nails, and place my hand in his side, I will not believe." **644**

Eight days later, his disciples were again in the house, and Thomas was with them. The doors were shut, but Jesus came and stood among them, and said, "Peace be with you." Then he said to Thomas, "Put your finger here, and see my hands; and put out your hand, and place it in my side; do not be faithless, but believing."

(2) **Matthew 28:17** And when they saw him they worshiped him; but some doubted. **644**

(1) **Luke 24:30** When he was at table with them, he took the bread and blessed, and broke it, and gave it to them. **645**

(2) **Luke 24:39–43** ". . . See my hands and my feet, that it is I myself; handle me, and see; for a spirit has not flesh and bones as you see that I have." And when he had said this, he showed them his hands and his feet. And while they still disbelieved for joy, and wondered, he said to them, "Have you anything here to eat?" They gave him a piece of broiled fish, and he took it and ate before them. **645**

(3) **John 20:20** When he had said this, he showed them his hands and his side. Then the disciples were glad when they saw the Lord. **645**

(4) **John 20:27** Then he said to Thomas, "Put your finger here, and see my hands; and put out your hand, and place it in my side; do not be faithless, but believing." **645**

(5) **John 21:9** When they got out on land, they saw a charcoal fire there, with fish lying on it, and bread. **645**

(6) **John 21:13–15** Jesus came and took the bread and gave it to them, and so with the fish. This was now the third time that Jesus was revealed to the disciples after he was raised from the dead. **645**

When they had finished breakfast, Jesus said to Simon Peter, "Simon, son of John, do you love me more than these?" He said to him, "Yes, Lord; you know that I love you." He said to him, "Feed my lambs."

(7) **Matthew 28:9** And behold, Jesus met them and said, "Hail!" And they came up and took hold of his feet and worshiped him. **645**

(8) **Matthew 28:16–17** Now the eleven disciples went to Galilee, to the mountain to which Jesus had directed them. And when they saw him they worshiped him; but some doubted. **645**

645 (9) **Luke 24:15** While they were talking and discussing together, Jesus himself drew near and went with them.

645 (10) **Luke 24:36** As they were saying this, Jesus himself stood among them.

645 (11) **John 20:14** Saying this, she turned round and saw Jesus standing, but she did not know that it was Jesus.

645 (12) **John 20:17** Jesus said to her, "Do not hold me, for I have not yet ascended to the Father; but go to my brethren and say to them, I am ascending to my Father and your Father, to my God and your God."

645 (13) **John 20:19** On the evening of that day, the first day of the week, the doors being shut where the disciples were, for fear of the Jews, Jesus came and stood among them and said to them, "Peace be with you."

645 (14) **John 20:26** Eight days later, his disciples were again in the house, and Thomas was with them. The doors were shut, but Jesus came and stood among them, and said, "Peace be with you."

645 (15) **John 21:4** Just as day was breaking, Jesus stood on the beach; yet the disciples did not know that it was Jesus.

645 (16) **Mark 16:12** After this he appeared in another form to two of them, as they were walking into the country.

645 (17) **John 20:14–16** Saying this, she turned round and saw Jesus standing, but she did not know that it was Jesus. Jesus said to her, "Woman, why are you weeping? Whom do you seek?" Supposing him to be the gardener, she said to him, "Sir, if you have carried him away, tell me where you have laid him, and I will take him away." Jesus said to her, "Mary." She turned and said to him in Hebrew, "Rabboni!" (which means Teacher).

645 (18) **John 21:4** Just as day was breaking, Jesus stood on the beach; yet the disciples did not know that it was Jesus.

645 (19) **John 21:7** That disciple whom Jesus loved said to Peter, "It is the Lord!" When Simon Peter heard that it was the Lord, he put on his clothes, for he was stripped for work, and sprang into the sea.

646 **1 Corinthians 15:35–50** But some one will ask, "How are the dead raised? With what kind of body do they come?" You foolish man! What you sow does not come to life unless it dies. And what you sow is not the body which is to be, but a bare kernel, perhaps of wheat or of some other grain. But God gives it a body as he has chosen, and to each kind of seed its own body. For not all flesh is alike, but there is one kind for men, another for animals, another for birds, and another for fish. There are celestial bodies and there are terrestrial bodies; but the glory of the celestial is one, and the glory of the terrestrial is another. There is one glory of the sun, and another glory of the moon, and another glory of the stars; for star differs from star in glory.

So is it with the resurrection of the dead. What is sown is perishable, what is raised is imperishable. It is sown in dishonor, it is raised in glory. It is sown in weakness, it is raised in power. It is sown a physical body, it is raised a spiritual body. If there is a physical body, there is also a spiritual body. Thus it is written, "The first man Adam became a living being"; the last Adam became a life-giving spirit. But it is not the spiritual which is first but the physical, and then the spiritual. The first man was from the earth, a man of dust; the second man is from heaven. As was the man of dust, so are those who are of the dust; and as is the man of heaven, so are those who are of heaven. Just as we have borne the image of the man of dust, we shall also bear the image of the man of heaven. I tell you this, brethren: flesh and blood cannot inherit the kingdom of God, nor does the perishable inherit the imperishable.

John 14:22 Judas (not Iscariot) said to him, "Lord, how is it that you will manifest **647**
yourself to us, and not to the world?"

(1) **Acts 2:24** But God raised him up, having loosed the pangs of death, because it **648**
was not possible for him to be held by it.

(2) **Romans 6:4** We were buried therefore with him by baptism into death, so that **648**
as Christ was raised from the dead by the glory of the Father, we too might walk in newness of life.

(3) **2 Corinthians 13:4** For he was crucified in weakness, but lives by the power **648**
of God. For we are weak in him, but in dealing with you we shall live with him by the power of God.

(4) **Philippians 3:10** . . . that I may know him and the power of his resurrection, **648**
and may share his sufferings, becoming like him in his death. . . .

(5) **Ephesians 1:19–22** . . . and what is the immeasurable greatness of his power in **648**
us who believe, according to the working of his great might which he accomplished in Christ when he raised him from the dead and made him sit at his right hand in the heavenly places, far above all rule and authority and power and dominion, and above every name that is named, not only in this age but also in that which is to come; and he has put all things under his feet and has made him the head over all things for the church. . . .

(6) **Hebrews 7:16** . . . who has become a priest, not according to a legal require- **648**
ment concerning bodily descent but by the power of an indestructible life.

(1) **Mark 8:31** And he began to teach them that the Son of man must suffer many **649**
things, and be rejected by the elders and the chief priests and the scribes, and be killed, and after three days rise again.

(2) **Mark 9:9–31** And as they were coming down the mountain, he charged them **649**
to tell no one what they had seen, until the Son of man should have risen from the dead. So they kept the matter to themselves, questioning what the rising from the dead meant. And they asked him, "Why do the scribes say that first Elijah must come?" And he said to them, "Elijah does come first to restore all things; and how is it written of the Son of man, that he should suffer many things and be treated with contempt? But I tell you that Elijah has come, and they did to him whatever they pleased, as it is written of him."

And when they came to the disciples, they saw a great crowd about them, and scribes arguing with them. And immediately all the crowd, when they saw him, were greatly amazed, and ran up to him and greeted him. And he asked them, "What are you discussing with them?" And one of the crowd answered him, "Teacher, I brought my son to you, for he has a dumb spirit; and wherever it seizes him, it dashes him down; and he foams and grinds his teeth and becomes rigid; and I asked your disciples to cast it out, and they were not able." And he answered them, "O faithless generation, how long am I to be with you? How long am I to bear with you? Bring him to me." And they brought the boy to him; and when the spirit saw him, immediately it convulsed the boy, and he fell on the ground and rolled about, foaming at the mouth. And Jesus asked his father, "How long has he had this?" And he said, "From childhood. And it has often cast him into the fire and into the water, to destroy him; but if you can do anything, have pity on us and help us." And Jesus said to him, "If you can! All things are possible to him who believes." Immediately the father of the child cried out and said, "I believe; help my unbelief!" And when Jesus saw that a crowd came running together, he rebuked the unclean spirit, saying to it, "You dumb and deaf spirit, I command you, come out of him, and never enter him again." And after crying out and convulsing him terribly, it came out, and the boy was like a corpse; so that most of them said, "He is dead." But Jesus took him by the hand and lifted him up, and he arose. And when he had entered the house, his disciples asked him privately, "Why could we not cast it out?" And he said to them, "This kind cannot be driven out by anything but prayer."

They went on from there and passed through Galilee. And he would not have any one know it; for he was teaching his disciples, saying to them, "The Son of man will be delivered into the hands of men, and they will kill him; and when he is killed, after three days he will rise."

649 (3) **Mark 10:34** ". . . and they will mock him, and spit upon him, and scourge him, and kill him; and after three days he will rise."

650 (1) ***Statuta Ecclesiae antiquae* (mid- or late fifth century): DS 325**
An examination of faith to be made before episcopal ordination

Whoever is to be ordained bishop must first be examined to determine whether . . . he has sure knowledge of the senses of Scripture, competence in Church dogmas, and, above all, can declare the teachings of the faith in simple words, i.e., affirming that the Father and the Son and the Holy Spirit are one God and proclaiming the entire deity to be, in the Trinity, coessential, consubstantial, coeternal, and co-omnipotent; that each individual person in the Trinity is fully God and all three persons are one God; that [he believes] the divine Incarnation was effected neither in the Father nor in the Son, but alone in the Son so that he who was Son in the divinity of God the Father became in man the son of a human mother, true God from the Father and true man from a mother, taking flesh from the womb of a mother, and a rational human soul while in both natures, i.e., man and God being one person, one Son, one Christ, one Lord creator of all things that are, and author and Lord and creator [ruler] with the Father and the Holy Spirit of all creatures, who suffered in a true suffering of the flesh, died the true death of his body, rose in a true resurrection of his flesh and a true taking back of his soul, in which he will come to judge the living and the dead. He is also to be asked if he believes there is one and the same author and God of the Old and New Testament, i.e., of the Law and the Prophets and the Apostles; that the devil is evil not by condition but by choice. He is also to be asked if he believes that the resurrection is of this flesh that we bear and not another; if he believes in the future judgment where each will receive punishment or glory for what he has done in the body; if he does not disapprove of marriage; if he does not condemn a second marriage; if he does not find fault with eating meat; if he will give

Communion to reconciled penitents; if in baptism all sins, i.e., both original sin and those which have been voluntarily committed, are remitted; if outside the Catholic Church there is no salvation.

If after having been examined in all these things he shall have been found fully instructed, then with the consent of the clerics and the laity and with all the bishops of the province gathered together . . . let him be ordained bishop.

(2) **Pope Anastasius II, letter to Laurence, bishop of Lignido (497): DS 359** 650
Whoever say Christ is a rarified [*subtilem*] man, or that God can suffer, or turned into flesh, or not to have had a co-united body, or to have brought this body from heaven, or that it is a phantasm, or that God the Word was mortal and needed to be raised up by the Father, or that he took up a body without a soul or a man without senses, or that the two natures of Christ were made one by being mixed together and not confessing our Lord Jesus Christ to be two unmixed natures but one person, according to which there is one Christ, one and the same Son—the Catholic and apostolic Church declares them anathema.

(3) **Pope St. Hormisdas, letter to the Emperor Justin (26 March 521): DS 369** 650
For the same is God and man, not, as the infidels say, by the introduction of a fourth person, but the Son of God himself, God and man, the same is power and weakness, humility and majesty, redeeming and sold, nailed to the Cross and bestowing the kingdom of heaven, taking our weakness so that it could be abolished, having enormous power so that death could not destroy him. He was buried because he willed to be born a man, and he rose because he was like the Father: suffering wounds and savior of the sick, one of the dead and lifegiver to those who obey, descending to hell and not leaving the bosom of the Father. Hence he soon took up again by his singular strength and admirable power the soul which, sharing our common condition, he yielded up.

(4) **Council of Toledo XI (675): DS 539** [The Redemption] In this form of as- 650
sumed human nature we believe according to the truth of the Gospels that He was conceived without sin, born without sin, and died without sin, who alone *for us became sin* [II Cor. 5:21], that is, a sacrifice for our sin. And yet He endured His passion without detriment to His divinity, for our sins, and condemned to death and to the cross, He accepted the true death of the body; also on the third day, restored by His own power, He arose from the grave.

(1) **Matthew 28:6** He is not here; for he has risen, as he said. Come, see the place 652
where he lay.

(2) **Mark 16:7** ". . . But go, tell his disciples and Peter that he is going before you 652
to Galilee; there you will see him, as he told you."

(3) **Luke 24:6–7** ". . . Remember how he told you, while he was still in Galilee, 652
that the Son of man must be delivered into the hands of sinful men, and be crucified, and on the third day rise."

(4) **Luke 24:26–27** ". . . Was it not necessary that the Christ should suffer these 652
things and enter into his glory?" And beginning with Moses and all the prophets, he interpreted to them in all the scriptures the things concerning himself.

652 (5) **Luke 24:44–48** Then he said to them, "These are my words which I spoke to you, while I was still with you, that everything written about me in the law of Moses and the prophets and the psalms must be fulfilled." Then he opened their minds to understand the scriptures, and said to them, "Thus it is written, that the Christ should suffer and on the third day rise from the dead, and that repentance and forgiveness of sins should be preached in his name to all nations, beginning from Jerusalem. You are witnesses of these things.

652 (6) **1 Corinthians 15:3–4** For I delivered to you as of first importance what I also received, that Christ died for our sins in accordance with the scriptures, that he was buried, that he was raised on the third day in accordance with the scriptures. . . .

652 (7) **Nicene Creed** [Editor's note: the Nicene Creed may be found in the CCC following paragraph 184.]

653 **Psalm 2:7**

I will tell of the decree of the Lord:
He said to me, "You are my son,
today I have begotten you. . . ."

654 (1) **Romans 4:25** . . . who was put to death for our trespasses and raised for our justification.

654 (2) **Ephesians 2:4–5** But God, who is rich in mercy, out of the great love with which he loved us, even when we were dead through our trespasses, made us alive together with Christ (by grace you have been saved). . . .

654 (3) **1 Peter 1:3** Blessed be the God and Father of our Lord Jesus Christ! By his great mercy we have been born anew to a living hope through the resurrection of Jesus Christ from the dead. . . .

655 **Colossians 3:1–3** If then you have been raised with Christ, seek the things that are above, where Christ is, seated at the right hand of God. Set your minds on things that are above, not on things that are on earth. For you have died, and your life is hid with Christ in God.

658 (1) **Romans 6:4** We were buried therefore with him by baptism into death, so that as Christ was raised from the dead by the glory of the Father, we too might walk in newness of life.

658 (2) **Romans 8:11** If the Spirit of him who raised Jesus from the dead dwells in you, he who raised Christ Jesus from the dead will give life to your mortal bodies also through his Spirit which dwells in you.

659 (1) **Luke 24:31** And their eyes were opened and they recognized him; and he vanished out of their sight.

659 (2) **John 20:19** On the evening of that day, the first day of the week, the doors being shut where the disciples were, for fear of the Jews, Jesus came and stood among them and said to them, "Peace be with you."

659 (3) **John 20:26** Eight days later, his disciples were again in the house, and Thomas was with them. The doors were shut, but Jesus came and stood among them, and said, "Peace be with you."

(4) **Acts 1:3** To them he presented himself alive after his passion by many proofs, 659
appearing to them during forty days, and speaking of the kingdom of God.

(5) **Acts 10:41** . . . not to all the people but to us who were chosen by God as 659
witnesses, who ate and drank with him after he rose from the dead.

(6) **Mark 16:12** After this he appeared in another form to two of them, as they 659
were walking into the country.

(7) **Luke 24:15** While they were talking and discussing together, Jesus himself drew 659
near and went with them.

(8) **John 20:14–15** Saying this, she turned round and saw Jesus standing, but she 659
did not know that it was Jesus. Jesus said to her, "Woman, why are you weeping? Whom do you seek?" Supposing him to be the gardener, she said to him, "Sir, if you have carried him away, tell me where you have laid him, and I will take him away."

(9) **John 21:4** Just as day was breaking, Jesus stood on the beach; yet the disciples 659
did not know that it was Jesus.

(10) **Acts 1:9** And when he had said this, as they were looking on, he was lifted 659
up, and a cloud took him out of their sight.

(11) **Acts 2:33** Being therefore exalted at the right hand of God, and having received 659
from the Father the promise of the Holy Spirit, he has poured out this which you see and hear.

(12) **Acts 7:56** . . . and he said, "Behold, I see the heavens opened, and the Son of 659
man standing at the right hand of God."

(13) **Luke 9:34–35** As he said this, a cloud came and overshadowed them; and they 659
were afraid as they entered the cloud. And a voice came out of the cloud, saying, "This is my Son, my Chosen; listen to him!"

(14) **Luke 24:51** While he blessed them, he parted from them, and was carried up 659
into heaven.

(15) **Exodus 13:22** . . . the pillar of cloud by day and the pillar of fire by night did 659
not depart from before the people.

(16) **Mark 16:19** So then the Lord Jesus, after he had spoken to them, was taken 659
up into heaven, and sat down at the right hand of God.

(17) **Psalm 110:1** 659

The Lord says to my lord:
"Sit at my right hand,
till I make your enemies your footstool."

(18) **1 Corinthians 9:1** Am I not free? Am I not an apostle? Have I not seen Jesus 659
our Lord? Are not you my workmanship in the Lord?

(19) **Galatians 1:16** . . . was pleased to reveal his Son to me, in order that I might 659
preach him among the Gentiles, I did not confer with flesh and blood. . . .

661 (1) **John 16:28** ". . . I came from the Father and have come into the world; again, I am leaving the world and going to the Father."

661 (2) **Ephesians 4:8–10** Therefore it is said,
"When he ascended on high he led a host of captives,
and he gave gifts to men."
(In saying, "He ascended," what does it mean but that he had also descended into the lower parts of the earth? He who descended is he who also ascended far above all the heavens, that he might fill all things.)

662 **Revelation 4:6–11** . . . and before the throne there is as it were a sea of glass, like crystal.

And round the throne, on each side of the throne, are four living creatures, full of eyes in front and behind: the first living creature like a lion, the second living creature like an ox, the third living creature with the face of a man, and the fourth living creature like a flying eagle. And the four living creatures, each of them with six wings, are full of eyes all round and within, and day and night they never cease to sing,
"Holy, holy, holy, is the Lord God Almighty,
who was and is and is to come!"
And whenever the living creatures give glory and honor and thanks to him who is seated on the throne, who lives for ever and ever, the twenty-four elders fall down before him who is seated on the throne and worship him who lives for ever and ever; they cast their crowns before the throne, singing,
"Worthy art thou, our Lord and God,
to receive glory and honor and power,
for thou didst create all things,
and by thy will they existed and were created."

665 (1) **Acts 1:11** . . . and said, "Men of Galilee, why do you stand looking into heaven? This Jesus, who was taken up from you into heaven, will come in the same way as you saw him go into heaven."

665 (2) **Colossians 3:3** For you have died, and your life is hid with Christ in God.

668 (1) **Ephesians 4:10** (. . . He who descended is he who also ascended far above all the heavens, that he might fill all things.)

668 (2) **1 Corinthians 15:24** Then comes the end, when he delivers the kingdom to God the Father after destroying every rule and every authority and power.

668 (3) **1 Corinthians 15:27–28** "For God has put all things in subjection under his feet." But when it says, "All things are put in subjection under him," it is plain that he is excepted who put all things under him. When all things are subjected to him, then the Son himself will also be subjected to him who put all things under him, that God may be everything to every one.

669 (1) **Ephesians 1:22** . . . and he has put all things under his feet and has made him the head over all things for the church. . . .

669 (2) **Ephesians 4:11–13** And his gifts were that some should be apostles, some prophets, some evangelists, some pastors and teachers, to equip the saints for the work of ministry, for building up the body of Christ, until we all attain to the unity of the faith and of the knowledge of the Son of God, to mature manhood, to the measure of the stature of the fulness of Christ. . . .

(1) **1 Peter 4:7** The end of all things is at hand; therefore keep sane and sober for your prayers. **670**

(2) **1 Corinthians 10:11** Now these things happened to them as a warning, but they were written down for our instruction, upon whom the end of the ages has come. **670**

(3) **Mark 16:17–18** ". . . And these signs will accompany those who believe: in my name they will cast out demons; they will speak in new tongues; they will pick up serpents, and if they drink any deadly thing, it will not hurt them; they will lay their hands on the sick, and they will recover." **670**

(4) **Mark 16:20** And they went forth and preached everywhere, while the Lord worked with them and confirmed the message by the signs that attended it. Amen. **670**

(1) **Matthew 25:31** "When the Son of man comes in his glory, and all the angels with him, then he will sit on his glorious throne. . . ." **671**

(2) **2 Thessalonians 2:7** For the mystery of lawlessness is already at work; only he who now restrains it will do so until he is out of the way. **671**

(3) **2 Peter 3:13** But according to his promise we wait for new heavens and a new earth in which righteousness dwells. **671**

(4) **Romans 8:19–22** For the creation waits with eager longing for the revealing of the sons of God; for the creation was subjected to futility, not of its own will but by the will of him who subjected it in hope; because the creation itself will be set free from its bondage to decay and obtain the glorious liberty of the children of God. We know that the whole creation has been groaning in travail together until now. . . . **671**

(5) **1 Corinthians 15:28** When all things are subjected to him, then the Son himself will also be subjected to him who put all things under him, that God may be everything to every one. **671**

(6) **1 Corinthians 11:26** For as often as you eat this bread and drink the cup, you proclaim the Lord's death until he comes. **671**

(7) **2 Peter 3:11–12** Since all these things are thus to be dissolved, what sort of persons ought you to be in lives of holiness and godliness, waiting for and hastening the coming of the day of God, because of which the heavens will be kindled and dissolved, and the elements will melt with fire! **671**

(1) **Acts 1:6–7** So when they had come together, they asked him, "Lord, will you at this time restore the kingdom to Israel?" He said to them, "It is not for you to know times or seasons which the Father has fixed by his own authority. . . ." **672**

(2) **Isaiah 11:1–9** **672**

There shall come forth a shoot from the stump of Jesse,
  and a branch shall grow out of his roots.
And the Spirit of the Lord shall rest upon him,
  the spirit of wisdom and understanding,
  the spirit of counsel and might,
  the spirit of knowledge and the fear of the Lord.
And his delight shall be in the fear of the Lord.

He shall not judge by what his eyes see,
    or decide by what his ears hear;
but with righteousness he shall judge the poor,
    and decide with equity for the meek of the earth;
and he shall smite the earth with the rod of his mouth,
    and with the breath of his lips he shall slay the wicked.
Righteousness shall be the girdle of his waist,
    and faithfulness the girdle of his loins.

The wolf shall dwell with the lamb,
    and the leopard shall lie down with the kid,
and the calf and the lion and the fatling together,
    and a little child shall lead them.
The cow and the bear shall feed;
    their young shall lie down together;
    and the lion shall eat straw like the ox.
The sucking child shall play over the hole of the asp,
    and the weaned child shall put his hand on the adder's den.
They shall not hurt or destroy
    in all my holy mountain;
for the earth shall be full of the knowledge of the Lord
    as the waters cover the sea.

672 (3) **Acts 1:8** ". . . But you shall receive power when the Holy Spirit has come upon you; and you shall be my witnesses in Jerusalem and in all Judea and Samaria and to the end of the earth."

672 (4) **1 Corinthians 7:26** I think that in view of the present distress it is well for a person to remain as he is.

672 (5) **Ephesians 5:16** . . . making the most of the time, because the days are evil.

672 (6) **1 Peter 4:17** For the time has come for judgment to begin with the household of God; and if it begins with us, what will be the end of those who do not obey the Gospel of God?

672 (7) **Matthew 25:1–13** "Then the kingdom of heaven shall be compared to ten maidens who took their lamps and went to meet the bridegroom. Five of them were foolish, and five were wise. For when the foolish took their lamps, they took no oil with them; but the wise took flasks of oil with their lamps. As the bridegroom was delayed, they all slumbered and slept. But at midnight there was a cry, 'Behold, the bridegroom! Come out to meet him.' Then all those maidens rose and trimmed their lamps. And the foolish said to the wise, 'Give us some of your oil, for our lamps are going out.' But the wise replied, 'Perhaps there will not be enough for us and for you; go rather to the dealers and buy for yourselves.' And while they went to buy, the bridegroom came, and those who were ready went in with him to the marriage feast; and the door was shut. Afterward the other maidens came also, saying, 'Lord, lord, open to us.' But he replied, 'Truly I say to you, I do not know you.' Watch therefore, for you know neither the day nor the hour. . . ."

672 (8) **Mark 13:33–37** ". . . Take heed, watch; for you do not know when the time will come. It is like a man going on a journey, when he leaves home and puts his servants in charge, each with his work, and commands the doorkeeper to be on the watch. Watch therefore—for you do not know when the master of the house will come, in the evening, or at midnight, or at cockcrow, or in the morning—lest he come suddenly and find you asleep. And what I say to you I say to all: Watch."

(9) **1 John 2:18** Children, it is the last hour; and as you have heard that antichrist 672
is coming, so now many antichrists have come; therefore we know that it is the last hour.

(10) **1 John 4:3** . . . and every spirit which does not confess Jesus is not of God. 672
This is the spirit of antichrist, of which you heard that it was coming, and now it is in the world already.

(11) **1 Timothy 4:1** Now the Spirit expressly says that in later times some will 672
depart from the faith by giving heed to deceitful spirits and doctrines of demons. . . .

(1) **Revelation 22:20** He who testifies to these things says, "Surely I am coming 673
soon." Amen. Come, Lord Jesus!

(2) **Mark 13:32** "But of that day or that hour no one knows, not even the angels 673
in heaven, nor the Son, but only the Father. . . ."

(3) **Matthew 24:44** Therefore you also must be ready; for the Son of man is coming 673
at an hour you do not expect.

(4) **1 Thessalonians 5:2** For you yourselves know well that the day of the Lord 673
will come like a thief in the night.

(5) **2 Thessalonians 2:3–12** Let no one deceive you in any way; for that day will 673
not come, unless the rebellion comes first, and the man of lawlessness is revealed, the son of perdition, who opposes and exalts himself against every so-called god or object of worship, so that he takes his seat in the temple of God, proclaiming himself to be God. Do you not remember that when I was still with you I told you this? And you know what is restraining him now so that he may be revealed in his time. For the mystery of lawlessness is already at work; only he who now restrains it will do so until he is out of the way. And then the lawless one will be revealed, and the Lord Jesus will slay him with the breath of his mouth and destroy him by his appearing and his coming.

The coming of the lawless one by the activity of Satan will be with all power and with pretended signs and wonders, and with all wicked deception for those who are to perish, because they refused to love the truth and so be saved. Therefore God sends upon them a strong delusion, to make them believe what is false, so that all may be condemned who did not believe the truth but had pleasure in unrighteousness.

(1) **Matthew 23:39** ". . . For I tell you, you will not see me again, until you say, 674
'Blessed is he who comes in the name of the Lord.'"

(2) **Luke 21:24** . . . they will fall by the edge of the sword, and be led captive among 674
all nations; and Jerusalem will be trodden down by the Gentiles, until the times of the Gentiles are fulfilled.

(1) **Luke 18:8** ". . . I tell you, he will vindicate them speedily. Nevertheless, when 675
the Son of man comes, will he find faith on earth?"

675 (2) **Matthew 24:12** And because wickedness is multiplied, most men's love will grow cold.

675 (3) **Luke 21:12** But before all this they will lay their hands on you and persecute you, delivering you up to the synagogues and prisons, and you will be brought before kings and governors for my name's sake.

675 (4) **John 15:19–20** ". . . If you were of the world, the world would love its own; but because you are not of the world, but I chose you out of the world, therefore the world hates you. Remember the word that I said to you, 'A servant is not greater than his master.' If they persecuted me, they will persecute you; if they kept my word, they will keep yours also. . . ."

675 (5) **2 Thessalonians 2:4–12** . . . who opposes and exalts himself against every so-called god or object of worship, so that he takes his seat in the temple of God, proclaiming himself to be God. Do you not remember that when I was still with you I told you this? And you know what is restraining him now so that he may be revealed in his time. For the mystery of lawlessness is already at work; only he who now restrains it will do so until he is out of the way. And then the lawless one will be revealed, and the Lord Jesus will slay him with the breath of his mouth and destroy him by his appearing and his coming.

The coming of the lawless one by the activity of Satan will be with all power and with pretended signs and wonders, and with all wicked deception for those who are to perish, because they refused to love the truth and so be saved. Therefore God sends upon them a strong delusion, to make them believe what is false, so that all may be condemned who did not believe the truth but had pleasure in unrighteousness.

675 (6) **1 Thessalonians 5:2–3** For you yourselves know well that the day of the Lord will come like a thief in the night. When people say, "There is peace and security," then sudden destruction will come upon them as travail comes upon a woman with child, and there will be no escape.

675 (7) **2 John 7** For many deceivers have gone out into the world, men who will not acknowledge the coming of Jesus Christ in the flesh; such a one is the deceiver and the antichrist.

675 (8) **1 John 2:18** Children, it is the last hour; and as you have heard that antichrist is coming, so now many antichrists have come; therefore we know that it is the last hour.

675 (9) **1 John 2:22** Who is the liar but he who denies that Jesus is the Christ? This is the antichrist, he who denies the Father and the Son.

676 (1) **Congregation for the Doctrine of the Faith, Decree of 19 July 1944: DS 3839** In recent times on several occasions this Supreme Sacred Congregation of the Holy Office has been asked what must be thought of the system of mitigated Millenarianism, which teaches, for example, that Christ the Lord before the final judgment, whether or not preceded by the resurrection of the many just, will come visibly to rule over this world. The answer is : The system of mitigated Millenarianism cannot be taught safely.

(2) Pius XI, encyclical *Divini Redemptoris* (1937) 676

To the Patriarchs, Primates, Archbishops, Bishops, and other Ordinaries in Peace and Communion with the Apostolic See.

Venerable Brethren, Health and Apostolic Benediction.

The promise of a Redeemer brightens the first page of the history of mankind, and the confident hope aroused by this promise softened the keen regret for a paradise which had been lost. It was this hope that accompanied the human race on its weary journey, until in the fullness of time the expected Savior came to begin a new universal civilization, the Christian civilization, far superior even to that which up to this time had been laboriously achieved by certain more privileged nations.

Nevertheless, the struggle between good and evil remained in the world as a sad legacy of the original fall. Nor has the ancient tempter ever ceased to deceive mankind with false promises. It is on this account that one convulsion following upon another has marked the passage of the centuries, down to the revolution of our own days. This modern revolution, it may be said, has actually broken out or threatens everywhere, and it exceeds in amplitude and violence anything yet experienced in the preceding persecutions launched against the Church. Entire peoples find themselves in danger of falling back into a barbarism worse than that which oppressed the greater part of the world at the coming of the Redeemer.

This all too imminent danger, Venerable Brethren, as you have already surmised, is bolshevistic and atheistic Communism, which aims at upsetting the social order and at undermining the very foundations of Christian civilization.

I. ATTITUDE OF THE CHURCH TOWARDS COMMUNISM

Previous Condemnations

In the face of such a threat, the Catholic Church could not and does not remain silent. This Apostolic See, above all, has not refrained from raising its voice, for it knows that its proper and social mission is to defend truth, justice and all those eternal values which Communism ignores or attacks. Ever since the days when groups of "intellectuals" were formed in an arrogant attempt to free civilization from the bonds of morality and religion, Our Predecessors overtly and explicitly drew the attention of the world to the consequences of the de-Christianization of human society. With reference to Communism, Our Venerable Predecessor, Pius IX, of holy memory, as early as 1846 pronounced a solemn condemnation, which he confirmed in the words of the Syllabus directed against "that infamous doctrine of so-called Communism which is absolutely contrary to the natural law itself, and if once adopted would utterly destroy the rights, property and possessions of all men, and even society itself." Later on, another of Our predecessors, the immortal Leo XIII, in his Encyclical *Quod Apostolici Muneris,* defined Communism as "the fatal plague which insinuates itself into the very marrow of human society only to bring about its ruin." With clear intuition he pointed out that the atheistic movements existing among the masses of the Machine Age had their origin in that school of philosophy which for centuries had sought to divorce science from the life of the Faith and of the Church.

Acts of Present Pontificate

During Our Pontificate We too have frequently and with urgent insistence denounced the current trend to atheism which is alarmingly on the increase. In 1924 when Our relief-mission returned from the Soviet Union We condemned Communism in a special Allocution which We addressed to the whole world. In our Encyclicals *Miserentissimus Redemptor*, *Quadragesimo Anno*, *Caritate Christi*, *Acerba Animi*, *Dilectissima Nobis,* We raised a solemn protest against the persecutions unleashed in Russia, in Mexico and now in Spain. Our two Allocutions of last year, the first on the occasion of the opening of the International Catholic Press Exposition, and the second during Our audience to the Spanish refugees, along with Our message of last Christmas, have evoked a world-wide echo which is not yet spent. In fact, the most persistent enemies of the Church, who from Moscow are directing the struggle against Christian civilization, themselves bear witness, by their unceasing attacks in word and act, that even to this hour the Papacy has continued faithfully to protect the sanctuary of the Christian religion, and that it has called public attention to the perils of Communism more frequently and more effectively than any other public authority on earth.

Need of Another Solemn Pronouncement

To Our great satisfaction, Venerable Brethren, you have, by means of individual and even joint pastoral Letters, accurately transmitted and explained to the Faithful these admonitions. Yet despite Our frequent and paternal warning the peril only grows greater from day to day because of the pressure exerted by clever agitators. Therefore We believe it to be Our duty to raise Our voice once more, in a still more solemn missive, in accord with the tradition of this Apostolic See, the Teacher of Truth, and in accord with the desire of the whole Catholic world, which makes the appearance of such a document but natural. We trust that the echo of Our voice will reach every mind free from prejudice and every heart sincerely desirous of the good of mankind. We wish this the more because Our words are now receiving sorry confirmation from the spectacle of the bitter fruits of subversive ideas, which We foresaw and foretold, and which are in fact multiplying fearfully in the countries already stricken, or threatening every other country of the world.

Hence We wish to expose once more in a brief synthesis the principles of atheistic Communism as they are manifested chiefly in bolshevism. We wish also to indicate its method of action and to contrast with its false principles the clear doctrine of the Church, in order to inculcate anew and with greater insistence the means by which the Christian civilization, the true *civitas humana*, can be saved from the satanic scourge, and not merely saved, but better developed for the well-being of human society.

II. COMMUNISM IN THEORY AND PRACTICE

The Communism of today, more emphatically than similar movements in the past, conceals in itself a false messianic idea. A pseudo-ideal of justice, of equality and fraternity in labor impregnates all its doctrine and activity with a deceptive mysticism, which communicates a zealous and contagious enthusiasm to the multitudes entrapped by delusive promises. This is especially true in an age like ours, when unusual misery has resulted from the unequal distribution of the goods of this world. This pseudo-ideal is even boastfully advanced as if it were responsible for a certain economic progress. As a matter of fact, when such progress is at all real, its true causes are quite different, as for instance the intensification of industrialism in countries which were formerly almost without it, the exploitation of immense natural resources, and the use of the most brutal methods to insure the achievement of gigantic projects with a minimum of expense.

1. Doctrine

The doctrine of modern Communism, which is often concealed under the most seductive trappings, is in substance based on the principles of dialectical and historical materialism previously advocated by Marx, of which the theoreticians of bolshevism claim to possess the only genuine interpretation. According to this doctrine there is in the world only one reality, matter, the blind forces of which evolve into plant, animal and man. Even human society is nothing but a phenomenon and form of matter, evolving in the same way. By a law of inexorable necessity and through a perpetual conflict of forces, matter moves towards the final synthesis of a classless society. In such a doctrine, as is evident, there is no room for the idea of God; there is no difference between matter and spirit, between soul and body; there is neither survival of the soul after death nor any hope in a future life. Insisting on the dialectical aspect of their materialism, the Communists claim that the conflict which carries the world towards its final synthesis can be accelerated by man. Hence they endeavor to sharpen the antagonisms which arise between the various classes of society. Thus the class struggle with its consequent violent hate and destruction takes on the aspects of a crusade for the progress of humanity. On the other hand, all other forces whatever, as long as they resist such systematic violence, must be annihilated as hostile to the human race.

Man and the Family under Communism

Communism, moreover, strips man of liberty, robs human personality of all its dignity, and removes all the moral restraints that check the eruptions of blind impulse. There is no recognition of any right of the individual in his relations to the collectivity; no natural right is accorded to human personality, which is a mere cog-wheel in the Communist system. In man's relations with other individuals, besides, Communists hold the principle of absolute equality, rejecting all hierarchy and divinely-constituted authority, including the authority of parents. What men call authority and subordination is derived from the community as its first and only font. Nor is the individual granted any property rights over material goods or the means of production, for inasmuch as these are the source of further wealth, their possession would give one man power over another. Precisely on this score, all forms of private property must be eradicated, for they are at the origin of all economic enslavement.

Refusing to human life any sacred or spiritual character, such a doctrine logically makes of marriage and the family a purely artificial and civil institution, the outcome of a specific economic system. There exists no matrimonial bond of a juridico-moral nature that is not subject to the whim of the individual or of the collectivity. Naturally, therefore, the notion of an indissoluble marriage-tie is scouted. Communism is particularly characterized by the rejection of any link that binds woman to the family and the home, and her emancipation is proclaimed as a basic principle. She is withdrawn from the family and the care of her children, to be thrust instead into public life and collective production under the same conditions as man. The care of home and children then devolves upon the collectivity. Finally, the right of education is denied to parents, for it is conceived as the exclusive prerogative of the community, in whose name and by whose mandate alone parents may exercise this right.

Communist Society

What would be the condition of a human society based on such materialistic tenets? It would be a collectivity with no other hierarchy than that of the economic system. It would have only one mission: the production of material things by means of collective labor, so that the goods of this world might be enjoyed in a paradise where each would "give according to his powers" and would "receive according to his needs." Communism recognizes in the collectivity the right, or rather, unlimited discretion, to draft individuals for the labor of the collectivity with no regard for their personal welfare; so that even violence could be legitimately exercised to dragoon the recalcitrant against their wills. In the Communistic commonwealth morality and law would be nothing but a derivation of the existing economic order, purely earthly in origin and unstable in character. In a word, the Communists claim to inaugurate a new era and a new civilization which is the result of blind evolutionary forces culminating in a humanity without God.

When all men have finally acquired the collectivist mentality in this Utopia of a really classless society, the political State, which is now conceived by Communists merely as the instrument by which the proletariat is oppressed by the capitalists, will have lost all reason for its existence and will "wither away." However, until that happy consummation is realized, the State and the powers of the State furnish Communism with the most efficacious and most extensive means for the achievement of its goal.

Such, Venerable Brethren, is the new gospel which bolshevistic and atheistic Communism offers the world as the glad tidings of deliverance and salvation! It is a system full of errors and sophisms. It is in opposition both to reason and to Divine Revelation. It subverts the social order, because it means the destruction of its foundations; because it ignores the true origin and purpose of the State; because it denies the rights, dignity and liberty of human personality.

2. Spread of Communism Explained

How is it possible that such a system, long since rejected scientifically and now proved erroneous by experience, how is it, We ask, that such a system could spread so rapidly in all parts of the world? The explanation lies in the fact that too few have been able to grasp the nature of Communism. The majority instead succumb to its deception, skillfully concealed by the most extravagant promises. By pretending to desire only the betterment of the condition of the working classes, by urging the removal of the very real abuses chargeable to the liberalistic economic order, and by demanding a more equitable distribution of this world's goods (objectives entirely and undoubtedly legitimate), the Communist takes advantage of the present world-wide economic crisis to draw into the sphere of his influence even those sections of the populace which on principle reject all forms of materialism and terrorism. And as every error contains its element of truth, the partial truths to which We have referred are astutely presented according to the needs of time and place, to conceal, when convenient, the repulsive crudity and inhumanity of Communistic principles and tactics. Thus the Communist ideal wins over many of the better-minded members of the community. These in turn become the apostles of the movement among the younger intelligentsia who are still too immature to recognize the intrinsic errors of the system. The preachers of Communism are also proficient in exploiting racial antagonisms and political divisions and oppositions. They take advantage of the lack of orientation characteristic of modern agnostic science in order to burrow into the universities, where they bolster up the principles of their doctrine with pseudo-scientific arguments.

Liberalism Prepares the Way

If we would explain the blind acceptance of Communism by so many thousands of workmen, we must remember that the way had been already prepared for it by the religious and moral destitution in which wage-earners had been left by liberal economics. Even on Sundays and holy days, labor-shifts were given no time to attend to their essential religious duties. No one thought of building churches within convenient distance of factories, nor of facilitating the work of the priest. On the contrary, laicism was actively and persistently promoted, with the result that we are now reaping the fruits of the errors so often denounced by Our Predecessors and by Ourselves. It can surprise no one that the Communistic fallacy should be spreading in a world already to a large extent de-Christianized.

Shrewd and Widespread Propaganda

There is another explanation for the rapid diffusion of the Communistic ideas now seeping into every nation, great and small, advanced and backward, so that no corner of the earth is free from them. This explanation is to be found in a propaganda so truly diabolical that the world has perhaps never witnessed its like before. It is directed from one common center. It is shrewdly adapted to the varying conditions of diverse peoples. It has at its disposal great financial resources, gigantic organizations, international congresses, and countless trained workers. It makes use of pamphlets and reviews, of cinema, theater and radio, of schools and even universities. Little by little it penetrates into all classes of the people and even reaches the better-minded groups of the community, with the result that few are aware of the poison which increasingly pervades their minds and hearts.

Silence of the Press

A third powerful factor in the diffusion of Communism is the conspiracy of silence on the part of a large section of the non-Catholic press of the world. We say conspiracy, because it is impossible otherwise to explain how a press, usually so eager to exploit even the little daily incidents of life has been able to remain silent for so long about the horrors perpetrated in Russia, in Mexico and even in a great part of Spain; and that it should have relatively so little to say concerning a world organization as vast as Russian Communism. This silence is due in part to short-sighted political policy, and is favored by various occult forces which for a long time have been working for the overthrow of the Christian Social Order.

3. Sad Consequences

Meanwhile the sorry effects of this propaganda are before our eyes. Where Communism has been able to assert its power—and here We are thinking with special affection of the people of Russia and Mexico—it has striven by every possible means, as its champions openly boast, to destroy Christian civilization and the Christian religion by banishing every remembrance of them from the hearts of men, especially of the young. Bishops and priests were exiled, condemned to forced labor, shot and done to death in inhuman fashion; laymen suspected of defending their religion were vexed, persecuted, dragged off to trial and thrown into prison.

Communist Horrors in Spain

Even where the scourge of Communism has not yet had time enough to exercise to the full its logical effects, as witness Our beloved Spain, it has, alas, found compensation in the fiercer violence of its attack. Not only this or that church or isolated monastery was sacked, but as far as possible every church and every monastery was destroyed. Every vestige of the Christian religion was eradicated, even though intimately linked with the rarest monuments of art and science. The fury of Communism has not confined itself to the indiscriminate slaughter of bishops, of thousands of priests and religious of both sexes; it searches out above all those who have been devoting their lives to the welfare of the working classes and the poor. But the majority of its victims have been laymen of all conditions and classes. Even up to the present moment, masses of them are slain almost daily for no other offense than the fact that they are good Christians or at least opposed to atheistic Communism. And this fearful destruction has been carried out with a hatred and a savage barbarity one would not have believed possible in our age. No man of good sense, nor any statesman conscious of his responsibility can fail to shudder at the thought that what is happening today in Spain may perhaps be repeated tomorrow in other civilized countries.

Logical Result of System

Nor can it be said that these atrocities are a transitory phenomenon, the usual accompaniment of all great revolutions, the isolated excesses common to every war. No, they are the natural fruit of a system which lacks all inner restraint. Some restraint is necessary for man considered either as an individual or in society. Even the barbaric peoples had this inner check in the natural law written by God in the heart of every man. And where this natural law was held in higher esteem, ancient nations rose to a grandeur that still fascinates—more than it should—certain superficial students of human history. But tear the very idea of God from the hearts of men, and they are necessarily urged by their passions to the most atrocious barbarity.

Struggle against All That Is Divine

This, unfortunately, is what we now behold. For the first time in history we are witnessing a struggle, cold-blooded in purpose and mapped out to the least detail, between man and "all that is called God." Communism is by its nature anti-religious. It considers religion as "the opiate of the people" because the principles of religion which speak of a life beyond the grave dissuade the proletariat from the dream of a Soviet paradise which is of this world.

Terrorism

But the law of nature and its Author cannot be flouted with impunity. Communism has not been able, and will not be able, to achieve its objectives even in the merely economic sphere. It is true that in Russia it has been a contributing factor in rousing men and materials from the inertia of centuries, and in obtaining by all manner of means, often without scruple, some measure of material success. Nevertheless We know from reliable and even very recent testimony that not even there, in spite of slavery imposed on millions of men, has Communism reached its promised goal. After all, even the sphere of economics needs some morality, some moral sense of responsibility, which can find no place in a system so thoroughly materialistic as Communism. Terrorism is the only possible substitute, and it is terrorism that reigns today in Russia, where former comrades in revolution are exterminating each other. Terrorism, having failed despite all to stem the tide of moral corruption, cannot even prevent the dissolution of society itself.

Concern for Oppressed Russians

In making these observations it is no part of Our intention to condemn en masse the peoples of the Soviet Union. For them We cherish the warmest paternal affection. We are well aware that not a few of them groan beneath the yoke imposed on them by men who in very large part are strangers to the real interests of the country. We recognize that many others were deceived by fallacious hopes. We blame only the system, with its authors and abettors who considered Russia the best-prepared field for experimenting with a plan elaborated decades ago, and who from there continue to spread it from one end of the world to the other.

III. DOCTRINE OF THE CHURCH IN CONTRAST

We have exposed the errors and the violent, deceptive tactics of bolshevistic and atheistic Communism. It is now time, Venerable Brethren, to contrast with it the true notion, already familiar to you, of the *civitas humana* or human society, as taught by reason and Revelation through the mouth of the Church, *Magistra Gentium*.

1. God the Supreme Reality

Above all other reality there exists one supreme Being: God, the omnipotent Creator of all things, the all-wise and just Judge of all men. This supreme reality, God, is the absolute condemnation of the impudent falsehoods of Communism. In truth, it is not because men believe in God that He exists; rather because He exists do all men whose eyes are not deliberately closed to the truth believe in Him and pray to Him.

2. Man and Family according to Reason and Faith

In the Encyclical on Christian Education We explained the fundamental doctrine concerning man as it may be gathered from reason and Faith. Man has a spiritual and immortal soul. He is a person, marvelously endowed by his Creator with gifts of body and mind. He is a true "microcosm," as the ancients said, a world in miniature, with a value far surpassing that of the vast inanimate cosmos. God alone is his last end, in this life and the next. By sanctifying grace he is raised to the dignity of a son of God, and incorporated into the Kingdom of God in the Mystical Body of Christ. In consequence he has been endowed by God with many and varied prerogatives: the right to life, to bodily integrity, to the necessary means of existence; the right to tend toward his ultimate goal in the path marked out for him by God; the right of association and the right to possess and use property.

Just as matrimony and the right to its natural use are of divine origin, so likewise are the constitution and fundamental prerogatives of the family fixed and determined by the Creator. In the Encyclical on Christian Marriage and in Our other Encyclical on Education, cited above, we have treated these topics at considerable length.

Man and Society

But God has likewise destined man for civil society according to the dictates of his very nature. In the plan of the Creator, society is a natural means which man can and must use to reach his destined end. Society is for man and not vice versa. This must not be understood in the sense of liberalistic individualism, which subordinates society to the selfish use of the individual; but only in the sense that by means of an organic union with society and by mutual collaboration the attainment of earthly happiness is placed within the reach of all. In a further sense, it is society which affords the opportunities for the development of all the individual and social gifts bestowed on human nature. These natural gifts have a value surpassing the immediate interests of the moment, for in society they reflect the divine perfection, which would not be true were man to live alone. But on final analysis, even in this latter function, society is made for man, that he may recognize this reflection of God's perfection, and refer it in praise and adoration to the Creator. Only man, the human person, and not society in any form is endowed with reason and a morally free will.

Mutual Rights and Duties

Man cannot be exempted from his divinely imposed obligations toward civil society, and the representatives of authority have the right to coerce him when he refuses without reason to do his duty. Society, on the other hand, cannot defraud man of his God-granted rights, the most important of which We have indicated above. Nor can society systematically void these rights by making their use impossible. It is therefore according to the dictates of reason that ultimately all material things should be ordained to man as a person, that through his mediation they may find their way to the Creator. In this wise we can apply to man, the human person, the words of the Apostle of the Gentiles, who writes to the Corinthians on the Christian economy of salvation: "All things are yours, and you are Christ's, and Christ is God's." While Communism impoverishes human personality by inverting the terms of the relation of man to society, to what lofty heights is man not elevated by reason and Revelation!

Socio-Economic Order

The directive principles concerning the social-economic order have been expounded in the social Encyclical of Leo XIII on the question of labor. Our own Encyclical on the Reconstruction of the Social Order adapted these principles to present needs. Then, insisting anew on the age-old doctrine of the Church concerning the individual and social character of private property, We explained clearly the right and dignity of labor, the relations of mutual aid and collaboration which should exist between those who possess capital and those who work, the salary due in strict justice to the worker for himself and for his family.

In this same Encyclical of Ours We have shown that the means of saving the world of today from the lamentable ruin into which a moral liberalism has plunged us are neither the class-struggle nor terror, nor yet the autocratic abuse of State power, but rather the infusion of social justice and the sentiment of Christian love into the social-economic order. We have indicated how a sound prosperity is to be restored according to the true principles of a sane corporative system which respects the proper hierarchic structure of society; and how all the occupational groups should be fused into a harmonious unity inspired by the principle of the common good. And the genuine and chief function of public and civil authority consists precisely in the efficacious furthering of this harmony and coordination of all social forces.

Social Hierarchy and State Rights

In view of this organized common effort towards peaceful living, Catholic doctrine vindicates to the State the dignity and authority of a vigilant and provident defender of those divine and human rights on which the Sacred Scriptures and the Fathers of the Church insist so often. It is not true that all have equal rights in civil society. It is not true that there exists no lawful social hierarchy. Let it suffice to refer to the Encyclicals of Leo XIII already cited, especially to that on State powers, and to the other on the Christian Constitution of States. In these documents the Catholic will find the principles of reason and the Faith clearly explained, and these principles will enable him to defend himself against the errors and perils of a Communistic conception of the State. The enslavement of man despoiled of his rights, the denial of the transcendental origin of the State and its authority, the horrible abuse of public power in the service of a collectivistic terrorism, are the very contrary of all that corresponds with natural ethics and the will of the Creator. Both man and civil society derive their origin from the Creator, Who has mutually ordained them one to the other. Hence neither can be exempted from their correlative obligations, nor deny or diminish each other's rights. The Creator Himself has regulated this mutual relationship in its fundamental lines, and it is by an unjust usurpation that Communism arrogates to itself the right to enforce, in place of the divine law based on the immutable principles of truth and charity, a partisan political program which derives from the arbitrary human will and is replete with hate.

3. Beauty of Church Doctrine

In teaching this enlightening doctrine the Church has no other intention than to realize the glad tidings sung by the Angels above the cave of Bethlehem at the Redeemer's birth: "Glory to God . . . and . . . peace to men . . . ," true peace and true happiness, even here below as far as is possible, in preparation for the happiness of heaven—but to men of good will. This doctrine is equally removed from all extremes of error and all exaggerations of parties or systems which stem from error. It maintains a constant equilibrium of truth and justice, which it vindicates in theory and applies and promotes in practice, bringing into harmony the rights and duties of all parties. Thus authority is reconciled with liberty, the dignity of the individual with that of the State, the human personality of the subject with the divine delegation of the superior; and in this way a balance is struck between the due dependence and well-ordered love of a man for himself, his family and country, and his love of other families and other peoples, founded on the love of God, the Father of all, their first principle and last end. The Church does not separate a proper regard for temporal welfare from solicitude for the eternal. If she subordinates the former to the latter according to the words of her divine Founder, "Seek ye first the Kingdom of God and His justice, and all these things shall be added unto you," she is nevertheless so far from being unconcerned with human affairs, so far from hindering civil progress and material advancement, that she actually fosters and promotes them in the most sensible and efficacious manner. Thus even in the sphere of social-economics, although the Church has never proposed a definite technical system, since this is not her field, she has nevertheless clearly outlined the guiding principles which, while susceptible of varied concrete applications according to the diversified conditions of times and places and peoples, indicate the safe way of securing the happy progress of society.

The wisdom and supreme utility of this doctrine are admitted by all who really understand it. With good reason outstanding statesmen have asserted that, after a study of various social systems, they have found nothing sounder than the principles expounded in the Encyclicals *Rerum Novarum* and *Quadragesimo Anno*. In non-Catholic, even in non-Christian countries, men recognize the great value to society of the social doctrine of the Church. Thus, scarcely a month ago, an eminent political figure of the Far East, a non-Christian, did not hesitate to affirm publicly that the Church, with her doctrine of peace and Christian brotherhood, is rendering a signal contribution to the difficult task of establishing and maintaining peace among the nations. Finally, We know from reliable information that flows into this Center of Christendom from all parts of the world, that the Communists themselves, where they are not utterly depraved, recognize the superiority of the social doctrine of the Church, when once explained to them, over the doctrines of their leaders and their teachers. Only those blinded by passion and hatred close their eyes to the light of truth and obstinately struggle against it.

4. Alleged Conflict between Doctrine and Practice

But the enemies of the Church, though forced to acknowledge the wisdom of her doctrine, accuse her of having failed to act in conformity with her principles, and from this conclude to the necessity of seeking other solutions. The utter falseness and injustice of this accusation is shown by the whole history of Christianity. To refer only to a single typical trait, it was Christianity that first affirmed the real and universal brotherhood of all men of whatever race and condition. This doctrine she proclaimed by a method, and with an amplitude and conviction, unknown to preceding centuries; and with it she potently contributed to the abolition of slavery. Not bloody revolution, but the inner force of her teaching made the proud Roman matron see in her slave a sister in Christ. It is Christianity that adores the Son of God, made Man for love of man, and become not only the "Son of a Carpenter" but Himself a "Carpenter." It was Christianity that raised manual labor to its true dignity, whereas it had hitherto been so despised that even the moderate Cicero did not hesitate to sum up the general opinion of his time in words of which any modern sociologist would be ashamed: "All artisans are engaged in sordid trades, for there can be nothing ennobling about a workshop."

Faithful to these principles, the Church has given new life to human society. Under her influence arose prodigious charitable organizations, great guilds of artisans and workingmen of every type. These guilds, ridiculed as "medieval" by the liberalism of the last century, are today claiming the admiration of our contemporaries in many countries who are endeavoring to revive them in some modern form. And when others systems hindered her work and raised obstacles to the salutary influence of the Church, she was never done warning them of their error. We need but recall with what constant firmness and energy Our Predecessor, Leo XIII, vindicated for the workingman the right to organize, which the dominant liberalism of the more powerful States relentlessly denied him. Even today the authority of this Church doctrine is greater than it seems; for the influence of ideas in the realm of facts, though invisible and not easily measured, is surely of predominant importance.

It may be said in all truth that the Church, like Christ, goes through the centuries doing good to all. There would be today neither Socialism nor Communism if the rulers of the nations had not scorned the teachings and maternal warnings of the Church. On the bases of liberalism and laicism they wished to build other social edifices which, powerful and imposing as they seemed at first, all too soon revealed the weakness of their foundations, and today are crumbling one after another before our eyes, as everything must crumble that is not grounded on the one corner stone which is Christ Jesus.

IV. DEFENSIVE AND CONSTRUCTIVE PROGRAM

This, Venerable Brethren, is the doctrine of the Church, which alone in the social as in all other fields can offer real light and assure salvation in the face of Communistic ideology. But this doctrine must be consistently reduced to practice in every-day life, according to the admonition of St. James the Apostle: "Be ye doers of the word and not hearers only, deceiving your own selves." The most urgent need of the present day is therefore the energetic and timely application of remedies which will effectively ward off the catastrophe that daily grows more threatening. We cherish the firm hope that the fanaticism with which the sons of darkness work day and night at their materialistic and atheistic propaganda will at least serve the holy purpose of stimulating the sons of light to a like and even greater zeal for the honor of the Divine Majesty.

What then must be done, what remedies must be employed to defend Christ and Christian civilization from this pernicious enemy? As a father in the midst of his family, We should like to speak quite intimately of those duties which the great struggle of our day imposes on all the children of the Church; and We would address Our paternal admonition even to those sons who have strayed far from her.

1. Renewal of Christian Life

As in all the stormy periods of the history of the Church, the fundamental remedy today lies in a sincere renewal of private and public life according to the principles of the Gospel by all those who belong to the Fold of Christ, that they may be in truth the salt of the earth to preserve human society from total corruption.

With heart deeply grateful to the Father of Light, from Whom descends "every best gift and every perfect gift," We see on all sides consoling signs of this spiritual renewal. We see it not only in so many singularly chosen souls who in these last years have been elevated to the sublime heights of sanctity, and in so many others who with generous hearts are making their way towards the same luminous goal, but also in the new flowering of a deep and practical piety in all classes of society even the most cultured, as We pointed out in Our recent Motu Proprio *In multis solaciis* of October 28 last, on the occasion of the reorganization of the Pontifical Academy of Sciences.

Nevertheless We cannot deny that there is still much to be done in the way of spiritual renovation. Even in Catholic countries there are still too many who are Catholics hardly more than in name. There are too many who fulfill more or less faithfully the more essential obligations of the religion they boast of professing, but have no desire of knowing it better, of deepening their inward conviction, and still less of bringing into conformity with the external gloss the inner splendor of a right and unsullied conscience, that recognizes and performs all its duties under the eye of God. We know how much Our Divine Savior detested this empty pharisaic show, He Who wished that all should adore the Father "in spirit and in truth." The Catholic who does not live really and sincerely according to the Faith he professes will not long be master of himself in these days when the winds of strife and persecution blow so fiercely, but will be swept away defenseless in this new deluge which threatens the world. And thus, while he is preparing his own ruin, he is exposing to ridicule the very name of Christian.

Detachment from Worldly Goods

And here We wish, Venerable Brethren, to insist more particularly on two teachings of Our Lord which have a special bearing on the present condition of the human race: detachment from earthly goods and the precept of charity. "Blessed are the poor in spirit" were the first words that fell from the lips of the Divine Master in His sermon on the mount. This lesson is more than ever necessary in these days of materialism athirst for the goods and pleasures of this earth. All Christians, rich or poor, must keep their eye fixed on heaven, remembering that "we have not here a lasting city, but we seek one that is to come." The rich should not place their happiness in things of earth nor spend their best efforts in the acquisition of them. Rather, considering themselves only as stewards of their earthly goods, let them be mindful of the account they must render of them to their Lord and Master, and value them as precious means that God has put into their hands for doing good; let them not fail, besides, to distribute of their abundance to the poor, according to the evangelical precept. Otherwise there shall be verified of them and their riches the harsh condemnation of St. James the Apostle: "Go to now, ye rich men; weep and howl in your miseries which shall come upon you. Your riches are corrupted, and your garments are moth-eaten; your gold and silver is cankered; and the rust of them shall be for a testimony against you and shall eat your flesh like fire. You have stored up to yourselves wrath against the last days. . . ."

But the poor too, in their turn, while engaged, according to the laws of charity and justice, in acquiring the necessities of life and also in bettering their condition, should always remain "poor in spirit," and hold spiritual goods in higher esteem than earthly property and pleasures. Let them remember that the world will never be able to rid itself of misery, sorrow and tribulation, which are the portion even of those who seem most prosperous. Patience, therefore, is the need of all, that Christian patience which comforts the heart with the divine assurance of eternal happiness. "Be patient, therefore, brethren," we repeat with St. James, "until the coming of the Lord. Behold the husbandman waiteth for the precious fruit of the earth, patiently bearing until he receive the early and the later rain. Be you therefore also patient and strengthen your hearts, for the coming of the Lord is at hand." Only thus will be fulfilled the consoling promise of the Lord: "Blessed are the poor!" These words are no vain consolation, a promise as empty as those of the Communists. They are the words of life, pregnant with a sovereign reality. They are fully verified here on earth, as well as in eternity. Indeed, how many of the poor, in anticipation of the Kingdom of Heaven, already proclaimed their own: "for yours is the Kingdom of Heaven," find in these words a happiness which so many of the wealthy, uneasy with their riches and ever thirsting for more, look for in vain!

Christian Charity

Still more important as a remedy for the evil we are considering, or certainly more directly calculated to cure it, is the precept of charity. We have in mind that Christian charity, "patient and kind," which avoids all semblance of demeaning paternalism, and all ostentation; that charity which from the very beginning of Christianity won to Christ the poorest of the poor, the slaves. And We are grateful to all those members of charitable associations, from the conferences of St. Vincent de Paul to the recent great relief-organizations, which are perseveringly practicing the spiritual and corporal works of mercy. The more the working men and the poor realize what the spirit of love animated by the virtue of Christ is doing for them, the more readily will they abandon the false persuasion that Christianity has lost its efficacy and that the Church stands on the side of the exploiters of their labor.

But when on the one hand We see thousands of the needy, victims of real misery for various reasons beyond their control, and on the other so many round about them who spend huge sums of money on useless things and frivolous amusement, We cannot fail to remark with sorrow not only that justice is poorly observed, but that the precept of charity also is not sufficiently appreciated, is not a vital thing in daily life. We desire therefore, Venerable Brethren, that this divine precept, this precious mark of identification left by Christ to His true disciples, be ever more fully explained by pen and word of mouth; this precept which teaches us to see in those who suffer Christ Himself, and would have us love our brothers as Our Divine Savior has loved us, that is, even at the sacrifice of ourselves, and, if need be, of our very life. Let all then frequently meditate on those words of the final sentence, so consoling yet so terrifying, which the Supreme Judge will pronounce on the day of the Last Judgment: "Come, ye blessed of my Father . . . for I was hungry and you gave me to eat; I was thirsty and you gave me to drink. . . . Amen, I say to you, as long as you did it to one of these my least brethren you did it to me." And the reverse: "Depart from me, you cursed, into everlasting fire . . . for I was hungry and you gave me not to eat; I was thirsty and you gave me not to drink. . . . Amen, I say to you, as long as you did it not to one of these least, neither did you do it to me." To be sure of eternal life, therefore, and to be able to help the poor effectively, it is imperative to return to a more moderate way of life, to renounce the joys, often sinful, which the world today holds out in such abundance; to forget self for love of the neighbor. There is a divine regenerating force in this "new precept" (as Christ called it) of Christian charity. Its faithful observance will pour into the heart an inner peace which the world knows not, and will finally cure the ills which oppress humanity.

Duties of Strict Justice

But charity will never be true charity unless it takes justice into constant account. The Apostle teaches that "he that loveth his neighbor hath fulfilled the law" and he gives the reason: "For, *Thou shalt not commit adultery, Thou shalt not kill, Thou shalt not steal*...and if there be any other commandment, it is comprised in this word: *Thou shalt love thy neighbor as thyself.*" According to the Apostle, then, all the commandments, including those which are of strict justice, as those which forbid us to kill or to steal, may be reduced to the single precept of true charity. From this it follows that a "charity" which deprives the workingman of the salary to which he has a strict title in justice, is not charity at all, but only its empty name and hollow semblance. The wage-earner is not to receive as alms what is his due in justice. And let no one attempt with trifling charitable donations to exempt himself from the great duties imposed by justice. Both justice and charity often dictate obligations touching on the same subject-matter, but under different aspects; and the very dignity of the workingman makes him justly and acutely sensitive to the duties of others in his regard.

Therefore We turn again in a special way to you, Christian employers and industrialists, whose problem is often so difficult for the reason that you are saddled with the heavy heritage of an unjust economic regime whose ruinous influence has been felt through many generations. We bid you be mindful of your responsibility. It is unfortunately true that the manner of acting in certain Catholic circles has done much to shake the faith of the working-classes in the religion of Jesus Christ. These groups have refused to understand that Christian charity demands the recognition of certain rights due to the workingman, which the Church has explicitly acknowledged. What is to be thought of the action of those Catholic employers who in one place succeeded in preventing the reading of Our Encyclical *Quadragesimo Anno* in their local churches? Or of those Catholic industrialists who even to this day have shown themselves hostile to a labor movement that We Ourselves recommended? Is it not deplorable that the right of private property defended by the Church should so often have been used as a weapon to defraud the workingman of his just salary and his social rights?

Social Justice

In reality, besides commutative justice, there is also social justice with its own set obligations, from which neither employers nor workingmen can escape. Now it is of the very essence of social justice to demand for each individual all that is necessary for the common good. But just as in the living organism it is impossible to provide for the good of the whole unless each single part and each individual member is given what it needs for the exercise of its proper functions, so it is impossible to care for the social organism and the good of society as a unit unless each single part and each individual member—that is to say, each individual man in the dignity of his human personality—is supplied with all that is necessary for the exercise of his social functions. If social justice be satisfied, the result will be an intense activity in economic life as a whole, pursued in tranquility and order. This activity will be proof of the health of the social body, just as the health of the human body is recognized in the undisturbed regularity and perfect efficiency of the whole organism.

But social justice cannot be said to have been satisfied as long as workingmen are denied a salary that will enable them to secure proper sustenance for themselves and for their families; as long as they are denied the opportunity of acquiring a modest fortune and forestalling the plague of universal pauperism; as long as they cannot make suitable provision through public or private insurance for old age, for periods of illness and unemployment. In a word, to repeat what has been said in Our Encyclical *Quadragesimo Anno*: "Then only will the economic and social order be soundly established and attain its ends, when it offers, to all and to each, all those goods which the wealth and resources of nature, technical science and the corporate organization of social affairs can give. These goods should be sufficient to supply all necessities and reasonable comforts, and to uplift men to that higher standard of life which, provided it be used with prudence, is not only not a hindrance but is of singular help to virtue."

It happens all too frequently, however, under the salary system, that individual employers are helpless to ensure justice unless, with a view to its practice, they organize institutions the object of which is to prevent competition incompatible with fair treatment for the workers. Where this is true, it is the duty of contractors and employers to support and promote such necessary organizations as normal instruments enabling them to fulfil their obligations of justice. But the laborers too must be mindful of their duty to love and deal fairly with their employers, and persuade themselves that there is no better means of safeguarding their own interests.

If, therefore, We consider the whole structure of economic life, as We have already pointed out in Our Encyclical *Quadragesimo Anno*, the reign of mutual collaboration between justice and charity in social-economic relations can only be achieved by a body of professional and interprofessional organizations, built on solidly Christian foundations, working together to effect, under forms adapted to different places and circumstances, what has been called the Corporation.

Social Study and Propaganda

To give to this social activity a greater efficacy, it is necessary to promote a wider study of social problems in the light of the doctrine of the Church and under the aegis of her constituted authority. If the manner of acting of some Catholics in the social-economic field has left much to be desired, this has often come about because they have not known and pondered sufficiently the teachings of the Sovereign Pontiffs on these questions. Therefore, it is of the utmost importance to foster in all classes of society an intensive program of social education adapted to the varying degrees of intellectual culture. It is necessary with all care and diligence to procure the widest possible diffusion of the teachings of the Church, even among the working-classes. The minds of men must be illuminated with the sure light of Catholic teaching, and their wills must be drawn to follow and apply it as the norm of right living in the conscientious fulfilment of their manifold social duties. Thus they will oppose that incoherence and discontinuity in Christian life which We have many times lamented. For there are some who, while exteriorly faithful to the practice of their religion, yet in the field of labor and industry, in the professions, trade and business, permit a deplorable cleavage in their conscience, and live a life too little in conformity with the clear principles of justice and Christian charity. Such lives are a scandal to the weak, and to the malicious a pretext to discredit the Church.

In this renewal the Catholic Press can play a prominent part. Its foremost duty is to foster in various attractive ways an ever better understanding of social doctrine. It should, too, supply accurate and complete information on the activity of the enemy and the means of resistance which have been found most effective in various quarters. It should offer useful suggestions and warn against the insidious deceits with which Communists endeavor, all too successfully, to attract even men of good faith.

2. Distrust of Communist Tactics

On this point We have already insisted in Our Allocution of May 12th of last year, but We believe it to be a duty of special urgency, Venerable Brethren, to call your attention to it once again. In the beginning Communism showed itself for what it was in all its perversity; but very soon it realized that it was thus alienating the people. It has therefore changed its tactics, and strives to entice the multitudes by trickery of various forms, hiding its real designs behind ideas that in themselves are good and attractive. Thus, aware of the universal desire for peace, the leaders of Communism pretend to be the most zealous promoters and propagandists in the movement for world amity. Yet at the same time they stir up a class-warfare which causes rivers of blood to flow, and, realizing that their system offers no internal guarantee of peace, they have recourse to unlimited armaments. Under various names which do not suggest Communism, they establish organizations and periodicals with the sole purpose of carrying their ideas into quarters otherwise inaccessible. They try perfidiously to worm their way even into professedly Catholic and religious organizations. Again, without receding an inch from their subversive principles, they invite Catholics to collaborate with them in the realm of so-called humanitarianism and charity; and at times even make proposals that are in perfect harmony with the Christian spirit and the doctrine of the Church. Elsewhere they carry their hypocrisy so far as to encourage the belief that Communism, in countries where faith and culture are more strongly entrenched, will assume another and much milder form. It will not interfere with the practice of religion. It will respect liberty of conscience. There are some even who refer to certain changes recently introduced into soviet legislation as a proof that Communism is about to abandon its program of war against God.

See to it, Venerable Brethren, that the Faithful do not allow themselves to be deceived! Communism is intrinsically wrong, and no one who would save Christian civilization may collaborate with it in any undertaking whatsoever. Those who permit themselves to be deceived into lending their aid towards the triumph of Communism in their own country will be the first to fall victims of their error. And the greater the antiquity and grandeur of the Christian civilization in the regions where Communism successfully penetrates, so much more devastating will be the hatred displayed by the godless.

Prayer and Penance

But "unless the Lord keep the city, he watcheth in vain that keepeth it." And so, as a final and most efficacious remedy, We recommend, Venerable Brethren, that in your dioceses you use the most practical means to foster and intensify the spirit of prayer joined with Christian penance. When the Apostles asked the Savior why they had been unable to drive the evil spirit from a demoniac, Our Lord answered: "This kind is not cast out but by prayer and fasting." So, too, the evil which today torments humanity can be conquered only by a world-wide crusade of prayer and penance. We ask especially the Contemplative Orders, men and women, to redouble their prayers and sacrifices to obtain from heaven efficacious aid for the Church in the present struggle. Let them implore also the powerful intercession of the Immaculate Virgin who, having crushed the head of the serpent of old, remains the sure protectress and invincible "Help of Christians."

V. MINISTERS AND COWORKERS IN CATHOLIC SOCIAL ACTION

To apply the remedies thus briefly indicated to the task of saving the world as We have traced it above, Jesus Christ, our Divine King, has chosen priests as the first-line ministers and messengers of His gospel. Theirs is the duty, assigned to them by a special vocation, under the direction of their Bishops and in filial obedience to the Vicar of Christ on earth, of keeping alight in the world the torch of Faith, and of filling the hearts of the Faithful with that supernatural trust which has aided the Church to fight and win so many other battles in the name of Christ: "This is the victory which overcometh the world, our Faith."

To priests in a special way We recommend anew the oft-repeated counsel of Our Predecessor, Leo XIII, to go to the workingman. We make this advice Our own, and faithful to the teachings of Jesus Christ and His Church, We thus complete it: "Go to the workingman, especially where he is poor; and in general, go to the poor." The poor are obviously more exposed than others to the wiles of agitators who, taking advantage of their extreme need, kindle their hearts to envy of the rich and urge them to seize by force what fortune seems to have denied them unjustly. If the priest will not go to the workingman and to the poor, to warn them or to disabuse them of prejudice and false theory, they will become an easy prey for the apostles of Communism.

Indisputably much has been done in this direction, especially after the publication of the Encyclicals *Rerum Novarum* and *Quadragesimo Anno*. We are happy to voice Our paternal approval of the zealous pastoral activity manifested by so many Bishops and priests who have with due prudence and caution been planning and applying new methods of apostolate more adapted to modern needs. But for the solution of our present problem, all this effort is still inadequate. When our country is in danger, everything not strictly necessary, everything not bearing directly on the urgent matter of unified defense, takes second place. So we must act in today's crisis. Every other enterprise, however attractive and helpful, must yield before the vital need of protecting the very foundation of the Faith and of Christian civilization. Let our parish priests, therefore, while providing of course for the normal needs of the Faithful, dedicate the better part of their endeavors and their zeal to winning back the laboring masses to Christ and to His Church. Let them work to infuse the Christian spirit into quarters where it is least at home. The willing response of the masses, and results far exceeding their expectations, will not fail to reward them for their strenuous pioneer labor. This has been and continues to be our experience in Rome and in other capitals, where zealous parish communities are being formed as new churches are built in the suburban districts, and real miracles are being worked in the conversion of people whose hostility to religion has been due solely to the fact that they did not know it.

But the most efficacious means of apostolate among the poor and lowly is the priest's example, the practice of all those sacerdotal virtues which We have described in Our Encyclical *Ad Catholici Sacerdotii*. Especially needful, however, for the present situation is the shining example of a life which is humble, poor and disinterested, in imitation of a Divine Master Who could say to the world with divine simplicity: "The foxes have holes and the birds of the air nests, but the Son of Man hath not where to lay His head." A priest who is really poor and disinterested in the Gospel sense may work among his flock marvels recalling a Saint Vincent de Paul, a Cure of Ars, a Cottolengo, a Don Bosco and so many others; while an avaricious and selfish priest, as We have noted in the above-mentioned Encyclical, even though he should not plunge with Judas to the abyss of treason, will never be more than empty "sounding brass" and useless "tinkling cymbal." Too often, indeed, he will be a hindrance rather than an instrument of grace in the midst of his people. Furthermore, where a secular priest or religious is obliged by his office to administer temporal property, let him remember that he is not only to observe scrupulously all that charity and justice prescribe, but that he has a special obligation to conduct himself in very truth as a father of the poor.

1. Catholic Action

After this appeal to the clergy, We extend Our paternal invitation to Our beloved sons among the laity who are doing battle in the ranks of Catholic Action. On another occasion We have called this movement so dear to Our heart "a particularly providential assistance" in the work of the Church during these troublous times. Catholic Action is in effect a *social* apostolate also, inasmuch as its object is to spread the Kingdom of Jesus Christ not only among individuals, but also in families and in society. It must, therefore, make it a chief aim to train its members with special care and to prepare them to fight the battles of the Lord. This task of formation, now more urgent and indispensable than ever, which must always precede direct action in the field, will assuredly be served by study-circles, conferences, lecture-courses and the various other activities undertaken with a view to making known the Christian solution of the social problem.

The militant leaders of Catholic Action, thus properly prepared and armed, will be the first and immediate apostles of their fellow workmen. They will be an invaluable aid to the priest in carrying the torch of truth, and in relieving grave spiritual and material suffering, in many sectors where inveterate anti-clerical prejudice or deplorable religious indifference has proved a constant obstacle to the pastoral activity of God's ministers. In this way they will collaborate, under the direction of especially qualified priests, in that work of spiritual aid to the laboring classes on which We set so much store, because it is the means best calculated to save these, Our beloved children, from the snares of Communism.

In addition to this individual apostolate which, however useful and efficacious, often goes unheralded, Catholic Action must organize propaganda on a large scale to disseminate knowledge of the fundamental principles on which, according to the Pontifical documents, a Christian Social Order must build.

Auxiliary Organizations

Ranged with Catholic Action are the groups which We have been happy to call its auxiliary forces. With paternal affection We exhort these valuable organizations also to dedicate themselves to the great mission of which We have been treating, a cause which today transcends all others in vital importance.

Homogeneous Groups

We are thinking likewise of those associations of workmen, farmers, technicians, doctors, employers, students and others of like character, groups of men and women who live in the same cultural atmosphere and share the same way of life. Precisely these groups and organizations are destined to introduce into society that order which We have envisaged in Our Encyclical *Quadragesimo Anno*, and thus to spread in the vast and various fields of culture and labor the recognition of the Kingdom of Christ.

Even where the State, because of changed social and economic conditions, has felt obliged to intervene directly in order to aid and regulate such organizations by special legislative enactments, supposing always the necessary respect for liberty and private initiative, Catholic Action may not urge the circumstance as an excuse for abandoning the field. Its members should contribute prudently and intelligently to the study of the problems of the hour in the light of Catholic doctrine. They should loyally and generously participate in the formation of the new institutions, bringing to them the Christian spirit which is the basic principle of order wherever men work together in fraternal harmony.

Appeal to Catholic Workers

Here We should like to address a particularly affectionate word to Our Catholic workingmen, young and old. They have been given, perhaps as a reward for their often heroic fidelity in these trying days, a noble and an arduous mission. Under the guidance of their Bishops and priests, they are to bring back to the Church and to God those immense multitudes of their brother-workmen who, because they were not understood or treated with the respect to which they were entitled, in bitterness have strayed far from God. Let Catholic workingmen show these their wandering brethren by word and example that the Church is a tender Mother to all those who labor and suffer, and that she has never failed, and never will fail, in her sacred maternal duty of protecting her children. If this mission, which must be fulfilled in mines, in factories, in shops, wherever they may be laboring, should at times require great sacrifices, Our workmen will remember that the Savior of the world has given them an example not only of toil but of self-immolation.

2. Need for Unity

To all Our children, finally, of every social rank and every nation, to every religious and lay organization in the Church, We make another and more urgent appeal for union. Many times Our paternal heart has been saddened by the divergencies—often idle in their causes, always tragic in their consequences—which array in opposing camps the sons of the same Mother Church. Thus it is that the radicals, who are not so very numerous, profiting by this discord are able to make it more acute, and end by pitting Catholics one against the other. In view of the events of the past few months, Our warning must seem superfluous. We repeat it nevertheless once more, for those who have not understood, or perhaps do not desire to understand. Those who make a practice of spreading dissension among Catholics assume a terrible responsibility before God and the Church.

Invitation to All Believers

But in this battle joined by the powers of darkness against the very idea of Divinity, it is Our fond hope that, besides the host which glories in the name of Christ, all those —and they comprise the overwhelming majority of mankind—who still believe in God and pay Him homage may take a decisive part. We therefore renew the invitation extended to them five years ago in Our Encyclical *Caritate Christi*, invoking their loyal and hearty collaboration "in order to ward off from mankind the great danger that threatens all alike." Since, as We then said, "belief in God is the unshakable foundation of all social order and of all responsibility on earth, it follows that all those who do not want anarchy and terrorism ought to take energetic steps to prevent the enemies of religion from attaining the goal they have so brazenly proclaimed to the world."

3. Duties of the Christian State

Such is the positive task, embracing at once theory and practice, which the Church undertakes in virtue of the mission, confided to her by Christ, of constructing a Christian society, and, in our own times, of resisting unto victory the attacks of Communism. It is the duty of the Christian State to concur actively in this spiritual enterprise of the Church, aiding her with the means at its command, which although they be external devices, have nonetheless for their prime object the good of souls.

This means that all diligence should be exercised by States to prevent within their territories the ravages of an anti-God campaign which shakes society to its very foundations. For there can be no authority on earth unless the authority of the Divine Majesty be recognized; no oath will bind which is not sworn in the Name of the Living God. We repeat what We have said with frequent insistence in the past, especially in Our Encyclical *Caritate Christi*: "How can any contract be maintained, and what value can any treaty have, in which every guarantee of conscience is lacking? And how can there be talk of guarantees of conscience when all faith in God and all fear of God have vanished? Take away this basis, and with it all moral law falls, and there is no remedy left to stop the gradual but inevitable destruction of peoples, families, the State, civilization itself."

Provisions for the Common Good

It must likewise be the special care of the State to create those material conditions of life without which an orderly society cannot exist. The State must take every measure necessary to supply employment, particularly for the heads of families and for the young. To achieve this end demanded by the pressing needs of the common welfare, the wealthy classes must be induced to assume those burdens without which human society cannot be saved nor they themselves remain secure. However, measures taken by the State with this end in view ought to be of such a nature that they will really affect those who actually possess more than their share of capital resources, and who continue to accumulate them to the grievous detriment of others.

Prudent and Sober Administration

The State itself, mindful of its responsibility before God and society, should be a model of prudence and sobriety in the administration of the commonwealth. Today more than ever the acute world crisis demands that those who dispose of immense funds, built up on the sweat and toil of millions, keep constantly and singly in mind the common good. State functionaries and all employees are obliged in conscience to perform their duties faithfully and unselfishly, imitating the brilliant example of distinguished men of the past and of our own day, who with unremitting labor sacrificed their all for the good of their country. In international trade-relations let all means be sedulously employed for the removal of those artificial barriers to economic life which are the effects of distrust and hatred. All must remember that the peoples of the earth form but one family in God.

Unrestricted Freedom for the Church

At the same time the State must allow the Church full liberty to fulfill her divine and spiritual mission, and this in itself will be an effectual contribution to the rescue of nations from the dread torment of the present hour. Everywhere today there is an anxious appeal to moral and spiritual forces; and rightly so, for the evil we must combat is at its origin primarily an evil of the spiritual order. From this polluted source the monstrous emanations of the communistic system flow with satanic logic. Now, the Catholic Church is undoubtedly preeminent among the moral and religious forces of today. Therefore the very good of humanity demands that her work be allowed to proceed unhindered.

Those who act otherwise, and at the same time fondly pretend to attain their objective with purely political or economic means, are in the grip of a dangerous error. When religion is banished from the school, from education and from public life, when the representatives of Christianity and its sacred rites are held up to ridicule, are we not really fostering the materialism which is the fertile soil of Communism? Neither force, however well organized it be, nor earthly ideals however lofty or noble, can control a movement whose roots lie in the excessive esteem for the goods of this world.

We trust that those rulers of nations, who are at all aware of the extreme danger threatening every people today, may be more and more convinced of their supreme duty not to hinder the Church in the fulfillment of her mission. This is the more imperative since, while this mission has in view man's happiness in heaven, it cannot but promote his true felicity in time.

The Erring Recalled

We cannot conclude this Encyclical Letter without addressing some words to those of Our children who are more or less tainted with the Communist plague. We earnestly exhort them to hear the voice of their loving Father. We pray the Lord to enlighten them that they may abandon the slippery path which will precipitate one and all to ruin and catastrophe, and that they recognize that Jesus Christ, Our Lord, is their only Savior: "For there is no other name under heaven given to man, whereby we must be saved."

CONCLUSION

Saint Joseph, Model and Patron

To hasten the advent of that "peace of Christ in the kingdom of Christ" so ardently desired by all, We place the vast campaign of the Church against world Communism under the standard of St. Joseph, her mighty Protector. He belongs to the working-class, and he bore the burdens of poverty for himself and the Holy Family, whose tender and vigilant head he was. To him was entrusted the Divine Child when Herod loosed his assassins against Him. In a life of faithful performance of everyday duties, he left an example for all those who must gain their bread by the toil of their hands. He won for himself the title of "The Just," serving thus as a living model of that Christian justice which should reign in social life.

With eyes lifted on high, our Faith sees the new heavens and the new earth described by Our first Predecessor, St. Peter. While the promises of the false prophets of this earth melt away in blood and tears, the great apocalyptic prophecy of the Redeemer shines forth in heavenly splendor: "Behold, I make all things new."

Venerable Brethren, nothing remains but to raise Our paternal hands to call down upon you, upon your clergy and people, upon the whole Catholic family, the Apostolic Benediction.

Given at Rome, at St. Peter's, on the feast of St. Joseph, patron of the universal Church, on the 19th of March, 1937, the 16th year of our Pontificate.

(3) ***Gaudium et spes* 20–21** Modern atheism often takes on a systematic form also **676**
which, in addition to other causes, so insists on man's desire for autonomy as to object to any dependence on God at all. Those who profess this kind of atheism maintain that freedom consists in this, that man is an end to himself, and the sole maker, with supreme control, of his own history (*propriae suae historiae solus artifex et demiurgus*). They claim that his outlook cannot be reconciled with the assertion of a Lord who is

author and end of all things, or that at least it makes such an affirmation altogether unnecessary. The sense of power which modern technical progress begets in man may encourage this outlook.

Among the various kinds of present-day atheism, that one should not go unnoticed which looks for man's autonomy through his economic and social emancipation. It holds that religion, of its very nature, thwarts such emancipation by raising man's hopes in a future life, thus both deceiving him and discouraging him from working for a better form of life on earth. That is why those who hold such views, wherever they gain control of the state, violently attack religion, and in order to spread atheism, especially in the education of young people, make use of all the means by which the civil authority can bring pressure to bear on its subjects.

The Church, as given over to the service of both God and man, cannot cease from reproving, with sorrow yet with the utmost firmness, as she has done in the past, those harmful teachings and ways of acting which are in conflict with reason and with common human experience, and which cast man down from the noble state to which he is born.

She tries nevertheless to seek out the secret motives which lead the atheistic mind to deny God. Well knowing how important are the problems raised by atheism, and urged by her love for all men, she considers that these motives deserve an earnest and more thorough scrutiny.

The Church holds that to acknowledge God is in no way to oppose the dignity of man, since such dignity is grounded and brought to perfection in God. Man has in fact been placed in society by God, who created him as an intelligent and free being; but over and above this he is called as a son to intimacy with God and to share in his happiness. She further teaches that hope in a life to come does not take away from the importance of the duties of this life on earth but rather adds to it by giving new motives for fulfilling those duties. When, on the other hand, man is left without this divine support and without hope of eternal life his dignity is deeply wounded, as may so often be seen today. The problems of life and death, of guilt and of suffering, remain unsolved, so that men are not rarely cast into despair.

Meanwhile, every man remains a question to himself, one that is dimly perceived and left unanswered. For there are times, especially in the major events of life, when no man can altogether escape from such self-questioning. God alone, who calls man to deeper thought and to more humble probing, can fully and with complete certainty supply an answer to this questioning.

Atheism must be countered both by presenting true teaching in a fitting manner and by the full and complete life of the Church and of her members. For it is the function of the Church to render God the Father and his incarnate Son present and as it were visible, while ceaselessly renewing and purifying herself under the guidance of the Holy Spirit. This is brought about chiefly by the witness of a living and mature faith, one namely that is so well formed that it can see difficulties clearly and overcome them. Many martyrs have borne, and continue to bear, a splendid witness to this faith. This faith should show its fruitfulness by penetrating the whole life, even the worldly activities, of those who believe, and by urging them to be loving and just especially towards those in need. Lastly, what does most to show God's presence clearly is the brotherly love of the faithful who, being all of one mind and spirit, work together for the faith of the Gospel and present themselves as a sign of unity.

Although the Church altogether rejects atheism, she nevertheless sincerely proclaims that all men, those who believe as well as those who do not, should help to establish right order in this world where all live together. This certainly cannot be done without a dialogue that is sincere and prudent. The Church therefore deplores the discrimination between believers and unbelievers which some civil authorities unjustly practice in defiance of the fundamental rights of the human person. She demands effective freedom for the faithful to be allowed to build up God's temple in this world also. She courteously invites atheists to weigh the merits of the Gospel of Christ with an open mind.

For the Church knows full well that her message is in harmony with the most secret desires of the human heart, since it champions the dignity of man's calling, giving hope once more to those who already despair of their higher destiny. Her message, far from impairing man, helps him to develop himself by bestowing light, life, and freedom. Apart from this message nothing is able to satisfy the heart of man: "Thou hast made us for thyself, O Lord, and our heart is restless until it rest in thee."

(1) **Revelation 19:1–9** After this I heard what seemed to be the loud voice of a 677
great multitude in heaven, crying,

"Hallelujah! Salvation and glory and power belong to our God,
for his judgments are true and just;
he has judged the great harlot who corrupted the earth with her fornication,
and he has avenged on her the blood of his servants."

Once more they cried,

"Hallelujah! The smoke from her goes up for ever and ever."

And the twenty-four elders and the four living creatures fell down and worshiped God who is seated on the throne, saying, "Amen. Hallelujah!" And from the throne came a voice crying,

"Praise our God, all you his servants,
you who fear him, small and great."

Then I heard what seemed to be the voice of a great multitude, like the sound of many waters and like the sound of mighty thunderpeals, crying,

"Hallelujah! For the Lord our God the Almighty reigns.
Let us rejoice and exult and give him the glory,
for the marriage of the Lamb has come,
and his Bride has made herself ready;
it was granted her to be clothed with fine linen, bright and pure"—

for the fine linen is the righteous deeds of the saints.

And the angel said to me, "Write this: Blessed are those who are invited to the marriage supper of the Lamb." And he said to me, "These are true words of God."

(2) **Revelation 13:8** . . . and all who dwell on earth will worship it, every one whose 677
name has not been written before the foundation of the world in the book of life of the Lamb that was slain.

(3) **Revelation 20:7–10** And when the thousand years are ended, Satan will be 677
loosed from his prison and will come out to deceive the nations which are at the four corners of the earth, that is, Gog and Magog, to gather them for battle; their number is like the sand of the sea. And they marched up over the broad earth and surrounded the camp of the saints and the beloved city; but fire came down from heaven and consumed them, and the devil who had deceived them was thrown into the lake of fire and sulfur where the beast and the false prophet were, and they will be tormented day and night for ever and ever.

(4) **Revelation 21:2–4** And I saw the holy city, new Jerusalem, coming down out 677
of heaven from God, prepared as a bride adorned for her husband; and I heard a loud voice from the throne saying, "Behold, the dwelling of God is with men. He will dwell with them, and they shall be his people, and God himself will be with them; he

will wipe away every tear from their eyes, and death shall be no more, neither shall there be mourning nor crying nor pain any more, for the former things have passed away."

677 (5) **Revelation 20:12** And I saw the dead, great and small, standing before the throne, and books were opened. Also another book was opened, which is the book of life. And the dead were judged by what was written in the books, by what they had done.

677 (6) **2 Peter 3:12–13** . . . waiting for and hastening the coming of the day of God, because of which the heavens will be kindled and dissolved, and the elements will melt with fire! But according to his promise we wait for new heavens and a new earth in which righteousness dwells.

678 (1) **Daniel 7:10**

A stream of fire issued
    and came forth from before him;
a thousand thousands served him,
    and ten thousand times ten thousand stood before him;
the court sat in judgment,
    and the books were opened.

678 (2) **Joel 3–4 (2:28–3:21 RSV)**

"And it shall come to pass afterward,
    that I will pour out my spirit on all flesh;
your sons and your daughters shall prophesy,
    your old men shall dream dreams,
    and your young men shall see visions.
Even upon the menservants and maidservants
    in those days, I will pour out my spirit.

"And I will give portents in the heavens and on the earth, blood and fire and columns of smoke. The sun shall be turned to darkness, and the moon to blood, before the great and terrible day of the Lord comes. And it shall come to pass that all who call upon the name of the Lord shall be delivered; for in Mount Zion and in Jerusalem there shall be those who escape, as the Lord has said, and among the survivors shall be those whom the Lord calls.

"For behold, in those days and at that time, when I restore the fortunes of Judah and Jerusalem, I will gather all the nations and bring them down to the valley of Jehoshaphat, and I will enter into judgment with them there, on account of my people and my heritage Israel, because they have scattered them among the nations, and have divided up my land, and have cast lots for my people, and have given a boy for a harlot, and have sold a girl for wine, and have drunk it.

"What are you to me, O Tyre and Sidon, and all the regions of Philistia? Are you paying me back for something? If you are paying me back, I will requite your deed upon your own head swiftly and speedily. For you have taken my silver and my gold, and have carried my rich treasures into your temples. You have sold the people of Judah and Jerusalem to the Greeks, removing them far from their own border. But now I will stir them up from the place to which you have sold them, and I will requite your deed upon your own head. I will sell your sons and your daughters into the hand of the sons of Judah, and they will sell them to the Sabeans, to a nation far off; for the Lord has spoken."

Proclaim this among the nations:

Prepare war,
stir up the mighty men.
Let all the men of war draw near,
let them come up.
Beat your plowshares into swords,
and your pruning hooks into spears;
let the weak say, "I am a warrior."

Hasten and come,
all you nations round about,
gather yourselves there.
Bring down thy warriors, O Lord.
Let the nations bestir themselves,
and come up to the valley of Jehoshaphat;
for there I will sit to judge
all the nations round about.

Put in the sickle,
for the harvest is ripe.
Go in, tread,
for the wine press is full.
The vats overflow,
for their wickedness is great.

Multitudes, multitudes,
in the valley of decision!
For the day of the Lord is near
in the valley of decision.
The sun and the moon are darkened,
and the stars withdraw their shining.

And the Lord roars from Zion,
and utters his voice from Jerusalem,
and the heavens and the earth shake.
But the Lord is a refuge to his people,
a stronghold to the people of Israel.

"So you shall know that I am the Lord your God,
who dwell in Zion, my holy mountain.
And Jerusalem shall be holy
and strangers shall never again pass through it.

"And in that day
the mountains shall drip sweet wine,
and the hills shall flow with milk,
and all the stream beds of Judah
shall flow with water;
and a fountain shall come forth from the house of the Lord
and water the valley of Shittim.

"Egypt shall become a desolation
and Edom a desolate wilderness,
for the violence done to the people of Judah,
because they have shed innocent blood in their land.
But Judah shall be inhabited for ever,
and Jerusalem to all generations.

I will avenge their blood, and I will not clear the guilty,
for the Lord dwells in Zion."

678 (3) **Malachi 3:19 (4:1 RSV)** "For behold, the day comes, burning like an oven, when all the arrogant and all evildoers will be stubble; the day that comes shall burn them up, says the Lord of hosts, so that it will leave them neither root nor branch. . . ."

678 (4) **Matthew 3:7–12** But when he saw many of the Pharisees and Sadducees coming for baptism, he said to them, "You brood of vipers! Who warned you to flee from the wrath to come? Bear fruit that befits repentance, and do not presume to say to yourselves, 'We have Abraham as our father'; for I tell you, God is able from these stones to raise up children to Abraham. Even now the axe is laid to the root of the trees; every tree therefore that does not bear good fruit is cut down and thrown into the fire.

"I baptize you with water for repentance, but he who is coming after me is mightier than I, whose sandals I am not worthy to carry; he will baptize you with the Holy Spirit and with fire. His winnowing fork is in his hand, and he will clear his threshing floor and gather his wheat into the granary, but the chaff he will burn with unquenchable fire."

678 (5) **Mark 12:38–40** And in his teaching he said, "Beware of the scribes, who like to go about in long robes, and to have salutations in the market places and the best seats in the synagogues and the places of honor at feasts, who devour widows' houses and for a pretense make long prayers. They will receive the greater condemnation."

678 (6) **Luke 12:1–3** In the meantime, when so many thousands of the multitude had gathered together that they trod upon one another, he began to say to his disciples first, "Beware of the leaven of the Pharisees, which is hypocrisy. Nothing is covered up that will not be revealed, or hidden that will not be known. Therefore whatever you have said in the dark shall be heard in the light, and what you have whispered in private rooms shall be proclaimed upon the housetops. . . ."

678 (7) **John 3:20–21** For every one who does evil hates the light, and does not come to the light, lest his deeds should be exposed. But he who does what is true comes to the light, that it may be clearly seen that his deeds have been wrought in God.

678 (8) **Romans 2:16** . . . on that day when, according to my gospel, God judges the secrets of men by Christ Jesus.

678 (9) **1 Corinthians 4:5** Therefore do not pronounce judgment before the time, before the Lord comes, who will bring to light the things now hidden in darkness and will disclose the purposes of the heart. Then every man will receive his commendation from God.

678 (10) **Matthew 11:20–24** Then he began to upbraid the cities where most of his mighty works had been done, because they did not repent. "Woe to you, Chorazin! woe to you, Bethsaida! for if the mighty works done in you had been done in Tyre and Sidon, they would have repented long ago in sackcloth and ashes. But I tell you, it shall be more tolerable on the day of judgment for Tyre and Sidon than for you. And you, Capernaum, will you be exalted to heaven? You shall be brought down to Hades. For if the mighty works done in you had been done in Sodom, it would have remained until this day. But I tell you that it shall be more tolerable on the day of judgment for the land of Sodom than for you."

(11) **Matthew 12:41–42** The men of Nineveh will arise at the judgment with this 678
generation and condemn it; for they repented at the preaching of Jonah, and behold, something greater than Jonah is here. The queen of the South will arise at the judgment with this generation and condemn it; for she came from the ends of the earth to hear the wisdom of Solomon, and behold, something greater than Solomon is here.

(12) **Matthew 5:22** ". . . But I say to you that every one who is angry with his 678
brother shall be liable to judgment; whoever insults his brother shall be liable to the council, and whoever says, 'You fool!' shall be liable to the hell of fire. . . ."

(13) **Matthew 7:1–5** "Judge not, that you be not judged. For with the judgment 678
you pronounce you will be judged, and the measure you give will be the measure you get. Why do you see the speck that is in your brother's eye, but do not notice the log that is in your own eye? Or how can you say to your brother, 'Let me take the speck out of your eye,' when there is the log in your own eye? You hypocrite, first take the log out of your own eye, and then you will see clearly to take the speck out of your brother's eye. . . ."

(1) **John 5:27** . . . and has given him authority to execute judgment, because he is 679
the Son of man.

(2) **Matthew 25:31** "When the Son of man comes in his glory, and all the angels 679
with him, then he will sit on his glorious throne. . . ."

(3) **Acts 10:42** And he commanded us to preach to the people, and to testify that 679
he is the one ordained by God to be judge of the living and the dead.

(4) **Acts 17:31** ". . . because he has fixed a day on which he will judge the world in 679
righteousness by a man whom he has appointed, and of this he has given assurance to all men by raising him from the dead."

(5) **2 Timothy 4:1** I charge you in the presence of God and of Christ Jesus who 679
is to judge the living and the dead, and by his appearing and his kingdom. . . .

(6) **John 3:17** For God sent the Son into the world, not to condemn the world, 679
but that the world might be saved through him.

(7) **John 5:26** For as the Father has life in himself, so he has granted the Son also 679
to have life in himself. . . .

(8) **John 3:18** He who believes in him is not condemned; he who does not believe 679
is condemned already, because he has not believed in the name of the only Son of God.

(9) **John 12:48** He who rejects me and does not receive my sayings has a judge; 679
the word that I have spoken will be his judge on the last day.

(10) **Matthew 12:32** And whoever says a word against the Son of man will be 679
forgiven; but whoever speaks against the Holy Spirit will not be forgiven, either in this age or in the age to come.

679 (11) **1 Corinthians 3:12–15** Now if any one builds on the foundation with gold, silver, precious stones, wood, hay, straw—each man's work will become manifest; for the Day will disclose it, because it will be revealed with fire, and the fire will test what sort of work each one has done. If the work which any man has built on the foundation survives, he will receive a reward. If any man's work is burned up, he will suffer loss, though he himself will be saved, but only as through fire.

679 (12) **Hebrews 6:4–6** For it is impossible to restore again to repentance those who have once been enlightened, who have tasted the heavenly gift, and have become partakers of the Holy Spirit, and have tasted the goodness of the word of God and the powers of the age to come, if they then commit apostasy, since they crucify the Son of God on their own account and hold him up to contempt.

679 (13) **Hebrews 10:26–31** For if we sin deliberately after receiving the knowledge of the truth, there no longer remains a sacrifice for sins, but a fearful prospect of judgment, and a fury of fire which will consume the adversaries. A man who has violated the law of Moses dies without mercy at the testimony of two or three witnesses. How much worse punishment do you think will be deserved by the man who has spurned the Son of God, and profaned the blood of the covenant by which he was sanctified, and outraged the Spirit of grace? For we know him who said, "Vengeance is mine, I will repay." And again, "The Lord will judge his people." It is a fearful thing to fall into the hands of the living God.

689 **Galatians 4:6** And because you are sons, God has sent the Spirit of his Son into our hearts, crying, "Abba! Father!"

690 (1) **John 3:34** For he whom God has sent utters the words of God, for it is not by measure that he gives the Spirit. . . .

690 (2) **John 7:39** Now this he said about the Spirit, which those who believed in him were to receive; for as yet the Spirit had not been given, because Jesus was not yet glorified.

690 (3) **John 17:22** The glory which thou hast given me I have given to them, that they may be one even as we are one. . . .

690 (4) **John 16:14** He will glorify me, for he will take what is mine and declare it to you.

691 **Matthew 28:19** Go therefore and make disciples of all nations, baptizing them in the name of the Father and of the Son and of the Holy Spirit. . . .

692 **1 John 2:1** My little children, I am writing this to you so that you may not sin; but if any one does sin, we have an advocate [consoler] with the Father, Jesus Christ the righteous. . . .

693 (1) **Galatians 3:14** . . . that in Christ Jesus the blessing of Abraham might come upon the Gentiles, that we might receive the promise of the Spirit through faith.

693 (2) **Ephesians 1:13** In him you also, who have heard the word of truth, the gospel of your salvation, and have believed in him, were sealed with the promised Holy Spirit. . . .

(1) **John 19:34** But one of the soldiers pierced his side with a spear, and at once there came out blood and water. 694

(2) **1 John 5:8** There are three witnesses, the Spirit, the water, and the blood; and these three agree. 694

(3) **John 4:10–14** Jesus answered her, "If you knew the gift of God, and who it is that is saying to you, 'Give me a drink,' you would have asked him, and he would have given you living water." The woman said to him, "Sir, you have nothing to draw with, and the well is deep; where do you get that living water? Are you greater than our father Jacob, who gave us the well, and drank from it himself, and his sons, and his cattle?" Jesus said to her, "Every one who drinks of this water will thirst again, but whoever drinks of the water that I shall give him will never thirst; the water that I shall give him will become in him a spring of water welling up to eternal life." 694

(4) **John 7:38** ". . . He who believes in me, as the scripture has said, 'Out of his heart shall flow rivers of living water.'" 694

(5) **Exodus 17:1–6** All the congregation of the people of Israel moved on from the wilderness of Sin by stages, according to the commandment of the Lord, and camped at Rephidim; but there was no water for the people to drink. Therefore the people found fault with Moses, and said, "Give us water to drink." And Moses said to them, "Why do you find fault with me? Why do you put the Lord to the proof?" But the people thirsted there for water, and the people murmured against Moses, and said, "Why did you bring us up out of Egypt, to kill us and our children and our cattle with thirst?" So Moses cried to the Lord, "What shall I do with this people? They are almost ready to stone me." And the Lord said to Moses, "Pass on before the people, taking with you some of the elders of Israel; and take in your hand the rod with which you struck the Nile, and go. Behold, I will stand before you there on the rock at Horeb; and you shall strike the rock, and water shall come out of it, that the people may drink." And Moses did so, in the sight of the elders of Israel. 694

(6) **Isaiah 55:1** 694

"Ho, every one who thirsts, come to the waters;
and he who has no money,
come, buy and eat!
Come, buy wine and milk
without money and without price. . . ."

(7) **Zechariah 14:8** On that day living waters shall flow out from Jerusalem, half of them to the eastern sea and half of them to the western sea; it shall continue in summer as in winter. 694

(8) **1 Corinthians 10:4** . . . and all drank the same supernatural drink. For they drank from the supernatural Rock which followed them, and the Rock was Christ. 694

(9) **Revelation 21:6** And he said to me, "It is done! I am the Alpha and the Omega, the beginning and the end. To the thirsty I will give from the fountain of the water of life without payment. . . ." 694

(10) **Revelation 22:17** The Spirit and the Bride say, "Come." And let him who hears say, "Come." And let him who is thirsty come, let him who desires take the water of life without price. 694

695 (1) **1 John 2:20** But you have been anointed by the Holy One, and you all know.

695 (2) **1 John 2:27** . . . but the anointing which you received from him abides in you, and you have no need that any one should teach you; as his anointing teaches you about everything, and is true, and is no lie, just as it has taught you, abide in him.

695 (3) **2 Corinthians 1:21** But it is God who establishes us with you in Christ, and has commissioned [anointed] us. . . .

695 (4) **Exodus 30:22–32** Moreover, the Lord said to Moses, "Take the finest spices: of liquid myrrh five hundred shekels, and of sweet-smelling cinnamon half as much, that is, two hundred and fifty, and of aromatic cane two hundred and fifty, and of cassia five hundred, according to the shekel of the sanctuary, and of olive oil a hin; and you shall make of these a sacred anointing oil blended as by the perfumer; a holy anointing oil it shall be. And you shall anoint with it the tent of meeting and the ark of the testimony, and the table and all its utensils, and the lampstand and its utensils, and the altar of incense, and the altar of burnt offering with all its utensils and the laver and its base; you shall consecrate them, that they may be most holy; whatever touches them will become holy. And you shall anoint Aaron and his sons, and consecrate them, that they may serve me as priests. And you shall say to the people of Israel, 'This shall be my holy anointing oil throughout your generations. It shall not be poured upon the bodies of ordinary men, and you shall make no other like it in composition; it is holy, and it shall be holy to you. . . .'"

695 (5) **1 Samuel 16:13** Then Samuel took the horn of oil, and anointed him in the midst of his brothers; and the Spirit of the Lord came mightily upon David from that day forward. And Samuel rose up, and went to Ramah.

695 (6) **Luke 4:18–19**

"The Spirit of the Lord is upon me,
because he has anointed me to preach good news to the poor.
He has sent me to proclaim release to the captives
and recovering of sight to the blind,
to set at liberty those who are oppressed,
to proclaim the acceptable year of the Lord."

695 (7) **Isaiah 61:1**

The Spirit of the Lord God is upon me,
  because the Lord has anointed me
to bring good tidings to the afflicted;
  he has sent me to bind up the brokenhearted,
to proclaim liberty to the captives,
  and the opening of the prison to those who are bound. . . .

695 (8) **Luke 2:11** . . . for to you is born this day in the city of David a Savior, who is Christ the Lord.

695 (9) **Luke 2:26–27** And it had been revealed to him by the Holy Spirit that he should not see death before he had seen the Lord's Christ. And inspired by the Spirit he came into the temple; and when the parents brought in the child Jesus, to do for him according to the custom of the law. . . .

(10) **Luke 4:1** And Jesus, full of the Holy Spirit, returned from the Jordan, and was led by the Spirit. . . . **695**

(11) **Luke 6:19** And all the crowd sought to touch him, for power came forth from him and healed them all. **695**

(12) **Luke 8:46** But Jesus said, "Some one touched me; for I perceive that power has gone forth from me." **695**

(13) **Romans 1:4** . . . and designated Son of God in power according to the Spirit of holiness by his resurrection from the dead, Jesus Christ our Lord. . . . **695**

(14) **Romans 8:11** If the Spirit of him who raised Jesus from the dead dwells in you, he who raised Christ Jesus from the dead will give life to your mortal bodies also through his Spirit which dwells in you. **695**

(15) **Acts 2:36** ". . . Let all the house of Israel therefore know assuredly that God has made him both Lord and Christ, this Jesus whom you crucified." **695**

(1) **1 Kings 18:38–39** Then the fire of the Lord fell, and consumed the burnt offering, and the wood, and the stones, and the dust, and licked up the water that was in the trench. And when all the people saw it, they fell on their faces; and they said, "The Lord, he is God; the Lord, he is God." **696**

(2) **St. John of the Cross, *Llama de amor viva* (The Living Flame of Love)** **696**

O living flame of love
That tenderly wounds my soul
In its deepest center! Since
Now You are not oppressive,
Now Consummate! If it be Your will:
Tear through the veil of this sweet encounter!

O sweet cautery,
O delightful wound!
O gentle hand! O delicate touch
That tastes of eternal life
And pays every debt!
In killing You changed death to life.

O lamps of fire!
In whose splendors
The deep caverns of feeling,
Once obscure and blind,
Now give forth, so rarely, so exquisitely,
Both warmth and light to their Beloved.

How gently and lovingly
You will wake in my heart,
Where in secret You dwell alone;
And by Your sweet breathing,
Filled with good and glory,
How tenderly You swell my heart with love!

697 (1) **Exodus 24:15–18** Then Moses went up on the mountain, and the cloud covered the mountain. The glory of the Lord settled on Mount Sinai, and the cloud covered it six days; and on the seventh day he called to Moses out of the midst of the cloud. Now the appearance of the glory of the Lord was like a devouring fire on the top of the mountain in the sight of the people of Israel. And Moses entered the cloud, and went up on the mountain. And Moses was on the mountain forty days and forty nights.

697 (2) **Exodus 33:9–10** When Moses entered the tent, the pillar of cloud would descend and stand at the door of the tent, and the Lord would speak with Moses. And when all the people saw the pillar of cloud standing at the door of the tent, all the people would rise up and worship, every man at his tent door.

697 (3) **Exodus 40:36–38** Throughout all their journeys, whenever the cloud was taken up from over the tabernacle, the people of Israel would go onward; but if the cloud was not taken up, then they did not go onward till the day that it was taken up. For throughout all their journeys the cloud of the Lord was upon the tabernacle by day, and fire was in it by night, in the sight of all the house of Israel.

697 (4) **1 Corinthians 10:1–2** I want you to know, brethren, that our fathers were all under the cloud, and all passed through the sea, and all were baptized into Moses in the cloud and in the sea. . . .

697 (5) **1 Kings 8:10–12** And when the priests came out of the holy place, a cloud filled the house of the Lord, so that the priests could not stand to minister because of the cloud; for the glory of the Lord filled the house of the Lord.

Then Solomon said,

"The Lord has set the sun in the heavens,
but has said that he would dwell in thick darkness. . . ."

697 (6) **Acts 1:9** And when he had said this, as they were looking on, he was lifted up, and a cloud took him out of their sight.

697 (7) **Luke 21:27** And then they will see the Son of man coming in a cloud with power and great glory.

698 (1) **2 Corinthians 1:22** . . . he has put his seal upon us and given us his Spirit in our hearts as a guarantee.

698 (2) **Ephesians 1:13** In him you also, who have heard the word of truth, the gospel of your salvation, and have believed in him, were sealed with the promised Holy Spirit. . . .

698 (3) **Ephesians 4:30** And do not grieve the Holy Spirit of God, in whom you were sealed for the day of redemption.

699 (1) **Mark 6:5** And he could do no mighty work there, except that he laid his hands upon a few sick people and healed them.

699 (2) **Mark 8:23** And he took the blind man by the hand, and led him out of the village; and when he had spit on his eyes and laid his hands upon him, he asked him, "Do you see anything?"

(3) **Mark 10:16** And he took them in his arms and blessed them, laying his hands upon them. 699

(4) **Mark 16:18** ". . . they will pick up serpents, and if they drink any deadly thing, it will not hurt them; they will lay their hands on the sick, and they will recover." 699

(5) **Acts 5:12** Now many signs and wonders were done among the people by the hands of the apostles. And they were all together in Solomon's Portico. 699

(6) **Acts 14:3** So they remained for a long time, speaking boldly for the Lord, who bore witness to the word of his grace, granting signs and wonders to be done by their hands. 699

(7) **Acts 8:17–19** Then they laid their hands on them and they received the Holy Spirit. Now when Simon saw that the Spirit was given through the laying on of the apostles' hands, he offered them money, saying, "Give me also this power, that any one on whom I lay my hands may receive the Holy Spirit." 699

(8) **Acts 13:3** Then after fasting and praying they laid their hands on them and sent them off. 699

(9) **Acts 19:6** And when Paul had laid his hands upon them, the Holy Spirit came on them; and they spoke with tongues and prophesied. 699

(10) **Hebrews 6:2** . . . with instruction about ablutions, the laying on of hands, the resurrection of the dead, and eternal judgment. 699

(1) **Genesis 8:8–12** Then he sent forth a dove from him, to see if the waters had subsided from the face of the ground; but the dove found no place to set her foot, and she returned to him to the ark, for the waters were still on the face of the whole earth. So he put forth his hand and took her and brought her into the ark with him. He waited another seven days, and again he sent forth the dove out of the ark; and the dove came back to him in the evening, and lo, in her mouth a freshly plucked olive leaf; so Noah knew that the waters had subsided from the earth. Then he waited another seven days, and sent forth the dove; and she did not return to him any more. 701

(2) **Matthew 3:16** And when Jesus was baptized, he went up immediately from the water, and behold, the heavens were opened and he saw the Spirit of God descending like a dove, and alighting on him. . . . 701

(1) **2 Corinthians 3:14** But their minds were hardened; for to this day, when they read the old covenant, that same veil remains unlifted, because only through Christ is it taken away. 702

(2) **John 5:39** You search the scriptures, because you think that in them you have eternal life; and it is they that bear witness to me. . . . 702

(3) **John 5:46** If you believed Moses, you would believe me, for he wrote of me. 702

(4) **Luke 24:44** Then he said to them, "These are my words which I spoke to you, while I was still with you, that everything written about me in the law of Moses and the prophets and the psalms must be fulfilled." 702

703 (1) **Psalm 33:6**
By the word of the Lord the heavens were made,
and all their host by the breath of his mouth.

703 (2) **Psalm 104:30**
When thou sendest forth thy Spirit, they are created;
and thou renewest the face of the ground.

703 (3) **Genesis 1:2** The earth was without form and void, and darkness was upon the face of the deep; and the Spirit of God was moving over the face of the waters.

703 (4) **Genesis 2:7** . . . then the Lord God formed man of dust from the ground, and breathed into his nostrils the breath of life; and man became a living being.

703 (5) **Qoheleth 3:20–21 (Ecclesiastes: RSV)** All go to one place; all are from the dust, and all turn to dust again. Who knows whether the spirit of man goes upward and the spirit of the beast goes down to the earth?

703 (6) **Ezekiel 37:10** So I prophesied as he commanded me, and the breath came into them, and they lived, and stood upon their feet, an exceedingly great host.

705 (1) **John 1:14** And the Word became flesh and dwelt among us, full of grace and truth; we have beheld his glory, glory as of the only Son from the Father.

705 (2) **Philippians 2:7** . . . but emptied himself, taking the form of a servant, being born in the likeness of men.

706 (1) **Genesis 18:1–15** And the Lord appeared to him by the oaks of Mamre, as he sat at the door of his tent in the heat of the day. He lifted up his eyes and looked, and behold, three men stood in front of him. When he saw them, he ran from the tent door to meet them, and bowed himself to the earth, and said, "My lord, if I have found favor in your sight, do not pass by your servant. Let a little water be brought, and wash your feet, and rest yourselves under the tree, while I fetch a morsel of bread, that you may refresh yourselves, and after that you may pass on—since you have come to your servant." So they said, "Do as you have said." And Abraham hastened into the tent to Sarah, and said, "Make ready quickly three measures of fine meal, knead it, and make cakes." And Abraham ran to the herd, and took a calf, tender and good, and gave it to the servant, who hastened to prepare it. Then he took curds, and milk, and the calf which he had prepared, and set it before them; and he stood by them under the tree while they ate.

They said to him, "Where is Sarah your wife?" And he said, "She is in the tent." The Lord said, "I will surely return to you in the spring, and Sarah your wife shall have a son." And Sarah was listening at the tent door behind him. Now Abraham and Sarah were old, advanced in age; it had ceased to be with Sarah after the manner of women. So Sarah laughed to herself, saying, "After I have grown old, and my husband is old, shall I have pleasure?" The Lord said to Abraham, "Why did Sarah laugh, and say, 'Shall I indeed bear a child, now that I am old?' Is anything too hard for the Lord? At the appointed time I will return to you, in the spring, and Sarah shall have a son." But Sarah denied, saying, "I did not laugh"; for she was afraid. He said, "No, but you did laugh."

(2) **Luke 1:26–38** In the sixth month the angel Gabriel was sent from God to 706
a city of Galilee named Nazareth, to a virgin betrothed to a man whose name was Joseph, of the house of David; and the virgin's name was Mary. And he came to her and said, "Hail, O favored one, the Lord is with you!" But she was greatly troubled at the saying, and considered in her mind what sort of greeting this might be. And the angel said to her, "Do not be afraid, Mary, for you have found favor with God. And behold, you will conceive in your womb and bear a son, and you shall call his name Jesus.

He will be great, and will be called the Son of the Most High;
and the Lord God will give to him the throne of his father David,
and he will reign over the house of Jacob for ever;
and of his kingdom there will be no end."

And Mary said to the angel, "How shall this be, since I have no husband?" And the angel said to her,

"The Holy Spirit will come upon you,
and the power of the Most High will overshadow you;
therefore the child to be born will be called holy,
the Son of God.

And behold, your kinswoman Elizabeth in her old age has also conceived a son; and this is the sixth month with her who was called barren. For with God nothing will be impossible." And Mary said, "Behold, I am the handmaid of the Lord; let it be to me according to your word." And the angel departed from her.

(3) **Luke 1:54–55** 706

". . . He has helped his servant Israel,
in remembrance of his mercy,
as he spoke to our fathers,
to Abraham and to his posterity for ever."

(4) **John 1:12–13** But to all who received him, who believed in his name, he gave 706
power to become children of God; who were born, not of blood nor of the will of the flesh nor of the will of man, but of God.

(5) **Romans 4:16–21** That is why it depends on faith, in order that the promise may 706
rest on grace and be guaranteed to all his descendants—not only to the adherents of the law but also to those who share the faith of Abraham, for he is the father of us all, as it is written, "I have made you the father of many nations"—in the presence of the God in whom he believed, who gives life to the dead and calls into existence the things that do not exist. In hope he believed against hope, that he should become the father of many nations; as he had been told, "So shall your descendants be." He did not weaken in faith when he considered his own body, which was as good as dead because he was about a hundred years old, or when he considered the barenness of Sarah's womb. No distrust made him waver concerning the promise of God, but he grew strong in his faith as he gave glory to God, fully convinced that God was able to do what he had promised.

(6) **Genesis 12:3** ". . . I will bless those who bless you, and him who curses you I 706
will curse; and by you all the families of the earth shall bless themselves."

(7) **Galatians 3:16** Now the promises were made to Abraham and to his offspring. 706
It does not say, "And to offsprings," referring to many; but, referring to one, "And to your offspring," which is Christ.

706 (8) **John 11:52** . . . and not for the nation only, but to gather into one the children of God who are scattered abroad.

706 (9) **Genesis 22:17–19** ". . . I will indeed bless you, and I will multiply your descendants as the stars of heaven and as the sand which is on the seashore. And your descendants shall possess the gate of their enemies, and by your descendants shall all the nations of the earth bless themselves, because you have obeyed my voice." So Abraham returned to his young men, and they arose and went together to Beersheba; and Abraham dwelt at Beersheba.

706 (10) **Luke 1:73** . . . the oath which he swore to our father Abraham. . . .

706 (11) **John 3:16** For God so loved the world that he gave his only Son, that whoever believes in him should not perish but have eternal life.

706 (12) **Romans 8:32** He who did not spare his own Son but gave him up for us all, will he not also give us all things with him?

706 (13) **Galatians 3:14** . . . that in Christ Jesus the blessing of Abraham might come upon the Gentiles, that we might receive the promise of the Spirit through faith.

708 (1) **Exodus 19–20** On the third new moon after the people of Israel had gone forth out of the land of Egypt, on that day they came into the wilderness of Sinai. And when they set out from Rephidim and came into the wilderness of Sinai, they encamped in the wilderness; and there Israel encamped before the mountain. And Moses went up to God, and the Lord called to him out of the mountain, saying, "Thus you shall say to the house of Jacob, and tell the people of Israel: You have seen what I did to the Egyptians, and how I bore you on eagles' wings and brought you to myself. Now therefore, if you will obey my voice and keep my covenant, you shall be my own possession among all peoples; for all the earth is mine, and you shall be to me a kingdom of priests and a holy nation. These are the words which you shall speak to the children of Israel."

So Moses came and called the elders of the people, and set before them all these words which the Lord had commanded him. And all the people answered together and said, "All that the Lord has spoken we will do." And Moses reported the words of the people to the Lord. And the Lord said to Moses, "Lo, I am coming to you in a thick cloud, that the people may hear when I speak with you, and may also believe you for ever."

Then Moses told the words of the people to the Lord. And the Lord said to Moses, "Go to the people and consecrate them today and tomorrow, and let them wash their garments, and be ready by the third day; for on the third day the Lord will come down upon Mount Sinai in the sight of all the people. And you shall set bounds for the people round about, saying, 'Take heed that you do not go up into the mountain or touch the border of it; whoever touches the mountain shall be put to death; no hand shall touch him, but he shall be stoned or shot; whether beast or man, he shall not live.' When the trumpet sounds a long blast, they shall come up to the mountain." So Moses went down from the mountain to the people, and consecrated the people; and they washed their garments. And he said to the people, "Be ready by the third day; do not go near a woman."

On the morning of the third day there were thunders and lightnings, and a thick cloud upon the mountain, and a very loud trumpet blast, so that all the people who were in the camp trembled. Then Moses brought the people out of the camp to meet

God; and they took their stand at the foot of the mountain. And Mount Sinai was wrapped in smoke, because the Lord descended upon it in fire; and the smoke of it went up like the smoke of a kiln, and the whole mountain quaked greatly. And as the sound of the trumpet grew louder and louder, Moses spoke, and God answered him in thunder. And the Lord came down upon Mount Sinai, to the top of the mountain; and the Lord called Moses to the top of the mountain, and Moses went up. And the Lord said to Moses, "Go down and warn the people, lest they break through to the Lord to gaze and many of them perish. And also let the priests who come near to the Lord consecrate themselves, lest the Lord break out upon them." And Moses said to the Lord, "The people cannot come up to Mount Sinai; for thou thyself didst charge us, saying 'Set bounds about the mountain, and consecrate it.' " And the Lord said to him, "Go down, and come up bringing Aaron with you; but do not let the priests and the people break through to come up to the Lord, lest he break out against them." So Moses went down to the people and told them.

And God spoke all these words, saying, "I am the Lord your God, who brought you out of the land of Egypt, out of the house of bondage.

"You shall have no other gods before me.

"You shall not make for yourself a graven image, or any likeness of anything that is in heaven above, or that is in the earth beneath, or that is in the water under the earth; you shall not bow down to them or serve them; for I the Lord your God am a jealous God, visiting the iniquity of the fathers upon the children to the third and the fourth generation of those who hate me, but showing steadfast love to thousands of those who love me and keep my commandments.

"You shall not take the name of the Lord your God in vain; for the Lord will not hold him guiltless who takes his name in vain.

"Remember the sabbath day, to keep it holy. Six days you shall labor, and do all your work; but the seventh day is a sabbath to the Lord your God; in it you shall not do any work, you, or your son, or your daughter, your manservant, or your maidservant, or your cattle, or the sojourner who is within your gates; for in six days the Lord made heaven and earth, the sea, and all that is in them, and rested the seventh day; therefore the Lord blessed the sabbath day and hallowed it.

"Honor your father and your mother, that your days may be long in the land which the Lord your God gives you.

"You shall not kill.

"You shall not commit adultery.

"You shall not steal.

"You shall not bear false witness against your neighbor.

"You shall not covet your neighbor's house; you shall not covet your neighbor's wife, or his manservant, or his maidservant, or his ox, or his ass, or anything that is your neighbor's."

Now when all the people perceived the thunderings and the lightnings and the sound of the trumpet and the mountain smoking, the people were afraid and trembled; and they stood afar off, and said to Moses, "You speak to us, and we will hear; but let not God speak to us, lest we die." And Moses said to the people, "Do not fear; for God has come to prove you, and that the fear of him may be before your eyes, that you may not sin."

And the people stood afar off, while Moses drew near to the thick darkness where God was. And the Lord said to Moses, "Thus you shall say to the people of Israel: 'You have seen for yourselves that I have talked with you from heaven. You shall not make gods of silver to be with me, nor shall you make for yourselves gods of gold. An altar of earth you shall make for me and sacrifice on it your burnt offerings and your peace offerings, your sheep and your oxen; in every place where I cause my name to be remembered I will come to you and bless you. And if you make me an altar of stone, you shall not build it of hewn stones; for if you wield your tool upon it you profane it. And you shall not go up by steps to my altar, that your nakedness be not exposed on it.' . . ."

708 (2) **Deuteronomy 1–11** These are the words that Moses spoke to all Israel beyond the Jordan in the wilderness, in the Arabah over against Suph, between Paran and Tophel, Laban, Hazeroth, and Dizahab. It is eleven days' journey from Horeb by the way of Mount Seir to Kadeshbarnea. And in the fortieth year, on the first day of the eleventh month, Moses spoke to the people of Israel according to all that the Lord had given him in commandment to them, after he had defeated Sihon the king of the Amorites, who lived in Heshbon, and Og the king of Bashan, who lived in Ashtaroth and in Edrei. Beyond the Jordan, in the land of Moab, Moses undertook to explain this law, saying, "The Lord our God said to us in Horeb, 'You have stayed long enough at this mountain; turn and take your journey, and go to the hill country of the Amorites, and to all their neighbors in the Arabah, in the hill country and in the lowland, and in the Negeb, and by the seacoast, the land of the Canaanites, and Lebanon, as far as the great river, the river Euphrates. Behold, I have set the land before you; go in and take possession of the land which the Lord swore to your fathers, to Abraham, to Isaac, and to Jacob, to give them and to their descendants after them.'

"At that time I said to you, 'I am not able alone to bear you; the Lord your God has multiplied you, and behold, you are this day as the stars of heaven for multitude. May the Lord, the God of your fathers, make you a thousand times as many as you are, and bless you, as he has promised you! How can I bear alone the weight and burden of you and your strife? Choose wise, understanding, and experienced men, according to your tribes, and I will appoint them as your heads.' And you answered me, 'The thing that you have spoken is good for us to do.' So I took the heads of your tribes, wise and experienced men, and set them as heads over you, commanders of thousands, commanders of hundreds, commanders of fifties, commanders of tens, and officers, throughout your tribes. And I charged your judges at that time, 'Hear the cases between your brethren, and judge righteously between a man and his brother or the alien that is with him. You shall not be partial in judgment; you shall hear the small and the great alike; you shall not be afraid of the face of man, for the judgment is God's; and the case that is too hard for you, you shall bring to me, and I will hear it.' And I commanded you at that time all the things that you should do.

"And we set out from Horeb, and went through all that great and terrible wilderness which you saw, on the way to the hill country of the Amorites, as the Lord our God commanded us; and we came to Kadeshbarnea. And I said to you, 'You have come to the hill country of the Amorites, which the Lord our God gives us. Behold, the Lord your God has set the land before you; go up, take possession, as the Lord, the God of your fathers, has told you; do not fear or be dismayed.' Then all of you came near me, and said, 'Let us send men before us, that they may explore the land for us, and bring us word again of the way by which we must go up and the cities into which we shall come.' The thing seemed good to me, and I took twelve men of you, one man for each tribe; and they turned and went up into the hill country, and came to the Valley of Eschol and spied it out. And they took in their hands some of the fruit of the land and brought it down to us, and brought us word again, and said, 'It is a good land which the Lord our God gives us.'

"Yet you would not go up, but rebelled against the command of the Lord your God; and you murmured in your tents, and said, 'Because the Lord hated us he has brought us forth out of the land of Egypt, to give us into the hands of the Amorites, to destroy us. Whither are we going up? Our brethren have made our hearts melt, saying, "The people are greater and taller than we; the cities are great and fortified up to heaven; and moreover we have seen the sons of the Anakim there."' Then I said to you, 'Do not be in dread or afraid of them. The Lord your God who goes before you will himself fight for you, just as he did for you in Egypt before your eyes, and in the wilderness, where you have seen how the Lord your God bore you, as a man bears his son, in all the way that you went until you came to this place.' Yet in spite of this word you did not believe the Lord your God, who went before you in the way to seek you out a place to pitch your tents, in fire by night, to show you by what way you should go, and in the cloud by day.

"And the Lord heard your words, and was angered, and he swore, 'Not one of these men of this evil generation shall see the good land which I swore to give to your fathers, except Caleb the son of Jephunneh; he shall see it, and to him and to his children I will give the land upon which he has trodden, because he has wholly followed the Lord!' The Lord was angry with me also on your account, and said, 'You shall not go in there; Joshua the son of Nun, who stands before you, he shall enter; encourage him, for he shall cause Israel to inherit it. Moreover your little ones, who you said would become a prey, and your children, who this day have no knowledge of good or evil, shall go in there, and to them I will give it, and they shall possess it. But as for you, turn, and journey into the wilderness in the direction of the Red Sea.'

"Then you answered me, 'We have sinned against the Lord; we will go up and fight, just as the Lord our God commanded us.' And every man of you girded on his weapons of war, and thought it easy to go up into the hill country. And the Lord said to me, 'Say to them, Do not go up or fight, for I am not in the midst of you; lest you be defeated before your enemies.' So I spoke to you, and you would not hearken; but you rebelled against the command of the Lord, and were presumptuous and went up into the hill country. Then the Amorites who lived in that hill country came out against you and chased you as bees do and beat you down in Seir as far as Hormah. And you returned and wept before the Lord; but the Lord did not hearken to your voice or give ear to you. So you remained at Kadesh many days, the days that you remained there.

"Then we turned, and journeyed into the wilderness in the direction of the Red Sea, as the Lord told me; and for many days we went about Mount Seir. Then the Lord said to me, "You have been going about this mountain country long enough; turn northward. And command the people, You are about to pass through the territory of your brethren the sons of Esau, who live in Seir; and they will be afraid of you. So take good heed; do not contend with them; for I will not give you any of their land, no, not as much as for the sole of the foot to tread on, because I have given Mount Seir to Esau as a possession. You shall purchase food from them for money, that you may eat; and you shall also buy water of them for money, that you may drink. For the Lord your God has blessed you in all the work of your hands; he knows your going through this great wilderness; these forty years the Lord your God has been with you; you have lacked nothing.' So we went on, away from our brethren the sons of Esau who live in Seir, away from the Arabah road from Elath and Eziongeber.

"And we turned and went in the direction of the wilderness of Moab. And the Lord said to me, 'Do not harass Moab or contend with them in battle, for I will not give you any of their land for a possession, because I have given Ar to the sons of Lot for a possession.' (The Emim formerly lived there, a people great and many, and tall as the Anakim; like the Anakim they are also known as Rephaim, but the Moabites call them Emim. The Horites also lived in Seir formerly, but the sons of Esau dispossessed them, and destroyed them from before them, and settled in their stead; as Israel did to the land of their possession, which the Lord gave to them.) 'Now rise up, and go over the brook Zered.' So we went over the brook Zered. And the time from our leaving Kadeshbarnea until we crossed the brook Zered was thirty-eight years, until the entire generation, that is, the men of war, had perished from the camp, as the Lord had sworn to them. For indeed the hand of the Lord was against them, to destroy them from the camp, until they had perished.

"So when all the men of war had perished and were dead from among the people, the Lord said to me, 'This day you are to pass over the boundary of Moab at Ar; and when you approach the frontier of the sons of Ammon, do not harass them or contend with them, for I will not give you any of the land of the sons of Ammon as a possession, because I have given it to the sons of Lot for a possession.' (That also is known as a land of Rephaim; Rephaim formerly lived there, but the Ammonites call them Zamzummim, a people great and many, and tall as the Anakim; but the Lord destroyed them before them; and they dispossessed them, and settled in their stead; as he did for the sons of Esau, who live in Seir, when he destroyed the Horites before them, and they dispossessed them, and settled in their stead even to this day. As for the Avvim, who lived in villages as far as Gaza, the Caphtorim, who came from Caphtor, destroyed them and settled in their stead.) 'Rise up, take your journey, and go over the valley of the Arnon; behold, I have given into your hand Sihon the Amorite, king of Heshbon, and his land; begin to take possession, and contend with him in battle. This day I will begin to put the dread and fear of you upon the peoples that are under the whole heaven, who shall hear the report of you and shall tremble and be in anguish because of you.'

"So I sent messengers from the wilderness of Kedemoth to Sihon the king of Heshbon, with words of peace, saying, 'Let me pass through your land; I will go only by the road, I will turn aside neither to the right nor to the left. You shall sell me food for money, that I may eat, and give me water for money, that I may drink; only let me pass through on foot, as the sons of Esau who live in Seir and the Moabites who live in Ar did for me, until I go over the Jordan into the land which the Lord our God gives to us.' But Sihon the king of Heshbon would not let us pass by him; for the Lord your God hardened his spirit and made his heart obstinate, that he might give him into your hand, as at this day. And the Lord said to me, 'Behold, I have begun to give Sihon and his land over to you; begin to take possession, that you may occupy his land.' Then Sihon came out against us, he and all his people, to battle at Jahaz. And the Lord our God gave him over to us; and we defeated him and his sons and all his people. And we captured all his cities at that time and utterly destroyed every city, men, women, and children; we left none remaining; only the cattle we took as spoil for ourselves, with the booty of the cities which we captured. From Aroer, which is on the edge of the valley of the Arnon, and from the city that is in the valley, as far as Gilead, there was not a city too high for us; the Lord our God gave all into our hands. Only to the land of the sons of Ammon you did not draw near, that is, to all the banks of the river Jabbok and the cities of the hill country, and wherever the Lord our God forbade us.

"Then we turned and went up the way to Bashan; and Og the king of Bashan came out against us, he and all his people, to battle at Edrei. But the Lord said to me. 'Do not fear him; for I have given him and all his people and his land into your hand; and you shall do to him as you did to Sihon the king of the Amorites, who dwelt at Heshbon.' So the Lord our God gave into our hand Og also, the king of Bashan, and all his people; and we smote him until no survivor was left to him. And we took all his cities at that time—there was not a city which we did not take from them—

sixty cities, the whole region of Argob, the kingdom of Og in Bashan. All these were cities fortified with high walls, gates, and bars, besides very many unwalled villages. And we utterly destroyed them, as we did to Sihon the king of Heshbon, destroying every city, men, women, and children. But all the cattle and the spoil of the cities we took as our booty. So we took the land at that time out of the hand of the two kings of the Amorites who were beyond the Jordan, from the valley of the Arnon to Mount Hermon (the Sidonians call Hermon Sirion, while the Amorites call it Senir), all the cities of the tableland and all Gilead and all Bashan, as far as Salecah and Edrei, cities of the kingdom of Og in Bashan. (For only Og the king of Bashan was left of the remnant of the Rephaim; behold, his bedstead was a bedstead of iron; is it not in Rabbah of the Ammonites? Nine cubits was its length, and four cubits its breadth, according to the common cubit.)

"When we took possession of this land at that time, I gave to the Reubenites and the Gadites the territory beginning at Aroer, which is on the edge of the valley of the Arnon, and half the hill country of Gilead with its cities; the rest of Gilead, and all Bashan, the kingdom of Og, that is, all the region of Argob, I gave to the half-tribe of Manasseh. (The whole of that Bashan is called the land of Rephaim. Jair the Manassite took all the region of Argob, that is, Bashan, as far as the border of the Geshurites and the Maacathites, and called the villages after his own name, Havvothjair, as it is to this day.) To Machir I gave Gilead, and to the Reubenites and the Gadites I gave the territory from Gilead as far as the valley of the Arnon, with the middle of the valley as a boundary, as far over as the river Jabbok, the boundary of the Ammonites; the Arabah also, with the Jordan as the boundary, from Chinnereth as far as the sea of the Arabah, the Salt Sea, under the slopes of Pisgah on the east.

"And I commanded you at that time, saying, 'The Lord your God has given you this land to possess; all your men of valor shall pass over armed before your brethren the people of Israel. But your wives, your little ones, and your cattle (I know that you have many cattle) shall remain in the cities which I have given you, until the Lord gives rest to your brethren, as to you, and they also occupy the land which the Lord your God gives them beyond the Jordan; then you shall return every man to his possession which I have given you.' And I commanded Joshua at that time, 'Your eyes have seen all that the Lord your God has done to these two kings; so will the Lord do to all the kingdoms into which you are going over. You shall not fear them; for it is the Lord your God who fights for you.'

"And I besought the Lord at that time, saying, 'O Lord God, thou hast only begun to show thy servant thy greatness and thy mighty hand; for what god is there in heaven or on earth who can do such works and mighty acts as thine? Let me go over, I pray, and see the good land beyond the Jordan, that goodly hill country, and Lebanon.' But the Lord was angry with me on your account, and would not hearken to me; and the Lord said to me, 'Let it suffice you; speak no more to me of this matter. Go up to the top of Pisgah, and lift up your eyes westward and northward and southward and eastward, and behold it with your eyes; for you shall not go over this Jordan. But charge Joshua, and encourage and strengthen him; for he shall go over at the head of this people, and he shall put them in possession of the land which you shall see.' So we remained in the valley opposite Bethpeor.

"And now, O Israel, give heed to the statutes and the ordinances which I teach you, and do them; that you may live, and go in and take possession of the land which the Lord, the God of your fathers, gives you. You shall not add to the word which I command you, nor take from it; that you may keep the commandments of the Lord your God which I command you. Your eyes have seen what the Lord did at Baalpeor; for the Lord your God destroyed from among you all the men who followed the Baal of Peor; but you who held fast to the Lord your God are all alive this day. Behold,

I have taught you statutes and ordinances, as the Lord my God commanded me, that you should do them in the land which you are entering to take possession of it. Keep them and do them; for that will be your wisdom and your understanding in the sight of the peoples, who, when they hear all these statutes, will say, 'Surely this great nation is a wise and understanding people.' For what great nation is there that has a God so near to it as the Lord our God is to us, whenever we call upon him? And what great nation is there, that has statutes and ordinances so righteous as all this law which I set before you this day?

"Only take heed, and keep your soul diligently, lest you forget the things which your eyes have seen, and lest they depart from your heart all the days of your life; make them known to your children and your children's children—how on the day that you stood before the Lord your God at Horeb, the Lord said to me, 'Gather the people to me, that I may let them hear my words, so that they may learn to fear me all the days that they live upon the earth, and that they may teach their children so.' And you came near and stood at the foot of the mountain, while the mountain burned with fire to the heart of heaven, wrapped in darkness, cloud, and gloom. Then the Lord spoke to you out of the midst of the fire; you heard the sound of words, but saw no form; there was only a voice. And he declared to you his covenant, which he commanded you to perform, that is, the ten commandments; and he wrote them upon two tables of stone. And the Lord commanded me at that time to teach you statutes and ordinances, that you might do them in the land which you are going over to possess.

"Therefore take good heed to yourselves. Since you saw no form on the day that the Lord spoke to you at Horeb out of the midst of the fire, beware lest you act corruptly by making a graven image for yourselves, in the form of any figure, the likeness of male or female, the likeness of any beast that is on the earth, the likeness of any winged bird that flies in the air, the likeness of anything that creeps on the ground, the likeness of any fish that is in the water under the earth. And beware lest you lift up your eyes to heaven, and when you see the sun and the moon and the stars, all the host of heaven, you be drawn away and worship them and serve them, things which the Lord your God has allotted to all the peoples under the whole heaven. But the Lord has taken you, and brought you forth out of the iron furnace, out of Egypt, to be a people of his own possession, as at this day. Furthermore the Lord was angry with me on your account, and he swore that I should not cross the Jordan, and that I should not enter the good land which the Lord your God gives you for an inheritance. For I must die in this land, I must not go over the Jordan; but you shall go over and take possession of that good land. Take heed to yourselves, lest you forget the covenant of the Lord your God, which he made with you, and make a graven image in the form of anything which the Lord your God has forbidden you. For the Lord your God is a devouring fire, a jealous God.

"When you beget children and children's children, and have grown old in the land, if you act corruptly by making a graven image in the form of anything, and by doing what is evil in the sight of the Lord your God, so as to provoke him to anger, I call heaven and earth to witness against you this day, that you will soon utterly perish from the land which you are going over the Jordan to possess; you will not live long upon it, but will be utterly destroyed. And the Lord will scatter you among the peoples, and you will be left few in number among the nations where the Lord will drive you. And there you will serve gods of wood and stone, the work of men's hands, that neither see, nor hear, nor eat, nor smell. But from there you will seek the Lord your God, and you will find him, if you search after him with all your heart and with all your soul. When you are in tribulation, and all these things come upon you in the latter days, you will return to the Lord your God and obey his voice, for the Lord your God is a merciful God; he will not fail you or destroy you or forget the covenant with your fathers which he swore to them.

"For ask now of the days that are past, which were before you, since the day that God created man upon the earth, and ask from one end of heaven to the other, whether such a great thing as this has ever happened or was ever heard of. Did any people ever hear the voice of a god speaking out of the midst of the fire, as you have heard, and still live? Or has any god ever attempted to go and take a nation for himself from the midst of another nation, by trials, by signs, by wonders, and by war, by a mighty hand and an outstretched arm, and by great terrors, according to all that the Lord your God did for you in Egypt before your eyes? To you it was shown, that you might know that the Lord is God; there is no other besides him. Out of heaven he let you hear his voice, that he might discipline you; and on earth he let you see his great fire, and you heard his words out of the midst of the fire. And because he loved your fathers and chose their descendants after them, and brought you out of Egypt with his own presence, by his great power, driving out before you nations greater and mightier than yourselves, to bring you in, to give you their land for an inheritance, as at this day; know therefore this day, and lay it to your heart, that the Lord is God in heaven above and on the earth beneath; there is no other. Therefore you shall keep his statutes and his commandments, which I command you this day, that it may go well with you, and with your children after you, and that you may prolong your days in the land which the Lord your God gives you for ever."

Then Moses set apart three cities in the east beyond the Jordan, that the manslayer might flee there, who kills his neighbor unintentionally, without being at enmity with him in time past, and that by fleeing to one of these cities he might save his life: Bezer in the wilderness on the tableland for the Reubenites, and Ramoth in Gilead for the Gadites, and Golan in Bashan for the Manassites.

This is the law which Moses set before the children of Israel; these are the testimonies, the statutes, and the ordinances, which Moses spoke to the children of Israel when they came out of Egypt, beyond the Jordan in the valley opposite Bethpeor, in the land of Sihon the king of the Amorites, who lived at Heshbon, whom Moses and the children of Israel defeated when they came out of Egypt. And they took possession of his land and the land of Og the king of Bashan, the two kings of the Amorites, who lived to the east beyond the Jordan; from Aroer, which is on the edge of the valley of the Arnon, as far as Mount Sirion (that is, Hermon), together with all the Arabah on the east side of the Jordan as far as the Sea of the Arabah, under the slopes of Pisgah.

And Moses summoned all Israel, and said to them, "Hear, O Israel, the statutes and the ordinances which I speak in your hearing this day, and you shall learn them and be careful to do them. The Lord our God made a covenant with us in Horeb. Not with our fathers did the Lord make this covenant, but with us, who are all of us here alive this day. The Lord spoke with you face to face at the mountain, out of the midst of the fire, while I stood between the Lord and you at that time, to declare to you the word of the Lord; for you were afraid because of the fire, and you did not go up into the mountain. He said:

" 'I am the Lord your God, who brought you out of the land of Egypt, out of the house of bondage.

" 'You shall have no other gods before me.

" 'You shall not make for yourself a graven image, or any likeness of anything that is in heaven above, or that is on the earth beneath, or that is in the water under the earth; you shall not bow down to them or serve them; for I the Lord your God am a jealous God, visiting the iniquity of the fathers upon the children to the third and fourth generation of those who hate me, but showing steadfast love to thousands of those who love me and keep my commandments.

" 'You shall not take the name of the Lord your God in vain: for the Lord will not hold him guiltless who takes his name in vain.

" 'Observe the sabbath day, to keep it holy, as the Lord your God commanded you. Six days you shall labor, and do all your work; but the seventh day is a sabbath to the Lord your God; in it you shall not do any work, you, or your son, or your daughter, or your manservant, or your maidservant, or your ox, or your ass, or any of your cattle, or the sojourner who is within your gates, that your manservant and your maidservant may rest as well as you. You shall remember that you were a servant in the land of Egypt, and the Lord your God brought you out thence with a mighty hand and an outstretched arm; therefore the Lord your God commanded you to keep the sabbath day.

" 'Honor your father and your mother, as the Lord your God commanded you; that your days may be prolonged, and that it may go well with you, in the land which the Lord your God gives you.

" 'You shall not kill.

" 'Neither shall you commit adultery.

" 'Neither shall you steal.

" 'Neither shall you bear false witness against your neighbor.

" 'Neither shall you covet your neighbor's wife; and you shall not desire your neighbor's house, his field, or his manservant, or his maidservant, his ox, or his ass, or anything that is your neighbor's.'

"These words the Lord spoke to all your assembly at the mountain out of the midst of the fire, the cloud, and the thick darkness, with a loud voice; and he added no more. And he wrote them upon two tables of stone, and gave them to me. And when you heard the voice out of the midst of the darkness, while the mountain was burning with fire, you came near to me, all the heads of your tribes, and your elders; and you said, 'Behold, the Lord our God has shown us his glory and greatness, and we have heard his voice out of the midst of the fire; we have this day seen God speak with man and man still live. Now therefore why should we die? For this great fire will consume us; if we hear the voice of the Lord our God any more, we shall die. For who is there of all flesh, that has heard the voice of the living God speaking out of the midst of fire, as we have, and has still lived? Go near, and hear all that the Lord our God will say; and speak to us all that the Lord our God will speak to you; and we will hear and do it.'

"And the Lord heard your words, when you spoke to me; and the Lord said to me, 'I have heard the words of this people, which they have spoken to you; they have rightly said all that they have spoken. Oh that they had such a mind as this always, to fear me and to keep all my commandments, that it might go well with them and with their children for ever! Go and say to them, "Return to your tents." But you, stand here by me, and I will tell you all the commandment and the statutes and the ordinances which you shall teach them, that they may do them in the land which I give them to possess.' You shall be careful to do therefore as the Lord your God has commanded you; you shall not turn aside to the right hand or to the left. You shall walk in all the way which the Lord your God has commanded you, that you may live, and that it may go well with you, and that you may live long in the land which you shall possess.

"Now this is the commandment, the statutes and the ordinances which the Lord your God commanded me to teach you, that you may do them in the land to which you are going over, to possess it; that you may fear the Lord your God, you and your son and your son's son, by keeping all his statutes and his commandments, which I command you, all the days of your life; and that your days may be prolonged. Hear therefore, O Israel, and be careful to do them; that it may go well with you, and that you may multiply greatly, as the Lord, the God of your fathers, has promised you, in a land flowing with milk and honey.

"Hear, O Israel: The Lord our God is one Lord; and you shall love the Lord your God with all your heart, and with all your soul, and with all your might. And these words which I command you this day shall be upon your heart; and you shall teach them diligently to your children, and shall talk of them when you sit in your house, and when you walk by the way, and when you lie down, and when you rise. And you shall bind them as a sign upon your hand, and they shall be as frontlets between your eyes. And you shall write them on the doorposts of your house and your gates.

"And when the Lord your God brings you into the land which he swore to your fathers, to Abraham, to Isaac, and to Jacob, to give you, with great and goodly cities, which you did not build, and houses full of all good things, which you did not fill, and cisterns hewn out, which you did not hew, and vineyards and olive trees, which you did not plant, and when you eat and are full, then take heed lest you forget the Lord, who brought you out of the land of Egypt, out of the house of bondage. You shall fear the Lord your God; you shall serve him, and swear by his name. You shall not go after other gods, of the gods of the peoples who are round about you; for the Lord your God in the midst of you is a jealous God; lest the anger of the Lord your God be kindled against you, and he destroy you from off the face of the earth.

"You shall not put the Lord your God to the test, as you tested him at Massah. You shall diligently keep the commandments of the Lord your God, and his testimonies, and his statutes, which he has commanded you. And you shall do what is right and good in the sight of the Lord, that it may go well with you, and that you may go in and take possession of the good land which the Lord swore to give to your fathers by thrusting out all your enemies from before you, as the Lord has promised.

"When your son asks you in time to come, 'What is the meaning of the testimonies and the statutes and the ordinances which the Lord our God has commanded you?' then you shall say to your son, 'We were Pharaoh's slaves in Egypt; and the Lord brought us out of Egypt with a mighty hand; and the Lord showed signs and wonders, great and grievous, against Egypt and against Pharaoh and all his household, before our eyes; and he brought us out from there, that he might bring us in and give us the land which he swore to give to our fathers. And the Lord commanded us to do all these statutes, to fear the Lord our God, for our good always, that he might preserve us alive, as at this day. And it will be righteousness for us, if we are careful to do all this commandment before the Lord our God, as he has commanded us.'

"When the Lord your God brings you into the land which you are entering to take possession of it, and clears away many nations before you, the Hittites, the Girgashites, the Amorites, the Canaanites, the Perizzites, the Hivites, and the Jebusites, seven nations greater and mightier than yourselves, and when the Lord your God gives them over to you, and you defeat them; then you must utterly destroy them; you shall make no covenant with them, and show no mercy to them. You shall not make marriages with them, giving your daughters to their sons or taking their daughters for your sons. For they would turn away your sons from following me, to serve other gods; then the anger of the Lord would be kindled against you, and he would destroy you quickly. But thus shall you deal with them: you shall break down their altars, and dash in pieces their pillars, and hew down their Asherim, and burn their graven images with fire.

"For you are a people holy to the Lord your God; the Lord your God has chosen you to be a people for his own possession, out of all the peoples that are on the face of the earth. It was not because you were more in number than any other people that the Lord set his love upon you and chose you, for you were the fewest of all peoples; but it is because the Lord loves you, and is keeping the oath which he swore to your fathers, that the Lord has brought you out with a mighty hand, and redeemed you from the house of bondage, from the hand of Pharaoh king of Egypt. Know therefore that the Lord your God is God, the faithful God who keeps covenant and steadfast love with those who love him and keep his commandments, to a thousand generations, and requites to their face those who hate him, by destroying them; he will not be slack with him who hates him, he will requite him to his face. You shall therefore be careful to do the commandment, and the statutes, and the ordinances, which I command you this day.

"And because you hearken to these ordinances, and keep and do them, the Lord your God will keep you with the covenant and the steadfast love which he swore to your fathers to keep; he will love you, bless you, and multiply you; he will also bless the fruit of your body and the fruit of your ground, your grain and your wine and your oil, the increase of your cattle and the young of your flock, in the land which he swore to your fathers to give you. You shall be blessed above all peoples; there shall not be male or female barren among you, or among your cattle. And the Lord will take away from you all sickness; and none of the evil diseases of Egypt, which you knew, will he inflict upon you, but he will lay them upon all who hate you. And you shall destroy all the peoples that the Lord your God will give over to you, your eye shall not pity them; neither shall you serve their gods, for that would be a snare to you.

"If you say in your heart, 'These nations are greater than I; how can I dispossess them?' you shall not be afraid of them, but you shall remember what the Lord your God did to Pharaoh and to all Egypt, the great trials which your eyes saw, the signs, the wonders, the mighty hand, and the outstretched arm, by which the Lord your God brought you out; so will the Lord your God do to all the peoples of whom you are afraid. Moreover the Lord your God will send hornets among them, until those who are left and hide themselves from you are destroyed. You shall not be in dread of them; for the Lord your God is in the midst of you, a great and terrible God. The Lord your God will clear away these nations before you little by little; you may not make an end of them at once, lest the wild beasts grow too numerous for you. But the Lord your God will give them over to you, and throw them into great confusion, until they are destroyed. And he will give their kings into your hand, and you shall make their name perish from under heaven; not a man shall be able to stand against you, until you have destroyed them. The graven images of their gods you shall burn with fire; you shall not covet the silver or the gold that is on them, or take it for yourselves, lest you be ensnared by it; for it is an abomination to the Lord your God. And you shall not bring an abominable thing into your house, and become accursed like it; you shall utterly detest and abhor it; for it is an accursed thing.

"All the commandment which I command you this day you shall be careful to do, that you may live and multiply, and go in and possess the land which the Lord swore to give to your fathers. And you shall remember all the way which the Lord your God has led you these forty years in the wilderness, that he may humble you, testing you to know what was in your heart, whether you would keep his commandments, or not. And he humbled you and let you hunger and fed you with manna, which you did not know, nor did your fathers know; that he might make you know that man does not live by bread alone, but that man lives by everything that proceeds out of the mouth of the Lord. Your clothing did not wear out upon you, and your foot did not swell, these forty years. Know then in your heart that, as a man disciplines his son, the Lord your God disciplines you. So you shall keep the commandments of the

Lord your God, by walking in his ways and by fearing him. For the Lord your God is bringing you into a good land, a land of brooks of water, of fountains and springs, flowing forth in valleys and hills, a land of wheat and barley, of vines and fig trees and pomegranates, a land of olive trees and honey, a land in which you will eat bread without scarcity, in which you will lack nothing, a land whose stones are iron, and out of whose hills you can dig copper. And you shall eat and be full, and you shall bless the Lord your God, for the good land he has given you.

"Take heed lest you forget the Lord your God, by not keeping his commandments and his ordinances and his statutes, which I command you this day: lest, when you have eaten and are full, and have built goodly houses and live in them, and when your herds and flocks multiply, and your silver and gold is multiplied, and all that you have is multiplied, then your heart be lifted up, and you forget the Lord your God, who brought you out of the land of Egypt, out of the house of bondage, who led you through the great and terrible wilderness, with its fiery serpents and scorpions and thirsty ground where there was no water, who brought you water out of the flinty rock, who fed you in the wilderness with manna which your fathers did not know, that he might humble you and test you, to do you good in the end. Beware lest you say in your heart, 'My power and the might of my hand have gotten me this wealth.' You shall remember the Lord your God, for it is he who gives you power to get wealth; that he may confirm his covenant which he swore to your fathers, as at this day. And if you forget the Lord your God and go after other gods and serve them and worship them, I solemnly warn you this day that you shall surely perish. Like the nations that the Lord makes to perish before you, so shall you perish, because you would not obey the voice of the Lord your God.

"Hear, O Israel; you are to pass over the Jordan this day, to go in to dispossess nations greater and mightier than yourselves, cities great and fortified up to heaven, a people great and tall, the sons of the Anakim, whom you know, and of whom you have heard it said, 'Who can stand before the sons of Anak?' Know therefore this day that he who goes over before you as a devouring fire is the Lord your God; he will destroy them and subdue them before you; so you shall drive them out, and make them perish quickly, as the Lord has promised you.

"Do not say in your heart, after the Lord your God has thrust them out before you, 'It is because of my righteousness that the Lord has brought me in to possess this land'; whereas it is because of the wickedness of these nations that the Lord is driving them out before you. Not because of your righteousness or the uprightness of your heart are you going in to possess their land; but because of the wickedness of these nations the Lord your God is driving them out from before you, and that he may confirm the word which the Lord swore to your fathers, to Abraham, to Isaac, and to Jacob.

"Know therefore, that the Lord your God is not giving you this good land to possess because of your righteousness; for you are a stubborn people. Remember and do not forget how you provoked the Lord your God to wrath in the wilderness; from the day you came out of the land of Egypt, until you came to this place, you have been rebellious against the Lord. Even at Horeb you provoked the Lord to wrath, and the Lord was so angry with you that he was ready to destroy you. When I went up the mountain to receive the tables of stone, the tables of the covenant which the Lord made with you, I remained on the mountain forty days and forty nights; I neither ate bread nor drank water. And the Lord gave me the two tables of stone written with the finger of God; and on them were all the words which the Lord had spoken with you on the mountain out of the midst of the fire on the day of the assembly. And at the end of forty days and forty nights the Lord gave me the two tables of stone, the tables of the covenant. Then the Lord said to me, 'Arise, go down quickly from here; for your people whom you have brought from Egypt have acted corruptly; they have turned aside quickly out of the way which I commanded them; they have made themselves a molten image.'

"Furthermore the Lord said to me, 'I have seen this people, and behold, it is a stubborn people; let me alone, that I may destroy them and blot out their name from under heaven; and I will make of you a nation mightier and greater than they.' So I turned and came down from the mountain, and the mountain was burning with fire; and the two tables of the covenant were in my two hands. And I looked, and behold, you had sinned against the Lord your God; you had made yourselves a molten calf; you had turned aside quickly from the way which the Lord had commanded you. So I took hold of the two tables, and cast them out of my two hands, and broke them before your eyes. Then I lay prostrate before the Lord as before, forty days and forty nights; I neither ate bread nor drank water, because of all the sin which you had committed, in doing what was evil in the sight of the Lord, to provoke him to anger. For I was afraid of the anger and hot displeasure which the Lord bore against you, so that he was ready to destroy you. But the Lord hearkened to me that time also. And the Lord was so angry with Aaron that he was ready to destroy him; and I prayed for Aaron also at the same time. Then I took the sinful thing, the calf which you had made, and burned it with fire and crushed it, grinding it very small, until it was as fine as dust; and I threw the dust of it into the brook that descended out of the mountain.

"At Taberah also, and at Massah, and at Kibrothhattaavah, you provoked the Lord to wrath. And when the Lord sent you from Kadeshbarnea, saying, 'Go up and take possession of the land which I have given you,' then you rebelled against the commandment of the Lord your God, and did not believe him or obey his voice. You have been rebellious against the Lord from the day that I knew you.

"So I lay prostrate before the Lord for these forty days and forty nights, because the Lord had said he would destroy you. And I prayed to the Lord, 'O Lord God, destroy not thy people and thy heritage, whom thou hast redeemed through thy greatness, whom thou hast brought out of Egypt with a mighty hand. Remember thy servants, Abraham, Isaac, and Jacob; do not regard the stubbornness of this people, or their wickedness, or their sin, lest the land from which thou didst bring us say, "Because the Lord was not able to bring them into the land which he promised them, and because he hated them, he has brought them out to slay them in the wilderness." For they are thy people and thy heritage, whom thou didst bring out by thy great power and by thy outstretched arm.'

"At that time the Lord said to me, 'Hew two tables of stone like the first, and come up to me on the mountain, and make an ark of wood. And I will write on the tables the words that were on the first tables which you broke, and you shall put them in the ark.' So I made an ark of acacia wood, and hewed two tables of stone like the first, and went up the mountain with the two tables in my hand. And he wrote on the tables, as at the first writing, the ten commandments which the Lord had spoken to you on the mountain out of the midst of the fire on the day of the assembly; and the Lord gave them to me. Then I turned and came down from the mountain, and put the tables in the ark which I had made; and there they are, as the Lord commanded me.

(The people of Israel journeyed from Beeroth Benejaakan to Moserah. There Aaron died, and there he was buried; and his son Eleazar ministered as priest in his stead. From there they journeyed to Gudgodah, and from Gudgodah to Jotbathah, a land with brooks of water. At that time the Lord set apart the tribe of Levi to carry the ark of the covenant of the Lord, to stand before the Lord to minister to him and to bless in his name, to this day. Therefore Levi has no portion or inheritance with his brothers; the Lord is his inheritance, as the Lord your God said to him.)

"I stayed on the mountain, as at the first time, forty days and forty nights, and the Lord hearkened to me that time also; the Lord was unwilling to destroy you. And the Lord said to me, 'Arise, go on your journey at the head of the people, that they may go in and possess the land, which I swore to their fathers to give them.'

"And now, Israel, what does the Lord your God require of you, but to fear the Lord your God, to walk in all his ways, to love him, to serve the Lord your God with all your heart and with all your soul, and to keep the commandments and statutes of the Lord, which I command you this day for your good? Behold, to the Lord your God belong heaven and the heaven of heavens, the earth with all that is in it; yet the Lord set his heart in love upon your fathers and chose their descendants after them, you above all peoples, as at this day. Circumcise therefore the foreskin of your heart, and be no longer stubborn. For the Lord your God is God of gods and Lord of lords, the great, the mighty, and the terrible God, who is not partial and takes no bribe. He executes justice for the fatherless and the widow, and loves the sojourner, giving him food and clothing. Love the sojourner therefore; for you were sojourners in the land of Egypt. You shall fear the Lord your God; you shall serve him and cleave to him, and by his name you shall swear. He is your praise; he is your God, who has done for you these great and terrible things which your eyes have seen. Your fathers went down to Egypt seventy persons; and now the Lord your God has made you as the stars of heaven for multitude.

"You shall therefore love the Lord your God, and keep his charge, his statutes, his ordinances, and his commandments always. And consider this day (since I am not speaking to your children who have not known or seen it), consider the discipline of the Lord your God, his greatness, his mighty hand and his outstretched arm, his signs and his deeds which he did in Egypt to Pharaoh the king of Egypt and to all his land; and what he did to the army of Egypt, to their horses and to their chariots; how he made the water of the Red Sea overflow them as they pursued after you, and how the Lord has destroyed them to this day; and what he did to you in the wilderness, until you came to this place; and what he did to Dathan and Abiram the sons of Eliab, son of Reuben; how the earth opened its mouth and swallowed them up, with their households, their tents, and every living thing that followed them, in the midst of all Israel; for your eyes have seen all the great work of the Lord which he did.

"You shall therefore keep all the commandment which I command you this day, that you may be strong, and go in and take possession of the land which you are going over to possess, and that you may live long in the land which the Lord swore to your fathers to give to them and to their descendants, a land flowing with milk and honey. For the land which you are entering to take possession of it is not like the land of Egypt, from which you have come, where you sowed your seed and watered it with your feet, like a garden of vegetables; but the land which you are going over to possess is a land of hills and valleys, which drinks water by the rain from heaven, a land which the Lord your God cares for; the eyes of the Lord your God are always upon it, from the beginning of the year to the end of the year.

"And if you will obey my commandments which I command you this day, to love the Lord your God, and to serve him with all your heart and with all your soul, he will give the rain for your land in its season, the early rain and the later rain, that you may gather in your grain and your wine and your oil. And he will give grass in your fields for your cattle, and you shall eat and be full. Take heed lest your heart be deceived, and you turn aside and serve other gods and worship them, and the anger of the Lord be kindled against you, and he shut up the heavens, so that there be no rain, and the land yield no fruit, and you perish quickly off the good land which the Lord gives you.

"You shall therefore lay up these words of mine in your heart and in your soul; and you shall bind them as a sign upon your hand, and they shall be as frontlets between your eyes. And you shall teach them to your children, talking of them when you are sitting in your house, and when you are walking by the way, and when you lie down, and when you rise. And you shall write them upon the doorposts of your house and upon your gates, that your days and the days of your children may be multiplied in the land which the Lord swore to your fathers to give them, as long as the heavens are above the earth. For if you will be careful to do all this commandment which I command you to do, loving the Lord your God, walking in all his ways, and cleaving to him, then the Lord will drive out all these nations before you, and you will dispossess nations greater and mightier than yourselves. Every place on which the sole of your foot treads shall be yours; your territory shall be from the wilderness and Lebanon and from the River, the river Euphrates, to the western sea. No man shall be able to stand against you; the Lord your God will lay the fear of you and the dread of you upon all the land that you shall tread, as he promised you.

"Behold, I set before you this day a blessing and a curse: the blessing, if you obey the commandments of the Lord your God, which I command you this day, and the curse, if you do not obey the commandments of the Lord your God, but turn aside from the way which I command you this day, to go after other gods which you have not known. And when the Lord your God brings you into the land which you are entering to take possession of it, you shall set the blessing on Mount Gerizim and the curse on Mount Ebal. Are they not beyond the Jordan, west of the road, toward the going down of the sun, in the land of the Canaanites who live in the Arabah, over against Gilgal, beside the oak of Moreh? For you are to pass over the Jordan to go in to take possession of the land which the Lord your God gives you; and when you possess it and live in it, you shall be careful to do all the statutes and the ordinances which I set before you this day. . . ."

708 (3) **Deuteronomy 29–30** These are the words of the covenant which the Lord commanded Moses to make with the people of Israel in the land of Moab, besides the covenant which he had made with them at Horeb.

And Moses summoned all Israel and said to them: "You have seen all that the Lord did before your eyes in the land of Egypt, to Pharaoh and to all his servants and to all his land, the great trials which your eyes saw, the signs, and those great wonders; but to this day the Lord has not given you a mind to understand, or eyes to see, or ears to hear. I have led you forty years in the wilderness; your clothes have not worn out upon you, and your sandals have not worn off your feet; you have not eaten bread, and you have not drunk wine or strong drink; that you may know that I am the Lord your God. And when you came to this place, Sihon the king of Heshbon and Og the king of Bashan came out against us to battle, but we defeated them; we took their land, and gave it for an inheritance to the Reubenites, the Gadites, and the half-tribe of the Manassites. Therefore be careful to do the words of this covenant, that you may prosper in all that you do.

"You stand this day all of you before the Lord your God; the heads of your tribes, your elders, and your officers, all the men of Israel, your little ones, your wives, and the sojourner who is in your camp, both he who hews your wood and he who draws your water, that you may enter into the sworn covenant of the Lord your God, which the Lord your God makes with you this day; that he may establish you this day as his people, and that he may be your God, as he promised you, and as he swore to your fathers, to Abraham, to Isaac, and to Jacob. Nor is it with you only that I make this sworn covenant, but with him who is not here with us this day as well as with him who stands here with us this day before the Lord our God.

"You know how we dwelt in the land of Egypt, and how we came through the midst of the nations through which you passed; and you have seen their detestable things, their idols of wood and stone, of silver and gold, which were among them. Beware lest there be among you a man or woman or family or tribe, whose heart turns away this day from the Lord our God to go and serve the gods of those nations; lest there be among you a root bearing poisonous and bitter fruit, one who, when he hears the words of this sworn covenant, blesses himself in his heart, saying, 'I shall be safe, though I walk in the stubbornness of my heart.' This would lead to the sweeping away of moist and dry alike. The Lord would not pardon him, but rather the anger of the Lord and his jealousy would smoke against that man, and the curses written in this book would settle upon him, and the Lord would blot out his name from under heaven. And the Lord would single him out from all the tribes of Israel for calamity, in accordance with all the curses of the covenant written in this book of the law. And the generation to come, your children who rise up after you, and the foreigner who comes from a far land, would say, when they see the afflictions of that land and the sicknesses with which the Lord has made it sick—the whole land brimstone and salt, and a burnt-out waste, unsown, and growing nothing, where no grass can sprout, an overthrow like that of Sodom and Gomorrah, Admah and Zeboiim, which the Lord overthrew in his anger and wrath—yea, all the nations would say, 'Why has the Lord done thus to this land? What means the heat of this great anger?' Then men would say, 'It is because they forsook the covenant of the Lord, the God of their fathers, which he made with them when he brought them out of the land of Egypt, and went and served other gods and worshiped them, gods whom they had not known and whom he had not allotted to them; therefore the anger of the Lord was kindled against this land, bringing upon it all the curses written in this book; and the Lord uprooted them from their land in anger and fury and great wrath, and cast them into another land, as at this day.'

"The secret things belong to the Lord our God; but the things that are revealed belong to us and to our children for ever, that we may do all the words of this law.

"And when all these things come upon you, the blessing and the curse, which I have set before you, and you call them to mind among all the nations where the Lord your God has driven you, and return to the Lord your God, you and your children, and obey his voice in all that I command you this day, with all your heart and with all your soul; then the Lord your God will restore your fortunes, and have compassion upon you, and he will gather you again from all the peoples where the Lord your God has scattered you. If your outcasts are in the uttermost parts of heaven, from there the Lord your God will gather you, and from there he will fetch you; and the Lord your God will bring you into the land which your fathers possessed, that you may possess it; and he will make you more prosperous and numerous than your fathers. And the Lord your God will circumcise your heart and the heart of your offspring, so that you will love the Lord your God with all your heart and with all your soul, that you may live. And the Lord your God will put all these curses upon your foes and enemies who persecuted you. And you shall again obey the voice of the Lord, and keep all his commandments which I command you this day. The Lord your God will make you abundantly prosperous in all the work of your hand, in the fruit of your body, and in the fruit of your cattle, and in the fruit of your ground; for the Lord will again take delight in prospering you, as he took delight in your fathers, if you obey the voice of the Lord your God, to keep his commandments and his statutes which are written in this book of the law, if you turn to the Lord your God with all your heart and with all your soul.

"For this commandment which I command you this day is not too hard for you, neither is it far off. It is not in heaven, that you should say, 'Who will go up for us to heaven, and bring it to us, that we may hear it and do it?' Neither is it beyond the sea, that you should say, 'Who will go over the sea for us, and bring it to us, that we may hear it and do it?' But the word is very near you; it is in your mouth and in your heart, so that you can do it.

"See, I have set before you this day life and good, death and evil. If you obey the commandments of the Lord your God which I command you this day, by loving the Lord your God, by walking in his ways, and by keeping his commandments and his statutes and his ordinances, then you shall live and multiply, and the Lord your God will bless you in the land which you are entering to take possession of it. But if your heart turns away, and you will not hear, but are drawn away to worship other gods and serve them, I declare to you this day, that you shall perish; you shall not live long in the land which you are going over the Jordan to enter and possess. I call heaven and earth to witness against you this day, that I have set before you life and death, blessing and curse; therefore choose life, that you and your descendants may live, loving the Lord your God, obeying his voice, and cleaving to him; for that means life to you and length of days, that you may dwell in the land which the Lord swore to your fathers, to Abraham, to Isaac, and to Jacob, to give them."

708 (4) **Romans 3:20** For no human being will be justified in his sight by works of the law, since through the law comes knowledge of sin.

709 (1) **1 Peter 2:9** But you are a chosen race, a royal priesthood, a holy nation, God's own people, that you may declare the wonderful deeds of him who called you out of darkness into his marvelous light.

709 (2) **2 Samuel 7** Now when the king dwelt in his house, and the Lord had given him rest from all his enemies round about, the king said to Nathan the prophet, "See now, I dwell in a house of cedar, but the ark of God dwells in a tent." And Nathan said to the king, "Go, do all that is in your heart; for the Lord is with you."

But that same night the word of the Lord came to Nathan, "Go and tell my servant David, 'Thus says the Lord: Would you build me a house to dwell in? I have not dwelt in a house since the day I brought up the people of Israel from Egypt to this day, but I have been moving about in a tent for my dwelling. In all places where I have moved with all the people of Israel, did I speak a word with any of the judges of Israel, whom I commanded to shepherd my people Israel, saying, "Why have you not built me a house of cedar?"' Now therefore thus you shall say to my servant David, 'Thus says the Lord of hosts, I took you from the pasture, from following the sheep, that you should be prince over my people Israel; and I have been with you wherever you went, and have cut off all your enemies from before you; and I will make for you a great name, like the name of the great ones of the earth. And I will appoint a place for my people Israel, and will plant them, that they may dwell in their own place, and be disturbed no more; and violent men shall afflict them no more, as formerly, from the time that I appointed judges over my people Israel; and I will give you rest from all your enemies. Moreover the Lord declares to you that the Lord will make you a house. When your days are fulfilled and you lie down with your fathers, I will raise up your offspring after you, who shall come forth from your body, and I will establish his kingdom. He shall build a house for my name, and I will establish the throne of his kingdom for ever. I will be his father, and he shall be my son. When he commits iniquity, I will chasten him with the rod of men, with the stripes of the sons of men; but I will not take my steadfast love from him, as I took it from Saul, whom I put away from before you. And your house and your kingdom shall be made sure for ever before me; your throne shall be established for ever.'" In accordance with all these words, and in accordance with all this vision, Nathan spoke to David.

Then King David went in and sat before the Lord, and said, "Who am I, O Lord God, and what is my house, that thou hast brought me thus far? And yet this was a small thing in thy eyes, O Lord God; thou hast spoken also of thy servant's house for a great while to come, and hast shown me future generations, O Lord God! And what more can David say to thee? For thou knowest thy servant, O Lord God! Because of thy promise, and according to thy own heart, thou hast wrought all this greatness, to make thy servant know it. Therefore thou art great, O Lord God; for there is none like thee, and there is no God besides thee, according to all that we have heard with our ears. What other nation on earth is like thy people Israel, whom God went to redeem to be his people, making himself a name, and doing for them great and terrible things, by driving out before his people a nation and its gods? And thou didst establish for thyself thy people Israel to be thy people for ever; and thou, O Lord, didst become their God. And now, O Lord God, confirm for ever the word which thou hast spoken concerning thy servant and concerning his house, and do as thou hast spoken; and thy name will be magnified for ever, saying, 'The Lord of hosts is God over Israel,' and the house of thy servant David will be established before thee. For thou, O Lord of hosts, the God of Israel, hast made this revelation to thy servant, saying, 'I will build you a house'; therefore thy servant has found courage to pray this prayer to thee. And now, O Lord God, thou art God, and thy words are true, and thou hast promised this good thing to thy servant; now therefore may it please thee to bless the house of thy servant, that it may continue for ever before thee; for thou, O Lord God, hast spoken, and with thy blessing shall the house of thy servant be blessed for ever."

(3) **Psalm 89** 709

I will sing of thy steadfast love, O Lord, for ever;
with my mouth I will proclaim thy faithfulness to all generations.
For thy steadfast love was established for ever,
thy faithfulness is firm as the heavens.
Thou hast said, "I have made a covenant with my chosen one,
I have sworn to David my servant:
'I will establish your descendants for ever,
and build your throne for all generations.'" *Selah*

Let the heavens praise thy wonders, O Lord,
thy faithfulness in the assembly of the holy ones!
For who in the skies can be compared to the Lord?
Who among the heavenly beings is like the Lord,
a God feared in the council of the holy ones,
great and terrible above all that are round about him?
O Lord God of hosts,
who is mighty as thou art, O Lord,
with thy faithfulness round about thee?
Thou dost rule the raging of the sea;
when its waves rise, thou stillest them.
Thou didst crush Rahab like a carcass,
thou didst scatter thy enemies with thy mighty arm.
The heavens are thine, the earth also is thine;
the world and all that is in it, thou hast founded them.

The north and the south, thou hast created them;
    Tabor and Hermon joyously praise thy name.
Thou hast a mighty arm;
    strong is thy hand, high thy right hand.
Righteousness and justice are the foundation of thy throne;
    steadfast love and faithfulness go before thee.
Blessed are the people who know the festal shout,
    who walk, O Lord, in the light of thy countenance,
who exult in thy name all the day,
    and extol thy righteousness.
For thou art the glory of their strength;
    by thy favor our horn is exalted.
For our shield belongs to the Lord,
    our king to the Holy One of Israel.

Of old thou didst speak in a vision
    to thy faithful one, and say:
"I have set the crown upon one who is mighty,
    I have exalted one chosen from the people.
I have found David, my servant;
    with my holy oil I have anointed him;
so that my hand shall ever abide with him,
    my arm also shall strengthen him.
The enemy shall not outwit him,
    the wicked shall not humble him.
I will crush his foes before him
    and strike down those who hate him.
My faithfulness and my steadfast love shall be with him,
    and in my name shall his horn be exalted.
I will set his hand on the sea
    and his right hand on the rivers.
He shall cry to me, 'Thou art my Father,
    my God, and the Rock of my salvation.'
And I will make him the first-born,
    the highest of the kings of the earth.
My steadfast love I will keep for him for ever,
    and my covenant will stand firm for him.
I will establish his line for ever
    and his throne as the days of the heavens.
If his children forsake my law
    and do not walk according to my ordinances,
if they violate my statutes
    and do not keep my commandments,
then I will punish their transgression with the rod
    and their iniquity with scourges;
but I will not remove from him my steadfast love,
    or be false to my faithfulness.
I will not violate my covenant,
    or alter the word that went forth from my lips.
Once for all I have sworn by my holiness;
    I will not lie to David.
His line shall endure for ever,

his throne as long as the sun before me.
Like the moon it shall be established for ever;
it shall stand firm while the skies endure." *Selah*

But now thou hast cast off and rejected,
thou art full of wrath against thy anointed.
Thou hast renounced the covenant with thy servant;
thou hast defiled his crown in the dust.
Thou hast breached all his walls;
thou hast laid his strongholds in ruins.
All that pass by despoil him;
he has become the scorn of his neighbors.
Thou hast exalted the right hand of his foes;
thou hast made all his enemies rejoice.
Yea, thou hast turned back the edge of his sword,
and thou hast not made him stand in battle.
Thou hast removed the scepter from his hand,
and cast his throne to the ground.
Thou hast cut short the days of his youth;
thou hast covered him with shame. *Selah*

How long, O Lord? Wilt thou hide thyself for ever?
How long will thy wrath burn like fire?
Remember, O Lord, what the measure of life is,
for what vanity thou hast created all the sons of men!
What man can live and never see death?
Who can deliver his soul from the power of Sheol? *Selah*

Lord, where is thy steadfast love of old,
which by thy faithfulness thou didst swear to David?
Remember, O Lord, how thy servant is scorned;
how I bear in my bosom the insults of the peoples,
with which thy enemies taunt, O Lord,
with which they mock the footsteps of thy anointed.

Blessed be the Lord for ever! Amen and Amen.

(4) **Luke 1:32–33** 709
". . . He will be great, and will be called the Son of the Most High;
and the Lord God will give to him the throne of his father David,
and he will reign over the house of Jacob for ever;
and of his kingdom there will be no end."

Luke 24:26 ". . . Was it not necessary that the Christ should suffer these things 710
and enter into his glory?"

(1) **Zephaniah 2:3** 711
Seek the Lord, all you humble of the land,
who do his commands;
seek righteousness, seek humility;
perhaps you may be hidden
on the day of the wrath of the Lord.

711 (2) **Luke 2:25** Now there was a man in Jerusalem, whose name was Simeon, and this man was righteous and devout, looking for the consolation of Israel, and the Holy Spirit was upon him.

711 (3) **Luke 2:38** And coming up at that very hour she gave thanks to God, and spoke of him to all who were looking for the redemption of Jerusalem.

712 **Isaiah 6–12** In the year that King Uzziah died I saw the Lord sitting upon a throne, high and lifted up; and his train filled the temple. Above him stood the seraphim; each had six wings: with two he covered his face, and with two he covered his feet, and with two he flew. And one called to another and said:

"Holy, holy, holy is the Lord of hosts;
the whole earth is full of his glory."

And the foundations of the thresholds shook at the voice of him who called, and the house was filled with smoke. And I said: "Woe is me! For I am lost; for I am a man of unclean lips, and I dwell in the midst of a people of unclean lips; for my eyes have seen the King, the Lord of hosts!"

Then flew one of the seraphim to me, having in hand a burning coal which he had taken with tongs from the altar. And he touched my mouth, and said: "Behold, this has touched your lips; your guilt is taken away, and your sin forgiven." And I heard the voice of the Lord saying, "Whom shall I send, and who will go for us?" Then I said, "Here am I! Send me." And he said, "Go, and say to this people:

'Hear and hear, but do not understand;
see and see, but do not perceive.'
Make the heart of this people fat,
    and their ears heavy,
    and shut their eyes;
lest they see with their eyes,
    and hear with their ears,
and understand with their hearts,
    and turn and be healed."

Then I said, "How long, O Lord?" And he said:

"Until cities lie waste
    without inhabitant,
and houses without men,
    and the land is utterly desolate,
and the Lord removes men far away,
    and the forsaken places are many in the midst of the land.
And though a tenth remain in it,
    it will be burned again,
like a terebinth or an oak,
    whose stump remains standing
    when it is felled."
The holy seed is its stump.

In the days of Ahaz the son of Jotham, son of Uzziah, king of Judah, Rezin the king of Syria and Pekah the son of Remaliah the king of Israel came up to Jerusalem to wage war against it, but they could not conquer it. When the house of David was told, "Syria is in league with Ephraim," his heart and the heart of his people shook as the trees of the forest shake before the wind.

And the Lord said to Isaiah, "Go forth to meet Ahaz, you and Shearjashub your son, at the end of the conduit of the upper pool on the highway to the Fuller's Field, and say to him, 'Take heed, be quiet, do not fear, and do not let your heart be faint because of these two smoldering stumps of firebrands, at the fierce anger of Rezin and Syria and the son of Remaliah. Because Syria, with Ephraim and the son of Remaliah, has devised evil against you, saying, "Let us go up against Judah and terrify it, and let us conquer it for ourselves, and set up the son of Tabeel as king in the midst of it," thus says the Lord God:

It shall not stand,
and it shall not come to pass.
For the head of Syria is Damascus,
and the head of Damascus is Rezin.

(Within sixty-five years Ephraim will be broken to pieces so that it will no longer be a people.)

And the head of Ephraim is Samaria,
and the head of Samaria is the son of Remaliah.
If you will not believe,
surely you shall not be established.'"

Again the Lord spoke to Ahaz, "Ask a sign of the Lord your God; let it be deep as Sheol or high as heaven." But Ahaz said, "I will not ask, and I will not put the Lord to the test." And he said, "Hear then, O house of David! Is it too little for you to weary men, that you weary my God also? Therefore the Lord himself will give you a sign. Behold a young woman [Gk.: virgin] shall conceive and bear a son, and shall call his name Immanuel. He shall eat curds and honey when he knows how to refuse the evil and choose the good. For before the child knows how to refuse the evil and choose the good, the land before whose two kings you are in dread will be deserted. The Lord will bring upon you and upon your people and upon your father's house such days as have not come since the day that Ephraim departed from Judah—the king of Assyria."

In that day the Lord will whistle for the fly which is at the sources of the streams of Egypt, and for the bee which is in the land of Assyria. And they will all come and settle in the steep ravines, and in the clefts of the rocks, and on all the thornbushes, and on all the pastures.

In that day the Lord will shave with a razor which is hired beyond the River—with the king of Assyria—the head and the hair of the feet, and it will sweep away the beard also.

In that day a man will keep alive a young cow and two sheep; and because of the abundance of milk which they give, he will eat curds; for every one that is left in the land will eat curds and honey.

In that day every place where there used to be a thousand vines, worth a thousand shekels of silver, will become briers and thorns. With bow and arrows men will come there, for all the land will be briers and thorns; and as for the hills which used to be hoed with a hoe, you will not come there for fear of briers and thorns; but they will become a place where cattle are let loose and where sheep tread.

Then the Lord said to me, "Take a large tablet and write upon it in common characters, 'Belonging to Mahershalalhashbaz.'" And I got reliable witnesses, Uriah the priest and Zechariah the son of Jeberechiah, to attest for me. And I went to the prophetess, and she conceived and bore a son. Then the Lord said to me, "Call his name Mahershalalhashbaz; for before the child knows how to cry 'My father' or 'My mother', the wealth of Damascus and the spoil of Samaria will be carried away before the king of Assyria."

The Lord spoke to me again: "Because this people have refused the waters of Shiloah that flow gently, and melt in fear before Rezin and the son of Remaliah; therefore, behold, the Lord is bringing up against them the waters of the River, mighty and many, the king of Assyria and all his glory; and it will rise over all its channels and go over all its banks; and it will sweep on into Judah, it will overflow and pass on, reaching even to the neck; and its outspread wings will fill the breadth of your land, O Immanuel."

Be broken, you peoples, and be dismayed;
give ear, all you far countries;
gird yourselves and be dismayed;
gird yourselves and be dismayed.
Take counsel together, but it will come to naught;
speak a word, but it will not stand,
for God is with us.

For the Lord spoke thus to me with his strong hand upon me, and warned me not to walk in the way of this people, saying: "Do not call conspiracy all that this people call conspiracy, and do not fear what they fear, nor be in dread. But the Lord of hosts, him you shall regard as holy; let him be your fear, and let him be your dread. And he will become a sanctuary, and a stone of offense, and a rock of stumbling to both houses of Israel, a trap and a snare to the inhabitants of Jerusalem. And many shall stumble thereon; they shall fall and be broken; they shall be snared and taken."

Bind up the testimony, seal the teaching among my disciples. I will wait for the Lord, who is hiding his face from the house of Jacob, and I will hope in him. Behold, I and the children whom the Lord has given me are signs and portents in Israel from the Lord of hosts, who dwells on Mount Zion. And when they say to you, "Consult the mediums and the wizards who chirp and mutter," should not a people consult their God? Should they consult the dead on behalf of the living? To the teaching and to the testimony! Surely for this word which they speak there is no dawn. They will pass through the land, greatly distressed and hungry; and when they are hungry, they will be enraged and will curse their king and their God, and turn their faces upward; and they will look to the earth, but behold, distress and darkness, the gloom of anguish; and they will be thrust into thick darkness.

But there will be no gloom for her that was in anguish. In the former time he brought into contempt the land of Zebulun and the land of Naphtali, but in the latter time he will make glorious the way of the sea, the land beyond the Jordan, Galilee of the nations.

The people who walked in darkness
have seen a great light;
those who dwelt in a land of deep darkness,
on them has light shined.
Thou hast multiplied the nation,
thou hast increased its joy;
they rejoice before thee
as with joy at the harvest,
as men rejoice when they divide the spoil.
For the yoke of his burden,
and the staff for his shoulder,
the rod of his oppressor,
thou hast broken as on the day of Midian.
For every boot of the tramping warrior in battle tumult
and every garment rolled in blood
will be burned as fuel for the fire.
For to us a child is born,
to us a son is given;
and the government will be upon his shoulder,
and his name will be called

"Wonderful Counselor, Mighty God,
Everlasting Father, Prince of Peace."
Of the increase of his government and of peace
there will be no end,
upon the throne of David, and over his kingdom,
to establish it, and to uphold it
with justice and with righteousness
from this time forth and for evermore.
The zeal of the Lord of hosts will do this.

The Lord has sent a word against Jacob,
and it will light upon Israel;
and all the people will know,
Ephraim and the inhabitants of Samaria,
who say in pride and in arrogance of heart:
"The bricks have fallen,
but we will build with dressed stones;
the sycamores have been cut down,
but we will put cedars in their place."
So the Lord raises adversaries against them,
and stirs up their enemies.
The Syrians on the east and the Philistines on the west
devour Israel with open mouth.
For all this his anger is not turned away
and his hand is stretched out still.
The people did not turn to him who smote them,
nor seek the Lord of hosts.
So the Lord cut off from Israel head and tail,
palm branch and reed in one day—
the elder and honored man is the head,
and the prophet who teaches lies is the tail;
for those who lead this people lead them astray,
and those who are led by them are swallowed up.
Therefore the Lord does not rejoice over their young men,
and has no compassion on their fatherless and widows;
for every one is godless and an evildoer,
and every mouth speaks folly.
For all this his anger is not turned away
and his hand is stretched out still.

For wickedness burns like a fire,
it consumes briers and thorns;
it kindles the thickets of the forest,
and they roll upward in a column of smoke.
Through the wrath of the Lord of hosts
the land is burned,
and the people are like fuel for the fire;
no man spares his brother.
They snatch on the right, but are still hungry,
and they devour on the left, but are not satisfied;
each devours his neighbor's flesh,
Manasseh Ephraim, and Ephraim Manasseh,
and together they are against Judah.

For all this his anger is not turned away
and his hand is stretched out still.

Woe to those who decree iniquitous decrees,
and the writers who keep writing oppression,
to turn aside the needy from justice
and to rob the poor of my people of their right,
that widows may be their spoil,
and that they may make the fatherless their prey!
What will you do on the day of punishment,
in the storm which will come from afar?
To whom will you flee for help,
and where will you leave your wealth?
Nothing remains but to crouch among the prisoners
or fall among the slain.
For all this his anger is not turned away
and his hand is stretched out still.

Ah, Assyria, the rod of my anger,
the staff of my fury!
Against a godless nation I send him,
and against the people of my wrath I command him,
to take spoil and seize plunder,
and to tread them down like the mire of the streets.
But he does not so intend,
and his mind does not so think;
but it is in his mind to destroy,
and to cut off nations not a few;
for he says:
"Are not my commanders all kings?
Is not Calno like Carchemish?
Is not Hamath like Arpad?
Is not Samaria like Damascus?
As my hand has reached to the kingdoms of the idols
whose graven images were greater than those of Jerusalem and Samaria,
shall I not do to Jerusalem and her idols
as I have done to Samaria and her images?"

When the Lord has finished all his work on Mount Zion and on Jerusalem he will punish the arrogant boasting of the king of Assyria and his haughty pride. For he says:

"By the strength of my hand I have done it,
and by my wisdom, for I have understanding;
I have removed the boundaries of peoples,
and have plundered their treasures;
like a bull I have brought down those who sat on thrones.
My hand has found like a nest
the wealth of the peoples;
and as men gather eggs that have been forsaken
so I have gathered all the earth;
and there was none that moved a wing,
or opened the mouth, or chirped."

Shall the axe vaunt itself over him who hews with it,
or the saw magnify itself against him who wields it?

As if a rod should wield him who lifts it,
or as if a staff should lift him who is not wood!
Therefore the Lord, the Lord of hosts,
will send wasting sickness among his stout warriors,
and under his glory a burning will be kindled,
like the burning of fire.
The light of Israel will become a fire,
and his Holy One a flame;
and it will burn and devour
his thorns and briers in one day.
The glory of his forest and of his fruitful land
the Lord will destroy, both soul and body,
and it will be as when a sick man wastes away.
The remnant of the trees of his forest will be so few
that a child can write them down.

In that day the remnant of Israel and the survivors of the house of Jacob will no more lean upon him that smote them, but will lean upon the Lord, the Holy One of Israel, in truth. A remnant will return, the remnant of Jacob, to the mighty God. For though your people Israel be as the sand of the sea, only a remnant of them will return. Destruction is decreed, overflowing with righteousness. For the Lord, the Lord of hosts, will make a full end, as decreed, in the midst of all the earth.

Therefore thus says the Lord, the Lord of hosts: "O my people, who dwell in Zion, be not afraid of the Assyrians when they smite with the rod and lift up their staff against you as the Egyptians did. For in a very little while my indignation will come to an end, and my anger will be directed to their destruction. And the Lord of hosts will wield against them a scourge, as when he smote Midian at the rock of Oreb; and his rod will be over the sea, and he will lift it as he did in Egypt. And in that day his burden will depart from your shoulder, and his yoke will be destroyed from your neck."

He has gone up from Rimmon,
he has come to Aiath;
he has passed through Migron,
at Michmash he stores his baggage;
they have crossed over the pass,
at Geba they lodge for the night;
Ramah trembles,
Gibeah of Saul has fled.
Cry aloud, O daughter of Gallim!
Hearken, O Laishah!
Answer her, O Anathoth!
Madmenah is in flight,
the inhabitants of Gebim flee for safety.
This very day he will halt at Nob,
he will shake his fist
at the mount of the daughter of Zion,
the hill of Jerusalem.

Behold, the Lord, the Lord of hosts
will lop the boughs with terrifying power;
the great in height will be hewn down,
and the lofty will be brought low.

He will cut down the thickets of the forest with an axe,
    and Lebanon with its majestic trees will fall.

There shall come forth a shoot
    from the stump of Jesse,
and a branch shall grow out of his roots.
And the Spirit of the Lord shall rest upon him,
    the spirit of wisdom and understanding,
    the spirit of counsel and might,
    the spirit of knowledge and the fear of the Lord.
And his delight shall be in the fear of the Lord.

He shall not judge by what his eyes see,
    or decide by what his ears hear;
but with righteousness he shall judge the poor,
    and decide with equity for the meek of the earth;
and he shall smite the earth with the rod of his mouth,
    and with the breath of his lips he shall slay the wicked.
Righteousness shall be the girdle of his waist,
    and faithfulness the girdle of his loins.

The wolf shall dwell with the lamb,
    and the leopard shall lie down with the kid,
and the calf and the lion and the fatling together,
    and a little child shall lead them.
The cow and the bear shall feed;
    their young shall lie down together;
    and the lion shall eat straw like the ox.
The sucking child shall play over the hole of the asp,
    and the weaned child shall put his hand on the adder's den.
They shall not hurt or destroy
    in all my holy mountain;
for the earth shall be full of the knowledge of the Lord
    as the waters cover the sea.

In that day the root of Jesse shall stand as an ensign to the peoples; him shall the nations seek, and his dwellings shall be glorious.

In that day the Lord will extend his hand yet a second time to recover the remnant which is left of his people, from Assyria, from Egypt, from Pathros, from Ethiopia, from Elam, from Shinar, from Hamath, and from the coastlands of the sea.

He will raise an ensign for the nations,
    and will assemble the outcasts of Israel,
and gather the dispersed of Judah
    from the four corners of the earth.
The jealousy of Ephraim shall depart,
    and those who harass Judah shall be cut off;
Ephraim shall not be jealous of Judah,
    and Judah shall not harass Ephraim.
But they shall swoop down upon the shoulder of the Philistines in the west,
    and together they shall plunder the people of the east.
They shall put forth their hand against Edom and Moab,
    and the Ammonites shall obey them.
And the Lord will utterly destroy
    the tongue of the sea of Egypt;

and will wave his hand over the River
with his scorching wind,
and smite it into seven channels
that men may cross dryshod.
And there will be a highway from Assyria
for the remnant which is left of his people,
as there was for Israel
when they came up from the land of Egypt.

You will say in that day:
"I will give thanks to thee, O Lord,
for though thou wast angry with me,
thy anger turned away,
and thou didst comfort me.

"Behold, God is my salvation;
I will trust, and will not be afraid;
for the Lord God is my strength and my song,
and he has become my salvation."

With joy you will draw water from the wells of salvation. And you will say in that day:

"Give thanks to the Lord,
call upon his name;
make known his deeds among the nations,
proclaim that his name is exalted.

"Sing praises to the Lord, for he has done gloriously;
let this be known in all the earth.
Shout, and sing for joy, O inhabitant of Zion,
for great in your midst is the Holy One of Israel."

(1) **Isaiah 42:1–9** 713

Behold my servant, whom I uphold,
my chosen, in whom my soul delights;
I have put my Spirit upon him,
he will bring forth justice to the nations.
He will not cry or lift up his voice,
or make it heard in the street;
a bruised reed he will not break,
and a dimly burning wick he will not quench;
he will faithfully bring forth justice.
He will not fail or be discouraged
till he has established justice in the earth;
and the coastlands wait for his law.

Thus says God, the Lord,
who created the heavens and stretched them out,
who spread forth the earth and what comes from it,
who gives breath to the people upon it
and spirit to those who walk in it:
"I am the Lord, I have called you in righteousness,
I have taken you by the hand and kept you;
I have given you as a covenant to the people,
a light to the nations,
to open the eyes that are blind,

to bring out the prisoners from the dungeon,
from the prison those who sit in darkness.
I am the Lord, that is my name;
my glory I give to no other,
nor my praise to graven images.
Behold, the former things have come to pass,
and new things I now declare;
before they spring forth
I tell you of them."

713 (2) **Matthew 12:18–21**
"Behold, my servant whom I have chosen,
my beloved with whom my soul is well pleased.
I will put my Spirit upon him,
and he shall proclaim justice to the Gentiles.
He will not wrangle or cry aloud,
nor will any one hear his voice in the streets;
he will not break a bruised reed
or quench a smoldering wick,
till he brings justice to victory;
and in his name will the Gentiles hope."

713 (3) **John 1:32–34** And John bore witness, "I saw the Spirit descend as a dove from heaven, and it remained on him. I myself did not know him; but he who sent me to baptize with water said to me, 'He on whom you see the Spirit descend and remain, this is he who baptizes with the Holy Spirit.' And I have seen and have borne witness that this is the Son of God."

713 (4) **Isaiah 49:1–6**
Listen to me, O coastlands,
and hearken, you peoples from afar.
The Lord called me from the womb,
from the body of my mother he named my name.
He made my mouth like a sharp sword,
in the shadow of his hand he hid me;
he made me a polished arrow,
in his quiver he hid me away.
And he said to me, "You are my servant,
Israel, in whom I will be glorified."
But I said, "I have labored in vain,
I have spent my strength for nothing and vanity;
yet surely my right is with the Lord,
and my recompense with my God."
And now the Lord says,
who formed me from the womb to be his servant,
to bring Jacob back to him,
and that Israel might be gathered to him,
for I am honored in the eyes of the Lord,
and my God has become my strength—
he says:
"It is too light a thing that you should be my servant
to raise up the tribes of Jacob
and to restore the preserved of Israel;

I will give you as a light to the nations,
that my salvation may reach to the end of the earth."

(5) **Matthew 3:17** . . . and lo, a voice from heaven, saying, "This is my beloved **713**
Son, with whom I am well pleased."

(6) **Luke 2:32** **713**
". . . a light for revelation to the Gentiles,
and for glory to thy people Israel."

(7) **Isaiah 50:4–10** **713**
The Lord has given me
the tongue of those who are taught,
that I may know how to sustain with a word
him that is weary.
Morning by morning he wakens,
he wakens my ear
to hear as those who are taught.
The Lord God has opened my ear,
and I was not rebellious,
I turned not backward.
I gave my back to the smiters,
and my cheeks to those who pulled out the beard;
I hid not my face
from shame and spitting.

For the Lord God helps me;
therefore I have not been confounded;
therefore I have set my face like a flint,
and I know that I shall not be put to shame;
he who vindicates me is near.
Who will contend with me?
Let us stand up together.
Who is my adversary?
Let him come near to me.
Behold, the Lord God helps me;
who will declare me guilty?
Behold, all of them will wear out like a garment;
the moth will eat them up.

Who among you fears the Lord
and obeys the voice of his servant,
who walks in darkness
and has no light,
yet trusts in the name of the Lord
and relies upon his God?

(8) **Isaiah 52:13–53:12** **713**
Behold, my servant shall prosper,
he shall be exalted and lifted up,
and shall be very high.
As many were astonished at him—
his appearance was so marred, beyond human semblance,
and his form beyond that of the sons of men—

so shall he startle many nations;
kings shall shut their mouths because of him;
for that which has not been told them they shall see,
and that which they have not heard they shall understand.

Who has believed what we have heard?
And to whom has the arm of the Lord been revealed?
For he grew up before him like a young plant,
and like a root out of dry ground;
he had no form or comeliness that we should look at him,
and no beauty that we should desire him.
He was despised and rejected by men;
a man of sorrows, and acquainted with grief;
and as one from whom men hide their faces
he was despised, and we esteemed him not.

Surely he has borne our griefs
and carried our sorrows;
yet we esteemed him stricken,
smitten by God, and afflicted.
But he was wounded for our transgressions,
he was bruised for our iniquities;
upon him was the chastisement that made us whole,
and with his stripes we are healed.
All we like sheep have gone astray;
we have turned every one to his own way;
and the Lord has laid on him
the iniquity of us all.

He was oppressed, and he was afflicted,
yet he opened not his mouth;
like a lamb that is led to the slaughter,
and like a sheep that before its shearers is dumb,
so he opened not his mouth.
By oppression and judgment he was taken away;
and as for his generation, who considered
that he was cut off out of the land of the living,
stricken for the transgression of my people?
And they made his grave with the wicked
and with a rich man in his death,
although he had done no violence,
and there was no deceit in his mouth.

Yet it was the will of the Lord to bruise him;
he has put him to grief;
when he makes himself an offering for sin,
he shall see his offspring, he shall prolong his days;
the will of the Lord shall prosper in his hand;
he shall see the fruit of the travail of his soul and be satisfied;
by his knowledge shall the righteous one, my servant,
make many to be accounted righteous;
and he shall bear their iniquities.
Therefore I will divide him a portion with the great,
and he shall divide the spoil with the strong;

because he poured out his soul to death,
and was numbered with the transgressors;
yet he bore the sin of many,
and made intercession for the transgressors.

Luke 4:18–19 714
"The Spirit of the Lord is upon me,
because he has anointed me to
preach good news to the poor.
He has sent me to proclaim release
to the captives
and recovering of sight to the blind,
to set at liberty those who are oppressed,
to proclaim the acceptable year of the Lord."

(1) **Ezekiel 11:19** And I will give them one heart, and put a new spirit within them; 715
I will take the stony heart out of their flesh. . . .

(2) **Ezekiel 36:25–28** I will sprinkle clean water upon you, and you shall be clean 715
from all your uncleannesses, and from all your idols I will cleanse you. A new heart I will give you, and a new spirit I will put within you; and I will take out of your flesh the heart of stone and give you a heart of flesh. And I will put my spirit within you, and cause you to walk in my statutes and be careful to observe my ordinances. You shall dwell in the land which I gave to your fathers; and you shall be my people, and I will be your God.

(3) **Ezekiel 37:1–14** The hand of the Lord was upon me, and he brought me out 715
by the Spirit of the Lord, and set me down in the midst of the valley; it was full of bones. And he led me round among them; and behold, there were very many upon the valley; and lo, they were very dry. And he said to me, "Son of man, can these bones live?" And I answered, "O Lord God, thou knowest." Again he said to me, "Prophesy to these bones, and say to them, O dry bones, hear the word of the Lord. Thus says the Lord God to these bones: Behold, I will cause breath to enter you, and you shall live. And I will lay sinews upon you, and will cause flesh to come upon you, and cover you with skin, and put breath in you, and you shall live; and you shall know that I am the Lord."

So I prophesied as I was commanded; and as I prophesied, there was a noise, and behold, a rattling; and the bones came together, bone to its bone. And as I looked, there were sinews on them, and flesh had come upon them, and skin had covered them; but there was no breath in them. Then he said to me, "Prophesy to the breath, prophesy, son of man, and say to the breath, Thus says the Lord God: Come from the four winds, O breath, and breathe upon these slain, that they may live." So I prophesied as he commanded me, and the breath came into them, and they lived, and stood upon their feet, an exceedingly great host.

Then he said to me, "Son of man, these bones are the whole house of Israel. Behold, they say, 'Our bones are dried up, and our hope is lost; we are clean cut off.' Therefore prophesy, and say to them, Thus says the Lord God: Behold, I will open your graves, and raise you from your graves, O my people; and I will bring you home into the land of Israel. And you shall know that I am the Lord, when I open your graves, and raise you from your graves, O my people. And I will put my Spirit within you, and you shall live, and I will place you in your own land; then you shall know that I, the Lord, have spoken, and I have done it, says the Lord."

715 (4) **Jeremiah 31:31–34** "Behold, the days are coming, says the Lord, when I will make a new covenant with the house of Israel and the house of Judah, not like the covenant which I made with their fathers when I took them by the hand to bring them out of the land of Egypt, my covenant which they broke, though I was their husband, says the Lord. But this is the covenant which I will make with the house of Israel after those days, says the Lord: I will put my law within them, and I will write it upon their hearts; and I will be their God, and they shall be my people. And no longer shall each man teach his neighbor and each his brother, saying, 'Know the Lord,' for they shall all know me, from the least of them to the greatest, says the Lord; for I will forgive their iniquity, and I will remember their sin no more."

715 (5) **Joel 3:1–5 (2:28–32 RSV)**

"And it shall come to pass afterward,
that I will pour out my spirit on all flesh;
your sons and your daughters shall prophesy,
your old men shall dream dreams,
and your young men shall see visions.
Even upon the menservants and maidservants
in those days, I will pour out my spirit.

"And I will give portents in the heavens and on the earth, blood and fire and columns of smoke. The sun shall be turned to darkness, and the moon to blood, before the great and terrible day of the Lord comes. And it shall come to pass that all who call upon the name of the Lord shall be delivered; for in Mount Zion and in Jerusalem there shall be those who escape, as the Lord has said, and among the survivors shall be those whom the Lord calls. . . ."

715 (6) **Acts 2:17–21**

". . . 'And in the last days it shall be, God declares,
that I will pour out my Spirit upon all flesh,
and your sons and your daughters shall prophesy,
and your young men shall see visions,
and your old men shall dream dreams;
yea, and on my menservants and my maidservants in those days
I will pour out my Spirit; and they shall prophesy.
And I will show wonders in the heaven above
and signs on the earth beneath,
blood, and fire, and vapor of smoke;
the sun shall be turned into darkness
and the moon into blood,
before the day of the Lord comes,
the great and manifest day.
And it shall be that whoever calls on the name of the Lord shall be saved.'"

716 (1) **Zephaniah 2:3**

Seek the Lord, all you humble of the land,
who do his commands;
seek righteousness, seek humility;
perhaps you may be hidden
on the day of the wrath of the Lord.

(2) **Psalm 22:27 (22:26: RSV)** 716
The afflicted shall eat and be satisfied;
those who seek him shall praise the Lord!
May your hearts live for ever!

(3) **Psalm 34:3 (34:2: RSV)** 716
My soul makes its boast in the Lord;
let the afflicted hear and be glad.

(4) **Isaiah 49:13** 716
Sing for joy, O heavens, and exult, O earth;
break forth, O mountains, into singing!
For the Lord has comforted his people,
and will have compassion on his afflicted.

(5) **Isaiah 61:1** 716
The Spirit of the Lord God is upon me,
because the Lord has anointed me
to bring good tidings to the afflicted;
he has sent me to bind up the brokenhearted,
to proclaim liberty to the captives,
and the opening of the prison to those who are bound. . . .

Luke 1:68 717
"Blessed be the Lord God of Israel,
for he has visited and reedemed his people. . . ."

Luke 1:78 718
. . . through the tender mercy of our God,
when the day shall dawn upon us from on high. . . .

(1) **Matthew 11:13–14** For all the prophets and the law prophesied until John; 719
and if you are willing to accept it, he is Elijah who is to come.

(2) **Isaiah 40:1–3** 719
Comfort, comfort my people,
says your God.
Speak tenderly to Jerusalem,
and cry to her
that her warfare is ended,
that her iniquity is pardoned,
that she has received from the Lord's hand
double for all her sins.
A voice cries:
"In the wilderness prepare the way of the Lord,
make straight in the desert a highway for our God. . . ."

(3) **John 15:26** But when the Counselor comes, whom I shall send to you from the 719
Father, even the Spirit of truth, who proceeds from the Father, he will bear witness
to me. . . .

(4) **John 5:35** He was a burning and shining lamp, and you were willing to rejoice 719
for a while in his light.

719 (5) **1 Peter 1:10–12** In this is love, not that we loved God but that he loved us and sent his Son to be the expiation for our sins. Beloved, if God so loved us, we also ought to love one another. No man has ever seen God; if we love one another, God abides in us and his love is perfected in us.

720 **John 3:5** Jesus answered, "Truly, truly, I say to you, unless one is born of water and the Spirit, he cannot enter the kingdom of God. . . ."

721 (1) **Proverbs 8:1–9:6**

Does not wisdom call,
  does not understanding raise her voice?
On the heights beside the way,
  in the paths she takes her stand;
beside the gates in front of the town,
  at the entrance of the portals she cries aloud:
"To you, O men, I call,
  and my cry is to the sons of men.
O simple ones, learn prudence;
  O foolish men, pay attention.
Hear, for I will speak noble things,
  and from my lips will come what is right;
for my mouth will utter truth;
  wickedness is an abomination to my lips.
All the words of my mouth are righteous;
  there is nothing twisted or crooked in them.
They are all straight to him who understands
  and right to those who find knowledge.
Take my instruction instead of silver,
  and knowledge rather than choice gold;
for wisdom is better than jewels,
  and all that you may desire cannot compare with her.
I, wisdom, dwell in prudence,
  and I find knowledge and discretion.
The fear of the Lord is hatred of evil.
Pride and arrogance and the way of evil
  and perverted speech I hate.
I have counsel and sound wisdom,
  I have insight, I have strength.
By me kings reign,
  and rulers decree what is just;
by me princes rule,
  and nobles govern the earth.
I love those who love me,
  and those who seek me diligently find me.
Riches and honor are with me,
  enduring wealth and prosperity.
My fruit is better than gold, even fine gold,
  and my yield than choice silver.
I walk in the way of righteousness,
  in the paths of justice,
endowing with wealth those who love me,
  and filling their treasuries.

The Lord created me at the beginning of his work,
the first of his acts of old.
Ages ago I was set up,
at the first, before the beginning of the earth.
When there were no depths I was brought forth,
when there were no springs abounding with water.
Before the mountains had been shaped,
before the hills, I was brought forth;
before he had made the earth with its fields,
or the first of the dust of the world.
When he established the heavens, I was there,
when he drew a circle on the face of the deep,
when he made firm the skies above,
when he established the fountains of the deep,
when he assigned to the sea its limit,
so that the waters might not transgress his command,
when he marked out the foundations of the earth,
then I was beside him, like a master workman;
and I was daily his delight,
rejoicing before him always,
rejoicing in his inhabited world
and delighting in the sons of men.

And now, my sons, listen to me:
happy are those who keep my ways.
Hear instruction and be wise,
and do not neglect it.
Happy is the man who listens to me,
watching daily at my gates,
waiting beside my doors.
For he who finds me finds life
and obtains favor from the Lord;
but he who misses me injures himself;
all who hate me love death."

Wisdom has built her house,
she has set up her seven pillars.
She has slaughtered her beasts, she has mixed her wine,
she has also set her table.
She has sent out her maids to call
from the highest places in the town,
"Whoever is simple, let him turn in here!"
To him who is without sense she says,
"Come, eat of my bread
and drink of the wine I have mixed.
Leave simpleness, and live,
and walk in the way of insight."

(2) **Sirach 24** 721
Wisdom will praise herself,
and will glory in the midst of her people.
In the assembly of the Most High she will open her mouth,
and in the presence of his host she will glory:

"I came forth from the mouth of the Most High,
and covered the earth like a mist.
I dwelt in high places,
and my throne was in a pillar of cloud.
Alone I have made the circuit of the vault of heaven
and have walked in the depths of the abyss.
In the waves of the sea, in the whole earth,
and in every people and nation I have gotten a possession.
Among all these I sought a resting place;
I sought in whose territory I might lodge.

"Then the Creator of all things gave me a commandment,
and the one who created me assigned a place for my tent.
And he said, 'Make your dwelling in Jacob,
and in Israel receive your inheritance.'
From eternity, in the beginning, he created me,
and for eternity I shall not cease to exist.
In the holy tabernacle I ministered before him,
and so I was established in Zion.
In the beloved city likewise he gave me a resting place,
and in Jerusalem was my dominion.
So I took root in an honored people,
in the portion of the Lord, who is their inheritance.

"I grew tall like a cedar in Lebanon,
and like a cypress on the heights of Hermon.
I grew tall like a palm tree in Engedi,
and like rose plants in Jericho;
like a beautiful olive tree in the field,
and like a plane tree I grew tall.
Like cassia and camel's thorn I gave forth the aroma of spices,
and like choice myrrh I spread a pleasant odor,
like galbanum, onycha, and stacte,
and like the fragrance of frankincense in the tabernacle.
Like a terebinth I spread out my branches,
and my branches are glorious and graceful.
Like a vine I caused loveliness to bud,
and my blossoms became glorious and abundant fruit.

"Come to me, you who desire me,
and eat your fill of my produce.
For the remembrance of me is sweeter than honey,
and my inheritance sweeter than the honeycomb.
Those who eat me will hunger for more,
and those who drink me will thirst for more.
Whoever obeys me will not be put to shame,
and those who work with my help will not sin."

All this is the book of the covenant of the Most High God,
the law which Moses commanded us
as an inheritance for the congregations of Jacob.
It fills men with wisdom, like the Pishon,
and like the Tigris at the time of the first fruits.
It makes them full of understanding, like the Euphrates,
and like the Jordan at harvest time.

It makes instruction shine forth like light,
like the Gihon at the time of vintage.
Just as the first man did not know her perfectly,
the last one has not fathomed her;
for her thought is more abundant than the sea,
and her counsel deeper than the great abyss.

I went forth like a canal from a river
and like a water channel into a garden.
I said, "I will water my orchard and drench my garden plot";
and lo, my canal became a river, and my river became a sea.
I will again make instruction shine forth like the dawn,
and I will make it shine afar;
I will again pour out teaching like prophecy,
and leave it to all future generations.
Observe that I have not labored for myself alone,
but for all who seek instruction.

(1) **Zephaniah 3:14** 722
Sing aloud, O daughter of Zion;
shout, O Israel!
Rejoice and exult with all your heart,
O daughter of Jerusalem!

(2) **Zechariah 2:14 (2:10 RSV)** Sing and rejoice, O daughter of Zion; for lo, I 722
come and I dwell in the midst of you, says the Lord.

(3) **Luke 1:46–55** And Mary said, 722
"My soul magnifies the Lord,
and my spirit rejoices in God my Savior,
for he has regarded the low estate of his handmaiden.
For behold, henceforth all generations will call me blessed;
for he who is mighty has done great things for me,
and holy is his name.
And his mercy is on those who fear him
from generation to generation.
He has shown strength with his arm,
he has scattered the proud in the imagination of their hearts,
he has put down the mighty from their thrones,
and exalted those of low degree;
he has filled the hungry with good things,
and the rich he has sent empty away.
He has helped his servant Israel,
in remembrance of his mercy,
as he spoke to our fathers,
to Abraham and to his posterity for ever."

(1) **Luke 1:26–38** In the sixth month the angel Gabriel was sent from God to 723
a city of Galilee named Nazareth, to a virgin betrothed to a man whose name was Joseph, of the house of David; and the virgin's name was Mary. And he came to her and said, "Hail, O favored one, the Lord is with you!" But she was greatly troubled at the saying and considered in her mind what sort of greeting this might be. And the angel said to her, "Do not be afraid, Mary, for you have found favor with God.

And behold, you will conceive in your womb and bear a son, and you shall call his name Jesus.

He will be great, and will be called the Son of the Most High;
and the Lord God will give to him the throne of his father David,
and he will reign over the house of Jacob for ever;
and of his kingdom there will be no end."

And Mary said to the angel, "How shall this be, since I have no husband?" And the angel said to her,

"The Holy Spirit will come upon you,
and the power of the Most High will overshadow you;
therefore the child to be born will be called holy,
the Son of God.

And behold, your kinswoman Elizabeth in her old age has also conceived a son; and this is the sixth month with her who was called barren. For with God nothing will be impossible." And Mary said, "Behold, I am the handmaid of the Lord; let it be to me according to your word." And the angel departed from her.

723 (2) **Romans 4:18–21** In hope he believed against hope, that he should become the father of many nations; as he had been told, "So shall your descendants be." He did not weaken in faith when he considered his own body, which was as good as dead because he was about a hundred years old, or when he considered the barenness of Sarah's womb. No distrust made him waver concerning the promise of God, but he grew strong in his faith as he gave glory to God, fully convinced that God was able to do what he had promised.

723 (3) **Galatians 4:26–28** But the Jerusalem above is free, and she is our mother. For it is written,

"Rejoice, O barren one who does not bear;
break forth and shout, you who are not in travail;
for the children of the desolate one
are many more than the children of
her that is married."

Now we, brethren, like Isaac, are children of promise.

724 (1) **Luke 1:15–19**

". . . for he will be great before the Lord,
and he shall drink no wine nor strong drink,
and he will be filled with the Holy Spirit,
even from his mother's womb.
And he will turn many of the sons of Israel to the Lord their God,
and he will go before him in the spirit and power of Elijah,
to turn the hearts of the fathers to the children,
and the disobedient to the wisdom of the just,
to make ready for the Lord a people prepared."

And Zechariah said to the angel, "How shall I know this? For I am an old man, and my wife is advanced in years." And the angel answered him, "I am Gabriel, who stand in the presence of God; and I was sent to speak to you, and to bring you this good news. . . ."

724 (2) **Matthew 2:11** . . . and going into the house they saw the child with Mary his mother, and they fell down and worshiped him. Then, opening their treasures, they offered him gifts, gold and frankincense and myrrh.

Luke 2:14 725
"Glory to God in the highest,
and on earth peace among men with whom he is pleased!"

John 19:25–27 So the soldiers did this. But standing by the cross of Jesus were 726
his mother, and his mother's sister, Mary the wife of Clopas, and Mary Magdalene. When Jesus saw his mother, and the disciple whom he loved standing near, he said to his mother, "Woman, behold, your son!" Then he said to the disciple, "Behold, your mother!" And from that hour the disciple took her to his own home.

(1) **John 6:27** ". . . Do not labor for the food which perishes, but for the food 728
which endures to eternal life, which the Son of man will give to you; for on him has God the Father set his seal."

(2) **John 6:51** ". . . I am the living bread which came down from heaven; if any 728
one eats of this bread, he will live for ever; and the bread which I shall give for the life of the world is my flesh."

(3) **John 6:62–63** Then what if you were to see the Son of man ascending where 728
he was before? It is the spirit that gives life, the flesh is of no avail; the words that I have spoken to you are spirit and life.

(4) **John 3:5–8** Jesus answered, "Truly, truly, I say to you, unless one is born of 728
water and the Spirit, he cannot enter the kingdom of God. That which is born of the flesh is flesh, and that which is born of the Spirit is spirit. Do not marvel that I said to you, 'You must be born anew.' The wind blows where it wills, and you hear the sound of it, but you do not know whence it comes or whither it goes; so it is with every one who is born of the Spirit."

(5) **John 4:10** Jesus answered her, "If you knew the gift of God, and who it is that 728
is saying to you, 'Give me a drink,' you would have asked him, and he would have given you living water."

(6) **John 4:14** ". . . but whoever drinks of the water that I shall give him will never 728
thirst; the water that I shall give him will become in him a spring of water welling up to eternal life."

(7) **John 4:23–24** ". . . But the hour is coming, and now is, when the true worshipers 728
will worship the Father in spirit and truth, for such the Father seeks to worship him. God is spirit, and those who worship him must worship in spirit and truth."

(8) **John 7:37–39** On the last day of the feast, the great day, Jesus stood up and 728
proclaimed, "If any one thirst, let him come to me and drink. He who believes in me, as the scripture has said, 'Out of his heart shall flow rivers of living water.'" Now this he said about the Spirit, which those who believed in him were to receive; for as yet the Spirit had not been given, because Jesus was not yet glorified.

(9) **Luke 11:13** ". . . If you then, who are evil, know how to give good gifts to your 728
children, how much more will the heavenly Father give the Holy Spirit to those who ask him!"

728 (10) **Matthew 10:19–20** When they deliver you up, do not be anxious how you are to speak or what you are to say; for what you are to say will be given to you in that hour; for it is not you who speak, but the Spirit of your Father speaking through you.

729 (1) **John 14:16–17** And I will pray the Father, and he will give you another Counselor, to be with you for ever, even the Spirit of truth, whom the world cannot receive, because it neither sees him nor knows him; you know him, for he dwells with you, and will be in you.

729 (2) **John 14:26** But the Counselor, the Holy Spirit, whom the Father will send in my name, he will teach you all things, and bring to your remembrance all that I have said to you.

729 (3) **John 15:26** But when the Counselor comes, whom I shall send to you from the Father, even the Spirit of truth, who proceeds from the Father, he will bear witness to me. . . .

729 (4) **John 16:7–15** ". . . Nevertheless I tell you the truth: it is to your advantage that I go away, for if I do not go away, the Counselor will not come to you; but if I go, I will send him to you. And when he comes, he will convince the world concerning sin and righteousness and judgment: concerning sin, because they do not believe in me; concerning righteousness, because I go to the Father, and you will see me no more; concerning judgment, because the ruler of this world is judged.

"I have yet many things to say to you, but you cannot bear them now. When the Spirit of truth comes, he will guide you into all the truth; for he will not speak on his own authority, but whatever he hears he will speak, and he will declare to you the things that are to come. He will glorify me, for he will take what is mine and declare it to you. All that the Father has is mine; therefore I said that he will take what is mine and declare it to you. . . ."

729 (5) **John 17:26** ". . . I made known to them thy name, and I will make it known, that the love with which thou hast loved me may be in them, and I in them."

730 (1) **John 13:1** Now before the feast of the Passover, when Jesus knew that his hour had come to depart out of this world to the Father, having loved his own who were in the world, he loved them to the end.

730 (2) **John 17:1** When Jesus had spoken these words, he lifted up his eyes to heaven and said, "Father, the hour has come; glorify thy Son that the Son may glorify thee. . . ."

730 (3) **Luke 23:46** Then Jesus, crying with a loud voice, said, "Father, into thy hands I commit my spirit!" And having said this he breathed his last.

730 (4) **John 19:30** When Jesus had received the vinegar, he said, "It is finished"; and he bowed his head and gave up his spirit.

730 (5) **John 20:22** And when he had said this, he breathed on them, and said to them, "Receive the Holy Spirit. . . ."

730 (6) **Matthew 28:19** Go therefore and make disciples of all nations, baptizing them in the name of the Father and of the Son and of the Holy Spirit. . . .

(7) **Luke 24:47–48** . . . and that repentance and forgiveness of sins should be 730
preached in his name to all nations, beginning from Jerusalem. You are witnesses of these things.

(8) **Acts 1:8** ". . . But you shall receive power when the Holy Spirit has come upon 730
you; and you shall be my witnesses in Jerusalem and in all Judea and Samaria and to the end of the earth."

Acts 2:33–36 ". . . Being therefore exalted at the right hand of God, and having 731
received from the Father the promise of the Holy Spirit, he has poured out this which you see and hear. For David did not ascend into the heavens; but he himself says,

'The Lord said to my Lord, Sit at my right hand,
till I make thy enemies a stool for they feet.'

Let all the house of Israel therefore know assuredly that God has made him both Lord and Christ, this Jesus whom you crucified."

(1) **Romans 8:23** . . . and not only the creation, but we ourselves, who have the first 735
fruits of the Spirit, groan inwardly as we wait for adoption as sons, the redemption of our bodies.

(2) **2 Corinthians 1:21** But it is God who establishes us with you in Christ, and 735
has commissioned us. . . .

(3) **1 Corinthians 13** If I speak in the tongues of men and of angels, but have not 735
love, I am a noisy gong or a clanging cymbal. And if I have prophetic powers and understand all mysteries and all knowledge, and if I have all faith, so as to remove mountains, but have not love, I am nothing. If I give away all I have, and if I deliver my body to be burned, but have not love, I gain nothing.

Love is patient and kind; love is not jealous or boastful; it is not arrogant or rude. Love does not insist on its own way; it is not irritable or resentful; it does not rejoice at wrong but rejoices in the right. Love bears all things, believes all things, hopes all things, endures all things.

Love never ends; as for prophecies, they will pass away; as for tongues, they will cease; as for knowledge, it will pass away. For our knowledge is imperfect and our prophesy is imperfect; but when the perfect comes, the imperfect will pass away. When I was a child, I spoke like a child, I thought like a child, I reasoned like a child; when I became a man, I gave up childish ways. For now we see in a mirror dimly, but then face to face. Now I know in part; then I shall understand fully, even as I have been fully understood. So faith, hope, love abide, these three; but the greatest of these is love.

Matthew 16:24–26 Then Jesus told his disciples, "If any man would come after 736
me, let him deny himself and take up his cross and follow me. For whoever would save his life will lose it, and whoever loses his life for my sake will find it. For what will it profit a man, if he gains the whole world and forfeits his life? Or what shall a man give in return for his life? . . ."

Psalm 2:6–7 745

"I have set my king
on Zion, my holy hill."

I will tell of the decree of the Lord:
He said to me, "You are my son,
today I have begotten you. . . ."

746 **Acts 2:36** ". . . Let all the house of Israel therefore know assuredly that God has made him both Lord and Christ, this Jesus whom you crucified."

748 **Mark 16:15** And he said to them, "Go into all the world and preach the gospel to the whole creation. . . ."

751 (1) **Acts 19:39** But if you seek anything further, it shall be settled in the regular assembly.

751 (2) **Exodus 19** On the third new moon after the people of Israel had gone forth out of the land of Egypt, on that day they came into the wilderness of Sinai. And when they set out from Rephidim and came into the wilderness of Sinai, they encamped in the wilderness; and there Israel encamped before the mountain. And Moses went up to God, and the Lord called to him out of the mountain, saying, "Thus you shall say to the house of Jacob, and tell the people of Israel: You have seen what I did to the Egyptians, and how I bore you on eagles' wings and brought you to myself. Now therefore, if you will obey my voice and keep my covenant, you shall be my own possession among all peoples; for all the earth is mine, and you shall be to me a kingdom of priests and a holy nation. These are the words which you shall speak to the children of Israel."

So Moses came and called the elders of the people, and set before them all these words which the Lord had commanded him. And all the people answered together and said, "All that the Lord has spoken we will do." And Moses reported the words of the people to the Lord. And the Lord said to Moses, "Lo, I am coming to you in a thick cloud, that the people may hear when I speak with you, and may also believe you for ever."

Then Moses told the words of the people to the Lord. And the Lord said to Moses, "Go to the people and consecrate them today and tomorrow, and let them wash their garments, and be ready by the third day; for on the third day the Lord will come down upon Mount Sinai in the sight of all the people. And you shall set bounds for the people round about, saying, 'Take heed that you do not go up into the mountain or touch the border of it; whoever touches the mountain shall be put to death; no hand shall touch him, but he shall be stoned or shot; whether beast or man, he shall not live.' When the trumpet sounds a long blast, they shall come up to the mountain." So Moses went down from the mountain to the people, and consecrated the people; and they washed their garments. And he said to the people, "Be ready by the third day; do not go near a woman."

On the morning of the third day there were thunders and lightnings, and a thick cloud upon the mountain, and a very loud trumpet blast, so that all the people who were in the camp trembled. Then Moses brought the people out of the camp to meet God; and they took their stand at the foot of the mountain. And Mount Sinai was wrapped in smoke, because the Lord descended upon it in fire; and the smoke of it went up like the smoke of a kiln, and the whole mountain quaked greatly. And as the sound of the trumpet grew louder and louder, Moses spoke, and God answered him in thunder. And the Lord came down upon Mount Sinai, to the top of the mountain; and the Lord called Moses to the top of the mountain, and Moses went up. And the Lord said to Moses, "Go down and warn the people, lest they break through to the Lord to gaze and many of them perish. And also let the priests who come near to the Lord consecrate themselves, lest the Lord break out upon them." And Moses said to the Lord, "The people cannot come up to Mount Sinai; for thou thyself didst charge us, saying 'Set bounds about the mountain, and consecrate it.'" And the Lord said to him, "Go down, and come up bringing Aaron with you; but do not let the priests and the people break through to come up to the Lord, lest he break out against them." So Moses went down to the people and told them.

(1) **1 Corinthians 11:18** For, in the first place, when you assemble as a church, I hear that there are divisions among you; and I partly believe it. . . . **752**

(2) **1 Corinthians 14:19** . . . nevertheless, in church I would rather speak five words with my mind, in order to instruct others, than ten thousand words in a tongue. **752**

(3) **1 Corinthians 14:28** But if there is no one to interpret, let each of them keep silence in church and speak to himself and to God. **752**

(4) **1 Corinthians 14:34–35** . . . the women should keep silence in the churches. For they are not permitted to speak, but should be subordinate, as even the law says. If there is anything they desire to know, let them ask their husbands at home. For it is shameful for a woman to speak in church. **752**

(5) **1 Corinthians 1:2** To the church of God which is at Corinth, to those sanctified in Christ Jesus, called to be saints together with all those who in every place call on the name of our Lord Jesus Christ, both their Lord and ours. . . . **752**

(6) **1 Corinthians 16:1** Now concerning the contribution for the saints: as I directed the churches of Galatia, so you also are to do. **752**

(7) **1 Corinthians 15:9** For I am the least of the apostles, unfit to be called an apostle, because I persecuted the church of God. **752**

(8) **Galatians 1:13** For you have heard of my former life in Judaism, how I persecuted the church of God violently and tried to destroy it. . . . **752**

(9) **Philippians 3:6** . . . as to zeal a persecutor of the church, as to righteousness under the law blameless. **752**

(1) **Ephesians 1:22** . . . and he has put all things under his feet and has made him the head over all things for the church. . . . **753**

(2) **Colossians 1:18** He is the head of the body, the church; he is the beginning, the first-born from the dead, that in everything he might be pre-eminent. **753**

(3) ***Lumen gentium* 9** At all times and in every race, anyone who fears God and does what is right has been acceptable to him (cf. Acts 10:35). He has, however, willed to make men holy and save them, not as individuals without any bond or link between them, but rather to make them into a people who might acknowledge him and serve him in holiness. He therefore chose the Israelite race to be his own people and established a covenant with it. He gradually instructed this people—in its history manifesting both himself and the decree of his will—and made it holy unto himself. All these things, however, happened as a preparation and figure of that new and perfect covenant which was to be ratified in Christ, and of the fuller revelation which was to be given through the word of God made flesh. "Behold the days are coming, says the Lord, when I will make a new covenant with the house of Israel and the house of Judah. . . . I will put my law within them, and I will write it upon their **753**

hearts, and they shall be my people. . . . For they shall all know me from the least of them to the greatest, says the Lord" (Jer. 31:31–34). Christ instituted this new covenant, namely the new covenant in his blood (cf. 1 Cor. 11:25); he called a race made up of Jews and Gentiles which would be one, not according to the flesh, but in the Spirit, and this race would be the new People of God. For those who believe in Christ, who are reborn, not from a corruptible seed, but from an incorruptible one through the word of the living God (cf. 1 Pet. 1:23), not from flesh, but from water and the Holy Spirit (cf. Jn. 3:5–6), are finally established as "a chosen race, a royal priesthood, a holy nation . . . who in times past were not a people, but now are the People of God" (1 Pet. 2:9–10).

That messianic people has as its head Christ, "who was delivered up for our sins and rose again for our justification" (Rom. 4:25), and now, having acquired the name which is above all names, reigns gloriously in heaven. The state of this people is that of the dignity and freedom of the sons of God, in whose hearts the Holy Spirit dwells as in a temple. Its law is the new commandment to love as Christ loved us (cf. Jn. 13:34). Its destiny is the kingdom of God which has been begun by God himself on earth and which must be further extended until it is brought to perfection by him at the end of time when Christ our life (cf. Col. 3:4), will appear and "creation itself also will be delivered from its slavery to corruption into the freedom of the glory of the sons of God" (Rom. 8:21). Hence that messianic people, although it does not actually include all men, and at times may appear as a small flock, is, however, a most sure seed of unity, hope and salvation for the whole human race. Established by Christ as a communion of life, love and truth, it is taken up by him also as the instrument for the salvation of all; as the light of the world and the salt of the earth (cf. Mt. 5:13–16) it is sent forth into the whole world.

As Israel according to the flesh which wandered in the desert was already called the Church of God (2 Esd. 13:1; cf. Num. 20:4; Deut. 23:1 ff.), so too, the new Israel, which advances in this present era in search of a future and permanent city (cf. Heb. 13:14), is called also the Church of Christ (cf. Mt. 16:18). It is Christ indeed who had purchased it with his own blood (cf. Acts 20:28); he has filled it with his Spirit; he has provided means adapted to its visible and social union. All those, who in faith look towards Jesus, the author of salvation and the principle of unity and peace, God has gathered together and established as the Church, that it may be for each and everyone the visible sacrament of this saving unity. Destined to extend to all regions of the earth, it enters into human history, though it transcends at once all times and all racial boundaries. Advancing through trials and tribulations, the Church is strengthened by God's grace, promised to her by the Lord so that she may not waver from perfect fidelity, but remain the worthy bride of the Lord, ceaselessly renewing herself through the action of the Holy Spirit until, through the cross, she may attain to that light which knows no setting.

754 (1) **John 10:1–10** "Truly, truly, I say to you, he who does not enter the sheepfold by the door but climbs in by another way, that man is a thief and a robber; but he who enters by the door is the shepherd of the sheep. To him the gatekeeper opens; the sheep hear his voice, and he calls his own sheep by name and leads them out. When he has brought out all his own, he goes before them, and the sheep follow him, for they know his voice. A stranger they will not follow, but they will flee from him, for they do not know the voice of strangers." This figure Jesus used with them, but they did not understand what he was saying to them.

So Jesus again said to them, "Truly, truly, I say to you, I am the door of the sheep. All who came before me are thieves and robbers; but the sheep did not heed them. I am the door; if any one enters by me, he will be saved, and will go in and out and find pasture. The thief comes only to steal and kill and destroy; I came that they may have life, and have it abundantly. . . ."

(2) **Isaiah 40:11** 754

He will feed his flock like a shepherd,
  he will gather the lambs in his arms,
he will carry them in his bosom,
  and gently lead those that are with young.

(3) **Ezekiel 34:11–31** "For thus says the Lord God: Behold, I, I myself will search 754
for my sheep, and will seek them out. As a shepherd seeks out his flock when some of his sheep have been scattered abroad, so will I seek out my sheep; and I will rescue them from all places where they have been scattered on a day of clouds and thick darkness. And I will bring them out from the peoples, and gather them from the countries, and will bring them into their own land; and I will feed them on the mountains of Israel, by the fountains, and in all the inhabited places of the country. I will feed them with good pasture, and upon the mountain heights of Israel shall be their pasture; there they shall lie down in good grazing land, and on fat pasture they shall feed on the mountains of Israel. I myself will be the shepherd of my sheep, and I will make them lie down, says the Lord God. I will seek the lost, and I will bring back the strayed, and I will bind up the crippled, and I will strengthen the weak, and the fat and the strong I will watch over; I will feed them in justice.

"As for you, my flock, thus says the Lord God: Behold, I judge between sheep and sheep, rams and he-goats. Is it not enough for you to feed on the good pasture, that you must tread down with your feet the rest of your pasture; and to drink of clear water, that you must foul the rest with your feet? And must my sheep eat what you have trodden with your feet, and drink what you have fouled with your feet?

"Therefore, thus says the Lord God to them: Behold, I, I myself will judge between the fat sheep and the lean sheep. Because you push with side and shoulder, and thrust at all the weak with your horns, till you have scattered them abroad, I will save my flock, they shall no longer be a prey; and I will judge between sheep and sheep. And I will set up over them one shepherd, my servant David, and he shall feed them: he shall feed them and be their shepherd. And I, the Lord, will be their God, and my servant David shall be prince among them; I, the Lord, have spoken.

"I will make with them a covenant of peace and banish wild beasts from the land, so that they may dwell securely in the wilderness and sleep in the woods. And I will make them and the places round about my hill a blessing; and I will send down the showers in their season; they shall be showers of blessing. And the trees of the field shall yield their fruit, and the earth shall yield its increase, and they shall be secure in their land; and they shall know that I am the Lord, when I break the bars of their yoke, and deliver them from the hand of those who enslaved them. They shall no more be a prey to the nations, nor shall the beasts of the land devour them; they shall dwell securely, and none shall make them afraid. And I will provide for them prosperous plantations so that they shall no more be consumed with hunger in the land, and no longer suffer the reproach of the nations. And they shall know that I, the Lord their God, am with them, and that they, the house of Israel, are my people, says the Lord God. And you are my sheep, the sheep of my pasture, and I am your God, says the Lord God."

(4) **John 10:11** I am the good shepherd. The good shepherd lays down his life for 754
the sheep.

754 (5) **1 Peter 5:4** And when the chief Shepherd is manifested you will obtain the unfading crown of glory.

754 (6) **John 10:11–16** I am the good shepherd. The good shepherd lays down his life for the sheep. He who is a hireling and not a shepherd, whose own the sheep are not, sees the wolf coming and leaves the sheep and flees; and the wolf snatches them and scatters them. He flees because he is a hireling and cares nothing for the sheep. I am the good shepherd; I know my own and my own know me, as the Father knows me and I know the Father; and I lay down my life for the sheep. And I have other sheep, that are not of this fold; I must bring them also, and they will heed my voice. So there shall be one flock, one shepherd.

756 **1 Timothy 3:15** . . . if I am delayed, you may know how one ought to behave in the household of God, which is the church of the living God, the pillar and bulwark of the truth.

760 (1) **Aristides, *Apologia* 16, 6** As men who know God, they ask from Him petitions which are proper for Him to give and for them to receive: and thus they accomplish the course of their lives. And because they acknowledge the goodnesses of God towards them, lo! on account of them there flows forth the beauty that is in the world. And truly they are of the number of those that have found the truth by going about and seeking it, and as far as we have comprehended, we have understood that they only are near to the knowledge of the truth.

But the good deeds which they do, they do not proclaim in the ears of the multitude, and they take care that no one shall perceive them, and hide their gift, as he who has found a treasure and hides it. And they labor to become righteous as those that expect to see their Messiah and receive from Him the promises made to them with great glory.

But their sayings and their ordinances, O king, and the glory of their service, and the expectation of their recompense of reward, according to the doing of each one of them, which they expect in another world, thou art able to know from their writings. It sufficeth for us that we have briefly made known to your majesty concerning the conversation and the truth of the Christians. For truly great and wonderful is their teaching to him that is willing to examine and understand it. And truly this people is a new people, and there is something divine mingled with it. Take now their writings and read in them, and lo! ye will find that not of myself have I brought these things forward nor as their advocate have I said them, but as I have read in their writings, these things I firmly believe, and those things also that are to come. And therefore I was constrained to set forth the truth to them that take pleasure therein and seek after the world to come.

And I have no doubt that the world stands by reason of the intercession of Christians. But the rest of the peoples are deceived and deceivers, rolling themselves before the elements of the world, according as the sight of their understanding is unwilling to pass by them; and they grope as if in the dark, because they are unwilling to know the truth, and like drunken men they stagger and thrust one another and fall down.

760 (2) **Justin, *Apologiae* II, 7** Therefore God postpones the collapse and dissolution of the universe (through which the bad angels, the demons, and men would cease to exist), because of the Christian seed, which He knows to be the cause in nature [of the world's preservation]. If such were not the case, it would be impossible for you to do the things you do and be influenced by the evil demons; but the fire of judgment would descend and would completely dissolve everything, just as the flood

waters once left no one but him, with his family, whom we call Noe and you call Deucalion, from whom in turn so many have been born, some of them bad, others good. In this manner, we claim that the world will finally be destroyed by fire, and not, as the Stoics believe, because all things change into one another according to their disgraceful doctrine of metamorphosis. Nor do we teach [as do the Stoics] that men act and suffer according to the dictates of fate, but that by his own free will each man acts either well or evilly; and that through the influence of evil demons good men, such as Socrates and the like, are persecuted and imprisoned, while Sardanapalus, Epicurus, and the like seem to be endowed with wealth and glory. But the Stoics, ignorant of this demoniacal influence, claimed that everything takes place by the necessity of fate. But, since God from the very beginning created the race of angels and men with free will, they will justly pay the penalty in everlasting fire for the sins they have committed. Indeed, every creature is capable, by nature, of vice and of virtue. Nor would any action of theirs be worthy of praise unless they had the power to incline to either [vice or virtue]. The truth of this is shown everywhere by those legislators and philosophers who, acting according to right reason, have ordered some things to be done and others to be avoided. The Stoic philosophers also, in their moral teaching, always respect the same principles, so it is easily seen how wrong they are in their teaching on principles and incorporeal beings. For, if they state that human acts occur by fate, they will admit either that God is nothing else than those things which continually turn and change and dissolve into the same elements, and will seem to understand only corruptible things, and to affirm that God himself both in part and in whole is in every sin; or else that neither vice nor virtue is anything—which is against every sound idea, reason, and mind.

(3) **Tertullian,** ***Apologeticus*** **31, 3; 32, 1** But it is clearly and expressly said: 'Pray 760
for kings, for princes and for rulers, that all may be peaceful for you!' For, when the empire is shaken, and its other members are shaken, we, too, although we are considered outsiders by the crowd, are naturally involved in some part of the disaster.

There is also another, even greater, obligation for us to pray for the emperors; yes, even for the continuance of the empire in general and for Roman interests. We realize that the tremendous force which is hanging over the whole world, and the very end of the world with its threat of dreadful afflictions, is arrested for a time by the continued existence of the Roman Empire. This event we have no desire to experience, and, in praying that it may be deferred, we favor the continuance of Rome.

(4) **St. Epiphanius,** ***Panarion seu adversus LXXX haereses*** **I, 1, 5** And the Stoic 760
notion of deity is as follows. They claim that God is mind, or a mind of the whole visible vault—I mean the vault of heaven, earth and the rest—like a soul in a body. But they also divide the one Godhead into many individual beings: sun, moon and stars, soul, air and the rest. And <they have a doctrine of> reincarnations of souls and transmigrations from body to body, with <souls> being removed <from> bodies, entering (others) in turn, and being born over again—with their great deceit they finish off with this impiety. And they think that the soul is a part of God, and immortal.

Zeno was the founder of their Stoa, and there is much confused chatter about him. Some have said that he was <a son> of a Cleanthes of Tyre. But others claim that he was a Citean, a Cypriote islander, and that he lived at Rome for a while, but later offered this doctrine at Athens, at the Stoa as it is called. Some, however, say that there are two Zenos, Zeno of Elis and the one just mentioned. Both taught the same doctrine anyhow, even though there might be two of them. And so like the other sects, this (other) Zeno also maintains that matter is contemporaneous with God, and that there is a fate and fortune by which all things are directed and influenced.

Now then, I shall <administer> a remedy for Zeno's condition, as far as this brief discussion of mine can do it. For rather than overload the content of the treatise, <I need only> give <the main points>. However, skimming the surface so as not to digress, I shall address Zeno:

Mister, where did you get the guidance for your teaching? Or which Holy Spirit has spoken to you from heaven about your imposture? For you have to say that there are two contemporaries, matter and God. Your count will be wrong and prove untenable. For you admit that there is some sort of creator whom you also call "almighty," though you divide him into a plurality of gods. But what can he be creator of, if matter is contemporaneous with him? Matter in itself must be in control of itself, if it did not originate from any cause and is not subject to one. And if the creator took his material from it, and acquired it on loan, there must be a weakness (in him). And this must be an interest-free loan to a bankrupt, who provided for his own creation's existence, not from his own resources, but from property mortgaged to someone else.

And there is plenty wrong with your false notion of transmigration, you self-appointed sage who promises men knowledge! For if the soul is a part of God and immortal, and yet you associate wretched bodies with the fashioning of it—though you claim that its essence is from God! Not just <human> bodies—bodies of four-footed beasts too, and things that crawl, and vermin of foul origin! And what could be worse?

You further introduce fate as the cause of whatever happens to man and other beings. But I shall expose your invention succinctly with one argument. If cleverness, understanding, the generation of the rational and irrational, and everything else, is a matter of fate, then no more laws! Fate is in control of adulterers and the rest. Rather than the man, who does the deed under necessity, the stars, which have imposed necessity, must pay the penalty.

Moreover, I shall say some more on this subject, in a different way. No more diatribes! No more sophists, rhetoricians, and grammarians, no more doctors and the other professions, and the countless manual trades! No one should give instruction any more, if people's acquisition of the sciences depends on fate, not education. For if fate has made him educated and erudite, one should not learn from a teacher. Let the thread-spinning Fates weave knowledge into him naturally, as your imposture with its boastful oratory says.

761 (1) ***Lumen gentium* 9:** see 753 (3).

761 (2) ***Lumen gentium* 13** All men are called to belong to the new People of God. This People therefore, whilst remaining one and only one, is to be spread throughout the whole world and to all ages in order that the design of God's will may be fulfilled: he made human nature one in the beginning and has decreed that all his children who were scattered should be finally gathered together as one (cf. John 11:52). It was for this purpose that God sent his Son, whom he appointed heir of all things (cf. Heb. 1:2), that he might be teacher, king and priest of all, the head of the new and universal People of God's sons. This, too, is why God sent the Spirit of his Son, the Lord and Giver of Life. The Spirit is, for the Church and for each and every believer, the principle of their union and unity in the teaching of the apostles and fellowship, in the breaking of bread and prayer (cf. Acts 2:42 Gk.).

The one People of God is accordingly present in all the nations of the earth, since its citizens, who are taken from all nations, are of a kingdom whose nature is not earthly but heavenly. All the faithful scattered throughout the world are in communion with each other in the Holy Spirit so that 'he who dwells in Rome knows those in most distant parts to be his members' (*qui Romae sedet, Indos scit membrum suum esse*). Since the kingdom of Christ is not of this world (cf. Jn. 18:36), the Church or People of God which establishes this kingdom does not take away anything from the temporal welfare of any people. Rather she fosters and takes to herself, in so far as they are good, the abilities, the resources and customs of peoples. In so taking them to herself she purifies, strengthens and elevates them. The Church indeed is mindful that she must work with that king to whom the nations were given for an inheritance (cf. Ps. 2:8) and to whose city gifts are brought (cf. Ps. 71[72]:10; Is. 60:4–7; Apoc. 21:24). This character of universality which adorns the People of God is a gift from the Lord himself whereby the Catholic ceaselessly and efficaciously seeks for the return of all humanity and all its goods under Christ the Head in the unity of his Spirit.

In virtue of this catholicity each part contributes its own gifts to other parts and to the whole Church, so that the whole and each of the parts are strengthened by the common sharing of all things and by the common effort to attain to fullness in unity. Hence it is that the People of God is not only an assembly of various peoples, but in itself is made up of different ranks. This diversity among its members is either by reason of their duties—some exercise the sacred ministry for the good of their brethren—or it is due to their condition and manner of life—many enter the religious state and, intending to sanctity by the narrower way, stimulate their brethren by their example. Holding a rightful place in the communion of the Church there are also particular Churches that retain their own traditions, without prejudice to the Chair of Peter which presides over the whole assembly of charity, and protects their legitimate variety while at the same time taking care that these differences do not hinder unity, but rather contribute to it. Finally, between all the various parts of the Church there is a bond of close communion whereby spiritual riches, apostolic workers and temporal resources are shared. For the members of the People of God are called upon to share their goods, and the words of the apostle apply also to each of the Churches, 'according to the gift that each has received, administer it to one another as good stewards of the manifold grace of God' (1 Pet. 5:10).

All men are called to this catholic unity which prefigures and promotes universal peace. And in different ways to it belong, or are related: the Catholic faithful, others who believe in Christ, and finally all mankind, called by God's grace to salvation.

(3) ***Lumen gentium* 16** Finally, those who have not yet received the Gospel are **761**
related to the People of God in various ways. There is, first, that people to which the covenants and promises were made, and from which Christ was born according to the flesh (cf. Rom. 9:4–5): in view of the divine choice, they are a people most dear for the sake of the fathers, for the gifts of God are without repentance (cf. Rom. 11:29–32). But the plan of salvation also includes those who acknowledge the Creator, in the first place amongst whom are the Moslems: these profess to hold the faith of Abraham, and together with us they adore the one, merciful God, mankind's judge on the last day. Nor is God remote from those who in shadows and images seek the unknown God, since he gives to all men life and breath and all things (cf. Acts 17:25–28), and since the Savior wills all men to be saved (cf. 1 Tim. 2:4). Those who, through no fault of their own, do not know the Gospel of Christ or his Church, but who nevertheless seek God with a sincere heart, and, moved by grace, try in their actions to do his will as they know it through the dictates of their conscience—those too may achieve eternal salvation. Nor shall divine providence deny the assistance necessary for salvation to those who, without any fault of theirs, have not yet arrived at an explicit knowledge of God, and who, not without grace, strive to lead a good life. Whatever good or truth is found amongst them is considered by the Church to be a preparation for the Gospel and given by him who enlightens all men that they

may at length have life. But very often, deceived by the Evil One, men have become vain in their reasonings, have exchanged the truth of God for a lie and served the world rather than the Creator (cf. Rom. 1:21 and 25). Or else, living and dying in this world without God, they are exposed to ultimate despair. Hence to procure the glory of God and the salvation of all these, the Church, mindful of the Lord's command, "preach the Gospel to every creature" (Mk. 16:16) takes zealous care to foster the missions.

762 (1) **Genesis 12:2** And I will make of you a great nation, and I will bless you, and make your name great, so that you will be a blessing.

762 (2) **Genesis 15:5–6** And he brought him outside and said, "Look toward heaven, and number the stars, if you are able to number them." Then he said to him, "So shall your descendants be." And he believed the Lord; and he reckoned it to him as righteousness.

762 (3) **Exodus 19:5–6** ". . . Now therefore, if you will obey my voice and keep my covenant, you shall be my own possession among all peoples; for all the earth is mine, and you shall be to me a kingdom of priests and a holy nation. These are the words which you shall speak to the children of Israel."

762 (4) **Deuteronomy 7:6** "For you are a people holy to the Lord your God; the Lord your God has chosen you to be a people for his own possession, out of all the peoples that are on the face of the earth. . . ."

762 (5) **Isaiah 2:2–5**

It shall come to pass in the latter days
  that the mountain of the house of the Lord
shall be established as the highest of the mountains,
  and shall be raised above the hills;
and all the nations shall flow to it,
  and many peoples shall come, and say:
"Come, let us go up to the mountain of the Lord,
  to the house of the God of Jacob;
that he may teach us his ways
  and that we may walk in his paths."
For out of Zion shall go forth the law,
  and the word of the Lord from Jerusalem.
He shall judge between the nations,
  and shall decide for many peoples;
and they shall beat their swords into plowshares,
  and their spears into pruning hooks;
nation shall not lift up sword against nation,
  neither shall they learn war any more.

O house of Jacob,
  come, let us walk
  in the light of the Lord.

762 (6) **Micah 4:1–4**

It shall come to pass in the latter days
  that the mountain of the house of the Lord
shall be established as the highest of the mountains,
  and shall be raised up above the hills;

and peoples shall flow to it,
    and many nations shall come, and say:
"Come, let us go up to the mountain of the Lord,
    to the house of the God of Jacob;
that he may teach us his ways
    and we may walk in his paths."
For out of Zion shall go forth the law,
    and the word of the Lord from Jerusalem.
He shall judge between many peoples,
    and shall decide for strong nations afar off;
and they shall beat their swords into plowshares,
    and their spears into pruning hooks;
nation shall not lift up sword against nation,
    neither shall they learn war any more;
but they shall sit every man under his vine and under his fig tree,
    and none shall make them afraid;
    for the mouth of the Lord of hosts has spoken.

(7) **Hosea 1** The word of the Lord that came to Hosea the son of Beeri, in the days **762**
of Uzziah, Jotham, Ahaz, and Hezekiah, kings of Judah, and in the days of Jeroboam the son of Joash, king of Israel.

When the Lord first spoke through Hosea, the Lord said to Hosea, "Go, take to yourself a wife of harlotry and have children of harlotry, for the land commits great harlotry by forsaking the Lord." So he went and took Gomer the daughter of Diblaim, and she conceived and bore him a son.

And the Lord said to him, "Call his name Jezreel; for yet a little while, and I will punish the house of Jehu for the blood of Jezreel, and I will put an end to the kingdom of the house of Israel. And on that day, I will break the bow of Israel in the valley of Jezreel."

She conceived again and bore a daughter. And the Lord said to him, "Call her name Not pitied, for I will no more have pity on the house of Israel, to forgive them at all. But I will have pity on the house of Judah, and I will deliver them by the Lord their God; I will not deliver them by bow, nor by sword, nor by war, nor by horses, nor by horsemen."

When she had weaned Not pitied, she conceived and bore a son. And the Lord said, "Call his name Not my people, for you are not my people and I am not your God."

Yet the number of the people of Israel shall be like the sand of the sea, which can be neither measured nor numbered; and in the place where it was said to them, "You are not my people," it shall be said to them, "Sons of the living God." And the people of Judah and the people of Israel shall be gathered together, and they shall appoint for themselves one head; and they shall go up from the land, for great shall be the day of Jezreel.

(8) **Isaiah 1:2–4** **762**

Hear, O heavens, and give ear, O earth;
    for the Lord has spoken:
"Sons have I reared and brought up,
    but they have rebelled against me.
The ox knows its owner,
    and the ass its master's crib;

but Israel does not know,
    my people does not understand."

Ah, sinful nation,
    a people laden with iniquity,
offspring of evildoers,
    sons who deal corruptly!
They have forsaken the Lord,
    they have despised the Holy One of Israel,
    they are utterly estranged.

762 (9) **Jeremiah 2** The word of the Lord came to me, saying, "Go and proclaim in the hearing of Jerusalem, Thus says the Lord,
I remember the devotion of your youth,
    your love as a bride,
how you followed me in the wilderness,
    in a land not sown.
Israel was holy to the Lord,
    the first fruits of his harvest.
All who ate of it became guilty;
    evil came upon them,
                says the Lord."

Hear the word of the Lord, O house of Jacob, and all the families of the house of Israel. Thus says the Lord:
"What wrong did your fathers find in me
    that they went far from me,
and went after worthlessness, and became worthless?
They did not say, 'Where is the Lord
    who brought us up from the land of Egypt,
who led us in the wilderness,
    in a land of deserts and pits,
in a land of drought and deep darkness,
    in a land that none passes through,
    where no man dwells?'
And I brought you into a plentiful land
    to enjoy its fruits and its good things.
But when you came in you defiled my land,
    and made my heritage an abomination.
The priests did not say, 'Where is the Lord?'
    Those who handle the law did not know me;
the rulers transgressed against me;
    the prophets prophesied by Baal,
    and went after things that do not profit.

"Therefore I still contend with you,
                says the Lord,
    and with your children's children I will contend.
For cross to the coasts of Cyprus and see,
    or send to Kedar and examine with care;
    see if there has been such a thing.
Has a nation changed its gods,
    even though they are no gods?

But my people have changed their glory
    for that which does not profit.
Be appalled, O heavens, at this,
    be shocked, be utterly desolate,
                says the Lord,
for my people have committed two evils:
    they have forsaken me,
the fountain of living waters,
    and hewed out cisterns for themselves,
broken cisterns,
    that can hold no water.

"Is Israel a slave? Is he a homeborn servant?
    Why then has he become a prey?
The lions have roared against him,
    they have roared loudly.
They have made his land a waste;
    his cities are in ruins, without inhabitant.
Moreover, the men of Memphis and Tahpanhes
    have broken the crown of your head.
Have you not brought this upon yourself
    by forsaking the Lord your God,
    when he led you in the way?
And now what do you gain by going to Egypt,
    to drink the waters of the Nile?
Or what do you gain by going to Assyria,
    to drink the waters of the Euphrates?
Your wickedness will chasten you,
    and your apostasy will reprove you.
Know and see that it is evil and bitter
    for you to forsake the Lord your God;
    the fear of me is not in you,
                says the Lord God of hosts.

"For long ago you broke your yoke
    and burst your bonds;
    and you said, 'I will not serve.'
Yea, upon every high hill
    and under every green tree
    you bowed down as a harlot.
Yet I planted you a choice vine,
    wholly of pure seed.
How then have you turned degenerate
    and become a wild vine?
Though you wash yourself with lye
    and use much soap,
    the stain of your guilt is still before me,
                says the Lord God.
    How can you say, 'I am not defiled,
    I have not gone after the Baals'?
Look at your way in the valley;
    know what you have done—
a restive young camel interlacing her tracks,

a wild ass used to the wilderness,
in her heat sniffing the wind!
Who can restrain her lust?
None who seek her need weary themselves;
in her month they will find her.
Keep your feet from going unshod
and your throat from thirst.
But you said, 'It is hopeless,
for I have loved strangers,
and after them I will go.'

"As a thief is shamed when caught,
so the house of Israel shall be shamed:
they, their kings, their princes,
their priests, and their prophets,
who say to a tree, 'You are my father,'
and to a stone, 'You gave me birth.'
For they have turned their back to me,
and not their face.
But in the time of their trouble they say,
'Arise and save us!'
But where are your gods
that you made for yourself?
Let them arise, if they can save you,
in your time of trouble;
for as many as your cities
are your gods, O Judah.

"Why do you complain against me?
You have all rebelled against me,
says the Lord.
In vain have I smitten your children,
they took no correction;
your own sword devoured your prophets
like a ravening lion.
And you, O generation, heed the
word of the Lord.
Have I been a wilderness to Israel,
or a land of thick darkness?
Why then do my people say, 'We are free,
we will come no more to thee'?
Can a maiden forget her ornaments,
or a bride her attire?

Yet my people have forgotten me
days without number.

"How well you direct your course
to seek lovers!
So that even to wicked women
you have taught your ways.
Also on your skirts is found
the lifeblood of guiltless poor;
you did not find them breaking in.
Yet in spite of all these things

you say, 'I am innocent;
 surely his anger has turned from me.'
Behold, I will bring you to judgment
 for saying, 'I have not sinned.'
How lightly you gad about,
 changing your way!
You shall be put to shame by Egypt
 as you were put to shame by Assyria.
From it too you will come away
 with your hands upon your head,
for the Lord has rejected those in whom you trust,
 and you will not prosper by them. . . ."

(10) **Isaiah 55:3** 762
Incline your ear, and come to me;
 hear, that your soul may live;
and I will make with you an everlasting covenant,
 my steadfast, sure love for David.

(1) ***Lumen gentium* 3:** see 542. 763

(2) ***Ad gentes divinitus* 3** This universal plan of God for salvation of mankind is 763
not carried out solely in a secret manner, as it were, in the minds of men, nor by the efforts, even religious, through which they in many ways seek God in an attempt to touch him and find him, although God is not far from any of us (cf. Acts 17:27); their efforts need to be enlightened and corrected, although in the loving providence of God they may lead one to the true God and be a preparation for the Gospel. However, in order to establish a relationship of peace and communion with himself, and in order to bring about brotherly union among men, and they sinners, God decided to enter into the history of mankind in a new and definitive manner, by sending his own Son in human flesh, so that through him he might snatch men from the power of darkness and of Satan (cf. Col. 1:13; Acts 10:38) and in him reconcile the world to himself. He appointed him, through whom he made the world, to be heir of all things, that he might restore all things in him (cf. Eph. 1:10).

Jesus Christ was sent into the world as the true Mediator between God and men. Since he is God, all the fullness of the divine nature dwells in him bodily (Col. 2:9); as man he is the new Adam, full of grace and truth (Jn. 1:14), who has been constituted head of a restored humanity. So the Son of God entered the world by means of a true incarnation that he might make men sharers in the divine nature; though rich, he was made poor for our sake, that by his poverty we might become rich (2 Cor. 8:9). The Son of man did not come to be served, but to serve and to give his life as a ransom for many, that is for all (cf. Mk. 10:45). The fathers of the Church constantly proclaim that what was not assumed by Christ was not healed. Now Christ took a complete human nature just as it is found in us poor unfortunates, but one that was without sin (cf. Heb. 4:15; 9:28). Christ, whom the Father sanctified and sent into the world (cf. Jn. 10:36), said of himself: "The Spirit of the Lord is upon me, because he anointed me; to bring good news to the poor he sent me, to heal the broken-hearted, to proclaim to the captive release, and sight to the blind" (Lk. 4:8); and on another occasion: "The Son of man has come to seek and to save what was lost" (Lk. 9:10).

Now, what was once preached by the Lord, or fulfilled in him for the salvation of mankind, must be proclaimed and spread to the ends of the earth (Acts 1:8), starting from Jerusalem (cf. Lk. 24:27), so that what was accomplished for the salvation of all men may, in the course of time, achieve its universal effect.

764 (1) **Matthew 10:16** "Behold, I send you out as sheep in the midst of wolves; so be wise as serpents and innocent as doves. . . ."

764 (2) **Matthew 26:31** Then Jesus said to them, "You will all fall away because of me this night; for it is written, 'I will strike the shepherd, and the sheep of the flock will be scattered.' . . ."

764 (3) **John 10:1–21** "Truly, truly, I say to you, he who does not enter the sheepfold by the door but climbs in by another way, that man is a thief and a robber; but he who enters by the door is the shepherd of the sheep. To him the gatekeeper opens; the sheep hear his voice, and he calls his own sheep by name and leads them out. When he has brought out all his own, he goes before them, and the sheep follow him, for they know his voice. A stranger they will not follow, but they will flee from him, for they do not know the voice of strangers." This figure Jesus used with them, but they did not understand what he was saying to them.

So Jesus again said to them, "Truly, truly, I say to you, I am the door of the sheep. All who came before me are thieves and robbers; but the sheep did not heed them. I am the door; if any one enters by me, he will be saved, and will go in and out and find pasture. The thief comes only to steal and kill and destroy; I came that they may have life, and have it abundantly. I am the good shepherd. The good shepherd lays down his life for the sheep. He who is a hireling and not a shepherd, whose own the sheep are not, sees the wolf coming and leaves the sheep and flees; and the wolf snatches them and scatters them. He flees because he is a hireling and cares nothing for the sheep. I am the good shepherd; I know my own and my own know me, as the Father knows me and I know the Father; and I lay down my life for the sheep. And I have other sheep, that are not of this fold; I must bring them also, and they will heed my voice. So there shall be one flock, one shepherd. For this reason the Father loves me, because I lay down my life, that I may take it again. No one takes it from me, but I lay it down of my own accord. I have power to lay it down, and I have power to take it again; this charge I have received from my Father."

There was again a division among the Jews because of these words. Many of them said, "He has a demon, and he is mad; why listen to him?" Others said, "These are not the sayings of one who has a demon. Can a demon open the eyes of the blind?"

764 (4) **Matthew 12:49** And stretching out his hand toward his disciples, he said, "Here are my mother and my brothers! . . ."

764 (5) **Matthew 5–6** Seeing the crowds , he went up on the mountain, and when he sat down his disciples came to him. And he opened his mouth and taught them, saying:

"Blessed are the poor in spirit, for theirs is the kingdom of heaven.
"Blessed are those who mourn, for they shall be comforted.
"Blessed are the meek, for they shall inherit the earth.
"Blessed are those who hunger and thirst for righteousness, for they
shall be satisfied.
"Blessed are the merciful, for they shall obtain mercy.
"Blessed are the pure in heart, for they shall see God.
"Blessed are the peacemakers, for they shall be called sons of God.
"Blessed are those who are persecuted for righteousness' sake, for
theirs is the kingdom of heaven.

"Blessed are you when men revile you and persecute you and utter all kinds of evil against you falsely on my account. Rejoice and be glad, for your reward is great in heaven, for so men persecuted the prophets who were before you.

"You are the salt of the earth; but if salt has lost its taste, how shall its saltness be restored? It is no longer good for anything except to be thrown out and trodden under foot by men.

"You are the light of the world. A city set on a hill cannot be hid. Nor do men light a lamp and put it under a bushel, but on a stand, and it gives light to all in the house. Let your light so shine before men, that they may see your good works and give glory to your Father who is in heaven.

"Think not that I have come to abolish the law and the prophets; I have come not to abolish them but to fulfil them. For truly, I say to you, till heaven and earth pass away, not an iota, not a dot, will pass from the law until all is accomplished. Whoever then relaxes one of the least of these commandments and teaches men so, shall be called least in the kingdom of heaven; but he who does them and teaches them shall be called great in the kingdom of heaven. For I tell you, unless your righteousness exceeds that of the scribes and Pharisees, you will never enter the kingdom of heaven.

"You have heard that it was said to the men of old, 'You shall not kill; and whoever kills shall be liable to judgment.' But I say to you that every one who is angry with his brother shall be liable to judgment; whoever insults his brother shall be liable to the council, and whoever says, 'You fool!' shall be liable to the hell of fire. So if you are offering your gift at the altar, and there remember that your brother has something against you, leave your gift there before the altar and go; first be reconciled to your brother, and then come and offer your gift. Make friends quickly with your accuser, while you are going with him to court, lest your accuser hand you over to the judge, and the judge to the guard, and you be put in prison; truly, I say to you, you will never get out till you have paid the last penny.

"You have heard that it was said, 'You shall not commit adultery.' But I say to you that every one who looks at a woman lustfully has already committed adultery with her in his heart. If your right eye causes you to sin, pluck it out and throw it away; it is better that you lose one of your members than that your whole body be thrown into hell. And if your right hand causes you to sin, cut it off and throw it away; it is better that you lose one of your members than that your whole body go into hell.

"It was also said, 'Whoever divorces his wife, let him give her a certificate of divorce.' But I say to you that every one who divorces his wife, except on the ground of unchastity, makes her an adulteress; and whoever marries a divorced woman commits adultery.

"Again you have heard that it was said to the men of old, 'You shall not swear falsely, but shall perform to the Lord what you have sworn.' But I say to you, Do not swear at all, either by heaven, for it is the throne of God, or by the earth, for it is his footstool, or by Jerusalem, for it is the city of the great King. And do not swear by your head, for you cannot make one hair white or black. Let what you say be simply 'Yes' or 'No'; anything more than this comes from evil.

"You have heard that it was said, 'An eye for an eye and a tooth for a tooth.' But I say to you, Do not resist one who is evil. But if any one strikes you on the right cheek, turn to him the other also; and if any one would sue you and take your coat, let him have your cloak as well; and if any one forces you to go one mile, go with him two miles. Give to him who begs from you, and do not refuse him who would borrow from you.

"You have heard that it was said, 'You shall love your neighbor and hate your enemy.' But I say to you, Love your enemies and pray for those who persecute you, so that you may be sons of your Father who is in heaven; for he makes his sun rise on the evil and on the good, and sends rain on the just and on the unjust. For if you love those who love you, what reward have you? Do not even the tax collectors do the same? And if you salute only your brethren, what more are you doing than others? Do not even the Gentiles do the same? You, therefore, must be perfect, as your heavenly Father is perfect.

"Beware of practicing your piety before men in order to be seen by them; for then you will have no reward from your Father who is in heaven.

"Thus, when you give alms, sound no trumpet before you, as the hypocrites do in the synagogues and in the streets, that they may be praised by men. Truly, I say to you, they have received their reward. But when you give alms, do not let your left hand know what your right hand is doing, so that your alms may be in secret; and your Father who sees in secret will reward you.

"And when you pray, you must not be like the hypocrites; for they love to stand and pray in the synagogues and at the street corners, that they may be seen by men. Truly, I say to you, they have received their reward. But when you pray, go into your room and shut the door and pray to your Father who is in secret; and your Father who sees in secret will reward you.

"And in praying do not heap up empty phrases as the Gentiles do; for they think that they will be heard for their many words. Do not be like them, for your Father knows what you need before you ask him. Pray then like this:

Our Father who art in heaven,
Hallowed be thy name.
Thy kingdom come.
Thy will be done,
 On earth as it is in heaven.
Give us this day our daily bread;
And forgive us our debts,
 As we also have forgiven our debtors;
And lead us not into temptation,
 But deliver us from evil.

For if you forgive men their trespasses, your heavenly Father also will forgive you; but if you do not forgive men their trespasses, neither will your Father forgive your trespasses.

"And when you fast, do not look dismal, like the hypocrites, for they disfigure their faces that their fasting may be seen by men. Truly, I say to you, they have received their reward. But when you fast, anoint your head and wash your face, that your fasting may not be seen by men but by your Father who is in secret; and your Father who sees in secret will reward you.

"Do not lay up for yourselves treasures on earth, where moth and rust consume and where thieves break in and steal, but lay up for yourselves treasures in heaven, where neither moth nor rust consumes and where thieves do not break in and steal. For where your treasure is, there will your heart be also.

"The eye is the lamp of the body. So, if your eye is sound, your whole body will be full of light; but if your eye is not sound, your whole body will be full of darkness. If then the light in you is darkness, how great is the darkness!

"No one can serve two masters; for either he will hate the one and love the other, or he will be devoted to the one and despise the other. You cannot serve God and mammon.

"Therefore I tell you, do not be anxious about your life, what you shall eat or what you shall drink, nor about your body, what you shall put on. Is not life more than food, and the body more than clothing? Look at the birds of the air: they neither sow nor reap nor gather into barns, and yet your heavenly Father feeds them. Are you not of more value than they? And which of you by being anxious can add one cubit to his span of life? And why are you anxious about clothing? Consider the lilies of the field, how they grow; they neither toil nor spin; yet I tell you, even Solomon in all his glory was not arrayed like one of these. But if God so clothes the grass of the field, which today is alive and tomorrow is thrown into the oven, will he not much more clothe you, O men of little faith? Therefore do not be anxious, saying, 'What shall we eat?' or 'What shall we drink?' or 'What shall we wear?' For the Gentiles seek all these things; and your heavenly Father knows that you need them all. But seek first his kingdom and his righteousness, and all these things shall be yours as well.

"Therefore do not be anxious about tomorrow, for tomorrow will be anxious for itself. Let the day's own trouble be sufficient for the day. . . ."

(1) **Mark 3:14–15** And he appointed twelve, to be with him, and to be sent out to preach and have authority to cast out demons. . . . 765

(2) **Matthew 19:28** Jesus said to them, "Truly, I say to you, in the new world, when the Son of man shall sit on his glorious throne, you who have followed me will also sit on twelve thrones, judging the twelve tribes of Israel. . . ." 765

(3) **Luke 22:30** . . . that you may eat and drink at my table in my kingdom, and sit on thrones judging the twelve tribes of Israel. 765

(4) **Revelation 21:12–14** It had a great, high wall, with twelve gates, and at the gates twelve angels, and on the gates the names of the twelve tribes of the sons of Israel were inscribed; on the east three gates, on the north three gates, on the south three gates, and on the west three gates. And the wall of the city had twelve foundations, and on them the twelve names of the twelve apostles of the Lamb. 765

(5) **Mark 6:7** And he called to him the twelve, and began to send them out two by two, and gave them authority over the unclean spirits. 765

(6) **Luke 10:1–2** After this the Lord appointed seventy others, and sent them on ahead of him, two by two, into every town and place where he himself was about to come. And he said to them, "The harvest is plentiful, but the laborers are few; pray therefore the Lord of the harvest to send out laborers into his harvest. . . ." 765

(7) **Matthew 10:25** . . . it is enough for the disciple to be like his teacher, and the servant like his master. If they have called the master of the house Beelzebul, how much more will they malign those of his household. 765

(8) **John 15:20** ". . . Remember the word that I said to you, 'A servant is not greater than his master.' If they persecuted me, they will persecute you; if they kept my word, they will keep yours also. . . ." 765

St. Ambrose, *Expositio evangelii secundum Lucam* 2, 85–89 Moses also taught me that no one but God made the world: for *in the beginning God made the heavens and the earth*. He also taught me that God made man as his own work and it is not without purpose that he established him: *God fashioned him from the clay of the earth and breathed upon his face the breath of life*, so that you would see that in fashioning man God used a kind of bodily activity. He also taught that God made woman: for *he made Adam sleepy, and he fell asleep, and he took a rib from his side and covered it with his flesh. And the Lord God fashioned the rib which he took from Adam into woman.* And it is not in vain, as I said, that Moses shows God working upon Adam and Eve with 766 a kind of bodily hands. God commanded the world to be, and it came to be, and Scripture shows the work of the world accomplished by a single word; and then with man, the prophet makes a point of showing, so to speak, God's own hands at work. The works God has fashioned compel me to understand in these things something mysteriously more than I read there. The Apostle comes to my aid in my difficulty, and what I did not understand: *bone of my bone and flesh of my flesh, and she was called woman because she was taken from man*, he reveals to me in the Holy Spirit, saying *this is a great mystery*. What mystery? *That they shall be two in one flesh* and *that a man shall leave his father and mother and cleave to his wife* and *that we are members of his Body, of his flesh and of his bones*. Who is this man for whose sake the woman leaves her parents? The Church, who is gathered together from the gentile peoples, leaves her parents; of her is it said prophetically *forget your own people and your father's house*. For the sake of which man, unless perhaps him of whom John says: *a man is coming after me who came to be before me*? From whose side, while asleep, God took a rib; for it is he who slept, took his repose, and rose because the Lord took him up. What is this rib if not his power? For when the soldier opened his side, immediately there poured forth blood and water for the life of the world. This life of the world is Christ's rib, the rib of the second Adam; for *the first Adam is a living soul, the last Adam is a life-giving spirit*; the last Adam is Christ and Christ's rib is the life of the Church. *Therefore we are members of his Body, of his flesh, and of his bones*. And perhaps this is the rib of which it is said: *I felt power go out of me*; this is the rib which went forth from Christ without diminishing his Body; for it is not a physical but a spiritual rib, and the Spirit is not itself divided in being given, but gives to each as he wills. This is Eve, the mother of all the living. For if you understand *you are seeking the living among the dead*, you will understand that the dead are those without Christ, those not sharing in life; this means not sharing in Christ, for Christ is life. Therefore the mother of the living is the Church whom God built upon that supreme cornerstone who is Jesus Christ, in whom the whole structure is adorned and grows into a temple.

Let God come, therefore; let him build up woman. The one as a helpmate for Adam, and the other for Christ. Not because Christ needs help, but because we seek and desire to attain to the grace of Christ through the Church. And even now she is being built up and formed, the woman is being fashioned and created. And so Scripture used a new expression, that we are being built up upon the foundation of the apostles and prophets. And now a spiritual house is rising up to be a holy priesthood. Come, Lord God, build this woman, build the city. And may your servant come also, for I believe in your word: *it is he who will build a city for me*. Behold the woman who is mother of all. Behold the spiritual house, the city which lives for ever for it knows not death. For this city is Jerusalem, which is now seen on earth but will be exalted above Elijah—for Elijah was but one person—lifted up above Henoch in whom death was not found; for he *was snatched up so that malice would not change his heart*; but this woman is loved by Christ as glorious, holy, immaculate, without wrinkle. And how much better is it that the whole Body is lifted up, and not just Elijah! For this is the hope of the Church. She will indeed be snatched up, lifted up, taken to heaven. Yes, Elijah was taken up in a chariot of fire, and so the Church will be taken up. You don't believe me? Believe Paul then, in whom Christ spoke. *We will be taken up*, he says, *in the clouds, before Christ in the air, and we will be forever with the Lord*. Therefore for the building up of the Church many were sent; the patriarchs were sent; the prophets were sent; the archangel Gabriel was sent; countless angels were assigned to this and a multitude of the heavenly host praised God because the building of this city was approaching. Many were sent to her, but Christ alone built her. In truth he was not alone for the Father was always present; and though he himself built her, he did not claim all the merit for himself. It is written of the Temple of God which Solomon built, and which is a figure of the Church, that there were 70,000 carriers and 80,000 hewers of stone. Let those angels come. Let the hewers of stone come. May they hew what is superfluous in our stones, polish what is rough. Let the carriers come who bear on their shoulders for it is written: *they will be borne upon their shoulders.*

(1) **Matthew 28:19–20** ". . . Go therefore and make disciples of all nations, baptizing them in the name of the Father and of the Son and of the Holy Spirit, teaching them to observe all that I have commanded you; and lo, I am with you always, to the close of the age." 767

(2) ***Ad gentes divinitus* 2** The Church on earth is by its very nature missionary since, according to the plan of the Father, it has its origin in the mission of the Son and the Holy Spirit. This plan flows from "fountain-like love," the love of God the Father. As the principle without principle from whom the Son is generated and from whom the Holy Spirit proceeds through the Son, God in his great and merciful kindness freely creates us and, moreover, graciously calls us to share in his life and glory. He generously pours out, and never ceases to pour out, his divine goodness, so that he who is creator of all things might at last become "all in all" (1 Cor. 15:28), thus simultaneously assuring his own glory and our happiness. It pleased God to call men to share in his life and not merely singly, without any bond between them, but he formed them into a people, in which his children who had been scattered were gathered together (cf. Jn. 11:52). 767

(3) ***Ad gentes divinitus* 5–6** From the beginning of his ministry the Lord Jesus "called to himself those whom he wished and he caused twelve of them to be with him and to be sent out preaching" (Mk. 3:13; cf. Mt. 10:1–42). Thus the apostles were both the seeds of the new Israel and the beginning of the sacred hierarchy. Later, before he was assumed into heaven (cf. Acts 1:11), after he had fulfilled in himself the mysteries of our salvation and the renewal of all things by his death and resurrection, the Lord, who had received all power in heaven and on earth (cf. Mt. 28:18), founded his Church as the sacrament of salvation; and just as he had been sent by the Father (cf. Jn. 20:21), so he sent the apostles into the whole world, commanding them: "Go, therefore, and make disciples of all nations, baptizing them in the name of the Father and of the Son and of the Holy Spirit; teaching them to observe all that I have commanded you" (Mt. 28:19 ff.); "Go into the whole world, preach the Gospel to every creature. He who believes and is baptized shall be saved; but he who does not believe, shall be condemned" (Mk. 16:15 ff.). Hence the Church has an obligation to proclaim the faith and salvation which comes from Christ, both by reason of the express command which the order of bishops inherited from the apostles, an obligation in the discharge of which they are assisted by priests, and one which they share with the successor of St. Peter, the supreme pastor of the Church, and also by reason of the life which Christ infuses into his members: "From him the whole body, being closely joined and knit together through every joint of the system, according to the functioning in due measure of each single part, derives its increase to the building up of itself in love" (Eph. 4:16). The mission of the Church is carried out by means of that activity through which, in obedience to Christ's command and moved by the grace and love of the Holy Spirit, the Church makes itself fully present to all men and peoples in order to lead them to the faith, freedom and peace of Christ by the example of its life and teaching, by the sacraments and other means of grace. Its aim is to open up for all men a free and sure path to full participation in the mystery of Christ. 767

Since this mission continues and, in the course of history, unfolds the mission of Christ, who was sent to evangelize the poor, then the Church, urged on by the Spirit of Christ, must walk the road Christ himself walked, a way of poverty and obedience, of service and self-sacrifice even to death, a death from which he emerged victorious by his resurrection. So it was that the apostles walked in hope and by much trouble and suffering filled up what was lacking in the sufferings of Christ for his body, which is the Church. Often, too, the seed was the blood of Christians.

This task which must be carried out by the order of bishops, under the leadership of Peter's successor and with the prayers and cooperation of the whole Church, is one and the same everywhere and in all situations, although, because of circumstances, it may not always be exercised in the same way. The differences which must be recognized in this activity of the Church, do not flow from the inner nature of the mission itself, but from the circumstances in which it is exercised.

These circumstances depend either on the Church itself or on the peoples, classes or men to whom its mission is directed. Although the Church possesses in itself the totality and fullness of the means of salvation, it does not always, in fact cannot, use every one of them immediately, but it has to make beginnings and work by slow stages to give effect to God's plan. Sometimes after a successful start it has cause to mourn a setback, or it may linger in a state of semi-fulfillment and insufficiency. With regard to peoples, classes and men it is only by degrees that it touches and penetrates them and so raises them to a catholic perfection. In each situation and circumstance a proper line of action and effective means should be adopted.

The special undertakings in which preachers of the Gospel, sent by the Church, and going into the whole world, carry out the work of preaching the Gospel and implanting the Church among people who do not yet believe in Christ, are generally called "missions." Such undertakings are accomplished by missionary activity and are, for the most part, carried out in defined territories recognized by the Holy See. The special end of this missionary activity is the evangelization and the implanting of the Church among peoples or groups in which it has not yet taken root. All over the world indigenous particular churches ought to grow from the seed of the word of God, churches which would be adequately organized and would possess their own proper strength and maturity. With their own hierarchy and faithful, and sufficiently endowed with means adapted to the living of a full Christian life, they should contribute to the good of the whole Church. The principal instrument in this work of implanting the Church is the preaching of the Gospel of Jesus Christ. It was to announce this Gospel that the Lord sent his disciples into the whole world, that men, having been reborn by the word of God (cf. 1 Pet. 1:23), might through baptism, be joined to the Church which, as the Body of the Word Incarnate, lives and is nourished by the word of God and the Eucharist (cf. Acts 4:23).

Various stages, which are sometimes intermingled, are to be found in this missionary activity of the Church; first there is the beginning or planting and then a time of freshness and youthfulness. Nor does the Church's missionary activity cease once this point has been passed; the obligation to carry on the work devolves on the particular churches already constituted, an obligation to preach the Gospel to all who are still outside.

Moreover, it often happens that, owing to various cases, the groups among whom the Church operates are utterly changed so that an entirely new situation arises. Then the Church must consider whether these new circumstances require that she should once again exercise her missionary activity. The situation, however, is often of such a nature that for the time being there is no possibility of directly and immediately preaching the Gospel. In that case missionaries, patiently, prudently, and with great faith, can and ought at least bear witness to the love and kindness of Christ and thus prepare a way for the Lord, and in some way make him present.

It is clear, therefore, that missionary activity flows immediately from the very nature of the Church. Missionary activity extends the saving faith of the Church, it expands and perfects its catholic unity, it is sustained by its apostolicity, it activates the collegiate sense of its hierarchy, and bears witness to its sanctity which it both extends and promotes. Missionary work among the nations differs from the pastoral care of the faithful and likewise from efforts aimed at restoring Christian unity. Nevertheless, these two latter are very closely connected with the Church's missionary endeavor because the division of Christians is injurious to the holy work of preaching the Gospel to every creature, and deprives many people of access to the faith. Because of the Church's mission, all baptized people are called upon to come together in one flock that they might bear unanimous witness to Christ their Lord before the nations. And if they cannot yet fully bear witness to one faith, they should at least be imbued with mutual respect and love.

(1) ***Lumen gentium* 8** The one mediator, Christ, established and ever sustains here 769
on earth his holy Church, the community of faith, hope and charity, as a visible organization through which he communicates truth and grace to all men. But, the society structured with hierarchical organs and the mystical body of Christ, the visible society and the spiritual community, the earthly Church and the Church endowed with heavenly riches, are not to be thought of as two realities. On the contrary, they form one complex reality which comes together from a human and a divine element. For this reason the Church is compared, in a powerful analogy, to the mystery of the incarnate Word. As the assumed nature, inseparably united to him, serves the divine Word as a living organ of salvation, so, in a somewhat similar way, does the social structure of the Church serve the Spirit of Christ who vivifies it, in the building up of the body (cf. Eph. 4:15).

This is the sole Church of Christ which in the Creed we profess to be one, holy, catholic, and apostolic, which our Savior, after his resurrection, entrusted to Peter's pastoral care (Jn. 21:17), commissioning him and the other apostles to extend and rule it (cf. Mt. 28:18, etc.), and which he raised up for all ages as "the pillar and mainstay of the truth" (1 Tim. 3:15). This Church, constituted and organized as a society in the present world, subsists in the Catholic Church, which is governed by the successor of Peter and by the bishops in communion with him. Nevertheless, many elements of sanctification and of truth are found outside its visible confines. Since these are gifts belonging to the Church of Christ, they are forces impelling towards Catholic unity.

Just as Christ carried out the work of redemption in poverty and oppression, so the Church is called to follow the same path if she is to communicate the fruits of salvation to men. Christ Jesus, "though he was by nature God . . . emptied himself, taking the nature of a slave" (Phil. 2:6, 7), and "being rich, became poor" (2 Cor. 8:9) for our sake. Likewise, the Church, although she needs human resources to carry out her mission, is not set up to seek earthly glory, but to proclaim, and this by her own example, humility and self-denial. Christ was sent by the Father "to bring good news to the poor . . . to heal the contrite of heart" (Lk. 4:18), "to seek and to save what was lost" (Lk. 19:10). Similarly, the Church encompasses with her love all those who are afflicted by human misery and she recognizes in those who are poor and who suffer, the image of her poor and suffering founder. She does all in her power to relieve their need and in them she strives to serve Christ. Christ, "holy, innocent and undefiled" (Heb. 7:26) knew nothing of sin (2 Cor. 5:21), but came only to expiate the sins of the people (cf. Heb. 2:17). The Church, however, clasping sinners to her bosom, at once holy and always in need of purification, follows constantly the path of penance and renewal.

The Church, "like a stranger in a foreign land, presses forward amid the persecutions of the world and the consolations of God," announcing the cross and death of the Lord until he comes (cf. 1 Cor. 11:26). But by the power of the risen Lord she is given strength to overcome, in patience and in love, her sorrows and her difficulties, both those that are from within and those that are from without, so that she may reveal in the world, faithfully, however darkly, the mystery of her Lord until, in the consummation, it shall be manifested in full light.

769 (2) ***Lumen gentium* 6** In the Old Testament the revelation of the kingdom is often made under the forms of symbols. In similar fashion the inner nature of the Church is now made known to us in various images. Taken either from the life of the shepherd or from cultivation of the land, from the art of building or from family life and marriage, these images have their preparation in the books of the prophets.

The Church is, accordingly, a sheepfold, the sole and necessary gateway to which is Christ (Jn. 10:1–10). It is also a flock, of which God foretold that he would himself be the shepherd (cf. Is. 40:11; Ex. 34:11 f.), and whose sheep, although watched over by human shepherds, are nevertheless at all times led and brought to pasture by Christ himself, the Good Shepherd and prince of shepherds (cf. Jn. 10:11; 1 Pet. 5:4), who gave his life for his sheep (cf. Jn. 10:11–16).

The Church is a cultivated field, the tillage of God (1 Cor. 3:9). On that land the ancient olive tree grows whose holy roots were the prophets and in which the reconciliation of Jews and Gentiles has been brought about and will be brought about again (Rom. 11:13–26). That land, like a choice vineyard, has been planted by the heavenly cultivator (Mt. 21:33–43; cf. Is. 5:1 f.). Yet the true vine is Christ who gives life and fruitfulness to the branches, that is, to us, who through the Church remain in Christ without whom we can do nothing (Jn. 15:1–5).

Often, too, the Church is called the building of God (1 Cor. 3:9). The Lord compared himself to the stone which the builders rejected, but which was made into the cornerstone (Mt. 21:42; cf. Acts 4:11; 1 Pet. 2:7; Ps. 117:22). On this foundation the Church is built by the apostles (cf. 1 Cor. 3:11) and from it the Church receives solidity and unity. This edifice has many names to describe it; the house of God in which his family dwells; the household of God in the Spirit (Eph. 2:19, 22); the dwelling-place of God among men (Apoc. 21:3); and, especially, the holy temple. This temple, symbolized in places of worship built out of stone, is praised by the Fathers and, not without reason, is compared in the liturgy to the Holy City, the New Jerusalem. As living stones we here on earth are built into it (1 Pet. 2:5). It is this holy city that is seen by John as it comes down out of heaven from God when the world is made anew, prepared like a bride adorned for her husband (Apoc. 21:1 f.).

The Church, further, which is called "that Jerusalem which is above" and "our mother" (Gal. 4:26; cf. Apoc. 12:17), is described as the spotless spouse of the spotless lamb (Apoc. 19:7; 21:2 and 9; 22:17). It is she whom Christ "loved and for whom he delivered himself up that he might sanctify her" (Eph. 5:26). It is she whom he unites to himself by an unbreakable alliance, and whom he constantly "nourishes and cherishes" (Eph. 5:29). It is she whom, once purified, he willed to be joined to himself, subject in love and fidelity (cf. Eph. 5:24), and whom, finally, he filled with heavenly gifts for all eternity, in order that we may know the love of God and of Christ for us, a love which surpasses all understanding (cf. Eph. 3:19). While on earth she journeys in a foreign land away from the Lord (cf. 2 Cor. 5:6), the Church sees herself as an exile. She seeks and is concerned about those things which are above, where Christ is seated at the right hand of God, where the life of the Church is hidden with Christ in God until she appears in glory with her Spouse (cf. Col. 3:1–4).

(1) **Ephesians 3:9–11** . . . and to make all men see what is the plan of the mystery 772
hidden for ages in God who created all things; that through the church the manifold wisdom of God might now be made known to the principalities and powers in the heavenly places. This was according to the eternal purpose which he has realized in Christ Jesus our Lord. . . .

(2) **Ephesians 5:25–27** Husbands, love your wives, as Christ loved the church and 772
gave himself up for her, that he might sanctify her, having cleansed her by the washing of water with the word, that he might present the church to himself in splendor, without spot or wrinkle or any such thing, that she might be holy and without blemish.

(1) ***Lumen gentium* 48** The Church, to which we are all called in Christ Jesus, 773
and in which by the grace of God we acquire holiness, will receive its perfection only in the glory of heaven, when will come the time of the renewal of all things (Acts 3:21). At that time, together with the human race, the universe itself, which is so closely related to man and which attains its destiny through him, will be perfectly reestablished in Christ (cf. Eph. 1:10; Col. 1:20; 2 Pet. 3:10–13).

Christ lifted up from the earth, has drawn all men to himself (cf. Jn. 12:32). Rising from the dead (cf. Rom. 6:9) he sent his life-giving Spirit upon his disciples and through him set up his Body which is the Church as the universal sacrament of salvation. Sitting at the right hand of the Father he is continually active in the world in order to lead men to the Church and, through it, join them more closely to himself; and, by nourishing them with his own Body and Blood, make them partakers of his glorious life. The promised and hoped for restoration, therefore, has already begun in Christ. It is carried forward in the sending of the Holy Spirit and through him continues in the Church in which, through our faith, we learn the meaning of our earthly life, while we bring to term, with hope of future good, the task allotted to us in the world by the Father, and so work out our salvation (cf. Phil. 2:12).

Already the final age of the world is with us (cf. 1 Cor. 10:11) and the renewal of the world is irrevocably under way; it is even now anticipated in a certain real way, for the Church on earth is endowed already with a sanctity that is real though imperfect. However, until there be realized new heavens and a new earth in which justice dwells (cf. 2 Pet. 3:13) the pilgrim Church, in its sacraments and institutions, which belong to this present age, carries the mark of this world which will pass, and she herself takes her place among the creatures which groan and travail yet and await the revelation of the sons of God (cf. Rom. 8:19–22).

So it is, united with Christ in the Church and marked with the Holy Spirit "who is the guarantee of our inheritance" (Eph. 1:14) that we are truly called and indeed are children of God (cf. 1 Jn. 3:1) though we have not yet appeared with Christ in glory (cf. Col. 3:4) in which we will be like to God, for we will see him as he is (cf. 1 Jn. 3:2). "While we are at home in the body we are away from the Lord" (2 Cor. 5:6) and having the first fruits of the Spirit we groan inwardly (cf. Rom. 8:23) and we desire to be with Christ (cf. Phil. 1:23). That same charity urges us to live more for him who died for us and who rose again (cf. 2 Cor. 5:15). We make it our aim, then, to please the Lord in all things (cf. 2 Cor. 5:9) and we put on the armor of God that we may be able to stand against the wiles of the devil and resist in the evil day (cf. Eph. 6:11–13). Since we know neither the day nor the hour, we should follow the advice of the Lord and watch constantly so that, when the single course of our earthly life is completed (cf. Heb. 9:27), we may merit to enter with him into the marriage feast and be numbered among the blessed (cf. Mt. 25:31–46) and not, like the wicked and slothful servants (cf. Mt. 25:26), be ordered to depart into the eternal fire (cf. Mt. 25:41), into the outer darkness where "men will weep and gnash their teeth" (Mt. 22:13 and 25:30). Before we reign with Christ in glory we must all appear "before the judgment seat of Christ, so that each one may receive good or evil, according to what he has done in the body" (2 Cor. 5:10), and at the end of the world "they will come forth, those who have done good, to the resurrection of life, and those who have done evil, to the resurrection of judgment" (Jn. 5:29; cf. Mt. 25:46). We reckon then that "the sufferings of this present time are not worth comparing with the glory that is to be revealed to us" (Rom. 8:18; cf. 2 Tim. 2:11–12), and strong in faith we look for "the blessed hope, the appearing of the glory of our great God and Savior Jesus Christ" (Tit. 2:13) "who will change our lowly body to be like his glorious body" (Phil. 3:21) and who will come "to be glorified in his saints, and to be marvelled at in all who have believed" (2 Th. 1:10).

773 (2) ***Mulieris dignitatem* 27** The Second Vatican Council renewed the Church's awareness of the universality of the priesthood. In the New Covenant there is only one sacrifice and only one priest: Christ. *All the baptized share in the one priesthood of Christ*, both men and women, inasmuch as they must "present their bodies as a living sacrifice, holy and acceptable to God (cf. Rom 12:1), give witness to Christ in every place, and give an explanation to anyone who asks the reason for the hope in eternal life that is in them (cf. 1 Pt 3:15)." Universal participation in Christ's sacrifice, in which the Redeemer has offered to the Father the whole world and humanity in particular, brings it about that all in the Church are "a kingdom of priests" (Rev 5:10; cf. 1 Pt 2:9), who not only share in the priestly mission but also in the prophetic and kingly mission of Christ the Messiah. Furthermore, this participation determines the organic unity of the Church, the People of God, with Christ. It expresses at the same time the "great mystery" described in the Letter to the Ephesians: *the Bride united to her Bridegroom*; united, because she lives his life; united, because she shares in his threefold mission (*tria munera Christi*); united *in such a manner as to respond* with a "sincere gift" of self *to the inexpressible gift of the love of the Bridegroom*, the Redeemer of the world. This concerns everyone in the Church, women as well as men. It obviously concerns those who share in the "ministerial priesthood," which is characterized by service. In the context of the "great mystery" of Christ and of the Church, all are called to respond—as a bride—with the gift of their lives to the inexpressible gift of the love of Christ, who alone, as the Redeemer of the world, is the Church's Bridegroom. The "royal priesthood," which is universal, at the same time expresses the gift of the Bride.

This is of *fundamental importance for understanding the Church in her* own *essence*, so as to avoid applying to the Church—even in her dimension as an "institution" made up of human beings and forming part of history—criteria of understanding and judgment which do not pertain to her nature. Although the Church possesses a "hierarchical" structure, nevertheless this structure is totally ordered to the holiness of Christ's members. And holiness is measured according to the "great mystery" in which the Bride responds with the gift of love to the gift of the Bridegroom. She does this "in the Holy Spirit," since "God's love has been poured into our hearts through the Holy Spirit who has been given to us" (Rom 5:5). The Second Vatican Council, confirming the teaching of the whole of tradition, recalled that in the hierarchy of holiness it is *precisely the "woman,"* Mary of Nazareth, who is the "figure" of the Church. She "precedes" everyone on the path to holiness: in her person "the Church has already reached that perfection whereby she exists without spot or wrinkle (cf. Eph 5:27)." In this sense, one can say that the Church is both "Marian" and "Apostolic-Petrine."

In the history of the Church, even from earliest times, there were side-by-side with men *a number of women*, for whom the response of the Bride to the Bridegroom's redemptive love acquired full expressive force. First we see those women who had personally encountered Christ and followed him. After his departure, together with the Apostles, they "devoted themselves to prayer" in the Upper Room in Jerusalem until the day of Pentecost. On that day the Holy Spirit spoke through "the sons and daughters" of the People of God, thus fulfilling the words of the prophet Joel (cf. Acts 2:17). These women, and others afterwards, played *an active and important role in the life of the early Church*, in building up from its foundations the first Christian community—and subsequent communities—*through their own charisms and their varied service*. The apostolic writings note their names, such as Phoebe, "a deaconess of the Church at Cenchreae" (cf. Rom 16:1), Prisca with her husband Aquila (cf. 2 Tim 4:19), Euodia and Syntyche (cf. Phil 4:2), Mary, Tryphaena, Persis, and Tryphosa (cf. Rom 16:6, 12). St. Paul speaks of their "hard work" for Christ, and this hard work indicates the various fields of the Church's apostolic service, beginning with the "domestic Church." For in the latter, "sincere faith" passes from the mother to her children and grandchildren, as was the case in the house of Timothy (cf. 2 Tim 1:5).

The same thing is repeated down the centuries, from one generation to the next, as *the history of the Church* demonstrates. By defending the dignity of women and their vocation, the Church has shown honor and gratitude for those women who—faithful to the Gospel—have shared in every age in the apostolic mission of the whole People of God. They are the holy martyrs, virgins, and mothers of families, who bravely bore witness to their faith and passed on the Church's faith and tradition by bringing up their children in the spirit of the Gospel.

In every age and in every country we find many "perfect" women (cf. Prov 31:10) who, despite persecution, difficulties and discrimination, have shared in the Church's mission. It suffices to mention: Monica, the mother of Augustine, Macrina, Olga of Kiev, Matilda of Tuscany, Hedwig of Silesia, Jadwiga of Cracow, Elizabeth of Thuringia, Birgitta of Sweden, Joan of Arc, Rose of Lima, Elizabeth Ann Seton and Mary Ward.

The witness and the achievements of Christian women have had a significant impact on the life of the Church as well as of society. Even in the face of serious social discrimination, holy women have acted "freely," strengthened by their union with Christ. Such union and freedom rooted in God explain, for example, the great work of St. Catherine of Siena in the life of the Church, and the work of St. Teresa of Jesus in the monastic life.

In our own days too the Church is constantly enriched by the witness of the many women who fulfill their vocation to holiness. Holy women are an incarnation of the feminine ideal; they are also a model for all Christians, a model of the "*sequela Christi*," an example of how the Bride must respond with love to the love of the Bridegroom.

***Lumen gentium* 17** As he had been sent by the Father, the Son himself sent the apostles (cf. Jn. 20:21) saying, "go, therefore, and make disciples of all nations, baptizing them in the name of the Father, and of the Son, and of the Holy Spirit, teaching them to observe all that I have commanded you; and behold I am with you all days even unto the consummation of the world" (Mt. 28:18–20). The Church has received this solemn command of Christ from the apostles, and she must fulfil it to the very ends of the earth (cf. Acts 1:8). Therefore, she makes the words of the apostle her own, "Woe to me if I do not preach the Gospel" (1 Cor. 9:16), and accordingly never ceases to send heralds of the Gospel until such time as the infant Churches are fully established, and can themselves continue the work of evangelization. For the Church is driven by the Holy Spirit to do her part for the full realization of the plan of God, who has constituted Christ as the source of salvation for the whole world. By her 776 proclamation of the Gospel, she draws her hearers to receive and profess the faith, she prepares them for baptism, snatches them from the slavery of error, and she incorporates them into Christ so that in love for him they grow to full maturity. The effect of her work is that whatever good is found sown in the minds and hearts of men or in the rites and customs of peoples, these not only are preserved from destruction, but are purified, raised up, and perfected for the glory of God, the confusion of the devil, and the happiness of man. Each disciple of Christ has the obligation of spreading the faith to the best of his ability. But if any believer can baptize, it is for the priests to complete the building up of the body in the eucharistic sacrifice, thus fulfilling the words of the prophet, "From the rising of the sun, even to going down, my name is great among the gentiles. And in every place there is a sacrifice, and there is offered to my name a clean offering" (Mal. 1:11). Thus the Church prays and likewise labors so that into the People of God, the Body of the Lord and the Temple of the Holy Spirit, may pass the fullness of the whole world, and that in Christ, the head of all things, all honor and glory may be rendered to the Creator, the Father of the universe.

778 **Revelation 14:4** It is these who have not defiled themselves with women, for they are chaste; it is these who follow the Lamb wherever he goes; these have been redeemed from mankind as first fruits for God and the Lamb. . . .

782 (1) **John 13:34** A new commandment I give to you, that you love one another; even as I have loved you, that you also love one another.

782 (2) **Matthew 5:13–16** "You are the salt of the earth; but if salt has lost its taste, how shall its saltness be restored? It is no longer good for anything except to be thrown out and trodden under foot by men.

"You are the light of the world. A city set on a hill cannot be hid. Nor do men light a lamp and put it under a bushel, but on a stand, and it gives light to all in the house. Let your light so shine before men, that they may see your good works and give glory to your Father who is in heaven. . . ."

783 ***Redemptoris hominis* 18–21** This necessarily brief look at man's situation in the modern world makes us direct our thoughts and our hearts to Jesus Christ, and to the mystery of the Redemption, in which the question of man is inscribed with a special vigor of truth and love. If Christ "united Himself with each man," the Church lives more profoundly her own nature and mission by penetrating into the depths of this mystery and into its rich universal language. It was not without reason that the Apostle speaks of Christ's Body, the Church. If this Mystical Body of Christ is God's People—as the Second Vatican Council was to say later, on the basis of the whole of the biblical and patristic tradition—this means that in it each man receives within himself that breath of life that comes from Christ. In this way, turning to man and his real problems, his hopes and sufferings, his achievements and falls—this too also makes the Church as a body, an organism, a social unit perceive the same divine influences, the light and strength of the Spirit that come from the crucified and risen Christ, and it is for this very reason that she lives her life. The Church has only one life: that which is given her by her Spouse and Lord. Indeed, precisely because Christ united Himself with her in His mystery of Redemption, the Church must be strongly united with each man.

This union of Christ with man is in itself a mystery. From the mystery is born "the new man," called to become a partaker of God's life, and newly created in Christ for the fullness of grace and truth. Christ's union with man is power and the source of power, as St. John stated so incisively in the prologue of his Gospel: "(The Word) gave power to become children of God." Man is transformed inwardly by this power as the source of a new life that does not disappear and pass away but lasts to eternal life. This life, which the Father has promised and offered to each man in Jesus Christ, His eternal and only Son, who, "when the time had fully come," became incarnate and was born of the Virgin Mary, is the final fulfillment of man's vocation. It is in a way the fulfillment of the "destiny" that God has prepared for him from eternity. This "divine destiny" is advancing, in spite of all the enigmas, the unsolved riddles, the twists and turns of "human destiny" in the world of time. Indeed, while all this, in spite of all the riches of life in time, necessarily and inevitably leads to the frontier of death and the goal of the destruction of the human body, beyond that goal we see Christ. "I am the resurrection and the life, he who believes in me . . . shall never die." In Jesus Christ, who was crucified and laid in the tomb and then rose again, "our hope of resurrection dawned . . . the bright promise of immortality," on the way to which man, through the death of the body, shares with the whole of visible creation the necessity to which matter is subject. We intend and are trying to fathom ever more deeply the language of the truth that man's Redeemer enshrined in the phrase "It is the spirit that gives life, the flesh is of no avail." In spite of appearances, these words express the highest affirmation of man—the affirmation of the body given life by the Spirit.

The Church lives these realities; she lives by this truth about man, which enables him to go beyond the bounds of temporariness and at the same time to think with particular love and solicitude of everything within the dimensions of this temporariness that affect man's life and the life of the human spirit, in which is expressed that never-ending restlessness referred to in the words of St. Augustine: "You made us for Yourself, Lord, and our heart is restless until it rests in You." In this creative restlessness beats and pulsates what is most deeply human—the search for truth, the insatiable need for the good, hunger for freedom, nostalgia for the beautiful, and the voice of conscience. Seeking to see man as it were with "the eyes of Christ Himself," the Church becomes more and more aware that she is the guardian of a great treasure, which she may not waste but must continually increase. Indeed, the Lord Jesus said: "He who does not gather with me scatters." This treasure of humanity enriched by the inexpressible mystery of divine filiation and by the grace of "adoption as sons" in the only Son of God, through whom we call God "Abba, Father," is also a powerful force unifying the Church above all inwardly and giving meaning to all her activity. Through this force the Church is united with the Spirit of Christ, that Holy Spirit promised and continually communicated by the Redeemer and whose descent, which was revealed on the day of Pentecost, endures for ever. Thus the powers of the Spirit, the gifts of the Spirit, and the fruits of the Holy Spirit are revealed in men. The present-day Church seems to repeat with ever greater fervor and with holy insistence: "Come, Holy Spirit!" Come! Come! "Heal our wounds, our strength renew; On our dryness pour Your dew; Wash the stains of guilt away; Bend the stubborn heart and will; Melt the frozen, warm the chill; Guide the steps that go astray."

This appeal to the Spirit, intended precisely to obtain the Spirit, is the answer to all the "materialisms" of our age. It is these materialisms that give birth to so many forms of insatiability in the human heart. This appeal is making itself heard on various sides and seems to be bearing fruit also in different ways. Can it be said that the Church is not alone in making this appeal? Yes it can, because the "need" for what is spiritual is expressed also by people who are outside the visible confines of the Church. Is not this confirmed by the truth concerning the Church that the recent Council so acutely emphasized at the point in the Dogmatic Constitution *Lumen Gentium* where it teaches that the Church is a "sacrament or sign and means of intimate union with God, and of the unity of all mankind"? This invocation addressed to the Spirit to obtain the Spirit is really a constant self-insertion into the full magnitude of the mystery of the Redemption, in which Christ, united with the Father and with each man, continually communicates to us the Spirit who places within us the sentiments of the Son and directs us towards the Father. This is why the Church of our time—a time particularly hungry for the Spirit, because it is hungry for justice, peace, love, goodness, fortitude, responsibility, and human dignity—must concentrate and gather around that Mystery, finding in it the light and the strength that are indispensable for her mission. For if, as was already said, man is the way for the Church's daily life, the Church must be always aware of the dignity of the divine adoption received by man in Christ through the grace of the Holy Spirit and of his destination to grace and glory. By reflecting ever anew on all this, and by accepting it with a faith that is more and more aware and a love that is more and more firm, the Church also makes herself better fitted for the service to man to which Christ the Lord calls her when He says: "The Son of man came not to be served but to serve." The Church performs this ministry by sharing in the "triple office" belonging to her Master and Redeemer. This teaching, with its biblical foundation, was brought fully to the fore by the Second Vatican Council, to the great advantage of the Church's life. For when we become aware that we share in Christ's triple mission, His triple office as priest, as prophet and as king, we also become more aware of what must receive service from the whole of the Church as the society and community of the People of God on earth, and we likewise understand how each one of us must share in this mission and service.

In the light of the sacred teaching of the Second Vatican Council, the Church thus appears before us as the social subject of responsibility for divine truth. With deep emotion we hear Christ Himself saying: "The word which you hear is not mine but the Father's who sent me." In this affirmation by our Master do we not notice responsibility for the revealed truth, which is the "property" of God Himself, since even He, "the only Son," who lives "in the bosom of the Father," when transmitting that truth as a prophet and teacher, feels the need to stress that He is acting in full fidelity to its divine source? The same fidelity must be a constitutive quality of the Church's faith, both when she is teaching it and when she is professing it. Faith as a specific supernatural virtue infused into the human spirit makes us sharers in knowledge of God as a response to His revealed Word. Therefore, it is required, when the Church professes and teaches the faith, that she should adhere strictly to divine truth, and should translate it into living attitudes of "obedience in harmony with reason." Christ Himself, concerned for this fidelity to divine truth, promised the Church the special assistance of the Spirit of truth, gave the gift of infallibility to those whom He entrusted with the mandate of transmitting and teaching that truth—as has besides been clearly defined by the First Vatican Council and has then been repeated by the Second Vatican Council—and He furthermore endowed the whole of the People of God with a special sense of the faith.

Consequently, we have become sharers in this mission of the prophet Christ, and in virtue of that mission we together with Him are serving divine truth in the Church. Being responsible for that truth also means loving it and seeking the most exact understanding of it, in order to bring it closer to ourselves and others in all its saving power, its splendor and its profundity joined with simplicity. This love and this aspiration to understand the truth must go hand in hand, as is confirmed by the histories of the saints in the Church. These received most brightly the authentic light that illuminates divine truth and brings close God's very reality, because they approached this truth with veneration and love—love in the first place for Christ, the living Word of divine truth, and then love for His human expression in the Gospel, tradition and theology. Today we still need above all that understanding and interpretation of God's Word; we need that theology. Theology has always had and continues to have great importance for the Church, the People of God, to be able to share creatively and fruitfully in Christ's mission as prophet. Therefore, when theologians, as servants of divine truth, dedicate their studies and labors to ever deeper understanding of that truth, they can never lose sight of the meaning of their service in the Church, which is enshrined in the concept *intellectus fidei.* This concept has, so to speak, a two-way function, in line with St. Augustine's expression: *intellege, ut credas—crede, ut intellegas,* and it functions correctly when they seek to serve the magisterium, which in the Church is entrusted to the bishops joined by the bond of hierarchical communion with Peter's successor, when they place themselves at the service of their solicitude in teaching and giving pastoral care, and when they place themselves at the service of the apostolic commitments of the whole of the People of God.

As in preceding ages, and perhaps more than in preceding ages, theologians and all men of learning in the Church are today called to unite faith with learning and wisdom, in order to help them to combine with each other, as we read in the prayer in the liturgy of the memorial of St. Albert, Doctor of the Church. This task has grown enormously today because of the advance of human learning, its methodology, and the achievements in knowledge of the world and of man. This concerns both the exact sciences and the human sciences, as well as philosophy, which, as the Second Vatican Council recalled is closely linked with theology.

In this field of human knowledge, which is continually being broadened and yet differentiated, faith too must be investigated deeply, manifesting the magnitude of revealed mystery and tending towards an understanding of truth, which has in God its one supreme source. If it is permissible and even desirable that the enormous work to be done in this direction should take into consideration a certain pluralism of methodology, the work cannot however depart from the fundamental unity in the teaching of faith and morals which is that work's end. Accordingly, close collaboration by theology with the magisterium is indispensable. Every theologian must be particularly aware of what Christ Himself stated when He said: "The word which you hear is not mine but the Father's who sent me." Nobody, therefore, can make of theology as it were a simple collection of his own personal ideas, but everybody must be aware of being in close union with the mission of teaching truth for which the Church is responsible.

The sharing in the prophetic office of Christ Himself shapes the life of the whole of the Church in her fundamental dimension. A particular share in this office belongs to the pastors of the Church, who teach and continually and in various ways proclaim and transmit the doctrine concerning the Christian faith and morals. This teaching, both in its missionary and its ordinary aspect, helps to assemble the People of God around Christ, prepares for participation in the Eucharist and points out the ways for sacramental life. In 1977 the synod of the bishops dedicated special attention to catechesis in the modern world, and the mature results of its deliberations, experiences and suggestions will shortly find expression—in keeping with the proposal made by the participants in the synod—in a special papal document. Catechesis certainly constitutes a permanent and also fundamental form of activity by the Church, one in which her prophetic charism is manifested: witnessing and teaching go hand in hand. And although here we are speaking in the first place of priests, it is however impossible not to mention also the great number of men and women religious dedicating themselves to catechetical activity for the love of the divine Master. Finally, it would be difficult not to mention the many lay people who find expression in this activity for their faith and their apostolic responsibility.

Furthermore, increasing care must be taken that the various forms of catechesis and its various fields—beginning with the fundamental field, family catechesis, that is the catechesis by parents of their children—should give evidence of the universal sharing by the whole of the People of God in the prophetic office of Christ Himself. Linked with this fact, the Church's responsibility for divine truth must be increasingly shared in various ways by all. What shall we say at this point with regard to the specialists in the various disciplines, those who represent the natural sciences and letters, doctors, jurists, artists and technicians, teachers at various levels and with different specializations? As members of the People of God, they all have their own part to play in Christ's prophetic mission and service of divine truth, among other ways by an honest attitude towards truth, whatever field it may belong to, while educating others in truth and teaching them to mature in love and justice. Thus, a sense of responsibility for truth is one of the fundamental points of encounter between the Church and each man and also one of the fundamental demands determining man's vocation in the community of the Church. The present-day Church, guided by a sense of responsibility for truth, must persevere in fidelity to her own nature, which involves the prophetic mission that comes from Christ Himself: "As the Father has sent me, even so I send you. . . . Receive the Holy Spirit."

In the mystery of the Redemption, that is to say in Jesus Christ's saving work, the Church not only shares in the Gospel of her Master through fidelity to the word and service of truth, but she also shares, through a submission filled with hope and love, in the power of His redeeming action expressed and enshrined by Him in a sacramental form, especially in the Eucharist. The Eucharist is the center and summit of the whole of sacramental life, through which each Christian receives the saving power of the Redemption, beginning with the mystery of Baptism, in which we are buried into the death of Christ, in order to become sharers in His resurrection, as the Apostle teaches. In the light of this teaching, we see still more clearly the reason why the entire sacramental life of the Church and of each Christian reaches its summit and fullness in the Eucharist. For by Christ's will there is in this sacrament a continual renewing of the mystery of the sacrifice of Himself that Christ offered to the Father on the altar of the cross, a sacrifice that the Father accepted, giving, in return for this total self-giving by His Son, who "became obedient unto death," His own paternal gift, that is to say the grant of new immortal life in the resurrection, since the Father is the first source and the giver of life from the beginning. That new life, which involves the bodily glorification of the crucified Christ, became an efficacious sign of the new gift granted to humanity, the gift that is the Holy Spirit, through whom the divine life that the Father has in Himself and gives to His Son is communicated to all men who are united with Christ.

The Eucharist is the most perfect sacrament of this union. By celebrating and also partaking of the Eucharist we unite ourselves with Christ on earth and in heaven who intercedes for us with the Father but we always do so through the redeeming act of His sacrifice, through which he has redeemed us, so that we have been "bought with a price." The "price" of our redemption is likewise a further proof of the value that God Himself sets on man and of our dignity in Christ. For by becoming "children of God," adopted sons, we also become in His likeness "a kingdom and priests" and obtain "a royal priesthood," that is to say we share in that unique and irreversible restoration of man and the world to the Father that was carried out once for all by Him, who is both the eternal Son and also true Man. The Eucharist is the sacrament in which our new being is most completely expressed and in which Christ Himself unceasingly and in an ever new manner "bears witness" in the Holy Spirit to our spirit that each of us, as a sharer in the mystery of the Redemption, has access to the fruits of the filial reconciliation with God that He Himself actuated and continually actuates among us by means of the Church's ministry.

It is an essential truth, not only of doctrine but also of life, that the Eucharist builds the Church, building it as the authentic community of the People of God, as the assembly of the faithful, bearing the same mark of unity that was shared by the apostles and the first disciples of the Lord. The Eucharist builds ever anew this community and unity, ever building and regenerating it on the basis of the sacrifice of Christ, since it commemorates His death on the cross, the price by which He redeemed us. Accordingly, in the Eucharist we touch in a way the very mystery of the body and the blood of the Lord, as is attested by the very words used at its institution, the words that, because of that institution, have become the words with which those called to this ministry in the Church unceasingly celebrate the Eucharist.

The Church lives by the Eucharist, by the fullness of this sacrament, the stupendous content and meaning of which have often been expressed in the Church's magisterium from the most distant times down to our own days. However, we can say with certainty that, although this teaching is sustained by the acuteness of theologians, by men of deep faith and prayer, and by ascetics and mystics, in complete fidelity to the Eucharistic mystery, it still reaches no more than the threshold, since it is incapable of grasping and translating into words what the Eucharist is in all its fullness, what is expressed by it and what is actuated by it. Indeed, the Eucharist is the ineffable sacrament! The essential commitment and, above all, the visible grace and source of supernatural strength for the Church as the People of God is to persevere and advance constantly in Eucharistic life and Eucharistic piety and to develop spiritually in the climate of the Eucharist. With all the greater reason, then, it is not permissible for us, in thought, life or action, to take away from this truly most holy sacrament its full magnitude and its essential meaning. It is at one and the same time a sacrifice-sacrament, a communion-sacrament, and a presence-sacrament. And, although it is true that the Eucharist always was and must continue to be the most profound revelation of the human brotherhood of Christ's disciples and confessors, it cannot be treated merely as an "occasion" for manifesting this brotherhood. When celebrating the sacrament of the body and blood of the Lord, the full magnitude of the divine mystery must be respected, as must the full meaning of this sacramental sign in which Christ is really present and is received, the soul is filled with grace and the pledge of future glory is given. This is the source of the duty to carry out rigorously the liturgical rites and everything that is a manifestation of community worship offered to God Himself, all the more so because in this sacramental sign He entrusts Himself to us with limitless trust, as if not taking into consideration our human weakness, our unworthiness, the force of habit, routine, or even the possibility of insult. Every member of the Church, especially bishops and priests, must be vigilant in seeing that this sacrament of love shall be at the center of the life of the People of God, so that through all the manifestations of worship due to it Christ shall be given back "love for love" and truly become "the life of our souls." Nor can we, on the other hand, ever forget the following words of St. Paul: "Let a man examine himself, and so eat of the bread and drink of the cup."

This call by the Apostle indicates at least indirectly the close link between the Eucharist and Penance. Indeed, if the first word of Christ's teaching, the first phrase of the Gospel Good News, was "Repent, and believe in the gospel" (*Metanoeite*), the sacrament of the passion, cross and resurrection seems to strengthen and consolidate in an altogether special way this call in our souls. The Eucharist and Penance thus become in a sense two closely connected dimensions of authentic life in accordance with the spirit of the Gospel, of truly Christian life. The Christ who calls to the Eucharistic banquet is always the same Christ who exhorts us to penance and repeats His "Repent." Without this constant ever renewed endeavor for conversion, partaking of the Eucharist would lack its full redeeming effectiveness and there would be a loss or at least a weakening of the special readiness to offer God the spiritual sacrifice in which our sharing in the priesthood of Christ is expressed in an essential and universal manner. In Christ, priesthood is linked with His sacrifice, His self-giving to the Father; and, precisely because it is without limit, that self-giving gives rise in us human beings subject to numerous limitations to the need to turn to God in an ever more mature way and with a constant, ever more profound, conversion.

In the last years much has been done to highlight in the Church's practice—in conformity with the most ancient tradition of the Church—the community aspect of penance and especially of the sacrament of Penance. We cannot however forget that conversion is a particularly profound inward act in which the individual cannot be replaced by others and cannot make the community be a substitute for him. Although the participation by the fraternal community of the faithful in the penitential celebration is a great help for the act of personal conversion, nevertheless, in the final analysis, it is necessary that in this act there should be a pronouncement by the individual himself with the whole depth of his conscience and with the whole of his sense of guilt and of trust in God, placing himself like the Psalmist before God to confess: "Against you . . . have I sinned." In faithfully observing the centuries-old practice of the sacrament of Penance—the practice of individual confession with a personal act of sorrow and the intention to amend and make satisfaction—the Church is therefore defending the human soul's individual right: man's right to a more personal encounter with the crucified forgiving Christ, with Christ saying, through the minister of the sacrament of reconciliation: "Your sins are forgiven"; "Go, and do not sin again." As is evident, this is also a right on Christ's part with regard to every human being redeemed by Him: His right to meet each one of us in that key moment in the soul's life constituted by the moment of conversion and forgiveness. By guarding the sacrament of Penance, the Church expressly affirms her faith in the mystery of the Redemption as a living and life-giving reality that fits in with man's inward truth, with human guilt and also with the desires of the human conscience. "Blessed are those who hunger and thirst for righteousness, for they shall be satisfied." The sacrament of Penance is the means to satisfy man with the righteousness that comes from the Redeemer Himself.

In the Church, gathering particularly today in a special way around the Eucharist and desiring that the authentic Eucharistic community should become a sign of the gradually maturing unity of all Christians, there must be a lively-felt need for penance, both in its sacramental aspect, and in what concerns penance as a virtue. This second aspect was expressed by Paul VI in the Apostolic Constitution *Paenitemini*. One of the Church's tasks is to put into practice the teaching *Paenitemini* contains; this subject must be investigated more deeply by us in common reflection, and many more decisions must be made about it in a spirit of pastoral collegiality and with respect for the different traditions in this regard and the different circumstances of the lives of the people of today. Nevertheless, it is certain that the Church of the new advent, the Church that is continually preparing for the new coming of the Lord, must be the Church of the Eucharist and of Penance. Only when viewed in this spiritual aspect of her life and activity is she seen to be the Church of the divine mission, the Church *in statu missionis*, as the Second Vatican Council has shown her to be.

In building up from the very foundations the picture of the Church as the People of God—by showing the threefold mission of Christ Himself, through participation in which we become truly God's People—the Second Vatican Council highlighted, among other characteristics of the Christian vocation, the one that can be described as "kingly." To present all the riches of the Council's teaching we would here have to make reference to numerous chapters and paragraphs of the Constitution *Lumen Gentium* and of many other documents by the Council. However, one element seems to stand out in the midst of all these riches: the sharing in Christ's kingly mission, that is to say the fact of rediscovering in oneself and others the special dignity of our vocation that can be described as "kingship." This dignity is expressed in readiness to serve, in keeping with the example of Christ, who "came not to be served but to serve." If, in the light of this attitude of Christ's, "being a king" is truly possible only by "being a servant," then "being a servant" also demands so much spiritual maturity that it must really be described as "being a king." In order to be able to serve others worthily and effectively we must be able to master ourselves, possess the virtues that make this mastery possible. Our sharing in Christ's kingly mission—His "kingly function" (*munus*)—is closely linked with every sphere of both Christian and human morality.

In presenting the complete picture of the People of God and recalling the place among that people held not only by priests but also by the laity, not only by the representatives of the hierarchy but also by those of the institutes of consecrated life, the Second Vatican Council did not deduce this picture merely from a sociological premise. The Church as a human society can of course be examined and described according to the categories used by the sciences with regard to any human society. But these categories are not enough. For the whole of the community of the People of God and for each member of it what is in question is not just a specific "social membership"; rather, for each and every one what is essential is a particular "vocation." Indeed, the Church as the People of God is also—according to the teaching of St. Paul mentioned above, of which Pius XII reminded us in wonderful terms—"Christ's Mystical Body." Membership in that body has for its source a particular call, united with the saving action of grace. Therefore, if we wish to keep in mind this community of the People of God, which is so vast and so extremely differentiated, we must see first and foremost Christ saying in a way to each member of the community: "Follow me." It is the community of the disciples, each of whom in a different way—at times very consciously and consistently, at other times not very consciously and very inconsistently—is following Christ. This shows also the deeply "personal" aspect and dimension of this society, which, in spite of all the deficiencies of its community life—in the human meaning of this word—is a community precisely because all its members form it together with Christ Himself, at least because they bear in their souls the indelible mark of a Christian.

The Second Vatican Council devoted very special attention to showing how this "ontological" community of disciples and confessors must increasingly become, even from the "human" point of view, a community aware of its own life and activity. The initiatives taken by the Council in this field have been followed up by the many further initiatives of a synodal, apostolic and organizational kind. We must, however, always keep in mind the truth that every initiative serves true renewal in the Church and helps to bring the authentic light that is Christ insofar as the initiative is based on adequate awareness of the individual Christian's vocation and of responsibility for this singular, unique and unrepeatable grace by which each Christian in the community of the People of God builds up the Body of Christ. This principle, the key rule for the whole of Christian practice—apostolic and pastoral practice, practice of interior and social life—must with due proportion be applied to the whole of humanity and to each human being. The Pope, too, and every bishop must apply this principle to himself. Priests and religious must be faithful to this principle. It is the basis on which their lives must be built by married people, parents, and women and men of different conditions and professions, from those who occupy the highest posts in society to those who perform the simplest tasks. It is precisely the principle of the "kingly service" that imposes on each one of us, in imitation of Christ's example, the duty to demand of himself exactly what we have been called to, what we have personally obliged ourselves to by God's grace, in order to respond to our vocation. This fidelity to the vocation received from God through Christ involves the joint responsibility for the Church for which the Second Vatican Council wishes to educate all Christians. Indeed, in the Church as the community of the People of God under the guidance of the Holy Spirit's working, each member has "his own special gift," as St. Paul teaches. Although this "gift" is a personal vocation and a form of participation in the Church's saving work, it also serves others, builds the Church and the fraternal communities in the various spheres of human life on earth.

Fidelity to one's vocation, that is to say persevering readiness for "kingly service," has particular significance for these many forms of building, especially with regard to the more exigent tasks, which have more influence on the life of our neighbor and of the whole of society. Married people must be distinguished for fidelity to their vocation, as is demanded by the indissoluble nature of the sacramental institution of marriage. Priests must be distinguished for a similar fidelity to their vocation, in view of the indelible character that the sacrament of Orders stamps on their souls. In receiving this sacrament, we in the Latin Church knowingly and freely commit ourselves to live in celibacy, and each one of us must therefore do all he can, with God's grace, to be thankful for this gift and faithful to the bond that he has accepted forever. He must do so as married people must, for they must endeavor with all their strength to persevere in their matrimonial union, building up the family community through this witness of love and educating new generations of men and women, capable in their turn of dedicating the whole of their lives to their vocation, that is to say to the "kingly service" of which Jesus Christ has offered us the example and most beautiful model. His Church, made up of all of us, is "for men" in the sense that, by basing ourselves on Christ's example and collaborating with the grace that He has gained for us, we are able to attain to "being kings," that is to say we are able to produce a mature humanity in each one of us. Mature humanity means full use of the gift of freedom received from the Creator when He called to existence the man made "in his image, after his likeness." This gift finds its full realization in the unreserved giving of the whole of one's human person, in a spirit of the love of a spouse, to Christ and, with Christ, to all those to whom He sends men and women totally consecrated to Him in accordance with the evangelical counsels. This is the ideal of the religious life, which has been undertaken by the orders and congregations both ancient and recent, and by the secular institutes.

Nowadays it is sometimes held, though wrongly, that freedom is an end in itself, that each human being is free when he makes use of freedom as he wishes, and that this must be our aim in the lives of individuals and societies. In reality, freedom is a great gift only when we know how to use it consciously for everything that is our true good. Christ teaches us that the best use of freedom is charity, which takes concrete form in self-giving and in service. For this "freedom Christ has set us free" and ever continues to set us free. The Church draws from this source the unceasing inspiration, the call and the drive for her mission and her service among all mankind. The full truth about human freedom is indelibly inscribed on the mystery of the Redemption. The Church truly serves mankind when she guards this truth with untiring attention, fervent love and mature commitment and when in the whole of her own community she transmits it and gives it concrete form in human life through each Christian's fidelity to his vocation. This confirms what we have already referred to, namely that man is and always becomes the "way" for the Church's daily life.

786 (1) **John 12:32** ". . . and I, when I am lifted up from the earth, will draw all men to myself."

(2) ***Lumen gentium* 36** Christ, made obedient unto death and because of this exalted by the Father (cf. Ph. 2:8–9), has entered into the glory of his kingdom. All things are subjected to him until he subjects himself and all created things to the Father, so that God may be all in all (cf. 1 Cor. 15:27–28). He communicated this power to the disciples that they be constituted in royal liberty and, by self-abnegation of a holy life, overcome the reign of sin in themselves (cf. Rom. 6:12)—that indeed by serving Christ in others they may in humility and patience bring their brethren to that king to serve whom is to reign. The Lord also desires that his kingdom be spread by the lay faithful: the kingdom of truth and life, the kingdom of holiness and grace, the kingdom of justice, love and peace. In this kingdom creation itself will be delivered from the slavery of corruption into the freedom of the glory of the sons of God (cf. Rom. 8:21). Clearly, a great promise, a great commission is given to the disciples: "all things are yours, you are Christ's, and Christ is God's" (1 Cor. 3:23). 786

The faithful must, then, recognize the inner nature, the value and the ordering of the whole of creation to the praise of God. By their secular activity they help one another achieve greater holiness of life, so that the world may be filled with the spirit of Christ and may the more effectively attain its destiny in justice, in love and in peace. The laity enjoy a principal role in the universal fulfillment of this task. Therefore, by their competence in secular disciplines and by their activity, interiorly raised up by grace, let them work earnestly in order that created goods through human labor, technical skill and civil culture may serve the utility of all men according to the plan of the creator and the light of his word. May these goods be more suitably distributed among all men and in their own way may they be conducive to universal progress in human and Christian liberty. Thus, through the members of the Church, will Christ increasingly illuminate the whole of human society with his saving light.

Moreover, by uniting their forces, let the laity so remedy the institutions and conditions of the world when the latter are an inducement to sin, that these may be conformed to the norms of justice, favoring rather than hindering the practice of virtue. By so doing they will impregnate culture and human works with a moral value. In this way the field of the world is better prepared for the seed of the divine word and the doors of the Church are opened more widely through which the message of peace may enter the world.

Because of the very economy of salvation the faithful should learn to distinguish carefully between the rights and the duties which they have as belonging to the Church and those which fall to them as members of the human society. They will strive to unite the two harmoniously, remembering that in every temporal affair they are to be guided by a Christian conscience, since not even in temporal business may any human activity be withdrawn from God's dominion. In our times it is most necessary that this distinction and harmony should shine forth as clearly as possible in the manner in which the faithful act, in order that the mission of the Church may correspond more fully with the special circumstances of the world today. But just as it must be recognized that the terrestrial city, rightly concerned with secular affairs, is governed by its own principles, thus also the ominous doctrine which seeks to build society with no regard for religion, and attacks and utterly destroys the religious liberty of its citizens, is rightly to be rejected.

(1) **Mark 1:16–20** And passing along by the Sea of Galilee, he saw Simon and Andrew the brother of Simon casting a net in the sea; for they were fisherman. And Jesus said to them, "Follow me and I will make you become fishers of men." And immediately they left their nets and followed him. And going on a little farther, he saw James the son of Zebedee and John his brother, who were in their boat mending 787

the nets. And immediately he called them; and they left their father Zebedee in the boat with the hired servants, and followed him.

787 (2) **Mark 3:13–19** And he went up on the mountain, and called to him those whom he desired; and they came to him. And he appointed twelve, to be with him, and to be sent out to preach and have authority to cast out demons: Simon whom he surnamed Peter; James the son of Zebedee and John the brother of James, whom he surnamed Boanerges, that is, sons of thunder; Andrew, and Philip, and Bartholomew, and Matthew, and Thomas, and James the son of Alphaeus, and Thaddaeus, and Simon the Cananaean, and Judas Iscariot, who betrayed him.

Then he went home. . . .

787 (3) **Matthew 13:10–17** Then the disciples came and said to him, "Why do you speak to them in parables?" And he answered them, "To you it has been given to know the secrets of the kingdom of heaven, but to them it has not been given. For to him who has will more be given and he will have abundance; but from him who has not, even what he has will be taken away. This is why I speak to them in parables, because seeing they do not see, and hearing they do not hear, nor do they understand. With them indeed is fulfilled the prophecy of Isaiah which says:

'You shall indeed hear but never understand,
and you shall indeed see but never perceive.
For this people's heart has grown dull,
and their ears are heavy of hearing,
and their eyes they have closed,
lest they should perceive with their eyes,
and hear with their ears,
and understand with their heart,
and turn for me to heal them.'

But blessed are your eyes, for they see, and your ears, for they hear. Truly, I say to you, many prophets and righteous men longed to see what you see, and did not see it, and to hear what you hear, and did not hear it. . . ."

787 (4) **Luke 10:17–20** The seventy returned with joy, saying, "Lord, even the demons are subject to us in your name!" And he said to them, "I saw Satan fall like lightning from heaven. Behold, I have given you authority to tread upon serpents and scorpions, and over all the power of the enemy; and nothing shall hurt you. Nevertheless do not rejoice in this, that the spirits are subject to you; but rejoice that your names are written in heaven."

787 (5) **Luke 22:28–30** "You are those who have continued with me in my trials; and I assign to you, as my Father assigned to me, a kingdom, that you may eat and drink at my table in my kingdom, and sit on thrones judging the twelve tribes of Israel. . . ."

788 (1) **John 14:18** "I will not leave you desolate; I will come to you. . . ."

788 (2) **John 20:22** And when he had said this, he breathed on them, and said to them, "Receive the Holy Spirit. . . ."

788 (3) **Matthew 28:20** ". . . teaching them to observe all that I have commanded you; and lo, I am with you always, to the close of the age."

788 (4) **Acts 2:33** Being therefore exalted at the right hand of God, and having received from the Father the promise of the Holy Spirit, he has poured out this which you see and hear.

(1) **Romans 6:4–5** We were buried therefore with him by baptism into death, so 790
that as Christ was raised from the dead by the glory of the Father, we too might walk in newness of life.

For if we have been united with him in a death like his, we shall certainly be united with him in a resurrection like his.

(2) **1 Corinthians 12:13** For by one Spirit we were all baptized into one body— 790
Jews or Greeks, slaves or free—and all were made to drink of one Spirit.

(1) **Colossians 2:19** . . . and not holding fast to the Head, from whom the whole 794
body, nourished and knit together through its joints and ligaments, grows with a growth that is from God.

(2) **Ephesians 4:11–16** And his gifts were that some should be apostles, some 794
prophets, some evangelists, some pastors and teachers, to equip the saints for the work of ministry, for building up the body of Christ, until we all attain to the unity of the faith and of the knowledge of the Son of God, to mature manhood, to the measure of the stature of the fulness of Christ; so that we may no longer be children, tossed to and fro and carried about with every wind of doctrine, by the cunning of men, by their craftiness in deceitful wiles. Rather, speaking the truth in love, we are to grow up in every way into him who is the head, into Christ, from whom the whole body, joined and knit together by every joint with which it is supplied, when each part is working properly, makes bodily growth and upbuilds itself in love.

(1) **Matthew 22:1–14** And again Jesus spoke to them in parables, saying, "The 796
kingdom of heaven may be compared to a king who gave a marriage feast for his son, and sent his servants to call those who were invited to the marriage feast; but they would not come. Again he sent other servants, saying, 'Tell those who are invited, Behold, I have made ready my dinner, my oxen and my fat calves are killed, and everything is ready; come to the marriage feast.' But they made light of it and went off, one to his farm, another to his business, while the rest seized his servants, treated them shamefully, and killed them. The king was angry, and he sent his troops and destroyed those murderers and burned their city. Then he said to his servants, 'The wedding is ready, but those invited were not worthy. Go therefore to the thoroughfares, and invite to the marriage feast as many as you find.' And those servants went out into the streets and gathered all whom they found, both bad and good; so the wedding hall was filled with guests.

"But when the king came in to look at the guests, he saw there a man who had no wedding garment; and he said to him, 'Friend, how did you get in here without a wedding garment?' And he was speechless. Then the king said to the attendants, 'Bind him hand and foot, and cast him into the outer darkness; there men will weep and gnash their teeth.' For many are called, but few are chosen."

(2) **Matthew 25:1–13** "Then the kingdom of heaven shall be compared to ten 796
maidens who took their lamps and went to meet the bridegroom. Five of them were foolish, and five were wise. For when the foolish took their lamps, they took no oil with them; but the wise took flasks of oil with their lamps. As the bridegroom was delayed, they all slumbered and slept. But at midnight there was a cry, 'Behold, the bridegroom! Come out to meet him.' Then all those maidens rose and trimmed their lamps. And the foolish said to the wise, 'Give us some of your oil, for our lamps are going out.' But the wise replied, 'Perhaps there will not be enough for us and for you; go rather to the dealers and buy for yourselves.' And while they went to buy,

the bridegroom came, and those who were ready went in with him to the marriage feast; and the door was shut. Afterward the other maidens came also, saying, 'Lord, lord, open to us.' But he replied, 'Truly, I say to you, I do not know you.' Watch therefore, for you know neither the day nor the hour. . . ."

796 (3) **1 Corinthians 6:15–17** Do you not know that your bodies are members of Christ? Shall I therefore take the members of Christ and make them members of a prostitute? Never! Do you not know that he who joins himself to a prostitute becomes one body with her? For, as it is written, "The two shall become one flesh." But he who is united to the Lord becomes one spirit with him.

796 (4) **2 Corinthians 11:2** I feel a divine jealousy for you, for I betrothed you to Christ to present you as a pure bride to her one husband.

796 (5) **Revelation 22:17** The Spirit and the Bride say, "Come." And let him who hears say, "Come." And let him who is thirsty come, let him who desires take the water of life without price.

796 (6) **Ephesians 1:4** . . . even as he chose us in him before the foundation of the world, that we should be holy and blameless before him.

796 (7) **Ephesians 5:27** . . . that he might present the church to himself in splendor, without spot or wrinkle or any such thing, that she might be holy and without blemish.

796 (8) **Ephesians 5:29** For no man ever hates his own flesh, but nourishes and cherishes it, as Christ does the church. . . .

797 (1) **1 Corinthians 3:16–17** Do you not know that you are God's temple and that God's Spirit dwells in you? If any one destroys God's temple, God will destroy him. For God's temple is holy, and that temple you are.

797 (2) **Ephesians 2:21** . . . in whom the whole structure is joined together and grows into a holy temple in the Lord. . . .

798 (1) **Ephesians 4:16** . . . from whom the whole body, joined and knit together by every joint with which it is supplied, when each part is working properly, makes bodily growth and upbuilds itself in love.

798 (2) **1 Corinthians 12:13** For by one Spirit we were all baptized into one body—Jews or Greeks, slaves or free—and all were made to drink of one Spirit.

798 (3) ***Apostolicam actuositatem* 3** From the fact of their union with Christ the head flows the laymen's right and duty to be apostles. Inserted as they are in the Mystical Body of Christ by baptism and strengthened by the power of the Holy Spirit in confirmation, it is by the Lord himself that they are assigned to the apostolate. If they are consecrated a kingly priesthood and a holy nation (cf. 1 Pet. 2:4–10), it is in order that they may in all their actions offer spiritual sacrifices and bear witness to Christ all the world over. Charity, which is, as it were, the soul of the whole apostolate, is given to them and nourished in them by the sacraments, the Eucharist above all.

The apostolate is lived in faith, hope and charity poured out by the Holy Spirit into the hearts of all the members of the Church. And the precept of charity, which is the Lord's greatest commandment, urges all Christians to work for the glory of God through the coming of his kingdom and for the communication of eternal life to all men, that they may know the only true God and Jesus Christ whom he has sent (cf. Jn. 17:3).

On all Christians, accordingly, rests the noble obligation of working to bring all men throughout the whole world to hear and accept the divine message of salvation.

The Holy Spirit sanctifies the People of God through the ministry and the sacraments. However, for the exercise of the apostolate he gives the faithful special gifts besides (cf. 1 Cor. 12:7), "allotting them to each one as he wills" (1 Cor. 12:11), so that each and all, putting at the service of others the grace received may be "as good stewards of God's varied gifts," (1 Pet. 4:10), for the building up of the whole body in charity (cf. Eph. 4:16). From the reception of these charisms, even the most ordinary ones, there arises for each of the faithful the right and duty of exercising them in the Church and in the world for the good of men and the development of the Church, of exercising them in the freedom of the Holy Spirit who "breathes where he wills" (Jn. 3:8), and at the same time in communion with his brothers in Christ, and with his pastors especially. It is for the pastors to pass judgment on the authenticity and good use of these gifts, not certainly with a view to quenching the Spirit but to testing everything and keeping what is good (cf. 1 Th. 5:12, 19, 21).

1 Corinthians 13: see 735 (3). **800**

(1) ***Lumen gentium* 30** Having made clear the functions of the hierarchy, the holy Council is pleased to turn its attention to the state of those Christians who are called the laity. Everything that has been said of the People of God is addressed equally to laity, religious and clergy. Because of their situation and mission, however, certain things pertain particularly to the laity, both men and women, the foundations of which must be more fully examined owing to the special circumstances of our time. The pastors, indeed, know well how much the laity contribute to the welfare of the whole Church. For they know that they themselves were not established by Christ to undertake alone the whole salvific mission of the Church to the world, but that it is their exalted office so to be shepherds of the faithful and also recognize the latter's contribution and charisms that everyone in his own way will, with one mind, cooperate in the common task. For all must "practice the truth in love, and so grow up in all things in him who is the head, Christ. For from him the whole body—being closely joined and knit together through every joint of the system according to the functioning in due measure of each single part—derives its increase to the building up of itself in love" (Eph. 4:15–16). **801**

(2) **1 Thessalonians 5:12** But we beseech you, brethren, to respect those who labor among you and are over you in the Lord and admonish you. . . . **801**

(3) **1 Thessalonians 5:19–21** Do not quench the Spirit, do not despise prophesying, but test everything; hold fast what is good. . . . **801**

(4) ***Christifideles laici* 24** The Holy Spirit, while bestowing diverse ministries in Church communion, enriches it still further with particular gifts or promptings of grace, called *charisms*. These can take a great variety of forms both as a manifestation of the absolute freedom of the Spirit who abundantly supplies them, and as a response to the varied needs of the Church in history. The description and the classification given to these gifts in the New Testament are an indication of their rich variety. "To each is given the manifestation of the Spirit for the common good. To one is given **801**

through the Spirit the utterance of wisdom, and to another the utterance of knowledge according to the same Spirit, to another faith by the same Spirit, to another gifts of healing by the one Spirit, to another the working of miracles, to another prophecy, to another the ability to distinguish between spirits, to another various kinds of tongues, to another the interpretation of tongues" (1 Cor 12:7–10; cf. 1 Cor 12:4–6, 28–31; Rom 12:6–8; 1 Pt 4:10–11).

Whether they be exceptional and great or simple and ordinary, the charisms are *graces of the Holy Spirit that have,* directly or indirectly, *a usefulness for the ecclesial community,* ordered as they are to the building up of the Church, to the well-being of humanity and to the needs of the world.

Even in our own times there is no lack of a fruitful manifestation of various charisms among the faithful, women and men. These charisms are given to individual persons and can even be shared by others in such ways as to continue in time a precious and effective heritage, serving as a source of a particular spiritual affinity among persons. In referring to the apostolate of the lay faithful the Second Vatican Council writes: "For the exercise of the apostolate the Holy Spirit who sanctifies the People of God through the ministry and the sacraments gives the faithful special gifts as well (cf. 1 Cor 12:7), 'allotting them to each one as he wills' (cf. 1 Cor 12:11), so that each might place 'at the service of others the grace received' and become 'good stewards of God's varied grace' (1 Pt 4:10), and build up thereby the whole body in charity (cf. Eph 4:16)."

By a logic which looks to the divine source of this giving, as the Council recalls, the gifts of the Spirit demand that those who have received them exercise them for the growth of the whole Church.

The charisms are *received in gratitude* both on the part of the one who receives them, and also on the part of the entire Church. They are in fact a singularly rich source of grace for the vitality of the apostolate and for the holiness of the whole Body of Christ, provided that they be gifts that come truly from the Spirit and are exercised in full conformity with the authentic promptings of the Spirit. In this sense the *discernment of charisms* is always necessary. Indeed, the Synod Fathers have stated: "The action of the Holy Spirit, who breathes where he will, is not always easily recognized and received. We know that God acts in all Christians, and we are aware of the benefits which flow from charisms both for individuals and for the whole Christian community. Nevertheless, at the same time we are also aware of the power of sin and how it can disturb and confuse the life of the faithful and of the community."

For this reason no charism dispenses a person from reference and submission to the *Pastors of the Church.* The Council clearly states: "Judgment as to their [charisms'] genuineness and proper use belongs to those who preside over the Church, and to whose special competence it belongs, not indeed to extinguish the Spirit, but to test all things and hold fast to what is good (cf. 1 Thes 5:12 and 19:21)," so that all the charisms might work together, in their diversity and complementarity, for the common good.

811 **Congregation for the Doctrine of the Faith, letter to the bishops of England (16 September 1864): DS 2888** The true Church of Jesus Christ was established by divine authority, and is known by a fourfold mark, which we assert in the Creed must be believed; and each one of these marks so clings to the others that it cannot be separated from them; hence it happens that that Church which truly is, and is called Catholic should at the same time shine with the prerogatives of unity, sanctity, and apostolic succession. Therefore, the Catholic Church alone is conspicuous and perfect in the unity of the whole world and of all nations, particularly in that unity whose beginning, root, and unfailing origin are that supreme authority and "higher

principality" of blessed PETER, the prince of the Apostles, and of his successors in the Roman Chair. No other Church is Catholic except the one which, founded on the one PETER, grows into one "body compacted and fitly joined together" [Eph. 4:16] in the unity of faith and charity. . . .

(1) ***Unitatis redintegratio* 2** What has revealed the love of God among us is that the only-begotten Son of God has been sent by the Father into the world, so that, being made man, he might by his redemption of the entire human race give new life to it and unify it. Before offering himself up as a spotless victim upon the altar of the cross, he prayed to his Father for those who believe: "that all may be one, as you, Father, are in me, and I in you; I pray that they may be one in us, that the world may believe that you sent me" (Jn. 17:21). In his Church he instituted the wonderful sacrament of the Eucharist by which the unity of the Church is both signified and brought about. He gave his followers a new commandment to love one another, and promised the Spirit, their Advocate, who, as Lord and life-giver, should remain with them forever. 815

After being lifted up on the cross and glorified, the Lord Jesus poured forth the Spirit whom he had promised, and through whom he has called and gathered together the people of the New Covenant, which is the Church, into a unity of faith, hope and charity, as the Apostle teaches us: "There is one body and one Spirit, just as you were called to the one hope of your calling; one Lord, one faith, one baptism" (Eph. 4:4–5). For "all you who have been baptized into Christ have put on Christ . . . for you are all one in Christ Jesus" (Gal. 3:27–28). It is the Holy Spirit, dwelling in those who believe and pervading and ruling over the entire Church, who brings about that wonderful communion of the faithful and joins them together so intimately in Christ that he is the principle of the Church's unity. By distributing various kinds of spiritual gifts and ministries, he enriches the Church of Jesus Christ with different functions "in order to equip the saints for the work of service, so as to build up the body of Christ" (Eph. 4:12).

In order to establish this his holy Church everywhere in the world till the end of time, Christ entrusted to the College of the Twelve the task of teaching, ruling and sanctifying. Among their number he chose Peter. And after Peter's confession of faith, he determined that on him he would build his Church; to him he promised the keys of the kingdom of heaven, and after his profession of love, entrusted all his sheep to him to be confirmed in faith and shepherded in perfect unity, with himself, Christ Jesus, forever remaining the chief corner-stone and shepherd of our souls.

It is through the faithful preaching of the Gospel by the Apostles and their successors—the bishops with Peter's successor at their head—through their administering the sacraments, and through their governing in love, that Jesus Christ wishes his people to increase, under the action of the Holy Spirit; and he perfects its fellowship in unity: in the confession of one faith, in the common celebration of divine worship, and in the fraternal harmony of the family of God.

The Church, then, God's only flock, like a standard lifted on high for the nations to see it, ministers the Gospel of peace to all mankind, as it makes its pilgrim way in hope toward its goal, the fatherland above.

This is the sacred mystery of the unity of the Church, in Christ and through Christ, with the Holy Spirit energizing its various functions. The highest exemplar and source of this mystery is the unity, in the Trinity of Persons, of one God, the Father and the Son in the Holy Spirit.

(2) ***Lumen gentium* 14** This holy Council first of all turns its attention to the 815
Catholic faithful. Basing itself on scripture and tradition, it teaches that the Church,

a pilgrim now on earth, is necessary for salvation: the one Christ is mediator and the way of salvation; he is present to us in his body which is the Church. He himself explicitly asserted the necessity of faith and baptism (cf. Mk. 16:16; Jn. 3:5), and thereby affirmed at the same time the necessity of the Church which men enter through baptism as through a door. Hence they could not be saved who, knowing that the Catholic Church was founded as necessary by God through Christ, would refuse either to enter it, or to remain in it.

Fully incorporated into the Church are those who, possessing the Spirit of Christ, accept all the means of salvation given to the Church together with her entire organization, and who—by the bonds constituted by the profession of faith, the sacraments, ecclesiastical government, and communion—are joined in the visible structure of the Church of Christ, who rules her through the Supreme Pontiff and the bishops. Even though incorporated into the Church, one who does not however persevere in charity is not saved. He remains indeed in the bosom of the Church, but "in body" not "in heart." All children of the Church should nevertheless remember that their exalted condition results, not from their own merits, but from the grace of Christ. If they fail to respond in thought, word and deed to that grace, not only shall they not be saved, but they shall be the more severely judged.

Catechumens who, moved by the Holy Spirit, desire with an explicit intention to be incorporated into the Church, are by that very intention joined to her. With love and solicitude mother Church already embraces them as her own.

815 (3) **CIC Canon 205** Those baptized are fully in communion with the Catholic Church on this earth who are joined with Christ in its visible structure by the bonds of profession of faith, of the sacraments and of ecclesiastical governance.

817 **CIC Canon 751** Heresy is the obstinate post-baptismal denial of some truth which must be believed with divine and catholic faith, or it is likewise an obstinate doubt concerning the same; apostasy is the total repudiation of the Christian faith; schism is the refusal of submission to the Roman Pontiff or of communion with the members of the Church subject to him.

819 (1) ***Lumen gentium* 15** The Church knows that she is joined in many ways to the baptized who are honored by the name of Christian, but who do not however profess the Catholic faith in its entirety or have not preserved unity or communion under the successor of Peter. For there are many who hold sacred scripture in honor as a rule of faith and of life, who have a sincere religious zeal, who lovingly believe in God the Father Almighty and in Christ, the Son of God and the Savior, who are sealed by baptism which unites them to Christ, and who indeed recognize and receive other sacraments in their own Churches or ecclesiastical communities. Many of them possess the episcopate, celebrate the holy Eucharist and cultivate devotion of the Virgin Mother of God. There is furthermore a sharing in prayer and spiritual benefits; these Christians are indeed in some real way joined to us in the Holy Spirit for, by his gifts and graces, his sanctifying power is also active in them and he has strengthened some of them even to the shedding of their blood. And so the Spirit stirs up desires and actions in all of Christ's disciples in order that all may be peaceably united, as Christ ordained, in one flock under one shepherd. Mother Church never ceases to pray, hope and work that this may be achieved, and she exhorts her children to purification and renewal so that the sign of Christ may shine more brightly over the face of the Church.

(2) *Unitatis redintegratio* 3 In this one and only Church of God from its very beginnings there arose certain rifts, which the Apostle strongly censures as damnable. But in subsequent centuries much more serious dissensions appeared and large communities became separated from full communion with the Catholic Church—for which, often enough, men of both sides were to blame. However, one cannot charge with the sin of the separation those who at present are born into these communities and in them are brought up in the faith of Christ, and the Catholic Church accepts them with respect and affection as brothers. For men who believe in Christ and have been properly baptized are put in some, though imperfect, communion with the Catholic Church. Without doubt, the differences that exist in varying degrees between them and the Catholic Church—whether in doctrine and sometimes in discipline, or concerning the structure of the Church—do indeed create many obstacles, sometimes serious ones, to full ecclesiastical communion. The ecumenical movement is striving to overcome these obstacles. But even in spite of them it remains true that all who have been justified by faith in baptism are incorporated into Christ; they therefore have a right to be called Christians, and with good reason are accepted as brothers by the children of the Catholic Church. 819

Moreover, some, even very many, of the most significant elements and endowments which together go to build up and give life to the Church itself, can exist outside the visible boundaries of the Catholic Church: the written Word of God; the life of grace; faith, hope and charity, with the other interior gifts of the Holy Spirit, as well as visible elements. All of these, which come from Christ and lead back to him, belong by right to the one Church of Christ.

The brethren divided from us also carry out many liturgical actions of the Christian religion. In ways that vary according to the condition of each Church or community, these liturgical actions most certainly can truly engender a life of grace, and, one must say, can aptly give access to the communion of salvation.

It follows that the separated Churches and communities as such, though we believe they suffer from the defects already mentioned, have been by no means deprived of significance and importance in the mystery of salvation. For the Spirit of Christ has not refrained from using them as means of salvation which derive their efficacy from the very fullness of grace and truth entrusted to the Catholic Church.

Nevertheless, our separated brethren, whether considered as individuals or as communities and Churches, are not blessed with that unity which Jesus Christ wished to bestow on all those to whom he has given new birth into one body, and whom he has quickened to newness of life—that unity which the Holy Scriptures and the ancient Tradition of the Church proclaim. For it is through Christ's Catholic Church alone, which is the universal help towards salvation, that the fullness of the means of salvation can be obtained. It was to the apostolic college alone, of which Peter is the head, that we believe that Our Lord entrusted all the blessings of the New Covenant, in order to establish on earth the one Body of Christ into which all those should be fully incorporated who belong in any way to the people of God. During its pilgrimage on earth, this people, though still in its members liable to sin, is growing in Christ and is guided by God's gentle wisdom, according to his hidden designs, until it shall happily arrive at the fullness of eternal glory in the heavenly Jerusalem.

(1) **Hebrews 7:25** Consequently he is able for all time to save those who draw near to God through him, since he always lives to make intercession for them. 820

(2) *Unitatis redintegratio* 1 The restoration of unity among all Christians is one of the principal concerns of the Second Vatican Council. Christ the Lord founded one Church and one Church only. However, many Christian communions present 820

themselves to men as the true inheritors of Jesus Christ; all indeed profess to be followers of the Lord but they differ in mind and go their different ways, as if Christ himself were divided. Certainly, such division openly contradicts the will of Christ, scandalizes the world, and damages that most holy cause, the preaching of the Gospel to every creature.

The Lord of Ages nevertheless wisely and patiently follows out the plan of his grace on our behalf, sinners that we are. In recent times he has begun to bestow more generously upon divided Christians remorse over their divisions and longing for unity.

Everywhere large numbers have felt the impulse of this grace, and among our separated brethren also there increases from day to day a movement, fostered by the grace of the Holy Spirit, for the restoration of unity among all Christians. Taking part in this movement, which is called ecumenical, are those who invoke the Triune God and confess Jesus as Lord and Savior. They do this not merely as individuals but also as members of the corporate groups in which they have heard the Gospel, and which each regards as his Church and indeed, God's. And yet, almost everyone, though in different ways, longs for the one visible Church of God, a Church truly universal and sent forth to the whole world that the world may be converted to the Gospel and so be saved, to the glory of God.

The sacred Council gladly notes all this. It has already declared its teaching on the Church, and now, moved by a desire for the restoration of unity among all the followers of Christ, it wishes to set before all Catholics guidelines, helps and methods, by which they too can respond to the grace of this divine call.

820 (3) ***Lumen gentium* 8:** see 769 (1).

821 (1) ***Unitatis redintegratio* 6** Every renewal of the Church essentially consists in an increase of fidelity to her own calling. Undoubtedly this explains the dynamism of the movement toward unity.

Christ summons the Church, as she goes her pilgrim way, to that continual reformation of which she always has need, insofar as she is an institution of men here on earth. Consequently, if, in various times and circumstances, there have been deficiencies in moral conduct or in Church discipline, or even in the way that Church teaching has been formulated—to be carefully distinguished from the deposit of faith itself—these should be set right at the opportune moment and in the proper way.

Church renewal therefore has notable ecumenical importance. Already this renewal is taking place in various spheres of the Church's life: the biblical and liturgical movements, the preaching of the Word of God and catechetics, the apostolate of the laity, new forms of religious life and the spirituality of married life, and the Church's social teaching and activity. All these should be considered as promises and guarantees for the future progress of ecumenism.

821 (2) ***Unitatis redintegratio* 9** We must become familiar with the outlook of our separated brethren. Study is absolutely required for this, and it should be pursued in fidelity to the truth and with a spirit of good will. Catholics who already have a proper grounding need to acquire a more adequate understanding of the respective doctrines of our separated brethren, their history, their spiritual and liturgical life, their religious psychology and cultural background. Most valuable for this purpose are meetings of the two sides—especially for discussion of theological problems—where each can treat with the other on an equal footing, provided that those who take part in them under the guidance of the authorities are truly competent. From such dialogue will emerge still more clearly what the situation of the Catholic Church really is. In this way, too, we will better understand the outlook of our separated brethren and more aptly present our own belief.

(3) ***Unitatis redintegratio* 10** Sacred theology and other branches of knowledge, especially those of a historical nature, must be taught with due regard for the ecumenical point of view, so that they may correspond as exactly as possible with the facts. **821**

It is important that future pastors and priests should have mastered a theology that has been carefully elaborated in this way and not polemically, especially in what concerns the relations of separated brethren with the Catholic Church. For it is upon the formation which priests receive that so largely depends the necessary instruction and spiritual formation of the faithful and of religious.

Moreover, Catholics engaged in missionary work in the same territories as other Christians ought to know, particularly in these times, the problems and the benefits which affect their apostolate because of the ecumenical movement.

(4) ***Unitatis redintegratio* 4:** see 94 (3). **821**

(5) ***Unitatis redintegratio* 9:** see 821 (2). **821**

(6) ***Unitatis redintegratio* 11** The manner and order in which Catholic belief is expressed should in no way become an obstacle to dialogue with our brethren. It is, of course, essential that the doctrine be clearly presented in its entirety. Nothing is so foreign to the spirit of ecumenism as a false irenicism which harms the purity of Catholic doctrine and obscures its genuine and certain meaning. **821**

At the same time, Catholic belief must be explained more profoundly and precisely, in such a way and in such terms that our separated brethren can also really understand it.

Furthermore, in ecumenical dialogue, Catholic theologians, standing fast by the teaching of the Church yet searching together with separated brethren into the divine mysteries, should do so with love for the truth, with charity, and with humility. When comparing doctrines with one another, they should remember that in Catholic doctrine there exists an order or "hierarchy" of truths, since they vary in their relation to the foundation of the Christian faith. Thus the way will be opened whereby this kind of "fraternal rivalry" will incite all to a deeper realization and a clearer expression of the unfathomable riches of Christ.

(7) ***Unitatis redintegratio* 12** Before the whole world let all Christians confess their faith in God, one and three, in the incarnate Son of God, our Redeemer and Lord. United in their efforts, and with mutual respect, let them bear witness to our common hope which does not play us false. Since cooperation in social matters is so widespread today, all men without exception are called to work together; with much greater reason is this true of all who believe in God, but most of all, it is especially true of all Christians, since they bear the seal of Christ's name. Cooperation among Christians vividly expresses that bond which already unites them, and it sets in clearer relief the features of Christ the Servant. Such cooperation, which has already begun in many countries, should be developed more and more, particularly in regions where social and technological evolution is taking place. It should contribute to a just appreciation of the dignity of the human person, to the promotion of the blessings of peace, the application of Gospel principles to social life, and the advancement of the arts and sciences in a truly Christian spirit. It should use every possible means to relieve the afflictions of our times, such as famine and natural disasters, illiteracy and poverty, **821**

lack of housing, and the unequal distribution of wealth. Through such cooperation, all believers in Christ are able to learn easily how they can understand each other better and esteem each other more, and how the road to the unity of Christians may be made smooth.

827 (1) ***Unitatis redintegratio* 3:** see 819 (2).

827 (2) ***Unitatis redintegratio* 6:** see 821 (1).

827 (3) **Hebrews 2:17** Therefore he had to be made like his brethren in every respect, so that he might become a merciful and faithful high priest in the service of God, to make expiation for the sins of the people.

827 (4) **Hebrews 7:26** For it was fitting that we should have such a high priest, holy, blameless, unstained, separated from sinners, exalted above the heavens.

827 (5) **2 Corinthians 5:21** For our sake he made him to be sin who knew no sin, so that in him we might become the righteousness of God.

827 (6) **1 John 1:8–10** If we say we have no sin, we deceive ourselves, and the truth is not in us. If we confess our sins, he is faithful and just, and will forgive our sins and cleanse us from all unrighteousness. If we say we have not sinned, we make him a liar, and his word is not in us.

827 (7) **Matthew 13:24–30** Another parable he put before them, saying, "The kingdom of heaven may be compared to a man who sowed good seed in his field; but while men were sleeping, his enemy came and sowed weeds among the wheat, and went away. So when the plants came up and bore grain, then the weeds appeared also. And the servants of the householder came and said to him, 'Sir, did you not sow good seed in your field? How then has it weeds?' He said to them, 'An enemy has done this.' The servants said to him, 'Then do you want us to go and gather them?' But he said, 'No; lest in gathering the weeds you root up the wheat along with them. Let both grow together until the harvest; and at harvest time I will tell the reapers, Gather the weeds first and bind them in bundles to be burned, but gather the wheat into my barn.' "

828 (1) ***Lumen gentium* 40** The Lord Jesus, divine teacher and model of all perfection, preached holiness of life (of which he is the author and maker) to each and every one of his disciples without distinction: "You, therefore, must be perfect, as your heavenly Father is perfect" (Mt. 5:48). For he sent the Holy Spirit to all to move them interiorly to love God with their whole heart, with their whole soul, with their whole understanding, and with their whole strength (cf. Mk. 12:30), and to love one another as Christ loved them (cf. Jn. 13:34; 15:12). The followers of Christ, called by God not in virtue of their works but by his design and grace, and justified in the Lord Jesus, have been made sons of God in the baptism of faith and partakers of the divine nature, and so are truly sanctified. They must therefore hold on to and perfect in their lives that sanctification which they have received from God. They are told by the apostle to live "as is fitting among saints" (Eph. 5:3), and to put on "as God's chosen ones, holy and beloved, compassion, kindness, lowliness, meekness, and patience" (Col. 3:12), to have the fruits of the Spirit for their sanctification (cf. Gal. 5:22; Rom. 6:22). But since we all offend in many ways (cf. Jas. 3:2), we constantly need God's mercy and must pray every day: "And forgive us our debts" (Mt. 6:12).

It is therefore quite clear that all Christians in any state or walk of life are called to the fullness of Christian life and to the perfection of love, and by this holiness a more human manner of life is fostered also in earthly society. In order to reach this perfection the faithful should use the strength dealt out to them by Christ's gift, so that, following in his footsteps and conformed to his image, doing the will of God in everything, they may wholeheartedly devote themselves to the glory of God and to the service of their neighbor. Thus the holiness of the People of God will grow in fruitful abundance, as is clearly shown in the history of the Church through the life of so many saints.

(2) ***Lumen gentium* 48–51** The Church, to which we are all called in Christ Jesus, 828
and in which by the grace of God we acquire holiness, will receive its perfection only in the glory of heaven, when will come the time of the renewal of all things (Acts 3:21). At that time, together with the human race, the universe itself, which is so closely related to man and which attains its destiny through him, will be perfectly reestablished in Christ (cf. Eph. 1:10; Col. 1:20; 2 Pet. 3:10–13).

Christ lifted up from the earth, has drawn all men to himself (cf. Jn. 12:32). Rising from the dead (cf. Rom. 6:9) he sent his life-giving Spirit upon his disciples and through him set up his Body which is the Church as the universal sacrament of salvation. Sitting at the right hand of the Father he is continually active in the world in order to lead men to the Church and, through it, join them more closely to himself; and, by nourishing them with his own Body and Blood, make them partakers of his glorious life. The promised and hoped for restoration, therefore, has already begun in Christ. It is carried forward in the sending of the Holy Spirit and through him continues in the Church, in which through our faith, we learn the meaning of our earthly life, while we bring to term, with hope of future good, the task allotted to us in the world by the Father, and so work out our salvation (cf. Phil. 2:12).

Already the final age of the world is with us (cf. 1 Cor. 10:11) and the renewal of the world is irrevocably under way; it is even now anticipated in a certain real way, for the Church on earth is endowed already with a sanctity that is real though imperfect. However, until there be realized new heavens and a new earth in which justice dwells (cf. 2 Pet. 3:13) the pilgrim Church, in its sacraments and institutions, which belong to this present age, carries the mark of this world which will pass, and she herself takes her place among the creatures which groan and travail yet and await the revelation of the sons of God (cf. Rom. 8:19–22).

So it is, united with Christ in the Church and marked with the Holy Spirit "who is the guarantee of our inheritance" (Eph. 1:14) that we are truly called and indeed are children of God (cf. 1 Jn. 3:1) though we have not yet appeared with Christ in glory (cf. Col. 3:4) in which we will be like to God, for we will see him as he is (cf. 1 Jn. 3:2). "While we are at home in the body we are away from the Lord" (2 Cor. 5:6) and having the first fruits of the Spirit we groan inwardly (cf. Rom. 8:23) and we desire to be with Christ (cf. Phil. 1:23). That same charity urges us to live more for him who died for us and who rose again (cf. 2 Cor. 5:15). We make it our aim, then, to please the Lord in all things (cf. 2 Cor. 5:9) and we put on the armor of God that we may be able to stand against the wiles of the devil and resist in the evil day (cf. Eph. 6:11–13). Since we know neither the day nor the hour, we should follow the advice of the Lord and watch constantly so that, when the single course of our earthly life is completed (cf. Heb. 9:27), we may merit to enter with him into the marriage feast and be numbered among the blessed (cf. Mt. 25:31–46) and not, like the wicked and slothful servants (cf. Mt. 25:26), be ordered to depart into the eternal fire (cf. Mt. 25:41), into the outer darkness where "men will weep and gnash their teeth" (Mt. 22:13 and 25:30). Before we reign with Christ in glory we must all appear "before the judgment seat of Christ, so that each one may receive good or evil, according to what he has done in the body" (2 Cor. 5:10), and at the end of the world "they will come forth, those who have done good, to the resurrection of life, and those who have done evil, to the resurrection of judgment" (Jn. 5:29; cf. Mt. 25:46). We reckon then that "the sufferings of this present time are not worth comparing with the glory that is to be revealed to us" (Rom. 8:18; cf. 2 Tim. 2:11–12), and strong in faith we look for "the blessed hope, the appearing of the glory of our great God and Savior Jesus Christ" (Tit. 2:13) "who will change our lowly body to be like his glorious body" (Phil. 3:21) and who will come "to be glorified in his saints, and to be marvelled at in all who have believed" (2 Th. 1:10).

When the Lord will come in glory, and all his angels with him (cf. Mt. 25:31), death will be no more and all things will be subject to him (cf. 1 Cor. 15:26–27). But at the present time some of his disciples are pilgrims on earth. Others have died and are being purified, while still others are in glory, contemplating "in full light, God himself triune and one, exactly as he is." All of us, however, in varying degrees and in different ways share in the same charity towards God and our neighbors, and we all sing the one hymn of glory to our God. All, indeed, who are of Christ and who have his Spirit form one Church and in Christ cleave together (Eph. 4:16). So it is that the union of the wayfarers with the brethren who sleep in the peace of Christ is in no way interrupted, but on the contrary, according to the constant faith of the Church, this union is reinforced by an exchange of spiritual goods. Being more closely united to Christ, those who dwell in heaven fix the whole Church more firmly in holiness, add to the nobility of the worship that the Church offers to God here on earth, and in many ways help in a broader building up of the Church (cf. 1 Cor. 12:12–27). Once received into their heavenly home and being present to the Lord (cf. 2 Cor. 5:8), through him and with him and in him they do not cease to intercede with the Father for us, as they proffer the merits which they acquired on earth through the one mediator between God and men, Christ Jesus (cf. 1 Tim. 2:5), serving God in all things and completing in their flesh what is lacking in Christ's afflictions for the sake of his Body, that is, the Church (cf. Col. 1:24). So by their brotherly concern is our weakness greatly helped.

In full consciousness of this communion of the whole Mystical Body of Jesus Christ, the Church in its pilgrim members, from the very earliest days of the Christian religion, has honored with great respect the memory of the dead; and, "because it is a holy and a wholesome thought to pray for the dead that they may be loosed from their sins" (2 Mac. 12:46) she offers her suffrages for them. The Church has always believed that the apostles and Christ's martyrs, who gave the supreme witness of faith and charity by the shedding of their blood, are closely united with us in Christ; she has always venerated them, together with the Blessed Virgin Mary and the holy angels, with a special love, and has asked piously for the help of their intercession. Soon there were added to these others who had chosen to imitate more closely the virginity and poverty of Christ, and still others whom the outstanding practice of the Christian virtues and the wonderful graces of God recommended to the pious devotion and imitation of the faithful.

To look on the life of those who have faithfully followed Christ is to be inspired with a new reason for seeking the city which is to come (cf. Heb. 13:14 and 11:10), while at the same time we are taught to know a most safe path by which, despite the vicissitudes of the world, and in keeping with the state of life and condition proper to each of us, we will be able to arrive at perfect union with Christ, that is, holiness. God shows to men, in a vivid way, his presence and his face in the lives of those companions of ours in the human condition who are more perfectly transformed into the image of Christ (cf. 2 Cor. 3:18). He speaks to us in them and offers us a sign of this kingdom, to which we are powerfully attracted, so great a cloud of witnesses is there given (cf. Heb. 12:1) and such a witness to the truth of the Gospel.

It is not merely by the title of example that we cherish the memory of those in heaven; we seek, rather, that by this devotion to the exercise of fraternal charity the union of the whole Church in the Spirit may be strengthened (cf. Eph. 4:1–6). Exactly as Christian communion between men on their earthly pilgrimage brings us closer to Christ, so our community with the saints joins us to Christ, from whom as from its fountain and head issues all grace and the life of the People of God itself. It is most fitting, therefore, that we love those friends and co-heirs of Jesus Christ who are also our brothers and outstanding benefactors, and that we give due thanks to God for them, "humbly invoking them, and having recourse to their prayers, their aid and help in obtaining from God through his Son, Jesus Christ, Our Lord, our only Redeemer and Savior, the benefits we need." Every authentic witness of love, indeed, offered by us to those who are in heaven tends to and terminates in Christ, "the crown of all the saints," and through him in God who is wonderful in his saints and is glorified in them.

It is especially in the sacred liturgy that our union with the heavenly Church is best realized; in the liturgy, through the sacramental signs, the power of the Holy Spirit acts on us, and with community rejoicing we celebrate together the praise of the divine majesty, when all those of every tribe and tongue and people and nation (cf. Apoc. 5:9) who have been redeemed by the blood of Christ and gathered together into one Church glorify, in one common song of praise, the one and triune God. When, then, we celebrate the eucharistic sacrifice we are most closely united to the worship of the heavenly Church; when in the fellowship of communion we honor and remember the glorious Mary ever virgin, St. Joseph, the holy apostles and martyrs and all the saints.

This sacred council accepts loyally the venerable faith of our ancestors in the living communion which exists between us and our brothers who are in the glory of heaven or who are yet being purified after their death; and it proposes again the decrees of the Second Council of Nicea, of the Council of Florence, and of the Council of Trent. At the same time, in keeping with its pastoral preoccupations, this council urges all concerned to remove or correct any abuses, excesses or defects which may have crept in here or there, and so restore all things that Christ and God be more fully praised. Let us teach the faithful, therefore, that the authentic cult of the saints does not consist so much in a multiplicity of external acts, but rather in a more intense practice of our love, whereby, for our own greater good and that of the Church, we seek from the saints "example in their way of life, fellowship in their communion, and the help of their intercession." On the other hand, let the faithful be taught that our communion with these in heaven, provided that it is understood in the full light of faith, in no way diminishes the worship of adoration given to God the Father, through Christ, in the Spirit; on the contrary, it greatly enriches it.

For if we continue to love one another and to join in praising the Most Holy Trinity —all of us who are sons of God and form one family in Christ (cf. Heb. 3:6)—we will be faithful to the deepest vocation of the Church and will share in a foretaste of the liturgy of perfect glory. At the hour when Christ will appear, when the glorious resurrection of the dead will occur, the glory of God will light up the heavenly city, and the Lamb will be its lamp (cf. Apoc. 21:24). Then the whole Church of the saints in the supreme happiness of charity will adore God and "the Lamb who was slain" (cf. Apoc. 5:12), proclaiming with one voice: "To him who sits upon the throne and to the Lamb be blessing and honor and glory and might for ever and ever" (Apoc. 5:13–14).

829 **Ephesians 5:26–27** . . . that he might sanctify her, having cleansed her by the washing of water with the word, that he might present the church to himself in splendor, without spot or wrinkle or any such thing, that she might be holy and without blemish.

830 ***Ad gentes divinitus* 4** To do this, Christ sent the Holy Spirit from the Father to exercise inwardly his saving influence, and to promote the spread of the Church. Without doubt, the Holy Spirit was at work in the world before Christ was glorified. On the day of Pentecost, however, he came down on the disciples that he might remain with them forever (cf. Jn. 14:16); on that day the Church was openly displayed to the crowds and the spread of the Gospel among the nations, through preaching, was begun. Finally, on that day was foreshadowed the union of all peoples in the catholicity of the faith by means of the Church of the New Alliance, a Church which speaks every language, understands and embraces all tongues in charity, and thus overcomes the dispersion of Babel. The "acts of the apostles" began with Pentecost, just as Christ was conceived in the Virgin Mary with the coming of the Holy Spirit and was moved to begin his ministry by the descent of the same Holy Spirit, who came down upon him while he was praying. Before freely laying down his life for the world, the Lord Jesus organized the apostolic ministry and promised to send the Holy Spirit, in such a way that both would be always and everywhere associated in the fulfillment of the work of salvation. Throughout the ages the Holy Spirit makes the entire Church "one in communion and ministry; and provides her with different hierarchical and charismatic gifts," giving life to ecclesiastical structures, being as it were their soul, and inspiring in the hearts of the faithful that same spirit of mission which impelled Christ himself. He even at times visibly anticipates apostolic action, just as in various ways he unceasingly accompanies and directs it.

831 **Matthew 28:19** Go therefore and make disciples of all nations, baptizing them in the name of the Father and of the Son and of the Holy Spirit. . . .

833 (1) ***Christus Dominus* 11** A diocese is a section of the People of God entrusted to a bishop to be guided by him with the assistance of his clergy so that, loyal to its pastor and formed by him into one community in the Holy Spirit through the Gospel and the Eucharist, it constitutes one particular church in which the one, holy, catholic and apostolic Church of Christ is truly present and active.

Individual bishops to whom the care of particular dioceses is committed care for their flocks under the authority of the Supreme Pontiff, in the name of God, as their proper, ordinary and immediate pastors, sanctifying and governing them. They should, however, recognize the rights which are conferred by law on Patriarchs or other hierarchical authorities.

Bishops should devote themselves to their apostolic office as witnesses of Christ to all men. They should not limit themselves to those who already acknowledge the Prince of Pastors but should also devote their energies wholeheartedly to those who have strayed in any way from the path of truth or who have no knowledge of the gospel of Christ and of his saving mercy, so that ultimately all men may walk "in all goodness, justice and truth" (Eph. 5:9).

833 (2) **CIC Canons 368–69**

Can. 368—Particular churches in which and from which exists the one and unique Catholic Church are first of all dioceses; to which unless otherwise evident are likened a territorial prelature, a territorial abbacy, an apostolic vicariate, an apostolic prefecture, and an apostolic administration which has been erected on a stable basis.

Can. 369—A diocese is a portion of the people of God which is entrusted for pastoral care to a bishop with the cooperation of the presbyterate so that, adhering to its pastor and gathered by him in the Holy Spirit through the gospel and the Eucharist, it constitutes a particular church in which the one, holy, catholic and apostolic Church of Christ is truly present and operative.

(1) ***Lumen gentium* 13:** see 761 (2). 834

(2) **Vatican Council I (1870): DS 3057** Therefore, whoever succeeds Peter in this chair, he according to the institution of Christ himself, holds the primacy of Peter over the whole Church. "Therefore the disposition of truth remains, and blessed Peter persevering in the accepted fortitude of the rock does not abandon the guidance of the Church which he has received." For this reason "it has always been necessary because of mightier pre-eminence for every church to come to the Church of Rome, that is those who are the faithful everywhere," so that in this See, from which the laws of "venerable communion" emanate over all, they as members associated in one head, coalesce into one bodily structure. 834

***Unitatis redintegratio* 13–18** We now turn our attention to the two principal types of division which affect the seamless robe of Christ. 838

The first divisions occurred in the East, either because of the dispute over the dogmatic formulae of the Councils of Ephesus and Chalcedon, or later by the dissolving of ecclesiastical communion between the Eastern Patriarchates and the Roman See.

Still other divisions arose in the West more than four centuries later. These stemmed from the events which are commonly referred to as the Reformation. As a result, many communions, national or confessional, were separated from the Roman See. Among those in which Catholic traditions and institutions in part continue to exist, the Anglican communion occupies a special place.

These various divisions, however, differ greatly from one another not only by reason of their origin, place and time, but still more by reason of the nature and seriousness of questions concerning faith and Church order. Therefore, without minimizing the differences between the various Christian bodies, and without overlooking the bonds which continue to exist among them in spite of the division, the Council has decided to propose the following considerations for prudent ecumenical action.

For many centuries the Churches of the East and of the West went their own ways, though a brotherly communion of faith and sacramental life bound them together. If disagreements in faith and discipline arose among them, the Roman See acted by common consent as moderator.

This Council gladly reminds everyone of one highly significant fact among others: in the East there flourish many particular local Churches; among them the Patriarchal Churches hold first place, and of them many glory in taking their origins from the apostles themselves. Hence, of primary concern and care among the Orientals has been, and still is, the preservation in a communion of faith and charity of those family ties which ought to exist between local Churches, as between sisters.

From their very origins the Churches of the East have had a treasury from which the Church of the West has drawn largely for its liturgy, spiritual tradition and jurisprudence. Nor must we underestimate the fact that the basic dogmas of the Christian faith concerning the Trinity and the Word of God made flesh from the Virgin Mary were defined in Ecumenical Councils held in the East. To preserve this faith, these Churches have suffered, and still suffer much.

However, the heritage handed down by the apostles was received differently and in different forms, so that from the very beginnings of the Church its development varied from region to region and also because of differing mentalities and ways of life. These reasons, plus external causes, as well as the lack of charity and mutual understanding, left the way open to divisions.

For this reason the Council urges all, but especially those who commit themselves to the work for the restoration of the full communion that is desired between the Eastern Churches and the Catholic Church, to give due consideration to this special feature of the origin and growth of the Churches of the East, and to the character of the relations which obtained between them and the Roman See before the separation, and to form for themselves a correct evaluation of these facts. The careful observation of this will greatly contribute to the dialogue in view.

Everyone knows with what love the Eastern Christians celebrate the sacred liturgy, especially the eucharistic mystery, source of the Church's life and pledge of future glory. In this mystery the faithful, united with their bishops, have access to God the Father through the Son, the Word made flesh who suffered and was glorified, in the outpouring of the Holy Spirit. And so, made "sharers of the divine nature" (2 Pet. 1:4), they enter into communion with the most holy Trinity. Hence, through the celebration of the Eucharist of the Lord in each of these Churches, the Church of God is built up and grows in stature, and through concelebration, their communion with one another is made manifest.

In this liturgical worship, the Eastern Christians pay high tribute, in beautiful hymns of praise, to Mary ever Virgin, whom the ecumenical Synod of Ephesus solemnly proclaimed to be the holy Mother of God in order that Christ might by truly and properly acknowledged as Son of God and Son of Man, according to the scriptures. They also give homage to the saints, among them the Fathers of the universal Church.

These Churches, although separated from us, yet possess true sacraments, above all —by apostolic succession—the priesthood and the Eucharist, whereby they are still joined to us in closest intimacy. Therefore some worship in common (*communicatio in sacris*), given suitable circumstances and the approval of Church authority, is not merely possible but is encouraged.

Moreover, in the East are to be found the riches of those spiritual traditions which are given expression in monastic life especially. From the glorious times of the holy Fathers, that monastic spirituality flourished in the East which later flowed over into the Western world, and there provided a source from which Latin monastic life took its rise and has often drawn fresh vigor ever since. Therefore, it is earnestly recommended that Catholics avail themselves more often of the spiritual riches of the Eastern Fathers which lift up the whole man to the contemplation of divine mysteries.

Everyone should realize that it is of supreme importance to understand, venerate, preserve and foster the rich liturgical and spiritual heritage of the Eastern Churches in order faithfully to preserve the fullness of Christian tradition, and to bring about reconciliation between Eastern and Western Christians.

From the earliest times the Churches of the East followed their own disciplines, sanctioned by the holy Fathers, by Synods, and even by Ecumenical Councils. Far from being an obstacle to the Church's unity, such diversity of customs and observances only adds to her beauty and contributes greatly to carrying out her mission, as has already been stated. To remove all shadow of doubt, then, this holy Synod solemnly declares that the Churches of the East, while keeping in mind the necessary unity of the whole Church, have the power to govern themselves according to their own disciplines, since these are better suited to the character of their faithful and better adapted to foster the good of souls. The perfect observance of this traditional principle—which indeed has not always been observed—is a prerequisite for any restoration of union.

What has already been said about legitimate variety we are pleased to apply to differences in theological expressions of doctrine. In the study of revealed truth East and West have used different methods and approaches in understanding and confessing divine things. It is hardly surprising, then, if sometimes one tradition has come nearer to a full appreciation of some aspects of a mystery of revelation than the other, or has expressed them better. In such cases, these various theological formulations are often to be considered complementary rather than conflicting. With regard to the authentic theological traditions of the Orientals, we must recognize that they are admirably rooted in Holy Scripture, are fostered and given expression in liturgical life, are nourished by the living tradition of the apostles and by the works of the Fathers and spiritual writers of the East; they are directed toward a right ordering of life, indeed, toward a full contemplation of Christian truth.

This sacred Council thanks God that many Eastern children of the Catholic Church preserve this heritage and wish to express it more faithfully and completely in their lives, and are already living in full communion with their brethren who follow the tradition of the West. But it declares that this entire heritage of spirituality and liturgy, of discipline and theology, in various traditions, belongs to the full catholic and apostolic character of the Church.

After taking all these factors into consideration, this sacred Council confirms what previous Councils and Roman Pontiffs have proclaimed: in order to restore communion and unity or preserve them, one must "impose no burden beyond what is indispensable" (Acts 15:28). It is the Council's urgent desire that every effort should be made toward the gradual realization of this unity in the various organizations and living activities of the Church, especially by prayer and by fraternal dialogue on points of doctrine and the more pressing pastoral problems of our time. Similarly, to the pastors and faithful of the Catholic Church, it commends close relations with those no longer living in the East but far from their homeland, so that friendly collaboration with them may increase in a spirit of love, without bickering or rivalry. If this task is carried on wholeheartedly, the Council hopes that with the removal of the wall dividing the Eastern and Western Church at last there may be but one dwelling, firmly established on the cornerstone, Christ Jesus, who will make both one.

***Nostra aetate* 4** Sounding the depths of the mystery which is the Church, this sacred 839
Council remembers the spiritual ties which link the people of the New Covenant to the stock of Abraham.

The Church of Christ acknowledges that in God's plan of salvation the beginning of her faith and election is to be found in the patriarchs, Moses and the prophets. She professes that all Christ's faithful, who as men of faith are sons of Abraham (cf. Gal. 3:7), are included in the same patriarch's call and that the salvation of the Church is mystically prefigured in the exodus of God's chosen people from the land of bondage. On this account the Church cannot forget that she received the revelation of the Old Testament by way of that people with whom God in his inexpressible mercy established the ancient covenant. Nor can she forget that she draws nourishment from that good olive tree onto which the wild olive branches of the Gentiles have been grafted (cf. Rom. 11:17–24). The Church believes that Christ who is our peace has through his cross reconciled Jews and Gentiles and made them one in himself (cf. Eph. 2:14–16).

Likewise, the Church keeps ever before her mind the words of the apostle Paul about his kinsmen: "they are Israelites, and to them belong the sonship, the glory, the covenants, the giving of the law, the worship, and the promises; to them belong the patriarchs, and of their race according to the flesh, is the Christ" (Rom. 9:4–5), the son of the Virgin Mary. She is mindful, moreover, that the apostles, the pillars on which the Church stands, are of Jewish descent, as are many of those early disciples who proclaimed the Gospel of Christ to the world.

As holy Scripture testifies, Jerusalem did not recognize God's moment when it came (cf. Lk. 19:42). Jews for the most part did not accept the Gospel; on the contrary, many opposed the spreading of it (cf. Rom. 11:28). Even so, the apostle Paul maintains that the Jews remain very dear to God, for the sake of the patriarchs, since God does not take back the gifts he bestowed or the choice he made. Together with the prophets and that same apostle, the Church awaits the day, known to God alone, when all peoples will call on God with one voice and "serve him shoulder to shoulder" (Soph. 3:9; cf. Is. 66:23; Ps. 65:4; Rom. 11:11–32).

Since Christians and Jews have such a common spiritual heritage, this sacred Council wishes to encourage and further mutual understanding and appreciation. This can be obtained, especially, by way of biblical and theological enquiry and through friendly discussions.

Even though the Jewish authorities and those who followed their lead pressed for the death of Christ (cf. John 19:6), neither all Jews indiscriminately at that time, nor Jews today, can be charged with the crimes committed during his passion. It is true that the Church is the new people of God, yet the Jews should not be spoken of as rejected or accursed as if this followed from holy Scripture. Consequently, all must take care, lest in catechizing or in preaching the Word of God, they teach anything which is not in accord with the truth of the Gospel message or the spirit of Christ.

Indeed, the Church reproves every form of persecution against whomsoever it may be directed. Remembering, then, her common heritage with the Jews and moved not by any political consideration, but solely by the religious motivation of Christian charity, she deplores all hatreds, persecutions, displays of antisemitism leveled at any time or from any source against the Jews.

The Church always held and continues to hold that Christ out of infinite love freely underwent suffering and death because of the sins of all men, so that all might attain salvation. It is the duty of the Church, therefore, in her preaching to proclaim the cross of Christ as the sign of God's universal love and the source of all grace.

841 ***Nostra aetate* 3** The Church has also a high regard for the Muslims. They worship God, who is one, living and subsistent, merciful and almighty, the Creator of heaven and earth, who has also spoken to men. They strive to submit themselves without reserve to the hidden decrees of God, just as Abraham submitted himself to God's plan, to whose faith Muslims eagerly link their own. Although not acknowledging him as God, they venerate Jesus as a prophet, his virgin Mother they also honor, and even at times devoutly invoke. Further, they await the day of judgment and the reward of God following the resurrection of the dead. For this reason they highly esteem an upright life and worship God, especially by way of prayer, alms-deeds and fasting.

Over the century many quarrels and dissensions have arisen between Christians and Muslims. The sacred Council now pleads with all to forget the past, and urges that a sincere effort be made to achieve mutual understanding; for the benefit of all men, let them together preserve and promote peace, liberty, social justice and moral values.

843 (1) ***Nostra aetate* 2:** see 282.

843 (2) ***Evangelii nuntiandi* 53** This proclamation is relevant also for immense sections of the human race who profess non-Christian religions in which the spiritual life of innumerable human communities finds valid expression. In these we hear re-echoed,

as it were, the voices of those who for a thousand years have sought God in a manner which, while imperfect, has always been sincere and upright. These religions, possessing as they do, a splendid patrimony of religious writings, have taught generations of men how to pray. They are adorned by innumerable 'seeds of the Word' and therefore truly constitute a genuine 'preparation for the gospel', to adopt the excellent expression of the second Vatican council inspired by the work of Eusebius of Caesarea. But this consideration gives rise to many very complex questions which call for the greatest prudence. Theologians have still to study these important and difficult questions in the light of Christian tradition and the magisterium of the church so that new paths may be opened to missionaries both now and in the future which they may follow in their approach to non-Christian religions.

Neither our respect for these religions nor the high esteem in which we hold them nor the complexity of the questions involved should deter the church from proclaiming the message of Jesus Christ to these non-Christians. On the contrary she holds that these multitudes of men have the right to know the riches of the mystery of Christ. It is in these, we believe, that the whole human family can find in the most comprehensive form and beyond all their expectations everything for which they have been groping, as it were, about God, about man and his ultimate destiny, about life and death and about truth itself. Accordingly, even in the face of the most admirable forms of natural religion, the church judges that it is her special function, by virtue of the religion of Jesus Christ which she proclaims in her evangelization, to bring men into contact with God's plan, with his living presence, with his solicitude. In this way she presents to men the mystery of the divine paternity which extends to the human race; in other words, by virtue of our religion a true and living relationship with God is established which other religions cannot achieve even though they seem, as it were, to have their arms raised up towards heaven. The church therefore seeks to foster and maintain her missionary zeal: it is, in fact, her aim to increase it in these present times. She feels bound by a duty to all peoples in the discharge of which she will spare no pains in her efforts to spread the good news of Jesus Our Savior. She is constantly training new generations of missionaries for this purpose. This is a fact to which we are glad to advert in these days when there are some who think and say that all eagerness and zeal for the apostolate is extinguished and that the age of missionary work is past. In reply to this assertion the synod of bishops has declared that the missionary proclamation has lost none of its vigor and that the church will always strive to fulfil its function in this regard.

1 Peter 3:20–21 . . . who formerly did not obey, when God's patience waited in the days of Noah, during the building of the ark, in which a few, that is, eight persons, were saved through water. Baptism, which corresponds to this, now saves you, not as a removal of dirt from the body but as an appeal to God for a clear conscience, through the resurrection of Jesus Christ. . . . **845**

(1) **St. Cyprian, Epistle 73, 21** Can the power of baptism, I ask, be greater or stronger than the confession and suffering of a man who confesses Christ before men and is baptized in his own blood? Yet, not even this sort of baptism can benefit the heretic who, though he has confessed Christ, is put to death outside the Church. Otherwise one would have to suppose that the supporters and spokesmen of the heretics successfully proclaim them martyrs when they are killed for a confession of Christ that is false, and that they assign to them the crown and glory for a martyr's sufferings despite the explicit testimony of the Apostle that even if they are burnt and put to death it will profit them nothing. **846**

If, then, not even the baptism of blood and of public confession will profit the heretic for salvation—for there is no salvation outside the Church—how much more must this be so if in some lair, in some den of thieves, a man is bathed in polluted and spurious water, and so far from putting off his old sins, he loads himself with yet more fresh and graver ones.

Baptism, we conclude, cannot be common to us and to heretics, for we have in common with them neither God the Father nor Christ the Son nor the Holy Spirit nor faith nor Church itself. It is essential, therefore, that when they come from heresy to the Church, they should be baptized; if they are to be made ready for the kingdom of God by divine regeneration in the one, genuine, and lawful baptism of the holy Church, they must be born of both sacraments. As it is written: *Unless a man is born of water and the Spirit, he cannot enter the kingdom of God.*

846 (2) **St. Cyprian, *De Unitatis***

The Unity of the Catholic Church

1. Since the Lord warns us in these words: 'Ye are the salt of the earth,' and since He bids us to be simple unto harmlessness, and yet to be prudent with our simplicity, what else, most beloved brethren, befits us than to have foresight and watching with an anxious heart alike to perceive the snares of the crafty enemy and to beware lest we, who have put on Christ the wisdom of God the Father, seem to be less wise in guarding our salvation. For persecution alone is not to be feared, nor the advances which are made in open attack to overwhelm and cast down the servants of God. To be cautious is easier when the object of fear is manifest, and the soul is prepared for the contest beforehand, when the adversary declares himself. The enemy is more to be feared and guarded against when he creeps up secretly, when deceiving us under the appearance of peace he steals forward by hidden approaches, from which too he receives the name of serpent (creeper, crawler, stealer). This is always his cunning; this is his blind and dark deceit for circumventing men. Thus from the very beginning of the world did he deceive and, flattering with lying words, mislead the inexperienced soul with its reckless incredulity. Thus trying to tempt the Lord himself, as if he would creep up again and deceive, he approaches secretly. Yet he was understood and driven back and so cast down, because he was discovered and unmasked.

2. In this an example has been given us to flee the way of the old man; to walk in the footsteps of the conquering Christ, that we may not heedlessly be turned back again unto the snare of death, but that, on guard against the danger, we may receive and possess immortality. But how can we possess immortality, unless we keep those commandments of Christ by which death is overcome and conquered, He Himself warning us in these words: 'If thou wilt enter into life, keep the commandments,' and again: 'If you do what I command you, I no longer call you servant but friends.' These, finally, He calls strong and steadfast, these grounded upon a rock of firm foundation, these firmly established against all the tempests and storms of the world with an unmoveable and unshaken firmness. 'He who hears my words,' He says, 'and does them, I shall liken him to a wise man who built his house upon a rock. The rain descended and the floods came, the winds blew and beat upon that house, but it did not fall, for it was founded upon a rock.' Therefore, we ought to stand firm upon His words, and to learn and do whatever He taught and did. But how does he say that he believes in Christ who does not do what Christ ordered him to do? Or, whence shall he attain the reward of faith, who does not keep the faith of the commandment? He will necessarily waver and wander, and caught up by the breath of error will be blown as the dust which the wind stirs up, nor will he make any advance in his walk toward salvation, who does not hold to the truth of the saving way.

3. But not only must we guard against things which are open and manifest but also against those which deceive with the subtlety of clever fraud. Now what is more clever, or what more subtle than that the enemy, detected and cast down by the coming of Christ, after light had come to the Gentiles, and the saving splendor had shone forth for the preservation of man, that the deaf might receive the hearing of spiritual grace, the blind open their eyes to the Lord, the weak grow strong with eternal health, the lame run to the church, the dumb supplicate with clear voices and prayers, seeing the idols abandoned and his shrines and temples deserted because of the great populace of believers, devise a new fraud, under the very title of Christian name to deceive the incautious? He invented heresies and schisms with which to overthrow the faith, to corrupt the truth, to divide unity. Those whom he cannot hold in the blindness of the old way, he circumvents and deceives by the error of a new way. He snatches men from the Church itself, and, while they seem to themselves to have already approached the light and to have escaped the night of the world, he again pours forth other shadows upon the unsuspecting, so that, although they do not stand with the Gospel of Christ and with the observation of Him and with the law, they call themselves Christians, and, although they walk in darkness, they think that they have light, while the adversary cajoles and deceives, who, as the Apostle says, transforms himself into an angel of light, and adorns his ministers as those of justice who offer night for day, death for salvation, despair under the offer of hope, perfidy under the pretext of faith, antichrist under the name of Christ, so that while they tell plausible lies, they frustrate the truth by their subtlety. This happens, most beloved brethren, because there is no return to the source of truth, and the Head is not sought, and the doctrine of the heavenly Master is not kept.

4. If anyone considers and examines these things, there is no need of a lengthy discussion and arguments. Proof for faith is easy in a brief statement of the truth. The Lord speaks to Peter: 'I say to thee,' He says, 'thou art Peter, and upon this rock I will build my church, and the gates of hell shall not prevail against it. And I will give thee the keys of the kingdom of heaven; and whatever thou shalt bind on earth shall be bound also in heaven, and whatever thou shalt loose on earth shall be loosed also in heaven.' Upon him, being one, He builds His Church, and although after His resurrection He bestows equal power upon all the Apostles, and says: 'As the Father has sent me, I also send you. Receive ye the Holy Spirit: if you forgive the sins of anyone, they will be forgiven him; if you retain the sins of anyone, they will be retained,' yet that He might display unity, He established by His authority the origin of the same unity as beginning from one. Surely the rest of the Apostles also were that which Peter was, endowed with an equal partnership of office and of power, but the beginning proceeds from unity, that the Church of Christ may be shown to be one. This one Church, also, the Holy Spirit in the Canticle of Canticles designates in the person of the Lord and says: 'One is my dove, my perfect one is but one, she is the only one of her mother, the chosen one of her that bore her.' Does he who does not hold this unity think that he holds the faith? Does he who strives against the Church and resists her think that he is in the Church, when too the blessed Apostle Paul teaches this same thing and sets forth the sacrament of unity saying: 'One body and one Spirit, one hope of your calling, one Lord, one faith, one baptism, one God'?

5. This unity we ought to hold firmly and defend, especially we bishops who watch over the Church, that we may prove that also the episcopate itself is one and undivided. Let no one deceive the brotherhood by lying; let no one corrupt the faith by a perfidious prevarication of the truth. The episcopate is one, the parts of which are held together by the individual bishops. The Church is one which with increasing fecundity extend far and wide into the multitude, just as the rays of the sun are

many but the light is one, and the branches of the tree are many but the strength is one founded in its tenacious root, and, when many streams flow from one source, although a multiplicity of waters seems to have been diffused from the abundance of the overflowing supply nevertheless unity is preserved in their origin. Take away a ray of light from the body of the sun, its unity does not take on any division of its light; break a branch from a tree, the branch thus broken will not be able to bud; cut off a stream from its source, the stream thus cut off dries up. Thus too the Church bathed in the light of the Lord projects its rays over the whole world, yet there is one light which is diffused everywhere, and the unity of the body is not separated. She extends her branches over the whole earth in fruitful abundance; she extends her richly flowing streams far and wide; yet her head is one, and her source is one, and she is the one mother copious in the results of her fruitfulness. By her womb we are born; by her milk we are nourished; by her spirit we are animated.

6. The spouse of Christ cannot be defiled; she is uncorrupted and chaste. She knows one home, with chase modesty she guards the sanctity of one couch. She keeps us for God; she assigns the children whom she has created to the kingdom. Whoever is separated from the Church and is joined with an adulteress is separated from the promises of the Church, nor will he who has abandoned the Church arrive at the rewards of Christ. He is a stranger; he is profane; he is an enemy. He cannot have God as a father who does not have the Church as a mother. If whoever was outside the ark of Noe was able to escape, he too who is outside the Church escapes. The Lord warns, saying: 'He who is not with me is against me, and who does not gather with me, scatters.' He who breaks the peace and concord of Christ acts against Christ; he who gathers somewhere outside the Church scatters the Church of Christ. The Lord says: 'I and the Father are one.' And again of the Father and Son and the Holy Spirit it is written: 'And these three are one.' Does anyone believe that this unity which comes from divine strength, which is closely connected with the divine sacraments, can be broken asunder in the Church and be separated by the divisions of colliding wills? He who does not hold this unity, does not hold the law of God, does not hold the faith of the Father and the Son, does not hold life and salvation.

7. This sacrament of unity, this bond of concord inseparably connected is shown, when in the Gospel the tunic of the Lord Jesus Christ is not at all divided and is not torn, but by those who cast lots for the garment of Christ, who rather might have put on Christ, a sound garment is received, and an undamaged and undivided tunic is possessed. Divine Scripture speaks and says: 'Now of the tunic, since it was woven throughout from the upper part without seam, they said to one another: "Let us not tear it, but let us cast lots for it, whose it shall be."' He bore the unity that came down from the upper part, that is, that came down from heaven and the Father, which could not all be torn by him who received and possessed it, but he obtained it whole once for all and a firmness inseparably solid. He cannot possess the garment of Christ who tears and divides the Church of Christ. Then on the other hand when at the death of Solomon his kingdom and people were torn asunder, Ahias the prophet met King Jeroboam in the field and tore his garment into twelve pieces, saying: 'Take to thee ten pieces, for thus saith the Lord: "Behold I rend the kingdom out of the hand of Solomon, and will give thee ten sceptres, but two sceptres shall remain to him for the sake of my servant David and for the sake of Jerusalem the city which I have chosen, that I may place my name there."' When the twelve tribes of Israel were torn asunder, the prophet Ahias rent his garment. But because the people of Christ cannot be torn asunder, His tunic woven and united throughout was not divided by those who possessed it. Undivided, joined, connected it shows the coherent concord of us who have put on Christ. By the sacrament and sign of His garment, He has declared the unity of the Church.

8. Who then is so profane and lacking in faith, who so insane by the fury of discord as either to believe that the unity of God, the garment of the Lord, the Church of Christ, can be torn asunder or to dare to do so? He Himself warns us in His Gospel, and teaches saying: 'And there shall be one flock and one shepherd.' And does anyone think that there can be either many shepherds or many flocks in one place? Likewise the Apostle Paul insinuating this same unity upon us beseeches and urges us in these words: 'I beseech you, brethren,' he says, 'by the name of our Lord Jesus Christ, that you all say the same thing, and that there be no dissensions among you: but that you be perfectly united in the same mind and in the same judgment.' And again he says: 'Bearing with one another in love, careful to preserve the unity of the Spirit, in the bond of peace.' Do you think that you can stand and live, withdrawing from the Church, and building for yourself other abodes and different dwellings, when it was said to Rhaab, in whom the Church was prefigured: 'You shall gather your father and your mother and your brethren and the entire house of your father to your own self in your house, and it will be that everyone who goes out of the door of your house shall be his own accuser'; likewise, when the sacrament of the Passover contains nothing else in the law of the Exodus than that the lamb which is slain in the figure of Christ be eaten in one house? God speaks, saying: 'In one house it shall be eaten, you shall not carry the flesh outside of the house.' The flesh of Christ and the holy of the Lord cannot be carried outside, and there is no other house for believers except the one Church. This house, this hospice of unanimity the Holy Spirit designates and proclaims, when He says: 'God who makes those of one mind to dwell in his house.' In the house of God, in the Church of Christ, those of one mind dwell; they persevere in concord and simplicity.

9. So the Holy Spirit came in a dove. It is a simple and happy animal, not bitter with gall, not cruel with its bites, not violent with lacerating claws; it loves the hospitalities of men; when they give birth they bring forth their offspring together; when they go and come they cling together; they spend their lives in mutual intercourse; they recognize the concord of peace by the kiss of the beak; they fulfill the law of unanimity in all things. This is the simplicity which ought to be known in the Church; this the charity to be attained, that the love of the brethren imitate the doves, that their gentleness and tenderness equal that of the lambs and the sheep. What is the savagery of wolves doing in the breast of a Christian, and the madness of dogs and the lethal poison of snakes and the bloody cruelties of beasts? Congratulations are due, when such as these are separated from the Church, lest they prey upon the doves and sheep with their cruel and venemous contagion. Bitterness cannot cling and join with sweetness, darkness with light, rains with clear water, fighting with peace, sterility with fecundity, drought with running waters, storm with calm. Let no one think that the good can depart from the Church; the wind does not ravage the wheat, nor does the storm overturn the tree strongly and solidly rooted; the light straws are tossed about by the tempest; the feeble trees are thrown down by the onrush of the whirlwind. The Apostle Paul execrates and strikes at these, when he says: 'They have gone forth from us, but they were not of us. For if they had been of us, they would have continued with us.'

10. Hence heresies have both frequently arisen and are arising, while the perverse mind has no peace, while discordant perfidy does not maintain unity. Indeed the Lord permits and suffers these things to happen, while the choice of one's own liberty remains, so that, while the norm of truth examines our hearts and minds, the sound faith of those who are approved may become manifest in a clear light. Through the Apostle the Holy Spirit forewarns and says: 'For there must be factions, so that those who are approved among you may be made manifest.' Thus the faithful are approved; thus the perfidious are disclosed; thus also before the day of judgment, already here

too the souls of the just and the unjust are divided and the chaff is separated from the wheat. From these are those who of their own accord set themselves over daring strangers without divine appointment, who establish themselves as prelates without any law of ordination, who assume the name of bishop for themselves, although no one gives them the episcopacy; whom the Holy Spirit in the psalms designates as sitting in the chair of pestilence, the plague and disease of the faith, deceiving with a serpent's tongue and masters in corrupting truth, vomiting lethal poisons from their pestilential tongues, whose speech creeps about like cancer, whose discussions inject a deadly virus within the breast and heart of everyone.

11. Against such people the Lord cries out; from these He restrains and recalls His wandering people saying: 'Hearken not to the words of false prophets, since the visions of their hearts frustrate them. They speak, but not from the mouth of the Lord. They say to them who reject the word of God: Peace shall be to you and to all who walk in their own desires. To everyone who walks in the errors of his own heart [they say]: "Evil shall not come upon you." I have not spoken to them, yet they have prophesied. If they had stood in my counsel and had heard my words, and if they had taught my people, I would have turned them from their evil thoughts.' These same people does the Lord again designate and point out, when He says: 'They have abandoned me to the fountain of living water, and have dug for themselves broken cisterns which cannot hold water.' Although there cannot be another baptism than the one, they think that they baptize; although the fountain of life has been deserted, they promise the grace of the life-giving and saving water. There men are not washed but rather are made foul, nor are their sins purged but on the contrary piled high. That nativity generates sons not for God but for the devil. Being born through a lie they do not obtain the promises of truth; begotten of perfidy they lose the grace of faith. They cannot arrive at the reward of peace who have broken the peace of the Lord by the madness of discord.

12. Let not certain ones deceive themselves by an empty interpretation of what the Lord has said: 'Whenever two or three have gathered together in my name, I am with them.' Corrupters and false interpreters of the Gospel quote the last words and pass over earlier ones, being mindful of part and craftily suppressing part. As they themselves have been cut off from the Church, so they cut off a sentence of one chapter. For when the Lord urged unanimity and peace upon His disciples, He said: 'I say to you that if two of you agree upon earth concerning anything whatsoever that you shall ask, it shall be granted you by my Father who is in heaven. For wherever two or three have gathered together in my name, I am with them,' showing that the most is granted not to the multitude but to the unanimity of those that pray. 'If two of you,' He says, 'agree upon earth'; He placed unanimity first; He set the concord of peace first; He taught that we should agree faithfully and firmly. But how can he agree with anyone, who does not agree with the body of the Church herself and with the universal brotherhood? How can two or three be gathered in the name of Christ, who it is clear are separated from Christ and His gospel? For we did not withdraw from them, but they from us, and when thereafter heresies and schisms arose, while they were establishing diverse meeting places for themselves, they abandoned the source and origin of truth. The Lord, moreover, is speaking of His Church, and He is speaking to those who are in the Church, that if they are in agreement, if, according to what He has commanded and admonished, although two or three are gathered together, they pray with unanimity, although they are two or three, they can obtain from the majesty of God, what they demand. 'Wherever two or three have gathered, I,' He said, 'am with them,' namely, with the simple and the peaceful, with those who fear God and keep the commandments of God. He said that He was with these although two or three, just as also He was with the three children in the fiery furnace,

and, because they remained simple toward God and in unanimity among themselves, He animated them in the midst of flames with the breath of dew; just as he was present with the two apostles shut up in prison, because they were simple, because they were of one mind, He opened the doors of the prison and returned them again to the market-place that they might pass on the word to the multitude which they were faithfully preaching. When then He lays it down in His commandments and says: 'Where there are two or three, I am with them,' He who established and made the Church did not separate men from the Church, but rebuking the faithless for their discord and commanding peace to the faithful by His word, He shows that He is with two or three who pray with one mind rather than with a great many who are in disagreement, and that more can be obtained by the harmonious prayer of a few than by the discordant supplication of many.

13. So too when He gave the law of prayer, He added, saying: 'And when you stand up to pray, forgive whatever you have against anyone, that your Father also who is in heaven may forgive you your offenses.' And He calls back from the altar one who comes to the sacrifice with dissension, and He orders Him first to be reconciled with his brother and then return with peace and offer his gift to God, because God did not look with favor upon the gifts of Cain; for he could not have God at peace with him, who through envious discord did not have peace with his brother. What peace then do the enemies of the brethren promise themselves? What sacrifices do the imitators of priests believe that they celebrate? Do they who are gathered together outside the Church of Christ think that Christ is with them when they have been gathered together?

14. Even if such men are slain in confession of the Name that stain is not washed away by blood; the inexpiable and serious fault of discord is purged not even by martyrdom. He cannot be a martyr who is not in the Church. He will not be able to arrive in the kingdom who deserted her who is to rule. Christ gave us peace; He ordered us to be in agreement and of one mind; He commanded us to keep the bonds of love and charity uncorrupted and inviolate. He cannot display himself a martyr who has not maintained fraternal charity. The Apostle Paul teaches and bears witness to this when he says: 'If I have faith so that I remove mountains, but not so that I have charity, I am nothing; and if I distribute all my goods for food, and if I hand over my body so that I am burned, but not so that I have charity, I accomplish nothing. Charity is noble, charity is kind, charity envieth not, is not puffed up, is not provoked; does not act perversely, thinks no evil, loves all things, believes all things, hopes all things, bears all things. Charity never will fall away.' 'Never,' he says, 'will charity fall away.' For she will always be in the kingdom and will endure forever in the unity of the brotherhood clinging to it. Discord cannot come to the kingdom of heaven; to the rewards of Christ who said: 'This is my commandment that you love one another, even as I have loved you.' He will not be able to attain it who has violated the love of Christ by perfidious dissension. He who does not have charity does not have God. The words of the blessed Apostle John are: 'God,' he says, 'is love, and he who abides in love, abides in God and God abides in him.' They cannot abide with God who have been unwilling to be of one mind in God's Church. Although they burn when given over to flames and fire, or lay down their lives when thrown to the beasts, that crown of faith will not be theirs, but the punishment of perfidy, and no glorious ending of religious valor but the destruction of desperation. Such a man can be slain; he cannot be crowned. Thus he professes himself to be a Christian, just as the devil often falsely declares himself to be even Christ, although the Lord forewarned of this saying: 'Many will come in my name saying: "I am the Christ," and will deceive many.' Just as He is not Christ, although he deceives in His name, so he cannot seem a Christian who does not abide in His Gospel and in the true faith.

15. For both to prophesy and to drive out demons, and to perform great miracles on earth is certainly a sublime and admirable thing, yet whoever is found in all this does not attain the kingdom of heaven unless he walk in the observance of the right and just way. The Lord gives warning and says: 'Many will say to me in that day: "Lord, Lord, have we not prophesied in Thy name and cast out devils in thy name and worked great miracles in thy name?" And then I will say to them: "I never knew you. Depart from me ye workers of iniquity."' There is need of righteousness that one may deserve well of God as judge; His precepts and admonitions must be obeyed that our merits may receive their reward. The Lord in the Gospel, when he was directing the way of our hope and faith, in a brief summary said: 'The Lord thy God is one Lord,' and 'Thou shalt love the Lord thy God with thy whole heart, and with thy whole soul and with thy whole strength. This is the first, and the second is like unto it: Thou shalt love thy neighbor as thyself. On these two commandments depend the whole law and the prophets.' He taught at the same time unity and love by the authority of His teaching; He included all the prophets and the law in two commandments. But what unity does he preserve, what love does he guard or consider, who mad with the fury of discord splits the Church, destroys the faith, disturbs the peace, dissipates charity, profanes the sacrament?

16. This evil, most faithful brethren, began long ago, but now the dangerous destruction of the same evil has increased, and the venemous plague of heretical perversity and schisms has begun to rise and to spread more, because even so it was to be at the decline of the world, for the Holy Spirit proclaimed it to us and forewarned us through the Apostle: 'In the last days,' he says, 'dangerous times will come, men will be lovers of self, haughty, proud, covetous, blasphemous, disobedient to parents, ungrateful, impious, without affection, without law, slanderers, incontinent, merciless, not loving the good, treacherous, stubborn, puffed up with pride, loving pleasure more than God, having a semblance of piety, but denying its power. Of such are they who make their way into houses and captivate silly women who are sin-laden and led away by various lusts; ever learning, yet never attaining knowledge of the truth. Just as Jannes and Mambres resisted Moses, so these resist the truth. But they will make no further progress, for their folly will be obvious to all, as was that of those others.' Whatever things were foretold are being fulfilled and, as the end of the world now approaches, have come with the testing of men and the times alike. More and more, as the adversary raves, error deceives, stupidity raises its head, envy inflames, covetousness blinds, impiety depraves, pride puffs up, discord exasperates, anger rushes headlong.

17. Yet let not the extreme and precipitous perfidy of many move or disturb us, but rather let it strengthen our faith by the truth of things foretold. As certain ones begin to be such, because these things were predicted beforehand, thus let other brethren beware of matters of a similar sort, because these also were predicted, as the Lord instructed us saying: 'Be on your guard therefore; behold I have told you all things beforehand.' I beseech you, avoid men of this sort, and ward off from your side and from your hearing their pernicious conversation as the contagion of death, as it is written: 'Hedge in thy ears with thorns, and hear not a wicked tongue.' And again: 'Evil communications corrupt good manners.' The Lord teaches and admonishes that we must withdraw from such. 'They are blind guides,' He says, 'of the blind. But if a blind man guide a blind man, both shall fall into a pit.' Such a one is to be turned away from, and whoever has separated himself from the Church is to be shunned. Such a man is perverted and sins and is condemned by his very self. Does he seem to himself to be with Christ, who acts contrary to the priests of Christ, who separates himself from association with His clergy and His people? That man bears arms against the Church; he fights against God's plan. An enemy of the altar, a rebel against the sac-

rifice of Christ, for the faith faithless, for religion sacrilegious, a disobedient servant, an impious son, a hostile brother, despising the bishops and abandoning the priests of God, he dares to set up another altar, to compose another prayer with unauthorized words, to profane the truth of the Lord's offering by false sacrifices, and not to know that he who struggles against God's plan on account of his rash daring is punished by divine censure.

18. Thus Core, Dathan, and Abiron, who tried to assume for themselves in opposition to Moses and Aaron the freedom to sacrifice, immediately paid the penalty for their efforts. The earth, breaking its bonds, opened up into a deep chasm, and the opening of the receding ground swallowed up the standing and the living, and not only did the anger of the indignant God strike those who had been the authors [of the revolt], but fire that went out from the Lord in speedy revenge also consumed two hundred and fifty others, participants and sharers in the same madness, who had been joined together with them in the daring, clearly warning and showing that whatever the wicked attempt by human will to destroy God's plan is done against God. Thus Ozias the king also, when, carrying the censer and violently assuming to himself the right to sacrifice contrary to the law of God, although Azarias, the priest, resisted him, he was unwilling to give way and obey, was confounded by the divine indignation and was polluted on his forehead by the spot of leprosy, being marked for his offense against the Lord where they are signed who merited well of the Lord. And the sons of Aaron, who place a strange fire on the altar, which the Lord had not ordered, were immediately extinguished in the sight of the avenging Lord.

19. These, certainly, they imitate and follow, who despise God's tradition and seek after strange doctrines and introduce teachings of human disposition. These the Lord rebukes and reproves in His Gospel when He says: 'You reject the commandment of God that you may establish your own tradition.' This crime is worse than that which the lapsed seem to have committed, who while established in penance for their crime beseech God with full satisfactions. Here the Church is sought and entreated, there the Church is resisted; here there can have been necessity, there the will is held in wickedness; here he who lapsed harmed only himself, there he who tried to cause a heresy or schism deceived many by dragging them with him; here there is the loss of one soul, there danger to a great many. Certainly this one knows that he has sinned and bewails and laments; that one swelling in his sin and taking pleasure in his very crimes separates children from their Mother, entices sheep from their shepherd, and disturbs the sacraments of God. And whereas the lapsed has sinned once, the former sins daily. Finally, the lapsed later, after achieving martyrdom, can receive the promises of the kingdom; the former, if he is killed outside the Church, cannot arrive at the rewards of the Church.

20. Let no one marvel, most beloved brethren, that even certain of the confessors proceed to these lengths, that some also sin so wickedly and so grievously. For neither does confession [of Christ] make one immune from the snares of the devil, nor does it defend him who is still placed in the world, with a perpetual security against worldly temptations and dangers and onsets and attacks; otherwise never might we have seen afterwards among the confessors the deceptions and debaucheries and adulteries which now with groaning and sorrow we see among some. Whoever that confessor is, he is not greater or better or dearer to God than Solomon, who, however, as long as he walked in the ways of the Lord, so long retained the grace which he had received from the Lord; after he had abandoned the way of the Lord, he lost also the grace of the Lord. And so it is written: 'Hold what you have, lest another receive thy crown.' Surely the Lord would not make this threat, that the crown of righteousness can be taken away, unless, when righteousness departs, the crown also must depart.

21. Confession is the beginning of glory, not already the merit of the crown; nor does it achieve praise, but it initiates dignity, and since it is written; 'He that shall persevere to the end, he shall be saved,' whatever has taken place before the end is a step by which the ascent is made to the summit of salvation, not the end by which the topmost point is held secure. He is a confessor, but after the confession the danger is greater, because the adversary is the more provoked. He is a confessor; for this reason he ought to stand with the Gospel of the Lord, for by the Gospel he has obtained glory from the Lord. 'To whom much is given, of him much is required'; and to whom the more dignity is allotted, from him the more service is demanded. Let no one perish through the example of a confessor, let no one learn injustice, no one insolence, no one perfidy from the habits of a confessor. He is a confessor; let him be humble and quiet, in his actions let him be modest with discipline, so that he who is called a confessor of Christ may imitate the Christ whom he confesses. For since he says: 'Everyone that exalts himself shall be humbled, and everyone that humbles himself shall be exalted,' and since he himself has been exalted by the Father, because He, the Word and the Power and the Wisdom of God the Father humbled Himself on earth, how can He love pride who even by His law enjoined humility upon us and Himself received from the Father the highest name as the reward of humility? He is a confessor of Christ, but only if afterwards the majesty and dignity of Christ be not blasphemed by him. Let not the tongue which has confessed Christ be abusive nor boisterous; let it not be heard resounding with insults and contentions; let it not after words of praise shoot forth a serpent's poisons against the brethren and priests of God. But if he later become blameworthy and abominable, if he dissipates his confession by evil conversation, if he pollutes his life with unseemly foulness, if, finally, abandoning the Church where he became a confessor and breaking the concord of its unity, he change his first faith for a later faithlessness, he cannot flatter himself by reason of his confession as if elected to the reward of glory, when by this very fact the merits of punishment have grown the more.

22. For the Lord chose even Judas among the Apostles, and yet later Judas betrayed the Lord. Nevertheless, the firmness and faith of the Apostles did not on this account fall, because the traitor Judas defected from their fellowship. So also in this case the sanctity and dignity of the confessors was not immediately diminished, because the faith of some of them was broken. The blessed Apostle speaks in his letter saying: 'For what if some of them have fallen away from the faith? Has their infidelity made of no effect the faith of God? God forbid. For God is true, but every man a liar.' The greater and better part of the confessors stand firm in the strength of their faith and in the truth of the Lord's law and teaching, neither do they depart from the peace of the Church, who remember that they have obtained grace in the Church from God's esteem, and by this very fact do they obtain greater praise for their faith, that they separated themselves from the perfidy of those who had been joined with them in the fellowship of confession, and withdrew from the contagion of their crime. Moreover, illumined by the light of the Gospel, shining with the pure white light of the Lord, they are as praiseworthy in preserving the peace of Christ as they were victorious in their encounter with the devil.

23. Indeed, I desire, most beloved brethren, and I likewise advise and entreat, that, if it can be done, no one of the brethren perish, and that our rejoicing Mother enclose in her bosom one body of people in agreement. If, however, saving counsel cannot recall certain leaders of schisms and authors of dissensions who persist in their blind and obstinate madness to the way of salvation, yet the rest of you either taken by your simplicity, or induced by error, or deceived by some craftiness of misleading cunning, free yourselves from the snare of deceit, liberate your wandering steps from errors, recognize the right way of the heavenly road. The words of the Apostle giving

testimony are: 'We charge you in the name of the Lord Jesus Christ that you withdraw from all brethren who walk disorderly and not according to the tradition which they received from us.' And again he says: 'Let no one deceive you with vain words; for because of these things comes the wrath of God upon the children of disobedience. Be ye not, therefore, partakers with them.' We must withdraw, rather flee from those who fall away, lest, while one is joined with them as they walk wickedly, and passes over the paths of error and crime, wandering apart from the way of the true road, he himself also be caught in a like crime. God is one and Christ one and His Church one and the faith one and the people one joined together by the tie of concord into a solid unity of body. The unity cannot be torn asunder, nor can the one body be separated by a division of its structure, nor torn into bits by the wrenching asunder of its entrails by laceration. Whatever departs from the parent-stem will not be able to breathe and live apart; it loses the substance of health.

24. The Holy Spirit warns us, saying: 'Who is the man that desireth life; who loveth to see the best days? Keep thy tongue from evil, and thy lips from speaking guile. Turn away from evil and do good; seek after peace, and pursue it.' The son of peace ought to seek and follow peace; he who knows and loves the bond of charity ought to restrain his tongue from the evil of dissension. Among his divine commands and salutary instructions the Lord now very near His passion added the following: 'Peace I leave you, my peace I give you.' This inheritance He gave us, all the gifts and rewards of His promise He assured us in the conservation of peace. If we are heirs of Christ, let us remain in the peace of Christ; if we are sons of God, we ought to be peace-makers. 'Blessed,' He said, 'are the peace-makers, for they shall be called the sons of God.' The sons of God should be peace-makers, gentle in heart, simple in speech, harmonious in affection, clinging to one another faithfully in the bonds of unanimity.

25. This unanimity existed of old among the Apostles; thus the new assembly of believers, guarding the commandments of the Lord, maintained their charity. Scripture proves this in the following words: 'But the multitude of those who believed acted with one soul and one mind.' And again, 'And all were persevering with one mind in prayer with the women and Mary the mother of Jesus and His brethren.' Thus they prayed with efficacious prayers; thus they were able with confidence to obtain whatever they asked of God's mercy.

26. But with us unanimity has been so diminished that even the liberality of our good works has been lessened. Then they sold their homes and estates, and, laying up treasures for themselves in heaven, they offered to the Apostles the proceeds to be distributed for use among the poor. But now we do not even give a tenth of our patrimony, and, although the Lord orders us to sell, we rather buy and increase. So has the vigor of faith withered in us; so has the strength of believers languished. And therefore the Lord, looking upon our times, says in His Gospel: 'When the Son of man comes, do you think that He will find faith on the earth?' We see that what he foretold is coming to pass. There is no faith in the fear of God, in the law of justice, in love, in works. No one considers fear of the future; no one thinks of the day of the Lord and the anger of God and the punishments to come upon unbelievers and the eternal torments decreed for the faithless. Whatever our conscience would fear, if it believed, because it does not believe, it does not fear at all. But if it did believe, it would also be on guard; if it were on guard, it would also escape.

27. Let us rouse ourselves in so far as we can, most beloved brethren, and, breaking the sleep of old inertia let us awake to the observing and keeping of the Lord's precepts. Let us be such as He Himself ordered us to be when He said: 'Let your loins be girt, and your lamps brightly burning, and you yourself like to men waiting for their Lord, when He shall come from the wedding, that when He comes and knocks,

they may open to Him. Blessed are those servants whom the Lord, when He comes, shall find watching.' We ought to be girt, lest, when the day of departure come, it finds us burdened and entangled. Let our light shine forth in good works and glow, so that it may lead us from the night of this world to the light of eternal brightness. Let us always with solicitude and caution await the sudden coming of the Lord, so that, when He knocks, our faith may be vigilant, ready to receive from the Lord the reward of its vigilance. If these mandates are kept, if these warnings and precepts are maintained, we cannot be overtaken while sleeping by the deceit of the devil; we will reign as vigilant servants with Christ as our Lord.

847 Congregation for the Doctrine of the Faith, Letter to the Archbishop of Boston, 8 August 1949: DS 3866–72

THE SUPREME SACRED CONGREGATION OF THE HOLY OFFICE

From the Headquarters of the Holy Office

August 8, 1949
Protocol Number 122/49.

Your Excellency:

This Supreme Sacred Congregation has followed very attentively the rise and the course of the grave controversy stirred up by certain associates of "St. Benedict Center" and "Boston College" in regard to the interpretation of that axiom: "*Outside the Church there is no salvation.*"

After having examined all the documents that are necessary or useful in this matter, among them information from your Chancery, as well as appeals and reports in which the associates of "St. Benedict Center" explain their opinions and complaints, and also many other documents pertinent to the controversy, officially collected, the same Sacred Congregation is convinced that the unfortunate controversy arose from the fact that the axiom: "outside the Church there is no salvation," was not correctly understood and weighed, and that the same controversy was rendered more bitter by serious disturbance of discipline arising from the fact that some of the associates of the institutions mentioned above refused reverence and obedience to legitimate authorities.

Accordingly, the Most Eminent and Most Reverend Cardinals of this Supreme Congregation, in a plenary session, held on Wednesday, July 27, 1949, decreed, and the August Pontiff in an audience on the following Thursday, July 28, 1949, deigned to give his approval, that the following explanations pertinent to the doctrine, and also that invitations and exhortations relevant to discipline be given:

We are bound by divine and Catholic faith to believe all those things which are contained in the word of God, whether it be Scripture or Tradition, and are proposed by the Church to be believed as divinely revealed, not only through solemn judgment but also through the ordinary and universal teaching office (Denzinger, n. 1792).

Now, among those things which the Church has always preached and will never cease to preach is contained also that infallible statement by which we are taught that there is no salvation outside the Church.

However, this dogma must be understood in that sense in which the Church herself understands it. For, it was not to private judgments that Our Savior gave for explanation those things that are contained in the deposit of faith, but to the teaching authority of the Church.

Now, in the first place, the Church teaches that in this matter there is question of a most strict command of Jesus Christ. For He explicitly enjoined on His apostles to teach all nations to observe all things whatsoever He Himself had commanded (Matt., 28:19–20).

Now, among the commandments of Christ, that one holds not the least place, by which we are commanded to be incorporated by Baptism into the Mystical Body of Christ, which is the Church, and to remain united to Christ and to His Vicar, through whom He Himself in a visible manner governs the Church on earth.

Therefore, no one will be saved who, knowing the Church to have been divinely established by Christ, nevertheless refuses to submit to the Church or withholds obedience from the Roman Pontiff, the Vicar of Christ on earth.

Not only did the Savior command that all nations should enter the Church, but He also decreed the Church to be a means of salvation, without which no one can enter the kingdom of eternal glory.

In His infinite mercy God has willed that the effects, necessary for one to be saved, of those helps to salvation which are directed toward man's final end, not by intrinsic necessity, but only by divine institution, can also be obtained in certain circumstances when those helps are used only in *desire* and *longing*. This we see clearly stated in the Sacred Council of Trent, both in reference to the Sacrament of Regeneration and in reference to the Sacrament of Penance (Denzinger, nn. 797, 807).

The same in its own degree must be asserted of the Church, in as far as she is the general help to salvation. Therefore, that one may obtain eternal salvation, it is not always required that he be incorporated into the Church *actually* as a member, but it is necessary that at least he be united to her by *desire* and *longing*.

However, this desire need not always be explicit, as it is in catechumens; but when a person is involved in invincible ignorance, God accepts also an *implicit desire*, so called because it is included in that good disposition of soul whereby a person wishes his will to be conformed to the will of God.

These things are clearly taught in that dogmatic letter which was issued by the Sovereign Pontiff, Pope Pius XII, on June 29, 1943, "On the Mystical Body of Jesus Christ" (AAS, Vol. 35, an. 1943, p. 193 ff.). For in this letter the Sovereign Pontiff clearly distinguishes between those who are *actually* incorporated into the Church as members, and those who are united to the Church only *by desire*.

Discussing the members of which the Mystical Body is composed here on earth, the same August Pontiff says: "Actually only those are to be included as members of the Church who have been baptized and profess the true faith, and who have not been so unfortunate as to separate themselves from the unity of the Body, or been excluded by legitimate authority for grave faults committed."

Toward the end of this same Encyclical Letter, when most affectionately inviting to unity those who do not belong to the body of the Catholic Church, he mentions those who "are related to the Mystical Body of the Redeemer by a certain unconscious *yearning* and *desire*," and these he by no means excludes from eternal salvation, but on the other hand states that they are in a condition "in which they cannot be sure of their salvation" since "they still remain deprived of those many heavenly gifts and helps which can only be enjoyed in the Catholic Church" (AAS, loc. cit., 243).

With these wise words he reproves both those who exclude from eternal salvation all united to the Church *only by implicit desire*, and those who falsely assert that men can be saved equally well in every religion (cf. Pope Pius IX, Allocution "Singulari quadam," in Denzinger, nn. 1641, ff.—also Pope Pius IX in the Encyclical Letter "Quanto conficiamur moerore" in Denzinger, n. 1677).

But it must not be thought that any kind of desire of entering the Church suffices that one may be saved. It is necessary that the desire by which one is related to the Church be animated by perfect charity. Nor can an implicit desire produce its effect, unless a person has supernatural faith: "For he who comes to God must believe that God exists and is a rewarder of those who seek Him" (Hebrews, 11:6). The Council of Trent declares (Session VI, chap. 8): "Faith is the beginning of man's salvation, the foundation and root of all justification, without which it is impossible to please God and attain to the fellowship of His children" (Denzinger, n. 801).

From what has been said it is evident that those things which are proposed in the periodical "From the Housetops," fascicle 3, as the genuine teaching of the Catholic Church are far from being such and are very harmful both to those within the Church and those without.

From these declarations which pertain to doctrine certain conclusions follow which regard discipline and conduct, and which cannot be unknown to those who vigorously defend the necessity by which all are bound of belonging to the true Church and of submitting to the authority of the Roman Pontiff and of the Bishops "whom the Holy Ghost has placed . . . to rule the Church" (Acts, 20:28).

Hence, one cannot understand how the St. Benedict Center can consistently claim to be a Catholic school and wish to be accounted such, and yet not conform to the prescriptions of Canons 1381 and 1382 of the Code of Canon Law, and continue to exist as a source of discord and rebellion against ecclesiastical authority and as a source of the disturbance of many consciences.

Furthermore, it is beyond understanding how a member of a religious institute, namely Father Feeney, presents himself as a "Defender of the faith," and at the same time does not hesitate to attack the catechetical instruction proposed by lawful authorities, and has not even feared to incur grave sanctions threatened by the sacred canons because of his serious violations of his duties as a religious, a priest and an ordinary member of the Church.

Finally, it is in no wise to be tolerated that certain Catholics shall claim for themselves the right to publish a periodical, for the purpose of spreading theological doctrines, without the permission of competent Church Authority, called the "imprimatur," which is prescribed by the sacred canons.

Therefore, let them who in grave peril are ranged against the Church seriously bear in mind that after "Rome has spoken" they cannot be excused even by reasons of good faith. Certainly, their bond and duty of obedience toward the Church is much graver than that of those who as yet are related to the Church "only by an unconscious desire." Let them realize that they are children of the Church, lovingly nourished by her with the milk of doctrine and the sacraments, and hence, having heard the clear voice of their Mother, they cannot be excused from culpable ignorance, and therefore to them applies without any restriction that principle: submission to the Catholic Church and to the Sovereign Pontiff is required as necessary for salvation.

In sending this letter, I declare my profound esteem, and remain

Your Excellency's most devoted
F. Cardinal Marchetti-Selvaggiani

A. Ottaviani
Assessor

To His Excellency
Most Reverend Richard James Cushing
Archbishop of Boston

848 **1 Corinthians 9:16** For if I preach the gospel, that gives me no ground for boasting. For necessity is laid upon me. Woe to me if I do not preach the gospel!

850 ***Redemptoris missio* 23** The different versions of the "missionary mandate" contain common elements as well as characteristics proper to each. Two elements, however, are found in all the versions. First, there is the universal dimension of the task entrusted to the apostles, who are sent to "all nations" (Mt 28:19); "into all the world

and . . . to the whole creation" (Mk 16:15); to "all nations" (Lk 24:47); "to the end of the earth" (Acts 1:8). Secondly, there is the assurance given to the apostles by the Lord that they will not be alone in the task, but will receive the strength and the means necessary to carry out their mission. The reference here is to the presence and power of the Spirit and the help of Jesus himself: "And they went forth and preached everywhere, while the Lord worked with them" (Mk 16:20).

As for the different emphases found in each version, Mark presents mission as proclamation or *kerygma*: "Preach the Gospel" (Mk 16:15). His aim is to lead his readers to repeat Peter's profession of faith: "You are the Christ" (Mk 8:29), and to say with the Roman centurion who stood before the body of Jesus on the Cross: "Truly this man was the Son of God!" (Mk 15:39) In Matthew, the missionary emphasis is placed on the foundation of the Church and on her teaching (cf. Mt 28:19–20; 16:18). According to him, the mandate shows that the proclamation of the Gospel must be completed by a specific ecclesial and sacramental catechesis. In Luke, mission is presented as witness (cf. Lk 24:48; Acts 1:8), centered especially on the Resurrection (cf. Acts 1:22). The missionary is invited to believe in the transforming power of the Gospel and to proclaim what Luke presents so well, that is, conversion to God's love and mercy, the experience of a complete liberation which goes to the root of all evil, namely sin.

John is the only Evangelist to speak explicitly of a "mandate," a word equivalent to "mission." He directly links the mission which Jesus entrusts to his disciples with the mission which he himself has received from the Father: "As the Father has sent me, even so I send you" (Jn 20:21). Addressing the Father, Jesus says: "As you sent me into the world, so I have sent them into the world" (Jn 17:18). The entire missionary sense of John's Gospel is expressed in the "priestly prayer": "This is eternal life, that they know you the only true God, and Jesus Christ whom you have sent" (Jn 17:3). The ultimate purpose of mission is to enable people to share in the communion which exists between the Father and the Son. The disciples are to live in unity with one another, remaining in the Father and the Son, so that the world may know and believe (cf. Jn 17:21–23). This is a very important missionary text. It makes us understand that we are missionaries above all because of *what we are* as a Church whose innermost life is unity in love, even before we become missionaries *in word or deed.*

The four Gospels therefore bear witness to a certain pluralism within the fundamental unity of the same mission, a pluralism which reflects different experiences and situations within the first Christian communities. It is also the result of the driving force of the Spirit himself; it encourages us to pay heed to the variety of missionary charisms and to the diversity of circumstances and peoples. Nevertheless, all the Evangelists stress that the mission of the disciples is to cooperate in the mission of Christ: "Lo, I am with you always, to the close of the age" (Mt 28:20). Mission, then, is based not on human abilities but on the power of the Risen Lord.

(1) ***Apostolicam actuositatem* 6** The Church's mission is concerned with the salvation of men; and men win salvation through the grace of Christ and faith in him. 851
The apostolate of the Church therefore, and of each of its members, aims primarily at announcing to the world by word and action the message of Christ and communicating to it the grace of Christ. The principal means of bringing this about is the ministry of the word and of the sacraments. Committed in a special way to the clergy, it leaves room however for a highly important part for the laity, the part namely of "helping on the cause of truth" (3 Jn. 8). It is in this sphere most of all that the lay apostolate and the pastoral ministry complete each other.

Laymen have countless opportunities for exercising the apostolate of evangelization and sanctification. The very witness of a Christian life, and good works done in a supernatural spirit, are effective in drawing men to the faith and to God; and that is what the Lord has said: "Your light must shine so brightly before men that they can see your good works and glorify your Father who is in heaven" (Mt. 5:16).

This witness of life, however, is not the sole element in the apostolate; the true apostle is on the lookout for occasions of announcing Christ by word, either to unbelievers to draw them towards the faith, or to the faithful to instruct them, strengthen them, incite them to a more fervent life; "for Christ's love urges us on" (2 Cor. 5:14), and in the hearts of all should the apostle's words find echo: "Woe to me if I do not preach the Gospel" (1 Cor. 9:16).

At a time when new questions are being put and when grave errors aiming at undermining religion, the moral order and human society itself are rampant, the Council earnestly exhorts the laity to take a more active part, each according to his talents and knowledge and in fidelity to the mind of the Church, in the explanation and defense of Christian principles and in the correct application of them to the problems of our times.

851 (2) ***Redemptoris missio* 11** What then should be said of the objections already mentioned regarding the mission *ad gentes?* While respecting the beliefs and sensitivities of all, we must first clearly affirm our faith in Christ, the one Savior of humanity, a faith we have received as a gift from on high, not as a result of any merit of our own. We say with Paul, "I am not ashamed of the Gospel: it is the power of God for salvation to everyone who has faith" (Rom 1:16). Christian martyrs of all times —including our own—have given and continue to give their lives in order to bear witness to this faith, in the conviction that every human being needs Jesus Christ, who has conquered sin and death and reconciled mankind to God.

Confirming his words by miracles and by his Resurrection from the dead, Christ proclaimed himself to be the Son of God dwelling in intimate union with the Father, and was recognized as such by his disciples. The Church offers men the Gospel, that prophetic message which responds to the needs and aspirations of the human heart and always remains "Good News." The Church cannot fail to proclaim that Jesus came to reveal the face of God and to merit salvation for all mankind by his Cross and Resurrection.

To the question, "*why mission?*" we reply with the Church's faith and experience that true liberation consists in opening oneself to the love of Christ. In him, and only in him, are we set free from all alienation and doubt, from slavery to the power of sin and death. Christ is truly "our peace" (Eph 2:14); "the love of Christ impels us" (2 Cor 5:14), giving meaning and joy to our life. *Mission is an issue of faith*, an accurate indicator of our faith in Christ and his love for us.

The temptation today is to reduce Christianity to merely human wisdom, a pseudo-science of well-being. In our heavily secularized world a "gradual secularization of salvation" has taken place, so that people strive for the good of man, but man who is truncated, reduced to his merely horizontal dimension. We know, however, that Jesus came to bring integral salvation, one which embraces the whole person and all mankind and opens up the wondrous prospect of divine filiation. *Why mission?* Because to us, as to St. Paul, "this grace was given, to preach to the Gentiles the unsearchable riches of Christ" (Eph 3:8). Newness of life in him is the "Good News" for men and women of every age: all are called to it and destined for it. Indeed, all people are searching for it, albeit at times in a confused way, and have a right to know the value of this gift and to approach it freely. The Church, and every individual Christian within her, may not keep hidden or monopolize this newness and richness which has been received from God's bounty in order to be communicated to all mankind.

This is why the Church's mission derives not only from the Lord's mandate but also from the profound demands of God's life within us. Those who are incorporated in the Catholic Church ought to sense their privilege and for that very reason their greater obligation of *bearing witness to the faith and to the Christian life* as a service to their brothers and sisters and as a fitting response to God. They should be ever mindful that "they owe their distinguished status not to their own merits but to Christ's special grace; and if they fail to respond to this grace in thought, word and deed, not only will they not be saved, they will be judged more severely."

(1) ***Lumen gentium* 15:** see 819 (1). 853

(2) ***Redemptoris missio* 12–20** "It is 'God, who is rich in mercy' whom Jesus Christ 853
has revealed to us as Father: it is his very Son who, in himself, has manifested him and made him known to us." I wrote this at the beginning of my Encyclical *Dives in Misericordia*, to show that Christ is the revelation and incarnation of the Father's mercy. Salvation consists in believing and accepting the mystery of the Father and of his love, made manifest and freely given in Jesus through the Spirit. In this way the kingdom of God comes to be fulfilled: the kingdom prepared for in the Old Testament, brought about by Christ and in Christ, and proclaimed to all peoples by the Church, which works and prays for its perfect and definitive realization.

The Old Testament attests that God chose and formed a people for himself, in order to reveal and carry out his loving plan. But at the same time God is the Creator and Father of all people; he cares and provides for them, extending his blessing to all (cf. Gen 12:3); he has established a covenant with all of them (cf. Gen 9:1–17). Israel experiences a personal and saving God (cf. Dt 4:37; 7:6–8; Is 43:1–7) and becomes his witness and interpreter among the nations. In the course of her history, Israel comes to realize that her election has a universal meaning (cf. for example Is 2:2–5; 25:6–8; 60:1–6; Jer 3:17; 16:19).

Jesus of Nazareth brings God's plan to fulfillment. After receiving the Holy Spirit at his Baptism, Jesus makes clear his messianic calling: he goes about Galilee "preaching the Gospel of God and saying: 'The time is fulfilled, and the kingdom of God is at hand; repent and believe in the Gospel'" (Mk 1:14–15; cf. Mt 4:17; Lk 4:43). The proclamation and establishment of God's kingdom are the purpose of his mission: "I was sent for this purpose" (Lk 4:43). But that is not all. Jesus himself is the "Good News," as he declares at the very beginning of his mission in the synagogue at Nazareth, when he applies to himself the words of Isaiah about the Anointed One sent by the Spirit of the Lord (cf. Lk 4:14–21). Since the "Good News" is Christ, there is an identity between the message and the messenger, between saying, doing and being. His power, the secret of the effectiveness of his actions, lies in his total identification with the message he announces: he proclaims the "Good News" not just by what he says or does, but by what he is.

The ministry of Jesus is described in the context of his journeys within his homeland. Before Easter, the scope of his mission was focused on Israel. Nevertheless, Jesus offers a new element of extreme importance. The eschatological reality is not relegated to a remote "end of the world," but is already close and at work in our midst. The kingdom of God is at hand (cf. Mk 1:15); its coming is to be prayed for (cf. Mt 6:10); faith can glimpse it already at work in signs such as miracles (cf. Mt 11:4–5) and exorcisms (cf. Mt 12:25–28), in the choosing of the Twelve (cf. Mk 3:13–19), and in the proclamation of the Good News to the poor (cf. Lk 4:18). Jesus' encounters with Gentiles make it clear that entry into the kingdom comes through faith and conversion (cf. Mk 1:15), and not merely by reason of ethnic background.

The kingdom which Jesus inaugurates is the kingdom of God. Jesus himself reveals who this God is, the One whom he addresses by the intimate term "Abba," Father (cf. Mk 14:36). God, as revealed above all in the parables (cf. Lk 15:3–32; Mt 20:1–16), is sensitive to the needs and sufferings of every human being: he is a Father filled with love and compassion, who grants forgiveness and freely bestows the favors asked of him.

St. John tells us that "God is love" (1 Jn 4:8, 16). Every person therefore is invited to "repent" and to "believe" in God's merciful love. The kingdom will grow insofar as every person learns to turn to God in the intimacy of prayer as to a Father (cf. Lk 11:2; Mt 23:9) and strives to do his will (cf. Mt 7:21).

Jesus gradually reveals the characteristics and demands of the kingdom through his words, his actions and his own person.

The kingdom of God is meant for all mankind, and all people are called to become members of it. To emphasize this fact, Jesus drew especially near to those on the margins of society, and showed them special favor in announcing the Good News. At the beginning of his ministry he proclaimed that he was "anointed . . . to preach good news to the poor" (Lk 4:18). To all who are victims of rejection and contempt Jesus declares: "Blessed are you poor" (Lk 6:20). What is more, he enables such individuals to experience liberation even now, by being close to them, going to eat in their homes (cf. Lk 5:30; 15:2), treating them as equals and friends (cf. Lk 7:34), and making them feel loved by God, thus revealing his tender care for the needy and for sinners (cf. Lk 15:1–32).

The liberation and salvation brought by the kingdom of God come to the human person both in his physical and spiritual dimensions. Two gestures are characteristic of Jesus' mission: healing and forgiving. Jesus' many healings clearly show his great compassion in the face of human distress, but they also signify that in the kingdom there will no longer be sickness or suffering, and that his mission, from the very beginning, is meant to free people from these evils. In Jesus' eyes, healings are also a sign of spiritual salvation, namely liberation from sin. By performing acts of healing, he invites people to faith, conversion and the desire for forgiveness (cf. Lk 5:24). Once there is faith, healing is an encouragement to go further: it leads to salvation (cf. Lk 18:42–43). The acts of liberation from demonic possession—the supreme evil and symbol of sin and rebellion against God—are signs that indeed "the kingdom of God has come upon you" (Mt 12:28).

The kingdom aims at transforming human relationships; it grows gradually as people slowly learn to love, forgive and serve one another. Jesus sums up the whole Law, focusing it on the commandment of love (cf. Mt 22:34–40; Lk 10:25–28). Before leaving his disciples, he gives them a "new commandment": "Love one another; even as I have loved you" (Jn 13:34; cf. 15:12). Jesus' love for the world finds its highest expression in the gift of his life for mankind (cf. Jn 15:13), which manifests the love which the Father has for the world (cf. Jn 3:16). The kingdom's nature, therefore, is one of communion among all human beings—with one another and with God.

The kingdom is the concern of everyone: individuals, society, and the world. Working for the kingdom means acknowledging and promoting God's activity, which is present in human history and transforms it. Building the kingdom means working for liberation from evil in all its forms. In a word, the kingdom of God is the manifestation and the realization of God's plan of salvation in all its fullness.

By raising Jesus from the dead, God has conquered death, and in Jesus he has definitely inaugurated his kingdom. During his earthly life, Jesus was the Prophet of the kingdom; after his Passion, Resurrection and Ascension into heaven he shares in God's power and in his dominion over the world (cf. Mt 28:18; Acts 2:36; Eph 1:18–21). The Resurrection gives a universal scope to Christ's message, his actions and whole mission. The disciples recognize that the kingdom is already present in the person of Jesus and is slowly being established within man and the world through a mysterious connection with him.

Indeed, after the Resurrection, the disciples preach the kingdom by proclaiming Jesus crucified and risen from the dead. In Samaria, Philip "preached good news about the kingdom of God and the name of Jesus Christ" (Acts 8:12). In Rome, we find Paul "preaching the kingdom of God and teaching about the Lord Jesus Christ" (Acts 28:31). The first Christians also proclaim "the kingdom of Christ and of God" (Eph 5:5; cf. Rev 11:15; 12:10), or "the kingdom of our Lord and Savior Jesus Christ" (2 Pt 1:11). The preaching of the early Church was centered on the proclamation of Jesus Christ, with whom the kingdom was identified. Now, as then, there is a need to unite *the proclamation of the kingdom of God* (the content of Jesus' own "*kerygma*") and *the proclamation of the Christ-event* (the "*kerygma*" of the apostles). The two proclamations are complementary; each throws light on the other.

Nowadays the kingdom is much spoken of, but not always in a way consonant with the thinking of the Church. In fact, there are ideas about salvation and mission which can be called "anthropocentric" in the reductive sense of the word, inasmuch as they are focused on man's earthly needs. In this view, the kingdom tends to become something completely human and secularized; what counts are programs and struggles for a liberation which is socio-economic, political and even cultural, but within a horizon that is closed to the transcendent. Without denying that on this level too there are values to be promoted, such a notion nevertheless remains within the confines of a kingdom of man, deprived of its authentic and profound dimensions. Such a view easily translates into one more ideology of purely earthly progress. The kingdom of God, however, "is not of this world . . . is not from the world" (Jn 18:36).

There are also conceptions which deliberately emphasize the kingdom and which describe themselves as "kingdom-centered." They stress the image of a Church which is not concerned about herself, but which is totally concerned with bearing witness to and serving the kingdom. It is a "Church for others" just as Christ is the "man for others." The Church's task is described as though it had to proceed in two directions: on the one hand promoting such "values of the kingdom" as peace, justice, freedom, brotherhood, etc., while on the other hand fostering dialogue between peoples, cultures and religions, so that through a mutual enrichment they might help the world to be renewed and to journey ever closer towards the kingdom.

Together with positive aspects, these conceptions often reveal negative aspects as well. First, they are silent about Christ: the kingdom of which they speak is "theocentrically" based, since, according to them, Christ cannot be understood by those who lack Christian faith, whereas different peoples, cultures and religions are capable of finding common ground in the one divine reality, by whatever name it is called. For the same reason they put great stress on the mystery of creation, which is reflected in the diversity of cultures and beliefs, but they keep silent about the mystery of redemption. Furthermore, the kingdom, as they understand it, ends up either leaving very little room for the Church or undervaluing the Church in reaction to a presumed "ecclesiocentrism" of the past, and because they consider the Church herself only a sign, for that matter a sign not without ambiguity.

This is not the kingdom of God as we know it from Revelation. The kingdom cannot be detached either from Christ or from the Church.

As has already been said, Christ not only proclaimed the kingdom, but in him the kingdom itself became present and was fulfilled. This happened not only through his words and his deeds: "Above all, . . . the kingdom is made manifest in the very person of Christ, Son of God and Son of Man, who came 'to serve and to give his life as a ransom for many' (Mk 10:45)." The kingdom of God is not a concept, a doctrine, or a program subject to free interpretation, but it is before all else *a person* with the face and name of Jesus of Nazareth, the image of the invisible God. If the kingdom is separated from Jesus, it is no longer the kingdom of God which he revealed. The result is a distortion of the meaning of the kingdom, which runs the risk of being transformed into a purely human or ideological goal, and a distortion of the identity of Christ, who no longer appears as the Lord to whom everything must one day be subjected (cf. 1 Cor 15:27).

Likewise, one may not separate the kingdom from the Church. It is true that the Church is not an end unto herself, since she is ordered towards the kingdom of God of which she is the seed, sign and instrument. Yet, while remaining distinct from Christ and the kingdom, the Church is indissolubly united to both. Christ endowed the Church, his Body, with the fullness of the benefits and means of salvation. The Holy Spirit dwells in her, enlivens her with his gifts and charisms, sanctifies, guides and constantly renews her. The result is a unique and special relationship which, while not excluding the action of Christ and the Spirit outside the Church's visible boundaries, confers upon her a specific and necessary role; hence the Church's special connection with the kingdom of God and of Christ, which she has "the mission of announcing and inaugurating among all peoples."

It is within this overall perspective that the reality of the kingdom is understood. Certainly, the kingdom demands the promotion of human values, as well as those which can properly be called "evangelical," since they are intimately bound up with the "Good News." But this sort of promotion, which is at the heart of the Church, must not be detached from or opposed to other fundamental tasks, such as proclaiming Christ and his Gospel, and establishing and building up communities which make present and active within mankind the living image of the kingdom. One need not fear falling thereby into a form of "ecclesiocentrism." Pope Paul VI, who affirmed the existence of "a profound link between Christ, the Church and evangelization," also said that the Church "is not an end unto herself, but rather is fervently concerned to be completely of Christ, in Christ and for Christ, as well as completely of men, among men and for men."

The Church is effectively and concretely at the service of the kingdom. This is seen especially in her preaching, which is a call to conversion. Preaching constitutes the Church's first and fundamental way of serving the coming of the kingdom in individuals and in human society. Eschatological salvation begins even now in newness of life in Christ: "To all who believed in him, who believed in his name, he gave power to become children of God" (Jn 1:12).

The Church, then, serves the kingdom by establishing communities and founding new particular churches, and by guiding them to mature faith and charity in openness towards others, in service to individuals and society, and in understanding and esteem for human institutions.

The Church serves the kingdom by spreading throughout the world the "Gospel values" which are an expression of the kingdom and which help people to accept God's plan. It is true that the inchoate reality of the kingdom can also be found beyond the confines of the Church among peoples everywhere, to the extent that they live "Gospel values" and are open to the working of the Spirit who breathes when and where he wills (cf. Jn 3:8). But it must immediately be added that this temporal dimension of the kingdom remains incomplete unless it is related to the kingdom of Christ present in the Church and straining towards eschatological fullness.

The many dimensions of the kingdom of God do not weaken the foundations and purposes of missionary activity, but rather strengthen and extend them. The Church is the sacrament of salvation for all mankind, and her activity is not limited only to those who accept her message. She is a dynamic force in mankind's journey towards the eschatological kingdom, and is the sign and promoter of Gospel values. The

Church contributes to mankind's pilgrimage of conversion to God's plan through her witness and through such activities as dialogue, human promotion, commitment to justice and peace, education and the care of the sick, and aid to the poor and to children. In carrying on these activities, however, she never loses sight of the priority of the transcendent and spiritual realities which are premises of eschatological salvation.

Finally, the Church serves the kingdom by her intercession, since the kingdom by its very nature is God's gift and work, as we are reminded by the Gospel parables and by the prayer which Jesus taught us. We must ask for the kingdom, welcome it and make it grow within us; but we must also work together so that it will be welcomed and will grow among all people, until the time when Christ "delivers the kingdom to God the Father" and "God will be everything to everyone" (cf. 1 Cor 15:24, 28).

(1) ***Redemptoris missio* 42–47** People today put more trust in witnesses than in 854
teachers, in experience than in teaching, and in life and action than in theories. The witness of a Christian life is the first and irreplaceable form of mission: Christ, whose mission we continue, is the "witness" *par excellence* (Rev 1:5; 3:14) and the model of all Christian witness. The Holy Spirit accompanies the Church along her way and associates her with the witness he gives to Christ (cf. Jn 15:26–27).

The first form of witness is *the very life of the missionary, of the Christian family*, and *of the ecclesial community*, which reveal a new way of living. The missionary who, despite all his or her human limitations and defects, lives a simple life, taking Christ as the model, is a sign of God and of transcendent realities. But everyone in the Church, striving to imitate the Divine Master, can and must bear this kind of witness; in many cases it is the only possible way of being a missionary.

The evangelical witness which the world finds most appealing is that of concern for people, and of charity towards the poor, the weak and those who suffer. The complete generosity underlying this attitude and these actions stands in marked contrast to human selfishness. It raises precise questions which lead to God and to the Gospel. A commitment to peace, justice, human rights and human promotion is also a witness to the Gospel when it is a sign of concern for persons and is directed towards integral human development.

Christians and Christian communities are very much a part of the life of their respective nations and can be a sign of the Gospel in their fidelity to their native land, people and national culture, while always preserving the freedom brought by Christ. Christianity is open to universal brotherhood, for all men and women are sons and daughters of the same Father and brothers and sisters in Christ.

The Church is called to bear witness to Christ by taking courageous and prophetic stands in the face of the corruption of political or economic power; by not seeking her own glory and material wealth; by using her resources to serve the poorest of the poor and by imitating Christ's own simplicity of life. The Church and her missionaries must also bear the witness of humility, above all with regard to themselves —a humility which allows them to make a personal and communal examination of conscience in order to correct in their behavior whatever is contrary to the Gospel and disfigures the face of Christ.

Proclamation is the permanent priority of mission. The Church cannot elude Christ's explicit mandate, nor deprive men and women of the "Good News" about their being loved and saved by God. "Evangelization will always contain—as the foundation, center and at the same time the summit of its dynamism—a clear proclamation that, in Jesus Christ . . . salvation is offered to all men, as a gift of God's grace and mercy." All forms of missionary activity are directed to this proclamation, which reveals and gives access to the mystery hidden for ages and made known in Christ (cf. Eph 3:3–9; Col 1:25–29), the mystery which lies at the heart of the Church's mission and life, as the hinge on which all evangelization turns.

In the complex reality of mission, initial proclamation has a central and irreplaceable role, since it introduces man "into the mystery of the love of God, who invites him to enter into a personal relationship with himself in Christ" and opens the way to conversion. Faith is born of preaching, and every ecclesial community draws its origin and life from the personal response of each believer to that preaching. Just as the whole economy of salvation has its center in Christ, so too all missionary activity is directed to the proclamation of his mystery.

The subject of proclamation is Christ who was crucified, died and is risen: through him is accomplished our full and authentic liberation from evil, sin and death; through him God bestows "new life" that is divine and eternal. This is the "Good News" which changes man and his history, and which all peoples have a right to hear. This proclamation is to be made within the context of the lives of the individuals and peoples who receive it. It is to be made with an attitude of love and esteem towards those who hear it, in language which is practical and adapted to the situation. In this proclamation the Spirit is at work and establishes a communion between the missionary and his hearers, a communion which is possible inasmuch as both enter into communion with God the Father through Christ.

Proclamation, because it is made in union with the entire ecclesial community, is never a merely personal act. The missionary is present and carries out his work by virtue of a mandate he has received; even if he finds himself alone, he remains joined by invisible but profound bonds to the evangelizing activity of the whole Church. Sooner or later, his hearers come to recognize in him the community which sent him and which supports him.

Proclamation is inspired by faith, which gives rise to enthusiasm and fervor in the missionary. As already mentioned, the Acts of the Apostles uses the word *parrhesia* to describe this attitude, a word which means to speak frankly and with courage. This term is found also in St. Paul: "We had courage in our God to declare to you the Gospel of God in the face of great opposition" (1 Th 2:2); "Pray . . . also for me, that utterance may be given me in opening my mouth boldly to proclaim the mystery of the Gospel for which I am an ambassador in chains; that I may declare it boldly, as I ought to speak" (Eph 6:18–20).

In proclaiming Christ to non-Christians, the missionary is convinced that, through the working of the Spirit, there already exists in individuals and peoples an expectation, even if an unconscious one, of knowing the truth about God, about man, and about how we are to be set free from sin and death. The missionary's enthusiasm in proclaiming Christ comes from the conviction that he is responding to that expectation, and so he does not become discouraged or cease his witness even when he is called to manifest his faith in an environment that is hostile or indifferent. He knows that the Spirit of the Father is speaking through him (cf. Mt 10:17–20; Lk 12:11–12) and he can say with the apostles: "We are witnesses to these things, and so is the Holy Spirit" (Acts 5:32). He knows that he is not proclaiming a human truth, but the "word of God," which has an intrinsic and mysterious power of its own (cf. Rom 1:16).

The supreme test is the giving of one's life, to the point of accepting death in order to bear witness to one's faith in Jesus Christ. Throughout Christian history, martyrs, that is, "witnesses," have always been numerous and indispensable to the spread of the Gospel. In our own age, there are many: bishops, priests, men and women religious, lay people—often unknown heroes who give their lives to bear witness to the faith. They are *par excellence* the heralds and witnesses of the faith.

The proclamation of the Word of God has *Christian conversion* as its aim: a complete and sincere adherence to Christ and his Gospel through faith. Conversion is a gift of God, a work of the Blessed Trinity. It is the Spirit who opens people's hearts so that they can believe in Christ and "confess him" (cf. 1 Cor 12:3); of those who draw near to him through faith Jesus says: "No one can come to me unless the Father who sent me draws him" (Jn 6:44).

From the outset, conversion is expressed in faith which is total and radical, and which neither limits nor hinders God's gift. At the same time, it gives rise to a dynamic and lifelong process which demands a continual turning away from "life according to the flesh" to "life according to the Spirit" (cf. Rom 8:3–13). Conversion means accepting, by a personal decision, the saving sovereignty of Christ and becoming his disciple.

The Church calls all people to this conversion, following the example of John the Baptist, who prepared the way for Christ by "preaching a baptism of repentance for the forgiveness of sins" (Mk 1:4), as well as the example of Christ himself, who "after John was arrested, . . . came into Galilee preaching the Gospel of God and saying: 'The time is fulfilled, and the kingdom of God is at hand; *repent* and believe in the Gospel'" (Mk 1:14–15).

Nowadays the call to conversion which missionaries address to non-Christians is put into question or passed over in silence. It is seen as an act of "proselytizing"; it is claimed that it is enough to help people to become more human or more faithful to their own religion, that it is enough to build communities capable of working for justice, freedom, peace and solidarity. What is overlooked is that every person has the right to hear the "Good News" of the God who reveals and gives himself in Christ, so that each one can live out in its fullness his or her proper calling. This lofty reality is expressed in the words of Jesus to the Samaritan woman: "If you knew the gift of God," and in the unconscious but ardent desire of the woman: "Sir, give me this water, that I may not thirst" (Jn 4:10, 15).

The apostles, prompted by the Spirit, invited all to change their lives, to be converted and to be baptized. Immediately after the event of Pentecost, Peter spoke convincingly to the crowd: "When they heard this, they were cut to the heart, and said to Peter and the rest of the Apostles, 'Brethren, what shall we do?' And Peter said to them, '*Repent*, and be baptized every one of you in the name of Jesus Christ for the forgiveness of your sins; and you shall receive the gift of the Holy Spirit'" (Acts 2:37–38). That very day some three thousand persons were baptized. And again, after the healing of the lame man, Peter spoke to the crowd and repeated: "*Repent* therefore, and turn again, that your sins may be blotted out!" (Acts 3:19).

Conversion to Christ is joined to Baptism not only because of the Church's practice, but also by the will of Christ himself, who sent the apostles to make disciples of all nations and to baptize them (cf. Mt 28:19). Conversion is also joined to Baptism because of the intrinsic need to receive the fullness of new life in Christ. As Jesus says to Nicodemus: "Truly, truly, I say to you, unless one is born of water and the Spirit, he cannot enter the kingdom of God" (Jn 3:5). In Baptism, in fact, we are born anew to the life of God's children, united to Jesus Christ and anointed in the Holy Spirit. Baptism is not simply a seal of conversion, and a kind of external sign indicating conversion and attesting to it. Rather, it is the sacrament which signifies and effects rebirth from the Spirit, establishes real and unbreakable bonds with the Blessed Trinity, and makes us members of the Body of Christ, which is the Church.

All this needs to be said, since not a few people, precisely in those areas involved in the mission *ad gentes*, tend to separate conversion to Christ from Baptism, regarding Baptism as unnecessary. It is true that in some places sociological considerations associated with Baptism obscure its genuine meaning as an act of faith. This is due to a variety of historical and cultural factors which must be removed where they still exist, so that the sacrament of spiritual rebirth can be seen for what it truly is. Local ecclesial communities must devote themselves to this task. It is also true that many profess an interior commitment to Christ and his message yet do not wish to be committed sacramentally, since, owing to prejudice or because of the failings of Christians, they find it difficult to grasp the true nature of the Church as a mystery of faith and love. I wish to encourage such people to be fully open to Christ, and to remind them that, if they feel drawn to Christ, it was he himself who desired that the Church should be the "place" where they would in fact find him. At the same time, I invite the Christian faithful, both individually and as communities, to bear authentic witness to Christ through the new life they have received.

Certainly, every convert is a gift to the Church and represents a serious responsibility for her, not only because converts have to be prepared for Baptism through the catechumenate and then be guided by religious instruction, but also because—especially in the case of adults—such converts bring with them a kind of new energy, an enthusiasm for the faith, and a desire to see the Gospel lived out in the Church. They would be greatly disappointed if, having entered the ecclesial community, they were to find a life lacking fervor and without signs of renewal! We cannot preach conversion unless we ourselves are converted anew every day.

854 (2) ***Redemptoris missio* 48–49** Conversion and Baptism give entry into a Church already in existence or require the establishment of new communities which confess Jesus as Savior and Lord. This is part of God's plan, for it pleases him "to call human beings to share in his own life not merely as individuals, without any unifying bond between them, but rather to make them into a people in which his children, who had been widely scattered, might be gathered together in unity."

The mission *ad gentes* has this objective: to found Christian communities and develop churches to their full maturity. This is a central and determining goal of missionary activity, so much so that the mission is not completed until it succeeds in building a new particular church which functions normally in its local setting. The Decree *Ad Gentes* deals with this subject at length, and since the Council, a line of theological reflection has developed which emphasizes that the whole mystery of the Church is contained in each particular church, provided it does not isolate itself but remains in communion with the universal Church and becomes missionary in its own turn. Here we are speaking of a great and lengthy process, in which it is hard to identify the precise stage at which missionary activity properly so-called comes to an end and is replaced by pastoral activity. Even so, certain points must remain clear.

It is necessary first and foremost to strive to establish Christian communities everywhere, communities which are "a sign of the presence of God in the world" and which grow until they become churches. Notwithstanding the high number of dioceses, there are still very large areas where there are no local churches or where their number is insufficient in relation to the vastness of the territory and the density of the population. There is still much to be done in implanting and developing the Church. This phase of ecclesial history, called the *plantatio Ecclesiae*, has not reached its end; indeed, for much of the human race it has yet to begin.

Responsibility for this task belongs to the universal Church and to the particular churches, to the whole people of God and to all its missionary forces. Every church, even one made up of recent converts, is missionary by its very nature, and is both evangelized and evangelizing. Faith must always be presented as a gift of God to be lived out in community (families, parishes, associations), and to be extended to others through witness in word and deed. The evangelizing activity of the Christian community, first in its own locality, and then elsewhere as part of the Church's universal mission, is the clearest sign of a mature faith. A radical conversion in thinking is required in order to become missionary, and this holds true both for individuals and entire communities. The Lord is always calling us to come out of ourselves and to share with others the goods we possess, starting with the most precious gift of all—our faith. The effectiveness of the Church's organizations, movements, parishes and apostolic works must be measured in the light of this missionary imperative. Only by becoming missionary will the Christian community be able to overcome its internal divisions and tensions, and rediscover its unity and its strength of faith.

Missionary personnel coming from other churches and countries must work in communion with their local counterparts for the development of the Christian community. In particular, it falls to missionary personnel—in accordance with the directives of the bishops and in cooperation with those responsible at the local level—to foster the spread of the faith and the expansion of the Church in non-Christian environments and among non-Christian groups, and to encourage a missionary sense within the particular churches, so that pastoral concern will always be combined with concern for the mission *ad gentes*. In this way, every church will make its own the solicitude of Christ the Good Shepherd, who fully devotes himself to his flock, but at the same time is mindful of the "other sheep, that are not of this fold" (Jn 10:16).

(3) ***Redemptoris missio* 52–54** As she carries out missionary activity among the nations, the Church encounters different cultures and becomes involved in the process of inculturation. The need for such involvement has marked the Church's pilgrimage throughout her history, but today it is particularly urgent. 854

The process of the Church's insertion into peoples' cultures is a lengthy one. It is not a matter of purely external adaptation, for inculturation "means the intimate transformation of authentic cultural values through their integration in Christianity and the insertion of Christianity in the various human cultures." The process is thus a profound and all-embracing one, which involves the Christian message and also the Church's reflection and practice. But at the same time it is a difficult process, for it must in no way compromise the distinctiveness and integrity of the Christian faith.

Through inculturation the Church makes the Gospel incarnate in different cultures and at the same time introduces peoples, together with their cultures, into her own community. She transmits to them her own values, at the same time taking the good elements that already exist in them and renewing them from within. Through inculturation the Church, for her part, becomes a more intelligible sign of what she is, and a more effective instrument of mission.

Thanks to this action within the local churches, the universal Church herself is enriched with forms of expression and values in the various sectors of Christian life, such as evangelization, worship, theology and charitable works. She comes to know and to express better the mystery of Christ, all the while being motivated to continual renewal. During my pastoral visits to the young churches I have repeatedly dealt with these themes, which are present in the Council and the subsequent Magisterium.

Inculturation is a slow journey which accompanies the whole of missionary life. It involves those working in the Church's mission *ad gentes*, the Christian communities as they develop, and the bishops, who have the task of providing discernment and encouragement for its implementation.

Missionaries, who come from other churches and countries, must immerse themselves in the cultural milieu of those to whom they are sent, moving beyond their own cultural limitations. Hence they must learn the language of the place in which they work, become familiar with the most important expressions of the local culture, and discover its values through direct experience. Only if they have this kind of awareness will they be able to bring to people the knowledge of the hidden mystery (cf. Rom 16:25–27; Eph 3:5) in a credible and fruitful way. It is not of course a matter of missionaries renouncing their own cultural identity, but of understanding, appreciating, fostering and evangelizing the culture of the environment in which they are working, and therefore of equipping themselves to communicate effectively with it, adopting a manner of living which is a sign of gospel witness and of solidarity with the people.

Developing ecclesial communities, inspired by the Gospel, will gradually be able to express their Christian experience in original ways and forms that are consonant with their own cultural traditions, provided that those traditions are in harmony with the objective requirements of the faith itself. To this end, especially in the more delicate areas of inculturation, particular churches of the same region should work in communion with each other and with the whole Church, convinced that only through attention both to the universal Church and to the particular churches will they be capable of translating the treasure of faith into a legitimate variety of expressions. Groups which have been evangelized will thus provide the elements for a "translation" of the gospel message, keeping in mind the positive elements acquired down the centuries from Christianity's contact with different cultures and not forgetting the dangers of alterations which have sometimes occurred.

In this regard, certain guidelines remain basic. Properly applied, inculturation must be guided by two principles: "compatibility with the Gospel and communion with the universal Church." Bishops, as guardians of the "deposit of faith," will take care to ensure fidelity and, in particular, to provide discernment, for which a deeply balanced approach is required. In fact there is a risk of passing uncritically from a form of alienation from culture to an overestimation of culture. Since culture is a human creation and is therefore marked by sin, it too needs to be "healed, ennobled and perfected."

This kind of process needs to take place gradually, in such a way that it really is an expression of the community's Christian experience. As Pope Paul VI said in Kampala: "It will require an incubation of the Christian 'mystery' in the genius of your people in order that its native voice, more clearly and frankly, may then be raised harmoniously in the chorus of other voices in the universal Church." In effect, inculturation must involve the whole people of God, and not just a few experts, since the people reflect the authentic *sensus fidei* which must never be lost sight of. Inculturation needs to be guided and encouraged, but not forced, lest it give rise to negative reactions among Christians. It must be an expression of the community's life, one which must mature within the community itself, and not be exclusively the result of erudite research. The safeguarding of traditional values is the work of a mature faith.

855 ***Redemptoris missio* 50** This solicitude will serve as a motivation and stimulus for a renewed commitment to ecumenism. The relationship between *ecumenical activity* and *missionary activity* makes it necessary to consider two closely associated factors. On the one hand, we must recognize that "the division among Christians damages the holy work of preaching the Gospel to every creature and is a barrier for many in their approach to the faith." The fact that the Good News of reconciliation is preached by Christians who are divided among themselves weakens their witness. It is thus urgent to work for the unity of Christians, so that missionary activity can be more effective. At the same time we must not forget that efforts towards unity are themselves a sign of the work of reconciliation which God is bringing about in our midst.

On the other hand, it is true that some kind of communion, though imperfect, exists among all those who have received Baptism in Christ. On this basis the Council established the principle that "while all appearance of indifferentism and confusion is ruled out, as well as any appearance of unhealthy rivalry, Catholics should collaborate in a spirit of fellowship with their separated brothers and sisters in accordance with the norms of the Decree on Ecumenism: by a common profession of faith in God and in Jesus Christ before the nations—to the extent that this is possible—and by their cooperation in social and technical as well as in cultural and religious matters."

Ecumenical activity and harmonious witness to Jesus Christ by Christians who belong to different churches and ecclesial communities has already borne abundant fruit. But it is ever more urgent that they work and bear witness together at this time when Christian and para-Christian sects are sowing confusion by their activity. The expansion of these sects represents a threat for the Catholic Church and for all the ecclesial communities with which she is engaged in dialogue. Wherever possible, and in the light of local circumstances, the response of Christians can itself be an ecumenical one.

***Redemptoris missio* 55** Inter-religious dialogue is a part of the Church's evangelizing 856
mission. Understood as a method and means of mutual knowledge and enrichment, dialogue is not in opposition to the mission *ad gentes;* indeed, it has special links with that mission and is one of its expressions. This mission, in fact, is addressed to those who do not know Christ and his Gospel, and who belong for the most part to other religions. In Christ, God calls all peoples to himself and he wishes to share with them the fullness of his revelation and love. He does not fail to make himself present in many ways, not only to individuals but also to entire peoples through their spiritual riches, of which their religions are the main and essential expression, even when they contain "gaps, insufficiencies and errors." All of this has been given ample emphasis by the Council and the subsequent Magisterium, without detracting in any way from the fact that *salvation comes from Christ and that dialogue does not dispense from evangelization.*

In the light of the economy of salvation, the Church sees no conflict between proclaiming Christ and engaging in inter-religious dialogue. Instead, she feels the need to link the two in the context of her mission *ad gentes.* These two elements must maintain both their intimate connection and their distinctiveness; therefore they should not be confused, manipulated or regarded as identical, as though they were interchangeable.

I recently wrote to the bishops of Asia: "Although the Church gladly acknowledges whatever is true and holy in the religious traditions of Buddhism, Hinduism and Islam as a reflection of that truth which enlightens all people, this does not lessen her duty and resolve to proclaim without fail Jesus Christ who is 'the way, and the truth and the life.'. . . The fact the followers of other religions can receive God's grace and be saved by Christ apart from the ordinary means which he has established does not thereby cancel the call to faith and baptism which God wills for all people." Indeed Christ himself "while expressly insisting on the need for faith and baptism, at the same time confirmed *the need for the Church,* into which people enter through Baptism as through a door." Dialogue should be conducted and implemented with the conviction that *the Church is the ordinary means of salvation* and that *she alone* possesses the fullness of the means of salvation.

(1) **Matthew 28:16–20** Now the eleven disciples went to Galilee, to the mountain 857
to which Jesus had directed them. And when they saw him they worshiped him; but some doubted. And Jesus came and said to them, "All authority in heaven and on earth has been given to me. Go therefore and make disciples of all nations, baptizing them in the name of the Father and of the Son and of the Holy Spirit, teaching them to observe all that I have commanded you; and lo, I am with you always, to the close of the age."

857 (2) **Acts 1:8** "... But you shall receive power when the Holy Spirit has come upon you; and you shall be my witnesses in Jerusalem and in all Judea and Samaria and to the end of the earth."

857 (3) **1 Corinthians 9:1** Am I not free? Am I not an apostle? Have I not seen Jesus our Lord? Are not you my workmanship in the Lord?

857 (4) **1 Corinthians 15:7–8** Then he appeared to James, then to all the apostles. Last of all, as to one untimely born, he appeared also to me.

857 (5) **Galatians 1:1** Paul an apostle—not from men nor through man, but through Jesus Christ and God the Father, who raised him from the dead. . . .

857 (6) **Acts 2:42** And they devoted themselves to the apostles' teaching and fellowship, to the breaking of bread and the prayers.

857 (7) **2 Timothy 1:13–14** Follow the pattern of the sound words which you have heard from me, in the faith and love which are in Christ Jesus; guard the truth that has been entrusted to you by the Holy Spirit who dwells within us.

858 (1) **John 13:20** "... Truly, truly, I say to you, he who receives any one whom I send receives me; and he who receives me receives him who sent me."

858 (2) **John 17:18** As thou didst send me into the world, so I have sent them into the world.

858 (3) **Luke 10:16** "He who hears you hears me, and he who rejects you rejects me, and he who rejects me rejects him who sent me."

859 **John 15:5** I am the vine, you are the branches. He who abides in me, and I in him, he it is that bears much fruit, for apart from me you can do nothing.

860 **Matthew 28:20** "... teaching them to observe all that I have commanded you; and lo, I am with you always, to the close of the age."

861 (1) **St. Clement of Rome, *Epistula ad Corinthios* 42** The Apostles preached to us the Gospel received from Jesus Christ, and Jesus Christ was God's Ambassador. Christ, in other words, comes with a message from God, and the Apostles with a message from Christ. Both these orderly arrangements, therefore, originate from the will of God. And so, after receiving their instructions and being fully assured through the Resurrection of our Lord Jesus Christ, as well as confirmed in faith by the word of God, they went forth, equipped with the fullness of the Holy Spirit, to preach the good news that the Kingdom of God was close at hand. From land to land, accordingly, and from city to city they preached, and from among their earliest converts appointed men whom they had tested by the Spirit to act as bishops and deacons for the future believers. And this was no innovation, for, a long time before the Scripture had spoken about bishops and deacons; for somewhere it says: I will establish their overseers in observance of the law and their ministers in fidelity.

861 (2) **St. Clement of Rome, *Epistula ad Corinthios* 44** Our Apostles, too, were given to understand by our Lord Jesus Christ that the office of the bishop would give rise to intrigues. For this reason, equipped as they were with perfect foreknowledge, they

appointed the men mentioned before, and afterwards laid down a rule once for all to this effect: when these men die, other approved men shall succeed to their sacred ministry. Consequently, we deem it an injustice to eject from the sacred ministry the persons who were appointed either by them, or later, with the consent of the whole Church, by other men in high repute and have ministered to the flock of Christ faultlessly, humbly, quietly and unselfishly, and have moreover, over a long period of time, earned the esteem of all. Indeed, it will be no small sin for us if we oust men who have irreproachably and piously offered the sacrifices proper to the episcopate. Happy the presbyters who have before now completed life's journey and taken their departure in mature age and laden with fruit! They, surely, do not have to fear that anyone will dislodge them from the place built for them. Yes, we see that you removed some, their good conduct notwithstanding, from the sacred ministry on which their faultless discharge had shed luster.

John 15:5 I am the vine, you are the branches. He who abides in me, and I in him, **864**
he it is that bears much fruit, for apart from me you can do nothing.

Ephesians 4:3–5 . . . eager to maintain the unity of the Spirit in the bond of peace. **866**
There is one body and one Spirit, just as you were called to the one hope that belongs to your call, one Lord, one faith, one baptism. . . .

Matthew 16:18 And I tell you, you are Peter, and on this rock I will build my **869**
church, and the powers of death shall not prevail against it.

***Lumen gentium* 31** The term "laity" is here understood to mean all the faithful **871**
except those in Holy Orders and those who belong to a religious state approved by the Church. That is, the faithful who by Baptism are incorporated into Christ, are placed in the People of God, and in their own way share the priestly, prophetic and kingly office of Christ, and to the best of their ability carry on the mission of the whole Christian people in the Church and in the world.

Their secular character is proper and peculiar to the laity. Although those in Holy Orders may sometimes be engaged in secular activities, or even practice a secular profession, yet by reason of their particular vocation, they are principally and expressly ordained to the sacred ministry. At the same time, religious give outstanding and striking testimony that the world cannot be transfigured and offered to God without the spirit of the beatitudes. But by reason of their special vocation it belongs to the laity to seek the kingdom of God by engaging in temporal affairs and directing them according to God's will. They live in the world, that is, they are engaged in each and every work and business of the earth and in the ordinary circumstances of social and family life which, as it were, constitute their very existence. There they are called by God that, being led by the spirit to the Gospel, they may contribute to the sanctification of the world, as from within like leaven, by fulfilling their own particular duties. Thus, especially by the witness of their life, resplendent in faith, hope and charity they must manifest Christ to others. It pertains to them in a special way so to illuminate and order all temporal things with which they are so closely associated that these may be effected and grow according to Christ and may be to the glory of the Creator and Redeemer.

***Lumen gentium* 32** By divine institution holy Church is ordered and governed with **872**
a wonderful diversity. "For just as in one body we have many members, yet all the members have not the same function, so we the many, are one body in Christ, but severally members one of another" (Rom. 12:4–5).

There is, therefore, one chosen People of God: "one Lord, one faith, one baptism" (Eph. 4:5); there is a common dignity of members deriving from their rebirth in Christ, a common grace as sons, a common vocation to perfection, one salvation, one hope and undivided charity. In Christ and in the Church there is, then, no inequality arising from race or nationality, social condition or sex, for "there is neither Jew nor Greek; there is neither slave nor freeman; there is neither male nor female. For you are all 'one' in Christ Jesus" (Gal. 3:28 Greek; cf. Col. 3:11).

In the Church not everyone marches along the same path, yet all are called to sanctity and have obtained an equal privilege of faith through the justice of God (cf. 2 Pet. 1:1). Although by Christ's will some are established as teachers, dispensers of the mysteries and pastors for the others, there remains, nevertheless, a true equality between all with regard to the dignity and to the activity which is common to all the faithful in the building up of the Body of Christ. The distinction which the Lord has made between the sacred ministers and the rest of the People of God involves union, for the pastors and the other faithful are joined together by a close relationship: the pastors of the Church—following the example of the Lord—should minister to each other and to the rest of the faithful; the latter should eagerly collaborate with the pastors and teachers. And so amid variety all will bear witness to the wonderful unity in the Body of Christ: this very diversity of graces, of ministries and of works gathers the sons of God into one, for "all these things are the work of the one and the same Spirit" (1 Cor. 12:11).

As the laity through the divine choice have Christ as their brother, who, though Lord of all, came not to be served but to serve (cf. Mt. 20:28), they also have as brothers those in the sacred ministry who by teaching, by sanctifying and by ruling with the authority of Christ so nourish the family of God that the new commandment of love may be fulfilled by all. As St. Augustine very beautifully puts it: "When I am frightened by what I am to you, then I am consoled by what I am with you. To you I am the bishop, with you I am a Christian. The first is an office, the second a grace; the first a danger, the second salvation."

876 (1) **Romans 1:1** Paul, a servant of Jesus Christ, called to be an apostle, set apart for the gospel of God. . . .

876 (2) **1 Corinthians 9:19** For though I am free from all men, I have made myself a slave to all, that I might win the more.

877 **John 17:21–23** . . . that they may all be one; even as thou, Father, art in me, and I in thee, that they also may be in us, so that the world may believe that thou hast sent me. The glory which thou hast given me I have given to them, that they may be one even as we are one, I in them and thou in me, that they may become perfectly one, so that the world may know that thou hast sent me and hast loved them even as thou hast loved me.

878 (1) **Matthew 4:19** And he said to them, "Follow me, and I will make you fishers of men."

878 (2) **Matthew 4:21** And going on from there he saw two other brothers, James the son of Zebedee and John his brother, in the boat with Zebedee their father, mending their nets, and he called them.

878 (3) **John 1:43** The next day Jesus decided to go to Galilee. And he found Philip and said to him, "Follow me."

CIC Canon 330 Just as, by the Lord's decision, Saint Peter and the other Apostles constitute one college, so in a similar way the Roman Pontiff, successor of Peter, and the bishops, successors of the Apostles, are joined together. 880

(1) **Matthew 16:18–19** ". . . And I tell you, you are Peter, and on this rock I will build my church, and the powers of death shall not prevail against it. I will give you the keys of the kingdom of heaven, and whatever you bind on earth shall be bound in heaven, and whatever you loose on earth shall be loosed in heaven." 881

(2) **John 21:15–17** When they had finished breakfast, Jesus said to Simon Peter, "Simon, son of John, do you love me more than these?" He said to him, "Yes, Lord; you know that I love you." He said to him, "Feed my lambs." A second time he said to him, "Simon, son of John, do you love me?" He said to him, "Yes, Lord; you know that I love you." He said to him, "Tend my sheep." He said to him the third time, "Simon, son of John, do you love me?" Peter was grieved because he said to him the third time, "Do you love me?" And he said to him, "Lord, you know everything; you know that I love you." Jesus said to him, "Feed my sheep. . . ." 881

(1) ***Christus Dominus* 2** In this Church of Christ the Roman Pontiff, as the successor of Peter, to whom Christ entrusted the care of his sheep and his lambs, has been granted by God supreme, full, immediate and universal power in the care of souls. As pastor of all the faithful his mission is to promote the common good of the universal Church and the particular good of all the churches. He is therefore endowed with the primacy of ordinary power over all the churches. 882

The bishops also have been designated by the Holy Spirit to take the place of the apostles as pastors of souls and, together with the Supreme Pontiff and subject to his authority, they are commissioned to perpetuate the work of Christ, the eternal Pastor. For Christ commanded the apostles and their successors and gave them the power to teach all peoples, to sanctify men in truth and to give them spiritual nourishment. By virtue, therefore, of the Holy Spirit who has been given to them, bishops have been constituted true and authentic teachers of the faith and have been made pontiffs and pastors.

(2) ***Christus Dominus* 9** In exercising his supreme, full and immediate authority over the universal Church the Roman Pontiff employs the various departments of the Roman Curia, which act in his name and by his authority for the good of the churches and in the service of the sacred pastors. It is the earnest desire of the Fathers of the sacred Council that these departments, which have indeed rendered excellent service to the Roman Pontiff and to the pastors of the Church, should be reorganized and modernized, should be more in keeping with different regions and rites, especially in regard to their number, their names, their competence, their procedures and methods of coordination. It is hoped also that, in view of the pastoral role proper to bishops, the functions of the legates of the Roman Pontiff should be more precisely determined. 882

CIC Canon 336 The college of bishops, whose head is the Supreme Pontiff and whose members are the bishops by virtue of sacramental consecration and hierarchical communion with the head and members of the college, and in which the apostolic body endures, together with its head, and never without its head, is also the subject of supreme and full power over the universal Church. 883

886 (1) ***Christus Dominus* 3** United in one college or body for the instruction and direction of the universal Church, the bishops, sharing in the solicitude of all the churches, exercise this their episcopal function, which they have received by virtue of their episcopal consecration in communion with the Supreme Pontiff and subject to his authority. They exercise this function individually as regards that portion of the Lord's flock which has been entrusted to each one of them, each bishop having responsibility for the particular church assigned to him. On occasion a number of bishops will cooperate to provide for the common needs of their churches.

Accordingly the sacred Synod, having regard to the conditions of human society which have brought about a new order of things, has promulgated the following decrees in order to determine more exactly the pastoral functions of bishops.

886 (2) **Galatians 2:10** . . . only they would have us remember the poor, which very thing I was eager to do.

887 ***Canon of the Apostles* 34** Account these worthy to be esteemed your rulers and your kings, and bring them tribute as to kings; for by you they and their families ought to be maintained. As Samuel made constitutions for the people concerning a king, in the first book of Kings, and Moses did so concerning priests in Leviticus, so do we also make constitutions for you concerning bishops. For if there the multitude distributed the inferior services in proportion to so great a king, ought not therefore the bishop much more now to receive of you those things which are determined by God for the sustenance of himself and of the rest of the clergy belonging to him? But if we may add somewhat further, let the bishop receive more than the other received of old: for he only managed the affairs of the soldiery, being entrusted with war and peace for the preservation of men's bodies; but the other is entrusted with the exercise of the priestly office in relation to God, in order to preserve both body and soul from dangers. By how much, therefore, the soul is more valuable than the body, so much the priestly office is beyond the kingly. For it binds and looses those that are worthy of punishment or of remission. Wherefore you ought to love the bishop as your father, and fear him as your king, and honor him as your lord, bringing to him your fruits and the works of your hands, for a blessing upon you, giving to him your first-fruits, and your tithes, and your oblations, and your gifts, as to the priest of God; the first-fruits of your wheat, and wine, and oil, and autumnal fruits, and wool, and all things which the Lord God gives thee. And thy offering shall be accepted as a savor of a sweet smell to the Lord thy God; and the Lord will bless the works of thy hands, and will multiply the good things of the land. "For a blessing is upon the head of him that giveth."

888 **Matthew 16:15** He said to them, "But who do you say that I am?"

889 ***Dei Verbum* 10** Sacred Tradition and sacred Scripture make up a single sacred deposit of the Word of God, which is entrusted to the Church. By adhering to it the entire holy people, united to its pastors, remains always faithful to the teaching of the apostles, to the brotherhood, to the breaking of bread and the prayers (cf. Acts 2:42 Greek). So, in maintaining, practicing and professing the faith that has been handed on there should be a remarkable harmony between the bishops and the faithful.

But the task of giving an authentic interpretation of the Word of God, whether in its written form or in the form of Tradition, has been entrusted to the living teaching office of the Church alone. Its authority in this matter is exercised in the name of Jesus Christ. Yet this Magisterium is not superior to the Word of God, but is its servant. It teaches only what has been handed on to it. At the divine command and with the help of the Holy Spirit, it listens to this devotedly, guards it with dedication and expounds it faithfully. All that it proposes for belief as being divinely revealed is drawn from this single deposit of faith.

It is clear, therefore, that, in the supremely wise arrangement of God, sacred Tradition, sacred Scripture and the Magisterium of the Church are so connected and associated that one of them cannot stand without the others. Working together, each in its own way under the action of the one Holy Spirit, they all contribute effectively to the salvation of souls.

(1) **Vatican Council I (1870): DS 3074** . . . that the Roman Pontiff, when he 891
speaks *ex cathedra*, that is, when carrying out the duty of the pastor and teacher of all Christians in accord with his supreme apostolic authority he explains a doctrine of faith or morals to be held by the universal Church, through the divine assistance promised him in blessed Peter, operates with that infallibility with which the divine Redeemer wished that His Church be instructed in defining doctrine on faith and morals; and so such definitions of the Roman Pontiff from himself, but not from the consensus of the Church, are unalterable.

(2) ***Lumen gentium* 25** Among the more important duties of bishops that of preach- 891
ing the Gospel has pride of place. For the bishops are heralds of the faith, who draw new disciples to Christ; they are authentic teachers, that is, teachers endowed with the authority of Christ, who preach the faith to the people assigned to them, the faith which is destined to inform their thinking and direct their conduct; and under the light of the Holy Spirit they make that faith shine forth, drawing from the storehouse of revelation new things and old (cf. Mt. 13:52); they make it bear fruit and with watchfulness they ward off whatever errors threaten their flock (cf. 2 Tim. 4:14). Bishops who teach in communion with the Roman Pontiff are to be revered by all as witnesses of divine and Catholic truth; the faithful, for their part, are obliged to submit to their bishops' decision, made in the name of Christ, in matters of faith and morals, and to adhere to it with a ready and respectful allegiance of mind. This loyal submission of the will and intellect must be given, in a special way, to the authentic teaching authority of the Roman Pontiff, even when he does not speak *ex cathedra* in such wise, indeed, that his supreme teaching authority be acknowledged with respect, and that one sincerely adhere to decisions made by him, conformably with his manifest mind and intention, which is made known principally either by the character of the documents in question, or by the frequency with which a certain doctrine is proposed, or by the manner in which the doctrine is formulated.

Although the bishops, taken individually, do not enjoy the privilege of infallibility, they do, however, proclaim infallibly the doctrine of Christ on the following conditions: namely, when, even though dispersed throughout the world but preserving for all that amongst themselves and with Peter's successor the bond of communion, in their authoritative teaching concerning matters of faith and morals, they are in agreement that a particular teaching is to be held definitively and absolutely. This is still more clearly the case when, assembled in an ecumenical council, they are, for the universal Church, teachers of and judges in matters of faith and morals, whose decisions must be adhered to with the loyal and obedient assent of faith.

This infallibility, however, with which the divine redeemer wished to endow his Church in defining doctrine pertaining to faith and morals, is co-extensive with the deposit of revelation, which must be religiously guarded and loyally and courageously expounded. The Roman Pontiff, head of the college of bishops, enjoys this infallibility in virtue of his office, when, as supreme pastor and teacher of all the faithful—

who confirms his brethren in the faith (cf. Lk. 22:32)—he proclaims in an absolute decision a doctrine pertaining to faith or morals. For that reason his definitions are rightly said to be irreformable by their very nature and not by reason of the assent of the Church, in as much as they were made with the assistance of the Holy Spirit promised to him in the person of blessed Peter himself; and as a consequence they are in no way in need of the approval of others, and do not admit of appeal to any other tribunal. For in such a case the Roman Pontiff does not utter a pronouncement as a private person, but rather does he expound and defend the teaching of the Catholic faith as the supreme teacher of the universal Church, in whom the Church's charism of infallibility is present in a singular way. The infallibility promised to the Church is also present in the body of bishops when, together with Peter's successor, they exercise the supreme teaching office. Now, the assent of the Church can never be lacking to such definitions on account of the same Holy Spirit's influence, through which Christ's whole flock is maintained in the unity of the faith and makes progress in it.

Furthermore, when the Roman Pontiff, or the body of bishops together with him, define a doctrine, they make the definition in conformity with revelation itself, to which all are bound to adhere and to which they are obliged to submit; and this revelation is transmitted integrally either in written form or in oral tradition through the legitimate succession of bishops and above all through the watchful concern of the Roman Pontiff himself; and through the light of the Spirit of truth it is scrupulously preserved in the Church and unerringly explained. The Roman Pontiff and the bishops, by reason of their office and the seriousness of the matter, apply themselves with zeal to the work of enquiring by every suitable means into this revelation and of giving apt expression to its contents; they do not, however, admit any new public revelation as pertaining to the divine deposit of faith.

900 ***Lumen gentium* 33** Gathered together in the People of God and established in the one Body of Christ under one head, the laity—no matter who they are—have, as living members, the vocation of applying to the building up of the Church and to its continual sanctification all the powers which they have received from the goodness of the Creator and from the grace of the Redeemer.

The apostolate of the laity is a sharing in the salvific mission of the Church. Through Baptism and Confirmation all are appointed to this apostolate by the Lord himself. Moreover, by the sacraments, and especially by the Eucharist, that love of God and man which is the soul of the apostolate is communicated and nourished. The laity, however, are given this special vocation: to make the Church present and fruitful in those places and circumstances where it is only through them that she can become the salt of the earth. Thus, every lay person, through those gifts given to him, is at once the witness and the living instrument of the mission of the Church itself "according to the measure of Christ's bestowal" (Eph. 4:7).

Besides this apostolate which belongs to absolutely every Christian, the laity can be called in different ways to more immediate cooperation in the apostolate of the hierarchy, like those men and women who helped the apostle Paul in the Gospel, laboring much in the Lord (cf. Phil. 4:3; Rom. 16:3 ff.). They have, moreover, the capacity of being appointed by the hierarchy to some ecclesiastical offices with a view to a spiritual end.

All the laity, then, have the exalted duty of working for the ever greater spread of the divine plan of salvation to all men, of every epoch and all over the earth. Therefore may the way be clear for them to share diligently in the salvific work of the Church according to their ability and the needs of the times.

(1) ***Lumen gentium* 10** Christ the Lord, high priest taken from among men (cf. Heb. 5:1–5), made the new people "a kingdom of priests to God, his Father" (Apoc. 1:6; cf. 5:9–10). The baptized, by regeneration and the anointing of the Holy Spirit, are consecrated to be a spiritual house and a holy priesthood, that through all the works of Christian men they may offer spiritual sacrifices and proclaim the perfection of him who has called them out of darkness into his marvellous light (cf. 1 Pet. 2:4–10). Therefore all the disciples of Christ, persevering in prayer and praising God (cf. Acts 2:42–47), should present themselves as a sacrifice, living, holy and pleasing to God (cf. Rom. 12:1). They should everywhere on earth bear witness to Christ and give an answer to everyone who asks a reason for the hope of an eternal life which is theirs (cf. 1 Pet. 3:15). 901

Though they differ essentially and not only in degree, the common priesthood of the faithful and the ministerial or hierarchical priesthood are none the less ordered one to another; each in its own proper way shares in the one priesthood of Christ. The ministerial priest, by the sacred power that he has, forms and rules the priestly people; in the person of Christ he effects the eucharistic sacrifice and offers it to God in the name of all the people. The faithful indeed, by virtue of their royal priesthood, participate in the offering of the Eucharist. They exercise that priesthood, too, by the reception of the sacraments, prayer and thanksgiving, the witness of a holy life, abnegation and active charity.

(2) **1 Peter 2:5** . . . and like living stones be yourselves built into a spiritual house, to be a holy priesthood, to offer spiritual sacrifices acceptable to God through Jesus Christ. 901

CIC Canon 230, §1 Lay men who possess the age and qualifications determined by decree of the conference of bishops can be installed on a stable basis in the ministries of lector and acolyte in accord with the prescribed liturgical rite; the conferral of these ministries, however, does not confer on these lay men a right to obtain support or remuneration from the Church. 903

***Ad gentes divinitus* 15** When the Holy Spirit, who calls all men to Christ and arouses in their hearts the submission of faith by the seed of the word and the preaching of the Gospel, brings those who believe in Christ to a new life through the womb of the baptismal font, he gathers them into one people of God which is a "chosen race, a royal priesthood, a holy nation, a purchased people" (1 Pet. 2:9). 905

Therefore, missionaries, the fellow workers of God (cf. 1 Cor. 3:9), should raise up communities of the faithful, so that walking worthy of the calling to which they have been called (cf. Eph. 4:1) they might carry out the priestly, prophetic and royal offices entrusted to them by God. In this way the Christian community will become a sign of God's presence in the world. Through the eucharistic sacrifice it goes continually to the Father with Christ, carefully nourished with the word of God it bears witness to Christ, it walks in charity and is enlivened by an apostolic spirit.

From the start the Christian community should be so organized that it is able to provide for its own needs as far as possible.

This community of the faithful, endowed with the cultural riches of its own nation, must be deeply rooted in the people; families imbued with the spirit of the Gospel should flourish and be helped with suitable schools; groups and associations should be set up so that the spirit of the lay apostolate might pervade the whole of society. Finally, let charity shine out between Catholics of different rites.

The ecumenical spirit should be nourished among neophytes; they must appreciate that their brothers who believe in Christ are disciples of Christ, and having been reborn in baptism share in many of the blessings of the people of God. Insofar as religious conditions permit, ecumenical action should be encouraged, so that, while avoiding every form of indifferentism or confusion and also senseless rivalry, Catholics might collaborate with their separated brethren, insofar as it is possible, by a common profession before the nations of faith in God and in Jesus Christ, and by a common, fraternal effort in social, cultural, technical and religious matters, in accordance with the Decree on Ecumenism. Let them cooperate, especially, because of Christ their common Lord. May his name unite them! There should be collaboration of this type not only between private persons, but also, subject to the judgment of the local ordinary, between churches or ecclesiastical communities in their undertakings.

The Christian faithful who have been gathered into the Church from every nation and "are not marked off from the rest of men either by country, by language, or by political institutions," should live for God and Christ according to the honorable usages of their race. As good citizens they should sincerely and actively foster love of country and, while utterly rejecting racial hatred or exaggerated nationalism, work for universal love among men.

In achieving all this, the laity, that is Christians who have been incorporated into Christ and live in the world, are of primary importance and worthy of special care. It is for them, imbued with the Spirit of Christ, to be a leaven animating and directing the temporal order from within, so that everything is always carried out in accordance with the will of Christ.

However, it is not sufficient for the Christian people to be present or established in a particular nation, nor sufficient that it should merely exercise the apostolate of good example; it has been established and it is present so that it might by word and deed proclaim Christ to non-Christian fellow countrymen and help them towards a full reception of Christ.

Various types of ministry are necessary for the implanting and growth of the Christian community, and once these forms of service have been called forth from the body of the faithful, by the divine call, they are to be carefully fostered and nurtured by all. Among these functions are those of priests, deacons and catechists, and also that of Catholic Action. Brothers and nuns, likewise, play an indispensable role in planting and strengthening the kingdom of Christ in souls, and in the work of further extending it, both by their prayers and active work.

906 (1) CIC Canon 229

§1. Lay persons are bound by the obligation and possess the right to acquire a knowledge of Christian doctrine adapted to their capacity and condition so that they can live in accord with that doctrine, announce it, defend it when necessary, and be enabled to assume their role in exercising the apostolate.

§2. Lay persons also possess the right to acquire that deeper knowledge of the sacred sciences which are taught in ecclesiastical universities or faculties or in institutes of religious sciences by attending classes and obtaining academic degrees.

§3. Likewise, the prescriptions as to the required suitability having been observed, lay persons are capable of receiving from legitimate ecclesiastical authority a mandate to teach the sacred sciences.

906 (2) CIC Canon 774

§1. Under the supervision of legitimate ecclesiastical authority this concern for catechesis pertains to all the members of the Church in proportion to each one's role.

§2. Parents above others are obliged to form their children in the faith and practice of the Christian life by word and example; godparents and those who take the place of parents are bound by an equivalent obligation.

(3) **CIC Canon 776** In virtue of his office the pastor is bound to provide for the catechetical formation of adults, young people and children, to which end he is to employ the services of the clerics attached to the parish, members of institutes of consecrated life and of societies of apostolic life, with due regard for the character of each institute, and lay members of the Christian faithful, above all catechists; all of these are not to refuse to furnish their services willingly unless they are legitimately impeded. The pastor is to promote and foster the role of parents in the family catechesis mentioned in can. 774, §2. 906

(4) **CIC Canon 780** Local ordinaries are to see to it that catechists are duly prepared to fulfill their task correctly, namely, that continuing formation is made available to them, that they acquire a proper knowledge of the Church's teaching, and that they learn in theory and in practice the norms proper to the pedagogical disciplines. 906

(5) **CIC Canon 823, §1** In order for the integrity of the truths of the faith and morals to be preserved, the pastors of the Church have the duty and the right to be vigilant lest harm be done to the faith or morals of the Christian faithful through writings or the use of the instruments of social communication; they likewise have the duty and the right to demand that writings to be published by the Christian faithful which touch upon faith or morals be submitted to their judgment; they also have the duty and right to denounce writings which harm correct faith or good morals. 906

Philippians 2:8–9 And being found in human form he humbled himself and became obedient unto death, even death on a cross. Therefore God has highly exalted him and bestowed on him the name which is above every name. . . . 908

(1) **CIC Canon 443, §4** Presbyters and other members of the Christian faithful can also be called to particular councils with only a consultative vote; their number is not to exceed half of the number of those mentioned in §§1–3 [Diocesan, coadjutor, auxiliary, and titular bishops]. 911

(2) **CIC Canon 463** 911

§1. The following persons are to be called to the diocesan synod as its members and are obliged to participate in it:

1° the coadjutor bishop and the auxiliary bishops;

2° the vicars general, the episcopal vicars and the judicial vicar;

3° the canons of the cathedral church;

4° the members of the presbyteral council;

5° lay members of the Christian faithful and members of institutes of consecrated life, to be selected by the pastoral council in a manner and number to be determined by the diocesan bishop or, where such a council does not exist, in a manner determined by the diocesan bishop;

6° the rector of the diocesan major seminary;

7° the vicars forane;

8° at least one presbyter to be selected from each vicariate forane by all who have the care of souls there; also to be selected is another presbyter who would take the place of the first one selected if he were impeded;

9° some superiors of the religious institutes and societies of apostolic life which have a house in the diocese, to be selected in a manner and number determined by the diocesan bishop.

§2. Others can be called as members to the diocesan synod by the diocesan bishop; these can be clerics, members of institutes of consecrated life, or lay members of the Christian faithful.

911 (3) **CIC Canon 492, §1** In each diocese a finance council is to be established by the bishop, over which he himself or his delegate presides, and which is to be composed of at least three members of the Christian faithful truly skilled in financial affairs as well as in civil law, of outstanding integrity and appointed by the bishop.

911 (4) **CIC Canon 511** In each diocese, to the extent that pastoral circumstances recommend it, a pastoral council is to be established whose responsibility it is to investigate under the authority of the bishop all those things which pertain to pastoral works, to ponder them and to propose practical conclusions about them.

911 (5) **CIC Canon 517, §2** If the diocesan bishop should decide that due to a dearth of priests a participation in the exercise of the pastoral care of a parish is to be entrusted to a deacon or to some other person who is not a priest or to a community of persons, he is to appoint some priest endowed with the powers and faculties of a pastor to supervise the pastoral care.

911 (6) **CIC Canon 536** §1. After the diocesan bishop has listened to the presbyteral council and if he judges it opportune, a pastoral council is to be established in each parish; the pastor presides over it, and through it the Christian faithful along with those who share in the pastoral care of the parish in virtue of their office give their help in fostering pastoral activity.

§2. This pastoral council possesses a consultative vote only and is governed by norms determined by the diocesan bishop.

911 (7) **CIC Canon 1421, §2** The conference of bishops can permit lay persons to be appointed judges; when it is necessary, one of them can be employed to form a collegiate tribunal.

915 (1) ***Lumen gentium* 42–43** 'God is love, and he who abides in love abides in God, and God abides in him' (1 Jn. 4:16). God has poured out his love in our hearts through the Holy Spirit who has been given to us (cf. Rom. 5:5); therefore the first and most necessary gift is charity, by which we love God above all things and our neighbor because of him. But if charity is to grow and fructify in the soul like a good seed, each of the faithful must willingly hear the word of God and carry out his will with deeds, with the help of his grace; he must frequently partake of the sacraments, chiefly the Eucharist, and take part in the liturgy; he must constantly apply himself to prayer, self-denial, active brotherly service and the practice of all virtues. This is because love, as the bond of perfection and fullness of the law (cf. Col. 3:14; Rom. 13:10), governs, gives meaning to, and perfects all the means of sanctification. Hence the true disciple of Christ is marked by love both of God and of his neighbor.

Since Jesus, the Son of God, showed his love by laying down his life for us, no one has greater love than he who lays down his life for him and for his brothers (cf. 1 Jn. 3:16, Jn. 15:13). Some Christians have been called from the beginning, and will always be called, to give this greatest testimony of love to all, especially to persecutors. Martyrdom makes the disciple like his master, who willingly accepted death for the salvation of the world, and through it he is conformed to him by the shedding of blood. Therefore the Church considers it the highest gift and supreme test of love. And while it is given to few, all however must be prepared to confess Christ before men and to follow him along the way of the cross amidst the persecutions which the Church never lacks.

Likewise the Church's holiness is fostered in a special way by the manifold counsels which the Lord proposes to his disciples in the Gospel for them to observe. Towering among these counsels is that precious gift of divine grace given to some by the Father (cf. Mt. 19:11; 1 Cor. 7:7) to devote themselves to God alone more easily with an undivided heart (cf. 1 Cor. 7:32–24) in virginity or celibacy. This perfect continence for love of the kingdom of heaven has always been held in high esteem by the Church as a sign and stimulus of love, and as a singular source of spiritual fertility in the world.

The Church bears in mind too the apostle's admonition when calling the faithful to charity and exhorting them to have the same mind which Christ Jesus showed, who "emptied himself, taking the form of a servant . . . and became obedient unto death" (Phil. 2:7–8) and for our sakes "became poor, though he was rich" (2 Cor. 8:9). Since the disciples must always imitate this love and humility of Christ and bear witness of it, Mother Church rejoices that she has within herself many men and women who pursue more closely the Savior's self-emptying and show it forth more clearly, by undertaking poverty with the freedom of God's sons, and renouncing their own will: they subject themselves to man for the love of God, thus going beyond what is of precept in the matter of perfection, so as to conform themselves more fully to the obedient Christ.

Therefore all the faithful are invited and obliged to holiness and the perfection of their own state of life. Accordingly let all of them see that they direct their affections rightly, lest they be hindered in their pursuit of perfect love by the use of worldly things and by an adherence to riches which is contrary to the spirit of evangelical poverty, following the apostle's advice: Let those who use this world not fix their abode in it, for the form of this world is passing away (cf. 1 Cor. 7:31, Greek text).

The teaching and example of Christ provide the foundation for the evangelical counsels of chaste self-dedication to God, of poverty and of obedience. The Apostles and Fathers of the Church commend them, and so do her doctors and pastors. They therefore constitute a gift of God which the Church has received from her Lord and which by his grace she always safeguards.

Guided by the Holy Spirit, Church authority has been at pains to give a right interpretation of the counsels, to regulate their practice, and also to set up stable forms of living embodying them. From the God-given seed of the counsels a wonderful and wide-spreading tree has grown up in the field of the Lord, branching out into various forms of religious life lived in solitude or in community. Different religious families have come into existence in which spiritual resources are multiplied for the progress in holiness of their members and for the good of the entire Body of Christ.

Members of these families enjoy many helps towards holiness of life. They have a stable and more solidly based way of Christian life. They receive well-proven teaching on seeking after perfection. They are bound together in brotherly communion in the army of Christ. Their Christian freedom is fortified by obedience. Thus they are enabled to live securely and to maintain faithfully the religious life to which they have pledged themselves. Rejoicing in spirit they advance on the road of love.

This form of life has its own place in relation to the divine and hierarchical structure of the Church. Not, however, as though it were a kind of middle way between the clerical and lay conditions of life. Rather it should be seen as a form of life to which some Christians, both clerical and lay, are called by God so that they may enjoy a special gift of grace in the life of the Church and may contribute, each in his own way, to the saving mission of the Church.

(2) ***Perfectae caritatis* 1** In the constitution, *Lumen Gentium*, the holy synod has 915
already shown that the pursuit of perfect charity by means of the evangelical counsels traces its origins to the teaching and the example of the Divine Master, and that it

is a very clear symbol of the heavenly kingdom. Now however it proposes to deal with the life and discipline of those institutes whose members make profession of chastity, poverty and obedience, and to make provision for their needs, as our times recommend.

From the very beginning of the Church there were men and women who set out to follow Christ with greater liberty, and to imitate him more closely, by practicing the evangelical counsels. They led lives dedicated to God, each in his own way. Many of them, under the inspiration of the Holy Spirit, became hermits or founded religious families. These the Church, by virtue of her authority, gladly accepted and approved. Thus, in keeping with the divine purpose, a wonderful variety of religious communities came into existence. This has considerably contributed towards enabling the Church not merely to be equipped for every good work (cf. 2 Tim. 3:17) and to be prepared for the work of the ministry unto the building-up of the Body of Christ (cf. Eph. 4:12), but also to appear adorned with the manifold gifts of her children, like a bride adorned for her husband (cf. Apoc. 21:2), and to manifest in herself the multiform wisdom of God (cf. Eph. 3:10).

Amid such a great variety of gifts, however, all those who are called by God to the practice of the evangelical counsels, and who make faithful profession of them, bind themselves to the Lord in a special way. They follow Christ who, virginal and poor (cf. Mt. 8:20; Lk. 9:58), redeemed and sanctified men by obedience unto death on the cross (cf. Phil. 2:8). Under the impulse of love, which the Holy Spirit pours into their hearts (cf. Rom. 5:5), they live more and more for Christ and for his Body, the Church (cf. Col. 1:24). The more fervently, therefore, they join themselves to Christ by this gift of their whole life, the fuller does the Church's life become and the more vigorous and fruitful its apostolate.

In order that the Church of today may benefit more fully from lives consecrated by the profession of the counsels and from the vital function which they perform, the holy synod makes the following provisions. They deal only with the general principles of the up-to-date renewal of the life and discipline of religious orders and, while leaving their special characters intact, of societies of common life without vows, and of secular institutes. Particular norms for their exposition and application will be determined after the council by the competent authority.

916 (1) ***Perfectae caritatis* 5** The members of each institute should recall, first of all, that when they made professions of the evangelical counsels they were responding to a divine call, to the end that, not merely being dead to sin (cf. Rom. 6:11) but renouncing the world also, they might live for God alone. They have dedicated their whole lives to his service. This constitutes a special consecration, which is deeply rooted in their baptismal consecration and is a fuller expression of it. Since this gift of themselves has been accepted by the Church, they should be aware that they are dedicated to its service also. This service of God should stimulate and foster the exercise of the virtues by them, especially the virtues of humility and obedience, fortitude and chastity, by which they share in Christ's emptying of himself (cf. Phil. 2:7–8) and at the same time in his life in the spirit (cf. Rom. 9:1–13).

Religious, therefore, faithful to their profession and leaving all things for Christ's sake (cf. Mk. 10:28), should follow him, regarding this as the one thing that is necessary (cf. Lk. 10:39) and should be solicitous for all that is his (cf. Cor. 7:32).

The members of each institute, therefore, ought to seek God before all else, and solely; they should join contemplation, by which they cleave to God by mind and heart, to apostolic love, by which they endeavor to be associated with the work of redemption and to spread the kingdom of God.

(2) **CIC Canon 573** 916

§1. Life consecrated by the profession of the evangelical counsels is a stable form of living by which faithful, following Christ more closely under the action of the Holy Spirit, are totally dedicated to God who is loved most of all, so that, having dedicated themselves to His honor, the upbuilding of the Church and the salvation of the world by a new and special title, they strive for the perfection of charity in service to the Kingdom of God and, having become an outstanding sign in the Church, they may foretell the heavenly glory.

§2. Christian faithful who profess the evangelical counsels of chastity, poverty and obedience by vows or other sacred bonds according to the proper laws of institutes freely assume this form of living in institutes of consecrated life canonically erected by competent church authority and through the charity to which these counsels lead they are joined to the Church and its mystery in a special way.

CIC Canon 605 Approving new forms of consecrated life is reserved to the Apostolic See alone. Diocesan bishops, however, should strive to discern new gifts of consecrated life granted to the Church by the Holy Spirit and they should aid their promoters so that they can express their proposals as well as possible and protect them with suitable statutes, utilizing especially the general norms contained in this section. 919

1 Corinthians 7:34–36 . . . and his interests are divided. And the unmarried woman or girl is anxious about the affairs of the Lord, how to be holy in body and spirit; but the married woman is anxious about worldly affairs, how to please her husband. I say this for your own benefit, not to lay any restraint upon you, but to promote good order and to secure your undivided devotion to the Lord. If any one thinks that he is not behaving properly toward his betrothed, if his passions are strong, and it has to be, let him do as he wishes: let them marry—it is no sin. 922

(1) **CIC Canon 604, §1** Similar to these forms of consecrated life is the order of virgins, who, committed to the holy plan of following Christ more closely, are consecrated to God by the diocesan bishop according to the approved liturgical rite, are betrothed mystically to Christ, the Son of God, and are dedicated to the service of the Church. 924

(2) **Rite of Consecration to a Life of Virginity, Introduction 2** Those who consecrate their chastity under the inspiration of the Holy Spirit do so for the sake of more fervent love of Christ and of greater freedom in the service of their brothers and sisters. 924

They are to spend their time in works of penance and of mercy, in apostolic activity and in prayer, according to their state of life and spiritual gifts.

To fulfill their duty of prayer they are strongly advised to celebrate the liturgy of the hours each day, especially morning prayer and evening prayer. In this way, by joining their voices to those of Christ the High Priest and of his Church, they will offer unending praise to the heavenly Father and pray for the salvation of the whole world.

(3) **CIC Canon 604, §2** In order to observe their commitment more faithfully and to perform by mutual support service to the Church which is in harmony with their state these virgins can form themselves into associations. 924

925 (1) **CIC Canon 607**

§1. Religious life, as a consecration of the whole person, manifests in the Church a wonderful marriage brought about by God, a sign of the future age. Thus religious bring to perfection their full gift as a sacrifice offered to God by which their whole existence becomes a continuous worship of God in love.

§2. A religious institute is a society in which members, according to proper law, pronounce public vows either perpetual or temporary, which are to be renewed when they have lapsed, and live a life in common as brothers or sisters.

§3. The public witness to be rendered by religious to Christ and to the Church entails a separation from the world proper to the character and purpose of each institute.

925 (2) **CIC Canon 573**

§1. Life consecrated by the profession of the evangelical counsels is a stable form of living by which faithful, following Christ more closely under the action of the Holy Spirit, are totally dedicated to God who is loved most of all, so that, having dedicated themselves to His honor, the upbuilding of the Church and the salvation of the world by a new and special title, they strive for the perfection of charity in service to the Kingdom of God and, having become an outstanding sign in the Church, they may foretell the heavenly glory.

§2. Christian faithful who profess the evangelical counsels of chastity, poverty and obedience by vows or other sacred bonds according to the proper laws of institutes freely assume this form of living in institutes of consecrated life canonically erected by competent church authority and through the charity to which these counsels lead they are joined to the Church and its mystery in a special way.

925 (3) ***Unitatis redintegratio* 15** Everyone knows with what love the Eastern Christians celebrate the sacred liturgy, especially the eucharistic mystery, source of the Church's life and pledge of future glory. In this mystery the faithful, united with their bishops, have access to God the Father through the Son, the Word made flesh who suffered and was glorified, in the outpouring of the Holy Spirit. And so, made "sharers of the divine nature" (2 Pet. 1:4), they enter into communion with the most holy Trinity. Hence, through the celebration of the Eucharist of the Lord in each of these Churches, the Church of God is built up and grows in stature, and through concelebration, their communion with one another is made manifest.

In this liturgical worship, the Eastern Christians pay high tribute, in beautiful hymns of praise, to Mary ever Virgin, whom the ecumenical Synod of Ephesus solemnly proclaimed to be the holy Mother of God in order that Christ might be truly and properly acknowledged as Son of God and Son of Man, according to the scriptures. They also give homage to the saints, among them the Fathers of the universal Church.

These Churches, although separated from us, yet possess true sacraments, above all—by apostolic succession—the priesthood and the Eucharist, whereby they are still joined to us in closest intimacy. Therefore some worship in common (*communicatio in sacris*), given suitable circumstances and the approval of Church authority, is not merely possible but is encouraged.

Moreover, in the East are to be found the riches of those spiritual traditions which are given expression in monastic life especially. From the glorious times of the holy Fathers, that monastic spirituality flourished in the East which later flowed over into the Western world, and there provided a source from which Latin monastic life took its rise and has often drawn fresh vigor ever since. Therefore, it is earnestly recommended that Catholics avail themselves more often of the spiritual riches of the Eastern Fathers which lift up the whole man to the contemplation of divine mysteries.

Everyone should realize that it is of supreme importance to understand, venerate, preserve and foster the rich liturgical and spiritual heritage of the Eastern Churches in order faithfully to preserve the fullness of Christian tradition, and to bring about reconciliation between Eastern and Western Christians.

(1) ***Christus Dominus* 33–35** All religious (including for the purposes of this sec- 927
tion members of other institutes professing the evangelical counsels) are under an obligation, in accordance with the particular vocation of each, to work zealously and diligently for the building up and growth of the whole Mystical Body of Christ and for the good of the particular churches. It is their duty to promote these objectives primarily by means of prayer, works of penance, and by the example of their own lives. The sacred Synod earnestly exhorts them to develop an ever-increasing esteem and zeal for these practices. But, with due consideration for the special character of each religious institute, they should apply themselves more zealously to the external works of the apostolate.

Religious priests, who have been raised to the priesthood to be prudent cooperators with the episcopal order, are able nowadays to give more help to bishops in view of the more pressing needs of souls. Thus they may be said in a certain sense to belong to the diocesan clergy inasmuch as they share in the care of souls and in the practice of apostolic works under the authority of the bishops. The other members, too, of religious institutes, both men and women, also belong in a special sense to the diocesan family and render valuable help to the sacred hierarchy, and in view of the growing needs of the apostolate they can and should constantly increase the aid they give.

In order, however, that the works of the apostolate may always be carried out harmoniously in the individual dioceses and that the unity of diocesan discipline be preserved intact, the following fundamental principles are decreed:

(1) Religious should at all times treat the bishops, as the successors of the apostles, with loyal respect and reverence. Moreover, whenever legitimately called upon to do apostolic work, they must carry out these duties in such a way as to be the auxiliaries of the bishop and subject to him. Furthermore, religious should comply promptly and faithfully with the requests or desires of the bishops when they are asked to undertake a greater share in the ministry of salvation. Due consideration should be given to the character of the particular institute and to its constitutions, which may, if necessary, be adapted for this purpose in accord with the principles of this decree of the Council.

Especially in view of the urgent needs of souls and of the lack of diocesan clergy, those religious institutes which are not dedicated to a purely contemplative life may be called upon by the bishop to help in various pastoral ministries. The special character of each religious institute should be taken into consideration. Superiors should make every effort to cooperate, even taking responsibility for parishes on a temporary basis.

(2) Religious who are engaged in the external apostolate should be inspired by the spirit of their own institute, should remain faithful to the observance of their rule, and should be obedient to their superiors. Bishops should not fail for their part to insist on this obligation.

(3) The privilege of exemption whereby religious are reserved to the control of the Supreme Pontiff, or of some other ecclesiastical authority, and are exempted from the jurisdiction of bishops, relates primarily to the internal organization of their institutes. Its purpose is to ensure that everything is suitably and harmoniously arranged within them, and the perfection of the religious life promoted. The privilege ensures also that the Supreme Pontiff may employ these religious for the good of the

universal Church, or that some other competent authority may do so for the good of the churches under its jurisdiction. This exemption, however, does not prevent religious being subject to the jurisdiction of the bishops in the individual dioceses in accordance with the general law, insofar as is required for the performance of their pastoral duties and the proper care of souls.

(4) All religious, whether exempt or non-exempt, are subject to the authority of the local ordinary in the following matters: public worship, without prejudice, however, to the diversity of rites; the care of souls; preaching to the people; the religious and moral education, catechetical instruction and liturgical formation of the faithful, especially of children. They are also subject to diocesan rules regarding the comportment proper to the clerical state and also the various activities relating to the exercise of their sacred apostolate. Catholic schools conducted by religious are also subject to the local ordinaries as regards their general policy and supervision without prejudice, however, to the right of the religious to manage them. Likewise, religious are obliged to observe all those prescriptions which episcopal councils or conferences legitimately decree as binding on all.

(5) Organized cooperation should be encouraged between the various religious institutes and between them and the diocesan clergy. There should be the closest possible coordination of all apostolic works and activities. This will depend mainly on a supernatural attitude of heart and mind grounded on charity. It is the responsibility of the Apostolic See to foster this coordination in regard to the universal Church; it is for each bishop to do so in his own diocese, and for the patriarchs and episcopal synods and conferences in their territories.

There should be consultations beforehand between bishops or episcopal conferences and religious superiors or conferences of major superiors, with regard to apostolic activities to be undertaken by religious.

(6) In order to promote harmonious and fruitful relations between the bishops and religious, the bishops and superiors should meet at regular intervals and as often as seems opportune to discuss business matters of general concern in their territory.

927 (2) **CIC Canon 591** In order to provide better for the good of institutes and the needs of the apostolate, the Supreme Pontiff, by reason of his primacy over the universal Church and considering the common good, can exempt institutes of consecrated life from the governance of local ordinaries and subject them either to himself alone or to another ecclesiastical authority.

927 (3) ***Ad gentes divinitus* 18** Right from the planting of the Church the religious life should be carefully fostered, because not only does it provide valuable and absolutely necessary help for missionary activity, but through the deeper consecration made to God in the Church it clearly shows and signifies the intimate nature of the Christian vocation.

Religious institutes which are working for the implanting of the Church and which are deeply imbued with those mystical graces which are part of the Church's religious tradition, should strive to give them expression and to hand them on in a manner in keeping with the character and outlook of each nation. They should carefully consider how traditions of asceticism and contemplation, the needs of which have been sown by God in certain ancient cultures before the preaching of the Gospel, might be incorporated into the Christian religious life.

Different forms of religious life should be promoted in the new churches, so that they might manifest different aspects of Christ's mission and the life of the Church, devote themselves to various pastoral works, and prepare their members to exercise them properly. However, episcopal conferences should take care that congregations pursuing the same apostolic end are not multiplied, with consequent damage to the religious life and the apostolate.

The various undertakings aimed at establishing the contemplative life are worthy of special mention; some aim at implanting the rich tradition of their own order and retaining the essential elements of the monastic life, others are returning to the more simple forms of early monasticism. All, however, are eagerly seeking a real adaptation to local conditions. The contemplative life should be restored everywhere, because it belongs to the fullness of the Church's presence.

(4) ***Ad gentes divinitus* 40** Religious institutes of the contemplative and active life have up to this time played, and still play, the greatest part in the evangelization of the world. This sacred Synod willingly acknowledges their merits and thanks God for all that has been done for the glory of God and the service of souls; it exhorts them to continue untiringly in the work they have begun, since they know that the virtue of charity which they are obliged to practice more perfectly because of their vocation, impels and obliges them to a spirit and a work that is truly Catholic. 927

Institutes of the contemplative life, by their prayers, penances and trials, are of the greatest importance in the conversion of souls since it is in answer to prayer that God sends workers into his harvest (cf. Mt. 9:38), opens the minds of non-Christians to hear the Gospel (cf. Acts 16:14), and makes fruitful the word of salvation in their hearts (cf. 1 Cor. 3:7). Indeed these institutes are requested to establish houses in missionary territories, as quite a few have already done, so that by living their life there in a manner adapted to the genuinely religious traditions of the people, they might bear an outstanding witness among non-Christians to the majesty and love of God, and to union in Christ.

Institutes of the active life, whether or not they pursue a strictly missionary ideal, should sincerely examine themselves before God as to whether they might be able to extend their work for the expansion of the kingdom of God among the nations; whether they might be able to leave certain ministries to others so as to spend their strength for the missions; whether they might be able to begin work in the missions, adapting their constitutions if necessary, in accordance, however, with the mind of the founder; whether their members engage in missionary work to the full extent of their possibilities; whether their form of life bears witness to the Gospel in a manner adapted to the mentality and circumstances of the people.

Since, under the inspiration of the Holy Spirit, secular institutes are growing daily in the Church, their work, under the authority of the bishop, can be fruitful in many ways for the missions especially as an example of total dedication to the evangelization of the world.

CIC Canon 713, §2 Lay members share in the Church's evangelizing task in the world and of the world through their witness of a Christian life and fidelity toward their consecration, and through their efforts to order temporal things according to God and inform the world by the power of the gospel. Also, they cooperate in serving the ecclesial community, according to their particular secular way of life. 929

CIC Canon 731 §1. Comparable to institutes of consecrated life are societies of apostolic life whose members without religious vows pursue the particular apostolic purpose of the society, and leading a life as brothers or sisters in common according to a particular manner of life, strive for the perfection of charity through the observance of the constitutions. 930

§2. Among these there are societies in which the members embrace the evangelical counsels by some bond defined in the constitutions.

931 ***Redemptoris missio* 69** From the inexhaustible and manifold richness of the Spirit come the vocations of the *Institutes of Consecrated Life*, whose members, "because of the dedication to the service of the Church deriving from their very consecration, have an obligation to play a special part in missionary activity, in a manner appropriate to their Institute." History witnesses to the outstanding service rendered by religious families in the spread of the faith and the formation of new churches: from the ancient monastic institutions, to the medieval Orders, up to the more recent congregations.

(a) Echoing the Council, I invite *institutes of contemplative life* to establish communities in the young churches, so as to "bear glorious witness among non-Christians to the majesty and love of God, as well as to unity in Christ." This presence is beneficial throughout the non-Christian world, especially in those areas where religious traditions hold the contemplative life in great esteem for its asceticism and its search for the Absolute.

(b) To *institutes of active life*, I would recommend the immense opportunities for works of charity, for the proclamation of the Gospel, for Christian education, cultural endeavors and solidarity with the poor and those suffering from discrimination, abandonment and oppression. Whether they pursue a strictly missionary goal or not, such institutes should ask themselves how willing and able they are to broaden their action in order to extend God's kingdom. In recent times many institutes have responded to this request, which I hope will be given even greater consideration and implementation for a more authentic service. The Church needs to make known the great Gospel values of which she is the bearer. No one witnesses more effectively to these values than those who profess the consecrated life in chastity, poverty and obedience, in a total gift of self to God and in complete readiness to serve man and society after the example of Christ.

934 **CIC Canon 207** §1. Among the Christian faithful by divine institution there exist in the Church sacred ministers, who are also called clerics in law, and other Christian faithful, who are also called laity.

§2. From both groups there exist Christian faithful who are consecrated to God in their own special manner and serve the salvific mission of the Church through the profession of the evangelical counsels by means of vows or other sacred bonds recognized and sanctioned by the Church. Such persons also are of service to the saving mission of the Church; although their state does not belong to the hierarchical structure of the Church, they nevertheless do belong to its life and holiness.

943 ***Lumen gentium* 36:** see 786 (2).

952 (1) **Luke 16:1** He also said to the disciples, "There was a rich man who had a steward, and charges were brought to him that this man was wasting his goods. . . ."

952 (2) **Luke 16:3** ". . . And the steward said to himself, 'What shall I do, since my master is taking the stewardship away from me? I am not strong enough to dig, and I am ashamed to beg. . . .' "

953 **1 Corinthians 10:24** Let no one seek his own good, but the good of his neighbor.

956 **Jordan of Saxony, *Lib.* 93** Also, before his death he told his friars with assurance that they were going to regard him as more useful to them dead than alive. Undoubtedly he knew to Whom he had entrusted the investment of his effort and of his fruitful life, not doubting that for the rest there was laid up for him a crown of justice, and, once he received it, he would become more powerful in intercession to the degree to which he would have by then entered more securely into the powers of his Lord.

Hebrews 3:6 . . . but Christ was faithful over God's house as a son. And we are his house if we hold fast our confidence and pride in our hope. 959

(1) **Pius XII, *Proclamation of the Dogma of the Assumption of the Blessed Virgin Mary* (1950): DS 3903** Accordingly, after We directed Our prayers in supplication to God again and again, invoked the light of the Spirit of Truth, for the glory of Almighty God, who lavishes His special benevolence on the Virgin Mary, for the honor of her Son, the immortal King of the Ages and the victor over sin and death, for the increasing glory of the same august Mother, and for the joy and exultation of the whole Church, by the authority of our Lord Jesus Christ, of the Blessed Apostles, Peter and Paul, and by Our own authority We pronounce, declare, and define that the dogma was revealed by God, that the Immaculate Mother of God, the ever Virgin Mary, after completing her course of life upon earth, was assumed to the glory of heaven both in body and soul. 966

(2) **Revelation 19:16** On his robe and on his thigh he has a name inscribed, King of kings and Lord of lords. 966

(1) ***Marialis cultis* 42** We wish now, venerable Brothers, to dwell for a moment on the renewal of the pious practice which has been called "the compendium of the entire Gospel": the Rosary. To this our predecessors have devoted close attention and care. On many occasions they have recommended its frequent recitation, encouraged its diffusion, explained its nature, recognized its suitability for fostering contemplative prayer—prayer of both praise and petition—and recalled its intrinsic effectiveness for promoting Christian life and apostolic commitment. 971

We too, from the first General Audience of our Pontificate on 13 July 1963, have shown our great esteem for the pious practice of the Rosary. Since that time we have underlined its value on many different occasions, some ordinary, some grave. Thus, at a moment of anguish and uncertainty we published the Letter *Christi Matri* (15 September 1966), in order to obtain prayers to Our Lady of the Rosary, to implore from God the supreme benefit of peace. We renewed this appeal in our Apostolic Exhortation *Recurrens Mensis October* (7 October 1969), in which we also commemorated the fourth centenary of the Apostolic Letter *Consueverunt Romani Pontifices* of our predecessor Saint Pius V, who in that document explained and in a certain sense established the traditional form of the Rosary.

(2) ***Sacrosanctum concilium* 103** In celebrating this annual cycle of the mysteries of Christ, Holy Church honors the Blessed Mary, Mother of God, with a special love. She is inseparably linked with her son's saving work. In her the Church admires and exalts the most excellent fruit of redemption, and joyfully contemplates, as in a faultless image, that which she herself desires and hopes wholly to be. 971

Romans 4:25 . . . who was put to death for our trespasses and raised for our justification. 977

Matthew 18:21–22 Then Peter came up and said to him, "Lord, how often shall my brother sin against me, and I forgive him? As many as seven times?" Jesus said to him, "I do not say to you seven times, but seventy times seven. . . ." 982

St. Ambrose, *De Poenitentia* 1, 15 That faithful teacher, having promised one of two things, gave each. He came with a rod, for he separated the guilty man from the holy fellowship. And well is he said to be delivered to Satan who is separated from 983 the body of Christ. But he came in love and with the spirit of meekness, whether because he so delivered him up as to save his soul, or because he afterwards restored to the sacraments him whom he had before separated.

For it is needful to separate one who has grievously fallen, lest a little leaven corrupt the whole lump. And the old leaven must be purged out, or the old man in each person; that is, the outward man and his deeds, he who among the people has grown old in sin and hardened in vices. And well did he say purged, not cast forth, for what is purged is not considered wholly valueless, for to this end is it purged, that what is of value be separated from the worthless, but that which is cast forth is considered to have in itself nothing of value.

The Apostle then judged that the sinner should then at once be restored to the heavenly sacraments if he himself wished to be cleansed. And well is it said "Purge," for he is purged as by certain things done by the whole people, and is washed in the tears of the multitude, and redeemed from sin by the weeping of the multitude, and is purged in the inner man. For Christ granted to His Church that one should be redeemed by means of all, as she herself was found worthy of the coming of the Lord Jesus, in order that through One all might be redeemed.

This is Paul's meaning which the words make more obscure. Let us consider the exact words of the Apostle: "Purge out," says he, "the old leaven, that ye may be a new lump, even as ye are unleavened." Either that the whole Church takes up the burden of the sinner, with whom she has to suffer in weeping and prayer and pain, and, as it were, covers herself with his leaven, in order that by means of all that which is to be done away in the individual doing penance may be purged by a kind of contribution and commixture of compassion and mercy offered with manly vigor. Or one may understand it as that woman in the Gospel teaches us, who is a type of the Church, when she hid the leaven in her meal, till all was leavened, and the whole could be used as pure.

The Lord taught me in the Gospel what leaven is when He said: "Do ye not understand that I said not concerning bread, Beware of the leaven of the Pharisees and Sadducees?" Then, it is said, they understood that He spake not of bread, but that they should beware of the doctrine of the Pharisees and Sadducees. This leaven, then —that is, the doctrine of the Pharisees and the contentiousness of the Sadducees—the Church hides in her meal, when she softened the hard letter of the Law by a spiritual interpretation, and ground it as it were in the mill of her explanations, bringing out as it were from the husks of the letter the inner secrets of the mysteries, and setting forth the belief in the Resurrection, wherein the mercy of God is proclaimed, and wherein it is believed that the life of those who are dead is restored.

Now this comparison seems to be not unfitly brought forward in this place, since the kingdom of heaven is redemption from sin, and therefore we all, both bad and good, are mingled with the meal of the Church that we all may be a new lump. But that no one may be afraid that an admixture of evil leaven might injure the lump, the Apostle said: "That ye may be a new lump, even as ye are unleavened;" that is to say, This mixture will render you again such, as in the pure integrity of your innocence. If we thus have compassion, we are not stained with the sins of others, but we gain the restoration of another to the increase of our own grace, so that our integrity remains as it was. And therefore he adds: "For Christ our Passover is sacrificed for us;" that is, the Passion of the Lord profited all, and gave redemption to sinners who repented of the sins they had committed.

Let us then keep the feast on good food, doing penance yet joyful in our redemption, for no food is sweeter than kindness and gentleness. Let no envy towards the sinner who is saved be mingled with our feasts and joy, lest that envious brother, as is set forth in the Gospel, exclude himself from the house of his Father, because he grieved at the reception of his brother, at whose lasting exile he was wont to rejoice.

And you Novatians cannot deny that you are like him, who, as you say, do not come together to the Church because by penance a hope of return had been given to those who had lapsed. But this is only a pretense, for Novatian contrived his schism through grief at his loss of the episcopal office.

But do you not understand that the Apostle also prophesied of you and says to you: "And ye are puffed up and did not rather mourn, that he who did this deed might be taken away from among you"? He is, then, wholly taken away when his sin is done away, but the Apostle does not say that the sinner is to be shut out of the Church who counsels his cleansing.

(1) **John 6:39–40** ". . . and this is the will of him who sent me, that I should lose nothing of all that he has given me, but raise it up at the last day. For this is the will of my Father, that every one who sees the Son and believes in him should have eternal life; and I will raise him up at the last day." **989**

(2) **1 Thessalonians 4:14** For since we believe that Jesus died and rose again, even so, through Jesus, God will bring with him those who have fallen asleep. **989**

(3) **1 Corinthians 6:14** And God raised the Lord and will also raise us up by his power. **989**

(4) **2 Corinthians 4:14** . . . knowing that he who raised the Lord Jesus will raise us also with Jesus and bring us with you into his presence. **989**

(5) **Philippians 3:10–11** . . . that I may know him and the power of his resurrection, and may share his sufferings, becoming like him in his death, that if possible I may attain the resurrection from the dead. **989**

(1) **Genesis 6:3** Then the Lord said, "My spirit shall not abide in man for ever, for he is flesh, but his days shall be a hundred and twenty years." **990**

(2) **Psalm 56:5 (56:4: RSV)** **990**

In God, whose word I praise,
in God I trust without a fear.
What can flesh do to me?

(3) **Isaiah 40:6** **990**

A voice says, "Cry!"
And I said, "What shall I cry?"
All flesh is grass,
and all its beauty is like the flower of the field.

(1) **2 Maccabees 7:29** ". . . Do not fear this butcher, but prove worthy of your brothers. Accept death, so that in God's mercy I may get you back again with your brothers." **992**

(2) **Daniel 12:1–13** "At that time shall arise Michael, the great prince who has charge of your people. And there shall be a time of trouble, such as never has been since there was a nation till that time; but at that time your people shall be delivered, every one whose name shall be found written in the book. And many of those who **992**

sleep in the dust of the earth shall awake, some to everlasting life, and some to shame and everlasting contempt. And those who are wise shall shine like the brightness of the firmament; and those who turn many to righteousness, like the stars for ever and ever. But you, Daniel, shut up the words, and seal the book, until the time of the end. Many shall run to and fro, and knowledge shall increase."

Then I Daniel looked, and behold, two others stood, one on this bank of the stream and one on that bank of the stream. And I said to the man clothed in linen, who was above the waters of the stream, "How long shall it be till the end of these wonders?" The man clothed in linen, who was above the waters of the stream, raised his right hand and his left hand toward heaven; and I heard him swear by him who lives for ever that it would be for a time, two times, and half a time; and that when the shattering of the power of the holy people comes to an end all these things would be accomplished. I heard, but I did not understand. Then I said, "O my lord, what shall be the issue of these things?" He said, "Go your way, Daniel, for the words are shut up and sealed until the time of the end. Many shall purify themselves, and make themselves white, and be refined; but the wicked shall do wickedly; and none of the wicked shall understand; but those who are wise shall understand. And from the time that the continual burnt offering is taken away, and the abomination that makes desolate is set up, there shall be a thousand two hundred and ninety days. Blessed is he who waits and comes to the thousand three hundred and thirty-five days. But go your way till the end; and you shall rest, and shall stand in your allotted place at the end of the days."

993 (1) **John 11:24** Martha said to him, "I know that he will rise again in the resurrection at the last day."

993 (2) **Acts 23:6** But when Paul perceived that one part were Sadducees and the other Pharisees, he cried out in the council, "Brethren, I am a Pharisee, a son of Pharisees; with respect to the hope and the resurrection of the dead I am on trial."

994 (1) **John 5:24–25** ". . . Truly, truly, I say to you, he who hears my word and believes him who sent me, has eternal life; he does not come into judgment, but has passed from death to life.

"Truly, truly, I say to you, the hour is coming, and now is, when the dead will hear the voice of the Son of God, and those who hear will live. . . ."

994 (2) **John 6:40** ". . . For this is the will of my Father, that every one who sees the Son and believes in him should have eternal life; and I will raise him up at the last day."

994 (3) **John 6:54** . . . he who eats my flesh and drinks my blood has eternal life, and I will raise him up at the last day.

994 (4) **Mark 5:21–42** And when Jesus had crossed again in the boat to the other side, a great crowd gathered about him; and he was beside the sea. Then came one of the rulers of the synagogue, Jairus by name; and seeing him, he fell at his feet, and besought him, saying, "My little daughter is at the point of death. Come and lay your hands on her, so that she may be made well, and live." And he went with him.

And a great crowd followed him and thronged about him. And there was a woman who had had a flow of blood for twelve years, and who had suffered much under many physicians, and had spent all that she had, and was no better but rather grew worse. She had heard the reports about Jesus, and came up behind him in the crowd and touched his garment. For she said, "If I touch even his garments, I shall be made well." And immediately the hemorrhage ceased; and she felt in her body that she was healed of her disease. And Jesus, perceiving in himself that power had gone forth from him, immediately turned about in the crowd, and said, "Who touched my garments?" And his disciples said to him, "You see the crowd pressing around you, and yet you say, 'Who touched me?' " And he looked around to see who had done it. But the woman, knowing what had been done to her, came in fear and trembling and fell down before him, and told him the whole truth. And he said to her, "Daughter, your faith has made you well; go in peace, and be healed of your disease."

While he was still speaking, there came from the ruler's house some who said, "Your daughter is dead. Why trouble the Teacher any further?" But ignoring what they said, Jesus said to the ruler of the synagogue, "Do not fear, only believe." And he allowed no one to follow him except Peter and James and John the brother of James. When they came to the house of the ruler of the synagogue, he saw a tumult, and people weeping and wailing loudly. And when he had entered, he said to them, "Why do you make a tumult and weep? The child is not dead but sleeping." And they laughed at him. But he put them all outside, and took the child's father and mother and those who were with him, and went in where the child was. Taking her by the hand he said to her, "Talitha cumi"; which means, "Little girl, I say to you, arise." And immediately the girl got up and walked (she was twelve years of age), and they were immediately overcome with amazement.

(5) **Luke 7:11–17** Soon afterward he went to a city called Nain, and his disciples 994
and a great crowd went with him. As he drew near to the gate of the city, behold, a man who had died was being carried out, the only son of his mother, and she was a widow; and a large crowd from the city was with her. And when the Lord saw her, he had compassion on her and said to her, "Do not weep." And he came and touched the bier, and the bearers stood still. And he said, "Young man, I say to you, arise." And the dead man sat up, and began to speak. And he gave him to his mother. Fear seized them all; and they glorified God, saying, "A great prophet has arisen among us!" and "God has visited his people!" And this report concerning him spread through the whole of Judea and all surrounding country.

(6) **John 11** Now a certain man was ill, Lazarus of Bethany, the village of Mary and 994
her sister Martha. It was Mary who anointed the Lord with ointment and wiped his feet with her hair, whose brother Lazarus was ill. So the sisters went to him, saying, "Lord, he whom you love is ill." But when Jesus heard it he said, "This illness is not unto death; it is for the glory of God, so that the Son of God may be glorified by means of it."

Now Jesus loved Martha and her sister and Lazarus. So when he heard that he was ill, he stayed two days longer in the place where he was. Then after this he said to the disciples, "Let us go into Judea again." The disciples said to him, "Rabbi, the Jews were but now seeking to stone you, and are you going there again?' " Jesus answered, "Are there not twelve hours in the day? If any one walks in the day, he does not stumble, because he sees the light of this world. But if any one walks in the night, he stumbles, because the light is not in him." Thus he spoke, and then he said to them, "Our friend Lazarus has fallen asleep, but I go to awake him out of sleep." The disciples said to him, "Lord, if he has fallen asleep, he will recover." Now Jesus had spoken of his death, but they thought that he meant taking rest in sleep. Then Jesus told them plainly, "Lazarus is dead; and for your sake I am glad that I was not there, so that you may believe. But let us go to him." Thomas, called the Twin, said to his fellow disciples, "Let us also go, that we may die with him."

Now when Jesus came, he found that Lazarus had already been in the tomb four days. Bethany was near Jerusalem, about two miles off, and many of the Jews had come to Martha and Mary to console them concerning their brother. When Martha heard that Jesus was coming, she went and met him, while Mary sat in the house. Martha said to Jesus, "Lord, if you had been here, my brother would not have died. And even now I know that whatever you ask from God, God will give you." Jesus said to her, "Your brother will rise again." Martha said to him, "I know that he will rise again in the resurrection at the last day." Jesus said to her, "I am the resurrection and the life; he who believes in me, though he die, yet shall he live, and whoever lives and believes in me shall never die. Do you believe this?" She said to him, "Yes, Lord; I believe that you are the Christ, the Son of God, he who is coming into the world."

When she had said this, she went and called her sister Mary, saying quietly, "The Teacher is here and is calling for you." And when she heard it, she rose quickly and went to him. Now Jesus had not yet come to the village, but was still in the place where Martha had met him. When the Jews who were with her in the house, consoling her, saw Mary rise quickly and go out, they followed her, supposing that she was going to the tomb to weep there. Then Mary, when she came where Jesus was and saw him, fell at his feet, saying to him, "Lord, if you had been here, my brother would not have died." When Jesus saw her weeping, and the Jews who came with her also weeping, he was deeply moved in spirit and troubled; and he said, "Where have you laid him?" They said to him, "Lord, come and see." Jesus wept. So the Jews said, "See how he loved him!" But some of them said, "Could not he who opened the eyes of the blind man have kept this man from dying?"

Then Jesus, deeply moved again, came to the tomb; it was a cave, and a stone lay upon it. Jesus said, "Take away the stone." Martha, the sister of the dead man, said to him, "Lord, by this time there will be an odor, for he has been dead four days." Jesus said to her, "Did I not tell you that if you would believe you would see the glory of God?" So they took away the stone. And Jesus lifted up his eyes and said, "Father, I thank thee that thou hast heard me. I knew that thou hearest me always, but I have said this on account of the people standing by, that they may believe that thou didst send me." When he had said this, he cried with a loud voice, "Lazarus, come out." The dead man came out, his hands and feet bound with bandages, and his face wrapped with a cloth. Jesus said to them, "Unbind him, and let him go."

Many of the Jews therefore, who had come with Mary and had seen what he did, believed in him; but some of them went to the Pharisees and told them what Jesus had done. So the chief priests and the Pharisees gathered the council, and said, "What are we to do? For this man performs many signs. If we let him go on thus, every one will believe in him, and the Romans will come and destroy both our holy place and our nation." But one of them, Caiaphas, who was high priest that year, said to them, "You know nothing at all; you do not understand that it is expedient for you that one man should die for the people, and that the whole nation should not perish." He did not say this of his own accord, but being high priest that year he prophesied that Jesus should die for the nation, and not for the nation only, but to gather into one the children of God who are scattered abroad. So from that day on they took counsel how to put him to death.

Jesus therefore no longer went about openly among the Jews, but went from there to the country near the wilderness, to a town called Ephraim; and there he stayed with the disciples.

Now the Passover of the Jews was at hand, and many went up from the country to Jerusalem before the Passover, to purify themselves. They were looking for Jesus and saying to one another as they stood in the temple, "What do you think? That he will not come to the feast?" Now the chief priests and the Pharisees had given orders that if any one knew where he was, he should let them know, so that they might arrest him.

(7) **Mark 10:34** ". . . and they will mock him, and spit upon him, and scourge him, **994**
and kill him; and after three days he will rise."

(8) **John 2:19–22** Jesus answered them, "Destroy this temple, and in three days I **994**
will raise it up." The Jews then said, "It has taken forty-six years to build this temple, and will you raise it up in three days?" But he spoke of the temple of his body. When therefore he was raised from the dead, his disciples remembered that he had said this; and they believed the scripture and the word which Jesus had spoken.

Acts 4:33 And with great power the apostles gave their testimony to the resurrection **995**
of the Lord Jesus, and great grace was upon them all.

(1) **Acts 17:32** Now when they heard of the resurrection of the dead, some mocked; **996**
but others said, "We will hear you again about this."

(2) **1 Corinthians 15:12–13** Now if Christ is preached as raised from the dead, **996**
how can some of you say that there is no resurrection of the dead? But if there is no resurrection of the dead, then Christ has not been raised. . . .

Daniel 12:2 And many of those who sleep in the dust of the earth shall awake, **998**
some to everlasting life, and some to shame and everlasting contempt.

Philippians 3:20 But our commonwealth is in heaven, and from it we await a Savior, **1003**
the Lord Jesus Christ. . . .

(1) **Philippians 1:23** I am hard pressed between the two. My desire is to depart and **1005**
be with Christ, for that is far better.

(2) **Paul VI, *The* Credo *of the People of God* 28** We believe in eternal life. We **1005**
believe that the souls of all those who die in the grace of Christ—whether they must still make expiation in the fire of Purgatory, or whether from the moment they leave their bodies they are received by Jesus into Paradise like the good thief—go to form that People of God which succeeds death, death which will be totally destroyed on the day of the Resurrection when these souls are reunited with their bodies.

(1) **Genesis 2:17** ". . . but of the tree of the knowledge of good and evil you shall **1006**
not eat, for in the day that you eat of it you shall die."

(2) **Romans 6:3–9** Do you not know that all of us who have been baptized into **1006**
Christ Jesus were baptized into his death? We were buried therefore with him by baptism into death, so that as Christ was raised from the dead by the glory of the Father, we too might walk in newness of life.

For if we have been united with him in a death like his, we shall certainly be united with him in a resurrection like his. We know that our old self was crucified with him so that the sinful body might be destroyed, and we might no longer be enslaved to sin. For he who has died is freed from sin. But if we have died with Christ, we believe that we shall also live with him. For we know that Christ being raised from the dead will never die again; death no longer has dominion over him.

1006 (3) **Philippians 3:10–11** . . . that I may know him and the power of his resurrection, and may share his sufferings, becoming like him in his death, that if possible I may attain the resurrection from the dead.

1008 (1) **Genesis 2:17** ". . . but of the tree of the knowledge of good and evil you shall not eat, for in the day that you eat of it you shall die."

1008 (2) **Genesis 3:3** ". . . but God said, 'You shall not eat of the fruit of the tree which is in the midst of the garden, neither shall you touch it, lest you die.'"

1008 (3) **Genesis 3:19**

". . . In the sweat of your face
you shall eat bread
till you return to the ground,
for out of it you were taken;
you are dust,
and to dust you shall return."

1008 (4) **Wisdom 1:13**

. . . because God did not make death,
and he does not delight in the death of the living. . . .

1008 (5) **Romans 5:12** Therefore as sin came into the world through one man and death through sin, and so death spread to all men because all men sinned. . . .

1008 (6) **Romans 6:23** For the wages of sin is death, but the free gift of God is eternal life in Christ Jesus our Lord.

1008 (7) **Council of Trent (1546): DS 1511** If anyone does not confess that the first man Adam, when he had transgressed the commandment of God in Paradise, immediately lost his holiness and the justice in which he had been established, and that he incurred through the offense of that prevarication the wrath and indignation of God and hence the death with which God had previously threatened him, and with death captivity under his power, who thenceforth "had the empire of death" [Heb. 2:14], that is of the devil, and that through that offense of prevarication the entire Adam was transformed in body and soul for the worse, let him be anathema.

1008 (8) **Wisdom 2:23–24**

. . . for God created man for incorruption,
and made him in the image of his own eternity,
but through the devil's envy death entered the world,
and those who belong to his party experience it.

1008 (9) **1 Corinthians 15:26** The last enemy to be destroyed is death.

1009 (1) **Mark 14:33–34** And he took with him Peter and James and John, and began to be greatly distressed and troubled. And he said to them, "My soul is very sorrowful, even to death; remain here, and watch."

1009 (2) **Hebrews 5:7–8** In the days of his flesh, Jesus offered up prayers and supplications, with loud cries and tears, to him who was able to save him from death, and he was heard for his godly fear. Although he was a Son, he learned obedience through what he suffered. . . .

(3) **Romans 5:19–21** For as by one man's disobedience many were made sinners, 1009
so by one man's obedience many will be made righteous. Law came in, to increase the trespass; but where sin increased, grace abounded all the more, so that, as sin reigned in death, grace also might reign through righteousness to eternal life through Jesus Christ our Lord.

Luke 23:46 Then Jesus, crying with a loud voice, said, "Father, into thy hands I 1011
commit my spirit!" And having said this he breathed his last.

1 Thessalonians 4:13–14 But we would not have you ignorant, brethren, concern- 1012
ing those who are asleep, that you may not grieve as others do who have no hope. For since we believe that Jesus died and rose again, even so, through Jesus, God will bring with him those who have fallen asleep.

1 Corinthians 15:42–44 So is it with the resurrection of the dead. What is sown is 1017
perishable, what is raised is imperishable. It is sown in dishonor, it is raised in glory. It is sown in weakness, it is raised in power. It is sown a physical body, it is raised a spiritual body. If there is a physical body, there is also a spiritual body.

(1) **2 Timothy 1:9–10** . . . who saved us and called us with a holy calling, not in 1021
virtue of our works but in virtue of his own purpose and the grace which he gave us in Christ Jesus ages ago, and now has manifested through the appearing of our Savior Christ Jesus, who abolished death and brought life and immortality to light through the gospel.

(2) **Luke 16:22** The poor man died and was carried by the angels to Abraham's 1021
bosom. The rich man also died and was buried. . . .

(3) **Luke 23:43** And he said to him, "Truly, I say to you, today you will be with 1021
me in Paradise."

(4) **Matthew 16:26** For what will it profit a man, if he gains the whole world and 1021
forfeits his life? Or what shall a man give in return for his life?

(5) **2 Corinthians 5:8** We are of good courage, and we would rather be away from 1021
the body and at home with the Lord.

(6) **Philippians 1:23** I am hard pressed between the two. My desire is to depart 1021
and be with Christ, for that is far better.

(7) **Hebrews 9:27** And just as it is appointed for men to die once, and after that 1021
comes judgment. . . .

(8) **Hebrews 12:23** . . . and to the assembly of the first-born who are enrolled 1021
in heaven, and to a judge who is God of all, and to the spirits of just men made perfect. . . .

(1) **Council of Lyons II (1274): DS 857–58** However, the souls of those who 1022
after having received holy baptism have incurred no stain of sin whatever, also those souls who, after contracting the stain of sin, either while remaining in their bodies or being divested of them, have been cleansed, as we have said above, are received immediately into heaven. The souls of those who die in mortal sin or with original sin only, however, immediately descend to hell, yet to be punished with different punishments.

1022 (2) **Council of Florence (1439): DS 1304–6** [*De novissimis*] It has likewise defined, that, if those truly penitent have departed in the love of God, before they have made satisfaction by worthy fruits of penance for sins of commission and omission, the souls of these are cleansed after death by purgatorial punishments; and so that they may be released from punishments of this kind, the suffrages of the living faithful are of advantage to them, namely, the sacrifices of Masses, prayers, and almsgiving, and other works of piety, which are customarily performed by the faithful for other faithful according to the institutions of the Church. And that the souls of those, who after the reception of baptism have incurred no stain of sin at all, and also those, who after the contraction of the stain of sin whether in their bodies, or when released from the same bodies, as we have said before, are purged, are immediately received into heaven, and see clearly the one and triune God Himself, just as He is, yet according to the diversity of merits, one more perfectly than another. Moreover, the souls of those who depart in actual mortal sin or in original sin only, descend immediately into hell but to undergo punishments of different kinds.

1022 (3) **Council of Trent (1563): DS 1820** Since the Catholic Church, instructed by the Holy Spirit, in conformity with the sacred writings and the ancient tradition of the Fathers in sacred councils, and very recently in this ecumenical Synod, has taught that there is a purgatory, and that the souls detained there are assisted by the suffrages of the faithful, and especially by the acceptable sacrifice of the altar, the holy Synod commands the bishops that they insist that the sound doctrine of purgatory, which has been transmitted by the holy Fathers and holy Councils, be believed by the faithful of Christ, be maintained, taught, and everywhere preached. Let the more difficult and subtle "questions," however, and those which do not make for "edification" [cf. I Tim. 1:4], and from which there is very often no increase in piety, be excluded from popular discourses to uneducated people. Likewise, let them not permit uncertain matters, or those that have the appearance of falsehood, to be brought out and discussed publicly. Those matters on the contrary, which tend to a certain curiosity or superstition, or that savor of filthy lucre, let them prohibit as scandals and stumbling blocks to the faithful. . . .

1022 (4) **Benedict XII, *Benedictus Deus* (1336): DS 1000–1001** By this edict which will prevail forever, with apostolic authority we declare: that according to the common arrangement of God, souls of all the saints who departed from this world before the passion of our Lord Jesus Christ; also of the holy apostles, the martyrs, the confessors, virgins, and the other faithful who died after the holy baptism of Christ had been received by them, in whom nothing was to be purged, when they departed, nor will there be when they shall depart also in the future; or if then there was or there will be anything to be purged in these when after their death they have been purged; and the souls of children departing before the use of free will, reborn and baptized in that same baptism of Christ, when all have been baptized, immediately after their death and that aforesaid purgation in those who were in need of a purgation of this kind, even before the resumption of their bodies and the general judgment after the ascension of our Savior, our Lord Jesus Christ, into heaven, have been, are, and will be in heaven, in the kingdom of heaven and in celestial paradise with Christ, united in the company of the holy angels, and after the passion and death of our Lord Jesus Christ have seen and see the divine essence by intuitive vision, and even face to face, with no mediating creature, serving in the capacity of an object seen, but divine essence immediately revealing itself plainly, clearly, and openly, to them, and seeing thus they enjoy the same divine essence, and also that from such vision and enjoyment their souls, which now have departed, are truly blessed and they have eternal life and rest; and also [the souls] of those who afterwards will depart, will see that same divine essence, and will enjoy it before the general judgment; and that such vision of the divine essence and its enjoyment makes void the acts of faith and hope in them, inasmuch as faith and hope are proper theological virtues; and that after there has begun or will be such intuitive and face-to-face vision and enjoyment in these, the same vision and enjoyment without any interruption [intermission] or departure of the aforesaid vision and enjoyment exist continuously and will continue even up to the last judgment and from then even unto eternity.

(5) **John XXII, *Ne super his* (1334): DS 990** On the subject of these [opinions] which have rather often been expressed both by Us and by some other persons in Our presence in citing Sacred Scripture and original statements by the Saints or by reasoning in some other fashion in regard to the purified souls separated from their bodies (whether before the resumption of their bodies they see the divine essence by that vision which, to be precise, the Apostle calls "face to face"), so that they [the opinions] may not be able to be foisted upon the ears of the faithful in a manner other than that in which they have been said and have been understood and are understood and are said by Us, note that We are declaring Our intention, which We hold and have held in respect to these matters along with the holy Catholic Church, in this present series of remarks as follows. 1022

(6) **Benedict XII, *Benedictus Deus* (1336): DS 1002** Moreover, we declare that according to the common arrangement of God, the souls of those who depart in actual mortal sin immediately after their death descend to hell where they are tortured by infernal punishments, and that nevertheless on the day of judgment all men with their bodies will make themselves ready to render an account of their own deeds before the tribunal of Christ, "so that everyone may receive the proper things of the body according as he has done whether it be good or evil" [II Cor. 5:10]. 1022

(1) **1 Corinthians 13:12** For now we see in a mirror dimly, but then face to face. Now I know in part; then I shall understand fully, even as I have been fully understood. 1023

(2) **Revelation 22:4** . . . they shall see his face, and his name shall be on their foreheads. 1023

(3) ***Lumen gentium* 49** When the Lord will come in glory, and all his angels with him (cf. Mt. 25:31), death will be no more and all things will be subject to him (cf. 1 Cor. 15:26–27). But at the present time some of his disciples are pilgrims on earth. Others have died and are being purified, while still others are in glory, contemplating "in full light, God himself triune and one, exactly as he is." All of us, however, in varying degrees and in different ways share in the same charity towards God and our neighbors, and we all sing the one hymn of glory to our God. All, indeed, who are of Christ and who have his Spirit form one Church and in Christ cleave together (Eph. 4:16). So it is that the union of the wayfarers with the brethren who sleep in the peace of Christ is in no way interrupted, but on the contrary, according to the constant faith of the Church, this union is reinforced by an exchange of spiritual goods. Being more closely united to Christ, those who dwell in heaven fix the whole Church more firmly in holiness, add to the nobility of the worship that the Church offers to God here on earth, and in many ways help in a broader building up of the Church (cf. 1 Cor. 12:12–27). Once received into their heavenly home and being present to the Lord (cf. 2 Cor. 5:8), through him and with him and in him they do 1023

not cease to intercede with the Father for us, as they proffer the merits which they acquired on earth through the one mediator between God and men, Christ Jesus (cf. 1 Tim. 2:5), serving God in all things and completing in their flesh what is lacking in Christ's afflictions for the sake of his Body, that is, the Church (cf. Col. 1:24). So by their brotherly concern is our weakness greatly helped.

1025 (1) **John 14:3** And when I go and prepare a place for you, I will come again and will take you to myself, that where I am you may be also.

1025 (2) **1 Thessalonians 4:17** . . . then we who are alive, who are left, shall be caught up together with them in the clouds to meet the Lord in the air; and so we shall always be with the Lord.

1025 (3) **Revelation 2:17** "'. . . He who has an ear, let him hear what the Spirit says to the churches. To him who conquers I will give some of the hidden manna, and I will give him a white stone, with a new name written on the stone which no one knows except him who receives it.'. . . "

1029 (1) **Matthew 25:21** ". . . His master said to him, 'Well done, good and faithful servant; you have been faithful over a little, I will set you over much; enter into the joy of your master.'. . . "

1029 (2) **Matthew 25:23** ". . . His master said to him, 'Well done, good and faithful servant; you have been faithful over a little, I will set you over much; enter into the joy of your master.'. . . "

1031 (1) **Council of Florence (1439): DS 1304** [*De novissimis*] It has likewise defined, that, if those truly penitent have departed in the love of God, before they have made satisfaction by worthy fruits of penance for sins of commission and omission, the souls of these are cleansed after death by purgatorial punishments; and so that they may be released from punishments of this kind, the suffrages of the living faithful are of advantage to them, namely, the sacrifices of Masses, prayers, and almsgiving, and other works of piety, which are customarily performed by the faithful for other faithful according to the institutions of the Church.

1031 (2) **Council of Trent (1563): DS 1820** Since the Catholic Church, instructed by the Holy Spirit, in conformity with the sacred writings and the ancient tradition of the Fathers in sacred councils, and very recently in this ecumenical Synod, has taught that there is a purgatory, and that the souls detained there are assisted by the suffrages of the faithful, and especially by the acceptable sacrifice of the altar, the holy Synod commands the bishops that they insist that the sound doctrine of purgatory, which has been transmitted by the holy Fathers and holy Councils, be believed by the faithful of Christ, be maintained, taught, and everywhere preached. Let the more difficult and subtle "questions," however, and those which do not make for "edification" [cf. I Tim. 1:4], and from which there is very often no increase in piety, be excluded from popular discourses to uneducated people. Likewise, let them not permit uncertain matters, or those that have the appearance of falsehood, to be brought out and discussed publicly. Those matters on the contrary, which tend to a certain curiosity or superstition, or that savor of filthy lucre, let them prohibit as scandals and stumbling blocks to the faithful. . . .

(3) **Council of Trent (1547): DS 1580** If anyone shall say that after the reception of the grace of justification, to every penitent sinner the guilt is so remitted and the penalty of eternal punishment so blotted out that no penalty of temporal punishment remains to be discharged either in this world or in the world to come in purgatory before the entrance to the kingdom of heaven can be opened: let him be anathema. 1031

(4) **Benedict XII, *Benedictus Deus* (1336): DS 1000** By this edict which will prevail forever, with apostolic authority we declare: that according to the common arrangement of God, souls of all the saints who departed from this world before the passion of our Lord Jesus Christ; also of the holy apostles, the martyrs, the confessors, virgins, and the other faithful who died after the holy baptism of Christ had been received by them, in whom nothing was to be purged, when they departed, nor will there be when they shall depart also in the future; or if then there was or there will be anything to be purged in these when after their death they have been purged; and the souls of children departing before the use of free will, reborn and baptized in that same baptism of Christ, when all have been baptized, immediately after their death and that aforesaid purgation in those who were in need of a purgation of this kind, even before the resumption of their bodies and the general judgment after the ascension of our Savior, our Lord Jesus Christ, into heaven, have been, are, and will be in heaven, in the kingdom of heaven and in celestial paradise with Christ, united in the company of the holy angels, and after the passion and death of our Lord Jesus Christ have seen and see the divine essence by intuitive vision, and even face to face, with no mediating creature, serving in the capacity of an object seen, but divine essence immediately revealing itself plainly, clearly, and openly, to them, and seeing thus they enjoy the same divine essence, and also that from such vision and enjoyment their souls, which now have departed, are truly blessed and they have eternal life and rest; and also [the souls] of those who afterwards will depart, will see that same divine essence, and will enjoy it before the general judgment. . . . 1031

(5) **1 Corinthians 3:15** If any man's work is burned up, he will suffer loss, though he himself will be saved, but only as through fire. 1031

(6) **1 Peter 1:7** . . . so that the genuineness of your faith, more precious than gold which though perishable is tested by fire, may redound to praise and glory and honor at the revelation of Jesus Christ. 1031

(7) **Matthew 12:31** Therefore I tell you, every sin and blasphemy will be forgiven men, but the blasphemy against the Spirit will not be forgiven. 1031

(1) **Council of Lyons II (1274): DS 856** Because if they die truly repentant in charity before they have made satisfaction by worthy fruits of penance for (sins) committed and omitted, their souls are cleansed after death by purgatorial or purifying punishments, as Brother John has explained to us. And to relieve punishments of this kind, the offerings of the living faithful are of advantage to these, namely, the sacrifices of Masses, prayers, alms, and other duties of piety, which have customarily been performed by the faithful for the other faithful according to the regulations of the Church. 1032

(2) **Job 1:5** And when the days of the feast had run their course, Job would send and sanctify them, and he would rise early in the morning and offer burnt offerings according to the number of them all; for Job said, "It may be that my sons have sinned, and cursed God in their hearts." Thus Job did continually. 1032

1033 **Matthew 25:31–46** "When the Son of man comes in his glory, and all the angels with him, then he will sit on his glorious throne. Before him will be gathered all the nations, and he will separate them one from another as a shepherd separates the sheep from the goats, and he will place the sheep at his right hand, but the goats at the left. Then the King will say to those at his right hand, 'Come, O blessed of my Father, inherit the kingdom prepared for you from the foundation of the world; for I was hungry and you gave me food, I was thirsty and you gave me drink, I was a stranger and you welcomed me, I was naked and you clothed me, I was sick and you visited me, I was in prison and you came to me.' Then the righteous will answer him, 'Lord, when did we see thee hungry and feed thee, or thirsty and give thee drink? And when did we see thee a stranger and welcome thee, or naked and clothe thee? And when did we see thee sick or in prison and visit thee?' And the King will answer them, 'Truly, I say to you, as you did it to one of the least of these my brethren, you did it to me.' Then he will say to those at his left hand, 'Depart from me, you cursed, into the eternal fire prepared for the devil and his angels; for I was hungry and you gave me no food, I was thirsty and you gave me no drink, I was a stranger and you did not welcome me, naked and you did not clothe me, sick and in prison and you did not visit me.' Then they also will answer, 'Lord, when did we see thee hungry or thirsty or a stranger or naked or sick or in prison, and did not minister to thee?' Then he will answer them, 'Truly, I say to you, as you did it not to one of the least of these, you did it not to me.' And they will go away into eternal punishment, but the righteous into eternal life."

1034 (1) **Matthew 5:22** ". . . But I say to you that every one who is angry with his brother shall be liable to judgment; whoever insults his brother shall be liable to the council, and whoever says, 'You fool!' shall be liable to the hell of fire. . . ."

1034 (2) **Matthew 5:29** If your right eye causes you to sin, pluck it out and throw it away; it is better that you lose one of your members than that your whole body be thrown into hell.

1034 (3) **Matthew 10:28** And do not fear those who kill the body but cannot kill the soul; rather fear him who can destroy both soul and body in hell.

1034 (4) **Matthew 13:42** . . . and throw them into the furnace of fire; there men will weep and gnash their teeth.

1034 (5) **Matthew 13:50** . . . and throw them into the furnace of fire; there men will weep and gnash their teeth.

1034 (6) **Mark 9:43–48** And if your hand causes you to sin, cut it off; it is better for you to enter life maimed than with two hands to go to hell, to the unquenchable fire. And if your foot causes you to sin, cut it off; it is better for you to enter life lame than with two feet to be thrown into hell. And if your eye causes you to sin, pluck it out; it is better for you to enter the kingdom of God with one eye than with two eyes to be thrown into hell, where their worm does not die, and the fire is not quenched.

1035 (1) **From the Creed "Quicumque": DS 76** But it is necessary for eternal salvation that he faithfully believe also the incarnation of our Lord Jesus Christ. Accordingly it is the right faith, that we believe and confess, that our Lord Jesus Christ, the Son of God is God and man. He is God begotten of the substance of the Father before time, and he is man born of the substance of his mother in time: perfect God, perfect man, consisting of a rational soul and a human body, equal to the Father according to his Godhead, less than the Father according to humanity. Although he is God and man, yet he is not two, but he is one Christ; one, however, not by the conversion of the Divinity into a human body, but by the assumption of humanity in the Godhead; one absolutely not by confusion of substance, but by unity of person. For just as the rational soul and body are one man, so God and man are one Christ. He suffered for our salvation, descended into hell, on the third day arose again from the dead, ascended to heaven, sits at the right hand of God the Father almighty; thence he shall come to judge the living and the dead; at his coming all men have to arise again with their bodies and will render an account of their own deeds: and those who have done good, will go into life everlasting, but those who have done evil, into eternal fire.—This is the Catholic faith; unless every one believes this faithfully and firmly, he cannot be saved.

(2) **Emperor Justinian, *Canons against Origen* (543): DS 409** If anyone says or 1035
holds that the Lord Christ in the future age will be crucified in behalf of the demons, just as (He was) for the sake of men, let him be anathema.

(3) **Emperor Justinian, *Canons against Origen* (543): DS 411** If anyone says or 1035
holds that the punishment of the demons and of impious men is temporary, and that it will have an end at some time, that is to say, there will be a complete restoration of the demons or of impious men, let him be anathema.

(4) **Lateran Council IV (1215): DS 801** And finally the only begotten Son of 1035
God, Jesus Christ, incarnate by the whole Trinity in common, conceived of Mary ever Virgin with the Holy Spirit cooperating, made true man, formed of a rational soul and human flesh, one Person in two natures, clearly pointed out the way of life. And although He according to divinity is immortal and impassible, the very same according to humanity was made passible and mortal, who, for the salvation of the human race, having suffered on the wood of the Cross and died, descended into hell, arose from the dead and ascended into heaven. But He descended in soul, and He arose in the flesh, and He ascended equally in both, to come at the end of time, to judge the living and the dead, and to render to each according to his works, to the wicked as well as to the elect, all of whom will rise with their bodies which they now bear, that they may receive according to their works, whether these works have been good or evil, the latter everlasting punishment with the devil, and the former everlasting glory with Christ.

(5) **Lateran Council IV (1215): DS 858** The souls of those who die in mortal sin 1035
or with original sin only, however, immediately descend to hell, yet to be punished with different punishments.

(6) **Benedict XII, *Benedictus Deus* (1336): DS 1002** Moreover, we declare that 1035
according to the common arrangement of God, the souls of those who depart in actual mortal sin immediately after their death descend to hell where they are tortured by infernal punishments, and that nevertheless on the day of judgment all men with their bodies will make themselves ready to render an account of their own deeds before the tribunal of Christ, "so that everyone may receive the proper things of the body according as he has done whether it be good or evil" [II Cor. 5:10].

(7) **Council of Florence: DS 1351** It firmly believes, professes, and proclaims 1035
that those not living within the Catholic Church, not only pagans, but also Jews and

heretics and schismatics cannot become participants in eternal life, but will depart "into everlasting fire which was prepared for the devil and his angels" [Matt. 25:41], unless before the end of life the same have been added to the flock; and that the unity of the ecclesiastical body is so strong that only to those remaining in it are the sacraments of the Church of benefit for salvation, and do fastings, almsgiving, and other functions of piety and exercises of Christian service produce eternal reward, and that no one, whatever almsgiving he has practiced, even if he has shed blood for the name of Christ, can be saved, unless he has remained in the bosom and unity of the Catholic Church.

1035 (8) **Council of Trent (1547): DS 1575** If anyone shall say that in every good work the just one sins at least venially, or (what is more intolerable) mortally, and therefore deserves eternal punishments, and that it is only because God does not impute those works unto damnation that he is not damned, let him be anathema.

1035 (9) **Paul VI, *The* Credo *of the People of God* 12** He dwelt among us full of grace and truth. He announced and established the Kingdom of God, enabling us to know the Father. He gave us the commandment that we should love one another as he loved us. He taught us the way of the Gospel Beatitudes, according to which we were to be poor in spirit and humble, bearing suffering in patience, thirsting after justice, merciful, clean of heart, peaceful, enduring persecution for justice's sake. He suffered under Pontius Pilate, the Lamb of God taking to himself the sins of the world, and he died for us, nailed to the Cross, saving us by his redeeming blood. After he had been buried he rose from the dead of his own power, lifting us by his resurrection to that sharing in the divine life which is grace. He ascended into heaven whence he will come again to judge the living and the dead, each according to his merits. Those who have responded to the love and compassion of God will go into eternal life. Those who have refused them to the end will be consigned to the fire that is never extinguished.

1037 (1) **Council of Orange II (529): DS 397** [III. Predestination] According to the Catholic faith we believe this also, that after grace has been received through baptism, all the baptized with the help and cooperation of Christ can and ought to fulfill what pertains to the salvation of the soul, if they will labor faithfully. We not only do not believe that some have been truly predestined to evil by divine power, but also with every execration we pronounce anathema upon those, if there are [any such], who wish to believe so great an evil. This, too, we profess and believe unto salvation, that in every good work we do not begin, and afterwards are helped by the mercy of God, but He Himself, with no preceding good services [on our part], previously inspires us with faith and love of Him, so that we may both faithfully seek the sacraments of baptism, and after baptism with His help be able to perform those [acts] which are pleasing to Him. So very clearly we should believe that the faith—so admirable —both of that famous thief, whom the Lord restored to his native land of paradise [Luke 23:43], and of Cornelius the centurion, to whom the angel of the Lord was sent [Acts 10:3], and of Zacheus, who deserved to receive the Lord Himself [Luke 19:6], was not from nature, but a gift of God's bounty.

1037 (2) **Council of Trent (1547): DS 1567** If anyone shall say that the grace of justification is attained by those only who are predestined unto life, but that all others, who are called, are called indeed, but do not receive grace, as if they are by divine power predestined to evil: let him be anathema.

(1) **John 12:49** For I have not spoken on my own authority; the Father who sent me has himself given me commandment what to say and what to speak. 1039

(2) **Psalm 50:3** 1039

Our God comes, he does not keep silence,
before him is a devouring fire,
round about him a mighty tempest.

Song of Solomon 8:6 1040

Set me as a seal upon your heart,
as a seal upon your arm;
for love is strong as death,
jealousy is cruel as the grave.
Its flashes are flashes of fire,
a most vehement flame.

Revelation 21:1 Then I saw a new heaven and a new earth; for the first heaven and the first earth had passed away, and the sea was no more. 1043

Revelation 21:5 And he who sat upon the throne said, "Behold, I make all things new." Also he said, "Write this, for these words are trustworthy and true." 1044

(1) ***Lumen gentium* 1** Christ is the light of humanity; and it is, accordingly, the heart-felt desire of this sacred Council, being gathered together in the Holy Spirit, that, by proclaiming his Gospel to every creature (cf. Mk 16:15), it may bring to all men that light of Christ which shines out visibly from the Church. Since the Church, in Christ, is in the nature of sacrament—a sign and instrument, that is, of communion with God and of unity among all men—she here proposes, for the benefit of the faithful and of the whole world, to set forth, as clearly as possible, and in the tradition laid down by earlier Councils, her own nature and universal mission. The condition of the modern world lends greater urgency to this duty of the Church; for, while men of the present day are drawn ever more closely together by social, technical and cultural bonds, it still remains for them to achieve full unity in Christ. 1045

(2) **Revelation 21:27** But nothing unclean shall enter it, nor any one who practices abomination or falsehood, but only those who are written in the Lamb's book of life. 1045

Council of Trent (1547): DS 1549 And whereas "in many things we all offend" [Jas. 3:2; can. 23], each one should have before his eyes the severity and judgment as well as mercy and goodness; neither ought anyone to judge himself, even though he be "not conscious to himself of anything," since the whole life of men must be judged and examined not by the judgment of men, but of God, who "will bring to light the hidden things of darkness, and will make manifest the counsels of the hearts, and then shall every man have praise from God" [I Cor. 4:4 ff.], "who," as it is written, "will render to every man according to his works" [Rom. 2:6]. 1059

Revelation 22:21 The grace of the Lord Jesus be with all the saints. Amen. 1061

(1) **Matthew 6:2** "Thus, when you give alms, sound no trumpet before you, as the hypocrites do in the synagogues and in the streets, that they may be praised by men. Truly, I say to you, they have received their reward. . . ." 1063

1063 (2) **Matthew 6:5** "And when you pray, you must not be like the hypocrites; for they love to stand and pray in the synagogues and at the street corners, that they may be seen by men. Truly, I say to you, they have received their reward. . . ."

1063 (3) **Matthew 6:16** "And when you fast, do not look dismal, like the hypocrites, for they disfigure their faces that their fasting may be seen by men. Truly, I say to you, they have received their reward. . . ."

1063 (4) **John 5:19** Jesus said to them, "Truly, truly, I say to you, the Son can do nothing of his own accord, but only what he sees the Father doing; for whatever he does, that the Son does likewise. . . ."

II

THE CELEBRATION OF THE CHRISTIAN MYSTERY

Ephesians 3:4 When you read this you can perceive my insight into the mystery of Christ. . . . 1066

John 17:4 I glorified thee on earth, having accomplished the work which thou gavest me to do. . . . 1069

(1) **Luke 1:23** And when his time of service was ended, he went to his home. 1070

(2) **Acts 13:2** While they were worshiping the Lord and fasting, the Holy Spirit said, "Set apart for me Barnabas and Saul for the work to which I have called them." 1070

(3) **Romans 15:16** . . . to be a minister of Christ Jesus to the Gentiles in the priestly service of the gospel of God, so that the offering of the Gentiles may be acceptable, sanctified by the Holy Spirit. 1070

(4) **Romans 15:27** . . . they were pleased to do it, and indeed they are in debt to them, for if the Gentiles have come to share in their spiritual blessings, they ought also to be of service to them in material blessings. 1070

(5) **2 Corinthians 9:12** . . . for the rendering of this service not only supplies the wants of the saints but also overflows in many thanksgivings to God. 1070

(6) **Philippians 2:14–17** Do all things without grumbling or questioning, that you may be blameless and innocent, children of God without blemish in the midst of a crooked and perverse generation, among whom you shine as lights in the world, holding fast the word of life, so that in the day of Christ I may be proud that I did not run in vain or labor in vain. Even if I am to be poured as a libation upon the sacrificial offering of your faith, I am glad and rejoice with you all. 1070

(7) **Philippians 2:25** I have thought it necessary to send to you Epaphroditus my brother and fellow worker and fellow soldier, and your messenger and minister to my need. . . . 1070

(8) **Philippians 2:30** . . . for he nearly died for the work of Christ, risking his life to complete your service to me. 1070

(9) **Hebrews 8:2** . . . a minister in the sanctuary and the true tent which is set up not by man but by the Lord. 1070

(10) **Hebrews 8:6** But as it is, Christ has obtained a ministry which is as much more excellent than the old as the covenant he mediates is better, since it is enacted on better promises. 1070

1073 **Ephesians 3:16–17** . . . that according to the riches of his glory he may grant you to be strengthened with might through his Spirit in the inner man, and that Christ may dwell in your hearts through faith; that you, being rooted and grounded in love. . . .

1075 ***Sacrosanctum concilium* 3–4** That is why the sacred Council judges that the following principles concerning the promotion and reform of the liturgy should be called to mind, and that practical norms should be established.

Among these principles and norms there are some which can and should be applied both to the Roman rite and also to all the other rites. The practical norms which follow, however, should be taken as applying only to the Roman rite except for those which, in the very nature of things, affect other rites as well.

Finally, in faithful obedience to tradition, the sacred Council declares that Holy Mother Church holds all lawfully recognized rites to be of equal right and dignity; that she wishes to preserve them in the future and to foster them in every way. The Council also desires that, where necessary, the rites be revised carefully in the light of sound tradition, and that they be given new vigor to meet present-day circumstances and needs.

1076 (1) ***Sacrosanctum concilium* 6** Accordingly, just as Christ was sent by the Father so also he sent the apostles, filled with the Holy Spirit. This he did so that they might preach the Gospel to every creature and proclaim that the Son of God by his death and resurrection had freed us from the power of Satan and from death, and brought us into the Kingdom of his Father. But he also willed that the work of salvation which they preached should be set in train through the sacrifice and sacraments, around which the entire liturgical life revolves. Thus by Baptism men are grafted into the paschal mystery of Christ; they die with him, are buried with him, and rise with him. They receive the spirit of adoption as sons "in which we cry, Abba, Father" (Rom. 8:15) and thus become true adorers such as the Father seeks. In like manner as often as they eat the Supper of the Lord they proclaim the death of the Lord until he comes. That was why on the very day of Pentecost when the Church appeared before the world those "who received the word" of Peter "were baptized." And "they continued steadfastly in the teaching of the apostles and in the communion of the breaking of bread and in prayers . . . praising God and being in favor with all the people" (Acts 2:41–47). From that time onward the Church has never failed to come together to celebrate the paschal mystery, reading those things "which were in all the scriptures concerning him" (Lk. 24:27), celebrating the Eucharist in which "the victory and triumph of his death are again made present," and at the same time "giving thanks to God for his inexpressible gift" (2 Cor. 9:15) in Christ Jesus, "in praise of his glory" (Eph. 1:12) through the power of the Holy Spirit.

1076 (2) ***Lumen gentium* 2** The eternal Father, in accordance with the utterly gratuitous and mysterious design of his wisdom and goodness, created the whole universe, and chose to raise up men to share in his own divine life; and when they had fallen in Adam, he did not abandon them, but at all times held out to them the means of salvation, bestowed in consideration of Christ, the Redeemer, "who is the image of the invisible God, the firstborn of every creature" (Col. 1:15). All the elect, before time began, the Father "foreknew and also predestined to become conformed to the image of his Son, that he should be the firstborn among many brethren" (Rom. 8:29). He determined to call together in a holy Church those who should believe in Christ. Already present in figure at the beginning of the world, this Church was prepared in marvellous fashion in the history of the people of Israel and in the old Alliance.

Established in this last age of the world, and made manifest in the outpouring of the Spirit, it will be brought to glorious completion at the end of time. At that moment, as the Fathers put it, all the just from the time of Adam, "from Abel, the just one, to the last of the elect" will be gathered together with the Father in the universal Church.

(1) **John 13:1** Now before the feast of the Passover, when Jesus knew that his hour 1085
had come to depart out of this world to the Father, having loved his own who were in the world, he loved them to the end.

(2) **John 17:1** When Jesus had spoken these words, he lifted up his eyes to heaven and 1085
said, "Father, the hour has come; glorify thy Son that the Son may glorify thee. . . ."

John 20:21–23 Jesus said to them again, "Peace be with you. As the Father has 1087
sent me, even so I send you." And when he had said this, he breathed on them, and said to them, "Receive the Holy Spirit. . . ."

***Lumen gentium* 50** In full consciousness of this communion of the whole Mystical 1090
Body of Jesus Christ, the Church in its pilgrim members, from the very earliest days of the Christian religion, has honored with great respect the memory of the dead; and, "because it is a holy and a wholesome thought to pray for the dead that they may be loosed from their sins" (2 Mac. 12:46) she offers her suffrages for them. The Church has always believed that the apostles and Christ's martyrs, who gave the supreme witness of faith and charity by the shedding of their blood, are closely united with us in Christ; she has always venerated them, together with the Blessed Virgin Mary and the holy angels, with a special love, and has asked piously for the help of their intercession. Soon there were added to these others who had chosen to imitate more closely the virginity and poverty of Christ, and still others whom the outstanding practice of the Christian virtues and the wonderful graces of God recommended to the pious devotion and imitation of the faithful.

To look on the life of those who have faithfully followed Christ is to be inspired with a new reason for seeking the city which is to come (cf. Heb. 13:14 and 11:10), while at the same time we are taught to know a most safe path by which, despite the vicissitudes of the world, and in keeping with the state of life and condition proper to each of us, we will be able to arrive at perfect union with Christ, that is, holiness. God shows to men, in a vivid way, his presence and his face in the lives of those companions of ours in the human condition who are more perfectly transformed into the image of Christ (cf. 2 Cor. 3:18). He speaks to us in them and offers us a sign of this kingdom, to which we are powerfully attracted, so great a cloud of witnesses is there given (cf. Heb 12:1) and such a witness to the truth of the Gospel.

It is not merely by the title of example that we cherish the memory of those in heaven; we seek, rather, that by this devotion to the exercise of fraternal charity the union of the whole Church in the Spirit may be strengthened (cf. Eph. 4:1–6). Exactly as Christian communion between men on their earthly pilgrimage brings us closer to Christ, so our community with the saints joins us to Christ, from whom as from its fountain and head issues all grace and the life of the People of God itself. It is most fitting, therefore, that we love those friends and co-heirs of Jesus Christ who are also our brothers and outstanding benefactors, and that we give due thanks to God for them, "humbly invoking them, and having recourse to their prayers, their aid and help in obtaining from God through his Son, Jesus Christ, Our Lord, our only Redeemer and Savior, the benefits we need." Every authentic witness of love, indeed, offered by us to those who are in heaven tends to and terminates in Christ, "the crown of all the saints," and through him in God who is wonderful in his saints and is glorified in them.

It is especially in the sacred liturgy that our union with the heavenly Church is best realized; in the liturgy, through the sacramental signs, the power of the Holy Spirit acts on us, and with community rejoicing we celebrate together the praise of the divine majesty, when all those of every tribe and tongue and people and nation (cf. Apoc. 5:9) who have been redeemed by the blood of Christ and gathered together into one Church glorify, in one common song of praise, the one and triune God. When, then, we celebrate the eucharistic sacrifice we are most closely united to the worship of the heavenly Church; when in the fellowship of communion we honor and remember the glorious Mary ever virgin, St. Joseph, the holy apostles and martyrs and all the saints.

1094 (1) ***Dei Verbum* 14–16** God, with loving concern contemplating, and making preparation for, the salvation of the whole human race, in a singular undertaking chose for himself a people to whom he would entrust his promises. By his covenant with Abraham (cf. Gen. 15:18) and, through Moses, with the race of Israel (cf. Ex. 24:8), he did acquire a people for himself, and to them he revealed himself in words and deeds as the one, true, living God, so that Israel might experience the ways of God with men. Moreover, by listening to the voice of God speaking to them through the prophets, they had daily to understand his ways more fully and more clearly, and make them more widely known among the nations (cf. Ps. 21:28–29, 95:1–3; Is. 2:1–4; Jer. 3:17). Now the economy of salvation, foretold, recounted and explained by the sacred authors, appears as the true Word of God in the books of the Old Testament, that is why these books, divinely inspired, preserve a lasting value: "For whatever was written in former days was written for our instruction, that by steadfastness and the encouragement of the Scriptures we might have hope" (Rom. 15:4).

The economy of the Old Testament was deliberately so oriented that it should prepare for and declare in prophecy the coming of Christ, redeemer of all men, and of the messianic kingdom (cf. Lk. 24:44; Jn. 5:39; 1 Pet. 1:10), and should indicate it by means of different types (cf. 1 Cor. 10:11). For in the context of the human situation before the era of salvation established by Christ, the books of the Old Testament provide an understanding of God and man and make clear to all men how a just and merciful God deals with mankind. These books, even though they contain matters imperfect and provisional, nevertheless show us authentic divine teaching. Christians should accept with veneration these writings which give expression to a lively sense of God, which are a storehouse of sublime teaching on God and of sound wisdom on human life, as well as a wonderful treasury of prayers; in them, too, the mystery of our salvation is present in a hidden way.

God, the inspirer and author of the books of both Testaments, in his wisdom has so brought it about that the New should be hidden in the Old and that the Old should be made manifest in the New. For, although Christ founded the New Covenant in his blood (cf. Lk. 22:20; 1 Cor. 11:25), still the books of the Old Testament, all of them caught up into the Gospel message, attain and show forth their full meaning in the New Testament (cf. Mt. 5:17; Lk. 24:27; Rom. 16:25–26; 2 Cor. 3:14–16) and, in their turn, shed light on it and explain it.

1094 (2) **Luke 24:13–49** That very day two of them were going to a village named Emmaus, about seven miles from Jerusalem, and talking with each other about all these things that had happened. While they were talking and discussing together, Jesus himself drew near and went with them. But their eyes were kept from recognizing him. And he said to them, "What is this conversation which you are holding with each other as you walk?" And they stood still, looking sad. Then one of them, named Cleopas, answered him, "Are you the only visitor to Jerusalem who does not know the things that have happened there in these days?" And he said to them, "What things?" And they said to him, "Concerning Jesus of Nazareth, who was a prophet mighty in deed and word before God and all the people, and how our chief priests and rulers delivered him up to be condemned to death, and crucified him. But we had hoped that he was the one to redeem Israel. Yes, and besides all this, it is now the third day since this happened. Moreover, some women of our company amazed us. They were at the tomb early in the morning and did not find his body; and they came back saying that they had even seen a vision of angels, who said that he was alive. Some of those who were with us went to the tomb, and found it just as the women had said; but him they did not see." And he said to them, "O foolish men, and slow of heart to believe all that the prophets have spoken! Was it not necessary that the Christ should suffer these things and enter into his glory?" And beginning with Moses and all the prophets, he interpreted to them in all the scriptures the things concerning himself.

So they drew near to the village to which they were going. He appeared to be going further, but they constrained him, saying, "Stay with us, for it is toward evening and the day is now far spent." So he went in to stay with them. When he was at table with them, he took the bread and blessed, and broke it, and gave it to them. And their eyes were opened and they recognized him; and he vanished out of their sight. They said to each other, "Did not our hearts burn within us while he talked to us on the road, while he opened to us the scriptures?" And they rose that same hour and returned to Jerusalem; and they found the eleven gathered together and those who were with them, who said, "The Lord has risen indeed, and has appeared to Simon!" Then they told what had happened on the road, and how he was known to them in the breaking of the bread.

As they were saying this, Jesus himself stood among them. But they were startled and frightened, and supposed that they saw a spirit. And he said to them, "Why are you troubled, and why do questionings rise in your hearts? See my hands and my feet, that it is I myself; handle me, and see; for a spirit has not flesh and bones as you see that I have." And while they still disbelieved for joy, and wondered, he said to them, "Have you anything here to eat?" They gave him a piece of broiled fish, and he took it and ate before them.

Then he said to them, "These are my words which I spoke to you, while I was still with you, that everything written about me in the law of Moses and the prophets and the psalms must be fulfilled." Then he opened their minds to understand the scriptures, and said to them, "Thus it is written, that the Christ should suffer and on the third day rise from the dead, and that repentance and forgiveness of sins should be preached in his name to all nations, beginning from Jerusalem. You are witnesses of these things. And behold, I send the promise of my Father upon you; but stay in the city, until you are clothed with power from on high."

(3) **2 Corinthians 3:14–16** But their minds were hardened; for to this day, when 1094
they read the old covenant, that same veil remains unlifted, because only through Christ is it taken away. Yes, to this day whenever Moses is read a veil lies over their minds; but when a man turns to the Lord the veil is removed.

(4) **1 Peter 3:21** Baptism, which corresponds to this, now saves you, not as a re- 1094
moval of dirt from the body but as an appeal to God for a clear conscience, through the resurrection of Jesus Christ. . . .

1094 (5) **1 Corinthians 10:1–6** I want you to know, brethren, that our fathers were all under the cloud, and all passed through the sea, and all were baptized into Moses in the cloud and in the sea, and all ate the same supernatural food and all drank the same supernatural drink. For they drank from the supernatural Rock which followed them, and the Rock was Christ. Nevertheless with most of them God was not pleased; for they were overthrown in the wilderness.

Now these things are warnings for us, not to desire evil as they did.

1099 **John 14:26** But the Counselor, the Holy Spirit, whom the Father will send in my name, he will teach you all things, and bring to your remembrance all that I have said to you.

1105 **Romans 12:1** I appeal to you therefore, brethren, by the mercies of God, to present your bodies as a living sacrifice, holy and acceptable to God, which is your spiritual worship.

1107 (1) **Ephesians 1:14** . . . which is the guarantee of our inheritance until we acquire possession of it, to the praise of his glory.

1107 (2) **2 Corinthians 1:22** . . . he has put his seal upon us and given us his Spirit in our hearts as a guarantee.

1108 (1) **John 15:1–17** "I am the true vine, and my Father is the vinedresser. Every branch of mine that bears no fruit, he takes away, and every branch that does bear fruit he prunes, that it may bear more fruit. You are already made clean by the word which I have spoken to you. Abide in me, and I in you. As the branch cannot bear fruit by itself, unless it abides in the vine, neither can you, unless you abide in me. I am the vine, you are the branches. He who abides in me, and I in him, he it is that bears much fruit, for apart from me you can do nothing. If a man does not abide in me, he is cast forth as a branch and withers; and the branches are gathered, thrown into the fire and burned. If you abide in me, and my words abide in you, ask whatever you will, and it shall be done for you. By this my Father is glorified, that you bear much fruit, and so prove to be my disciples. As the Father has loved me, so have I loved you; abide in my love. If you keep my commandments, you will abide in my love, just as I have kept my Father's commandments and abide in his love. These things I have spoken to you, that my joy may be in you, and that your joy may be full.

"This is my commandment, that you love one another as I have loved you. Greater love has no man than this, that a man lay down his life for his friends. You are my friends if you do what I command you. No longer do I call you servants, for the servant does not know what his master is doing; but I have called you friends, for all that I have heard from my Father I have made known to you. You did not choose me, but I chose you and appointed you that you should go and bear fruit and that your fruit should abide; so that whatever you ask the Father in my name, he may give it to you. This I command you, to love one another. . . ."

1108 (2) **Galatians 5:22–23** But the fruit of the Spirit is love, joy, peace, patience, kindness, goodness, faithfulness, gentleness, self-control; against such there is no law.

1108 (3) **1 John 1:3–7** . . . that which we have seen and heard we proclaim also to you, so that you may have fellowship with us; and our fellowship is with the Father and with his Son Jesus Christ. And we are writing this that our joy may be complete.

This is the message we have heard from him and proclaim to you, that God is light and in him is no darkness at all. If we say we have fellowship with him while we walk in darkness, we lie and do not live according to the truth; but if we walk in the light, as he is in the light, we have fellowship with one another, and the blood of Jesus his Son cleanses us from all sin.

(1) ***Sacrosanctum concilium* 6:** see 1076 (1). 1113

(2) **Council of Lyons II (1274): DS 860** The same holy Roman Church also 1113
holds and teaches that the ecclesiastical sacraments are seven: namely, one is baptism, concerning which we have spoken above; another is the sacrament of confirmation which the bishops confer through the imposition of hands when anointing the reborn; another is penance; another the Eucharist; another the sacrament of orders; another is matrimony; another extreme unction, which according to the doctrine of St. James is given to the sick. The same Roman Church prepares the sacrament of the Eucharist from unleavened bread, holding and teaching that in the same sacrament the bread is changed into the body, and the wine into the blood of Jesus Christ. But concerning matrimony it holds that neither one man is permitted to have many wives nor one woman many husbands at the same time. But she (the Church) says that second and third marriages successively are permissible for one freed from a legitimate marriage through the death of the other party, if another canonical impediment for some reason is not an obstacle.

(3) **Council of Florence (1439): DS 1310** In the fifth place we have reduced under 1113
this very brief formula the truth of the sacraments of the Church for the sake of an easier instruction of the Armenians, the present as well as the future. There are seven sacraments of the new Law: namely, baptism, confirmation, Eucharist, penance, extreme unction, orders, and matrimony, which differ a great deal from the sacraments of the Old Law. For those of the Old Law did not effect grace, but only pronounced that it should be given through the passion of Christ; these sacraments of ours contain grace, and confer it upon those who receive them worthily.

(4) **Council of Trent (1547): DS 1601** If anyone shall say that the sacraments 1113
of the New Law were not all instituted by Jesus Christ our Lord, or that there are more or less than seven, namely baptism, confirmation, Eucharist, penance, extreme unction, order, and matrimony, or even that anyone of these seven is not truly and strictly speaking a sacrament: let him be anathema.

(1) **Luke 5:17** On one of those days, as he was teaching, there were Pharisees and 1116
teachers of the law sitting by, who had come from every village of Galilee and Judea and from Jerusalem; and the power of the Lord was with him to heal.

(2) **Luke 6:19** And all the crowd sought to touch him, for power came forth from 1116
him and healed them all.

(3) **Luke 8:46** But Jesus said, "Some one touched me; for I perceive that power 1116
has gone forth from me."

(1) **Matthew 13:52** And he said to them, "Therefore every scribe who has been 1117
trained for the kingdom of heaven is like a householder who brings out of his treasure what is new and what is old."

1117 (2) **1 Corinthians 4:1** This is how one should regard us, as servants of Christ and stewards of the mysteries of God.

1118 **St. Thomas Aquinas, *Summa theologiae* III, 64, 2, ad 3**

article 2. are the sacraments of divine institution alone?

THE SECOND POINT: 1. It seems that the sacraments are not of divine institution alone. For those things which are divinely instituted are handed down to us in sacred Scripture. Now certain rites are performed in the sacraments of which there is no mention in sacred Scripture, as in the case of the chrism with which men are confirmed and the oil with which priests are anointed and of many other things, both words and actions, which we use in the sacraments. Therefore the sacraments are not of divine institution alone.

2. Sacraments are a certain kind of signs. Now sensible things have certain significances by nature. Nor can it be said that God takes pleasure in some significances and not in others, for he himself approves of everything which he has made. Yet the power to attract men to something by certain signs seems to be a property of the demons. For Augustine tells us that *the demons proffer their seductions through creatures even though it is not they but God who is the author of these, giving each of them its own special attraction according to their diverse kinds, an attraction consisting not, as for animals, in their value as food, but as for spiritual beings in their force as signs. Therefore it seems that the sacraments do not need to be of divine institution.*

3. The Apostles acted as vicars of God upon earth. Hence St. Paul tells us, *If I have pardoned anything, for your sakes have I done it in the person of Christ.* In other words he acts as though Christ himself had done the pardoning. On this showing, then, it seems that the Apostles and their successors are able to institute new sacraments.

ON THE OTHER HAND, it is he who imparts strength and power to something who is its institutor, as is clear in the case of the institutors of laws. Now as will be apparent from what has already been said, the power of the sacrament comes from God alone. Therefore God alone can institute a sacrament.

REPLY: From what has been said above, it is evident that sacraments act as instruments in producing spiritual effects. Now an instrument derives its power from the principal agent, and with regard to the sacraments the agent is twofold, namely he who institutes the sacrament and he who uses the sacrament once instituted by applying it in order to cause it to take effect. Furthermore the power of the sacrament cannot derive from him who uses that sacrament. For the only active contribution which he makes is as a minister. Hence the only remaining alternative is that the power of the sacrament derives from him who is the institutor of that sacrament. Since, therefore, the power of the sacrament is derived from God alone, it follows that God alone is the institutor of the sacraments.

Hence: 1. Those rites of human institution which are enacted in the sacraments do not belong to them as of necessity. Their purpose is, rather, to impart a certain solemnity to the sacraments so as to excite devotion and reverence in those receiving them. But those things which belong to a given sacrament of necessity are instituted by Christ himself who is God and man. And while it is true that not all of them are handed down in Scripture, still the Church possesses them from the family tradition of the Apostles. Thus St. Paul says, *The rest I will set in order when I come.*

2. Sensible things have of their very nature a certain aptitude to signify spiritual effects. Nevertheless it is by divine institution that a special determination is imparted to this aptitude restricting it to one special significance. And this is why Hugh of St. Victor says that *a sacrament conveys its meaning as a result of institution.* Nevertheless God chooses certain things before others to convey the significances of the sacra-

ments not because his good pleasure is specially restricted to them but so that the significance can be more suitably conveyed.

3. The Apostles and their successors are the vicars of God with regard to the rule of the Church as instituted through faith and with regard to the sacraments of the faith. Hence just as it is not lawful for them to constitute any other Church so too it is not lawful for them either to hand down any other faith or to institute any other sacraments. The Church is rather said to have been built up with *the sacraments which flowed from the side of Christ hanging on the Cross.*

article 3. did Christ as man have the power actively to produce the interior effect of the sacraments?

THE THIRD POINT: 1. It seems that as man Christ did have the power actively to produce the interior effect of the sacraments. For John the Baptist says, *He who sent me to baptize with water said to me: He upon whom you shall see the Spirit descending and remaining upon him, he it is who baptizes in the Holy Spirit.* Now to baptize in the Holy Spirit is to confer the interior grace of the Holy Spirit. And the Holy Spirit descended upon Christ as man and not as God. For as God it is he himself who gives the Holy Spirit. Therefore it seems that as man Christ did have the power to cause the interior effect of the sacraments.

2. In *Matthew* our Lord says, *That you may know that the Son of Man has power on earth to forgive sins.* Now the remission of sins is an interior effect of the sacrament. Therefore it seems that as man Christ does actively produce the interior effect of the sacraments.

3. The function of instituting the sacraments belongs to him who works as the principal agent in producing the interior effect of the sacrament. Now it is manifest that Christ instituted the sacraments. Therefore it is he himself who works interiorly to produce the effect of the sacraments.

4. No one can confer the effect of a sacrament without that sacrament unless he produces the effect of the sacrament by his own power. Now Christ conferred the effect of a sacrament without the sacrament, as is clear in the case of Magdalen to whom he said, *Your sins are forgiven you.* Therefore it seems that Christ actively produces the interior effect of the sacrament as man.

5. That in the power of which the sacrament is made to take effect is the principal agent with regard to the interior effect. Now sacraments derive their power from the Passion of Christ and the invocation of his name, as we are told in 1 *Corinthians*, *Was Paul then crucified for you? Or were you baptized in the name of Paul?* Therefore it is as man that Christ actively produces the interior effect of the sacrament.

ON THE OTHER HAND, we have the following statement of Augustine, *In the sacraments the divine power works interiorly to produce salvation.* Now the divine power is the power of Christ as God and not as man. Therefore it is not as man but as God that Christ works to produce the interior effect of the sacrament.

REPLY: Christ operates the interior effect of the sacraments both as man and as God, but in different ways. For as God he works in the sacraments by his power as their author. As man, however, he works to produce the interior effect of the sacraments through merit and by way of efficient causality, but still by a causality that is instrumental. For it has been established that the Passion of Christ, which belongs to him in his human nature, is the cause of our justification in the way both of merit and of efficient causality, operating not indeed as a principal agent or through the power belonging to the author of it, but as an instrument in virtue of the fact that his humanity is the instrument of his divinity, as has been argued above.

However since it is an instrument that is conjoined to his divinity in his person it possesses a certain priority and causality in relation to the separated instruments which are the ministers of the Church and the sacraments themselves, as is clear from the foregoing arguments. Hence just as Christ, as God, has the power of *authority* in the sacraments so too as man he has the power of principal minister or the power of *excellence*. Now this consists in four elements. First in the fact that, as has been stated above, it is the merit and power of his Passion that operates in the sacraments. Moreover it is through faith that the power of the Passion is applied to us, as we are told in the passage in *Romans* running, *whom God set forth to be a propitiation through faith in his blood*, and it is this faith that we affirm by invoking Christ's name. And because of this it follows that the second element in the power of excellence which Christ has in the sacraments consists in the fact that the sacraments are consecrated in his name. The third element consists in the fact that because the sacraments derive their power from their institution it is a property of the excellence of Christ's power that he himself, who gave the sacraments their power, was able to institute them. The fourth element consists in the fact that because a cause does not depend upon its effect, but *vice versa*, it is a property of the excellence of Christ's power that he himself was able to confer the sacramental effect without the external sacrament itself.

And from this our reply to the objections will be clear. For, as has been said, both sets of argument put forward are true in a certain sense.

1120 (1) ***Lumen gentium* 10, 2** Though they differ essentially and not only in degree, the common priesthood of the faithful and the ministerial or hierarchical priesthood are none the less ordered one to another; each in its own proper way shares in the one priesthood of Christ. The ministerial priest, by the sacred power that he has, forms and rules the priestly people; in the person of Christ he effects the eucharistic sacrifice and offers it to God in the name of all the people. The faithful indeed, by virtue of their royal priesthood, participate in the offering of the Eucharist. They exercise that priesthood, too, by the reception of the sacraments, prayer and thanksgiving, the witness of a holy life, abnegation and active charity.

1120 (2) **John 20:21–23** Jesus said to them again, "Peace be with you. As the Father has sent me, even so I send you." And when he had said this, he breathed on them, and said to them, "Receive the Holy Spirit. . . ."

1120 (3) **Luke 24:47** . . . and that repentance and forgiveness of sins should be preached in his name to all nations, beginning from Jerusalem.

1120 (4) **Matthew 28:18–20** And Jesus came and said to them, "All authority in heaven and on earth has been given to me. Go therefore and make disciples of all nations, baptizing them in the name of the Father and of the Son and of the Holy Spirit, teaching them to observe all that I have commanded you; and lo, I am with you always, to the close of the age."

1121 **Council of Trent (1547), *Decretum de sacramentis*: DS 1609** Can. 9. If anyone shall say that in the three sacraments, namely, baptism, confirmation, and orders, there is not imprinted on the soul a sign, that is, a certain spiritual and indelible mark, on account of which they cannot be repeated: let him be anathema.

1124 ***Dei Verbum* 8** Thus, the apostolic preaching, which is expressed in a special way in the inspired books, was to be preserved in a continuous line of succession until the end of time. Hence the apostles, in handing on what they themselves had received, warn the faithful to maintain the traditions which they had learned either by word of mouth or by letter (cf. 2 Th. 2:15); and they warn them to fight hard for the faith that had been handed on to them once and for all (cf. Jude 3). What was handed on by the apostles comprises everything that serves to make the People of God live their lives in holiness and increase their faith. In this way the Church, in her doctrine, life and worship, perpetuates and transmits to every generation all that she herself is, all that she believes.

The Tradition that comes from the apostles makes progress in the Church, with the help of the Holy Spirit. There is a growth in insight into the realities and words that are being passed on. This comes about in various ways. It comes through the contemplation and study of believers who ponder these things in their hearts (cf. Lk. 2:19 and 51). It comes from the intimate sense of spiritual realities which they experience. And it comes from the preaching of those who have received, along with their right of succession in the episcopate, the sure charism of truth. Thus, as the centuries go by, the Church is always advancing towards the plenitude of divine truth, until eventually the words of God are fulfilled in her.

The sayings of the Holy Fathers are a witness to the life-giving presence of this Tradition, showing how its riches are poured out in the practice and life of the Church, in her belief and her prayer. By means of the same Tradition the full canon of the sacred books is known to the Church and the holy Scriptures themselves are more thoroughly understood and constantly actualized in the Church. Thus God, who spoke in the past, continues to converse with the spouse of his beloved Son. And the Holy Spirit, through whom the living voice of the Gospel rings out in the Church—and through her in the world—leads believers to the full truth, and makes the Word of Christ dwell in them in all its richness (cf. Col. 3:16).

(1) ***Unitatis redintegratio* 2:** see 815 (1). **1126**

(2) ***Unitatis redintegratio* 15:** see 925 (3). **1126**

(1) **Council of Trent (1547): DS 1605** If anyone shall say that these sacraments have been instituted for the nourishing of faith alone: let him be anathema. **1127**

(2) **Council of Trent (1547): DS 1606** If anyone shall say that the sacraments of the New Law do not contain the grace which they signify, or that they do not confer that grace on those who do not place an obstacle in the way, as though they were only outward signs of grace or justice, received through faith, and certain marks of the Christian profession by which the faithful among men are distinguished from the unbelievers: let him be anathema. **1127**

Council of Trent (1547): DS 1608 If anyone shall say that by the said sacraments of the New Law, grace is not conferred from the work which has been worked [*ex opere operato*], but that faith alone in the divine promise suffices to obtain grace: let him be anathema. **1128**

(1) **Council of Trent (1547): DS 1604** If anyone shall say that the sacraments of the New Law are not necessary for salvation, but are superfluous, and that, although all are not necessary for every individual, without them or without the desire of them through faith alone men obtain from God the grace of justification: let him be anathema. **1129**

(2) **2 Peter 1:4** . . . by which he has granted to us his precious and very great promises, that through these you may escape from the corruption that is in the world because of passion, and become partakers of the divine nature. **1129**

1137 (1) **Ezekiel 1:26–28** And above the firmament over their heads there was the likeness of a throne, in appearance like sapphire; and seated above the likeness of a throne was a likeness as it were of a human form. And upward from what had the appearance of his loins I saw as it were gleaming bronze, like the appearance of fire enclosed round about; and downward from what had the appearance of his loins I saw as it were the appearance of fire, and there was brightness round about him. Like the appearance of the bow that is in the cloud on the day of rain, so was the appearance of the brightness round about.

1137 (2) **John 1:29** The next day he saw Jesus coming toward him, and said, "Behold, the Lamb of God, who takes away the sin of the world! . . . "

1137 (3) **Hebrews 4:4–15** For he has somewhere spoken of the seventh day in this way, "And God rested on the seventh day from all his works." And again in this place he said,

> "They shall never enter my rest."

Since therefore it remains for some to enter it, and those who formerly received the good news failed to enter because of disobedience, again he sets a certain day, "Today," saying through David so long afterward, in the words already quoted,

> "Today, when you hear his voice,
> do not harden your hearts."

For if Joshua had given them rest, God would not speak later of another day. So then, there remains a sabbath rest for the people of God; for whoever enters God's rest also ceases from his labors as God did from his.

Let us therefore strive to enter that rest, that no one fall by the same sort of disobedience. For the word of God is living and active, sharper than any two-edged sword, piercing to the division of soul and spirit, of joints and marrow, and discerning the thoughts and intentions of the heart. And before him no creature is hidden, but all are open and laid bare to the eyes of him with whom we have to do.

Since then we have a great high priest who has passed through the heavens, Jesus, the Son of God, let us hold fast our confession. For we have not a high priest who is unable to sympathize with our weaknesses, but one who in every respect has been tempted as we are, yet without sin.

1137 (4) **Hebrews 10:19–21** Therefore, brethren, since we have confidence to enter the sanctuary by the blood of Jesus, by the new and living way which he opened for us through the curtain, that is, through his flesh, and since we have a great priest over the house of God. . . .

1137 (5) **Revelation 21:6** And he said to me, "It is done! I am the Alpha and the Omega, the beginning and the end. To the thirsty I will give from the fountain of the water of life without payment. . . ."

1137 (6) **John 4:10–14** Jesus answered her, "If you knew the gift of God, and who it is that is saying to you, 'Give me a drink,' you would have asked him, and he would have given you living water." The woman said to him, "Sir, you have nothing to draw with, and the well is deep; where do you get that living water? Are you greater than our father Jacob, who gave us the well, and drank from it himself, and his sons, and his cattle?" Jesus said to her, "Every one who drinks of this water will thirst again, but whoever drinks of the water that I shall give him will never thirst; the water that I shall give him will become in him a spring of water welling up to eternal life."

(1) **Revelation 4–5** After this I looked, and lo, in heaven an open door! And the 1138
first voice, which I had heard speaking to me like a trumpet, said, "Come up hither, and I will show you what must take place after this." At once I was in the Spirit, and lo, a throne stood in heaven, with one seated on the throne! And he who sat there appeared like jasper and carnelian, and round the throne was a rainbow that looked like an emerald. Round the throne were twenty-four thrones, and seated on the thrones were twenty-four elders, clad in white garments, with golden crowns upon their heads. From the throne issue flashes of lightning, and voices and peals of thunder, and before the throne burn seven torches of fire, which are the seven spirits of God; and before the throne there is as it were a sea of glass, like crystal.

And round the throne, on each side of the throne, are four living creatures, full of eyes in front and behind: the first living creature like a lion, the second living creature like an ox, the third living creature with the face of a man, and the fourth living creature like a flying eagle. And the four living creatures, each of them with six wings, are full of eyes all round and within, and day and night they never cease to sing,

"Holy, holy, holy, is the Lord God Almighty,
who was and is and is to come!"

And whenever the living creatures give glory and honor and thanks to him who is seated on the throne, who lives for ever and ever, the twenty-four elders fall down before him who is seated on the throne and worship him who lives for ever and ever; they cast their crowns before the throne, singing,

"Worthy art thou, our Lord and God,
to receive glory and honor and power,
for thou didst create all things,
and by thy will they existed and were created."

And I saw in the right hand of him who was seated on the throne a scroll written within and on the back, sealed with seven seals; and I saw a strong angel proclaiming with a loud voice, "Who is worthy to open the scroll and break its seals?" And no one in heaven or on earth or under the earth was able to open the scroll or to look into it, and I wept much that no one was found worthy to open the scroll or to look into it. Then one of the elders said to me, "Weep not; lo, the Lion of the tribe of Judah, the Root of David, has conquered, so that he can open the scroll and its seven seals."

And between the throne and the four living creatures and among the elders, I saw a Lamb standing, as though it had been slain, with seven horns and with seven eyes, which are the seven spirits of God sent out into all the earth; and he went and took the scroll from the right hand of him who was seated on the throne. And when he had taken the scroll, the four living creatures and the twenty-four elders fell down before the Lamb, each holding a harp, and with golden bowls full of incense, which are the prayers of the saints; and they sang a new song, saying,

"Worthy art thou to take the scroll and to open its seals,
for thou wast slain and by thy blood didst ransom men for God
from every tribe and tongue and people and nation,
and hast made them a kingdom and priests to our God,
and they shall reign on earth."

Then I looked, and I heard around the throne and the living creatures and the elders the voice of many angels, numbering myriads of myriads and thousands of thousands, saying with a loud voice, "Worthy is the Lamb who was slain, to receive power and wealth and wisdom and might and honor and glory and blessing!" And I heard every creature in heaven and on earth and under the earth and in the sea, and all therein, saying, "To him who sits upon the throne and to the Lamb be blessing and honor and glory and might for ever and ever!" And the four living creatures said, "Amen!" and the elders fell down and worshiped.

1138 (2) **Revelation 7:1–8** After this I saw four angels standing at the four corners of the earth, holding back the four winds of the earth, that no wind might blow on earth or sea or against any tree. Then I saw another angel ascend from the rising of the sun, with the seal of the living God, and he called with a loud voice to the four angels who had been given power to harm earth and sea, saying, "Do not harm the earth or the sea or the trees, till we have sealed the servants of our God upon their foreheads." And I heard the number of the sealed, a hundred and forty-four thousand sealed, out of every tribe of the sons of Israel, twelve thousand sealed out of the tribe of Judah, twelve thousand of the tribe of Reuben, twelve thousand of the tribe of Gad, twelve thousand of the tribe of Asher, twelve thousand of the tribe of Naphtali, twelve thousand of the tribe of Manasseh, twelve thousand of the tribe of Simeon, twelve thousand of the tribe of Levi, twelve thousand of the tribe of Issachar, twelve thousand of the tribe of Zebulun, twelve thousand of the tribe of Joseph, twelve thousand sealed out of the tribe of Benjamin.

1138 (3) **Revelation 14:1** Then I looked, and lo, on Mount Zion stood the Lamb, and with him a hundred and forty-four thousand who had his name and his Father's name written on their foreheads.

1138 (4) **Isaiah 6:2–3** Above him stood the seraphim; each had six wings: with two he covered his face, and with two he covered his feet, and with two he flew. And one called to another and said:

"Holy, holy, holy is the Lord of hosts;
the whole earth is full of his glory."

1138 (5) **Revelation 12** And a great portent appeared in heaven, a woman clothed with the sun, with the moon under her feet, and on her head a crown of twelve stars; she was with child and she cried out in her pangs of birth, in anguish for delivery. And another portent appeared in heaven; behold, a great red dragon, with seven heads and ten horns, and seven diadems upon his heads. His tail swept down a third of the stars of heaven, and cast them to the earth. And the dragon stood before the woman who was about to bear a child, that he might devour her child when she brought it forth; she brought forth a male child, one who is to rule all the nations with a rod of iron, but her child was caught up to God and to his throne, and the woman fled into the wilderness, where she has a place prepared by God, in which to be nourished for one thousand two hundred and sixty days.

Now war arose in heaven, Michael and his angels fighting against the dragon; and the dragon and his angels fought, but they were defeated and there was no longer any place for them in heaven. And the great dragon was thrown down, that ancient serpent, who is called the Devil and Satan, the deceiver of the whole world—he was thrown down to the earth, and his angels were thrown down with him. And I heard a loud voice in heaven, saying, "Now the salvation and the power and the kingdom of our God and the authority of his Christ have come, for the accuser of our brethren has been thrown down, who accuses them day and night before our God. And they have conquered him by the blood of the Lamb and by the word of their testimony, for they loved not their lives even unto death. Rejoice then, O heaven and you that dwell therein! But woe to you, O earth and sea, for the devil has come down to you in great wrath, because he knows that his time is short!"

And when the dragon saw that he had been thrown down to the earth, he pursued the woman who had borne the male child. But the woman was given the two wings of the great eagle that she might fly from the serpent into the wilderness, to the place where she is to be nourished for a time, and times, and half a time. The serpent poured water like a river out of his mouth after the woman, to sweep her away with the flood. But the earth came to the help of the woman, and the earth opened its mouth and swallowed the river which the dragon had poured from his mouth. Then the dragon was angry with the woman, and went off to make war on the rest of her offspring, on those who keep the commandments of God and bear testimony to Jesus. And he stood on the sand of the sea.

(6) **Revelation 21:9** Then came one of the seven angels who had the seven bowls full of the seven last plagues, and spoke to me, saying, "Come, I will show you the Bride, the wife of the Lamb." 1138

(1) **1 Peter 2:4–5** Come to him, to that living stone, rejected by men but in God's sight chosen and precious; and like living stones be yourselves built into a spiritual house, to be a holy priesthood, to offer spiritual sacrifices acceptable to God through Jesus Christ. 1141

(2) ***Lumen gentium* 10** Christ the Lord, high priest taken from among men (cf. Heb. 5:1–5), made the new people "a kingdom of priests to God, his Father" (Apoc. 1:6; cf. 5:9–10). The baptized, by regeneration and the anointing of the Holy Spirit, are consecrated to be a spiritual house and a holy priesthood, that through all the works of Christian men they may offer spiritual sacrifices and proclaim the perfection of him who has called them out of darkness into his marvellous light (cf. 1 Pet. 2:4–10). Therefore all the disciples of Christ, persevering in prayer and praising God (cf. Acts 2:42–47), should present themselves as a sacrifice, living, holy and pleasing to God (cf. Rom. 12:1). They should everywhere on earth bear witness to Christ and give an answer to everyone who asks a reason for the hope of an eternal life which is theirs (cf. 1 Pet. 3:15). 1141

Though they differ essentially and not only in degree, the common priesthood of the faithful and the ministerial or hierarchical priesthood are none the less ordered one to another; each in its own proper way shares in the one priesthood of Christ. The ministerial priest, by the sacred power that he has, forms and rules the priestly people; in the person of Christ he effects the eucharistic sacrifice and offers it to God in the name of all the people. The faithful indeed, by virtue of their royal priesthood, participate in the offering of the Eucharist. They exercise that priesthood, too, by the reception of the sacraments, prayer and thanksgiving, the witness of a holy life, abnegation and active charity.

(3) ***Lumen gentium* 34** Since he wishes to continue his witness and his service through the laity also, the supreme and eternal priest, Christ Jesus, vivifies them with his spirit and ceaselessly impels them to accomplish every good and perfect work. 1141

To those whom he intimately joins to his life and mission he also gives a share in his priestly office, to offer spiritual worship for the glory of the Father and the salvation of man. Hence the laity, dedicated as they are to Christ and anointed by the Holy Spirit, are marvellously called and prepared so that even richer fruits of the Spirit may be produced in them. For all their works, prayers and apostolic undertakings, family and married life, daily work, relaxation of mind and body, if they are accomplished in the Spirit—indeed even the hardships of life if patiently borne—all these become spiritual sacrifices acceptable to God through Jesus Christ (cf. 1 Pet. 2:5). In the celebration of the Eucharist these may most fittingly be offered to the Father along with the body of the Lord. And so, worshipping everywhere by their holy actions, the laity consecrate the world itself to God.

1141 (4) ***Presbyterorum ordinis* 2** The Lord Jesus "whom the Father consecrated and sent into the world" (Jn. 10:36) makes his whole Mystical Body sharer in the anointing of the Spirit wherewith he has been anointed: for in that Body all the faithful are made a holy and kingly priesthood, they offer spiritual sacrifices to God through Jesus Christ, and they proclaim the virtues of him who has called them out of darkness into his admirable light. Therefore there is no such thing as a member that has not a share in the mission of the whole Body. Rather, every single member ought to reverence Jesus in his heart and by the spirit of prophecy give testimony of Jesus.

However, the Lord also appointed certain men as ministers, in order that they might be united in one body in which "all the members have not the same function" (Rom. 12:4). These men were to hold in the community of the faithful the sacred power of Order, that of offering sacrifice and forgiving sins, and were to exercise the priestly office publicly on behalf of men in the name of Christ. Thus Christ sent the apostles as he himself had been sent by the Father, and then through the apostles made their successors, the bishops, sharers in his consecration and mission.

The function of the bishops' ministry was handed over in a subordinate degree to priests so that they might be appointed in the order of the priesthood and be co-workers of the episcopal order for the proper fulfilment of the apostolic mission that had been entrusted to it by Christ.

Because it is joined with the episcopal order the office of priests shares in the authority by which Christ himself builds up and sanctifies and rules his Body. Hence the priesthood of priests, while presupposing the sacraments of initiation, is nevertheless conferred by its own particular sacrament. Through that sacrament priests by the anointing of the Holy Spirit are signed with a special character and so are configured to Christ the priest in such a way that they are able to act in the person of Christ the head.

Since they share in the function of the apostles in their own degree, priests are given the grace by God to be the ministers of Jesus Christ among the nations, fulfilling the sacred task of the Gospel, that the oblation of the gentiles may be made acceptable and sanctified in the Holy Spirit. For it is by the apostolic herald of the Gospel that the People of God is called together and gathered so that all who belong to this people, sanctified as they are by the Holy Spirit, may offer themselves "a living sacrifice, holy and acceptable to God" (Rom. 12:1). Through the ministry of priests the spiritual sacrifice of the faithful is completed in union with the sacrifice of Christ the only mediator, which in the Eucharist is offered through the priests' hands in the name of the whole Church in an unbloody and sacramental manner until the Lord himself come. The ministry of priests is directed to this and finds its consummation in it. For their ministration, which begins with the announcement of the Gospel, draws its force and power from the sacrifice of Christ and tends to this, that "the whole redeemed city, that is, the whole assembly and community of the saints should be offered as a universal sacrifice to God through the High Priest who offered himself in his passion for us that we might be the body of so great a Head."

Therefore the object that priests strive for by their ministry and life is the procuring of the glory of God the Father in Christ. That glory consists in men's conscious, free, and grateful acceptance of God's plan as completed in Christ and their manifestation of it in their whole life. Thus priests, whether they devote themselves to prayer and adoration, or preach the Word, or offer the eucharistic sacrifice and administer the other sacraments, or exercise other services for the benefit of men, are contributing at once to the increase of God's glory and men's growth in the divine life. And all these activities, since they flow from the pasch of Christ, will find their consummation in the glorious coming of the same Lord, when he shall have delivered up the kingdom to God and the Father.

(1) ***Presbyterorum ordinis* 2**: see 1141 (4). 1142

(2) ***Presbyterorum ordinis* 15** Among the virtues especially demanded by the ministry of priests must be reckoned that disposition of mind by which they are always prepared to seek not their own will but the will of him who has sent them. The divine task for the fulfilment of which they have been set apart by the Holy Spirit transcends all human strength and human wisdom; for "God chose what is weak in the world to shame the strong" (1 Cor. 1:27). 1142

Therefore the true minister of Christ is conscious of his own weakness and labors in humility. He proves what is well-pleasing to God and, bound as it were in the Spirit, he is guided in all things by the will of him who wishes all men to be saved. He is able to discover and carry out that will in the course of his daily routine by humbly placing himself at the service of all those who are entrusted to his care by God in the office that has been committed to him and the variety of events that make up his life.

The priestly ministry, being the ministry of the Church itself, can only be fulfilled in the hierarchical union of the whole body of the Church. Hence pastoral charity urges priests to act within this communion and by obedience to dedicate their own will to the service of God and their fellow-Christians. They will accept and carry out in the spirit of faith the commands and suggestions of the Pope and of their bishop and other superiors. They will most gladly spend themselves and be spent in whatever office is entrusted to them, even the humbler and poorer. By acting in this way they preserve and strengthen the indispensable unity with their brothers in the ministry and especially with those whom the Lord has appointed the visible rulers of his Church. They also work towards the building up of the Body of Christ, which grows "by what every joint supplieth." This obedience, which leads to the more mature freedom of the sons of God, by its nature demands that priests in the exercise of their duties should be moved by charity prudently to seek new methods of advancing the good of the Church. At the same time it also demands that while putting forward their schemes with confidence and being insistent in making known the needs of the flock entrusted to them, they should always be prepared to submit to the judgment of those who exercise the chief function in ruling God's Church.

By this humility and by responsible and willing obedience priests conform themselves to Christ. They reproduce the sentiment of Jesus Christ who "emptied himself, taking the form of a servant . . . and became obedient unto death" (Phil 2:7–9), and who by this obedience overcame and redeemed the disobedience of Adam, as the apostle declares: "For as by one man's disobedience many were made sinners, so by one man's obedience many will be made righteous" (Rom. 5:19).

(1) **Wisdom 13:1** 1147

For all men who are ignorant of God were foolish by nature;
and they were unable from the good things that are seen to know him who exists. . . .
nor did they recognize the craftsman while paying heed to his works;

(2) **Romans 1:19–20** For what can be known about God is plain to them, because God has shown it to them. Ever since the creation of the world his invisible nature, namely, his eternal power and deity, has been clearly perceived in the things that have been made. So they are without excuse. . . . 1147

(3) **Acts 14:17** ". . . yet he did not leave himself without witness, for he did good and gave you from heaven rains and fruitful seasons, satisfying your hearts with food and gladness." 1147

1151 (1) **Luke 8:10** . . . he said, "To you it has been given to know the secrets of the kingdom of God; but for others they are in parables, so that seeing they may not see, and hearing they may not understand. . . ."

1151 (2) **John 9:6** As he said this, he spat on the ground and made clay of the spittle and anointed the man's eyes with the clay. . . .

1151 (3) **Mark 7:33–35** And taking him aside from the multitude privately, he put his fingers into his ears, and he spat and touched his tongue; and looking up to heaven, he sighed, and said to him, "Ephphatha," that is, "Be opened." And his ears were opened, his tongue was released, and he spoke plainly.

1151 (4) **Mark 8:22–25** And they came to Bethsaida. And some people brought to him a blind man, and begged him to touch him. And he took the blind man by the hand, and led him out of the village; and when he had spit on his eyes and laid his hands upon him, he asked him, "Do you see anything?" And he looked up and said, "I see men; but they look like trees, walking." Then again he laid his hands upon his eyes; and he looked intently and was restored, and saw everything clearly.

1151 (5) **Luke 9:31** . . . who appeared in glory and spoke of his departure, which he was to accomplish at Jerusalem.

1151 (6) **Luke 22:7–20** Then came the day of Unleavened Bread, on which the passover lamb had to be sacrificed. So Jesus sent Peter and John, saying, "Go and prepare the passover for us, that we may eat it." They said to him, "Where will you have us prepare it?" He said to them, "Behold, when you have entered the city, a man carrying a jar of water will meet you; follow him into the house which he enters, and tell the householder, 'The Teacher says to you, Where is the guest room, where I am to eat the passover with my disciples? And he will show you a large upper room furnished; there make ready." And they went, and found it as he had told them; and they prepared the passover.

And when the hour came, he sat at table, and the apostles with him. And he said to them, "I have earnestly desired to eat this passover with you before I suffer; for I tell you I shall not eat it until it is fulfilled in the kingdom of God." And he took a cup, and when he had given thanks he said, "Take this, and divide it among yourselves; for I tell you that from now on I shall not drink of the fruit of the vine until the kingdom of God comes." And he took bread, and when he had given thanks he broke it and gave it to them, saying, "This is my body which is given for you. Do this in remembrance of me." And likewise the cup after supper, saying, "This cup which is poured out for you is the new covenant in my blood. . . ."

1156 (1) **St. Augustine, *Enarratio in Psalmos* 72, 1** Listen! Listen, most beloved vitals of the body of Christ: your hope is the Lord your God, and you do not look back upon follies and deceptive lunacies; and you who are still looking back, listen so that you may not look back. This psalm has the inscription (that is, the title): "The hymns of David, son of Jesse, have ended. A psalm of Asaph himself." We have so many psalms in the titles of which is written the name "David"; nowhere is "son of Jesse" added, except in this one alone. And it must be believed that this has not been done in vain, nor pointlessly; for God gives us a nudge everywhere, and calls the devout pursuit of charity to our understanding. What is: "The hymns of David, son of Jesse, have ended"? Hymns are the praises of God accompanied by singing; hymns are songs containing the praise of God. If it is praise, and it is not directed to God, it is not a hymn; if it is praise, and praise of God, and is not sung, it is not a hymn. It is fitting, then, if it is a hymn, that it have these three qualities: first, praise; second, direction to God; third, song. What, then, is: "The hymns have ceased"? The praises which are sung to God have ceased. This seems to announce a distressing fact and, so to speak, one full of grief. For he who sings praise, does not only praise, but also praises with merriment; he who sings praise, does not only sing, but also loves Him of Whom he sings. In the praise of one making his public declaration of faith there is preaching; in the song of one who loves there is affection. It says, therefore, "the hymns of David have ended," and it adds: "the son of Jesse." For David, the son of Jesse, was the King of Israel at a certain time in the Old Testament; and at that time the New Testament was hidden there, as the fruit is hidden in the root. For if you seek the fruit in the root, you will not find it; however, you do not find fruit on the branches except that which has come forth from the root. At that time, therefore, to the first people who came from the seed of Abraham in a carnal sense —for the second people (belonging to the New Testament) also belong to the seed of Abraham, but now in a spiritual sense; to that first people, then, while still carnal, when a few prophets understood both what was desired by God and when it needed to be publicly proclaimed, they foretold these future times and the coming of our Lord Jesus Christ. And just as Christ Himself, Who was to be born according to the flesh, had been hidden in the root in the seed of the patriarchs, and was to be revealed at a certain time as though when the fruit appears, as it was written, "A shoot from the root of Jesse has burst into flower," so also the New Testament itself, which had been hidden in Christ in those earlier times, was known only to the prophets and to a very few devout persons, not from a manifestation of contemporary events, but from a revelation of things to come. For what need is there, brothers, that I make mention of one particular detail, that Abraham, when he sends his faithful servant to arrange the betrothal of a wife for his only son, makes him swear to him, and in the oath says to him: "Place your hand beneath my thigh and swear"? What was in the thigh [translator's note: euphemism for "groin"] of Abraham, where he put his hand while swearing? What was there, except that even then it was promised to him: "In your seed all the nations will be blessed." Under the name of "thigh" the flesh is signified. Of the flesh of Abraham, through Isaac and Jacob and (not to belabor the point) through Mary [came] our Lord Jesus Christ.

(2) **Colossians 3:16** Let the word of Christ dwell in you richly, teach and admonish one another in all wisdom, and sing psalms and hymns and spiritual songs with thankfulness in your hearts to God. 1156

***Sacrosanctum concilium* 112** The musical tradition of the universal Church is a treasure of inestimable value, greater even than that of any other art. The main reason for this pre-eminence is that, as a combination of sacred music and words, it forms a necessary or integral part of the solemn liturgy. 1157

Sacred scripture, indeed, has bestowed praise upon sacred song. So have the Fathers of the Church and the Roman pontiffs who in more recent times, led by St. Pius X, have explained more precisely the ministerial function exercised by sacred music in the service of the Lord.

Therefore sacred music is to be considered the more holy, the more closely connected it is with the liturgical action, whether making prayer more pleasing, promoting unity of minds, or conferring greater solemnity upon the sacred rites. The Church, indeed, approves of all forms of true art which have the requisite qualities, and admits them into divine worship.

Accordingly, the sacred Council, keeping to the norms and precepts of ecclesiastical tradition and discipline as having regard to the purpose of sacred music, which is the glory of God and the sanctification of the faithful, decrees as follows. . . .

1158 ***Sacrosanctum concilium* 119** In certain countries, especially in mission lands, there are people who have their own musical tradition, and this plays a great part in their religious and social life. For this reason their music should be held in proper esteem and a suitable place is to be given to it, not only in forming their religious sense but also in adapting worship to their native genius, as indicated in Articles 39 and 40.

Therefore, in the musical training of missionaries, great care should be taken to see that they become competent in promoting the traditional music of those peoples both in the schools and in sacred services, as far as may be practicable.

1161 (1) **Romans 8:29** For those whom he foreknew he also predestined to be conformed to the image of his Son, in order that he might be the first-born among many brethren.

1161 (2) **1 John 3:2** Beloved, we are God's children now; it does not yet appear what we shall be, but we know that when he appears we shall be like him, for we shall see him as he is.

1165 (1) **Matthew 6:11** Give us this day our daily bread. . . .

1165 (2) **Hebrews 3:7–4:11** Therefore, as the Holy Spirit says,
"Today, when you hear his voice,
do not harden your hearts as in the rebellion,
on the day of testing in the wilderness,
where your fathers put me to the test
and saw my works for forty years.
Therefore I was provoked with that generation,
and said, 'They always go astray in their hearts;
they have not known my ways.'
As I swore in my wrath,
'They shall never enter my rest.' "

Take care, brethren, lest there be in any of you an evil, unbelieving heart, leading you to fall away from the living God. But exhort one another every day, as long as it is called "today," that none of you may be hardened by the deceitfulness of sin. For we share in Christ, if only we hold our first confidence firm to the end, while it is said,
"Today, when you hear his voice,
do not harden your hearts as in the rebellion."

Who were they that heard and yet were rebellious? Was it not all those who left Egypt under the leadership of Moses? And with whom was he provoked forty years? Was it not with those who sinned, whose bodies fell in the wilderness? And to whom did he swear that they should never enter his rest, but to those who were disobedient? So we see that they were unable to enter because of unbelief.

Therefore, while the promise of entering his rest remains, let us fear lest any of you be judged to have failed to reach it. For good news came to us just as to them; but the message which they heard did not benefit them, because it did not meet with faith in the hearers. For we who have believed enter that rest, as he has said,
"As I swore in my wrath,
'They shall never enter my rest,' "

although his works were finished from the foundation of the world. For he has somewhere spoken of the seventh day in this way, "And God rested on the seventh day from all his works." And again in this place he said,

"They shall never enter my rest."

Since therefore it remains for some to enter it, and those who formerly received the good news failed to enter because of disobedience, again he sets a certain day, "Today," saying through David so long afterward, in the words already quoted,

"Today, when you hear his voice,
do not harden your hearts."

For if Joshua had given them rest, God would not speak later of another day. So then, there remains a sabbath rest for the people of God; for whoever enters God's rest also ceases from his labors as God did from his.

Let us therefore strive to enter that rest, that no one fall by the same sort of disobedience.

(3) **Psalm 95:7** **1165**

For he is our God,
and we are the people of his pasture,
and the sheep of his hand.

O that today you would hearken to his voice!

(1) **John 21:12** Jesus said to them, "Come and have breakfast." Now none of the disciples dared ask him, "Who are you?" They knew it was the Lord. **1166**

(2) **Luke 24:30** When he was at the table with them, he took the bread and blessed, and broke it, and gave it to them. **1166**

(1) ***Sacrosanctum concilium* 108** The minds of the faithful should be directed primarily toward the feasts of the Lord whereby the mysteries of salvation are celebrated throughout the year. For this reason, the Proper of the Time shall be given due preference over the feasts of the saints so that the entire cycle of the mysteries of salvation may be suitably recalled. **1173**

(2) ***Sacrosanctum concilium* 111** The saints have been traditionally honored in the Church, and their authentic relics and images held in veneration. For the feasts of the saints proclaim the wonderful works of Christ in his servants and offer to the faithful fitting examples for their imitation. **1173**

Lest the feasts of the saints should take precedence over the feasts which commemorate the very mysteries of salvation, many of them should be left to be celebrated by a particular Church, or nation, or family of religious. Only those should be extended to the universal Church which commemorate saints who are truly of universal importance.

***Sacrosanctum concilium*, chapter IV** Jesus Christ, High Priest of the New and Eternal Covenant, taking human nature, introduced into this earthly exile that hymn which is sung throughout all ages in the halls of heaven. He attaches to himself the entire community of mankind and has them join him in singing his divine song of praise. **1174**

For he continues his priestly work through his Church. The Church, by celebrating the Eucharist and by other means, especially the celebration of the divine office, is ceaselessly engaged in praising the Lord and interceding for the salvation of the entire world.

The divine office, in keeping with the ancient Christian tradition, is so devised that the whole course of the day and night is made holy by the praise of God. Therefore, when this wonderful song of praise is correctly celebrated by priests and others deputed to it by the Church, or by the faithful praying together with a priest in the approved form, then it is truly the voice of the Bride herself addressed to her Bridegroom. It is the very prayer which Christ himself together with his Body addresses to the Father.

Hence all who take part in the divine office are not only performing a duty for the Church, they are also sharing in what is the greatest honor for Christ's Bride; for by offering these praises to God they are standing before God's throne in the name of the Church, their Mother.

Priests who are engaged in the sacred pastoral ministry will pray the divine office the more fervently, the more alive they are to the need to heed St. Paul's exhortation, "Pray without ceasing" (1 Th. 5:17). For only the Lord, who said, "Without me you can do nothing," can make their work effective and fruitful. That is why the apostles when instituting deacons said, "We will devote ourselves to prayer and to the ministry of the word" (Acts 6:4).

In order that the divine office may be better and more perfectly prayed, whether by priests or by other members of the Church, in existing circumstances, the sacred Council, continuing the restoration so happily begun by the Apostolic See, decrees as follows concerning the office of the Roman rite:

Since the purpose of the office is to sanctify the day, the traditional sequence of the hours is to be restored so that, as far as possible, they may again become also in fact what they have been in name. At the same time account must be taken of the conditions of modern life in which those who are engaged in apostolic work must live.

Therefore, in the revision of the office these norms are to be observed:

(a) By the venerable tradition of the universal Church, Lauds as morning prayer, and Vespers as evening prayer, are the two hinges on which the daily office turns. They must be considered as the chief hours and are to be celebrated as such.

(b) Compline is to be drawn up so as suitably to mark the close of the day.

(c) The hour called Matins, although it should retain the character of nocturnal prayer when recited in choir, shall be so adapted that it may be recited at any hour of the day, and it shall be made up of fewer psalms and longer readings.

(d) The hour of Prime is to be suppressed.

(e) In choir the minor hours of Terce, Sect, and None are to be observed. Outside of choir it will be lawful to select any one of the three most suited to the time of the day.

The divine office, because it is the public prayer of the Church, is a source of piety and a nourishment for personal prayer. For this reason, priests and others who take part in the divine office are earnestly exhorted in the Lord to attune their minds to their voices when praying it. To achieve this more fully, they should take steps to improve their understanding of the liturgy and of the Bible, especially of the psalms. When the Roman office is being revised, its venerable centuries-old treasures are to be so adapted that those to whom it is handed on may profit from it more fully and more easily.

So that it may be possible in practice to observe the course of the hours proposed in Article 89, the psalms are no longer to be distributed throughout one week but through a longer period of time.

The task of revising the psalter, already happily begun, is to be finished as soon as possible. It shall take into account the style of Christian Latin, the liturgical use of the psalms—including the singing of the psalms—and the entire tradition of the Latin Church.

As regards the readings, the following points shall be observed:

(a) Readings from sacred scripture shall be so arranged that the riches of the divine word may be easily accessible in more abundant measure;

(b) Readings taken from the works of the fathers, doctors, and ecclesiastical writers shall be better selected;

(c) The accounts of the martyrdom or lives of the saints are to be made historically accurate.

Hymns are to be restored to their original form, as far as may be desirable. They are to be purged of whatever smacks of mythology or accords ill with Christian piety. Also, as occasion may warrant, other selections are to be made from the treasury of hymns.

So that the day may be truly sanctified and that the hours themselves may be recited with spiritual advantage, it is best that each of them be prayed at the time which corresponds most closely with its true canonical time.

Communities obliged to choral office are bound to celebrate the office in choir every day in addition to the conventual Mass. In particular:

(a) Orders of canons, monks, and nuns, and of other regulars bound by law or constitutions to choral office, must say the entire office;

(b) Cathedral or collegiate chapters are bound to recite those parts of the office imposed on them by general or particular law;

(c) All members of the above communities who are in major orders or who are solemnly professed, except for lay brothers, are bound to recite individually those canonical hours which they do not pray in choir.

Clerics not bound to office in choir, but who are in major orders, are bound to pray the entire office every day, either in common or individually, as laid down in Article 89.

The rubrics shall determine when it is appropriate to substitute a liturgical service for the divine office.

In particular cases, and for adequate reasons, ordinaries may dispense their subjects, wholly or in part, from the obligation of reciting the divine office, or they may change it to another obligation.

Any religious who in virtue of their constitutions recite parts of the divine office, are thereby joining in the public prayer of the Church.

The same can be said of those who, in virtue of their constitutions, recite any "little office", provided it be drawn up after the pattern of the divine office, and be duly approved.

Since the divine office is the voice of the Church, that is, of the whole mystical body publicly praising God, it is recommended that clerics who are not obliged to attend office in choir, especially priests who live together or who assemble for any purpose, should pray at least some part of the divine office in common.

All who pray the divine office, whether in choir or in common, should fulfil the task entrusted to them as perfectly as possible. This refers not only to the internal devotion of mind but also to the external manner of celebration.

It is, moreover, fitting that whenever possible the office be sung, both in choir and in common.

Pastors of souls should see to it that the principal hours, especially Vespers, are celebrated in common in church on Sundays and on the more solemn feasts. The laity, too, are encouraged to recite the divine office, either with the priests, or among themselves, or even individually.

In accordance with the age-old tradition of the Latin rite, the Latin language is to be retained by clerics in the divine office. But in individual cases the ordinary has the power to grant the use of a vernacular translation to those clerics for whom the use of Latin constitutes a grave obstacle to their praying the office properly. The vernacular version, however, must be one that is drawn up in accordance with the provisions of Article 36.

The competent superior has the power to grant the use of the vernacular for the divine office, even in choir, to religious, including men who are not clerics. The vernacular version, however, must be one that is approved.

Any cleric bound to the divine office fulfils his obligation if he prays the office in the vernacular together with a group of the faithful or with those mentioned in par. 2 above, provided that the text used has been approved.

1175 (1) ***Sacrosanctum concilium* 86** Priests who are engaged in the sacred pastoral ministry will pray the divine office the more fervently, the more alive they are to the need to heed St. Paul's exhortation, "Pray without ceasing" (1 Th. 5:17). For only the Lord, who said, "Without me you can do nothing," can make their work effective and fruitful. That is why the apostles when instituting deacons said, "We will devote ourselves to prayer and to the ministry of the word" (Acts 6:4).

1175 (2) ***Sacrosanctum concilium* 96** Clerics not bound to office in choir, but who are in major orders, are bound to pray the entire office every day, either in common or individually, as laid down in Article 89.

1175 (3) ***Sacrosanctum concilium* 98** Any religious who in virtue of their constitutions recite parts of the divine office, are thereby joining in the public prayer of the Church.

The same can be said of those who, in virtue of their constitutions, recite any "little office", provided it be drawn up after the pattern of the divine office, and be duly approved.

1175 (4) ***Presbyterorum ordinis* 5** God, who alone is the holy one and sanctifier, has willed to take men as allies and helpers to become humble servants in his work of sanctification. The purpose then for which priests are consecrated by God through the ministry of the bishop is that they should be made sharers in a special way in Christ's priesthood and, by carrying out sacred functions, act as his ministers who through his Spirit continually exercises his priestly function for our benefit in the liturgy. By Baptism priests introduce men into the People of God; by the sacrament of Penance they reconcile sinners with God and the Church; by the Anointing of the Sick they relieve those who are ill; and especially by the celebration of Mass they offer Christ's sacrifice sacramentally. But in the celebration of all the sacraments—as St. Ignatius Martyr already asserted in the early Church—priests are hierarchically united with the bishop in various ways and so make him present in a certain sense in individual assemblies of the faithful.

But the other sacraments, and indeed all ecclesiastical ministries and works of the apostolate are bound up with the Eucharist and are directed towards it. For in the most blessed Eucharist is contained the whole spiritual good of the Church, namely Christ himself our Pasch and the living bread which gives life to men through his flesh—that flesh which is given life and gives life through the Holy Spirit. Thus men are invited and led to offer themselves, their works and all creation with Christ. For this reason the Eucharist appears as the source and the summit of all preaching of the Gospel: catechumens are gradually led up to participation in the Eucharist, while the faithful who have already been consecrated in baptism and confirmation are fully incorporated in the Body of Christ by the reception of the Eucharist.

Therefore the eucharistic celebration is the center of the assembly of the faithful over which the priest presides. Hence priests teach the faithful to offer the divine victim to God the Father in the sacrifice of the Mass and with the victim to make an offering of their whole life. In the spirit of Christ the pastor, they instruct them to submit their sins to the Church with a contrite heart in the sacrament of Penance, so that they may be daily more and more converted to the Lord, remembering his words: "Repent, for the kingdom of heaven is at hand" (Mt. 4:17). They teach them to take part in the celebrations of the sacred liturgy in such a way as to achieve sincere prayer in them also. They guide them to the exercise of an ever more perfect spirit of prayer throughout their lives in proportion to each one's graces and needs. They lead all the faithful on to the observance of the duties of their particular state in life, and those who are more advanced to the carrying out of the evangelical counsels in the way suited to their individual cases. Finally they train the faithful so that they will be able to sing in their hearts to the Lord with psalms and hymns and spiritual canticles, giving thanks always for all things in the name of our Lord Jesus Christ to God the Father.

By their fulfilment of the Divine Office priests themselves should extend to the different hours of the day the praise and thanksgiving they offer in the celebration of the Eucharist. By the Office they pray to God in the name of the Church for the whole people entrusted to them and in fact for the whole world.

The house of prayer in which the most holy Eucharist is celebrated and reserved, where the faithful assemble, and where is worshipped the presence of the Son of God our Savior, offered for us on the sacrificial altar for the help and consolation of the faithful—this house ought to be in good taste and a worthy place for prayer and sacred ceremonial. In it pastors and faithful are called upon to respond with grateful hearts to the gifts of him who through his humanity is unceasingly pouring the divine life into the members of his Body. Priests ought to go to the trouble of properly cultivating liturgical knowledge and art so that by means of their liturgical ministry God the Father, Son, and Holy Spirit may be daily more perfectly praised by the Christian communities entrusted to their care.

***Dignitatis humanae* 4** The freedom or immunity from coercion in religious mat- 1180
ters which is the right of individuals must also be accorded to men when they act in community. Religious communities are a requirement of the nature of man and of religion itself.

Therefore, provided the just requirements of public order are not violated, these groups have a right to immunity so that they may organize themselves according to their own principles. They must be allowed to honor the supreme Godhead with public worship, help their members to practice their religion and strengthen them with religious instruction, and promote institutions in which members may work together to organize their own lives according to their religious principles.

Religious communities also have the right not to be hindered by legislation or administrative action on the part of the civil authority in the selection, training, appointment and transfer of their own ministers, in communicating with religious authorities and communities in other parts of the world, in erecting buildings for religious purposes, and in the acquisition and use of the property they need.

Religious communities have the further right not to be prevented from publicly teaching and bearing witness to their beliefs by the spoken or written word. However, in spreading religious belief and in introducing religious practices everybody must at all times avoid any action which seems to suggest coercion or dishonest or unworthy persuasion especially when dealing with the uneducated or the poor. Such a manner of acting must be considered an abuse of one's own right and an infringement of the rights of others.

Also included in the right to religious freedom is the right of religious groups not to be prevented from freely demonstrating the special value of their teaching for the organization of society and the inspiration of all human activity. Finally, rooted in the social nature of man and in the very nature of religion is the right of men, prompted by their own religious sense, freely to hold meetings or establish educational, cultural, charitable and social organizations.

1181 (1) ***Sacrosanctum concilium* 122–27** The fine arts are rightly classed among the noblest activities of man's genius; this is especially true of religious art and of its highest manifestation, sacred art. Of their nature the arts are directed toward expressing in some way the infinite beauty of God in works made by human hands. Their dedication to the increase of God's praise and of his glory is more complete, the more exclusively they are devoted to turning men's minds devoutly toward God.

For that reason holy Mother Church has always been the patron of the fine arts and has ever sought their noble ministry, to the end especially that all things set apart for use in divine worship should be worthy, becoming, and beautiful, signs and symbols of things supernatural. And to this end she has trained artists. In fact the Church has, with good reason, always claimed the right to pass judgment on the arts, deciding which of the works of artists are in accordance with faith, piety, and the laws religiously handed down, and are to be considered suitable for sacred use.

The Church has been particularly careful to see that sacred furnishings should worthily and beautifully serve the dignity of worship. She has admitted changes in material style, or ornamentation prompted by the progress of technical arts with the passage of time.

Wherefore it has pleased the Fathers to issue the following decrees on these matters:

The Church has not adopted any particular style of art as her own. She has admitted styles from every period, in keeping with the natural characteristics and conditions of peoples and the needs of the various rites. Thus in the course of the centuries she has brought into existence a treasury of art which must be preserved with every care. The art of our own times from every race and country shall also be given free scope in the Church, provided it bring to the task the reverence and honor due to the sacred buildings and rites. Thus it is enabled to join its voice to that wonderful chorus of praise in honor of the Catholic faith sung by great men in past ages.

Ordinaries are to take care that in encouraging and favoring truly sacred art, they should seek for noble beauty rather than sumptuous display. The same principle applies also to sacred vestments and ornaments.

Bishops should be careful to ensure that works of art which are repugnant to faith, morals, and Christian piety, and which offend true religious sense either by depraved forms or through lack of artistic merit or because of mediocrity or pretense, be removed from the house of God and from other sacred places.

And when churches are to be built, let great care be taken that they be suitable for the celebration of liturgical services and for the active participation of the faithful.

The practice of placing sacred images in churches so that they be venerated by the faithful is to be maintained. Nevertheless their number should be moderate and their relative positions should reflect right order. For otherwise the Christian people may find them incongruous and they may foster devotion of doubtful orthodoxy.

When passing judgment on works of art, local ordinaries should ask the opinion of the diocesan commission on sacred art and—when occasion demands—the opinions of others who are experts, and the commissions mentioned in Articles 44, 45 and 46.

Ordinaries should ensure that sacred furnishings and works of value are not disposed of or destroyed, for they are ornaments of God's house.

Bishops, either personally or through suitable priests who are gifted with a knowledge and love of art, should have a special concern for artists, so as to imbue them with the spirit of sacred art and of the sacred liturgy.

It is also desirable that schools or academies of sacred art should be established in those parts of the world where they would be useful for the training of artists.

All artists who, prompted by their talents, desire to serve God's glory in holy Church should ever remember that they are engaged in a kind of holy imitation of God the Creator: that they are concerned with works destined to be used in Catholic worship, for the edification of the faithful and to foster their piety and religious formation.

(2) ***Sacrosanctum concilium* 7** To accomplish so great a work Christ is always present 1181
in his Church, especially in her liturgical celebrations. He is present in the Sacrifice of the Mass not only in the person of his minister, "the same now offering, through the ministry of priests, who formerly offered himself on the cross," but especially in the eucharistic species. By his power he is present in the sacraments so that when anybody baptizes it is really Christ himself who baptizes. He is present in his word since it is he himself who speaks when the holy scriptures are read in the Church. Lastly, he is present when the Church prays and sings, for he has promised "where two or three are gathered together in my name there am I in the midst of them" (Mt. 18:20).

Christ, indeed, always associates the Church with himself in this great work in which God is perfectly glorified and men are sanctified. The Church is his beloved Bride who calls to her Lord, and through him offers worship to the eternal Father.

The liturgy, then, is rightly seen as an exercise of the priestly office of Jesus Christ. It involves the presentation of man's sanctification under the guise of signs perceptible by the senses and its accomplishment in ways appropriate to each of these signs. In it full public worship is performed by the Mystical Body of Jesus Christ, that is, by the Head and his members.

From this it follows that every liturgical celebration, because it is an action of Christ the Priest and of his Body, which is the Church, is a sacred action surpassing all others. No other action of the Church can equal its efficacy by the same title and to the same degree.

(1) **Hebrews 13:10** We have an altar from which those who serve the tent have no 1182
right to eat.

(2) **General Introduction to the Roman Missal 259** At the altar the sacrifice of 1182
the cross is made present under sacramental signs. It is also the table of the Lord and the people of God are called together to share in it. The altar is, as well, the center of the thanksgiving that the eucharist accomplishes.

***Sacrosanctum concilium* 128** The canons and ecclesiastical statutes which govern 1183
the provision of external things which pertain to sacred worship should be revised as soon as possible, together with the liturgical books, as laid down in Article 25. These laws refer especially to the worthy and well-planned construction of sacred buildings, the shape and construction of altars, the nobility, placing, and security of the eucharistic tabernacle, the suitability and dignity of the baptistry, the proper ordering of sacred images, and the scheme of decoration and embellishment. Laws which seem

less suited to the reformed liturgy should be amended or abolished. Those which are helpful are to be retained, or introduced if lacking.

In this matter, especially as regards the material and form of sacred furnishing and vestments, in accordance with Article 22 of this Constitution, powers are given to territorial episcopal conferences to adapt such things to the needs and customs of their different regions.

1201 **Paul VI, *Evangelii nuntiandi* 63–64** The individual churches—which are involved not only with men but also with their aspirations, their wealth and their poverty, with their manner of praying and living and their outlook on the world—must make their own the substance of the evangelical message. Without any sacrifice of the essential truths they must transpose this message into an idiom which will be understood by the people they serve and thus proclaim it.

The churches must make this transposition with all the judgment, care, reverence and competence which the nature of the task demands in fields relating to the sacred liturgy, to catechetics, to the formulation of theological principles, to the secondary ecclesial structures and to the ministry. When we speak of idiom we must be understood to mean not so much an explanation of the words or a literary style as an anthropological and cultural adaptation.

This is a question which calls for no small measure of prudence, because evangelization will lose much of its power and efficacy if it does not take into consideration the people to whom it is addressed, if it does not make use of their language, their signs and their symbols, if it does not offer an answer to the questions which are relevant to them, if, in a word, it does not reach and influence their way of life. On the other hand there is the danger that evangelization may lose its very nature and its savor if on the pretext of transposing its content into another language that content is rendered meaningless or is corrupted, or if in the effort to adapt the universal truth to some particular region this truth is in fact rejected and unity destroyed. For without unity there cannot be universality. In fact it is only a church which is conscious of her universal mission and which in practice always shows herself to be universal that can have a message to deliver which can be understood by all and knows no territorial boundaries.

When there is due consideration for the needs of the particular church the universal church will certainly be invigorated and this must be regarded as important and urgent because it is in accordance with the inherent desire of peoples and communities for an ever increasing recognition of their own natural predispositions.

If this invigoration is to be achieved it is essential that the individual churches should be wholeheartedly receptive to the universal church. It is especially worthy of note that those Christians who are most simple and faithful to the gospel are keenly conscious of the true significance of the gospel and have a spontaneous appreciation of this universal dimension. They have an instinctive and eager desire for it. They see themselves as a part of it, are in the fullest harmony with it and are really troubled when, on account of some ideology which they do not understand, they find themselves confined within the bounds of a church lacking this universality, circumscribed by local boundaries and restricted in her horizons.

Furthermore, it is a clear lesson of history that if any individual church, even when acting with the best of intentions and relying on arguments based on theology, social theory or pastoral considerations, or moved by the desire for a certain liberty of action, cuts herself off from the universal church and the visible center of her life, she can rarely if ever avoid two equally grave dangers. There is on the one hand the danger of an arid isolation and on the other hand the danger of a rapid disintegration as each of her constituent parts separates from her just as she has separated from the principal center. From this arises the danger of losing her liberty since, being separated from her and from the other churches which gave her strength and vigor, she can easily become the prey of various forces which may seek to reduce her to servitude and exploit her.

The individual churches should be united to the universal church by enduring bonds, bonds of charity and loyalty, of ready obedience to the magisterium of Peter, of unity in the law of prayer: *lex orandi* which is also the law of belief: *lex credendi* and finally by solicitude for the preservation of that unity which constitutes universality. The stronger these bonds are, the better fitted she will be to transpose the treasure of the faith into a legitimate variety of ways of communicating her message, whether it be the profession of faith, forms of prayer or worship, Christian life and conduct or the spiritual vigor of the people to whom it is addressed. And her evangelization will be all the more authentic since she will be able to draw from the universal patrimony all that is profitable for her people and will be able to give the universal church the experience and the life of her people to the advantage of all.

(1) ***Lumen gentium* 23** Collegiate unity is also apparent in the mutual relations of each bishop to individual dioceses and with the universal Church. The Roman Pontiff, as the successor of Peter, is the perpetual and visible source and foundation of the unity both of the bishops and of the whole company of the faithful. The individual bishops are the visible source and foundation of unity in their own particular Churches, which are constituted after the model of the universal Church; it is in these and formed out of them that the one and unique Catholic Church exists. And for that reason precisely each bishop represents his own Church, whereas all, together with the pope, represent the whole Church in a bond of peace, love and unity. 1202

Individual bishops, in so far as they are set over particular Churches, exercise their pastoral office over the portion of the People of God assigned to them, not over other Churches nor the Church universal. But in so far as they are members of the episcopal college and legitimate successors of the apostles, by Christ's arrangement and decree, each is bound to have such care and solicitude for the whole Church which, though it be not exercised by any act of jurisdiction, does for all that redound in an eminent degree to the advantage of the universal Church. For all the bishops have the obligation of fostering and safeguarding the unity of the faith and of upholding the discipline which is common to the whole Church; of schooling the faithful in a love of the whole Mystical Body of Christ and, in a special way, of the poor, the suffering, and those who are undergoing persecution for the sake of justice (cf. Mt. 5:10); finally, of promoting all that type of active apostolate which is common to the whole Church, especially in order that the faith may increase and the light of truth may rise in its fullness on all men. Besides, it is an established fact of experience that, in ruling well their own Churches as portions of the universal Church, they contribute efficaciously to the welfare of the whole Mystical Body, which, from another point of view, is a corporate body of Churches.

The task of announcing the Gospel in the whole world belongs to the body of pastors, to whom, as a group, Christ gave a general injunction and imposed a general obligation, to which already Pope Celestine called the attention of the Fathers of the Council of Ephesus. Consequently, the bishops, each for his own part, in so far as the due performance of their own duty permits, are obliged to enter into collaboration with one another and with Peter's successor, to whom, in a special way, the noble task of propagating the Christian name was entrusted. Thus, they should come to the aid of the missions by every means in their power, supplying both harvest workers and also spiritual and material aids, either directly and personally themselves, or by arousing the fervent cooperation of the faithful. Lastly, in accordance with the venerable example of former times, bishops should gladly extend their fraternal assistance, in the fellowship of an all-pervading charity, to other Churches, especially to neighboring ones and to those most in need of help.

It has come about through divine providence that, in the course of time, different Churches set up in various places by the apostles and their successors joined together in a multiplicity of organically united groups which, whilst safeguarding the unity of the faith and the unique divine structure of the universal Church, have their own discipline, enjoy their own liturgical usage and inherit a theological and spiritual patrimony. Some of these, notably the ancient patriarchal Churches, as mothers in the faith, gave birth to other daughter-Churches, as it were, and down to our own days they are linked with these by bonds of a more intimate charity in what pertains to the sacramental life and in a mutual respect for rights and obligations. This multiplicity of local Churches, unified in a common effort, shows all the more resplendently the catholicity of the undivided Church. In a like fashion the episcopal conferences at the present time are in a position to contribute in many and fruitful ways to the concrete realization of the collegiate spirit.

1202 (2) ***Unitatis redintegratio* 4:** see 94 (3).

1204 (1) ***Sacrosanctum concilium* 37–40** Even in the liturgy the Church does not wish to impose a rigid uniformity in matters which do not involve the faith or the good of the whole community. Rather does she respect and foster the qualities and talents of the various races and nations. Anything in these people's way of life which is not indissolubly bound up with superstition and error she studies with sympathy, and, if possible, preserves intact. She sometimes even admits such things into the liturgy itself, provided they harmonize with its true and authentic spirit.

Provided that the substantial unity of the Roman rite is preserved, provision shall be made, when revising the liturgical books, for legitimate variations and adaptations to different groups, regions and peoples, especially in mission countries. This should be borne in mind when drawing up the rites and determining rubrics.

Within the limits set by the typical editions of the liturgical books it shall be for the competent territorial ecclesiastical authority mentioned in Article 22:2, to specify adaptations, especially as regards the administration of the sacraments, sacramentals, processions, liturgical language, sacred music and the arts, according, however, to the fundamental norms laid down in this Constitution.

In some places and circumstances, however, an even more radical adaptation of the liturgy is needed, and this entails greater difficulties. For this reason:

(1) The competent territorial ecclesiastical authority mentioned in Article 22:2 must, in this matter, carefully and prudently consider which elements from the traditions and cultures of individual peoples might appropriately be admitted into divine worship. Adaptations which are considered useful or necessary should then be submitted to the Holy See, by whose consent they may be introduced.

(2) To ensure that adaptations may be made with all the circumspection necessary, the Apostolic See will grant power to this same territorial ecclesiastical authority to permit and to direct, as the case requires, the necessary preliminary experiments over a determined period of time among certain groups suitable for the purpose.

(3) Because liturgical laws usually involve special difficulties with respect to adaptation, especially in mission lands, men who are experts in the matters in question must be employed to formulate them.

1204 (2) ***Catechesi tradendae* 53** Now a second question. As I said recently to the members of the Biblical Commission: "The term 'acculturation' or 'inculturation' may be a neologism, but it expresses very well one factor of the great mystery of the Incarnation." We can say of catechesis, as well as of evangelization in general, that it is called to bring the power of the Gospel into the very heart of culture and cultures. For this purpose, catechesis will seek to know these cultures and their essential components; it will learn their most significant expressions; it will respect their particular values and riches. In this manner it will be able to offer these cultures the knowledge of the hidden mystery and help them to bring forth from their own living tradition original expressions of Christian life, celebration and thought. Two things must however be kept in mind.

On the one hand the Gospel message cannot be purely and simply isolated from the culture in which it was first inserted (the biblical world or, more concretely, the cultural milieu in which Jesus of Nazareth lived), nor, without serious loss, from the cultures in which it has already been expressed down the centuries; it does not spring spontaneously from any cultural soil; it has always been transmitted by means of an apostolic dialogue which inevitably becomes part of a certain dialogue of cultures.

On the other hand, the power of the Gospel everywhere transforms and regenerates. When that power enters into a culture, it is no surprise that it rectifies many of its elements. There would be no catechesis if it were the Gospel that had to change when it came into contact with the cultures.

To forget this would simply amount to what St. Paul very forcefully calls "emptying the cross of Christ of its power."

It is a different matter to take, with wise discernment, certain elements, religious or otherwise, that form part of the cultural heritage of a human group and use them to help its members to understand better the whole of the Christian mystery. Genuine catechists know that catechesis "takes flesh" in the various cultures and milieux: one has only to think of the peoples with their great differences, of modern youth, of the great variety of circumstances in which people find themselves today. But they refuse to accept an impoverishment of catechesis through a renunciation or obscuring of its message, by adaptations, even in language, that would endanger the "precious deposit" of the faith, or by concessions in matters of faith or morals. They are convinced that true catechesis eventually enriches these cultures by helping them to go beyond the defective or even inhuman features in them, and by communicating to their legitimate values the fullness of Christ.

***Sacrosanctum concilium* 21** In order that the Christian people may more certainly 1205
derive an abundance of graces from the sacred liturgy, holy Mother Church desires to undertake with great care a general restoration of the liturgy itself. For the liturgy is made up of unchangeable elements divinely instituted, and of elements subject to change. These latter not only may be changed but ought to be changed with the passage of time, if they have suffered from the intrusion of anything out of harmony with the inner nature of the liturgy or have become less suitable. In this restoration both texts and rites should be drawn up so as to express more clearly the holy things which they signify. The Christian people, as far as is possible, should be able to understand them with ease and take part in them fully, actively, and as a community.

Therefore, the sacred Council establishes the following general norms. . . .

St. Thomas Aquinas, *Summa theologiae* III, 65, 1 1210

article 1. ought there to be seven sacraments?

THE FIRST POINT: 1. It seems that there ought not to be seven sacraments. For the sacraments draw their efficacy from divine power and from the power of Christ's Passion. Now divine power is single and Christ's Passion is single. For, as we are told, *by one offering he has perfected forever those that are sanctified.* Therefore there should not have been more than one sacrament.

2. A sacrament is designed as a remedy to counteract the harmful effects of sin. Now these are of two kinds, namely penalty and guilt. Therefore two sacraments would be sufficient.

3. Sacraments fall under the activities of the ecclesiastical hierarchy, as Dionysius makes clear. Now as he himself says, the hierarchy of the Church has three activities, namely *purgation, illumination, and perfection.* Therefore there should be no more than three sacraments.

4. Augustine tells us that the sacraments of the New Law are fewer in number than those of the Old. Now there was no sacrament in the Old Law corresponding to confirmation or extreme unction. Therefore these should not be numbered among the sacraments of the New Law either.

5. Among all the kinds of sin lust is not graver than the rest, as is clear from the arguments put forward in the *Secunda Pars.* Now no special sacrament has been instituted to counteract the effects of other sins. Therefore matrimony should not have been instituted either to counteract the effects of lust.

6. On the other hand, it seems that there are many sacraments. For sacraments are defined as sacred signs of a special kind. Now in the Church many other sanctifying acts are performed by means of sacred signs, such as holy water, the consecrating of altars, and other acts of this kind. Therefore there are more than seven sacraments.

7. Hugh of St. Victor asserts that the sacraments of the Old Law consisted of offerings, tithes, and sacrifices. Now the Church's sacrifice constitutes one sacrament, that namely which is called the Eucharist. Therefore offerings and tithes ought to be called sacraments too.

8. There are three main kinds of sin: original, mortal, and venial. Now baptism is designed to overcome original sin while penance is designed to overcome mortal sin. Therefore there ought to be another sacrament besides the seven, one namely designed to overcome venial sin.

REPLY: As we have already argued, the sacraments of the Church are designed to achieve two effects: to render man perfect in all that pertains to the worship of God as expressed in the religion of Christian living, and also as a remedy to counteract the harmful effects of sin. Now from both points of view it is fitting to have seven sacraments.

For just as physical things have a certain resemblance to spiritual realities, so too there is a certain correspondence between spiritual living and physical living. Now in respect of his physical life a man may be perfected in two ways: first in his own person as an individual, second in the relationship which he bears to the whole social community in which he is living. For man is by nature a social animal.

In respect of his own person there are two ways in which man is perfected in his physical life: first positively in that he directly achieves some positive further fulness of life, or second indirectly in that various obstacles to this fulness of life are removed such as sicknesses or conditions of this kind. With regard to the direct achieving of a positive further fulness of life this takes place in three ways: first through generation, for it is through this that man begins to be and to live, and the factor corresponding to this in the life of the spirit is baptism, which is spiritual regeneration, as we are told in that passage of *Titus* which runs, *through the washing of regeneration* etc. The second way is through growth, for it is by this that the individual is brought to his due fulness in size, weight, and strength. And the factor corresponding to this in the life of the spirit is confirmation, for it is in this that the Holy Spirit and strength are conferred. This is why the disciples, who have already been baptized, are told in *Luke, Wait in the city until you have received power from on high.* The third way of directly achieving some positive further fulness of life at the physical level is through nutrition, for it is by this that life and strength in man are maintained. And the factor corresponding to this in the spiritual life is the Eucharist. This is why we are told in *John, Except ye eat the flesh of the Son of Man and drink his blood ye have not life in yourselves.*

This would, in fact, be enough for man if the life he had, both at the physical and at the spiritual levels, were not subject to noxious influences. But from time to time man falls into physical disorders and spiritual ones too, namely sins. And because of this he needs a cure from such disorders. The cure provided contains two elements: the first is the actual healing by which health is restored. And the factor corresponding to this in the life of the spirit is penance, in accordance with the verse in the *Psalms, Heal my soul for I have sinned against you.* The second element is the restoration of the sufferer's former strength by means of a suitable diet and exercise. And the factor corresponding to this in the life of the spirit is extreme unction, for it is this that removes the remaining effects of sin and renders man ready for final glory. This is why we are told in *James, And if he be in sins they shall be forgiven him.*

Now let us turn to the two ways in which man is brought to his due perfection in relation to the community as a whole. One way in which this is achieved is for him to be given the power of presiding over a group of many individuals and of performing acts which affect the community at large. And the factor corresponding to this in the life of the spirit is the sacrament of order, in accordance with that passage in *Hebrews* which reminds us that priests offer sacrifices not merely on their own behalf but for the people as well. Another way in which man achieves a further fulness of perfection in relation to the community as a whole is connected with natural propagation. And in the physical and spiritual life alike this takes place within Matrimony, the reason being that it is not merely a sacrament but a function of nature as well.

These considerations likewise make it clear what the number of the sacraments should be from the point of view of their function as supplying a remedy against the harmful effects of sin. For baptism is designed as a remedy against lack of spiritual life; confirmation as a remedy against that weakness to which the soul is subject for some little time after birth; the Eucharist against the soul's proneness to sin; penance against actual sin committed after baptism; extreme unction against those elements of sin which remain, those namely which, whether through negligence or ignorance, are not sufficiently removed by penance; order against the breaking up of ties which bind the multitude into a community; matrimony as a remedy against personal lust and at the same time to make good the losses in the community incurred through death.

Some, however, regard the number of the sacraments as appropriate because it corresponds in a certain sense to the virtues, and also to the harmful effects of the penal consequences they entail. Such as these argue that baptism corresponds to faith and is designed to counteract original sin; extreme unction corresponds to hope and is designed to counteract venial sin; the Eucharist corresponds to charity and is designed to counteract the penal consequences of bad will; order corresponds to prudence and is designed to counteract ignorance; penance corresponds to justice and is designed to counteract mortal sin; matrimony corresponds to temperance and is designed to counteract concupiscence, confirmation corresponds to fortitude and is designed to counteract weakness.

Hence: 1. The same principal agent may use various instruments to produce various effects according to the requirements of the various operations involved. In the same way the divine power and the Passion of Christ produce their effects in us through various sacraments as through so many different instruments.

2. Faults and their penal consequences differ among themselves in two ways: first in virtue of the fact that there are different categories of faults and penalties; second, according to the different conditions of life of the individuals involved and their place in society. And from this point of view it is fitting that a number of sacraments should have been instituted, as is clear from what has been said.

3. In actions within a hierarchically composed community the agents, the subjects of the actions concerned, and the actions themselves have all to be taken into consideration. Now in the present context the agents are the Church's ministers, and these are catered for in the sacrament of order. Again the subjects are those who come to receive the sacraments. And it is matrimony that ensures that there shall be such. But the actions themselves which are involved here consist of *purgation, illumination, and perfection,* and of these purgation is the only one which is incapable of constituting a sacrament of the New Law and conferring grace. However it is catered for in certain of the sacramentals, namely catechesis and exorcism. Moreover as Dionysius explains, purgation and illumination taken together have their special corresponding sacrament in baptism. And in order to cater for the relapser there is also, and secondarily, a special correspondence between these two actions taken together and the sacraments of penance and extreme unction. As for the third action, perfection, in its aspect as a strengthening force it has confirmation to correspond to it while in its aspect as the attainment of the end in view it has a special connection with the Eucharist.

4. In the sacrament of confirmation the fulness of the Holy Spirit is bestowed for the purpose of strengthening the subject. In extreme unction man is made ready so that he can enter straightway into glory. Now neither of these functions is provided for in the Old Testament. And this is why there could be nothing in the Old Law to correspond to these sacraments. Nonetheless it remains true that the sacraments of the Old Law were more numerous because of the diversity of sacrifices and ceremonies included.

5. There are two reasons why it should be fitting for a special sacrament to have been instituted in order to provide a remedy against sexual concupiscence: the first is that this kind of concupiscence is destructive not only of the person but of nature itself. The second is that because of its vehemence it is liable to overpower the reason.

6. The name 'sacrament' is not given to holy water or other kinds of consecration because they do not produce the effect proper to a sacrament, namely the attainment of grace. Rather they have the force of making the subject ready in certain ways for the sacraments. They do this either by removing obstacles, as in the case of holy water, which is designed to guard against the devil's wiles, or against venial sins, or alternatively they produce a certain positive fitness for the performance of the sacraments as in the case of the consecrating of an altar or a sacred vessel out of reverence for the Eucharist.

7. Offerings and tithes, whether under the natural law or under the law of Moses, are designed not merely to supply the needs of the ministers and the poor, but also to have a figurative value. And for this reason they did constitute sacraments. Now, however, they have not survived in so far as their figurative value is concerned. Hence they are not sacraments.

8. The blotting out of venial sins does not require the infusion of grace. Hence no sacrament of the New Law has been instituted directly against venial sin, seeing that grace is infused in any one of these sacraments. For venial sin is removed by certain of the sacramentals, for instance holy water and others of the same kind. Some, however, argue that extreme unction is designed to counteract venial sin. But on this point more will be said in the appropriate place.

Rite of Christian Initiation of Adults, Introduction 1–2 The rite of Christian 1212
initiation presented here is designed for adults who, after hearing the mystery of Christ proclaimed, consciously and freely seek the living God and enter the way of faith and conversion as the Holy Spirit opens their hearts. By God's help they will be strengthened spiritually during their preparation and at the proper time will receive the sacraments fruitfully.

This rite includes not simply the celebration of the sacraments of baptism, confirmation, and eucharist, but also all the rites belonging to the catechumenate. Endorsed by the ancient practice of the Church, a catechumenate that would be suited to contemporary missionary activity in all regions was so widely requested that the Second Vatican Council decreed its restoration, revision, and adaptation to local traditions.

(1) **Council of Florence (1439): DS 1314** Holy baptism, which is the gateway to 1213
the spiritual life, holds the first place among all the sacraments; through it we are made members of Christ and of the body of the Church. And since death entered into the universe through the first man, "unless we are born of water and the Spirit, we cannot," as the Truth says, "enter into the kingdom of heaven" (cf. John 3:5). The matter of this sacrament is real and natural water; it makes no difference whether cold or warm. The form is: *I baptize thee in the name of the Father and of the Son and of the Holy Ghost.* Yet we do not deny that through these words: *Such a* (this) *servant of Christ is baptized in the name of the Father and of the Holy Ghost* or: *Such a one is baptized by my hands in the name of the Father and of the Son and of the Holy Ghost*, a true baptism is administered since the principal causes, from which baptism has its power is the Holy Trinity; the instrumental cause, however, is the minister, who bestows the sacrament externally; if the act which is performed through the minister himself, is expressed with the invocation of the Holy Trinity, the sacrament is effected.

(2) **CIC Canon 204, §1** The Christian faithful are those who, inasmuch as they have 1213
been incorporated in Christ through baptism, have been constituted as the people of God; for this reason, since they have become sharers in Christ's priestly, prophetic and royal office in their own manner, they are called to exercise the mission which God has entrusted to the Church to fulfill in the world, in accord with the condition proper to each one.

(3) **CIC Canon 849** Baptism, the gate to the sacraments, necessary for salvation 1213
in fact or at least in intention, by which men and women are freed from their sins, are reborn as children of God and, configured to Christ by an indelible character, are incorporated in the Church, is validly conferred only by washing with true water together with the required form of words.

(4) **CCEO Canon 675, §1** In baptism a person through washing with natural water 1213
with the invocation of the name of God the Father, Son and Holy Spirit, is freed from sin, reborn to new life, puts on Christ and is incorporated in the Church which is His Body.

(1) **Romans 6:3–4** Do you not know that all of us who have been baptized into 1214
Christ Jesus were baptized into his death? We were buried therefore with him by baptism into death, so that as Christ was raised from the dead by the glory of the Father, we too might walk in newness of life.

(2) **Colossians 2:12** . . . and you were buried with him in baptism, in which you 1214
were also raised with him through faith in the working of God, who raised him from the dead.

1218 **Genesis 1:2** The earth was without form and void, and darkness was upon the face of the deep; and the Spirit of God was moving over the face of the waters.

1223 (1) **Matthew 3:13** Then Jesus came from Galilee to the Jordan to John, to be baptized by him.

1223 (2) **Mark 16:15–16** And he said to them, "Go into all the world and preach the gospel to the whole creation. He who believes and is baptized will be saved; but he who does not believe will be condemned. . . ."

1224 **Philippians 2:7** . . . but emptied himself, taking the form of a servant, being born in the likeness of men.

1225 (1) **Luke 12:50** I have a baptism to be baptized with; and how I am constrained until it is accomplished!

1225 (2) **John 19:34** But one of the soldiers pierced his side with a spear, and at once there came out blood and water.

1225 (3) **1 John 5:6–8** This is he who came by water and blood, Jesus Christ, not with the water only but with the water and the blood. And the Spirit is the witness, because the Spirit is the truth. There are three witnesses, the Spirit, the water, and the blood; and these three agree.

1225 (4) **John 3:5** Jesus answered, "Truly, truly, I say to you, unless one is born of water and the Spirit, he cannot enter the kingdom of God."

1226 (1) **Acts 2:41** So those who received his word were baptized, and there were added that day about three thousand souls.

1226 (2) **Acts 8:12–13** But when they believed Philip as he preached good news about the kingdom of God and the name of Jesus Christ, they were baptized, both men and women. Even Simon himself believed, and after being baptized he continued with Philip. And seeing signs and great miracles performed, he was amazed.

1226 (3) **Acts 10:48** And he commanded them to be baptized in the name of Jesus Christ. Then they asked him to remain for some days.

1226 (4) **Acts 16:15** And when she was baptized, with her household, she besought us, saying, "If you have judged me to be faithful to the Lord, come to my house and stay." And she prevailed upon us.

1227 (1) **Colossians 2:12** . . . and you were buried with him in baptism, in which you were also raised with him through faith in the working of God, who raised him from the dead.

1227 (2) **1 Corinthians 6:11** And such were some of you. But you were washed, you were sanctified, you were justified in the name of the Lord Jesus Christ and in the Spirit of our God.

1227 (3) **1 Corinthians 12:13** For by one Spirit we were all baptized into one body—Jews or Greeks, slaves or free—and all were made to drink of one Spirit.

(1) **1 Peter 1:23** You have been born anew, not of perishable seed but of imperishable, through the living and abiding word of God. . . . 1228

(2) **Ephesians 5:26** . . . that he might sanctify her, having cleansed her by the washing of water with the word. . . . 1228

(1) **Rite of Christian Initiation of Adults:** see 1212. 1232

(2) ***Sacrosanctum concilium*** **37–40:** see 1204 (1). 1232

(1) ***Ad gentes divinitus*** **14** Those who have received from God the gift of faith in Christ, through the Church, should be admitted with liturgical rites to the catechumenate which is not a mere exposition of dogmatic truths and norms of morality, but a period of formation in the whole Christian life, an apprenticeship of sufficient duration, during which the disciples will be joined to Christ their teacher. The catechumens should be properly initiated into the mystery of salvation and the practice of the evangelical virtues, and they should be introduced into the life of faith, liturgy and charity of the People of God by successive sacred rites. 1233

Then, having been delivered from the powers of darkness through the sacraments of Christian initiation (cf. Col. 1:13), and having died, been buried, and risen with Christ (cf. Rom. 6:4–11; Col. 2:12–13; 1 Pet. 3:21–22; Mk. 16:16), they receive the Spirit of adoption of children (cf. 1 Th. 3:5–7; Acts 8:14–17) and celebrate with the whole people of God the memorial of the Lord's death and resurrection.

It is desirable that the liturgy of Lent and Paschal time should be restored in such a way that it will serve to prepare the hearts of the catechumens for the celebration of the Paschal Mystery, at whose solemn ceremonies they are reborn to Christ in baptism.

This Christian initiation, which takes place during the catechumenate, should not be left entirely to the priests and catechists, but should be the concern of the whole Christian community, especially of the sponsors, so that from the beginning the catechumens will feel that they belong to the people of God. Since the life of the Church is apostolic, the catechumens must learn to cooperate actively in the building up of the Church and in its work of evangelization, both by the example of their lives and the profession of their faith.

The juridical status of catechumens should be clearly defined in the new Code of Canon Law. Since they are already joined to the Church they are already of the household of Christ and are quite frequently already living a life of faith, hope and charity.

(2) **CIC Canon 851** 1233

It is necessary that the celebration of baptism be properly prepared. Thus:

1° an adult who intends to receive baptism is to be admitted to the catechumenate and, to the extent possible, be led through the several stages to sacramental initiation, in accord with the order of initiation adapted by the conference of bishops and the special norms published by it;

2° the parents of an infant who is to be baptized and likewise those who are to undertake the office of sponsor are to be properly instructed in the meaning of this sacrament and the obligations which are attached to it; personally or through others the pastor is to see to it that the parents are properly formed by pastoral directions and by common prayer, gathering several families together and where possible visiting them.

1233 (3) **CIC Canon 865**
§1. To be baptized, it is required that an adult have manifested the will to receive baptism, be sufficiently instructed in the truths of faith and in Christian obligations and be tested in the Christian life by means of the catechumenate; the adult is also to be exhorted to have sorrow for personal sins.
§2. An adult in danger of death may be baptized if, having some knowledge of the principal truths of faith, the person has in any way manifested an intention of receiving baptism and promises to observe the commandments of the Christian religion.

1233 (4) **CIC Canon 866** Unless a grave reason prevents it, an adult who is baptized is to be confirmed immediately after baptism and participate in the celebration of the Eucharist, also receiving Communion.

1233 (5) **CIC Canon 851, 2°** The parents of an infant who is to be baptized and likewise those who are to undertake the office of sponsor are to be properly instructed in the meaning of this sacrament and the obligations which are attached to it; personally or through others the pastor is to see to it that the parents are properly formed by pastoral directions and by common prayer, gathering several families together and where possible visiting them.

1233 (6) **CIC Canon 868**
§1. For the licit baptism of an infant it is necessary that:
1° the parents or at least one of them or the person who lawfully takes their place gives consent;
2° there be a founded hope that the infant will be brought up in the Catholic religion; if such a hope is altogether lacking, the baptism is to be put off according to the prescriptions of particular law and the parents are to be informed of the reason.
§2. The infant of Catholic parents, in fact of non-Catholic parents also, who is in danger of death is licitly baptized even against the will of the parents.

1237 **Romans 6:17** But thanks be to God, that you who were once slaves of sin have become obedient from the heart to the standard of teaching to which you were committed. . . .

1241 **Rite of Baptism of Children 62** Then the celebrant says:
The God of power and Father of our Lord Jesus Christ has freed you from sin and brought you to new life through water and the Holy Spirit.
He now anoints you with the chrism of salvation, so that, united with his people, you may remain for ever a member of Christ who is Priest, Prophet, and King.
All: Amen.
Next, the celebrant anoints each child on the crown of the head with chrism, in silence.
If the number of children is large and other priests or deacons are present, these may anoint some of the children with chrism.

1243 **Philippians 2:15** . . . that you may be blameless and innocent, children of God without blemish in the midst of a crooked and perverse generation, among whom you shine as lights in the world. . . .

1246 **CCEO Canon 679** Every person not yet baptized and only such a person is capable of receiving baptism.

(1) **Rite of Christian Initiation of Adults 19** The rite of election or enrollment of names (nos. 118–137) should as a rule be celebrated on the First Sunday of Lent. As circumstances suggest or require, it may be anticipated somewhat or even celebrated on a weekday. 1248

(2) **Rite of Christian Initiation of Adults 98** During the period of the catechumenate, a rite of anointing the catechumens, through use of the oil of catechumens, may be celebrated wherever this seems beneficial or desirable. The presiding celebrant for such a first anointing of the catechumens is a priest or a deacon. 1248

(1) **CIC Canon 206** 1249

§1. Catechumens are in union with the Church in a special manner, that is, under the influence of the Holy Spirit, they ask to be incorporated into the Church by explicit choice and are therefore united with the Church by that choice just as by a life of faith, hope and charity which they lead; the Church already cherishes them as its own.

§2. The Church has special care for catechumens; the Church invites them to lead the evangelical life and introduces them to the celebration of sacred rites, and grants them various prerogatives which are proper to Christians.

(2) **CIC Canon 788, §3** It is the responsibility of the conference of bishops to issue statutes by which the catechumenate is regulated; these statutes are to determine what things are to be expected of catechumens and define what prerogatives are recognized as theirs. 1249

(1) **Council of Trent (1546): DS 1514** "If anyone denies that infants newly born from their mothers' wombs are to be baptized," even though they be born of baptized parents, "or says they are baptized indeed for the remission of sins, but that they derive nothing of original sin from Adam, which must be expiated by the laver of regeneration" for the attainment of life everlasting, whence it follows, that in them the form of baptism for the remission of sins is understood to be not true, but false: let him be anathema. For what the Apostle has said: "By one man sin entered into the world, and by sin death, and so death passed upon all men, in whom all have sinned" [Rom. 5:12], is not to be understood otherwise than as the Catholic Church spread everywhere has always understood it. For by reason of this rule of faith from a tradition of the apostles even infants, who could not as yet commit any sins of themselves, are for this reason truly baptized for the remission of sins, so that in them there may be washed away by regeneration, what they have contracted by generation. "For unless a man be born again of water and the Holy Ghost, he cannot enter into the kingdom of God" [John 3:5]. 1250

(2) **Colossians 1:12–14** . . . giving thanks to the Father, who has qualified us to share in the inheritance of the saints in light. He has delivered us from the dominion of darkness and transferred us to the kingdom of his beloved Son, in whom we have redemption, the forgiveness of sins. 1250

(3) **CIC Canon 867** 1250

§1. Parents are obliged to see to it that infants are baptized within the first weeks after birth; as soon as possible after the birth or even before it parents are to go to the pastor to request the sacrament for their child and to be properly prepared for it.

§2. An infant in danger of death, is to be baptized without any delay.

1250 (4) **CCEO Canon 681**

§1. For an infant to be licitly baptized it is necessary that:

1° there is a founded hope that the infant will be educated in the Catholic Church, with due regard for §5;

2° the parents, or at least one of them, or the person who lawfully takes their place, consent.

§2. An abandoned infant or a foundling, unless his baptism is certainly established, should be baptized.

§3. Those who lack the use of reason from infancy are to be baptized as infants.

§4. An infant either of Catholic parents or even of non-Catholics, who is in a critical situation wherein death is prudently foreseen before he or she reaches the use of reason is licitly baptized.

§5. The infant of non-Catholic Christians is licitly baptized, if the parents, or one of them or the one who legitimately takes their place, requests it and if it is physically or morally impossible to approach their own minister.

1250 (5) **CCEO Canon 686, §1** Parents are held to the obligation that the infant be baptized as soon as possible according to legitimate custom.

1251 (1) ***Lumen gentium* 11** The sacred nature and organic structure of the priestly community is brought into operation through the sacraments and the exercise of virtues. Incorporated into the Church by Baptism, the faithful are appointed by their baptismal character to Christian religious worship; reborn as sons of God, they must profess before men the faith they have received from God through the Church. By the sacrament of Confirmation they are more perfectly bound to the Church and are endowed with the special strength of the Holy Spirit. Hence they are, as true witnesses of Christ, more strictly obliged to spread the faith by word and deed. Taking part in the eucharistic sacrifice, the source and summit of the Christian life, they offer the divine victim to God and themselves along with it. And so it is that, both in the offering and in Holy Communion, each in his own way, though not of course indiscriminately, has his own part to play in the liturgical action. Then, strengthened by the body of Christ in the eucharistic communion, they manifest in a concrete way that unity of the People of God which this holy sacrament aptly signifies and admirably realizes.

Those who approach the sacrament of Penance obtain pardon from God's mercy for the offense committed against him, and are, at the same time, reconciled with the Church which they have wounded by their sins and which by charity, by example and by prayer labors for their conversion. By the sacred anointing of the sick and the prayer of the priests the whole Church commends those who are ill to the suffering and glorified Lord that he may raise them up and save them (cf. Jas. 5:14–16). And indeed she exhorts them to contribute to the good of the People of God by freely uniting themselves to the passion and death of Christ (cf. Rom. 8:17; Col. 1:24; 2 Tim. 2:11–12; 1 Pet. 4:13). Those among the faithful who have received Holy Orders are appointed to nourish the Church with the word and grace of God in the name of Christ. Finally, in virtue of the sacrament of Matrimony by which they signify and share (cf. Eph. 5:32) the mystery of the unity and faithful love between Christ and the Church, Christian married couples help one another to attain holiness in their married life and in the rearing of their children. Hence by reason of their state in life and of their position they have their own gifts in the People of God (cf. 1 Cor. 7:7). From the marriage of Christians there comes the family in which new citizens of human society are born and, by the grace of the Holy Spirit in Baptism, those are made children of God so that the People of God may be perpetuated throughout the centuries. In what might be regarded as the domestic Church, the parents, by word and example, are the first heralds of the faith with regard to their children. They must foster the vocation which is proper to each child, and this with special care if it be to religion.

Strengthened by so many and such great means of salvation, all the faithful, whatever their condition or state—though each in his own way—are called by the Lord to that perfection of sanctity by which the Father himself is perfect.

(2) ***Lumen gentium* 41** The forms and tasks of life are many but holiness is one— 1251
that sanctity which is cultivated by all who act under God's Spirit and, obeying the Father's voice and adoring God the Father in spirit and in truth, follow Christ, poor, humble and cross-bearing, that they may deserve to be partakers of his glory. Each one, however, according to his own gifts and duties must steadfastly advance along the way of a living faith, which arouses hope and works through love.

In the first place, the shepherds of Christ's flock, in the image of the high and eternal priest, shepherd and bishop of our souls, should carry out their ministry with holiness and eagerness, with humility and fortitude; thus fulfilled, this ministry will also be for them an outstanding means of sanctification. Called to the fullness of the priesthood, they are endowed with a sacramental grace, so that by prayer, sacrifice and preaching, and through every form of episcopal care and service, they may fulfil the perfect duty of pastoral love. They should not be afraid to lay down their life for their sheep and, being a model to their flock (cf. 1 Pet. 5:3), they must foster a growing holiness in the Church, also by their own example.

Priests, who resemble the episcopal rank, forming the spiritual crown of the bishops, partake of their grace of office through Christ the eternal and only Mediator; they should grow in the love of God and of their neighbor by the daily exercise of their duty, should keep the bond of priestly fellowship, should abound in every spiritual good and bear a living witness of God to all, imitating those priests who, in the course of centuries, left behind them an outstanding example of holiness, often in a humble and hidden service. Their praise lives on in God's Church. They have the duty to pray and offer sacrifice for their people and for the whole People of God, appreciating what they do and imitating what they touch with their hands. Rather than be held back by perils and hardships in their apostolic labors they should rise to greater holiness, nourishing and fostering their action with an overflowing contemplation, for the delight of the entire Church of God. Let all priests, especially those who by special title of ordination are called diocesan priests, remember that their faithful union and generous cooperation with their bishop greatly helps their sanctification.

The ministers of lesser rank also partake in a special way of the mission and grace of the high priest, and in the first place the deacons who, waiting upon the mysteries of Christ and of the Church, should keep themselves free from every vice, should please God and give a good example to all in everything (cf. 1 Tim. 3:8–10 and 12–13). Clerics, called by the Lord and set aside as his portion and preparing themselves for the ministerial duties under the watchful eye of the shepherds, are bound to conform their minds and hearts to such high calling, persevering in prayer, fervent in love, thinking about whatever is true, just and of good repute, doing everything for the glory and honor of God. Close to them are those laymen chosen by God, who are called by the bishop to give themselves fully to apostolic works, and carry out a very fruitful activity in the Lord's field.

Christian married couples and parents, following their own way, should support one another in grace all through life with faithful love, and should train their children (lovingly received from God) in Christian doctrine and evangelical virtues. Because in this way they present to all an example of unfailing and generous love, they build up the brotherhood of charity, and they stand as witnesses and cooperators of the fruitfulness of mother Church, as a sign of, and a share in that love with which Christ loved his bride and gave himself for her. In a different way, a similar example is given by widows and single people, who can also greatly contribute to the holiness and activity of the Church. And those who engage in human work, often of a heavy kind, should perfect themselves through it, help their fellow-citizens, and promote the betterment of the whole of human society and the whole of creation; indeed, with their active charity, rejoicing in hope and bearing one another's burdens, they should imitate Christ who plied his hands with carpenter's tools and is always working with the Father for the salvation of all; and they should rise to a higher sanctity, truly apostolic, by their everyday work itself.

In a special way also, those who are weighed down by poverty, infirmity, sickness and other hardships should realize that they are united to Christ, who suffers for the salvation of the world; let those feel the same who suffer persecution for the sake of justice, those whom the Lord declared blessed in the Gospel and whom "the God of all grace, who has called us to his eternal glory in Christ Jesus, will himself restore, establish, strengthen and settle" (1 Pet. 5:10).

Accordingly all Christians, in the conditions, duties and circumstances of their life and through all these, will sanctify themselves more and more if they receive all things with faith from the hand of the heavenly Father and cooperate with the divine will, thus showing forth in that temporal service the love with which God has loved the world.

1251 (3) ***Gaudium et spes* 48** The intimate partnership of life and the love which constitutes the married state has been established by the creator and endowed by him with its own proper laws: it is rooted in the contract of its partners, that is, in their irrevocable personal consent. It is an institution confirmed by the divine law and receiving its stability, even in the eyes of society, from the human act by which the partners mutually surrender themselves to each other; for the good of the partners, of the children, and of society this sacred bond no longer depends on human decision alone. For God himself is the author of marriage and has endowed it with various benefits and with various ends in view: all of these have a very important bearing on the continuation of the human race, on the personal development and eternal destiny of every member of the family, on the dignity, stability, peace, and prosperity of the family and of the whole human race. By its very nature the institution of marriage and married love is ordered to the procreation and education of the offspring and it is in them that it finds its crowning glory. Thus the man and woman, who "are no longer two but one" (Mt. 19:6), help and serve each other by their marriage partnership; they become conscious of their unity and experience it more deeply from day to day. The intimate union of marriage, as a mutual giving of two persons, and the good of the children demand total fidelity from the spouses and require an unbreakable unity between them.

Christ our Lord has abundantly blessed this love, which is rich in its various features, coming as it does from the spring of divine love and modeled on Christ's own union with the Church. Just as of old God encountered his people with a covenant of love and fidelity, so our Savior, the spouse of the Church, now encounters Christian spouses through the sacrament of marriage. He abides with them in order that by their mutual self-giving spouses will love each other with enduring fidelity, as he loved the Church and delivered himself for it. Authentic married love is caught up into divine love and is directed and enriched by the redemptive power of Christ and the salvific action of the Church, with the result that the spouses are effectively led to God and are helped and strengthened in their lofty role as fathers and mothers. Spouses, therefore, are fortified and, as it were, consecrated for the duties and dignity of their state by a special sacrament; fulfilling their conjugal and family role by virtue of this sacrament, spouses are penetrated with the spirit of Christ and their whole life is suffused by faith, hope, and charity; thus they increasingly further their own perfection and their mutual sanctification, and together they render glory to God.

Inspired by the example and family prayer of their parents, children, and in fact everyone living under the family roof, will more easily set out upon the path of a truly human training, of salvation, and of holiness. As for the spouses, when they are given the dignity and role of fatherhood and motherhood, they will eagerly carry out their duties of education, especially religious education, which primarily devolves on them.

Children as living members of the family contribute in their own way to the sanctification of their parents. With sentiments of gratitude, affection and trust, they will repay their parents for the benefits given to them and will come to their assistance as devoted children in times of hardship and in the loneliness of old age. Widowhood, accepted courageously as a continuation of the calling to marriage, will be honored by all. Families will generously share their spiritual treasures with other families. The Christian family springs from marriage, which is an image and a sharing in the partnership of love between Christ and the Church; it will show forth to all men Christ's living presence in the world and the authentic nature of the Church by the love and generous fruitfulness of the spouses, by their unity and fidelity, and by the loving way in which all members of the family cooperate with each other.

(4) **CIC Canon 868** 1251

§1. For the licit baptism of an infant it is necessary that:

1° the parents or at least one of them or the person who lawfully takes their place gives consent;

2° there be a founded hope that the infant will be brought up in the Catholic religion; if such a hope is altogether lacking, the baptism is to be put off according to the prescriptions of particular law and the parents are to be informed of the reason.

§2. The infant of Catholic parents, in fact of non-Catholic parents also, who is in danger of death is licitly baptized even against the will of the parents.

(1) **Acts 16:15** And when she was baptized, with her household, she besought us, 1252
saying, "If you have judged me to be faithful to the Lord, come to my house and stay." And she prevailed upon us.

(2) **Acts 16:33** And he took them the same hour of the night, and washed their 1252
wounds, and he was baptized at once, with all his family.

(3) **Acts 18:8** Crispus, the ruler of the synagogue, believed in the Lord, together 1252
with all his household; and many of the Corinthians hearing Paul believed and were baptized.

(4) **1 Corinthians 1:16** (I did baptize also the household of Stephanas. Beyond 1252
that, I do not know whether I baptized any one else.)

1252 (5) **Congregation for the Doctrine of the Faith, instruction *Pastoralis actio***
Pastoral work with regard to infant baptism was greatly assisted by the promulgation of the new Ritual, prepared in accordance with the directives of the Second Vatican Council. The pace of change in society, however, is making it difficult for the young to be brought up in the faith and to persevere in it, and the resulting problems encountered by Christian parents and pastors have not been completely eliminated.

Many parents are distressed to see their children abandoning the faith and no longer receiving the sacraments, in spite of their own efforts to give them a Christian upbringing, and some pastors are asking themselves whether they should not be stricter before admitting infants to baptism. Some think it better to delay the baptism of children until the completion of a catechumenate of greater or less duration, while others are asking for a reexamination of the teaching on the necessity of baptism, at least for infants, and wish the celebration of the sacrament to be put off until such an age when an individual can make a personal commitment, perhaps even until the beginning of adult life.

However, this questioning of traditional sacramental pastoral practice cannot fail to raise in the Church justified fears of jeopardizing so essential a doctrine as that of the necessity of baptism. In particular, many parents are scandalized at finding baptism refused or delayed when, with full awareness of their duty, they request it for their children.

In view of this situation and in response to the many petitions received, the Sacred Congregation for the Doctrine of the Faith, in consultation with various Episcopal Conferences, has prepared the present Instruction. The purpose of the document is to recall the principal points of doctrine in this field which justify the Church's constant practice down the centuries and demonstrate its permanent value in spite of the difficulties raised today. The document will then indicate some general guidelines for pastoral action.

Both in the East and in the West the practice of baptizing infants is considered a rule of immemorial tradition. Origen, and later Saint Augustine, considered it a "tradition received from the Apostles". When the first direct evidence of infant baptism appears in the second century, it is never presented as an innovation. Saint Irenaeus, in particular, considers it a matter of course that the baptized should include "infants and small children" as well as adolescents, young adults and older people. The oldest known ritual, describing at the start of the third century the *Apostolic Tradition*, contains the following rule: "First baptize the children. Those of them who can speak for themselves should do so. The parents or someone of their family should speak for the others." At a Synod of African Bishops Saint Cyprian stated that "God's mercy and grace should not be refused to anyone born", and the Synod, recalling that "all human beings" are "equal", whatever be "their size or age", declared it lawful to baptize children "by the second or third day after their birth".

Admittedly there was a certain decline in the practice of infant baptism during the fourth century. At that time even adults postponed their Christian initiation out of apprehension about future sins and fear of public penance, and many parents put off the baptism of their children for the same reasons. But it must also be noted that Fathers and Doctors such as Basil, Gregory of Nyssa, Ambrose, John Chrysostom, Jerome and Augustine, who were themselves baptized as adults on account of this state of affairs, vigorously reacted against such negligence and begged adults not to postpone baptism, since it is necessary for salvation. Several of them insisted that baptism should be administered to infants.

Popes and Councils also often intervened to remind Christians of their duty to have their children baptized.

At the close of the fourth century the ancient custom of baptizing children as well as adults "for the forgiveness of sins" was used against the teachings of Pelagius. As Origen and Saint Cyprian had noted, before Saint Augustine, this custom confirmed the Church's belief in original sin, and this in turn showed still more clearly the necessity of infant baptism. There were interventions on those lines by Pope Siricius and Pope Innocent I. Later, the Council of Carthage in 418 condemned "whoever says that newborn infants should not be baptized", and it taught that, on account of the Church's "rule of faith" concerning original sin, "even babies, who are yet unable to commit any sin personally, are truly baptized for the forgiveness of sins, for the purpose of cleansing by rebirth what they have received by birth".

This teaching was constantly reaffirmed and defended during the Middle Ages. In particular, the Council of Vienne in 1312 stressed that the sacrament of baptism has for its effect, in the case of infants, not just the forgiveness of sins but also the granting of grace and the virtues. The Council of Florence in 1442 rebuked those who wanted baptism postponed and declared that infants should receive "as soon as is convenient" (*quam primum commode*) the sacrament "through which they are rescued from the devil's power and adopted as God's children".

The Council of Trent repeated the Council of Carthage's condemnation, and, referring to the words of Jesus to Nicodemus, it declared that "since the promulgation of the Gospel" nobody can be justified "without being washed for rebirth or wishing to be". One of the errors anathematized by the Council is the Anabaptist view that "it is better that the baptism (of children) be omitted than to baptize in the faith of the Church alone those who do not believe by their own act."

The various regional councils and synods held after the Council of Trent taught with equal firmness the necessity of baptizing children. Pope Paul VI also solemnly recalled the centuries-old teaching on this matter, declaring that "baptism should be conferred even on infants who are yet unable to commit any sin personally, in order that, having been born without supernatural grace, they may be born again of water and the Holy Spirit to divine life in Christ Jesus."

The texts of the Magisterium quoted above were chiefly concerned with refuting errors. They are far from exhausting the riches of the doctrine on baptism expressed in the New Testament, the catechesis of the Fathers and the teaching of the Doctors of the Church: baptism is a manifestation of the Father's prevenient love, a sharing in the Son's Paschal Mystery, and a communication of new life in the Spirit; it brings people into the inheritance of God and joins them to the Body of Christ, the Church.

In view of this, Christ's warning in Saint John's Gospel, "unless one is born of water and the Spirit, he cannot enter the kingdom of God", must be taken as an invitation of universal and limitless love, the words of a Father calling all his children and wishing them to have the greatest of blessings. This pressing and irrevocable call cannot leave us indifferent or neutral, since its acceptance is a condition for achieving our destiny.

The Church must respond to the mission that Christ gave to the Apostles after his Resurrection. Saint Matthew's Gospel reports it in a particularly solemn form: "All authority in heaven and on earth has been given to me. Go therefore and make disciples of all nations, baptizing them in the name of the Father and of the Son and of the Holy Spirit." Transmitting the faith and administering baptism are closely linked in this command of the Lord, and they are an integral part of the Church's mission, which is universal and cannot cease to be universal.

This is how the Church has understood her mission from the beginning, and not only with regard to adults. She has always understood the words of Jesus to Nicodemus to mean that "children should not be deprived of baptism." Jesus' words are so universal and absolute in form that the Fathers employed them to establish the necessity of baptism, and the Magisterium applied them expressly to infants: the sacrament is for them too entry into the people of God and the gateway to personal salvation.

The Church has thus shown by her teaching and practice that she knows no other way apart from baptism for ensuring children's entry into eternal happiness. Accordingly, she takes care not to neglect the mission that the Lord has given her of providing rebirth "of water and the Spirit" for all those who can be baptized. As for children who die without baptism, the Church can only entrust them to God's mercy, as she does in the funeral rite provided for them.

The fact that infants cannot yet profess personal faith does not prevent the Church from conferring this sacrament on them, since in reality it is in her own faith that she baptizes them. This point of doctrine was clearly defined by Saint Augustine: "When children are presented to be given spiritual grace", he wrote, "it is not so much those holding them in their arms who present them—although, if these people are good Christians, they are included among those who present the children—as the whole company of saints and faithful Christians. . . . It is done by the whole of Mother Church which is in the saints, since it is as a whole that she gives birth to each and every one of them." This teaching is repeated by Saint Thomas Aquinas and all the theologians after him: the child who is baptized believes not on its own account, by a personal act, but through others, "through the Church's faith communicated to it". This same teaching is also expressed in the new Rite of Baptism, when the celebrant asks the parents and godparents to profess the faith of the Church, the faith in which the children are baptized.

Although the Church is truly aware of the efficacy of her faith operating in the baptism of children, and aware of the validity of the sacrament that she confers on them, she recognizes limits to her practice, since, apart from cases of danger of death, she does not admit a child to baptism without its parents' consent and a serious assurance that after baptism it will be given a Catholic upbringing. This is because she is concerned both for the natural rights of the parents and for the requirements of the development of faith in the child.

It is in the light of the teaching recalled above that we must judge certain views which are expressed today about infant baptism and which question its legitimacy as a general rule.

Noting that in the New Testament writings baptism follows the preaching of the Gospel, presupposes conversion and goes with a profession of faith, and furthermore that the effects of grace (forgiveness of sins, justification, rebirth and sharing in divine life) are generally linked with faith rather than with the sacrament, some people propose that the order "preaching, faith, sacrament" should become the rule. Apart from cases of danger of death, they would apply this rule to children, and would institute an obligatory catechumenate for them.

It is beyond doubt that the preaching of the Apostles was normally directed to adults, and the first to be baptized were people converted to the Christian faith. As these facts are related in the books of the New Testament, they could give rise to the opinion that it is only the faith of adults that is considered in these texts. However, as was mentioned above, the practice of baptizing children rests on an immemorial tradition originating from the Apostles, the importance of which cannot be ignored; besides, baptism is never administered without faith; in the case of infants, it is the faith of the Church.

Furthermore, in accordance with the teaching of the Council of Trent on the sacraments, baptism is not just a sign of faith but also a cause of faith. It produces in the baptized "interior enlightenment", and so the Byzantine liturgy is right to call it the sacrament of enlightenment, or simply enlightenment, meaning that the faith received pervades the soul and causes the veil of blindness to fall before the brightness of Christ.

It is also said that, since every grace is intended for a person, it should be consciously accepted and appropriated by the person who receives it, something that an infant is quite incapable of doing.

But in reality the child is a person long before it can show it by acts of consciousness and freedom. As a person, the child is already capable of becoming, through the sacrament of baptism, a child of God and a coheir with Christ. Later, when consciousness and freedom awake, these will have at their disposal the powers placed in the child's soul by the grace of baptism.

Some people also object that baptizing infants is a restriction of their freedom. They say that it is contrary to the dignity of the children as persons to impose on them future religious obligations that they may perhaps later be led to reject. In this view it would be better to confer the sacrament only at an age when free commitment has become possible; until then parents and teachers should restrain themselves and avoid exercising any pressure.

Such an attitude is simply an illusion: there is no such thing as a pure human freedom, immune from being influenced in any way. Even on the natural level, parents make choices for their child that are essential for its life and for its orientation towards true values. A so-called neutral attitude on the part of the family with regard to the child's religious life would in fact be a negative choice that would deprive the child of an essential good.

Above all, those who claim that the sacrament of baptism compromises a child's freedom forget that every individual, baptized or not, is, as a creature, bound by indefeasible duties to God, duties which baptism ratifies and ennobles through the adoption as a child of God. They also forget that the New Testament presents entry into the Christian life not as a form of slavery or constraint but as admittance to true freedom.

It can happen that, when a child grows up, it will reject the obligations derived from its baptism. Although its parents may be hurt as a result, they should not reproach themselves for having had the child baptized and giving it a Christian upbringing, as was their right and their duty. In spite of appearances, the seeds of faith sown in the child's soul may one day come to life again, and the parents will contribute to this by their patience and love, by their prayers and by the authentic witness of their own faith.

In view of the link between the person and society, some people hold that infant baptism is still suitable in a homogeneous type of society, in which values, judgments and customs form a coherent system; but they hold that it is inappropriate in today's pluralistic societies, which are characterized by instability of values and conflicts of ideas. In the present situation, they say baptism should be delayed until the candidate's personality has sufficiently matured.

The Church is well aware that she must take the social reality into account. But the criteria of homogeneity and pluralism are merely pointers and cannot be set up as normative principles; they are inadequate for settling a strictly religious question, which by its nature is a matter for the Church and the Christian family.

While the criterion of the homogeneous society would legitimize infant baptism if the society is Christian, it would also lead one to consider it as illegitimate when Christian families are in a minority, whether within an ethnic group that is still predominantly pagan or in a militantly atheistic regime. This obviously cannot be admitted.

The criterion of the pluralistic society is not more valid than the preceding criterion, since in this type of society the family and the Church can act freely and accordingly provide a Christian education.

Besides, a study of history clearly shows that if these "sociological" criteria had been applied in the first centuries of the Church they would have paralyzed all her missionary expansion. It is worth adding that all too often pluralism is being invoked in a paradoxical way, in order to impose on the faithful behavior patterns that in reality are an obstacle to the exercise of their Christian freedom.

In a society whose mentality, customs and laws are no longer inspired by the Gospel it is therefore of great importance that in questions connected with infant baptism the Church's own nature and mission should be taken into consideration before all else.

In spite of being intermingled with human society and in spite of being made up of different nationalities and cultures, the People of God has its own identity, characterized by unity of faith and sacraments. Animated as it is by a single spirit and a single hope, it is an organic whole, capable of producing within the various groups of humanity the structures necessary for its growth. It is in this context that the Church's sacramental pastoral practice, in particular with regard to infant baptism, must be placed; her practice must not depend only on criteria borrowed from the human sciences.

A final criticism of infant baptism would have it that the practice comes from a pastoral usage lacking missionary impetus and concerned more with administering a sacrament than with stirring up faith and fostering commitment to spreading the Gospel. It is asserted that, by retaining infant baptism, the Church is yielding to the temptation of numbers and social establishment, and that she is encouraging the maintenance of a magical concept of the sacraments, while she really ought to engage in missionary activity, bring the faith of Christians to maturity, foster their free conscious commitment, and consequently admit a number of stages in her sacramental pastoral practice.

Undoubtedly, the Church's apostolate should aim at stirring up lively faith and fostering a truly Christian life; but the requirements of pastoral practice with regard to administering the sacraments to adults cannot be applied unchanged to children who, as mentioned above, are baptized "in the faith of the Church". Besides, we must not treat lightly the necessity of the sacrament: it is a necessity that has lost none of its importance and urgency, especially when what is at stake is ensuring that the child receives the infinite blessing of eternal life.

With regard to preoccupation with numbers, if this preoccupation is properly understood it is not a temptation or an evil for the Church but a duty and a blessing. The Church, described by Saint Paul as Christ's "body" and his "fullness", is the visible sacrament of Christ in the world, with the mission of extending to everyone the sacramental link between her and her glorified Savior. Accordingly, she cannot fail to wish to give to everyone, children no less than adults, the first and basic sacrament of baptism.

If it is understood in this way, the practice of infant baptism is truly evangelical, since it has the force of witness, manifesting God's initiative and the gratuitous character of the love with which he surrounds our lives: "not that we loved God but that he loved us. . . . We love, because he first loved us." Even in the case of adults, the demands that the reception of baptism involves should not make us forget that "he saved us, not because of deeds done by us in righteousness, but in virtue of his own mercy, by the washing of regeneration and renewal in the Holy Spirit."

While certain suggestions being put forward today cannot be accepted—suggestions such as the definitive abandonment of infant baptism and freedom to choose, whatever the reasons, between immediate baptism and deferred baptism—one cannot deny the need for a pastoral effort pursued in greater depth and renewed in certain aspects. It is appropriate to indicate the principles and fundamental guidelines at this point.

In the first place it is important to recall that the baptism of infants must be considered a serious duty. The questions which it poses to pastors can be settled only by faithful attention to the teaching and constant practice of the Church.

Concretely, pastoral practice regarding infant baptism must be governed by two great principles, the second of which is subordinate to the first.

1. Baptism, which is necessary for salvation, is the sign and the means of God's prevenient love, which frees us from original sin and communicates to us a share in divine life. Considered in itself, the gift of these blessings to infants must not be delayed.

2. Assurances must be given that the gift thus granted can grow by an authentic education in the faith and Christian life, in order to fulfill the true meaning of the sacrament. As a rule, these assurances are to be given by the parents or close relatives, although various substitutions are possible within the Christian community. But if these assurances are not really serious there can be grounds for delaying the sacrament; and if they are certainly non-existent the sacrament should even be refused.

On the basis of these two principles, concrete cases will be examined in a pastoral dialogue between the priest and the family. The rules for dialogue with parents who are practicing Christians are given in the Introduction to the Ritual. It is sufficient to recall here two of the more significant points.

In the first place, much importance is given to the presence and active participation of the parents in the celebration. The parents now have priority over the godparents, although the presence of the latter continues to be required, since their assistance in the child's education is valuable and can sometimes be essential.

Secondly, preparation for the baptism has an important place. The parents must give thought to the baptism; they should inform their pastors of the coming birth and prepare themselves spiritually. The pastors, for their part, will visit the families or gather them together and give them catechesis and appropriate advice. They will also urge the families to pray for the children that they are expecting.

As for the time of the actual celebration, the indications in the Ritual should be followed: "The first consideration is the welfare of the child, that it may not be deprived of the benefit of the sacrament; then the health of the mother must be considered, so that, as far as possible she too may be present. Then, as long as they do not interfere with the greater good of the child, there are pastoral considerations such as allowing sufficient time to prepare the parents and for planning the actual celebration to bring out its paschal character." Accordingly, "if the child is in danger of death, it is to be baptized without delay"; otherwise, as a rule "an infant should be baptized within the first weeks after birth."

It sometimes happens that pastors are approached by parents who have little faith and practice their religion only occasionally, or even by non-Christian parents who request baptism for their children for reasons that deserve consideration.

In this case the pastor will endeavor by means of a clear-sighted and understanding dialogue to arouse the parents' interest in the sacrament they are requesting and make them aware of the responsibility that they are assuming.

In fact the Church can only accede to the desire of these parents if they give an assurance that, once the child is baptized, it will be given the benefit of the Christian upbringing required by the sacrament. The Church must have a well-founded hope that the baptism will bear fruit.

If the assurances given—for example, the choice of godparents who will take sincere care of the child, or the support of the community of the faithful—are sufficient, the priest cannot refuse to celebrate the sacrament without delay, as in the case of children of Christian families. If on the other hand they are insufficient, it will be prudent to delay baptism. However the pastors should keep in contact with the parents so as to secure, if possible, the conditions required on their part for the celebration of the sacrament. If even this solution fails, it can be suggested, as a last recourse, that the child be enrolled in a catechumenate to be given when the child reaches school age.

These rules have already been made and are already in force, but they require some clarifications.

In the first place it must be clear that the refusal of baptism is not a means of exercising pressure. Nor can one speak of refusal, still less of discrimination, but rather of educational delay, according to individual cases, aimed at helping the family to grow in faith or to become more aware of its responsibilities.

With regard to the assurances, any pledge giving a well-founded hope for the Christian upbringing of the children deserves to be considered as sufficient.

Enrollment for a future catechumenate should not be accompanied by a specially created rite which would easily be taken as an equivalent of the sacrament itself. It should also be clear that this enrollment is not admittance to the catechumenate and that the infants enrolled cannot be considered catechumens with all the prerogatives attached to being such. They must be presented later on for a catechumenate suited to their age. In this regard, it must be stated clearly that the existence in the Rite of Christian Initiation of Adults of a Rite of Initiation for Children of Catechetical Age in no way means that the Church considers it preferable or normal to delay baptism until that age.

Finally, in areas where families of little faith or non-Christian families make up the majority, so as to justify the local setting up by the Bishops' Conference of a joint pastoral plan which provides for postponing baptism beyond the time fixed by the general law, Christian families living in these areas retain the full right to have their children baptized earlier. The sacrament is therefore to be administered in accordance with the Church's will and as the faith and generosity of these families deserve.

The pastoral effort brought into play on the occasion of the baptism of infants should be part of a broader activity extending to the families and to the whole of the Christian community.

From this viewpoint it is important to intensify pastoral care of engaged couples at meetings in preparation for marriage, and likewise the pastoral care of young couples. The whole ecclesial community must be called upon as circumstances demand, especially teachers, married couples, family action movements, religious congregations and secular institutes. Priests must give this apostolate an important place in their ministry. In particular, they will remind parents of their responsibilities in awakening their children's faith and educating it. It is in fact for parents to begin the religious initiation of the child, to teach it to love Christ as a close friend and to form its conscience. This task will be all the more fruitful and easy if it builds on the grace of baptism present in the child's heart.

As is clearly indicated in the Ritual, the parish community, especially the group of Christians that constitute the family's human environment, should play a part in the pastoral practice regarding baptism. "Christian instruction and the preparation for baptism are a vital concern of God's people, the Church, which hands on and nourishes the faith it has received from the Apostles." This active participation by the Christian people, which has already come into use in the case of adults, is also required for the baptism of infants, in which "the people of God, that is the Church, made present in the local community, has an important part to play." In addition, the community itself will as a rule draw great profit, both spiritual and apostolic, from the baptism ceremony. Finally, the community's work will continue, after the liturgical celebration, through the contribution of the adults to the education of the young in faith, both by the witness of their own Christian lives and by their participation in various catechetical activities.

In addressing the Bishops, the Congregation for the Doctrine of the Faith is fully confident that, as part of the mission that they have received from the Lord, they will take care to recall the Church's teaching on the necessity of infant baptism, promote an appropriate pastoral practice, and bring back to the traditional practice those who, perhaps under the pressure of comprehensible pastoral concerns, have departed from it. The Congregation also hopes that the teaching and guidelines contained in this Instruction will reach all pastors, Christian parents and the ecclesial community, so that all will become aware of their responsibilities and make their contribution, through the baptism of children and their Christian education, to the growth of the Church, the Body of Christ.

Mark 16:16 He who believes and is baptized will be saved; but he who does not 1253
believe will be condemned.

(1) **CIC Canons 872–74** 1255

Can. 872—Insofar as possible one to be baptized is to be given a sponsor who is to assist an adult in Christian initiation, or, together with the parents, to present an infant at the baptism, and who will help the baptized to lead a Christian life in harmony with baptism, and to fulfill faithfully the obligations connected with it.

Can. 873—Only one male or one female sponsor or one of each sex is to be employed.

Can. 874—§1. To be admitted to the role of sponsor, a person must:

1° be designated by the one to be baptized, by the parents or the one who takes their place or, in their absence, by the pastor or minister and is to have the qualifications and intention of performing this role;

2° have completed the sixteenth year, unless a different age has been established by the diocesan bishop or it seems to the pastor or minister that an exception is to be made for a just cause;

3° be a Catholic who has been confirmed and has already received the sacrament of the Most Holy Eucharist and leads a life in harmony with the faith and the role to be undertaken;

4° not be bound by any canonical penalty legitimately imposed or declared;

5° not be the father or the mother of the one to be baptized.

§2. A baptized person who belongs to a non-Catholic ecclesial community may not be admitted except as a witness to baptism and together with a Catholic sponsor.

(2) ***Sacrosanctum concilium* 67** The rite for the baptism of infants is to be revised, 1255
its revision taking into account the fact that those to be baptized are infants. The role of parents and godparents, and also their duties, should be brought out more clearly in the rite itself.

(1) **CIC Canon 861, §1** The ordinary minister of baptism is a bishop, presbyter 1256
or deacon, with due regard for the prescription of can. 530, n. 1.

(2) **CCEO Canon 677, §1** Baptism is administered ordinarily by a priest; but, 1256
with due regard for particular law, the proper pastor of the person to be baptized, or another priest with the permission of the same pastor or the local hierarch, is competent for its administration, which permission, for a serious reason is lawfully presumed.

1256 (3) **1 Timothy 2:4** . . . who desires all men to be saved and to come to the knowledge of the truth.

1257 (1) **John 3:5** Jesus answered, "Truly, truly, I say to you, unless one is born of water and the Spirit, he cannot enter the kingdom of God. . . ."

1257 (2) **Matthew 28:19–20** "Go therefore and make disciples of all nations, baptizing them in the name of the Father and of the Son and of the Holy Spirit, teaching them to observe all that I have commanded you; and lo, I am with you always, to the close of the age."

1257 (3) **Council of Trent (1547): DS 1618** If anyone shall say that baptism is optional, that is, not necessary for salvation: let him be anathema.

1257 (4) ***Lumen gentium* 14** This holy Council first of all turns its attention to the Catholic faithful. Basing itself on scripture and tradition, it teaches that the Church, a pilgrim now on earth, is necessary for salvation: the one Christ is mediator and the way of salvation; he is present to us in his body which is the Church. He himself explicitly asserted the necessity of faith and baptism (cf. Mk. 16:16; Jn. 3:5), and thereby affirmed at the same time the necessity of the Church which men enter through baptism as through a door. Hence they could not be saved who, knowing that the Catholic Church was founded as necessary by God through Christ, would refuse either to enter it, or to remain in it.

Fully incorporated into the Church are those who, possessing the Spirit of Christ, accept all the means of salvation given to the Church together with her entire organization, and who—by the bonds constituted by the profession of faith, the sacraments, ecclesiastical government, and communion—are joined in the visible structure of the Church of Christ, who rules her through the Supreme Pontiff and the bishops. Even though incorporated into the Church, one who does not however persevere in charity is not saved. He remains indeed in the bosom of the Church, but "in body" not "in heart". All children of the Church should nevertheless remember that their exalted condition results, not from their own merits, but from the grace of Christ. If they fail to respond in thought, word and deed to that grace, not only shall they not be saved, but they shall be the more severely judged.

Catechumens who, moved by the Holy Spirit, desire with an explicit intention to be incorporated into the Church, are by that very intention joined to her. With love and solicitude mother Church already embraces them as her own.

1257 (5) ***Ad gentes divinitus* 5** From the beginning of his ministry the Lord Jesus "called to himself those whom he wished and he caused twelve of them to be with him and to be sent out preaching" (Mk. 3:13; cf. Mt. 10:1–42). Thus the apostles were both the seeds of the new Israel and the beginning of the sacred hierarchy. Later, before he was assumed into heaven (cf. Acts 1:11), after he had fulfilled in himself the mysteries of our salvation and the renewal of all things by his death and resurrection, the Lord, who had received all power in heaven and on earth (cf. Mt. 28:18), founded his Church as the sacrament of salvation; and just as he had been sent by the Father (cf. Jn. 20:21), so he sent the apostles into the whole world, commanding them: "Go, therefore, and make disciples of all nations, baptizing them in the name of the Father and of the Son and of the Holy Spirit; teaching them to observe all that I have commanded you" (Mt. 28:19 ff.); "Go into the whole world, preach the Gospel to every creature. He who believes and is baptized shall be saved; but he who does not believe, shall be condemned" (Mk. 16:15 ff.). Hence the Church has an obligation to proclaim the faith and salvation which comes from Christ, both by reason of the express command which the order of bishops inherited from the apostles, an obligation in the discharge of which they are assisted by priests, and one which they share with the successor of St. Peter, the supreme pastor of the Church, and also by reason of the life which Christ infuses into his members: "From him the whole body, being closely joined and knit together through every joint of the system, according to the functioning in due measure of each single part, derives its increase to the building up of itself in love" (Eph. 4:16). The mission of the Church is carried out by means of that activity through which, in obedience to Christ's command and moved by the grace and love of the Holy Spirit, the Church makes itself fully present to all men and peoples in order to lead them to the faith, freedom and peace of Christ by the example of its life and teaching, by the sacraments and other means of grace. Its aim is to open up for all men a free and sure path to full participation in the mystery of Christ.

Since this mission continues and, in the course of history, unfolds the mission of Christ, who was sent to evangelize the poor, then the Church, urged on by the Spirit of Christ, must walk the road Christ himself walked, a way of poverty and obedience, of service and self-sacrifice even to death, a death from which he emerged victorious by his resurrection. So it was that the apostles walked in hope and by much trouble and suffering filled up what was lacking in the sufferings of Christ for his body, which is the Church. Often, too, the seed was the blood of Christians.

(6) **Mark 16:16** He who believes and is baptized will be saved; but he who does **1257**
not believe will be condemned.

(1) ***Lumen gentium* 16** Finally, those who have not yet received the Gospel are **1260**
related to the People of God in various ways. There is, first, that people to which the covenants and promises were made, and from which Christ was born according to the flesh (cf. Rom. 9:4–5): in view of the divine choice, they are a people most dear for the sake of the fathers, for the gifts of God are without repentance (cf. Rom. 11:29–32). But the plan of salvation also includes those who acknowledge the Creator, in the first place amongst whom are the Moslems: these profess to hold the faith of Abraham, and together with us they adore the one, merciful God, mankind's judge on the last day. Nor is God remote from those who in shadows and images seek the unknown God, since he gives to all men life and breath and all things (cf. Acts 17:25–28), and since the Savior wills all men to be saved (cf. 1 Tim. 2:4). Those who, through no fault of their own, do not know the Gospel of Christ or his Church, but who nevertheless seek God with a sincere heart, and, moved by grace, try in their actions to do his will as they know it through the dictates of their conscience—those too may achieve eternal salvation. Nor shall divine providence deny the assistance necessary for salvation to those who, without any fault of theirs, have not yet arrived at an explicit knowledge of God, and who, not without grace, strive to lead a good life. Whatever good or truth is found amongst them is considered by the Church to be a preparation for the Gospel and given by him who enlightens all men that they may at length have life. But very often, deceived by the Evil One, men have become vain in their reasonings, have exchanged the truth of God for a lie and served the world rather than the Creator (cf. Rom. 1:21 and 25). Or else, living and dying in this world without God, they are exposed to ultimate despair. Hence to procure the glory of God and the salvation of all these, the Church, mindful of the Lord's command, "preach the Gospel to every creature" (Mk. 16:16), takes zealous care to foster the missions.

1260 (2) ***Ad gentes divinitus* 7** The reason for missionary activity lies in the will of God, "who wishes all men to be saved and to come to the knowledge of the truth. For there is one God and one Mediator between God and men, himself a man, Jesus Christ, who gave himself as a ransom for all" (1 Tim. 2:4–5), "neither is there salvation in any other" (Acts 4:12). Everyone, therefore, ought to be converted to Christ, who is known through the preaching of the Church, and they ought, by baptism, to become incorporated into him, and into the Church which is his body. Christ himself explicitly asserted the necessity of faith and baptism (cf. Mk. 16:16; Jn. 3:5), and thereby affirmed at the same time the necessity of the Church, which men enter through baptism as through a door. Hence those cannot be saved, who, knowing that the Catholic Church was founded through Jesus Christ, by God, as something necessary, still refuse to enter it, or to remain in it. So, although in ways known to himself God can lead those who, through no fault of their own, are ignorant of the Gospel to that faith without which it is impossible to please him (Heb. 11:6), the Church, nevertheless, still has the obligation and also the sacred right to evangelize. And so, today as always, missionary activity retains its full force and necessity.

By means of this activity the mystical Body of Christ unceasingly gathers and directs its energies towards its own increase (Eph. 4:11–16). The members of the Church are impelled to engage in this activity because of the charity with which they love God and by which they desire to share with all men in the spiritual goods of this life and the life to come.

Finally, by this missionary activity God is fully glorified, when men fully and consciously accept the work of salvation which he accomplished in Christ. By means of it God's plan is realized, a plan to which Christ lovingly and obediently submitted for the glory of the Father who sent him in order that the whole human race might become one people of God, form one body of Christ, and be built up into one temple of the Holy Spirit; all of which, as an expression of brotherly concord, answers to a profound longing in all men. And thus, finally, the intention of the creator in creating man in his own image and likeness will be truly realized, when all who possess human nature, and have been regenerated in Christ through the Holy Spirit, gazing together on the glory of God, will be able to say "Our Father."

1261 **1 Timothy 2:4** . . . who desires all men to be saved and to come to the knowledge of the truth.

1262 (1) **Acts 2:38** And Peter said to them, "Repent, and be baptized every one of you in the name of Jesus Christ for the forgiveness of your sins; and you shall receive the gift of the Holy Spirit. . . ."

1262 (2) **John 3:5** Jesus answered, "Truly, truly, I say to you, unless one is born of water and the Spirit, he cannot enter the kingdom of God. . . ."

1263 **Council of Florence (1439): DS 1316** The effect of this sacrament is the remission of every sin, original and actual, also of every punishment which is due to the sin itself. Therefore, no satisfaction must be enjoined for past sins upon those who immediately attain to the kingdom of heaven and the vision of God.

1265 (1) **Galatians 4:5–7** . . . to redeem those who were under the law, so that we might receive adoption as sons. And because you are sons, God has sent the Spirit of his Son into our hearts, crying, "Abba! Father!" So through God you are no longer a slave but a son, and if a son then an heir.

(2) **1 Corinthians 6:15** Do you not know that your bodies are members of Christ? Shall I therefore take the members of Christ and make them members of a prostitute? Never! **1265**

(3) **1 Corinthians 12:27** Now you are the body of Christ and individually members of it. **1265**

(4) **Romans 8:17** . . . and if children, then heirs, heirs of God and fellow heirs with Christ, provided we suffer with him in order that we may also be glorified with him. **1265**

(5) **1 Corinthians 6:19** Do you not know that your body is a temple of the Holy Spirit within you, which you have from God? You are not your own. . . . **1265**

(1) **1 Corinthians 6:19:** see 1265 (5) above. **1269**

(2) **2 Corinthians 5:15** And he died for all, that those who live might live no longer for themselves but for him who for their sake died and was raised. **1269**

(3) **Ephesians 5:21** Be subject to one another out of reverence for Christ. **1269**

(4) **1 Corinthians 16:15–16** Now, brethren, you know that the household of Stephanas were the first converts in Achaia, and they have devoted themselves to the service of the saints; I urge you to be subject to such men and to every fellow worker and laborer. **1269**

(5) **1 Thessalonians 5:12–13** But we beseech you, brethren, to respect those who labor among you and are over you in the Lord and admonish you, and to esteem them very highly in love because of their work. Be at peace among yourselves. **1269**

(6) **John 13:12–15** When he had washed their feet, and taken his garments, and resumed his place, he said to them, "Do you know what I have done to you? You call me Teacher and Lord; and you are right, for so I am. If I then, your Lord and Teacher, have washed your feet, you also ought to wash one another's feet. For I have given you an example, that you also should do as I have done to you. . . ." **1269**

(7) ***Lumen gentium* 37** Like all Christians, the laity have the right to receive in abundance the help of the spiritual goods of the Church, especially that of the word of God and the sacraments from the pastors. To the latter the laity should disclose their needs and desires with that liberty and confidence which befits children of God and brothers of Christ. By reason of the knowledge, competence or pre-eminence which they have the laity are empowered—indeed sometimes obliged—to manifest their opinion on those things which pertain to the good of the Church. If the occasion should arise this should be done through the institutions established by the Church for that purpose and always with truth, courage and prudence and with reverence and charity towards those who, by reason of their office, represent the person of Christ. **1269**

Like all Christians, the laity should promptly accept in Christian obedience what is decided by the pastors who, as teachers and rulers of the Church, represent Christ. In this they will follow Christ's example who, by his obedience unto death, opened the blessed way of the liberty of the sons of God to all men. Nor should they fail to commend to God in their prayers those who have been placed over them, who indeed keep watch as having to render an account of our souls, that they may do this with joy and not with grief (cf. Heb. 13:17).

The pastors, indeed, should recognize and promote the dignity and responsibility of the laity in the Church. They should willingly use their prudent advice and confidently assign duties to them in the service of the Church, leaving them freedom and scope for acting. Indeed, they should give them the courage to undertake works on their own initiative. They should with paternal love consider attentively in Christ initial moves, suggestions and desires proposed by the laity. Moreover the pastors must respect and recognize the liberty which belongs to all in the terrestrial city.

Many benefits for the Church are to be expected from this familiar relationship between the laity and the pastors. The sense of their own responsibility is strengthened in the laity, their zeal is encouraged, they are more ready to unite their energies to the work of their pastors. The latter, helped by the experience of the laity, are in a position to judge more clearly and more appropriately in spiritual as well as in temporal matters. Strengthened by all her members, the Church can thus more effectively fulfil her mission for the life of the world.

1269 (8) **CIC Canons 208–23**

Can. 208—In virtue of their rebirth in Christ there exists among all the Christian faithful a true equality with regard to dignity and the activity whereby all cooperate in the building up of the Body of Christ in accord with each one's own condition and function.

Can. 209—§1. The Christian faithful are bound by an obligation, even in their own patterns of activity, always to maintain communion with the Church.

§2. They are to fulfill with great diligence the duties which they owe to the universal Church and to the particular church to which they belong according to the prescriptions of law.

Can. 210—All the Christian faithful must make an effort, in accord with their own condition, to live a holy life and to promote the growth of the Church and its continual sanctification.

Can. 211—All the Christian faithful have the duty and the right to work so that the divine message of salvation may increasingly reach the whole of humankind in every age and in every land.

Can. 212—§1. The Christian faithful, conscious of their own responsibility, are bound by Christian obedience to follow what the sacred pastors, as representatives of Christ, declare as teachers of the faith or determine as leaders of the Church.

§2. The Christian faithful are free to make known their needs, especially spiritual ones, and their desires to the pastors of the Church.

§3. In accord with the knowledge, competence and preeminence which they possess, they have the right and even at times a duty to manifest to the sacred pastors their opinion on matters which pertain to the good of the Church, and they have a right to make their opinion known to the other Christian faithful, with due regard for the integrity of faith and morals and reverence toward their pastors, and with consideration for the common good and the dignity of persons.

Can. 213—The Christian faithful have the right to receive assistance from the sacred pastors out of the spiritual goods of the Church, especially the word of God and the sacraments.

Can. 214—The Christian faithful have the right to worship God according to the prescriptions of their own rite approved by the legitimate pastors of the Church, and to follow their own form of spiritual life consonant with the teaching of the Church.

Can. 215—The Christian faithful are at liberty freely to found and to govern associations for charitable and religious purposes or for the promotion of the Christian vocation in the world; they are free to hold meetings to pursue these purposes in common.

Can. 216—All the Christian faithful, since they participate in the mission of the Church, have the right to promote or to sustain apostolic action by their own undertakings in accord with each one's state and condition; however, no undertaking shall assume the name Catholic unless the consent of competent ecclesiastical authority is given.

Can. 217—The Christian faithful since they are called by baptism to lead a life in conformity with the teaching of the gospel, have the right to a Christian education by which they will be properly instructed so as to develop the maturity of a human person and at the same time come to know and live the mystery of salvation.

Can. 218—Those who are engaged in the sacred disciplines enjoy a lawful freedom of inquiry and of prudently expressing their opinions on matters in which they have expertise, while observing a due respect for the magisterium of the Church.

Can. 219—All the Christian faithful have the right to be free from any kind of coercion in choosing a state in life.

Can. 220—No one is permitted to damage unlawfully the good reputation which another person enjoys nor to violate the right of another person to protect his or her own privacy.

Can. 221—§1. The Christian faithful can legitimately vindicate and defend the rights which they enjoy in the Church before a competent ecclesiastical court in accord with the norm of law.

§2. The Christian faithful also have the right, if they are summoned to judgment by competent authority, that they be judged in accord with the prescriptions of the law to be applied with equity.

§3. The Christian faithful have the right not to be punished with canonical penalties except in accord with the norm of law.

Can. 222—§1. The Christian faithful are obliged to assist with the needs of the Church so that the Church has what is necessary for divine worship, for apostolic works and works of charity and for the decent sustenance of ministers.

§2. They are also obliged to promote social justice and, mindful of the precept of the Lord, to assist the poor from their own resources.

Can. 223—§1. In exercising their rights the Christian faithful, both as individuals and when gathered in associations, must take account of the common good of the Church and of the rights of others as well as their own duties toward others.

§2. In the interest of the common good, ecclesiastical authority has competence to regulate the exercise of the rights which belong to the Christian faithful.

(9) **CCEO Canon 675, §2** Only by the actual reception of baptism is a person made capable for the other sacraments. **1269**

(1) ***Lumen gentium* 17** As he had been sent by the Father, the Son himself sent the apostles (cf. Jn. 20:21) saying, "go, therefore, and make disciples of all nations, baptizing them in the name of the Father, and of the Son, and of the Holy Spirit, teaching them to observe all that I have commanded you; and behold I am with you all days even unto the consummation of the world" (Mt. 28:18–20). The Church has received this solemn command of Christ from the apostles, and she must fulfil it to the very ends of the earth (cf. Acts 1:8). Therefore, she makes the words of the apostle her own, "Woe to me if I do not preach the Gospel" (1 Cor. 9:16), and accordingly never ceases to send heralds of the Gospel until such time as the infant Churches are fully established, and can themselves continue the work of evangelization. For the Church is driven by the Holy Spirit to do her part for the full realization of the plan of God, who has constituted Christ as the source of salvation for the whole world. By her proclamation of the Gospel, she draws her hearers to receive and profess the **1270**

faith, she prepares them for baptism, snatches them from the slavery of error, and she incorporates them into Christ so that in love for him they grow to full maturity. The effect of her work is that whatever good is found sown in the minds and hearts of men or in the rites and customs of peoples, these not only are preserved from destruction, but are purified, raised up, and perfected for the glory of God, the confusion of the devil, and the happiness of man. Each disciple of Christ has the obligation of spreading the faith to the best of his ability. But if any believer can baptize, it is for the priests to complete the building up of the body in the eucharistic sacrifice, thus fulfilling the words of the prophet, "From the rising of the sun, even to going down, my name is great among the gentiles. And in every place there is a sacrifice, and there is offered to my name a clean offering" (Mal. 1:11). Thus the Church prays and likewise labors so that into the People of God, the Body of the Lord and the Temple of the Holy Spirit, may pass the fullness of the whole world, and that in Christ, the head of all things, all honor and glory may be rendered to the Creator, the Father of the universe.

1270 (2) ***Ad gentes divinitus* 7** The reason for missionary activity lies in the will of God, "who wishes all men to be saved and to come to the knowledge of the truth. For there is one God and one Mediator between God and men, himself a man, Jesus Christ, who gave himself as a ransom for all" (1 Tim. 2:4–5), "neither is there salvation in any other" (Acts 4:12). Everyone, therefore, ought to be converted to Christ, who is known through the preaching of the Church, and they ought, by baptism, to become incorporated into him, and into the Church which is his body. Christ himself explicitly asserted the necessity of faith and baptism (cf. Mk. 16:16; Jn. 3:5), and thereby affirmed at the same time the necessity of the Church, which men enter through baptism as through a door. Hence those cannot be saved, who, knowing that the Catholic Church was founded through Jesus Christ, by God, as something necessary, still refuse to enter it, or to remain in it. So, although in ways known to himself God can lead those who, through no fault of their own, are ignorant of the Gospel to that faith without which it is impossible to please him (Heb. 11:6), the Church, nevertheless, still has the obligation and also the sacred right to evangelize. And so, today as always, missionary activity retains its full force and necessity.

By means of this activity the mystical Body of Christ unceasingly gathers and directs its energies towards its own increase (Eph. 4:11–16). The members of the Church are impelled to engage in this activity because of the charity with which they love God and by which they desire to share with all men in the spiritual goods of this life and the life to come.

Finally, by this missionary activity God is fully glorified, when men fully and consciously accept the work of salvation which he accomplished in Christ. By means of it God's plan is realized, a plan to which Christ lovingly and obediently submitted for the glory of the Father who sent him in order that the whole human race might become one people of God, form one body of Christ, and be built up into one temple of the Holy Spirit; all of which, as an expression of brotherly concord, answers to a profound longing in all men. And thus, finally, the intention of the creator in creating man in his own image and likeness will be truly realized, when all who possess human nature, and have been regenerated in Christ through the Holy Spirit, gazing together on the glory of God, will be able to say "Our Father."

1270 (3) ***Ad gentes divinitus* 23** Although the obligation of spreading the faith falls individually on every disciple of Christ, still the Lord Christ has always called from the number of his disciples those whom he has chosen that they might be with him so that he might send them to preach to the nations (cf. Mk. 3:13 ff.). So the Holy Spirit, who shares his gifts as he wills for the common good (cf. 1 Cor. 12:11), implants in the hearts of individuals a missionary vocation and at the same time raises up institutes in the Church who take on the duty of evangelization, which pertains to the whole Church, and make it as it were their own special task.

Those people who are endowed with the proper natural temperament, have the necessary qualities and outlook, and are ready to undertake missionary work, have a special vocation, whether they are natives of the place or foreigners, priests, religious or lay people. Having been sent by legitimate authority they go forth in faith and obedience to those who are far from Christ, as ministers of the Gospel, set aside for the work to which they have been called (cf. Acts 13:2) "that the offering up of the Gentiles may become acceptable, being sanctified by the Holy Spirit" (Rom. 16:16).

(1) **Romans 8:29** For those whom he foreknew he also predestined to be conformed to the image of his Son, in order that he might be the first-born among many brethren. 1272

(2) **Council of Trent (1547): DS 1609–19** If anyone shall say that in the three sacraments, namely, baptism, confirmation, and orders, there is not imprinted on the soul a sign, that is, a certain spiritual and indelible mark, on account of which they cannot be repeated: let him be anathema. 1272

If anyone shall say that all Christians have power to administer the word and all the sacraments: let him be anathema.

If anyone shall say that in ministers, when they effect and confer the sacraments, the intention at least of doing what the Church does is not required: let him be anathema.

If anyone shall say that a minister who is in mortal sin, although he observes all the essentials which pertain to the performance or conferring of the sacrament, neither performs nor confers the sacrament: let him be anathema.

If anyone shall say that the received and approved rites of the Catholic Church accustomed to be used in the solemn administration of the sacraments may be disdained or omitted by the minister without sin and at pleasure, or may be changed by any pastor of the churches to other new ones: let him be anathema.

If anyone shall say that the baptism of John had the same force as the baptism of Christ: let him be anathema.

If anyone shall say that real and natural water is not necessary for baptism, and on that account those words of our Lord Jesus Christ: "Unless a man be born again of water and the Holy Spirit" (John 3:5), are distorted into some sort of metaphor: let him be anathema.

If anyone shall say that in the Roman Church (which is the mother and the teacher of all churches) there is not the true doctrine concerning the sacrament of baptism: let him be anathema.

If anyone shall say that the baptism, which is also given by heretics in the name of the Father and of the Son and of the Holy Spirit, with the intention of doing what the Church does, is not true baptism: let him be anathema.

If anyone shall say that baptism is optional, that is, not necessary for salvation: let him be anathema.

If anyone shall say that one who is baptized cannot, even if he wishes, lose grace, however much he may sin, unless he is unwilling to believe: let him be anathema.

(1) ***Lumen gentium* 11:** see 1251 (1). 1273

1273 (2) ***Lumen gentium* 10** Christ the Lord, high priest taken from among men (cf. Heb. 5:1–5), made the new people "a kingdom of priests to God, his Father" (Apoc. 1:6; cf. 5:9–10). The baptized, by regeneration and the anointing of the Holy Spirit, are consecrated to be a spiritual house and a holy priesthood, that through all the works of Christian men they may offer spiritual sacrifices and proclaim the perfection of him who has called them out of darkness into his marvellous light (cf. 1 Pet. 2:4–10). Therefore all the disciples of Christ, persevering in prayer and praising God (cf. Acts 2:42–47), should present themselves as a sacrifice, living, holy and pleasing to God (cf. Rom. 12:1). They should everywhere on earth bear witness to Christ and give an answer to everyone who asks a reason for the hope of an eternal life which is theirs (cf. 1 Pet. 3:15).

Though they differ essentially and not only in degree, the common priesthood of the faithful and the ministerial or hierarchical priesthood are none the less ordered one to another; each in its own proper way shares in the one priesthood of Christ. The ministerial priest, by the sacred power that he has, forms and rules the priestly people; in the person of Christ he effects the eucharistic sacrifice and offers it to God in the name of all the people. The faithful indeed, by virtue of their royal priesthood, participate in the offering of the Eucharist. They exercise that priesthood, too, by the reception of the sacraments, prayer and thanksgiving, the witness of a holy life, abnegation and active charity.

1274 (1) **Ephesians 1:13–14** In him you also, who have heard the word of truth, the gospel of your salvation, and have believed in him, were sealed with the promised Holy Spirit, which is the guarantee of our inheritance until we acquire possession of it, to the praise of his glory.

1274 (2) **2 Corinthians 1:21–22** But it is God who establishes us with you in Christ, and has commissioned us; he has put his seal upon us and given us his Spirit in our hearts as a guarantee.

1280 (1) **Council of Trent (1547): DS 1609** If anyone shall say that in the three sacraments, namely, baptism, confirmation, and orders, there is not imprinted on the soul a sign, that is, a certain spiritual and indelible mark, on account of which they cannot be repeated: let him be anathema.

1280 (2) **Council of Trent (1547): DS 1624** If anyone shall say that baptism truly and rightly administered must be repeated for him who has denied the faith of Christ among infidels, when he is converted to repentance: let him be anathema.

1281 ***Lumen gentium* 16:** see 1260 (1).

1285 (1) **Rite of Confirmation, Introduction 1** Those who have been baptized continue on the path of Christian initiation through the sacrament of confirmation. In this sacrament they receive the Holy Spirit whom the Lord sent upon the apostles on Pentecost.

1285 (2) **Rite of Confirmation, Introduction 2** This giving of the Holy Spirit conforms believers more fully to Christ and strengthens them so that they may bear witness to Christ for the building up of his Body in faith and love. They are so marked with the character or seal of the Lord that the sacrament of confirmation cannot be repeated.

1286 (1) **Isaiah 11:2**

And the Spirit of the Lord shall rest upon him,
the spirit of wisdom and understanding,

the spirit of counsel and might,
the spirit of knowledge and the fear of the Lord.

(2) **Isaiah 61:1** 1286
The Spirit of the Lord God is upon me,
because the Lord has anointed me
to bring good tidings to the afflicted;
he has sent me to bind up the brokenhearted,
to proclaim liberty to the captives,
and the opening of the prison to those who are bound. . . .

(3) **Luke 4:16–22** And he came to Nazareth, where he had been brought up; and 1286
he went to the synagogue, as his custom was, on the sabbath day. And he stood up to read; and there was given to him the book of the prophet Isaiah. He opened the book and found the place where it was written,
"The Spirit of the Lord is upon me,
because he has anointed me to preach good news to the poor.
He has sent me to proclaim release to the captives
and recovering of sight to the blind,
to set at liberty those who are oppressed,
to proclaim the acceptable year of the Lord."
And he closed the book, and gave it back to the attendant, and sat down; and the eyes of all in the synagogue were fixed on him. And he began to say to them, "Today this scripture has been fulfilled in your hearing."

(4) **Matthew 3:13–17** Then Jesus came from Galilee to the Jordan to John, to be 1286
baptized by him. John would have prevented him, saying, "I need to be baptized by you, and do you come to me?" But Jesus answered him, "Let it be so now; for thus it is fitting for us to fulfil all righteousness." Then he consented. And when Jesus was baptized, he went up immediately from the water, and behold, the heavens were opened and he saw the Spirit of God descending like a dove, and alighting on him; and lo, a voice from heaven, saying, "This is my beloved Son, with whom I am well pleased."

(5) **John 1:33–34** ". . . I myself did not know him; but he who sent me to baptize 1286
with water said to me, 'He on whom you see the Spirit descend and remain, this is he who baptizes with the Holy Spirit.' And I have seen and have borne witness that this is the Son of God."

(1) **Ezekiel 36:25–27** I will sprinkle clean water upon you, and you shall be clean 1287
from all your uncleannesses, and from all your idols I will cleanse you. A new heart I will give you, and a new spirit I will put within you; and I will take out of your flesh the heart of stone and give you a heart of flesh. And I will put my spirit within you, and cause you to walk in my statutes and be careful to observe my ordinances.

(2) **Joel 3:1–2 (2:28–29 RSV)** 1287
"And it shall come to pass afterward,
that I will pour out my spirit on all flesh;
your sons and your daughters shall prophesy,
your old men shall dream dreams,
and your young men shall see visions.
Even upon the menservants and maidservants
in those days, I will pour out my spirit. . . ."

1287 (3) **Luke 12:12** ". . . for the Holy Spirit will teach you in that very hour what you ought to say."

1287 (4) **John 3:5–8** Jesus answered, "Truly, truly, I say to you, unless one is born of water and the Spirit, he cannot enter the kingdom of God. That which is born of the flesh is flesh, and that which is born of the Spirit is spirit. Do not marvel that I said to you, 'You must be born anew.' The wind blows where it wills, and you hear the sound of it, but you do not know whence it comes or whither it goes; so it is with every one who is born of the Spirit."

1287 (5) **John 7:37–39** On the last day of the feast, the great day, Jesus stood up and proclaimed, "If any one thirst, let him come to me and drink. He who believes in me, as the scripture has said, 'Out of his heart shall flow rivers of living water.'" Now this he said about the Spirit, which those who believed in him were to receive; for as yet the Spirit had not been given, because Jesus was not yet glorified.

1287 (6) **John 16:7–15** ". . . Nevertheless I tell you the truth: it is to your advantage that I go away, for if I do not go away, the Counselor will not come to you; but if I go, I will send him to you. And when he comes, he will convince the world concerning sin and righteousness and judgment: concerning sin, because they do not believe in me; concerning righteousness, because I go to the Father, and you will see me no more; concerning judgment, because the ruler of this world is judged.

"I have yet many things to say to you, but you cannot bear them now. When the Spirit of truth comes, he will guide you into all the truth; for he will not speak on his own authority, but whatever he hears he will speak, and he will declare to you the things that are to come. He will glorify me, for he will take what is mine and declare it to you. All that the Father has is mine; therefore I said that he will take what is mine and declare it to you. . . ."

1287 (7) **Acts 1:8** ". . . But you shall receive power when the Holy Spirit has come upon you; and you shall be my witnesses in Jerusalem and in all Judea and Samaria and to the end of the earth."

1287 (8) **John 20:22** And when he had said this, he breathed on them, and said to them, "Receive the Holy Spirit. . . ."

1287 (9) **Acts 2:1–4** When the day of Pentecost had come, they were all together in one place. And suddenly a sound came from heaven like the rush of a mighty wind, and it filled all the house where they were sitting. And there appeared to them tongues as of fire, distributed and resting on each one of them. And they were all filled with the Holy Spirit and began to speak in other tongues, as the Spirit gave them utterance.

1287 (10) **Acts 2:17–18**

". . . 'And in the last days it shall be, God declares,
that I will pour out my Spirit upon all flesh,
and your sons and your daughters shall prophesy,
and your young men shall see visions,
and your old men shall dream dreams;
yea, and on my menservants and my maidservants in those days
I will pour out my Spirit; and they shall prophesy. . . .'"

1287 (11) **Acts 2:38** And Peter said to them, "Repent, and be baptized every one of you in the name of Jesus Christ for the forgiveness of your sins; and you shall receive the gift of the Holy Spirit. . . ."

(1) **Acts 8:15–17** . . . who came down and prayed for them that they might receive 1288
the Holy Spirit; for it had not yet fallen on any of them, but they had only been baptized in the name of the Lord Jesus. Then they laid their hands on them and they received the Holy Spirit.

(2) **Acts 19:5–6** On hearing this, they were baptized in the name of the Lord Jesus. 1288
And when Paul had laid his hands upon them, the Holy Spirit came on them; and they spoke with tongues and prophesied.

(3) **Hebrews 6:2** . . . with instruction about ablutions, the laying on of hands, the 1288
resurrection of the dead, and eternal judgment.

(1) **CCEO Canon 695, §1** Chrismation with holy myron must be administered in 1290
conjunction with baptism, except in a case of true necessity, in which case, however, it is to be seen that it is administered as soon as possible.

(2) **CCEO Canon 696, §1** All presbyters of the Eastern Churches can validly ad- 1290
minister this sacrament either along with baptism or separately to all the Christian faithful of any Church *sui iuris* including the Latin Church.

St. Hippolytus, *Traditio apostolica* 21 And at the hour when the cock crows they 1291
shall first <*of all*> pray over the water.

When they come to the water, let the water be pure and flowing.

And they shall put off their clothes.

And they shall baptize the little children first. And if they can answer for themselves, let them answer. But if they cannot, let their parents answer or someone from their family.

And next they shall baptize the grown men; and last the women, who shall [*all*] have loosed their hair and laid aside the gold ornaments [*which they were wearing*]. Let no one go down to the water having any alien object with them.

And at the time determined for baptizing the bishop shall give thanks over the oil and put it into a vessel and it is called the Oil of Thanksgiving.

And he shall take [*also*] other oil and exorcise over it, and it is called Oil of Exorcism.

And let a deacon carry the Oil of Exorcism and stand on the left hand [*of the presbyter*] <*who will do the anointing*>. And another deacon shall take the Oil of Thanksgiving and stand on the right hand.

And when the presbyter takes hold of each one of those who are to be baptized, let him bid him renounce saying:

I renounce thee, Satan, and all thy service and all thy works.

And when he has said this let him anoint him with the Oil of Exorcism saying:

Let all evil spirits depart far from thee.

[*And also turning him to the East, let him say:*

I consent to Thee, O Father and Son and Holy Ghost, before whom all creation trembleth and is moved. Grant me to do all Thy wills (sic) without blame.]

Then after these things let him give him over to the presbyter who stands at the water [*to baptize*];

[*And a presbyter takes his right hand and he turns his face to the East. Before he descends into the water, while he still turns his face to the East, standing above the water he says after receiving the Oil of Exorcism, thus: I believe and bow me unto Thee and all Thy service, O Father, Son and Holy Ghost. And so he descends into the water.*]

And let them stand in the water naked. And let a deacon likewise go down with him into the water.

[*And let him say to him and instruct him: Dost thou believe in one God the Father Almighty and His only-begotten Son Jesus Christ our Lord and our Savior, and His Holy Spirit, Giver of life to all creatures, the Trinity of one substance, one Godhead, one Lordship, one Kingdom, one Faith, one Baptism in the Holy Catholic Apostolic Church for life eternal* [*Amen*]? *And he who is baptized shall say again thus: Verily, I believe.*]

And [*when*] he [*who is to be baptized*] goes down to the water, let him who baptizes lay hand on him saying thus:

Dost thou believe in God the Father Almighty?

And he who is being baptized shall say:

I believe.

Let him forthwith baptize him once, having his hand laid upon his head.

And after <*this*> let him say:

Dost thou believe in Christ Jesus, the Son of God,
Who was born of Holy Spirit and the Virgin Mary,
Who was crucified in the days of Pontius Pilate,
And died, [*and was buried*]
And rose the third day living from the dead
And ascended into the heavens,
And sat down at the right hand of the Father,
And will come to judge the living and the dead?

And when he says: I believe, let him baptize him the second time.

And again let him say:

Dost thou believe in <*the*> Holy Spirit in the Holy Church,
And the resurrection of the flesh?

And he who is being baptized shall say: I believe. And so let him baptize him the third time.

And afterwards when he comes up [*from the water*] he shall be anointed by the presbyter with the Oil of Thanksgiving saying:

I anoint thee with holy oil in the Name of Jesus Christ.

And so each one drying himself [*with a towel*] they shall now put on their clothes, and after this let them be together in the assembly.

1293 (1) **Deuteronomy 11:14** . . . he will give the rain for your land in its season, the early rain and the later rain, that you may gather in your grain and your wine and your oil.

1293 (2) **Psalm 23:5**

Thou preparest a table before me
in the presence of my enemies;
thou anointest my head with oil,
my cup overflows.

1293 (3) **Psalm 104:15**

. . . and wine to gladden the heart of man,
oil to make his face shine,
and bread to strengthen man's heart.

1293 (4) **Isaiah 1:6**

From the sole of the foot even to the head,
there is no soundness in it,
but bruises and sores
and bleeding wounds;

they are not pressed out, or bound up,
or softened with oil.

(5) **Luke 10:34** . . . and went to him and bound up his wounds, pouring on oil and 1293
wine; then he set him on his own beast and brought him to an inn, and took care of him.

(1) **Genesis 38:18** He said, "What pledge shall I give you?" She replied, "Your 1295
signet and your cord, and your staff that is in your hand." So he gave them to her, and went in to her, and she conceived by him.

(2) **Genesis 41:42** Then Pharaoh took his signet ring from his hand and put it on 1295
Joseph's hand, and arrayed him in garments of fine linen, and put a gold chain about his neck. . . .

(3) **Deuteronomy 32:34** 1295
"Is not this laid up in store with me,
sealed up in my treasuries? . . ."

(4) **Song of Solomon 8:6** 1295
Set me as a seal upon your heart,
as a seal upon your arm;
for love is strong as death,
jealousy is cruel as the grave.
Its flashes are flashes of fire,
a most vehement flame.

(5) **1 Kings 21:8** So she wrote letters in Ahab's name and sealed them with his seal, 1295
and she sent the letters to the elders and the nobles who dwelt with Naboth in his city.

(6) **Jeremiah 32:10** I signed the deed, sealed it, got witnesses, and weighed the 1295
money on scales.

(7) **Isaiah 29:11** And the vision of all this has become to you like the words of a 1295
book that is sealed. When men give it to one who can read, saying, "Read this," he says, "I cannot, for it is sealed."

(1) **John 6:27** ". . . Do not labor for the food which perishes, but for the food 1296
which endures to eternal life, which the Son of man will give to you; for on him has God the Father set his seal."

(2) **Ephesians 1:13** In him you also, who have heard the word of truth, the gospel 1296
of your salvation, and have believed in him, were sealed with the promised Holy Spirit. . . .

(3) **Ephesians 4:30** And do not grieve the Holy Spirit of God, in whom you were 1296
sealed for the day of redemption.

(4) **Revelation 7:2–3** Then I saw another angel ascend from the rising of the sun, 1296
with the seal of the living God, and he called with a loud voice to the four angels who had been given power to harm earth and sea, saying, "Do not harm the earth or the sea or the trees, till we have sealed the servants of our God upon their foreheads."

1296 (5) **Revelation 9:4** . . . they were told not to harm the grass of the earth or any green growth or any tree, but only those of mankind who have not the seal of God upon their foreheads. . . .

1296 (6) **Ezekiel 9:4–6** And the Lord said to him, "Go through the city, through Jerusalem, and put a mark upon the foreheads of the men who sigh and groan over all the abominations that are committed in it." And to the others he said in my hearing, "Pass through the city after him, and smite; your eye shall not spare, and you shall show no pity; slay old men outright, young men and maidens, little children and women, but touch no one upon whom is the mark. And begin at my sanctuary." So they began with the elders who were before the house.

1298 (1) ***Sacrosanctum concilium* 71** The rite of Confirmation is to be revised also so that the intimate connection of this sacrament with the whole of the Christian initiation may more clearly appear. For this reason the renewal of baptismal promises should fittingly precede the reception of this sacrament.

Confirmation may be conferred within Mass when convenient. For conferring outside Mass, a formula introducing the rite should be drawn up.

1298 (2) **CIC Canon 866** Unless a grave reason prevents it, an adult who is baptized is to be confirmed immediately after baptism and participate in the celebration of the Eucharist, also receiving Communion.

1301 **St. Hippolytus, *Traditio apostolica* 21:** see 1291.

1303 (1) ***Lumen gentium* 11** The sacred nature and organic structure of the priestly community is brought into operation through the sacraments and the exercise of virtues. Incorporated into the Church by Baptism, the faithful are appointed by their baptismal character to Christian religious worship; reborn as sons of God, they must profess before men the faith they have received from God through the Church. By the sacrament of Confirmation they are more perfectly bound to the Church and are endowed with the special strength of the Holy Spirit. Hence they are, as true witnesses of Christ, more strictly obliged to spread the faith by word and deed. Taking part in the eucharistic sacrifice, the source and summit of the Christian life, they offer the divine victim to God and themselves along with it. And so it is that, both in the offering and in Holy Communion, each in his own way, though not of course indiscriminately, has his own part to play in the liturgical action. Then, strengthened by the body of Christ in the eucharistic communion, they manifest in a concrete way that unity of the People of God which this holy sacrament aptly signifies and admirably realizes.

Those who approach the sacrament of Penance obtain pardon from God's mercy for the offense committed against him, and are, at the same time, reconciled with the Church which they have wounded by their sins and which by charity, by example and by prayer labors for their conversion. By the sacred anointing of the sick and the prayer of the priests the whole Church commends those who are ill to the suffering and glorified Lord that he may raise them up and save them (cf. Jas. 5:14–16). And indeed she exhorts them to contribute to the good of the People of God by freely uniting themselves to the passion and death of Christ (cf. Rom. 8:17; Col. 1:24; 2 Tim. 2:11–12; 1 Pet. 4:13). Those among the faithful who have received Holy Orders are appointed to nourish the Church with the word and grace of God in the name of Christ. Finally, in virtue of the sacrament of Matrimony by which they signify and share (cf. Eph. 5:32) the mystery of the unity and faithful love between Christ and the Church, Christian married couples help one another to attain holiness in their married life and in the rearing of their children. Hence by reason of their state in life and of their position they have their own gifts in the People of God (cf. 1 Cor. 7:7). From the marriage of Christians there comes the family in which new citizens of human society are born and, by the grace of the Holy Spirit in Baptism, those are made children of God so that the People of God may be perpetuated throughout the centuries. In what might be regarded as the domestic Church, the parents, by word and example, are the first heralds of the faith with regard to their children. They must foster the vocation which is proper to each child, and this with special care if it be to religion.

Strengthened by so many and such great means of salvation, all the faithful whatever their condition or state—though each in his own way—are called by the Lord to that perfection of sanctity by which the Father himself is perfect.

(2) **Council of Florence (1439): DS 1319** The effect of this sacrament, because in it the Holy Spirit is given for strength, was thus given to the Apostles on the day of Pentecost, so that the Christian might boldly confess the name of Christ. The one to be confirmed, therefore, must be anointed on the forehead, which is the seat of reverence, so that he may not be ashamed to confess the name of Christ and especially His Cross, which is indeed a "stumbling block to the Jews and unto the Gentiles foolishness" [cf. I Cor. 1:23] according to the Apostle; for which reason one is signed with the sign of the cross. **1303**

(3) ***Lumen gentium* 11:** see 1303 (1). **1303**

(4) ***Lumen gentium* 12** The holy People of God shares also in Christ's prophetic office: it spreads abroad a living witness to him, especially by a life of faith and love and by offering to God a sacrifice of praise, the fruit of lips praising his name (cf. Heb. 13:15). The whole body of the faithful who have an anointing that comes from the holy one (cf. 1 Jn. 2:20 and 27) cannot err in matters of belief. This characteristic is shown in the supernatural appreciation of the faith (*sensus fidei*) of the whole people, when, "from the bishops to the last of the faithful" they manifest a universal consent in matters of faith and morals. By this appreciation of the faith, aroused and sustained by the Spirit of truth, the People of God, guided by the sacred teaching authority (*magisterium*), and obeying it, receives not the mere word of men, but truly the word of God (cf. 1 Th. 2:13), the faith once for all delivered to the saints (cf. Jude 3). The People unfailingly adheres to this faith, penetrates it more deeply with right judgment, and applies it more fully in daily life. **1303**

It is not only through the sacraments and the ministrations of the Church that the Holy Spirit makes holy the People, leads them and enriches them with his virtues. Allotting his gifts according as he wills (cf. 1 Cor. 12:11), he also distributes special graces among the faithful of every rank. By these gifts he makes them fit and ready to undertake various tasks and offices for the renewal and building up of the Church, as it is written, "the manifestation of the Spirit is given to everyone for profit" (1 Cor. 12:7). Whether these charisms be very remarkable or more simple and widely diffused, they are to be received with thanksgiving and consolation since they are fitting and useful for the needs of the Church. Extraordinary gifts are not to be rashly desired, nor is it from them that the fruits of apostolic labors are to be presumptuously expected. Those who have charge over the Church should judge the genuineness and proper use of these gifts, through their office, not indeed to extinguish the Spirit, but to test all things and hold fast to what is good (cf. 1 Th. 5:12 and 19–21).

1304 (1) **Council of Trent (1547): DS 1609** If anyone shall say that in the three sacraments, namely, baptism, confirmation, and orders, there is not imprinted on the soul a sign, that is, a certain spiritual and indelible mark, on account of which they cannot be repeated: let him be anathema.

1304 (2) **Luke 24:48–49** ". . . You are witnesses of these things. And behold, I send the promise of my Father upon you; but stay in the city, until you are clothed with power from on high."

1306 **CIC Canon 889, §1** All baptized persons who have not been confirmed and only they are capable of receiving confirmation.

1307 (1) **CIC Canon 891** The sacrament of confirmation is to be conferred on the faithful at about the age of discretion unless the conference of bishops determines another age or there is danger of death or in the judgment of the minister a grave cause urges otherwise.

1307 (2) **CIC Canon 883, 3°** [The following have the faculty of administering confirmation by the law itself:] with regard to those in danger of death, the pastor or indeed any presbyter.

1308 **Wisdom 4:8**

For old age is not honored for length of time,
nor measured by number of years. . . .

1309 **Rite of Confirmation, Introduction 3** One of the highest responsibilities of the people of God is to prepare the baptized for confirmation. Pastors have the special responsibility to see that all the baptized reach the completion of Christian initiation and therefore that they are carefully prepared for confirmation.

Adult catechumens who are to be confirmed immediately after baptism have the help of the Christian community and, in particular, the formation that is given to them during the catechumenate. Catechists, sponsors, and members of the local Church participate in the catechumenate by means of catechesis and community celebrations of the rites of initiation. For those who were baptized in infancy and are confirmed only as adults the plan for the catechumenate is used with appropriate adaptations.

The initiation of children into the sacramental life is ordinarily the responsibility and concern of Christian parents. They are to form and gradually increase a spirit of faith in the children and, at times with the help of catechism classes, prepare them for the fruitful reception of the sacraments of confirmation and the eucharist. The role of the parents is also expressed by their active participation in the celebration of the sacraments.

1310 **Acts 1:14** All these with one accord devoted themselves to prayer, together with the women and Mary the mother of Jesus, and with his brothers.

1311 (1) **Rite of Confirmation, Introduction 5** As a rule there should be a sponsor for each of those to be confirmed. These sponsors bring the candidates to receive the sacrament, present them to the minister for the anointing, and will later help them to fulfill their baptismal promises faithfully under the influence of the Holy Spirit whom they have received.

In view of contemporary pastoral circumstances, it is desirable that the godparent at baptism, if available, also be the sponsor at confirmation. This change expresses more clearly the link between baptism and confirmation and also makes the function and responsibility of the sponsor more effective.

Nonetheless the option of choosing a special sponsor for confirmation is not excluded. Even the parents themselves may present their children for confirmation. It is for the local Ordinary to determine diocesan practice in the light of local conditions and circumstances.

(2) **Rite of Confirmation, Introduction 6** Pastors will see that the sponsors, chosen by the candidates or their families, are spiritually fit to take on this responsibility and have these qualities: 1311

a. sufficient maturity to fulfill their function;
b. membership in the Catholic Church and their own reception of Christian initiation through baptism, confirmation, and eucharist;
c. freedom from any impediment of law to their fulfilling the office of sponsor.

(3) **CIC Canon 893** §1. To perform the role of sponsor, it is necessary that a person fulfill the conditions mentioned in can. 874. 1311

§2. It is desirable that the one who undertook the role of sponsor at baptism be sponsor for confirmation.

(1) ***Lumen gentium* 26** The bishop, invested with the fullness of the sacrament of Orders, is "the steward of the grace of the supreme priesthood," above all in the Eucharist, which he himself offers, or ensures that it is offered, from which the Church ever derives its life and on which it thrives. This Church of Christ is really present in all legitimately organized local groups of the faithful, which, in so far as they are united to their pastors, are also quite appropriately called Churches in the New Testament. For these are in fact, in their own localities, the new people called by God, in the power of the Holy Spirit and as the result of full conviction (cf. 1 Thess. 1:5). In them the faithful are gathered together through the preaching of the Gospel of Christ, and the mystery of the Lord's Supper is celebrated "so that, by means of the flesh and blood of the Lord the whole brotherhood of the Body may be welded together." In each altar community, under the sacred ministry of the bishop, a manifest symbol is to be seen of that charity and "unity of the mystical body, without which there can be no salvation." In these communities, though they may often be small and poor, or existing in the diaspora, Christ is present through whose power and influence the One, Holy, Catholic and Apostolic Church is constituted. For "the sharing in the body and blood of Christ has no other effect than to accomplish our transformation into that which we receive." 1312

Moreover, every legitimate celebration of the Eucharist is regulated by the bishop, to whom is confided the duty of presenting to the divine majesty the cult of the Christian religion and of ordering it in accordance with the Lord's injunctions and the Church's regulations, as further defined for the diocese by his particular decision.

Thus the bishops, by praying and toiling for the people, apportion in many different forms and without stint that which flows from the abundance of Christ's holiness. By the ministry of the word they impart to those who believe the strength of God unto salvation (cf. Rom. 1:16), and through the sacraments, the frequent and fruitful distribution of which they regulate by their authority, they sanctify the faithful. They control the conferring of Baptism, through which a sharing in the priesthood of Christ is granted. They are the original ministers of Confirmation; it is they who confer sacred Orders and regulate the discipline of Penance, and who diligently exhort and instruct their flocks to take the part that is theirs, in a spirit of faith and reverence, in the liturgy and above all in the holy sacrifice of the Mass. Finally, by the example of their manner of life they should exercise a powerful influence for good on those over whom they are placed, by abstaining from all wrongdoing in their conduct, and, as far as they are able, with the help of the Lord, changing it for the better, so that together with the flock entrusted to them, they may attain to eternal life.

1312 (2) **CIC Canon 883, 2°** [The following have the faculty of administering confirmation by the law itself:] . . . with regard to the person in question, the presbyter who by reason of office or mandate of the diocesan bishop baptizes one who is no longer an infant or one already baptized whom he admits into the full communion of the Catholic Church. . . .

1313 (1) **CIC Canon 882** The ordinary minister of confirmation is the bishop; a presbyter who has this faculty by virtue of either the common law or a special concession of competent authority also confers this sacrament validly.

1313 (2) **CIC Canon 884, §2** For a grave cause, a bishop and likewise a presbyter who has the faculty to confirm by virtue of law or special concession of competent authority may in individual cases associate presbyters with themselves so that they may administer the sacrament.

1314 **CIC Canon 883, 3°** [The following have the faculty of administering confirmation by the law itself:] . . . with regard to those in danger of death, the pastor or indeed any presbyter.

1326 **1 Corinthians 15:28** When all things are subjected to him, then the Son himself will also be subjected to him who put all things under him, that God may be everything to every one.

1328 (1) **Luke 22:19** And he took bread, and when he had given thanks he broke it and gave it to them, saying, "This is my body which is given for you. Do this in remembrance of me."

1328 (2) **1 Corinthians 11:24** . . . and when he had given thanks, he broke it, and said, "This is my body which is for you. Do this in remembrance of me."

1328 (3) **Matthew 26:26** Now as they were eating, Jesus took bread, and blessed, and broke it, and gave it to the disciples and said, "Take, eat; this is my body."

1328 (4) **Mark 14:22** And as they were eating, he took bread, and blessed, and broke it, and gave it to them, and said, "Take; this is my body."

1329 (1) **1 Corinthians 11:20** When you meet together, it is not the Lord's supper that you eat.

1329 (2) **Revelation 19:9** And the angel said to me, "Write this: Blessed are those who are invited to the marriage supper of the Lamb." And he said to me, "These are true words of God."

1329 (3) **Matthew 14:19** Then he ordered the crowds to sit down on the grass; and taking the five loaves and the two fish he looked up to heaven, and blessed, and broke and gave the loaves to the disciples, and the disciples gave them to the crowds.

(4) **Matthew 15:36** . . . he took the seven loaves and the fish, and having given 1329
thanks he broke them and gave them to the disciples, and the disciples gave them to the crowds.

(5) **Mark 8:6** And he commanded the crowd to sit down on the ground; and he 1329
took the seven loaves, and having given thanks he broke them and gave them to his disciples to set before the people; and they set them before the crowd.

(6) **Mark 8:19** ". . . When I broke the five loaves for the five thousand, how many 1329
baskets full of broken pieces did you take up?" They said to him, "Twelve."

(7) **Matthew 26:26** Now as they were eating, Jesus took bread, and blessed, and 1329
broke it, and gave it to the disciples and said, "Take, eat; this is my body."

(8) **1 Corinthians 11:24** . . . and when he had given thanks, he broke it, and said, 1329
"This is my body which is for you. Do this in remembrance of me."

(9) **Luke 24:13–35** That very day two of them were going to a village named Em- 1329
maus, about seven miles from Jerusalem, and talking with each other about all these things that had happened. While they were talking and discussing together, Jesus himself drew near and went with them. But their eyes were kept from recognizing him. And he said to them, "What is this conversation which you are holding with each other as you walk?" And they stood still, looking sad. Then one of them, named Cleopas, answered him, "Are you the only visitor to Jerusalem who does not know the things that have happened there in these days?" And he said to them, "What things?" And they said to him, "Concerning Jesus of Nazareth, who was a prophet mighty in deed and word before God and all the people, and how our chief priests and rulers delivered him up to be condemned to death, and crucified him. But we had hoped that he was the one to redeem Israel. Yes, and besides all this, it is now the third day since this happened. Moreover, some women of our company amazed us. They were at the tomb early in the morning and did not find his body; and they came back saying that they had even seen a vision of angels, who said that he was alive. Some of those who were with us went to the tomb, and found it just as the women had said; but him they did not see." And he said to them, "O foolish men, and slow of heart to believe all that the prophets have spoken! Was it not necessary that the Christ should suffer these things and enter into his glory?" And beginning with Moses and all the prophets, he interpreted to them in all the scriptures the things concerning himself.

So they drew near to the village to which they were going. He appeared to be going further, but they constrained him, saying, "Stay with us, for it is toward evening and the day is now far spent." So he went in to stay with them. When he was at table with them, he took the bread and blessed, and broke it, and gave it to them. And their eyes were opened and they recognized him; and he vanished out of their sight. They said to each other, "Did not our hearts burn within us while he talked to us on the road, while he opened to us the scriptures?" And they rose that same hour and returned to Jerusalem; and they found the eleven gathered together and those who were with them, who said, "The Lord has risen indeed, and has appeared to Simon!" Then they told what had happened on the road, and how he was known to them in the breaking of the bread.

(10) **Acts 2:42** And they devoted themselves to the apostles' teaching and fellow- 1329
ship, to the breaking of bread and the prayers.

1329 (11) **Acts 2:46** And day by day, attending the temple together and breaking bread in their homes, they partook of food with glad and generous hearts. . . .

1329 (12) **Acts 20:7** On the first day of the week, when we were gathered together to break bread, Paul talked with them, intending to depart on the morrow; and he prolonged his speech until midnight.

1329 (13) **Acts 20:11** And when Paul had gone up and had broken bread and eaten, he conversed with them a long while, until daybreak, and so departed.

1329 (14) **1 Corinthians 10:16–17** The cup of blessing which we bless, is it not a participation in the blood of Christ? The bread which we break, is it not a participation in the body of Christ? Because there is one bread, we who are many are one body, for we all partake of the one bread.

1329 (15) **1 Corinthians 11:17–34** But in the following instructions I do not commend you, because when you come together it is not for the better but for the worse. For, in the first place, when you assemble as a church, I hear that there are divisions among you; and I partly believe it, for there must be factions among you in order that those who are genuine among you may be recognized. When you meet together, it is not the Lord's supper that you eat. For in eating, each one goes ahead with his own meal, and one is hungry and another is drunk. What! Do you not have houses to eat and drink in? Or do you despise the church of God and humiliate those who have nothing? What shall I say to you? Shall I commend you in this? No, I will not.

For I received from the Lord what I also delivered to you, that the Lord Jesus on the night when he was betrayed took bread, and when he had given thanks, he broke it, and said. "This is my body which is for you. Do this in remembrance of me." In the same way also the cup, after supper, saying, "This cup is the new covenant in my blood. Do this, as often as you drink it, in remembrance of me. For as often as you eat this bread and drink the cup, you proclaim the Lord's death until he comes.

Whoever, therefore, eats the bread or drinks the cup of the Lord in an unworthy manner will be guilty of profaning the body and blood of the Lord. Let a man examine himself, and so eat of the bread and drink of the cup. For any one who eats and drinks without discerning the body eats and drinks judgment upon himself. That is why many of you are weak and ill, and some have died. But if we judged ourselves truly, we should not be judged. But when we are judged by the Lord, we are chastened so that we may not be condemned along with the world.

So then, my brethren, when you come together to eat, wait for one another—if any one is hungry, let him eat at home—lest you come together to be condemned. About the other things I will give directions when I come.

1330 (1) **1 Peter 2:5** . . . and like living stones be yourselves built into a spiritual house, to be a holy priesthood, to offer spiritual sacrifices acceptable to God through Jesus Christ.

1330 (2) **Psalm 116:13**

I will lift up the cup of salvation
  and call on the name of the Lord. . . .

1330 (3) **Psalm 116:17**

I will offer to thee the sacrifice of thanksgiving
  and call on the name of the Lord.

(4) **Malachi 1:11** For from the rising of the sun to its setting my name is great 1330
among the nations, and in every place incense is offered to my name, and a pure
offering; for my name is great among the nations, says the Lord of hosts.

1 Corinthians 10:16–17 The cup of blessing which we bless, is it not a participation 1331
in the blood of Christ? The bread which we break, is it not a participation in the
body of Christ? Because there is one bread, we who are many are one body, for we
all partake of the one bread.

(1) **Psalm 104:13–15** 1333

From thy lofty abode thou waterest the mountains;
    the earth is satisfied with the fruit of thy work.
Thou dost cause the grass to grow for the cattle,
    and plants for man to cultivate,
that he may bring forth food from the earth,
    and wine to gladden the heart of man,
oil to make his face shine,
    and bread to strengthen man's heart.

(2) ***Roman Missal*, Eucharistic Prayer I, 95** 1333

Look with favor on these offerings
and accept them as once you accepted the gifts of your servant Abel,
the sacrifice of Abraham, our father in faith,
and the bread and wine offered by your priest Melchisedech.

Deuteronomy 8:3 And he humbled you and let you hunger and fed you with manna, 1334
which you did not know, nor did your fathers know; that he might make you know
that man does not live by bread alone, but that man lives by everything that proceeds
out of the mouth of the Lord.

(1) **Matthew 14:13–21** Now when Jesus heard this, he withdrew from there in a 1335
boat to a lonely place apart. But when the crowds heard it, they followed him on foot
from the towns. As he went ashore he saw a great throng; and he had compassion on
them, and healed their sick. When it was evening, the disciples came to him and said,
"This is a lonely place, and the day is now over; send the crowds away to go into the
villages and buy food for themselves." Jesus said, "They need not go away; you give
them something to eat." They said to him, "We have only five loaves here and two
fish." And he said, "Bring them here to me." Then he ordered the crowds to sit down
on the grass; and taking the five loaves and the two fish he looked up to heaven, and
blessed, and broke and gave the loaves to the disciples, and the disciples gave them
to the crowds. And they all ate and were satisfied. And they took up twelve baskets
full of the broken pieces left over. And those who ate were about five thousand men,
besides women and children.

(2) **Matthew 15:32–39** Then Jesus called his disciples to him and said, "I have 1335
compassion on the crowd, because they have been with me now three days, and have
nothing to eat; and I am unwilling to send them away hungry, lest they faint on the
way." And the disciples said to him, "Where are we to get bread enough in the desert
to feed so great a crowd?" And Jesus said to them, "How many loaves have you?"
They said, "Seven, and a few small fish." And commanding the crowd to sit down on
the ground, he took the seven loaves and the fish, and having given thanks he broke
them and gave them to the disciples, and the disciples gave them to the crowds. And

they all ate and were satisfied; and they took up seven baskets full of the broken pieces left over. Those who ate were four thousand men, besides women and children. And sending away the crowds, he got into the boat and went to the region of Magadan.

1335 (3) **John 2:11** This, the first of his signs, Jesus did at Cana in Galilee, and manifested his glory; and his disciples believed in him.

1335 (4) **Mark 14:25** ". . . Truly, I say to you, I shall not drink again of the fruit of the vine until that day when I drink it new in the kingdom of God."

1337 (1) **John 13:1–17** Now before the feast of the Passover, when Jesus knew that his hour had come to depart out of this world to the Father, having loved his own who were in the world, he loved them to the end. And during supper, when the devil had already put it into the heart of Judas Iscariot, Simon's son, to betray him, Jesus, knowing that the Father had given all things into his hands, and that he had come from God and was going to God, rose from supper, laid aside his garments, and girded himself with a towel. Then he poured water into a basin, and began to wash the disciples' feet, and to wipe them with the towel with which he was girded. He came to Simon Peter; and Peter said to him, "Lord, do you wash my feet?" Jesus answered him, "What I am doing you do not know now, but afterward you will understand." Peter said to him, "You shall never wash my feet." Jesus answered him, "If I do not wash you, you have no part in me." Simon Peter said to him, "Lord, not my feet only but also my hands and my head!" Jesus said to him, "He who has bathed does not need to wash, except for his feet, but he is clean all over; and you are clean, but not every one of you." For he knew who was to betray him; that was why he said, "You are not all clean."

When he had washed their feet, and taken his garments, and resumed his place, he said to them, "Do you know what I have done to you? You call me Teacher and Lord; and you are right, for so I am. If I then, your Lord and Teacher, have washed your feet, you also ought to wash one another's feet. For I have given you an example, that you also should do as I have done to you. Truly, truly, I say to you, a servant is not greater than his master; nor is he who is sent greater than he who sent him. If you know these things, blessed are you if you do them. . . ."

1337 (2) **John 13:34–35** ". . . A new commandment I give to you, that you love one another; even as I have loved you, that you also love one another. By this all men will know that you are my disciples, if you have love for one another."

1338 **John 6** After this Jesus went to the other side of the Sea of Galilee, which is the Sea of Tiberias. And a multitude followed him, because they saw the signs which he did on those who were diseased. Jesus went up on the mountain, and there sat down with his disciples. Now the Passover, the feast of the Jews, was at hand. Lifting up his eyes, then, and seeing that a multitude was coming to him, Jesus said to Philip, "How are we to buy bread, so that these people may eat?" This he said to test him, for he himself knew what he would do. Philip answered him, "Two hundred denarii would not buy enough bread for each of them to get a little." One of his disciples, Andrew, Simon Peter's brother, said to him, "There is a lad here who has five barley loaves and two fish; but what are they among so many?" Jesus said, "Make the people sit down." Now there was much grass in the place; so the men sat down, in number about five thousand. Jesus then took the loaves, and when he had given thanks, he distributed them to those who were seated; so also the fish, as much as they wanted. And when they had eaten their fill, he told his disciples, "Gather up the fragments left over, that nothing may be lost." So they gathered them up and filled twelve baskets with fragments from the five barley loaves, left by those who had eaten. When the people saw the sign which he had done, they said, "This is indeed the prophet who is to come into the world!"

Perceiving then that they were about to come and take him by force to make him king, Jesus withdrew again to the mountain by himself.

When evening came, his disciples went down to the sea, got into a boat, and started across the sea to Capernaum. It was now dark, and Jesus had not yet come to them. The sea rose because a strong wind was blowing. When they had rowed about three or four miles, they saw Jesus walking on the sea and drawing near to the boat. They were frightened, but he said to them, "It is I; do not be afraid." Then they were glad to take him into the boat, and immediately the boat was at the land to which they were going.

On the next day the people who remained on the other side of the sea saw that there had been only one boat there, and that Jesus had not entered the boat with his disciples, but that his disciples had gone away alone. However, boats from Tiberias came near the place where they ate the bread after the Lord had given thanks. So when the people saw that Jesus was not there, nor his disciples, they themselves got into the boats and went to Capernaum, seeking Jesus.

When they found him on the other side of the sea, they said to him, "Rabbi, when did you come here?" Jesus answered them, "Truly, truly, I say to you, you seek me, not because you saw signs, but because you ate your fill of the loaves. Do not labor for the food which perishes, but for the food which endures to eternal life, which the Son of man will give to you; for on him has God the Father set his seal." Then they said to him, "What must we do, to be doing the works of God?" Jesus answered them, "This is the work of God, that you believe in him whom he has sent." So they said to him, "Then what sign do you do, that we may see, and believe you? What work do you perform? Our fathers ate the manna in the wilderness; as it is written, 'He gave them bread from heaven to eat.'" Jesus then said to them, "Truly, truly, I say to you, it was not Moses who gave you the bread from heaven; my Father gives you the true bread from heaven. For the bread of God is that which comes down from heaven, and gives life to the world." They said to him, "Lord, give us this bread always."

Jesus said to them, "I am the bread of life; he who comes to me shall not hunger, and he who believes in me shall never thirst. But I said to you that you have seen me and yet do not believe. All that the Father gives me will come to me; and him who comes to me I will not cast out. For I have come down from heaven, not to do my own will, but the will of him who sent me; and this is the will of him who sent me, that I should lose nothing of all that he has given me, but raise it up at the last day. For this is the will of my Father, that every one who sees the Son and believes in him should have eternal life; and I will raise him up at the last day."

The Jews then murmured at him, because he said, "I am the bread which came down from heaven." They said, "Is not this Jesus, the son of Joseph, whose father and mother we know? How does he now say, 'I have come down from heaven'?" Jesus answered them, "Do not murmur among yourselves. No one can come to me unless the Father who sent me draws him; and I will raise him up at the last day. It is written in the prophets, 'And they shall all be taught by God.' Every one who has heard and learned from the Father comes to me. Not that any one has seen the Father except him who is from God; he has seen the Father. Truly, truly, I say to you, he who believes has eternal life. I am the bread of life. Your fathers ate the manna in the wilderness, and they died. This is the bread which comes down from heaven, that a man may eat of it and not die. I am the living bread which came down from heaven; if any one eats of this bread, he will live for ever; and the bread which I shall give for the life of the world is my flesh."

The Jews then disputed among themselves, saying, "How can this man give us his flesh to eat?" So Jesus said to them, "Truly, truly, I say to you, unless you eat the flesh of the Son of man and drink his blood, you have no life in you; he who eats my flesh and drinks my blood has eternal life, and I will raise him up at the last day. For my flesh is food indeed, and my blood is drink indeed. He who eats my flesh and drinks my blood abides in me, and I in him. As the living Father sent me, and I live because of the Father, so he who eats me will live because of me. This is the bread which came down from heaven, not such as the fathers ate and died; he who eats this bread will live for ever." This he said in the synagogue, as he taught at Capernaum.

Many of his disciples, when they heard it, said, "This is a hard saying; who can listen to it?" But Jesus, knowing in himself that his disciples murmured at it, said to them, "Do you take offense at this? Then what if you were to see the Son of man ascending where he was before? It is the spirit that gives life, the flesh is of no avail; the words that I have spoken to you are spirit and life. But there are some of you that do not believe." For Jesus knew from the first who those were that did not believe, and who it was that would betray him. And he said, "This is why I told you that no one can come to me unless it is granted him by the Father."

After this many of his disciples drew back and no longer went about with him. Jesus said to the twelve, "Do you also wish to go away?" Simon Peter answered him, "Lord, to whom shall we go? You have the words of eternal life; and we have believed, and have come to know, that you are the Holy One of God." Jesus answered them, "Did I not choose you, the twelve, and one of you is a devil?" He spoke of Judas the son of Simon Iscariot, for he, one of the twelve, was to betray him.

1339 (1) **Matthew 26:17–29** Now on the first day of Unleavened Bread the disciples came to Jesus, saying, "Where will you have us prepare for you to eat the passover?" He said, "Go into the city to a certain one, and say to him, 'The Teacher says, My time is at hand; I will keep the passover at your house with my disciples.'" And the disciples did as Jesus had directed them, and they prepared the passover.

When it was evening, he sat at table with the twelve disciples; and as they were eating, he said, "Truly, I say to you, one of you will betray me." And they were very sorrowful, and began to say to him one after another, "Is it I, Lord?" He answered, "He who has dipped his hand in the dish with me, will betray me. The Son of man goes as it is written of him, but woe to that man by whom the Son of man is betrayed! It would have been better for that man if he had not been born." Judas, who betrayed him, said, "Is it I, Master?" He said to him, "You have said so."

Now as they were eating, Jesus took bread, and blessed, and broke it, and gave it to the disciples and said, "Take, eat; this is my body." And he took a cup, and when he had given thanks he gave it to them, saying, "Drink of it, all of you; for this is my blood of the covenant, which is poured out for many for the forgiveness of sins. I tell you I shall not drink again of this fruit of the vine until that day when I drink it new with you in my Father's kingdom."

1339 (2) **Mark 14:12–25** And on the first day of Unleavened Bread, when they sacrificed the passover lamb, his disciples said to him, "Where will you have us go and prepare for you to eat the passover?" And he sent two of his disciples, and said to them, "Go into the city, and a man carrying a jar of water will meet you; follow him, and wherever he enters, say to the householder, 'The Teacher says, Where is my guest room, where I am to eat the passover with my disciples?' And he will show you a large upper room furnished and ready; there prepare for us." And the disciples set out and went to the city, and found it as he had told them; and they prepared the passover.

And when it was evening he came with the twelve. And as they were at table eating, Jesus said, "Truly, I say to you, one of you will betray me, one who is eating with me." They began to be sorrowful, and to say to him one after another, "Is it I?" He said to them, "It is one of the twelve, one who is dipping bread into the dish with me. For the Son of man goes as it is written of him, but woe to that man by whom the Son of man is betrayed! It would have been better for that man if he had not been born."

And as they were eating, he took bread, and blessed, and broke it, and gave it to them, and said, "Take; this is my body." And he took a cup and when he had given thanks he gave it to them, and they all drank of it. And he said to them, "This is my blood of the covenant, which is poured out for many. Truly, I say to you, I shall not drink again of the fruit of the vine until that day when I drink it new in the kingdom of God."

(3) **1 Corinthians 11:23–26** For I received from the Lord what I also delivered to 1339
you, that the Lord Jesus on the night when he was betrayed took bread, and when he had given thanks, he broke it, and said, "This is my body which is for you. Do this in remembrance of me." In the same way also the cup, after supper, saying, "This cup is the new covenant in my blood. Do this, as often as you drink it, in remembrance of me." For as often as you eat this bread and drink the cup, you proclaim the Lord's death until he comes.

1 Corinthians 11:26 For as often as you eat this bread and drink the cup, you 1341
proclaim the Lord's death until he comes.

1 Corinthians 11:26: see 1341 above. 1344

***Dei Verbum* 21** The Church has always venerated the divine Scriptures as she ven- 1346
erated the Body of the Lord, in so far as she never ceases, particularly in the sacred liturgy, to partake of the bread of life and to offer it to the faithful from the one table of the Word of God and the Body of Christ. She has always regarded, and continues to regard the Scriptures, taken together with sacred Tradition, as the supreme rule of her faith. For, since they are inspired by God and committed to writing once and for all time, they present God's own Word in an unalterable form, and they make the voice of the Holy Spirit sound again and again in the words of the prophets and apostles. It follows that all the preaching of the Church, as indeed the entire Christian religion, should be nourished and ruled by sacred Scripture. In the sacred books the Father who is in heaven comes lovingly to meet his children, and talks with them. And such is the force and power of the Word of God that it can serve the Church as her support and vigor, and the children of the Church as strength for their faith, food for the soul, and a pure and lasting fount of spiritual life. Scripture verifies in the most perfect way the words: "The Word of God is living and active" (Heb. 4:12), and "is able to build you up and to give you the inheritance among all those who are sanctified" (Acts 20:32; cf. 1 Th. 2:13).

Luke 24:13–35 That very day two of them were going to a village named Emmaus, 1347
about seven miles from Jerusalem, and talking with each other about all these things that had happened. While they were talking and discussing together, Jesus himself drew near and went with them. But their eyes were kept from recognizing him. And he said to them, "What is this conversation which you are holding with each other

as you walk?" And they stood still, looking sad. Then one of them, named Cleopas, answered him, "Are you the only visitor to Jerusalem who does not know the things that have happened there in these days?" And he said to them, "What things?" And they said to him, "Concerning Jesus of Nazareth, who was a prophet mighty in deed and word before God and all the people, and how our chief priests and rulers delivered him up to be condemned to death, and crucified him. But we had hoped that he was the one to redeem Israel. Yes, and besides all this, it is now the third day since this happened. Moreover, some women of our company amazed us. They were at the tomb early in the morning and did not find his body; and they came back saying that they had even seen a vision of angels, who said that he was alive. Some of those who were with us went to the tomb, and found it just as the women had said; but him they did not see." And he said to them, "O foolish men, and slow of heart to believe all that the prophets have spoken! Was it not necessary that the Christ should suffer these things and enter into his glory?" And beginning with Moses and all the prophets, he interpreted to them in all the scriptures the things concerning himself.

So they drew near to the village to which they were going. He appeared to be going further, but they constrained him, saying, "Stay with us, for it is toward evening and the day is now far spent." So he went in to stay with them. When he was at table with them, he took the bread and blessed, and broke it, and gave it to them. And their eyes were opened and they recognized him; and he vanished out of their sight. They said to each other, "Did not our hearts burn within us while he talked to us on the road, while he opened to us the scriptures?" And they rose that same hour and returned to Jerusalem; and they found the eleven gathered together and those who were with them, who said, "The Lord has risen indeed, and has appeared to Simon!" Then they told what had happened on the road, and how he was known to them in the breaking of the bread.

1349 **1 Thessalonians 2:13** And we also thank God constantly for this, that when you received the word of God which you heard from us, you accepted it not as the word of men but as what it really is, the word of God, which is at work in you believers.

1350 **Malachi 1:11** For from the rising of the sun to its setting my name is great among the nations, and in every place incense is offered to my name, and a pure offering; for my name is great among the nations, says the Lord of hosts.

1351 (1) **1 Corinthians 16:1** Now concerning the contribution for the saints: as I directed the churches of Galatia, so you also are to do.

1351 (2) **2 Corinthians 8:9** For you know the grace of our Lord Jesus Christ, that though he was rich, yet for your sake he became poor, so that by his poverty you might become rich.

1353 ***Roman Missal*, Roman Canon 90**

Bless and approve our offering;
make it acceptable to you,
an offering in spirit and in truth.
Let it become for us
the body and blood of Jesus Christ,
your only Son, our Lord.
[Through Christ our Lord. Amen.]

1363 **Exodus 13:3** And Moses said to the people, "Remember this day, in which you came out from Egypt, out of the house of bondage, for by strength of hand the Lord brought you out from this place; no leavened bread shall be eaten. . . ."

Hebrews 7:25–27 Consequently he is able for all time to save those who draw near to God through him, since he always lives to make intercession for them. 1364

For it was fitting that we should have such a high priest, holy, blameless, unstained, separated from sinners, exalted above the heavens. He has no need, like those high priests, to offer sacrifices daily, first for his own sins and then for those of the people; he did this once for all when he offered up himself.

Romans 12:5 . . . so we, though many, are one body in Christ, and individually 1372
members one of another.

(1) ***Lumen gentium* 48** The Church, to which we are all called in Christ Jesus, 1373
and in which by the grace of God we acquire holiness, will receive its perfection only in the glory of heaven, when will come the time of the renewal of all things (Acts 3:21). At that time, together with the human race, the universe itself, which is so closely related to man and which attains its destiny through him, will be perfectly reestablished in Christ (cf. Eph. 1:10; Col. 1:20; 2 Pet. 3:10–13).

Christ lifted up from the earth, has drawn all men to himself (cf. Jn. 12:32). Rising from the dead (cf. Rom. 6:9) he sent his life-giving Spirit upon his disciples and through him set up his Body which is the Church as the universal sacrament of salvation. Sitting at the right hand of the Father he is continually active in the world in order to lead men to the Church and, through it, join them more closely to himself; and, by nourishing them with his own Body and Blood, make them partakers of his glorious life. The promised and hoped for restoration, therefore, has already begun in Christ. It is carried forward in the sending of the Holy Spirit and through him continues in the Church in which, through our faith, we learn the meaning of our earthly life, while we bring to term, with hope of future good, the task allotted to us in the world by the Father, and so work out our salvation (cf. Phil. 2:12).

Already the final age of the world is with us (cf. 1 Cor. 10:11) and the renewal of the world is irrevocably under way; it is even now anticipated in a certain real way, for the Church on earth is endowed already with a sanctity that is real though imperfect. However, until there be realized new heavens and a new earth in which justice dwells (cf. 2 Pet. 3:13) the pilgrim Church, in its sacraments and institutions, which belong to this present age, carries the mark of this world which will pass, and she herself takes her place among the creatures which groan and travail yet and await the revelation of the sons of God (cf. Rom. 8:19–22).

So it is, united with Christ in the Church and marked with the Holy Spirit "who is the guarantee of our inheritance" (Eph. 1:14) that we are truly called and indeed are children of God (cf. 1 Jn. 3:1) though we have not yet appeared with Christ in glory (cf. Col. 3:4) in which we will be like to God, for we will see him as he is (cf. 1 Jn. 3:2). "While we are at home in the body we are away from the Lord" (2 Cor. 5:6) and having the first fruits of the Spirit we groan inwardly (cf. Rom. 8:23) and we desire to be with Christ (cf. Phil. 1:23). That same charity urges us to live more for him who died for us and who rose again (cf. 2 Cor. 5:15). We make it our aim, then, to please the Lord in all things (cf. 2 Cor. 5:9) and we put on the armor of God that we may be able to stand against the wiles of the devil and resist in the evil day (cf. Eph. 6:11–13). Since we know neither the day nor the hour, we should follow the advice of the Lord and watch constantly so that, when the single course of our earthly life is completed (cf. Heb. 9:27), we may merit to enter with him into the marriage feast and be numbered among the blessed (cf. Mt. 25:31–46) and not, like the wicked and slothful servants (cf. Mt. 25:26), be ordered to depart into the eternal fire (cf. Mt. 25:41), into the outer darkness where "men will weep and gnash their teeth" (Mt. 22:13 and 25:30). Before we reign with Christ in glory we must all appear "before the judgment seat of Christ, so that each one may receive good or evil, according to what he has done in the body" (2 Cor. 5:10), and at the end of the world "they will come forth, those who have done good, to the resurrection of life, and those who have done evil, to the resurrection of judgment" (Jn. 5:29; cf. Mt. 25:46). We reckon then that "the sufferings of this present time are not worth comparing with the glory that is to be revealed to us" (Rom. 8:18; cf. 2 Tim. 2:11–12), and strong in faith we look for "the blessed hope, the appearing of the glory of our great God and Savior Jesus Christ" (Tit. 2:13) "who will change our lowly body to be like his glorious body" (Phil. 3:21) and who will come "to be glorified in his saints, and to be marvelled at in all who have believed" (2 Th. 1:10).

1373 (2) **Matthew 25:31–46** "When the Son of man comes in his glory, and all the angels with him, then he will sit on his glorious throne. Before him will be gathered all the nations, and he will separate them one from another as a shepherd separates the sheep from the goats, and he will place the sheep at his right hand, but the goats at the left. Then the King will say to those at his right hand, 'Come, O blessed of my Father, inherit the kingdom prepared for you from the foundation of the world; for I was hungry and you gave me food, I was thirsty and you gave me drink, I was a stranger and you welcomed me, I was naked and you clothed me, I was sick and you visited me, I was in prison and you came to me.' Then the righteous will answer him, 'Lord, when did we see thee hungry and feed thee, or thirsty and give thee drink? And when did we see thee a stranger and welcome thee, or naked and clothe thee? And when did we see thee sick or in prison and visit thee?' And the King will answer them, 'Truly, I say to you, as you did it to one of the least of these my brethren, you did it to me.' Then he will say to those at his left hand, 'Depart from me, you cursed, into the eternal fire prepared for the devil and his angels; for I was hungry and you gave me no food, I was thirsty and you gave me no drink, I was a stranger and you did not welcome me, naked and you did not clothe me, sick and in prison and you did not visit me.' Then they also will answer, 'Lord, when did we see thee hungry or thirsty or a stranger or naked or sick or in prison, and did not minister to thee?' Then he will answer them, 'Truly, I say to you, as you did it not to one of the least of these, you did it not to me.' And they will go away into eternal punishment, but the righteous into eternal life."

1377 **Council of Trent (1551): DS 1641** Therefore, it is very true that as much is contained under either species as under both. For Christ whole and entire exists under the species of bread and under any part whatsoever of that species, likewise the whole (Christ) is present under the species of wine and under its parts [can. 3].

1380 **Galatians 2:20** I have been crucified with Christ; it is no longer I who live, but Christ who lives in me; and the life I now live in the flesh I live by faith in the Son of God, who loved me and gave himself for me.

1386 **Matthew 8:8** But the centurion answered him, "Lord, I am not worthy to have you come under my roof; but only say the word, and my servant will be healed. . . ."

1387 **CIC Canon 919**

§1. One who is to receive the Most Holy Eucharist is to abstain from any food or drink, with the exception only of water and medicine, for at least the period of one hour before Holy Communion.

§2. A priest who celebrates the Most Holy Eucharist two or three times on the same day may take something before the second or third celebration even if the period of one hour does not intervene.

§3. Those who are advanced in age or who suffer from any infirmity, as well as those who take care of them, can receive the Most Holy Eucharist even if they have taken something during the previous hour.

CIC Canon 917 A person who has received the Most Holy Eucharist may receive it again on the same day only during the celebration of the Eucharist in which the person participates, with due regard for the prescription of can. 921 §2 [even if they have received Communion in the same day, those who are in danger of death are strongly urged to receive again]. 1388

CIC Canon 920 1389

§1. All the faithful, after they have been initiated into the Most Holy Eucharist, are bound by the obligation of receiving Communion at least once a year.

§2. This precept must be fulfilled during the Easter season unless it is fulfilled for a just cause at some other time during the year.

1 Corinthians 11:26 For as often as you eat this bread and drink the cup, you proclaim the Lord's death until he comes. 1393

Council of Trent (1551): DS 1638 Our Savior, therefore, when about to depart from this world to the Father, instituted this sacrament in which He poured forth, as it were, the riches of His divine love for men, "making a remembrance of his wonderful works" [Ps. 110:4], and He commanded us in the consuming of it to cherish His "memory" [I Cor. 11:24], and "to show forth his death until He come" to judge the world [I Cor. 11:26]. But He wished that this sacrament be received as the spiritual food of souls [Matt. 26:26], by which they may be nourished and strengthened [can. 5], living by the life of Him who said: "He who eateth me, the same also shall live by me" [John 6:58], and as an antidote, whereby we may be freed from daily faults and be preserved from mortal sins. He wished, furthermore, that this be a pledge of our future glory and of everlasting happiness, and thus be a symbol of that one "body" of which He Himself is the "head" [I Cor. 11:3; Eph. 5:23], and to which He wished us to be united, as members, by the closest bond of faith, hope, and charity, that we might "all speak the same thing and there might be no schisms among us" [cf. I Cor. 1:10]. 1394

1 Corinthians 12:13 For by one Spirit we were all baptized into one body—Jews or Greeks, slaves or free—and all were made to drink of one Spirit. 1396

Matthew 25:40 ". . . And the King will answer them, 'Truly, I say to you, as you did it to one of the least of these my brethren, you did it to me.' . . ." 1397

***Sacrosanctum concilium* 47** At the Last Supper, on the night he was betrayed, our Savior instituted the eucharistic sacrifice of his Body and Blood. This he did in order to perpetuate the sacrifice of the Cross throughout the ages until he should come again, and so to entrust to his beloved Spouse, the Church, a memorial of his death and resurrection: a sacrament of love, a sign of unity, a bond of charity, a paschal banquet in which Christ is consumed, the mind is filled with grace, and a pledge of future glory is given to us. 1398

CIC Canon 844, §3 Catholic ministers may licitly administer the sacraments of penance, Eucharist and anointing of the sick to members of the oriental churches which do not have full communion with the Catholic Church, if they ask on their 1399 own for the sacraments and are properly disposed. This holds also for members of other churches, which in the judgment of the Apostolic See are in the same condition as the oriental churches as far as these sacraments are concerned.

1401 **CIC Canon 844, §4** If the danger of death is present or other grave necessity, in the judgment of the diocesan bishop or the conference of bishops, Catholic ministers may licitly administer these sacraments to other Christians who do not have full communion with the Catholic Church, who cannot approach a minister of their own community and on their own ask for it, provided they manifest Catholic faith in these sacraments and are properly disposed.

1403 (1) **Luke 22:18** ". . . for I tell you that from now on I shall not drink of the fruit of the vine until the kingdom of God comes."

1403 (2) **Mark 14:25** ". . . Truly, I say to you, I shall not drink again of the fruit of the vine until that day when I drink it new in the kingdom of God."

1404 **Titus 2:13** . . . awaiting our blessed hope, the appearing of the glory of our great God and Savior Jesus Christ. . . .

1413 (1) **Council of Trent (1551): DS 1640** For the apostles had not yet received the Eucharist from the hand of the Lord [Matt. 26:26; Mark 14:22] when He Himself truly said that what He was offering was His body; and this belief has always been in the Church of God, that immediately after the consecration the true body of our Lord and His true blood together with His soul and divinity exist under the species of bread and wine; but the body indeed under the species of bread, and the blood under the species of wine by the force of the words, but the body itself under both by force of that natural connection and concomitance by which the parts of Christ the Lord, "who hath now risen from the dead to die no more" [Rom. 6:9], are mutually united, the divinity also because of that admirable hypostatic union [can. 1 and 3] with His body and soul.

1413 (2) **Council of Trent (1551): DS 1651** If anyone denies that in the sacrament of the most holy Eucharist there are truly, really, and substantially contained the body and blood together with the soul and divinity of our Lord Jesus Christ, and therefore the whole Christ, but shall say that He is in it as by a sign or figure, or force, let him be anathema.

1421 **Mark 2:1–12** And when he returned to Capernaum after some days, it was reported that he was at home. And many were gathered together, so that there was no longer room for them, not even about the door; and he was preaching the word to them. And they came, bringing to him a paralytic carried by four men. And when they could not get near him because of the crowd, they removed the roof above him; and when they had made an opening, they let down the pallet on which the paralytic lay. And when Jesus saw their faith, he said to the paralytic, "My son, your sins are forgiven." Now some of the scribes were sitting there, questioning in their hearts, "Why does this man speak thus? It is blasphemy! Who can forgive sins but God alone?" And immediately Jesus, perceiving in his spirit that they thus questioned within themselves, said to them, "Why do you question thus in your hearts? Which is easier, to say to the paralytic, 'Your sins are forgiven,' or to say, 'Rise, take up your pallet and walk'? But that you may know that the Son of man has authority on earth to forgive sins"—he said to the paralytic—"I say to you, rise, take up your pallet and go home." And he rose, and immediately took up the pallet and went out before them all; so that they were all amazed and glorified God, saying, "We never saw anything like this!"

(1) **Mark 1:15** . . . and saying, "The time is fulfilled, and the kingdom of God is at hand; repent, and believe in the gospel." 1423

(2) **Luke 15:18** I will arise and go to my father, and I will say to him, "Father, I have sinned against heaven and before you. . . ." 1423

(1) **Luke 11:4** ". . . and forgive us our sins, for we ourselves forgive every one who is indebted to us; and lead us not into temptation." 1425

(2) **Matthew 6:12** 1425

And forgive us our debts,
As we also have forgiven our debtors. . . .

(1) **Council of Trent (1546): DS 1515** If anyone denies that by the grace of our Lord Jesus Christ, which is conferred in baptism, the guilt of original sin is remitted, or even asserts that the whole of that which has the true and proper nature of sin is not taken away, but says that it is only touched in person or is not imputed, let him be anathema. 1426

(2) **Council of Trent (1547): DS 1545** To men, therefore, who have been justified in this respect, whether they have preserved uninterruptedly the grace received, or have recovered it when lost, the words of the Apostle are to be submitted: "Abound in every good work, knowing that your labor is not in vain in the Lord" [I Cor. 15:58]; "for God is not unjust, that he should forget your work and the love, which you have shown in his name" [Heb. 6:10], and: "Do not lose your confidence, which has a great reward" [Heb. 10:35]. And therefore to those who work well "unto the end" [Matt. 10:22], and who trust in God, life eternal is to be proposed, both as a grace mercifully promised to the sons of God through Christ Jesus, "and as a recompense" which is according to the promise of God Himself to be faithfully given to their good works and merits [can. 26 and 32]. For this is that "crown of justice which after his fight and course" the Apostle declared "was laid up for him, to be rendered to him by the just judge and not only to him, but also to all that love his coming" [II Tim. 4:7 ff.]. 1426

(3) ***Lumen gentium* 40** The Lord Jesus, divine teacher and model of all perfection, preached holiness of life (of which he is the author and maker) to each and every one of his disciples without distinction: "You, therefore, must be perfect, as your heavenly Father is perfect" (Mt. 5:48). For he sent the Holy Spirit to all to move them interiorly to love God with their whole heart, with their whole soul, with their whole understanding, and with their whole strength (cf. Mk. 12:30), and to love one another as Christ loved them (cf. Jn. 13:34; 15:12). The followers of Christ, called by God, not in virtue of their works but by his design and grace, and justified in the Lord Jesus, have been made sons of God in the baptism of faith and partakers of the divine nature, and so are truly sanctified. They must therefore hold on to and perfect in their lives that sanctification which they have received from God. They are told by the apostle to live "as is fitting among saints" (Eph. 5:3), and to put on "as God's chosen ones, holy and beloved, compassion, kindness, lowliness, meekness, and patience" (Col. 3:12), to have the fruits of the Spirit for their sanctification (cf. Gal. 5:22; Rom. 6:22). But since we all offend in many ways (cf. Jas. 3:2), we constantly need God's mercy and must pray every day: "And forgive us out debts" (Mt. 6:12). 1426

It is therefore quite clear that all Christians in any state or walk of life are called to the fullness of Christian life and to the perfection of love, and by this holiness a more human manner of life is fostered also in earthly society. In order to reach this perfection the faithful should use the strength dealt out to them by Christ's gift, so that, following in his footsteps and conformed to his image, doing the will of God in everything, they may wholeheartedly devote themselves to the glory of God and to the service of their neighbor. Thus the holiness of the People of God will grow in fruitful abundance, as is clearly shown in the history of the Church through the life of so many saints.

1427 **Acts 2:38** And Peter said to them, "Repent, and be baptized every one of you in the name of Jesus Christ for the forgiveness of your sins; and you shall receive the gift of the Holy Spirit. . . ."

1428 (1) **John 6:44** No one can come to me unless the Father who sent me draws him; and I will raise him up at the last day.

1428 (2) **John 12:32** ". . . and I, when I am lifted up from the earth, will draw all men to myself."

1428 (3) **1 John 4:10** In this is love, not that we loved God but that he loved us and sent his Son to be the expiation for our sins.

1429 (1) **Luke 22:61** And the Lord turned and looked at Peter. And Peter remembered the word of the Lord, how he had said to him, "Before the cock crows today, you will deny me three times."

1429 (2) **John 21:15–17** When they had finished breakfast, Jesus said to Simon Peter, "Simon, son of John, do you love me more than these?" He said to him, "Yes, Lord; you know that I love you." He said to him, "Feed my lambs." A second time he said to him, "Simon, son of John, do you love me?" He said to him, "Yes, Lord; you know that I love you." He said to him, "Tend my sheep." He said to him the third time, "Simon, son of John, do you love me?" Peter was grieved because he said to him the third time, "Do you love me?" And he said to him, "Lord, you know everything; you know that I love you." Jesus said to him, "Feed my sheep. . . ."

1430 (1) **Joel 2:12–13**

"Yet even now," says the Lord,
"return to me with all your heart,
with fasting, with weeping, and with mourning;
and rend your hearts and not your garments."
Return to the Lord, your God,
for he is gracious and merciful,
slow to anger, and abounding in steadfast love,
and repents of evil.

1430 (2) **Isaiah 1:16–17**

Wash yourselves; make yourselves clean;
remove the evil of your doings
from before my eyes;
cease to do evil,
learn to do good;
seek justice,
correct oppression;
defend the fatherless,
plead for the widow.

(3) **Matthew 6:1–6** "Beware of practicing your piety before men in order to be seen by them; for then you will have no reward from your Father who is in heaven. 1430

"Thus, when you give alms, sound no trumpet before you, as the hypocrites do in the synagogues and in the streets, that they may be praised by men. Truly, I say to you, they have received their reward. But when you give alms, do not let your left hand know what your right hand is doing, so that your alms may be in secret; and your Father who sees in secret will reward you.

"And when you pray, you must not be like the hypocrites; for they love to stand and pray in the synagogues and at the street corners, that they may be seen by men. Truly, I say to you, they have received their reward. But when you pray, go into your room and shut the door and pray to your Father who is in secret; and your Father who sees in secret will reward you. . . ."

(4) **Matthew 6:16–18** "And when you fast, do not look dismal, like the hypocrites, for they disfigure their faces that their fasting may be seen by men. Truly, I say to you, they have received their reward. But when you fast, anoint your head and wash your face, that your fasting may not be seen by men but by your Father who is in secret; and your Father who sees in secret will reward you. . . ." 1430

(1) **Council of Trent (1551): DS 1676–78** Contrition, which has the first place among the aforementioned acts of the penitent, is a sorrow of the soul and a detestation of sin committed, with a determination of not sinning in the future. This feeling of contrition is, moreover, necessary at all times to obtain the forgiveness of sins, and thus for a person who has fallen after baptism it especially prepares for the remission of sins, if it is united with trust in divine mercy and with the desire of performing the other things required to receive this sacrament correctly. The holy Synod, therefore, declares that this contrition includes not only cessation from sin and a resolution and a beginning of a new life, but also hatred of the old, according to this statement: "Cast away from you all your transgressions, by which you have transgressed, and make to yourselves a new heart and a new spirit" [Ezech. 18:31]. And certainly, he who has considered those lamentations of the saints: "To Thee only have I sinned, and have done evil before Thee" [Ps. 50:6]; "I have labored in my groanings; I shall wash my bed every night" [Ps. 6:7]; "I will recount to Thee all my years in the bitterness of my soul" [Isa. 38:15], and others of this kind, will readily understand that they emanate from a certain vehement hatred of past life and from a profound detestation of sins. 1431

The Council teaches, furthermore, that though it sometimes happens that this contrition is perfect because of charity and reconciles man to God, before this sacrament is actually received, this reconciliation nevertheless must not be ascribed to the contrition itself without the desire of the sacrament which is included in it. That imperfect contrition [can. 5] which is called attrition, since it commonly arises either from the consideration of the baseness of sin or from fear of hell and its punishments, if it renounces the desire of sinning with the hope of pardon, the Synod declares, not only does not make a person a hypocrite and a greater sinner, but is even a gift of God and an impulse of the Holy Spirit, not indeed as already dwelling in the penitent, but only moving him, assisted by which the penitent prepares a way for himself unto justice. And though without the sacrament of penance it cannot *per se* lead the sinner to justification, nevertheless it does dispose him to obtain the grace of God in the sacrament of penance. For the Ninivites, struck in a salutary way by this fear in consequence of the preaching of Jonas which was full of terror, did penance and obtained mercy from the Lord [cf. Jonas 3]. For this reason, therefore, do some falsely accuse Catholic writers, as if they taught that the sacrament of penance confers grace without any pious endeavor on the part of those who receive it, a thing which the Church of God has never taught or pronounced. Moreover, they also falsely teach that contrition is extorted and forced, and that it is not free and voluntary [can. 5].

1431 (2) **Council of Trent (1551): DS 1705** If anyone says that this contrition, which is evoked by examination, recollection, and hatred of sins "whereby one recalls his years in the bitterness of his soul" [Isa. 38:15], by pondering on the gravity of one's sins, the multitude, the baseness, the loss of eternal happiness, and the incurring of eternal damnation, together with the purpose of a better life, is not a true and a beneficial sorrow, and does not prepare for grace, but makes a man a hypocrite, and a greater sinner; finally that this sorrow is forced and not free and voluntary: let him be anathema.

1431 (3) ***Roman Catechism* II, 5, 4** The faithful, therefore, are first to be admonished and exhorted to labor most strenuously and studiously to attain this inward penance of the heart, which we call a virtue, without which exterior penance will avail them very little. Inward penance consists in turning ourselves to God from the heart, and in detesting and holding in hatred our past transgressions, with, at the same time, a firm and deliberate resolution of correcting our evil course of life and corrupt morals, not without the hope of obtaining pardon from the mercy of God. It is accompanied with grief and sadness, which latter is a perturbation and affection, and is called by many a passion, joined, as it were as a companion, to detestation of sins. Wherefore, with many of the holy Fathers, the definition of penance is comprised in this anguish of mind.

1432 (1) **Ezekiel 36:26–27** A new heart I will give you, and a new spirit I will put within you; and I will take out of your flesh the heart of stone and give you a heart of flesh. And I will put my spirit within you, and cause you to walk in my statutes and be careful to observe my ordinances.

1432 (2) **John 19:37** And again another scripture says, "They shall look on him whom they have pierced."

1432 (3) **Zechariah 12:10** "And I will pour out on the house of David and the inhabitants of Jerusalem a spirit of compassion and supplication, so that, when they look on him whom they have pierced, they shall mourn for him, as one mourns for an only child, and weep bitterly over him, as one weeps over a first-born. . . ."

1433 (1) **John 16:8–9** And when he comes, he will convince the world concerning sin and righteousness and judgment: concerning sin, because they do not believe in me. . . .

1433 (2) **John 15:26** But when the Counselor comes, whom I shall send to you from the Father, even the Spirit of truth, who proceeds from the Father, he will bear witness to me. . . .

1433 (3) **Acts 2:36–38** ". . . Let all the house of Israel therefore know assuredly that God has made him both Lord and Christ, this Jesus whom you crucified."

Now when they heard this they were cut to the heart, and said to Peter and the rest of the apostles, "Brethren, what shall we do?" And Peter said to them, "Repent, and be baptized every one of you in the name of Jesus Christ for the forgiveness of your sins; and you shall receive the gift of the Holy Spirit. . . ."

(4) ***Dominum et vivificantem* 27–48** When Jesus during the discourse in the Upper Room foretells the coming of the Holy Spirit "at the price of" his own departure, and promises "I will send him to you", in the very same context he adds "And when he comes, he *will convince the world concerning sin and righteousness and judgment.*" The same Counsellor and Spirit of truth who has been promised as the one who "will teach" and "bring to remembrance", who "will bear witness", and "guide into all the truth", in the words just quoted is foretold as the one who "will convince the world concerning sin and righteousness and judgment". 1433

The *context* too seems significant. Jesus links this foretelling of the Holy Spirit to the words indicating his "departure" through the Cross, and indeed emphasizes the need for this departure: "It is to your advantage that I go away, for if I do not go away, the Counsellor will not come to you."

But what counts more is *the explanation that Jesus himself adds* to these three words: sin, righteousness, judgment. For he says this: "He will convince the world concerning sin and righteousness and judgment: concerning sin, because they do not believe in me; concerning righteousness, because I go to the Father, and you will see me no more; concerning judgment, because the ruler of this world is judged." In the mind of Jesus, sin, righteousness and judgment have *a very precise meaning*, different from the meaning that one might be inclined to attribute to these words independently of the speaker's explanation. This explanation also indicates how one is to understand the "convincing the world" which is proper to the action of the Holy Spirit. Both the meaning of the individual words and the fact that Jesus linked them together in the same phrase are important here.

"*Sin*", in this passage, means the incredulity that Jesus encountered among "his own", beginning with the people of his own town of Nazareth. Sin means the rejection of his mission, a rejection that will cause people to condemn him to death. When he speaks next of "*righteousness*", Jesus seems to have in mind that definitive justice, which the Father will restore to him when he grants him the glory of the Resurrection and Ascension into heaven: "I go to the Father". In its turn, and in the context of "sin" and "righteousness" thus understood, "*judgment*" means that the Spirit of truth will show the guilt of the "world" in condemning Jesus to death on the Cross. Nevertheless, Christ did not come into the world only to judge it and condemn it: he came to save it. Convincing about sin and righteousness has as its purpose the salvation of the world, the salvation of men. Precisely this truth seems to be emphasized by the assertion that "judgment" concerns only the "prince of this world", Satan, the one who from the beginning has been exploiting the work of creation against salvation, against the covenant and the union of man with God: he is "already judged" from the start. If the Spirit-Counsellor is to convince the world precisely concerning judgment, it is in order to continue in the world the salvific work of Christ.

Here we wish to concentrate our attention principally on this mission of the Holy Spirit, which is "*to convince the world concerning sin*", but at the same time respecting the general context of Jesus' words in the Upper Room. The Holy Spirit, who takes from the Son the work of the Redemption of the world, by this very fact takes the task of the salvific "convincing of sin". This convincing is in permanent reference to "righteousness": that is to say to definitive salvation in God, to the fulfilment of the economy that has as its center the crucified and glorified Christ. And this salvific economy of God in a certain sense removes man from "judgment", that is from the damnation which has been inflicted on the sin of Satan, "the prince of this world", the one who because of his sin has become "the ruler of this world of darkness". And here we see that, through this reference to "judgment", vast horizons open up for understanding "sin" and also "righteousness". The Holy Spirit, by showing sin against the background of Christ's Cross in the economy of salvation (one could say "sin saved"), enables us to understand how his mission is also "to convince" of the sin that has already been definitively judged ("sin condemned").

All the words uttered by the Redeemer in the Upper Room on the eve of his Passion *become part of the era of the Church*: first of all, the words about the Holy Spirit as the Paraclete and Spirit of truth. These words become part of it in an ever new way, in every generation, in every age. This is confirmed, as far as our own age is concerned, by the teaching of the Second Vatican Council as a whole, and especially in the *Pastoral Constitution Gaudium et Spes*. Many passages of this document indicate clearly that the Council, by opening itself to the light of the Spirit of truth, is seen to be the *authentic depositary* of the predictions and promises made by Christ to the Apostles and to the Church in the farewell discourse: in a particular way as the depositary of the predictions that the Holy Spirit would "convince the world concerning sin and righteousness and judgment".

This is already indicated by the text in which *the Council explains how it understands the "world"*: "The Council focuses its attention on the world of men, the whole human family along with the sum of those realities in the midst of which that family lives. It gazes upon the world which is the theatre of man's history, and carries the marks of his energies, his tragedies, and his triumphs; that world which the Christian sees as created and sustained by its Maker's love, *fallen indeed into the bondage of sin*, yet *emancipated now by Christ*. He was crucified and rose again *to break the stranglehold of personified Evil*, so that this world might be fashioned anew according to God's design and reach its fulfilment." This very rich text needs to be read in conjunction with the other passages in the Constitution that seek to show *with all the realism of faith* the situation of sin in the contemporary world and that also seek to explain its essence, beginning from different points of view.

When on the eve of the Passover Jesus speaks of the Holy Spirit as the one who "will convince the world concerning sin", on the one hand this statement must be given *the widest possible meaning*, insofar as it includes all the sin in the history of humanity. But on the other hand, when Jesus explains that this sin consists in the fact that "they do not believe in him", this meaning seems to *apply only* to those who rejected the messianic mission of the Son of Man and condemned him to death of the Cross. But one can hardly fail to notice that this more "limited" and historically specified meaning of sin expands, until it assumes a universal dimension *by reason of the universality* of the *Redemption*, accomplished through the Cross. The revelation of the mystery of the Redemption opens the way to an understanding in which *every sin* wherever and whenever committed has a reference to the Cross of Christ—and therefore indirectly also to the sin of those who "have not believed in him", and who condemned Jesus Christ to death on the Cross.

From this point of view we must return to the event of Pentecost.

Christ's prophecies in the farewell discourse found their most exact and direct *confirmation* on the day of Pentecost, in particular the prediction which we are dealing with: "The Counsellor . . . will convince the world concerning sin." On that day, the *promised Holy Spirit came down* upon the Apostles gathered in prayer together with Mary the Mother of Jesus, in the same Upper Room, as we read in the *Acts of the Apostles*: "And they were all filled with the Holy Spirit and began to speak in other tongues, as the Spirit gave them utterance", "thus bringing back to unity the scattered races and offering to the Father the first-fruits of all the nations."

The connection between Christ's prediction and this event is clear. We perceive here the first and fundamental fulfilment of the promise of the Paraclete. He comes, sent by the Father, *"after" the departure of Christ*, "at the price of" that departure. This is first a departure through the Cross, and later, forty days after the Resurrection, through his Ascension into heaven. Once more, at the moment of the Ascension, Jesus orders the Apostles "not to depart from Jerusalem, but to wait for the promise of the Father"; "but before many days you shall be *baptized with the Holy Spirit*"; "but you shall receive power when the Holy Spirit has come upon you; and you shall be witnesses in Jerusalem and in all Judaea and Samaria and to the end of the earth."

These last words contain an echo or reminder of the prediction made in the Upper Room. And on the day of Pentecost this prediction is fulfilled with total accuracy. Acting under the influence of the Holy Spirit, who had been received by the Apostles while they were praying in the Upper Room, *Peter comes forwards and speaks* before a multitude of people of different languages, gathered for the feast. He proclaims what *he* certainly *would not have had the courage to say before*: "Men of Israel, . . . Jesus of Nazareth, a man attested to you by God with mighty works and wonders and signs which God did through him in your midst . . . this Jesus, delivered up according to the definite plan and foreknowledge of God, you *crucified* and killed by the hands of lawless men. But God raised him up, having loosed the pangs of death, because it was not possible for him to be held by it."

Jesus had foretold and promised: "he will bear witness to me, . . . and you also are my witnesses." In the first discourse of Peter in Jerusalem this "witness" *finds its clear beginning*: it is the witness to Christ crucified and risen. The witness of the Spirit-Paraclete and of the Apostles. And in the very content of that first witness, the Spirit of truth, through the lips of Peter, "*convinces the world concerning sin*": first of all, concerning the sin which is the rejection of Christ even to his condemnation to death, to death on the Cross of Golgotha. Similar proclamations will be repeated, according to the text of the Acts of the Apostles, on other occasions and in various places.

Beginning from this initial witness at Pentecost and for all future time, the action of the Spirit of truth who "convinces the world concerning the sin" of the rejection of Christ *is linked* inseparably with the witness to be borne to the Paschal Mystery: *the mystery of the Crucified and Risen One*. And in this link the same "convincing concerning sin" reveals its own salvific dimension. For it is a "convincing" that has [as] its purpose not merely *the accusation* of the world and still less its *condemnation*. Jesus Christ did not come into the world to judge it and condemn it but *to save it*. This is emphasized in this first discourse, when Peter exclaims: "Let all the house of Israel therefore know assuredly that God has made him both Lord and Christ, this Jesus whom you crucified." And then, when those present ask Peter and the Apostles: "Brethren, what shall we do?", this is Peter's answer: "*Repent*, and be baptized every one of you in the name of Jesus Christ *for the forgiveness of your sins*; and you shall receive the gift of the Holy Spirit."

In this way "convincing concerning *sin*" becomes at the same time a convincing *concerning the remission of sins*, in the power of the Holy Spirit. Peter in his discourse in Jerusalem calls people to conversion, as Jesus called his listeners to conversion at the beginning of his messianic activity. Conversion *requires convincing of sin*; it includes the interior judgment of the conscience, and this, being a proof of the action of the Spirit of truth in man's inmost being, becomes at the same time a new beginning of the bestowal of grace and love: "Receive the Holy Spirit." Thus in this "convincing concerning sin" we discover *a double gift*: the gift of the truth of conscience and the gift of the certainty of redemption. The Spirit of truth is the Counsellor.

The convincing concerning sin, through the ministry of the *apostolic* kerygma in the early Church, is *referred*—under the impulse of the Spirit poured out at Pentecost —*to the redemptive power* of Christ crucified and risen. Thus the promise concerning the Holy Spirit made before Easter is fulfilled: "He will take what is mine and declare it to you." When therefore, during the Pentecost event, Peter speaks *of the sin of those who "have not believed"* and have sent Jesus of Nazareth to an ignominious death, he bears witness to victory over sin: a victory achieved, in a certain sense, through the greatest sin that man could commit: *the killing of Jesus, the Son of God, consubstantial with the Father*! Similarly, the death of the Son of God conquers human death: "I will be your death, O death", as the sin of having crucified *the Son of God "conquers" human sin*! That sin which was committed in Jerusalem on Good Friday—and also every human sin. For the greatest sin on man's part is matched, in the heart of the Redeemer, *by the oblation of supreme love* that conquers the evil of all the sins of man. On the basis of this certainty the Church in the Roman liturgy does not hesitate to repeat every year, at the Easter Vigil, "O happy fault!", in the deacon's proclamation of the Resurrection when he sings the "*Exsultet*".

However, no one but *he himself, the Spirit of truth, can "convince the world"*, man or the human conscience of this ineffable truth. He is the Spirit who "searches even the depths of God". Faced with the mystery of sin we have to search "the depths of God" *to their very depth*. It is not enough to search the human conscience, the intimate mystery of man, but we have to penetrate the inner mystery of God, those "depths of God" that are summarized thus: to the Father—in the Son—through the Holy Spirit. It is precisely the Holy Spirit who "searches" the "depths of God", and from them draws *God's response* to man's sin. With this response there closes the process of "convincing concerning sin", as the event of Pentecost shows.

By convincing the "world" concerning the sin of Golgotha, concerning the death of the innocent Lamb, as happens on the day of Pentecost, the Holy Spirit also convinces of every sin, committed in any place and at any moment in human history: *for he demonstrates its relationship with the Cross of Christ.* The "convincing" is the demonstration of the evil of sin, of every sin, in relation to the Cross of Christ. Sin, shown in this relationship, *is recognized in the entire dimension of evil* proper to it, through the "*mysterium iniquitatis*" which is hidden within it. Man does not know this dimension—he is absolutely ignorant of it apart from the Cross of Christ. So he cannot be "convinced" of it except by *the Holy Spirit*: the Spirit of truth, but who is also the Counsellor.

For sin, shown in relation to the Cross of Christ, is at the same time *identified in the full dimension of the "mysterium pietatis"*, as indicated by the Post-Synodal Apostolic Exhortation *Reconciliatio et Paenitentia.* Man is also absolutely ignorant of this dimension of sin apart from the Cross of Christ. And he cannot be "convinced" of this dimension either except *by the Holy Spirit*: the one who "searches the depths of God".

This is the dimension of sin that we find in the witness concerning the beginning, commented on in the *Book of Genesis*. It is the sin that according to the revealed Word of God constitutes *the principle and root of all the others.* We find ourselves faced with the original reality of sin in human history and at the same time in the whole of the economy of salvation. It can be said that in this sin the "*mysterium iniquitatis*" has its beginning, but it can also be said that this is the sin concerning which the redemptive power of the "*mysterium pietatis*" becomes particularly clear and efficacious. This is expressed by Saint Paul, when he *contrasts* the "*disobedience*" of the first Adam with the "obedience" of Christ, the second Adam: "Obedience unto death".

According to the witness concerning the beginning, sin in its original reality takes place in man's will—and conscience—first of all as "disobedience", that is, as opposition of the will of man to the will of God. This original disobedience presupposes *a rejection*, or at least *a turning away from the truth contained in the Word of God*, who creates the world. This Word is the same Word who was "in the beginning with God", who "was God", and without whom "nothing has been made of all that is", since "the world was made through him". He is the Word who is also the eternal law, the source of every law which regulates the world and especially human acts. When therefore on the eve of his Passion Jesus Christ speaks of the sin of those who "*do not believe in him*", in these words of his, full of sorrow, there is *as it were a distant echo of that sin* which in its original form is obscurely *inscribed* in the mystery of creation. For the one who is speaking is not only the Son of Man but the one who is also "the first-born of all creation", "for in him all things were created . . . through him and for him". In the light of this truth we can understand that the "disobedience" in the mystery of the beginning presupposes in a certain sense the same "non-faith", that same "*they have not believed*", which will be repeated in the Paschal Mystery. As we have said, it is a matter of a rejection or at least a turning away from the truth contained in the Word of the Father. The rejection expresses itself in practice as "disobedience", in an act committed as an effect of the temptation which comes from the "father of lies". Therefore, at the root of human sin is the lie which is a radical *rejection of the truth* contained in the Word of the Father, through whom is expressed the loving omnipotence of the Creator: the omnipotence and also the love "of God the Father, Creator of heaven and earth".

"*The Spirit of God*", who according to the biblical description of creation "was moving over the face of the water", signifies the same "Spirit who searches the depths of God": "*searches the depths*" *of the Father and of the Word-Son* in the mystery of creation. Not only is he the direct witness of their mutual love from which creation derives, but he himself is this love. He himself, as love, is the eternal uncreated gift. In him is *the source and the beginning of every giving of gifts to creatures.* The witness concerning the beginning, which we find in the whole of Revelation, beginning with the *Book of Genesis*, is unanimous on this point. To create means to call into existence from nothing: therefore, to create means *to give* existence. And if the visible world is created for man, therefore the world is given to man. And at the same time that same man in his own humanity receives as a gift a special "*image and likeness*" to God. This means not only rationality and freedom as constitutive properties of human nature, but also, from the very beginning, the capacity of having a *personal relationship* with God, as "I" and "you", and therefore the *capacity of having a covenant*, which will take place in God's salvific communication with man. Against the background of the "image and likeness" of God, "the gift of the Spirit" ultimately means *a call to friendship*, in which the transcendent "depths of God" become in some way opened to participation on the part of man. The Second Vatican Council teaches: "The invisible God out of the abundance of his love speaks to men as friends and lives among them, so that he may invite and take them into fellowship with himself."

The Spirit, therefore, who "searches everything, even the depths of God", knows from the beginning "the secrets of man". For this reason he alone *can fully "convince concerning the sin" that happened at the beginning*, that sin which is the root of all other sins and the sources of man's sinfulness on earth, a source which never ceases to be active. The Spirit of truth knows the original reality of the sin caused in the will of man by the "father of lies", he who already "has been judged". The Holy Spirit therefore convinces the world of sin in connection with this "judgment", but by constantly *guiding toward the "righteousness"* that has been revealed to man together with the Cross of Christ: through "obedience unto death".

Only the Holy Spirit can convince concerning the sin of the human beginning, precisely he who is the love of the Father and of the Son, he who is gift, whereas *the sin of the human beginning consists in untruthfulness and in the rejection of the gift and the love* which determine the beginning of the world and of man.

According to the witness concerning the beginning which we find in the Scriptures and in Tradition, after the first (and also more complete) description in the *Book of Genesis*, sin in its original form is understood as "disobedience" and this means simply and directly *transgression of a prohibition laid down by God*. But in the light of the whole context it is also obvious that the ultimate roots of this disobedience are to be sought in the whole real situation of man. Having been called into existence, the human being—man and woman—is a creature. The "image of God", consisting in rationality and freedom, expresses the greatness and dignity of the human subject, who is a person. But this *personal subject* is also always *a creature*: in his existence and essence he depends on the Creator. According to the *Book of Genesis*, "the tree of the knowledge of good and evil" was to express and constantly remind man of the "limit" impassable for a created being. God's prohibition is to be understood in this sense: the Creator forbids man and woman to eat of the fruit of the tree of the knowledge of good and evil. The words of the enticement, that is to say the temptation, as formulated in the sacred text, are an inducement to transgress this prohibition—that is to say to *go beyond* that "limit": "When you eat of it your eyes will be opened, and you will be like God ('like gods'), knowing good and evil."

"Disobedience" means precisely going beyond that limit, which remains impassable to the will and the freedom of man as a created being. For God the Creator is the one definitive source of the moral order in the world created by him. Man cannot decide by himself what is good and what is evil—cannot "know good and evil, like God". In the created world *God* indeed remains the first and sovereign source *for deciding about good and evil*, through the intimate truth of being, which is the reflection *of the Word*, the eternal Son, consubstantial with the Father. To man, created to the image of God, the Holy Spirit gives the gift of *conscience*, so that in this conscience the image may faithfully reflect its model, which is both Wisdom and eternal Law, the source of the moral order in man and in the world. "Disobedience", as the original dimension of sin, means the *rejection of this source*, through man's claim to become an independent and exclusive source for deciding about good and evil. The Spirit who "searches the depths of God", and who at the same time is for man the light of conscience and the source of the moral order, knows in all its fullness this dimension of the sin inscribed in the mystery of man's beginning. And the Spirit does not cease "*convincing the world of it*" in connection with the Cross of Christ on Golgotha.

According to the witness of the beginning, God in creation has revealed himself as omnipotence, which is love. At the same time he has revealed to man that, as the "image and likeness" of his Creator, he is *called to participate in truth and love*. This participation means a life in union with God, who is "eternal life". But man, under the influence of the "father of lies", has separated himself from this participation. To what degree? Certainly not to the degree of the sin of a pure spirit, to the degree of the sin of Satan. The human spirit is incapable of reaching such a degree. In the very description given in *Genesis it is easy to see the difference of degree* between the "breath of evil" on the part of the one who "has sinned (or remains in sin) from the beginning" and already "has been judged", and the evil of disobedience on the part of man.

Man's disobedience, nevertheless, always means a *turning away from God*, and in a certain sense *the closing up* of human freedom in his regard. It also means a certain opening of this freedom—of the human mind and will—to the one who is the "father of lies". This act of conscious choice is not only "disobedience" but also involves a *certain consent to the motivation* which was contained in the first temptation to sin and which is unceasingly renewed during the whole history of man on earth: "For God knows that when you eat of it your eyes will be opened, and you will be like God, knowing good and evil."

Here we find ourselves at the very center of what could be called the "anti-Word", that is to say "the anti-truth". For *the truth about man* becomes *falsified: who man is* and what are *the impassable limits* of his being and freedom. This "anti-truth" is possible because at the same time there is a complete *falsification* of the *truth about who God is*. God the Creator is placed in a state of suspicion, indeed of accusation, in the mind of the creature. For the first time in human history there appears the perverse "genius of suspicion". He seeks to *"falsify" Good itself, the absolute Good*, which precisely in the work of creation has manifested itself as the Good which gives in an inexpressible way: as *bonum diffusivum sui*, as *creative love*. Who can completely "*convince* concerning sin", or concerning this motivation of man's original disobedience, except the one who alone is the gift and the source of all giving of gifts, except the Spirit, who "searches the depths of God" and is the love of the Father and the Son?

For in spite of all the witness of creation and of the salvific economy inherent in it, the spirit of darkness is capable of showing *God as an enemy* of his own creature, and in the first place as an enemy of man, *as a source of danger and threat to man*. In this way *Satan* manages to sow in man's soul the seed of opposition to the one who "from the beginning" would be considered as man's enemy—and not as Father. Man is challenged to become the adversary of God!

The analysis of sin in its original dimension indicates that, through the influence of the "father of lies", *throughout the history of humanity there will be a constant pressure on man to reject God*, even to the point of hating him: "*Love of self to the point of contempt for God*", as Saint Augustine puts it. Man will be inclined to see in God primarily a limitation of himself, and not the source of his own freedom and the fullness of good. We see this confirmed in the modern age, when the atheistic ideologies seek *to root out religion* on the grounds that religion causes the radical "*alienation*" *of man*, as if man were dispossessed of his own humanity when, accepting the idea of God, he attributes to God what belongs to man, and exclusively to man! Hence a process of thought and historico-sociological practice in which the rejection of God has reached the point of declaring his "death". An absurdity, both in concept and expression! But the ideology of the "death of God" is more a threat to *man*, as the Second Vatican Council indicates when it analyzes the question of the "independence of earthly affairs" and writes "For without the Creator the creature would disappear . . . when God is forgotten the creature itself grows unintelligible." The ideology of the "death of God" easily demonstrates in its effects that on the "theoretical and practical" levels it is the ideology of the "death of man".

The Spirit who searches the depths of God was called by Jesus in his discourse in the Upper Room *the Paraclete*. *For from the beginning the Spirit "is invoked"* in order to "convince the world concerning sin". He is invoked in a definitive way through the Cross of Christ. Convincing concerning sin means showing the evil that sin contains, and this is equivalent to revealing the *mystery of iniquity*. It is not possible to grasp the evil of sin in all its sad reality without "searching the depths of God". From the very beginning, the obscure mystery of sin has appeared in the world against the background of a reference to the Creator of human freedom. Sin has appeared as an act of the will of the creature-man *contrary* to the will of God, *to the salvific will of God*; indeed, sin has appeared in opposition to the truth, on the basis of the lie which has now been definitively "judged": the lie that has placed in a state of accusation, a state of permanent suspicion, creative and salvific love itself. Man has followed the "father of lies", setting himself up in opposition to the Father of life and the Spirit of truth.

Therefore, will not "convincing concerning sin" also have to mean *revealing suffering*? *Revealing the pain*, unimaginable and inexpressible, which on account of sin the Book of Genesis in its anthropomorphic vision seems to glimpse in the "depths of God" and in a certain sense in the very heart of the ineffable Trinity? The Church, taking her inspiration from Revelation, believes and professes that *sin is an offense against God*. What corresponds, in the inscrutable intimacy of the Father, the Word and the Holy Spirit, to this "offense", this rejection of the Spirit who is love and gift? The concept of God as the necessarily most perfect being certainly excludes from God any pain deriving from deficiencies or wounds; but in the "depths of God" there is a Father's love that, faced with man's sin, in the language of the Bible reacts so deeply as to say: "I am sorry that I have made him." "The Lord saw that the wickedness of man was great in the earth. . . . And *the Lord was sorry that he had made man on the earth*. . . . The Lord said: '*I am sorry that I have made them*.'" But more often the Sacred Book speaks to us of a Father who feels compassion for man, as though sharing his pain. In a word, this inscrutable and indescribable *fatherly "pain" will bring about* above all the wonderful *economy of redemptive love* in Jesus Christ, so that through the *mysterium pietatis* love can reveal itself in the history of man as stronger than sin. So that the "gift" may prevail!

The Holy Spirit who in the words of Jesus "convinces concerning sin" is the love of the Father and the Son, and as such is the Trinitarian gift, and at the same time the eternal source of every divine giving of gifts to creatures. Precisely in him we can picture as personified and actualized in a transcendent way that mercy which the Patristic and theological tradition, following the line of the Old and New Testaments, attributes to God. In man, mercy includes sorrow and compassion for the misfortunes of one's neighbor. In God, the Spirit-love expresses the consideration of human sin in a fresh outpouring of salvific love. From God, in the unity of the Father with the Son, the economy of salvation is born, the economy which fills the history of man with the gifts of the Redemption. Whereas sin, by rejecting love, has caused the "suffering" of man which in some way has affected the whole of creation, *the Holy Spirit* will enter into human and cosmic suffering with a new outpouring of love, which will redeem the world. And on the lips of Jesus the Redeemer, in whose humanity the "suffering" of God is concretized, there will be heard a word which manifests the eternal love full of mercy: "*Misereor*". Thus on the part of the Holy Spirit "convincing of sin" becomes a manifestation before creation, which is "subjected to futility", and above all in the depth of human consciences, that *sin* is *conquered through the sacrifice of the Lamb of God* who has become even "unto death" the *obedient servant* who, by making up for man's *disobedience*, accomplishes the redemption of the world. In this way the Spirit of truth, the Paraclete, "convinces concerning sin".

The redemptive value of Christ's sacrifice is expressed in very significant words by the author of the *Letter to the Hebrews*, who after recalling the sacrifices of the Old Covenant in which "the blood of goats and bulls . . ." purifies in "the flesh", adds: "How much more shall the blood of Christ, *who through the eternal spirit offered himself without blemish to God*, purify your conscience from dead works to serve the living God?". Though we are aware of other possible interpretations, our considerations on the presence of the Holy Spirit in the whole of Christ's life lead us to see this text as an invitation to reflect on the presence of the same Spirit also in the redemptive sacrifice of the Incarnate Word.

To begin with we reflect on the first words dealing with this sacrifice, and then separately on the "purification of conscience" which it accomplishes. For it is a sacrifice offered "*through the eternal Spirit*", that "derives" from it the power to "convince concerning sin". It is the same Holy Spirit, whom, according to the promise made in the Upper Room, *Jesus Christ* "will bring" to the Apostles on the day of his Resurrection, when he presents himself to them with the wounds of the crucifixion, and whom "he will give" them "*for the remission of sins*": "Receive the Holy Spirit; if you forgive the sins of any, they are forgiven."

We know that "God anointed Jesus of Nazareth with the Holy Spirit and with power", as Simon Peter said in the house of the centurion Cornelius. We know of the Paschal Mystery of his "departure", from the *Gospel of John*. The words of the

Letter to the Hebrews now explain to us how Christ "offered himself without blemish to God", and how he did this "with an eternal Spirit". In the sacrifice of the Son of Man the Holy Spirit is present and active just as he acted in Jesus' conception, in his coming into the world, in his hidden life and in his public ministry. According to the *Letter to the Hebrews*, on the way to his "departure" through Gethsemani and Golgotha, the same *Christ Jesus* in his own humanity *opened himself totally* to this *action of the Spirit-Paraclete*, who from suffering enables eternal salvific love to spring forth. Therefore he "was heard for his godly fear. Although he was a Son, he learned obedience through what he suffered." In this way *this Letter* shows how *humanity, subjected to sin* in the descendants of the first Adam, in Jesus Christ became *perfectly subjected to God* and united to him, and at the same time full of compassion towards men. Thus there is *a new humanity*, which in Jesus Christ through the suffering of the Cross has returned to the love which was betrayed by Adam through sin. This new humanity is discovered precisely in the divine source of the original outpouring of gifts: in the Spirit, who "searches . . . the depths of God" and is himself love and gift.

The Son of God Jesus Christ, as man, in the ardent prayer of his Passion, enabled the Holy Spirit, who had already penetrated the inmost depths of his humanity, *to transform that humanity into a perfect sacrifice* through the act of his death as the victim of love on the Cross. He made this offering by himself. As the one priest, "he offered himself without blemish to God". In his humanity he was worthy to become this sacrifice, for *he alone* was "without blemish". But he offered it "through the eternal Spirit", which means that the Holy Spirit acted in a special way in this absolute self-giving of the Son of Man, in order to transform this suffering into redemptive love.

The Old Testament on several occasions speaks of "fire from heaven" which burnt the oblations presented by men. By analogy one can say that the Holy Spirit is the *"fire from heaven" which works in the depth of the mystery of the Cross.* Proceeding from the Father, he directs towards the Father the sacrifice of the Son, bringing it into the *divine reality of the Trinitarian communion.* If sin caused suffering, now the pain of God in Christ crucified acquires through the Holy Spirit its full human expression. Thus there is a paradoxical mystery of love: in Christ there suffers a God who has been rejected by his own creature: "They do not believe in me!"; but at the same time, *from the depth* of this *suffering*—and indirectly from the depth of the very sin "of not having believed"—the Spirit *draws a new measure of the gift made to man and to creation* from the beginning. In the depth of the mystery of the Cross love is at work, that love which brings man back again to share in the life that is in God himself.

The Holy Spirit as Love and Gift *comes down, in a certain sense, into the very heart of the sacrifice* which is offered on the Cross. Referring here to the biblical tradition we can say: *he consumes this sacrifice with the fire of the love* which unites the Son with the Father in the Trinitarian communion. And since the sacrifice of the Cross is an act proper to Christ, also in this sacrifice he *"receives" the Holy Spirit.* He receives the Holy Spirit in such a way that afterwards—and he alone with God the Father—can *"give him" to the Apostles, to the Church, to humanity.* He alone "sends" the Spirit from the Father. He alone presents himself before the Apostles in the Upper Room, "breathes upon them" and says: "Receive the Holy Spirit; if you forgive the sins of any, they are forgiven", as John the Baptist had foretold: "He will baptize you with the Holy Spirit and with fire." With those words of Jesus the Holy Spirit is *revealed and at the same time made present* as the Love that works in the depths of the Paschal Mystery, as the source of the salvific power of the Cross of Christ, and as the gift of new and eternal life.

This truth about the Holy Spirit finds daily *expression in the Roman liturgy*, when before Communion the priest pronounces those significant words: "Lord Jesus Christ, Son of the living God, by the will of the Father *and the work of the Holy Spirit* your death brought life to the world. . . ." And in the Third Eucharistic Prayer, referring to the same salvific plan, the priest asks God that the Holy Spirit may "*make us an everlasting gift to you*".

We have said that, at the climax of the Paschal Mystery, the Holy Spirit is definitively revealed and made present in a new way. The Risen Christ says to the Apostles: "Receive the Holy Spirit." Thus the Holy Spirit is *revealed*, for the words of Christ constitute the confirmation of what he had promised and foretold during the discourse in the Upper Room. And with this the Paraclete is also *made present* in a new way. In fact, he was already at work from the beginning in the mystery of creation and throughout the history of the Old Covenant of God with man. His action was fully confirmed by the sending of the Son of Man as the Messiah, who came in the power of the Holy Spirit. At the climax of Jesus' messianic mission, the Holy Spirit becomes present in the Paschal Mystery *in all his divine subjectivity*: as the one who is now to continue the salvific work rooted in the sacrifice of the Cross. Of course Jesus entrusts this work to humanity: to the Apostles, to the Church. Nevertheless, in these men and through them the Holy Spirit remains the transcendent principal agent of the accomplishment of this work in the human spirit and in the history of the world: the invisible and at the same time omnipresent Paraclete! The Spirit who "blows where he wills".

The words of the Risen Christ on the "first day of the week" *give particular emphasis to the presence of the Paraclete-Counsellor* as the one who "convinces the world concerning sin, righteousness and judgment". For it is only in this relationship that it is possible to explain the words which Jesus directly relates to the "gift" of the Holy Spirit to the Apostles. He says: "Receive the Holy Spirit. If you forgive the sins of any, they are forgiven; if you retain the sins of any, they are retained." Jesus confers on the Apostles the power to forgive sins, so that they may pass it on to their successors in the Church. But this power granted to men presupposes and includes the saving action of the Holy Spirit. By becoming "the light of hearts", that is to say the light of consciences, the Holy Spirit "convinces concerning sin", which is to say, *he makes man realize his own evil* and at the same time *directs him towards what is good*. Thanks to the multiplicity of the Spirit's gifts, by reason of which he is invoked as the "sevenfold one", every kind of human sin can be reached by God's saving power. In reality—as Saint Bonaventure says—"by virtue of the seven gifts of the Holy Spirit all evils are destroyed and all good things are produced."

Thus *the conversion of the human heart*, which is an indispensable condition for the forgiveness of sins, is brought about by the influence of the Counsellor. Without a true conversion, which implies inner contrition, and without a sincere and firm purpose of amendment, sins remain "unforgiven", in the words of Jesus, and with him the Tradition of the Old and New Covenants. For the first words uttered by Jesus at the beginning of his ministry, according to the *Gospel of Mark*, are these: "Repent, and believe in the Gospel." A confirmation of this exhortation is the "convincing concerning sin" that the Holy Spirit undertakes in a new way by virtue of the Redemption accomplished by the Blood of the Son of Man. Hence the *Letter to the Hebrews* says that this "blood purifies the conscience". It therefore, so to speak, *opens to the Holy Spirit* the door into man's inmost being, namely into the sanctuary of human consciences.

The Second Vatican Council mentioned the Catholic teaching on conscience when it spoke about man's vocation and in particular about the dignity of the human person. It is precisely the *conscience* in particular which determines this dignity. For the conscience is "the *most secret core and sanctuary* of a man, where he is alone with God, whose voice echoes in his depths." It "can . . . speak to his heart more specifically: do this, shun that." This capacity to command what is good and to forbid evil, placed in man by the Creator, *is the main characteristic of the personal subject*. But at the same time, "in the depths of his conscience, man detects a law which he does not impose upon himself, but which holds him to obedience." The conscience therefore is not an independent and exclusive capacity to decide what is good and what is evil. Rather there is profoundly imprinted upon it *a principle of obedience* vis-à-vis the *objective norm* which establishes and conditions the correspondence of its decisions with the commands and prohibitions which are at the basis of human behavior, as from the passage of the *Book of Genesis* which we have already considered. Precisely in this sense the conscience is the "secret sanctuary" in which "*God's voice echoes*". The conscience is "the voice of God" even when man recognizes in it nothing more than the principle of the moral order which it is not humanly possible to doubt, even without any direct reference to the Creator. It is precisely in reference to this that the conscience always finds its foundation and justification.

The Gospel's "convincing concerning sin" under the influence of the Spirit of truth can be accomplished in man in no other way except *through the conscience*. If the conscience is upright, it serves "*to resolve according to truth* the moral problems which arise both in the life of individuals and from social relationships"; then "persons and groups turn aside from blind choice and try to be guided by the objective standards of moral conduct."

A result of an upright conscience is, first of all, *to call good and evil by their proper name*, as we read in the same Pastoral Constitution: "Whatever is opposed to life itself, such as any type of murder, genocide, abortion, euthanasia, or wilful self-destruction, whatever violates the integrity of the human person, such as mutilation, torments inflicted on body or mind, attempts to coerce the will itself; whatever insults human dignity, such as subhuman living conditions, arbitrary imprisonment, deportation, slavery, prostitution, the selling of women and children; as well as disgraceful working conditions, where people are treated as mere tools for profit, rather than as free and responsible persons"; and having called by name *the many different sins that are so frequent and widespread in our time*, the Constitution adds: "All these things and others of their kind are infamies indeed. They poison human society, but they do more harm to those who practice them than those who suffer from the injury. Moreover, they are a supreme dishonor to the Creator."

By calling by their proper name the sins that most dishonor man, and by showing that they are a moral evil that weighs negatively on any balance-sheet of human progress, the Council also describes all this as a stage in "a dramatic struggle between good and evil, between light and darkness", which characterizes "all of human life, whether individual or collective". The 1983 Assembly of the *Synod of Bishops* on reconciliation and penance specified even more clearly the personal and social significance of human sin.

In the Upper Room, on the eve of his Passion and again on the evening of Easter Day, Jesus Christ spoke of the Holy Spirit as the one who bears witness that *in human history sin continues to exist*. Yet sin has been *subjected* to the *saving power of the Redemption*. "Convincing the world concerning sin" does not end with the fact that sin is called by its right name and identified for what it is throughout its entire range. In convincing the world concerning sin *the Spirit of truth comes into contact with the voice of human consciences*.

By following this path we come *to a demonstration of the roots of sin*, which are to be found in man's inmost being, as described by the same Pastoral Constitution: "The truth is that the imbalances under which the modern world labors are linked with that more basic *imbalance* rooted *in the heart of man*. For in man himself many elements wrestle with one another. Thus, on the one hand, as a creature he experiences his limitations in a multitude of ways. On the other, he feels himself to be boundless in his desires and summoned to a higher life. Pulled by manifold attractions, he is constantly forced to choose among them and to renounce some. Indeed, as a weak and sinful being, *he often does what he would not, and fails to do what he would*." The Conciliar text is here referring to the well-known words of Saint Paul.

The "convincing concerning sin" which accompanies the human conscience in every careful reflection upon itself thus leads to the discovery of sin's roots in man, as also to the discovery of the way in which the conscience has been conditioned in the course of history. In this way we discover that original reality of sin of which we have already spoken. The *Holy Spirit "convinces concerning sin"* in relation to the mystery of man's origins, showing the fact that man is a *created being*, and therefore in complete ontological and ethical dependence upon the Creator. The Holy Spirit reminds us, at the same time, of the hereditary sinfulness of human nature. But the Holy Spirit the Counsellor "convinces concerning sin" *always in relation to the Cross of Christ*. In the context of this relationship Christianity rejects any "fatalism" regarding sin. As the Council teaches: "A monumental struggle against the powers of darkness pervades the whole history of man. The battle was joined from the very origins of the world and will continue until the last day, as the Lord has attested." "But *the Lord himself came to free and strengthen man*." Man, therefore, far from allowing himself to be "ensnared" in his sinful condition, by relying upon the voice of his own conscience "is obliged to wrestle constantly if he is to cling to what is good. Nor can he achieve his own interior integrity without valiant efforts and *the help of God's grace*." The Council rightly sees sin as *a factor of alienation* which weighs heavily on man's personal and social life. But at the same time it never tires of reminding us of the possibility of victory.

The Spirit of truth, who "convinces the world concerning sin", comes into contact with that laborious effort on the part of the human conscience which the Conciliar texts speak of so graphically. This *laborious effort of conscience* also determines the paths of human conversion: turning one's back on sin, in order to restore truth and love in man's very heart. We know that recognizing evil in ourselves sometimes demands a great effort. We know that *conscience* not only commands and forbids but also *judges* in the light of interior dictates and prohibitions. It is also the *source of remorse*: man suffers interiorly because of the evil he has committed. Is not this suffering as it were a distant echo of the "repentance at having created man" which in anthropomorphic language the Sacred Book attributes to God? Is it not an echo of that "reprobation" which is interiorized in the "heart" of the Trinity and by virtue of the eternal love is translated into the suffering of the Cross, into Christ's obedience unto death? When the Spirit of truth permits the human conscience *to share in that suffering*, the suffering of the conscience becomes particularly profound, but also particularly salvific. Then, by means of an act of perfect contrition, the authentic conversion of the heart is accomplished: this is the evangelical "metanoia".

The laborious effort of the human heart, the laborious effort of the conscience in which this "metanoia" or conversion takes place, is *a reflection* of that process whereby *reprobation is transformed into salvific love*, a love which is capable of suffering. The hidden giver of this saving power is the Holy Spirit: he whom the Church calls "the light of consciences" penetrates and fills "the depths of the human heart". Through just such a conversion in the Holy Spirit *a person becomes open to forgiveness, to the remission of sins*. And in all this wonderful dynamism of conversion-forgiveness there is confirmed the truth of what Saint Augustine writes concerning the mystery of man, when he comments on the words of the Psalm: "*The abyss calls to the abyss*." Precisely with regard to these "unfathomable depths" of man, of the human conscience, the mission of the Son and the Holy Spirit is accomplished. The *Holy Spirit "comes"* by virtue of Christ's "departure" in the Paschal Mystery: he comes in *each concrete case of conversion-forgiveness*, by virtue of the sacrifice of the Cross. For in this sacrifice "the blood of Christ . . . purifies your conscience from dead works to serve the living God." Thus there are continuously fulfilled the words about the Holy Spirit as "another Counsellor", the words spoken in the Upper Room to the Apostles and indirectly spoken to everyone: "You know him, for *he dwells with you* and will be in you".

Against the background of what has been said so far, certain other words of Jesus, shocking and disturbing ones, become easier to understand. We might call them *the words of "unforgiveness"*. They are reported for us by the Synoptics in connection with a particular sin which is called "blasphemy against the Holy Spirit". This is how they are reported in their three versions: *Matthew*: "Whoever says a word against the Son of Man will be forgiven; but whoever speaks against the Holy Spirit will not be forgiven, either in this age or in the age to come." *Mark*: "All sins will be forgiven the sons of men, and whatever blasphemies they utter; but whoever blasphemes against the Holy Spirit never has forgiveness, but is guilty of an eternal sin." *Luke*: "Every one who speaks a word against the Son of Man will be forgiven; but he who blasphemes against the Holy Spirit will not be forgiven."

Why is blasphemy against the Holy Spirit unforgivable? *How should this blasphemy be understood?* Saint Thomas Aquinas replies that it is a question of a sin that is "unforgivable by its very nature, insofar as it excludes the elements through which the forgiveness of sin takes place".

According to such an exegesis, "blasphemy" does not properly consist in offending against the Holy Spirit in words; it consists rather *in the refusal to accept the salvation which God offers to man through the Holy Spirit*, working through the power of the Cross. If man rejects the "convincing concerning sin" which comes from the Holy Spirit and which has the power to save, he also rejects the "coming" of the Counsellor—that "coming" which was accomplished in the Paschal Mystery, in union with the redemptive power of Christ's Blood: the Blood which "purifies the conscience from dead works."

We know that the result of such a purification is the forgiveness of sins. Therefore, whoever rejects the Spirit and the Blood remains in "dead works", in sin. And the blasphemy against the Holy Spirit consists precisely *in the radical refusal to accept this forgiveness*, of which he is the intimate giver and which presupposes the genuine conversion which he brings about in the conscience. If Jesus says that blasphemy against the Holy Spirit cannot be forgiven either in this life or in the next, it is because this "*non-forgiveness*" is linked, as to its cause, to "*non-repentance*", in other words to the radical refusal to be converted. This means the refusal to come to the sources of Redemption, which nevertheless remain "always" open in the economy of salvation in which the mission of the Holy Spirit is accomplished. The Spirit has infinite power to draw from these sources: "he will take what is mine", Jesus said. In this way he brings to completion in human souls the work of the Redemption accomplished by Christ, and distributes its fruits. Blasphemy against the Holy Spirit, then, is the sin committed by the person who claims to have a *"right" to persist in evil*—in any sin at all—and who thus rejects Redemption. One closes oneself up in sin, thus making impossible one's conversion, and consequently the remission of sins, which one considers not essential or not important for one's life. This is a state of spiritual ruin, because blasphemy against the Holy Spirit does not allow one to escape from one's self-imposed imprisonment and open oneself to the divine sources of the purification of consciences and of the remission of sins.

The action of the Spirit of truth, which works towards the salvific "convincing concerning sin", encounters in a person in this condition an interior resistance, as it were an impenetrability of conscience, a state of mind which could be described as fixed by reason of a free choice. This is what Sacred Scripture usually calls "hardness of heart". In our own time this attitude of mind and heart is perhaps reflected in *the loss of the sense of sin*, to which the Apostolic Exhortation *Reconciliatio et Paenitentia* devotes many pages. Pope Pius XII had already declared that "the sin of the century is the loss of the sense of sin", and this loss goes hand in hand with the "loss of the sense of God". In the Exhortation just mentioned we read: "In fact, God is the origin and the supreme end of man, and man carries in himself a divine seed. Hence it is the reality of God that reveals and illustrates the mystery of man. It is therefore vain to hope that there will take root a sense of sin against man and against human values, if there is no sense of offense against God, namely the true sense of sin."

Hence the Church constantly implores from God the grace that *integrity of human consciences* will not be lost, that their healthy *sensitivity* with regard to good and evil will not be blunted. This integrity and sensitivity are profoundly linked to the intimate action of the Spirit of truth. In this light the exhortations of Saint Paul assume particular eloquence: "*Do not quench the Spirit*"; "*Do not grieve the Holy Spirit.*" But above all the Church constantly implores with the greatest fervor *that there will be no increase* in the world of the sin that the Gospel calls "blasphemy against the Holy Spirit". Rather, she prays that it will *decrease* in human souls—and consequently in the forms and structures of society itself—and that it will make room for that openness of conscience necessary for the saving action of the Holy Spirit. The Church prays that the dangerous sin against the Spirit will give way to a holy readiness to accept his mission as the Counsellor, when he comes to "convince the world concerning sin, and righteousness and judgment".

In his farewell discourse Jesus linked these *three areas of "convincing"* as elements of the mission of the Paraclete: sin, righteousness and judgment. They mark out the area of that *mysterium pietatis* that in human history is opposed to sin, to the *mystery of iniquity*. On the one hand, as Saint Augustine says, there is "love of self to the point of contempt of God"; on the other, "love of God to the point of contempt of self". The Church constantly lifts up her prayer and renders her service in order that the history of consciences and the history of societies in the great human family *will not descend towards the pole of sin*, by the rejection of God's commandments "to the point of contempt of God", but rather *will rise towards the love* in which the Spirit that gives life is revealed.

Those who let themselves be "convinced concerning sin" by the Holy Spirit, also allow themselves to be convinced "concerning righteousness and judgment". The Spirit of truth who helps human beings, human consciences, to know *the truth concerning sin*, at the same time enables them to know *the truth about that righteousness* which entered human history in Jesus Christ. In this way, those who are "convinced concerning sin" and who are converted through the action of the Counsellor are, in a sense, led out of the range of the "judgment": that "judgment" by which "the ruler of this world is judged". In the depths of its divine-human mystery, conversion means the breaking of every fetter by which sin binds man to the whole of the *mystery of iniquity*. Those who are converted, therefore, are led by the Holy Spirit out of the range of the "judgment", and *introduced into that righteousness* which is in Christ Jesus, and is in him precisely because he receives it from the Father, as a reflection of the holiness of the Trinity. This is the righteousness of the Gospel and of the Redemption, the righteousness of the Sermon on the Mount and of the Cross, which effects the purifying of the conscience through the Blood of the Lamb. It is the righteousness which *the Father gives to the Son and to all those united with him in truth and in love.*

In this righteousness the Holy Spirit, the Spirit of the Father and the Son, who "convinces the world concerning sin", reveals himself and makes himself present in man as *the Spirit of eternal life.*

(1) **Tobit 12:8** Prayer is good when accompanied by fasting, almsgiving, and righteousness. A little with righteousness is better than much with wrongdoing. It is better to give alms than to treasure up gold. 1434

(2) **Matthew 6:1–18** "Beware of practicing your piety before men in order to be seen by them; for then you will have no reward from your Father who is in heaven. 1434

"Thus, when you give alms, sound no trumpet before you, as the hypocrites do in the synagogues and in the streets, that they may be praised by men. Truly, I say to you, they have received their reward. But when you give alms, do not let your left hand know what your right hand is doing, so that your alms may be in secret; and your Father who sees in secret will reward you.

"And when you pray, you must not be like the hypocrites; for they love to stand and pray in the synagogues and at the street corners, that they may be seen by men. Truly, I say to you, they have received their reward. But when you pray, go into your room and shut the door and pray to your Father who is in secret; and your Father who sees in secret will reward you.

"And in praying do not heap up empty phrases as the Gentiles do; for they think that they will be heard for their many words. Do not be like them, for your Father knows what you need before you ask him. Pray then like this:

Our Father who art in heaven,
Hallowed be thy name.
Thy kingdom come.
Thy will be done,
On earth as it is in heaven.
Give us this day our daily bread;
And forgive us our debts,
As we also have forgiven our debtors;
And lead us not into temptation,
But deliver us from evil.

For if you forgive men their trespasses, your heavenly Father also will forgive you; but if you do not forgive men their trespasses, neither will your Father forgive your trespasses.

"And when you fast, do not look dismal, like the hypocrites, for they disfigure their faces that their fasting may be seen by men. Truly, I say to you, they have received their reward. But when you fast, anoint your head and wash your face, that your fasting may not be seen by men but by your Father who is in secret; and your Father who sees in secret will reward you. . . ."

(3) **James 5:20** . . . let him know that whoever brings back a sinner from the error of his way will save his soul from death and will cover a multitude of sins. 1434

(1) **Amos 5:24** 1435

But let justice roll down like waters,
and righteousness like an ever-flowing stream.

1435 (2) **Isaiah 1:17**

. . . learn to do good;
seek justice,
correct oppression;
defend the fatherless,
plead for the widow.

1435 (3) **Luke 9:23** And he said to all, "If any man would come after me, let him deny himself and take up his cross daily and follow me. . . ."

1438 (1) ***Sacrosanctum concilium* 109–110** The two elements which are especially characteristic of Lent—the recalling of baptism or the preparation for it, and penance—should be given greater emphasis in the liturgy and in liturgical catechesis. It is by means of them that the Church prepares the faithful for the celebration of Easter, while they hear God's word more frequently and devote more time to prayer.

(a) More use is to be made of the baptismal features which are proper to the Lenten liturgy. Some of them which were part of an earlier tradition are to be restored where opportune.

(b) The same may be said of the penitential elements. But catechesis, as well as pointing out the social consequences of sin, must impress on the minds of the faithful the distinctive character of penance as a detestation of sin because it is an offense against God. The role of the Church in penitential practices is not to be passed over, and the need to pray for sinners should be emphasized.

During Lent, penance should be not only internal and individual but also external and social. The practice of penance should be encouraged in ways suited to the present day, to different regions, and to individual circumstances. It should be recommended by the authorities mentioned in Article 22.

But the paschal fast must be kept sacred. It should be celebrated everywhere on Good Friday, and where possible should be prolonged throughout Holy Saturday so that the faithful may attain the joys of the Sunday of the resurrection with uplifted and responsive minds.

1438 (2) **CIC Canons 1249–53**

Can. 1249—All members of the Christian faithful in their own way are bound to do penance in virtue of divine law; in order that all may be joined in a common observance of penance, penitential days are prescribed in which the Christian faithful in a special way pray, exercise works of piety and charity, and deny themselves by fulfilling their responsibilities more faithfully and especially by observing fast and abstinence according to the norm of the following canons.

Can. 1250—All Fridays through the year and the time of Lent are penitential days and times throughout the universal Church.

Can. 1251—Abstinence from eating meat or another food according to the prescriptions of the conference of bishops is to be observed on Fridays throughout the year unless they are solemnities; abstinence and fast are to be observed on Ash Wednesday and on the Friday of the Passion and Death of Our Lord Jesus Christ.

Can. 1252—All persons who have completed their fourteenth year are bound by the law of abstinence; all adults are bound by the law of fast up to the beginning of their sixtieth year. Nevertheless, pastors and parents are to see to it that minors who are not bound by the law of fast and abstinence are educated in an authentic sense of penance.

Can. 1253—It is for the conference of bishops to determine more precisely the observance of fast and abstinence and to substitute in whole or in part for fast and abstinence other forms of penance, especially works of charity and exercises of piety.

(3) **CCEO Canons 880–83** 1438

Can. 880—§1. Only the supreme authority of the Church can establish, transfer or suppress feast days and days of penance which are common to all of the Eastern Churches, with due regard for §3.

§2. The authority of a Church *sui iuris* which is competent to establish particular law can constitute, transfer or suppress feast days and days of penance for that Church *sui iuris*, however having sought the opinions of the other Churches *sui iuris* and with due regard for can. 40, §1.

§3. Holy days of obligation common to all the Eastern Churches, beyond Sundays, are the Nativity of our Lord Jesus Christ, the Epiphany, the Ascension, the Dormition of the Holy Mary Mother of God and the Holy Apostles Peter and Paul except for the particular law of a Church *sui iuris* approved by the Apostolic See which suppresses holy days of obligation or transfers them to a Sunday.

Can. 881—§1. The Christian faithful are bound by the obligation to participate on Sundays and feast days in the Divine Liturgy, or according to the prescriptions or legitimate customs of their own Church *sui iuris*, in the celebration of the divine praises.

§2. In order for the Christian faithful to fulfill this obligation more easily, the available time runs from the evening of the vigil until the end of the Sunday or feast day.

§3. The Christian faithful are strongly recommended to receive the Divine Eucharist on these days and indeed more frequently, even daily.

§4. The Christian faithful should abstain from those labors or business matters which impede the worship to be rendered to God, the joy which is proper to the Lord's day, or to the proper relaxation of mind and body.

Can. 882—On the days of penance the Christian faithful are obliged to observe fast or abstinence in the manner established by the particular law of their Church *sui iuris*.

Can. 883—§1. The Christian faithful who are outside the territorial boundaries of their own Church *sui iuris* can adopt fully for themselves the feast days and days of penance which are in force where they are staying.

§2. In families in which the parents are enrolled in different Churches *sui iuris*, it is permitted to observe the norms of one or the other Church, in regard to feast days and days of penance.

Luke 15:11–24 And he said, "There was a man who had two sons; and the younger 1439
of them said to his father, 'Father, give me the share of property that falls to me.' And he divided his living between them. Not many days later, the younger son gathered all he had and took his journey into a far country, and there he squandered his property in loose living. And when he had spent everything, a great famine arose in that country, and he began to be in want. So he went and joined himself to one of the citizens of that country, who sent him into his fields to feed swine. And he would gladly have fed on the pods that the swine ate; and no one gave him anything. But when he came to himself he said, 'How many of my father's hired servants have bread enough and to spare, but I perish here with hunger! I will arise and go to my father, and I will say to him, "Father, I have sinned against heaven and before you; I am no longer worthy to be called your son; treat me as one of your hired servants."' And he arose and came to his father. But while he was yet at a distance, his father saw him

and had compassion, and ran and embraced him and kissed him. And the son said to him, 'Father, I have sinned against heaven and before you; I am no longer worthy to be called your son.' But the father said to his servants, 'Bring quickly the best robe, and put it on him; and put a ring on his hand, and shoes on his feet; and bring the fatted calf and kill it, and let us eat and make merry; for this my son was dead, and is alive again; he was lost, and is found.' And they began to make merry. . . ."

1440 ***Lumen gentium* 11:** see 1303 (1).

1441 (1) **Mark 2:7** "Why does this man speak thus? It is blasphemy! Who can forgive sins but God alone?"

1441 (2) **John 20:21–23** Jesus said to them again, "Peace be with you. As the Father has sent me, even so I send you." And when he had said this, he breathed on them, and said to them, "Receive the Holy Spirit. . . ."

1443 (1) **Luke 15** Now the tax collectors and sinners were all drawing near to hear him. And the Pharisees and the scribes murmured, saying, "This man receives sinners and eats with them."

So he told them this parable: "What man of you, having a hundred sheep, if he has lost one of them, does not leave the ninety-nine in the wilderness, and go after the one which is lost, until he finds it? And when he has found it, he lays it on his shoulders, rejoicing. And when he comes home, he calls together his friends and his neighbors, saying to them, 'Rejoice with me, for I have found my sheep which was lost.' Just so, I tell you, there will be more joy in heaven over one sinner who repents than over ninety-nine righteous persons who need no repentance.

"Or what woman, having ten silver coins, if she loses one coin, does not light a lamp and sweep the house and seek diligently until she finds it? And when she has found it, she calls together her friends and neighbors, saying, 'Rejoice with me, for I have found the coin which I had lost.' Just so, I tell you, there is joy before the angels of God over one sinner who repents."

And he said, "There was a man who had two sons; and the younger of them said to his father, 'Father, give me the share of property that falls to me.' And he divided his living between them. Not many days later, the younger son gathered all he had and took his journey into a far country, and there he squandered his property in loose living. And when he had spent everything, a great famine arose in that country, and he began to be in want. So he went and joined himself to one of the citizens of that country, who sent him into his fields to feed swine. And he would gladly have fed on the pods that the swine ate; and no one gave him anything. But when he came to himself he said, 'How many of my father's hired servants have bread enough and to spare, but I perish here with hunger! I will arise and go to my father, and I will say to him, "Father, I have sinned against heaven and before you; I am no longer worthy to be called your son; treat me as one of your hired servants."' And he arose and came to his father. But while he was yet at a distance, his father saw him and had compassion, and ran and embraced him and kissed him. And the son said to him, 'Father, I have sinned against heaven and before you; I am no longer worthy to be called your son.' But the father said to his servants, 'Bring quickly the best robe, and put it on him; and put a ring on his hand, and shoes on his feet; and bring the fatted calf and kill it, and let us eat and make merry; for this my son was dead, and is alive again; he was lost, and is found.' And they began to make merry.

"Now his elder son was in the field; and as he came and drew near to the house, he heard music and dancing. And he called one of the servants and asked what this meant. And he said to him, 'Your brother has come, and your father has killed the fatted calf, because he has received him safe and sound.' But he was angry and refused to go in. His father came out and entreated him, but he answered his father, 'Lo, these many years I have served you, and I never disobeyed your command; yet you never gave me a kid, that I might make merry with my friends. But when this son of yours came, who has devoured your living with harlots, you killed for him the fatted calf!' And he said to him, 'Son, you are always with me, and all that is mine is yours. It was fitting to make merry and be glad, for this your brother was dead, and is alive; he was lost, and is found.'"

(2) **Luke 19:9** And Jesus said to him, "Today salvation has come to this house, 1443
since he also is a son of Abraham. . . ."

(1) **Matthew 18:18** Truly, I say to you, whatever you bind on earth shall be bound 1444
in heaven, and whatever you loose on earth shall be loosed in heaven.

(2) **Matthew 28:16–20** Now the eleven disciples went to Galilee, to the mountain 1444
to which Jesus had directed them. And when they saw him they worshiped him; but some doubted. And Jesus came and said to them, "All authority in heaven and on earth has been given to me. Go therefore and make disciples of all nations, baptizing them in the name of the Father and of the Son and of the Holy Spirit, teaching them to observe all that I have commanded you; and lo, I am with you always, to the close of the age."

Council of Trent (1547): DS 1542 Those who by sin have fallen away from the 1446
received grace of justification, will again be able to be justified [can. 29] when, roused by God through the sacrament of penance, they by the merit of Christ shall have attended to the recovery of the grace lost. For this manner of justification is the reparation of one fallen, which the holy Fathers have aptly called a second plank after the shipwreck of lost grace. For on behalf of those who after baptism fall into sin, Christ Jesus instituted the sacrament of penance, when He said: "Receive ye the Holy Ghost; whose sins you shall forgive, they are forgiven them, and whose sins you shall retain, they are retained" [I John 20:22, 23].

Council of Trent (1551): DS 1673 Furthermore, the holy Council teaches that 1450
the form of the sacrament of penance, in which its force chiefly consists, is set down in these words of the minister: "I absolve thee, etc."; to which indeed certain prayers are laudably added according to the custom of holy Church; yet in no way do they pertain to the essence of this form, nor are they necessary for the administration of the sacrament. The matter, as it were, of this sacrament, on the other hand, consists in the acts of the penitent himself, namely contrition, confession, and satisfaction [can. 4]. These, inasmuch as by the institution of God they are required in the penitent for the integrity of the sacrament for the full and perfect remission of sins, are for this reason called the parts of penance.

Council of Trent (1551): DS 1677 The Council teaches, furthermore, that though 1452
it sometimes happens that this contrition is perfect because of charity and reconciles man to God, before this sacrament is actually received, this reconciliation nevertheless must not be ascribed to the contrition itself without the desire of the sacrament which is included in it.

(1) **Council of Trent (1551): DS 1678** That imperfect contrition [can. 5] which is 1453
called attrition, since it commonly arises either from the consideration of the baseness

of sin or from fear of hell and its punishments, if it renounces the desire of sinning with the hope of pardon, the Synod declares, not only does not make a person a hypocrite and a greater sinner, but is even a gift of God and an impulse of the Holy Spirit, not indeed as already dwelling in the penitent, but only moving him, assisted by which the penitent prepares a way for himself unto justice. And though without the sacrament of penance it cannot *per se* lead the sinner to justification, nevertheless it does dispose him to obtain the grace of God in the sacrament of penance. For the Ninivites, struck in a salutary way by this fear in consequence of the preaching of Jonas which was full of terror, did penance and obtained mercy from the Lord [cf. Jonas 3]. For this reason, therefore, do some falsely accuse Catholic writers, as if they taught that the sacrament of penance confers grace without any pious endeavor on the part of those who receive it, a thing which the Church of God has never taught or pronounced. Moreover, they also falsely teach that contrition is extorted and forced, and that it is not free and voluntary [can. 5].

1453 (2) **Council of Trent (1551): DS 1705** If anyone says that this contrition, which is evoked by examination, recollection, and hatred of sins "whereby one recalls his years in the bitterness of his soul" [Isa. 38:15], by pondering on the gravity of one's sins, the multitude, the baseness, the loss of eternal happiness, and the incurring of eternal damnation, together with the purpose of a better life, is not a true and a beneficial sorrow, and does not prepare for grace, but makes a man a hypocrite, and a greater sinner; finally that this sorrow is forced and not free and voluntary: let him be anathema.

1454 (1) **Matthew 5–7** Seeing the crowds, he went up on the mountain, and when he sat down his disciples came to him. And he opened his mouth and taught them, saying:

"Blessed are the poor in spirit, for theirs is the kingdom of heaven.

"Blessed are those who mourn, for they shall be comforted.

"Blessed are the meek, for they shall inherit the earth.

"Blessed are those who hunger and thirst for righteousness, for they shall be satisfied.

"Blessed are the merciful, for they shall obtain mercy.

"Blessed are the pure in heart, for they shall see God.

"Blessed are the peacemakers, for they shall be called sons of God.

"Blessed are those who are persecuted for righteousness' sake, for theirs is the kingdom of heaven.

"Blessed are you when men revile you and persecute you and utter all kinds of evil against you falsely on my account. Rejoice and be glad, for your reward is great in heaven, for so men persecuted the prophets who were before you.

"You are the salt of the earth; but if salt has lost its taste, how shall its saltness be restored? It is no longer good for anything except to be thrown out and trodden under foot by men.

"You are the light of the world. A city set on a hill cannot be hid. Nor do men light a lamp and put it under a bushel, but on a stand, and it gives light to all in the house. Let your light so shine before men, that they may see your good works and give glory to your Father who is in heaven.

"Think not that I have come to abolish the law and the prophets; I have come not to abolish them but to fulfil them. For truly, I say to you, till heaven and earth pass away, not an iota, not a dot, will pass from the law until all is accomplished. Whoever then relaxes one of the least of these commandments and teaches men so, shall be called least in the kingdom of heaven; but he who does them and teaches them shall be called great in the kingdom of heaven. For I tell you, unless your righteousness exceeds that of the scribes and Pharisees, you will never enter the kingdom of heaven.

"You have heard that it was said to the men of old, 'You shall not kill; and whoever kills shall be liable to judgment.' But I say to you that every one who is angry with his brother shall be liable to judgment; whoever insults his brother shall be liable to the council, and whoever says, 'You fool!' shall be liable to the hell of fire. So if you are offering your gift at the altar, and there remember that your brother has something against you, leave your gift there before the altar and go; first be reconciled to your brother, and then come and offer your gift. Make friends quickly with your accuser, while you are going with him to court, lest your accuser hand you over to the judge, and the judge to the guard, and you be put in prison; truly, I say to you, you will never get out till you have paid the last penny.

"You have heard that it was said, 'You shall not commit adultery.' But I say to you that every one who looks at a woman lustfully has already committed adultery with her in his heart. If your right eye causes you to sin, pluck it out and throw it away; it is better that you lose one of your members than that your whole body be thrown into hell. And if your right hand causes you to sin, cut it off and throw it away; it is better that you lose one of your members than that your whole body go into hell.

"It was also said, 'Whoever divorces his wife, let him give her a certificate of divorce.' But I say to you that every one who divorces his wife, except on the ground of unchastity, makes her an adulteress; and whoever marries a divorced woman commits adultery.

"Again you have heard that it was said to the men of old, 'You shall not swear falsely, but shall perform to the Lord what you have sworn.' But I say to you, Do not swear at all, either by heaven, for it is the throne of God, or by the earth, for it is his footstool, or by Jerusalem, for it is the city of the great King. And do not swear by your head, for you cannot make one hair white or black. Let what you say be simply 'Yes' or 'No'; anything more than this comes from evil.

"You have heard that it was said, 'An eye for an eye and a tooth for a tooth.' But I say to you, Do not resist one who is evil. But if any one strikes you on the right cheek, turn to him the other also; and if any one would sue you and take your coat, let him have your cloak as well; and if any one forces you to go one mile, go with him two miles. Give to him who begs from you, and do not refuse him who would borrow from you.

"You have heard that it was said, 'You shall love your neighbor and hate your enemy.' But I say to you, Love your enemies and pray for those who persecute you, so that you may be sons of your Father who is in heaven; for he makes his sun rise on the evil and on the good, and sends rain on the just and on the unjust. For if you love those who love you, what reward have you? Do not even the tax collectors do the same? And if you salute only your brethren, what more are you doing than others? Do not even the Gentiles do the same? You, therefore, must be perfect, as your heavenly Father is perfect.

"Beware of practicing your piety before men in order to be seen by them; for then you will have no reward from your Father who is in heaven.

"Thus, when you give alms, sound no trumpet before you, as the hypocrites do in the synagogues and in the streets, that they may be praised by men. Truly, I say to you, they have received their reward. But when you give alms, do not let your left hand know what your right hand is doing, so that your alms may be in secret; and your Father who sees in secret will reward you.

"And when you pray, you must not be like the hypocrites; for they love to stand and pray in the synagogues and at the street corners, that they may be seen by men. Truly, I say to you, they have received their reward. But when you pray, go into your room and shut the door and pray to your Father who is in secret; and your Father who sees in secret will reward you.

"And in praying do not heap up empty phrases as the Gentiles do; for they think that they will be heard for their many words. Do not be like them, for your Father knows what you need before you ask him. Pray then like this:

Our Father who art in heaven,
Hallowed be thy name.
Thy kingdom come.
Thy will be done,
On earth as it is in heaven.
Give us this day our daily bread;
And forgive us our debts,
As we also have forgiven our debtors;
And lead us not into temptation,
But deliver us from evil.

For if you forgive men their trespasses, your heavenly Father also will forgive you; but if you do not forgive men their trespasses, neither will your Father forgive your trespasses.

"And when you fast, do not look dismal, like the hypocrites, for they disfigure their faces that their fasting may be seen by men. Truly, I say to you, they have received their reward. But when you fast, anoint your head and wash your face, that your fasting may not be seen by men but by your Father who is in secret; and your Father who sees in secret will reward you.

"Do not lay up for yourselves treasures on earth, where moth and rust consume and where thieves break in and steal, but lay up for yourselves treasures in heaven, where neither moth nor rust consumes and where thieves do not break in and steal. For where your treasure is, there will your heart be also.

"The eye is the lamp of the body. So, if your eye is sound, your whole body will be full of light; but if your eye is not sound, your whole body will be full of darkness. If then the light in you is darkness, how great is the darkness!

"No one can serve two masters; for either he will hate the one and love the other, or he will be devoted to the one and despise the other. You cannot serve God and mammon.

"Therefore I tell you, do not be anxious about your life, what you shall eat or what you shall drink, nor about your body, what you shall put on. Is not life more than food, and the body more than clothing? Look at the birds of the air: they neither sow nor reap nor gather into barns, and yet your heavenly Father feeds them. Are you not of more value than they? And which of you by being anxious can add one cubit to his span of life? And why are you anxious about clothing? Consider the lilies of the field, how they grow; they neither toil nor spin; yet I tell you, even Solomon in all his glory was not arrayed like one of these. But if God so clothes the grass of the field, which today is alive and tomorrow is thrown into the oven, will he not much more clothe you, O men of little faith? Therefore do not be anxious, saying, 'What shall we eat?' or 'What shall we drink?' or 'What shall we wear?' For the Gentiles seek all these things; and your heavenly Father knows that you need them all. But seek first his kingdom and his righteousness, and all these things shall be yours as well.

"Therefore do not be anxious about tomorrow, for tomorrow will be anxious for itself. Let the day's own trouble be sufficient for the day.

"Judge not, that you be not judged. For with the judgment you pronounce you will be judged, and the measure you give will be the measure you get. Why do you see the speck that is in your brother's eye, but do not notice the log that is in your own eye? Or how can you say to your brother, 'Let me take the speck out of your eye,' when there is the log in your own eye? You hypocrite, first take the log out of your own eye, and then you will see clearly to take the speck out of your brother's eye.

"Do not give dogs what is holy; and do not throw your pearls before swine, lest they trample them under foot and turn to attack you.

"Ask, and it will be given you; seek, and you will find; knock, and it will be opened to you. For every one who asks receives, and he who seeks finds, and to him who knocks it will be opened. Or what man of you, if his son asks him for bread, will give him a stone? Or if he asks for a fish, will give him a serpent? If you then, who are evil, know how to give good gifts to your children, how much more will your Father who is in heaven give good things to those who ask him! So whatever you wish that men would do to you, do so to them; for this is the law and the prophets.

"Enter by the narrow gate; for the gate is wide and the way is easy, that leads to destruction, and those who enter by it are many. For the gate is narrow and the way is hard, that leads to life, and those who find it are few.

"Beware of false prophets, who come to you in sheep's clothing but inwardly are ravenous wolves. You will know them by their fruits. Are grapes gathered from thorns, or figs from thistles? So, every sound tree bears good fruit, but the bad tree bears evil fruit. A sound tree cannot bear evil fruit, nor can a bad tree bear good fruit. Every tree that does not bear good fruit is cut down and thrown into the fire. Thus you will know them by their fruits.

"Not every one who says to me, 'Lord, Lord,' shall enter the kingdom of heaven, but he who does the will of my Father who is in heaven. On that day many will say to me, 'Lord, Lord, did we not prophesy in your name, and cast out demons in your name, and do many mighty works in your name?' And then will I declare to them, 'I never knew you; depart from me, you evildoers.'

"Every one then who hears these words of mine and does them will be like a wise man who built his house upon the rock; and the rain fell, and the floods came, and the winds blew and beat upon that house, but it did not fall, because it had been founded on the rock. And every one who hears these words of mine and does not do them will be like a foolish man who built his house upon the sand; and the rain fell, and the floods came, and the winds blew and beat against that house, and it fell; and great was the fall of it."

And when Jesus finished these sayings, the crowds were astonished at his teaching, for he taught them as one who had authority, and not as their scribes.

(2) **Romans 12–15** I appeal to you therefore, brethren, by the mercies of God, 1454
to present your bodies as a living sacrifice, holy and acceptable to God, which is your spiritual worship. Do not be conformed to this world but be transformed by the renewal of your mind, that you may prove what is the will of God, what is good and acceptable and perfect.

For by the grace given to me I bid every one among you not to think of himself more highly than he ought to think, but to think with sober judgment, each according to the measure of faith which God has assigned him. For as in one body we have many members, and all the members do not have the same function, so we, though many, are one body in Christ, and individually members one of another. Having gifts that differ according to the grace given to us, let us use them: if prophecy, in proportion to our faith; if service, in our serving; he who teaches, in his teaching; he who exhorts, in his exhortation; he who contributes, in liberality; he who gives aid, with zeal; he who does acts of mercy, with cheerfulness.

Let love be genuine; hate what is evil, hold fast to what is good; love one another with brotherly affection; outdo one another in showing honor. Never flag in zeal, be aglow with the Spirit, serve the Lord. Rejoice in your hope, be patient in tribulation, be constant in prayer. Contribute to the needs of the saints, practice hospitality.

Bless those who persecute you; bless and do not curse them. Rejoice with those who rejoice, weep with those who weep. Live in harmony with one another; do not be haughty, but associate with the lowly; never be conceited. Repay no one evil for evil, but take thought for what is noble in the sight of all. If possible, so far as it depends upon you, live peaceably with all. Beloved, never avenge yourselves, but leave it to the wrath of God; for it is written, "Vengeance is mine, I will repay, says the Lord." No, "if your enemy is hungry, feed him; if he is thirsty, give him drink; for by doing so you will heap burning coals upon his head." Do not be overcome by evil, but overcome evil with good.

Let every person be subject to the governing authorities. For there is no authority except from God, and those that exist have been instituted by God. Therefore he who resists the authorities resists what God has appointed, and those who resist will incur judgment. For rulers are not a terror to good conduct, but to bad. Would you have no fear of him who is in authority? Then do what is good, and you will receive his approval, for he is God's servant for your good. But if you do wrong, be afraid, for he does not bear the sword in vain; he is the servant of God to execute his wrath on the wrongdoer. Therefore one must be subject, not only to avoid God's wrath but also for the sake of conscience. For the same reason you also pay taxes, for the authorities are ministers of God, attending to this very thing. Pay all of them their dues, taxes to whom taxes are due, revenue to whom revenue is due, respect to whom respect is due, honor to whom honor is due.

Owe no one anything, except to love one another; for he who loves his neighbor has fulfilled the law. The commandments, "You shall not commit adultery, You shall not kill, You shall not steal, You shall not covet," and any other commandment, are summed up in this sentence, "You shall love your neighbor as yourself." Love does no wrong to a neighbor; therefore love is the fulfilling of the law.

Besides this you know what hour it is, how it is full time now for you to wake from sleep. For salvation is nearer to us now than when we first believed; the night is far gone, the day is at hand. Let us then cast off the works of darkness and put on the armor of light; let us conduct ourselves becomingly as in the day, not in reveling and drunkenness, not in debauchery and licentiousness, not in quarreling and jealousy. But put on the Lord Jesus Christ, and make no provision for the flesh, to gratify its desires.

As for the man who is weak in faith, welcome him, but not for disputes over opinions. One believes he may eat anything, while the weak man eats only vegetables. Let not him who eats despise him who abstains, and let not him who abstains pass judgment on him who eats; for God has welcomed him. Who are you to pass judgment on the servant of another? It is before his own master that he stands or falls. And he will be upheld, for the Master is able to make him stand.

One man esteems one day as better than another, while another man esteems all days alike. Let every one be fully convinced in his own mind. He who observes the day, observes it in honor of the Lord. He also who eats, eats in honor of the Lord, since he gives thanks to God; while he who abstains, abstains in honor of the Lord and gives thanks to God. None of us lives to himself, and none of us dies to himself. If we live, we live to the Lord, and if we die, we die to the Lord; so then, whether we live or whether we die, we are the Lord's. For to this end Christ died and lived again, that he might be Lord both of the dead and of the living.

Why do you pass judgment on your brother? Or you, why do you despise your brother? For we shall all stand before the judgment seat of God; for it is written,

"As I live, says the Lord, every knee shall bow to me,
and every tongue shall give praise to God."

So each of us shall give account of himself to God.

Then let us no more pass judgment on one another, but rather decide never to put a stumbling block or hindrance in the way of a brother. I know and am persuaded in the Lord Jesus that nothing is unclean in itself; but it is unclean for any one who thinks it unclean. If your brother is being injured by what you eat, you are no longer walking in love. Do not let what you eat cause the ruin of one for whom Christ died. So do not let your good be spoken of as evil. For the kingdom of God is not food and drink but righteousness and peace and joy in the Holy Spirit; he who thus serves Christ is acceptable to God and approved by men. Let us then pursue what makes for peace and for mutual upbuilding. Do not, for the sake of food, destroy the work of God. Everything is indeed clean, but it is wrong for any one to make others fall by what he eats; it is right not to eat meat or drink wine or do anything that makes your brother stumble. The faith that you have, keep between yourself and God; happy is he who has no reason to judge himself for what he approves. But he who has doubts is condemned, if he eats, because he does not act from faith; for whatever does not proceed from faith is sin.

We who are strong ought to bear with the failings of the weak, and not to please ourselves; let each of us please his neighbor for his good, to edify him. For Christ did not please himself; but, as it is written, "The reproaches of those who reproached thee fell on me." For whatever was written in former days was written for our instruction, that by steadfastness and by the encouragement of the scriptures we might have hope. May the God of steadfastness and encouragement grant you to live in such harmony with one another, in accord with Christ Jesus, that together you may with one voice glorify the God and Father of our Lord Jesus Christ.

Welcome one another, therefore, as Christ has welcomed you, for the glory of God. For I tell you that Christ became a servant to the circumcised to show God's truthfulness, in order to confirm the promises given to the patriarchs, and in order that the Gentiles might glorify God for his mercy. As it is written,

"Therefore I will praise thee among the Gentiles,
and sing to thy name";

and again it is said,

"Rejoice, O Gentiles, with his people";

and again,

"Praise the Lord, all Gentiles,
and let all the peoples praise him";

and further Isaiah says,

"The root of Jesse shall come,
he who rises to rule the Gentiles;
in him shall the Gentiles hope."

May the God of hope fill you with all joy and peace in believing, so that by the power of the Holy Spirit you may abound in hope.

I myself am satisfied about you, my brethren, that you yourselves are full of goodness, filled with all knowledge, and able to instruct one another. But on some points I have written to you very boldly by way of reminder, because of the grace given me by God to be a minister of Christ Jesus to the Gentiles in the priestly service of the gospel of God, so that the offering of the Gentiles may be acceptable, sanctified by the Holy Spirit. In Christ Jesus, then, I have reason to be proud of my work for God. For I will not venture to speak of anything except what Christ has wrought through me to win obedience from the Gentiles, by word and deed, by the power of signs and wonders, by the power of the Holy Spirit, so that from Jerusalem and as far round as

Illyricum I have fully preached the gospel of Christ, thus making it my ambition to preach the gospel, not where Christ has already been named, lest I build on another man's foundation, but as it is written,

"They shall see who have never been told of him,
and they shall understand who have never heard of him."

This is the reason why I have so often been hindered from coming to you. But now, since I no longer have any room for work in these regions, and since I have longed for many years to come to you, I hope to see you in passing as I go to Spain, and to be sped on my journey there by you, once I have enjoyed your company for a little. At present, however, I am going to Jerusalem with aid for the saints. For Macedonia and Achaia have been pleased to make some contribution for the poor among the saints at Jerusalem; they were pleased to do it, and indeed they are in debt to them, for if the Gentiles have come to share in their spiritual blessings, they ought also to be of service to them in material blessings. When therefore I have completed this, and have delivered to them what has been raised, I shall go on by way of you to Spain; and I know that when I come to you I shall come in the fulness of the blessing of Christ.

I appeal to you, brethren, by our Lord Jesus Christ and by the love of the Spirit, to strive together with me in your prayers to God on my behalf, that I may be delivered from the unbelievers in Judea, and that my service for Jerusalem may be acceptable to the saints, so that by God's will I may come to you with joy and be refreshed in your company. The God of peace be with you all. Amen.

1454 (3) **1 Corinthians 12–13** Now concerning spiritual gifts, brethren, I do not want you to be uninformed. You know that when you were heathen, you were led astray to dumb idols, however you may have been moved. Therefore I want you to understand that no one speaking by the Spirit of God ever says "Jesus be cursed!" and no one can say "Jesus is Lord" except by the Holy Spirit.

Now there are varieties of gifts, but the same Spirit; and there are varieties of service, but the same Lord; and there are varieties of working, but it is the same God who inspires them all in every one. To each is given the manifestation of the Spirit for the common good. To one is given through the Spirit the utterance of wisdom, and to another the utterance of knowledge according to the same Spirit, to another faith by the same Spirit, to another gifts of healing by the one Spirit, to another the working of miracles, to another prophecy, to another the ability to distinguish between spirits, to another various kinds of tongues, to another the interpretation of tongues. All these are inspired by one and the same Spirit, who apportions to each one individually as he wills.

For just as the body is one and has many members, and all the members of the body, though many, are one body, so it is with Christ. For by one Spirit we were all baptized into one body—Jews or Greeks, slaves or free—and all were made to drink of one Spirit.

For the body does not consist of one member but of many. If the foot should say, "Because I am not a hand, I do not belong to the body," that would not make it any less a part of the body. And if the ear should say, "Because I am not an eye, I do not belong to the body," that would not make it any less a part of the body. If the whole body were an eye, where would be the hearing? If the whole body were an ear, where would be the sense of smell? But as it is, God arranged the organs in the body, each one of them, as he chose. If all were a single organ, where would the body be? As it is, there are many parts, yet one body. The eye cannot say to the hand, "I have no need of you," nor again the head to the feet, "I have no need of you." On the contrary, the parts of the body which seem to be weaker are indispensable, and those parts of the body which we think less honorable we invest with the greater honor, and our unpresentable parts are treated with greater modesty, which our more presentable parts do not require. But God has so composed the body, giving the greater honor to the inferior part, that there may be no discord in the body, but that the members may have the same care for one another. If one member suffers, all suffer together; if one member is honored, all rejoice together.

Now you are the body of Christ and individually members of it. And God has appointed in the church first apostles, second prophets, third teachers, then workers of miracles, then healers, helpers, administrators, speakers in various kinds of tongues. Are all apostles? Are all prophets? Are all teachers? Do all work miracles? Do all possess gifts of healing? Do all speak with tongues? Do all interpret? But earnestly desire the higher gifts.

And I will show you a still more excellent way.

If I speak in the tongues of men and of angels, but have not love, I am a noisy gong or a clanging cymbal. And if I have prophetic powers, and understand all mysteries and all knowledge, and if I have all faith, so as to remove mountains, but have not love, I am nothing. If I give away all I have, and if I deliver my body to be burned, but have not love, I gain nothing.

Love is patient and kind; love is not jealous or boastful; it is not arrogant or rude. Love does not insist on its own way; it is not irritable or resentful; it does not rejoice at wrong, but rejoices in the right. Love bears all things, believes all things, hopes all things, endures all things.

Love never ends; as for prophecies, they will pass away; as for tongues, they will cease; as for knowledge, it will pass away. For our knowledge is imperfect and our prophecy is imperfect; but when the perfect comes, the imperfect will pass away. When I was a child, I spoke like a child, I thought like a child, I reasoned like a child; when I became a man, I gave up childish ways. For now we see in a mirror dimly, but then face to face. Now I know in part; then I shall understand fully, even as I have been fully understood. So faith, hope, love abide, these three; but the greatest of these is love.

(4) **Galatians 5** For freedom Christ has set us free; stand fast therefore, and do not 1454
submit again to a yoke of slavery.

Now I, Paul, say to you that if you receive circumcision, Christ will be of no advantage to you. I testify again to every man who receives circumcision that he is bound to keep the whole law. You are severed from Christ, you who would be justified by the law; you have fallen away from grace. For through the Spirit, by faith, we wait for the hope of righteousness. For in Christ Jesus neither circumcision nor uncircumcision is of any avail, but faith working through love. You were running well; who hindered you from obeying the truth? This persuasion is not from him who calls you. A little leaven leavens the whole lump. I have confidence in the Lord that you will take no other view than mine; and he who is troubling you will bear his judgment, whoever he is. But if I, brethren, still preach circumcision, why am I still persecuted? In that case the stumbling block of the cross has been removed. I wish those who unsettle you would mutilate themselves!

For you were called to freedom, brethren; only do not use your freedom as an opportunity for the flesh, but through love be servants of one another. For the whole law is fulfilled in one word, "You shall love your neighbor as yourself." But if you bite and devour one another take heed that you are not consumed by one another.

But I say, walk by the Spirit, and do not gratify the desires of the flesh. For the desires of the flesh are against the Spirit, and the desires of the Spirit are against the flesh; for these are opposed to each other, to prevent you from doing what you would. But if you are led by the Spirit you are not under the law. Now the works of the flesh are plain: fornication, impurity, licentiousness, idolatry, sorcery, enmity, strife, jealousy, anger, selfishness, dissension, party spirit, envy, drunkenness, carousing, and the like. I warn you, as I warned you before, that those who do such things shall not inherit the kingdom of God. But the fruit of the Spirit is love, joy, peace, patience, kindness, goodness, faithfulness, gentleness, self-control; against such there is no law. And those who belong to Christ Jesus have crucified the flesh with its passions and desires.

If we live by the Spirit, let us also walk by the Spirit. Let us have no self-conceit, no provoking of one another, no envy of one another.

1454 (5) **Ephesians 4–6** I therefore, a prisoner for the Lord, beg you to lead a life worthy of the calling to which you have been called, with all lowliness and meekness, with patience, forbearing one another in love, eager to maintain the unity of the Spirit in the bond of peace. There is one body and one Spirit, just as you were called to the one hope that belongs to your call, one Lord, one faith, one baptism, one God and Father of us all, who is above all and through all and in all. But the grace was given to each of us according to the measure of Christ's gift. Therefore it is said,

"When he ascended on high he led a host of captives,
and he gave gifts to men."

(In saying, "He ascended," what does it mean but that he had also descended into the lower parts of the earth? He who descended is he who also ascended far above all the heavens, that he might fill all things.) And his gifts were that some should be apostles, some prophets, some evangelists, some pastors and teachers, to equip the saints for the work of ministry, for building up the body of Christ, until we all attain to the unity of the faith and of the knowledge of the Son of God, to mature manhood, to the measure of the stature of the fulness of Christ; so that we may no longer be children, tossed to and fro and carried about with every wind of doctrine, by the cunning of men, by their craftiness in deceitful wiles. Rather, speaking the truth in love, we are to grow up in every way into him who is the head, into Christ, from whom the whole body, joined and knit together by every joint with which it is supplied, when each part is working properly, makes bodily growth and upbuilds itself in love.

Now this I affirm and testify in the Lord, that you must no longer live as the Gentiles do, in the futility of their minds; they are darkened in their understanding, alienated from the life of God because of the ignorance that is in them, due to their hardness of heart; they have become callous and have given themselves up to licentiousness, greedy to practice every kind of uncleanness. You did not so learn Christ! —assuming that you have heard about him and were taught in him, as the truth is in Jesus. Put off your old nature which belongs to your former manner of life and is corrupt through deceitful lusts, and be renewed in the spirit of your minds, and put on the new nature, created after the likeness of God in true righteousness and holiness.

Therefore, putting away falsehood, let every one speak the truth with his neighbor, for we are members one of another. Be angry but do not sin; do not let the sun go down on your anger, and give no opportunity to the devil. Let the thief no longer steal, but rather let him labor, doing honest work with his hands, so that he may be able to give to those in need. Let no evil talk come out of your mouths, but only such as is good for edifying, as fits the occasion, that it may impart grace to those who hear. And do not grieve the Holy Spirit of God, in whom you were sealed for the day of redemption. Let all bitterness and wrath and anger and clamor and slander be put away from you, with all malice, and be kind to one another, tenderhearted, forgiving one another, as God in Christ forgave you.

Therefore be imitators of God, as beloved children. And walk in love, as Christ loved us and gave himself up for us, a fragrant offering and sacrifice to God.

But fornication and all impurity or covetousness must not even be named among you, as is fitting among saints. Let there be no filthiness, nor silly talk, nor levity, which are not fitting; but instead let there be thanksgiving. Be sure of this, that no fornicator or impure man, or one who is covetous (that is, an idolater), has any inheritance in the kingdom of Christ and of God. Let no one deceive you with empty words, for it is because of these things that the wrath of God comes upon the sons of disobedience. Therefore do not associate with them, for once you were darkness, but now you are light in the Lord; walk as children of light (for the fruit of light is found in all that is good and right and true), and try to learn what is pleasing to the Lord. Take no part in the unfruitful works of darkness, but instead expose them. For it is a shame even to speak of the things that they do in secret; but when anything is exposed by the light it becomes visible, for anything that becomes visible is light. Therefore it is said,

"Awake, O sleeper, and arise from the dead,
and Christ shall give you light."

Look carefully then how you walk, not as unwise men but as wise, making the most of the time, because the days are evil. Therefore do not be foolish, but understand what the will of the Lord is. And do not get drunk with wine, for that is debauchery; but be filled with the Spirit, addressing one another in psalms and hymns and spiritual songs, singing and making melody to the Lord with all your heart, always and for everything giving thanks in the name of our Lord Jesus Christ to God the Father.

Be subject to one another out of reverence for Christ. Wives, be subject to your husbands, as to the Lord. For the husband is the head of the wife as Christ is the head of the church, his body, and is himself its Savior. As the church is subject to Christ, so let wives also be subject in everything to their husbands. Husbands, love your wives, as Christ loved the church and gave himself up for her, that he might sanctify her, having cleansed her by the washing of water with the word, that he might present the church to himself in splendor, without spot or wrinkle or any such thing, that she might be holy and without blemish. Even so husbands should love their wives as their own bodies. He who loves his wife loves himself. For no man ever hates his own flesh, but nourishes and cherishes it, as Christ does the church, because we are members of his body. "For this reason a man shall leave his father and mother and be joined to his wife, and the two shall become one flesh." This mystery is a profound one, and I am saying that it refers to Christ and the church; however, let each one of you love his wife as himself, and let the wife see that she respects her husband.

Children, obey your parents in the Lord, for this is right. "Honor your father and mother" (this is the first commandment with a promise), "that it may be well with you and that you may live long on the earth." Fathers, do not provoke your children to anger, but bring them up in the discipline and instruction of the Lord.

Slaves, be obedient to those who are your earthly masters, with fear and trembling, in singleness of heart, as to Christ; not in the way of eye-service, as men-pleasers, but as servants of Christ, doing the will of God from the heart, rendering service with a good will as to the Lord and not to men, knowing that whatever good any one does, he will receive the same again from the Lord, whether he is a slave or free. Masters, do the same to them, and forbear threatening, knowing that he who is both their Master and yours is in heaven, and that there is no partiality with him.

Finally, be strong in the Lord and in the strength of his might. Put on the whole armor of God, that you may be able to stand against the wiles of the devil. For we are not contending against flesh and blood, but against the principalities, against the powers, against the world rulers of this present darkness, against the spiritual hosts of wickedness in the heavenly places. Therefore take the whole armor of God, that you may be able to withstand in the evil day, and having done all, to stand. Stand therefore, having girded your loins with truth, and having put on the breastplate of righteousness, and having shod your feet with the equipment of the gospel of peace; besides all these, taking the shield of faith, with which you can quench all the flaming darts of the evil one. And take the helmet of salvation, and the sword of the Spirit, which is the word of God. Pray at all times in the Spirit, with all prayer and supplication. To that end keep alert with all perseverance, making supplication for all the saints, and also for me, that utterance may be given me in opening my mouth boldly to proclaim the mystery of the gospel, for which I am an ambassador in chains; that I may declare it boldly, as I ought to speak.

Now that you also may know how I am and what I am doing, Tychicus the beloved brother and faithful minister in the Lord will tell you everything. I have sent him to you for this very purpose, that you may know how we are, and that he may encourage your hearts.

Peace be to the brethren, and love with faith, from God the Father and the Lord Jesus Christ. Grace be with all who love our Lord Jesus Christ with love undying.

1456 (1) **Exodus 20:17** "You shall not covet your neighbor's house; you shall not covet your neighbor's wife, or his manservant, or his maidservant, or his ox, or his ass, or anything that is your neighbor's."

1456 (2) **Matthew 5:28** But I say to you that every one who looks at a woman lustfully has already committed adultery with her in his heart.

1457 (1) **CIC Canon 989** After having attained the age of discretion, each of the faithful is bound by an obligation faithfully to confess serious sins at least once a year.

1457 (2) **Council of Trent (1551): DS 1683** Moreover, as regards the manner of confessing secretly to a priest alone, although Christ has not prohibited that one confess sins publicly in expiation for his crimes and for his own humiliation, and as an example to others, as well as for the edification of the Church offended, yet this is not commanded by divine precept, nor would it be advisedly enjoined by any human law that offenses, especially secret ones, be disclosed by a public confession [can. 6]. Therefore, since secret sacramental confession, which the holy Church has used from the beginning and which she still uses, has always been recommended by the most holy and most ancient Fathers in emphatic and unanimous agreement, the empty calumny of those who do not fear to teach that this is foreign to the divine mandate and is a human invention, and that it had its origin in the Fathers assembled in the Lateran Council [can. 8] is manifestly disproved; for neither did the Church through the Lateran Council decree that the faithful of Christ should confess, a matter which she recognized was necessary and instituted by divine law, but that the precept of confession should be fulfilled at least once a year by each and all, when they have reached the years of discretion. Hence, this salutary custom of confessing to the great benefit of souls is now observed in the whole Church during that sacred and especially acceptable time of Lent, a custom which this holy Council completely approves and sanctions as pious and worthy to be retained [can. 8].

(3) **Council of Trent (1551): DS 1708** If anyone says that the confession of all sins as the Church observes is impossible, and is a human tradition to be abolished by the pious, or that each and all of the faithful of Christ of either sex are not bound to it once a year, according to the constitution of the great Lateran Council, and for this reason the faithful of Christ must be persuaded not to confess during the Lenten season; let him be anathema. **1457**

(4) **Council of Trent (1551): DS 1647** Now ecclesiastical usage declares that this examination is necessary, that no one conscious of mortal sin, however contrite he may seem to himself, should approach the Holy Eucharist without a previous sacramental confession. This, the holy Synod has decreed, is always to be observed by all Christians, even by those priests on whom by their office it may be incumbent to celebrate, provided the recourses of a confessor be not lacking to them. But if in an urgent necessity a priest should celebrate without previous confession, let him confess as soon as possible. **1457**

(5) **Council of Trent (1551): DS 1661** If anyone says that faith alone is sufficient preparation for receiving the sacrament of the most Holy Eucharist: let him be anathema. And that so great a Sacrament may not be unworthily received, and therefore unto death and condemnation, this holy Council ordains and declares that sacramental confession must necessarily be made beforehand by those whose conscience is burdened by mortal sin, however contrite they may consider themselves. If anyone moreover teaches the contrary or preaches or obstinately asserts, or even publicly by disputation shall presume to defend the contrary, by that fact itself he is excommunicated. **1457**

(6) **CIC Canon 916** A person who is conscious of grave sin is not to celebrate Mass or to receive the Body of the Lord without prior sacramental confession unless a grave reason is present and there is no opportunity of confessing: in this case the person is to be mindful of the obligation to make an act of perfect contrition, including the intention of confessing as soon as possible. **1457**

(7) **CCEO Canon 711** A person who is conscious of serious sin is not to celebrate the Divine Liturgy nor receive the Divine Eucharist unless a serious reason is present and there is no opportunity of receiving the sacrament of penance; in this case the person should make an act of perfect contrition, including the intention of confessing as soon as possible. **1457**

(8) **CIC Canon 914** It is the responsibility, in the first place, of parents and those who take the place of parents as well as of the pastor to see that children who have reached the use of reason are correctly prepared and are nourished by the divine food as early as possible, preceded by sacramental confession; it is also for the pastor to be vigilant lest any children come to the Holy Banquet who have not reached the use of reason or whom he judges are not sufficiently disposed. **1457**

(1) **Council of Trent (1551): DS 1680** From this it is gathered that all mortal sins of which they have knowledge after a careful self-examination must be enumerated in confession by the penitents, even though they are most secret and have been committed only against the two last precepts of the decalogue [Exod. 20:17; Matt. 5:28], sins which sometimes wound the soul more grievously, and are more dangerous than those which are committed openly. For venial sins, by which we are not excluded from the grace of God and into which we fall more frequently, although they may **1458**

rightly and profitably and without any presumption be declared in confession [can. 7], as the practice of pious persons indicates, may be passed over in silence without guilt and may be expiated by many other remedies. But since all mortal sins, even those of thought, make men children of wrath [Eph. 2:3] and enemies of God, it is necessary to ask pardon for all of them from God by an open and humble confession. While, therefore, the faithful of Christ strive to confess all sins which occur to their memory, they undoubtedly lay all of them before the divine mercy to be forgiven [can. 7]. While those who do otherwise and knowingly conceal certain sins, lay nothing before the divine bounty for forgiveness by the priest. "For if one who is ill is ashamed to make known his wound to the physician, the physician does not remedy what he does not know."

1458 (2) **CIC Canon 988, §2** It is to be recommended to the Christian faithful that venial sins also be confessed.

1458 (3) **Luke 6:36** Be merciful, even as your Father is merciful.

1459 **Council of Trent (1551): DS 1712** If anyone says that the whole punishment, together with the guilt, is always pardoned by God, and that the satisfaction of penitents is nothing other than faith, by which they perceive that Christ has made satisfaction for them: let him be anathema.

1460 (1) **Romans 3:25** . . . whom God put forward as an expiation by his blood, to be received by faith. This was to show God's righteousness, because in his divine forbearance he had passed over former sins. . . .

1460 (2) **1 John 2:1–2** My little children, I am writing this to you so that you may not sin; but if any one does sin, we have an advocate with the Father, Jesus Christ the righteous; and he is the expiation for our sins, and not for ours only but also for the sins of the whole world.

1460 (3) **Council of Trent (1551): DS 1690** Indeed the nature of divine justice seems to demand that those who have sinned through ignorance before baptism may be received into grace in one manner, and in another those who at one time freed from the servitude of sin and the devil, and on receiving the gift of the Holy Spirit, did not fear to "violate the temple of God knowingly" [I Cor. 3:17], "and to grieve the Holy Spirit" [Eph. 4:30]. And it befits divine clemency that sins be not thus pardoned us without any satisfaction, lest, seizing the occasion [Rom. 7:8], and considering sins trivial, we, offering injury and "affront to the Holy Spirit" [Heb. 10:29], fall into graver ones, "treasuring up to ourselves wrath against the day of wrath" [Rom. 2:5; Jas. 5:3]. For, without doubt, these satisfactions greatly restrain from sin, and as by a kind of rein act as a check, and make penitents more cautious and vigilant in the future; they also remove the remnants of sin, and destroy vicious habits acquired by living evilly through acts contrary to virtue. Neither was there ever in the Church of God any way considered more secure for warding off impending punishment by the Lord than that men perform these works of penance [Matt. 3:28; 4:17; 11:21 etc.] with true sorrow of soul. Add to this that, while we suffer by making satisfaction for our sins, we are made conformable to Christ Jesus, "who made satisfaction for our sins" [Rom. 5:10; I John 2:1 f.], from whom is all our sufficiency [II Cor. 3:5], having also a most certain pledge from Him that "if we suffer with Him, we shall also be glorified" [cf. Rom. 8:17].

1460 (4) **Philippians 4:13** I can do all things in him who strengthens me.

(5) **1 Corinthians 1:31** . . . therefore, as it is written, "Let him who boasts, boast 1460
of the Lord."

(6) **2 Corinthians 10:17** "Let him who boasts, boast of the Lord." 1460

(7) **Galatians 6:14** But far be it from me to glory except in the cross of our Lord 1460
Jesus Christ, by which the world has been crucified to me, and I to the world.

(8) **Luke 3:8** ". . . Bear fruits that befit repentance, and do not begin to say to 1460
yourselves, 'We have Abraham as our father'; for I tell you, God is able from these stones to raise up children to Abraham. . . ."

(1) **John 20:23** ". . . If you forgive the sins of any, they are forgiven; if you retain 1461
the sins of any, they are retained."

(2) **2 Corinthians 5:18** All this is from God, who through Christ reconciled us to 1461
himself and gave us the ministry of reconciliation. . . .

(1) ***Lumen gentium* 26, 3** Thus the bishops, by praying and toiling for the peo- 1462
ple, apportion in many different forms and without stint that which flows from the abundance of Christ's holiness. By the ministry of the word they impart to those who believe the strength of God unto salvation (cf. Rom. 1:16), and through the sacraments, the frequent and fruitful distribution of which they regulate by their authority, they sanctify the faithful. They control the conferring of Baptism, through which a sharing in the priesthood of Christ is granted. They are the original ministers of Confirmation; it is they who confer sacred Orders and regulate the discipline of Penance, and who diligently exhort and instruct their flocks to take the part that is theirs, in a spirit of faith and reverence, in the liturgy and above all in the holy sacrifice of the Mass. Finally, by the example of their manner of life they should exercise a powerful influence for good on those over whom they are placed, by abstaining from all wrongdoing in their conduct, and, as far as they are able, with the help of the Lord, changing it for the better, so that together with the flock entrusted to them, they may attain to eternal life.

(2) **CIC Canon 844** 1462

§1. Catholic ministers may licitly administer the sacraments to Catholic members of the Christian faithful only and, likewise, the latter may licitly receive the sacraments only from Catholic ministers with due regard for §§2, 3, and 4 of this canon, and can. 861, §2.

§2. Whenever necessity requires or genuine spiritual advantage suggests, and provided that the danger of error or indifferentism is avoided, it is lawful for the faithful for whom it is physically or morally impossible to approach a Catholic minister, to receive the sacraments of penance, Eucharist, and anointing of the sick from non-Catholic ministers in whose churches these sacraments are valid.

§3. Catholic ministers may licitly administer the sacraments of penance, Eucharist and anointing of the sick to members of the oriental churches which do not have full communion with the Catholic Church, if they ask on their own for the sacraments and are properly disposed. This holds also for members of other churches, which in the judgment of the Apostolic See are in the same condition as the oriental churches as far as these sacraments are concerned.

§4. If the danger of death is present or other grave necessity, in the judgment of the diocesan bishop or the conference of bishops, Catholic ministers may licitly administer these sacraments to other Christians who do not have full communion with the Catholic Church, who cannot approach a minister of their own community and on their own ask for it, provided they manifest Catholic faith in these sacraments and are properly disposed.

§5. For the cases in §§2, 3, and 4, neither the diocesan bishop nor the conference of bishops is to enact general norms except after consultation with at least the local competent authority of the interested non-Catholic church or community.

1462 (3) **CIC Canons 967–69**

Can. 967—§1. Besides the Roman Pontiff, cardinals by the law itself possess the faculty to hear the confessions of the Christian faithful anywhere in the world; likewise, bishops possess this faculty and licitly use it anywhere unless the diocesan bishop denies it in a particular case.

§2. Those who enjoy the faculty of hearing confessions habitually whether in virtue of office or by grant from the ordinary of the place of incardination or the place in which they have a domicile can exercise the same faculty everywhere unless the local ordinary denies it in a particular case, with due regard for the prescriptions of can. 974, §§2 and 3.

§3. Those who have been granted the faculty to hear confessions in virtue of an office or by a grant from the competent superior in accord with the norms of cann. 968, §2 and 969, §2 can by the law itself use the faculty anywhere in respect to members and others who stay day and night in a house of the institute or society; such persons also exercise this faculty licitly unless some major superior has denied it concerning his own subjects in a particular case.

Can. 968—§1. In virtue of their office any local ordinary, canon penitentiary, as well as the pastor of a parish and those who take the place of the pastor of a parish possess the faculty to hear confessions within their jurisdiction.

§2. In virtue of their office superiors of a clerical religious institute or society of apostolic life of pontifical right who in accord with the norms of their constitutions possess executive power of governance enjoy the faculty to hear the confessions of their subjects and others staying in the religious house day and night, with due regard for the prescription of can. 630, §4.

Can. 969—§1. The local ordinary alone is competent to confer upon any presbyters whatsoever the faculty to hear the confessions of any of the faithful; however, presbyters who are members of religious institutes should not use such a faculty without at least the presumed permission of their superior.

§2. The superior of a religious institute or of a society of apostolic life of pontifical right mentioned in can. 968, §2, is competent to confer on any presbyter whatsoever the faculty to hear the confessions of his subjects and others staying day and night in the house.

1462 (4) **CIC Canon 972** The faculty to hear confessions can be granted by the competent authority mentioned in can. 969 for an indefinite or for a definite period of time.

1462 (5) **CCEO Canon 722, §§3–4**

§3. For presbyters to act validly, they must be previously granted the faculty of administering the sacrament of penance, which is conferred either by the law itself or by a special grant made by a competent authority.

§4. Priests who are endowed with this faculty by virtue of their office or by virtue of the grant of the local hierarch of the eparchy in which they are enrolled or in which they have domicile, can validly administer the sacrament of penance anywhere to any Christian faithful, unless the local hierarch in a special case expressly denies it; the same faculties are licitly used observing the norms made by the eparchial bishop and also with at least the presumed permission of the rector of the church or the superior, if it is the case of a house of an institute of consecrated life.

(1) **CIC Canon 1331** 1463

§1. An excommunicated person is forbidden:

1° to have any ministerial participation in celebrating the Eucharistic Sacrifice or in any other ceremonies whatsoever of public worship;

2° to celebrate the sacraments and sacramentals and to receive the sacraments;

3° to discharge any ecclesiastical offices, ministries or functions whatsoever, or to place acts of governance.

§2. If the excommunication has been imposed or declared, the guilty party:

1° wishing to act against the prescriptions of §1, n. 1, is to be prevented from doing so or the liturgical action is to stop unless a serious cause intervenes;

2° invalidly places acts of governance which are only illicit in accord with the norms of §1, n. 3;

3° is forbidden to enjoy privileges formerly granted;

4° cannot validly acquire a dignity, office or other function in the Church;

5° cannot appropriate the revenues from any dignity, office, function or pension in the Church.

(2) **CIC Canons 1354–57** 1463

Can. 1354—§1. Besides the persons enumerated in cann. 1355–1356, all who can dispense from a law which includes a penalty and all who can exempt one from a precept which threatens a penalty can also remit that penalty.

§2. Furthermore, a law or a precept which establishes a penalty can also give the power of remission to other persons.

§3. If the Apostolic See reserves to itself or to another the remission of a penalty, such a reservation is to be interpreted strictly.

Can. 1355—§1. Unless it is reserved to the Apostolic See, the following can remit an imposed or declared penalty established by law:

1° the ordinary who set in motion the trial in order to impose or declare the penalty or who imposed or declared it by decree personally or through another;

2° the ordinary of the place where the offender lives, after consulting with the ordinary mentioned in n. 1, unless this is impossible due to extraordinary circumstances.

§2. Unless it is reserved to the Apostolic See an ordinary can remit an automatic (*latae sententiae*) penalty established by law but not declared for his own subjects and those who are living in his territory or who committed an offense there; any bishop, however, can also do this in the act of sacramental confession.

Can. 1356—§1. The following can remit an inflicted (*ferendae sententiae*) or automatic (*latae sententiae*) penalty established by a precept not issued by the Holy See:

1° the ordinary of the place where the offender lives;

2° if the penalty has been imposed or declared, the ordinary who set in motion the trial in order to impose or declare the penalty or who imposed or declared it by decree personally or through another.

§2. Before such a remission occurs, the author of the precept is to be consulted unless this is impossible due to extraordinary circumstances.

Can. 1357—§1. With due regard for the prescriptions of cann. 508 and 976, any confessor can remit in the internal sacramental forum an automatic (*latae sententiae*) censure of excommunication or interdict which has not been declared if it would be hard on the penitent to remain in a state of serious sin during the time necessary for the competent superior to provide.

§2. In granting a remission, the confessor is to impose on the penitent the burden of having recourse within a month to a superior or a priest endowed with faculties and obeying his mandates under pain of reincidence of the penalty; in the meantime he should impose an appropriate penance and the reparation of any scandal or damage to the extent that it is imperative; recourse can also be made by the confessor without mentioning any names.

§3. After they have recovered, those absolved in accord with can. 976 from an imposed or declared censure or one reserved to the Holy See are bound by the same obligation of recourse.

1463 (3) **CCEO Canon 1431**

§1. Those punished with a minor excommunication are deprived of the reception of the Divine Eucharist. In addition they can be excluded from participation in the Divine Liturgy, and even from entering the church while divine worship is publicly celebrated there.

§2. The sentence or the decree by which this penalty is imposed must determine its extent and, as the case may be, its duration.

1463 (4) **CCEO Canon 1434**

§1. In addition to all things mentioned in can. 1431, §1, a major excommunication forbids one to receive other sacraments, to administer sacraments and sacramentals, to exercise any offices, ministries and functions, to place acts of governance, which, if they are nonetheless placed, are null by law itself.

§2. One punished with a major excommunication is to be turned away from participating in the Divine Liturgy and in other public celebrations of divine worship.

§3. One punished with a major excommunication is forbidden to make use of privileges previously granted. He cannot validly obtain dignities, offices, ministries, or any other function in the Church or a pension, and he cannot acquire the revenues attached to them. Moreover, he is deprived of active and passive voice.

1463 (5) **CCEO Canon 1420**

§1. A penalty imposed in virtue of common law can be remitted by:

1° The hierarch who has initiated the penal trial or has imposed the penalty by decree;

2° the hierarch of the place where the guilty party lives, but after consultation with the hierarch mentioned in n. 1.

§2. These norms apply also in respect to penalties imposed in virtue of particular law or a penal precept, unless the particular law of a Church *sui iuris* provides otherwise.

§3. A penalty, however, imposed by the Apostolic See can be remitted only by the Apostolic See, unless the remitting of the penalty is delegated to the patriarch or to others.

(6) **CIC Canon 976** Even though he lacks the faculty to hear confessions, any priest validly and licitly absolves from any kind of censures and sins any penitent who is in danger of death, even if an approved priest is present. 1463

(7) **CCEO Canon 725** Any priest can validly and licitly absolve any penitent in danger of death from any sin, even if there is present a priest endowed with the faculty of administering the sacrament of penance. 1463

(1) **CIC Canon 986** 1464

§1. All to whom the care of souls is committed by reason of an office are obliged to provide that the confessions of the faithful entrusted to their care be heard when they reasonably ask to be heard and that the opportunity be given to them to come to individual confession on days and hours set for their convenience.

§2. In urgent necessity any confessor is obliged to hear the confessions of the Christian faithful, and in danger of death any priest is so obliged.

(2) **CCEO Canon 735** All to whom the care of souls is committed by reason of an office are obliged to provide that the confessions of the faithful entrusted to their care be heard when they reasonably ask to be heard and that the opportunity be given to them to come to individual confession on days and hours set for their convenience. 1464

(3) ***Presbyterorum ordinis* 13** Priests will acquire holiness in their own distinctive way by exercising their functions sincerely and tirelessly in the Spirit of Christ. 1464

Since they are ministers of the Word of God, they read and hear every day the Word of God which they must teach to others. If they strive at the same time to make it part of their own lives, they will become daily more perfect disciples of the Lord, according to the saying of the apostle Paul to Timothy: "Practice these duties, devote yourself to them; so that all may see your progress. Take heed to thyself and to your teaching; hold to that, for in doing so you will save both yourself and your hearers" (1 Tim. 4:15–16). For by seeking more effective ways of conveying to others what they have meditated on they will savor more profoundly the "unsearchable riches of Christ" (Eph. 3:8) and the many-sided wisdom of God. By keeping in mind that it is the Lord who opens hearts and that the excellence comes not from themselves but from the power of God they will be more intimately united with Christ the Teacher and will be guided by his Spirit in the very act of teaching the Word. And by this close union with Christ they share in the charity of God, the mystery of which was kept hidden from all ages to be revealed in Christ.

Priests as ministers of the sacred mysteries, especially in the sacrifice of the Mass, act in a special way on the person of Christ who gave himself as a victim to sanctify men. And this is why they are invited to imitate what they handle, so that as they celebrate the mystery of the Lord's death they may take care to mortify their members from vices and concupiscences.

In the mystery of the eucharistic sacrifice, in which priests fulfil their principal function, the work of our redemption is continually carried out. For this reason the daily celebration of it is earnestly recommended. This celebration is an act of Christ and the Church even if it is impossible for the faithful to be present. So when priests unite themselves with the act of Christ the Priest they daily offer themselves completely to God, and by being nourished with Christ's Body they share in the charity of him who gives himself as food to the faithful.

In the same way they are united with the intention and the charity of Christ when they administer the sacraments. They do this in a special way when they show themselves to be always available to administer the sacrament of Penance whenever it is reasonably requested by the faithful. In reciting the Divine Office they lend their voice to the Church which perseveres in prayer in the name of the whole human race, in union with Christ who "always lives to make intercession for them" (Heb. 7:25).

While they govern and shepherd the People of God they are encouraged by the love of the Good Shepherd to give their lives for their sheep. They, too, are prepared for the supreme sacrifice, following the example of those priests who even in our own times have not shrunk from laying down their lives. Since they are the instructors in the faith and have themselves "confidence to enter the sanctuary by the blood of Jesus" (Heb. 10:19), they approach God "with a true heart in full assurance of faith" (Heb. 10:22). They set up a steadfast hope for their faithful people, so that they may be able to comfort all who are in distress by the exhortation wherewith God also exhorts them. As rulers of the community they cultivate the form of asceticism suited to a pastor of souls, renouncing their own convenience, seeking not their own good, but that of the many, that they may be saved, always making further progress towards a more perfect fulfilment of their pastoral work and, where the need arises, prepared to break new ground in pastoral methods under the guidance of the Spirit of love who breathes where he will.

1466 ***Presbyterorum ordinis* 13:** see previous document.

1467 (1) **CIC Canon 1388, §1** A confessor who directly violates the seal of confession incurs an automatic (*latae sententiae*) excommunication reserved to the Apostolic See; if he does so only indirectly, he is to be punished in accord with the seriousness of the offense.

1467 (2) **CCEO Canon 1456** §1. A confessor who has directly violated the seal of confession, is to be punished with a major excommunication, with due regard for can. 728, §1, n. 1; but if he broke the seal in another manner, he is to be punished with an appropriate penalty.

§2. One who has attempted in any way to gain information from confession, or who has given such information to others, shall be punished with a minor excommunication or suspension.

1468 **Luke 15:32** "'. . . It was fitting to make merry and be glad, for this your brother was dead, and is alive; he was lost, and is found.'"

1469 (1) **1 Corinthians 12:26** If one member suffers, all suffer together; if one member is honored, all rejoice together.

1469 (2) ***Lumen gentium* 48–50** The Church, to which we are all called in Christ Jesus, and in which by the grace of God we acquire holiness, will receive its perfection only in the glory of heaven, when will come the time of the renewal of all things (Acts 3:21). At that time, together with the human race, the universe itself, which is so closely related to man and which attains its destiny through him, will be perfectly reestablished in Christ (cf. Eph. 1:10; Col. 1:20; 2 Pet. 3:10–13).

Christ lifted up from the earth, has drawn all men to himself (cf. Jn. 12:32). Rising from the dead (cf. Rom. 6:9) he sent his life-giving Spirit upon his disciples and through him set up his Body which is the Church as the universal sacrament of salvation. Sitting at the right hand of the Father he is continually active in the world in order to lead men to the Church and, through it, join them more closely to himself; and, by nourishing them with his own Body and Blood, make them partakers of his glorious life. The promised and hoped for restoration, therefore, has already begun in Christ. It is carried forward in the sending of the Holy Spirit and through him continues in the Church, in which through our faith, we learn the meaning of our earthly life, while we bring to term, with hope of future good, the task allotted to us in the world by the Father, and so work out our salvation (cf. Phil. 2:12).

Already the final age of the world is with us (cf. 1 Cor. 10:11) and the renewal of the world is irrevocably under way; it is even now anticipated in a certain real way, for the Church on earth is endowed already with a sanctity that is real though imperfect. However, until there be realized new heavens and a new earth in which justice dwells (cf. 2 Pet. 3:13) the pilgrim Church, in its sacraments and institutions, which belong to this present age, carries the mark of this world which will pass, and she herself takes her place among the creatures which groan and travail yet and await the revelation of the sons of God (cf. Rom. 8:19–22).

So it is, united with Christ in the Church and marked with the Holy Spirit "who is the guarantee of our inheritance" (Eph. 1:14) that we are truly called and indeed are children of God (cf. 1 Jn. 3:1) though we have not yet appeared with Christ in glory (cf. Col. 3:4) in which we will be like to God, for we will see him as he is (cf. 1 Jn. 3:2). "While we are at home in the body we are away from the Lord" (2 Cor. 5:6) and having the first fruits of the Spirit we groan inwardly (cf. Rom. 8:23) and we desire to be with Christ (cf. Phil. 1:23). That same charity urges us to live more for him who died for us and who rose again (cf. 2 Cor. 5:15). We make it our aim, then, to please the Lord in all things (cf. 2 Cor. 5:9) and we put on the armor of God that we may be able to stand against the wiles of the devil and resist in the evil day (cf. Eph. 6:11–13). Since we know neither the day nor the hour, we should follow the advice of the Lord and watch constantly so that, when the single course of our earthly life is completed (cf. Heb. 9:27), we may merit to enter with him into the marriage feast and be numbered among the blessed (cf. Mt. 25:31–46) and not, like the wicked and slothful servants (cf. Mt. 25:26), be ordered to depart into the eternal fire (cf. Mt. 25:41), into the outer darkness where "men will weep and gnash their teeth" (Mt. 22:13 and 25:30). Before we reign with Christ in glory we must all appear "before the judgment seat of Christ, so that each one may receive good or evil, according to what he has done in the body" (2 Cor. 5:10), and at the end of the world "they will come forth, those who have done good, to the resurrection of life, and those who have done evil, to the resurrection of judgment" (Jn. 5:29; cf. Mt. 25:46). We reckon then that "the sufferings of this present time are not worth comparing with the glory that is to be revealed to us" (Rom. 8:18; cf. 2 Tim. 2:11–12), and strong in faith we look for "the blessed hope, the appearing of the glory of our great God and Savior Jesus Christ" (Tit. 2:13) "who will change our lowly body to be like his glorious body" (Phil. 3:21) and who will come "to be glorified in his saints, and to be marvelled at in all who have believed" (2 Th. 1:10).

When the Lord will come in glory, and all his angels with him (cf. Mt. 25:31), death will be no more and all things will be subject to him (cf. 1 Cor. 15:26–27). But at the present time some of his disciples are pilgrims on earth. Others have died and are being purified, while still others are in glory, contemplating "in full light, God himself triune and one, exactly as he is." All of us, however, in varying degrees and in different ways share in the same charity towards God and our neighbors, and we all sing the one hymn of glory to our God. All, indeed, who are of Christ and who have his Spirit form one Church and in Christ cleave together (Eph. 4:16). So it is that the union of the wayfarers with the brethren who sleep in the peace of Christ is in no way interrupted, but on the contrary, according to the constant faith of the Church, this union is reinforced by an exchange of spiritual goods. Being more closely united to Christ, those who dwell in heaven fix the whole Church more firmly in holiness, add to the nobility of the worship that the Church offers to God here on earth, and in many ways help in a broader building up of the Church (cf. 1 Cor. 12:12–27). Once received into their heavenly home and being present to the Lord (cf. 2 Cor. 5:8), through him and with him and in him they do not cease to intercede with the Father for us, as they proffer the merits which they acquired on earth through the one mediator between God and men, Christ Jesus (cf. 1 Tim. 2:5), serving God in all things and completing in their flesh what is lacking in Christ's afflictions for the sake of his Body, that is, the Church (cf. Col. 1:24). So by their brotherly concern is our weakness greatly helped.

In full consciousness of this communion of the whole Mystical Body of Jesus Christ, the Church in its pilgrim members, from the very earliest days of the Christian religion, has honored with great respect the memory of the dead; and, "because it is a holy and a wholesome thought to pray for the dead that they may be loosed from their sins" (2 Mac. 12:46) she offers her suffrages for them. The Church has always believed that the apostles and Christ's martyrs, who gave the supreme witness of faith and charity by the shedding of their blood, are closely united with us in Christ; she has always venerated them, together with the Blessed Virgin Mary and the holy angels, with a special love, and has asked piously for the help of their intercession. Soon there were added to these others who had chosen to imitate more closely the virginity and poverty of Christ, and still others whom the outstanding practice of the Christian virtues and the wonderful graces of God recommended to the pious devotion and imitation of the faithful.

To look on the life of those who have faithfully followed Christ is to be inspired with a new reason for seeking the city which is to come (cf. Heb. 13:14 and 11:10), while at the same time we are taught to know a most safe path by which, despite the vicissitudes of the world, and in keeping with the state of life and condition proper to each of us, we will be able to arrive at perfect union with Christ, that is, holiness. God shows to men, in a vivid way, his presence and his face in the lives of those companions of ours in the human condition who are more perfectly transformed into the image of Christ (cf. 2 Cor. 3:18). He speaks to us in them and offers us a sign of this kingdom, to which we are powerfully attracted, so great a cloud of witnesses is there given (cf. Heb 12:1) and such a witness to the truth of the Gospel.

It is not merely by the title of example that we cherish the memory of those in heaven; we seek, rather, that by this devotion to the exercise of fraternal charity the union of the whole Church in the Spirit may be strengthened (cf. Eph. 4:1–6). Exactly as Christian communion between men on their earthly pilgrimage brings us closer to Christ, so our community with the saints joins us to Christ, from whom as from its fountain and head issues all grace and the life of the People of God itself. It is most fitting, therefore, that we love those friends and co-heirs of Jesus Christ who are also our brothers and outstanding benefactors, and that we give due thanks to God for them, "humbly invoking them, and having recourse to their prayers, their aid and help in obtaining from God through his Son, Jesus Christ, Our Lord, our only Redeemer and Savior, the benefits we need." Every authentic witness of love, indeed, offered by us to those who are in heaven tends to and terminates in Christ, "the crown of all the saints," and through him in God who is wonderful in his saints and is glorified in them.

It is especially in the sacred liturgy that our union with the heavenly Church is best realized; in the liturgy, through the sacramental signs, the power of the Holy Spirit acts on us, and with community rejoicing we celebrate together the praise of the divine majesty, when all those of every tribe and tongue and people and nation (cf. Apoc. 5:9) who have been redeemed by the blood of Christ and gathered together into one Church glorify, in one common song of praise, the one and triune God.

When, then, we celebrate the eucharistic sacrifice we are most closely united to the worship of the heavenly Church; when in the fellowship of communion we honor and remember the glorious Mary ever virgin, St. Joseph, the holy apostles and martyrs and all the saints.

(1) **1 Corinthians 5:11** But rather I wrote to you not to associate with any one who bears the name of brother if he is guilty of immorality or greed, or is an idolater, reviler, drunkard, or robber—not even to eat with such a one. 1470

(2) **Galatians 5:19–21** Now the works of the flesh are plain: fornication, impurity, licentiousness, idolatry, sorcery, enmity, strife, jealousy, anger, selfishness, dissension, party spirit, envy, drunkenness, carousing, and the like. I warn you, as I warned you before, that those who do such things shall not inherit the kingdom of God. 1470

(3) **Revelation 22:15** Outside are the dogs and sorcerers and fornicators and murderers and idolaters, and every one who loves and practices falsehood. 1470

Paul VI, apostolic constitution *Indulgentiarum doctrina* norm 3 Partial as well as plenary indulgences can always be applied to the dead by way of suffrage. 1471

(1) **Council of Trent (1551): DS 1712–13** If anyone says that the whole punishment, together with the guilt, is always pardoned by God, and that the satisfaction of penitents is nothing other than faith, by which they perceive that Christ has made satisfaction for them: let him be anathema. 1472

If anyone says that for sins, as far as temporal punishment is concerned, there is very little satisfaction made to God through the merits of Christ by the punishments inflicted by Him and patiently borne, or by those enjoined by the priest, but voluntarily undertaken, as by fasts, prayers, almsgiving, or also by other works of piety, and that therefore the best penance is only a new life: let him be anathema.

(2) **Council of Trent (1563): DS 1820** Since the Catholic Church, instructed by the Holy Spirit, in conformity with the sacred writings and the ancient tradition of the Fathers in sacred councils, and very recently in this ecumenical Synod, has taught that there is a purgatory, and that the souls detained there are assisted by the suffrages of the faithful, and especially by the acceptable sacrifice of the altar, the holy Synod commands the bishops that they insist that the sound doctrine of purgatory, which has been transmitted by the holy Fathers and holy Councils, be believed by the faithful of Christ, be maintained, taught, and everywhere preached. Let the more difficult and subtle "questions," however, and those which do not make for "edification" [cf. I Tim. 1:4], and from which there is very often no increase in piety, be excluded from popular discourses to uneducated people. Likewise, let them not permit uncertain matters, or those that have the appearance of falsehood, to be brought out and discussed publicly. Those matters on the contrary, which tend to a certain curiosity or superstition, or that savor of filthy lucre, let them prohibit as scandals and stumbling blocks to the faithful. . . . 1472

Paul VI, apostolic constitution *Indulgentiarum doctrina*, 8 The taking away of the temporal punishment due to sins when their guilt has already been forgiven has been called specifically "indulgence." 1478

While it has something in common with other ways of eliminating the vestiges of sin, an indulgence is clearly different from them.

In fact, in granting an indulgence the Church uses its power as minister of Christ's Redemption. It not only prays. It intervenes with its authority to dispense to the faithful, provided they have the right dispositions, the treasury of satisfaction which Christ and the saints won for the remission of temporal punishment.

The authorities of the Church have two aims in granting indulgences. The first is to help the faithful to expiate their sins. The second is to encourage them to do works of piety, penitence and charity, particularly those which lead to growth in faith and which help the common good.

Further, if the faithful offer indulgences by way of intercession for the dead they cultivate charity in an excellent way. While they raise their minds in heaven they bring a wiser order into the things of this world.

The teaching authority, the Magisterium of the Church, has defended and explained the teaching about indulgences in various documents. Unfortunately, the practice of indulgences has on occasions been improperly applied. This has been either through "untimely and superfluous indulgences" which humiliated the power of the keys and weakened penitential satisfaction or it has been through the collection of "unlawful profits" which blasphemously took away the good name of indulgences. The Church deplored and corrected these improper uses. It "teaches and commands that the usage of indulgences—a usage most beneficial to Christians and approved by the authority of the Sacred Councils—should be kept in the Church; and it condemns with anathema those who say that indulgences are useless or that the Church does not have the power to grant them."

1482 ***Sacrosanctum concilium* 26–27** Liturgical services are not private functions but are celebrations of the Church which is "the sacrament of unity," namely, "the holy people united and arranged under their bishops."

Therefore, liturgical services pertain to the whole Body of the Church. They manifest it, and have effects upon it. But they also touch individual members of the Church in different ways, depending on their orders, their role in the liturgical services, and their actual participation in them.

It must be emphasized that rites which are meant to be celebrated in common, with the faithful present and actively participating, should as far as possible be celebrated in that way rather than by an individual and quasi-privately.

This applies with special force to the celebration of Mass (even though every Mass has of itself a public and social nature) and to the administration of the sacraments.

1483 (1) **CIC Canon 962, §1** For a member of the Christian faithful validly to enjoy sacramental absolution given to many at one time, it is required that this person not only be suitably disposed but also at the same time intend to confess individually the serious sins which at present cannot be so confessed.

1483 (2) **CIC Canon 961, §2** It is for the diocesan bishop to judge whether the conditions required in §1, n. 2, are present; he can determine general cases of such necessity in the light of criteria agreed upon with other members of the conference of bishops.

1483 (3) **CIC Canon 961, §1** Absolution cannot be imparted in a general manner to a number of penitents at once without previous individual confession unless:

1° the danger of death is imminent and there is not time for the priest or priests to hear the confessions of the individual penitents;

2° a serious necessity exists, that is, when in light of the number of penitents a supply of confessors is not readily available rightly to hear the confessions of individuals within a suitable time so that the penitents are forced to be deprived of sacramental grace or holy communion for a long time through no fault of their own; it is not considered a sufficient necessity if confessors cannot be readily available only because of the great number of penitents as can occur on the occasion of some great feast or pilgrimage.

Mark 2:17 And when Jesus heard it, he said to them, "Those who are well have no need of a physician, but those who are sick; I came not to call the righteous, but sinners." 1484

(1) **Psalm 6:3 (6:2: RSV)** 1502

Be gracious to me, O Lord, for I am languishing;
O Lord, heal me, for my bones are troubled.

(2) **Psalm 38** 1502

O Lord, rebuke me not in thy anger,
nor chasten me in thy wrath!
For thy arrows have sunk into me,
and thy hand has come down on me.

There is no soundness in my flesh
because of thy indignation;
there is no health in my bones
because of my sin.
For my iniquities have gone over my head;
they weigh like a burden too heavy for me.

My wounds grow foul and fester
because of my foolishness,
I am utterly bowed down and prostrate;
all the day I go about mourning.
For my loins are filled with burning,
and there is no soundness in my flesh.
I am utterly spent and crushed;
I groan because of the tumult of my heart.

Lord, all my longing is known to thee,
my sighing is not hidden from thee.
My heart throbs, my strength fails me;
and the light of my eyes—it also has gone from me.
My friends and companions stand aloof from my plague,
and my kinsmen stand afar off.

Those who seek my life lay their snares,
those who seek my hurt speak of ruin,
and meditate treachery all the day long.

But I am like a deaf man, I do not hear,
like a dumb man who does not open his mouth.
Yea, I am like a man who does not hear,
and in whose mouth are no rebukes.

But for thee, O Lord, do I wait;
it is thou, O Lord my God, who wilt answer.
For I pray, "Only let them not rejoice over me,
who boast against me when my foot slips!"

For I am ready to fall,
and my pain is ever with me.

I confess my iniquity,
I am sorry for my sin.
Those who are my foes without cause are mighty,
and many are those who hate me wrongfully.
Those who render me evil for good
are my adversaries because I follow after good.

Do not forsake me, O Lord!
O my God, be not far from me!
Make haste to help me,
O Lord, my salvation!

1502 (3) **Isaiah 38** In those days Hezekiah became sick and was at the point of death. And Isaiah the prophet the son of Amoz came to him, and said to him, "Thus says the Lord: Set your house in order; for you shall die, you shall not recover." Then Hezekiah turned his face to the wall, and prayed to the Lord, and said, "Remember now, O Lord, I beseech thee, how I have walked before thee in faithfulness and with a whole heart, and have done what is good in thy sight." And Hezekiah wept bitterly. Then the word of the Lord came to Isaiah: "Go and say to Hezekiah, Thus says the Lord, the God of David your father: I have heard your prayer, I have seen your tears; behold, I will add fifteen years to your life. I will deliver you and this city out of the hand of the king of Assyria, and defend this city.

"This is the sign to you from the Lord, that the Lord will do this thing that he has promised: Behold, I will make the shadow cast by the declining sun on the dial of Ahaz turn back ten steps." So the sun turned back on the dial the ten steps by which it had declined.

A writing of Hezekiah king of Judah, after he had been sick and had recovered from his sickness:

I said, In the noontide of my days
I must depart;
I am consigned to the gates of Sheol
for the rest of my years.
I said, I shall not see the Lord
in the land of the living;
I shall look upon man no more
among the inhabitants of the world.
My dwelling is plucked up and removed from me
like a shepherd's tent;
like a weaver I have rolled up my life;
he cuts me off from the loom;
from day to night thou dost bring me to an end;
I cry for help until morning;
like a lion he breaks all my bones;
from day to night thou dost bring me to an end.

Like a swallow or a crane I clamor,
I moan like a dove.
My eyes are weary with looking upward.
O Lord, I am oppressed; be thou my security!
But what can I say? For he has spoken to me,
and he himself has done it.
All my sleep has fled
because of the bitterness of my soul.

O Lord, by these things men live,
and in all these is the life of my spirit.
Oh, restore me to health and make me live!
Lo, it was for my welfare
that I had great bitterness;
but thou hast held back my life
from the pit of destruction,
for thou hast cast all my sins
behind thy back.
For Sheol cannot thank thee,
death cannot praise thee;
those who go down to the pit cannot hope
for thy faithfulness.
The living, the living, he thanks thee,
as I do this day;
the father makes known to the children
thy faithfulness.

The Lord will save me,
and we will sing to stringed instruments
all the days of our life,
at the house of the Lord.

Now Isaiah had said, "Let them take a cake of figs, and apply it to the boil, that he may recover." Hezekiah also had said, "What is the sign that I shall go up to the house of the Lord?"

(4) **Psalm 32:5** 1502
I acknowledged my sin to thee,
and I did not hide my iniquity;
I said, "I will confess my transgressions to the Lord";
then thou didst forgive the guilt of my sin.

(5) **Psalm 38:5 (38:4: RSV)** 1502
For my iniquities have gone over my head;
they weigh like a burden too heavy for me.

(6) **Psalm 39:9 (39:8: RSV)** 1502
Deliver me from all my transgressions.
Make me not the scorn of the fool!

(7) **Psalm 39:12 (39:11: RSV)** 1502
When thou dost chasten man
with rebukes for sin,
thou dost consume like a moth what is dear to him;
surely every man is a mere breath! *Selah!*

(8) **Psalm 107:20** 1502
. . . he sent forth his word, and healed them,
and delivered them from destruction.

(9) **Mark 2:5–12** And when Jesus saw their faith, he said to the paralytic, "My son, 1502
your sins are forgiven." Now some of the scribes were sitting there, questioning in
their hearts, "Why does this man speak thus? It is blasphemy! Who can forgive sins

but God alone?" And immediately Jesus, perceiving in his spirit that they thus questioned within themselves, said to them, "Why do you question thus in your hearts? Which is easier, to say to the paralytic, 'Your sins are forgiven,' or to say, 'Rise, take up your pallet and walk?' But that you may know that the Son of man has authority on earth to forgive sins"—he said to the paralytic—"I say to you, rise, take up your pallet and go home." And he rose, and immediately took up the pallet and went out before them all; so that they were all amazed and glorified God, saying, "We never saw anything like this!"

1502 (10) **Isaiah 53:11**

. . . he shall see the fruit of the travail of his soul and be satisfied;
by his knowledge shall the righteous one, my servant,
make many to be accounted righteous;
and he shall bear their iniquities.

1502 (11) **Isaiah 33:24**

And no inhabitant will say, "I am sick";
the people who dwell there will be forgiven their iniquity.

1503 (1) **Matthew 4:24** So his fame spread throughout all Syria, and they brought him all the sick, those afflicted with various diseases and pains, demoniacs, epileptics, and paralytics, and he healed them.

1503 (2) **Mark 2:5–12** And when Jesus saw their faith, he said to the paralytic, "My son, your sins are forgiven." Now some of the scribes were sitting there, questioning in their hearts, "Why does this man speak thus? It is blasphemy! Who can forgive sins but God alone?" And immediately Jesus, perceiving in his spirit that they thus questioned within themselves, said to them, "Why do you question thus in your hearts? Which is easier, to say to the paralytic, 'Your sins are forgiven,' or to say, 'Rise, take up your pallet and walk?' But that you may know that the Son of man has authority on earth to forgive sins"—he said to the paralytic—"I say to you, rise, take up your pallet and go home." And he rose, and immediately took up the pallet and went out before them all; so that they were all amazed and glorified God, saying, "We never saw anything like this!"

1503 (3) **Mark 2:17** And when Jesus heard it, he said to them, "Those who are well have no need of a physician, but those who are sick; I came not to call the righteous, but sinners."

1504 (1) **Mark 5:34** And he said to her, "Daughter, your faith has made you well; go in peace, and be healed of your disease."

1504 (2) **Mark 5:36** But ignoring what they said, Jesus said to the ruler of the synagogue, "Do not fear, only believe."

1504 (3) **Mark 9:23** And Jesus said to him, "If you can! All things are possible to him who believes."

1504 (4) **Mark 7:32–36** And they brought to him a man who was deaf and had an impediment in his speech; and they besought him to lay his hand upon him. And taking him aside from the multitude privately, he put his fingers into his ears, and he spat and touched his tongue; and looking up to heaven, he sighed, and said to him, "Ephphatha," that is, "Be opened." And his ears were opened, his tongue was released, and he spoke plainly. And he charged them to tell no one; but the more he charged them, the more zealously they proclaimed it.

(5) **Mark 8:22–25** And they came to Bethsaida. And some people brought to him 1504
a blind man, and begged him to touch him. And he took the blind man by the hand, and led him out of the village; and when he had spit on his eyes and laid his hands upon him, he asked him, "Do you see anything?" And he looked up and said, "I see men; but they look like trees, walking." Then again he laid his hands upon his eyes; and he looked intently and was restored, and saw everything clearly.

(6) **John 9:6–7** As he said this, he spat on the ground and made clay of the spittle 1504
and anointed the man's eyes with the clay, saying to him, "Go, wash in the pool of Siloam" (which means Sent). So he went and washed and came back seeing.

(7) **Mark 1:41** Moved with pity, he stretched out his hand and touched him, and 1504
said to him, "I will; be clean."

(8) **Mark 3:10** . . . for he had healed many, so that all who had diseases pressed 1504
upon him to touch him.

(9) **Mark 6:56** And wherever he came, in villages, cities, or country, they laid the 1504
sick in the market places, and besought him that they might touch even the fringe of his garment; and as many as touched it were made well.

(1) **Isaiah 53:4** 1505

Surely he has borne our griefs
and carried our sorrows;
yet we esteemed him stricken,
smitten by God, and afflicted.

(2) **Isaiah 53:4–6** 1505

Surely he has borne our griefs
and carried our sorrows;
yet we esteemed him stricken,
smitten by God, and afflicted.
But he was wounded for our transgressions,
he was bruised for our iniquities;
upon him was the chastisement that made us whole,
and with his stripes we are healed.
All we like sheep have gone astray;
we have turned every one to his own way;
and the Lord has laid on him
the iniquity of us all.

Matthew 10:38 . . . and he who does not take his cross and follow me is not worthy 1506
of me.

(1) **Acts 9:34** And Peter said to him, "Aeneas, Jesus Christ heals you; rise and make 1507
your bed." And immediately he rose.

(2) **Acts 14:3** So they remained for a long time, speaking boldly for the Lord, who 1507
bore witness to the word of his grace, granting signs and wonders to be done by their hands.

1507 (3) **Matthew 1:21** ". . . she will bear a son, and you shall call his name Jesus, for he will save his people from their sins."

1507 (4) **Acts 4:12** ". . . And there is salvation in no one else, for there is no other name under heaven given among men by which we must be saved."

1508 (1) **1 Corinthians 12:9** . . . to another faith by the same Spirit, to another gifts of healing by the one Spirit. . . .

1508 (2) **1 Corinthians 12:28** And God has appointed in the church first apostles, second prophets, third teachers, then workers of miracles, then healers, helpers, administrators, speakers in various kinds of tongues.

1508 (3) **1 Corinthians 12:30** Do all possess gifts of healing? Do all speak with tongues? Do all interpret?

1509 (1) **John 6:54** . . . he who eats my flesh and drinks my blood has eternal life, and I will raise him up at the last day.

1509 (2) **John 6:58** ". . . This is the bread which came down from heaven, not such as the fathers ate and died; he who eats this bread will live for ever."

1509 (3) **1 Corinthians 11:30** That is why many of you are weak and ill, and some have died.

1510 (1) **Council of Constantinople II (553): DS 216** Truly since your love has wished to take counsel regarding this just as concerning other (matters), my son Celestine, the deacon, has also added in his letter that what was written in the epistle of the blessed Apostle James has been proposed by your love: *If anyone among you is sick, let him call the priests, and let them pray over him, anointing him with oil in the name of the Lord: and the prayer of faith shall save the sufferer, and the Lord shall raise him up, and if he has committed sin, he shall pardon him* [Jas. 5:14 f.]. There is no doubt that this anointing ought to be interpreted or understood of the sick faithful, who can be anointed with the holy oil of chrism, which prepared by a bishop, is permitted not only to priests, but also to all as Christians for anointing in their own necessity or in the necessity of their (people). Moreover, we see that addition to be superfluous; that what is undoubtedly permitted the presbyters is questioned regarding bishops. For, on this account it was said to priests, because the bishops being hindered by other business cannot go to all the sick. But if a bishop, to whom it belongs to prepare the chrism, is able (to do it) or thinks someone is worthy to be visited by him, he can both bless and anoint with the chrism without delay. For, that cannot be administered to penitents, because it is a kind of sacrament. For, how is it supposed that one species (of sacrament) can be granted to those to whom the rest of the sacraments are denied?

1510 (2) **Council of Florence (1439): DS 1324–25** The fifth sacrament is extreme unction, whose matter is the olive oil blessed by the bishop. This sacrament should be given only to the sick of whose death there is fear; and he should be anointed in the following places: on the eyes because of sight, on the ears because of hearing, on the nostrils because of smell, on the mouth because of taste and speech, on the hands because of touch, on the feet because of gait, on the loins because of the delight that flourishes there. The form of this sacrament is the following: *Per istam sanctam unctionem et suam piissimam misericordiam indulgeat tibi Dominus, quidquid per visum,* etc. (Through this holy anointing and his most kind mercy may the Lord forgive you whatever through it, etc.). And similarly on the other members. The minister of this sacrament is the priest. Now the effect is the healing of the mind and, moreover, in so far as it is expedient, of the body itself also. On this sacrament blessed James, the Apostle says: "Is any man sick among you? Let him bring in the priests of the church, and let them pray over him, anointing him with oil in the name of the Lord. And the prayer of faith shall save the sick man; and the Lord shall raise him up: and if he be in sins, they shall be forgiven him" [Jas. 5:14, 15].

(3) **Council of Trent (1551): DS 1695–96** This sacred unction for the sick, how- 1510
ever, was instituted by Christ our Lord as truly and properly a sacrament of the New Testament, alluded to in Mark [Mark 6:13], indeed, but recommended to the faithful and promulgated by James the Apostle and brother of the Lord [can. 1]. "Is any man," he says, "sick among you?" "Let him bring in the priests of the Church, and let them pray over him, anointing him with oil in the name of the Lord and the prayer of faith shall save the sick man, and the Lord shall raise him up; and if he be in sins, they shall be forgiven him" [Jas. 5:14, 15]. In these words, as the Church has learned from apostolic tradition transmitted from hand to hand, he teaches the matter, form, proper ministration, and effect of this salutary sacrament. For the Church has understood that the matter is the oil blessed by the bishop, since the unction very appropriately represents the grace of the Holy Spirit, with which the soul of the sick person is visibly anointed; and that these words are the form: "By this anointing, etc."

Furthermore, the significance and effect of this sacrament are explained in these words: "And the prayer of faith shall save the sick man, and the Lord shall raise him up, and if he be in sins they shall be forgiven him" [Jas. 5:15]. For the thing signified is the grace of the Holy Spirit, whose anointing wipes away sins, if there be any still to be expiated, and the remains of sin, and relieves, and strengthens the soul of the sick person [can. 2] by exciting in him great confidence in divine mercy, supported by which the sick person bears more lightly the miseries and pains of his illness, and resists more easily the temptations of the evil spirit who "lies in wait for his heel" [Gen. 3:15], and sometimes attains bodily health, when it is expedient for the salvation of the soul.

(4) **Council of Trent (1551): DS 1716–17** If anyone says that extreme unction 1510
is not truly and properly a sacrament instituted by our Lord Jesus Christ [cf. Mark 6:13], and promulgated by blessed James the Apostle [Jas. 5:14], but is only a rite accepted by the Fathers, or a human fiction: let him be anathema.

If anyone says that the sacred anointing of the sick does not confer grace nor remit sins, nor alleviate the sick, but that it has already ceased, as if it had at one time only been a healing grace: let him be anathema.

(1) **Mark 6:13** And they cast out many demons, and anointed with oil many that 1511
were sick and healed them.

(2) **James 5:14–15** Is any among you sick? Let him call for the elders of the church, 1511
and let them pray over him, anointing him with oil in the name of the Lord; and the prayer of faith will save the sick man, and the Lord will raise him up; and if he has committed sins, he will be forgiven.

Council of Trent (1551): DS 1696 Furthermore, the significance and effect of this 1512
sacrament are explained in these words: "And the prayer of faith shall save the sick

man, and the Lord shall raise him up, and if he be in sins they shall be forgiven him" [Jas. 5:15]. For the thing signified is the grace of the Holy Spirit, whose anointing wipes away sins, if there be any still to be expiated, and the remains of sin, and relieves, and strengthens the soul of the sick person [can. 2] by exciting in him great confidence in divine mercy, supported by which the sick person bears more lightly the miseries and pains of his illness, and resists more easily the temptations of the evil spirit who "lies in wait for his heel" [Gen. 3:15], and sometimes attains bodily health, when it is expedient for the salvation of the soul.

1513 (1) ***Sacrosanctum concilium* 73** "Extreme Unction," which may also and more fittingly be called "Anointing of the Sick," is not a sacrament for those only who are at the point of death. Hence, as soon as anyone of the faithful begins to be in danger of death from sickness or old age, the fitting time for him to receive this sacrament has certainly already arrived.

1513 (2) **CIC Canon 847, §1** In the administration of sacraments in which the sacred oils are to be used, the minister must use oils pressed from olives or from other plants that have been recently consecrated or blessed by the bishop, with due regard for the prescription of can. 999, n. 2; he is not to use old oils unless there is some necessity.

1514 (1) **CIC Canon 1004, §1** The anointing of the sick can be administered to a member of the faithful who, after having reached the use of reason, begins to be in danger due to sickness or old age.

1514 (2) **CIC Canon 1005** This sacrament is to be administered when there is a doubt whether the sick person has attained the use of reason, whether the person is dangerously ill, or whether the person is dead.

1514 (3) **CIC Canon 1007** The anointing of the sick is not to be conferred upon those who obstinately persist in manifest serious sin.

1514 (4) **CCEO Canon 738** The Christian faithful freely receive anointing of the sick whenever they are gravely ill; pastors of souls and persons who are close to the sick are to see to it that they are supported by this sacrament at an opportune time.

1516 (1) **Council of Trent (1551): DS 1697** And now, as regards the prescribing of those who can receive and administer this sacrament, this, too, was clearly expressed in the words above. For it is also indicated there that the proper ministers of this sacrament are the presbyters of the Church [can. 4], under which name in that place are to be understood not the elders by age or the foremost in rank among the people, but either bishops or priests duly ordained by them with the "imposition of the hands of the priesthood" [1 Tim. 4:14; can. 4].

1516 (2) **Council of Trent (1551): DS 1719** If anyone says that the priests of the Church, whom blessed James exhorts to be brought to anoint the sick, are not the priests ordained by a bishop, but the elders by age in each community, and that for this reason a priest alone is not the proper minister of extreme unction: let him be anathema.

1516 (3) **CIC Canon 1003**

§1. Every priest, and only a priest, validly administers the anointing of the sick.

§2. All priests to whom the care of souls has been committed have the duty and the right to administer the anointing of the sick to all the faithful committed to their pastoral office; for a reasonable cause any other priest can administer this sacrament with at least the presumed consent of the aforementioned priest.

§3. Every priest is allowed to carry blessed oil with him so that he can administer the sacrament of the anointing of the sick in case of necessity.

(4) **CCEO Canon 739, §1** All priests, and only priests, validly administer the anointing of the sick. 1516

***Sacrosanctum concilium* 27** It must be emphasized that rites which are meant to be celebrated in common, with the faithful present and actively participating, should as far as possible be celebrated in that way rather than by an individual and quasi-privately. 1517

This applies with special force to the celebration of Mass (even though every Mass has of itself a public and social nature) and to the administration of the sacraments.

James 5:15 . . . and the prayer of faith will save the sick man, and the Lord will raise him up; and if he has committed sins, he will be forgiven. 1519

(1) **Hebrews 2:15** . . . and deliver all those who through fear of death were subject to lifelong bondage. 1520

(2) **Council of Florence (1439): DS 1325** The minister of this sacrament is the priest. Now the effect is the healing of the mind and, moreover, in so far as it is expedient, of the body itself also. On this sacrament blessed James, the Apostle says: "Is any man sick among you? Let him bring in the priests of the church, and let them pray over him, anointing him with oil in the name of the Lord. And the prayer of faith shall save the sick man; and the Lord shall raise him up: and if he be in sins, they shall be forgiven him" [Jas. 5:14, 15]. 1520

(3) **Council of Trent (1551): DS 1717** If anyone says that the sacred anointing of the sick does not confer grace nor remit sins, nor alleviate the sick, but that it has already ceased, as if it had at one time only been a healing grace: let him be anathema. 1520

John 13:1 Now before the feast of the Passover, when Jesus knew that his hour had come to depart out of this world to the Father, having loved his own who were in the world, he loved them to the end. 1524

***Lumen gentium* 10** Christ the Lord, high priest taken from among men (cf. Heb. 5:1–5), made the new people "a kingdom of priests to God, his Father" (Apoc. 1:6; cf. 5:9–10). The baptized, by regeneration and the anointing of the Holy Spirit, are consecrated to be a spiritual house and a holy priesthood, that through all the works of Christian men they may offer spiritual sacrifices and proclaim the perfection of him who has called them out of darkness into his marvellous light (cf. 1 Pet. 2:4–10). Therefore all the disciples of Christ, persevering in prayer and praising God (cf. Acts 2:42–47), should present themselves as a sacrifice, living, holy and pleasing to God (cf. Rom. 12:1). They should everywhere on earth bear witness to Christ and give an answer to everyone who asks a reason for the hope of an eternal life which is theirs (cf. 1 Pet. 3:15). 1535

Though they differ essentially and not only in degree, the common priesthood of the faithful and the ministerial or hierarchical priesthood are none the less ordered one to another; each in its own proper way shares in the one priesthood of Christ. The ministerial priest, by the sacred power that he has, forms and rules the priestly people; in the person of Christ he effects the eucharistic sacrifice and offers it to God in the name of all the people. The faithful indeed, by virtue of their royal priesthood, participate in the offering of the Eucharist. They exercise that priesthood, too, by the reception of the sacraments, prayer and thanksgiving, the witness of a holy life, abnegation and active charity.

1537 (1) **Hebrews 5:6**

"... as he says also in another place,
"Thou art a priest for ever,
after the order of Melchizedek.""

1537 (2) **Hebrews 7:11** Now if perfection had been attainable through the Levitical priesthood (for under it the people received the law), what further need would there have been for another priest to arise after the order of Melchizedek, rather than one named after the order of Aaron?

1537 (3) **Psalm 110:4**

The Lord has sworn
and will not change his mind,
"You are a priest for ever
after the order of Melchizedek."

1538 ***Lumen gentium* 10:** see 1535.

1539 (1) **Isaiah 61:6**

... but you shall be called the priests of the Lord,
men shall speak of you as the ministers of our God;
you shall eat the wealth of the nations,
and in their riches you shall glory.

1539 (2) **Numbers 1:48–53** For the Lord said to Moses, "Only the tribe of Levi you shall not number, and you shall not take a census of them among the people of Israel; but appoint the Levites over the tabernacle of the testimony, and over all its furnishings, and over all that belongs to it; they are to carry the tabernacle and all its furnishings, and they shall tend it, and shall encamp around the tabernacle. When the tabernacle is to set out, the Levites shall take it down; and when the tabernacle is to be pitched, the Levites shall set it up. And if any one else comes near, he shall be put to death. The people of Israel shall pitch their tents by their companies, every man by his own camp and every man by his own standard; but the Levites shall encamp around the tabernacle of the testimony, that there may be no wrath upon the congregation of the people of Israel; and the Levites shall keep charge of the tabernacle of the testimony."

1539 (3) **Joshua 13:33** But to the tribe of Levi Moses gave no inheritance; the Lord God of Israel is their inheritance, as he said to them.

1539 (4) **Exodus 29:1–30** "Now this is what you shall do to them to consecrate them, that they may serve me as priests. Take one young bull and two rams without blemish, and unleavened bread, unleavened cakes mixed with oil, and unleavened wafers spread with oil. You shall make them of fine wheat flour. And you shall put them in one basket and bring them in the basket, and bring the bull and the two rams. You shall bring Aaron and his sons to the door of the tent of meeting, and wash them with water. And you shall take the garments, and put on Aaron the coat and the robe of the ephod, and the ephod, and the breastpiece, and gird him with the skilfully woven band of the ephod; and you shall set the turban on his head, and put the holy crown upon the turban. And you shall take the anointing oil, and pour it on his head and anoint him. Then you shall bring his sons, and put coats on them, and you shall gird them with girdles and bind caps on them; and the priesthood shall be theirs by a perpetual statute. Thus you shall ordain Aaron and his sons.

"Then you shall bring the bull before the tent of meeting. Aaron and his sons shall lay their hands upon the head of the bull, and you shall kill the bull before the Lord, at the door of the tent of meeting, and shall take part of the blood of the bull and put it upon the horns of the altar with your finger, and the rest of the blood you shall pour out at the base of the altar. And you shall take all the fat that covers the entrails, and the appendage of the liver, and the two kidneys with the fat that is on them, and burn them upon the altar. But the flesh of the bull, and its skin, and its dung, you shall burn with fire outside the camp; it is a sin offering.

"Then you shall take one of the rams, and Aaron and his sons shall lay their hands upon the head of the ram, and you shall slaughter the ram, and shall take its blood and throw it against the altar round about. Then you shall cut the ram into pieces, and wash its entrails and its legs, and put them with its pieces and its head, and burn the whole ram upon the altar; it is a burnt offering to the Lord; it is a pleasing odor, an offering by fire to the Lord.

"You shall take the other ram; and Aaron and his sons shall lay their hands upon the head of the ram, and you shall kill the ram, and take part of its blood and put it upon the tip of the right ear of Aaron and upon the tips of the right ears of his sons, and upon the thumbs of their right hands, and upon the great toes of their right feet, and throw the rest of the blood against the altar round about. Then you shall take part of the blood that is on the altar, and of the anointing oil, and sprinkle it upon Aaron and his garments, and upon his sons and his sons' garments with him; and he and his garments shall be holy, and his sons and his sons' garments with him.

"You shall also take the fat of the ram, and the fat tail, and the fat that covers the entrails, and the appendage of the liver, and the two kidneys with the fat that is on them, and the right thigh (for it is a ram of ordination), and one loaf of bread, and one cake of bread with oil, and one wafer, out of the basket of unleavened bread that is before the Lord; and you shall put all these in the hands of Aaron and in the hands of his sons, and wave them for a wave offering before the Lord. Then you shall take them from their hands, and burn them on the altar in addition to the burnt offering, as a pleasing odor before the Lord; it is an offering by fire to the Lord.

"And you shall take the breast of the ram of Aaron's ordination and wave it for a wave offering before the Lord; and it shall be your portion. And you shall consecrate the breast of the wave offering, and the thigh of the priests' portion, which is waved, and which is offered from the ram of ordination, since it is for Aaron and for his sons. It shall be for Aaron and his sons as a perpetual due from the people of Israel, for it is the priests' portion to be offered by the people of Israel from their peace offerings; it is their offering to the Lord.

"The holy garments of Aaron shall be for his sons after him, to be anointed in them and ordained in them. The son who is priest in his place shall wear them seven days, when he comes into the tent of meeting to minister in the holy place. . . ."

(5) **Leviticus 8** The Lord said to Moses, "Take Aaron and his sons with him, and 1539
the garments, and the anointing oil, and the bull of the sin offering, and the two rams, and the basket of unleavened bread; and assemble all the congregation at the door of the tent of meeting." And Moses did as the Lord commanded him; and the congregation was assembled at the door of the tent of meeting.

And Moses said to the congregation, "This is the thing which the Lord has commanded to be done." And Moses brought Aaron and his sons, and washed them with water. And he put on him the coat, and girded him with the girdle, and clothed him with the robe, and put the ephod upon him, and girded him with the skilfully woven band of the ephod, binding it to him therewith. And he placed the breastpiece on him, and in the breastpiece he put the Urim and the Thummim. And he set the turban upon his head, and on the turban, in front, he set the golden plate, the holy crown, as the Lord commanded Moses.

Then Moses took the anointing oil, and anointed the tabernacle and all that was in it, and consecrated them. And he sprinkled some of it on the altar seven times, and anointed the altar and all its utensils, and the laver and its base, to consecrate them. And he poured some of the anointing oil on Aaron's head, and anointed him, to consecrate him. And Moses brought Aaron's sons, and clothed them with coats, and girded them with girdles, and bound caps on them, as the Lord commanded Moses.

Then he brought the bull of the sin offering; and Aaron and his sons laid their hands upon the head of the bull of the sin offering. And Moses killed it, and took the blood, and with his finger put it on the horns of the altar round about, and purified the altar, and poured out the blood at the base of the altar, and consecrated it, to make atonement for it. And he took all the fat that was on the entrails, and the appendage of the liver, and the two kidneys with their fat, and Moses burned them on the altar. But the bull, and its skin, and its flesh, and its dung, he burned with fire outside the camp, as the Lord commanded Moses.

Then he presented the ram of the burnt offering; and Aaron and his sons laid their hands on the head of the ram. And Moses killed it, and threw the blood upon the altar round about. And when the ram was cut into pieces, Moses burned the head and the pieces and the fat. And when the entrails and the legs were washed with water, Moses burned the whole ram on the altar, as a burnt offering, a pleasing odor, an offering by fire to the Lord, as the Lord commanded Moses.

Then he presented the other ram, the ram of ordination; and Aaron and his sons laid their hands on the head of the ram. And Moses killed it, and took some of its blood and put it on the tip of Aaron's right ear and on the thumb of his right hand and on the great toe of his right foot. And Aaron's sons were brought, and Moses put some of the blood on the tips of their right ears and on the thumbs of their right hands and on the great toes of their right feet; and Moses threw the blood upon the altar round about. Then he took the fat, and the fat tail, and all the fat that was on the entrails, and the appendage of the liver, and the two kidneys with their fat, and the right thigh; and out of the basket of unleavened bread which was before the Lord he took one unleavened cake, and one cake of bread with oil, and one wafer, and placed them on the fat and on the right thigh; and he put all these in the hands of Aaron and in the hands of his sons, and waved them as a wave offering before the Lord. Then Moses took them from their hands, and burned them on the altar with the burnt offering, as an ordination offering, a pleasing odor, an offering by fire to the Lord. And Moses took the breast, and waved it for a wave offering before the Lord; it was Moses' portion of the ram of ordination, as the Lord commanded Moses.

Then Moses took some of the anointing oil and of the blood which was on the altar, and sprinkled it upon Aaron and his garments, and also upon his sons and his sons' garments; so he consecrated Aaron and his garments, and his sons and his sons' garments with him.

And Moses said to Aaron and his sons, "Boil the flesh at the door of the tent of meeting, and there eat it and the bread that is in the basket of ordination offerings, as I commanded, saying, 'Aaron and his sons shall eat it'; and what remains of the flesh and the bread you shall burn with fire. And you shall not go out from the door of the tent of meeting for seven days, until the days of your ordination are completed, for it will take seven days to ordain you. As has been done today, the Lord has commanded to be done to make atonement for you. At the door of the tent of meeting you shall remain day and night for seven days, performing what the Lord has charged, lest you die; for so I am commanded." And Aaron and his sons did all the things which the Lord commanded by Moses.

(1) **Malachi 2:7–9** ". . . For the lips of a priest should guard knowledge, and men should seek instruction from his mouth, for he is the messenger of the Lord of hosts. But you have turned aside from the way; you have caused many to stumble by your instruction; you have corrupted the covenant of Levi, says the Lord of hosts, and so I make you despised and abased before all the people, inasmuch as you have not kept my ways but have shown partiality in your instruction." 1540

(2) **Hebrews 5:3** Because of this he is bound to offer sacrifice for his own sins as well as for those of the people. 1540

(3) **Hebrews 7:27** He has no need, like those high priests, to offer sacrifices daily, first for his own sins and then for those of the people; he did this once for all when he offered up himself. 1540

(4) **Hebrews 10:1–4** For since the law has but a shadow of the good things to come instead of the true form of these realities, it can never, by the same sacrifices which are continually offered year after year, make perfect those who draw near. Otherwise, would they not have ceased to be offered? If the worshipers had once been cleansed, they would no longer have any consciousness of sin. But in these sacrifices there is a reminder of sin year after year. For it is impossible that the blood of bulls and goats should take away sins. 1540

Numbers 11:24–25 So Moses went out and told the people the words of the Lord; and he gathered seventy men of the elders of the people, and placed them round about the tent. Then the Lord came down in the cloud and spoke to him, and took some of the spirit that was upon him and put it upon the seventy elders; and when the spirit rested upon them, they prophesied. But they did so no more. 1541

(1) **Hebrews 6:20** . . . where Jesus has gone as a forerunner on our behalf, having become a high priest for ever after the order of Melchizedek. 1544

(2) **Genesis 14:18** And Melchizedek king of Salem brought out bread and wine; he was priest of God Most High. 1544

(1) **Revelation 5:9–10** . . . and they sang a new song, saying, 1546
"Worthy art thou to take the scroll and to open its seals,
for thou wast slain and by thy blood didst ransom men for God
from every tribe and tongue and people and nation,
and hast made them a kingdom and priests to our God,
and they shall reign on earth."

(2) **1 Peter 2:5** . . . and like living stones be yourselves built into a spiritual house, to be a holy priesthood, to offer spiritual sacrifices acceptable to God through Jesus Christ. 1546

1546 (3) **1 Peter 2:9** But you are a chosen race, a royal priesthood, a holy nation, God's own people, that you may declare the wonderful deeds of him who called you out of darkness into his marvelous light.

1548 (1) ***Lumen gentium* 10**: see 1535.

1548 (2) ***Lumen gentium* 28** Christ, whom the Father hallowed and sent into the world (Jn. 10:36), has, through his apostles, made their successors, the bishops namely, sharers in his consecration and mission; and these, in their turn, duly entrusted in varying degrees various members of the Church with the office of their ministry. Thus the divinely instituted ecclesiastical ministry is exercised in different degrees by those who even from ancient times have been called bishops, priests and deacons. Whilst not having the supreme degree of the pontifical office, and notwithstanding the fact that they depend on the bishops in the exercise of their own proper power, the priests are for all that associated with them by reason of their sacerdotal dignity; and in virtue of the sacrament of Orders, after the image of Christ, the supreme and eternal priest (Heb. 5:1–10; 7:24; 9:11–28), they are consecrated in order to preach the Gospel and shepherd the faithful as well as to celebrate divine worship as true priests of the New Testament. On the level of their own ministry sharing in the unique office of Christ, the mediator (1 Tim. 2:5), they announce to all the word of God. However, it is in the eucharistic cult or in the eucharistic assembly of the faithful (*synaxis*) that they exercise in a supreme degree their sacred functions; there, acting in the person of Christ and proclaiming his mystery, they unite the votive offerings of the faithful to the sacrifice of Christ their head, and in the sacrifice of the Mass they make present again and apply, until the coming of the Lord (cf. 1 Cor. 11:26), the unique sacrifice of the New Testament, that namely of Christ offering himself once for all a spotless victim to the Father (cf. Heb. 9:11–28). And on behalf of the faithful who are moved to sorrow or are stricken with sickness they exercise in an eminent degree a ministry of reconciliation and comfort, whilst they carry the needs and supplications of the faithful to God the Father (cf. Heb. 5:1–4). Exercising, within the limits of the authority which is theirs, the office of Christ, the Shepherd and Head, they assemble the family of God as a brotherhood fired with a single ideal, and through Christ in the Spirit they lead it to God the Father. In the midst of the flock they adore him in spirit and in truth (cf. Jn. 4:24). In short, they labor in preaching and instruction (cf. 1 Tim. 5:17), firmly adhering to what they read and meditate in the law of God, inculcating that which they believe, and putting into practice what they preach.

The priests, prudent cooperators of the episcopal college and its support and mouthpiece, called to the service of the People of God, constitute, together with their bishop, a unique sacerdotal college (*presbyterium*) dedicated it is true to a variety of distinct duties. In each local assembly of the faithful they represent in a certain sense the bishop, with whom they are associated in all trust and generosity; in part they take upon themselves his duties and solicitude and in their daily toils discharge them. Those who, under the authority of the bishop, sanctify and govern that portion of the Lord's flock assigned to them render the universal Church visible in their locality and contribute efficaciously towards building up the whole body of Christ (cf. Eph. 4:12). And ever anxious for the good of the children of God they should be eager to lend their efforts to the pastoral work of the whole diocese, nay rather of the whole Church. By reason of this sharing in the priesthood and mission of the bishop the priests should see in him a true father and obey him with all respect. The bishop, on his side, should treat the priests, his helpers, as his sons and friends, just as Christ calls his disciples no longer servants but friends (cf. Jn. 15:15). All priests, then, whether diocesan or religious, by reason of the sacrament of Orders and of the ministry correspond to and cooperate with the body of bishops and, according to their vocation and the grace that is given them, they serve the welfare of the whole Church.

In virtue of their sacred ordination and of their common mission all priests are united together by bonds of intimate brotherhood, which manifests itself in a spontaneously and gladly given mutual help, whether spiritual or temporal, whether pastoral or personal, through the medium of reunions and community life, work and fraternal charity.

As to the faithful, they (the priests) should bestow their paternal attention and solicitude on them, whom they have begotten spiritually through baptism and instruction (cf. 1 Cor. 4:15; 1 Pet. 1:23). Gladly constituting themselves models of the flock (cf. 1 Pet. 5:3), they should preside over and serve their local community in such a way that it may deserve to be called by the name which is given to the unique People of God in its entirety, that is to say, the Church of God (cf. 1 Cor 1:2; 2 Cor. 1:1, and *passim*). They should be mindful that by their daily conduct and solicitude they display the reality of a truly priestly and pastoral ministry both to believers and unbelievers alike, to Catholics and non-Catholics; that they are bound to bear witness before all men of the truth and of the life, and as good shepherds seek after those too (cf. Lk. 15:4–7) who, whilst having been baptized in the Catholic Church, have given up the practice of the sacraments, or even fallen away from the faith.

Since the human race today is tending more and more towards civil, economic and social unity, it is all the more necessary that priests should unite their efforts and combine their resources under the leadership of the bishops and the Supreme Pontiff and thus eliminate division and dissension in every shape or form, so that all mankind may be led into the unity of the family of God.

(3) ***Sacrosanctum concilium* 33** Although the sacred liturgy is principally the wor- 1548
ship of the divine majesty it likewise contains much instruction for the faithful. For in the liturgy God speaks to his people, and Christ is still proclaiming his Gospel. And the people reply to God both by song and prayer.

Moreover the prayers addressed to God by the priest who, in the person of Christ, presides over the assembly, are said in the name of the entire holy people and of all present. And the visible signs which the sacred liturgy uses to signify invisible divine things have been chosen by Christ or by the Church. Thus not only when things are read "which were written for our instruction" (Rom. 15:4), but also when the Church prays or sings or acts, the faith of those taking part is nourished, and their minds are raised to God so that they may offer him their spiritual homage and receive his grace more abundantly.

Therefore in the revision of the liturgy the following general norms should be observed. . . .

(4) ***Christus Dominus* 11** A diocese is a section of the People of God entrusted to a 1548
bishop to be guided by him with the assistance of his clergy so that, loyal to its pastor and formed by him into one community in the Holy Spirit through the Gospel and the Eucharist, it constitutes one particular church in which the one, holy, catholic and apostolic Church of Christ is truly present and active.

Individual bishops to whom the care of particular dioceses is committed care for their flocks under the authority of the Supreme Pontiff, in the name of God, as their proper, ordinary and immediate pastors, sanctifying and governing them. They should, however, recognize the rights which are conferred by law on Patriarchs or other hierarchical authorities.

Bishops should devote themselves to their apostolic office as witnesses of Christ to all men. They should not limit themselves to those who already acknowledge the Prince of Pastors but should also devote their energies wholeheartedly to those who have strayed in any way from the path of truth or who have no knowledge of the gospel of Christ and of his saving mercy, so that ultimately all men may walk "in all goodness, justice and truth" (Eph. 5:9).

1548 (5) ***Presbyterorum ordinis* 2** The Lord Jesus "whom the Father consecrated and sent into the world" (Jn. 10:36) makes his whole Mystical Body sharer in the anointing of the Spirit wherewith he has been anointed: for in that Body all the faithful are made a holy and kingly priesthood, they offer spiritual sacrifices to God through Jesus Christ, and they proclaim the virtues of him who has called them out of darkness into his admirable light. Therefore there is no such thing as a member that has not a share in the mission of the whole Body. Rather, every single member ought to reverence Jesus in his heart and by the spirit of prophecy give testimony of Jesus.

However, the Lord also appointed certain men as ministers, in order that they might be united in one body in which "all the members have not the same function" (Rom. 12:4). These men were to hold in the community of the faithful the sacred power of Order, that of offering sacrifice and forgiving sins, and were to exercise the priestly office publicly on behalf of men in the name of Christ. Thus Christ sent the apostles as he himself had been sent by the Father, and then through the apostles made their successors, the bishops, sharers in his consecration and mission.

The function of the bishops' ministry was handed over in a subordinate degree to priests so that they might be appointed in the order of the priesthood and be co-workers of the episcopal order for the proper fulfilment of the apostolic mission that had been entrusted to it by Christ.

Because it is joined with the episcopal order the office of priests shares in the authority by which Christ himself builds up and sanctifies and rules his Body. Hence the priesthood of priests, while presupposing the sacraments of initiation, is nevertheless conferred by its own particular sacrament. Through that sacrament priests by the anointing of the Holy Spirit are signed with a special character and so are configured to Christ the priest in such a way that they are able to act in the person of Christ the head.

Since they share in the function of the apostles in their own degree, priests are given the grace by God to be the ministers of Jesus Christ among the nations, fulfilling the sacred task of the Gospel, that the oblation of the gentiles may be made acceptable and sanctified in the Holy Spirit. For it is by the apostolic herald of the Gospel that the People of God is called together and gathered so that all who belong to this people, sanctified as they are by the Holy Spirit, may offer themselves "a living sacrifice, holy and acceptable to God" (Rom. 12:1). Through the ministry of priests the spiritual sacrifice of the faithful is completed in union with the sacrifice of Christ the only mediator, which in the Eucharist is offered through the priests' hands in the name of the whole Church in an unbloody and sacramental manner until the Lord himself come. The ministry of priests is directed to this and finds its consummation in it. For their ministration, which begins with the announcement of the Gospel, draws its force and power from the sacrifice of Christ and tends to this, that "the whole redeemed city, that is, the whole assembly and community of the saints should be offered as a universal sacrifice to God through the High Priest who offered himself in his passion for us that we might be the body of so great a Head."

Therefore the object that priests strive for by their ministry and life is the procuring of the glory of God the Father in Christ. That glory consists in men's conscious, free, and grateful acceptance of God's plan as completed in Christ and their manifestation of it in their whole life. Thus priests, whether they devote themselves to prayer and adoration, or preach the Word, or offer the eucharistic sacrifice and administer the other sacraments, or exercise other services for the benefit of men, are contributing at once to the increase of God's glory and men's growth in the divine life. And all these activities, since they flow from the pasch of Christ, will find their consummation in the glorious coming of the same Lord, when he shall have delivered up the kingdom to God and the Father.

(6) ***Presbyterorum ordinis* 6** Priests exercise the function of Christ as Pastor and 1548
Head in proportion to their share of authority. In the name of the bishop they gather the family of God as a brotherhood endowed with the spirit of unity and lead it in Christ through the Spirit to God the Father. For the exercise of this ministry, as for the rest of the priests' functions, a spiritual power is given them, a power whose purpose is to build up. And in building up the Church priests ought to treat everybody with the greatest kindness after the model of our Lord. They should act towards people not according to what may please men, but according to the demands of Christian doctrine and life. They should teach them and warn them as their dearest children, according to the words of the apostle: "Be urgent in season and out of season, convince, rebuke, and exhort, be unfailing in patience and in teaching" (2 Tim. 4:2).

For this reason it is the priests' part as instructors of the people in the faith to see to it either personally or through others that each member of the faithful shall be led in the Holy Spirit to the full development of his own vocation in accordance with the Gospel teaching, and to sincere and active charity and the liberty with which Christ has set us free. Very little good will be achieved by ceremonies however beautiful, or societies however flourishing, if they are not directed towards educating people to reach Christian maturity. To encourage this maturity priests will make their help available to people to enable them to determine the solution to their problems and the will of God in the crises of life, great or small. Christians must also be trained so as not to live only for themselves. Rather, according to the demands of the new law of charity every man as he has received grace ought to minister it one to another, and in this way all should carry out their duties in a Christian way in the community of their fellow men.

Although priests owe service to everybody, the poor and the weaker ones have been committed to their care in a special way. It was with these that the Lord himself associated, and the preaching of the Gospel to them is given as a sign of his messianic mission. Priests will look after young people with special diligence. This applies also to married couples and parents. It is desirable that these should meet in friendly groups to help each other in the task of more easily and more fully living in a Christian way of life that is often difficult. Priests should keep in mind that all religious, men and women, being a particularly eminent group in the Lord's house, are deserving of having special care directed to their spiritual progress for the good of the whole Church. Finally, priests ought to be especially devoted to the sick and the dying, visiting them and comforting them in the Lord.

The pastor's task is not limited to individual care of the faithful. It extends by right also to the formation of a genuine Christian community. But if a community spirit is to be properly cultivated it must embrace not only the local church but the universal Church. A local community ought not merely to promote the care of the faithful within itself, but should be imbued with the missionary spirit and smooth the path to Christ for all men. But it must regard as its special charge those under instruction and the newly converted who are gradually educated in knowing and living the Christian life.

However, no Christian community is built up which does not grow from and hinge on the celebration of the most holy Eucharist. From this all education for community spirit must begin. This eucharistic celebration, to be full and sincere, ought to lead on the one hand to the various works of charity and mutual help, and on the other hand to missionary activity and the various forms of Christian witness.

In addition the ecclesial community exercises a truly motherly function in leading souls to Christ by its charity, its prayer, its example and its penitential works. For it constitutes an effective instrument for showing or smoothing the path towards Christ and his Church for those who have not yet found faith; while also encouraging, supporting and strengthening believers for their spiritual struggles.

In building up a community of Christians, priests can never be the servants of any human ideology or party. Rather their task as heralds of the Gospel and pastors of the Church is the attainment of the spiritual growth of the Body of Christ.

1549 (1) ***Lumen gentium* 21** In the person of the bishops, then, to whom the priests render assistance, the Lord Jesus Christ, supreme high priest, is present in the midst of the faithful. Though seated at the right hand of God the Father, he is not absent from the assembly of his pontiffs; on the contrary indeed, it is above all through their signal service that he preaches the Word of God to all peoples and administers without cease to the faithful the sacraments of faith; that through their paternal care (cf. 1 Cor. 4:15) he incorporates, by a supernatural rebirth, new members into his body; that finally, through their wisdom and prudence he directs and guides the people of the New Testament on their journey towards eternal beatitude. Chosen to shepherd the Lord's flock, these pastors are servants of Christ and stewards of the mysteries of God (cf. 1 Cor. 4:1), to whom is entrusted the duty of affirming the Gospel of the grace of God (cf. Rom. 15:16; Acts 20:24), and of gloriously promulgating the Spirit and proclaiming justification (cf. 2 Cor. 3:8–9).

In order to fulfil such exalted functions, the apostles were endowed by Christ with a special outpouring of the Holy Spirit coming upon them (cf. Acts 1:8; 2:4; Jn. 20:22–23), and, by the imposition of hands (cf. 1 Tim. 4:14; 2 Tim. 1:6–7), they passed on to their auxiliaries the gift of the Spirit, which is transmitted down to our day through episcopal consecration. The holy synod teaches, moreover, that the fullness of the sacrament of Orders is conferred by episcopal consecration, that fullness, namely, which both in the liturgical tradition of the Church and in the language of the Fathers of the Church is called the high priesthood, the acme of the sacred ministry. Now, episcopal consecration confers, together with the office of sanctifying, the duty also of teaching and ruling, which, however, of their very nature can be exercised only in hierarchical communion with the head and members of the college. In fact, from tradition, which is expressed especially in the liturgical rites and in the customs of both the Eastern and Western Church, it is abundantly clear that by the imposition of hands and through the words of the consecration, the grace of the Holy Spirit is given, and a sacred character is impressed in such wise that bishops, in a resplendent and visible manner, take the place of Christ himself, teacher, shepherd and priest, and act as his representatives (*in eius persona*). It is the right of bishops to admit newly elected members into the episcopal body by means of the sacrament of Orders.

1549 (2) **Ignatius of Antioch, *Epistula ad Magnesios* 6, 1** Since, then, in the persons mentioned before I have with the eyes of the faith looked upon your whole community and have come to love it, I exhort you to strive to do all things in harmony with God: the bishop is to preside in the place of God, while the presbyters are to function as the council of the Apostles, and the deacons, who are most dear to me, are entrusted with the ministry of Jesus Christ, who before time began was with the Father and has at last appeared.

(1) **Mark 10:43–45** ". . . But it shall not be so among you; but whoever would be great among you must be your servant, and whoever would be first among you must be slave of all. For the Son of man also came not to be served but to serve, and to give his life as a ransom for many." 1551

(2) **1 Peter 5:3** . . . not as domineering over those in your charge but being examples to the flock. 1551

(3) **John 21:15–17** When they had finished breakfast, Jesus said to Simon Peter, "Simon, son of John, do you love me more than these?" He said to him, "Yes, Lord; you know that I love you." He said to him, "Feed my lambs." A second time he said to him, "Simon, son of John, do you love me?" He said to him, "Yes, Lord; you know that I love you." He said to him, "Tend my sheep." He said to him the third time, "Simon, son of John, do you love me?" Peter was grieved because he said to him the third time, "Do you love me?" And he said to him, "Lord, you know everything; you know that I love you." Jesus said to him, "Feed my sheep. . . ." 1551

(1) ***Sacrosanctum concilium* 33:** see 1548 (3). 1552

(2) ***Lumen gentium* 10:** see 1535. 1552

***Lumen gentium* 22** Just as, in accordance with the Lord's decree, St. Peter and the rest of the apostles constitute a unique apostolic college, so in like fashion the Roman Pontiff, Peter's successor, and the bishops, the successors of the apostles, are related with and united to one another. Indeed, the very ancient discipline whereby the bishops installed throughout the whole world lived in communion with one another and with the Roman Pontiff in a bond of unity, charity and peace; likewise the holding of councils in order to settle conjointly, in a decision rendered balanced and equitable by the advice of many, all questions of major importance; all this points clearly to the collegiate character and structure of the episcopal order, and the holding of ecumenical councils in the course of the centuries bears this out unmistakably. Indeed, pointing to it also quite clearly is the custom, dating from very early times, of summoning a number of bishops to take part in the elevation of one newly chosen to the highest sacerdotal office. One is constituted a member of the episcopal body in virtue of the sacramental consecration and by the hierarchical communion with the head and members of the college. 1559

The college or body of bishops has for all that no authority unless united with the Roman Pontiff, Peter's successor, as its head, whose primatial authority, let it be added, over all, whether pastors or faithful, remains in its integrity. For the Roman Pontiff, by reason of his office as Vicar of Christ, namely, and as pastor of the entire Church, has full, supreme and universal power over the whole Church, a power which he can always exercise unhindered. The order of bishops is the successor to the college of the apostles in their role as teachers and pastors, and in it the apostolic college is perpetuated. Together with their head, the Supreme Pontiff, and never apart from him, they have supreme and full authority over the universal Church; but this power cannot be exercised without the agreement of the Roman Pontiff. The Lord made Peter alone the rock-foundation and holder of the keys of the Church (cf. Mt. 16:18–19), and constituted him shepherd of his whole flock (cf. Jn. 21:15 ff.). It is clear, however, that the office of binding and loosing which was given to Peter (Mt. 16:19), was also assigned to the college of the apostles united to its head (Mt. 18:18; 28:16–20). This college, in so far as it is composed of many members, is the expression of the multifariousness and universality of the People of God; and of the unity of the flock of Christ, in so far as it is assembled under one head. In it the bishops, whilst loyally respecting the primacy and pre-eminence of their head, exercise their own proper authority for the good of their faithful, indeed even for the good of the whole Church, the organic structure and harmony of which are strengthened by the continued influence of the Holy Spirit. The supreme authority over the whole Church, which this college possesses, is exercised in a solemn way in an ecumenical council. There never is an ecumenical council which is not confirmed or at least recognized as such by Peter's successor. And it is the prerogative of the Roman Pontiff to convoke such councils, to preside over them and to confirm them. This same collegiate power can be exercised in union with the pope by the bishops while living in different parts of the world, provided the head of the college summon them to collegiate action, or at least approve or freely admit the corporate action of the unassembled bishops, so that a truly collegiate act may result.

1560 (1) ***Lumen gentium* 23:** see 1202 (1).

1560 (2) ***Christus Dominus* 4** The bishops, by virtue of their sacramental consecration and their hierarchical communion with the head of the college and its other members, are constituted members of the episcopal body. "The order of bishops is the successor to the college of the apostles in their role as teachers and pastors, and in it the apostolic college is perpetuated. Together with their head, the Supreme Pontiff, and never apart from him, they have supreme and full authority over the universal Church, but this power cannot be exercised without the agreement of the Roman Pontiff." This authority "is exercised in a solemn way in an ecumenical council." Accordingly the sacred Synod decrees that all bishops who are members of the episcopal college have the right to take part in an ecumenical council. "This same collegiate power can be exercised in union with the Pope by the bishops whilst living in different parts of the world, provided the head of the college summon them to collegiate action, or at least approve or freely admit the corporate action of the unassembled bishops, so that a truly collegiate action may result."

1560 (3) ***Christus Dominus* 36** From the earliest ages of the Church, bishops in charge of particular churches, inspired by a spirit of fraternal charity and by zeal for the universal mission entrusted to the apostles, have pooled their resources and their aspirations in order to promote both the common good and the good of individual churches. With this end in view synods, provincial councils and, finally, plenary councils were established in which the bishops determined on a common program to be followed in various churches both for teaching the truths of the faith and for regulating ecclesiastical discipline.

This sacred Ecumenical Synod expresses its earnest hope that these admirable institutions—synods and councils—may flourish with renewed vigor so that the growth of religion and the maintenance of discipline in the various churches may increasingly be more effectively provided for in accordance with the needs of the times.

1560 (4) ***Christus Dominus* 37** It is often impossible, nowadays especially, for bishops to exercise their office suitably and fruitfully unless they establish closer understanding and cooperation with other bishops. Since episcopal conferences—many such have already been established in different countries—have produced outstanding examples of a more fruitful apostolate, this sacred Synod judges that it would be in the highest degree helpful if in all parts of the world the bishops of each country or region would meet regularly, so that by sharing their wisdom and experience and exchanging views they may jointly formulate a program for the common good of the Church.

Therefore, the sacred Synod makes the following decrees concerning episcopal conferences. . . .

(5) ***Ad gentes divinitus* 5** From the beginning of his ministry the Lord Jesus "called to himself those whom he wished and he caused twelve of them to be with him and to be sent out preaching" (Mk. 3:13; cf. Mt. 10:1–42). Thus the apostles were both the seeds of the new Israel and the beginning of the sacred hierarchy. Later, before he was assumed into heaven (cf. Acts 1:11), after he had fulfilled in himself the mysteries of our salvation and the renewal of all things by his death and resurrection, the Lord, who had received all power in heaven and on earth (cf. Mt. 28:18), founded his Church as the sacrament of salvation; and just as he had been sent by the Father (cf. Jn. 20:21), so he sent the apostles into the whole world, commanding them: "Go, therefore, and make disciples of all nations, baptizing them in the name of the Father and of the Son and of the Holy Spirit; teaching them to observe all that I have commanded you" (Mt. 28:19 ff.); "Go into the whole world, preach the Gospel to every creature. He who believes and is baptized shall be saved; but he who does not believe, shall be condemned" (Mk. 16:15 ff.). Hence the Church has an obligation to proclaim the faith and salvation which comes from Christ, both by reason of the express command which the order of bishops inherited from the apostles, an obligation in the discharge of which they are assisted by priests, and one which they share with the successor of St. Peter, the supreme pastor of the Church, and also by reason of the life which Christ infuses into his members: "From him the whole body, being closely joined and knit together through every joint of the system, according to the functioning in due measure of each single part, derives its increase to the building up of itself in love" (Eph. 4:16). The mission of the Church is carried out by means of that activity through which, in obedience to Christ's command and moved by the grace and love of the Holy Spirit, the Church makes itself fully present to all men and peoples in order to lead them to the faith, freedom and peace of Christ by the example of its life and teaching, by the sacraments and other means of grace. Its aim is to open up for all men a free and sure path to full participation in the mystery of Christ. 1560

Since this mission continues and, in the course of history, unfolds the mission of Christ, who was sent to evangelize the poor, then the Church, urged on by the Spirit of Christ, must walk the road Christ himself walked, a way of poverty and obedience, of service and self-sacrifice even to death, a death from which he emerged victorious by his resurrection. So it was that the apostles walked in hope and by much trouble and suffering filled up what was lacking in the sufferings of Christ for his body, which is the Church. Often, too, the seed was the blood of Christians.

(6) ***Ad gentes divinitus* 6** This task which must be carried out by the order of bishops, under the leadership of Peter's successor and with the prayers and cooperation of the whole Church, is one and the same everywhere and in all situations, although, because of circumstances, it may not always be exercised in the same way. The differences which must be recognized in this activity of the Church, do not flow from the inner nature of the mission itself, but from the circumstances in which it is exercised. 1560

These circumstances depend either on the Church itself or on the peoples, classes or men to whom its mission is directed. Although the Church possesses in itself the totality and fullness of the means of salvation, it does not always, in fact cannot, use every one of them immediately, but it has to make beginnings and work by slow stages to give effect to God's plan. Sometimes after a successful start it has cause to mourn a setback, or it may linger in a state of semi-fulfillment and insufficiency. With regard to peoples, classes and men it is only by degrees that it touches and penetrates them and so raises them to a catholic perfection. In each situation and circumstance a proper line of action and effective means should be adopted.

The special undertakings in which preachers of the Gospel, sent by the Church, and going into the whole world, carry out the work of preaching the Gospel and implanting the Church among people who do not yet believe in Christ, are generally called "missions." Such undertakings are accomplished by missionary activity and are, for the most part, carried out in defined territories recognized by the Holy See. The special end of this missionary activity is the evangelization and the implanting of the Church among peoples or groups in which it has not yet taken root. All over the world indigenous particular churches ought to grow from the seed of the word of God, churches which would be adequately organized and would possess their own proper strength and maturity. With their own hierarchy and faithful, and sufficiently endowed with means adapted to the living of a full Christian life, they should contribute to the good of the whole Church. The principal instrument in this work of implanting the Church is the preaching of the Gospel of Jesus Christ. It was to announce this Gospel that the Lord sent his disciples into the whole world, that men, having been reborn by the word of God (cf. 1 Pet. 1:23), might through baptism, be joined to the Church which, as the Body of the Word Incarnate, lives and is nourished by the word of God and the Eucharist (cf. Acts 4:23).

Various stages, which are sometimes intermingled, are to be found in this missionary activity of the Church; first there is the beginning or planting and then a time of freshness and youthfulness. Nor does the Church's missionary activity cease once this point has been passed; the obligation to carry on the work devolves on the particular churches already constituted, an obligation to preach the Gospel to all who are still outside.

Moreover, it often happens that, owing to various cases, the groups among whom the Church operates are utterly changed so that an entirely new situation arises. Then the Church must consider whether these new circumstances require that she should once again exercise her missionary activity. The situation, however, is often of such a nature that for the time being there is no possibility of directly and immediately preaching the Gospel. In that case missionaries, patiently, prudently, and with great faith, can and ought at least bear witness to the love and kindness of Christ and thus prepare a way for the Lord, and in some way make him present.

It is clear, therefore, that missionary activity flows immediately from the very nature of the Church. Missionary activity extends the saving faith of the Church, it expands and perfects its catholic unity, it is sustained by its apostolicity, it activates the collegiate sense of its hierarchy, and bears witness to its sanctity which it both extends and promotes. Missionary work among the nations differs from the pastoral care of the faithful and likewise from efforts aimed at restoring Christian unity. Nevertheless, these two latter are very closely connected with the Church's missionary endeavor because the division of Christians is injurious to the holy work of preaching the Gospel to every creature, and deprives many people of access to the faith. Because of the Church's mission, all baptized people are called upon to come together in one flock that they might bear unanimous witness to Christ their Lord before the nations. And if they cannot yet fully bear witness to one faith, they should at least be imbued with mutual respect and love.

1560 (7) ***Ad gentes divinitus* 38** All bishops, as members of the body of bishops which succeeds the college of the apostles, are consecrated not for one diocese alone, but for the salvation of the whole world. The command of Christ to preach the Gospel to every creature (Mk. 16:15) applies primarily and immediately to them—with Peter, and subject to Peter. From this arises that communion and cooperation of the churches which is so necessary today for the work of evangelization. Because of this communion, each church cares for all the others, they make known their needs to each other, they share their possessions, because the spread of the Body of Christ is the responsibility of the whole college of bishops.

By arousing, fostering and directing missionary work in his own diocese, with which he is one, the bishop makes present and, as it were, visible the missionary spirit and zeal of the people of God, so that the whole diocese becomes missionary.

It is the task of the bishop to raise up among his people, especially among those who are sick or afflicted, souls who with a generous heart will offer prayers and works of penance to God for the evangelization of the world. He should gladly foster vocations to missionary institutes among young people and clerics, and be grateful if God should choose some of them to play a part in the missionary activity of the Church. He should exhort and assist diocesan congregations to undertake their own work in the missions; he should promote the works of missionary institutes among his people, especially the pontifical works for the missions. It is right that these works should be given first place, because they are a means by which Catholics are imbued from infancy with a truly universal and missionary outlook and also a means for instigating an effective collecting of funds for all the missions, each according to its needs.

Since the need for workers in the vineyard of the Lord grows from day to day; and since diocesan priests themselves wish to play a greater part in the evangelization of the world, this sacred Synod desires that bishops, being conscious of the very grave shortage of priests which impedes the evangelization of many regions, would, after a proper training, send to those dioceses which lack clergy some of their best priests who offer themselves for mission work, where at least for a time they would exercise the missionary ministry in a spirit of service.

In order that the missionary activity of bishops might be more effectively exercised for the good of the whole Church, it is desirable that episcopal conferences should regulate all those matters which concern organized cooperation in their own regions.

In their conferences the bishops should consider the question of sending diocesan priests for the evangelization of the nations; the particular contribution, in proportion to its income, which each diocese will be obliged to make every year for the work of the missions; the direction and organization of ways and means for directly helping or, if need be, founding missionary institutes and seminaries of diocesan clergy for the missions; the fostering of closer links between such institutes and the dioceses.

It likewise pertains to episcopal conferences to found and promote agencies which will fraternally receive those who immigrate from missionary territories for reasons of work or study, and which will aid them by suitable pastoral attention. By means of these immigrants people who are distant become, in a sense, neighbors, while a wonderful opportunity is offered to communities which have long been Christian to speak with nations which have not yet heard the Gospel, and of showing them the true face of Christ by their own acts of kindness and assistance.

(1) ***Sacrosanctum concilium* 41** The bishop is to be considered as the High Priest **1561**
of his flock from whom the life in Christ of his faithful is in some way derived and upon whom it in some way depends.

Therefore all should hold in the greatest esteem the liturgical life of the diocese centered around the bishop, especially in his cathedral church. They must be convinced that the principal manifestation of the Church consists in the full, active participation of all God's holy people in the same liturgical celebrations, especially in the same Eucharist, in one prayer, at one altar, at which the bishop presides, surrounded by his college of priests and by his ministers.

1561 (2) ***Lumen gentium* 26** The bishop, invested with the fullness of the sacrament of Orders, is "the steward of the grace of the supreme priesthood," above all in the Eucharist, which he himself offers, or ensures that it is offered, from which the Church ever derives its life and on which it thrives. This Church of Christ is really present in all legitimately organized local groups of the faithful, which, in so far as they are united to their pastors, are also quite appropriately called Churches in the New Testament. For these are in fact, in their own localities, the new people called by God, in the power of the Holy Spirit and as the result of full conviction (cf. 1 Thess. 1:5). In them the faithful are gathered together through the preaching of the Gospel of Christ, and the mystery of the Lord's Supper is celebrated "so that, by means of the flesh and blood of the Lord the whole brotherhood of the Body may be welded together." In each altar community, under the sacred ministry of the bishop, a manifest symbol is to be seen of that charity and "unity of the mystical body, without which there can be no salvation." In these communities, though they may often be small and poor, or existing in the diaspora, Christ is present through whose power and influence the One, Holy, Catholic and Apostolic Church is constituted. For "the sharing in the body and blood of Christ has no other effect than to accomplish our transformation into that which we receive."

Moreover, every legitimate celebration of the Eucharist is regulated by the bishop, to whom is confided the duty of presenting to the divine majesty the cult of the Christian religion and of ordering it in accordance with the Lord's injunctions and the Church's regulations, as further defined for the diocese by his particular decision.

Thus the bishops, by praying and toiling for the people, apportion in many different forms and without stint that which flows from the abundance of Christ's holiness. By the ministry of the word they impart to those who believe the strength of God unto salvation (cf. Rom. 1:16), and through the sacraments, the frequent and fruitful distribution of which they regulate by their authority, they sanctify the faithful. They control the conferring of Baptism, through which a sharing in the priesthood of Christ is granted. They are the original ministers of Confirmation; it is they who confer sacred Orders and regulate the discipline of Penance, and who diligently exhort and instruct their flocks to take the part that is theirs, in a spirit of faith and reverence, in the liturgy and above all in the holy sacrifice of the Mass. Finally, by the example of their manner of life they should exercise a powerful influence for good on those over whom they are placed, by abstaining from all wrongdoing in their conduct, and, as far as they are able, with the help of the Lord, changing it for the better, so that together with the flock entrusted to them, they may attain to eternal life.

1565 **Acts 1:8** ". . . But you shall receive power when the Holy Spirit has come upon you; and you shall be my witnesses in Jerusalem and in all Judea and Samaria and to the end of the earth."

1566 ***Presbyterorum ordinis* 2:** see 1548 (5).

1569 (1) ***Christus Dominus* 15** In exercising their mission of sanctification bishops should be mindful of the fact that they have been chosen from among men and made their representatives before God to offer gifts and sacrifices in expiation of sins. It is the bishops who enjoy the fullness of the sacrament of orders, and both priests and deacons are dependent on them in the exercise of their power. The former, in order that they may be prudent cooperators with the episcopal order, have also been consecrated as true priests of the New Testament; the latter having been ordained for the ministry, serve the people of God in union with the bishop and his clergy. It is therefore bishops who are the principal dispensers of the mysteries of God, and it is their function to control, promote and protect the entire liturgical life of the Church entrusted to them.

They should therefore see to it that the faithful know and live the paschal mystery more deeply through the Eucharist, forming one closely-knit body, united by the charity of Christ; "devoting themselves to prayer and the ministry of the word" (Acts 6:4). They should aim to make of one mind in prayer all who are entrusted to their care, and to ensure their advancement in grace through the reception of the sacraments, and that they become faithful witnesses to the Lord.

As spiritual guides of their flocks, bishops should be zealous in promoting the sanctity of their clergy, their religious and their laity according to the vocation of each individual, remembering that they are under an obligation to give an example of sanctity in charity, humility and simplicity of life. Let them so sanctify the churches entrusted to them that the mind of the universal Church of Christ may be fully reflected in them. They should, therefore, make every effort to foster vocations to the priesthood and to the religious life, and encourage missionary vocations especially.

(2) **St. Hippolytus, *Traditio apostolica* 8** And when a presbyter is ordained the 1569
bishop shall lay his hand upon his head, the presbyters also touching him. And he shall pray over him according to the aforementioned form which we gave before over the bishop, praying and saying:

O God and Father of our Lord Jesus Christ—*<as far as "of thy Name"* (iii. 3) *but continuing>*—Look upon this thy servant and impart to him the spirit of grace and counsel, "that he may share" in the presbyterate "and govern" Thy people in a pure heart.

As Thou didst look upon the people of Thy choice and didst command Moses to choose presbyters whom Thou didst fill with the spirit which Thou hadst granted to Thy minister,

So now, O Lord, grant that there may be preserved among us unceasingly the Spirit of Thy grace, and make us worthy that in faith we may minister to Thee praising Thee in singleness of heart,

Through Thy Child Christ Jesus through Whom to Thee be glory, might *<and praise>*, to the Father and to the Son with *<the>* Holy Spirit in the holy Church now and for ever and world without end. Amen.

(1) ***Lumen gentium* 41:** see 1251 (2). 1570

(2) ***Apostolicam actuositatem* 16** The apostolate to be exercised by the individual 1570
—which flows abundantly from a truly Christian life (cf. Jn. 4:11)—is the starting point and condition of all types of lay apostolate, including the organized apostolate; nothing can replace it.

The individual apostolate is everywhere and always in place; in certain circumstances it is the only one appropriate, the only one possible. Every lay person, whatever his condition, is called to it, is obliged to it, even if he has not the opportunity or possibility of collaborating in associations.

The apostolate, through which the laity build up the Church, sanctify the world and get it to live in Christ, can take on many forms.

A special form of the individual apostolate is the witness of a whole lay life issuing from faith, hope and charity; it is a sign very much in keeping with our times, and a manifestation of Christ living in his faithful. Then, by the apostolate of the word, which in certain circumstances is absolutely necessary, the laity proclaim Christ, explain and spread his teachings, each one according to his condition and competence, and profess those teachings with fidelity.

Moreover, cooperating as citizens of this world in all that has to do with the constructing and conducting of the temporal order, the laity should, by the light of faith, try to find the higher motives that should govern their behavior in the home and in professional, cultural and social life; they should too, given the opportunity, let these motives be seen by others, conscious that by so doing they become cooperators with God the creator, redeemer and sanctifier, and give him glory.

Finally, the laity should vitalize their lives with charity and, to the extent of the capability of each give concrete expression to it in works.

All should remember that by public worship and by prayer, by penance and the willing acceptance of the toil and hardships of life by which they resemble the suffering Christ (cf. 2 Cor. 4:10; Col. 1:24), they can reach all men and contribute to the salvation of the entire world.

1570 (3) **Mark 10:45** ". . . For the Son of man also came not to be served but to serve, and to give his life as a ransom for many."

1570 (4) **Luke 22:27** For which is the greater, one who sits at table, or one who serves? Is it not the one who sits at table? But I am among you as one who serves.

1570 (5) **St. Polycarp, *Epistula ad Philippenses* 5, 2** Similarly, deacons must be blameless in the presence of His justice, like servants of God and Christ, not of men; not slanderers, not double-tongued, not money-lovers, temperate in all things, compassionate, careful, walking according to the truth of the Lord, who became the servant of all. If we be pleasing to Him in this world, we shall receive the future world in accordance with His promises to raise us up from the dead, and, if we act in a manner worthy of Him, 'we shall also reign with Him,' provided we believe.

1570 (6) ***Lumen gentium* 29** At a lower level of the hierarchy are to be found deacons, who receive the imposition of hands "not unto the priesthood, but unto the ministry." For, strengthened by sacramental grace they are dedicated to the People of God, in conjunction with the bishop and his body of priests, in the service of the liturgy, of the Gospel and of works of charity. It pertains to the office of a deacon, in so far as it may be assigned to him by the competent authority, to administer Baptism solemnly, to be custodian and distributor of the Eucharist, in the name of the Church, to assist at and to bless marriages, to bring Viaticum to the dying, to read the sacred scripture to the faithful, to instruct and exhort the people, to preside over the worship and the prayer of the faithful, to administer sacramentals, and to officiate at funeral and burial services. Dedicated to works of charity and functions of administration, deacons should recall the admonition of St. Polycarp: "Let them be merciful, and zealous, and let them walk according to the truth of the Lord, who became the servant of all."

Since, however, the laws and customs of the Latin Church in force today in many areas render it difficult to fulfil these functions, which are so extremely necessary for the life of the Church, it will be possible in the future to restore the diaconate as a proper and permanent rank of the hierarchy. But it pertains to the competent local episcopal conferences, of one kind or another, with the approval of the Supreme Pontiff, to decide whether and where it is opportune that such deacons be appointed. Should the Roman Pontiff think fit, it will be possible to confer this diaconal order even upon married men, provided they be of more mature age, and also on suitable young men, for whom, however, the law of celibacy must remain in force.

(7) ***Sacrosanctum concilium* 35, 4** Bible services should be encouraged, especially on the vigils of the more solemn feasts, on some weekdays of Advent and Lent, and on Sundays and holidays, especially in places where no priest is available. In this case a deacon or some other person authorized by the bishop should preside over the celebration. 1570

(8) ***Ad gentes divinitus* 16** The Church, with great joy, gives thanks for the priceless gift of the priestly vocation which God has given to so many young men from among those peoples but recently converted to Christ. For the Church is more firmly rooted in a people when the different communities of the faithful have ministers of salvation who are drawn from their own members—bishops, priests and deacons, serving their own brothers—so that these young churches gradually acquire a diocesan structure with their own clergy. 1570

Those things which have been decreed by this Council concerning the priestly vocation and priestly formation are to be religiously observed wherever the Church is being planted for the first time and also by the young churches. Special importance is to be attached to what has been said about closely combining spiritual, doctrinal and pastoral formation; about living a life in accordance with the Gospel without any thought of personal or family advantage; about fostering a deep appreciation of the mystery of the Church. In this way they will learn, in a wonderful manner, to give themselves fully to the service of Christ's Body, and to the work of the Gospel; they will learn to adhere to their bishop as loyal fellow workers, and to collaborate with their brothers.

To attain this general end, the whole of the student's formation is to be organized in the light of the mystery of salvation, as it is revealed in the Scriptures. They must discover and live this mystery of Christ and of human salvation as it is present in the liturgy.

These general requirements for priestly training, both pastoral and practical, which have been laid down by the Council, must be accompanied with a desire to face up to the particular nation's own way of thinking and acting. Therefore, the minds of the students must be opened and refined so that they will better understand and appreciate the culture of their own people; in philosophy and theology they should examine the relationship between the traditions and religion of their homeland and Christianity. In the same way, priestly formation must take account of the pastoral needs of the region; the students must learn the history, goal and method of missionary activity, as well as the peculiar social, economic and cultural conditions of their own people. They should be formed in the spirit of ecumenism and properly prepared for fraternal dialogue with non-Christians. All this demands that, as far as possible, studies for the priesthood should be undertaken in close contact with the way of life of their own people. Finally, care must be taken to train them in proper ecclesiastical and financial administration.

Suitable priests should be selected, who, after a period of pastoral work, would pursue higher studies even at foreign universities, especially at Rome, or at other institutes of learning. As members of the local clergy, with their learning and experience, they should be a great asset to these young churches in discharging the more difficult ecclesiastical duties.

Wherever it appears opportune to episcopal conferences, the diaconate should be restored as a permanent state of life, in accordance with the norms of the Constitution on the Church. It would help those men who carry out the ministry of a deacon—preaching the word of God as catechists, governing scattered Christian communities in the name of the bishop or parish priest, or exercising charity in the performance of social or charitable works—if they were to be strengthened by the imposition of hands which has come down from the apostles. They would be more closely bound to the altar and their ministry would be made more fruitful through the sacramental grace of the diaconate.

1573 **Pius XII, apostolic constitution *Sacramentum ordinis* (30 November 1947): DS 3858** It is established moreover, among all that the sacraments of the New Law, as sensible and efficient signs of invisible grace, owe and signify the grace which they effect, and effect the grace which they signify. Indeed the effects which should be produced and so signified by the sacred ordination of the diaconate, presbyterate, and episcopate, namely, power and grace, are found to have been sufficiently signified in all the rites of the universal Church of different times and regions by the imposition of hands, and by the words that determine this. Furthermore, there is no one who does [not] know that the Roman Church always considered valid the ordinations conferred in the Greek rite, without the handing over of the instruments, so that at the Council of Florence, in which the union of the Greeks with the Church of Rome was accomplished, it was not imposed on the Greeks that they change the rite of ordination, or that they insert in it the tradition of the instruments; rather, the Church wished that in the City itself (Rome) Greeks be ordained according to their own rite. From all this it is gathered that according to the mind of the Council of Florence the tradition of the instruments is not required for the substance and validity of this sacrament, according to the will of our Lord Jesus Christ Himself. But if, according to the will and prescription of the Church, the same should some day be held necessary for validity also, all would know that the Church is able even to change and to abrogate what she has established.

1575 (1) ***Roman Missal*, Preface of the Apostles I**

Father, all-powerful and ever-living God,
we do well always and everywhere to give you thanks.

You are the eternal Shepherd
who never leaves his flock untended.
Through the apostles
you watch over us and protect us always.
You made them shepherds of the flock
to share in the work of your Son,
and from their place in heaven they guide us still.

And so, with all the choirs of angels in heaven
we proclaim your glory
and join in their unending hymn of praise. . . .

1575 (2) ***Lumen gentium* 21:** see 1549 (1).

1575 (3) **Ephesians 4:11** And his gifts were that some should be apostles, some prophets, some evangelists, some pastors and teachers. . . .

1576 (1) **Innocent III, letter *Eius exemplo* (18 December 1208): DS 794** We approve, therefore, the baptism of infants, who, if they died after baptism, before they commit sin, we confess and believe are saved; and in baptism all sins, that original sin which was contracted as well as those which voluntarily have been committed, we believe are forgiven. We decree that confirmation performed by a bishop, that is, by the imposition of hands, is holy and must be received reverently. Firmly and without doubt with a pure heart we believe and simply in faithful words we affirm that the sacrifice, that is, the bread and wine [Other texts: in the sacrifice of the Eucharist those things which before consecration were bread and wine] after the consecration is the true body and blood of our Lord Jesus Christ, in which we believe nothing more by a good nor less by a bad priest is accomplished because it is accomplished not in the merits of the one who consecrates but in the word of the Creator and in the power of the Holy Spirit. Therefore, we firmly believe and we confess that however honest, religious, holy, and prudent anyone may be, he cannot nor ought he to consecrate the Eucharist nor to perform the sacrifice of the altar unless he be a priest, regularly ordained by a visible and perceptible bishop. And to this office three things are necessary, as we believe: namely, a certain person, that is a priest as we said above, properly established by a bishop for that office; and those solemn words which have been expressed by the holy Fathers in the canon; and the faithful intention of the one who offers himself; and so we firmly believe and declare that whosoever without the preceding episcopal ordination, as we said above, believes and contends that he can offer the sacrifice of the Eucharist is a heretic and is a participant and companion of the perdition of Core and his followers, and he must be segregated from the entire holy Roman Church. To sinners truly penitent, we believe that forgiveness is granted by God, and with them we communicate most gladly. We venerate the anointing of the sick with the consecrated oil. According to the Apostle [cf. I Cor. 7] we do not deny that carnal unions should be formed, but ordinarily we forbid absolutely the breaking of the contracts. Man also with his wife we believe and confess are saved, and we do not even condemn second or later marriages.

(2) **Lateran Council IV (1215): DS 802** One indeed is the universal Church of the faithful, outside which no one at all is saved, in which the priest himself is the sacrifice, Jesus Christ, whose body and blood are truly contained in the sacrament of the altar under the species of bread and wine; the bread (changed) into His body by the divine power of transubstantiation, and the wine into the blood, so that to accomplish the mystery of unity we ourselves receive from His (nature) what He Himself received from ours. And surely no one can accomplish this sacrament except a priest who has been rightly ordained according to the keys of the Church which Jesus Christ Himself conceded to the Apostles and to their successors. But the sacrament of baptism (which at the invocation of God and the indivisible Trinity, namely, of the Father and of the Son and of the Holy Spirit, is solemnized in water) rightly conferred by anyone in the form of the Church is useful unto salvation for little ones and for adults. And if, after the reception of baptism, anyone shall have lapsed into sin, through true penance he can always be restored. Moreover, not only virgins and the continent but also married persons pleasing to God through right faith and good work merit to arrive at a blessed eternity. 1576

(3) **CIC Canon 1012** The minister of sacred ordination is a consecrated bishop. 1576

(4) **CCEO Canon 744** Only a bishop validly administers sacred ordination by the imposition of hands and by the prayers prescribed by the Church. 1576

(5) **CCEO Canon 747** A candidate to the diaconate or presbyterate should be ordained by his own eparchial bishop or by another bishop with lawful dimissorial letters. 1576

(1) **Mark 3:14–19** And he appointed twelve, to be with him, and to be sent out to preach and have authority to cast out demons: Simon whom he surnamed Peter; James the son of Zebedee and John the brother of James, whom he surnamed Boanerges, that is, sons of thunder; Andrew, and Philip, and Bartholomew, and Matthew, and 1577

Thomas, and James the son of Alphaeus, and Thaddaeus, and Simon the Cananaean, and Judas Iscariot, who betrayed him. Then he went home. . . .

1577 (2) **Luke 6:12–16** In these days he went out to the mountain to pray; and all night he continued in prayer to God. And when it was day, he called his disciples, and chose from them twelve, whom he named apostles; Simon, whom he named Peter, and Andrew his brother, and James and John, and Philip, and Bartholomew, and Matthew, and Thomas, and James the son of Alphaeus, and Simon who was called the Zealot, and Judas the son of James, and Judas Iscariot, who became a traitor.

1577 (3) **1 Timothy 3:1–13** The saying is sure: If any one aspires to the office of bishop, he desires a noble task. Now a bishop must be above reproach, the husband of one wife, temperate, sensible, dignified, hospitable, an apt teacher, no drunkard, not violent but gentle, not quarrelsome, and no lover of money. He must manage his own household well, keeping his children submissive and respectful in every way; for if a man does not know how to manage his own household, how can he care for God's church? He must not be a recent convert, or he may be puffed up with conceit and fall into the condemnation of the devil; moreover he must be well thought of by outsiders, or he may fall into reproach and the snare of the devil.

Deacons likewise must be serious, not double-tongued, not addicted to much wine, not greedy for gain; they must hold the mystery of the faith with a clear conscience. And let them also be tested first; then if they prove themselves blameless let them serve as deacons. The women likewise must be serious, no slanderers, but temperate, faithful in all things. Let deacons be the husband of one wife, and let them manage their children and their households well; for those who serve well as deacons gain a good standing for themselves and also great confidence in the faith which is in Christ Jesus.

1577 (4) **2 Timothy 1:6** Hence I remind you to rekindle the gift of God that is within you through the laying on of my hands. . . .

1577 (5) **Titus 1:5–9** This is why I left you in Crete, that you might amend what was defective, and appoint elders in every town as I directed you, if any man is blameless, the husband of one wife, and his children are believers and not open to the charge of being profligate or insubordinate. For a bishop, as God's steward, must be blameless; he must not be arrogant or quick-tempered or a drunkard or violent or greedy for gain, but hospitable, a lover of goodness, master of himself, upright, holy, and self-controlled; he must hold firm to the sure word as taught, so that he may be able to give instruction in sound doctrine and also to confute those who contradict it.

1577 (6) **St. Clement of Rome, *Epistula ad Corinthios* 42, 4** From land to land, accordingly, and from city to city they preached, and from among their earliest converts appointed men whom they had tested by the Spirit to act as bishops and deacons for the future believers.

1577 (7) **St. Clement of Rome, *Epistula ad Corinthios* 44, 3** Consequently, we deem it an injustice to eject from the sacred ministry the persons who were appointed either by them, or later, with the consent of the whole Church, by other men in high repute and have ministered to the flock of Christ faultlessly, humbly, quietly and unselfishly, and have moreover, over a long period of time, earned the esteem of all.

(8) ***Mulieris dignitatem* 26–27** Against the broad background of the "great mystery" expressed in the spousal relationship between Christ and the Church, it is possible to understand adequately the calling of the "Twelve." *In calling only men as his Apostles*, Christ acted *in a completely free and sovereign manner*. In doing so, he exercised the same freedom with which, in all his behavior, he emphasized the dignity and the vocation of women, without conforming to the prevailing customs and to the traditions sanctioned by the legislation of the time. Consequently, the assumption that he called men to be apostles in order to conform with the widespread mentality of his times, does not at all correspond to Christ's way of acting. "Teacher, we know that you are true, and teach the way of God truthfully, and care for no man; for *you do not regard the position of men*" (Mt. 22:16). These words fully characterize *Jesus of Nazareth's behavior*. Here one also finds an explanation for the calling of the "Twelve." They are with Christ at the Last Supper. They alone receive the sacramental charge, "Do this in remembrance of me" (Lk 22:19; 1 Cor 11:24), which is joined to the institution of the Eucharist. On Easter Sunday night they receive the Holy Spirit for the forgiveness of sins: "Whose sins you forgive are forgiven them, and whose sins you retain are retained" (Jn 20:23). 1577

We find ourselves at the very heart of the Paschal Mystery, which completely reveals the spousal love of God. Christ is the Bridegroom because "he has given himself": his body has been "given," his blood has been "poured out" (cf. Lk 22:19–20). In this way "he loved them to the end" (Jn 13:1). The "sincere gift" contained in the Sacrifice of the Cross gives definitive prominence to the spousal meaning of God's love. As the redeemer of the world, Christ is the Bridegroom of the Church. *The Eucharist* is *the Sacrament of our Redemption*. It is *the Sacrament of the Bridegroom and of the Bride*. The Eucharist makes present and realizes anew in a sacramental manner the redemptive act of Christ, who "creates" the Church, his body. Christ is united with this "body" as the bridegroom with the bride. All this is contained in the Letter to the Ephesians. The perennial "unity of the two" that exists between man and woman from the very "beginning" is introduced into this "great mystery" of Christ and of the Church.

Since Christ, in instituting the Eucharist, linked it in such an explicit way to the priestly service of the Apostles, it is legitimate to conclude that he thereby wished to express the relationship between man and woman, between what is "feminine" and what is "masculine." It is a relationship willed by God both in the mystery of creation and in the mystery of Redemption. It is *the Eucharist* above all that expresses *the redemptive act of Christ the Bridegroom towards the Church the Bride*. This is clear and unambiguous when the sacramental ministry of the Eucharist, in which the priest acts "*in persona Christi*," is performed by a man. This explanation confirms the teaching of the Declaration *Inter Insigniores*, published at the behest of Paul VI in response to the question concerning the admission of women to the ministerial priesthood.

The Second Vatican Council renewed the Church's awareness of the universality of the priesthood. In the New Covenant there is only one sacrifice and only one priest: Christ. *All the baptized share in the one priesthood of Christ*, both men and women, inasmuch as they must "present their bodies as a living sacrifice, holy and acceptable to God (cf. Rom 12:1), give witness to Christ in every place, and give an explanation to anyone who asks the reason for the hope in eternal life that is in them (cf. 1 Pt 3:15)." Universal participation in Christ's sacrifice, in which the Redeemer has offered to the Father the whole world and humanity in particular, brings it about that all in the Church are "a kingdom of priests" (Rev 5:10; cf. 1 Pt 2:9), who not only share in the priestly mission but also in the prophetic and kingly mission of Christ the Messiah. Furthermore, this participation determines the organic unity of the Church, the People of God, with Christ. It expresses at the same time the "great mystery" described in the Letter to the Ephesians: *the Bride united to her Bridegroom*; united, because she lives his life; united, because she shares in his threefold mission (*tria munera Christi*); united *in such a manner as to respond* with a "sincere gift" of self *to the inexpressible gift of the love of the Bridegroom*, the Redeemer of the world. This concerns everyone in the Church, women as well as men. It obviously concerns those who share in the "ministerial priesthood," which is characterized by service. In the context of the "great mystery" of Christ and of the Church, all are called to respond —as a bride—with the gift of their lives to the inexpressible gift of the love of Christ, who alone, as the Redeemer of the world, is the Church's Bridegroom. The "royal priesthood," which is universal, at the same time expresses the gift of the Bride.

This is of *fundamental importance for understanding the Church in her* own *essence*, so as to avoid applying to the Church—even in her dimension as an "institution" made up of human beings and forming part of history—criteria of understanding and judgment which do not pertain to her nature. Although the Church possesses a "hierarchical" structure, nevertheless this structure is totally ordered to the holiness of Christ's members. And holiness is measured according to the "great mystery" in which the Bride responds with the gift of love to the gift of the Bridegroom. She does this "in the Holy Spirit," since "God's love has been poured into our hearts through the Holy Spirit who has been given to us" (Rom 5:5). The Second Vatican Council, confirming the teaching of the whole of tradition, recalled that in the hierarchy of holiness it is *precisely the "woman,"* Mary of Nazareth, who is the "figure" of the Church. She "precedes" everyone on the path to holiness: in her person "the Church has already reached that perfection whereby she exists without spot or wrinkle (cf. Eph 5:27)." In this sense, one can say that the Church is both "Marian" and "Apostolic-Petrine."

In the history of the Church, even from earliest times, there were side-by-side with men *a number of women*, for whom the response of the Bride to the Bridegroom's redemptive love acquired full expressive force. First we see those women who had personally encountered Christ and followed him. After his departure, together with the Apostles, they "devoted themselves to prayer" in the Upper Room in Jerusalem until the day of Pentecost. On that day the Holy Spirit spoke through "the sons and daughters" of the People of God, thus fulfilling the words of the prophet Joel (cf. Acts 2:17). These women, and others afterwards, played *an active and important role in the life of the early Church*, in building up from its foundations the first Christian community—and subsequent communities—*through their own charisms and their varied service*. The apostolic writings note their names, such as Phoebe, "a deaconess of the Church at Cenchreae" (cf. Rom 16:1), Prisca with her husband Aquila (cf. 2 Tim 4:19), Euodia and Syntyche (cf. Phil 4:2), Mary, Tryphaena, Persis, and Tryphosa (cf. Rom 16:6, 12). St. Paul speaks of their "hard work" for Christ, and this hard work indicates the various fields of the Church's apostolic service, beginning with the "domestic Church." For in the latter, "sincere faith" passes from the mother to her children and grandchildren, as was the case in the house of Timothy (cf. 2 Tim 1:5).

The same thing is repeated down the centuries, from one generation to the next, as *the history of the Church* demonstrates. By defending the dignity of women and their vocation, the Church has shown honor and gratitude for those women who—faithful to the Gospel—have shared in every age in the apostolic mission of the whole People of God. They are the holy martyrs, virgins, and mothers of families, who bravely bore witness to their faith and passed on the Church's faith and tradition by bringing up their children in the spirit of the Gospel.

In every age and in every country we find many "perfect" women (cf. Prov 31:10) who, despite persecution, difficulties and discrimination, have shared in the Church's mission. It suffices to mention: Monica, the mother of Augustine, Macrina, Olga of Kiev, Matilda of Tuscany, Hedwig of Silesia, Jadwiga of Cracow, Elizabeth of Thuringia, Birgitta of Sweden, Joan of Arc, Rose of Lima, Elizabeth Ann Seton and Mary Ward.

The witness and the achievements of Christian women have had a significant impact on the life of the Church as well as of society. Even in the face of serious social discrimination, holy women have acted "freely," strengthened by their union with Christ. Such union and freedom rooted in God explain, for example, the great work of St. Catherine of Siena in the life of the Church, and the work of St. Teresa of Jesus in the monastic life.

In our own days too the Church is constantly enriched by the witness of the many women who fulfill their vocation to holiness. Holy women are an incarnation of the feminine ideal; they are also a model for all Christians, a model of the "*sequela Christi*," an example of how the Bride must respond with love to the love of the Bridegroom.

(9) **Congregation for the Doctrine of the Faith, declaration *Inter insigniores*** 1577
Among the characteristics that mark our present age, Pope John XXIII indicated, in his Encyclical *Pacem in Terris* of 11 April 1963, "the part that women are now taking in public life. . . . This is a development that is perhaps of swifter growth among Christian nations, but it is also happening extensively, if more slowly, among nations that are heirs to different traditions and imbued with a different culture." Along the same lines, the Second Vatican Council, enumerating in its Pastoral Constitution *Gaudium et Spes* the forms of discrimination touching upon the basic rights of the person which must be overcome and eliminated as being contrary to God's plan, gives first place to discrimination based upon sex. The resulting equality will secure the building up of a world that is not levelled out and uniform but harmonious and unified, if men and women contribute to it their own resources and dynamism, as Pope Paul VI recently stated.

In the life of the Church herself, as history shows us, women have played a decisive role and accomplished tasks of outstanding value. One has only to think of the foundresses of the great religious families, such as Saint Clare and Saint Teresa of Avila. The latter, moreover, and Saint Catherine of Siena, have left writings so rich in spiritual doctrine that Pope Paul VI has included them among the Doctors of the Church. Nor could one forget the great number of women who have consecrated themselves to the Lord for the exercise of charity or for the missions, and the Christian wives who have had a profound influence on their families, particularly for the passing on of the faith to their children.

But our age gives rise to increased demands: "Since in our time women have an ever more active share in the whole life of society, it is very important that they participate more widely also in the various sectors of the Church's apostolate." This charge of the Second Vatican Council has already set in motion the whole process of change now taking place: these various experiences of course need to come to maturity. But as Pope Paul VI also remarked, a very large number of Christian communities are already benefitting from the apostolic commitment of women. Some of these women are called to take part in councils set up for pastoral reflection, at the diocesan or parish level; and the Apostolic See has brought women into some of its working bodies.

For some years now various Christian communities stemming from the sixteenth-century Reformation or of later origin have been admitting women to the pastoral office on a par with men. This initiative has led to petitions and writings by members of these communities and similar groups, directed towards making this admission a general thing; it has also led to contrary reactions. This therefore constitutes an ecumenical problem, and the Catholic Church must make her thinking known on it, all the more because in various sectors of opinion the question has been asked whether she too could not modify her discipline and admit women to priestly ordination. A number of Catholic theologians have even posed this question publicly, evoking studies not only in the sphere of exegesis, patrology and Church history but also in the field of the history of institutions and customs, of sociology and of psychology. The various arguments capable of clarifying this important problem have been submitted to a critical examination. As we are dealing with a debate which classical theology scarcely touched upon, the current argumentation runs the risk of neglecting essential elements.

For these reasons, in execution of a mandate received from the Holy Father and echoing the declaration which he himself made in his letter of 30 November 1975, the Sacred Congregation for the Doctrine of the Faith judges it necessary to recall that the Church, in fidelity to the example of the Lord, does not consider herself authorized to admit women to priestly ordination. The Sacred Congregation deems it opportune at the present juncture to explain this position of the Church. It is a position which will perhaps cause pain but whose positive value will become apparent in the long run, since it can be of help in deepening understanding of the respective roles of men and of women.

The Catholic Church has never felt that priestly or episcopal ordination can be validly conferred on women. A few heretical sects in the first centuries, especially Gnostic ones, entrusted the exercise of the priestly ministry to women: this innovation was immediately noted and condemned by the Fathers, who considered it as unacceptable in the Church. It is true that in the writings of the Fathers one will find the undeniable influence of prejudices unfavorable to women, but nevertheless, it should be noted that these prejudices had hardly any influence on their pastoral activity, and still less on their spiritual direction. But over and above considerations inspired by the spirit of the times, one finds expressed—especially in the canonical documents of the Antiochian and Egyptian traditions—this essential reason, namely, that by calling only men to the priestly Order and ministry in its true sense, the Church intends to remain faithful to the type of ordained ministry willed by the Lord Jesus Christ and carefully maintained by the Apostles.

The same conviction animates mediaeval theology, even if the Scholastic doctors, in their desire to clarify by reason the data of faith, often present arguments on this point that modern thought would have difficulty in admitting or would even rightly reject. Since that period and up to our own time, it can be said that the question has not been raised again, for the practice has enjoyed peaceful and universal acceptance.

The Church's tradition in the matter has thus been so firm in the course of the centuries that the Magisterium has not felt the need to intervene in order to formulate a principle which was not attacked, or to defend a law which was not challenged. But each time that this tradition had the occasion to manifest itself, it witnessed to the Church's desire to conform to the model left to her by the Lord.

The same tradition has been faithfully safeguarded by the Churches of the East. Their unanimity on this point is all the more remarkable since in many other questions their discipline admits of a great diversity. At the present time these same Churches refuse to associate themselves with requests directed towards securing the accession of women to priestly ordination.

Jesus Christ did not call any woman to become part of the Twelve. If he acted in this way, it was not in order to conform to the customs of his time, for his attitude towards women was quite different from that of his milieu, and he deliberately and courageously broke with it.

For example, to the great astonishment of his own disciples Jesus converses publicly with the Samaritan woman (cf. Jn 4:27); he takes no notice of the state of legal impurity of the woman who had suffered from haemorrhages (cf. Mt 9:20–22); he allows a sinful woman to approach him in the house of Simon the Pharisee (cf. Lk 7:37ff.); and by pardoning the woman taken in adultery, he means to show that one must not be more severe towards the fault of a woman than towards that of a man (cf. Jn 8:11). He does not hesitate to depart from the Mosaic Law in order to affirm the equality of the rights and duties of men and women with regard to the marriage bond (cf. Mk 10:2–11; Mt 19:3–9).

In his itinerant ministry Jesus was accompanied not only by the Twelve but also by a group of women: "Mary, surnamed the Magdalene, from whom seven demons had gone out, Joanna the wife of Herod's steward Chuza, Susanna, and several others who provided for them out of their own resources" (Lk 8:2–3). Contrary to the Jewish mentality, which did not accord great value to the testimony of women, as Jewish law attests, it was nevertheless women who were the first to have the privilege of seeing the risen Lord, and it was they who were charged by Jesus to take the first paschal message to the Apostles themselves (cf. Mt 28:7–10; Lk 24:9–10; Jn 20:11–18), in order to prepare the latter to become the official witnesses to the Resurrection.

It is true that these facts do not make the matter immediately obvious. This is no surprise, for the questions that the Word of God brings before us go beyond the obvious. In order to reach the ultimate meaning of the mission of Jesus and the ultimate meaning of Scripture, a purely historical exegesis of the texts cannot suffice. But it must be recognized that we have here a number of convergent indications that make all the more remarkable the fact that Jesus did not entrust the apostolic charge to women. Even his Mother, who was so closely associated with the mystery of her Son, and whose incomparable role is emphasized by the Gospels of Luke and John, was not invested with the apostolic ministry. This fact was to lead the Fathers to present her as the example of Christ's will in this domain; as Pope Innocent III repeated later, at the beginning of the thirteenth century, "Although the Blessed Virgin Mary surpassed in dignity and in excellence all the Apostles, nevertheless it was not to her but to them that the Lord entrusted the keys of the Kingdom of Heaven."

The apostolic community remained faithful to the attitude of Jesus towards women. Although Mary occupied a privileged place in the little circle of those gathered in the Upper Room after the Lord's Ascension (cf. Acts 1:14), it was not she who was called to enter the College of the Twelve at the time of the election that resulted in the choice of Matthias: those who were put forward were two disciples whom the Gospels do not even mention.

On the day of Pentecost, the Holy Spirit filled them all, men and women (cf. Acts 2:1; 1:14), yet the proclamation of the fulfilment of the prophecies in Jesus was made only by "Peter and the Eleven" (Acts 2:14).

When they and Paul went beyond the confines of the Jewish world, the preaching of the Gospel and the Christian life in the Greco-Roman civilization impelled them to break with Mosaic practices, sometimes regretfully. They could therefore have envisaged conferring ordination on women, if they had not been convinced of their duty of fidelity to the Lord on this point. In the Hellenistic world, the cult of a number of pagan divinities was entrusted to priestesses. In fact the Greeks did not share the ideas of the Jews: although their philosophers taught the inferiority of women, historians nevertheless emphasize the existence of a certain movement for the advancement of women during the Imperial period. In fact we know from the book of the Acts and from the Letters of Saint Paul that certain women worked with the Apostle for the Gospel (cf. Rom 16:3–12; Phil 4:3). Saint Paul lists their names with gratitude in the final salutations of the Letters. Some of them often exercised an important influence on conversions: Priscilla, Lydia and others; especially Priscilla, who took it on herself to complete the instruction of Apollos (cf. Acts 18:26); Phoebe, in the service of the

Church of Cenchreae (cf. Rom. 16:1). All these facts manifest within the Apostolic Church a considerable evolution vis-à-vis the customs of Judaism. Nevertheless at no time was there a question of conferring ordination on these women.

In the Pauline Letters, exegetes of authority have noted a difference between two formulas used by the Apostle: he writes indiscriminately "my fellow workers" (Rom 16:3; Phil 4:2–3) when referring to men and women helping him in his apostolate in one way or another; but he reserves the title "God's fellow workers" (1 Cor 3:9–9; cf. 1 Thess 3:2) to Apollos, Timothy and himself, thus designated because they are directly set apart for the apostolic ministry and the preaching of the Word of God. In spite of the so important role played by women on the day of the Resurrection, their collaboration was not extended by Saint Paul to the official and public proclamation of the message, since this proclamation belongs exclusively to the apostolic mission.

Could the Church today depart from this attitude of Jesus and the Apostles, which has been considered as normative by the whole tradition up to our own day? Various arguments have been put forward in favor of a positive reply to this question, and these must now be examined.

It has been claimed in particular that the attitude of Jesus and the Apostles is explained by the influence of their milieu and their times. It is said that, if Jesus did not entrust to women and not even to his Mother a ministry assimilating them to the Twelve, this was because historical circumstances did not permit him to do so. No one however has ever proved—and it is clearly impossible to prove—that this attitude is inspired only by social and cultural reasons. As we have seen, an examination of the Gospels shows on the contrary that Jesus broke with the prejudices of his time, by widely contravening the discriminations practiced with regard to women. One therefore cannot maintain that, by not calling women to enter the group of the Apostles, Jesus was simply letting himself be guided by reasons of expediency. For all the more reason, social and cultural conditioning did not hold back the Apostles working in the Greek milieu, where the same forms of discrimination did not exist.

Another objection is based upon the transitory character that one claims to see today in some of the prescriptions of Saint Paul concerning women, and upon the difficulties that some aspects of his teaching raise in this regard. But it must be noted that these ordinances, probably inspired by the customs of the period, concern scarcely more than disciplinary practices of minor importance, such as the obligation imposed upon women to wear a veil on the head (1 Cor 11:2–6); such requirements no longer have a normative value. However, the Apostle's forbidding of women "to speak" in the assemblies (cf. 1 Cor 14:34–35; 1 Tim 2:12) is of a different nature, and exegetes define its meaning in this way: Paul in no way opposes the right, which he elsewhere recognizes as possessed by women, to prophesy in the assembly (cf. 1 Cor 11:5); the prohibition solely concerns the official function of teaching in the Christian assembly. For Saint Paul this prescription is bound up with the divine plan of creation (cf. 1 Cor 11:7; Gen 2:18–24): it would be difficult to see in it the expression of a cultural fact. Nor should it be forgotten that we owe to Saint Paul one of the most vigorous texts in the New Testament on the fundamental equality of men and women, as children of God in Christ (cf. Gal. 3:28). Therefore there is no reason for accusing him of prejudices against women, when we note the trust that he shows towards them and the collaboration that he asks of them in his apostolate.

But over and above these objections taken from the history of apostolic times, those who support the legitimacy of change in the matter turn to the Church's practice in her sacramental discipline. It has been noted, in our day especially, to what extent the Church is conscious of possessing a certain power over the sacraments, even though they were instituted by Christ. She has used this power down the centuries in order to determine their signs and the conditions of their administration: recent decisions of Popes Pius XII and Paul VI are proof of this. However, it must be emphasized that this power, which is a real one, has definite limits. As Pope Pius XII recalled: "The Church has no power over the substance of the sacraments, that is to say, over what Christ the Lord, as the sources of Revelation bear witness, determined should be maintained in the sacramental sign." This was already the teaching of the Council of Trent, which declared: "In the Church there has always existed this power, that in the administration of the sacraments, provided that their substance remains unaltered, she can lay down or modify what she considers more fitting either for the benefit of those who receive them or for respect towards those same sacraments, according to varying circumstances, times or places."

Moreover, it must not be forgotten that the sacramental signs are not conventional ones. Not only is it true that, in many respects, they are natural signs because they respond to the deep symbolism of actions and things, but they are more than this: they are principally meant to link the person of every period to the supreme Event of the history of salvation, in order to enable that person to understand, through all the Bible's wealth of pedagogy and symbolism, what grace they signify and produce. For example, the sacrament of the Eucharist is not only a fraternal meal, but at the same time the memorial which makes present and actual Christ's sacrifice and his offering by the Church. Again, the priestly ministry is not just a pastoral service; it ensures the continuity of the functions entrusted by Christ to the Apostles and the continuity of the powers related to those functions. Adaptation to civilizations and times therefore cannot abolish, on essential points, the sacramental reference to constitutive events of Christianity and to Christ himself.

In the final analysis it is the Church, through the voice of her Magisterium, that, in these various domains, decides what can change and what must remain immutable. When she judges that she cannot accept certain changes, it is because she knows that she is bound by Christ's manner of acting. Her attitude, despite appearances, is therefore not one of archaism but of fidelity: it can be truly understood only in this light. The Church makes pronouncements in virtue of the Lord's promise and the presence of the Holy Spirit, in order to proclaim better the mystery of Christ and to safeguard and manifest the whole of its rich content.

This practice of the Church therefore has a normative character: in the fact of conferring priestly ordination only on men, it is a question of an unbroken tradition throughout the history of the Church, universal in the East and in the West, and alert to repress abuses immediately. This norm, based on Christ's example, has been and is still observed because it is considered to conform to God's plan for his Church.

Having recalled the Church's norm and the basis thereof, it seems useful and opportune to illustrate this norm by showing the profound fittingness that theological reflection discovers between the proper nature of the sacrament of Order, with its specific reference to the mystery of Christ, and the fact that only men have been called to receive priestly ordination. It is not a question here of bringing forward a demonstrative argument, but of clarifying this teaching by the analogy of faith.

The Church's constant teaching, repeated and clarified by the Second Vatican Council and again recalled by the 1971 Synod of Bishops and by the Sacred Congregation for the Doctrine of the Faith in its Declaration of 24 June 1973, declares that the bishop or the priest, in the exercise of his ministry, does not act in his own name, *in persona propria*: he represents Christ, who acts through him: "the priest truly acts in the place of Christ", as Saint Cyprian already wrote in the third century. It is this ability to represent Christ that Saint Paul considered as characteristic of his apostolic function (cf. 2 Cor 5:20; Gal 4:14). The supreme expression of this representation is found in the altogether special form it assumes in the celebration of the Eucharist, which is the source and center of the Church's unity, the sacrificial meal in which the People of God are associated in the sacrifice of Christ: the priest, who alone has the power to perform it, then acts not only through the effective power conferred on him by Christ, but *in persona Christi*, taking the role of Christ, to the point of being his very image, when he pronounces the words of consecration.

The Christian priesthood is therefore of a sacramental nature: the priest is a sign, the supernatural effectiveness of which comes from the ordination received, but a sign that must be perceptible and which the faithful must be able to recognize with ease. The whole sacramental economy is in fact based upon natural signs, on symbols imprinted upon the human psychology: "Sacramental signs", says Saint Thomas, "represent what they signify by natural resemblance". The same natural resemblance is required for persons as for things: when Christ's role in the Eucharist is to be expressed sacramentally, there would not be this "natural resemblance" which must exist between Christ and his minister if the role of Christ were not taken by a man: in such a case it would be difficult to see in the minister the image of Christ. For Christ himself was and remains a man.

Christ is of course the firstborn of all humanity, of women as well as men: the unity which he re-established after sin is such that there are no more distinctions between Jew and Greek, slave and free, male and female, but all are one in Christ Jesus (cf. Gal 3:28). Nevertheless, the Incarnation of the Word took place according to the male sex: this is indeed a question of fact, and this fact, while not implying an alleged natural superiority of man over woman, cannot be disassociated from the economy of salvation: it is, indeed, in harmony with the entirety of God's plan as God himself has revealed it, and of which the mystery of the Covenant is the nucleus.

For the salvation offered by God to men and women, the union with him to which they are called—in short, the Covenant—took on, from the Old Testament Prophets onwards, the privileged form of a nuptial mystery: for God the Chosen People is seen as his ardently loved spouse. Both Jewish and Christian tradition has discovered the depth of this intimacy of love by reading and rereading the Song of Songs; the divine Bridegroom will remain faithful even when the Bride betrays his love, when Israel is unfaithful to God (cf. Hos 1–3; Jer 2). When the "fullness of time" (Gal 4:4) comes, the Word, the Son of God, takes on flesh in order to establish and seal the new and eternal Covenant in his blood, which will be shed for many so that sins may be forgiven. His death will gather together again the scattered children of God: from his pierced side will be born the Church, as Eve was born from Adam's side. At that time there is fully and eternally accomplished the nuptial mystery proclaimed and hymned in the Old Testament: Christ is the Bridegroom; the Church is his bride, whom he loves because he has gained her by his blood and made her glorious, holy and without blemish, and henceforth he is inseparable from her. This nuptial theme, which is developed from the Letters of Saint Paul onwards (cf. 2 Cor 11:2; Eph 5:22–23) to the writings of Saint John (cf. especially Jn 3:29; Rev 19:7, 9), is present also in the Synoptic Gospels: the Bridegroom's friends must not fast as long as he is with them (cf. Mk 2:19); the Kingdom of Heaven is like a king who gave a feast for his son's wedding (cf. Mt 22:1–14). It is through this Scriptural language, all interwoven with symbols, and which expresses and affects man and woman in their profound identity, that there is revealed to us the mystery of God and Christ, a mystery which of itself is unfathomable.

That is why we can never ignore the fact that Christ is a man. And therefore, unless one is to disregard the importance of this symbolism for the economy of Revelation, it must be admitted that, in actions which demand the character of ordination and in which Christ himself, the author of the Covenant, the Bridegroom and Head of the Church, is represented, exercising his ministry of salvation—which is in the highest degree the case of the Eucharist—his role (this is the original sense of the word *persona*) must be taken by a man. This does not stem from any personal superiority of the latter in the order of values, but only from a difference of fact on the level of functions and service.

Could one say that, since Christ is now in the heavenly condition, from now on it is a matter of indifference whether he be represented by a man or by a woman, since "at the resurrection men and women do not marry" (Mt 2:30)? But this text does not mean that the distinction between man and woman, insofar as it determines the identity proper to the person, is suppressed in the glorified state; what holds for us holds also for Christ. It is indeed evident that in human beings the difference of sex exercises an important influence, much deeper than, for example, ethnic differences: the latter do not affect the human person as intimately as the difference of sex, which is directly ordained both for the communion of persons and for the generation of human beings. In Biblical Revelation this difference is the effect of God's will from the beginning: "male and female he created them" (Gen 1:27).

However, it will perhaps be further objected that the priest, especially when he presides at the liturgical and sacramental functions, equally represents the Church: he acts in her name with "the intention of doing what she does". In this sense, the theologians of the Middle Ages said that the minister also acts *in persona Ecclesiae*, that is to say, in the name of the whole Church and in order to represent her. And in fact, leaving aside the question of the participation of the faithful in a liturgical action, it is indeed in the name of the whole Church that the action is celebrated by the priest: he prays in the name of all, and in the Mass he offers the sacrifice of the whole Church. In the new Passover, the Church, under visible signs, immolates Christ through the ministry of the priest. And so, it is asserted, since the priest also represents the Church, would it not be possible to think that this representation could be carried out by a woman, according to the symbolism already explained? It is true that the priest represents the Church, which is the Body of Christ. But if he does so, it is precisely because he first represents Christ himself, who is the Head and Shepherd of the Church. The Second Vatican Council used this phrase to make more precise and to complete the expression *in persona Christi*. It is in this quality that the priest presides over the Christian assembly and celebrates the Eucharistic sacrifice "in which the whole Church offers and is herself wholly offered".

If one does justice to these reflections, one will better understand how well-founded is the basis of the Church's practice; and one will conclude that the controversies raised in our days over the ordination of women are for all Christians a pressing invitation to meditate on the mystery of the Church, to study in greater detail the meaning of the episcopate and the priesthood, and to rediscover the real and pre-eminent place of the priest in the community of the baptized, of which he indeed forms part but from which he is distinguished because, in the actions that call for the character of ordination, for the community he is—with all the effectiveness proper to the sacraments—the image and symbol of Christ himself who calls, forgives, and accomplishes the sacrifice of the Covenant.

It is opportune to recall that problems of sacramental theology, especially when they concern the ministerial priesthood, as is the case here, cannot be solved except in the light of Revelation. The human sciences, however valuable their contribution in their own domain, cannot suffice here, for they cannot grasp the realities of faith: the properly supernatural content of these realities is beyond their competence.

Thus one must note the extent to which the Church is a society different from other societies, original in her nature and in her structures. The pastoral charge in the Church is normally linked to the sacrament of Order: it is not a simple government, comparable to the modes of authority found in States. It is not granted by the people's spontaneous choice: even when it involves designation through election, it is the laying on of hands and the prayer of the successors of the Apostles which guarantee God's choice; and it is the Holy Spirit, given by ordination, who grants participation in the ruling power of the Supreme Pastor, Christ (cf. Acts 20:28). It is a charge of service and love: "If you love me, feed my sheep" (cf. Jn 21:15–17).

For this reason one cannot see how it is possible to propose the admission of women to the priesthood in virtue of the equality of rights of the human person, an equality which holds good also for Christians. To this end use is sometimes made of the text quoted above, from the Letter to the Galatians (3:28), which says that in Christ there is no longer any distinction between men and women. But this passage does not concern ministries: it only affirms the universal calling to divine filiation, which is the same for all. Moreover, and above all, to consider the ministerial priesthood as a human right would be to misjudge its nature completely: baptism does not confer any personal title to public ministry in the Church. The priesthood is not conferred for the honor or advantage of the recipient, but for the service of God and the Church; it is the object of a specific and totally gratuitous vocation: "You did not choose me, no, I chose you; and I commissioned you . . ." (Jn 15:16; cf. Heb 5:4).

It is sometimes said and written in books and periodicals that some women feel that they have a vocation to the priesthood. Such an attraction, however noble and understandable, still does not suffice for a genuine vocation. In fact a vocation cannot be reduced to a mere personal attraction, which can remain purely subjective. Since the priesthood is a particular ministry of which the Church has received the charge and the control, authentication by the Church is indispensable here and is a constitutive part of the vocation: Christ chose "those he wanted" (Mk 3:13). On the other hand, there is a universal vocation of all the baptized to the exercise of the royal priesthood by offering their lives to God and by giving witness for his praise.

Women who express a desire for the ministerial priesthood are doubtless motivated by the desire to serve Christ and the Church. And it is not surprising that, at a time when they are becoming more aware of the discriminations to which they have been subject, they should desire the ministerial priesthood itself. But it must not be forgotten that the priesthood does not form part of the rights of the individual, but stems from the economy of the mystery of Christ and the Church. The priestly office cannot become the goal of social advancement; no merely human progress of society or of the individual can of itself give access to it: it is of another order.

It therefore remains for us to meditate more deeply on the nature of the real equality of the baptized which is one of the great affirmations of Christianity: equality is in no way identity, for the Church is a differentiated body, in which each individual has his or her role. The roles are distinct, and must not be confused; they do not favor the superiority of some vis-à-vis the others, nor do they provide an excuse for jealousy; the only better gift, which can and must be desired, is love (cf. 1 Cor 12–13). The greatest in the Kingdom of Heaven are not the ministers but the saints.

The Church desires that Christian women should become fully aware of the greatness of their mission: today their role is of capital importance, both for the renewal and humanization of society and for the rediscovery by believers of the true face of the Church.

1578 **Hebrews 5:4** And one does not take the honor upon himself, but he is called by God, just as Aaron was.

1579 ***Presbyterorum ordinis* 16** Perfect and perpetual continence for the sake of the kingdom of heaven was recommended by Christ the Lord. It has been freely accepted and laudably observed by many Christians down through the centuries as well as in our own time, and has always been highly esteemed in a special way by the Church as a feature of priestly life. For it is at once a sign of pastoral charity and an incentive to it as well as being in a special way a source of spiritual fruitfulness in the world. It is true that it is not demanded of the priesthood by its nature. This is clear from the practice of the primitive Church and the tradition of the Eastern Churches where in addition to those—including all bishops—who choose from the gift of grace to preserve celibacy, there are also many excellent married priests. While recommending ecclesiastical celibacy this sacred Council does not by any means aim at changing that contrary discipline which is lawfully practiced in the Eastern Churches. Rather the Council affectionately exhorts all those who have received the priesthood in the married state to persevere in their holy vocation and continue to devote their lives fully and generously to the flock entrusted to them.

There are many ways in which celibacy is in harmony with the priesthood. For the whole mission of the priest is dedicated to the service of the new humanity which Christ, the victor over death, raises up in the world through his Spirit and which is born "not of blood nor of the will of the flesh nor of the will of man, but of God" (Jn 1:13). By preserving virginity or celibacy for the sake of the kingdom of heaven priests are consecrated in a new and excellent way to Christ. They more readily cling to him with undivided heart and dedicate themselves more freely in him and through him to the service of God and of men. They are less encumbered in their service of his kingdom and of the task of heavenly regeneration. In this way they become better fitted for a broader acceptance of fatherhood in Christ.

By means of celibacy, then, priests profess before men their willingness to be dedicated with undivided loyalty to the task entrusted to them, namely that of espousing the faithful to one husband and presenting them as a chaste virgin to Christ. They recall that mystical marriage, established by God and destined to be fully revealed in the future, but which the Church holds Christ as her only spouse. Moreover they are made a living sign of that world to come, already present through faith and charity, a world in which the children of the resurrection shall neither be married nor take wives.

For these reasons, based on the mystery of Christ and his mission, celibacy, which at first was recommended to priests, was afterwards in the Latin Church imposed by law on all who were to be promoted to holy Orders. This sacred Council approves and confirms this legislation so far as it concerns those destined for the priesthood, and feels confident in the Spirit that the gift of celibacy, so appropriate to the priesthood of the New Testament, is liberally granted by the Father, provided those who share Christ's priesthood through the sacrament of Order, and indeed the whole Church, ask for that gift humbly and earnestly.

This sacred Council also exhorts all priests who, with trust in God's grace, have of their own free choice accepted consecrated celibacy after the example of Christ, to hold fast to it with courage and enthusiasm, and to persevere faithfully in this state, appreciating that glorious gift that has been given them by the Father and is so clearly extolled by the Lord, and keeping before their eyes the great mysteries that are signified and fulfilled in it. And the more that perfect continence is considered by many people to be impossible in the world of today, so much the more humbly and perseveringly in union with the Church ought priests demand the grace of fidelity, which is never denied to those who ask.

At the same time they will employ all the helps to fidelity both supernatural and natural, which are available to everybody. Especially they should never neglect to follow the rules of ascetical practice which are approved by the experience of the Church and are as necessary as ever in the modern world. So this sacred Council asks that not only priests but all the faithful would cherish this precious gift of priestly celibacy, and that all of them would beg of God always to lavish this gift abundantly on his Church.

1580 ***Presbyterorum ordinis* 16:** see previous document.

1582 (1) **Council of Trent (1563): DS 1767** But since in the sacrament of orders, as also in baptism and in confirmation, a sign is imprinted [can. 4], which can neither be effaced nor taken away, justly does the holy Synod condemn the opinion of those who assert that the priests of the New Testament have only a temporary power, and that those at one time rightly ordained can again become laymen, if they do not exercise the ministry of the word of God [can. 1]. But if anyone should affirm that all Christians without distinction are priests of the New Testament, or that they are all endowed among themselves with an equal spiritual power, he seems to do nothing else than disarrange [can. 6] the ecclesiastical hierarchy, which is "as an army set in array" [cf. Cant. 6:3], just as if, contrary to the teaching of blessed Paul, all were apostles, all prophets, all evangelists, all pastors, all doctors [cf. I Cor. 12:29; Eph. 4:11].

1582 (2) ***Lumen gentium* 21:** see 1549 (1).

1582 (3) ***Lumen gentium* 28:** see 1548 (2).

1582 (4) ***Lumen gentium* 29:** see 1570 (6).

1582 (5) ***Presbyterorum ordinis* 2:** see 1548 (5).

1583 (1) **CIC Canons 290–93**

Can. 290—After it has been validly received, sacred ordination never becomes invalid. A cleric, however, loses the clerical state:

1° by a judicial decision or administrative decree which declares the invalidity of sacred ordination;

2° by the legitimate infliction of the penalty of dismissal;

3° by a rescript of the Apostolic See which is granted by the Apostolic See to deacons only for serious reasons and to presbyters only for the most serious reasons.

Can. 291—Besides the case mentioned in can. 290, n. 1, loss of the clerical state does not entail a dispensation from the obligation of celibacy, which is granted by the Roman Pontiff alone.

Can. 292—A cleric who loses the clerical state in accord with the norm of law also loses with it the rights which pertain to the clerical state; nor is he bound by any of the obligations of the clerical state, with due regard for the prescription of can. 291; he is prohibited from exercising the power of orders with due regard for the prescription of can. 976; and by the very fact he is deprived of all offices, functions and any delegated power.

Can. 293—A cleric who has lost the clerical state cannot become a member of the clergy again without a rescript of the Apostolic See.

1583 (2) **CIC Canon 1336, §1, 3°, 5°** §1. Besides other penalties which the law may establish, the following are expiatory penalties which can punish an offender in perpetuity, for a prescribed time or for an indeterminate time. . . .

3° a prohibition against exercising those things mentioned in n. 2 or a prohibition against exercising them in a certain place or outside a certain place; which prohibitions are never under pain of nullity. . . .

5° dismissal from the clerical state.

(3) **CIC Canon 1338, §2** There is no such penalty as deprivation of the power of orders, but only the prohibition against exercising it or some acts of orders; there is likewise no such penalty as a deprivation of academic degrees. 1583

(4) **Council of Trent (1563): DS 1774** If anyone says that by sacred ordination the Holy Spirit is not imparted, and that therefore the bishops say in vain: "Receive ye the Holy Spirit"; or that by it a character is not imprinted or that he who has once been a priest can again become a layman: let him be anathema. 1583

(1) **Council of Trent (1547): DS 1612** If anyone shall say that a minister who is in mortal sin, although he observes all the essentials which pertain to the performance or conferring of the sacrament, neither performs nor confers the sacrament: let him be anathema. 1584

(2) **Council of Constance (1415): DS 1154** If a bishop or priest is living in mortal sin, he does not ordain, nor consecrate, nor perform, nor baptize. 1584

(1) **Roman Pontifical Ordination of Bishops 26, Prayer of Consecration** 1586

God the Father of our Lord Jesus Christ,
Father of mercies and God of all consolation,
you dwell in heaven,
yet look with compassion on all that is humble.
You know all things before they come to be;
by your gracious word
you have established the plan of your Church.

From the beginning
you chose the descendants of Abraham to be your holy nation.
You established rulers and priests,
and did not leave your sanctuary without ministers to serve you.
From the creation of the world you have been pleased to be glorified
by those whom you have chosen.

So now pour out upon this chosen one
that power which is from you,
the governing Spirit
whom you gave to your beloved Son, Jesus Christ,
the Spirit given by him to the holy apostles,
who founded the Church in every place to be your temple
for the unceasing glory and praise of your name.

Father, you know all hearts.
You have chosen your servant for the office of bishop.
May he be a shepherd to your holy flock,
and a high priest blameless in your sight,
ministering to you night and day;
may he always gain the blessing of your favor
and offer the gifts of your holy Church.
Through the Spirit who gives the grace of the high priesthood
grant him the power
to forgive sins as you have commanded,
to assign ministries as you have decreed,
and to loose every bond by the authority which you gave to your apostles.

May he be pleasing to you by his gentleness and purity of heart,
presenting a fragrant offering to you,
through Jesus Christ, your Son,
through whom glory and power and honor are yours
with the Holy Spirit
in your holy Church,
now and for ever.
Amen.

1586 (2) ***Christus Dominus* 13** Bishops should present the doctrine of Christ in a manner suited to the needs of the times, that is, so it may be relevant to those difficulties and questions which men find especially worrying and intimidating. They should also safeguard this doctrine, teaching the faithful themselves to defend it and propagate it. In presenting this doctrine they should proclaim the maternal solicitude of the Church for all men, whether they be Catholics or not, and should be especially solicitous for the poor and weaker brethren whom the Lord has commissioned them to evangelize.

Since it is the mission of the Church to maintain close relation with the society in which she lives the bishops should make it their special care to approach men and to initiate and promote dialogue with them. These discussions on religious matters should be marked by charity of expression as well as by humility and courtesy, so that truth may be combined with charity, and understanding with love. The discussions should likewise be characterized by due prudence allied, however, with sincerity which by promoting friendship is conducive to a union of minds.

Bishops should also endeavor to use the various methods available nowadays for proclaiming Christian doctrine. There are, first of all, preaching and catechetical instruction, which always hold pride of place. There is also doctrinal instruction in schools, universities, conferences and meetings of every kind. Finally, there are public statements made by way of comment on events, as well as the press and other media of public communication, all of which should be employed for the promulgation of the gospel of Christ.

1586 (3) ***Christus Dominus* 16** In exercising his office of father and pastor the bishop should be with his people as one who serves, as a good shepherd who knows his sheep and whose sheep know him, as a true father who excels in his love and solicitude for all, to whose divinely conferred authority all readily submit. He should so unite and mold his flock into one family that all, conscious of their duties, may live and act in the communion of charity.

In order to accomplish these things effectively the bishop "being ready for every good work" (2 Tim. 2:21) and "enduring all things for the sake of the elect" (2 Tim. 2:10) should so arrange his own life as to accommodate it to the needs of the times. His priests, who assume a part of his duties and concerns, and who are ceaselessly devoted to their work, should be the objects of his particular affection. He should regard them as sons and friends. He should always be ready to listen to them and cultivate an atmosphere of easy familiarity with them, thus facilitating the pastoral work of the entire diocese.

A bishop should be solicitous for the welfare—spiritual, intellectual, and material—of his priests, so that they may live holy and pious lives, and exercise a faithful and fruitful ministry. With this end in view he should encourage courses and arrange for special conferences for his priests from time to time. These could take the form of extended retreats for the renewal of their spiritual lives or courses intended to deepen their knowledge of ecclesiastical studies, especially of sacred scripture and theology, of the more important social questions, or of new methods of pastoral activity.

A bishop should be compassionate and helpful to those priests who are in any kind of danger or who have failed in some respect.

In order to be able to provide for the welfare of the faithful as their individual circumstances demand, he should try to keep himself informed of their needs in the social circumstances in which they live. To this end he should employ suitable methods, especially social research. He should be solicitous for all men whatever their age, condition or nationality, whether they are natives, visitors or foreign immigrants. In exercising his ministry he should ensure that the faithful are duly involved in Church affairs; he should recognize their right and duty to play their part in building up the Mystical Body of Christ.

Bishops should show affectionate consideration in their relations with the separated brethren and should urge the faithful also to exercise all kindness and charity in their regard, encouraging ecumenism as it is understood by the Church. The non-baptized also should be the object of their solicitude so that on them too may shine the charity of Christ of whom bishops are the witnesses before all men.

(4) **St. Hippolytus, *Traditio apostolica* 3** God and Father of our Lord Jesus Christ, 1586
Father of mercies and God of all comfort, who dwellest on high yet hast respect to the lowly, who knowest all things before they come to pass. Thou hast appointed the borders of thy church by the word of thy grace, predestinating from the beginning the righteous race of Abraham. And making them princes and priests, and leaving not thy sanctuary without a ministry, thou hast from the beginning of the world been well pleased to be glorified among those whom thou hast chosen. Pour forth now that power, which is thine, of thy royal Spirit, which thou gavest to thy beloved Servant Jesus Christ, which he bestowed on his holy apostles, who established the church in every place, the church which thou hast sanctified unto unceasing glory and praise of thy name. Thou who knowest the hearts of all, grant to this thy servant, whom thou hast chosen to be bishop, [to feed thy holy flock] and to serve as thy high priest without blame, ministering night and day, to propitiate thy countenance without ceasing and to offer thee the gifts of thy holy church. And by the Spirit of high-priesthood to have authority to remit sins according to thy commandment, to assign the lots according to thy precept, to loose every bond according to the authority which thou gavest to thy apostles, and to please thee in meekness and purity of heart, offering to thee an odour of sweet savour. Through thy Servant Jesus Christ our Lord, through whom be to thee glory, might, honour, with [the] Holy Spirit in [the] holy church, both now and always and world without end. Amen.

St. Ignatius of Antioch, *Epistula ad Trallianos* 3, 1 Likewise, let all respect the 1593
deacons as representing Jesus Christ, the bishop as a type of the Father, and the presbyters as God's high council and as the Apostolic college. Apart from these, no church deserves the name.

***Gaudium et spes* 48, 1** The intimate partnership of life and the love which con- 1601
stitutes the married state has been established by the creator and endowed by him with its own proper laws: it is rooted in the contract of its partners, that is, in their irrevocable personal consent. It is an institution confirmed by the divine law and receiving its stability, even in the eyes of society, from the human act by which the partners mutually surrender themselves to each other; for the good of the partners, of the children, and of society this sacred bond no longer depends on human decision alone. For God himself is the author of marriage and has endowed it with various

benefits and with various ends in view: all of these have a very important bearing on the continuation of the human race, on the personal development and eternal destiny of every member of the family, on the dignity, stability, peace, and prosperity of the family and of the whole human race. By its very nature the institution of marriage and married love is ordered to the procreation and education of the offspring and it is in them that it finds its crowning glory. Thus the man and woman, who "are no longer two but one" (Mt. 19:6), help and serve each other by their marriage partnership; they become conscious of their unity and experience it more deeply from day to day. The intimate union of marriage, as a mutual giving of two persons, and the good of the children demand total fidelity from the spouses and require an unbreakable unity between them.

1602 (1) **Genesis 1:26–27** Then God said, "Let us make man in our image, after our likeness; and let them have dominion over the fish of the sea, and over the birds of the air, and over the cattle, and over all the earth, and over every creeping thing that creeps upon the earth." So God created man in his own image, in the image of God he created him; male and female he created them.

1602 (2) **Ephesians 5:31–32** "For this reason a man shall leave his father and mother and be joined to his wife, and the two shall become one flesh." This mystery is a profound one, and I am saying that it refers to Christ and the church. . . .

1603 ***Gaudium et spes* 47, 2** However, this happy picture of the dignity of these partnerships is not reflected everywhere, but is overshadowed by polygamy, the plague of divorce, so-called free love, and similar blemishes; furthermore, married love is too often dishonored by selfishness, hedonism, and unlawful contraceptive practices. Besides, the economic, social, psychological, and civil climate of today has a severely disturbing effect on family life. There are also the serious and alarming problems arising in many parts of the world as a result of population expansion. On all of these counts an anguish of conscience is being generated. And yet the strength and vigor of the institution of marriage and family shines forth time and again: for despite the hardships flowing from the profoundly changing conditions of society today, the true nature of marriage and of the family is revealed in one way or another.

1604 (1) **Genesis 1:27** So God created man in his own image, in the image of God he created him; male and female he created them.

1604 (2) **1 John 4:8** He who does not love does not know God; for God is love.

1604 (3) **1 John 4:16** So we know and believe the love God has for us. God is love, and he who abides in love abides in God, and God abides in him.

1604 (4) **Genesis 1:31** And God saw everything that he had made, and behold, it was very good. And there was evening and there was morning, a sixth day.

1605 **Genesis 2:18–25** Then the Lord God said, "It is not good that the man should be alone; I will make him a helper fit for him." So out of the ground the Lord God formed every beast of the field and every bird of the air, and brought them to the man to see what he would call them; and whatever the man called every living creature, that was its name. The man gave names to all cattle, and to the birds of the air, and to every beast of the field; but for the man there was not found a helper fit for him. So the Lord God caused a deep sleep to fall upon the man, and while he slept took one of his ribs and closed up its place with flesh; and the rib which the Lord God had taken from the man he made into a woman and brought her to the man. Then the man said,

"This at last is bone of my bones
 and flesh of my flesh;
she shall be called Woman,
 because she was taken out of Man."

Therefore a man leaves his father and his mother and cleaves to his wife, and they become one flesh. And the man and his wife were both naked, and were not ashamed.

(1) **Genesis 3:12** The man said, "The woman whom thou gavest to be with me, she gave me fruit of the tree, and I ate." **1607**

(2) **Genesis 2:22** . . . and the rib which the Lord God had taken from the man he made into a woman and brought her to the man. **1607**

(3) **Genesis 3:16b** **1607**

"... your desire shall be for your husband,
 and he shall rule over you."

(4) **Genesis 1:28** And God blessed them, and God said to them, "Be fruitful and multiply, and fill the earth and subdue it; and have dominion over the fish of the sea and over the birds of the air and over every living thing that moves upon the earth." **1607**

(5) **Genesis 3:16–19** To the woman he said, **1607**

"I will greatly multiply your pain in childbearing;
 in pain you shall bring forth children,
yet your desire shall be for your husband,
 and he shall rule over you."
And to Adam he said,
"Because you have listened to the voice of your wife,
 and have eaten of the tree
of which I commanded you,
 'You shall not eat of it,'
cursed is the ground because of you;
 in toil you shall eat of it all the days of your life;
thorns and thistles it shall bring forth to you;
 and you shall eat the plants of the field.
In the sweat of your face
 you shall eat bread
till you return to the ground,
 for out of it you were taken;
you are dust,
 and to dust you shall return."

Genesis 3:21 And the Lord God made for Adam and for his wife garments of skins, and clothed them. **1608**

(1) **Matthew 19:8** He said to them, "For your hardness of heart Moses allowed you to divorce your wives, but from the beginning it was not so. . . ." **1610**

1610 (2) **Deuteronomy 24:1** "When a man takes a wife and marries her, if then she finds no favor in his eyes because he has found some indecency in her, and he writes her a bill of divorce and puts it in her hand and sends her out of his house, and she departs out of his house. . . ."

1611 (1) **Hosea 1–3** The word of the Lord that came to Hosea the son of Beeri, in the days of Uzziah, Jotham, Ahaz, and Hezekiah, kings of Judah, and in the days of Jeroboam the son of Joash, king of Israel.

When the Lord first spoke through Hosea, the Lord said to Hosea, "Go, take to yourself a wife of harlotry and have children of harlotry, for the land commits great harlotry by forsaking the Lord." So he went and took Gomer the daughter of Diblaim, and she conceived and bore him a son.

And the Lord said to him, "Call his name Jezreel; for yet a little while, and I will punish the house of Jehu for the blood of Jezreel, and I will put an end to the kingdom of the house of Israel. And on that day, I will break the bow of Israel in the valley of Jezreel."

She conceived again and bore a daughter. And the Lord said to him, "Call her name Not pitied, for I will no more have pity on the house of Israel, to forgive them at all. But I will have pity on the house of Judah, and I will deliver them by the Lord their God; I will not deliver them by bow, nor by sword, nor by war, nor by horses, nor by horsemen."

When she had weaned Not pitied, she conceived and bore a son. And the Lord said, "Call his name Not my people, for you are not my people and I am not your God."

Yet the number of the people of Israel shall be like the sand of the sea, which can be neither measured nor numbered; and in the place where it was said to them, "You are not my people," it shall be said to them, "Sons of the living God." And the people of Judah and the people of Israel shall be gathered together, and they shall appoint for themselves one head; and they shall go up from the land, for great shall be the day of Jezreel.

Say to your brother, "My people," and to your sister, "She has obtained pity."

"Plead with your mother, plead—
    for she is not my wife,
    and I am not her husband—
that she put away her harlotry from her face,
    and her adultery from between her breasts;
lest I strip her naked
    and make her as in the day she was born,
and make her like a wilderness,
    and set her like a parched land,
    and slay her with thirst.
Upon her children also I will have no pity,
    because they are children of harlotry.
For their mother has played the harlot;
    she that conceived them has acted shamefully.
For she said, 'I will go after my lovers,
    who give me my bread and my water,
    my wool and my flax, my oil and my drink.'
Therefore I will hedge up her way with thorns;
    and I will build a wall against her,
    so that she cannot find her paths.
She shall pursue her lovers,

but not overtake them;
and she shall seek them,
but shall not find them.
Then she shall say, 'I will go
and return to my first husband,
for it was better with me then than now.'
And she did not know
that it was I who gave her
the grain, the wine, and the oil,
and who lavished upon her silver
and gold which they used for Baal.
Therefore I will take back
my grain in its time,
and my wine in its season;
and I will take away my wool and my flax,
which were to cover her nakedness.
Now I will uncover her lewdness
in the sight of her lovers,
and no one shall rescue her out of my hand.
And I will put an end to all her mirth,
her feasts, her new moons, her sabbaths,
and all her appointed feasts.
And I will lay waste her vines and her fig trees,
of which she said, 'These are my hire,
which my lovers have given me.'
I will make them a forest,
and the beasts of the field shall devour them.
And I will punish her for the feast days of the Baals
when she burned incense to them
and decked herself with her ring and jewelry,
and went after her lovers,
and forgot me, says the Lord.

"Therefore, behold, I will allure her,
and bring her into the wilderness,
and speak tenderly to her.
And there I will give her her vineyards,
and make the Valley of Achor a door of hope.
And there she shall answer as in the days of her youth,
as at the time when she came out of the land of Egypt.

"And in that day, says the Lord, you will call me, 'My husband,' and no longer will you call me, 'My Baal.' For I will remove the names of the Baals from her mouth, and they shall be mentioned by name no more. And I will make for you a covenant on that day with the beasts of the field, the birds of the air, and the creeping things of the ground; and I will abolish the bow, the sword, and war from the land; and I will make you lie down in safety. And I will betroth you to me for ever; I will betroth you to me in righteousness and in justice, in steadfast love, and in mercy. I will betroth you to me in faithfulness; and you shall know the Lord.

"And in that day, says the Lord,
I will answer the heavens
and they shall answer the earth;
and the earth shall answer the grain, the wine, and the oil,

and they shall answer Jezreel;
and I will sow him for myself in the land.
And I will have pity on Not pitied,
and I will say to Not my people, 'You are my people';
and he shall say, 'Thou art my God.'"

And the Lord said to me, "Go again, love a woman who is beloved of a paramour and is an adulteress; even as the Lord loves the people of Israel, though they turn to other gods and love cakes of raisins." So I bought her for fifteen shekels of silver and a homer and a lethech of barley. And I said to her, "You must dwell as mine for many days; you shall not play the harlot, or belong to another man; so will I also be to you." For the children of Israel shall dwell many days without king or prince, without sacrifice or pillar, without ephod or teraphim. Afterward the children of Israel shall return and seek the Lord their God, and David their king; and they shall come in fear to the Lord and to his goodness in the latter days.

1611 (2) **Isaiah 54**

"Sing, O barren one, who did not bear;
break forth into singing and cry aloud,
you who have not been in travail!
For the children of the desolate one will be more
than the children of her that is married, says the Lord.
Enlarge the place of your tent,
and let the curtains of your habitations be stretched out;
hold not back, lengthen your cords
and strengthen your stakes.
For you will spread abroad to the right and to the left,
and your descendants will possess the nations
and will people the desolate cities.

"Fear not, for you will not be ashamed;
be not confounded, for you will not be put to shame;
for you will forget the shame of your youth,
and the reproach of your widowhood you will remember no more.
For your Maker is your husband,
the Lord of hosts is his name;
and the Holy One of Israel is your Redeemer,
the God of the whole earth he is called.
For the Lord has called you
like a wife forsaken and grieved in spirit,
like a wife of youth when she is cast off,
says your God.
For a brief moment I forsook you,
but with great compassion I will gather you.
In overflowing wrath for a moment
I hid my face from you,
but with everlasting love I will have compassion on you,
says the Lord, your Redeemer.

"For this is like the days of Noah to me:
as I swore that the waters of Noah
should no more go over the earth,
so I have sworn that I will not be angry with you
and will not rebuke you.

For the mountains may depart
    and the hills be removed,
but my steadfast love shall not depart from you,
    and my covenant of peace shall not be removed,
    says the Lord, who has compassion on you.

"O afflicted one, storm-tossed, and not comforted,
    behold, I will set your stones in antimony,
    and lay your foundations with sapphires.
I will make your pinnacles of agate,
    your gates of carbuncles,
    and all your wall of precious stones.
All your sons shall be taught by the Lord,
    and great shall be the prosperity of your sons.
In righteousness you shall be established;
    you shall be far from oppression, for you shall not fear;
    and from terror, for it shall not come near you.
If any one stirs up strife,
    it is not from me;
whoever stirs up strife with you
    shall fall because of you.
Behold, I have created the smith
    who blows the fire of coals,
    and produces a weapon for its purpose.
I have also created the ravager to destroy;
    no weapon that is fashioned against you shall prosper,
    and you shall confute every tongue that rises against you in judgment.
This is the heritage of the servants of the Lord
    and their vindication from me, says the Lord."

(3) **Isaiah 62** 1611

For Zion's sake I will not keep silent,
    and for Jerusalem's sake I will not rest,
until her vindication goes forth as brightness,
    and her salvation as a burning torch.
The nations shall see your vindication,
    and all the kings your glory;
and you shall be called by a new name
    which the mouth of the Lord will give.
You shall be a crown of beauty in the hand of the Lord,
    and a royal diadem in the hand of your God.
You shall no more be termed Forsaken,
    and your land shall no more be termed Desolate;
but you shall be called My delight is in her,
    and your land Married;
for the Lord delights in you,
    and your land shall be married.
For as a young man marries a virgin,
    so shall your sons marry you,
and as the bridegroom rejoices over the bride,
    so shall your God rejoice over you.

Upon your walls, O Jerusalem,
I have set watchmen;
all the day and all the night
they shall never be silent.
You who put the Lord in remembrance,
take no rest,
and give him no rest
until he establishes Jerusalem
and makes it a praise in the earth.
The Lord has sworn by his right hand
and his mighty arm:
"I will not again give your grain
to be food for your enemies,
and foreigners shall not drink your wine
for which you have labored;
but those who garner it shall eat it
and praise the Lord,
and those who gather it shall drink it
in the courts of my sanctuary."

Go through, go through the gates,
prepare the way for the people;
build up, build up the highway,
clear it of stones,
lift up an ensign over the peoples.
Behold, the Lord has proclaimed
to the end of the earth:
Say to the daughter of Zion,
"Behold, your salvation comes;
behold, his reward is with him,
and his recompense before him."
And they shall be called The holy people,
The redeemed of the Lord;
and you shall be called Sought out,
a city not forsaken.

1611 (4) **Jeremiah 2–3** The word of the Lord came to me, saying, "Go and proclaim in the hearing of Jerusalem, Thus says the Lord,

I remember the devotion of your youth,
your love as a bride,
how you followed me in the wilderness,
in a land not sown.
Israel was holy to the Lord,
the first fruits of his harvest.
All who ate of it became guilty;
evil came upon them,
says the Lord."

Hear the word of the Lord, O house of Jacob, and all the families of the house of Israel. Thus says the Lord:

"What wrong did your fathers find in me
that they went far from me,
and went after worthlessness, and became worthless?

They did not say, 'Where is the Lord
who brought us up from the land of Egypt,
who led us in the wilderness,
in a land of deserts and pits,
in a land of drought and deep darkness,
in a land that none passes through,
where no man dwells?'
And I brought you into a plentiful land
to enjoy its fruits and its good things.
But when you came in you defiled my land,
and made my heritage an abomination.
The priests did not say, 'Where is the Lord?'
Those who handle the law did not know me;
the rulers transgressed against me;
the prophets prophesied by Baal,
and went after things that do not profit.

"Therefore I still contend with you,
says the Lord,
and with your children's children I will contend.
For cross to the coasts of Cyprus and see,
or send to Kedar and examine with care;
see if there has been such a thing.
Has a nation changed its gods,
even though they are no gods?
But my people have changed their glory
for that which does not profit.
Be appalled, O heavens, at this,
be shocked, be utterly desolate,
says the Lord,
for my people have committed two evils:
they have forsaken me,
the fountain of living waters,
and hewed out cisterns for themselves,
broken cisterns,
that can hold no water.

"Is Israel a slave? Is he a homeborn servant?
Why then has he become a prey?
The lions have roared against him,
they have roared loudly.
They have made his land a waste;
his cities are in ruins, without inhabitant.
Moreover, the men of Memphis and Tahpanhes
have broken the crown of your head.
Have you not brought this upon yourself
by forsaking the Lord your God,
when he led you in the way?
And now what do you gain by going to Egypt,
to drink the waters of the Nile?
Or what do you gain by going to Assyria,
to drink the waters of the Euphrates?

Your wickedness will chasten you,
    and your apostasy will reprove you.
Know and see that it is evil and bitter
    for you to forsake the Lord your God;
    the fear of me is not in you,
        says the Lord God of hosts.

"For long ago you broke your yoke
    and burst your bonds;
    and you said, 'I will not serve.'
Yea, upon every high hill
    and under every green tree
    you bowed down as a harlot.
Yet I planted you a choice vine,
    wholly of pure seed.
How then have you turned degenerate
    and become a wild vine?
Though you wash yourself with lye
    and use much soap,
    the stain of your guilt is still before me,
        says the Lord God.
How can you say, 'I am not defiled,
    I have not gone after the Baals'?
Look at your way in the valley;
    know what you have done—
a restive young camel interlacing her tracks,
    a wild ass used to the wilderness,
in her heat sniffing the wind!
    Who can restrain her lust?
None who seek her need weary themselves;
    in her month they will find her.
Keep your feet from going unshod
    and your throat from thirst.
But you said, 'It is hopeless,
    for I have loved strangers,
    and after them I will go.'

"As a thief is shamed when caught,
    so the house of Israel shall be shamed:
they, their kings, their princes,
    their priests, and their prophets,
who say to a tree, 'You are my father,'
    and to a stone, 'You gave me birth.'
For they have turned their back to me,
    and not their face.
But in the time of their trouble they say,
    'Arise and save us!'
But where are your gods
    that you made for yourself?
Let them arise, if they can save you,
    in your time of trouble;
for as many as your cities
    are your gods, O Judah.

"Why do you complain against me?
You have all rebelled against me,
says the Lord.
In vain have I smitten your children,
they took no correction;
your own sword devoured your prophets
like a ravening lion.
And you, O generation, heed the word of the Lord.
Have I been a wilderness to Israel,
or a land of thick darkness?
Why then do my people say, 'We are free,
we will come no more to thee'?
Can a maiden forget her ornaments,
or a bride her attire?
Yet my people have forgotten me
days without number.

"How well you direct your course
to seek lovers!
So that even to wicked women
you have taught your ways.
Also on your skirts is found
the lifeblood of guiltless poor;
you did not find them breaking in.
Yet in spite of all these things
you say, 'I am innocent;
surely his anger has turned from me.'
Behold, I will bring you to judgment
for saying, 'I have not sinned.'
How lightly you gad about,
changing your way!
You shall be put to shame by Egypt
as you were put to shame by Assyria.
From it too you will come away
with your hands upon your head,
for the Lord has rejected those in whom you trust,
and you will not prosper by them.

"If a man divorces his wife
and she goes from him
and becomes another man's wife,
will he return to her?
Would not that land be greatly polluted?
You have played the harlot with many lovers;
and would you return to me?
says the Lord.

Lift up your eyes to the bare heights, and see!
Where have you not been lain with?
By the waysides you have sat awaiting lovers
like an Arab in the wilderness.
You have polluted the land
with your vile harlotry.
Therefore the showers have been withheld,

and the spring rain has not come;
yet you have a harlot's brow,
you refuse to be ashamed.
Have you not just now called to me,
'My father, thou art the friend of my youth—
will he be angry for ever,
will he be indignant to the end?'
Behold, you have spoken,
but you have done all the evil that you could."

The Lord said to me in the days of King Josiah: "Have you seen what she did, that faithless one, Israel, how she went up on every high hill and under every green tree, and there played the harlot? And I thought, 'After she has done all this she will return to me'; but she did not return, and her false sister Judah saw it. She saw that for all the adulteries of that faithless one, Israel, I had sent her away with a decree of divorce; yet her false sister Judah did not fear, but she too went and played the harlot. Because harlotry was so light to her, she polluted the land, committing adultery with stone and tree. Yet for all this her false sister Judah did not return to me with her whole heart, but in pretense, says the Lord."

And the Lord said to me, "Faithless Israel has shown herself less guilty than false Judah. Go, and proclaim these words toward the north, and say,
'Return, faithless Israel,
says the Lord.

I will not look on you in anger,
for I am merciful,
says the Lord;
I will not be angry for ever.
Only acknowledge your guilt,
that you rebelled against the Lord your God
and scattered your favors among strangers under every green tree,
and that you have not obeyed my voice,
says the Lord.
Return, O faithless children,
says the Lord;
for I am your master;
I will take you, one from a city and two from a family,
and I will bring you to Zion.

" 'And I will give you shepherds after my own heart, who will feed you with knowledge and understanding. And when you have multiplied and increased in the land, in those days, says the Lord, they shall no more say, "The ark of the covenant of the Lord." It shall not come to mind, or be remembered, or missed; it shall not be made again. At that time Jerusalem shall be called the throne of the Lord, and all nations shall gather to it, to the presence of the Lord in Jerusalem, and they shall no more stubbornly follow their own evil heart. In those days the house of Judah shall join the house of Israel, and together they shall come from the land of the north to the land that I gave your fathers for a heritage.

" 'I thought
how I would set you among my sons,
and give you a pleasant land,
a heritage most beauteous of all nations.
And I thought you would call me, My Father,
and would not turn from following me.

Surely, as a faithless wife leaves her husband,
so have you been faithless to me, O house of Israel,
says the Lord.' "

A voice on the bare heights is heard,
the weeping and pleading of Israel's sons,
because they have perverted their way,
they have forgotten the Lord their God.
"Return, O faithless sons,
I will heal your faithlessness."
"Behold, we come to thee;
for thou art the Lord our God.
Truly the hills are a delusion,
the orgies on the mountains.
Truly in the Lord our God
is the salvation of Israel.

"But from our youth the shameful thing has devoured all for which our fathers labored, their flocks and their herds, their sons and their daughters. Let us lie down in our shame, and let our dishonor cover us; for we have sinned against the Lord our God, we and our fathers, from our youth even to this day; and we have not obeyed the voice of the Lord our God."

(5) **Jeremiah 31** "At that time, says the Lord, I will be the God of all the families **1611**
of Israel, and they shall be my people."

Thus says the Lord:
"The people who survived the sword
found grace in the wilderness;
when Israel sought for rest,
the Lord appeared to him from afar.
I have loved you with an everlasting love;
therefore I have continued my faithfulness to you.
Again I will build you, and you shall be built,
O virgin Israel!
Again you shall adorn yourself with timbrels,
and shall go forth in the dance of the merrymakers.
Again you shall plant vineyards
upon the mountains of Samaria;
the planters shall plant,
and shall enjoy the fruit.
For there shall be a day when watchmen will call
in the hill country of Ephraim:
'Arise, and let us go up to Zion,
to the Lord our God.' "

For thus says the Lord:
"Sing aloud with gladness for Jacob,
and raise shouts for the chief of the nations;
proclaim, give praise, and say,
'The Lord has saved his people,
the remnant of Israel.'
Behold, I will bring them from the north country,
and gather them from the farthest parts of the earth,

among them the blind and the lame,
the woman with child and her who is in travail, together;
a great company, they shall return here.
With weeping they shall come,
and with consolations I will lead them back,
I will make them walk by brooks of water,
in a straight path in which they shall not stumble;
for I am a father to Israel,
and Ephraim is my first-born.

"Hear the word of the Lord, O nations,
and declare it in the coastlands afar off;
say, 'He who scattered Israel will gather him,
and will keep him as a shepherd keeps his flock.'
For the Lord has ransomed Jacob,
and has redeemed him from hands too strong for him.
They shall come and sing aloud on the height of Zion,
and they shall be radiant over the goodness of the Lord,
over the grain, the wine, and the oil,
and over the young of the flock and the herd;
their life shall be like a watered garden,
and they shall languish no more.
Then shall the maidens rejoice in the dance,
and the young men and the old shall be merry.
I will turn their mourning into joy,
I will comfort them, and give them gladness for sorrow.
I will feast the soul of the priests with abundance,
and my people shall be satisfied with my goodness,
says the Lord."

Thus says the Lord:
"A voice is heard in Ramah,
lamentation and bitter weeping.
Rachel is weeping for her children;
she refuses to be comforted for her children,
because they are not."

Thus says the Lord:
"Keep your voice from weeping,
and your eyes from tears;
for your work shall be rewarded,
says the Lord,
and they shall come back from the land of the enemy.
There is hope for your future, says the Lord,
and your children shall come back to their own country.
I have heard Ephraim bemoaning,
'Thou hast chastened me, and I was chastened,
like an untrained calf;
bring me back that I may be restored,
for thou art the Lord my God.
For after I had turned away I repented;
and after I was instructed, I smote upon my thigh;
I was ashamed, and I was confounded,
because I bore the disgrace of my youth.'

Is Ephraim my dear son?
    Is he my darling child?
For as often as I speak against him,
    I do remember him still.
Therefore my heart yearns for him;
    I will surely have mercy on him,
                says the Lord.

"Set up waymarks for yourself,
    make yourself guideposts;
consider well the highway,
    the road by which you went.
Return, O virgin Israel,
    return to these your cities.
How long will you waver,
    O faithless daughter?
For the Lord has created a new thing on the earth:
    a woman protects a man."

Thus says the Lord of hosts, the God of Israel: "Once more they shall use these words in the land of Judah and in its cities when I restore their fortunes:

'The Lord bless you, O habitation of righteousness,
    O holy hill!'

And Judah and all its cities shall dwell there together, and the farmers and those who wander with their flocks. For I will satisfy the weary soul, and every languishing soul I will replenish."

Thereupon I awoke and looked, and my sleep was pleasant to me.

"Behold, the days are coming, says the Lord, when I will sow the house of Israel and the house of Judah with the seed of man and the seed of beast. And it shall come to pass that as I have watched over them to pluck up and break down, to overthrow, destroy, and bring evil, so I will watch over them to build and to plant, says the Lord. In those days they shall no longer say:

'The fathers have eaten sour grapes,
    and the children's teeth are set on edge.'

But every one shall die for his own sin; each man who eats sour grapes, his teeth shall be set on edge.

"Behold, the days are coming, says the Lord, when I will make a new covenant with the house of Israel and the house of Judah, not like the covenant which I made with their fathers when I took them by the hand to bring them out of the land of Egypt, my covenant which they broke, though I was their husband, says the Lord. But this is the covenant which I will make with the house of Israel after those days, says the Lord: I will put my law within them, and I will write it upon their hearts; and I will be their God, and they shall be my people. And no longer shall each man teach his neighbor and each his brother, saying, 'Know the Lord,' for they shall all know me from the least of them to the greatest, says the Lord; for I will forgive their iniquity, and I will remember their sin no more."

Thus says the Lord,

who gives the sun for light by day
    and the fixed order of the moon and the stars for light by night,
who stirs up the sea so that its waves roar—
    the Lord of hosts is his name:
"If this fixed order departs
    from before me, says the Lord,

then shall the descendants of Israel cease
from being a nation before me for ever."
Thus says the Lord:
"If the heavens above can be measured,
and the foundations of the earth below can be explored,
then I will cast off all the descendants of Israel
for all that they have done, says the Lord."

"Behold, the days are coming, says the Lord, when the city shall be rebuilt for the Lord from the tower of Hananel to the Corner Gate. And the measuring line shall go out farther, straight to the hill Gareb, and shall then turn to Goah. The whole valley of the dead bodies and the ashes, and all the fields as far as the brook Kidron, to the corner of the Horse Gate toward the east, shall be sacred to the Lord. It shall not be uprooted or overthrown any more for ever."

1611 (6) **Ezekiel 16:** see 219 (3).

1611 (7) **Ezekiel 23** The word of the Lord came to me: "Son of man, there were two women, the daughters of one mother; they played the harlot in Egypt; they played the harlot in their youth; there their breasts were pressed and their virgin bosoms handled. Oholah was the name of the elder and Oholibah the name of her sister. They became mine, and they bore sons and daughters. As for their names, Oholah is Samaria, and Oholibah is Jerusalem.

"Oholah played the harlot while she was mine; and she doted on her lovers the Assyrians, warriors clothed in purple, governors and commanders, all of them desirable young men, horsemen riding on horses. She bestowed her harlotries upon them, the choicest men of Assyria all of them; and she defiled herself with all the idols of every one on whom she doted. She did not give up her harlotry which she had practiced since her days in Egypt; for in her youth men had lain with her and handled her virgin bosom and poured out their lust upon her. Therefore I delivered her into the hands of her lovers, into the hands of the Assyrians, upon whom she doted. These uncovered her nakedness; they seized her sons and her daughters; and her they slew with the sword; and she became a byword among women, when judgment had been executed upon her.

"Her sister Oholibah saw this, yet she was more corrupt than she in her doting and in her harlotry, which was worse than that of her sister. She doted upon the Assyrians, governors and commanders, warriors clothed in full armor, horsemen riding on horses, all of them desirable young men. And I saw that she was defiled; they both took the same way. But she carried her harlotry further; she saw men portrayed upon the wall, the images of the Chaldeans portrayed in vermilion, girded with belts on their loins, with flowing turbans on their heads, all of them looking like officers, a picture of Babylonians whose native land was Chaldea. When she saw them she doted upon them, and sent messengers to them in Chaldea. And the Babylonians came to her into the bed of love, and they defiled her with their lust; and after she was polluted by them, she turned from them in disgust. When she carried on her harlotry so openly and flaunted her nakedness, I turned in disgust from her, as I had turned from her sister. Yet she increased her harlotry, remembering the days of her youth, when she played the harlot in the land of Egypt and doted upon her paramours there, whose members were like those of asses, and whose issue was like that of horses. Thus you longed for the lewdness of your youth, when the Egyptians handled your bosom and pressed your young breasts."

Therefore, O Oholibah, thus says the Lord God: "Behold, I will rouse against you your lovers from whom you turned in disgust, and I will bring them against you from every side: the Babylonians and all the Chaldeans, Pekod and Shoa and Koa, and all the Assyrians with them, desirable young men, governors and commanders all of them, officers and warriors, all of them riding on horses. And they shall come against you from the north with chariots and wagons and a host of peoples; they shall set themselves against you on every side with buckler, shield, and helmet, and I will commit the judgment to them, and they shall judge you according to their judgments. And I will direct my indignation against you, that they may deal with you in fury. They shall cut off your nose and your ears, and your survivors shall fall by the sword. They shall seize your sons and your daughters, and your survivors shall be devoured by fire. They shall also strip you of your clothes and take away your fine jewels. Thus I will put an end to your lewdness and your harlotry brought from the land of Egypt; so that you shall not lift up your eyes to the Egyptians or remember them any more. For thus says the Lord God: Behold, I will deliver you into the hands of those whom you hate, into the hands of those from whom you turned in disgust; and they shall deal with you in hatred, and take away all the fruit of your labor, and leave you naked and bare, and the nakedness of your harlotry shall be uncovered. Your lewdness and your harlotry have brought this upon you, because you played the harlot with the nations, and polluted yourself with their idols. You have gone the way of your sister; therefore I will give her cup into your hand. Thus says the Lord God:

"You shall drink your sister's cup
which is deep and large;
you shall be laughed at and held in derision,
for it contains much;
you will be filled with drunkenness and sorrow.
A cup of horror and desolation,
is the cup of your sister Samaria;
you shall drink it and drain it out,
and pluck out your hair,
and tear your breasts;

for I have spoken, says the Lord God. Therefore thus says the Lord God: Because you have forgotten me and cast me behind your back, therefore bear the consequences of your lewdness and harlotry."

The Lord said to me: "Son of man, will you judge Oholah and Oholibah? Then declare to them their abominable deeds. For they have committed adultery, and blood is upon their hands; with their idols they have committed adultery; and they have even offered up to them for food the sons whom they had borne to me. Moreover this they have done to me: they have defiled my sanctuary on the same day and profaned my sabbaths. For when they had slaughtered their children in sacrifice to their idols, on the same day they came into my sanctuary to profane it. And lo, this is what they did in my house. They even sent for men to come from far, to whom a messenger was sent, and lo, they came. For them you bathed yourself, painted your eyes, and decked yourself with ornaments; you sat upon a stately couch, with a table spread before it on which you had placed my incense and my oil. The sound of a carefree multitude was with her; and with men of the common sort drunkards were brought from the wilderness; and they put bracelets upon the hands of the women, and beautiful crowns upon their heads.

"Then I said, Do not men now commit adultery when they practice harlotry with her? For they have gone in to her, as men go in to a harlot. Thus they went in to Oholah and to Oholibah to commit lewdness. But righteous men shall pass judgment on them with the sentence of adulteresses, and with the sentence of women that shed blood; because they are adulteresses, and blood is upon their hands."

For thus says the Lord God: "Bring up a host against them, and make them an object of terror and a spoil. And the host shall stone them and dispatch them with their swords; they shall slay their sons and their daughters, and burn up their houses. Thus will I put an end to lewdness in the land, that all women may take warning and not commit lewdness as you have done. And your lewdness shall be requited upon you, and you shall bear the penalty for your sinful idolatry; and you shall know that I am the Lord God."

1611 (8) **Malachi 2:13–17** And this again you do. You cover the Lord's altar with tears, with weeping and groaning because he no longer regards the offering or accepts it with favor at your hand. You ask, "Why does he not?" Because the Lord was witness to the covenant between you and the wife of your youth, to whom you have been faithless, though she is your companion and your wife by covenant. Has not the one God made and sustained for us the spirit of life? And what does he desire? Godly offspring. So take heed to yourselves, and let none be faithless to the wife of his youth. "For I hate divorce, says the Lord God of Israel, and covering one's garment with violence, says the Lord of hosts. So take heed to yourselves and do not be faithless."

You have wearied the Lord with your words. Yet you say, "How have we wearied him?" By saying, "Every one who does evil is good in the sight of the Lord, and he delights in them." Or by asking, "Where is the God of justice?"

1612 ***Gaudium et spes* 22** In reality it is only in the mystery of the Word made flesh that the mystery of man truly becomes clear. For Adam, the first man, was a type of him who was to come, Christ the Lord. Christ the new Adam, in the very revelation of the mystery of the Father and of his love, fully reveals man to himself and brings to light his most high calling. It is no wonder, then, that all the truths mentioned so far should find in him their source and their most perfect embodiment.

He who is the "image of the invisible God" (Col. 1:15), is himself the perfect man who has restored in the children of Adam that likeness to God which had been disfigured ever since the first sin. Human nature, by the very fact that it was assumed, not absorbed, in him, has been raised in us also to a dignity beyond compare. For, by his incarnation, he, the son of God, has in a certain way united himself with each man. He worked with human hands, he thought with a human mind. He acted with a human will, and with a human heart he loved. Born of the Virgin Mary, he has truly been made one of us, like to us in all things except sin.

As an innocent lamb he merited life for us by his blood which he freely shed. In him God reconciled us to himself and to one another, freeing us from the bondage of the devil and of sin, so that each one of us could say with the apostle: the Son of God "loved me and gave himself for me" (Gal. 2:20). By suffering for us he not only gave us an example so that we might follow in his footsteps, but he also opened up a way. If we follow this path, life and death are made holy and acquire a new meaning.

Conformed to the image of the Son who is the firstborn of many brothers, the Christian man receives the "first fruits of the Spirit" (Rom. 8:23) by which he is able to fulfil the new law of love. By this Spirit, who is the "pledge of our inheritance" (Eph. 1:14), the whole man is inwardly renewed, right up to the "redemption of the body" (Rom. 8:23). "If the Spirit of him who raised Jesus from the dead dwells in you, he who raised Christ Jesus from the dead will give life to your mortal bodies also through his Spirit who dwells in you" (Rom. 8:11). The Christian is certainly bound both by need and by duty to struggle with evil through many afflictions and to suffer death; but, as one who has been made a partner in the paschal mystery, and as one who has been configured to the death of Christ, he will go forward, strengthened by hope, to the resurrection.

All this holds true not for Christians only but also for all men of good will in whose hearts grace is active invisibly. For since Christ died for all, and since all men are in fact called to one and the same destiny, which is divine, we must hold that the Holy Spirit offers to all the possibility of being made partners, in a way known to God, in the paschal mystery.

Such is the nature and the greatness of the mystery of man as enlightened for the faithful by the Christian revelation. It is therefore through Christ, and in Christ, that light is thrown on the riddle of suffering and death which, apart from his Gospel, overwhelms us. Christ has risen again, destroying death by his death, and has given life abundantly to us so that, becoming sons in the Son, we may cry out in the Spirit: Abba, Father!

John 2:1–11 On the third day there was a marriage at Cana in Galilee, and the mother of Jesus was there; Jesus also was invited to the marriage, with his disciples. When the wine gave out, the mother of Jesus said to him, "They have no wine." And Jesus said to her, "O woman, what have you to do with me? My hour has not yet come." His mother said to the servants, "Do whatever he tells you." Now six stone jars were standing there, for the Jewish rites of purification, each holding twenty or thirty gallons. Jesus said to them, "Fill the jars with water." And they filled them up to the brim. He said to them, "Now draw some out, and take it to the steward of the feast." So they took it. When the steward of the feast tasted the water now become wine, and did not know where it came from (though the servants who had drawn the water knew), the steward of the feast called the bridegroom and said to him, "Every man serves the good wine first; and when men have drunk freely, then the poor wine; but you have kept the good wine until now." This, the first of his signs, Jesus did at Cana in Galilee, and manifested his glory; and his disciples believed in him. **1613**

Matthew 19:8 He said to them, "For your hardness of heart Moses allowed you to divorce your wives, but from the beginning it was not so. . . ." **1614**

(1) **Mark 8:34** And he called to him the multitude with his disciples, and said to them, "If any man would come after me, let him deny himself and take up his cross and follow me. . . ." **1615**

(2) **Matthew 11:29–30** Take my yoke upon you, and learn from me; for I am gentle and lowly in heart, and you will find rest for your souls. For my yoke is easy, and my burden is light. **1615**

(3) **Matthew 19:11** But he said to them, "Not all men can receive this saying, but only those to whom it is given. . . ." **1615**

Genesis 2:25 And the man and his wife were both naked, and were not ashamed. **1616**

(1) **Ephesians 5:26–27** . . . that he might sanctify her, having cleansed her by the washing of water with the word, that he might present the church to himself in splendor, without spot or wrinkle or any such thing, that she might be holy and without blemish. **1617**

(2) **Council of Trent (1563): DS 1800** Since, therefore, matrimony in the evangelical law, by grace through Christ, excels the ancient marriages, our holy Fathers, the Councils, and the tradition of the universal Church have with good reason always taught that it is to be classed among the sacraments of the New Law; and since impious men of this age, madly raging against this teaching, have not only formed **1617**

false judgments concerning this venerable sacrament, but according to their custom, introducing under the pretext of the Gospel a carnal liberty, have in writing and in word asserted many things foreign to the mind of the Catholic Church and to the general opinion approved from the time of the apostles, not without great loss of the faithful of Christ, this holy and general Synod wishing to block their temerity has decided, lest their pernicious contagion attract more, that the more prominent heresies and errors of the aforesaid schismatics are to be destroyed, decreeing anathemas against these heretics and their errors.

1617 (3) **CIC Canon 1055, §2** For this reason a matrimonial contract cannot validly exist between baptized persons unless it is also a sacrament by that fact.

1618 (1) **Luke 14:26** "If any one comes to me and does not hate his own father and mother and wife and children and brothers and sisters, yes, and even his own life, he cannot be my disciple. . . ."

1618 (2) **Mark 10:28–31** Peter began to say to him, "Lo, we have left everything and followed you." Jesus said, "Truly, I say to you, there is no one who has left house or brothers or sisters or mother or father or children or lands, for my sake and for the gospel, who will not receive a hundredfold now in this time, houses and brothers and sisters and mothers and children and lands, with persecutions, and in the age to come eternal life. But many that are first will be last, and the last first."

1618 (3) **Revelation 14:4** It is these who have not defiled themselves with women, for they are chaste; it is these who follow the Lamb wherever he goes; these have been redeemed from mankind as first fruits for God and the Lamb. . . .

1618 (4) **1 Corinthians 7:32** I want you to be free from anxieties. The unmarried man is anxious about the affairs of the Lord, how to please the Lord. . . .

1618 (5) **Matthew 25:6** ". . . But at midnight there was a cry, 'Behold, the bridegroom! Come out to meet him.' . . ."

1619 (1) **Mark 12:25** For when they rise from the dead, they neither marry nor are given in marriage, but are like angels in heaven.

1619 (2) **1 Corinthians 7:31** . . . and those who deal with the world as though they had no dealings with it. For the form of this world is passing away.

1620 (1) **Matthew 19:3–12** And Pharisees came up to him and tested him by asking, "Is it lawful to divorce one's wife for any cause?" He answered, "Have you not read that he who made them from the beginning made them male and female, and said, 'For this reason a man shall leave his father and mother and be joined to his wife, and the two shall become one flesh'? So they are no longer two but one flesh. What therefore God has joined together, let not man put asunder." They said to him, "Why then did Moses command one to give a certificate of divorce, and to put her away?" He said to them, "For your hardness of heart Moses allowed you to divorce your wives, but from the beginning it was not so. And I say to you: whoever divorces his wife, except for unchastity, and marries another, commits adultery."

The disciples said to him, "If such is the case of a man with his wife, it is not expedient to marry." But he said to them, "Not all men can receive this saying, but only those to whom it is given. For there are eunuchs who have been so from birth, and there are eunuchs who have been made eunuchs by men, and there are eunuchs who have made themselves eunuchs for the sake of the kingdom of heaven. He who is able to receive this, let him receive it."

(2) ***Lumen gentium* 42** "God is love, and he who abides in love abides in God, and God abides in him" (1 Jn. 4:16). God has poured out his love in our hearts through the Holy Spirit who has been given to us (cf. Rom. 5:5); therefore the first and most necessary gift is charity, by which we love God above all things and our neighbor because of him. But if charity is to grow and fructify in the soul like a good seed, each of the faithful must willingly hear the word of God and carry out his will with deeds, with the help of his grace; he must frequently partake of the sacraments, chiefly the Eucharist, and take part in the liturgy; he must constantly apply himself to prayer, self-denial, active brotherly service and the practice of all virtues. This is because love, as the bond of perfection and fullness of the law (cf. Col. 3:14; Rom. 13:10), governs, gives meaning to, and perfects all the means of sanctification. Hence the true disciple of Christ is marked by love both of God and of his neighbor. 1620

Since Jesus, the Son of God, showed his love by laying down his life for us, no one has greater love than he who lays down his life for him and for his brothers (cf. 1 Jn. 3:16, Jn. 15:13). Some Christians have been called from the beginning, and will always be called, to give this greatest testimony of love to all, especially to persecutors. Martyrdom makes the disciple like his master, who willingly accepted death for the salvation of the world, and through it he is conformed to him by the shedding of blood. Therefore the Church considers it the highest gift and supreme test of love. And while it is given to few, all however must be prepared to confess Christ before men and to follow him along the way of the cross amidst the persecutions which the Church never lacks.

Likewise the Church's holiness is fostered in a special way by the manifold counsels which the Lord proposes to his disciples in the Gospel for them to observe. Towering among these counsels is that precious gift of divine grace given to some by the Father (cf. Mt. 19:11; 1 Cor. 7:7) to devote themselves to God alone more easily with an undivided heart (cf. 1 Cor. 7:32–24) in virginity or celibacy. This perfect continence for love of the kingdom of heaven has always been held in high esteem by the Church as a sign and stimulus of love, and as a singular source of spiritual fertility in the world.

The Church bears in mind too the apostle's admonition when calling the faithful to charity and exhorting them to have the same mind which Christ Jesus showed, who "emptied himself, taking the form of a servant . . . and became obedient unto death" (Phil. 2:7–8) and for our sakes "became poor, though he was rich" (2 Cor. 8:9). Since the disciples must always imitate this love and humility of Christ and bear witness of it, Mother Church rejoices that she has within herself many men and women who pursue more closely the Savior's self-emptying and show it forth more clearly, by undertaking poverty with the freedom of God's sons, and renouncing their own will: they subject themselves to man for the love of God, thus going beyond what is of precept in the matter of perfection, so as to conform themselves more fully to the obedient Christ.

Therefore all the faithful are invited and obliged to holiness and the perfection of their own state of life. Accordingly let all of them see that they direct their affections rightly, lest they be hindered in their pursuit of perfect love by the use of worldly things and by an adherence to riches which is contrary to the spirit of evangelical poverty, following the apostle's advice: Let those who use this world not fix their abode in it, for the form of this world is passing away (cf. 1 Cor. 7:31, Greek text).

(3) ***Perfectae caritatis* 12** Chastity "for the sake of the kingdom of heaven" (Mt. 1620
19:22), which religious profess, must be esteemed an exceptional gift of grace. It uniquely frees the heart of man (cf. 1 Cor. 7:32–35), so that he becomes more fervent in love for God and for all men. For this reason it is a special symbol of heavenly benefits, and for religious it is a most effective means of dedicating themselves whole-

heartedly to the divine service and the works of the apostolate. Thus for all Christ's faithful religious recall that wonderful marriage made by God, which will be fully manifested in the future age, and in which the Church has Christ for her only spouse.

Religious, therefore, at pains to be faithful to what they have professed, should believe our Lord's words and, relying on God's help, they should not presume on their own strength. They should practice mortification and custody of the senses. Nor should they neglect the natural means which promote health of mind and body. Thus, they should not be influenced by the false doctrines which allege that perfect continence is impossible or inimical to human development and, by a kind of spiritual instinct, they should reject whatever endangers chastity. Further, let all, and especially superiors, remember that chastity is preserved more securely when the members live a common life in true brotherly love.

The observance of perfect continence touches intimately the deeper inclinations of human nature. For this reason, candidates ought not to go forward, nor should they be admitted, to the profession of chastity except after really adequate testing, and unless they are sufficiently mature, psychologically and affectively. Not only should they be warned against the dangers to chastity which they may encounter, they should be taught to see that the celibacy they have dedicated to God is beneficial to their whole personality.

1620 (4) ***Optatam totius* 10** Students who follow the venerable tradition of priestly celibacy as laid down by the holy and permanent regulations of their own rite should be very carefully trained for this state. In it they renounce marriage for the sake of the kingdom of heaven (cf. Mt. 19:12) and hold fast to their Lord with that undivided love which is profoundly in harmony with the New Covenant; they bear witness to the resurrection in a future life (cf. Lk. 20:36) and obtain the most useful assistance towards the constant exercise of that perfect charity by which they can become all things to all men in their priestly ministry. They should keenly realize with what a sense of gratitude they should embrace this state, not only as a precept of ecclesiastical law, but as a precious gift of God which they should ask for humbly and to which they should hasten to respond freely and generously, under the inspiration and with the assistance of the Holy Spirit.

Students should have a proper knowledge of the duties and dignity of Christian marriage, which represents the love which exists between Christ and the Church (cf. Eph. 5:32). They should recognize the greater excellence of virginity consecrated to Christ, however, so that they may offer themselves to the Lord with fully deliberate and generous choice, and a complete surrender of body and soul.

They should be put on their guard against the dangers which threaten their chastity, especially in present-day society. They should learn how, with suitable natural and supernatural safeguards, to weave their renunciation of marriage into the pattern of their lives, so that not only will their daily conduct and activities suffer no harm from celibacy, but they themselves will acquire greater mastery of mind and body, will grow in maturity and receive greater measure of the blessedness promised by the Gospel.

1620 (5) ***Familiaris consortio* 16** Virginity or celibacy for the sake of the Kingdom of God not only does not contradict the dignity of marriage but presupposes it and confirms it. Marriage and virginity or celibacy are two ways of expressing and living the one mystery of the covenant of God with his people. When marriage is not esteemed, neither can consecrated virginity or celibacy exist; when human sexuality is not regarded as a great value given by the Creator, the renunciation of it for the sake of the Kingdom of Heaven loses its meaning.

Rightly indeed does Saint John Chrysostom say: "Whoever denigrates marriage also diminishes the glory of virginity. Whoever praises it makes virginity more admirable and resplendent. What appears good only in comparison with evil would not be particularly good. It is something better than what is admitted to be good that is the most excellent good."

In virginity or celibacy, the human being is awaiting, also in a bodily way, the eschatological marriage of Christ with the Church, giving himself or herself completely to the Church in the hope that Christ may give himself to the Church in the full truth of eternal life. The celibate person thus anticipates in his or her flesh the new world of the future resurrection.

By virtue of this witness, virginity or celibacy keeps alive in the Church a consciousness of the mystery of marriage and defends it from any reduction and impoverishment.

Virginity or celibacy, by liberating the human heart in a unique way, "so as to make it burn with greater love for God and all humanity", bears witness that the Kingdom of God and his justice is that pearl of great price which is preferred to every other value no matter how great, and hence must be sought as the only definitive value. It is for this reason that the Church, throughout her history, has always defended the superiority of this charism to that of marriage by reason of the wholly singular link which it has with the Kingdom of God.

In spite of having renounced physical fecundity, the celibate person becomes spiritually fruitful, the father and mother of many, cooperating in the realization of the family according to God's plan.

Christian couples therefore have the right to expect from celibate persons a good example and a witness of fidelity to their vocation until death. Just as fidelity at times becomes difficult for married people and requires sacrifice, mortification and self-denial, the same can happen to celibate persons, and their fidelity, even in the trials that may occur, should strengthen the fidelity of married couples.

These reflections on virginity or celibacy can enlighten and help those who, for reasons independent of their own will, have been unable to marry and have then accepted their situation in a spirit of service.

(1) ***Sacrosanctum concilium* 61** Thus, for well-disposed members of the faithful the 1621
liturgy of the sacraments and sacramentals sanctifies almost every event of their lives with the divine grace which flows from the paschal mystery of the Passion, Death and Resurrection of Christ. From this source all sacraments and sacramentals draw their power. There is scarcely any proper use of material things which cannot thus be directed toward the sanctification of men and the praise of God.

(2) ***Lumen gentium* 6** In the Old Testament the revelation of the kingdom is often 1621
made under the forms of symbols. In similar fashion the inner nature of the Church is now made known to us in various images. Taken either from the life of the shepherd or from cultivation of the land, from the art of building or from family life and marriage, these images have their preparation in the books of the prophets.

The Church is, accordingly, a sheepfold, the sole and necessary gateway to which is Christ (Jn. 10:1–10). It is also a flock, of which God foretold that he would himself be the shepherd (cf. Is. 40:11; Ex. 34:11 f.), and whose sheep, although watched over by human shepherds, are nevertheless at all times led and brought to pasture by Christ himself, the Good Shepherd and prince of shepherds (cf. Jn. 10:11; 1 Pet. 5:4), who gave his life for his sheep (cf. Jn. 10:11–16).

The Church is a cultivated field, the tillage of God (1 Cor. 3:9). On that land the ancient olive tree grows whose holy roots were the prophets and in which the reconciliation of Jews and Gentiles has been brought about and will be brought about again (Rom. 11:13–26). That land, like a choice vineyard, has been planted by the heavenly cultivator (Mt. 21:33–43; cf. Is. 5:1 f.). Yet the true vine is Christ who gives life and fruitfulness to the branches, that is, to us, who through the Church remain in Christ without whom we can do nothing (Jn. 15:1–5).

Often, too, the Church is called the building of God (1 Cor. 3:9). The Lord compared himself to the stone which the builders rejected, but which was made into the cornerstone (Mt. 21:42; cf. Acts 4:11; 1 Pet. 2:7; Ps. 117:22). On this foundation the Church is built by the apostles (cf. 1 Cor. 3:11) and from it the Church receives solidity and unity. This edifice has many names to describe it; the house of God in which his family dwells; the household of God in the Spirit (Eph. 2:19, 22); the dwelling-place of God among men (Apoc. 21:3); and, especially, the holy temple. This temple, symbolized in places of worship built out of stone, is praised by the Fathers and, not without reason, is compared in the liturgy to the Holy City, the New Jerusalem. As living stones we here on earth are built into it (1 Pet. 2:5). It is this holy city that is seen by John as it comes down out of heaven from God when the world is made anew, prepared like a bride adorned for her husband (Apoc. 21:1 f.).

The Church, further, which is called "that Jerusalem which is above" and "our mother" (Gal. 4:26; cf. Apoc. 12:17), is described as the spotless spouse of the spotless lamb (Apoc. 19:7; 21:2 and 9; 22:17). It is she whom Christ "loved and for whom he delivered himself up that he might sanctify her" (Eph. 5:26). It is she whom he unites to himself by an unbreakable alliance, and whom he constantly "nourishes and cherishes" (Eph. 5:29). It is she whom, once purified, he willed to be joined to himself, subject in love and fidelity (cf. Eph. 5:24), and whom, finally, he filled with heavenly gifts for all eternity, in order that we may know the love of God and of Christ for us, a love which surpasses all understanding (cf. Eph. 3:19). While on earth she journeys in a foreign land away from the Lord (cf. 2 Cor. 5:6), the Church sees herself as an exile. She seeks and is concerned about those things which are above, where Christ is seated at the right hand of God, where the life of the Church is hidden with Christ in God until she appears in glory with her Spouse (cf. Col. 3:1–4).

1621 (3) **1 Corinthians 10:17** Because there is one bread, we who are many are one body, for we all partake of the one bread.

1624 **Ephesians 5:32** This mystery is a profound one, and I am saying that it refers to Christ and the church. . . .

1627 (1) **CIC Canon 1057, §2** Matrimonial consent is an act of the will by which a man and a woman, through an irrevocable covenant, mutually give and accept each other in order to establish marriage.

1627 (2) **Genesis 2:24** Therefore a man leaves his father and his mother and cleaves to his wife, and they become one flesh.

1627 (3) **Mark 10:8** "'. . . and the two shall become one flesh.' So they are no longer two but one flesh. . . ."

1627 (4) **Ephesians 5:31** "For this reason a man shall leave his father and mother and be joined to his wife, and the two shall become one flesh."

1628 (1) **CIC Canon 1103** A marriage is invalid if it is entered into due to force or grave fear inflicted from outside the person, even when inflicted unintentionally, which is of such a type that the person is compelled to choose matrimony in order to be freed from it.

(2) **CIC Canon 1057, §1** Marriage is brought about through the consent of the parties, legitimately manifested between persons who are capable according to law of giving consent; no human power can replace this consent. **1628**

(1) **CIC Canons 1095–1107** **1629**

Can. 1095—They are incapable of contracting marriage:

1° who lack the sufficient use of reason;

2° who suffer from grave lack of discretion of judgment concerning essential matrimonial rights and duties which are to be mutually given and accepted;

3° who are not capable of assuming the essential obligations of matrimony due to causes of a psychic nature.

Can. 1096—§1. For matrimonial consent to be valid it is necessary that the contracting parties at least not be ignorant that marriage is a permanent consortium between a man and a woman which is ordered toward the procreation of offspring by means of some sexual cooperation.

§2. Such ignorance is not presumed after puberty.

Can. 1097—§1. Error concerning the person renders marriage invalid.

§2. Error concerning a quality of a person, even if such error is the cause of the contract, does not invalidate matrimony unless this quality was directly and principally intended.

Can. 1098—A person contracts invalidly who enters marriage deceived by fraud, perpetrated to obtain consent, concerning some quality of the other party which of its very nature can seriously disturb the partnership of conjugal life.

Can. 1099—Error concerning the unity, indissolubility or sacramental dignity of matrimony does not vitiate matrimonial consent so long as it does not determine the will.

Can. 1100—The knowledge or opinion of the nullity of a marriage does not necessarily exclude matrimonial consent.

Can. 1101—§1. The internal consent of the mind is presumed to be in agreement with the words or signs employed in celebrating matrimony.

§2. But if either or both parties through a positive act of the will should exclude marriage itself, some essential element or an essential property of marriage, it is invalidly contracted.

Can. 1102—§1. Marriage based on a condition concerning the future cannot be contracted validly.

§2. Marriage based on a condition concerning the past or the present is valid or invalid, insofar as the subject matter of the condition exists or not.

§3. The condition mentioned in §2 cannot be placed licitly without the written permission of the local ordinary.

Can. 1103—A marriage is invalid if it is entered into due to force or grave fear inflicted from outside the person, even when inflicted unintentionally, which is of such a type that the person is compelled to choose matrimony in order to be freed from it.

Can. 1104—§1. In order for marriage to be contracted validly, it is necessary that the contracting parties be present together, either in person or by proxy.

§2. Those to be married are to express their matrimonial consent in words; however, if they cannot speak, they are to express it by equivalent signs.

Can. 1105—§1. In order for marriage to be entered validly by proxy, it is required that:

1° there be a special mandate to contract marriage with a certain person;

2° the proxy be appointed by the person who gave the mandate and that the proxy fulfill this function in person.

§2. To be valid a mandate must be signed by the person who gave it as well as by the pastor or the local ordinary where the mandate was issued, or by a priest delegated by either of these, or at least by two witnesses, or it must be arranged by means of a document which is authentic according to civil law.

§3. If the person giving the mandate cannot write, this is to be noted in the mandate itself and another witness is to be added who also must sign the document; otherwise, the mandate is invalid.

§4. If the person who gave the mandate revokes it or becomes insane before the proxy has contracted the marriage in that person's name, the marriage is invalid even though either the proxy or the other contracting party was unaware of these developments.

Can. 1106—Marriage can be contracted through an interpreter; however, the pastor is not to assist at such a marriage unless he is convinced of the interpreter's trustworthiness.

Can. 1107—Even if a marriage was entered invalidly by reason of an impediment or lack of form, the consent which was furnished is presumed to continue until its revocation has been proved.

1629 (2) **CIC Canon 1071**

§1. Except in case of necessity, no one is to assist at the following marriages without the permission of the local ordinary:

1° the marriage of transients;

2° a marriage which cannot be recognized or celebrated in accord with the norm of civil law;

3° a marriage of a person who is bound by natural obligations toward another party or toward children, arising from a prior union;

4° a marriage of a person who has notoriously rejected the Catholic faith;

5° a marriage of a person who is bound by a censure;

6° a marriage of a minor child when the parents are unaware of it or are reasonably opposed to it;

7° a marriage to be entered by means of a proxy, mentioned in can. 1105.

§2. The local ordinary is not to grant permission for assisting at the marriage of a person who has notoriously rejected the Catholic faith unless the norms of can. 1125 have been observed, making any necessary adaptations.

1631 (1) **Council of Trent (1563): DS 1813–16** Although it is not to be doubted that clandestine marriages, made with the free consent of the contracting parties, are valid and true marriages, so long as the Church has not declared them invalid; and consequently that they are justly to be condemned, as the holy Synod condemns those with anathema, who deny that they are true and valid, and those also who falsely affirm that marriages contracted by minors without the consent of parents are invalid, and that parents can make them sanctioned or void, nevertheless the holy Church of God for very just reasons has always detested and forbidden them. But while the holy Synod recognizes that those prohibitions by reason of man's disobedience are no longer of any use, and considers the grave sins which have their origin in such clandestine marriage, especially, indeed, the sins of those who remain in the state of damnation, after abandoning the first wife, with whom they made a secret contract, while they publicly contract another, and live with her in continual adultery, since the Church, which does not judge what is hidden, cannot correct this evil, unless a more efficacious remedy be applied, therefore by continuing in the footsteps of the holy Lateran Council [IV] proclaimed under INNOCENT III, it commands that in the future, before a marriage is contracted, public announcement be made three times on three consecutive feast days in the Church during the celebration of the Masses, by the proper pastor of the contracting parties between whom the marriage is to be contracted; after these publications have been made, if no legitimate impediment is put in the way, one can proceed with the celebration of the marriage in the open church, where the parish priest, after the man and woman have been questioned, and their mutual consent has been ascertained, shall either say: "I join you together in matrimony, in the name of the Father and of the Son, and of the Holy Spirit," or use other words, according to the accepted rite of each province.

But if at some time there should be a probable suspicion that a marriage can be maliciously hindered, if so many publications precede it, then either one publication only may be made, or the marriage may be celebrated at once in the presence of the parish priest and of two or three witnesses; then before its consummation the publications should be made in the church, so that, if any impediments exist, they may the more easily be detected, unless the ordinary himself may judge it advisable that the publications be dispensed with, which the holy Synod leaves to his prudence and judgment.

Those who shall attempt to contract marriage otherwise than in the presence of the parish priest, or of another priest with the authorization of the parish priest or the ordinary, in the presence of two or three witnesses, the holy Synod renders absolutely incapable of thus contracting marriage, and declares that contracts of this kind are invalid and nil, inasmuch as by the present decree it invalidates and annuls them.

(2) **CIC Canon 1108** 1631

§1. Only those marriages are valid which are contracted in the presence of the local ordinary or the pastor or a priest or deacon delegated by either of them, who assist, and in the presence of two witnesses, according to the rules expressed in the following canons, with due regard for the exceptions mentioned in cann. 144, 1112, §1, 1116 and 1127, §§2 and 3.

§2. The one assisting at a marriage is understood to be only that person who, present at the ceremony, asks for the contractants' manifestation of consent and receives it in the name of the Church.

CIC Canon 1063 1632

Pastors of souls are obliged to see to it that their own ecclesial community furnishes the Christian faithful assistance so that the matrimonial state is maintained in a Christian spirit and makes progress toward perfection. This assistance is especially to be furnished through:

1° preaching, catechesis adapted to minors, youths and adults and even the use of the media of social communications so that through these means the Christian faithful may be instructed concerning the meaning of Christian marriage and the duty of Christian spouses and parents;

2° personal preparation for entering marriage so that through such preparation the parties may be predisposed toward the holiness and duties of their new state;

3° a fruitful liturgical celebration of marriage clarifying that the spouses signify and share in that mystery of unity and of fruitful love that exists between Christ and the Church;

4° assistance furnished to those already married so that, while faithfully maintaining and protecting the conjugal covenant, they may day by day come to lead holier and fuller lives in their families.

1635 (1) **CIC Canon 1124** Without the express permission of the competent authority, marriage is forbidden between two baptized persons, one of whom was baptized in the Catholic Church or received into it after baptism and has not left it by a formal act, and the other of whom is a member of a church or ecclesial community which is not in full communion with the Catholic Church.

1635 (2) **CIC Canon 1086**

§1. Marriage between two persons, one of whom is baptized in the Catholic Church or has been received into it and has not left it by means of a formal act, and the other of whom is non-baptized, is invalid.

§2. This impediment is not to be dispensed unless the conditions mentioned in cann. 1125 and 1126 are fulfilled.

§3. If at the time the marriage was contracted one party was commonly considered to be baptized or the person's baptism was doubted, the validity of the marriage is to be presumed in accord with the norm of can. 1060 until it is proven with certainty that one party was baptized and the other was not.

1635 (3) **CIC Canon 1125**

The local ordinary can grant this permission if there is a just and reasonable cause; he is not to grant it unless the following conditions have been fulfilled:

1° the Catholic party declares that he or she is prepared to remove dangers of falling away from the faith and makes a sincere promise to do all in his or her power to have all the children baptized and brought up in the Catholic Church;

2° the other party is to be informed at an appropriate time of these promises which the Catholic party has to make, so that it is clear that the other party is truly aware of the promise and obligation of the Catholic party;

3° both parties are to be instructed on the essential ends and properties of marriage, which are not to be excluded by either party.

1637 **1 Corinthians 7:16** Wife, how do you know whether you will save your husband? Husband, how do you know whether you will save your wife?

1638 **CIC Canon 1134** From a valid marriage arises a bond between the spouses which by its very nature is perpetual and exclusive; furthermore, in a Christian marriage the spouses are strengthened and, as it were, consecrated for the duties and the dignity of their state by a special sacrament.

1639 **Mark 10:9** What therefore God has joined together, let not man put asunder.

1640 **CIC Canon 1141** A ratified and consummated marriage cannot be dissolved by any human power or for any reason other than death.

1641 ***Lumen gentium* 41:** see 1251 (2).

1642 (1) **Galatians 6:2** Bear one another's burdens, and so fulfil the law of Christ.

1642 (2) ***Familiaris consortio* 13** The communion between God and his people finds its definitive fulfilment in Jesus Christ, the Bridegroom who loves and gives himself as the Savior of humanity, uniting it to himself as his body.

He reveals the original truth of marriage, the truth of the "beginning", and, freeing man from his hardness of heart, he makes man capable of realizing this truth in its entirety.

This revelation reaches its definitive fullness in the gift of love which the Word of God makes to humanity in assuming a human nature, and in the sacrifice which Jesus Christ makes of himself on the Cross for his bride, the Church. In this sacrifice there is entirely revealed that plan which God has imprinted on the humanity of man and woman since their creation; the marriage of baptized persons thus becomes a real symbol of that new and eternal covenant sanctioned in the blood of Christ. The Spirit which the Lord pours forth gives a new heart, and renders man and woman capable of loving one another as Christ has loved us. Conjugal love reaches that fullness to which it is interiorly ordained, conjugal charity, which is the proper and specific way in which the spouses participate in and are called to live the very charity of Christ who gave himself on the Cross.

In a deservedly famous page, Tertullian has well expressed the greatness of this conjugal life in Christ and its beauty: "How can I ever express the happiness of the marriage that is joined together by the Church, strengthened by an offering, sealed by a blessing, announced by angels and ratified by the Father? . . . How wonderful the bond between two believers, with a single hope, a single desire, a single observance, a single service! They are both brethren and both fellow-servants; there is no separation between them in spirit or flesh; in fact they are truly two in one flesh, and where the flesh is one, one is the spirit."

Receiving and meditating faithfully on the word of God, the Church has solemnly taught and continues to teach that the marriage of the baptized is one of the seven sacraments of the New Covenant.

Indeed, by means of baptism, man and woman are definitively placed within the new and eternal covenant, in the spousal covenant of Christ with the Church. And it is because of this indestructible insertion that the intimate community of conjugal life and love, founded by the Creator, is elevated and assumed into the spousal charity of Christ, sustained and enriched by his redeeming power.

By virtue of the sacramentality of their marriage, spouses are bound to one another in the most profoundly indissoluble manner. Their belonging to each other is the real representation, by means of the sacramental sign, of the very relationship of Christ with the Church.

Spouses are therefore the permanent reminder to the Church of what happened on the Cross; they are for one another and for the children witnesses to the salvation in which the sacrament makes them sharers. Of this salvation event marriage, like every sacrament, is a memorial, actuation and prophecy: "As a memorial, the sacrament gives them the grace and duty of commemorating the great works of God and of bearing witness to them before their children. As actuation, it gives them the grace and duty of putting into practice in the present, towards each other and their children, the demands of a love which forgives and redeems. As prophecy, it gives them the grace and duty of living and bearing witness to the hope of the future encounter with Christ."

Like each of the seven sacraments, so also marriage is a real symbol of the event of salvation, but in its own way. "The spouses participate in it as spouses, together, as a couple, so that the first and immediate effect of marriage (*res et sacramentum*) is not supernatural grace itself, but the Christian conjugal bond, a typically Christian communion of two persons because it represents the mystery of Christ's incarnation and the mystery of his covenant. The content of participation in Christ's life is also specific: conjugal love involves a totality, in which all the elements of the person enter —appeal of the body and instinct, power of feeling and affectivity, aspiration of the spirit and of will. It aims at a deeply personal unity, the unity that, beyond union in one flesh, leads to forming one heart and soul; it demands indissolubility and faithfulness in definitive mutual giving; and it is open to fertility (cf. *Humanae Vitae*, 9). In a word it is a question of the normal characteristics of all natural conjugal love, but with a new significance which not only purifies and strengthens them, but raises them to the extent of making them the expression of specifically Christian values."

1644 **Genesis 2:24** Therefore a man leaves his father and his mother and cleaves to his wife, and they become one flesh.

1645 ***Familiaris consortio* 19** The first communion is the one which is established and which develops between husband and wife: by virtue of the covenant of married life, the man and woman "are no longer two but one flesh" and they are called to grow continually in their communion through day-to-day fidelity to their marriage promise of total mutual self-giving.

The conjugal communion sinks its roots in the natural complementarity that exists between man and woman, and is nurtured through the personal willingness of the spouses to share their entire life-project, what they have and what they are: for this reason such communion is the fruit and the sign of a profoundly human need. But in the Lord Christ God takes up this human need, confirms it, purifies it and elevates it, leading it to perfection through the sacrament of Matrimony: the Holy Spirit who is poured out in the sacramental celebration offers Christian couples the gift of a new communion of love that is the living and real image of that unique unity which makes of the Church the indivisible Mystical Body of the Lord Jesus.

The gift of the Spirit is a commandment of life for Christian spouses and at the same time a stimulating impulse so that every day they may progress towards an ever richer union with each other on all levels—of the body, of the character, of the heart, of the intelligence and will, of the soul—revealing in this way to the Church and to the world the new communion of love, given by the grace of Christ.

Such a communion is radically contradicted by polygamy: this, in fact, directly negates the plan of God which was revealed from the beginning, because it is contrary to the equal personal dignity of men and women who in matrimony give themselves with a love that is total and therefore unique and exclusive. As the Second Vatican Council writes: "Firmly established by the Lord, the unity of marriage will radiate from the equal personal dignity of husband and wife, a dignity acknowledged by mutual and total love."

1648 ***Familiaris consortio* 20** Conjugal communion is characterized not only by its unity but also by its indissolubility: "As a mutual gift of two persons, this intimate union, as well as the good of children, imposes total fidelity on the spouses and argues for an unbreakable oneness between them."

It is a fundamental duty of the Church to reaffirm strongly, as the Synod Fathers did, the doctrine of the indissolubility of marriage. To all those who, in our times, consider it too difficult, or indeed impossible, to be bound to one person for the whole of life, and to those caught up in a culture that rejects the indissolubility of marriage and openly mocks the commitment of spouses to fidelity, it is necessary to reconfirm the good news of the definitive nature of that conjugal love that has in Christ its foundation and strength.

Being rooted in the personal and total self-giving of the couple, and being required by the good of the children, the indissolubility of marriage finds its ultimate truth in the plan that God has manifested in his revelation: he wills and he communicates the indissolubility of marriage as a fruit, a sign and a requirement of the absolutely faithful love that God has for man and that the Lord Jesus has for the Church.

Christ renews the first plan that the Creator inscribed in the hearts of man and woman, and in the celebration of the sacrament of matrimony offers "a new heart": thus the couples are not only able to overcome "hardness of heart", but also and above all they are able to share the full and definitive love of Christ, the new and eternal Covenant made flesh. Just as the Lord Jesus is the "faithful witness", the "yes" of the promises of God and thus the supreme realization of the unconditional faithfulness with which God loves his people, so Christian couples are called to participate truly in the irrevocable indissolubility that binds Christ to the Church his bride, loved by him to the end.

The gift of the sacrament is at the same time a vocation and commandment for the Christian spouses, that they may remain faithful to each other forever, beyond every trial and difficulty, in generous obedience to the holy will of the Lord: "What therefore God has joined together, let no man put asunder."

To bear witness to the inestimable value of the indissolubility and fidelity of marriage is one of the most precious and most urgent tasks of Christian couples in our time. So, with all my Brothers who participated in the Synod of Bishops, I praise and encourage those numerous couples who, though encountering no small difficulty, preserve and develop the value of indissolubility: thus, in a humble and courageous manner, they perform the role committed to them of being in the world a "sign"—a small and precious sign, sometimes also subjected to temptation, but always renewed —of the unfailing fidelity with which God and Jesus Christ love each and every human being. But it is also proper to recognize the value of the witness of those spouses who, even when abandoned by their partner, with the strength of faith and of Christian hope have not entered a new union: these spouses too give an authentic witness to fidelity, of which the world today has a great need. For this reason they must be encouraged and helped by the pastors and the faithful of the Church.

(1) ***Familiaris consortio* 83** Various reasons can unfortunately lead to the often ir- 1649
reparable breakdown of valid marriages. These include mutual lack of understanding and the inability to enter into interpersonal relationships. Obviously, separation must be considered as a last resort, after all other reasonable attempts at reconciliation have proved vain.

Loneliness and other difficulties are often the lot of separated spouses, especially when they are the innocent parties. The ecclesial community must support such people more than ever. It must give them much respect, solidarity, understanding and practical help, so that they can preserve their fidelity even in their difficult situation; and it must help them to cultivate the need to forgive which is inherent in Christian love, and to be ready perhaps to return to their former married life.

The situation is similar for people who have undergone divorce, but, being well aware that the valid marriage bond is indissoluble, refrain from becoming involved in a new union and devote themselves solely to carrying out their family duties and the responsibilities of Christian life. In such cases their example of fidelity and Christian consistency takes on particular value as a witness before the world and the Church. Here it is even more necessary for the Church to offer continual love and assistance, without there being any obstacle to admission to the sacraments.

(2) **CIC Canons 1151–55** 1649

Can. 1151—Spouses have the duty and the right to preserve conjugal living unless a legitimate cause excuses them.

Can. 1152—§1. Although it is earnestly recommended that a spouse, moved by Christian charity and a concern for the good of the family, not refuse pardon to an adulterous partner and not break up conjugal life, nevertheless, if the spouse has not expressly or tacitly condoned the misdeed of the other spouse, the former does have the right to sever conjugal living, unless he or she consented to the adultery, gave cause for it, or likewise committed adultery.

§2. Tacit condonation exists if the innocent spouse, after having become aware of the adultery, continued voluntarily to live with the other spouse in marital affection. Tacit condonation is presumed if the innocent spouse continued conjugal living for a period of six months and has not had recourse to ecclesiastical or civil authority.

§3. If the innocent spouse spontaneously severed conjugal living, that spouse within six months is to bring a suit for separation before the competent ecclesiastical authority; this authority, after having investigated all the circumstances, is to decide whether the innocent spouse can be induced to forgive the misdeed and not to prolong the separation permanently.

Can. 1152—§1. If either of the spouses causes serious danger of spirit or body to the other spouse or to the children, or otherwise renders common life too hard, that spouse gives the other a legitimate cause for separating in virtue of a decree of the local ordinary, or even on his or her own authority if there is danger in delay.

§2. In all cases, when the reason for the separation ceases to exist, conjugal living is to be restored unless ecclesiastical authority decides otherwise.

Can. 1154—After the separation of the spouses, suitable provision is to be made for the adequate support and education of the children.

Can. 1155—The innocent spouse can laudably readmit the other spouse to conjugal life, in which case the former renounces the right to separate.

1653 (1) ***Gravissimum educationis* 3** As it is the parents who have given life to their children, on them lies the gravest obligation of educating their family. They must therefore be recognized as being primarily and principally responsible for their education. The role of parents in education is of such importance that it is almost impossible to provide an adequate substitute. It is therefore the duty of parents to create a family atmosphere inspired by love and devotion to God and their fellow-men which will promote an integrated, personal and social education of their children. The family is therefore the principal school of the social virtues which are necessary to every society. It is therefore above all in the Christian family, inspired by the grace and the responsibility of the sacrament of matrimony, that children should be taught to know and worship God and to love their neighbor, in accordance with the faith which they have received in earliest infancy in the sacrament of Baptism. In it, also, they will have their first experience of a well-balanced human society and of the Church. Finally it is through the family that they are gradually initiated into association with their fellow-men in civil life and as members of the people of God. Parents should, therefore, appreciate how important a role the truly Christian family plays in the life and progress of the whole people of God.

The task of imparting education belongs primarily to the family, but it requires the help of society as a whole. As well as the rights of parents, and of those others to whom the parents entrust some share in their duty to educate, there are certain duties and rights vested in civil society inasmuch as it is its function to provide for the common good in temporal matters. It is its duty to promote the education of youth in various ways. It should recognize the duties and rights of parents, and of those others who play a part in education, and provide them with the requisite assistance. In accordance with the principle of subsidiarity, when the efforts of the parents and of other organizations are inadequate it should itself undertake the duty of education, with due consideration, however, for the wishes of the parents. Finally, insofar as the common good requires it, it should establish its own schools and institutes.

Education is, in a very special way, the concern of the Church, not only because the Church must be recognized as a human society capable of imparting education, but especially it has the duty of proclaiming the way of salvation to all men, of revealing the life of Christ to those who believe, and of assisting them with unremitting care so that they may be able to attain to the fulness of that life.

The Church as a mother is under an obligation, therefore, to provide for its children an education by virtue of which their whole lives may be inspired by the spirit of Christ. At the same time it will offer its assistance to all peoples for the promotion of a well-balanced perfection of the human personality, for the good of society in this world and for the development of a world more worthy of man.

(2) ***Familiaris consortio* 28** With the creation of man and woman in his own image 1653
and likeness, God crowns and brings to perfection the work of his hands: he calls them to a special sharing in his love and in his power as Creator and Father, through their free and responsible cooperation in transmitting the gift of human life: "God blessed them, and God said to them, 'Be fruitful and multiply, and fill the earth and subdue it.'"

Thus the fundamental task of the family is to serve life, to actualize in history the original blessing of the Creator—that of transmitting by procreation the divine image from person to person.

Fecundity is the fruit and the sign of conjugal love, the living testimony of the full reciprocal self-giving of the spouses: "While not making the other purposes of matrimony of less account, the true practice of conjugal love, and the whole meaning of the family life which results from it, have this aim: that the couple be ready with stout hearts to cooperate with the love of the Creator and the Savior, who through them will enlarge and enrich his own family day by day."

However, the fruitfulness of conjugal love is not restricted solely to the procreation of children, even understood in its specifically human dimension: it is enlarged and enriched by all those fruits of moral, spiritual and supernatural life which the father and mother are called to hand on to their children, and through the children to the Church and to the world.

(1) **Acts 18:8** Crispus, the ruler of the synagogue, believed in the Lord, together 1655
with all his household; and many of the Corinthians hearing Paul believed and were baptized.

(2) **Acts 16:31** And they said, "Believe in the Lord Jesus, and you will be saved, 1655
you and your household."

(3) **Acts 11:14** "'. . . he will declare to you a message by which you will be saved, 1655
you and all your household.'. . ."

***Familiaris consortio* 21** Conjugal communion constitutes the foundation on which 1656
is built the broader communion of the family, of parents and children, of brothers and sisters with each other, of relatives and other members of the household.

This communion is rooted in the natural bonds of flesh and blood, and grows to its specifically human perfection with the establishment and maturing of the still deeper and richer bonds of the spirit: the love that animates the interpersonal relationships of the different members of the family constitutes the interior strength that shapes and animates the family communion and community.

The Christian family is also called to experience a new and original communion which confirms and perfects natural and human communion. In fact the grace of

Jesus Christ, "the first-born among many brethren", is by its nature and interior dynamism "a grace of brotherhood", as Saint Thomas Aquinas calls it. The Holy Spirit, who is poured forth in the celebration of the sacraments, is the living source and inexhaustible sustenance of the supernatural communion that gathers believers and links them with Christ and with each other in the unity of the Church of God. The Christian family constitutes a specific revelation and realization of ecclesial communion, and for this reason too it can and should be called "the domestic Church".

All members of the family, each according to his or her own gift, have the grace and responsibility of building, day by day, the communion of persons, making the family "a school of deeper humanity": this happens where there is care and love for the little ones, the sick, the aged; where there is mutual service every day; where there is a sharing of goods, of joys and of sorrows.

A fundamental opportunity for building such a communion is constituted by the educational exchange between parents and children, in which each gives and receives. By means of love, respect and obedience towards their parents, children offer their specific and irreplaceable contribution to the construction of an authentically human and Christian family. They will be aided in this if parents exercise their unrenounceable authority as a true and proper "ministry", that is, as a service to the human and Christian well-being of their children, and in particular as a service aimed at helping them acquire a truly responsible freedom, and if parents maintain a living awareness of the "gift" they continually receive from their children.

Family communion can only be preserved and perfected through a great spirit of sacrifice. It requires, in fact, a ready and generous openness of each and all to understanding, to forbearance, to pardon, to reconciliation. There is no family that does not know how selfishness, discord, tension and conflict violently attack and at times mortally wound its own communion: hence there arise the many and varied forms of division in family life. But, at the same time, every family is called by the God of peace to have the joyous and renewing experience of "reconciliation", that is, communion reestablished, unity restored. In particular, participation in the sacrament of reconciliation and in the banquet of the one Body of Christ offers to the Christian family the grace and the responsibility of overcoming every division and of moving towards the fullness of communion willed by God, responding in this way to the ardent desire of the Lord: "that they may be one".

1658 **Matthew 11:28** Come to me, all who labor and are heavy laden, and I will give you rest.

1660 (1) **CIC Canon 1055, §1** The matrimonial covenant, by which a man and a woman establish between themselves a partnership of the whole of life, is by its nature ordered toward the good of the spouses and the procreation and education of offspring; this covenant between baptized persons has been raised by Christ the Lord to the dignity of a sacrament.

1660 (2) ***Gaudium et spes* 48, 1:** see 1601.

1661 **Council of Trent (1563): DS 1799** But the grace which was to perfect that natural love, and confirm the indissoluble union, and sanctify those united in marriage, Christ Himself, institutor and perfector of the venerable sacraments, merited for us by His passion. The Apostle Paul intimates this, when he says: "Men, love your wives as Christ loved the Church, and delivered himself up for it" [Eph. 5:25], directly adding: "This is a great Sacrament; but I speak in Christ and in the Church" [Eph. 5:32].

(1) **CIC Canon 1166** Somewhat in imitation of the sacraments, sacramentals are sacred signs by which spiritual effects especially are signified and are obtained by the intercession of the Church. **1667**

(2) **CCEO Canon 867** **1667**

§1. Through the sacramentals, which are sacred signs, by which in imitation of the sacraments effects, especially spiritual ones, are signified and obtained through the intercession of the Church, people are disposed to receive the principal effect of the sacraments and the various circumstances of life are sanctified.

§2. Concerning the sacramentals the norms of the particular law of the individual Church *sui iuris* should be observed.

(1) **Genesis 12:2** And I will make of you a great nation, and I will bless you, and make your name great, so that you will be a blessing. **1669**

(2) **Luke 6:28** . . . bless those who curse you, pray for those who abuse you. **1669**

(3) **Romans 12:14** Bless those who persecute you; bless and do not curse them. **1669**

(4) **1 Peter 3:9** Do not return evil for evil or reviling for reviling; but on the contrary bless, for to this you have been called, that you may obtain a blessing. **1669**

(5) ***Sacrosanctum concilium* 79** The sacramentals are to be revised, account being taken of the primary principle of enabling the faithful to participate intelligently, actively, and easily. The circumstances of our times must also be considered. When rituals are being revised as laid down in Article 63, new sacramentals may also be added as necessity requires. **1669**

Reserved blessings shall be very few. Reservations shall be in favor only of bishops or ordinaries.

Provision should be made for the administration of some sacramentals, at least in special circumstances and at the discretion of the ordinary, by qualified lay persons.

(6) **CIC Canon 1168** The minister of the sacramentals is a cleric who has been given the necessary power; in accord with the norm of the liturgical books and according to the judgment of the local ordinary, some sacramentals can also be administered by lay persons who are endowed with the appropriate qualities. **1669**

(7) ***De Benedictionibus* 16** The priest is the only proper minister of the anointing of the sick. **1669**

This office is ordinarily exercised by bishops, pastors and their assistants, priests who care for the sick or aged in hospitals, and superiors of clerical religious institutions.

(8) ***De Benedictionibus* 18** Other priests, with the consent of the ministers mentioned in no. 16, may confer the anointing. In case of necessity, a priest may presume this consent, but he should later inform the pastor or the chaplain of the hospital. **1669**

(1) **Mark 1:25–26** But Jesus rebuked him, saying, "Be silent, and come out of him!" And the unclean spirit, convulsing him and crying with a loud voice, came out of him. **1673**

(2) **Mark 3:15** . . . and have authority to cast out demons. . . . **1673**

1673 (3) **Mark 6:7** And he called to him the twelve, and began to send them out two by two, and gave them authority over the unclean spirits.

1673 (4) **Mark 6:13** And they cast out many demons, and anointed with oil many that were sick and healed them.

1673 (5) **Mark 16:17** And these signs will accompany those who believe: in my name they will cast out demons; they will speak in new tongues. . . .

1673 (6) **CIC Canon 1172**

§1. No one can legitimately perform exorcisms over the possessed unless he has obtained special and express permission from the local ordinary.

§2. Such permission from the local ordinary is to be granted only to a presbyter endowed with piety, knowledge, prudence and integrity of life.

1674 (1) **Council of Nicea II (787): DS 601** For, how much more frequently through the imaginal formation they are seen, so much more quickly are those who contemplate these, raised to the memory and desire of the originals of these, to kiss and to render honorable adoration to them, not however, to grant true *latria* according to our faith, which is proper to divine nature alone; but just as to the figure of the revered and life-giving Cross and to the holy gospels, and to the other sacred monuments, let an oblation of incense and lights be made to give honor to these as was the pious custom with the ancients. "For the honor of the image passes to the original"; and he who shows reverence to the image, shows reverence to the substance of Him depicted in it.

1674 (2) **Council of Nicea II (787): DS 603** For thus the doctrine of our Holy Fathers, that is, the tradition of the Catholic Church which has received the Gospel from and even to the end of the world is strengthened. Thus we follow Paul, who spoke in Christ [II Cor. 2:17], and all the divine apostolic group and the paternal sanctity *keeping the traditions* [II Thess. 2:14] which we have received. Thus prophetically we sing the triumphal hymns for the Church: *Rejoice exceedingly, O daughter of Sion, sing forth, O daughter of Jerusalem: be joyful and be happy with all your heart. The Lord has taken from you the injustices of those adverse to you: He has redeemed you from the power of your enemies. The Lord is king in your midst: You will not see more evils* [Wisd. 3:14 f.: LXX] *and peace to you unto time eternal.*

1674 (3) **Council of Trent (1563): DS 1822** That the holy bodies of the saints and also of the martyrs and of others living with Christ, who were the living "members of Christ and the temple of the Holy Spirit" [cf. I Cor. 3:16; 6:19; II Cor. 6:16], which are to be awakened by Him to eternal life and to be glorified, are to be venerated by the faithful, through which many benefits are bestowed by God on men, so that those who affirm that veneration and honor are not due to the relics of the saints, or that these and other memorials are honored by the faithful without profit, and that the places dedicated to the memory of the saints for the purpose of obtaining their help are visited in vain, let these be altogether condemned, just as the Church has for a long time condemned and now condemns them again.

1676 (1) ***Catechesi tradendae* 54** Another question of method concerns the utilization in catechetical instruction of valid elements in popular piety. I have in mind devotions practiced by the faithful in certain regions with moving fervor and purity of intention, even if the faith underlying them needs to be purified or rectified in many aspects.

I have in mind certain easily understood prayers that many simple people are fond of repeating. I have in mind certain acts of piety practiced with a sincere desire to do penance or to please the Lord. Underlying most of these prayers and practices, besides elements that should be discarded, there are other elements which, if they were properly used, could serve very well to help people advance towards knowledge of the mystery of Christ and of His message: the love and mercy of God, the Incarnation of Christ, His redeeming cross and resurrection, the activity of the Spirit in each Christian and in the Church, the mystery of the hereafter, the evangelical virtues to be practiced, the presence of the Christian in the world, etc. And why should we appeal to non-Christian or even anti-Christian elements, refusing to build on elements which, even if they need to be revised or improved, have something Christian at their root?

(2) ***Evangelii nuntiandi* 48** And now we must introduce another aspect of evan- 1676
gelization which cannot be ignored and which it is therefore opportune to consider. This is the practice of what is commonly known as popular religiosity. Both in those regions where the church has been established for many centuries and also where it is still in the process of being organized we find among the people particular customs expressive of their search for God and their faith. These customs have long been regarded as unhealthy and have sometimes been the object of contempt but in these days they are almost everywhere being reviewed and reconsidered. At the recent meeting of the synod the bishops, moved by an admirable zeal and a practical appreciation of pastoral realities, have endeavored to discern their full significance.

It must be admitted that popular religiosity has but a strictly limited value. It not infrequently opens the way to many false forms of religion and may verge on superstition. It is often confined to the lower forms of religious worship which do not lead souls to a generous adherence to the faith. It may lead to the establishment of sects and factions endangering the well-being of the ecclesial community.

But on the other hand, if it is prudently directed and especially when it is directed along the path and according to the methods of evangelization, it may be productive of great good. For it does indicate a certain thirst for God such as only those who are simple and poor in spirit can experience. It can arouse in men a capacity for self-dedication and for the exercise of heroism when there is question of professing the faith. It gives men a keen sensitivity by virtue of which they can appreciate the ineffable attributes of God: his fatherly compassion, his providence, his benevolence and loving presence. It can develop in the inmost depths of man habits of virtue rarely to be found otherwise in the same degree, such as patience, acceptance of the Cross in daily life, detachment, openness to other men and a spirit of ready service. It is on account of these qualities that we prefer to call it *popular piety* or the religion of the people rather than *religiosity*. It is a matter of pastoral charity for all those whom God has put in charge of ecclesial communities to establish principles for directing in the right channels this sentiment which can bear such excellent fruits and yet is fraught with danger. Above all we must be sympathetic in our approach, quick to appreciate its inherent nature and its desirable qualities and zealous to direct it so that the dangers arising out of its errors may be avoided. When it is wisely directed popular piety of this kind can make a constantly increasing contribution towards bringing the masses of our people into contact with God in Jesus Christ.

1 Corinthians 15:42–44 So is it with the resurrection of the dead. What is sown is 1683
perishable, what is raised is imperishable. It is sown in dishonor, it is raised in glory. It is sown in weakness, it is raised in power. It is sown a physical body, it is raised a spiritual body. If there is a physical body, there is also a spiritual body.

1684 *Sacrosanctum concilium* **81–82** Funeral rites should express more clearly the paschal character of Christian death, and should correspond more closely to the circumstances and traditions found in various regions. This also applies to the liturgical color to be used.

The rite for the Burial of Infants is to be revised, and a special Mass for the occasion should be provided.

1685 *Sacrosanctum concilium* **81** Funeral rites should express more clearly the paschal character of Christian death, and should correspond more closely to the circumstances and traditions found in various regions. This also applies to the liturgical color to be used.

1687 **1 Thessalonians 4:18** Therefore comfort one another with these words.

1689 (1) **Rite of Funerals 1** In the face of death, the Church confidently proclaims that God has created each person for eternal life and that Jesus, the Son of God, by his death and resurrection, has broken the chains of sin and death that bound humanity. Christ "achieved his task of redeeming humanity and giving perfect glory to God, principally by the paschal mystery of his blessed passion, resurrection from the dead, and glorious ascension."

1689 (2) **Rite of Funerals 57** The vigil in the form of the liturgy of the word consists of the introductory rites, the liturgy of the word, the prayer of intercession, and a concluding rite.

III

LIFE IN CHRIST

John 8:29 ". . . And he who sent me is with me; he has not left me alone, for I 1693
always do what is pleasing to him."

(1) **Romans 6:5** For if we have been united with him in a death like his, we shall 1694
certainly be united with him in a resurrection like his.

(2) **Colossians 2:12** . . . and you were buried with him in baptism, in which you 1694
were also raised with him through faith in the working of God, who raised him from the dead.

(3) **John 15:5** I am the vine, you are the branches. He who abides in me, and I in 1694
him, he it is that bears much fruit, for apart from me you can do nothing.

(4) **John 13:12–16** When he had washed their feet, and taken his garments, and 1694
resumed his place, he said to them, "Do you know what I have done to you? You call me Teacher and Lord; and you are right, for so I am. If I then, your Lord and Teacher, have washed your feet, you also ought to wash one another's feet. For I have given you an example, that you also should do as I have done to you. Truly, truly, I say to you, a servant is not greater than his master; nor is he who is sent greater than he who sent him. . . ."

(1) **1 Corinthians 6:19** Do you not know that your body is a temple of the Holy 1695
Spirit within you, which you have from God? You are not your own. . . .

(2) **Galatians 4:6** And because you are sons, God has sent the Spirit of his Son 1695
into our hearts, crying, "Abba! Father!"

(3) **Galatians 5:25** If we live by the Spirit, let us also walk by the Spirit. 1695

(4) **Ephesians 4:23** . . . and be renewed in the spirit of your minds. . . . 1695

Deuteronomy 30:15–20 "See, I have set before you this day life and good, death 1696
and evil. If you obey the commandments of the Lord your God which I command you this day, by loving the Lord your God, by walking in his ways, and by keeping his commandments and his statutes and his ordinances, then you shall live and multiply, and the Lord your God will bless you in the land which you are entering to take possession of it. But if your heart turns away, and you will not hear, but are drawn away to worship other gods and serve them, I declare to you this day, that you shall perish; you shall not live long in the land which you are going over the Jordan to enter and possess. I call heaven and earth to witness against you this day, that I have set before you life and death, blessing and curse; therefore choose life, that you and your descendants may live, loving the Lord your God, obeying his voice, and cleaving to him; for that means life to you and length of days, that you may dwell in the land which the Lord swore to your fathers, to Abraham, to Isaac, and to Jacob, to give them."

1697 ***Catechesi tradendae* 29** In the third chapter of his Apostolic Exhortation *Evangelii nuntiandi*, the same Pope recalled "the essential content, the living substance" of evangelization. Catechesis, too, must keep in mind each of these factors and also the living synthesis of which they are part.

I shall therefore limit myself here simply to recalling one or two points. Anyone can see, for instance, how important it is to make the child, the adolescent, the person advancing in faith understand "what can be known about God"; to be able in a way to tell them: "What you worship as unknown, this I proclaim to you"; to set forth briefly for them the mystery of the Word of God become man and accomplishing man's salvation by His Passover, that is to say, through His death and resurrection, but also by His preaching, by the signs worked by Him, and by the sacraments of His permanent presence in our midst. The synod fathers were indeed inspired when they asked that care should be taken not to reduce Christ to His humanity alone or His message to a no more than earthly dimension, but that He should be recognized as the Son of God, the Mediator giving us in the Spirit free access to the Father.

It is important to display before the eyes of the intelligence and of the heart, in the light of faith, the sacrament of Christ's presence constituted by the mystery of the Church, which is an assembly of human beings who are sinners and yet have at the same time been sanctified and who make up the family of God gathered together by the Lord under the guidance of those whom "the Holy Spirit has made . . . guardians, to feed the Church of God."

It is important to explain that the history of the human race, marked as it is by grace and sin, greatness and misery, is taken up by God in His Son Jesus, "foreshadowing in some way the age which is to come."

Finally, it is important to reveal frankly the demands—demands that involve self-denial but also joy—made by what the Apostle Paul liked to call "newness of life," "a new creation," being in Christ, and "eternal life in Christ Jesus," which is the same thing as life in the world but lived in accordance with the beatitudes and called to an extension and transfiguration hereafter.

Hence the importance in catechesis of personal moral commitments in keeping with the Gospel and of Christian attitudes, whether heroic or very simple, to life and the world—what we call the Christian or evangelical virtues. Hence also, in its endeavor to educate faith, the concern of catechesis not to omit but to clarify properly realities such as man's activity for his integral liberation, the search for a society with greater solidarity and fraternity, the fight for justice and the building of peace.

Besides, it is not to be thought that this dimension of catechesis is altogether new. As early as the patristic age, St. Ambrose and St. John Chrysostom—to quote only them—gave prominence to the social consequences of the demands made by the Gospel. Close to our own time, the catechism of St. Pius X explicitly listed oppressing the poor and depriving workers of their just wages among the sins that cry to God for vengeance. Since *Rerum novarum* especially, social concern has been actively present in the catechetical teaching of the Popes and Bishops. Many synod fathers rightly insisted that the rich heritage of the Church's social teaching should, in appropriate forms, find a place in the general catechetical education of the faithful.

1700 **Luke 15:11–32** And he said, "There was a man who had two sons; and the younger of them said to his father, 'Father, give me the share of property that falls to me.' And he divided his living between them. Not many days later, the younger son gathered all he had and took his journey into a far country, and there he squandered his property in loose living. And when he had spent everything, a great famine arose in that country, and he began to be in want. So he went and joined himself to one of the citizens of that country, who sent him into his fields to feed swine. And he would gladly have fed on the pods that the swine ate; and no one gave him anything. But when he came to himself he said, 'How many of my father's hired servants have bread enough and to spare, but I perish here with hunger! I will arise and go to my father, and I will say to him, "Father, I have sinned against heaven and before you; I am no longer worthy to be called your son; treat me as one of your hired servants." ' And he arose and came to his father. But while he was yet at a distance, his father saw him and had compassion, and ran and embraced him and kissed him. And the son said to him, 'Father, I have sinned against heaven and before you; I am no longer worthy to be called your son.' But the father said to his servants, 'Bring quickly the best robe, and put it on him; and put a ring on his hand, and shoes on his feet; and bring the fatted calf and kill it, and let us eat and make merry; for this my son was dead, and is alive again; he was lost, and is found.' And they began to make merry.

"Now his elder son was in the field; and as he came and drew near to the house, he heard music and dancing. And he called one of the servants and asked what this meant. And he said to him, 'Your brother has come, and your father has killed the fatted calf, because he has received him safe and sound.' But he was angry and refused to go in. His father came out and entreated him, but he answered his father, 'Lo, these many years I have served you, and I never disobeyed your command; yet you never gave me a kid, that I might make merry with my friends. But when this son of yours came, who has devoured your living with harlots, you killed for him the fatted calf!' And he said to him, 'Son, you are always with me, and all that is mine is yours. It was fitting to make merry and be glad, for this your brother was dead, and is alive; he was lost, and is found.' "

(1) **2 Corinthians 4:4** In their case the god of this world has blinded the minds of the unbelievers, to keep them from seeing the light of the gospel of the glory of Christ, who is the likeness of God. 1701

(2) ***Gaudium et spes* 22:** see 1612. 1701

***Gaudium et spes* 16** Deep within his conscience man discovers a law which he has not laid upon himself but which he must obey. Its voice, ever calling him to love and to do what is good and to avoid evil, tells him inwardly at the right moment: do this, shun that. For man has in his heart a law inscribed by God. His dignity lies in observing this law, and by it he will be judged. His conscience is man's most secret core, and his sanctuary. There he is alone with God whose voice echoes in his depths. By conscience, in a wonderful way, that law is made known which is fulfilled in the love of God and of one's neighbor. Through loyalty to conscience Christians are joined to other men in the search for truth and for the right solution to so many moral problems which arise both in the life of individuals and from social relationships. Hence, the more a correct conscience prevails, the more do persons and groups turn aside from blind choice and try to be guided by the objective standards of moral conduct. Yet it often happens that conscience goes astray through ignorance which it is unable to avoid, without thereby losing its dignity. This cannot be said of the man who takes little trouble to find out what is true and good, or when conscience is by degrees almost blinded through the habit of committing sin. 1713

(1) **Matthew 4:17** From that time Jesus began to preach, saying, "Repent, for the kingdom of heaven is at hand." 1720

(2) **1 John 3:2** Beloved, we are God's children now; it does not yet appear what we shall be, but we know that when he appears we shall be like him, for we shall see him as he is. 1720

1720 (3) **1 Corinthians 13:12** For now we see in a mirror dimly, but then face to face. Now I know in part; then I shall understand fully, even as I have been fully understood.

1720 (4) **Hebrews 4:7–11** . . . again he sets a certain day, "Today," saying through David so long afterward, in the words already quoted,

"Today, when you hear his voice,
do not harden your hearts."

For if Joshua had given them rest, God would not speak later of another day. So then, there remains a sabbath rest for the people of God; for whoever enters God's rest also ceases from his labors as God did from his.

Let us therefore strive to enter that rest, that no one fall by the same sort of disobedience.

1721 (1) **John 17:3** And this is eternal life, that they know thee the only true God, and Jesus Christ whom thou hast sent.

1721 (2) **Romans 8:18** I consider that the sufferings of this present time are not worth comparing with the glory that is to be revealed to us.

1724 **Matthew 13:3–23** And he told them many things in parables, saying: "A sower went out to sow. And as he sowed, some seeds fell along the path, and the birds came and devoured them. Other seeds fell on rocky ground, where they had not much soil, and immediately they sprang up, since they had no depth of soil, but when the sun rose they were scorched; and since they had no root they withered away. Other seeds fell upon thorns, and the thorns grew up and choked them. Other seeds fell on good soil and brought forth grain, some a hundredfold, some sixty, some thirty. He who has ears, let him hear."

Then the disciples came and said to him, "Why do you speak to them in parables?" And he answered them, "To you it has been given to know the secrets of the kingdom of heaven, but to them it has not been given. For to him who has will more be given, and he will have abundance; but from him who has not, even what he has will be taken away. This is why I speak to them in parables, because seeing they do not see, and hearing they do not hear, nor do they understand. With them indeed is fulfilled the prophecy of Isaiah which says:

'You shall indeed hear but never understand,
and you shall indeed see but never perceive.
For this people's heart has grown dull,
and their ears are heavy of hearing,
and their eyes they have closed,
lest they should perceive with their eyes,
and hear with their ears,
and understand with their heart,
and turn for me to heal them.'

But blessed are your eyes, for they see, and your ears, for they hear. Truly, I say to you, many prophets and righteous men longed to see what you see, and did not see it, and to hear what you hear, and did not hear it.

"Hear then the parable of the sower. When any one hears the word of the kingdom and does not understand it, the evil one comes and snatches away what is sown in his heart; this is what was sown along the path. As for what was sown on rocky ground, this is he who hears the word and immediately receives it with joy; yet he has no root in himself, but endures for a while, and when tribulation or persecution arises on account of the word, immediately he falls away. As for what was sown among thorns, this is he who hears the word, but the cares of the world and the delight in riches choke the word, and it proves unfruitful. As for what was sown on good soil, this is he who hears the word and understands it; he indeed bears fruit, and yields, in one case a hundredfold, in another sixty, and in another thirty."

Romans 6:17 But thanks be to God, that you who were once slaves of sin have become obedient from the heart to the standard of teaching to which you were committed. . . . **1733**

(1) **Genesis 4:10** And the Lord said, "What have you done? The voice of your brother's blood is crying to me from the ground. . . ." **1736**

(2) **2 Samuel 12:7–15** Nathan said to David, "You are the man. Thus says the Lord, the God of Israel, 'I anointed you king over Israel, and I delivered you out of the hand of Saul; and I gave you your master's house, and your master's wives into your bosom, and gave you the house of Israel and of Judah; and if this were too little, I would add to you as much more. Why have you despised the word of the Lord, to do what is evil in his sight? You have smitten Uriah the Hittite with the sword, and have taken his wife to be your wife, and have slain him with the sword of the Ammonites. Now therefore the sword shall never depart from your house, because you have despised me, and have taken the wife of Uriah the Hittite to be your wife.' Thus says the Lord, 'Behold, I will raise up evil against you out of your own house; and I will take your wives before your eyes, and give them to your neighbor, and he shall lie with your wives in the sight of this sun. For you did it secretly; but I will do this thing before all Israel, and before the sun.'" David said to Nathan, "I have sinned against the Lord." And Nathan said to David, "The Lord also has put away your sin; you shall not die. Nevertheless, because by this deed you have utterly scorned the Lord, the child that is born to you shall die." Then Nathan went to his house. **1736**

(1) ***Dignitatis humanae* 2** The Vatican Council declares that the human person has a right to religious freedom. Freedom of this kind means that all men should be immune from coercion on the part of individuals, social groups and every human power so that, within due limits, nobody is forced to act against his convictions nor is anyone to be restrained from acting in accordance with his convictions in religious matters in private or in public, alone or in associations with others. The Council further declares that the right to religious freedom is based on the very dignity of the human person as known through the revealed word of God and by reason itself. This right of the human person to religious freedom must be given such recognition in the constitutional order of society as will make it a civil right. **1738**

It is in accordance with their dignity that all men, because they are persons, that is, beings endowed with reason and free will and therefore bearing personal responsibility, are both impelled by their nature and bound by a moral obligation to seek the truth, especially religious truth. They are also bound to adhere to the truth once they come to know it and direct their whole lives in accordance with the demands of truth. But men cannot satisfy this obligation in a way that is in keeping with their own nature unless they enjoy both psychological freedom and immunity from external coercion. Therefore the right to religious freedom has its foundation not in the subjective attitude of the individual but in his very nature. For this reason the right to this immunity continues to exist even in those who do not live up to their obligation of seeking the truth and adhering to it. The exercise of this right cannot be interfered with as long as the just requirements of public order are observed.

1738 (2) ***Dignitatis humanae* 7** The right to freedom in matters of religion is exercised in human society. For this reason its use is subject to certain regulatory norms.

In availing of any freedom men must respect the moral principle of personal and social responsibility: in exercising their rights individual men and social groups are bound by the moral law to have regard for the rights of others, their own duties to others and the common good of all. All men must be treated with justice and humanity.

Furthermore, since civil society has the right to protect itself against possible abuses committed in the name of religious freedom the responsibility of providing such protection rests especially with the civil authority. However, this must not be done in an arbitrary manner or by the unfair practice of favoritism but in accordance with legal principles which are in conformity with the objective moral order. These principles are necessary for the effective protection of the rights of all citizens and for peaceful settlement of conflicts of rights. They are also necessary for an adequate protection of that just public peace which is to be found where men live together in good order and true justice. They are required too for the necessary protection of public morality. All these matters are basic to the common good and belong to what is called public order. For the rest, the principle of the integrity of freedom in society should continue to be upheld. According to this principle man's freedom should be given the fullest possible recognition and should not be curtailed except when and in so far as is necessary.

1741 **John 8:32** ". . . and you will know the truth, and the truth will make you free."

1743 **Sirach 15:14**

It was he who created man in the beginning,
and he left him in the power of his own inclination.

1753 **Matthew 6:2–4** "Thus, when you give alms, sound no trumpet before you, as the hypocrites do in the synagogues and in the streets, that they may be praised by men. Truly, I say to you, they have received their reward. But when you give alms, do not let your left hand know what your right hand is doing, so that your alms may be in secret; and your Father who sees in secret will reward you. . . ."

1764 **Mark 7:21** For from within, out of the heart of man, come evil thoughts, fornication, theft, murder, adultery. . . .

1766 **St. Augustine, *De Trinitate* VIII, 3, 4** Behold again, and see if thou canst. Thou certainly dost not love anything except what is good, since good is the earth, with the loftiness of its mountains, and the due measure of its hills, and the level surface of its plains; and good is an estate that is pleasant and fertile; and good is a house that is arranged in due proportions, and is spacious and bright; and good are animal and animate bodies; and good is air that is temperate and salubrious; and good is food that is agreeable and fit for health; and good is health, without pains or lassitude; and good is the countenance of man that is disposed in fit proportions, and is cheerful in look, and bright in color; and good is the mind of a friend, with the sweetness of agreement, and with the confidence of love; and good is a righteous man; and good are riches, since they are readily useful; and good is the heaven, with its sun, and moon, and stars; and good are the angels, by their holy obedience; and good is discourse that sweetly teaches and suitably admonishes the hearer; and good is a poem that is harmonious in its numbers and weighty in its sense. And why add yet more and more? This thing is good and that good, but take away this and that, and regard good itself if thou canst; so wilt thou see God, not good by a good that is other than Himself, but the good of all good. For in all these good things, whether those which I have mentioned, or any else that are to be discerned or thought, we could not say that one was better than another, when we judge truly, unless a conception of the good itself had been impressed upon us, such that according to it we might both approve some things as good, and prefer one good to another. So God is to be loved, not this and that good, but the good itself. For the good that must be sought for the soul is not one above which it is to fly by judging, but to which it is to cleave by loving; and what can this be except God? Not a good mind, or a good angel, or the good heaven, but the good good. For perhaps what I wish to say may be more easily perceived in this way. For when, for instance, a mind is called good, as there are two words, so from these words I understand two things—one whereby it is mind, and another whereby it is good. And itself had no share in making itself a mind, for there was nothing as yet to make itself to be anything; but to make itself to be a good mind, I see, must be brought about by the will: not because that by which it is mind is not itself anything good;—for how else is it already called, and most truly called, better than the body?—but it is not yet called a good mind, for this reason, that the action of the will still is wanted, by which it is to become more excellent; and if it has neglected this, then it is justly blamed, and is rightly called not a good mind. For it then differs from the mind which does perform this; and since the latter is praiseworthy, the former doubtless, which does not perform, it is blameable. But when it does this of set purpose, and becomes a good mind, it yet cannot attain to being so unless it turn itself to something which itself is not. And to what can it turn itself that it may become a good mind, except to the good which it loves, and seeks, and obtains? And if it turns itself back again from this, and becomes not good, then by the very act of turning away from the good, unless that good remain in it from which it turns away, it cannot again turn itself back thither if it should wish to amend.

St. Thomas Aquinas, *Summa theologiae* II–II, 24, 3 1767

article 3. is charity given us in proportion to our natural capacities?

THE THIRD POINT: 1. It appears so. For in *Matthew* we read that *he gave to each according to his ability*. Now prior to charity the only virtue man has is natural, for, as already explained, there is no virtue without charity. Therefore God infuses charity in proportion to the degree of natural virtue.

2. Moreover, wherever things are ordered towards each other, the second is proportioned to the first: for example, with material things form is proportioned to matter, and with divine gifts glory is proportioned to grace. Now since charity is a perfection of nature, it is related to natural capacity, as second to first, and it would in consequence seem to be given in proportion to it.

3. Besides, sharing in charity means the same for men and angels because, as appears from *Matthew* and *Luke*, beatitude has the same meaning for both. Now Peter Lombard asserts that with angels charity, as well as other gifts of grace, are bestowed in proportion to their natural capacities. The same therefore would seem to be the case with men.

ON THE OTHER HAND there is the text of *John*, *The Spirit breathes where he will*, and of 1 *Corinthians*, *All these things one and the same Spirit worketh dividing to everyone according as he will*. Consequently, charity is not given according to natural capacities but according to the will of the Spirit distributing his own gifts.

REPLY: A thing's quantity depends on its proper cause, because a more universal cause produces a greater effect. Now charity, as stated above, since it altogether transcends human nature, does not depend on any natural virtue, but solely on the grace of the Holy Spirit who infuses it. Accordingly its quantity does not depend on the quality of the nature or on the capacity of its natural virtue, but exclusively on the will of the Holy Spirit who distributes these gifts as he pleases. As St. Paul says, *To each of us is given grace according to the measure of the giving of Christ.*

Hence: 1. This ability, according to which God bestows his gifts, is either some disposition or preparation for them, or else the very effort which a man makes in receiving grace. But even this disposition or this effort is anticipated by the Holy Spirit, who moves man's soul now more, now less, as he sees fit. Hence St. Paul's phrase, *Who has made us worthy to be partakers of the lot of the saints in light.*

2. While it is true that a form is not out of proportion to its matter, it is also true that they both belong to the same genus. Similarly, grace and glory are referred to the same genus, for grace is nothing else than a certain beginning of glory in us. Charity and nature, however, do not belong to the same genus. Hence the comparison proves nothing.

3. Possessing an intellectual nature, an angel's condition is such that whatever it embraces it embraces with its whole being, as was explained in the *Prima Pars*. Accordingly, the higher the angel, the greater the effort made, for good, as in the case of those who continued steadfast, and for evil as with those who fell. Hence the higher angels by standing fast became better than others, while those who fell became worse. But man has a rational nature and such a nature is sometimes in potentiality and sometimes in act. And so it is not necessary that whatever he embraces he embrace with his whole being. In fact it can happen that a man with better natural gifts makes less of an effort than another, or the other way round. The cases therefore are not parallel.

1777 (1) **Romans 2:14–16** When Gentiles who have not the law do by nature what the law requires, they are a law to themselves, even though they do not have the law. They show that what the law requires is written on their hearts, while their conscience also bears witness and their conflicting thoughts accuse or perhaps excuse them on that day when, according to my gospel, God judges the secrets of men by Christ Jesus.

1777 (2) **Romans 1:32** Though they know God's decree that those who do such things deserve to die, they not only do them but approve those who practice them.

1785 (1) **Psalm 119:105**

Thy word is a lamp to my feet
and a light to my path.

1785 (2) ***Dignitatis humanae* 14** In order to satisfy the divine command: "Make disciples of all nations" (Mt. 28:19), the Catholic Church must spare no effort in striving "that the word of the Lord may speed on and triumph" (2 Th. 3:1).

The Church therefore earnestly urges her children first of all that "supplications, prayers, intercessions and thanksgivings be made for all men. . . . This is good and is acceptable in the sight of God our Savior, who desires all men to be saved and to come to the knowledge of the truth" (1 Tim. 2:1–4).

However, in forming their consciences the faithful must pay careful attention to the sacred and certain teaching of the Church. For the Catholic Church is by the will of Christ the teacher of truth. It is her duty to proclaim and teach with authority the truth which is Christ and, at the same time, to declare and confirm by her authority the principles of the moral order which spring from human nature itself. In addition, Christians should approach those who are outside wisely, "in the holy Spirit, genuine love, truthful speech" (2 Cor. 6:6–7), and should strive, even to the shedding of their blood, to spread the light of life with all confidence and apostolic courage.

The disciple has a grave obligation to Christ, his Master, to grow daily in his knowledge of the truth he has received from him, to be faithful in announcing it and vigorous in defending it without having recourse to methods which are contrary to the spirit of the Gospel. At the same time the love of Christ urges him to treat with love, prudence and patience those who are in error or ignorance with regard to the faith. He must take into account his duties towards Christ, the life-giving Word whom he must proclaim, the rights of the human person and the measure of grace which God has given to each man through Christ in calling him freely to accept and profess the faith.

(1) **Luke 6:31** And as you wish that men would do to you, do so to them. **1789**

(2) **Tobit 4:15** And what you hate, do not do to any one. Do not drink wine to excess or let drunkenness go with you on your way. **1789**

(1) **1 Timothy 3:9** . . . they must hold the mystery of the faith with a clear conscience. **1794**

(2) **2 Timothy 1:3** I thank God whom I serve with a clear conscience, as did my fathers, when I remember you constantly in my prayers. **1794**

(3) **1 Peter 3:21** Baptism, which corresponds to this, now saves you, not as a removal of dirt from the body but as an appeal to God for a clear conscience, through the resurrection of Jesus Christ. . . . **1794**

(4) **Acts 24:16** So I always take pains to have a clear conscience toward God and toward men. **1794**

Sirach 37:27–31 **1809**

My son, test your soul while you live;
see what is bad for it and do not give it that.
For not everything is good for every one,
and not every person enjoys everything.
Do not have an insatiable appetite for any luxury,
and do not give yourself up to food;
for overeating brings sickness,
and gluttony leads to nausea.
Many have died of gluttony,
but he who is careful to avoid it prolongs his life.

2 Peter 1:4 . . . by which he has granted to us his precious and very great promises, that through these you may escape from the corruption that is in the world because of passion, and become partakers of the divine nature. **1812**

1 Corinthians 13:13 So faith, hope, love abide, these three; but the greatest of these is love. **1813**

Council of Trent (1547): DS 1545 To men, therefore, who have been justified in this respect, whether they have preserved uninterruptedly the grace received, or have recovered it when lost, the words of the Apostle are to be submitted: "Abound in **1815**

every good work, knowing that your labor is not in vain in the Lord" [I Cor. 15:58]; "for God is not unjust, that he should forget your work and the love, which you have shown in his name" [Heb. 6:10], and: "Do not lose your confidence, which has a great reward" [Heb. 10:35]. And therefore to those who work well "unto the end" [Matt. 10:22], and who trust in God, life eternal is to be proposed, both as a grace mercifully promised to the sons of God through Christ Jesus, "and as a recompense" which is according to the promise of God Himself to be faithfully given to their good works and merits [can. 26 and 32]. For this is that "crown of justice which after his fight and course" the Apostle declared "was laid up for him, to be rendered to him by the just judge and not only to him, but also to all that love his coming" [II Tim. 4:7 ff.].

1816 ***Dignitatis humanae* 14:** see 1785 (2).

1819 (1) **Genesis 17:4–8** "Behold, my covenant is with you, and you shall be the father of a multitude of nations. No longer shall your name be Abram, but your name shall be Abraham; for I have made you the father of a multitude of nations. I will make you exceedingly fruitful; and I will make nations of you, and kings shall come forth from you. And I will establish my covenant between me and you and your descendants after you throughout their generations for an everlasting covenant, to be God to you and to your descendants after you. And I will give to you, and to your descendants after you, the land of your sojournings, all the land of Canaan, for an everlasting possession; and I will be their God."

1819 (2) **Genesis 22:1–18** After these things God tested Abraham, and said to him, "Abraham!" And he said, "Here am I." He said, "Take your son, your only son Isaac, whom you love, and go to the land of Moriah, and offer him there as a burnt offering upon one of the mountains of which I shall tell you." So Abraham rose early in the morning, saddled his ass, and took two of his young men with him, and his son Isaac; and he cut the wood for the burnt offering, and arose and went to the place of which God had told him. On the third day Abraham lifted up his eyes and saw the place afar off. Then Abraham said to his young men, "Stay here with the ass; I and the lad will go yonder and worship, and come again to you." And Abraham took the wood of the burnt offering, and laid it on Isaac his son; and he took in his hand the fire and the knife. So they went both of them together. And Isaac said to his father Abraham, "My father!" And he said, "Here am I, my son." He said, "Behold, the fire and the wood; but where is the lamb for a burnt offering?" Abraham said, "God will provide himself the lamb for a burnt offering, my son." So they went both of them together.

When they came to the place of which God had told him, Abraham built an altar there, and laid the wood in order, and bound Isaac his son, and laid him on the altar, upon the wood. Then Abraham put forth his hand, and took the knife to slay his son. But the angel of the Lord called to him from heaven, and said, "Abraham, Abraham!" And he said, "Here am I." He said, "Do not lay your hand on the lad or do anything to him; for now I know that you fear God, seeing you have not withheld your son, your only son, from me. And Abraham lifted up his eyes and looked, and behold, behind him was a ram, caught in a thicket by his horns; and Abraham went and took the ram, and offered it up as a burnt offering instead of his son. So Abraham called the name of that place The Lord will provide; as it is said to this day, "On the mount of the Lord it shall be provided."

And the angel of the Lord called to Abraham a second time from heaven, and said, "By myself I have sworn, says the Lord, because you have done this, and have not withheld your son, your only son, I will indeed bless you, and I will multiply your descendants as the stars of heaven and as the sand which is on the seashore. And your descendants shall possess the gate of their enemies, and by your descendants shall all the nations of the earth bless themselves, because you have obeyed my voice."

(1) **Romans 8:28–30** We know that in everything God works for good with those who love him, who are called according to his purpose. For those whom he foreknew he also predestined to be conformed to the image of his Son, in order that he might be the first-born among many brethren. And those whom he predestined he also called; and those whom he called he also justified; and those whom he justified he also glorified. **1821**

(2) **Matthew 7:21** "Not every one who says to me, 'Lord, Lord,' shall enter the kingdom of heaven, but he who does the will of my Father who is in heaven. . . ." **1821**

(3) **Council of Trent (1547): DS 1541** So also as regards the gift of perseverance [can. 16] of which it is written: He that "shall persevere to the end, he shall be saved" [Matt. 10:22; 24:13] (which gift cannot be obtained from anyone except from Him, "who is able to make him, who stands, stand" [Rom. 14:4], that he may stand perseveringly, and to raise him, who falls), let no one promise himself anything as certain with absolute certitude, although all ought to place and repose a very firm hope in God's help. For God, unless men be wanting in His grace, as He has begun a good work, so will He perfect it, "working to will and to accomplish" [Phil. 2:13; can. 22]. Nevertheless, let those "who think themselves to stand, take heed lest they fall" [I Cor. 10:12], and "with fear and trembling work out their salvation" [Phil. 2:12] in labors, in watchings, in almsdeeds, in prayers and oblations, in fastings and chastity [cf. II Cor. 6:3 ff.]. For they ought to fear, knowing that they are born again "unto the hope of glory" [cf. I Pet. 1:3], and not as yet unto glory in the combat that yet remains with the flesh, with the world, with the devil, in which they cannot be victors, unless with God's grace they obey the Apostle saying: "We are debtors, not to the flesh, to live according to the flesh. For if you live according to the flesh, you shall die. But if by the spirit you mortify the deeds of the flesh, you shall live" [Rom. 8:12 ff.]. **1821**

John 13:34 A new commandment I give to you, that you love one another; even as I have loved you, that you also love one another. **1823**

(1) **Matthew 22:40** ". . . On these two commandments depend all the law and the prophets." **1824**

(2) **Romans 13:8–10** Owe no one anything, except to love one another; for he who loves his neighbor has fulfilled the law. The commandments, "You shall not commit adultery, You shall not kill, You shall not steal, You shall not covet," and any other commandment, are summed up in this sentence, "You shall love your neighbor as yourself." Love does no wrong to a neighbor; therefore love is the fulfilling of the law. **1824**

(1) **Matthew 5:44** But I say to you, Love your enemies and pray for those who persecute you. . . . **1825**

(2) **Luke 10:27–37** And he answered, "You shall love the Lord your God with all your heart, and with all your soul, and with all your strength, and with all your mind; and your neighbor as yourself." And he said to him, "You have answered right; do this, and you will live." **1825**

But he, desiring to justify himself, said to Jesus, "And who is my neighbor?" Jesus replied, "A man was going down from Jerusalem to Jericho, and he fell among robbers, who stripped him and beat him, and departed, leaving him half dead. Now by chance a priest was going down that road; and when he saw him he passed by on the other side. So likewise a Levite, when he came to the place and saw him, passed by on the other side. But a Samaritan, as he journeyed, came to where he was; and when he saw him, he had compassion, and went to him and bound up his wounds, pouring on oil and wine; then he set him on his own beast and brought him to an inn, and took care of him. And the next day he took out two denarii and gave them to the innkeeper, saying, 'Take care of him; and whatever more you spend, I will repay you when I come back.' Which of these three, do you think, proved neighbor to the man who fell among the robbers?" He said, "The one who showed mercy on him." And Jesus said to him, "Go and do likewise."

1825 (3) **Mark 9:37** "Whoever receives one such child in my name receives me; and whoever receives me, receives not me but him who sent me."

1825 (4) **Matthew 25:40** ". . . And the King will answer them, 'Truly, I say to you, as you did it to one of the least of these my brethren, you did it to me.' . . ."

1825 (5) **Matthew 25:45** ". . . Then he will answer them, 'Truly, I say to you, as you did it not to one of the least of these, you did it not to me.' . . ."

1828 **1 John 4:19** We love, because he first loved us.

1831 **Isaiah 11:1–2**

There shall come forth a shoot from the stump of Jesse,
  and a branch shall grow out of his roots.
And the Spirit of the Lord shall rest upon him,
  the spirit of wisdom and understanding,
  the spirit of counsel and might,
  the spirit of knowledge and the fear of the Lord.

1846 **Luke 15:** see 1443 (1).

1850 **Philippians 2:6–9** . . . who, though he was in the form of God, did not count equality with God a thing to be grasped, but emptied himself, taking the form of a servant, being born in the likeness of men. And being found in human form he humbled himself and became obedient unto death, even death on a cross. Therefore God has highly exalted him and bestowed on him the name which is above every name. . . .

1851 **John 14:30** I will no longer talk much with you, for the ruler of this world is coming. He has no power over me. . . .

1852 (1) **Romans 1:28–32** And since they did not see fit to acknowledge God, God gave them up to a base mind and to improper conduct. They were filled with all manner of wickedness, evil, covetousness, malice. Full of envy, murder, strife, deceit, malignity, they are gossips, slanderers, haters of God, insolent, haughty, boastful, inventors of evil, disobedient to parents, foolish, faithless, heartless, ruthless. Though they know God's decree that those who do such things deserve to die, they not only do them but approve those who practice them.

(2) **1 Corinthians 6:9–10** Do you not know that the unrighteous will not inherit the kingdom of God? Do not be deceived; neither the immoral, nor idolaters, nor adulterers, nor sexual perverts, nor thieves, nor the greedy, nor drunkards, nor revilers, nor robbers will inherit the kingdom of God. 1852

(3) **Ephesians 5:3–5** But fornication and all impurity or covetousness must not even be named among you, as is fitting among saints. Let there be no filthiness, nor silly talk, nor levity, which are not fitting; but instead let there be thanksgiving. Be sure of this, that no fornicator or impure man, or one who is covetous (that is, an idolater), has any inheritance in the kingdom of Christ and of God. 1852

(4) **Colossians 3:5–8** Put to death therefore what is earthly in you: fornication, impurity, passion, evil desire, and covetousness, which is idolatry. On account of these the wrath of God is coming. In these you once walked, when you lived in them. But now put them all away: anger, wrath, malice, slander, and foul talk from your mouth. 1852

(5) **1 Timothy 1:9–10** . . . understanding this, that the law is not laid down for the just but for the lawless and disobedient, for the ungodly and sinners, for the unholy and profane, for murderers of fathers and murderers of mothers, for manslayers, immoral persons, sodomites, kidnapers, liars, perjurers, and whatever else is contrary to sound doctrine. . . . 1852

(6) **2 Timothy 3:2–5** For men will be lovers of self, lovers of money, proud, arrogant, abusive, disobedient to their parents, ungrateful, unholy, inhuman, implacable, slanderers, profligates, fierce, haters of good, treacherous, reckless, swollen with conceit, lovers of pleasure rather than lovers of God, holding the form of religion but denying the power of it. Avoid such people. 1852

1 John 5:16–17 If any one sees his brother committing what is not a mortal sin, he will ask, and God will give him life for those whose sin is not mortal. There is sin which is mortal; I do not say that one is to pray for that. All wrongdoing is sin, but there is sin which is not mortal. 1854

(1) **Mark 3:5–6** And he looked around at them with anger, grieved at their hardness of heart, and said to the man, "Stretch out your hand." He stretched it out, and his hand was restored. The Pharisees went out, and immediately held counsel with the Herodians against him, how to destroy him. 1859

(2) **Luke 16:19–31** "There was a rich man, who was clothed in purple and fine linen and who feasted sumptuously every day. And at his gate lay a poor man named Lazarus, full of sores, who desired to be fed with what fell from the rich man's table; moreover the dogs came and licked his sores. The poor man died and was carried by the angels to Abraham's bosom. The rich man also died and was buried; and in Hades, being in torment, he lifted up his eyes, and saw Abraham far off and Lazarus in his bosom. And he called out, 'Father Abraham, have mercy upon me, and send Lazarus to dip the end of his finger in water and cool my tongue; for I am in anguish in this flame.' But Abraham said, 'Son, remember that you in your lifetime received your good things, and Lazarus in like manner evil things; but now he is comforted here, and you are in anguish. And besides all this, between us and you a great chasm has been fixed, in order that those who would pass from here to you may not be able, and none may cross from there to us.' And he said, 'Then I beg you, father, to send him to my father's house, for I have five brothers, so that he may warn them, lest 1859

they also come into this place of torment.' But Abraham said, 'They have Moses and the prophets; let them hear them.' And he said, 'No, father Abraham; but if some one goes to them from the dead, they will repent.' He said to him, 'If they do not hear Moses and the prophets, neither will they be convinced if some one should rise from the dead.'"

1864 (1) **Matthew 12:32** And whoever says a word against the Son of man will be forgiven; but whoever speaks against the Holy Spirit will not be forgiven, either in this age or in the age to come.

1864 (2) **Luke 12:10** And every one who speaks a word against the Son of man will be forgiven; but he who blasphemes against the Holy Spirit will not be forgiven.

1864 (3) ***Dominum et vivificantem* 46** Against the background of what has been said so far, certain other words of Jesus, shocking and disturbing ones, become easier to understand. We might call them *the words of "unforgiveness"*. They are reported for us by the Synoptics in connection with a particular sin which is called "blasphemy against the Holy Spirit". This is how they are reported in their three versions: *Matthew*: "Whoever says a word against the Son of Man will be forgiven; but whoever speaks against the Holy Spirit will not be forgiven, either in this age or in the age to come." *Mark*: "All sins will be forgiven the sons of men, and whatever blasphemies they utter; but whoever blasphemes against the Holy Spirit never has forgiveness, but is guilty of an eternal sin." *Luke*: "Every one who speaks a word against the Son of Man will be forgiven; but he who blasphemes against the Holy Spirit will not be forgiven."

Why is blasphemy against the Holy Spirit unforgivable? *How should this blasphemy be understood?* Saint Thomas Aquinas replies that it is a question of a sin that is "unforgivable by its very nature, insofar as it excludes the elements through which the forgiveness of sin takes place."

According to such an exegesis, "blasphemy" does not properly consist in offending against the Holy Spirit in words; it consists rather *in the refusal to accept the salvation which God offers to man through the Holy Spirit*, working through the power of the Cross. If man rejects the "convincing concerning sin" which comes from the Holy Spirit and which has the power to save, he also rejects the "coming" of the Counsellor—that "coming" which was accomplished in the Paschal Mystery, in union with the redemptive power of Christ's Blood: the Blood which "purifies the conscience from dead works."

We know that the result of such a purification is the forgiveness of sins. Therefore, whoever rejects the Spirit and the Blood remains in "dead works", in sin. And the blasphemy against the Holy Spirit consists precisely in *the radical refusal to accept this forgiveness*, of which he is the intimate giver and which presupposes the genuine conversion which he brings about in the conscience. If Jesus says that blasphemy against the Holy Spirit cannot be forgiven either in this life or in the next, it is because this "*non-forgiveness*" is linked, as to its cause, to "*non-repentance*", in other words to the radical refusal to be converted. This means the refusal to come to the sources of Redemption, which nevertheless remain "always" open in the economy of salvation in which the mission of the Holy Spirit is accomplished. The Spirit has infinite power to draw from these sources: "he will take what is mine", Jesus said. In this way he brings to completion in human souls the work of the Redemption accomplished by Christ, and distributes its fruits. Blasphemy against the Holy Spirit, then, is the sin committed by the person who claims to have a *"right" to persist in evil*—in any sin at all—and who thus rejects Redemption. One closes oneself up in sin, thus making impossible one's conversion, and consequently the remission of sins, which one considers not essential or not important for one's life. This is a state of spiritual ruin, because blasphemy against the Holy Spirit does not allow one to escape from one's self-imposed imprisonment and open oneself to the divine sources of the purification of consciences and of the remission of sins.

Gregory the Great, *Moralia in Job* 31, 45 The leader of the devil's army is pride, whose progeny are the seven principal vices. While there are vices which attack us in an invisible warfare under the leadership of pride, some behave like officers and others like troops. For not all faults occupy the heart from the same quarter. But while the greater and less frequently-occurring faults can overcome a mind not on its guard, the lesser but more numerous faults pour in en mass. And once pride, the queen of vices, has fully conquered a heart, she soon hands it over to the seven principal vices, or to her generals. The army follows these generals for there is no doubt that persistence multitudes of vices follow them. We will better be able to demonstrate this if we enumerate these leaders and the army. Certainly the root of all evils is pride, of which Scripture says, "Pride is the origin of all sin" (Eccl. 10:15). The first of her progeny are certainly the seven principal vices which came forth from the virulent root, namely, vainglory, envy, anger, sloth, avarice, gluttony, lust. And because he grieved at our being held captive by pride's seven vices, our Redeemer wages a spiritual war of liberation for us, filled with a spirit of a sevenfold grace. **1866**

(1) **Genesis 4:10** And the Lord said, "What have you done? The voice of your brother's blood is crying to me from the ground. . . ." **1867**

(2) **Genesis 18:20** Then the Lord said, "Because the outcry against Sodom and Gomorrah is great and their sin is very grave. . . ." **1867**

(3) **Genesis 19:13** ". . . for we are about to destroy this place, because the outcry against its people has become great before the Lord, and the Lord has sent us to destroy it." **1867**

(4) **Exodus 3:7–10** Then the Lord said, "I have seen the affliction of my people who are in Egypt, and have heard their cry because of their taskmasters; I know their sufferings, and I have come down to deliver them out of the hand of the Egyptians, and to bring them up out of that land to a good and broad land, a land flowing with milk and honey, to the place of the Canaanites, the Hittites, the Amorites, the Perizzites, the Hivites, and the Jebusites. And now, behold, the cry of the people of Israel has come to me, and I have seen the oppression with which the Egyptians oppress them. Come, I will send you to Pharaoh that you may bring forth my people, the sons of Israel, out of Egypt. **1867**

(5) **Exodus 22:20–22** "Whoever sacrifices to any god, save to the Lord only, shall be utterly destroyed. **1867**

"You shall not wrong a stranger or oppress him, for you were strangers in the land of Egypt. You shall not afflict any widow or orphan. . . ."

(6) **Deuteronomy 24:14–15** "You shall not oppress a hired servant who is poor and needy, whether he is one of your brethren or one of the sojourners who are in your land within your towns; you shall give him his hire on the day he earns it, before the sun goes down (for he is poor, and sets his heart upon it); lest he cry against you to the Lord, and it be sin in you. . . ." **1867**

1867 (7) **James 5:4** Behold, the wages of the laborers who mowed your fields, which you kept back by fraud, cry out; and the cries of the harvesters have reached the ears of the Lord of hosts.

1869 ***Reconciliatio et paenitentia* 16** Sin, in the proper sense, is always a *personal* act, since it is an act of freedom on the part of an individual person, and not properly of a group or community. This individual may be conditioned, incited and influenced by numerous and powerful external factors. He may also be subjected to tendencies, defects and habits linked with his personal condition. In not a few cases such external and internal factors may attenuate, to a greater or lesser degree, the person's freedom and therefore his responsibility and guilt. But it is a truth of faith, also confirmed by our experience and reason, that the human person is free. This truth cannot be disregarded, in order to place the blame for individuals' sins on external factors such as structures, systems or other people. Above all, this would be to deny the person's dignity and freedom, which are manifested—even though in a negative and disastrous way—also in this responsibility for sin committed. Hence there is nothing so personal and untransferable in each individual as merit for virtue or responsibility for sin.

As a personal act, sin has its first and most important consequences in the *sinner himself*: that is, in his relationship with God, who is the very foundation of human life; and also in his spirit, weakening his will and clouding his intellect.

At this point we must ask what was being referred to by those who, during the preparation of the Synod and in the course of its actual work, frequently spoke of *social sin*.

The expression and the underlying concept in fact have various meanings.

To speak of *social sin* means in the first place to recognize that, by virtue of a human solidarity which is as mysterious and intangible as it is real and concrete, each individual's sin in some way affects others. This is the other aspect of that solidarity which on the religious level is developed in the profound and magnificent mystery of the *Communion of Saints*, thanks to which it has been possible to say that "every soul that rises above itself, raises up the world." To this *law of ascent* there unfortunately corresponds the *law of descent*. Consequently one can speak of a *communion of sin*, whereby a soul that lowers itself through sin drags down with itself the Church and, in some way, the whole world. In other words, there is no sin, not even the most intimate and secret one, the most strictly individual one, that exclusively concerns the person committing it. With greater or lesser violence, with greater or lesser harm, every sin has repercussions on the entire ecclesial body and the whole human family. According to this first meaning of the term, every sin can undoubtedly be considered as *social* sin.

Some sins however by their very matter constitute a direct attack on one's neighbor and, more exactly, in the language of the Gospel, against one's brother or sister. They are an offense against God because they are offenses against one's neighbor. These sins are usually called *social sins*, and this is the second meaning of the term. In this sense *social* sin is sin against love of neighbor, and in the law of Christ it is all the more serious in that it involves the second Commandment, which is "like unto the first." Likewise, the term *social* applies to every sin against justice in interpersonal relationships, committed either by the individual against the community or by the community against the individual. Also social is every sin against the rights of the human person, beginning with the right to life and including the life of the unborn, or against a person's physical integrity. Likewise *social* is every sin against others' freedom, especially against the supreme freedom to believe in God and adore him; *social* is every sin against the dignity and honor of one's neighbor. Also social is every sin against the common good and its exigencies in relation to the whole broad spectrum of the rights and duties of citizens. The term *social* can be applied to sins of commission or omission—on the part of political, economic or trade union leaders, who though in a position to do so do not work diligently and wisely for the improvement and transformation of society according to the requirements and potential of the given historic moment; as also on the part of workers who through absenteeism or non-cooperation fail to ensure that their industries can continue to advance the well-being of the workers themselves, of their families, and of the whole of society.

The third meaning of *social sin* refers to the relationships between the various human communities. These relationships are not always in accordance with the plan of God, who intends that there be justice in the world, and freedom and peace between individuals, groups and peoples. Thus the class struggle, whoever the person who leads it or on occasion seeks to give it a theoretical justification, is a *social evil.* Likewise, obstinate confrontation between blocs of nations, between one nation and another, between different groups within the same nation—all this too is a *social evil.* In both cases one may ask whether moral responsibility for these evils, and therefore sin, can be attributed to any person in particular. Now it has to be admitted that realities and situations such as those described, when they become generalized and reach vast proportions as social phenomena, almost always become anonymous, just as their causes are complex and not always identifiable. Hence if one speaks of *social sin* here, the expression obviously has an analogical meaning. However, to speak even analogically of *social sins* must not cause us to underestimate the responsibility of the individuals involved. It is meant to be an appeal to the consciences of all, so that each may shoulder his or her responsibility seriously and courageously in order to change those disastrous conditions and intolerable situations.

Having said this in the clearest and most unequivocal way, one must add at once that there is one meaning sometimes given to *social sin* that is not legitimate or acceptable, even though it is very common in certain quarters today. This usage contrasts *social sin* and *personal sin*, not without ambiguity, in a way that leads more or less unconsciously to the watering down and almost the abolition of *personal* sin, with the recognition only of *social* guilt and responsibilities. According to this usage, which can readily be seen to derive from non-Christian ideologies and systems—which have possibly been discarded today by the very people who formerly officially upheld them—practically every sin is a social sin, in the sense that blame for it is to be placed not so much on the moral conscience of an individual but rather on some vague entity or anonymous collectivity, such as the situation, the system, society, structures, or institutions.

Whenever the Church speaks of *situations* of sin, or when she condemns as *social sins* certain situations or the collective behavior of certain social groups, big or small, or even of whole nations and blocs of nations, she knows and she proclaims that such cases of *social sin* are the result of the accumulation and concentration of many personal sins. It is a case of the very *personal sins* of those who cause or support evil or who exploit it; of those who are in a position to avoid, eliminate or at least limit certain social evils but who fail to do so out of laziness, fear or the conspiracy of silence, through secret complicity or indifference; of those who take refuge in the supposed impossibility of changing the world, and also of those who sidestep the effort and sacrifice required, producing specious reasons of a higher order. The real responsibility, then, lies with individuals.

A situation—or likewise an institution, a structure, society itself—is not in itself the subject of moral acts. Hence a situation cannot in itself be good or bad.

At the heart of every *situation of sin* are always to be found sinful people. So true is this that even when such a situation can be changed in its structural and institutional aspects by the force of law, or—as unfortunately more often happens—by the law of force, the change in fact proves to be incomplete, of short duration, and ultimately vain and ineffective—not to say counterproductive—if the people directly or indirectly responsible for that situation are not converted.

1878 ***Gaudium et spes* 24, 3** Furthermore, the Lord Jesus, when praying to the Father "that they may all be one . . . even as we are one" (Jn. 17:21–22), has opened up new horizons closed to human reason by implying that there is a certain parallel between the union existing among the divine persons and the union of the sons of God in truth and love. It follows, then, that if man is the only creature on earth that God has wanted for its own sake, man can fully discover his true self only in a sincere giving of himself.

1879 ***Gaudium et spes* 25, 1** The social nature of man shows that there is an interdependence between personal betterment and the improvement of society. Insofar as man by his very nature stands completely in need of life in society, he is and he ought to be the beginning, the subject and the object of every social organization. Life in society is not something accessory to man himself: through his dealings with others, through mutual service, and through fraternal dialogue, man develops all his talents and becomes able to rise to his destiny.

1880 (1) **Luke 19:13** ". . . Calling ten of his servants, he gave them ten pounds, and said to them, 'Trade with these till I come.' . . ."

1880 (2) **Luke 19:15** When he returned, having received the kingdom, he commanded these servants, to whom he had given the money, to be called to him, that he might know what they had gained by trading.

1882 (1) ***Gaudium et spes* 25, 2** Among the social ties necessary for man's development some correspond more immediately to his innermost nature—the family, for instance, and the political community; others flow rather from his free choice. Nowadays for various reasons mutual relationships and interdependence increase from day to day and give rise to a variety of associations and organizations, both public and private. Socialization, as it is called, is not without its dangers, but it brings with it many advantages for the strengthening and betterment of human qualities and for the protection of human rights.

1882 (2) ***Centesimus annus* 12** The commemoration of *Rerum novarum* would be incomplete unless reference were also made to the situation of the world today. The document lends itself to such a reference, because the historical picture and the prognosis which it suggests have proved to be surprisingly accurate in the light of what has happened since then.

This is especially confirmed by the events which took place near the end of 1989 and at the beginning of 1990. These events, and the radical transformations which followed, can only be explained by the preceding situations which, to a certain extent, crystallized or institutionalized Leo XIII's predictions and the increasingly disturbing signs noted by his successors. Pope Leo foresaw the negative consequences—political, social and economic—of the social order proposed by "socialism," which at that time was still only a social philosophy and not yet a fully structured movement. It may seem surprising that "socialism" appeared at the beginning of the Pope's critique of solutions to the "question of the working class" at a time when "socialism" was not yet in the form of a strong and powerful State, with all the resources which that implies, as was later to happen. However, he correctly judged the danger posed to the masses by the attractive presentation of this simple and radical solution to the "question of the working class" of the time—all the more so when one considers the terrible situation of injustice in which the working classes of the recently industrialized nations found themselves.

Two things must be emphasized here: first, the great clarity in perceiving, in all its harshness, the actual condition of the working class—men, women and children; secondly, equal clarity in recognizing the evil of a solution which, by appearing to reverse the positions of the poor and the rich, was in reality detrimental to the very people whom it was meant to help. The remedy would prove worse than the sickness. By defining the nature of the socialism of his day as the suppression of private property, Leo XIII arrived at the crux of the problem.

His words deserve to be reread attentively: "To remedy these wrongs [the unjust distribution of wealth and the poverty of the workers], the socialists encourage the poor man's envy of the rich and strive to do away with private property, contending that individual possessions should become the common property of all. . . ; but their contentions are so clearly powerless to end the controversy that, were they carried into effect, the working man himself would be among the first to suffer. They are moreover emphatically unjust, for they would rob the lawful possessor, distort the functions of the State, and create utter confusion in the community." The evils caused by the setting up of this type of socialism as a state system—what would later be called "Real Socialism"—could not be better expressed.

Pius XI, encyclical *Quadragesimo anno* 1883

To Our Venerable Brethren, the Patriarchs, Primates, Archbishops, Bishops and other Ordinaries in Peace and Communion with the Holy See, and Likewise to All the Faithful of the Catholic World.

Venerable Brethren and Beloved Children, Health and Apostolic Benediction.

Forty years have passed since Leo XIII's peerless Encyclical, *On the Condition of Workers*, first saw the light, and the whole Catholic world, filled with grateful recollection, is undertaking to commemorate it with befitting solemnity.

Other Encyclicals of Our Predecessor had in a way prepared the path for that outstanding document and proof of pastoral care: namely, those on the family and the Holy Sacrament of Matrimony as the source of human society, on the origin of civil authority and its proper relations with the Church, on the chief duties of Christian citizens, against the tenets of Socialism, against false teachings on human liberty, and others of the same nature fully expressing the mind of Leo XIII. Yet the Encyclical, *On the Condition of Workers*, compared with the rest had this special distinction that at a time when it was most opportune and actually necessary to do so, it laid down for all mankind the surest rules to solve aright that difficult problem of human relations called "the social question."

The Occasion

For toward the close of the nineteenth century, the new kind of economic life that had arisen and the new developments of industry had gone to the point in most countries that human society was clearly becoming divided more and more into two classes. One class, very small in number, was enjoying almost all the advantages which modern inventions so abundantly provided; the other, embracing the huge multitude of working people, oppressed by wretched poverty, was vainly seeking escape from the straits wherein it stood.

Quite agreeable, of course, was this state of things to those who thought it in their abundant riches the result of inevitable economic laws and accordingly, as if it were for charity to veil the violation of justice which lawmakers not only tolerated but at times sanctioned, wanted the whole care of supporting the poor committed to charity alone. The workers, on the other hand, crushed by their hard lot, were barely enduring it and were refusing longer to bend their necks beneath so galling a yoke; and some of them, carried away by the heat of evil counsel, were seeking the overturn of everything, while others, whom Christian training restrained from such evil designs, stood firm in the judgment that much in this had to be wholly and speedily changed.

The same feeling those many Catholics, both priests and laymen, shared, whom a truly wonderful charity had long spurred on to relieve the unmerited poverty of the non-owning workers, and who could in no way convince themselves that so enormous and unjust an inequality in the distribution of this world's goods truly conforms to the designs of the all-wise Creator.

Those men were without question sincerely seeking an immediate remedy for this lamentable disorganization of States and a secure safeguard against worse dangers. Yet such is the weakness of even the best of human minds that, now rejected as dangerous innovators, now hindered in the good work by their very associates advocating other courses of action, and, uncertain in the face of various opinions, they were at a loss which way to turn.

In such a sharp conflict of mind, therefore, while the question at issue was being argued this way and that, nor always with calmness, all eyes as often before turned to the Chair of Peter, to that sacred depository of all truth whence words of salvation pour forth to all the world. And to the feet of Christ's Vicar on earth were flocking in unaccustomed numbers, men well versed in social questions, employers, and workers themselves, begging him with one voice to point out, finally, the safe road to them.

The wise Pontiff long weighed all this in his mind before God; he summoned the most experienced and learned to counsel; he pondered the issues carefully and from every angle. At last, admonished "by the consciousness of His Apostolic Office" lest silence on his part might be regarded as failure in his duty he decided, in virtue of the Divine Teaching Office entrusted to him, to address not only the whole Church of Christ but all mankind.

Therefore on the fifteenth day of May, 1891, that long awaited voice thundered forth; neither daunted by the arduousness of the problem nor weakened by age but with vigorous energy, it taught the whole human family to strike out in the social question upon new paths.

Chief Headings

You know, Venerable Brethren and Beloved Children, and understand full well the wonderful teaching which has made the Encyclical, *On the Condition of Workers*, illustrious forever. The Supreme Pastor in this Letter, grieving that so large a portion of mankind should "live undeservedly in miserable and wretched conditions," took it upon himself with great courage to defend "the cause of the workers whom the present age had handed over, each alone and defenseless, to the inhumanity of employers and the unbridled greed of competitors." He sought no help from either Liberalism or Socialism, for the one had proved that it was utterly unable to solve the social problem aright, and the other, proposing a remedy far worse than the evil itself, would have plunged human society into great dangers.

Since a problem was being treated "for which no satisfactory solution" is found "unless religion and the Church have been called upon to aid," the Pope, clearly exercising his right and correctly holding that the guardianship of religion and the stewardship over those things that are closely bound up with it had been entrusted especially to him and relying solely upon the unchangeable principles drawn from the treasury of right reason and Divine Revelation, confidently and *as one having authority*, declared and proclaimed "the rights and duties within which the rich and the proletariat—those who furnish material things and those who furnish work—ought to be restricted in relation to each other," and what the Church, heads of States and the people themselves directly concerned ought to do.

The Apostolic voice did not thunder forth in vain. On the contrary, not only did the obedient children of the Church hearken to it with marvelling admiration and hail it with the greatest applause, but many also who were wandering far from the truth, from the unity of the faith, and nearly all who since then either in private study or in enacting legislation have concerned themselves with the social and economic question.

Feeling themselves vindicated and defended by the Supreme Authority on earth, Christian workers received this Encyclical with special joy. So, too, did all those noble-hearted men who, long solicitous for the improvement of the condition of the workers, had up to that time encountered almost nothing but indifference from many, and even rankling suspicion, if not open hostility, from some. Rightly, therefore, have all these groups constantly held the Apostolic Encyclical from that time in such high honor that to signify their gratitude they are wont, in various places and in various ways, to commemorate it every year.

However in spite of such great agreement, there were some who were not a little disturbed; and so it happened that the teaching of Leo XIII, so noble and lofty and so utterly new to worldly ears, was held suspect by some, even among Catholics, and to certain ones it even gave offense. For it boldly attacked and overturned the idols of Liberalism, ignored long-standing prejudices, and was in advance of its time beyond all expectation, so that the slow of heart disdained to study this new social philosophy and the timid feared to scale so lofty a height. There were some also who stood, indeed, in awe at its splendor, but regarded it as a kind of imaginary ideal of perfection more desirable than attainable.

Scope of the Present Encyclical

Venerable Brethren and Beloved Children, as all everywhere and especially Catholic workers who are pouring from all sides into this Holy City, are celebrating with such enthusiasm the solemn commemoration of the fortieth anniversary of the Encyclical *On the Condition of Workers*, We deem it fitting on this occasion to recall the great benefits this Encyclical has brought to the Catholic Church and to all human society; to defend the illustrious Master's doctrine on the social and economic question against certain doubts and to develop it more fully as to some points; and lastly, summoning to court the contemporary economic regime and passing judgment on Socialism, to lay bare the root of the existing social confusion and at the same time point the only way to sound restoration: namely, the Christian reform of morals. All these matters which we undertake to treat will fall under three main headings, and this entire Encyclical will be devoted to their development.

I. BENEFITS FROM RERUM NOVARUM

To begin with the topic which we have proposed first to discuss, We cannot refrain, following the counsel of St. Ambrose who says that "no duty is more important than that of returning thanks," from offering our fullest gratitude to Almighty God for the immense benefits that have come through Leo's Encyclical to the Church and to human society. If indeed We should wish to review these benefits even cursorily, almost the whole history of the social question during the last forty years would have to be recalled to mind. These benefits can be reduced conveniently, however, to three main points, corresponding to the three kinds of help which Our Predecessor ardently desired for the accomplishment of his great work of restoration.

1. What the Church Has Done

In the first place Leo himself clearly stated what ought to be expected from the Church: "Manifestly it is the Church which draws from the Gospel the teachings through which the struggle can be composed entirely, or, after its bitterness is removed, can certainly become more tempered. It is the Church, again, that strives not only to instruct the mind, but to regulate by her precepts the life and morals of individuals, and that ameliorates the condition of the workers through her numerous and beneficent institutions."

Doctrinal Matters

The Church did not let these rich fountains lie quiescent in her bosom, but from them drew copiously for the common good of the longed-for peace. Leo himself and his Successors showing paternal charity and pastoral constancy always, in defense especially of the poor and the weak, proclaimed and urged without ceasing again and again by voice and pen the teaching on the social and economic question which *On the Condition of Workers* presented, and adapted it fittingly to the needs of time and of circumstance. And many bishops have done the same, who in their continual and able interpretation of this same teaching have illustrated it with commentaries and in accordance with the mind and instructions of the Holy See provided for its application to the conditions and institutions of diverse regions.

It is not surprising, therefore, that many scholars, both priests and laymen, led especially by the desire that the unchanged and unchangeable teaching of the Church should meet new demands and needs more effectively, have zealously undertaken to develop, with the Church as their guide and teacher, a social and economic science in accord with the conditions of our time.

And so, with Leo's Encyclical pointing the way and furnishing the light, a true Catholic social science has arisen, which is daily fostered and enriched by the tireless efforts of those chosen men whom We have termed auxiliaries of the Church. They do not, indeed, allow their science to lie hidden behind learned walls. As the useful and well attended courses instituted in Catholic universities, colleges, and seminaries, the social congresses and "weeks" that are held at frequent intervals with most successful results, the study groups that are promoted, and finally the timely and sound publications that are disseminated everywhere and in every possible way, clearly show, these men bring their science out into the full light and stress of life.

Nor is the benefit that has poured forth from Leo's Encyclical confined within these bounds; for the teaching which *On the Condition of Workers* contains has gradually and imperceptibly worked its way into the minds of those outside Catholic unity who do not recognize the authority of the Church. Catholic principles on the social question have, as a result, passed little by little into the patrimony of all human society, and We rejoice that the eternal truths which Our Predecessor of glorious memory proclaimed so impressively have been frequently invoked and defended not only in non-Catholic books and journals but in legislative halls and also courts of justice.

Furthermore, after the terrible war, when the statesmen of the leading nations were attempting to restore peace on the basis of a thorough reform of social conditions, did not they, among the norms agreed upon to regulate in accordance with justice and equity the labor of the workers, give sanction to many points that so remarkably coincide with Leo's principles and instructions as to seem consciously taken therefrom? The Encyclical *On the Condition of Workers*, without question, has become a memorable document and rightly to it may be applied the words of Isaias: "He shall set up a standard to the nations."

Practical Applications

Meanwhile, as Leo's teachings were being widely diffused in the minds of men, with learned investigations leading the way, they have come to be put into practice. In the first place, zealous efforts have been made, with active good will, to lift up that class which on account of the modern expansion of industry had increased to enormous numbers but not yet had obtained its rightful place or rank in human society and was, for that reason, all but neglected and despised—the workers, We mean—to whose improvement, to the great advantage of souls, the diocesan and regular clergy, though burdened with other pastoral duties, have under the leadership of the Bishops devoted themselves. This constant work, undertaken to fill the workers' souls with the Christian spirit, helped much also to make them conscious of their true dignity and render them capable, by placing clearly before them the rights and duties of their class, of legitimately and happily advancing and even of becoming leaders of their fellows.

From that time on, fuller means of livelihood have been more securely obtained; for not only did works of beneficence and charity begin to multiply at the urging of the Pontiff, but there have also been established everywhere new and continuously expanding organizations in which workers, draftsmen, farmers and employees of every kind, with the counsel of the Church and frequently under the leadership of her priests, give and receive mutual help and support.

2. What Civil Authority Has Done

With regard to civil authority, Leo XIII, boldly breaking through the confines imposed by Liberalism, fearlessly taught that government must not be thought a mere guardian of law and of good order, but rather must put forth every effort so that "through the entire scheme of laws and institutions . . . both public and individual well-being may develop spontaneously out of the very structure and administration of the State." Just freedom of action must, of course, be left both to individual citizens and to families, yet only on condition that the common good be preserved and wrong to any individual be abolished. The function of the rulers of the State, moreover, is to watch over the community and its parts; but in protecting private individuals in their rights, chief consideration ought to be given to the weak and the poor. "For the nation, as it were, of the rich is guarded by its own defenses and is in less need of governmental protection, whereas the suffering multitude, without the means to protect itself, relies especially on the protection of the State. Wherefore, since wage-workers are numbered among the great mass of the needy, the State must include them under its special care and foresight."

We, of course, do not deny that even before the Encyclical of Leo, some rulers of peoples have provided for certain of the more urgent needs of the workers and curbed more flagrant acts of injustice inflicted upon them. But after the Apostolic voice had sounded from the Chair of Peter throughout the world, rulers of nations, more fully alive at last to their duty, devoted their minds and attention to the task of promoting a more comprehensive and fruitful social policy.

And while the principles of Liberalism were tottering, which had long prevented effective action by those governing the State, the Encyclical *On the Condition of Workers* in truth impelled peoples themselves to promote a social policy on truer grounds and with greater intensity, and so strongly encouraged good Catholics to furnish valuable help to heads of States in this field that they often stood forth as illustrious champions of this new policy even in legislatures. Sacred ministers of the Church, thoroughly imbued with Leo's teaching, have, in fact, often proposed to the votes of the peoples' representatives the very social legislation that has been enacted in recent years and have resolutely demanded and promoted its enforcement.

A new branch of law, wholly unknown to the earlier time, has arisen from this continuous and unwearied labor to protect vigorously the sacred rights of the workers that flow from their dignity as men and as Christians. These laws undertake the protection of life, health, strength, family, homes, workshops, wages and labor hazards, in fine, everything which pertains to the condition of wage workers, with special concern for women and children. Even though these laws do not conform exactly everywhere and in all respects to Leo's recommendations, still it is undeniable that much in them savors of the Encyclical, *On the Condition of Workers*, to which great credit must be given for whatever improvement has been achieved in the workers' condition.

3. What the Concerned Parties Have Done

Finally, the wise Pontiff showed that "employers and workers themselves can accomplish much in this matter, manifestly through those institutions by the help of which the poor are opportunely assisted and the two classes of society are brought closer to each other." First place among these institutions, he declares, must be assigned to associations that embrace either workers alone or workers and employers together. He goes into considerable detail in explaining and commending these associations and expounds with a truly wonderful wisdom their nature, purpose, timeliness, rights, duties, and regulations.

These teachings were issued indeed most opportunely. For at that time in many nations those at the helm of State, plainly imbued with Liberalism, were showing little favor to workers' associations of this type; nay, rather they openly opposed them, and while going out of their way to recognize similar organizations of other classes and show favor to them, they were with criminal injustice denying the natural right to form associations to those who needed it most to defend themselves from ill treatment at the hands of the powerful. There were even some Catholics who looked askance at the efforts of workers to form associations of this type as if they smacked of a socialistic or revolutionary spirit.

Workers' Associations

The rules, therefore, which Leo XIII issued in virtue of his authority, deserve the greatest praise in that they have been able to break down this hostility and dispel these suspicions; but they have even a higher claim to distinction in that they encouraged Christian workers to found mutual associations according to their various occupations, taught them how to do so, and resolutely confirmed in the path of duty a goodly number of those whom socialist organizations strongly attracted by claiming to be the sole defenders and champions of the lowly and oppressed.

With respect to the founding of these societies, the Encyclical *On the Condition of Workers* most fittingly declared that "workers' associations ought to be so constituted and so governed as to furnish the most suitable and most convenient means to attain the object proposed, which consists in this, that the individual members of the association secure, so far as is possible, an increase in the goods of body, of soul, and of property," yet it is clear that "moral and religious perfection ought to be regarded as their principal goal, and that their social organization as such ought above all to be directed completely by this goal." For "when the regulations of associations are founded upon religion, the way is easy toward establishing the mutual relations of the members, so that peaceful living together and prosperity will result."

To the founding of these associations the clergy and many of the laity devoted themselves everywhere with truly praiseworthy zeal, eager to bring Leo's program to full realization. Thus associations of this kind have molded truly Christian workers who, in combining harmoniously the diligent practice of their occupation with the salutary precepts of religion, protect effectively and resolutely their own temporal interests and rights, keeping a due respect for justice and a genuine desire to work together with other classes of society for the Christian renewal of all social life.

These counsels and instructions of Leo XIII were put into effect differently in different places according to varied local conditions. In some places one and the same association undertook to attain all the ends laid down by the Pontiff; in others, because circumstances suggested or required it, a division of work developed and separate associations were formed. Of these, some devoted themselves to the defense of the rights and legitimate interests of their members in the labor market; others took over the work of providing mutual economic aid; finally still others gave all their attention to the fulfillment of religious and moral duties and other obligations of like nature.

This second method has especially been adopted where either the laws of a country, or certain special economic institutions, or that deplorable dissension of minds and hearts so widespread in contemporary society and an urgent necessity of combating with united purpose and strength the massed ranks of revolutionarists, have prevented Catholics from founding purely Catholic labor unions. Under these conditions, Catholics seem almost forced to join secular labor unions. These unions, however, should always profess justice and equity and give Catholic members full freedom to care for their own conscience and obey the laws of the Church. It is clearly the office of bishops, when they know that these associations are on account of circumstances necessary and are not dangerous to religion, to approve of Catholic workers joining them, keeping before their eyes, however, the principles and precautions laid down by Our Predecessor, Pius X of holy memory. Among these precautions the first and chief is this: Side by side with these unions there should always be associations zealously engaged in imbuing and forming their members in the teaching of religion and morality so that they in turn may be able to permeate the unions with that good spirit which should direct them in all their activity. As a result, the religious associations will bear good fruit even beyond the circle of their own membership.

To the Encyclical of Leo, therefore, must be given this credit, that these associations of workers have so flourished everywhere that while, alas, still surpassed in numbers by socialist and communist organizations, they already embrace a vast multitude of workers and are able, within the confines of each nation as well as in wider assemblies, to maintain vigorously the rights and legitimate demands of Catholic workers and insist also on the salutary Christian principles of society.

Associations in Other Classes

Leo's learned treatment and vigorous defense of the natural right to form associations began, furthermore, to find ready application to other associations also and not alone to those of the workers. Hence no small part of the credit must, it seems, be given to this same Encyclical of Leo for the fact that among farmers and others of the middle class most useful associations of this kind are seen flourishing to a notable degree and increasing day by day, as well as other institutions of a similar nature in which spiritual development and economic benefit are happily combined.

Associations of Employers

But if this cannot be said of organizations which Our same Predecessor intensely desired established among employers and managers of industry—and We certainly regret that they are so few—the condition is not wholly due to the will of men but to far graver difficulties that hinder associations of this kind which We know well and estimate at their full value. There is, however, strong hope that these obstacles also will be removed soon, and even now We greet with the deepest joy of Our soul, certain by no means insignificant attempts in this direction, the rich fruits of which promise a still richer harvest in the future.

Conclusion: Rerum Novarum
Magna Charta of the Social Order

All these benefits of Leo's Encyclical, Venerable Brethren and Beloved Children, which We have outlined rather than fully described, are so numerous and of such import as to show plainly that this immortal document does not exhibit a merely fanciful, even if beautiful, ideal of human society. Rather did Our Predecessor draw from the Gospel and, therefore, from an ever-living and life-giving fountain, teachings capable of greatly mitigating, if not immediately terminating that deadly internal struggle which is rending the family of mankind. The rich fruits which the Church of Christ and the whole human race have, by God's favor, reaped therefrom unto salvation prove that some of this good seed, so lavishly sown forty years ago, fell on good ground. On the basis of the long period of experience, it cannot be rash to say that Leo's Encyclical has proved itself the *Magna Charta* upon which all Christian activity in the social field ought to be based, as on a foundation. And those who would seem to hold in little esteem this Papal Encyclical and its commemoration either blaspheme what they know not, or understand nothing of what they are only superficially acquainted with, or if they do understand convict themselves formally of injustice and ingratitude.

Yet since in the course of these same years, certain doubts have arisen concerning either the correct meaning of some parts of Leo's Encyclical or conclusions to be deduced therefrom, which doubts in turn have even among Catholics given rise to controversies that are not always peaceful; and since, furthermore, new needs and changed conditions of our age have made necessary a more precise application of Leo's teaching or even certain additions thereto, We most gladly seize this fitting occasion, in accord with Our Apostolic Office through which We are debtors to all, to answer, so far as in Us lies, these doubts and these demands of the present day.

II. THE AUTHORITY OF THE CHURCH IN SOCIAL AND ECONOMIC MATTERS

Yet before proceeding to explain these matters, that principle which Leo XIII so clearly established must be laid down at the outset here, namely, that there resides in Us the right and duty to pronounce with supreme authority upon social and economic matters. Certainly the Church was not given the commission to guide men to an only fleeting and perishable happiness but to that which is eternal. Indeed "the Church holds that it is unlawful for her to mix without cause in these temporal concerns"; however, she can in no wise renounce the duty God entrusted to her to interpose her authority, not of course in matters of technique for which she is neither suitably equipped nor endowed by office, but in all things that are connected with the moral law. For as to these, the deposit of truth that God committed to Us and the grave duty of disseminating and interpreting the whole moral law, and of urging it in season and out of season, bring under and subject to Our supreme jurisdiction not only social order but economic activities themselves.

Even though economics and moral science employs each its own principles in its own sphere, it is, nevertheless, an error to say that the economic and moral orders are so distinct from and alien to each other that the former depends in no way on the latter. Certainly the laws of economics, as they are termed, being based on the very nature of material things and on the capacities of the human body and mind, determine the limits of what productive human effort cannot, and of what it can attain in the economic field and by what means. Yet it is reason itself that clearly shows, on the basis of the individual and social nature of things and of men, the purpose which God ordained for all economic life.

But it is only the moral law which, just as it commands us to seek our supreme and last end in the whole scheme of our activity, so likewise commands us to seek directly in each kind of activity those purposes which we know that nature, or rather God the Author of nature, established for that kind of action, and in orderly relationship to subordinate such immediate purposes to our supreme and last end. If we faithfully observe this law, then it will follow that the particular purposes, both individual and social, that are sought in the economic field will fall in their proper place in the universal order of purposes, and We, in ascending through them, as it were by steps, shall attain the final end of all things, that is God, to Himself and to us, the supreme and inexhaustible Good.

1. Right of Property

But to come down to particular points, We shall begin with ownership or the right of property. Venerable Brethren and Beloved Children, you know that Our Predecessor of happy memory strongly defended the right of property against the tenets of the Socialists of his time by showing that its abolition would result, not to the advantage of the working class, but to their extreme harm. Yet since there are some who calumniate the Supreme Pontiff, and the Church herself, as if she had taken and were still taking the part of the rich against the non-owning workers—certainly no accusation is more unjust than that—and since Catholics are at variance with one another concerning the true and exact mind of Leo, it has seemed best to vindicate this, that is, the Catholic teaching on this matter from calumnies and safeguard it from false interpretations.

Its Individual and Social Character

First, then, let it be considered as certain and established that neither Leo nor those theologians who have taught under the guidance and authority of the Church have ever denied or questioned the twofold character of ownership, called usually individual or social according as it regards either separate persons or the common good. For they have always unanimously maintained that nature, rather the Creator Himself, has given man the right of private ownership not only that individuals may be able to provide for themselves and their families but also that the goods which the Creator destined for the entire family of mankind may through this institution truly serve this purpose. All this can be achieved in no wise except through the maintenance of a certain and definite order.

Accordingly, twin rocks of shipwreck must be carefully avoided. For, as one is wrecked upon, or comes close to, what is known as "individualism" by denying or minimizing the social and public character of the right of property, so by rejecting or minimizing the private and individual character of this same right, one inevitably runs into "collectivism" or at least closely approaches its tenets. Unless this is kept in mind, one is swept from his course upon the shoals of that moral, juridical, and social modernism which We denounced in the Encyclical issued at the beginning of Our Pontificate. And, in particular, let those realize this who, in their desire for innovation, do not scruple to reproach the Church with infamous calumnies, as if she had allowed to creep into the teachings of her theologians a pagan concept of ownership which must be completely replaced by another that they with amazing ignorance call "Christian."

Obligations of Ownership

In order to place definite limits on the controversies that have arisen over ownership and its inherent duties there must be first laid down as foundation a principle established by Leo XIII: The right of property is distinct from its use. That justice called commutative commands sacred respect for the division of possessions and forbids invasion of others' rights through the exceeding of the limits of one's own property; but the duty of owners to use their property only in a right way does not come under this type of justice, but under other virtues, obligations of which "cannot be enforced by legal action." Therefore, they are in error who assert that ownership and its right use are limited by the same boundaries; and it is much farther still from the truth to hold that a right to property is destroyed or lost by reason of abuse or non-use.

Those, therefore, are doing a work that is truly salutary and worthy of all praise who, while preserving harmony among themselves and the integrity of the traditional teaching of the Church, seek to define the inner nature of these duties and their limits whereby either the right of property itself or its use, that is, the exercise of ownership, is circumscribed by the necessities of social living. On the other hand, those who seek to restrict the individual character of ownership to such a degree that in fact they destroy it are mistaken and in error.

Power of State in Ownership

It follows from what We have termed the individual and at the same time social character of ownership, that men must consider in this matter not only their own advantage but also the common good. To define these duties in detail when necessity requires and the natural law has not done so, is the function of those in charge of the State. Therefore, public authority, under the guiding light always of the natural and divine law, can determine more accurately upon consideration of the true requirements of the common good, what is permitted and what is not permitted to owners in the use of their property. Moreover, Leo XIII wisely taught "that God has left the limits of private possessions to be fixed by the industry of men and institutions of peoples." That history proves ownership, like other elements of social life, to be not absolutely unchanging, We once declared as follows: "What divers forms has property had, from that primitive form among rude and savage peoples, which may be observed in some places even in our time, to the form of possession in the patriarchal age; and so further to the various forms under tyranny (We are using the word tyranny in its classical sense); and then through the feudal and monarchical forms down to the various types which are to be found in more recent times." That the State is not permitted to discharge its duty arbitrarily is, however, clear. The natural right itself both of owning goods privately and of passing them on by inheritance ought always to remain intact and inviolate, since this indeed is a right that the State cannot take away: "For man is older than the State," and also "domestic living together is prior both in thought and in fact to uniting into a polity." Wherefore the wise Pontiff declared that it is grossly unjust for a State to exhaust private wealth through the weight of imposts and taxes. "For since the right of possessing goods privately has been conferred not by man's law, but by nature, public authority cannot abolish it, but can only control its exercise and bring it into conformity with the common weal." Yet when the State brings private ownership into harmony with the needs of the common good, it does not commit a hostile act against private owners but rather does them a friendly service; for it thereby effectively prevents the private possession of goods, which the Author of nature in His most wise providence ordained for the support of human life, from causing intolerable evils and thus rushing to its own destruction; it does not destroy private possessions, but safeguards them; and it does not weaken private property rights, but strengthens them.

Obligations Regarding Superfluous Income

Furthermore, a person's superfluous income, that is, income which he does not need to sustain life fittingly and with dignity, is not left wholly to his own free determination. Rather the Sacred Scriptures and the Fathers of the Church constantly declare in the most explicit language that the rich are bound by a very grave precept to practice almsgiving, beneficence, and munificence.

Expending larger incomes so that opportunity for gainful work may be abundant, provided, however, that this work is applied to producing really useful goods, ought to be considered, as We deduce from the principles of the Angelic Doctor, an outstanding exemplification of the virtue of munificence and one particularly suited to the needs of the times.

Titles in Acquiring Ownership

That ownership is originally acquired both by occupancy of a thing not owned by anyone and by labor, or, as is said, by specification, the tradition of all ages as well as the teaching of Our Predecessor Leo clearly testifies. For, whatever some idly say to the contrary, no injury is done to any person when a thing is occupied that is available to all but belongs to no one; however, only that labor which a man performs in his own name and by virtue of which a new form or increase has been given to a thing grants him title to these fruits.

2. Property ("Capital") and Labor

Far different is the nature of work that is hired out to others and expended on the property of others. To this indeed especially applies what Leo XIII says is "incontestable," namely, that "the wealth of nations originates from no other source than from the labor of workers." For is it not plain that the enormous volume of goods that makes up human wealth is produced by and issues from the hands of the workers that either toil unaided or have their efficiency marvelously increased by being equipped with tools or machines? Every one knows, too, that no nation has ever risen out of want and poverty to a better and nobler condition save by the enormous and combined toil of all the people, both those who manage work and those who carry out directions. But it is no less evident that, had not God the Creator of all things, in keeping with His goodness, first generously bestowed natural riches and resources—the wealth and forces of nature—such supreme efforts would have been idle and vain, indeed could never even have begun. For what else is work but to use or exercise the energies of mind and body on or through these very things? And in the application of natural resources to human use the law of nature, or rather God's will promulgated by it, demands that right order be observed. This order consists in this: that each thing have its proper owner. Hence it follows that unless a man is expending labor on his own property, the labor of one person and the property of another must be associated, for neither can produce anything without the other. Leo XIII certainly had this in mind when he wrote: "Neither capital can do without labor, nor labor without capital." Wherefore it is wholly false to ascribe to property alone or to labor alone whatever has been obtained through the combined effort of both, and it is wholly unjust for either, denying the efficacy of the other, to arrogate to itself whatever has been produced.

Unjust Claims of "Capital"

Property, that is, "capital," has undoubtedly long been able to appropriate too much to itself. Whatever was produced, whatever returns accrued, capital claimed for itself, hardly leaving to the worker enough to restore and renew his strength. For the doctrine was preached that all accumulation of capital falls by an absolutely insuperable economic law to the rich, and that by the same law the workers are given over and bound to perpetual want, to the scantiest of livelihoods. It is true, indeed, that things have not always and everywhere corresponded with this sort of teaching of the so-called Manchesterian Liberals; yet it cannot be denied that economic-social institutions have moved steadily in that direction. That these false ideas, these erroneous suppositions, have been vigorously assailed, and not by those alone who through them were being deprived of their innate right to obtain better conditions, will surprise no one.

Unjust Claims of Labor

And therefore, to the harassed workers there have come "intellectuals," as they are called, setting up in opposition to a fictitious law the equally fictitious moral principle that all products and profits, save only enough to repair and renew capital, belong by very right to the workers. This error, much more specious than that of certain of the Socialists who hold that whatever serves to produce goods ought to be transferred to the State, or, as they say "socialized," is consequently all the more dangerous and the more apt to deceive the unwary. It is an alluring poison which many have eagerly drunk whom open Socialism had not been able to deceive.

Principle of Just Distribution

Unquestionably, so as not to close against themselves the road to justice and peace through these false tenets, both parties ought to have been forewarned by the wise words of Our Predecessor: "However the earth may be apportioned among private owners, it does not cease to serve the common interests of all." This same doctrine We ourselves also taught above in declaring that the division of goods which results from private ownership was established by nature itself in order that created things may serve the needs of mankind in fixed and stable order. Lest one wander from the straight path of truth, this is something that must be continually kept in mind.

But not every distribution among human beings of property and wealth is of a character to attain either completely or to a satisfactory degree of perfection the end which God intends. Therefore, the riches that economic-social developments constantly increase ought to be so distributed among individual persons and classes that the common advantage of all, which Leo XIII had praised, will be safeguarded; in other words, that the common good of all society will be kept inviolate. By this law of social justice, one class is forbidden to exclude the other from sharing in the benefits. Hence the class of the wealthy violates this law no less, when, as if free from care on account of its wealth, it thinks it the right order of things for it to get everything and the worker nothing, than does the non-owning working class when, angered deeply at outraged justice and too ready to assert wrongly the one right it is conscious of, it demands for itself everything as if produced by its own hands, and attacks and seeks to abolish, therefore, all property and returns or incomes, of whatever kind they are or whatever the function they perform in human society, that have not been obtained by labor, and for no other reason save that they are of such a nature. And in this connection We must not pass over the unwarranted and unmerited appeal made by some to the Apostle when he said: "If any man will not work neither let him eat." For the Apostle is passing judgment on those who are unwilling to work, although they can and ought to, and he admonishes us that we ought diligently to use our time and energies of body and mind and not be a burden to others when we can provide for ourselves. But the Apostle in no wise teaches that labor is the sole title to a living or an income.

To each, therefore, must be given his own share of goods, and the distribution of created goods, which, as every discerning person knows, is laboring today under the gravest evils due to the huge disparity between the few exceedingly rich and the unnumbered propertyless, must be effectively called back to and brought into conformity with the norms of the common good, that is, social justice.

3. Redemption of the Non-Owning Workers

The redemption of the non-owning workers—this is the goal that Our Predecessor declared must necessarily be sought. And the point is the more emphatically to be asserted and more insistently repeated because the commands of the Pontiff, salutary as they are, have not infrequently been consigned to oblivion either because they were deliberately suppressed by silence or thought impracticable although they both can and ought to be put into effect. And these commands have not lost their force and wisdom for our time because that "pauperism" which Leo XIII beheld in all its horror is less widespread. Certainly the condition of the workers has been improved and made more equitable especially in the more civilized and wealthy countries where the workers can no longer be considered universally overwhelmed with misery and lacking the necessities of life. But since manufacturing and industry have so rapidly pervaded and occupied countless regions, not only in the countries called new, but also in the realms of the Far East that have been civilized from antiquity, the number of the non-owning working poor has increased enormously and their groans cry to God from the earth. Added to them is the huge army of rural wage workers, pushed to the lowest level of existence and deprived of all hope of ever acquiring "some property in land," and, therefore, permanently bound to the status of non-owning worker unless suitable and effective remedies are applied.

Conditions to Be Overcome by Wage Earner Ownership

Yet while it is true that the status of non-owning worker is to be carefully distinguished from pauperism, nevertheless the immense multitude of the non-owning workers on the one hand and the enormous riches of certain very wealthy men on the other establish an unanswerable argument that the riches which are so abundantly produced in our age of "industrialism," as it is called, are not rightly distributed and equitably made available to the various classes of the people.

Therefore, with all our strength and effort we must strive that at least in the future the abundant fruits of production will accrue equitably to those who are rich and will be distributed in ample sufficiency among the workers—not that these may become remiss in work, for man is born to labor as the bird to fly—but that they may increase their property by thrift, that they may bear, by wise management of this increase in property, the burdens of family life with greater ease and security, and that, emerging from the insecure lot in life in whose uncertainties non-owning workers are cast, they may be able not only to endure the vicissitudes of earthly existence but have also assurance that when their lives are ended they will provide in some measure for those they leave after them.

All these things which Our Predecessor has not only suggested but clearly and openly proclaimed, We emphasize with renewed insistence in our present Encyclical; and unless utmost efforts are made without delay to put them into effect, let no one persuade himself that public order, peace, and the tranquillity of human society can be effectively defended against agitators of revolution.

4. Just Wages and Salaries

As We have already indicated, following in the footsteps of Our Predecessor, it will be impossible to put these principles into practice unless the non-owning workers through industry and thrift advance to the state of possessing some little property. But except from pay for work, from what source can a man who has nothing else but work from which to obtain food and the necessaries of life set anything aside for himself through practicing frugality? Let us, therefore, explaining and developing wherever necessary Leo XIII's teachings and precepts, take up this question of wages and salaries which he called one "of very great importance."

Working for Wages Not Essentially Wrong

First of all, those who declare that a contract of hiring and being hired is unjust of its own nature, and hence a partnership-contract must take its place, are certainly in error and gravely misrepresent Our Predecessor whose Encyclical not only accepts working for wages or salaries but deals at some length with its regulation in accordance with the rules of justice.

We consider it more advisable, however, in the present condition of human society that, so far as is possible, the work-contract be somewhat modified by a partnership-contract, as is already being done in various ways and with no small advantage to workers and owners. Workers and other employees thus become sharers in ownership or management or participate in some fashion in the profits received.

The just amount of pay, however, must be calculated not on a single basis but on several, as Leo XIII already wisely declared in these words: "To establish a rule of pay in accord with justice, many factors must be taken into account."

By this statement he plainly condemned the shallowness of those who think that this most difficult matter is easily solved by the application of a single rule or measure—and one quite false.

For they are greatly in error who do not hesitate to spread the principle that labor is worth and must be paid as much as its products are worth, and that consequently the one who hires out his labor has the right to demand all that is produced through his labor. How far this is from the truth is evident from what We have already explained in treating of property and labor.

Individual and Social Character of Work

It is obvious that, as in the case of ownership, so in the case of work, especially work hired out to others, there is a social aspect also to be considered in addition to the personal or individual aspect. For man's productive effort cannot yield its fruits unless a truly social and organic body exists, unless a social and juridical order watches over the exercise of work, unless the various occupations, being interdependent, cooperate with and mutually complete one another, and, what is still more important, unless mind, material things, and work combine and form as it were a single whole. Therefore, where the social and individual nature of work is neglected, it will be impossible to evaluate work justly and pay it according to justice.

Three Points to Be Considered

Conclusions of the greatest importance follow from this twofold character which nature has impressed on human work, and it is in accordance with these that wages ought to be regulated and established.

a) Support of the worker and his family. In the first place, the worker must be paid a wage sufficient to support him and his family. That the rest of the family should also contribute to the common support, according to the capacity of each, is certainly right, as can be observed especially in the families of farmers, but also in the families of many craftsmen and small shopkeepers. But to abuse the years of childhood and the limited strength of women is grossly wrong. Mothers, concentrating on household duties, should work primarily in the home or in its immediate vicinity. It is an intolerable abuse, and to be abolished at all cost, for mothers on account of the father's low wage to be forced to engage in gainful occupations outside the home to the neglect of their proper cares and duties, especially the training of children. Every effort must therefore be made that fathers of families receive a wage large enough to meet ordinary family needs adequately. But if this cannot always be done under existing circumstances, social justice demands that changes be introduced as soon as possible whereby such a wage will be assured to every adult workingman.

It will not be out of place here to render merited praise to all who, with a wise and useful purpose, have tried and tested various ways of adjusting the pay for work to family burdens in such a way that, as these increase, the former may be raised and indeed, if the contingency arises, there may be enough to meet extraordinary needs.

b) Condition of the business. In determining the amount of the wage, the condition of a business and of the one carrying it on must also be taken into account; for it would be unjust to demand excessive wages which a business cannot stand without its ruin and consequent calamity to the workers. If, however, a business makes too little money, because of lack of energy or lack of initiative or because of indifference to technical and economic progress, that must not be regarded a just reason for reducing the compensation of the workers. But if the business in question is not making enough money to pay the workers an equitable wage because it is being crushed by unjust burdens or forced to sell its product at less than a just price, those who are thus the cause of the injury are guilty of grave wrong, for they deprive workers of their just wage and force them under the pinch of necessity to accept a wage less than fair.

Let, then, both workers and employers strive with united strength and counsel to overcome the difficulties and obstacles and let a wise provision on the part of public authority aid them in so salutary a work. If, however, matters come to an extreme crisis, it must be finally considered whether the business can continue or the workers are to be cared for in some other way. In such a situation, certainly most serious, a feeling of close relationship and a Christian concord of minds ought to prevail and function effectively among employers and workers.

c) Requirements of the common good. Lastly, the amount of the pay must be adjusted to the public economic good. We have shown above how much it helps the common good for workers and other employees, by setting aside some part of their income which remains after necessary expenditures, to attain gradually to the possession of a moderate amount of wealth. But another point, scarcely less important, and especially vital in our times, must not be overlooked: namely, that the opportunity to work be provided to those who are able and willing to work. This opportunity depends largely on the wage and salary rate, which can help as long as it is kept within proper limits, but which on the other hand can be an obstacle if it exceeds these limits. For everyone knows that an excessive lowering of wages, or their increase beyond due measure, causes unemployment. This evil, indeed, especially as we see it prolonged and injuring so many during the years of Our Pontificate, has plunged workers into misery and temptations, ruined the prosperity of nations, and put in jeopardy the public order, peace, and tranquillity of the whole world. Hence it is contrary to social justice when, for the sake of personal gain and without regard for the common good, wages and salaries are excessively lowered or raised; and this same social justice demands that wages and salaries be so managed, through agreement of plans and wills, in so far as can be done, as to offer to the greatest possible number the opportunity of getting work and obtaining suitable means of livelihood.

A right proportion among wages and salaries also contributes directly to the same result; and with this is closely connected a right proportion in the prices at which the goods are sold that are produced by the various occupations, such as agriculture, manufacturing, and others. If all these relations are properly maintained, the various occupations will combine and coalesce into, as it were, a single body and like members of the body mutually aid and complete one another. For then only will the social economy be rightly established and attain its purposes when all and each are supplied with all the goods that the wealth and resources of nature, technical achievement, and the social organization of economic life can furnish. And these goods ought indeed to be enough both to meet the demands of necessity and decent comfort and to advance people to that happier and fuller condition of life which, when it is wisely cared for, is not only no hindrance to virtue but helps it greatly.

5. Reconstruction of the Social Order

What We have thus far stated regarding an equitable distribution of property and regarding just wages concerns individual persons and only indirectly touches social order, to the restoration of which according to the principles of sound philosophy and to its perfection according to the sublime precepts of the law of the Gospel, Our Predecessor, Leo XIII, devoted all his thought and care.

Still, in order that what he so happily initiated may be solidly established, that what remains to be done may be accomplished, and that even more copious and richer benefits may accrue to the family of mankind, two things are especially necessary: reform of institutions and correction of morals.

When we speak of the reform of institutions, the State comes chiefly to mind, not as if universal well-being were to be expected from its activity, but because things have come to such a pass through the evil of what we have termed "individualism" that, following upon the overthrow and near extinction of that rich social life which was once highly developed through associations of various kinds, there remain virtually only individuals and the State. This is to the great harm of the State itself; for, with a structure of social governance lost, and with the taking over of all the burdens which the wrecked associations once bore, the State has been overwhelmed and crushed by almost infinite tasks and duties.

As history abundantly proves, it is true that on account of changed conditions many things which were done by small associations in former times cannot be done now save by large associations. Still, that most weighty principle, which cannot be set aside or changed, remains fixed and unshaken in social philosophy: Just as it is gravely wrong to take from individuals what they can accomplish by their own initiative and industry and give it to the community, so also it is an injustice and at the same time a grave evil and disturbance of right order to assign to a greater and higher association what lesser and subordinate organizations can do. For every social activity ought of its very nature to furnish help to the members of the body social, and never destroy and absorb them.

The supreme authority of the State ought, therefore, to let subordinate groups handle matters and concerns of lesser importance, which would otherwise dissipate its efforts greatly. Thereby the State will more freely, powerfully, and effectively do all those things that belong to it alone because it alone can do them: directing, watching, urging, restraining, as occasion requires and necessity demands. Therefore, those in power should be sure that the more perfectly a graduated order is kept among the various associations, in observance of the principle of "subsidiary function," the stronger social authority and effectiveness will be and the happier and more prosperous the condition of the State.

Mutual Cooperation

First and foremost, the State and every good citizen ought to look to and strive toward this end: that the conflict between the hostile classes be abolished and harmonious cooperation of the Industries and Professions be encouraged and promoted.

The social policy of the State, therefore, must devote itself to the reestablishment of the Industries and Professions. In actual fact, human society now, for the reason that it is founded on classes with divergent aims and hence opposed to one another and therefore inclined to enmity and strife, continues to be in a violent condition and is unstable and uncertain.

Labor, as Our Predecessor explained well in his Encyclical, is not a mere commodity. On the contrary, the worker's human dignity in it must be recognized. It therefore cannot be bought and sold like a commodity. Nevertheless, as the situation now stands, hiring and offering for hire in the so-called labor market separate men into two divisions, as into battle lines, and the contest between these divisions turns the labor market itself almost into a battlefield where, face to face, the opposing lines struggle bitterly. Everyone understands that this grave evil which is plunging all human society to destruction must be remedied as soon as possible. But complete cure will not come until this opposition has been abolished and well-ordered members of the social body—Industries and Professions—are constituted in which men may have their place, not according to the position each has in the labor market but according to the respective social functions which each performs. For under nature's guidance it comes to pass that just as those who are joined together by nearness of habitation establish towns, so those who follow the same industry or profession—whether in the economic or other field—form guilds or associations, so that many are wont to consider these self-governing organizations, if not essential, at least natural to civil society.

Because order, as St. Thomas well explains, is unity a rising from the harmonious arrangement of many objects, a true, genuine social order demands that the various members of a society be united together by some strong bond. This unifying force is present not only in the producing of goods or the rendering of services—in which the employers and employees of an identical Industry or Profession collaborate jointly—but also in that common good, to achieve which all Industries and Professions together ought, each to the best of its ability, to cooperate amicably. And this unity will be the stronger and more effective, the more faithfully individuals and the Industries and Professions themselves strive to do their work and excel in it.

It is easily deduced from what has been said that the interests common to the whole Industry or Profession should hold first place in these guilds. The most important among these interests is to promote the cooperation in the highest degree of each industry and profession for the sake of the common good of the country. Concerning matters, however, in which particular points, involving advantage or detriment to employers or workers, may require special care and protection, the two parties, when these cases arise, can deliberate separately or as the situation requires reach a decision separately.

The teaching of Leo XIII on the form of political government, namely, that men are free to choose whatever form they please, provided that proper regard is had for the requirements of justice and of the common good, is equally applicable in due proportion, it is hardly necessary to say, to the guilds of the various industries and professions.

Moreover, just as inhabitants of a town are wont to found associations with the widest diversity of purposes, which each is quite free to join or not, so those engaged in the same industry or profession will combine with one another into associations equally free for purposes connected in some manner with the pursuit of the calling itself. Since these free associations are clearly and lucidly explained by Our Predecessor of illustrious memory, We consider it enough to emphasize this one point: People are quite free not only to found such associations, which are a matter of private order and private right, but also in respect to them "freely to adopt the organization and the rules which they judge most appropriate to achieve their purpose." The same freedom must be asserted for founding associations that go beyond the boundaries of individual callings. And may these free organizations, now flourishing and rejoicing in their salutary fruits, set before themselves the task of preparing the way, in conformity with the mind of Christian social teaching, for those larger and more important guilds, Industries and Professions, which We mentioned before, and make every possible effort to bring them to realization.

Restoration of Guiding Principles of Economics

Attention must be given also to another matter that is closely connected with the foregoing. Just as the unity of human society cannot be founded on an opposition of classes, so also the right ordering of economic life cannot be left to a free competition of forces. For from this source, as from a poisoned spring, have originated and spread all the errors of individualist economic teaching. Destroying through forgetfulness or ignorance the social and moral character of economic life, it held that economic life must be considered and treated as altogether free from and independent of public authority, because in the market, i.e., in the free struggle of competitors, it would have a principle of self-direction which governs it much more perfectly than would the intervention of any created intellect. But free competition, while justified and certainly useful provided it is kept within certain limits, clearly cannot direct economic life—a truth which the outcome of the application in practice of the tenets of this evil individualistic spirit has more than sufficiently demonstrated. Therefore, it is most necessary that economic life be again subjected to and governed by a true and effective directing principle. This function is one that the economic dictatorship which has recently displaced free competition can still less perform, since it is a headstrong power and a violent energy that, to benefit people, needs to be strongly curbed and wisely ruled. But it cannot curb and rule itself. Loftier and nobler principles—social justice and social charity—must, therefore, be sought whereby this dictatorship may be governed firmly and fully. Hence, the institutions themselves of peoples and, particularly those of all social life, ought to be penetrated with this justice, and it is most necessary that it be truly effective, that is, establish a juridical and social order which will, as it were, give form and shape to all economic life. Social charity, moreover, ought to be as the soul of this order, an order which public authority ought to be ever ready effectively to protect and defend. It will be able to do this the more easily as it rids itself of those burdens which, as We have stated above, are not properly its own.

Furthermore, since the various nations largely depend on one another in economic matters and need one another's help, they should strive with a united purpose and effort to promote by wisely conceived pacts and institutions a prosperous and happy international cooperation in economic life.

If the members of the body social are, as was said, reconstituted, and if the directing principle of economic-social life is restored, it will be possible to say in a certain sense even of this body what the Apostle says of the mystical body of Christ: "The whole body (being closely joined and knit together through every joint of the system according to the functioning in due measure of each single part) derives its increase to the building up of itself in love."

Recently, as all know, there has been inaugurated a special system of syndicates and corporations of the various callings which in view of the theme of this Encyclical it would seem necessary to describe here briefly and comment upon appropriately.

The civil authority itself constitutes the syndicate as a juridical personality in such a manner as to confer on it simultaneously a certain monopoly-privilege, since only such a syndicate, when thus approved, can maintain the rights (according to the type of syndicate) of workers or employers, and since it alone can arrange for the placement of labor and conclude so-termed labor agreements. Anyone is free to join a syndicate or not, and only within these limits can this kind of syndicate be called free; for syndical dues and special assessments are exacted of absolutely all members of every specified calling or profession, whether they are workers or employers; likewise all are bound by the labor agreements made by the legally recognized syndicate. Nevertheless, it has been officially stated that this legally recognized syndicate does not prevent the existence, without legal status, however, of other associations made up of persons following the same calling.

The associations, or corporations, are composed of delegates from the two syndicates (that is, of workers and employers) respectively of the same industry or profession and, as true and proper organs and institutions of the State, they direct the syndicates and coordinate their activities in matters of common interest toward one and the same end.

Strikes and lock-outs are forbidden; if the parties cannot settle their dispute, public authority intervenes.

Anyone who gives even slight attention to the matter will easily see what are the obvious advantages in the system We have thus summarily described: The various classes work together peacefully, socialist organizations and their activities are repressed, and a special magistracy exercises a governing authority. Yet lest We neglect anything in a matter of such great importance and that all points treated may be properly connected with the more general principles which We mentioned above and with those which We intend shortly to add, We are compelled to say that to Our certain knowledge there are not wanting some who fear that the State, instead of confining itself as it ought to the furnishing of necessary and adequate assistance, is substituting itself for free activity; that the new syndical and corporative order savors too much of an involved and political system of administration; and that (in spite of those more general advantages mentioned above, which are of course fully admitted) it rather serves particular political ends than leads to the reconstruction and promotion of a better social order.

To achieve this latter lofty aim, and in particular to promote the common good truly and permanently, We hold it is first and above everything wholly necessary that God bless it and, secondly, that all men of good will work with united effort toward that end. We are further convinced, as a necessary consequence, that this end will be attained the more certainly the larger the number of those ready to contribute toward it their technical, occupational, and social knowledge and experience; and also, what is more important, the greater the contribution made thereto of Catholic principles and their application, not indeed by Catholic Action (which excludes strictly syndical or political activities from its scope) but by those sons of Ours whom Catholic Action imbues with Catholic principles and trains for carrying on an apostolate under the leadership and teaching guidance of the Church—of that Church which in this field also that We have described, as in every other field where moral questions are involved and discussed, can never forget or neglect through indifference its divinely imposed mandate to be vigilant and to teach.

What We have taught about the reconstruction and perfection of social order can surely in no wise be brought to realization without reform of morality, the very record of history clearly shows. For there was a social order once which, although indeed not perfect or in all respects ideal, nevertheless, met in a certain measure the requirements of right reason, considering the conditions and needs of the time. If that order has long since perished, that surely did not happen because the order could not have accommodated itself to changed conditions and needs by development and by a certain expansion, but rather because men, hardened by too much love of self, refused to open the order to the increasing masses as they should have done, or because, deceived by allurements of a false freedom and other errors, they became impatient of every authority and sought to reject every form of control.

There remains to Us, after again calling to judgment the economic system now in force and its most bitter accuser, Socialism, and passing explicit and just sentence upon them, to search out more thoroughly the root of these many evils and to point out that the first and most necessary remedy is a reform of morals.

III. THE GREAT CHANGES SINCE LEO'S TIME

Important indeed have the changes been which both the economic system and Socialism have undergone since Leo XIII's time.

That, in the first place, the whole aspect of economic life is vastly altered, is plain to all. You know, Venerable Brethren and Beloved Children, that the Encyclical of Our Predecessor of happy memory had in view chiefly that economic system, wherein, generally, some provide capital while others provide labor for a joint economic activity. And in a happy phrase he described it thus: "Neither capital can do without labor, nor labor without capital."

1. Changes in Economic Life

With all his energy Leo XIII sought to adjust this economic system according to the norms of right order; hence, it is evident that this system is not to be condemned in itself. And surely it is not of its own nature vicious. But it does violate right order when capital hires workers, that is, the non-owning working class, with a view to and under such terms that it directs business and even the whole economic system according to its own will and advantage, scorning the human dignity of the workers, the social character of economic activity and social justice itself, and the common good.

Even today this is not, it is true, the only economic system in force everywhere; for there is another system also, which still embraces a huge mass of humanity, significant in numbers and importance, as for example, agriculture wherein the greater portion of mankind honorably and honestly procures its livelihood. This group, too, is being crushed with hardships and with difficulties, to which Our Predecessor devotes attention in several places in his Encyclical and which We Ourselves have touched upon more than once in Our present Letter.

But, with the diffusion of modern industry throughout the whole world, the "capitalist" economic regime has spread everywhere to such a degree, particularly since the publication of Leo XIII's Encyclical, that it has invaded and pervaded the economic and social life of even those outside its orbit and is unquestionably impressing on it its advantages, disadvantages and vices, and, in a sense, is giving it its own shape and form.

Accordingly, when directing Our special attention to the changes which the capitalist economic system has undergone since Leo's time, We have in mind the good not only of those who dwell in regions given over to "capital" and industry, but of all mankind.

Domination Has Succeeded Free Competition

In the first place, it is obvious that not only is wealth concentrated in our times but an immense power and despotic economic dictatorship is consolidated in the hands of a few, who often are not owners but only the trustees and managing directors of invested funds which they administer according to their own arbitrary will and pleasure.

This dictatorship is being most forcibly exercised by those who, since they hold the money and completely control it, control credit also and rule the lending of money. Hence they regulate the flow, so to speak, of the life-blood whereby the entire economic system lives, and have so firmly in their grasp the soul, as it were, of economic life that no one can breathe against their will.

This concentration of power and might, the characteristic mark, as it were, of contemporary economic life, is the fruit that the unlimited freedom of struggle among competitors has of its own nature produced, and which lets only the strongest survive; and this is often the same as saying, those who fight the most violently, those who give least heed to their conscience.

This accumulation of might and of power generates in turn three kinds of conflict. First, there is the struggle for economic supremacy itself; then there is the bitter fight to gain supremacy over the State in order to use in economic struggles its resources and authority; finally there is conflict between States themselves, not only because countries employ their power and shape their policies to promote every economic advantage of their citizens, but also because they seek to decide political controversies that arise among nations through the use of their economic supremacy and strength.

Tragic Consequences

The ultimate consequences of the individualist spirit in economic life are those which you yourselves, Venerable Brethren and Beloved Children, see and deplore: Free competition has destroyed itself; economic dictatorship has supplanted the free market; unbridled ambition for power has likewise succeeded greed for gain; all economic life has become tragically hard, inexorable, and cruel. To these are to be added the grave evils that have resulted from an intermingling and shameful confusion of the functions and duties of public authority with those of the economic sphere—such as, one of the worst, the virtual degradation of the majesty of the State, which although it ought to sit on high like a queen and supreme arbitress, free from all partiality and intent upon the one common good and justice, is become a slave, surrendered and delivered to the passions and greed of men. And as to international relations, two different streams have issued from the one fountain-head: On the one hand, economic nationalism or even economic imperialism; on the other, a no less deadly and accursed internationalism of finance or international imperialism whose country is where profit is.

Remedies

In the second part of this Encyclical where We have presented Our teaching, We have described the remedies for these great evils so explicitly that We consider it sufficient at this point to recall them briefly. Since the present system of economy is founded chiefly upon ownership and labor, the principles of right reason, that is, of Christian social philosophy, must be kept in mind regarding ownership and labor and their association together, and must be put into actual practice. First, so as to avoid the reefs of individualism and collectivism, the twofold character, that is individual and social, both of capital or ownership and of work or labor must be given due and rightful weight. Relations of one to the other must be made to conform to the laws of strictest justice—commutative justice, as it is called—with the support, however, of Christian charity. Free competition, kept within definite and due limits, and still more economic dictatorship, must be effectively brought under public authority in these matters which pertain to the latter's function. The public institutions themselves, of peoples, moreover, ought to make all human society conform to the needs of the common good; that is, to the norm of social justice. If this is done, that most important division of social life, namely, economic activity, cannot fail likewise to return to right and sound order.

2. Changes of Socialism

Socialism, against which Our Predecessor, Leo XIII, had especially to inveigh, has since his time changed no less profoundly than the form of economic life. For Socialism, which could then be termed almost a single system and which maintained definite teachings reduced into one body of doctrine, has since then split chiefly into two sections, often opposing each other and even bitterly hostile, without either one however abandoning a position fundamentally contrary to Christian truth that was characteristic of Socialism.

a) The more violent section: Communism. One section of Socialism has undergone almost the same change that the capitalistic economic system, as We have explained above, has undergone. It has sunk into Communism. Communism teaches and seeks two objectives: Unrelenting class warfare and absolute extermination of private ownership. Not secretly or by hidden methods does it do this, but publicly, openly, and by employing every and all means, even the most violent. To achieve these objectives there is nothing which it does not dare, nothing for which it has respect or reverence; and when it has come to power, it is incredible and portent-like in its cruelty and inhumanity. The horrible slaughter and destruction through which it has laid waste vast regions of eastern Europe and Asia are the evidence; how much an enemy and how openly hostile it is to Holy Church and to God Himself is, alas, too well proved by facts and fully known to all. Although We, therefore, deem it superfluous to warn upright and faithful children of the Church regarding the impious and iniquitous character of Communism, yet We cannot without deep sorrow contemplate the heedlessness of those who apparently make light of these impending dangers, and with sluggish inertia allow the widespread propagation of doctrine which seeks by violence and slaughter to destroy society altogether. All the more gravely to be condemned is the folly of those who neglect to remove or change the conditions that inflame the minds of peoples, and pave the way for the overthrow and destruction of society.

b) The more moderate section: Socialism. The other section, which has kept the name Socialism, is surely more moderate. It not only professes the rejection of violence but modifies and tempers to some degree, if it does not reject entirely, the class struggle and the abolition of private ownership. One might say that, terrified by its own principles and by the conclusions drawn therefrom by Communism, Socialism inclines toward and in a certain measure approaches the truths which Christian tradition has always held sacred; for it cannot be denied that its demands at times come very near those that Christian reformers of society justly insist upon.

Class Struggle and Abolition of Ownership Diminished

For if the class struggle abstains from enmities and mutual hatred, it gradually changes into an honest discussion of differences founded on a desire for justice, and if this is not that blessed social peace which we all seek, it can and ought to be the point of departure from which to move forward to the mutual cooperation of the Industries and Professions. So also the war declared on private ownership, more and more abated, is being so restricted that now, finally, not the possession itself of the means of production is attacked but rather a kind of sovereignty over society which ownership has, contrary to all right, seized and usurped. For such sovereignty belongs in reality not to owners but to the public authority. If the foregoing happens, it can come even to the point that imperceptibly these ideas of the more moderate socialism will no longer differ from the desires and demands of those who are striving to remold human society on the basis of Christian principles. For certain kinds of property, it is rightly contended, ought to be reserved to the State since they carry with them a dominating power so great that it cannot without danger to the general welfare be entrusted to private individuals.

Such just demands and desire have nothing in them now which is inconsistent with Christian truth, and much less are they special to Socialism. Those who work solely toward such ends have, therefore, no reason to become socialists.

Is Middle Course Possible?

Yet let no one think that all the socialist groups or factions that are not communist have, without exception, recovered their senses to this extent either in fact or in name. For the most part they do not reject the class struggle or the abolition of ownership, but only in some degree modify them. Now if these false principles are modified and to some extent erased from the program, the question arises, or rather is raised without warrant by some, whether the principles of Christian truth cannot perhaps be also modified to some degree and be tempered so as to meet Socialism half-way and, as it were, by a middle course, come to agreement with it. There are some allured by the foolish hope that socialists in this way will be drawn to us. A vain hope! Those who want to be apostles among socialists ought to profess Christian truth whole and entire, openly and sincerely, and not connive at error in any way. If they truly wish to be heralds of the Gospel, let them above all strive to show to socialists that socialist claims, so far as they are just, are far more strongly supported by the principles of Christian faith and much more effectively promoted through the power of Christian charity.

But what if Socialism has really been so tempered and modified as to the class struggle and private ownership that there is in it no longer anything to be censured on these points? Has it thereby renounced its contradictory nature to the Christian religion? This is the question that holds many minds in suspense. And numerous are the Catholics who, although they clearly understand that Christian principles can never be abandoned or diminished, seem to turn their eyes to the Holy See and earnestly beseech Us to decide whether this form of Socialism has so far recovered from false doctrines that it can be accepted without the sacrifice of any Christian principle and in a certain sense be baptized. That We, in keeping with Our fatherly solicitude, may answer their petitions, We make this pronouncement: Whether considered as a doctrine, or an historical fact, or a movement, Socialism, if it remains truly Socialism, even after it has yielded to truth and justice on the points which we have mentioned, cannot be reconciled with the teachings of the Catholic Church because its concept of society itself is utterly foreign to Christian truth.

Socialist Concept of Society and of Man's Social Character Foreign to Christian Truth

For, according to Christian teaching, man, endowed with a social nature, is placed on this earth so that by leading a life in society and under an authority ordained of God he may fully cultivate and develop all his faculties unto the praise and glory of his Creator; and that by faithfully fulfilling the duties of his craft or other calling he may obtain for himself temporal and at the same time eternal happiness. Socialism, on the other hand, wholly ignoring and indifferent to this sublime end of both man and society, affirms that human association has been instituted for the sake of material advantage alone.

Because of the fact that goods are produced more efficiently by a suitable division of labor than by the scattered efforts of individuals, socialists infer that economic activity, only the material ends of which enter into their thinking, ought of necessity to be carried on socially. Because of this necessity, they hold that men are obliged, with respect to the producing of goods, to surrender and subject themselves entirely to society. Indeed, possession of the greatest possible supply of things that serve the advantages of this life is considered of such great importance that the higher goods of man, liberty not excepted, must take a secondary place and even be sacrificed to the demands of the most efficient production of goods. This damage to human dignity, undergone in the "socialized" process of production, will be easily offset, they say, by the abundance of socially produced goods which will pour out in profusion to individuals to be used freely at their pleasure for comforts and cultural development. Society, therefore, as Socialism conceives it, can on the one hand neither exist nor be thought of without an obviously excessive use of force; on the other hand, it fosters a liberty no less false, since there is no place in it for true social authority, which rests not on temporal and material advantages but descends from God alone, the Creator and last end of all things.

Catholic and Socialist: Contradictory Terms

If Socialism, like all errors, contains some truth (which, moreover, the Supreme Pontiffs have never denied), it is based nevertheless on a theory of human society peculiar to itself and irreconcilable with true Christianity. Religious socialism, Christian socialism, are contradictory terms; no one can be at the same time a good Catholic and a true socialist.

Socialism Pervading Morality and Culture

All these admonitions which have been renewed and confirmed by Our solemn authority must likewise be applied to a certain new kind of socialist activity, hitherto little known but now carried on among many socialist groups. It devotes itself above all to the training of the mind and character. Under the guise of affection it tries in particular to attract children of tender age and win them to itself, although it also embraces the whole population in its scope in order finally to produce true socialists who would shape human society to the tenets of Socialism.

Since in Our Encyclical, *The Christian Education of Youth*, We have fully taught the principles that Christian education insists on and the ends it pursues, the contradiction between these principles and ends and the activities and aims of this socialism that is pervading morality and culture is so clear and evident that no demonstration is required here. But they seem to ignore or underestimate the grave dangers that it carries with it who think it of no importance courageously and zealously to resist them according to the gravity of the situation. It belongs to Our Pastoral Office to warn these persons of the grave and imminent evil: let all remember that Liberalism is the father of this Socialism that is pervading morality and culture and that Bolshevism will be its heir.

Catholic Deserters to Socialism

Accordingly, Venerable Brethren, you can well understand with what great sorrow We observe that not a few of Our sons, in certain regions especially, although We cannot be convinced that they have given up the true faith and right will, have deserted the camp of the Church and gone over to the ranks of Socialism, some to glory openly in the name of socialist and to profess socialist doctrines, others through thoughtlessness or even, almost against their wills to join associations which are socialist by profession or in fact.

In the anxiety of Our paternal solicitude, We give Ourselves to reflection and try to discover how it could happen that they should go so far astray and We seem to hear what many of them answer and plead in excuse: The Church and those proclaiming attachment to the Church favor the rich, neglect the workers and have no concern for them; therefore, to look after themselves they had to join the ranks of socialism.

It is certainly most lamentable, Venerable Brethren, that there have been, nay, that even now there are men who, although professing to be Catholics, are almost completely unmindful of that sublime law of justice and charity that binds us not only to render to everyone what is his but to succor brothers in need as Christ the Lord Himself, and—what is worse—out of greed for gain do not scruple to exploit the workers. Even more, there are men who abuse religion itself, and under its name try to hide their unjust exactions in order to protect themselves from the manifestly just demands of the workers. The conduct of such We shall never cease to censure gravely. For they are the reason why the Church could, even though undeservedly, have the appearance of and be charged with taking the part of the rich and with being quite unmoved by the necessities and hardships of those who have been deprived, as it were, of their natural inheritance. The whole history of the Church plainly demonstrates that such appearances are unfounded and such charges unjust. The Encyclical itself, whose anniversary we are celebrating, is clearest proof that it is the height of injustice to hurl these calumnies and reproaches at the Church and her teaching.

Invitation to Return

Although pained by the injustice and downcast in fatherly sorrow, it is so far from Our thought to repulse or to disown children who have been miserably deceived and have strayed so far from the truth and salvation that We cannot but invite them with all possible solicitude to return to the maternal bosom of the Church. May they lend ready ears to Our voice, may they return whence they have left, to the home that is truly their Father's, and may they stand firm there where their own place is, in the ranks of those who, zealously following the admonitions which Leo promulgated and We have solemnly repeated, are striving to restore society according to the mind of the Church on the firmly established basis of social justice and social charity. And let them be convinced that nowhere, even on earth, can they find full happiness save with Him who, being rich, became poor for our sakes that through His poverty we might become rich, Who was poor and in labors from His youth, Who invited to Himself all that labor and are heavily burdened that He might refresh them fully in the love of His heart, and Who, lastly, without any respect for persons will require more of them to whom more has been given and "will render to everyone according to his conduct."

3. Moral Renovation

Yet, if we look into the matter more carefully and more thoroughly, we shall clearly perceive that, preceding this ardently desired social restoration, there must be a renewal of the Christian spirit, from which so many immersed in economic life have, far and wide, unhappily fallen away, lest all our efforts be wasted and our house be builded not on a rock but on shifting sand.

And so, Venerable Brethren and Beloved Sons, having surveyed the present economic system, We have found it laboring under the gravest of evils. We have also summoned Communism and Socialism again to judgment and have found all their forms, even the most modified, to wander far from the precepts of the Gospel.

"Wherefore," to use the words of Our Predecessor, "if human society is to be healed, only a return to Christian life and institutions will heal it." For this alone can provide effective remedy for that excessive care for passing things that is the origin of all vices; and this alone can draw away men's eyes, fascinated by and wholly fixed on the changing things of the world, and raise them toward Heaven. Who would deny that human society is in most urgent need of this cure now?

Chief Forms of Disorder: Loss of Souls

Minds of all, it is true, are affected almost solely by temporal upheavals, disasters, and calamities. But if we examine things critically with Christian eyes, as we should, what are all these compared with the loss of souls? Yet it is not rash by any means to say that the whole scheme of social and economic life is now such as to put in the way of vast numbers of mankind most serious obstacles which prevent them from caring for the one thing necessary; namely, their eternal salvation.

We, made Shepherd and Protector by the Prince of Shepherds, Who Redeemed them by His Blood, of a truly innumerable flock, cannot hold back Our tears when contemplating this greatest of their dangers. Nay rather, fully mindful of Our pastoral office and with paternal solicitude, We are continually meditating on how We can help them; and We have summoned to Our aid the untiring zeal of others who are concerned on grounds of justice or charity. For what will it profit men to become expert in more wisely using their wealth, even to gaining the whole world, if thereby they suffer the loss of their souls. What will it profit to teach them sound principles of economic life if in unbridled and sordid greed they let themselves be swept away by their passion for property, so that "hearing the commandments of the Lord they do all things contrary."

Causes of This Loss

The root and font of this defection in economic and social life from the Christian law, and of the consequent apostasy of great numbers of workers from the Catholic faith, are the disordered passions of the soul, the sad result of original sin which has so destroyed the wonderful harmony of man's faculties that, easily led astray by his evil desires, he is strongly incited to prefer the passing goods of this world to the lasting goods of Heaven. Hence arises that unquenchable thirst for riches and temporal goods, which has at all times impelled men to break God's laws and trample upon the rights of their neighbors, but which, on account of the present system of economic life, is laying far more numerous snares for human frailty. Since the instability of economic life, and especially of its structure, exacts of those engaged in it most intense and unceasing effort, some have become so hardened to the stings of conscience as to hold that they are allowed, in any manner whatsoever, to increase their profits and use means, fair or foul, to protect their hard-won wealth against sudden changes of fortune. The easy gains that a market unrestricted by any law opens to everybody attracts large numbers to buying and selling goods, and they, their one aim being to make quick profits with the least expenditure of work, raise or lower prices by their uncontrolled business dealings so rapidly according to their own caprice and greed that they nullify the wisest forecasts of producers. The laws passed to promote corporate business, while dividing and limiting the risk of business, have given occasion to the most sordid license. For We observe that consciences are little affected by this reduced obligation of accountability; that furthermore, by hiding under the shelter of a joint name, the worst of injustices and frauds are penetrated; and that, too, directors of business companies, forgetful of their trust, betray the rights of those whose savings they have undertaken to administer. Lastly, We must not omit to mention those crafty men who, wholly unconcerned about any honest usefulness of their work, do not scruple to stimulate the baser human desires and, when they are aroused, use them for their own profit.

Strict and watchful moral restraint enforced vigorously by governmental authority could have banished these enormous evils and even forestalled them; this restraint, however, has too often been sadly lacking. For since the seeds of a new form of economy were bursting forth just when the principles of rationalism had been implanted and rooted in many minds, there quickly developed a body of economic teaching far removed from the true moral law, and, as a result, completely free rein was given to human passions. Thus it came to pass that many, much more than ever before, were solely concerned with increasing their wealth by any means whatsoever, and that in seeking their own selfish interests before everything else they had no conscience about committing even the gravest of crimes against others. Those first entering upon this broad way that leads to destruction easily found numerous imitators of their iniquity by the example of their manifest success, by their insolent display of wealth, by their ridiculing the conscience of others, who, as they said, were troubled by silly scruples, or lastly by crushing more conscientious competitors.

With the rulers of economic life abandoning the right road, it was easy for the rank and file of workers everywhere to rush headlong also into the same chasm; and all the more so, because very many managements treated their workers like mere tools, with no concern at all for their souls, without indeed even the least thought of spiritual things. Truly the mind shudders at the thought of the grave dangers to which the morals of workers (particularly younger workers) and the modesty of girls and women are exposed in modern factories; when we recall how often the present economic scheme, and particularly the shameful housing conditions, create obstacles to the family bond and normal family life; when we remember how many obstacles are put in the way of the proper observance of Sundays and Holy Days; and when we reflect upon the universal weakening of that truly Christian sense through which even rude and unlettered men were wont to value higher things, and upon its substitution by the single preoccupation of getting in any way whatsoever one's daily bread. And thus bodily labor, which Divine Providence decreed to be performed, even after original sin, for the good at once of man's body and soul, is being everywhere changed into an instrument of perversion; for dead matter comes forth from the factory ennobled, while men there are corrupted and degraded.

Remedies

a) Christian Principles of Economics. No genuine cure can be furnished for this lamentable ruin of souls, which, so long as it continues, will frustrate all efforts to regenerate society, unless men return openly and sincerely to the teaching of the Gospel, to the precepts of Him Who alone has the words of everlasting life, words which will never pass away, even if Heaven and earth will pass away. All experts in social problems are seeking eagerly a structure so fashioned in accordance with the norms of reason that it can lead economic life back to sound and right order. But this order, which We Ourselves ardently long for and with all Our efforts promote, will be wholly defective and incomplete unless all the activities of men harmoniously unite to imitate and attain, in so far as it lies within human strength, the marvelous unity of the Divine plan. We mean that perfect order which the Church with great force and power preaches and which right human reason itself demands, that all things be directed to God as the first and supreme end of all created activity, and that all created good under God be considered as mere instruments to be used only in so far as they conduce to the attainment of the supreme end. Nor is it to be thought that gainful occupations are thereby belittled or judged less consonant with human dignity; on the contrary, we are taught to recognize in them with reverence the manifest will of the Divine Creator Who placed man upon the earth to work it and use it in a multitude of ways for his needs. Those who are engaged in producing goods, therefore, are not forbidden to increase their fortune in a just and lawful manner; for it is only fair that he who renders service to the community and makes it richer should also, through the increased wealth of the community, be made richer himself according to his position, provided that all these things be sought with due respect for the laws of God and without impairing the rights of others and that they be employed in accordance with faith and right reason. If these principles are observed by everyone, everywhere, and always, not only the production and acquisition of goods but also the use of wealth, which now is seen to be so often contrary to right order, will be brought back soon within the bounds of equity and just distribution. The sordid love of wealth, which is the shame and great sin of our age, will be opposed in actual fact by the gentle yet effective law of Christian moderation which commands man to seek first the Kingdom of God and His justice, with the assurance that, by virtue of God's kindness and unfailing promise, temporal goods also, in so far as he has need of them, shall be given him besides.

b) Role of charity. But in effecting all this, the law of charity, "which is the bond of perfection," must always take a leading role. How completely deceived, therefore, are those rash reformers who concern themselves with the enforcement of justice alone—and this, commutative justice—and in their pride reject the assistance of charity! Admittedly, no vicarious charity can substitute for justice which is due as an obligation and is wrongfully denied. Yet even supposing that everyone should finally receive all that is due him, the widest field for charity will always remain open. For justice alone can, if faithfully observed, remove the causes of social conflict but can never bring about union of minds and hearts. Indeed all the institutions for the establishment of peace and the promotion of mutual help among men, however perfect these may seem, have the principal foundation of their stability in the mutual bond of minds and hearts whereby the members are united with one another. If this bond is lacking, the best of regulations come to naught, as we have learned by too frequent experience. And so, then only will true cooperation be possible for a single common good when the constituent parts of society deeply feel themselves members of one great family and children of the same Heavenly Father; nay, that they are one body in Christ, "but severally members one of another," so that "if one member suffers anything, all the members suffer with it." For then the rich and others in positions of power will change their former indifference toward their poorer brothers into a solicitous and active love, listen with kindliness to their just demands, and freely forgive their possible mistakes and faults. And the workers, sincerely putting aside every feeling of hatred or envy which the promoters of social conflict so cunningly exploit, will not only accept without rancor the place in human society assigned them by Divine Providence, but rather will hold it in esteem, knowing well that everyone according to his function and duty is toiling usefully and honorably for the common good and is following closely in the footsteps of Him Who, being in the form of God, willed to be a carpenter among men and be known as the son of a carpenter.

Difficult Task

Therefore, out of this new diffusion throughout the world of the spirit of the Gospel, which is the spirit of Christian moderation and universal charity, We are confident there will come that longed-for and full restoration of human society in Christ, and that "Peace of Christ in the Kingdom of Christ," to accomplish which, from the very beginning of Our Pontificate, We firmly determined and resolved within Our heart to devote all Our care and all Our pastoral solicitude, and toward this same highly important and most necessary end now, you also, Venerable Brethren, who with Us rule the Church of God under the mandate of the Holy Ghost, are earnestly toiling with wholly praiseworthy zeal in all parts of the world, even in the regions of the holy missions to the infidels. Let well-merited acclamations of praise be bestowed upon you and at the same time upon all those, both clergy and laity, who We rejoice to see, are daily participating and valiantly helping in this same great work, Our beloved sons engaged in Catholic Action, who with a singular zeal are undertaking with Us the solution of the social problems in so far as by virtue of her divine institution this is proper to and devolves upon the Church. All these We urge in the Lord, again and again, to spare no labors and let no difficulties conquer them, but rather to become day by day more courageous and more valiant. Arduous indeed is the task which We propose to them, for We know well that on both sides, both among the upper and the lower classes of society, there are many obstacles and barriers to be overcome. Let them not, however, lose heart; to face bitter combats is a mark of Christians, and to endure grave labors to the end is a mark of them who, as good soldiers of Christ, follow Him closely.

Relying therefore solely on the all-powerful aid of Him "Who wishes all men to be saved," let us strive with all our strength to help those unhappy souls who have turned from God and, drawing them away from the temporal cares in which they are too deeply immersed, let us teach them to aspire with confidence to the things that are eternal. Sometimes this will be achieved much more easily than seems possible at first sight to expect. For if wonderful spiritual forces lie hidden, like sparks beneath ashes, within the secret recesses of even the most abandoned man—certain proof that his soul is naturally Christian—how much the more in the hearts of those many upon many who have been led into error rather through ignorance or environment.

Moreover, the ranks of the workers themselves are already giving happy and promising signs of a social reconstruction. To Our soul's great joy, We see in these ranks also the massed companies of young workers, who are receiving the counsel of Divine Grace with willing ears and striving with marvelous zeal to gain their comrades for Christ. No less praise must be accorded to the leaders of workers' organizations who, disregarding their own personal advantage and concerned solely about the good of their fellow members, are striving prudently to harmonize the just demands of their members with the prosperity of their whole occupation and also to promote these demands, and who do not let themselves be deterred from so noble a service by any obstacle or suspicion. Also, as anyone may see, many young men, who by reason of their talent or wealth will soon occupy high places among the leaders of society, are studying social problems with deeper interest, and they arouse the joyful hope that they will dedicate themselves wholly to the restoration of society.

Way to Proceed

The present state of affairs, Venerable Brethren, clearly indicates the way in which We ought to proceed. For We are now confronted, as more than once before in the history of the Church, with a world that in large part has almost fallen back into paganism. That these whole classes of men may be brought back to Christ Whom they have denied, we must recruit and train from among them, themselves, auxiliary soldiers of the Church who know them well and their minds and wishes, and can reach their hearts with a tender brotherly love. The first and immediate apostles to the workers ought to be workers; the apostles to those who follow industry and trade ought to be from among them themselves. It is chiefly your duty, Venerable Brethren, and of your clergy, to search diligently for these lay apostles both of workers and of employers, to select them with prudence, and to train and instruct them properly. A difficult task, certainly, is thus imposed on priests, and to meet it, all who are growing up as the hope of the Church, must be duly prepared by an intensive study of the social question. Especially is it necessary that those whom you intend to assign in particular to this work should demonstrate that they are men possessed of the keenest sense of justice, who will resist with true manly courage the dishonest demands or the unjust acts of anyone, who will excel in the prudence and judgment which avoids every extreme, and, above all, who will be deeply permeated by the charity of Christ, which alone has the power to subdue firmly but gently the hearts and wills of men to the laws of justice and equity. Upon this road so often tried by happy experience, there is no reason why we should hesitate to go forward with all speed.

These Our Beloved Sons who are chosen for so great a work, We earnestly exhort in the Lord to give themselves wholly to the training of the men committed to their care, and in the discharge of this eminently priestly and apostolic duty to make proper use of the resources of Christian education by teaching youth, forming Christian organizations, and founding study groups guided by principles in harmony with the Faith. But above all, let them hold in high esteem and assiduously employ for the good of their disciples that most valuable means of both personal and social restoration which, as We taught in Our Encyclical, *Mens Nostra*, is to be found in the Spiritual Exercises. In that Letter We expressly mentioned and warmly recommended not only the Spiritual Exercises for all the laity, but also the highly beneficial Workers' Retreats. For in that school of the spirit, not only are the best of Christians developed but true apostles also are trained for every condition of life and are enkindled with the fire of the heart of Christ. From this school they will go forth as did the Apostles from the Upper Room of Jerusalem, strong in faith, endowed with an invincible steadfastness in persecution, burning with zeal, interested solely in spreading everywhere the Kingdom of Christ.

Certainly there is the greatest need now of such valiant soldiers of Christ who will work with all their strength to keep the human family safe from the dire ruin into which it would be plunged were the teachings of the Gospel to be flouted, and that order of things permitted to prevail which tramples underfoot no less the laws of nature than those of God. The Church of Christ, built upon an unshakable rock, has nothing to fear for herself, as she knows for a certainty that the gates of hell shall never prevail against her. Rather, she knows full well, through the experience of many centuries, that she is wont to come forth from the most violent storms stronger than ever and adorned with new triumphs. Yet her maternal heart cannot but be moved by the countless evils with which so many thousands would be afflicted during storms of this kind, and above all by the consequent enormous injury to spiritual life which would work eternal ruin to so many souls redeemed by the Blood of Jesus Christ.

To ward off such great evils from human society nothing, therefore, is to be left untried; to this end may all our labors turn, to this all our energies, to this our fervent and unremitting prayers to God! For with the assistance of Divine Grace the fate of the human family rests in our hands. Venerable Brethren and Beloved Sons, let us not permit the children of this world to appear wiser in their generation than we who by the Divine Goodness are the children of the light. We find them, indeed, selecting and training with the greatest shrewdness alert and resolute devotees who spread their errors ever wider day by day through all classes of men and in every part of the world. And whenever they undertake to attack the Church of Christ more violently, We see them put aside their internal quarrels, assembling in full harmony in a single battle line with a completely united effort, and work to achieve their common purpose.

Close Union and Cooperation Urged

Surely there is not one that does not know how many and how great are the works that the tireless zeal of Catholics is striving everywhere to carry out, both for social and economic welfare as well as in the fields of education and religion. But this admirable and unremitting activity not infrequently shows less effectiveness because of the dispersion of its energies in too many different directions. Therefore, let all men of good will stand united, all who under the Shepherds of the Church wish to fight this good and peaceful battle of Christ; and under the leadership and teaching guidance of the Church let all strive according to the talent, powers, and position of each to contribute something to the Christian reconstruction of human society which Leo XIII inaugurated through his immortal Encyclical, *On the Condition of Workers*, seeking not themselves and their own interests, but those of Jesus Christ, not trying to press at all costs their own counsels, but ready to sacrifice them, however excellent, if the greater common good should seem to require it, so that in all and above all Christ may reign, Christ may command to Whom be "honor and glory and dominion forever and ever."

That this may happily come to pass, to all of you, Venerable Brethren and Beloved Children, who are members of the vast Catholic family entrusted to Us, but with the especial affection of Our heart to workers and to all others engaged in manual occupations, committed to us more urgently by Divine Providence, and to Christian employers and managements, with paternal love We impart the Apostolic Benediction.

Given at Rome, at Saint Peter's, the fifteenth day of May, in the year 1931, the tenth year of Our Pontificate.

***Centesimus annus* 41** Marxism criticized capitalist bourgeois societies, blaming 1887
them for the commercialization and alienation of human existence. This rebuke is of course based on a mistaken and inadequate idea of alienation, derived solely from the sphere of relationships of production and ownership, that is, giving them a materialistic foundation and moreover denying the legitimacy and positive value of market relationships even in their own sphere. Marxism thus ends up by affirming that only in a collective society can alienation be eliminated. However, the historical experience of socialist countries has sadly demonstrated that collectivism does not do away with alienation but rather increases it, adding to it a lack of basic necessities and economic inefficiency.

The historical experience of the West, for its part, shows that even if the Marxist analysis and its foundation of alienation are false, nevertheless alienation—and the loss of the authentic meaning of life—is a reality in Western societies too. This happens in consumerism, when people are ensnared in a web of false and superficial gratifications rather than being helped to experience their personhood in an authentic and concrete way. Alienation is found also in work, when it is organized so as to ensure maximum returns and profits with no concern whether the worker, through his own labor, grows or diminishes as a person, either through increased sharing in a genuinely supportive community or through increased isolation in a maze of relationships marked by destructive competitiveness and estrangement, in which he is considered only a means and not an end.

The concept of alienation needs to be led back to the Christian vision of reality, by recognizing in alienation a reversal of means and ends. When man does not recognize in himself and in others the value and grandeur of the human person, he effectively deprives himself of the possibility of benefitting from his humanity and of entering into that relationship of solidarity and communion with others for which God created him. Indeed, it is through the free gift of self that man truly finds himself. This gift is made possible by the human person's essential "capacity for transcendence." Man cannot give himself to a purely human plan for reality, to an abstract ideal or to a false utopia. As a person, he can give himself to another person or to other persons, and ultimately to God, who is the author of his being and who alone can fully accept his gift. A man is alienated if he refuses to transcend himself and to live the experience of self-giving and of the formation of an authentic human community oriented towards his final destiny, which is God. A society is alienated if its forms of social organization, production and consumption make it more difficult to offer this gift of self and to establish this solidarity between people.

Exploitation, at least in the forms analyzed and described by Karl Marx, has been overcome in Western society. Alienation, however, has not been overcome as it exists in various forms of exploitation, when people use one another, and when they seek an ever more refined satisfaction of their individual and secondary needs, while ignoring the principal and authentic needs which ought to regulate the manner of satisfying the other ones too. A person who is concerned solely or primarily with possessing and enjoying, who is no longer able to control his instincts and passions, or to subordinate them by obedience to the truth, cannot be free: *obedience to the truth* about God and man is the first condition of freedom, making it possible for a person to order his needs and desires and to choose the means of satisfying them according to a correct scale of values, so that the ownership of things may become an occasion of personal growth for him. This growth can be hindered as a result of manipulation by the means of mass communication, which impose fashions and trends of opinion through carefully orchestrated repetition, without it being possible to subject to critical scrutiny the premises on which these fashions and trends are based.

1888 ***Lumen gentium* 36** Christ, made obedient unto death and because of this exalted by the Father (cf. Ph. 2:8–9), has entered into the glory of his kingdom. All things are subjected to him until he subjects himself and all created things to the Father, so that God may be all in all (cf. 1 Cor. 15:27–28). He communicated this power to the disciples that they be constituted in royal liberty and, by self-abnegation of a holy life, overcome the reign of sin in themselves (cf. Rom. 6:12) that indeed by serving Christ in others they may in humility and patience bring their brethren to that king to serve whom is to reign. The Lord also desires that his kingdom be spread by the lay faithful: the kingdom of truth and life, the kingdom of holiness and grace, the kingdom of justice, love and peace. In this kingdom creation itself will be delivered from the slavery of corruption into the freedom of the glory of the sons of God (cf. Rom. 8:21). Clearly, a great promise, a great commission is given to the disciples: "all things are yours, you are Christ's, and Christ is God's" (1 Cor. 3:23).

The faithful must, then, recognize the inner nature, the value and the ordering of the whole of creation to the praise of God. By their secular activity they help one another achieve greater holiness of life, so that the world may be filled with the spirit of Christ and may the more effectively attain its destiny in justice, in love and in peace. The laity enjoy a principal role in the universal fulfillment of this task. Therefore, by their competence in secular disciplines and by their activity, interiorly raised up by grace, let them work earnestly in order that created goods through human labor, technical skill and civil culture may serve the utility of all men according to the plan of the creator and the light of his word. May these goods be more suitably distributed among all men and in their own way may they be conducive to universal progress in human and Christian liberty. Thus, through the members of the Church, will Christ increasingly illuminate the whole of human society with his saving light.

Moreover, by uniting their forces, let the laity so remedy the institutions and conditions of the world when the latter are an inducement to sin, that these may be conformed to the norms of justice, favoring rather than hindering the practice of virtue. By so doing they will impregnate culture and human works with a moral value. In this way the field of the world is better prepared for the seed of the divine word and the doors of the Church are opened more widely through which the message of peace may enter the world.

Because of the very economy of salvation the faithful should learn to distinguish carefully between the rights and the duties which they have as belonging to the Church and those which fall to them as members of the human society. They will strive to unite the two harmoniously, remembering that in every temporal affair they are to be guided by a Christian conscience, since not even in temporal business may any human activity be withdrawn from God's dominion. In our times it is most necessary that this distinction and harmony should shine forth as clearly as possible in the manner in which the faithful act, in order that the mission of the Church may correspond more fully with the special circumstances of the world today. But just as it must be recognized that the terrestrial city, rightly concerned with secular affairs, is governed by its own principles, thus also the ominous doctrine which seeks to build society with no regard for religion, and attacks and utterly destroys the religious liberty of its citizens, is rightly to be rejected.

(1) ***Centesimus annus* 3** I now wish to propose a "rereading" of Pope Leo's encyclical by issuing an invitation to "look back" at the text itself in order to discover anew the richness of the fundamental principles which it formulated for dealing with the question of the condition of workers. But this is also an invitation to "look around" at the "new things" which surround us and in which we find ourselves caught up, very different from the "new things" which characterized the final decade of the last century. Finally, it is an invitation to "look to the future" at a time when we can already glimpse the third millennium of the Christian era, so filled with uncertainties but also with promises—uncertainties and promises which appeal to our imagination and creativity, and which reawaken our responsibility, as disciples of the "one teacher" (cf. Mt 23:8), to show the way, to proclaim the truth and to communicate the life which is Christ (cf. Jn 14:6). **1896**

A rereading of this kind will not only confirm *the permanent value of such teaching*, but will manifest *the true meaning of the Church's Tradition* which, being ever living and vital, builds upon the foundation laid by our fathers in the faith, and particularly upon what "the Apostles passed down to the Church" in the name of Jesus Christ, who is her irreplaceable foundation (cf. 1 Cor 3:11).

It was out of an awareness of his mission as the successor of Peter that Pope Leo XIII proposed to speak out, and Peter's successor today is moved by that same awareness. Like Pope Leo and the popes before and after him, I take my inspiration from the Gospel image of "the scribe who has been trained for the kingdom of heaven," whom the Lord compares to "a householder who brings out of his treasure what is new and what is old" (Mt 13:52). The treasure is the great outpouring of the Church's Tradition, which contains "what is old"—received and passed on from the very beginning—and which enables us to interpret the "new things" in the midst of which the life of the Church and the world unfolds.

Among the things which become "old" as a result of being incorporated into Tradition, and which offer opportunities and material for enriching both Tradition and the life of faith, there is the fruitful activity of many millions of people, who, spurred on by the social Magisterium, have sought to make that teaching the inspiration for their involvement in the world. Acting either as individuals or joined together in various groups, associations and organizations, these people represent a *great movement for the defense of the human person* and the safeguarding of human dignity. Amid changing historical circumstances, this movement has contributed to the building up of a more just society or at least to the curbing of injustice.

The present encyclical seeks to show the fruitfulness of the principles enunciated by Leo XIII, which belong to the Church's doctrinal patrimony and, as such, involve the exercise of her teaching authority. But pastoral solicitude also prompts me to propose *an analysis of some events of recent history*. It goes without saying that part of the responsibility of pastors is to give careful consideration to current events in order to discern the new requirements of evangelization. However, such an analysis is not meant to pass definitive judgments, since this does not fall *per se* within the Magisterium's specific domain.

(2) ***Centesimus annus* 5** The "new things" to which the Pope devoted his attention were anything but positive. The first paragraph of the encyclical describes in strong terms the "new things" (*rerum novarum*) which gave it its name: "That *the spirit of revolutionary change* which has long been disturbing the nations of the world should have passed beyond the sphere of politics and made its influence felt in the related sphere of practical economics is not surprising. Progress in industry, the development of new trades, the changing relationship between employers and workers, the enormous wealth of a few as opposed to the poverty of the many, the increasing **1896**

self-reliance of the workers and their closer association with each other, as well as a notable decline in morality: all these elements have led to the conflict now taking place."

The Pope and the Church with him were confronted, as was the civil community, by a society which was torn by a conflict all the more harsh and inhumane because it knew no rule or regulation. It was *the conflict between capital and labor*, or—as the encyclical puts it—the worker question. It is precisely about this conflict, in the very pointed terms in which it then appeared, that the Pope did not hesitate to speak.

Here we find the first reflection for our times as suggested by the encyclical. In the face of a conflict which set man against man, almost as if they were "wolves," a conflict between the extremes of mere physical survival on the one side and opulence on the other, the Pope did not hesitate to intervene by virtue of his "apostolic office," that is, on the basis of the mission received from Jesus Christ himself to "feed his lambs and tend his sheep" (cf. Jn 21:15–17), and to "bind and loose" on earth for the kingdom of heaven (cf. Mt 16:19). The Pope's intention was certainly to restore peace, and the present-day reader cannot fail to note his severe condemnation, in no uncertain terms, of the class struggle. However, the Pope was very much aware that *peace is built on the foundation of justice:* what was essential to the encyclical was precisely its proclamation of the fundamental conditions for justice in the economic and social situation of the time.

In this way, Pope Leo XIII, in the footsteps of his predecessors, created a lasting paradigm for the Church. The Church, in fact, has something to say about specific human situations, both individual and communal, national and international. She formulates a genuine doctrine for these situations, a *corpus* which enables her to analyze social realities, to make judgments about them and to indicate directions to be taken for the just resolution of the problems involved.

In Pope Leo XIII's time such a concept of the Church's right and duty was far from being commonly admitted. Indeed, a twofold approach prevailed: one directed to this world and this life, to which faith ought to remain extraneous; the other directed towards a purely other-worldly salvation, which neither enlightens nor directs existence on earth. The Pope's approach in publishing *Rerum Novarum* gave the Church "citizenship status" as it were, amid the changing realities of public life, and this standing would be more fully confirmed later on. In effect, to teach and to spread her social doctrine pertains to the Church's evangelizing mission and is an essential part of the Christian message, since this doctrine points out the direct consequences of that message in the life of society and situates daily work and struggles for justice in the context of bearing witness to Christ the Savior. This doctrine is likewise a source of unity and peace in dealing with the conflicts which inevitably arise in social and economic life. Thus it is possible to meet these new situations without degrading the human person's transcendent dignity, either in oneself or in one's adversaries, and to direct those situations towards just solutions.

Today, at a distance of a hundred years, the validity of this approach affords me the opportunity to contribute to the development of Christian social doctrine. The "new evangelization," which the modern world urgently needs and which I have emphasized many times, must include among its essential elements *a proclamation of the Church's social doctrine.* As in the days of Pope Leo XIII, this doctrine is still suitable for indicating the right way to respond to the great challenges of today, when ideologies are being increasingly discredited. Now, as then, we need to repeat that there can be *no genuine solution of the "social question" apart from the Gospel*, and that the "new things" can find in the Gospel the context for their correct understanding and the proper moral perspective for judgment on them.

(1) Leo XIII, encyclical *Immortale Dei* 1898

To Our Venerable Brethren the Patriarchs, Primates, Archbishops, Bishops, and other Ordinaries in Peace and Communion with the Apostolic See.

The Catholic Church, that imperishable handiwork of our all-merciful God, has for her immediate and natural purpose the saving of souls and securing our happiness in heaven. Yet, in regard to things temporal, she is the source of benefits as manifold and great as if the chief end of her existence were to ensure the prospering of our earthly life. And, indeed, wherever the Church has set her foot she has straightway changed the face of things, and has attempered the moral tone of the people with a new civilization and with virtues before unknown. All nations which have yielded to her sway have become eminent by their gentleness, their sense of justice, and the glory of their high deeds.

And yet a hackneyed reproach of old date is leveled against her, that the Church is opposed to the rightful aims of the civil government, and is wholly unable to afford help in spreading that welfare and progress which justly and naturally are sought after by every well-regulated State. From the very beginning Christians were harassed by slanderous accusations of this nature, and on that account were held up to hatred and execration, for being (so they were called) enemies of the Empire. The Christian religion was moreover commonly charged with being the cause of the calamities that so frequently befell the State, whereas, in very truth, just punishment was being awarded to guilty nations by an avenging God. This odious calumny, with most valid reason, nerved the genius and sharpened the pen of St. Augustine, who, notably in his treatise, *The City of God*, set forth in so bright a light the worth of Christian wisdom in its relation to the public wealth that he seems not merely to have pleaded the cause of the Christians of his day, but to have refuted for all future times impeachments so grossly contrary to truth. The wicked proneness, however, to levy like charges and accusations has not been lulled to rest. Many, indeed, are they who have tried to work out a plan of civil society based on doctrines other than those approved by the Catholic Church. Nay, in these latter days a novel conception of law has begun here and there to gain increase and influence, the outcome, as it is maintained, of an age arrived at full stature, and the result of progressive liberty. But, though endeavors of various kinds have been ventured on, it is clear that no better mode has been devised for the building up and ruling the State than that which is the necessary growth of the teachings of the Gospel. We deem it, therefore, of the highest moment, and a strict duty of Our apostolic office, to contrast with the lessons taught by Christ the novel theories now advanced touching the State. By this means We cherish hope that the bright shining of the truth may scatter the mists of error and doubt, so that one and all may see clearly the imperious law of life which they are bound to follow and obey.

It is not difficult to determine what would be the form and character of the State were it governed according to the principles of Christian philosophy. Man's natural instinct moves him to live in civil society, for he cannot, if dwelling apart, provide himself with the necessary requirements of life, nor procure the means of developing his mental and moral faculties. Hence, it is divinely ordained that he should lead his life—be it family, or civil—with his fellow men, amongst whom alone his several wants can be adequately supplied. But, as no society can hold together unless some one be over all, directing all to strive earnestly for the common good, every body politic must have a ruling authority, and this authority, no less than society itself, has its source in nature, and has, consequently, God for its Author. Hence, it follows that all public power must proceed from God. For God alone is the true and supreme Lord of the world. Everything, without exception, must be subject to Him, and must serve him, so that whosoever holds the right to govern holds it from one sole and single source, namely, God, the sovereign Ruler of all. "There is no power but from God."

The right to rule is not necessarily, however, bound up with any special mode of government. It may take this or that form, provided only that it be of a nature of the government, rulers must ever bear in mind that God is the paramount ruler of the world, and must set Him before themselves as their exemplar and law in the administration of the State. For, in things visible God has fashioned secondary causes, in which His divine action can in some wise be discerned, leading up to the end to which the course of the world is ever tending. In like manner, in civil society, God has always willed that there should be a ruling authority, and that they who are invested with it should reflect the divine power and providence in some measure over the human race.

They, therefore, who rule should rule with evenhanded justice, not as masters, but rather as fathers, for the rule of God over man is most just, and is tempered always with a father's kindness. Government should, moreover, be administered for the well-being of the citizens, because they who govern others possess authority solely for the welfare of the State. Furthermore, the civil power must not be subservient to the advantage of any one individual or of some few persons, inasmuch as it was established for the common good of all. But, if those who are in authority rule unjustly, if they govern overbearingly or arrogantly, and if their measures prove hurtful to the people, they must remember that the Almighty will one day bring them to account, the more strictly in proportion to the sacredness of their office and preeminence of their dignity. "The mighty shall be mightily tormented." Then, truly, will the majesty of the law meet with the dutiful and willing homage of the people, when they are convinced that their rulers hold authority from God, and feel that it is a matter of justice and duty to obey them, and to show them reverence and fealty, united to a love not unlike that which children show their parents. "Let every soul be subject to higher powers." To despise legitimate authority, in whomsoever vested, is unlawful, as a rebellion against the divine will, and whoever resists that, rushes willfully to destruction. "He that resisteth the power resisteth the ordinance of God, and they that resist, purchase to themselves damnation." To cast aside obedience, and by popular violence to incite to revolt, is therefore treason, not against man only, but against God.

As a consequence, the State, constituted as it is, is clearly bound to act up to the manifold and weighty duties linking it to God, by the public profession of religion. Nature and reason, which command every individual devoutly to worship God in holiness, because we belong to Him and must return to Him, since from Him we came, bind also the civil community by a like law. For, men living together in society are under the power of God no less than individuals are, and society, no less than individuals, owes gratitude to God who gave it being and maintains it and whose ever-bounteous goodness enriches it with countless blessings. Since, then, no one is allowed to be remiss in the service due to God, and since the chief duty of all men is to cling to religion in both its teaching and practice—not such religion as they may have a preference for, but the religion which God enjoins, and which certain and most clear marks show to be the only one true religion—it is a public crime to act as though there were no God. So, too, is it a sin for the State not to have care for religion as a something beyond its scope, or as of no practical benefit; or out of many forms of religion to adopt that one which chimes in with the fancy; for we are bound absolutely to worship God in that way which He has shown to be His will. All who rule, therefore, would hold in honor the holy name of God, and one of their chief duties must be to favor religion, to protect it, to shield it under the credit and sanction of the laws, and neither to organize nor enact any measure that may compromise its safety. This is the bounden duty of rulers to the people over whom they rule. For one and all are we destined by our birth and adoption to enjoy, when this frail and fleeting life is ended, a supreme and final good in heaven, and to the attainment of this every endeavor should be directed. Since, then, upon this depends the full and perfect happiness of mankind, the securing of this end should be of all imaginable interests the most urgent. Hence, civil society, established for the common welfare, should not only safeguard the well-being of the community, but have also at heart the interests of its individual members, in such mode as not in any way to hinder, but in every manner to render as easy as may be, the possession of that highest and unchangeable good for which all should seek. Wherefore, for this purpose, care must especially be taken to preserve unharmed and unimpeded the religion whereof the practice is the link connecting man with God.

Now, it cannot be difficult to find out which is the true religion, if only it be sought with an earnest and unbiased mind; for proofs are abundant and striking. We have, for example, the fulfillment of prophecies, miracles in great numbers, the rapid spread of the faith in the midst of enemies and in face of overwhelming obstacles, the witness of the martyrs, and the like. From all these it is evident that the only true religion is the one established by Jesus Christ Himself, and which He committed to His Church to protect and to propagate.

For the only-begotten Son of God established on earth a society which is called the Church, and to it He handed over the exalted and divine office which He had received from His Father, to be continued through the ages to come. "As the Father hath sent Me, I also send you." "Behold I am with you all days, even to the consummation of the world." Consequently, as Jesus Christ came into the world that men "might have life and have it more abundantly," so also has the Church for its aim and end the eternal salvation of souls, and hence it is so constituted as to open wide its arms to all mankind, unhampered by any limit of either time or place. "Preach ye the Gospel to every creature."

Over this mighty multitude God has Himself set rulers with power to govern, and He has willed that one should be the head of all, and the chief and unerring teacher of truth, to whom He has given "the keys of the kingdom of heaven." "Feed My lambs, feed My sheep." "I have prayed for thee that thy faith fail not."

This society is made up of men, just as civil society is, and yet is supernatural and spiritual, on account of the end for which it was founded, and of the means by which it aims at attaining that end. Hence, it is distinguished and differs from civil society, and, what is of highest moment, it is a society chartered as of right divine, perfect in its nature and in its title, to possess in itself and by itself, through the will and loving kindness of its Founder, all needful provision for its maintenance and action. And just as the end at which the Church aims is by far the noblest of ends, so is its authority the most exalted of all authority, nor can it be looked upon as inferior to the civil power, or in any manner dependent upon it.

In very truth, Jesus Christ gave to His Apostles unrestrained authority in regard to things sacred, together with the genuine and most true power of making laws, as also with the twofold right of judging and of punishing, which flow from that power. "All power is given to Me in heaven and on earth: going therefore teach all nations . . . teaching them to observe all things whatsoever I have commanded you." And in another place: "If he will not hear them, tell the Church." And again: "In readiness to revenge all disobedience." And once more: "That . . . I may not deal more severely according to the power which the Lord hath given me, unto edification and not unto destruction." Hence, it is the Church, and not the State, that is to be man's guide to heaven. It is to the Church that God has assigned the charge of seeing to, and legislating for, all that concerns religion; of teaching all nations; of spreading the Christian faith as widely as possible; in short, of administering freely and without hindrance, in accordance with her own judgment, all matters that fall within its competence.

Now, this authority, perfect in itself, and plainly meant to be unfettered, so long assailed by a philosophy that truckles to the State, the Church has never ceased to claim for herself and openly to exercise. The Apostles themselves were the first to uphold it, when, being forbidden by the rulers of the synagogue to preach the Gospel, they courageously answered: "We must obey God rather than men." This same authority the holy Fathers of the Church were always careful to maintain by weighty arguments, according as occasion arose, and the Roman Pontiffs have never shrunk from defending it with unbending constancy. Nay, more, princes and all invested with power to rule have themselves approved it, in theory alike and in practice. It cannot be called in question that in the making of treaties, in the transaction of business matters, in the sending and receiving [of] ambassadors, and in the interchange of other kinds of official dealings they have been wont to treat with the Church as with a supreme and legitimate power. And, assuredly, all ought to hold that it was not without a singular disposition of God's providence that this power of the Church was provided with a civil sovereignty as the surest safeguard of her independence.

The Almighty, therefore, has given the charge of the human race to two powers, the ecclesiastical and the civil, the one being set over divine, and the other over human, things. Each in its kind is supreme, each has fixed limits within which it is contained, limits which are defined by the nature and special object of the province of each, so that there is, we may say, an orbit traced out within which the action of each is brought into play by its own native right. But, inasmuch as each of these two powers has authority over the same subjects, and as it might come to pass that one and the same thing—related differently, but still remaining one and the same thing—might belong to the jurisdiction and determination of both, therefore God, who foresees all things, and who is the author of these two powers, has marked out the course of each in right correlation to the other. "For the powers that are, are ordained of God." Were this not so, deplorable contentions and conflicts would often arise, and, not infrequently, men, like travelers at the meeting of two roads, would hesitate in anxiety and doubt, not knowing what course to follow. Two powers would be commanding contrary things, and it would be a dereliction of duty to disobey either of the two.

But it would be most repugnant to them to think thus of the wisdom and goodness of God. Even in physical things, albeit of a lower order, the Almighty has so combined the forces and springs of nature with tempered action and wondrous harmony that no one of them clashes with any other, and all of them most fitly and aptly work together for the great purpose of the universe. There must, accordingly, exist between these two powers a certain orderly connection, which may be compared to the union of the soul and body in man. The nature and scope of that connection can be determined only, as We have laid down, by having regard to the nature of each power, and by taking account of the relative excellence and nobleness of their purpose. One of the two has for its proximate and chief object the well-being of this mortal life; the other, the everlasting joys of heaven. Whatever, therefore, in things human is of a sacred character, whatever belongs either of its own nature or by reason of the end to which it is referred, to the salvation of souls, or to the worship of God, is subject to the power and judgment of the Church. Whatever is to be ranged under the civil and political order is rightly subject to the civil authority. Jesus Christ has Himself given command that what is Caesar's is to be rendered to Caesar, and that what belongs to God is to be rendered to God.

There are, nevertheless, occasions when another method of concord is available for the sake of peace and liberty: We mean when rulers of the State and the Roman Pontiff come to an understanding touching some special matter. At such times the Church gives signal proof of her motherly love by showing the greatest possible kindliness and indulgence.

Such, then, as We have briefly pointed out, is the Christian organization of civil society; not rashly or fancifully shaped out, but educed from the highest and truest principles, confirmed by natural reason itself.

In such organization of the State there is nothing that can be thought to infringe upon the dignity of rulers, and nothing unbecoming them; nay, so far from degrading the sovereign power in its due rights, it adds to it permanence and luster. Indeed, when more fully pondered, this mutual co-ordination has a perfection in which all other forms of government are lacking, and from which excellent results would flow, were the several component parts to keep their place and duly discharge the office and work appointed respectively for each. And, doubtless, in the constitution of the State such as We have described, divine and human things are equitably shared; the rights of citizens assured to them, and fenced round by divine, by natural, and by human law; the duties incumbent on each one being wisely marked out, and their fulfillment fittingly insured. In their uncertain and toilsome journey to the everlasting city all see that they have safe guides and helpers on their way, and are conscious that others have charge to protect their persons alike and their possessions, and to obtain or preserve for them everything essential for their present life. Furthermore, domestic society acquires that firmness and solidity so needful to it from the holiness of marriage, one and indissoluble, wherein the rights and duties of husband and wife are controlled with wise justice and equity; due honor is assured to the woman; the authority of the husband is conformed to the pattern afforded by the authority of God; the power of the father is tempered by a due regard for the dignity of the mother and her offspring; and the best possible provision is made for the guardianship, welfare, and education of the children.

In political affairs, and all matters civil, the laws aim at securing the common good, and are not framed according to the delusive caprices and opinions of the mass of the people, but by truth and by justice; the ruling powers are invested with a sacredness more than human, and are withheld from deviating from the path of duty, and from overstepping the bounds of rightful authority; and the obedience is not the servitude of man to man, but submission to the will of God, exercising His sovereignty through the medium of men. Now, this being recognized as undeniable, it is felt that the high office of rulers should be held in respect; that public authority should be constantly and faithfully obeyed; that no act of sedition should be committed; and that the civic order of the commonwealth should be maintained as sacred.

So, also, as to the duties of each one toward his fellow men, mutual forbearance, kindliness, generosity are placed in the ascendant; the man who is at once a citizen and a Christian is not drawn aside by conflicting obligations; and, lastly, the abundant benefits with which the Christian religion, of its very nature, endows even the mortal life of man are acquired for the community and civil society. And this to such an extent that it may be said in sober truth: "The condition of the commonwealth depends on the religion with which God is worshiped; and between one and the other there exists an intimate and abiding connection."

Admirably, according to his wont, does St. Augustine, in many passages, enlarge upon the nature of these advantages; but nowhere more markedly and to the point than when he addresses the Catholic Church in the following words: "Thou dost teach and train children with much tenderness, young men with much vigor, old men with much gentleness; as the age not of the body alone, but of the mind of each requires. Women thou dost subject to their husbands in chaste and faithful obedience, not for the gratifying of their lust, but for bringing forth children, and for having a share in the family concerns. Thou dost set husbands over their wives, not that they may play false to the weaker sex, but according to the requirements of sincere affection. Thou dost subject children to their parents in a kind of free service, and dost establish parents over their children with a benign rule. . . . Thou joinest together, not in society only, but in a sort of brotherhood, citizen with citizen, nation with nation, and the whole race of men, by reminding them of their common parentage. Thou teachest kings to look to the interests of their people, and dost admonish the people to be submissive to their kings. With all care dost thou teach all to whom honor is due, and affection, and reverence, and fear, consolation, and admonition and exhortation, and discipline, and reproach, and punishment. Thou showest that all these are not equally incumbent on all, but that charity is owing to all, and wrongdoing to none." And in another place, blaming the false wisdom of certain time-serving philosophers, he observes: "Let those who say that the teaching of Christ is hurtful to the State produce such armies as the maxims of Jesus have enjoined soldiers to bring into being; such governors of provinces; such husbands and wives; such parents and children; such masters and servants; such kings; such judges, and such payers and collectors of tribute, as the Christian teaching instructs them to become, and then let them dare to say that such teaching is hurtful to the State. Nay, rather will they hesitate to own that this discipline, if duly acted up to, is the very mainstay of the commonwealth."

There was once a time when States were governed by the philosophy of the Gospel. Then it was that the power and divine virtue of Christian wisdom had diffused itself throughout the laws, institutions, and morals of the people, permeating all ranks and relations of civil society. Then, too, the religion instituted by Jesus Christ, established firmly in befitting dignity, flourished everywhere, by the favor of princes and the legitimate protection of magistrates; and Church and State were happily united in concord and friendly interchange of good offices. The State, constituted in this wise, bore fruits important beyond all expectation, whose remembrance is still, and always will be, in renown, witnessed to as they are by countless proofs which can never be blotted out or ever obscured by any craft of any enemies. Christian Europe has subdued barbarous nations, and changed them from a savage to a civilized condition, from superstition to true worship. It victoriously rolled back the tide of Mohammedan conquest; retained the headship of civilization; stood forth in the front rank as the leader and teacher of all, in every branch of national culture; bestowed on the world the gift of true and many-sided liberty; and most wisely founded very numerous institutions for the solace of human suffering. And if we inquire how it was able to bring about so altered a condition of things, the answer is—beyond all question, in large measure, through religion, under whose auspices so many great undertakings were set on foot, through whose aid they were brought to completion.

A similar state of things would certainly have continued had the agreement of the two powers been lasting. More important results even might have been justly looked for, had obedience waited upon the authority, teaching, and counsels of the Church, and had this submission been specially marked by greater and more unswerving loyalty. For that should be regarded in the light of an ever-changeless law which Ivo of Chartres wrote to Pope Paschal II: "When kingdom and priesthood are at one, in complete accord, the world is well ruled, and the Church flourishes, and brings forth abundant fruit. But when they are at variance, not only smaller interests prosper not, but even things of greatest moment fall into deplorable decay."

But that harmful and deplorable passion for innovation which was aroused in the sixteenth century threw first of all into confusion the Christian religion, and next, by natural sequence, invaded the precincts of philosophy, whence it spread amongst all classes of society. From this source, as from a fountain-head, burst forth all those later tenets of unbridled license which, in the midst of the terrible upheavals of the last century, were wildly conceived and boldly proclaimed as the principles and foundation of that new conception of law which was not merely previously unknown, but was at variance on many points with not only the Christian, but even the natural law.

Amongst these principles the main one lays down that as all men are alike by race and nature, so in like manner all are equal in the control of their life; that each one is so far his own master as to be in no sense under the rule of any other individual; that each is free to think on every subject just as he may choose, and to do whatever he may like to do; that no man has any right to rule over other men. In a society grounded upon such maxims all government is nothing more nor less than the will of the people, and the people, being under the power of itself alone, is alone its own ruler. It does choose, nevertheless, some to whose charge it may commit itself, but in such wise that it makes over to them not the right so much as the business of governing, to be exercised, however, in its name.

The authority of God is passed over in silence, just as if there were no God; or as if He cared nothing for human society; or as if men, whether in their individual capacity or bound together in social relations, owed nothing to God; or as if there could be a government of which the whole origin and power and authority did not reside in God Himself. Thus, as is evident, a State becomes nothing but a multitude which is its own master and ruler. And since the people is declared to contain within itself the spring-head of all rights and of all power, it follows that the State does not consider itself bound by any kind of duty toward God. Moreover, it believes that it is not obliged to make public profession of any religion; or to inquire which of the very many religions is the only one true; or to prefer one religion to all the rest; or to show to any form of religion special favor; but, on the contrary, is bound to grant equal rights to every creed, so that public order may not be disturbed by any particular form of religious belief.

And it is a part of this theory that all questions that concern religion are to be referred to private judgment; that every one is to be free to follow whatever religion he prefers, or none at all if he disapprove of all. From this the following consequences logically flow: that the judgment of each one's conscience is independent of all law; that the most unrestrained opinions may be openly expressed as to the practice or omission of divine worship; and that every one has unbounded license to think whatever he chooses and to publish abroad whatever he thinks.

Now, when the State rests on foundations like those just named—and for the time being they are greatly in favor—it readily appears into what and how unrightful a position the Church is driven. For, when the management of public business is in harmony with doctrines of such a kind, the Catholic religion is allowed a standing in civil society equal only, or inferior, to societies alien from it; no regard is paid to the laws of the Church, and she who, by the order and commission of Jesus Christ, has the duty of teaching all nations, finds herself forbidden to take any part in the instruction of the people. With reference to matters that are of twofold jurisdiction, they who administer the civil power lay down the law at their own will, and in matters that appertain to religion defiantly put aside the most sacred decrees of the Church. They claim jurisdiction over the marriages of Catholics, even over the bond as well as the unity and the indissolubility of matrimony. They lay hands on the goods of the clergy, contending that the Church cannot possess property. Lastly, they treat the Church with such arrogance that, rejecting entirely her title to the nature and rights of a perfect society, they hold that she differs in no respect from other societies in the State, and for this reason possesses no right nor any legal power of action, save that which she holds by the concession and favor of the government. If in any State the Church retains her own agreement publicly entered into by the two powers, men forthwith begin to cry out that matters affecting the Church must be separated from those of the State.

Their object in uttering this cry is to be able to violate unpunished their plighted faith, and in all things to have unchecked control. And as the Church, unable to abandon her chiefest and most sacred duties, cannot patiently put up with this, and asks that the pledge given to her be fully and scrupulously acted up to, contentions frequently arise between the ecclesiastical and the civil power, of which the issue commonly is that the weaker power yields to the one which is stronger in human resources.

Accordingly, it has become the practice and determination under this condition of public polity (now so much admired by many) either to forbid the action of the Church altogether, or to keep her in check and bondage to the State. Public enactments are in great measure framed with this design. The drawing up of laws, the administration of State affairs, the godless education of youth, the spoliation and suppression of religious orders, the overthrow of the temporal power of the Roman Pontiff, all alike aim to this one end—to paralyze the action of Christian institutions, to cramp to the utmost the freedom of the Catholic Church, and to curtail her every single prerogative.

Now, natural reason itself proves convincingly that such concepts of the government of a State are wholly at variance with the truth. Nature itself bears witness that all power, of every kind, has its origin from God, who is its chief and most august source.

The sovereignty of the people, however, and this without any reference to God, is held to reside in the multitude; which is doubtless a doctrine exceedingly well calculated to flatter and to inflame many passions, but which lacks all reasonable proof, and all power of insuring public safety and preserving order. Indeed, from the prevalence of this teaching, things have come to such a pass that many hold as an axiom of civil jurisprudence that seditions may be rightfully fostered. For the opinion prevails that princes are nothing more than delegates chosen to carry out the will of the people; whence it necessarily follows that all things are as changeable as the will of the people, so that risk of public disturbance is ever hanging over our heads.

To hold, therefore, that there is no difference in matters of religion between forms that are unlike each other, and even contrary to each other, most clearly leads in the end to the rejection of all religion in both theory and practice. And this is the same thing as atheism, however it may differ from it in name. Men who really believe in the existence of God must, in order to be consistent with themselves and to avoid absurd conclusions, understand that differing modes of divine worship involving dissimilarity and conflict even on most important points cannot all be equally probable, equally good, and equally acceptable to God.

So, too, the liberty of thinking, and of publishing, whatsoever each one likes, without any hindrance, is not in itself an advantage over which society can wisely rejoice. On the contrary, it is the fountain-head and origin of many evils. Liberty is a power perfecting man, and hence should have truth and goodness for its object. But the character of goodness and truth cannot be changed at option. These remain ever one and the same, and are no less unchangeable than nature itself. If the mind assents to false opinions, and the will chooses and follows after what is wrong, neither can attain its native fullness, but both must fall from their native dignity into an abyss of corruption. Whatever, therefore, is opposed to virtue and truth may not rightly be brought temptingly before the eye of man, much less sanctioned by the favor and protection of the law. A well-spent life is the only way to heaven, whither all are bound, and on this account the State is acting against the laws and dictates of nature whenever it permits the license of opinion and of action to lead minds astray from truth and souls away from the practice of virtue. To exclude the Church, founded by God Himself, from life, from laws, from the education of youth, from domestic society is a grave and fatal error. A State from which religion is banished can never be well regulated; and already perhaps more than is desirable is known of the nature and tendency of the so-called *civil* philosophy of life and morals. The Church of Christ is the true and sole teacher of virtue and guardian of morals. She it is who preserves in their purity the principles from which duties flow, and, by setting forth most urgent reasons for virtuous life, bids us not only to turn away from wicked deeds, but even to curb all movements of the mind that are opposed to reason, even though they be not carried out in action.

To wish the Church to be subject to the civil power in the exercise of her duty is a great folly and a sheer injustice. Whenever this is the case, order is disturbed, for things natural are put above things supernatural; the many benefits which the Church, if free to act, would confer on society are either prevented or at least lessened in number; and a way is prepared for enmities and contentions between the two powers, with how evil result to both the issue of events has taught us only too frequently.

Doctrines such as these, which cannot be approved by human reason, and most seriously affect the whole civil order, Our predecessors the Roman Pontiffs (well aware of what their apostolic office required of them) have never allowed to pass uncondemned. Thus, Gregory XVI in his encyclical letter *Mirari Vos*, dated August 15, 1832, inveighed with weighty words against the sophisms which even at his time were being publicly inculcated—namely, that no preference should be shown for any particular form of worship; that it is right for individuals to form their own personal judgments about religion; that each man's conscience is his sole and all-sufficing guide; and that it is lawful for every man to publish his own views, whatever they may be, and even to conspire against the State. On the question of the separation of Church and State the same Pontiff writes as follows: "Nor can We hope for happier results either for religion or for the civil government from the wishes of those who desire that the Church be separated from the State, and the concord between the secular and ecclesiastical authority be dissolved. It is clear that these men, who yearn for a shameless liberty, live in dread of an agreement which has always been fraught with good, and advantageous alike to sacred and civil interests." To the like effect, also, as occasion presented itself, did Pius IX brand publicly many false opinions which were gaining ground, and afterwards ordered them to be condensed in summary form in order that in this sea of error Catholics might have a light which they might safely follow.

From these pronouncements of the Popes it is evident that the origin of public power is to be sought for in God Himself, and not in the multitude, and that it is repugnant to reason to allow free scope for sedition. Again, that it is not lawful for the State, any more than for the individual, either to disregard all religious duties or to hold in equal favor different kinds of religion; that the unrestrained freedom of thinking and of openly making known one's thoughts is not inherent in the rights of citizens, and is by no means to be reckoned worthy of favor and support. In like manner it is to be understood that the Church no less than the State itself is a society perfect in its own nature and its own right, and that those who exercise sovereignty ought not so to act as to compel the Church to become subservient or subject to them, or to hamper her liberty in the management of her own affairs, or to despoil her in any way of the other privileges conferred upon her by Jesus Christ. In matters, however, of mixed jurisdiction, it is in the highest degree consonant to nature, as also to the designs of God, that so far from one of the powers separating itself from the other, or still less coming into conflict with it, complete harmony, such as is suited to the end for which each power exists, should be preserved between them.

This, then, is the teaching of the Catholic Church concerning the constitution and government of the State. By the words and decrees just cited, if judged dispassionately, no one of the several forms of government is in itself condemned, inasmuch as none of them contains anything contrary to Catholic doctrine, and all of them are capable, if wisely and justly managed, to insure the welfare of the State. Neither is it blameworthy in itself, in any manner, for the people to have a share greater or less, in the government: for at certain times, and under certain laws, such participation may not only be of benefit to the citizens, but may even be of obligation. Nor is there any reason why any one should accuse the Church of being wanting in gentleness of action or largeness of view, or of being opposed to real and lawful liberty. The Church, indeed, deems it unlawful to place the various forms of divine worship on the same footing as the true religion, but does not, on that account, condemn those rulers who, for the sake of securing some great good or of hindering some great evil, allow patiently custom or usage to be a kind of sanction for each kind of religion having its place in the State. And, in fact, the Church is wont to take earnest heed that no one shall be forced to embrace the Catholic faith against his will, for, as St. Augustine wisely reminds us, "Man cannot believe otherwise than of his own will."

In the same way the Church cannot approve of that liberty which begets a contempt of the most sacred laws of God, and casts off the obedience due to lawful authority, for this is not liberty so much as license, and is most correctly styled by St. Augustine the "liberty of self-ruin," and by the Apostle St. Peter the "cloak of malice." Indeed, since it is opposed to reason, it is a true slavery, "for whosoever committeth sin is the slave of sin." On the other hand, that liberty is truly genuine, and to be sought after, which in regard to the individual does not allow men to be the slaves of error and of passion, the worst of all masters; which, too, in public administration guides the citizens in wisdom and provides for them increased means of well-being; and which, further, protects the State from foreign interference.

This honorable liberty, alone worthy of human beings, the Church approves most highly and has never slackened her endeavor to preserve, strong and unchanged, among nations. And, in truth, whatever in the State is of chief avail for the common welfare; whatever has been usefully established to curb the license of rulers who are opposed to the true interests of the people, or to keep in check the leading authorities from unwarrantably interfering in municipal or family affairs; whatever tends to uphold the honor, manhood, and equal rights of individual citizens—of all these things, as the monuments of past ages bear witness, the Catholic Church has always been the originator, the promoter, or the guardian. Ever, therefore, consistent with herself, while on the one hand she rejects that exorbitant liberty which in individuals and in nations ends in license or in thraldom, on the other hand, she willingly and most gladly welcomes whatever improvements the age brings forth, if these really secure the prosperity of life here below, which is, as it were, a stage in the journey to the life that will know no ending.

Therefore, when it is said that the Church is hostile to modern political regimes and that she repudiates the discoveries of modern research, the charge is a ridiculous and groundless calumny. Wild opinions she does repudiate, wicked and seditious projects she does condemn, together with that attitude of mind which points to the beginning of a willful departure from God. But, as all truth must necessarily proceed from God, the Church recognizes in all truth that is reached by research a trace of the divine intelligence. And as all truth in the natural order is powerless to destroy belief in the teachings of revelation, but can do much to confirm it, and as every newly discovered truth may serve to further the knowledge or the praise of God, it follows that whatsoever spreads the range of knowledge will always be willingly and even joyfully welcomed by the Church. She will always encourage and promote, as she does in other branches of knowledge, all study occupied with the investigation of nature. In these pursuits, should the human intellect discover anything not known before, the Church makes no opposition. She never objects to search being made for things that minister to the refinements and comforts of life. So far, indeed, from opposing these she is now, as she ever has been, hostile alone to indolence and sloth, and earnestly wishes that the talents of men may bear more and more abundant fruit by cultivation and exercise. Moreover, she gives encouragement to every kind of art and handicraft, and through her influence, directing all strivings after progress toward virtue and salvation, she labors to prevent man's intellect and industry from turning him away from God and from heavenly things.

All this, though so reasonable and full of counsel, finds little favor nowadays when States not only refuse to conform to the rules of Christian wisdom, but seem even anxious to recede from them further and further on each successive day. Nevertheless, since truth when brought to light is wont, of its own nature, to spread itself far and wide, and gradually take possession of the minds of men, We, moved by the great and holy duty of Our apostolic mission to all nations, speak, as We are bound to do, with freedom. Our eyes are not closed to the spirit of the times. We repudiate not the assured and useful improvements of our age, but devoutly wish affairs of State to take a safer course than they are now taking, and to rest on a more firm foundation without injury to the true freedom of the people; for the best parent and guardian of liberty amongst men is truth. "The truth shall make you free."

If in the difficult times in which Our lot is cast, Catholics will give ear to Us, as it behooves them to do, they will readily see what are the duties of each one in matters of opinion as well as action. As regards opinion, whatever the Roman Pontiffs have hitherto taught, or shall hereafter teach, must be held with a firm grasp of mind, and, so often as occasion requires, must be openly professed.

Especially with reference to the so-called "liberties" which are so greatly coveted in these days, all must stand by the judgment of the apostolic see, and have the same mind. Let no man be deceived by the honest outward appearance of these liberties, but let each one reflect whence these have had their origin, and by what efforts they are everywhere upheld and promoted. Experience has made Us well acquainted with their results to the State, since everywhere they have borne fruits which the good and wise bitterly deplore. If there really exist anywhere, or if we in imagination conceive, a State, waging wanton and tyrannical war against Christianity, and if we compare with it the modern form of government just described, this latter may seem the more endurable of the two. Yet, undoubtedly, the principles on which such a government is grounded are, as We have said, of a nature which no one can approve.

Secondly, action may relate to private and domestic matters, or to matters public. As to private affairs, the first duty is to conform life and conduct to the gospel precepts, and to refuse to shrink from this duty when Christian virtue demands some sacrifice slightly more difficult to make. All, moreover, are bound to love the Church as their common mother, to obey her laws, promote her honor, defend her rights, and to endeavor to make her respected and loved by those over whom they have authority. It is also of great moment to the public welfare to take a prudent part in the business of municipal administration, and to endeavor above all to introduce effectual measures, so that, as becomes a Christian people, public provision may be made for the instruction of youth in religion and true morality. Upon these things the well-being of every State greatly depends.

Furthermore, it is in general fitting and salutary that Catholics should extend their efforts beyond this restricted sphere, and give their attention to national politics. We say "in general" because these Our precepts are addressed to all nations. However, it may in some places be true that, for most urgent and just reasons, it is by no means expedient for Catholics to engage in public affairs or to take an active part in politics. Nevertheless, as We have laid down, to take no share in public matters would be as wrong as to have no concern for, or to bestow no labor upon, the common good, and the more so because Catholics are admonished, by the very doctrines which they profess, to be upright and faithful in the discharge of duty, while, if they hold aloof, men whose principles offer but small guarantee for the welfare of the State will the more readily seize the reins of government. This would tend also to the injury of the Christian religion, forasmuch as those would come into power who are badly disposed toward the Church, and those who are willing to befriend her would be deprived of all influence.

It follows clearly, therefore, that Catholics have just reasons for taking part in the conduct of public affairs. For in so doing they assume not nor should they assume the responsibility of approving what is blameworthy in the actual methods of government, but seek to turn these very methods, so far as is possible, to the genuine and true public good, and to use their best endeavors at the same time to infuse, as it were, into all the veins of the State the healthy sap and blood of Christian wisdom and virtue. The morals and ambitions of the heathens differed widely from those of the Gospel, yet Christians were to be seen living undefiled everywhere in the midst of pagan superstition, and, while always true to themselves, coming to the front boldly wherever an opening was presented. Models of loyalty to their rulers, submissive, so far as was permitted, to the sovereign power, they shed around them on every side a halo of sanctity; they strove to be helpful to their brethren, and to attract others to the wisdom of Jesus Christ, yet were bravely ready to withdraw from public life, nay, even to lay down their life, if they could not without loss of virtue retain honors, dignities, and offices. For this reason, Christian ways and manners speedily found their way not only into private houses but into the camp, the senate, and even into the imperial palaces. "We are but of yesterday," wrote Tertullian, "yet we swarm in all your institutions, we crowd your cities, islands, villages, towns, assemblies, the army itself, your wards and corporations, the palace, the senate, and the law courts." So that the Christian faith, when once it became lawful to make public profession of the Gospel, appeared in most of the cities of Europe, not like an infant crying in its cradle, but already grown up and full of vigor.

In these Our days it is well to revive these examples of Our forefathers. First and foremost, it is the duty of all Catholics worthy of the name and wishful to be known as most loving children of the Church, to reject without swerving whatever is inconsistent with so fair a title; to make use of popular institutions, so far as can honestly be done, for the advancement of truth and righteousness; to strive that liberty of action shall not transgress the bounds marked out by nature and the law of God; to endeavor to bring back all civil society to the pattern and form of Christianity which We have described. It is barely possible to lay down any fixed method by which such purposes are to be attained, because the means adopted must suit places and times widely differing from one another. Nevertheless, above all things, unity of aim must be preserved, and similarity must be sought after in all plans of action. Both these objects will be carried into effect without fail if all will follow the guidance of the apostolic see as their rule of life and obey the bishops whom the Holy Spirit has placed to rule the Church of God. The defense of Catholicism, indeed, necessarily demands that in the profession of doctrines taught by the Church all shall be of one mind and all steadfast in believing; and care must be taken never to connive, in any way, at false opinions, never to withstand them less strenuously than truth allows. In mere matters of opinion it is permissible to discuss things with moderation, with a desire of searching into the truth, without unjust suspicion or angry recriminations.

Hence, lest concord be broken by rash charges, let this be understood by all, that the integrity of Catholic faith cannot be reconciled with opinions verging on naturalism or rationalism, the essence of which is utterly to do away with Christian institutions and to install in society the supremacy of man to the exclusion of God. Further, it is unlawful to follow one line of conduct in private life and another in public, respecting privately the authority of the Church, but publicly rejecting it; for this would amount to joining together good and evil, and to putting man in conflict with himself; whereas he ought always to be consistent, and never in the least point nor in any condition of life to swerve from Christian virtue.

But in matters merely political, as, for instance, the best form of government, and this or that system of administration, a difference of opinion is lawful. Those, therefore, whose piety is in other respects known, and whose minds are ready to accept in all obedience the decrees of the apostolic see, cannot in justice be accounted as bad men because they disagree as to subjects We have mentioned; and still graver wrong will be done them, if—as We have more than once perceived with regret—they are accused of violating, or of wavering in, the Catholic faith.

Let this be well borne in mind by all who are in the habit of publishing their opinions, and above all by journalists. In the endeavor to secure interests of the highest order there is no room for intestine strife or party rivalries; since all should aim with one mind and purpose to make safe that which is the common object of all—the maintenance of religion and of the State. If, therefore, there have hitherto been dissensions, let them henceforth be gladly buried in oblivion. If rash or injurious acts have been committed, whoever may have been at fault, let mutual charity make amends, and let the past be redeemed by a special submission of all to the apostolic see. In this way Catholics will attain two most excellent results: they will become helpers to the Church in preserving and propagating Christian wisdom, and they will confer the greatest benefit on civil society, the safety of which is exceedingly imperiled by evil teachings and bad passions.

This, venerable brethren, is what We have thought it Our duty to expound to all nations of the Catholic world touching the Christian constitution of States and the duties of individual citizens. It behooves Us now with earnest prayer to implore the protection of heaven, beseeching God, who alone can enlighten the minds of men and move their will, to bring about those happy ends for which We yearn and strive, for His greater glory and the general salvation of mankind. As a happy augury of the divine benefits, and in token of Our paternal benevolence, to you, venerable brothers, and to the clergy and to the whole people committed to your charge and vigilance, We grant lovingly in the Lord the apostolic benediction.

Given at St. Peter's in Rome, the first day of November, 1885, the seventh year of Our pontificate.

(2) Leo XIII, encyclical *Diuturnum illud* 1898

To the Patriarchs, Primates, Archbishops, and Bishops of the Catholic world in Grace and Communion with the Apostolic See.

The long-continued and most bitter war waged against the divine authority of the Church has reached the culmination to which it was tending, the common danger, namely, of human society and especially of the civil power on which the public safety chiefly reposes. In our own times most particularly this result is apparent. For popular passions now reject, with more boldness than formerly, every restraint of authority. So great is the license on all sides, so frequent are seditions and tumults, that not only is obedience often refused to those who rule states, but a sufficiently safe guarantee of security does not seem to have been left to them.

For a long time, indeed, pains have been taken to render rulers the object of contempt and hatred to the multitude. The flames of envy thus excited have at last burst forth, and attempts have been several times made, at very short intervals, on the life of sovereign princes, either by secret plots or by open attacks. The whole of Europe was lately filled with horror at the horrible murder of a most powerful emperor. Whilst the minds of men are still filled with astonishment at the magnitude of the crime, abandoned men do not fear publicly to utter threats and intimidations against other European princes.

These perils to commonwealth, which are before Our eyes, fill Us with grave anxiety, when We behold the security of rulers and the tranquility of empires, together with the safety of nations, put in peril almost from hour to hour. Nevertheless, the divine power of the Christian religion has given birth to excellent principles of stability and order for the State, while at the same time it has penetrated into the customs and institutions of States. And of this power not the least nor last fruit is a just and wise proportion of mutual rights and duties in both princes and peoples. For in the precepts and example of Christ our Lord there is a wonderful force for restraining in their duty as much those who obey as those who rule; and for keeping between them that agreement which is most according to nature, and that concord of wills, so to speak, from which arises a course of administration tranquil and free from all disturbance. Wherefore, being, by the favor of God, entrusted with the government of the Catholic Church, and made guardian and interpreter of the doctrines of Christ, We judge that it belongs to Our jurisdiction, venerable brethren, publicly to set forth what Catholic truth demands of every one in this sphere of duty; thus making clear also by what way and by what means measures may be taken for the public safety in so critical a state of affairs.

Although man, when excited by a certain arrogance and contumacy, has often striven to cast aside the reins of authority, he has never yet been able to arrive at the state of obeying no one. In every association and community of men, necessity itself compels that some should hold pre-eminence, lest society, deprived of a prince or head by which it is ruled should come to dissolution and be prevented from attaining the end for which it was created and instituted. But, if it was not possible that political power should be removed from the midst of states, it is certain that men have used every art to take away its influence and to lessen its majesty, as was especially the case in the sixteenth century, when a fatal novelty of opinions infatuated many. Since that epoch, not only has the multitude striven after a liberty greater than is just, but it has seen fit to fashion the origin and construction of the civil society of men in accordance with its own will.

Indeed, very many men of more recent times, walking in the footsteps of those who in a former age assumed to themselves the name of philosophers, say that all power comes from the people; so that those who exercise it in the State do so not as their own, but as delegated to them by the people, and that, by this rule, it can be revoked by the will of the very people by whom it was delegated. But from these, Catholics dissent, who affirm that the right to rule is from God, as from a natural and necessary principle.

It is of importance, however, to remark in this place that those who may be placed over the State may in certain cases be chosen by the will and decision of the multitude, without opposition to or impugning of the Catholic doctrine. And by this choice, in truth, the ruler is designated, but the rights of ruling are not thereby conferred. Nor is the authority delegated to him, but the person by whom it is to be exercised is determined upon.

There is no question here respecting forms of government, for there is no reason why the Church should not approve of the chief power being held by one man or by more, provided only it be just, and that it tend to the common advantage. Wherefore, so long as justice be respected, the people are not hindered from choosing for themselves that form of government which suits best either their own disposition, or the institutions and customs of their ancestors.

But, as regards political power, the Church rightly teaches that it comes from God, for it finds this clearly testified in the sacred Scriptures and in the monuments of antiquity; besides, no other doctrine can be conceived which is more agreeable to reason, or more in accord with the safety of both princes and peoples.

In truth, that the source of human power is in God the books of the Old Testament in very many places clearly establish. "By me kings reign . . . by me princes rule, and the mighty decree justice." And in another place: "Give ear you that rule the people . . . for power is given you of the Lord and strength by the Most High." The same thing is contained in the Book of Ecclesiasticus: "Over every nation he hath set a ruler." These things, however, which they had learned of God, men were little by little untaught through heathen superstition, which even as it has corrupted the true aspect and often the very concept of things, so also it has corrupted the natural form and beauty of the chief power. Afterwards, when the Christian Gospel shed its light, vanity yielded to truth, and that noble and divine principle whence all authority flows began to shine forth. To the Roman governor, ostentatiously pretending that he had the power of releasing and of condemning, our Lord Jesus Christ answered: "Thou shouldst not have any power against me unless it were given thee from above." And St. Augustine, in explaining this passage, says: "Let us learn what He said, which also He taught by His Apostle, that there is no power but from God." The faithful voice of the Apostles, as an echo, repeats the doctrine and precepts of Jesus Christ. The teaching of Paul to the Romans, when subject to the authority of heathen princes, is lofty and full of gravity: "There is not power but from God," from which, as from its cause, he draws this conclusion: "The prince is the minister of God."

The Fathers of the Church have taken great care to proclaim and propagate this very doctrine in which they had been instructed. "We do not attribute," says St. Augustine, "the power of giving government and empires to any but the true God." On the same passage St. John Chrysostom says: "That there are kingdoms, and that some rule, while others are subject, and that none of these things is brought about by accident or rashly . . . is, I say, a work of divine wisdom." The same truth is testified by St. Gregory the Great, saying: "We confess that power is given from above to emperors and kings." Verily the holy doctors have undertaken to illustrate also the same precepts by the natural light of reason in such a way that they must appear to be altogether right and true, even to those who follow reason for their sole guide.

And, indeed, nature, or rather God who is the Author of nature, wills that man should live in a civil society; and this is clearly shown both by the faculty of language, the greatest medium of intercourse, and by numerous innate desires of the mind, and the many necessary things, and things of great importance, which men isolated cannot procure, but which they can procure when joined and associated with others. But now, a society can neither exist nor be conceived in which there is no one to govern the wills of individuals, in such a way as to make, as it were, one will out of many, and to impel them rightly and orderly to the common good; therefore, God has willed that in a civil society there should be some to rule the multitude. And this also is a powerful argument, that those by whose authority the State is administered must be able so to compel the citizens to obedience that it is clearly a sin in the latter not to obey. But no man has in himself or of himself the power of constraining the free will of others by fetters of authority of this kind. This power resides solely in God, the Creator and Legislator of all things; and it is necessary that those who exercise it should do it as having received it from God. "There is one lawgiver and judge, who is able to destroy and deliver." And this is clearly seen in every kind of power. That that which resides in priests comes from God is so acknowledged that among all nations they are recognized as, and called, the ministers of God. In like manner, the authority of fathers of families preserves a certain impressed image and form of the authority which is in God, "of whom all paternity in heaven and earth is named." But in this way different kinds of authority have between them wonderful resemblances, since, whatever there is of government and authority, its origin is derived from one and the same Creator and Lord of the world, who is God.

Those who believe civil society to have risen from the free consent of men, looking for the origin of its authority from the same source, say that each individual has given up something of his right, and that voluntarily every person has put himself into the power of the one man in whose person the whole of those rights has been centered. But it is a great error not to see, what is manifest, that men, as they are not a nomad race, have been created, without their own free will, for a natural community of life. It is plain, moreover, that the pact which they allege is openly a falsehood and a fiction, and that it has no authority to confer on political power such great force, dignity, and firmness as the safety of the State and the common good of the citizens require. Then only will the government have all those ornaments and guarantees, when it is understood to emanate from God as its august and most sacred source.

And it is impossible that any should be found not only more true but even more advantageous than this opinion. For the authority of the rulers of a State, if it be a certain communication of divine power, will by that very reason immediately acquire a dignity greater than human—not, indeed, that impious and most absurd dignity sometimes desired by heathen emperors when affecting divine honors, but a true and solid one received by a certain divine gift and benefaction. Whence it will behoove citizens to submit themselves and to be obedient to rulers, as to God, not so much through fear of punishment as through respect for their majesty; nor for the sake of pleasing, but through conscience, as doing their duty. And by this means authority will remain far more firmly seated in its place. For the citizens, perceiving the force of this duty, would necessarily avoid dishonesty and contumacy, because they must be persuaded that they who resist State authority resist the divine will; that they who refuse honor to rulers refuse it to God Himself.

This doctrine the Apostle Paul particularly inculcated on the Romans; to whom he wrote with so great authority and weight on the reverence to be entertained toward the higher powers, that it seems nothing could be prescribed more weightily: "Let every soul be subject to higher powers, for there is no power but from God, and those that are, are ordained of God. Therefore he that resisteth the power resisteth the ordinance of God, and they that resist purchase to themselves damnation . . . wherefore be subject of necessity, not only for wrath, but also for conscience' sake." And in agreement with this is the celebrated declaration of Peter, the Prince of the Apostles, on the same subject: "Be ye subject, therefore, to every human creature for God's sake; whether it be to the king as excelling, or to governors, as sent by him for the punishment of evildoers, and for the praise of the good, for so is the will of God."

The one only reason which men have for not obeying is when anything is demanded of them which is openly repugnant to the natural or the divine law, for it is equally unlawful to command to do anything in which the law of nature or the will of God is violated. If, therefore, it should happen to any one to be compelled to prefer one or the other, viz., to disregard either the commands of God or those of rulers, he must obey Jesus Christ, who commands us to "give to Caesar the things that are Caesar's, and to God the things that are God's," and must reply courageously after the example of the Apostles: "We ought to obey God rather than men." And yet there is no reason why those who so behave themselves should be accused of refusing obedience; for, if the will of rulers is opposed to the will and the laws of God, they themselves exceed the bounds of their own power and pervert justice; nor can their authority then be valid, which, when there is no justice, is null.

But in order that justice may be retained in government it is of the highest importance that those who rule States should understand that political power was not created for the advantage of any private individual; and that the administration of the State must be carried on to the profit of those who have been committed to their care, not to the profit of those to whom it has been committed. Let princes take example from the Most High God, by whom authority is given to them; and, placing before themselves His model in governing the State, let them rule over the people with equity and faithfulness, and let them add to that severity, which is necessary, a paternal charity. On this account they are warned in the oracles of the sacred Scriptures, that they will have themselves some day to render an account to the King of kings and Lord of lords; if they shall fail in their duty, that it will not be possible for them in any way to escape the severity of God: "The Most High will examine your work and search out your thoughts: because being ministers of his kingdom you have not judged rightly. . . . Horribly and speedily will he appear to you, for a most severe judgment shall be for them that bear rule. . . . For God will not accept any man's person, neither will he stand in awe of any man's greatness; for he made the little and the great, and he hath equally care of all. But a greater punishment is ready for the more mighty."

And if these precepts protect the State, all cause or desire for seditions is removed; the honor and security of rulers, the quiet and well-being of societies will be secure. The dignity also of the citizen is best provided for; for to them it has been permitted to retain even in obedience that greatness which conduces to the excellence of man. For they understand that, in the judgment of God, there is neither slave nor free man; that there is one Lord of all, rich "to all that call upon Him," but that they on this account submit to and obey their rulers, because these in a certain sort bring before them the image of God, "whom to serve is to reign."

But the Church has always so acted that the Christian form of civil government may not dwell in the minds of men, but that it may be exhibited also in the life and habits of nations. As long as there were at the helm of the States pagan emperors, who were prevented by superstition from rising to that form of imperial government which We have sketched, she studied how to instill into the minds of subjects, immediately on their embracing the Christian institutions, the teaching that they must be desirous of bringing their lives into conformity with them. Therefore, the pastors of souls, after the example of the Apostle Paul, were accustomed to teach the people with the utmost care and diligence "to be subject to princes and powers, to obey at a word," and to pray God for all men and particularly "for kings and all that are in a high station: for this is good and acceptable in the sight of God our Savior." And the Christians of old left the most striking proofs of this; for, when they were harassed in a very unjust and cruel way by pagan emperors, they nevertheless at no time omitted to conduct themselves obediently and submissively, so that, in fact, they seemed to vie with each other: those in cruelty, and these in obedience.

This great modesty, this fixed determination to obey, was so well known that it could not be obscured by the calumny and malice of enemies. On this account, those who were going to plead in public before the emperors for any persons bearing the

Christian name proved by this argument especially that it was unjust to enact laws against the Christians because they were in the sight of all men exemplary in their bearing according to the laws. Athenagoras thus confidently addresses Marcus Aurelius Antoninus and Lucius Aurelius Commodus, his son: "You allow us, who commit no evil, yea, who demean ourselves the most piously and justly of all toward God and likewise toward your government, to be driven about, plundered and exiled." In like manner, Tertullian openly praises the Christians because they were the best and surest friends of all to the Empire: "The Christian is the enemy of no one, much less of the emperor, whom he knows to be appointed by God, and whom he must, therefore, of necessity love, reverence and honor, and wish to be preserved together with the whole Roman Empire." Nor did he hesitate to affirm that, within the limits of the Empire, the number of enemies was wont to diminish just in proportion as the number of Christians increased. There is also a remarkable testimony to the same point in the Epistle to Diognetus, which confirms the statement that the Christians at that period were not only in the habit of obeying the laws, but in every office they of their own accord did more, and more perfectly, than they were required to do by the laws. "Christians observe these things which have obtained the sanction of the law, and in the character of their lives they even go beyond the law."

The case, indeed, was different when they were ordered by the edicts of emperors and the threats of praetors to abandon the Christian faith or in any way fail in their duty. At these times, undoubtedly, they preferred to displease men rather than God. Yet, even under these circumstances, they were so far from doing anything seditious or despising the imperial majesty that they took it on themselves only to profess themselves Christians, and declare that they would not in any way alter their faith. But they had no thought of resistance, calmly and joyfully they went to the torture of the rack, in so much that the magnitude of the torments gave place to their magnitude of mind. During the same period the force of Christian principles was observed in like manner in the army. For it was a mark of a Christian soldier to combine the greatest fortitude with the greatest attention to military discipline, and to add to nobility of mind immovable fidelity towards his prince. But, if anything dishonorable was required of him, as, for instance, to break the laws of God, or to turn his sword against innocent disciples of Christ, then, indeed, he refused to execute the orders, yet in such wise that he would rather retire from the army and die for his religion than oppose the public authority by means of sedition and tumult.

But afterward, when Christian rulers were at the head of States, the Church insisted much more on testifying and preaching how much sanctity was inherent in the authority of rulers. Hence, when people thought of princedom, the image of a certain sacred majesty would present itself to their minds, by which they would be impelled to greater reverence and love of rulers. And on this account she wisely provides that kings should commence their reign with the celebration of solemn rites; which, in the Old Testament, was appointed by divine authority.

But from the time when the civil society of men, raised from the ruins of the Roman Empire, gave hope of its future Christian greatness, the Roman Pontiffs, by the institution of the Holy Empire, consecrated the political power in a wonderful manner. Greatly, indeed, was the authority of rulers ennobled; and it is not to be doubted that what was then instituted would always have been a very great gain, both to ecclesiastical and civil society, if princes and peoples had ever looked to the same object as the Church. And, indeed, tranquility and a sufficient prosperity lasted so long as there was a friendly agreement between these two powers. If the people were turbulent, the Church was at once the mediator for peace. Recalling all to their duty, she subdued the more lawless passions partly by kindness and partly by authority. So, if, in ruling, princes erred in their government, she went to them and, putting before them the rights, needs, and lawful wants of their people, urged them to equity, mercy, and kindness. Whence it was often brought about that the dangers of civil wars and popular tumults were stayed.

On the other hand, the doctrines on political power invented by late writers have already produced great ills amongst men, and it is to be feared that they will cause the very greatest disasters to posterity. For an unwillingness to attribute the right of ruling to God, as its Author, is not less than a willingness to blot out the greatest splendor of political power and to destroy its force. And they who say that this power depends on the will of the people err in opinion first of all; then they place authority on too weak and unstable a foundation. For the popular passions, incited and goaded on by these opinions, will break out more insolently; and, with great harm to the common weal, descend headlong by an easy and smooth road to revolts and to open sedition. In truth, sudden uprisings and the boldest rebellions immediately followed in Germany the so-called Reformation, the authors and leaders of which, by their new doctrines, attacked at the very foundation religious and civil authority; and this with so fearful an outburst of civil war and with such slaughter that there was scarcely any place free from tumult and bloodshed. From this heresy there arose in the last century a false philosophy—a new right as it is called, and a popular authority, together with an unbridled license which many regard as the only true liberty. Hence we have reached the limit of horrors, to wit, communism, socialism, nihilism, hideous deformities of the civil society of men and almost its ruin. And yet too many attempt to enlarge the scope of these evils, and under the pretext of helping the multitude, already have fanned no small flames of misery. The things we thus mention are neither unknown nor very remote from us.

This, indeed, is all the graver because rulers, in the midst of such threatening dangers, have no remedies sufficient to restore discipline and tranquility. They supply themselves with the power of laws, and think to coerce, by the severity of their punishment, those who disturb their governments. They are right to a certain extent, but yet should seriously consider that no power of punishment can be so great that it alone can preserve the State. For fear, as St. Thomas admirably teaches, "is a weak foundation; for those who are subdued by fear would, should an occasion arise in which they might hope for immunity, rise more eagerly against their rulers, in proportion to the previous extent of their restraint through fear." And besides, "from too great fear many fall into despair; and despair drives men to attempt boldly to gain what they desire." That these things are so we see from experience. It is therefore necessary to seek a higher and more reliable reason for obedience, and to say explicitly that legal severity cannot be efficacious unless men are led on by duty, and moved by the salutary fear of God. But this is what religion can best ask of them, religion which by its power enters into the souls and bends the very wills of men causing them not only to render obedience to their rulers, but also to show their affection and good will, which is in every society of men the best guardian of safety.

For this reason the Roman Pontiffs are to be regarded as having greatly served the public good, for they have ever endeavored to break the turbulent and restless spirit of innovators, and have often warned men of the danger they are to civil society. In this respect we may worthily recall to mind the declaration of Clement VII to Ferdinand, King of Bohemia and Hungary: "In the cause of faith your own dignity and advantage and that of other rulers is included, since the faith cannot be shaken without your authority being brought down; which has been most clearly shown in several instances." In the same way the supreme forethought and courage of Our predecessors have been shown, especially of Clement XI, Benedict XIV, and Leo XII, who, when in their day the evil of vicious doctrine was more widely spreading and the boldness of the sects was becoming greater, endeavored by their authority to close the door against them. And We Ourselves have several times declared what great dangers are impending, and have pointed out the best ways of warding them off. To princes and other rulers of the State we have offered the protection of religion, and we have exhorted the people to make abundant use of the great benefits which the Church supplies. Our present object is to make rulers understand that this protection, which is stronger than any, is again offered to them; and We earnestly exhort them in our Lord to defend religion, and to consult the interest of their Lord to defend religion, and to consult the interest of their States by giving that liberty to the Church which cannot be taken away without injury and ruin to the commonwealth.

The Church of Christ, indeed, cannot be an object of suspicion to rulers, nor of hatred to the people; for it urges rulers to follow justice, and in nothing to decline from their duty; while at the same time it strengthens and in many ways supports their authority. All things that are of a civil nature the Church acknowledges and declares to be under the power and authority of the ruler; and in things whereof for different reasons the decision belongs both to the sacred and to the civil power, the Church wishes that there should be harmony between the two so that injurious contests may be avoided. As to what regards the people, the Church has been established for the salvation of all men and has ever loved them as a mother. For it is the Church which by the exercise of her charity has given gentleness to the minds of men, kindness to their manners, and justice to their laws. Never opposed to honest liberty, the Church has always detested a tyrant's rule. This custom which the Church has ever had of deserving well of mankind is notably expressed by St. Augustine when he says that "the Church teaches kings to study the welfare of their people, and people to submit to their kings, showing what is due to all: and that to all is due charity and to no one injustice."

For these reasons, venerable brethren, your work will be most useful and salutary if you employ with us every industry and effort which God has given you in order to avert the dangers and evils of human society. Strive with all possible care to make men understand and show forth in their lives what the Catholic Church teaches on government and the duty of obedience. Let the people be frequently urged by your authority and teaching to fly from the forbidden sects, to abhor all conspiracy, to have nothing to do with sedition, and let them understand that they who for God's sake obey their rulers render a reasonable service and a generous obedience. And as it is God "who gives safety to kings," and grants to the people "to rest in the beauty of peace and in the tabernacles of confidence and in wealthy repose," it is to Him that we must pray, beseeching Him to incline all minds to uprightness and truth, to calm angry passions, to restore the long-wished-for tranquility to the world.

That we may pray with greater hope, let us take as our intercessors and protectors of our welfare the Virgin Mary, the great Mother of God, the help of Christians, and protector of the human race; St. Joseph, her chaste spouse, in whose patronage the whole Church greatly trusts; and the Princes of the Apostles, Peter and Paul, the guardians and protectors of the Christian name.

Given at St. Peter's in Rome, the twenty-ninth day of June, 1881, the third year of Our pontificate.

1899 **1 Peter 2:13–17** Be subject for the Lord's sake to every human institution, whether it be to the emperor as supreme, or to governors as sent by him to punish those who do wrong and to praise those who do right. For it is God's will that by doing right you should put to silence the ignorance of foolish men. Live as free men, yet without using your freedom as a pretext for evil; but live as servants of God. Honor all men. Love the brotherhood. Fear God. Honor the emperor.

1 Timothy 2:1–2 First of all, then, I urge that supplications, prayers, intercessions, 1900
and thanksgivings be made for all men, for kings and all who are in high positions, that we may lead a quiet and peaceable life, godly and respectful in every way.

Gaudium et spes **74, 1** Individuals, families, and the various groups which make 1906
up the civil community, are aware of their inability to achieve a truly human life by their own unaided efforts; they see the need for a wider community where each one will make a specific contribution to an even broader implementation of the common good. For this reason they set up various forms of political communities. The political community, then, exists for the common good: this is its full justification and meaning and the source of its specific and basic right to exist. The common good embraces the sum total of all those conditions of social life which enable individuals, families, and organizations to achieve complete and efficacious fulfilment.

Gaudium et spes **26, 2** At the same time, however, there is a growing awareness 1908
of the sublime dignity of the human person, who stands above all things and whose rights and duties are universal and inviolable. He ought, therefore, to have ready access to all that is necessary for living a genuinely human life: for example, food, clothing, housing, the right freely to choose his state of life and set up a family, the right to education, work, to his good name, to respect, to proper knowledge, the right to act according to the dictates of conscience and to safeguard his privacy, and rightful freedom even in matters of religion.

Centesimus annus **43** The Church has no models to present; models that are real 1914
and truly effective can only arise within the framework of different historical situations, through the efforts of all those who responsibly confront concrete problems in all their social, economic, political and cultural aspects, as these interact with one another. For such a task the Church offers her social teaching as an *indispensable and ideal orientation*, a teaching which, as already mentioned, recognizes the positive value of the market and of enterprise, but which at the same time points out that these need to be oriented towards the common good. This teaching also recognizes the legitimacy of workers' efforts to obtain full respect for their dignity and to gain broader areas of participation in the life of industrial enterprises so that, while cooperating with others and under the direction of others, they can in a certain sense "work for themselves" through the exercise of their intelligence and freedom.

The integral development of the human person through work does not impede but rather promotes the greater productivity and efficiency of work itself, even though it may weaken consolidated power structures. A business cannot be considered only as a "society of capital goods"; it is also a "society of persons" in which people participate in different ways and with specific responsibilities, whether they supply the necessary capital for the company's activities or take part in such activities through their labor. To achieve these goals there is still need for a broad associated workers' movement, directed towards the liberation and promotion of the whole person.

In the light of today's "new things," we have reread *the relationship between individual or private property and the universal destination of material wealth*. Man fulfills himself by using his intelligence and freedom. In so doing he utilizes the things of this world as objects and instruments and makes them his own. The foundation of the right to private initiative and ownership is to be found in this activity. By means of his work man commits himself, not only for his own sake but also *for others* and *with others*. Each person collaborates in the work of others and for their good. Man works in order to provide for the needs of his family, his community, his nation, and ultimately all humanity. Moreover, he collaborates in the work of his fellow employees, as well as in the work of suppliers and in the customers' use of goods, in a progressively expanding chain of solidarity. Ownership of the means of production, whether in industry or agriculture, is just and legitimate if it serves useful work. It becomes illegitimate, however, when it is not utilized or when it serves to impede the work of others, in an effort to gain a profit which is not the result of the overall expansion of work and the wealth of society, but rather is the result of curbing them or of illicit exploitation, speculation or the breaking of solidarity among working people. Ownership of this kind has no justification, and represents an abuse in the sight of God and man.

The obligation to earn one's bread by the sweat of one's brow also presumes the right to do so. A society in which this right is systematically denied, in which economic policies do not allow workers to reach satisfactory levels of employment, cannot be justified from an ethical point of view, nor can that society attain social peace. Just as the person fully realizes himself in the free gift of self, so too ownership morally justifies itself in the creation, at the proper time and in the proper way, of opportunities for work and human growth for all.

1916 ***Gaudium et spes* 30, 1** The pace of change is so far-reaching and rapid nowadays that no one can allow himself to close his eyes to the course of events or indifferently ignore them and wallow in the luxury of a merely individualistic morality. The best way to fulfil one's obligations of justice and love is to contribute to the common good according to one's means and the needs of others, even to the point of fostering and helping public and private organizations devoted to bettering the conditions of life. There is a kind of person who boasts of grand and noble sentiments and lives in practice as if he could not care less about the needs of society. There are many in various countries who make light of social laws and directives and are not ashamed to resort to fraud and cheating to avoid paying just taxes and fulfilling other social obligations. There are others who neglect the norms of social conduct, such as those regulating public hygiene and speed limits, forgetting that they are endangering their own lives and the lives of others by their carelessness.

1930 ***Pacem in terris* 65** The common good requires that civil authorities maintain a careful balance between coordinating and protecting the rights of the citizens, on the one hand, and promoting them, on the other. It should not happen that certain individuals or social groups derive special advantage from the fact that their rights have received preferential protection. Nor should it happen that governments in seeking to protect these rights, become obstacles to their full expression and free use. *For this principle must always be retained: that State activity in the economic field, no matter what its breadth or depth may be, ought not to be exercised in such a way as to curtail an individual's freedom of personal initiative. Rather it should work to expand that freedom as much as possible by the effective protection of the essential personal rights of each and every individual.*

1933 **Matthew 5:43–44** "You have heard that it was said, 'You shall love your neighbor and hate your enemy.' But I say to you, Love your enemies, and pray for those who persecute you. . . ."

1936 (1) ***Gaudium et spes* 29, 2** Undoubtedly not all men are alike as regards physical capacity and intellectual and moral powers. But forms of social or cultural discrimination in basic personal rights on the grounds of sex, race, color, social conditions, language or religion, must be curbed and eradicated as incompatible with God's design. It is regrettable that these basic personal rights are not yet being respected everywhere, as is the case with women who are denied the chance freely to choose a husband, or a state of life, or to have access to the same educational and cultural benefits as are available to men.

(2) **Matthew 25:14–30** "For it will be as when a man going on a journey called his 1936
servants and entrusted to them his property; to one he gave five talents, to another two, to another one, to each according to his ability. Then he went away. He who had received the five talents went at once and traded with them; and he made five talents more. So also, he who had the two talents made two talents more. But he who had received the one talent went and dug in the ground and hid his master's money. Now after a long time the master of those servants came and settled accounts with them. And he who had received the five talents came forward, bringing five talents more, saying, 'Master, you delivered to me five talents; here I have made five talents more.' His master said to him, 'Well done, good and faithful servant; you have been faithful over a little, I will set you over much; enter into the joy of your master.' And he also who had the two talents came forward, saying, 'Master, you delivered to me two talents; here I have made two talents more.' His master said to him, 'Well done, good and faithful servant; you have been faithful over a little, I will set you over much; enter into the joy of your master.' He also who had received the one talent came forward, saying, 'Master, I knew you to be a hard man, reaping where you did not sow, and gathering where you did not winnow; so I was afraid, and I went and hid your talent in the ground. Here you have what is yours.' But his master answered him, 'You wicked and slothful servant! You knew that I reap where I have not sowed, and gather where I have not winnowed? Then you ought to have invested my money with the bankers, and at my coming I should have received what was my own with interest. So take the talent from him, and give it to him who has the ten talents. For to every one who has will more be given, and he will have abundance; but from him who has not, even what he has will be taken away. And cast the worthless servant into the outer darkness; there men will weep and gnash their teeth.'. . ."

(3) **Luke 19:11–27** As they heard these things, he proceeded to tell a parable, be- 1936
cause he was near to Jerusalem, and because they supposed that the kingdom of God was to appear immediately. He said therefore, "A nobleman went into a far country to receive a kingdom and then return. Calling ten of his servants, he gave them ten pounds, and said to them, 'Trade with these till I come.' But his citizens hated him and sent an embassy after him, saying, 'We do not want this man to reign over us.' When he returned, having received the kingdom, he commanded these servants, to whom he had given the money, to be called to him, that he might know what they had gained by trading. The first came before him, saying, 'Lord, your pound has made ten pounds more.' And he said to him, 'Well done, good servant! Because you have been faithful in a very little, you shall have authority over ten cities.' And the second came, saying, 'Lord, your pound has made five pounds.' And he said to him, 'And you are to be over five cities.' Then another came, saying, 'Lord, here is your pound, which I kept laid away in a napkin; for I was afraid of you, because you are a severe man; you take up what you did not lay down, and reap what you did not sow.' He said to him, 'I will condemn you out of your own mouth, you wicked servant! You knew that I was a severe man, taking up what I did not lay down and reaping what I did not sow? Why then did you not put my money into the bank, and at my coming I should have collected it with interest?' And he said to those who stood by, 'Take the pound from him, and give it to him who has ten pounds.' (And they said to him, 'Lord, he has ten pounds!') 'I tell you, that to every one who has will more be given; but from him who has not, even what he has will be taken away. But as for

these enemies of mine, who did not want me to reign over them, bring them here and slay them before me.' "

1939 (1) ***Sollicitudo rei socialis* 38–40** This path is *long and complex*, and what is more it is constantly threatened because of the intrinsic frailty of human resolutions and achievements, and because of the *mutability* of very unpredictable and external circumstances. Nevertheless, one must have the courage to set out on this path, and, where some steps have been taken or a part of the journey made, the courage to go on to the end.

In the context of these reflections, the decision to set out or to continue the journey involves, above all, a *moral* value which men and women of faith recognize as a demand of God's will, the only true foundation of an absolutely binding ethic.

One would hope that also men and women without an explicit faith would be convinced that the obstacles to integral development are not only economic but rest on *more profound attitudes* which human beings can make into absolute values. Thus one would hope that all those who, to some degree or other, are responsible for ensuring a "more human life" for their fellow human beings, whether or not they are inspired by a religious faith, will become fully aware of the urgent need to *change* the *spiritual attitudes* which define each individual's relationship with self, with neighbor, with even the remotest human communities, and with nature itself; and all of this in view of higher values such as the *common good* or, to quote the felicitous expression of the Encyclical *Populorum Progressio*, the full development "of the whole individual and of all people."

For *Christians*, as for all who recognize the precise theological meaning of the word "sin," a change of behavior or mentality or mode of existence is called "conversion," to use the language of the Bible (cf. Mk 13:3, 5; Is 30:15). This conversion specifically entails a relationship to God, to the sin committed, to its consequences and hence to one's neighbor, either an individual or a community. It is God, in "whose hands are the hearts of the powerful" and the hearts of all, who according to his own promise and by the power of his Spirit can transform "hearts of stone" into "hearts of flesh" (cf. Ezek 36:26).

On the path toward the desired conversion, toward the overcoming of the moral obstacles to development, it is already possible to point to the *positive* and *moral value* of the growing awareness of *interdependence* among individuals and nations. The fact that men and women in various parts of the world feel personally affected by the injustices and violations of human rights committed in distant countries, countries which perhaps they will never visit, is a further sign of a reality transformed into *awareness*, thus acquiring a *moral* connotation.

It is above all a question of *interdependence*, sensed as a *system determining* relationships in the contemporary world, in its economic, cultural, political and religious elements, and accepted as a *moral category*. When interdependence becomes recognized in this way, the correlative response as a moral and social attitude, as a "virtue," is *solidarity*. This then is not a feeling of vague compassion or shallow distress at the misfortunes of so many people, both near and far. On the contrary, it is *a firm and persevering determination* to commit oneself to the *common good*; that is to say to the good of all and of each individual, because we are *all* really responsible for *all*. This determination is based on the *solid* conviction that what is hindering full development is that desire for profit and that thirst for power already mentioned. These attitudes and "structures of sin" are only conquered—presupposing the help of divine grace—by a *diametrically opposed attitude*: a commitment to the good of one's neighbor with the readiness, in the gospel sense, to "lose oneself" for the sake of the other instead of exploiting him, and to "serve him" instead of oppressing him for one's own advantage (cf. Mt 10:40–42; 20:25; Mk 10:42–45; Lk 22:25–27).

The exercise of solidarity *within each society* is valid when its members recognize one another as persons. Those who are more influential, because they have a greater share of goods and common services, should feel *responsible* for the weaker and be ready to share with them all they possess. Those who are weaker, for their part, in the same spirit of *solidarity*, should not adopt a purely *passive* attitude or one that is *destructive* of the social fabric, but, while claiming their legitimate rights, should do what they can for the good of all. The intermediate groups, in their turn, should not selfishly insist on their particular interests, but respect the interests of others.

Positive signs in the contemporary world are the *growing awareness* of the solidarity of the poor among themselves, their *efforts to support one another*, and their *public demonstrations* on the social scene which, without recourse to violence, present their own needs and rights in the face of the inefficiency or corruption of the public authorities. By virtue of her own evangelical duty the Church feels called to take her stand beside the poor, to discern the justice of their requests, and to help satisfy them, without losing sight of the good of groups in the context of the common good.

The same criterion is applied by analogy in international relationships. Interdependence must be transformed into *solidarity*, based upon the principle that the goods of creation *are meant for all*. That which human industry produces through the processing of raw materials, with the contribution of work, must serve equally for the good of all.

Surmounting every type of *imperialism* and determination to preserve their *own hegemony*, the stronger and richer nations must have a sense of moral *responsibility* for the other nations, so that a *real international system* may be established which will rest on the foundation of the *equality* of all peoples and on the necessary respect for their legitimate differences. The economically weaker countries, or those still at subsistence level, must be enabled, with the assistance of other peoples and of the international community, to make a contribution of their own to the common good with their treasures of *humanity* and *culture*, which otherwise would be lost for ever.

Solidarity helps us to see the "other"—whether a *person, people or nation*—not just as some kind of instrument, with a work capacity and physical strength to be exploited at low cost and then discarded when no longer useful, but as our "neighbor," a "helper" (cf. Gen 2:18–20), to be made a sharer, on a par with ourselves, in the banquet of life to which all are equally invited by God. Hence the importance of reawakening the *religious awareness* of individuals and peoples.

Thus the exploitation, oppression and annihilation of others are excluded. These facts, in the present division of the world into opposing blocs, combine to produce the *danger of war* and an excessive preoccupation with personal security, often to the detriment of the autonomy, freedom of decision, and even the territorial integrity of the weaker nations situated within the so-called "areas of influence" or "safety belts."

The "structures of sin" and the sins which they produce are likewise radically opposed to *peace and development*, for development, in the familiar expression of Pope Paul's Encyclical, is "the new name for peace."

In this way, the solidarity which we propose is the *path to peace and at the same time to development*. For world peace is inconceivable unless the world's leaders come to recognize that *interdependence* in itself demands the abandonment of the politics of blocs, the sacrifice of all forms of economic, military or political imperialism, and the transformation of mutual distrust into *collaboration*. This is precisely the act proper to solidarity among individuals and nations.

The motto of the pontificate of my esteemed predecessor Pius XII was *Opus iustitiae pax*, peace as the fruit of justice. Today one could say, with the same exactness and the same power of biblical inspiration (cf. Is 32:17; Jas 3:18): *Opus solidaritatis pax*, peace as the fruit of solidarity.

The goal of peace, so desired by everyone, will certainly be achieved through the putting into effect of social and international justice, but also through the practice of the virtues which favor togetherness, and which teach us to live in unity, so as to build in unity, by giving and receiving, a new society and a better world.

Solidarity is undoubtedly a *Christian virtue*. In what has been said so far it has been possible to identify many points of contact between solidarity and *charity*, which is the distinguishing mark of Christ's disciples (cf. Jn 13:35).

In the light of faith, solidarity seeks to go beyond itself, to take on the *specifically Christian* dimension of total gratuity, forgiveness and reconciliation. One's neighbor is then not only a human being with his or her own rights and a fundamental equality with everyone else, but becomes the *living image* of God the Father, redeemed by the blood of Jesus Christ and placed under the permanent action of the Holy Spirit. One's neighbor must therefore be loved, even if an enemy, with the same love with which the Lord loves him or her; and for that person's sake one must be ready for sacrifice, even the ultimate one: to lay down one's life for the brethren (cf. 1 Jn 3:16).

At that point, awareness of the common fatherhood of God, of the brotherhood of all in Christ—"children in the Son"—and of the presence and life-giving action of the Holy Spirit will bring to our vision of the world *a new criterion* for interpreting it. Beyond human and natural bonds, already so close and strong, there is discerned in the light of faith a new *model* of the *unity* of the human race, which must ultimately inspire our *solidarity*. This supreme *model of unity*, which is a reflection of the intimate life of God, one God in three Persons, is what we Christians mean by the word "*communion*." This specifically Christian communion, jealously preserved, extended and enriched with the Lord's help, is the *soul* of the Church's vocation to be a "sacrament," in the sense already indicated.

Solidarity therefore must play its part in the realization of this divine plan, both on the level of individuals and on the level of national and international society. The "evil mechanisms" and "structures of sin" of which we have spoken can be overcome only through the exercise of the human and Christian solidarity to which the Church calls us and which she tirelessly promotes. Only in this way can such positive energies be fully released for the benefit of development and peace.

Many of the Church's canonized saints offer a *wonderful witness* of such solidarity and can serve as examples in the present difficult circumstances. Among them I wish to recall St. Peter Claver and his service to the slaves at Cartagena de Indias, and St. Maximilian Maria Kolbe who offered his life in place of a prisoner unknown to him in the concentration camp at Auschwitz.

1939 (2) ***Centesimus annus* 10** Another important aspect, which has many applications to our own day, is the concept of the relationship between the State and its citizens. *Rerum novarum* criticizes two social and economic systems: socialism and liberalism. The opening section, in which the right to private property is reaffirmed, is devoted to socialism. Liberalism is not the subject of a special section, but it is worth noting that criticisms of it are raised in the treatment of the duties of the State. The State cannot limit itself to "favoring one portion of the citizens," namely the rich and prosperous, nor can it "neglect the other," which clearly represents the majority of society. Otherwise, there would be a violation of that law of justice which ordains that every person should receive his due. "When there is question of defending the rights of individuals, the defenseless and the poor have a claim to special consideration. The richer class has many ways of shielding itself, and stands less in need of help from the State; whereas the mass of the poor have no resources of their own to fall back on, and must chiefly depend on the assistance of the State. It is for this reason that wage-earners, since they mostly belong to the latter class, should be specially cared for and protected by the government."

These passages are relevant today, especially in the face of the new forms of poverty in the world, and also because they are affirmations which do not depend on a specific notion of the State or on a particular political theory. Leo XIII is repeating an elementary principle of sound political organization, namely, the more that individuals are defenseless within a given society, the more they require the care and concern of others, and in particular the intervention of governmental authority.

In this way what we nowadays call the principle of solidarity, the validity of which both in the internal order of each nation and in the international order I have discussed in the encyclical *Sollicitudo rei socialis*, is clearly seen to be one of the fundamental principles of the Christian view of social and political organization. This principle is frequently stated by Pope Leo XIII, who uses the term "friendship," a concept already found in Greek philosophy. Pope Pius XI refers to it with the equally meaningful term "social charity." Pope Paul VI, expanding the concept to cover the many modern aspects of the social question, speaks of a "civilization of love."

(1) St. Thomas Aquinas, *Summa theologiae* I–II 90, 1 1951

Question 90. the nature of law

Here there are four points of inquiry: (1) whether law is a function of reason; (2) about its purpose; (3) its agent; (4) and its promulgation.

article 1. is law a function of mind?

THE FIRST POINT: 1. Law apparently is not a function of mind, since St. Paul says that *I see another law in my members, warring against the law of my mind.* What is mental does not enter into our members, for thought is not exercised through a physical organ. Hence law is not a function of reason.

2. Besides, in the reason there is but the faculty itself, a disposition it may have, or an activity. Law however, is not the very faculty, nor one of its dispositions, for these, as we have seen, are the intellectual virtues, nor an activity, for then it would lapse when reasoning is suspended, as during sleep. Law, therefore, does not belong to the reason.

3. Then also, law motions its subjects to act aright. Yet it has been stated that setting human activity into motion is properly the work of the will. Therefore law is the office of will rather than of mind; which accords with the words of the Jurist, *what has pleased the sovereign has the force of law.*

ON THE OTHER HAND the burden of law is to prescribe or prohibit. Such executive commanding issues from the reason, as already noted. Consequently law is a function of reason.

REPLY: Law is a kind of direction or measure for human activity through which a person is led to do something or held back. The word comes from *ligando,* because it is binding on how we should act. Now direction and measure come to human acts from reason, from which, as we have shown, they start. It is the function of reason to plan for an end, and this purpose, as Aristotle notes, is the original source of what we do. The originating principle in any class strikes the note for all there comprised, for instance, the unit of calculation in a numerical system, or the first motion that sets going a derivative series of motions. We are left with the conclusion, then, that law is something that belongs to reason.

Hence: 1. Taken as a rule and measure, law can be present in two manners, first, and this is proper to the reason, as in the ruling and measuring principle, and in this manner it is the reason alone; second, as in the subject ruled and measured, and in this manner law is present wherever it communicates a tendency to something, which tendency can be called derivatively, though not essentially, a 'law'. The inclination to concupiscence of our physical parts in this sense is called 'the law of members'.

1951 (2) **Tertullian, *Adversus Marcionem* 2, 4** The goodness of God having, therefore, provided man for the pursuit of the knowledge of Himself, added this to its original notification, that it first prepared a habitation for him, the vast fabric (of the world) to begin with, and then afterwards the vaster one (of a higher world), that he might on a great as well as on a smaller stage practice and advance in his probation, and so be promoted from the *good* which God had given him, that is, from his high position, to God's *best*; that is, to some higher abode. In this good work *God* employs a most excellent minister, even His own Word. "My heart" He says, "hath emitted my most excellent Word." Let Marcion take hence his first lesson on the noble fruit of this truly most excellent tree. But, like a most clumsy clown, he has grafted a good branch on a bad stock. The sapling, however, of his blasphemy shall be never strong: it shall wither with its planter, and thus shall be manifested the nature of the good tree. Look at the total result: how fruitful was the Word! God issued His *fiat*, and it was done: God also saw that it was good; not as if He were ignorant of the good until He saw it; but because it was good, He therefore saw it, and honoured it, and set His seal upon it; and consummated the goodness of His works by His vouchsafing to them that contemplation. Thus God blessed what He made good, in order that He might commend Himself to you as whole and perfect, good both in word and act. As yet the Word knew no malediction, because He was a stranger to malefaction. We shall see what reasons required *this* also of God. Meanwhile, the world consisted of all things good, plainly foreshowing how much good was preparing for him for whom all this was provided. Who indeed was so worthy of dwelling amongst the works of God, as he who was His own image and likeness? That image was wrought out by a goodness even more operative than its wont, with no imperious word, but with friendly hand preceded by an almost affable utterance: "Let us make man in our image, after our likeness." Goodness spake the word; Goodness formed man of the dust of the ground into so great a substance of the flesh, built up out of one material with so many qualities; Goodness breathed into him a soul, not dead, but living. Goodness gave him dominion over all things, which he was to enjoy and rule over, and even give names to. In addition to this, Goodness annexed pleasures to man; so that, while master of the whole world, he might tarry among higher delights, being translated into paradise, out of the world into the Church. The self-same Goodness provided also a help meet for him, that there might be nothing in his lot that was not good. For, said He, that the man be alone is not good. He knew full well what a blessing to him would be the sex of Mary, and also of the Church. The law, however, which you find fault with, and wrest into a subject of contention, was imposed on man by Goodness, aiming at his happiness, that he might cleave to God, and so not show himself an abject creature rather than a free one, nor reduce himself to the level of the other animals, his subjects, which were free from God, and exempt from all tedious subjection; but might, as the sole human being, boast that he alone was worthy of receiving laws from God; and as a rational being, capable of intelligence and knowledge, be restrained within the bounds of rational liberty, subject to Him who had subjected all things unto him. To secure the observance of this law, Goodness likewise took counsel by help of this sanction: "In the day that thou eatest thereof, thou shalt surely die." For it was a most benignant act of His thus to point out the issues of transgression, lest ignorance of the danger should encourage a neglect of obedience. Now, since it was given as a reason previous to the imposition of the law, it also amounted to a motive for subsequently observing it, that a penalty was annexed to its transgression; a penalty, indeed, which He who proposed it was still unwilling that it should be incurred. Learn then the goodness of our God amidst these things and up to this point; learn it from His excellent works, from His kindly blessings, from His indulgent bounties, from His gracious providences, from His laws and warnings, so good and merciful.

***Gaudium et spes* 10** The dichotomy affecting the modern world is, in fact, a symptom of the deeper dichotomy that is in man himself. He is the meeting point of many conflicting forces. In his condition as a created being he is subject to a thousand shortcomings, but feels untrammeled in his inclinations and destined for a higher form of life. Torn by a welter of anxieties he is compelled to choose between them and repudiate some among them. Worse still, feeble and sinful as he is, he often does the very thing he hates and does not do what he wants. And so he feels himself divided, and the result is a host of discords in social life. Many, it is true, fail to see the dramatic nature of this state of affairs in all its clarity for their vision is in fact blurred by materialism, or they are prevented from even thinking about it by the wretchedness of their plight. Others delude themselves that they have found peace in a world-view now fashionable. There are still others whose hopes are set on a genuine and total emancipation of mankind through human effort alone and look forward to some future earthly paradise where all the desires of their hearts will be fulfilled. Nor is it unusual to find people who having lost faith in life extol the kind of foolhardiness which would empty life of all significance in itself and invest it with a meaning of their own devising. Nonetheless, in the face of modern developments there is a growing body of men who are asking the most fundamental of all questions or are glimpsing them with a keener insight: What is man? What is the meaning of suffering, evil, death, which have not been eliminated by all this progress? What is the purpose of these achievements, purchased at so high a a price? What can man contribute to society? What can he expect from it? What happens after this earthly life is ended? 1958

The Church believes that Christ, who died and was raised for the sake of all, can show man the way and strengthen him through the Spirit in order to be worthy of his destiny: nor is there any other name under heaven given among men by which they can be saved. The Church likewise believes that the key, the center and the purpose of the whole of man's history is to be found in its Lord and Master. She also maintains that beneath all that changes there is much that is unchanging, much that has its ultimate foundation in Christ, who is the same yesterday, and today, and forever. And that is why the Council, relying on the inspiration of Christ, the image of the invisible God, the firstborn of all creation, proposes to speak to all men in order to unfold the mystery that is man and cooperate in tackling the main problems facing the world today.

Vatican Council I (1870): DS 3005 [*The necessity of revelation*]. Indeed, it must be attributed to this divine revelation that those things, which in divine things are impenetrable to human reason by itself, can, even in this present condition of the human race, be known readily by all with firm certitude and with no admixture of error. Nevertheless, it is not for this reason that revelation is said to be absolutely necessary, but because God in His infinite goodness has ordained man for a supernatural end, to participation, namely, in the divine goods which altogether surpass the understanding of the human mind, since "eye hath not seen, nor ear heard, neither hath it entered into the heart of man, what things God hath prepared for them that love Him" [1 Cor. 2:9; can. 2 and 3]. 1960

1963 (1) **Romans 7:12** So the law is holy, and the commandment is holy and just and good.

1963 (2) **Romans 7:14** We know that the law is spiritual; but I am carnal, sold under sin.

1963 (3) **Romans 7:16** Now if I do what I do not want, I agree that the law is good.

1963 (4) **Galatians 3:24** So that the law was our custodian until Christ came, that we might be justified by faith.

1963 (5) **Romans 7** Do you not know, brethren—for I am speaking to those who know the law—that the law is binding on a person only during his life? Thus a married woman is bound by law to her husband as long as he lives; but if her husband dies she is discharged from the law concerning the husband. Accordingly, she will be called an adulteress if she lives with another man while her husband is alive. But if her husband dies she is free from that law, and if she marries another man she is not an adulteress.

Likewise, my brethren, you have died to the law through the body of Christ, so that you may belong to another, to him who has been raised from the dead in order that we may bear fruit for God. While we were living in the flesh, our sinful passions, aroused by the law, were at work in our members to bear fruit for death. But now we are discharged from the law, dead to that which held us captive, so that we serve not under the old written code but in the new life of the Spirit.

What then shall we say? That the law is sin? By no means! Yet, if it had not been for the law, I should not have known sin. I should not have known what it is to covet if the law had not said, "You shall not covet." But sin, finding opportunity in the commandment, wrought in me all kinds of covetousness. Apart from the law sin lies dead. I was once alive apart from the law, but when the commandment came, sin revived and I died; the very commandment which promised life proved to be death to me. For sin, finding opportunity in the commandment, deceived me and by it killed me. So the law is holy, and the commandment is holy and just and good.

Did that which is good, then, bring death to me? By no means! It was sin, working death in me through what is good, in order that sin might be shown to be sin, and through the commandment might become sinful beyond measure. We know that the law is spiritual; but I am carnal, sold under sin. I do not understand my own actions. For I do not do what I want, but I do the very thing I hate. Now if I do what I do not want, I agree that the law is good. So then it is no longer I that do it, but sin which dwells within me. For I know that nothing good dwells within me, that is, in my flesh. I can will what is right, but I cannot do it. For I do not do the good I want, but the evil I do not want is what I do. Now if I do what I do not want, it is no longer I that do it, but sin which dwells within me.

So I find it to be a law that when I want to do right, evil lies close at hand. For I delight in the law of God, in my inmost self, but I see in my members another law at war with the law of my mind and making me captive to the law of sin which dwells in my members. Wretched man that I am! Who will deliver me from this body of death? Thanks be to God through Jesus Christ our Lord! So then, I of myself serve the law of God with my mind, but with my flesh I serve the law of sin.

1964 **Romans 5:5** . . . and hope does not disappoint us, because God's love has been poured into our hearts through the Holy Spirit which has been given to us.

1965 **Jeremiah 31:31–34** "Behold, the days are coming, says the Lord, when I will make a new covenant with the house of Israel and the house of Judah, not like the covenant which I made with their fathers when I took them by the hand to bring them out of the land of Egypt, my covenant which they broke, though I was their husband, says the Lord. But this is the covenant which I will make with the house of Israel after those days, says the Lord: I will put my law within them, and I will write it upon their hearts; and I will be their God, and they shall be my people. And no longer shall each man teach his neighbor and each his brother, saying, 'Know the Lord,' for they shall all know me from the least of them to the greatest, says the Lord; for I will forgive their iniquity, and I will remember their sin no more."

Matthew 5:17–19 "Think not that I have come to abolish the law and the prophets; 1967
I have come not to abolish them but to fulfil them. For truly, I say to you, till heaven and earth pass away, not an iota, not a dot, will pass from the law until all is accomplished. Whoever then relaxes one of the least of these commandments and teaches men so, shall be called least in the kingdom of heaven; but he who does them and teaches them shall be called great in the kingdom of heaven. . . ."

(1) **Matthew 15:18–19** But what comes out of the mouth proceeds from the heart, 1968
and this defiles a man. For out of the heart come evil thoughts, murder, adultery, fornication, theft, false witness, slander.

(2) **Matthew 5:44** But I say to you, Love your enemies and pray for those who 1968
persecute you. . . .

(3) **Matthew 5:48** You, therefore, must be perfect, as your heavenly Father is per- 1968
fect.

(1) **Matthew 6:1–6** "Beware of practicing your piety before men in order to be 1969
seen by them; for then you will have no reward from your Father who is in heaven.

"Thus, when you give alms, sound no trumpet before you, as the hypocrites do in the synagogues and in the streets, that they may be praised by men. Truly, I say to you, they have received their reward. But when you give alms, do not let your left hand know what your right hand is doing, so that your alms may be in secret; and your Father who sees in secret will reward you.

"And when you pray, you must not be like the hypocrites; for they love to stand and pray in the synagogues and at the street corners, that they may be seen by men. Truly, I say to you, they have received their reward. But when you pray, go into your room and shut the door and pray to your Father who is in secret; and your Father who sees in secret will reward you. . . ."

(2) **Matthew 6:16–18** "And when you fast, do not look dismal, like the hypocrites, 1969
for they disfigure their faces that their fasting may be seen by men. Truly, I say to you, they have received their reward. But when you fast, anoint your head and wash your face, that your fasting may not be seen by men but by your Father who is in secret; and your Father who sees in secret will reward you. . . ."

(3) **Matthew 6:9–13** Pray then like this: 1969

Our Father who art in heaven,
Hallowed be thy name.
Thy kingdom come.
Thy will be done,
    On earth as it is in heaven.

Give us this day our daily bread;
And forgive us our debts,
As we also have forgiven our debtors;
And lead us not into temptation,
But deliver us from evil.

1969 (4) **Luke 11:2–4** And he said to them, "When you pray, say:
"Father, hallowed be thy name. Thy kingdom come. Give us each day our daily bread; and forgive us our sins, for we ourselves forgive every one who is indebted to us; and lead us not into temptation."

1970 (1) **Matthew 7:13–14** "Enter by the narrow gate; for the gate is wide and the way is easy, that leads to destruction, and those who enter by it are many. For the gate is narrow and the way is hard, that leads to life, and those who find it are few. . . ."

1970 (2) **Matthew 7:21–27** "Not every one who says to me, 'Lord, Lord,' shall enter the kingdom of heaven, but he who does the will of my Father who is in heaven. On that day many will say to me, 'Lord, Lord, did we not prophesy in your name, and cast out demons in your name, and do many mighty works in your name?' And then will I declare to them, 'I never knew you; depart from me, you evildoers.'

"Every one then who hears these words of mine and does them will be like a wise man who built his house upon the rock; and the rain fell, and the floods came, and the winds blew and beat upon that house, but it did not fall, because it had been founded on the rock. And every one who hears these words of mine and does not do them will be like a foolish man who built his house upon the sand; and the rain fell, and the floods came, and the winds blew and beat against that house, and it fell; and great was the fall of it."

1970 (3) **Luke 6:31** And as you wish that men would do to you, do so to them.

1970 (4) **John 15:12** "This is my commandment, that you love one another as I have loved you. . . ."

1970 (5) **John 13:34** A new commandment I give to you, that you love one another; even as I have loved you, that you also love one another.

1971 (1) **Romans 14** As for the man who is weak in faith, welcome him, but not for disputes over opinions. One believes he may eat anything, while the weak man eats only vegetables. Let not him who eats despise him who abstains, and let not him who abstains pass judgment on him who eats; for God has welcomed him. Who are you to pass judgment on the servant of another? It is before his own master that he stands or falls. And he will be upheld, for the Master is able to make him stand.

One man esteems one day as better than another, while another man esteems all days alike. Let every one be fully convinced in his own mind. He who observes the day, observes it in honor of the Lord. He also who eats, eats in honor of the Lord, since he gives thanks to God; while he who abstains, abstains in honor of the Lord and gives thanks to God. None of us lives to himself, and none of us dies to himself. If we live, we live to the Lord, and if we die, we die to the Lord; so then, whether we live or whether we die, we are the Lord's. For to this end Christ died and lived again, that he might be Lord both of the dead and of the living.

Why do you pass judgment on your brother? Or you, why do you despise your brother? For we shall all stand before the judgment seat of God; for it is written,

"As I live, says the Lord, every knee shall bow to me,
and every tongue shall give praise to God."
So each of us shall give account of himself to God.

Then let us no more pass judgment on one another, but rather decide never to put a stumbling block or hindrance in the way of a brother. I know and am persuaded in the Lord Jesus that nothing is unclean in itself; but it is unclean for any one who thinks it unclean. If your brother is being injured by what you eat, you are no longer walking in love. Do not let what you eat cause the ruin of one for whom Christ died. So do not let your good be spoken of as evil. For the kingdom of God is not food and drink but righteousness and peace and joy in the Holy Spirit; he who thus serves Christ is acceptable to God and approved by men. Let us then pursue what makes for peace and for mutual upbuilding. Do not, for the sake of food, destroy the work of God. Everything is indeed clean, but it is wrong for any one to make others fall by what he eats; it is right not to eat meat or drink wine or do anything that makes your brother stumble. The faith that you have, keep between yourself and God; happy is he who has no reason to judge himself for what he approves. But he who has doubts is condemned, if he eats, because he does not act from faith; for whatever does not proceed from faith is sin.

(2) **1 Corinthians 5–10** It is actually reported that there is immorality among you, 1971
and of a kind that is not found even among pagans; for a man is living with his father's wife. And you are arrogant! Ought you not rather to mourn? Let him who has done this be removed from among you.

For though absent in body I am present in spirit, and as if present, I have already pronounced judgment in the name of the Lord Jesus on the man who has done such a thing. When you are assembled, and my spirit is present, with the power of our Lord Jesus, you are to deliver this man to Satan for the destruction of the flesh, that his spirit may be saved in the day of the Lord Jesus.

Your boasting is not good. Do you not know that a little leaven leavens the whole lump? Cleanse out the old leaven that you may be a new lump, as you really are unleavened. For Christ, our paschal lamb, has been sacrificed. Let us, therefore, celebrate the festival, not with the old leaven, the leaven of malice and evil, but with the unleavened bread of sincerity and truth.

I wrote to you in my letter not to associate with immoral men; not at all meaning the immoral of this world, or the greedy and robbers, or idolaters, since then you would need to go out of the world. But rather I wrote to you not to associate with any one who bears the name of brother if he is guilty of immorality or greed, or is an idolater, reviler, drunkard, or robber—not even to eat with such a one. For what have I to do with judging outsiders? Is it not those inside the church whom you are to judge? God judges those outside. "Drive out the wicked person from among you."

When one of you has a grievance against a brother, does he dare go to law before the unrighteous instead of the saints? Do you not know that the saints will judge the world? And if the world is to be judged by you, are you incompetent to try trivial cases? Do you not know that we are to judge angels? How much more, matters pertaining to this life! If then you have such cases, why do you lay them before those who are least esteemed by the church? I say this to your shame. Can it be that there is no man among you wise enough to decide between members of the brotherhood, but brother goes to law against brother, and that before unbelievers?

To have lawsuits at all with one another is defeat for you. Why not rather suffer wrong? Why not rather be defrauded? But you yourselves wrong and defraud, and that even your own brethren.

Do you not know that the unrighteous will not inherit the kingdom of God? Do not be deceived; neither the immoral, nor idolaters, nor adulterers, nor sexual perverts, nor thieves, nor the greedy, nor drunkards, nor revilers, nor robbers will inherit the kingdom of God. And such were some of you. But you were washed, you were sanctified, you were justified in the name of the Lord Jesus Christ and in the Spirit of our God.

"All things are lawful for me," but not all things are helpful. "All things are lawful for me," but I will not be enslaved by anything. "Food is meant for the stomach and the stomach for food"—and God will destroy both one and the other. The body is not meant for immorality, but for the Lord, and the Lord for the body. And God raised the Lord and will also raise us up by his power. Do you not know that your bodies are members of Christ? Shall I therefore take the members of Christ and make them members of a prostitute? Never! Do you not know that he who joins himself to a prostitute becomes one body with her? For, as it is written, "The two shall become one flesh." But he who is united to the Lord becomes one spirit with him. Shun immorality. Every other sin which a man commits is outside the body; but the immoral man sins against his own body. Do you not know that your body is a temple of the Holy Spirit within you, which you have from God? You are not your own; you were bought with a price. So glorify God in your body.

Now concerning the matters about which you wrote. It is well for a man not to touch a woman. But because of the temptation to immorality, each man should have his own wife and each woman her own husband. The husband should give to his wife her conjugal rights, and likewise the wife to her husband. For the wife does not rule over her own body, but the husband does; likewise the husband does not rule over his own body, but the wife does. Do not refuse one another except perhaps by agreement for a season, that you may devote yourselves to prayer; but then come together again, lest Satan tempt you through lack of self-control. I say this by way of concession, not of command. I wish that all were as I myself am. But each has his own special gift from God, one of one kind and one of another.

To the unmarried and the widows I say that it is well for them to remain single as I do. But if they cannot exercise self-control, they should marry. For it is better to marry than to be aflame with passion.

To the married I give charge, not I but the Lord, that the wife should not separate from her husband (but if she does, let her remain single or else be reconciled to her husband)—and that the husband should not divorce his wife.

To the rest I say, not the Lord, that if any brother has a wife who is an unbeliever, and she consents to live with him, he should not divorce her. If any woman has a husband who is an unbeliever, and he consents to live with her, she should not divorce him. For the unbelieving husband is consecrated through his wife, and the unbelieving wife is consecrated through her husband. Otherwise, your children would be unclean, but as it is they are holy. But if the unbelieving partner desires to separate, let it be so; in such a case the brother or sister is not bound. For God has called us to peace. Wife, how do you know whether you will save your husband? Husband, how do you know whether you will save your wife?

Only, let every one lead the life which the Lord has assigned to him, and in which God has called him. This is my rule in all the churches. Was any one at the time of his call already circumcised? Let him not seek to remove the marks of the circumcision. Was any one at the time of his call uncircumcised? Let him not seek circumcision. For neither circumcision counts for anything nor uncircumcision, but keeping the commandments of God. Every one should remain in the state in which he was called. Were you a slave when called? Never mind. But if you can gain your freedom, avail yourself of the opportunity. For he who was called in the Lord as a slave is a freedman of the Lord. Likewise he who was free when called is a slave of Christ. You were bought with a price; do not become slaves of men. So, brethren, in whatever state each was called, there let him remain with God.

Now concerning the unmarried, I have no command of the Lord, but I give my opinion as one who by the Lord's mercy is trustworthy. I think that in view of the present distress it is well for a person to remain as he is. Are you bound to a wife? Do not seek to be free. Are you free from a wife? Do not seek marriage. But if you marry, you do not sin, and if a girl marries she does not sin. Yet those who marry will have worldly troubles, and I would spare you that. I mean, brethren, the appointed time has grown very short; from now on, let those who have wives live as though they had none, and those who mourn as though they were not mourning, and those who rejoice as though they were not rejoicing, and those who buy as though they had no goods, and those who deal with the world as though they had no dealings with it. For the form of this world is passing away.

I want you to be free from anxieties. The unmarried man is anxious about the affairs of the Lord, how to please the Lord; but the married man is anxious about worldly affairs, how to please his wife, and his interests are divided. And the unmarried woman or girl is anxious about the affairs of the Lord, how to be holy in body and spirit; but the married woman is anxious about worldly affairs, how to please her husband. I say this for your own benefit, not to lay any restraint upon you, but to promote good order and to secure your undivided devotion to the Lord.

If any one thinks that he is not behaving properly toward his betrothed, if his passions are strong, and it has to be, let him do as he wishes: let them marry—it is no sin. But whoever is firmly established in his heart, being under no necessity but having his desire under control, and has determined this in his heart, to keep her as his betrothed, he will do well. So that he who marries his betrothed does well; and he who refrains from marriage will do better.

A wife is bound to her husband as long as he lives. If the husband dies, she is free to be married to whom she wishes, only in the Lord. But in my judgment she is happier if she remains as she is. And I think that I have the Spirit of God.

Now concerning food offered to idols: we know that "all of us possess knowledge." "Knowledge" puffs up, but love builds up. If any one imagines that he knows something, he does not yet know as he ought to know. But if one loves God, one is known by him.

Hence, as to the eating of food offered to idols, we know that "an idol has no real existence," and that "there is no God but one." For although there may be so-called gods in heaven or on earth—as indeed there are many "gods" and many "lords"—yet for us there is one God, the Father, from whom are all things and for whom we exist, and one Lord, Jesus Christ, through whom are all things and through whom we exist. However, not all possess this knowledge. But some, through being hitherto accustomed to idols, eat food as really offered to an idol; and their conscience, being weak, is defiled. Food will not commend us to God. We are no worse off if we do not eat, and no better off if we do. Only take care lest this liberty of yours somehow become a stumbling block to the weak. For if any one sees you, a man of knowledge, at table in an idol's temple, might he not be encouraged, if his conscience is weak, to eat food offered to idols? And so by your knowledge this weak man is destroyed, the brother for whom Christ died. Thus, sinning against your brethren and wounding their conscience when it is weak, you sin against Christ. Therefore, if food is a cause of my brother's falling, I will never eat meat, lest I cause my brother to fall.

Am I not free? Am I not an apostle? Have I not seen Jesus our Lord? Are not you my workmanship in the Lord? If to others I am not an apostle, at least I am to you; for you are the seal of my apostleship in the Lord.

This is my defense to those who would examine me. Do we not have the right to our food and drink? Do we not have the right to be accompanied by a wife, as the other apostles and the brothers of the Lord and Cephas? Or is it only Barnabas and I who have no right to refrain from working for a living? Who serves as a soldier at his own expense? Who plants a vineyard without eating any of its fruit? Who tends a flock without getting some of the milk?

Do I say this on human authority? Does not the law say the same? For it is written in the law of Moses, "You shall not muzzle an ox when it is treading out the grain." Is it for oxen that God is concerned? Does he not speak entirely for our sake? It was written for our sake, because the plowman should plow in hope and the thresher thresh in hope of a share in the crop. If we have sown spiritual good among you, is it too much if we reap your material benefits? If others share this rightful claim upon you, do not we still more?

Nevertheless, we have not made use of this right, but we endure anything rather than put an obstacle in the way of the gospel of Christ. Do you not know that those who are employed in the temple service get their food from the temple, and those who serve at the altar share in the sacrificial offerings? In the same way, the Lord commanded that those who proclaim the gospel should get their living by the gospel.

But I have made no use of any of these rights, nor am I writing this to secure any such provision. For I would rather die than have any one deprive me of my ground for boasting. For if I preach the gospel, that gives me no ground for boasting. For necessity is laid upon me. Woe to me if I do not preach the gospel! For if I do this of my own will, I have a reward; but if not of my own will, I am entrusted with a commission. What then is my reward? Just this: that in my preaching I may make the gospel free of charge, not making full use of my right in the gospel.

For though I am free from all men, I have made myself a slave to all, that I might win the more. To the Jews I became as a Jew, in order to win Jews; to those under the law I became as one under the law—though not being myself under the law—that I might win those under the law. To those outside the law I became as one outside the law—not being without law toward God but under the law of Christ—that I might win those outside the law. To the weak I became weak, that I might win the weak. I have become all things to all men, that I might by all means save some. I do it all for the sake of the gospel, that I may share in its blessings.

Do you not know that in a race all the runners compete, but only one receives the prize? So run that you may obtain it. Every athlete exercises self-control in all things. They do it to receive a perishable wreath, but we an imperishable. Well, I do not run aimlessly, I do not box as one beating the air; but I pommel my body and subdue it, lest after preaching to others I myself should be disqualified.

I want you to know, brethren, that our fathers were all under the cloud, and all passed through the sea, and all were baptized into Moses in the cloud and in the sea, and all ate the same supernatural food and all drank the same supernatural drink. For they drank from the supernatural Rock which followed them, and the Rock was Christ. Nevertheless with most of them God was not pleased; for they were overthrown in the wilderness.

Now these things are warnings for us, not to desire evil as they did. Do not be idolaters as some of them were; as it is written, "The people sat down to eat and drink and rose up to dance." We must not indulge in immorality as some of them did, and twenty-three thousand fell in a single day. We must not put the Lord to the test, as some of them did and were destroyed by serpents; nor grumble, as some of them did and were destroyed by the Destroyer. Now these things happened to them as a warning, but they were written down for our instruction, upon whom the end of the ages has come. Therefore let any one who thinks that he stands take heed lest he fall. No temptation has overtaken you that is not common to man. God is faithful, and he will not let you be tempted beyond your strength, but with the temptation will also provide the way of escape, that you may be able to endure it.

Therefore, my beloved, shun the worship of idols. I speak as to sensible men; judge for yourselves what I say. The cup of blessing which we bless, is it not a participation in the blood of Christ? The bread which we break, is it not a participation in the body of Christ? Because there is one bread, we who are many are one body, for we all partake of the one bread. Consider the people of Israel; are not those who eat the sacrifices partners in the altar? What do I imply then? That food offered to idols is anything, or that an idol is anything? No, I imply that what pagans sacrifice they offer to demons and not to God. I do not want you to be partners with demons. You cannot drink the cup of the Lord and the cup of demons. You cannot partake of the table of the Lord and the table of demons. Shall we provoke the Lord to jealousy? Are we stronger than he?

"All things are lawful," but not all things are helpful. "All things are lawful," but not all things build up. Let no one seek his own good, but the good of his neighbor. Eat whatever is sold in the meat market without raising any question on the ground of conscience. For "the earth is the Lord's, and everything in it." If one of the unbelievers invites you to dinner and you are disposed to go, eat whatever is set before you without raising any question on the ground of conscience. (But if some one says to you, "This has been offered in sacrifice," then out of consideration for the man who informed you, and for conscience' sake—I mean his conscience, not yours—do not eat it.) For why should my liberty be determined by another man's scruples? If I partake with thankfulness, why am I denounced because of that for which I give thanks?

So, whether you eat or drink, or whatever you do, do all to the glory of God. Give no offense to Jews or to Greeks or to the church of God, just as I try to please all men in everything I do, not seeking my own advantage, but that of many, that they may be saved.

(1) **James 1:25** But he who looks into the perfect law, the law of liberty, and perseveres, being no hearer that forgets but a doer that acts, he shall be blessed in his doing. 1972

(2) **James 2:12** So speak and so act as those who are to be judged under the law of liberty. 1972

(3) **Galatians 4:1–7** I mean that the heir, as long as he is a child, is no better than a slave, though he is the owner of all the estate; but he is under guardians and trustees until the date set by the father. So with us; when we were children, we were slaves to the elemental spirits of the universe. But when the time had fully come, God sent forth his Son, born of woman, born under the law, to redeem those who were under the law, so that we might receive adoption as sons. And because you are sons, God has sent the Spirit of his Son into our hearts, crying, "Abba! Father!" So through God you are no longer a slave but a son, and if a son then an heir. 1972

(4) **Galatians 4:21–31** Tell me, you who desire to be under law, do you not hear the law? For it is written that Abraham had two sons, one by a slave and one by a free 1972

woman. But the son of the slave was born according to the flesh, the son of the free woman through promise. Now this is an allegory: these women are two covenants. One is from Mount Sinai, bearing children for slavery; she is Hagar. Now Hagar is Mount Sinai in Arabia; she corresponds to the present Jerusalem, for she is in slavery with her children. But the Jerusalem above is free, and she is our mother. For it is written,

"Rejoice, O barren one who does not bear;
break forth and shout, you who are not in travail;
for the children of the desolate one
are many more than the children of
her that is married."

Now we, brethren, like Isaac, are children of promise. But as at that time he who was born according to the flesh persecuted him who was born according to the Spirit, so it is now. But what does the scripture say? "Cast out the slave and her son; for the son of the slave shall not inherit with the son of the free woman." So, brethren, we are not children of the slave but of the free woman.

1972 (5) **Romans 8:15** For you did not receive the spirit of slavery to fall back into fear, but you have received the spirit of sonship. When we cry, "Abba! Father!"

1973 St. Thomas Aquinas, *Summa theologiae* II–II, 184, 3

article 3. whether perfection in this life consists in observing precepts or counsels

THE THIRD POINT: 1. It seems that perfection of life on earth does not consist in observing precepts but the counsels. For the Lord said, *If thou wilt be perfect, go sell what thou hast, and give to the poor, and come, follow me.* But this is a counsel. Therefore perfection consists in counsels and not in precepts.

2. Further, all are bound to observe the commandments, since they are necessary for salvation. If therefore the perfection of the Christian life consisted in precepts, it would follow that perfection is necessary for salvation and that all are bound to it. But this is evidently false.

3. Further, the perfection of the Christian life consists in charity, as already stated. But the perfection of charity does not seem to consist in the observance of precepts because the beginning and increase of charity precede perfection, as Augustine says, and charity cannot begin without observance of the precepts, as stated in *John*, *If any one love me, he will keep my word.* Therefore perfection of life consists not in precepts but in the counsels.

ON THE OTHER HAND, *Deuteronomy* says, *Thou shalt love the Lord thy God with thy whole heart*; and *Leviticus* says, *Thou shalt love thy friend as thyself.* These are two precepts of which the Lord says, *On these two commandments dependeth the whole law and the prophets.* But the perfection of charity, which constitutes the perfection of the Christian life, consists in loving God with our whole heart and our neighbor as ourselves. Therefore it seems that perfection consists in observance of precepts.

REPLY: Perfection can consist in something in two ways, in itself and essentially or secondarily and accidentally. In itself and essentially the perfection of the Christian life consists in charity—primarily in the love of God and secondarily in the love of neighbor, concerning which the principal precepts of divine law are given, as we have stated. But the love of God and neighbor do not fall under a precept according to any limitation, so that what goes beyond that, would be a matter of a counsel. This is evident from the very form of the precept which treats of perfection, when it states, *Thou shalt love the Lord thy God with thy whole heart* (and, according to Aristotle, *the whole and the perfect are identical*) and when it says, *Love thy neighbor as thyself* (since each one loves himself to the greatest extent). This is so because *the end of the commandment is charity*, as St. Paul says, but there is no limitation on an end, but only on the means to the end, as Aristotle says. Thus, the doctor does not place limits on health, but on the medication or diet used for healing. Hence it is evident that perfection consists essentially in the precepts. Therefore Augustine asks, *Why then should not this perfection be commanded of man even if no man has it in this life?*

Secondarily and instrumentally, however, perfection consists in the counsels, all of which, like the precepts, are ordained to charity, but in different ways. For the precepts are aimed at the removal of those things contrary to charity, i.e., those things incompatible with charity. But the counsels are aimed at the removal of those impediments to the exercise of charity which are not incompatible with charity, such as marriage, secular occupations, etc. So Augustine says, *Whatever things God commands, such as, Thou shalt not commit adultery, and whatever are not commanded, but suggested by a special counsel, such as, It is good for a man not to touch a woman, are done aright when they are referred to the love of God and of neighbor for God's sake, both in this world and in the world to come.* And therefore Abbot Moses says, *Fastings, vigils, meditation on Scripture, penury and loss of one's wealth are not perfection, but instruments of perfection, since the goal of such asceticism does not consist in those things, but through them one attains the goal.* And he had said previously, *We endeavor to ascend by these steps to the perfection of charity.*

Hence: 1. In those words of the Lord one thing is stated as a way to perfection, namely, *Go and sell what thou hast and give to the poor*, and another thing is added as constituting perfection, *Come, follow me.* Hence Jerome says, *Since it is not enough merely to leave, Peter added that which is perfect: And have followed thee.* And Ambrose states, *He commands him to follow, not with steps of the body, but with devotion of the soul*, which is effected by charity. Therefore from the very manner of speaking it appears that the counsels are a certain type of instrument for attaining perfection, for it is said, *If you want to be perfect, go, and sell*, etc. as if to say, *Doing this, you will come to this end.*

2. Augustine observes that the perfection of charity is commanded of man in this life because *one does not run well if he does not know where he is running. But how can he know if he is not shown by any precept?* And since that which falls under precept can be accomplished in various ways, one does not become a transgressor of the precept by not fulfilling it in the best possible way; it suffices that he fulfil it in some way. Now the perfection of divine love falls under the precept in all its extension, so that even the perfection of heaven is not excluded, as Augustine says. But whoever attains the perfection of divine love to any degree, avoids transgression of the precept. The lowest degree of divine love consists in not loving anything more than God, contrary to God, or equal to God, and one who does not have this degree of perfection in no way fulfils the precept. But there is a degree of perfection of love which cannot be attained in this life, as stated above; and if one lacks this degree, he does not transgress the precept. Similarly, one does not transgress the precept by not attaining the intermediate degrees of perfection, as long as he reaches the lowest degree.

3. Just as a person has at birth a certain natural perfection by reason of his species and another perfection which comes with growth, so also there is a certain perfection which pertains to the very species of charity, namely, that God is loved above all things and nothing contrary to God is loved. There is also another perfection of charity, even in this life, attained by a certain spiritual growth, as when a person refrains even from lawful things to give himself more freely to the service of God.

Romans 10:4 For Christ is the end of the law, that every one who has faith may 1977
be justified.

1987 **Romans 6:3–4** Do you not know that all of us who have been baptized into Christ Jesus were baptized into his death? We were buried therefore with him by baptism into death, so that as Christ was raised from the dead by the glory of the Father, we too might walk in newness of life.

1988 (1) **1 Corinthians 12** Now concerning spiritual gifts, brethren, I do not want you to be uninformed. You know that when you were heathen, you were led astray to dumb idols, however you may have been moved. Therefore I want you to understand that no one speaking by the Spirit of God ever says "Jesus be cursed!" and no one can say, "Jesus is Lord" except by the Holy Spirit.

Now there are varieties of gifts, but the same Spirit; and there are varieties of service, but the same Lord; and there are varieties of working, but it is the same God who inspires them all in every one. To each is given the manifestation of the Spirit for the common good. To one is given through the Spirit the utterance of wisdom, and to another the utterance of knowledge according to the same Spirit, to another faith by the same Spirit, to another gifts of healing by the one Spirit, to another the working of miracles, to another prophecy, to another the ability to distinguish between spirits, to another various kinds of tongues, to another the interpretation of tongues. All these are inspired by one and the same Spirit, who apportions to each one individually as he wills.

For just as the body is one and has many members, and all the members of the body, though many, are one body, so it is with Christ. For by one Spirit we were all baptized into one body—Jews or Greeks, slaves or free—and all were made to drink of one Spirit.

For the body does not consist of one member but of many. If the foot should say, "Because I am not a hand, I do not belong to the body," that would not make it any less a part of the body. And if the ear should say, "Because I am not an eye, I do not belong to the body," that would not make it any less a part of the body. If the whole body were an eye, where would be the hearing? If the whole body were an ear, where would be the sense of smell? But as it is, God arranged the organs in the body, each one of them, as he chose. If all were a single organ, where would the body be? As it is, there are many parts, yet one body. The eye cannot say to the hand, "I have no need of you," nor again the head to the feet, "I have no need of you." On the contrary, the parts of the body which seem to be weaker are indispensable, and those parts of the body which we think less honorable we invest with the greater honor, and our unpresentable parts are treated with greater modesty, which our more presentable parts do not require. But God has so composed the body, giving the greater honor to the inferior part, that there may be no discord in the body, but that the members may have the same care for one another. If one member suffers, all suffer together; if one member is honored, all rejoice together.

Now you are the body of Christ and individually members of it. And God has appointed in the church first apostles, second prophets, third teachers, then workers of miracles, then healers, helpers, administrators, speakers in various kinds of tongues. Are all apostles? Are all prophets? Are all teachers? Do all work miracles? Do all possess gifts of healing? Do all speak with tongues? Do all interpret? But earnestly desire the higher gifts.

And I will show you a still more excellent way.

1988 (2) **John 15:1–4** "I am the true vine, and my Father is the vinedresser. Every branch of mine that bears no fruit, he takes away, and every branch that does bear fruit he prunes, that it may bear more fruit. You are already made clean by the word which I have spoken to you. Abide in me, and I in you. As the branch cannot bear fruit by itself, unless it abides in the vine, neither can you, unless you abide in me. . . ."

Council of Trent (1547): DS 1529 The causes of this justification are: the final cause indeed is the glory of God and of Christ and life eternal; the efficient cause is truly a merciful God who gratuitously "washes and sanctifies" [I Cor. 6:11], "signing and anointing with the Holy Spirit of promise, who is the pledge of our inheritance" [Eph. 1:13 f.]; but the meritorious cause is His most beloved only-begotten Son, our Lord Jesus Christ, "who when we were enemies" [cf. Rom. 5:10], "for the exceeding charity wherewith he loved us" [Eph. 2:4], merited justification for us [can. 10] by His most holy passion on the wood of the Cross, and made satisfaction for us to God the Father; the instrumental cause is the sacrament of baptism, which is the "sacrament of faith," without which no one is ever justified. Finally the unique formal cause is the "justice of God, not that by which He Himself is just, but by which He makes us just" [can. 10 and 11], that, namely, by which, when we are endowed with it by him, we are renewed in the spirit of our mind, and not only are we reputed, but we are truly called and are just, receiving justice within us, each one according to his own measure, which the "Holy Spirit distributes to everyone as he wills" [I Cor. 12:11], and according to each one's own disposition and cooperation. 1992

(1) **Romans 7:22** For I delight in the law of God, in my inmost self. . . . 1995

(2) **Ephesians 3:16** . . . that according to the riches of his glory he may grant you to be strengthened with might through his Spirit in the inner man. . . . 1995

(1) **John 1:12–18** But to all who received him, who believed in his name, he gave power to become children of God; who were born, not of blood nor of the will of the flesh nor of the will of man, but of God. 1996

And the Word became flesh and dwelt among us, full of grace and truth; we have beheld his glory, glory as of the only Son from the Father. (John bore witness to him, and cried, "This was he of whom I said, 'He who comes after me ranks before me, for he was before me.' ") And from his fulness have we all received, grace upon grace. For the law was given through Moses; grace and truth came through Jesus Christ. No one has ever seen God; the only Son, who is in the bosom of the Father, he has made him known.

(2) **John 17:3** And this is eternal life, that they know thee the only true God, and Jesus Christ whom thou hast sent. 1996

(3) **Romans 8:14–17** For all who are led by the Spirit of God are sons of God. For you did not receive the spirit of slavery to fall back into fear, but you have received the spirit of sonship. When we cry, "Abba! Father!" it is the Spirit himself bearing witness with our spirit that we are children of God, and if children, then heirs, heirs of God and fellow heirs with Christ, provided we suffer with him in order that we may also be glorified with him. 1996

(4) **2 Peter 1:3–4** His divine power has granted to us all things that pertain to life and godliness, through the knowledge of him who called us to his own glory and excellence, by which he has granted to us his precious and very great promises, that through these you may escape from the corruption that is in the world because of passion, and become partakers of the divine nature. 1996

1998 **1 Corinthians 2:7–9** But we impart a secret and hidden wisdom of God, which God decreed before the ages for our glorification. None of the rulers of this age understood this; for if they had, they would not have crucified the Lord of glory. But, as it is written,

"What no eye has seen, nor ear heard,
nor the heart of man conceived,
what God has prepared for those who love him". . . .

1999 (1) **John 4:14** ". . . but whoever drinks of the water that I shall give him will never thirst; the water that I shall give him will become in him a spring of water welling up to eternal life."

1999 (2) **John 7:38–39** ". . . He who believes in me, as the scripture has said, 'Out of his heart shall flow rivers of living water.' " Now this he said about the Spirit, which those who believed in him were to receive; for as yet the Spirit had not been given, because Jesus was not yet glorified.

2002 **Genesis 1:31** And God saw everything that he had made, and behold, it was very good. And there was evening and there was morning, a sixth day.

2003 (1) ***Lumen gentium* 12** The holy People of God shares also in Christ's prophetic office: it spreads abroad a living witness to him, especially by a life of faith and love and by offering to God a sacrifice of praise, the fruit of lips praising his name (cf. Heb. 13:15). The whole body of the faithful who have an anointing that comes from the holy one (cf. 1 Jn. 2:20 and 27) cannot err in matters of belief. This characteristic is shown in the supernatural appreciation of the faith (*sensus fidei*) of the whole people, when, "from the bishops to the last of the faithful" they manifest a universal consent in matters of faith and morals. By this appreciation of the faith, aroused and sustained by the Spirit of truth, the People of God, guided by the sacred teaching authority (*magisterium*), and obeying it, receives not the mere word of men, but truly the word of God (cf. 1 Th. 2:13), the faith once for all delivered to the saints (cf. Jude 3). The People unfailingly adheres to this faith, penetrates it more deeply with right judgment, and applies it more fully in daily life.

It is not only through the sacraments and the ministrations of the Church that the Holy Spirit makes holy the People, leads them and enriches them with his virtues. Allotting his gifts according as he wills (cf. 1 Cor. 12:11), he also distributes special graces among the faithful of every rank. By these gifts he makes them fit and ready to undertake various tasks and offices for the renewal and building up of the Church, as it is written, "the manifestation of the Spirit is given to everyone for profit" (1 Cor. 12:7). Whether these charisms be very remarkable or more simple and widely diffused, they are to be received with thanksgiving and consolation since they are fitting and useful for the needs of the Church. Extraordinary gifts are not to be rashly desired, nor is it from them that the fruits of apostolic labors are to be presumptuously expected. Those who have charge over the Church should judge the genuineness and proper use of these gifts, through their office not indeed to extinguish the Spirit, but to test all things and hold fast to what is good (cf. 1 Th. 5:12 and 19–21).

2003 (2) **1 Corinthians 12:** see 1988 (1).

2005 **Council of Trent (1547): DS 1533–34** Although it is necessary to believe that sins are neither forgiven, nor ever have been forgiven, except gratuitously by divine mercy for Christ's sake, yet it must not be said that sins are forgiven or have been forgiven to anyone who boasts of his confidence and certainty of the forgiveness of his sins and rests on that alone, since among heretics and schismatics this vain confidence, remote from all piety [can. 12], may exist, indeed in our own troubled times does exist, and is preached against the Catholic Church with vigorous opposition. But neither is this to be asserted, that they who are truly justified without any doubt whatever should decide for themselves that they are justified, and that no one is absolved from sins and is justified, except him who believes with certainty that he is absolved and justified, and that by this faith alone are absolution and justification effected [can. 14], as if he who does not believe this is doubtful of the promises of God and of the efficacy of the death and resurrection of Christ. For, just as no pious person should doubt the mercy of God, the merit of Christ, and the virtue and efficacy of the sacraments, so every one, when he considers himself and his own weakness and indisposition, may entertain fear and apprehension as to his own grace [can. 13], since no one can know with the certainty of faith, which cannot be subject to error, that he has obtained the grace of God.

Council of Trent (1547): DS 1548 Nor indeed is this to be omitted, that although 2009
in the sacred Writings so much is ascribed to good works, that even "he that shall give a drink of cold water to one of his least ones" Christ promises "shall not lose his reward" [Matt. 10:42], and the Apostle testifies that "that which is at present momentary and light of our tribulation, worketh for us above measure exceedingly an eternal weight of glory" [II Cor. 4:17]; nevertheless far be it that a Christian should either trust or "glory" in himself and not "in the Lord" [cf. I Cor. 1:31; II Cor. 10:17], whose goodness towards all men is so great that He wishes the things which are His gifts to be their own merits [can. 32].

2 Timothy 4 I charge you in the presence of God and of Christ Jesus who is to 2015
judge the living and the dead, and by his appearing and his kingdom: preach the word, be urgent in season and out of season, convince, rebuke, and exhort, be unfailing in patience and in teaching. For the time is coming when people will not endure sound teaching, but having itching ears they will accumulate for themselves teachers to suit their own likings, and will turn away from listening to the truth and wander into myths. As for you, always be steady, endure suffering, do the work of an evangelist, fulfil your ministry.

For I am already on the point of being sacrificed; the time of my departure has come. I have fought the good fight, I have finished the race, I have kept the faith. Henceforth there is laid up for me the crown of righteousness, which the Lord, the righteous judge, will award to me on that Day, and not only to me but also to all who have loved his appearing.

Do your best to come to me soon. For Demas, in love with this present world, has deserted me and gone to Thessalonica; Crescens has gone to Galatia, Titus to Dalmatia. Luke alone is with me. Get Mark and bring him with you; for he is very useful in serving me. Tychicus I have sent to Ephesus. When you come, bring the cloak that I left with Carpus at Troas, also the books, and above all the parchments. Alexander the coppersmith did me great harm; the Lord will requite him for his deeds. Beware of him yourself, for he strongly opposed our message. At my first defense no one took my part; all deserted me. May it not be charged against them! But the Lord stood by me and gave me strength to proclaim the message fully, that all the Gentiles might hear it. So I was rescued from the lion's mouth. The Lord will rescue me from every evil and save me for his heavenly kingdom. To him be the glory for ever and ever. Amen.

Greet Prisca and Aquila, and the household of Onesiphorus. Erastus remained at Corinth; Trophimus I left ill at Miletus. Do your best to come before winter. Eubulus sends greetings to you, as do Pudens and Linus and Claudia and all the brethren.

The Lord be with your spirit. Grace be with you.

2016 **Council of Trent (1547): DS 1576** If anyone shall say that the just ought not to expect and hope for an eternal recompense from God and the merit of Jesus Christ for the good works which have been performed in God, if by doing well and in keeping the divine commandments they persevere even to the end: let him be anathema.

2035 ***Lumen gentium* 25** Among the more important duties of bishops that of preaching the Gospel has pride of place. For the bishops are heralds of the faith, who draw new disciples to Christ; they are authentic teachers, that is, teachers endowed with the authority of Christ, who preach the faith to the people assigned to them, the faith which is destined to inform their thinking and direct their conduct; and under the light of the Holy Spirit they make that faith shine forth, drawing from the storehouse of revelation new things and old (cf. Mt. 13:52); they make it bear fruit and with watchfulness they ward off whatever errors threaten their flock (cf. 2 Tim. 4:14). Bishops who teach in communion with the Roman Pontiff are to be revered by all as witnesses of divine and Catholic truth; the faithful, for their part, are obliged to submit to their bishops' decision, made in the name of Christ, in matters of faith and morals, and to adhere to it with a ready and respectful allegiance of mind. This loyal submission of the will and intellect must be given, in a special way, to the authentic teaching authority of the Roman Pontiff, even when he does not speak *ex cathedra* in such wise, indeed, that his supreme teaching authority be acknowledged with respect, and that one sincerely adhere to decisions made by him, conformably with his manifest mind and intention, which is made known principally either by the character of the documents in question, or by the frequency with which a certain doctrine is proposed, or by the manner in which the doctrine is formulated.

Although the bishops, taken individually, do not enjoy the privilege of infallibility, they do, however, proclaim infallibly the doctrine of Christ on the following conditions: namely, when, even though dispersed throughout the world but preserving for all that amongst themselves and with Peter's successor the bond of communion, in their authoritative teaching concerning matters of faith and morals, they are in agreement that a particular teaching is to be held definitively and absolutely. This is still more clearly the case when, assembled in an ecumenical council, they are, for the universal Church, teachers of and judges in matters of faith and morals, whose decisions must be adhered to with the loyal and obedient assent of faith.

This infallibility, however, with which the divine redeemer wished to endow his Church in defining doctrine pertaining to faith and morals, is co-extensive with the deposit of revelation, which must be religiously guarded and loyally and courageously expounded. The Roman Pontiff, head of the college of bishops, enjoys this infallibility in virtue of his office, when, as supreme pastor and teacher of all the faithful—who confirms his brethren in the faith (cf. Lk. 22:32)—he proclaims in an absolute decision a doctrine pertaining to faith or morals. For that reason his definitions are rightly said to be irreformable by their very nature and not by reason of the assent of the Church, in as much as they were made with the assistance of the Holy Spirit promised to him in the person of blessed Peter himself; and as a consequence they are in no way in need of the approval of others, and do not admit of appeal to any other tribunal. For in such a case the Roman Pontiff does not utter a pronouncement as a private person, but rather does he expound and defend the teaching of the Catholic faith as the supreme teacher of the universal Church, in whom the Church's charism of infallibility is present in a singular way. The infallibility promised to the Church is also present in the body of bishops when, together with Peter's successor, they exercise the supreme teaching office. Now, the assent of the Church can never be lacking to such definitions on account of the same Holy Spirit's influence, through which Christ's whole flock is maintained in the unity of the faith and makes progress in it.

Furthermore, when the Roman Pontiff, or the body of bishops together with him, define a doctrine, they make the definition in conformity with revelation itself, to which all are bound to adhere and to which they are obliged to submit; and this revelation is transmitted integrally either in written form or in oral tradition through the legitimate succession of bishops and above all through the watchful concern of the Roman Pontiff himself; and through the light of the Spirit of truth it is scrupulously preserved in the Church and unerringly explained. The Roman Pontiff and the bishops, by reason of their office and the seriousness of the matter, apply themselves with zeal to the work of enquiring by every suitable means into this revelation and of giving apt expression to its contents; they do not, however, admit any new public revelation as pertaining to the divine deposit of faith.

***Dignitatis humanae* 14** In order to satisfy the divine command: "Make disciples of 2036
all nations" (Mt. 28:19), the Catholic Church must spare no effort in striving "that the word of the Lord may speed on and triumph" (2 Th. 3:1).

The Church therefore earnestly urges her children first of all that "supplications, prayers, intercessions and thanksgivings be made for all men. . . . This is good and is acceptable in the sight of God our Savior, who desires all men to be saved and to come to the knowledge of the truth" (1 Tim. 2:1–4).

However, in forming their consciences the faithful must pay careful attention to the sacred and certain teaching of the Church. For the Catholic Church is by the will of Christ the teacher of truth. It is her duty to proclaim and teach with authority the truth which is Christ and, at the same time, to declare and confirm by her authority the principles of the moral order which spring from human nature itself. In addition, Christians should approach those who are outside wisely, "in the holy Spirit, genuine love, truthful speech" (2 Cor. 6:6–7), and should strive, even to the shedding of their blood, to spread the light of life with all confidence and apostolic courage.

The disciple has a grave obligation to Christ, his Master, to grow daily in his knowledge of the truth he has received from him, to be faithful in announcing it and vigorous in defending it without having recourse to methods which are contrary to the spirit of the Gospel. At the same time the love of Christ urges him to treat with love, prudence and patience those who are in error or ignorance with regard to the faith. He must take into account his duties towards Christ, the life-giving Word whom he must proclaim, the rights of the human person and the measure of grace which God has given to each man through Christ in calling him freely to accept and profess the faith.

CIC Canon 213 The Christian faithful have the right to receive assistance from 2037
the sacred pastors out of the spiritual goods of the Church, especially the word of God and the sacraments.

1 Corinthians 2:10–15 . . . God has revealed to us through the Spirit. For the 2038
Spirit searches everything, even the depths of God. For what person knows a man's thoughts except the spirit of the man which is in him? So also no one comprehends the thoughts of God except the Spirit of God. Now we have received not the spirit

of the world, but the Spirit which is from God, that we might understand the gifts bestowed on us by God. And we impart this in words not taught by human wisdom but taught by the Spirit, interpreting spiritual truths to those who possess the Spirit.

The unspiritual man does not receive the gifts of the Spirit of God, for they are folly to him, and he is not able to understand them because they are spiritually discerned. The spiritual man judges all things, but is himself to be judged by no one.

2039 (1) **Romans 12:8** . . . he who exhorts, in his exhortation; he who contributes, in liberality; he who gives aid, with zeal; he who does acts of mercy, with cheerfulness.

2039 (2) **Romans 12:11** Never flag in zeal, be aglow with the Spirit, serve the Lord.

2042 (1) **CIC Canons 1246–48**

Can. 1246—§1. Sunday is the day on which the paschal mystery is celebrated in light of the apostolic tradition and is to be observed as the foremost holy day of obligation in the universal Church. Also to be observed are the day of the Nativity of Our Lord Jesus Christ, the Epiphany, the Ascension and the Most Holy Body and Blood of Christ, Holy Mary Mother of God and her Immaculate Conception and Assumption, Saint Joseph, the Apostles Saints Peter and Paul, and finally, All Saints.

§2. However, the conference of bishops can abolish certain holy days of obligation or transfer them to a Sunday with prior approval of the Apostolic See.

Can. 1247—On Sundays and other holy days of obligation the faithful are bound to participate in the Mass; they are also to abstain from those labors and business concerns which impede the worship to be rendered to God, the joy which is proper to the Lord's Day, or the proper relaxation of mind and body.

Can. 1248—§1. The precept of participating in the Mass is satisfied by assistance at a Mass which is celebrated anywhere in a Catholic rite either on the holy day or on the evening of the preceding day.

§2. If because of lack of a sacred minister or for other grave cause participation in the celebration of the Eucharist is impossible, it is specially recommended that the faithful take part in the liturgy of the word if it is celebrated in the parish church or in another sacred place according to the prescriptions of the diocesan bishop, or engage in prayer for an appropriate amount of time personally or in a family or, as occasion offers, in groups of families.

2042 (2) **CCEO Canon 881, §§1–2**

§1. The Christian faithful are bound by the obligation to participate on Sundays and feast days in the Divine Liturgy, or according to the prescriptions or legitimate customs of their own Church *sui iuris*, in the celebration of the divine praises.

§2. In order for the Christian faithful to fulfill this obligation more easily, the available time runs from the evening of the vigil until the end of the Sunday or feast day.

2042 (3) **CCEO Canon 881, §4** The Christian faithful should abstain from those labors or business matters which impede the worship to be rendered to God, the joy which is proper to the Lord's day, or to the proper relaxation of mind and body.

2042 (4) **CIC Canon 989** After having attained the age of discretion, each of the faithful is bound by an obligation faithfully to confess serious sins at least once a year.

2042 (5) **CCEO Canon 719** Anyone who is aware of serious sin is to receive the sacrament of penance as soon as possible; it is strongly recommended to all the Christian faithful that they receive this sacrament frequently especially during the times of fasts and penance observed in their own Church *sui iuris*.

(6) **CIC Canon 920** 2042

§1. All the faithful, after they have been initiated into the Most Holy Eucharist, are bound by the obligation of receiving Communion at least once a year.

§2. This precept must be fulfilled during the Easter season unless it is fulfilled for a just cause at some other time during the year.

(7) **CCEO Canon 708** The local hierarchs and the pastors are to see that with every diligence the Christian faithful are instructed concerning the obligation of receiving the Divine Eucharist in danger of death and also at those times which are established by a most praiseworthy custom or by particular law of their own Church *sui iuris*, especially at Easter time, during which Christ handed down the eucharistic mystery. 2042

(8) **CCEO Canon 881, §3** The Christian faithful are strongly recommended to receive the Divine Eucharist on these days and indeed more frequently, even daily. 2042

(1) **CIC Canon 1246** 2043

§1. Sunday is the day on which the paschal mystery is celebrated in light of the apostolic tradition and is to be observed as the foremost holy day of obligation in the universal Church. Also to be observed are the day of the Nativity of Our Lord Jesus Christ, the Epiphany, the Ascension and the Most Holy Body and Blood of Christ, Holy Mary Mother of God and her Immaculate Conception and Assumption, Saint Joseph, the Apostles Saints Peter and Paul, and finally, All Saints.

§2. However, the conference of bishops can abolish certain holy days of obligation or transfer them to a Sunday with prior approval of the Apostolic See.

(2) **CCEO Canon 881, §1** The Christian faithful are bound by the obligation to participate on Sundays and feast days in the Divine Liturgy, or according to the prescriptions or legitimate customs of their own Church *sui iuris*, in the celebration of the divine praises. 2043

(3) **CCEO Canon 881, §4** The Christian faithful should abstain from those labors or business matters which impede the worship to be rendered to God, the joy which is proper to the Lord's day, or to the proper relaxation of mind and body. 2043

(4) **CCEO Canon 880, §3** Holy days of obligation common to all the Eastern Churches, beyond Sundays, are the Nativity of our Lord Jesus Christ, the Epiphany, the Ascension, the Dormition of the Holy Mary Mother of God and the Holy Apostles Peter and Paul except for the particular law of a Church *sui iuris* approved by the Apostolic See which suppresses holy days of obligation or transfers them to a Sunday. 2043

(5) **CIC Canons 1249–51** 2043

Can. 1249—All members of the Christian faithful in their own way are bound to do penance in virtue of divine law; in order that all may be joined in a common observance of penance, penitential days are prescribed in which the Christian faithful in a special way pray, exercise works of piety and charity, and deny themselves by fulfilling their responsibilities more faithfully and especially by observing fast and abstinence according to the norm of the following canons.

Can. 1250—All Fridays through the year and the time of Lent are penitential days and times throughout the universal Church.

Can. 1251—Abstinence from eating meat or another food according to the prescriptions of the conference of bishops is to be observed on Fridays throughout the year unless they are solemnities; abstinence and fast are to be observed on Ash Wednesday and on the Friday of the Passion and Death of Our Lord Jesus Christ.

2043 (6) **CCEO Canon 882** On the days of penance the Christian faithful are obliged to observe fast or abstinence in the manner established by the particular law of their Church *sui iuris*.

2043 (7) **CIC Canon 222**

§1. The Christian faithful are obliged to assist with the needs of the Church so that the Church has what is necessary for divine worship, for apostolic works and works of charity and for the decent sustenance of ministers.

§2. They are also obliged to promote social justice and, mindful of the precept of the Lord, to assist the poor from their own resources.

2045 (1) **Ephesians 1:22** . . . and he has put all things under his feet and has made him the head over all things for the church. . . .

2045 (2) ***Lumen gentium* 39** The Church, whose mystery is set forth by this sacred Council, is held, as a matter of faith, to be unfailingly holy. This is because Christ, the Son of God, who with the Father and the Spirit is hailed as "alone holy," loved the Church as his Bride, giving himself up for her so as to sanctify her (cf. Eph. 5:25–26); he joined her to himself as his body and endowed her with the gift of the Holy Spirit for the glory of God. Therefore all in the Church, whether they belong to the hierarchy or are cared for by it, are called to holiness, according to the apostle's saying: 'For this is the will of God, your sanctification' (1 Th. 4:3; cf. Eph. 1:4). This holiness of the Church is constantly shown forth in the fruits of grace which the Spirit produces in the faithful and so it must be; it is expressed in many ways by the individuals who, each in his own state of life, tend to the perfection of love, thus helping others to grow in holiness; it appears in a manner peculiar to itself in the practice of the counsels which have been usually called "evangelical." This practice of the counsels prompted by the Holy Spirit, undertaken by many Christians whether privately or in a form or state sanctioned by the Church, gives and should give a striking witness and example of that holiness.

2053 (1) **Matthew 5:17** "Think not that I have come to abolish the law and the prophets; I have come not to abolish them but to fulfil them. . . ."

2053 (2) **Matthew 19:6–12** ". . . So they are no longer two but one flesh. What therefore God has joined together, let not man put asunder." They said to him, "Why then did Moses command one to give a certificate of divorce, and to put her away?" He said to them, "For your hardness of heart Moses allowed you to divorce your wives, but from the beginning it was not so. And I say to you: whoever divorces his wife, except for unchastity, and marries another, commits adultery."

The disciples said to him, "If such is the case of a man with his wife, it is not expedient to marry." But he said to them, "Not all men can receive this saying, but only those to whom it is given. For there are eunuchs who have been so from birth, and there are eunuchs who have been made eunuchs by men, and there are eunuchs who have made themselves eunuchs for the sake of the kingdom of heaven. He who is able to receive this, let him receive it."

2053 (3) **Matthew 19:21** Jesus said to him, "If you would be perfect, go, sell what you possess and give to the poor, and you will have treasure in heaven; and come, follow me."

2053 (4) **Matthew 19:23–29** And Jesus said to his disciples, "Truly, I say to you, it will be hard for a rich man to enter the kingdom of heaven. Again I tell you, it is easier for a camel to go through the eye of a needle than for a rich man to enter the kingdom of God." When the disciples heard this they were greatly astonished, saying, "Who then can be saved?" But Jesus looked at them and said to them, "With men this is impossible, but with God all things are possible." Then Peter said in reply, "Lo, we have left everything and followed you. What then shall we have?" Jesus said to them, "Truly, I say to you, in the new world, when the Son of man shall sit on his glorious throne, you who have followed me will also sit on twelve thrones, judging the twelve tribes of Israel. And every one who has left houses or brothers or sisters or father or mother or children or lands, for my name's sake, will receive a hundredfold, and inherit eternal life. . . ."

Matthew 5:46–47 For if you love those who love you, what reward have you? Do not even the tax collectors do the same? And if you salute only your brethren, what more are you doing than others? Do not even the Gentiles do the same? 2054

(1) **Deuteronomy 6:5** . . . and you shall love the Lord your God with all your heart, and with all your soul, and with all your might. 2055

(2) **Leviticus 19:18** You shall not take vengeance or bear any grudge against the sons of your own people, but you shall love your neighbor as yourself: I am the Lord. 2055

(1) **Deuteronomy 31:9** And Moses wrote this law, and gave it to the priests the sons of Levi, who carried the ark of the covenant of the Lord, and to all the elders of Israel. 2056

(2) **Deuteronomy 31:24** When Moses had finished writing the words of this law in a book, to the very end. . . . 2056

(3) **Exodus 20:1–17** And God spoke all these words, saying, 2056

"I am the Lord your God, who brought you out of the land of Egypt, out of the house of bondage.

"You shall have no other gods before me.

"You shall not make for yourself a graven image, or any likeness of anything that is in heaven above, or that is in the earth beneath, or that is in the water under the earth; you shall not bow down to them or serve them; for I the Lord your God am a jealous God, visiting the iniquity of the fathers upon the children to the third and the fourth generation of those who hate me, but showing steadfast love to thousands of those who love me and keep my commandments.

"You shall not take the name of the Lord your God in vain; for the Lord will not hold him guiltless who takes his name in vain.

"Remember the sabbath day, to keep it holy. Six days you shall labor, and do all your work; but the seventh day is a sabbath to the Lord your God; in it you shall not do any work, you, or your son, or your daughter, your manservant, or your maidservant, or your cattle, or the sojourner who is within your gates; for in six days the Lord made heaven and earth, the sea, and all that is in them, and rested the seventh day; therefore the Lord blessed the Sabbath day and hallowed it.

"Honor your father and your mother, that your days may be long in the land which the Lord your God gives you.

"You shall not kill.

"You shall not commit adultery.

"You shall not steal.

"You shall not bear false witness against your neighbor.

"You shall not covet your neighbor's house; you shall not covet your neighbor's wife, or his manservant, or his maidservant, or his ox, or his ass, or anything that is your neighbor's."

2056 (4) **Deuteronomy 5:6–22** "'I am the Lord your God, who brought you out of the land of Egypt, out of the house of bondage.

"'You shall have no other gods before me.

"'You shall not make for yourself a graven image, or any likeness of anything that is in heaven above, or that is on the earth beneath, or that is in the water under the earth; you shall not bow down to them or serve them; for I the Lord your God am a jealous God, visiting the iniquity of the fathers upon the children to the third and fourth generation of those who hate me, but showing steadfast love to thousands of those who love me and keep my commandments.

"'You shall not take the name of the Lord your God in vain: for the Lord will not hold him guiltless who takes his name in vain.

"'Observe the sabbath day, to keep it holy, as the Lord your God commanded you. Six days you shall labor, and do all your work; but the seventh day is a sabbath to the Lord your God; in it you shall not do any work, you, or your son, or your daughter, or your manservant, or your maidservant, or your ox, or your ass, or any of your cattle, or the sojourner who is within your gates, that your manservant and your maidservant may rest as well as you. You shall remember that you were a servant in the land of Egypt, and the Lord your God brought you out thence with a mighty hand and an outstretched arm; therefore the Lord your God commanded you to keep the sabbath day.

"'Honor your father and your mother, as the Lord your God commanded you; that your days may be prolonged, and that it may go well with you, in the land which the Lord your God gives you.

"'You shall not kill.

"'Neither shall you commit adultery.

"'Neither shall you steal.

"'Neither shall you bear false witness against your neighbor.

"'Neither shall you covet your neighbor's wife; and you shall not desire your neighbor's house, his field, or his manservant, or his maidservant, his ox, or his ass, or anything that is your neighbor's.'

"These words the Lord spoke to all your assembly at the mountain out of the midst of the fire, the cloud, and the thick darkness, with a loud voice; and he added no more. And he wrote them upon two tables of stone, and gave them to me. . . ."

2056 (5) **Hosea 4:2**

. . . there is swearing, lying, killing, stealing, and committing adultery;
they break all bounds and murder follows murder.

2056 (6) **Jeremiah 7:9** Will you steal, murder, commit adultery, swear falsely, burn incense to Baal, and go after other gods that you have not known . . . ?

2056 (7) **Ezekiel 18:5–9** "If a man is righteous and does what is lawful and right—if he does not eat upon the mountains or lift up his eyes to the idols of the house of Israel, does not defile his neighbor's wife or approach a woman in her time of impurity, does not oppress any one, but restores to the debtor his pledge, commits no robbery, gives his bread to the hungry and covers the naked with a garment, does not lend at interest or take any increase, withholds his hand from iniquity, executes true justice between man and man, walks in my statutes, and is careful to observe my ordinances—he is righteous, he shall surely live, says the Lord God. . . ."

(1) **Exodus 19:** see 751 (2). 2060

(2) **Exodus 24:7** Then he took the book of the covenant, and read it in the hearing of the people; and they said, "All that the Lord has spoken we will do, and we will be obedient." 2060

(1) **Exodus 20:2** "I am the Lord your God, who brought you out of the land of Egypt, out of the house of bondage. . . ." 2061

(2) **Deuteronomy 5:6** " 'I am the Lord your God, who brought you out of the land of Egypt, out of the house of bondage. . . .' " 2061

Council of Trent (1547): DS 1569–70 If anyone shall say that nothing except faith is commanded in the Gospel, that other things are indifferent, neither commanded nor prohibited, but free, or that the ten commandments in no way pertain to Christians: let him be anathema. 2068

If anyone shall say that a man who is justified and ever so perfect is not bound to observe the commandments of God and the Church, but only to believe, as if indeed the Gospel were a mere absolute promise of eternal life, without the condition of observation of the commandments: let him be anathema.

James 2:10–11 For whoever keeps the whole law but fails in one point has become guilty of all of it. For he who said, "Do not commit adultery," said also, "Do not kill." If you do not commit adultery but do kill, you have become a transgressor of the law. 2069

James 2:10–11: see previous document. 2079

(1) **Luke 10:27** And he answered, "You shall love the Lord your God with all your heart, and with all your soul, and with all your strength, and with all your mind; and your neighbor as yourself." 2083

(2) **Deuteronomy 5:6–9** " 'I am the Lord your God, who brought you out of the land of Egypt, out of the house of bondage. 2083

" 'You shall have no other gods before me.

" 'You shall not make for yourself a graven image, or any likeness of anything that is in heaven above, or that is on the earth beneath, or that is in the water under the earth; you shall not bow down to them or serve them; for I the Lord your God am a jealous God, visiting the iniquity of the fathers upon the children to the third and fourth generation of those who hate me. . . .' "

(1) **Exodus 19:16–25** On the morning of the third day there were thunders and lightnings, and a thick cloud upon the mountain, and a very loud trumpet blast, so that all the people who were in the camp trembled. Then Moses brought the people out of the camp to meet God; and they took their stand at the foot of the mountain. And Mount Sinai was wrapped in smoke, because the Lord descended upon it in fire; and the smoke of it went up like the smoke of a kiln, and the whole mountain quaked greatly. And as the sound of the trumpet grew louder and louder, Moses spoke, and God answered him in thunder. And the Lord came down upon Mount Sinai, to the top of the mountain; and the Lord called Moses to the top of the mountain, and Moses went up. And the Lord said to Moses, "Go down and warn the people, lest they break through to the Lord to gaze and many of them perish. And also let the 2085

priests who come near to the Lord consecrate themselves, lest the Lord break out upon them." And Moses said to the Lord, "The people cannot come up to Mount Sinai; for thou thyself didst charge us, saying 'Set bounds about the mountain, and consecrate it.'" And the Lord said to him, "Go down, and come up bringing Aaron with you; but do not let the priests and the people break through to come up to the Lord, lest he break out against them." So Moses went down to the people and told them.

2085 (2) **Exodus 24:15–18** Then Moses went up on the mountain, and the cloud covered the mountain. The glory of the Lord settled on Mount Sinai, and the cloud covered it six days; and on the seventh day he called to Moses out of the midst of the cloud. Now the appearance of the glory of the Lord was like a devouring fire on the top of the mountain in the sight of the people of Israel. And Moses entered the cloud, and went up on the mountain. And Moses was on the mountain forty days and forty nights.

2087 **Romans 1:18–32** For the wrath of God is revealed from heaven against all ungodliness and wickedness of men who by their wickedness suppress the truth. For what can be known about God is plain to them, because God has shown it to them. Ever since the creation of the world his invisible nature, namely, his eternal power and deity, has been clearly perceived in the things that have been made. So they are without excuse; for although they knew God they did not honor him as God or give thanks to him, but they became futile in their thinking and their senseless minds were darkened. Claiming to be wise, they became fools, and exchanged the glory of the immortal God for images resembling mortal man or birds or animals or reptiles.

Therefore God gave them up in the lusts of their hearts to impurity, to the dishonoring of their bodies among themselves, because they exchanged the truth about God for a lie and worshiped and served the creature rather than the Creator, who is blessed for ever! Amen.

For this reason God gave them up to dishonorable passions. Their women exchanged natural relations for unnatural, and the men likewise gave up natural relations with women and were consumed with passion for one another, men committing shameless acts with men and receiving in their own persons the due penalty for their error.

And since they did not see fit to acknowledge God, God gave them up to a base mind and to improper conduct. They were filled with all manner of wickedness, evil, covetousness, malice. Full of envy, murder, strife, deceit, malignity, they are gossips, slanderers, haters of God, insolent, haughty, boastful, inventors of evil, disobedient to parents, foolish, faithless, heartless, ruthless. Though they know God's decree that those who do such things deserve to die, they not only do them but approve those who practice them.

2093 **Deuteronomy 6:4–5** "Hear, O Israel: The Lord our God is one Lord; and you shall love the Lord your God with all your heart, and with all your soul, and with all your might. . . ."

2096 **Deuteronomy 6:13** You shall fear the Lord your God; you shall serve him, and swear by his name.

2097 **Luke 1:46–49** And Mary said,
"My soul magnifies the Lord,
and my spirit rejoices in God my Savior,

for he has regarded the low estate of his handmaiden.
For behold, henceforth all generations will call me blessed;
for he who is mighty has done great things for me,
and holy is his name. . . ."

(1) **Amos 5:21–25** **2100**

"I hate, I despise your feasts,
    and I take no delight in your solemn assemblies.
Even though you offer me your burnt offerings and cereal offerings,
    I will not accept them,
and the peace offerings of your fatted beasts
    I will not look upon.
Take away from me the noise of your songs;
    to the melody of your harps I will not listen.
But let justice roll down like waters,
    and righteousness like an ever-flowing stream.

"Did you bring to me sacrifices and offerings the forty years in the wilderness, O house of Israel? . . ."

(2) **Isaiah 1:10–20** **2100**

Hear the word of the Lord,
    you rulers of Sodom!
Give ear to the teaching of our God,
    you people of Gomorrah.
"What to me is the multitude of your sacrifices?
    says the Lord;
I have had enough of burnt offerings of rams
    and the fat of fed beasts;
I do not delight in the blood of bulls,
    or of lambs, or of he-goats.
"When you come to appear before me,
    who requires of you
    this trampling of my courts?
Bring no more vain offerings;
    incense is an abomination to me.
New moon and sabbath and the calling of assemblies—
    I cannot endure iniquity and solemn assembly.
Your new moons and your appointed feasts
    my soul hates;
they have become a burden to me,
    I am weary of bearing them.
When you spread forth your hands,
    I will hide my eyes from you;
even though you make many prayers,
    I will not listen;
    your hands are full of blood.
Wash yourselves; make yourselves clean;
    remove the evil of your doings
    from before my eyes;
cease to do evil,
    learn to do good;

seek justice,
  correct oppression;
defend the fatherless,
  plead for the widow.

"Come now, let us reason together,
  says the Lord:
though your sins are like scarlet,
  they shall be as white as snow;
though they are red like crimson,
  they shall become like wool.
If you are willing and obedient,
  you shall eat the good of the land;
But if you refuse and rebel,
  you shall be devoured by the sword;
  for the mouth of the Lord has spoken."

2100 (3) **Hosea 6:6**
For I desire steadfast love and not sacrifice,
  the knowledge of God, rather than burnt offerings.

2100 (4) **Hebrews 9:13–14** For if the sprinkling of defiled persons with the blood of goats and bulls and with the ashes of a heifer sanctifies for the purification of the flesh, how much more shall the blood of Christ, who through the eternal Spirit offered himself without blemish to God, purify your conscience from dead works to serve the living God.

2102 (1) **Acts 18:18** After this Paul stayed many days longer, and then took leave of the brethren and sailed for Syria, and with him Priscilla and Aquila. At Cenchreae he cut his hair, for he had a vow.

2102 (2) **Acts 21:23–24** Do therefore what we tell you. We have four men who are under a vow; take these men and purify yourself along with them and pay their expenses, so that they may shave their heads. Thus all will know that there is nothing in what they have been told about you but that you yourself live in observance of the law.

2103 (1) **CIC Canon 654** By religious profession members assume by public vow the observance of the three evangelical counsels, are consecrated to God through the ministry of the Church, and are incorporated into the institute with rights and duties defined by law.

2103 (2) **CIC Canon 692** Unless it has been rejected by the member in the act of notification, an indult legitimately granted and made known to the member brings with it, by the law itself, a dispensation from vows and from all obligations arising from profession.

2103 (3) **CIC Canons 1196–97**

Can. 1196—Besides the Roman Pontiff, the following persons can dispense from private vows for a just reason provided a dispensation does not injure a right acquired by others:

1° the local ordinary and the pastor as regards all their own subjects as well as travelers;

2° the superior of a religious institute or society of apostolic life if they are clerical of pontifical right as regards members, novices, and persons who stay day and night in a house of the institute or society;

3° persons to whom the power of dispensation has been delegated by the Apostolic See or by the local ordinary.

Can. 1197—The work promised in a private vow can be commuted to a greater or an equal good by the person who makes the vow; however, a person who has the power of dispensation according to the norm of can. 1196 can commute it to a lesser good.

(1) ***Dignitatis humanae* 1** Contemporary man is becoming increasingly conscious of the dignity of the human person; more and more people are demanding that men should exercise fully their own judgment and a responsible freedom in their actions and should not be subject to the pressure of coercion but be inspired by a sense of duty. At the same time they are demanding constitutional limitation of the powers of government to prevent excessive restriction of the rightful freedom of individuals and associations. This demand for freedom in human society is concerned chiefly with man's spiritual values, and especially with what concerns the free practice of religion in society. This Vatican Council pays careful attention to these spiritual aspirations and, with a view to declaring to what extent they are in accord with the truth and justice, searches the sacred tradition and teaching of the Church, from which it draws forth new things that are always in harmony with the old. **2105**

The sacred Council begins by professing that God himself has made known to the human race how men by serving him can be saved and reach happiness in Christ. We believe that this one true religion continues to exist in the Catholic and Apostolic Church, to which the Lord Jesus entrusted the task of spreading it among all men when he said to the apostles: "Go therefore and make disciples of all nations baptizing them in the name of the Father and of the Son and of the Holy Spirit, teaching them to observe all that I have commanded you" (Mt. 18:19–20). All men are bound to seek the truth, especially in what concerns God and his Church, and to embrace it and hold on to it as they come to know it.

The sacred Council likewise proclaims that these obligations bind man's conscience. Truth can impose itself on the mind of man only in virtue of its own truth, which wins over the mind with both gentleness and power. So while the religious freedom which men demand in fulfilling their obligation to worship God has to do with freedom from coercion in civil society, it leaves intact the traditional Catholic teaching on the moral duty of individuals and societies towards the true religion and the one Church of Christ. Furthermore, in dealing with this question of liberty the sacred Council intends to develop the teaching of recent popes on the inviolable rights of the human person and on the constitutional order of society.

(2) ***Apostolicam actuositatem* 13** The apostolate in one's social environment endeavors to infuse the Christian spirit into the mentality and behavior, laws and structures of the community in which one lives. To such a degree is it the special work and responsibility of lay people, that no one else can ever properly supply for them. In this area laymen can conduct the apostolate of like towards like. There the witness of their life is completed by the witness of their word. It is amid the surroundings of their work that they are best qualified to be of help to their brothers, in the surroundings of their profession, of their study, residence, leisure or local group. **2105**

The laity accomplish the Church's mission in the world principally by that blending of conduct and faith which makes them the light of the world; by that uprightness in all their dealings which is for every man such an incentive to love the true and the good and which is capable of inducing him at last to go to Christ and the Church; by that fraternal charity that makes them share the living conditions and labors, the sufferings and yearnings of their brothers, and thereby prepare all hearts, gently, imperceptibly, for the action of saving grace; by that full awareness of their personal responsibility in the development of society, which drives them on to perform their family, social and professional duties with Christian generosity. In this way their conduct makes itself gradually felt in the surroundings where they live and work.

This apostolate should reach out to every single person in that environment; and it must not exclude any good, spiritual or temporal, that can be done for them. Genuine apostles are not content, however, with just this; they are earnest also about revealing Christ by word to those around them. It is a fact that many men cannot hear the Gospel and come to acknowledge Christ except through the laymen they associate with.

2105 (3) **Leo XIII, encyclical *Immortale Dei*:** see 1898 (1).

2105 (4) **Pius XI, encyclical *Quas Primas***

To Our Venerable Brethren the Patriarchs, Primates, Archbishops, Bishops, and other Ordinaries in Peace and Communion with the Apostolic See.

Venerable Brethren, Greeting and the Apostolic Benediction.

In the first Encyclical Letter which We addressed at the beginning of Our Pontificate to the Bishops of the universal Church, We referred to the chief causes of the difficulties under which mankind was laboring. And We remember saying that these manifold evils in the world were due to the fact that the majority of men had thrust Jesus Christ and his holy law out of their lives; that these had no place either in private affairs or in politics: and we said further, that as long as individuals and states refused to submit to the rule of our Savior, there would be no really hopeful prospect of a lasting peace among nations. Men must look for the *peace of Christ in the Kingdom of Christ;* and that We promised to do as far as lay in Our power. *In the Kingdom of Christ,* that is, it seemed to Us that peace could not be more effectually restored nor fixed upon a firmer basis than through the restoration of the Empire of Our Lord. We were led in the meantime to indulge the hope of a brighter future at the sight of a more widespread and keener interest evinced in Christ and his Church, the one Source of Salvation, a sign that men who had formerly spurned the rule of our Redeemer and had exiled themselves from his kingdom were preparing, and even hastening, to return to the duty of obedience.

The many notable and memorable events which have occurred during this Holy Year have given great honor and glory to Our Lord and King, the Founder of the Church.

At the Missionary Exhibition men have been deeply impressed in seeing the increasing zeal of the Church for the spread of the kingdom of her Spouse to the most far distant regions of the earth. They have seen how many countries have been won to the Catholic name through the unremitting labor and self-sacrifice of missionaries, and the vastness of the regions which have yet to be subjected to the sweet and saving yoke of our King. All those who in the course of the Holy Year have thronged to this city under the leadership of their Bishops or priests had but one aim—namely, to expiate their sins—and at the tombs of the Apostles and in Our Presence to promise loyalty to the rule of Christ.

A still further light of glory was shed upon his kingdom, when after due proof of their heroic virtue, We raised to the honors of the altar six confessors and virgins. It was a great joy, a great consolation, that filled Our heart when in the majestic basilica of St. Peter Our decree was acclaimed by an immense multitude with the hymn of thanksgiving, *Tu Rex gloriae Christe.* We saw men and nations cut off from God, stirring up strife and discord and hurrying along the road to ruin and death, while the Church of God carries on her work of providing food for the spiritual life of men, nurturing and fostering generation after generation of men and women dedicated to Christ, faithful and subject to him in his earthly kingdom, called by him to eternal bliss in the kingdom of heaven.

Moreover, since this Jubilee Year marks the sixteenth centenary of the Council of Nicaea, We commanded that event to be celebrated, and We have done so in the Vatican basilica. There is a special reason for this in that the Nicene Synod defined and proposed for Catholic belief the dogma of the Consubstantiality of the Only-begotten with the Father, and added to the Creed the words "of whose kingdom there shall be no end," thereby affirming the kingly dignity of Christ.

Since this Holy Year therefore has provided more than one opportunity to enhance the glory of the kingdom of Christ, we deem it in keeping with our Apostolic office to accede to the desire of many of the Cardinals, Bishops, and faithful, made known to Us both individually and collectively, by closing this Holy Year with the insertion into the Sacred Liturgy of a special feast of *the Kingship of Our Lord Jesus Christ.* This matter is so dear to Our heart, Venerable Brethren, that I would wish to address to you a few words concerning it. It will be for you later to explain in a manner suited to the understanding of the faithful what We are about to say concerning the Kingship of Christ, so that the annual feast which We shall decree may be attended with much fruit and produce beneficial results in the future.

It has long been a common custom to give to Christ the metaphorical title of "King," because of the high degree of perfection whereby he excels all creatures. So he is said to reign "in the hearts of men," both by reason of the keenness of his intellect and the extent of his knowledge, and also because he is very truth, and it is from him that truth must be obediently received by all mankind. He reigns, too, in the wills of men, for in him the human will was perfectly and entirely obedient to the Holy Will of God, and further by his grace and inspiration he so subjects our free-will as to incite us to the most noble endeavors. He is *King of hearts*, too, by reason of his "charity which exceedeth all knowledge." And his mercy and kindness which draw all men to him, for never has it been known, nor will it ever be, that man be loved so much and so universally as Jesus Christ. But if we ponder this matter more deeply, we cannot but see that the title and the power of King belongs to Christ as man in the strict and proper sense too. For it is only as man that he may be said to have received from the Father "power and glory and a kingdom," since the Word of God, as consubstantial with the Father, has all things in common with him, and therefore has necessarily supreme and absolute dominion over all things created.

Do we not read throughout the Scriptures that Christ is the King? He it is that shall come out of Jacob to rule, who has been set by the Father as king over Sion, his holy mount, and shall have the Gentiles for his inheritance, and the utmost parts of the earth for his possession. In the nuptial hymn, where the future King of Israel is hailed as a most rich and powerful monarch, we read: "Thy throne, O God, is for ever and ever; the scepter of thy kingdom is a scepter of righteousness." There are many similar passages, but there is one in which Christ is even more clearly indicated. Here it is foretold that his kingdom will have no limits, and will be enriched with justice and peace: "in his days shall justice spring up, and abundance of peace. . . . And he shall rule from sea to sea, and from the river unto the ends of the earth."

The testimony of the Prophets is even more abundant. That of Isaias is well known: "For a child is born to us and a son is given to us, and the government is upon his shoulder, and his name shall be called Wonderful, Counsellor, God the mighty, the

Father of the world to come, the Prince of Peace. His empire shall be multiplied, and there shall be no end of peace. He shall sit upon the throne of David and upon his kingdom; to establish it and strengthen it with judgment and with justice, from henceforth and for ever." With Isaias the other Prophets are in agreement. So Jeremias foretells the "just seed" that shall rest from the house of David—the Son of David that shall rein as king, "and shall be wise, and shall execute judgment and justice in the earth." So, too, Daniel, who announces the kingdom that the God of heaven shall found, "that shall never be destroyed, and shall stand for ever." And again he says: "l beheld, therefore, in the vision of the night, and, lo! one like the son of man came with the clouds of heaven. And he came even to the Ancient of days: and they presented him before him. And he gave him power and glory and a kingdom: and all peoples, tribes, and tongues shall serve him. His power is an everlasting power that shall not be taken away, and his kingdom shall not be destroyed." The prophecy of Zachary concerning the merciful King "riding upon an ass and upon a colt the foal of an ass" entering Jerusalem as "the just and savior," amid the acclamations of the multitude, was recognized as fulfilled by the holy evangelists themselves.

This same doctrine of the Kingship of Christ which we have found in the Old Testament is even more clearly taught and confirmed in the New. The Archangel, announcing to the Virgin that she should bear a Son, says that "the Lord God shall give unto him the throne of David his father, and he shall reign in the house of Jacob for ever; and of his kingdom there shall be no end."

Moreover, Christ himself speaks of his own kingly authority: in his last discourse, speaking of the rewards and punishments that will be the eternal lot of the just and the damned; in his reply to the Roman magistrate, who asked him publicly whether he were a king or not; after his resurrection, when giving to his Apostles the mission of teaching and baptizing all nations, he took the opportunity to call himself king, confirming the title publicly, and solemnly proclaimed that all power was given him in heaven and on earth. These words can only be taken to indicate the greatness of his power, the infinite extent of his kingdom. What wonder, then, that he whom St. John calls the "prince of the kings of the earth" appears in the Apostle's vision of the future as he who "hath on his garment and on his thigh written 'King of kings and Lord of lords!'" It is Christ whom the Father "hath appointed heir of all things"; "for he must reign until at the end of the world he hath put all his enemies under the feet of God and the Father."

It was surely right, then, in view of the common teaching of the sacred books, that the Catholic Church, which is the kingdom of Christ on earth, destined to be spread among all men and all nations, should with every token of veneration salute her Author and Founder in her annual liturgy as King and Lord, and as King of Kings. And, in fact, she used these titles, giving expression with wonderful variety of language to one and the same concept, both in ancient psalmody and in the Sacramentaries. She uses them daily now in the prayers publicly offered to God, and in offering the Immaculate Victim. The perfect harmony of the Eastern liturgies with our own in this continual praise of Christ the King shows once more the truth of the axiom: *Legem credendi lex statuit supplicandi.* The rule of faith is indicated by the law of our worship.

The foundation of this power and dignity of Our Lord is rightly indicated by Cyril of Alexandria. "Christ," he says, "has dominion over all creatures, a dominion not seized by violence nor usurped, but his by essence and by nature." His kingship is founded upon the ineffable hypostatic union. From this it follows not only that Christ is to be adored by angels and men, but that to him as man angels and men are subject, and must recognize his empire; by reason of the hypostatic union Christ has power over all creatures. But a thought that must give us even greater joy and consolation is this that Christ is our King by acquired, as well as by natural right, for he is our Redeemer. Would that they who forget what they have cost their Savior might recall the words: "You were not redeemed with corruptible things, but with the precious blood of Christ, as of a lamb unspotted and undefiled." We are no longer our own property, for Christ has purchased us "with a great price"; our very bodies are the "members of Christ."

Let Us explain briefly the nature and meaning of this lordship of Christ. It consists, We need scarcely say, in a threefold power which is essential to lordship. This is sufficiently clear from the scriptural testimony already adduced concerning the universal dominion of our Redeemer, and moreover it is a dogma of faith that Jesus Christ was given to man, not only as our Redeemer, but also as a law-giver, to whom obedience is due. Not only do the gospels tell us that he made laws, but they present him to us in the act of making them. Those who keep them show their love for their Divine Master, and he promises that they shall remain in his love. He claimed judicial power as received from his Father, when the Jews accused him of breaking the Sabbath by the miraculous cure of a sick man. "For neither doth the Father judge any man; but hath given all judgement to the Son." In this power is included the right of rewarding and punishing all men living, for this right is inseparable from that of judging. Executive power, too, belongs to Christ, for all must obey his commands; none may escape them, nor the sanctions he has imposed.

This kingdom is spiritual and is concerned with spiritual things. That this is so the above quotations from Scripture amply prove, and Christ by his own action confirms it. On many occasions, when the Jews and even the Apostles wrongly supposed that the Messias would restore the liberties and the kingdom of Israel, he repelled and denied such a suggestion. When the populace thronged around him in admiration and would have acclaimed him King, he shrank from the honor and sought safety in flight. Before the Roman magistrate he declared that his kingdom was *not of this world.* The gospels present this kingdom as one which men prepare to enter by penance, and cannot actually enter except by faith and by baptism, which, though an external rite, signifies and produces an interior regeneration. This kingdom is opposed to none other than to that of Satan and to the power of darkness. It demands of its subjects a spirit of detachment from riches and earthly things, and a spirit of gentleness. They must hunger and thirst after justice, and more than this, they must deny themselves and carry the cross.

Christ as our Redeemer purchased the Church at the price of his own blood; as priest he offered himself, and continues to offer himself as a victim for our sins. Is it not evident, then, that his kingly dignity partakes in a manner of both these offices?

It would be a grave error, on the other hand, to say that Christ has no authority whatever in civil affairs, since, by virtue of the absolute empire over all creatures committed to him by the Father, all things are in his power. Nevertheless, during his life on earth he refrained from the exercise of such authority, and although he himself disdained to possess or to care for earthly goods, he did not, nor does he today, interfere with those who possess them. *Non eripit mortalia qui regna dat caelestia.*

Thus the empire of our Redeemer embraces all men. To use the words of Our immortal predecessor, Pope Leo XIII: "His empire includes not only Catholic nations, not only baptized persons who, though of right belonging to the Church, have been led astray by error, or have been cut off from her by schism, but also all those who are outside the Christian faith; so that truly the whole of mankind is subject to the power of Jesus Christ." Nor is there any difference in this matter between the individual and the family or the State; for all men, whether collectively or individually, are under the dominion of Christ. In him is the salvation of the individual, in him is the salvation of society. "Neither is there salvation in any other, for there is no other name under heaven given to men whereby we must be saved." He is the author of happiness and true prosperity for every man and for every nation. "For a nation is happy when its citizens are happy. What else is a nation but a number of men living in concord?" If, therefore, the rulers of nations wish to preserve their authority, to promote and increase the prosperity of their countries, they will not neglect the public duty of reverence and obedience to the rule of Christ. What We said at the beginning of Our Pontificate concerning the decline of public authority, and the lack of respect for the same, is equally true at the present day. "With God and Jesus Christ," we said, "excluded from political life, with authority derived not from God but from man, the very basis of that authority has been taken away, because the chief reason of the distinction between ruler and subject has been eliminated. The result is that human society is tottering to its fall, because it has no longer a secure and solid foundation."

When once men recognize, both in private and in public life, that Christ is King, society will at last receive the great blessings of real liberty, well-ordered discipline, peace and harmony. Our Lord's regal office invests the human authority of princes and rulers with a religious significance; it ennobles the citizen's duty of obedience. It is for this reason that St. Paul, while bidding wives revere Christ in their husbands, and slaves respect Christ in their masters, warns them to give obedience to them not as men, but as the vicegerents of Christ; for it is not meet that men redeemed by Christ should serve their fellow-men. "You are bought with a price; be not made the bond-slaves of men." If princes and magistrates duly elected are filled with the persuasion that they rule, not by their own right, but by the mandate and in the place of the Divine King, they will exercise their authority piously and wisely, and they will make laws and administer them, having in view the common good and also the human dignity of their subjects. The result will be a stable peace and tranquillity, for there will be no longer any cause of discontent. Men will see in their king or in their rulers men like themselves, perhaps unworthy or open to criticism, but they will not on that account refuse obedience if they see reflected in them the authority of Christ God and Man. Peace and harmony, too, will result; for with the spread and the universal extent of the kingdom of Christ men will become more and more conscious of the link that binds them together, and thus many conflicts will be either prevented entirely or at least their bitterness will be diminished.

If the kingdom of Christ, then, receives, as it should, all nations under its way, there seems no reason why we should despair of seeing that peace which the King of Peace came to bring on earth—he who came *to reconcile all things, who came not to be ministered unto but to minister*, who, though *Lord of all*, gave himself to us as a model of humility, and with his principal law united the precept of charity; who said also: "My yoke is sweet and my burden light." Oh, what happiness would be Ours if all men, individuals, families, and nations, would but let themselves be governed by Christ! "Then at length," to use the words addressed by our predecessor, Pope Leo XIII, twenty-five years ago to the bishops of the Universal Church, "then at length will many evils be cured; then will the law regain its former authority; peace with all its blessings be restored. Men will sheathe their swords and lay down their arms when all freely acknowledge and obey the authority of Christ, and every tongue confesses that the Lord Jesus Christ is in the glory of God the Father."

That these blessings may be abundant and lasting in Christian society, it is necessary that the kingship of our Savior should be as widely as possible recognized and understood, and to the end nothing would serve better than the institution of a special feast in honor of the Kingship of Christ. For people are instructed in the truths of faith, and brought to appreciate the inner joys of religion far more effectually by the annual celebration of our sacred mysteries than by any official pronouncement of the teaching of the Church. Such pronouncements usually reach only a few and the more learned among the faithful; feasts reach them all; the former speak but once, the latter speak every year—in fact, forever. The Church's teaching affects the mind primarily; her feasts affect both mind and heart, and have a salutary effect upon the whole of man's nature. Man is composed of body and soul, and he needs these external festivities so that the sacred rites, in all their beauty and variety, may stimulate him to drink more deeply of the fountain of God's teaching, that he may make it a part of himself, and use it with profit for his spiritual life.

History, in fact, tells us that in the course of ages these festivals have been instituted one after another according as the needs or the advantage of the people of Christ seemed to demand: as when they needed strength to face a common danger, when they were attacked by insidious heresies, when they needed to be urged to the pious consideration of some mystery of faith or of some divine blessing. Thus in the earliest days of the Christian era, when the people of Christ were suffering cruel persecution, the cult of the martyrs was begun in order, says St. Augustine, "that the feasts of the martyrs might incite men to martyrdom." The liturgical honors paid to confessors, virgins and widows produced wonderful results in an increased zest for virtue, necessary even in times of peace. But more fruitful still were the feasts instituted in honor of the Blessed Virgin. As a result of these men grew not only in their devotion to the Mother of God as an ever-present advocate, but also in their love of her as a mother bequeathed to them by their Redeemer. Not least among the blessings which have resulted from the public and legitimate honor paid to the Blessed Virgin and the saints is the perfect and perpetual immunity of the Church from error and heresy. We may well admire in this the admirable wisdom of the Providence of God, who, ever bringing good out of evil, has from time to time suffered the faith and piety of men to grow weak, and allowed Catholic truth to be attacked by false doctrines, but always with the result that truth has afterwards shone out with greater splendor, and that men's faith, aroused from its lethargy, has shown itself more vigorous than before.

The festivals that have been introduced into the liturgy in more recent years have had a similar origin, and have been attended with similar results. When reverence and devotion to the Blessed Sacrament had grown cold, the feast of Corpus Christi was instituted, so that by means of solemn processions and prayer of eight days' duration, men might be brought once more to render public homage to Christ. So, too, the feast of the Sacred Heart of Jesus was instituted at a time when men were oppressed by the sad and gloomy severity of Jansenism, which had made their hearts grow cold, and shut them out from the love of God and the hope of salvation.

If We ordain that the whole Catholic world shall revere Christ as King, We shall minister to the need of the present day, and at the same time provide an excellent remedy for the plague which now infects society. We refer to the plague of anti-clericalism, its errors and impious activities. This evil spirit, as you are well aware, Venerable Brethren, has not come into being in one day; it has long lurked beneath the surface. The empire of Christ over all nations was rejected. The right which the Church has from Christ himself, to teach mankind, to make laws, to govern peoples in all that pertains to their eternal salvation, that right was denied. Then gradually the religion of Christ came to be likened to false religions and to be placed ignominiously on the same level with them. It was then put under the power of the state and tolerated more or less at the whim of princes and rulers. Some men went even further, and wished to set up in the place of God's religion a natural religion consisting in some instinctive affection of the heart. There were even some nations who thought they could dispense with God, and that their religion should consist in impiety and the neglect of God. The rebellion of individuals and states against the authority of

Christ has produced deplorable consequences. We lamented these in the Encyclical *Ubi arcano*; we lament them today: the seeds of discord sown far and wide; those bitter enmities and rivalries between nations, which still hinder so much the cause of peace; that insatiable greed which is so often hidden under a pretense of public spirit and patriotism, and gives rise to so many private quarrels; a blind and immoderate selfishness, making men seek nothing but their own comfort and advantage, and measure everything by these; no peace in the home, because men have forgotten or neglect their duty; the unity and stability of the family undermined; society, in a word, shaken to its foundations and on the way to ruin. We firmly hope, however, that the feast of the Kingship of Christ, which in future will be yearly observed, may hasten the return of society to our loving Savior. It would be the duty of Catholics to do all they can to bring about this happy result. Many of these, however, have neither the station in society nor the authority which should belong to those who bear the torch of truth. This state of things may perhaps be attributed to a certain slowness and timidity in good people, who are reluctant to engage in conflict or oppose but a weak resistance; thus the enemies of the Church become bolder in their attacks. But if the faithful were generally to understand that it behoves them ever to fight courageously under the banner of Christ their King, then, fired with apostolic zeal, they would strive to win over to their Lord those hearts that are bitter and estranged from him, and would valiantly defend his rights.

Moreover, the annual and universal celebration of the feast of the Kingship of Christ will draw attention to the evils which anticlericalism has brought upon society in drawing men away from Christ, and will also do much to remedy them. While nations insult the beloved name of our Redeemer by suppressing all mention of it in their conferences and parliaments, we must all the more loudly proclaim his kingly dignity and power, all the more universally affirm his rights.

The way has been happily and providentially prepared for the celebration of this feast ever since the end of the last century. It is well known that this cult has been the subject of learned disquisitions in many books published in every part of the world, written in many different languages. The kingship and empire of Christ have been recognized in the pious custom, practiced by many families, of dedicating themselves to the Sacred Heart of Jesus; not only families have performed this act of dedication, but nations, too, and kingdoms. In fact, the whole of the human race was at the instance of Pope Leo XIII, in the Holy Year 1900, consecrated to the Divine Heart. It should be remarked also that much has been done for the recognition of Christ's authority over society by the frequent Eucharistic Congresses which are held in our age. These give an opportunity to the people of each diocese, district or nation, and to the whole world of coming together to venerate and adore Christ the King hidden under the Sacramental species. Thus by sermons preached at meetings and in churches, by public adoration of the Blessed Sacrament exposed and by solemn processions, men unite in paying homage to Christ, whom God has given them for their King. It is by a divine inspiration that the people of Christ bring forth Jesus from his silent hiding-place in the church, and carry him in triumph through the streets of the city, so that he whom men refused to receive when he came unto his own, may now receive in full his kingly rights.

For the fulfilment of the plan of which We have spoken, the Holy Year, which is now speeding to its close, offers the best possible opportunity. For during this year the God of mercy has raised the minds and hearts of the faithful to the consideration of heavenly blessings *which are above all understanding*, has either restored them once more to his grace, or inciting them anew to strive for higher gifts, has set their feet more firmly in the path of righteousness. Whether, therefore, We consider the many prayers that have been addressed to Us, or look to the events of the Jubilee Year, just past, We have every reason to think that the desired moment has at length arrived for enjoining that Christ be venerated by a special feast as King of all mankind. In this year, as We said at the beginning of this Letter, the Divine King, *truly wonderful in all his works, has been gloriously magnified,* for another company of his soldiers has been added to the list of saints. In this year men have looked upon strange things and strange labors, from which they have understood and admired the victories won by missionaries in the work of spreading his kingdom. In this year, by solemnly celebrating the centenary of the Council of Nicaea, We have commemorated the definition of the divinity of the word Incarnate, the foundation of Christ's empire over all men.

Therefore by Our Apostolic Authority We institute the Feast of the Kingship of Our Lord Jesus Christ to be observed yearly throughout the whole world on the last Sunday of the month of October—the Sunday, that is, which immediately precedes the Feast of All Saints. We further ordain that the dedication of mankind to the Sacred Heart of Jesus, which Our predecessor of saintly memory, Pope Pius X, commanded to be renewed yearly, be made annually on that day. This year, however, We desire that it be observed on the thirty-first day of the month on which day We Ourselves shall celebrate pontifically in honor of the kingship of Christ, and shall command that the same dedication be performed in Our presence. It seems to Us that We cannot in a more fitting manner close this Holy Year, nor better signify Our gratitude and that of the whole of the Catholic world to Christ the immortal King of ages, for the blessings showered upon Us, upon the Church, and upon the Catholic world during this holy period.

It is not necessary, Venerable Brethren, that We should explain to you at any length why We have decreed that this feast of the Kingship of Christ should be observed in addition to those other feasts in which his kingly dignity is already signified and celebrated. It will suffice to remark that although in all the feasts of our Lord the material object of worship is Christ, nevertheless their formal object is something quite distinct from his royal title and dignity. We have commanded its observance on a Sunday in order that not only the clergy may perform their duty by saying Mass and reciting the Office, but that the laity too, free from their daily tasks, may in a spirit of holy joy give ample testimony of their obedience and subjection to Christ. The last Sunday of October seemed the most convenient of all for this purpose, because it is at the end of the liturgical year, and thus the feast of the Kingship of Christ sets the crowning glory upon the mysteries of the life of Christ already commemorated during the year, and, before celebrating the triumph of all the Saints, we proclaim and extol the glory of him who triumphs in all the Saints and in all the Elect. Make it your duty and your task, Venerable Brethren, to see that sermons are preached to the people in every parish to teach them the meaning and the importance of this feast, that they may so order their lives as to be worthy of faithful and obedient subjects of the Divine King.

We would now, Venerable Brethren, in closing this letter, briefly enumerate the blessings which We hope and pray may accrue to the Church, to society, and to each one of the faithful, as a result of the public veneration of the Kingship of Christ.

When we pay honor to the princely dignity of Christ, men will doubtless be reminded that the Church, founded by Christ as a perfect society, has a natural and inalienable right to perfect freedom and immunity from the power of the state; and that in fulfilling the task committed to her by God of teaching, ruling, and guiding to eternal bliss those who belong to the kingdom of Christ, she cannot be subject to any external power. The State is bound to extend similar freedom to the orders and communities of religious of either sex, who give most valuable help to the Bishops of the Church by laboring for the extension and the establishment of the kingdom of Christ. By their sacred vows they fight against the threefold concupiscence of the world; by making profession of a more perfect life they render the holiness which her divine Founder willed should be a mark and characteristic of his Church more striking and more conspicuous in the eyes of all.

Nations will be reminded by the annual celebration of this feast that not only private individuals but also rulers and princes are bound to give public honor and obedience to Christ. It will call to their minds the thought of the last judgement, wherein Christ, who has been cast out of public life, despised, neglected and ignored, will most severely avenge these insults; for his kingly dignity demands that the State should take account of the commandments of God and of Christian principles, both in making laws and in administering justice, and also in providing for the young a sound moral education.

The faithful, moreover, by meditating upon these truths, will gain much strength and courage, enabling them to form their lives after the true Christian ideal. If to Christ our Lord is given all power in heaven and on earth; if all men, purchased by his precious blood, are by a new right subjected to his dominion; if this power embraces all men, it must be clear that not one of our faculties is exempt from his empire. He must reign in our minds, which should assent with perfect submission and firm belief to revealed truths and to the doctrines of Christ. He must reign in our wills, which should obey the laws and precepts of God. He must reign in our hearts, which should spurn natural desires and love God above all things, and cleave to him alone. He must reign in our bodies and in our members, which should serve as instruments for the interior sanctification of our souls, or to use the words of the Apostle Paul, *as instruments of justice unto God*. If all these truths are presented to the faithful for their consideration, they will prove a powerful incentive to perfection. It is Our fervent desire, Venerable Brethren, that those who are without the fold may seek after and accept the sweet yoke of Christ, and that we, who by the mercy of God are of the household of the faith, may bear that yoke, not as a burden but with joy, with love, with devotion; that having lived our lives in accordance with the laws of God's kingdom, we may receive full measure of good fruit, and counted by Christ good and faithful servants, we may be rendered partakers of eternal bliss and glory with him in his heavenly kingdom.

Let this letter, Venerable Brethren, be a token to you of Our fatherly love as the Feast of the Nativity of Our Lord Jesus Christ draws near; and receive the Apostolic Benediction as a pledge of divine blessings, which with loving heart, We impart to you, Venerable Brethren, to your clergy, and to your people.

Given at St. Peter's [in Rome], on the eleventh day of the month of December, in the Holy Year 1925, the fourth of Our Pontificate.

2108 (1) Leo XIII, encyclical *Libertas praestantissimum*

To the Patriarchs, Primates, Archbishops, and Bishops of the Catholic World in Grace and Communion with the Apostolic See.

Liberty, the highest of natural endowments, being the portion only of intellectual or rational natures, confers on man this dignity—that he is "in the hand of his counsel" and has power over his actions. But the manner in which such dignity is exercised is of the greatest moment, inasmuch as on the use that is made of liberty the highest good and the greatest evil alike depend. Man, indeed, is free to obey his reason, to seek moral good, and to strive unswervingly after his last end. Yet he is free also to turn aside to all other things; and, in pursuing the empty semblance of good, to disturb rightful order and to fall headlong into the destruction which he has voluntarily chosen. The Redeemer of mankind, Jesus Christ, having restored and exalted the original dignity of nature, vouchsafed special assistance to the will of man; and by the gifts of His grace here, and the promise of heavenly bliss hereafter, He raised it to a nobler state. In like manner, this great gift of nature has ever been, and always will be, deservingly cherished by the Catholic Church, for to her alone has been committed the charge of handing down to all ages the benefits purchased for us by Jesus Christ. Yet there are many who imagine that the Church is hostile to human liberty. Having a false and absurd notion as to what liberty is, either they pervert the very idea of freedom, or they extend it at their pleasure to many things in respect of which man cannot rightly be regarded as free.

We have on other occasions, and especially in Our encyclical letter *Immortale Dei*, in treating of the so-called *modern liberties*, distinguished between their good and evil elements; and We have shown that whatsoever is good in those liberties is as ancient as truth itself, and that the Church has always most willingly approved and practiced that good: but whatsoever has been added as new is, to tell the plain truth, of a vitiated kind, the fruit of the disorders of the age, and of an insatiate longing after novelties. Seeing, however, that many cling so obstinately to their own opinion in this matter as to imagine these modern liberties, cankered as they are, to be the greatest glory of our age, and the very basis of civil life, without which no perfect government can be conceived, We feel it a pressing duty, for the sake of the common good, to treat separately of this subject.

It is with *moral* liberty, whether in individuals or in communities, that We proceed at once to deal. But, first of all, it will be well to speak briefly of *natural* liberty; for, though it is distinct and separate from moral liberty, natural freedom is the fountain-head from which liberty of whatsoever kind flows, *sua vi suaque sponte*. The unanimous consent and judgment of men, which is the trusty voice of nature, recognizes this natural liberty in those only who are endowed with intelligence or reason; and it is by his use of this that man is rightly regarded as responsible for his actions. For, while other animate creatures follow their senses, seeking good and avoiding evil only by instinct, man has reason to guide him in each and every act of his life. Reason sees that whatever things that are held to be good upon earth may exist or may not, and discerning that none of them are of necessity for us, it leaves the will free to choose what it pleases. But man can judge of this contingency, as We say, only because he has a soul that is simple, spiritual, and intellectual—a soul, therefore, which is not produced by matter, and does not depend on matter for its existence; but which is created immediately by God, and, far surpassing the condition of things material, has a life and action of its own—so that, knowing the unchangeable and necessary reasons of what is true and good, it sees that no particular kind of good is necessary to us. When, therefore, it is established that man's soul is immortal and endowed with reason and not bound up with things material, the foundation of natural liberty is at once most firmly laid.

As the Catholic Church declares in the strongest terms the simplicity, spirituality, and immortality of the soul, so with unequalled constancy and publicity she ever also asserts its freedom. These truths she has always taught, and has sustained them as a dogma of faith, and whensoever heretics or innovators have attacked the liberty of man, the Church has defended it and protected this noble possession from destruction. History bears witness to the energy with which she met the fury of the Manichaeans and others like them; and the earnestness with which in later years she defended human liberty at the Council of Trent, and against the followers of Jansenius, is known to all. At no time, and in no place, has she held truce with *fatalism*.

Liberty, then, as We have said, belongs only to those who have the gift of reason or intelligence. Considered as to its nature, it is the faculty of choosing means fitted for the end proposed, for he is master of his actions who can choose one thing out of many. Now, since everything chosen as a means is viewed as good or useful, and since good, as such, is the proper object of our desire, it follows that freedom of choice is a property of the will, or, rather, is identical with the will in so far as it has in its action the faculty of choice. But the will cannot proceed to act until it is enlightened by the knowledge possessed by the intellect. In other words, the good wished by the will is necessarily good in so far as it is known by the intellect; and this the more, because in all voluntary acts choice is subsequent to a judgment upon the truth of the good presented, declaring to which good preference should be given. No sensible man can doubt that judgment is an act of reason, not of the will. The end, or object, both of the rational will and of its liberty is that good only which is in conformity with reason.

Since, however, both these faculties are imperfect, it is possible, as is often seen, that the reason should propose something which is not really good, but which has the appearance of good, and that the will should choose accordingly. For, as the possibility of error, and actual error, are defects of the mind and attest its imperfection, so the pursuit of what has a false appearance of good, though a proof of our freedom, just as a disease is a proof of our vitality, implies defect in human liberty. The will also, simply because of its dependence on the reason, no sooner desires anything contrary thereto than it abuses its freedom of choice and corrupts its very essence. Thus it is that the infinitely perfect God, although supremely free, because of the supremacy of His intellect and of His essential goodness, nevertheless cannot choose evil; neither can the angels and saints, who enjoy the beatific vision. St. Augustine and others urged most admirably against the Pelagians that, if the possibility of deflection from good belonged to the essence or perfection of liberty, then God, Jesus Christ, and the angels and saints, who have not this power, would have no liberty at all, or would have less liberty than man has in his state of pilgrimage and imperfection. This subject is often discussed by the Angelic Doctor in his demonstration that the possibility of sinning is not freedom, but slavery. It will suffice to quote his subtle commentary on the words of our Lord: "Whosoever committeth sin is the slave of sin." "Everything," he says, "is that which belongs to it naturally. When, therefore, it acts through a power outside itself, it does not act of itself, but through another, that is, as a slave. But man is by nature rational. When, therefore, he acts according to reason, he acts of himself and according to his free will; and this is liberty. Whereas, when he sins, he acts in opposition to reason, is moved by another, and is the victim of foreign misapprehensions. Therefore, 'Whosoever committeth sin is the slave of sin.'" Even the heathen philosophers clearly recognized this truth, especially they who held that the wise man alone is free; and by the term "wise man" was meant, as is well known, the man trained to live in accordance with his nature, that is, in justice and virtue.

Such, then, being the condition of human liberty, it necessarily stands in need of light and strength to direct its actions to good and to restrain them from evil. Without this, the freedom of our will would be our ruin. First of all, there must be *law*; that is, a fixed rule of teaching what is to be done and what is to be left undone. This rule cannot affect the lower animals in any true sense, since they act of necessity, following their natural instinct, and cannot of themselves act in any other way. On the other hand, as was said above, he who is free can either act or not act, can do this or do that, as he pleases, because his judgment precedes his choice. And his judgment not only decides what is right or wrong of its own nature, but also what is practically good and therefore to be chosen, and what is practically evil and therefore to be avoided. In other words, the reason prescribes to the will what it should seek after or shun, in order to the eventual attainment of man's last end, for the sake of which all his actions ought to be performed. This ordination of *reason* is called law. In man's free will, therefore, or in the moral necessity of our voluntary acts being in accordance with reason, lies the very root of the necessity of law. Nothing more foolish can be uttered or conceived than the notion that, because man is free by nature, he is therefore exempt from law. Were this the case, it would follow that to become free we must be deprived of reason; whereas the truth is that we are bound to submit to law precisely because we are free by our very nature. For, law is the guide of man's actions; it turns him toward good by its rewards, and deters him from evil by its punishments.

Foremost in this office comes the *natural law*, which is written and engraved in the mind of every man; and this is nothing but our reason, commanding us to do right and forbidding sin. Nevertheless, all prescriptions of human reason can have force of law only inasmuch as they are the voice and the interpreters of some higher power on which our reason and liberty necessarily depend. For, since the force of law consists in the imposing of obligations and the granting of rights, authority is the one and only foundation of all law—the power, that is, of fixing duties and defining rights, as also of assigning the necessary sanctions of reward and chastisement to each and all of its commands. But all this, clearly, cannot be found in man, if, as his own supreme legislator, he is to be the rule of his own actions. It follows, therefore, that the law of nature is the same thing as the *eternal law*, implanted in rational creatures, and inclining them *to their right action and end*; and can be nothing else but the eternal reason of God, the Creator and Ruler of all the world. To this rule of action and restraint of evil God has vouchsafed to give special and most suitable aids for strengthening and ordering the human will. The first and most excellent of these is the power of His divine *grace*, whereby the mind can be enlightened and the will wholesomely invigorated and moved to the constant pursuit of moral good, so that the use of our inborn liberty becomes at once less difficult and less dangerous. Not that the divine assistance hinders in any way the free movement of our will; just the contrary, for grace works inwardly in man and in harmony with his natural inclinations, since it flows from the very Creator of his mind and will, by whom all things are moved in conformity with their nature. As the Angelic Doctor points out, it is because divine grace comes from the Author of nature that it is so admirably adapted to be the safeguard of all natures, and to maintain the character, efficiency, and operations of each.

What has been said of the liberty of individuals is no less applicable to them when considered as bound together in civil society. For, what reason and the natural law do for individuals, that *human law*, promulgated for their good, does for the citizens of States. Of the laws enacted by men, some are concerned with what is good or bad by its very nature; and they command men to follow after what is right and to shun what is wrong, adding at the same time a suitable sanction. But such laws by no means derive their origin from civil society, because, just as civil society did not create human nature, so neither can it be said to be the author of the good which befits human nature, or of the evil which is contrary to it. Laws come before men live together in society, and have their origin in the natural, and consequently in the eternal, law. The precepts, therefore, of the natural law, contained bodily in the laws of men, have not merely the force of human law, but they possess that higher and more august sanction which belongs to the law of nature and the eternal law. And within the sphere of this kind of laws the duty of the civil legislator is, mainly, to keep the community in obedience by the adoption of a common discipline and by putting restraint upon refractory and viciously inclined men, so that, deterred from evil, they may turn to what is good, or at any rate may avoid causing trouble and disturbance to the State. Now, there are other enactments of the civil authority, which do not follow directly, but somewhat remotely, from the natural law, and decide many points which the law of nature treats only in a general and indefinite way. For instance, though nature commands all to contribute to the public peace and prosperity, whatever belongs to the manner, and circumstances, and conditions under which such service is to be rendered must be determined by the wisdom of men and not by nature herself. It is in the constitution of these particular rules of life, suggested by reason and prudence, and put forth by competent authority, that human law, properly so called, consists, binding all citizens to work together for the attainment of the common end proposed to the community, and forbidding them to depart from this end, and, in so far as human law is in conformity with the dictates of nature, leading to what is good, and deterring from evil.

From this it is manifest that the eternal law of God is the sole standard and rule of human liberty, not only in each individual man, but also in the community and civil society which men constitute when united. Therefore, the true liberty of human society does not consist in every man doing what he pleases, for this would simply end in turmoil and confusion, and bring on the overthrow of the State; but rather in this, that through the injunctions of the civil law all may more easily conform to the prescriptions of the eternal law. Likewise, the liberty of those who are in authority does not consist in the power to lay unreasonable and capricious commands upon their subjects, which would equally be criminal and would lead to the ruin of the commonwealth; but the binding force of human laws is in this, that they are to be regarded as applications of the eternal law, and incapable of sanctioning anything which is not contained in the eternal law, as in the principle of all law. Thus, St. Augustine most wisely says: "I think that you can see, at the same time, that there is nothing just and lawful in that temporal law, unless what men have gathered from this eternal law." If, then, by anyone in authority, something be sanctioned out of conformity with the principles of right reason, and consequently hurtful to the commonwealth, such an enactment can have no binding force of law, as being no rule of justice, but certain to lead men away from that good which is the very end of civil society.

Therefore, the nature of human liberty, however it be considered, whether in individuals or in society, whether in those who command or in those who obey, supposes the necessity of obedience to some supreme and eternal law, which is no other than the authority of God, commanding good and forbidding evil. And, so far from this most just authority of God over men diminishing, or even destroying their liberty, it protects and perfects it, for the real perfection of all creatures is found in the prosecution and attainment of their respective ends; but the supreme end to which human liberty must aspire is God.

These precepts of the truest and highest teaching, made known to us by the light of reason itself, the Church, instructed by the example and doctrine of her divine Author, has ever propagated and asserted; for she has ever made them the measure of her office and of her teaching to the Christian nations. As to morals, the laws of the Gospel not only immeasurably surpass the wisdom of the heathen, but are an invitation and an introduction to a state of holiness unknown to the ancients; and, bringing man nearer to God, they make him at once the possessor of a more perfect liberty. Thus, the powerful influence of the Church has ever been manifested in the custody and protection of the civil and political liberty of the people. The enumeration of its merits in this respect does not belong to our present purpose. It is sufficient to recall the fact that slavery, that old reproach of the heathen nations, was mainly abolished by the beneficent efforts of the Church. The impartiality of law and the true brotherhood of man were first asserted by Jesus Christ; and His apostles re-echoed His voice when they declared that in future there was to be neither Jew, nor Gentile, nor barbarian, nor Scythian, but all were brothers in Christ. So powerful, so conspicuous, in this respect is the influence of the Church that experience abundantly testifies how savage customs are no longer possible in any land where she has once set her foot; but that gentleness speedily takes the place of cruelty, and the light of truth quickly dispels the darkness of barbarism. Nor has the Church been less lavish in the benefits she has conferred on civilized nations in every age, either by resisting the tyranny of the wicked, or by protecting the innocent and helpless from injury, or, finally, by using her influence in the support of any form of government which commended itself to the citizens at home, because of its justice, or was feared by their enemies without, because of its power.

Moreover, the highest duty is to respect authority, and obediently to submit to just law; and by this the members of a community are effectually protected from the wrong-doing of evil men. Lawful power is from God, "and whosoever resisteth authority resisteth the ordinance of God"; wherefore, obedience is greatly ennobled when subjected to an authority which is the most just and supreme of all. But where the power to command is wanting, or where a law is enacted contrary to reason, or to the eternal law, or to some ordinance of God, obedience is unlawful, lest, while obeying man, we become disobedient to God. Thus, an effectual barrier being opposed to tyranny, the authority in the State will not have all its own way, but the interests and rights of all will be safeguarded—the rights of individuals, of domestic society, and of all the members of the commonwealth; all being free to live according to law and right reason; and in this, as We have shown, true liberty really consists.

If when men discuss the question of liberty they were careful to grasp its true and legitimate meaning, such as reason and reasoning have just explained, they would never venture to affix such a calumny on the Church as to assert that she is the foe of individual and public liberty. But many there are who follow in the footsteps of Lucifer, and adopt as their own his rebellious cry, "I will not serve"; and consequently substitute for true liberty what is sheer and most foolish license. Such, for instance, are the men belonging to that widely spread and powerful organization, who, usurping the name of liberty, style themselves *liberals*.

What *naturalists* or *rationalists* aim at in philosophy, that the supporters of *liberalism*, carrying out the principles laid down by naturalism, are attempting in the domain of morality and politics. The fundamental doctrine of rationalism is the supremacy of the human reason, which, refusing due submission to the divine and eternal reason, proclaims its own independence, and constitutes itself the supreme principle and source and judge of truth. Hence, these followers of liberalism deny the existence of any divine authority to which obedience is due, and proclaim that every man is the law to himself; from which arises that ethical system which they style *independent* morality, and which, under the guise of liberty, exonerates man from any obedience to the commands of God, and substitutes a boundless license. The end of all this it is not difficult to foresee, especially when society is in question. For, when once man is firmly persuaded that he is subject to no one, it follows that the efficient cause of the unity of civil society is not to be sought in any principle external to man, or superior to him, but simply in the free will of individuals; that the authority in the State comes from the people only; and that, just as every man's individual reason is his only rule of life, so the collective reason of the community should be the supreme guide in the management of all public affairs. Hence the doctrine of the supremacy of the greater number, and that all right and all duty reside in the majority. But, from what has been said, it is clear that all this is in contradiction to reason. To refuse any bond of union between man and civil society, on the one hand, and God the Creator and consequently the supreme Law-giver, on the other, is plainly repugnant to the nature, not only of man, but of all created things; for, of necessity, all effects must in some proper way be connected with their cause; and it belongs to the perfection of every nature to contain itself within that sphere and grade which the order of nature has assigned to it, namely, that the lower should be subject and obedient to the higher.

Moreover, besides this, a doctrine of such character is most hurtful both to individuals and to the State. For, once ascribe to human reason the only authority to decide what is true and what is good, and the real distinction between good and evil is destroyed; honor and dishonor differ not in their nature, but in the opinion and judgment of each one; pleasure is the measure of what is lawful; and, given a code of morality which can have little or no power to restrain or quiet the unruly propensities of man, a way is naturally opened to universal corruption. With reference also to public affairs: authority is severed from the true and natural principle whence it derives all its efficacy for the common good; and the law determining what it is right to do and avoid doing is at the mercy of a majority. Now, this is simply a road leading straight to tyranny. The empire of God over man and civil society once repudiated, it follows that religion, as a public institution, can have no claim to exist, and that everything that belongs to religion will be treated with complete indifference. Furthermore, with ambitious designs on sovereignty, tumult and sedition will be common amongst the people; and when duty and conscience cease to appeal to them, there will be nothing to hold them back but force, which of itself alone is powerless to keep their covetousness in check. Of this we have almost daily evidence in the conflict with *socialists* and members of other seditious societies, who labor unceasingly to bring about revolution. It is for those, then, who are capable of forming a just estimate of things to decide whether such doctrines promote that true liberty which alone is worthy of man, or rather, pervert and destroy it.

There are, indeed, some adherents of liberalism who do not subscribe to these opinions, which we have seen to be fearful in their enormity, openly opposed to the truth, and the cause of most terrible evils. Indeed, very many amongst them, compelled by the force of truth, do not hesitate to admit that such liberty is vicious, nay, is simple license, whenever intemperate in its claims, to the neglect of truth and justice; and therefore they would have liberty ruled and directed by right reason, and consequently subject to the natural law and to the divine eternal law. But here they think they may stop, holding that man as a free being is bound by no law of God except such as He makes known to us through our natural reason. In this they are plainly inconsistent. For if—as they must admit, and no one can rightly deny—the will of the Divine Law-giver is to be obeyed, because every man is under the power of God, and tends toward Him as his end, it follows that no one can assign limits to His legislative authority without failing in the obedience which is due. Indeed, if the human mind be so presumptuous as to define the nature and extent of God's rights and its own duties, reverence for the divine law will be apparent rather than real, and arbitrary judgment will prevail over the authority and providence of God. Man must, therefore, take his standard of a loyal and religious life from the eternal law; and from all and every one of those laws which God, in His infinite wisdom and power, has been pleased to enact, and to make known to us by such clear and unmistakable signs as to leave no room for doubt. And the more so because laws of this kind have the same origin, the same author, as the eternal law, are absolutely in accordance with right reason, and perfect the natural law. These laws it is that embody the government of God, who graciously guides and directs the intellect and the will of man lest these fall into error. Let, then, that continue to remain in a holy and inviolable union which neither can nor should be separated; and in all things—for this is the dictate of right reason itself—let God be dutifully and obediently served.

There are others, somewhat more moderate though not more consistent, who affirm that the morality of individuals is to be guided by the divine law, but not the morality of the State, for that in public affairs the commands of God may be passed over, and may be entirely disregarded in the framing of laws. Hence follows the fatal theory of the need of separation between Church and State. But the absurdity of such a position is manifest. Nature herself proclaims the necessity of the State providing means and opportunities whereby the community may be enabled to live properly, that is to say, according to the laws of God. For, since God is the source of all goodness and justice, it is absolutely ridiculous that the State should pay no attention to these laws or render them abortive by contrary enactments. Besides, those who are in authority owe it to the commonwealth not only to provide for its external well-being and the conveniences of life, but still more to consult the welfare of men's souls in the wisdom of their legislation. But, for the increase of such benefits, nothing more suitable can be conceived than the laws which have God for their author; and, therefore, they who in their government of the State take no account of these laws abuse political power by causing it to deviate from its proper end and from what nature itself prescribes. And, what is still more important, and what We have more than once pointed out, although the civil authority has not the same proximate end as the spiritual, nor proceeds on the same lines, nevertheless in the exercise of their separate powers they must occasionally meet. For their subjects are the same, and not infrequently they deal with the same objects, though in different ways. Whenever this occurs, since a state of conflict is absurd and manifestly repugnant to the most wise ordinance of God, there must necessarily exist some order or mode of procedure to remove the occasions of difference and contention, and to secure harmony in all things. This harmony has been not inaptly compared to that which exists between the body and the soul for the well-being of both one and the other, the separation of which brings irremediable harm to the body, since it extinguishes its very life.

To make this more evident, the growth of liberty ascribed to our age must be considered apart in its various details. And, first, let us examine that liberty in individuals which is so opposed to the virtue of religion, namely, the *liberty of worship*, as it is called. This is based on the principle that every man is free to profess as he may choose any religion or none.

But, assuredly, of all the duties which man has to fulfill, that, without doubt, is the chiefest and holiest which commands him to worship God with devotion and piety. This follows of necessity from the truth that we are ever in the power of God, are ever guided by His will and providence, and, having come forth from Him, must return to Him. Add to which, no true virtue can exist without religion, for moral virtue is concerned with those things which lead to God as man's supreme and ultimate good; and therefore religion, which (as St. Thomas says) "performs those actions which are directly and immediately ordained for the divine honor," rules and tempers all virtues. And if it be asked which of the many conflicting religions it is necessary to adopt, reason and the natural law unhesitatingly tell us to practice that one which God enjoins, and which men can easily recognize by certain exterior notes, whereby Divine Providence has willed that it should be distinguished, because, in a matter of such moment, the most terrible loss would be the consequence of error. Wherefore, when a liberty such as We have described is offered to man, the power is given him to pervert or abandon with impunity the most sacred of duties, and to exchange the unchangeable good for evil; which, as We have said, is no liberty, but its degradation, and the abject submission of the soul to sin.

This kind of liberty, if considered in relation to the State, clearly implies that there is no reason why the State should offer any homage to God, or should desire any public recognition of Him; that no one form of worship is to be preferred to another, but that all stand on an equal footing, no account being taken of the religion of the people, even if they profess the Catholic faith. But, to justify this, it must needs be taken as true that the State has no duties toward God, or that such duties, if they exist, can be abandoned with impunity, both of which assertions are manifestly false. For it cannot be doubted but that, by the will of God, men are united in civil society; whether its component parts be considered; or its form, which implies authority; or the object of its existence; or the abundance of the vast services which it renders to man. God it is who has made man for society, and has placed him in the company of others like himself, so that what was wanting to his nature, and beyond his attainment if left to his own resources, he might obtain by association with others. Wherefore, civil society must acknowledge God as its Founder and Parent, and must obey and reverence His power and authority. Justice therefore forbids, and reason itself forbids, the State to be godless; or to adopt a line of action which would end in godlessness—namely, to treat the various religions (as they call them) alike, and to bestow upon them promiscuously equal rights and privileges. Since, then, the profession of one religion is necessary in the State, that religion must be professed which alone is true, and which can be recognized without difficulty, especially in Catholic States, because the marks of truth are, as it were, engraven upon it. This religion, therefore, the rulers of the State must preserve and protect, if they would provide—as they should do—with prudence and usefulness for the good of the community. For public authority exists for the welfare of those whom it governs; and, although its proximate end is to lead men to the prosperity found in this life, yet, in so doing, it ought not to diminish, but rather to increase, man's capability of attaining to the supreme good in which his everlasting happiness consists: which never can be attained if religion be disregarded.

All this, however, We have explained more fully elsewhere. We now only wish to add the remark that liberty of so false a nature is greatly hurtful to the true liberty of both rulers and their subjects. Religion, of its essence, is wonderfully helpful to the State. For, since it derives the prime origin of all power directly from God Himself, with grave authority it charges rulers to be mindful of their duty, to govern without injustice or severity, to rule their people kindly and with almost paternal charity; it admonishes subjects to be obedient to lawful authority, as to the ministers of God; and it binds them to their rulers, not merely by obedience, but by reverence and affection, forbidding all seditions and venturesome enterprises calculated to disturb public order and tranquillity, and cause greater restrictions to be put upon the liberty of the people. We need not mention how greatly religion conduces to pure morals, and pure morals to liberty. Reason shows, and history confirms the fact, that the higher the morality of States, the greater are the liberty and wealth and power which they enjoy.

We must now consider briefly liberty of speech, and liberty of the press. It is hardly necessary to say that there can be no such right as this, if it be not used in moderation, and if it pass beyond the bounds and end of all true liberty. For right is a moral power which—as We have before said and must again and again repeat—it is absurd to suppose that nature has accorded indifferently to truth and falsehood, to justice and injustice. Men have a right freely and prudently to propagate throughout the State what things soever are true and honorable, so that as many as possible may possess them; but lying opinions, than which no mental plague is greater, and vices which corrupt the heart and moral life should be diligently repressed by public authority, lest they insidiously work the ruin of the State. The excesses of an unbridled intellect, which unfailingly end in the oppression of the untutored multitude, are no less rightly controlled by the authority of the law than are the injuries inflicted by violence upon the weak. And this all the more surely, because by far the greater part of the community is either absolutely unable, or able only with great difficulty, to escape from illusions and deceitful subtleties, especially such as flatter the passions. If unbridled license of speech and of writing be granted to all, nothing will remain sacred and inviolate; even the highest and truest mandates of natures, justly held to be the common and noblest heritage of the human race, will not be spared. Thus, truth being gradually obscured by darkness, pernicious and manifold error, as too often happens, will easily prevail. Thus, too, license will gain what liberty loses; for liberty will ever be more free and secure in proportion as license is kept in fuller restraint. In regard, however, to all matter of opinion which God leaves to man's free discussion, full liberty of thought and of speech is naturally within the right of everyone; for such liberty never leads men to suppress the truth, but often to discover it and make it known.

A like judgment must be passed upon what is called *liberty of teaching*. There can be no doubt that truth alone should imbue the minds of men, for in it are found the well-being, the end, and the perfection of every intelligent nature; and therefore nothing but truth should be taught both to the ignorant and to the educated, so as to bring knowledge to those who have it not, and to preserve it in those who possess it. For this reason it is plainly the duty of all who teach to banish error from the mind, and by sure safeguards to close the entry to all false convictions. From this it follows, as is evident, that the liberty of which We have been speaking is greatly opposed to reason, and tends absolutely to pervert men's minds, in as much as it claims for itself the right of teaching whatever it pleases—a liberty which the State cannot grant without failing in its duty. And the more so because the authority of teachers has great weight with their hearers, who can rarely decide for themselves as to the truth or falsehood of the instruction given to them.

Wherefore, this liberty, also, in order that it may deserve the name, must be kept within certain limits, lest the office of teaching be turned with impunity into an instrument of corruption. Now, truth, which should be the only subject matter of those who teach, is of two kinds: natural and supernatural. Of natural truths, such as the principles of nature and whatever is derived from them immediately by our reason, there is a kind of common patrimony in the human race. On this, as on a firm basis, morality, justice, religion, and the very bonds of human society rest: and to allow people to go unharmed who violate or destroy it would be most impious, most foolish, and most inhuman.

But with no less religious care must we preserve that great and sacred treasure of the truths which God Himself has taught us. By many and convincing arguments, often used by defenders of Christianity, certain leading truths have been laid down: namely, that some things have been revealed by God; that the only-begotten Son of God was made flesh, to bear witness to the truth; that a perfect society was founded by Him—the Church, namely, of which He is the head, and with which He has promised to abide till the end of the world. To this society He entrusted all the truths which He had taught, in order that it might keep and guard them and with lawful authority explain them; and at the same time He commanded all nations to hear the voice of the Church, as if it were His own, threatening those who would not hear it with everlasting perdition. Thus, it is manifest that man's best and surest teacher is God, the Source and Principle of all truth; and the only-begotten Son, who is in the bosom of the Father, the Way, the Truth, and the Life, the true Light which enlightens every man, and to whose teaching all must submit: "And they shall all be taught of God."

In faith and in the teaching of morality, God Himself made the Church a partaker of His divine authority, and through His heavenly gift she cannot be deceived. She is therefore the greatest and most reliable teacher of mankind, and in her swells an inviolable right to teach them. Sustained by the truth received from her divine Founder, the Church has ever sought to fulfill holily the mission entrusted to her by God; unconquered by the difficulties on all sides surrounding her, she has never ceased to assert her liberty of teaching, and in this way the wretched superstition of paganism being dispelled, the wide world was renewed unto Christian wisdom. Now, reason itself clearly teaches that the truths of divine revelation and those of nature cannot really be opposed to one another, and that whatever is at variance with them must necessarily be false. Therefore, the divine teaching of the Church, so far from being an obstacle to the pursuit of learning and the progress of science, or in any way retarding the advance of civilization, in reality brings to them the sure guidance of shining light. And for the same reason it is of no small advantage for the perfecting of human liberty, since our Savior Jesus Christ has said that by truth is man made free: "You shall know the truth, and the truth shall make you free." Therefore, there is no reason why genuine liberty should grow indignant, or true science feel aggrieved, at having to bear the just and necessary restraint of laws by which, in the judgment of the Church and of reason itself, human teaching has to be controlled.

The Church, indeed—as facts have everywhere proved—looks chiefly and above all to the defense of the Christian faith, while careful at the same time to foster and promote every kind of human learning. For learning is in itself good, and praiseworthy, and desirable; and further, all erudition which is the outgrowth of sound reason, and in conformity with the truth of things, serves not a little to confirm what we believe on the authority of God. The Church, truly, to our great benefit, has carefully preserved the monuments of ancient wisdom; has opened everywhere homes of science, and has urged on intellectual progress by fostering most diligently the arts by which the culture of our age is so much advanced. Lastly, we must not forget that a vast field lies freely open to man's industry and genius, containing all those things which have no necessary connection with Christian faith and morals, or as to which the Church, exercising no authority, leaves the judgment of the learned free and unconstrained.

From all this may be understood the nature and character of that liberty which the followers of liberalism so eagerly advocate and proclaim. On the one hand, they demand for themselves and for the State a license which opens the way to every perversity of opinion; and on the other, they hamper the Church in divers ways, restricting her liberty within narrowest limits, although from her teaching not only is there nothing to be feared, but in every respect very much to be gained.

Another liberty is widely advocated, namely, *liberty of conscience.* If by this is meant that everyone may, as he chooses, worship God or not, it is sufficiently refuted by the arguments already adduced. But it may also be taken to mean that every man in the State may follow the will of God and, from a consciousness of duty and free from every obstacle, obey His commands. This, indeed, is true liberty, a liberty worthy of the sons of God, which nobly maintains the dignity of man and is stronger than all violence or wrong—a liberty which the Church has always desired and held most dear. This is the kind of liberty the Apostles claimed for themselves with intrepid constancy, which the apologists of Christianity confirmed by their writings, and which the martyrs in vast numbers consecrated by their blood. And deservedly so; for this Christian liberty bears witness to the absolute and most just dominion of God over man, and to the chief and supreme duty of man toward God. It has nothing in common with a seditious and rebellious mind; and in no tittle derogates from obedience to public authority; for the right to command and to require obedience exists only so far as it is in accordance with the authority of God, and is within the measure that He has laid down. But when anything is commanded which is plainly at variance with the will of God, there is a wide departure from this divinely constituted order, and at the same time a direct conflict with divine authority; therefore, it is right not to obey.

By the patrons of liberalism, however, who make the State absolute and omnipotent, and proclaim that man should live altogether independently of God, the liberty of which We speak, which goes hand in hand with virtue and religion, is not admitted; and whatever is done for its preservation is accounted an injury and an offense against the State. Indeed, if what they say were really true, there would be no tyranny, no matter how monstrous, which we should not be bound to endure and submit to.

The Church most earnestly desires that the Christian teaching, of which We have given an outline, should penetrate every rank of society in reality and in practice; for it would be of the greatest efficacy in healing the evils of our day, which are neither few nor slight, and are the offspring in great part of the false liberty which is so much extolled, and in which the germs of safety and glory were supposed to be contained. The hope has been disappointed by the result. The fruit, instead of being sweet and wholesome, has proved cankered and bitter. If, then, a remedy is desired, let it be sought for in a restoration of sound doctrine, from which alone the preservation of order and, as a consequence, the defense of true liberty can be confidently expected.

Yet, with the discernment of a true mother, the Church weighs the great burden of human weakness, and well knows the course down which the minds and actions of men are in this our age being borne. For this reason, while not conceding any right to anything save what is true and honest, she does not forbid public authority to tolerate what is at variance with truth and justice, for the sake of avoiding some greater evil, or of obtaining or preserving some greater good. God Himself in His providence, though infinitely good and powerful, permits evil to exist in the world, partly that greater good may not be impeded, and partly that greater evil may not ensue. In the government of States it is not forbidden to imitate the Ruler of the world; and, as the authority of man is powerless to prevent every evil, it has (as St. Augustine says) to overlook and leave unpunished many things which are punished, and rightly, by Divine Providence. But if, in such circumstances, for the sake of the common good (and this is the only legitimate reason), human law may or even should tolerate evil, it may not and should not approve or desire evil for its own sake; for evil of itself, being a privation of good, is opposed to the common welfare which every legislator is bound to desire and defend to the best of his ability. In this, human law must endeavor to imitate God, who, as St. Thomas teaches, in allowing evil to exist in the world, "neither wills evil to be done, nor wills it not to be done, but wills only to permit it to be done; and this is good." This saying of the Angelic Doctor contains briefly the whole doctrine of the permission of evil.

But, to judge aright, we must acknowledge that, the more a State is driven to tolerate evil, the further is it from perfection; and that the tolerance of evil which is dictated by political prudence should be strictly confined to the limits which its justifying cause, the public welfare, requires. Wherefore, if such tolerance would be injurious to the public welfare, and entail greater evils on the State, it would not be lawful; for in such case the motive of good is wanting. And although in the extraordinary condition of these times the Church usually acquiesces in certain modern liberties, not because she prefers them in themselves, but because she judges it expedient to permit them, she would in happier times exercise her own liberty; and, by persuasion, exhortation, and entreaty would endeavor, as she is bound, to fulfill the duty assigned to her by God of providing for the eternal salvation of mankind. One thing, however, remains always true—that the liberty which is claimed for all to do all things is not, as We have often said, of itself desirable, inasmuch as it is contrary to reason that error and truth should have equal rights.

And as to *tolerance*, it is surprising how far removed from the equity and prudence of the Church are those who profess what is called liberalism. For, in allowing that boundless license of which We have spoken, they exceed all limits, and end at last by making no apparent distinction between truth and error, honesty and dishonesty.

And because the Church, the pillar and ground of truth, and the unerring teacher of morals, is forced utterly to reprobate and condemn tolerance of such an abandoned and criminal character, they calumniate her as being wanting in patience and gentleness, and thus fail to see that, in so doing, they impute to her as a fault what is in reality a matter for commendation. But, in spite of all this show of tolerance, it very often happens that, while they profess themselves ready to lavish liberty on all in the greatest profusion, they are utterly intolerant toward the Catholic Church, by refusing to allow her the liberty of being herself free.

And now to reduce for clearness' sake to its principal heads all that has been set forth with its immediate conclusions, the summing up in this briefly: that man, by a necessity of his nature, is wholly subject to the most faithful and ever-enduring power of God; and that, as a consequence, any liberty, except that which consists in submission to God and in subjection to His will, is unintelligible. To deny the existence of this authority in God, or to refuse to submit to it, means to act, not as a free man, but as one who treasonably abuses his liberty; and in such a disposition of mind the chief and deadly vice of liberalism essentially consists. The form, however, of the sin is manifold; for in more ways and degrees than one can the will depart from the obedience which is due to God or to those who share the divine power.

For, to reject the supreme authority to God, and to cast off all obedience to Him in public matters, or even in private and domestic affairs, is the greatest perversion of liberty and the worst kind of liberalism; and what We have said must be understood to apply to this alone in its fullest sense.

Next comes the system of those who admit indeed the duty of submitting to God, the Creator and Ruler of the world, inasmuch as all nature is dependent on His will, but who boldly reject all laws of faith and morals which are above natural reason, but are revealed by the authority of God; or who at least impudently assert that there is no reason why regard should be paid to these laws, at any rate publicly, by the State. How mistaken these men also are, and how inconsistent, we have seen above. From this teaching, as from its source and principle, flows that fatal principle of the separation of Church and State; whereas it is, on the contrary, clear that the two powers, though dissimilar in functions and unequal in degree, ought nevertheless to live in concord, by harmony in their action and the faithful discharge of their respective duties.

But this teaching is understood in two ways. Many wish the State to be separated from the Church wholly and entirely, so that with regard to every right of human society, in institutions, customs, and laws, the offices of State, and the education of youth, they would pay no more regard to the Church than if she did not exist; and, at most, would allow the citizens individually to attend to their religion in private if so minded. Against such as these, all the arguments by which We disprove the principle of separation of Church and State are conclusive; with this super-added, that it is absurd the citizen should respect the Church, while the State may hold her in contempt.

Others oppose not the existence of the Church, nor indeed could they; yet they despoil her of the nature and rights of a perfect society, and maintain that it does not belong to her to legislate, to judge, or to punish, but only to exhort, to advise, and to rule her subjects in accordance with their own consent and will. By such opinion they pervert the nature of this divine society, and attenuate and narrow its authority, its office of teacher, and its whole efficiency; and at the same time they aggrandize the power of the civil government to such extent as to subject the Church of God to the empire and sway of the State, like any voluntary association of citizens. To refute completely such teaching, the arguments often used by the defenders of Christianity, and set forth by Us, especially in the encyclical letter *Immortale Dei*, are of great avail; for by those arguments it is proved that, by a divine provision, all the rights which essentially belong to a society that is legitimate, supreme, and perfect in all its parts exist in the Church.

Lastly, there remain those who, while they do not approve the separation of Church and State, think nevertheless that the Church ought to adapt herself to the times and conform to what is required by the modern system of government. Such an opinion is sound, if it is to be understood of some equitable adjustment consistent with truth and justice; in so far, namely, that the Church, in the hope of some great good may show herself indulgent, and may conform to the times in so far as her sacred office permits. But it is not so in regard to practices and doctrines which a perversion of morals and a warped judgment have unlawfully introduced. Religion, truth, and justice must ever be maintained; and, as God has intrusted these great and sacred matters to her office as to dissemble in regard to what is false or unjust, or to connive at what is hurtful to religion.

From what has been said it follows that it is quite unlawful to demand, to defend, or to grant unconditional freedom of thought, of speech, or writing, or of worship, as if these were so many rights given by nature to man. For, if nature had really granted them, it would be lawful to refuse obedience to God, and there would be no restraint on human liberty. It likewise follows that freedom in these things may be tolerated wherever there is just cause, but only with such moderation as will prevent its degenerating into license and excess. And, where such liberties are in use, men should employ them in doing good, and should estimate them as the Church does; for liberty is to be regarded as legitimate in so far only as it affords greater facility for doing good, but no farther.

Whenever there exists, or there is reason to fear, an unjust oppression of the people on the one hand, or a deprivation of the liberty of the Church on the other, it is lawful to seek for such a change of government as will bring about due liberty of action. In such case, an excessive and vicious liberty is not sought, but only some relief, for the common welfare, in order that, while license for evil is allowed by the State, the power of doing good may not be hindered.

Again, it is not of itself wrong to prefer a democratic form of government, if only the Catholic doctrine be maintained as to the origin and exercise of power. Of the various forms of government, the Church does not reject any that are fitted to procure the welfare of the subject; she wishes only—and this nature itself requires—that they should be constituted without involving wrong to any one, and especially without violating the rights of the Church.

Unless it be otherwise determined, by reason of some exceptional condition of things, it is expedient to take part in the administration of public affairs. And the Church approves of every one devoting his services to the common good, and doing all that he can for the defense, preservation, and prosperity of his country.

Neither does the Church condemn those who, if it can be done without violation of justice, wish to make their country independent of any foreign or despotic power. Nor does she blame those who wish to assign to the State the power of self-government, and to its citizens the greatest possible measure of prosperity. The Church has always most faithfully fostered civil liberty, and this was seen especially in Italy, in the municipal prosperity, and wealth, and glory which were obtained at a time when the salutary power of the Church has spread, without opposition, to all parts of the State.

These things, venerable brothers, which, under the guidance of faith and reason, in the discharge of Our Apostolic office, We have now delivered to you, We hope, especially by your cooperation with Us, will be useful unto very many. In lowliness of heart We raise Our eyes in supplication to God, and earnestly beseech Him to shed mercifully the light of His wisdom and of His counsel upon men, so that, strengthened by these heavenly gifts, they may in matters of such moment discern what is true, and may afterwards, in public and private at all times and with unshaken constancy, live in accordance with the truth. As a pledge of these heavenly gifts, and in witness of Our good will to you, venerable brothers, and to the clergy and people committed to each of you, We most lovingly grant in the Lord the apostolic benediction.

Given at St. Peter's in Rome, the twentieth day of June, 1888, the tenth year of Our Pontificate.

2108 (2) **Pius XII, allocution of 6 December 1953**

It gives Us great satisfaction, beloved sons of the Union of Italian Catholic Jurists, to see you gather round Us here and to bid you heartfelt welcome.

In the beginning of October, another congress of jurists, dealing with International Penal Law, gathered in Our summer residence. Your convention is rather national in character, but the subject treated, "The national and international community," touches again the relationship between peoples and sovereign States. It is not by chance that congresses are multiplying for the study of international questions, be they scientific, economic, or political. The clear fact that relations between individuals of various nations and between nations themselves are growing in number and arousing deeper interest, makes daily more urgent a right ordering of international relations, both private and public; all the more so since this mutual approach is caused not only by vastly improved technological progress and free choice, but also by the more profound action of an intrinsic law of development. This movement, then, is not to be repressed, but fostered and promoted.

I. In this work of expansion, communities of States and peoples, whether already existing or about to exist, have naturally a special importance. They are communities in which sovereign States, that is to say, States which are subordinate to no other State, are united as a juridical community to attain definite juridical ends. It would give a false idea of these juridical communities to compare them to world empires of the past or of the present, in which are mingled different racial stocks, peoples, and States, willingly or unwillingly merged into a single conglomeration of States. In the present instance, however, States, remaining Sovereign, freely unite to form a juridical community.

In this connection, the history of the world, which shows repeated struggles for power, no doubt might make the establishment of a juridical community of free States seem almost Utopian. The conflicts of the past have too often arisen because of a desire to subjugate nations, and to extend the range of one's own power, or through the necessity of defending one's liberty and one's own independent existence. This time, on the contrary, it is precisely in order to prevent threatening conflicts that men turn to the idea of a supranational juridical community. Utilitarian considerations, certainly of considerable weight, move men to plan for peace; and finally perhaps it is precisely this mingling of men of different nations through technological progress that has awakened the belief, implanted in the hearts and souls of individuals, in a higher community of men, willed by the Creator, and rooted in the unity of their common origin, nature, and final destiny.

II. These, and other similar considerations, show that advance toward establishing a community of peoples does not look, as to its only and ultimate norm, to the will of the States, but rather to nature, to the Creator. The right to existence, the right to respect from others and to one's good name, the right to one's own culture and national character, the right to develop oneself, the right to demand observance of international treaties, and other like rights, are demanded by the law of nations, dictated by nature itself. The positive law of different peoples, also indispensable in the community of States, has, as its function, to define more exactly the rights derived from nature and to adapt them to concrete circumstances, and to take other steps directed, of course, toward the common good, on the basis of a positive agreement which, once freely made, has binding force.

In this community of nations, then, every State becomes a part of the system of international law, and hence of natural law, which is both support and crown of the whole. Thus the individual nation no longer is—nor in fact was it ever—"sovereign," in the sense of being entirely without restrictions. "Sovereignty," in the true sense of the word, means self-rule and exclusive competence in ways and means of handling the necessary affairs of a particular territory, always within the framework of international law, without, however, becoming dependent on the juridical system of any other State. Every State is immediately subject to international law. States which would lack this fulness of power, or whose independence of the power of any other State would not be guaranteed by international law, would not be sovereign. Yet no State could complain about a limitation of its sovereignty, if it were denied the power of acting arbitrarily and without regard for other States. Sovereignty is not a divinization of the State, nor omnipotence of the State in the Hegelian sense, not after the fashion of absolute juridical positivism.

III. There is no need to explain to you students of law, how the setting up, maintenance and operation of a real community of States, especially one that would embrace all peoples, give rise to many duties and problems, some of them extremely difficult and complicated, which cannot be solved by a simple 'yes' or 'no' answer. Such would be the question of race and origin, with their biological, psychological and social consequence; the question of language, the question of family life, with its relations, varying from nation to nation, between husband and wife, parents, the larger family group; the question of the equality or equal value of rights in what regards goods, contracts and persons, for the citizens of one sovereign State who either live for a short time in a foreign State, or retaining their own nationality, establish permanent residence there; the question of the right of immigration or of emigration, and other like questions.

The jurist, the statesman, the individual State, as well as the community of States, should here take account of all the inborn tendencies of individuals and communities in their contacts and reciprocal relationship, such as the tendency to adapt or to assimilate, and often even to absorb, or contrariwise, the tendency to exclude and to destroy anything that appears incapable of being assimilated, the tendency to expand, to embrace what is new, and on the contrary, the tendency to retreat and to hold aloof; the tendency to give oneself entirely, forgetful of self, and its opposite, selfishness, with no thought of giving service to others; the lust for power, the longing to keep others in subjection, and so on. All these instincts, either of self-aggrandizement or of self-defense, have their roots in the natural dispositions of individuals, of people, of races and of communities, because of the restrictions in which they are held. One never finds in them all that is good and just. God alone, the origin of all things, possesses within Himself, by reason of His infinity, all that is good.

From what we have said, it is easy to deduce the fundamental principle to be followed in dealing with these difficulties and tendencies; as far as is possible and lawful, to promote everything that leads easily to union and makes it more effective; to remove everything that disturbs it; to tolerate at times that which it is impossible to remedy, but which, on the other hand, must not be allowed to make shipwreck of the community, from which a higher good is sought. It is the application of this principle that causes difficulty.

IV. In this connection, We wish to treat with you, who are happy to profess yourselves Catholic jurists, concerning one of the questions which arises in a community of peoples, that is, the practical co-existence of Catholic with non-Catholic States.

Depending upon the religious belief of the great majority of citizens, or by reason of an explicit declaration of law, peoples and member States of the international community will be divided into Christians, non-Christians, those who are indifferent to religion, or wittingly without it, or even professed atheists. The interests of religion and morality will need for the whole extent of the international community a well-defined rule, which will hold for all the territory of the individual sovereign member-States of the international community. Allowing for probabilities and varying circumstances, this ruling of positive law will thus find expression: Within its own territory and for its own citizens, each State will regulate religious and moral affairs by its own laws; nevertheless, throughout the whole territory of the international community of States, the citizens of every member-State will be allowed their own beliefs and ethical and religious practices, in so far as these do not contravene the penal laws of the State in which they are residing.

For the jurist, the statesman, and the Catholic State arises here the question: Can they give their consent to such a ruling when there is question of entering and remaining in an international community?

Now, in regard to religious and moral interests, a two-fold question arises: the first deals with the objective truth and the obligation of conscience toward what is objectively true and good; the second deals with the practical attitude of the international community towards the individual sovereign State, and the attitude of the individual State toward the international community, in what concerns religion and morality. The first question can hardly be a matter for discussion and legal ruling between the individual States and the international community, especially in the case of a plurality of different religious beliefs within the international community. On the other hand, the second question can be of extreme importance and urgency.

V. Now to give the right answer to the second question. Above all, it must be clearly stated that no human authority, no State, no community of States, whatever be their religious character, can give a positive command or positive authorization to teach or to do that which would be contrary to religious truth or moral good. Such a command or such an authorization would have no binding force, and would remain without effect. No authority may give such a command, because it is contrary to nature to oblige the spirit and the will of man to error and evil, or to consider one or the other as indifferent. Not even God could give such a positive command or positive authorization, because it would be in contradiction to His absolute truth and sanctity.

Another question essentially different is this: Could the norm be established in a community of States, at least in certain circumstances, that the free exercise of a belief and of a religious or moral practice which has validity in one of the member States, be not hindered by laws or coercive measures of the State throughout the entire territory of the community of Nations? In other words, the question is raised whether in these circumstances "non impedire" or toleration is permissible, and whether consequently positive repression is not always a duty.

We have just spoken of the authority of God. Could God, although it would be possible and easy for Him to repress error and moral deviation, in some cases choose the "non impedire" without contradicting His infinite perfection? Could it be that, in certain circumstances, He would not even communicate the right to impede or to repress what is erroneous and false? A glance at things as they are gives an affirmative answer. It is plainly true that error and sin abound in the world to-day. God reprobates them, but He allows them to exist. Wherefore the statement that religious and moral error must always be impeded, when it is possible, because toleration of them is in itself immoral, is not valid absolutely and unconditionally. Moreover, God has not given even to human authority such an absolute and universal command in matters of faith and morality. Such a command is unknown to the common convictions of mankind, to the Christian conscience, to the sources of revelation and to the practice of the Church. Apart from other Scriptural texts which are adduced in support of this argument, Christ, in the parable of the cockle, gives the following advice: let the cockle grow in the field of the world together with the good seed until the harvest (cf. Matthew xiii, 24–30). The duty of repressing moral and religious error cannot, therefore, be an ultimate norm of action. It must be subordinate to higher and more general guiding principles, which, in some circumstances allow, and even perhaps seem to indicate as the better policy, toleration or error in order to promote a greater good.

Thus are made the two principles to which recourse must be had in concrete cases for the answer to the serious question concerning the attitude which the jurist, the statesman, and the sovereign Catholic State should adopt in a community of Nations with regard to a formula of religious and moral toleration just described. First, that which does not correspond with truth or with good morals objectively has no right to exist, to spread, or to be fostered. Secondly, nevertheless failure to prevent this with civil laws and coercive measures, can be justified in the interests of a higher and more general good.

Before all else, the Catholic statesman must judge if this condition is verified in the concrete—and this is, the "question of fact." In his decision, he will permit himself to be guided by weighing the dangerous consequences which stem from toleration, with those from which the community of Nations will be spared, if the formula of toleration be accepted. Moreover, he will be guided by the good which, with wise foresight, can be expected to accrue from toleration, to the international community as such, and indirectly, to the member State. In that which concerns religion and morality, he will also look for the judgment of the Church. For the Church, only he to whom Christ has entrusted the guidance of His whole Church is competent to speak in the last instance on these vital questions, touching international life; we mean the Roman Pontiff.

VI. The institution of a community of Nations which to-day has been partially realized, but, which is seeking always to be established and consolidated upon a higher and more perfect level, is an advance from the lower to the higher, that is, from a plurality of sovereign States to the greatest possible unity.

The Church of Christ has, in virtue of a mandate from her Divine Founder, a like universal mission. She must draw to herself and bind together, in religious unity, the men of all races and of all times. Here, however, the process is in a certain sense contrariwise; she descends from the higher to the lower. In the former case, the superior juridical unity of nations was, and still is, to be created. In the latter, the juridical community, with its universal end, its constitution, its powers, and those in whom these powers are invested, is already established from the beginning by the will and decree of Christ Himself. The duty of this universal community, from the outset, is to incorporate all men and all races (cf. Matt. xxviii, 19), and thereby to bring them to the full truth and the grace of Jesus Christ.

The Church in the fulfillment of this, her mission, has always been faced, and is still faced in large measure, by the same problems which the functioning of a community of sovereign States must overcome; only she feels them more acutely, for she is bound by the purpose of her mission, determined by her Founder Himself, a purpose which penetrates to the very depths of the spirit and heart of man. In this state of affairs, conflicts are inevitable, and history shows that there have always been conflicts, there still are, and according to the words of the Lord, there will be till the end of time. For the Church with her mission, has been and is confronted with men and nations of marvellous culture, with others of almost incredible lack of civilization, and with all possible intermediate degrees; diversity of extraction, of language, of philosophy, of religious belief, of national aspirations and characteristics; free peoples and enslaved peoples; peoples that have never belonged to the Church, and peoples that have been separated from her communion. The Church must live among them and with them; she can never declare before anyone that she is "not interested." The mandate imposed upon her by her Divine Founder renders it impossible for her to follow a policy of non-interference or laissez-faire. She has the duty to teach and educate in truth and goodness, which are wholly inflexible, and with this absolute obligation she must remain and work among men and nations who, in mental outlook, are completely different one from the other.

Let us return now, however, to the two propositions mentioned above; and in the first place, to the one which denies unconditionally everything that is religiously false and morally wrong. With regard to this point, there never has been and there is not now, in the Church, any wavering or any compromise, whether in theory or in practice. Her attitude has not changed in the course of history, nor can it change, whenever or wherever, under the most varied forms, she is confronted with the choice; either incense for idols or blood for Christ. This place where you are now gathered, Eternal Rome, with the remains of a greatness that was, and the glorious memories of its martyrs, is the most eloquent witness to the answer of the Church. Incense was not burned before idols, and so Christian blood flowed and hallowed the soil. But the temples of the gods lie in the cold devastation of ruin, and all tongues fervently repeat the ancient Creed of the Apostles.

With regard to the second proposition, that is to say, concerning tolerance in determined circumstances, and toleration even in cases in which one could proceed to repression, the Church—out of regard for those who, in good conscience though in invincible error, are of a different opinion—has been led to act and has acted with that tolerance, after she had become that State Church under Constantine the Great and the other Christian Emperors, always for higher and more cogent motives. So she acts to-day, and in the future likewise, she will be faced with the same necessity. In such individual cases the attitude of the Church is determined by consideration of what is demanded for safeguarding the "bonum commune." There is, on the one hand, the common good of the Church and the State in individual States, and on the other, the common good of the universal Church, the reign of God over the whole world. In considering the "pro" and "con" for resolving the "question of fact," as well as what concerns the final and supreme judgment in these matters, no other standards are valid for the Church but those which We have just indicated for the Catholic jurist and statesman.

VII. The ideas which We have set forth may be useful for the Catholic jurist and statesman also when, in their studies, or in the exercise of their profession, they come in contact with the agreements (Concordats, Treaties, Agreements, MODUS VIDENDI, etc.) which the Church (that is to say, for a long time now, the Apostolic See) has concluded and still continues with sovereign States. The Concordats are for her an expression of the collaboration between the Church and State. In principle, that is, in theory, she cannot approve complete separation of the two Powers. The Concordats, therefore, must assure to the Church a stable condition in right and in fact in the State with which they are concluded, and must guarantee to her full independence in the fulfillment of her divine mission. It is possible that the Church and the State proclaim in the Concordat their common religious conviction; but it may also happen that the Concordat have, together with other purposes, that of forestalling disputes with regard to questions of principle and of removing, from the very beginning, possible matters of conflict. When the Church has set her signature to a Concordat, it holds for everything contained therein. However, with the mutual acknowledgment of both high contracting parties, it may not hold in the same way for everything. It may signify an express approval, but it may also mean a simple tolerance, according to those two principles which regulate the coexistence of the Church and the faithful with the civil Powers and with men of another belief.

This, beloved sons, is what We had in mind to treat of with you at some length. For the rest, We are confident that the international community can banish every danger of war and establish peace, and, as far as the Church is concerned, can guarantee to her freedom of action everywhere, so that she may be able to establish in the spirit and the heart, in the thoughts and the actions of men, the Kingdom of Him Who is the Redeemer, the Lawgiver, the Judge, the Lord of the World, Jesus Christ, Who rules as God over all things, blessed forever (Rom. ix, 5).

Whilst then We follow, with fatherly interest and good wishes, your work for the greater good of nations and for the perfecting of international relations, from the fullness of Our heart We impart to you, as a pledge of God's choicest graces, the Apostolic Blessing.

(3) ***Dignitatis humanae* 2** The Vatican Council declares that the human person has a right to religious freedom. Freedom of this kind means that all men should be immune from coercion on the part of individuals, social groups and every human power so that, within due limits, nobody is forced to act against his convictions nor is anyone to be restrained from acting in accordance with his convictions in religious matters in private or in public, alone or in associations with others. The Council further declares that the right to religious freedom is based on the very dignity of the human person as known through the revealed word of God and by reason itself. This right of the human person to religious freedom must be given such recognition in the constitutional order of society as will make it a civil right. 2108

It is in accordance with their dignity that all men, because they are persons, that is, beings endowed with reason and free will and therefore bearing personal responsibility, are both impelled by their nature and bound by a moral obligation to seek the truth, especially religious truth. They are also bound to adhere to the truth once they come to know it and direct their whole lives in accordance with the demands of truth. But men cannot satisfy this obligation in a way that is in keeping with their own nature unless they enjoy both psychological freedom and immunity from external coercion. Therefore the right to religious freedom has its foundation not in the subjective attitude of the individual but in his very nature. For this reason the right to this immunity continues to exist even in those who do not live up to their obligation of seeking the truth and adhering to it. The exercise of this right cannot be interfered with as long as the just requirements of public order are observed.

(1) **Pius VI, *Quod aliquantum* 10 (1791)** And nevertheless, contrary to so certain an opinion in the Church, that national assembly has arrogated to itself the power of the Church, in so far as it made decisions which were so numerous and of such great importance, which are opposed both to the dogma and to the discipline of the Church, and in so far as it bound all bishops and clergy by an oath to carry out its decrees. But this should seem in no way surprising to those who easily understand from the very composition of the assembly that nothing is being set up by it as a 2109

goal and worked toward, other than that the Catholic religion be abolished, and with it the obedience owed to kings. Of course, it is decreed by that council that it be established in law that a human being placed in society should enjoy liberty in every respect, so that he ought not to be subjected to coercion, of course, in regard to religion, and that it is a matter within his choice to believe, to speak, to write, and even to publish whatever he wishes on the subject of religion itself; and it has declared that these quite freakish conclusions are derived from that equality of human beings among themselves and from the liberty of nature, and that they emanate from these. But what greater lunacy can be imagined than establishing an equality and a liberty among all persons which is of such a sort that no allowance is made for reason, with which the human race is particularly endowed by nature and is differentiated from other living beings? When God had created Man and had placed him in the paradise of delight, did He not at that same time impose upon him the penalty of death, if he ate from the tree of knowledge of good and evil? Did He not immediately, by this first command, restrict his freedom? Did He not at a later time, when Man had made himself guilty through disobedience, add more commands through Moses? And although He "would have left" him "under the control of his own judgment," so that he might be able to merit reward or punishment, nevertheless He added "orders and commands, so that they might preserve him, if he was willing to keep them."

2109 (2) **Pius IX, encyclical *Quanta cura***

To Our Venerable Brethren, all Patriarchs, Primates, Archbishops, and Bishops having favor and Communion of the Holy See.

Venerable Brethren, Health and Apostolic Benediction.

With how great care and pastoral vigilance the Roman Pontiffs, our predecessors, fulfilling the duty and office committed to them by the Lord Christ Himself in the person of most Blessed Peter, Prince of the Apostles, of feeding the lambs and the sheep, have never ceased sedulously to nourish the Lord's whole flock with words of faith and with salutary doctrine, and to guard it from poisoned pastures, is thoroughly known to all, and especially to you, Venerable Brethren. And truly the same, Our Predecessors, asserters of justice, being especially anxious for the salvation of souls, had nothing ever more at heart than by their most wise Letters and Constitutions to unveil and condemn all those heresies and errors which, being adverse to our Divine Faith, to the doctrine of the Catholic Church, to purity of morals, and to the eternal salvation of men, have frequently excited violent tempests, and have miserably afflicted both Church and State. For which cause the same Our Predecessors, have, with Apostolic fortitude, constantly resisted the nefarious enterprises of wicked men, who, like raging waves of the sea foaming out their own confusion, and promising liberty whereas they are the slaves of corruption, have striven by their deceptive opinions and most pernicious writings to raze the foundations of the Catholic religion and of civil society, to remove from among men all virtue and justice, to deprave persons, and especially inexperienced youth, to lead it into the snares of error, and at length to tear it from the bosom of the Catholic Church.

But now, as is well known to you, Venerable Brethren, already, scarcely had we been elevated to this Chair of Peter (by the hidden counsel of Divine Providence, certainly by no merit of our own), when, seeing with the greatest grief of Our soul a truly awful storm excited by so many evil opinions, and (seeing also) the most grievous calamities never sufficiently to be deplored which overspread the Christian people from so many errors, according to the duty of Our Apostolic Ministry, and following the illustrious example of Our Predecessors, We raised Our voice, and in many published Encyclical Letters and Allocutions delivered in Consistory, and other

Apostolic Letters, we condemned the chief errors of this most unhappy age, and we excited your admirable episcopal vigilance, and we again and again admonished and exhorted all sons of the Catholic Church, to us most dear, that they should altogether abhor and flee from the contagion of so dire a pestilence. And especially in our first Encyclical Letter written to you on Nov. 9, 1846, and in two Allocutions delivered by us in Consistory, the one on Dec. 9, 1854, and the other on June 9, 1862, we condemned the monstrous portents of opinion which prevail especially in this age, bringing with them the greatest loss of souls and detriment of civil society itself; which are grievously opposed also, not only to the Catholic Church and her salutary doctrine and venerable rights, but also to the eternal natural law engraven by God in all men's hearts, and to right reason; and from which almost all other errors have their origin.

But, although we have not omitted often to proscribe and reprobate the chief errors of this kind, yet the cause of the Catholic Church, and the salvation of souls entrusted to us by God, and the welfare of human society itself, altogether demand that we again stir up your pastoral solicitude to exterminate other evil opinions, which spring forth from the said errors as from a fountain. Which false and perverse opinions are on that ground the more to be detested, because they chiefly tend to this, that that salutary influence be impeded and (even) removed, which the Catholic Church, according to the institution and command of her Divine Author, should freely exercise even to the end of the world—not only over private individuals, but over nations, peoples, and their sovereign princes; and (tend also) to take away that mutual fellowship and concord of counsels between Church and State which has ever proved itself propitious and salutary, both for religious and civil interests. For you well know, venerable brethren, that at this time men are found not a few who, applying to civil society the impious and absurd principle of *naturalism*, as they call it, dare to teach that "the best constitution of public society and (also) civil progress altogether require that human society be conducted and governed without regard being had to religion any more than if it did not exist; or, at least, without any distinction being made between the true religion and false ones." And, against the doctrine of Scripture, of the Church, and of the Holy Fathers, they do not hesitate to assert that "that is the best condition of civil society, in which no duty is recognized, as attached to the civil power, of restraining by enacted penalties, offenders against the Catholic religion, except so far as public peace may require." From which totally false idea of social government they do not fear to foster that erroneous opinion, most fatal in its effects on the Catholic Church and the salvation of souls, called by Our Predecessor, Gregory XVI, *an insanity*, viz., that "liberty of conscience and worship is each man's personal right, which ought to be legally proclaimed and asserted in every rightly constituted society; and that a right resides in the citizens to an absolute liberty, which should be restrained by no authority whether ecclesiastical or civil, whereby they may be able openly and publicly to manifest and declare any of their ideas whatever, either by word of mouth, by the press, or in any other way." But, while they rashly affirm this, they do not think and consider that they are preaching *liberty of perdition*; and that "if human arguments are always allowed free room for discussion, there will never be wanting men who will dare to resist truth, and to trust in the flowing speech of human wisdom; whereas we know, from the very teaching of our Lord Jesus Christ, how carefully Christian faith and wisdom should avoid this most injurious babbling."

And, since where religion has been removed from civil society, and the doctrine and authority of divine revelation repudiated, the genuine notion itself of justice and human right is darkened and lost, and the place of true justice and legitimate right is supplied by material force, thence it appears why it is that some, utterly neglecting and disregarding the surest principles of sound reason, dare to proclaim that "the people's will, manifested by what is called public opinion or in some other way, constitutes a supreme law, free from all divine and human control; and that in the political order accomplished facts, from the very circumstance that they are accomplished, have the force of right." But who does not see and clearly perceive that human society, when set loose from the bonds of religion and true justice, can have, in truth, no other end than the purpose of obtaining and amassing wealth, and that (society under such circumstances) follows no other law in its actions, except the unchastened desire of ministering to its own pleasure and interests? For this reason, men of the kind pursue with bitter hatred the Religious Orders, although these have deserved extremely well of Christendom, civilization and literature, and cry out that the same have no legitimate reason for being permitted to exist; and thus (these evil men) applaud the calumnies of heretics. For, as Pius VI, Our Predecessor, taught most wisely, "the abolition of regulars is injurious to that state in which the Evangelical counsels are openly professed; it is injurious to a method of life praised in the Church as agreeable to Apostolic doctrine; it is injurious to the illustrious founders, themselves, whom we venerate on our altars, who did not establish these societies but by God's inspiration." And (these wretches) also impiously declare that permission should be refused to citizens and to the Church, "whereby they may openly give alms for the sake of Christian charity"; and that the law should be abrogated "whereby on certain fixed days servile works are prohibited because of God's worship"; and on the most deceptive pretext that the said permission and law are opposed to the principles of the best public economy. Moreover, not content with removing religion from public society, they wish to banish it also from private families. For, teaching and professing the most fatal error of *Communism and Socialism*, they assert that "domestic society or the family derives the whole principle of its existence from the civil law alone; and, consequently, that on civil law alone depend all rights of parents over their children, and especially that of providing for education." By which impious opinions and machinations these most deceitful men chiefly aim at this result, viz., that the salutary teaching and influence of the Catholic Church may be entirely banished from the instruction and education of youth, and that the tender and flexible minds of young men may be infected and depraved by every most pernicious error and vice. For all who have endeavored to throw into confusion things both sacred and secular, and to subvert the right order of society, and to abolish all rights, human and divine, have always (as we above hinted) devoted all their nefarious schemes, devices and efforts, to deceiving and depraving incautious youth and have placed all their hope in its corruption. For which reason they never cease by every wicked method to assail the clergy, both secular and regular, from whom (as the surest monuments of history conspicuously attest), so many great advantages have abundantly flowed to Christianity, civilization and literature, and to proclaim that "the clergy, as being hostile to the true and beneficial advance of science and civilization, should be removed from the whole charge and duty of instructing and educating youth."

Others meanwhile, reviving the wicked and so often condemned inventions of innovators, dare with signal impudence to subject to the will of the civil authority the supreme authority of the Church and of this Apostolic See given to her by Christ Himself, and to deny all those rights of the same Church and See which concern matters of the external order. For they are not ashamed of affirming "that the Church's laws do not bind in conscience unless when they are promulgated by the civil power; that acts and decrees of the Roman Pontiffs, referring to religion and the Church, need the civil power's sanction and approbation, or at least its consent; that the Apostolic Constitutions, whereby secret societies are condemned (whether an oath of secrecy be or be not required in such societies), and whereby their frequenters and favorers are smitten with anathema—have no force in those regions of the world wherein associations of the kind are tolerated by the civil government; that the excommunication pronounced by the Council of Trent and by Roman Pontiffs against those who assail and usurp the Church's rights and possessions, rests on a confusion between the spiritual and temporal orders, and (is directed) to the pursuit of a purely secular good; that the Church can decree nothing which binds the conscience of the faithful in regard to their use of temporal things; that the Church has no right of restraining by temporal punishments those who violate her laws; that it is conformable to the principles of sacred theology and public law to assert and claim for the civil government a right of property in those goods which are possessed by the Church, by the Religious Orders, and by other pious establishments." Nor do they blush openly and publicly to profess the maxim and principle of heretics from which arise so many perverse opinions and errors. For they repeat that the "ecclesiastical power is not by divine right distinct from, and independent of, the civil power, and that such distinction and independence cannot be preserved without the civil power's essential rights being assailed and usurped by the Church." Nor can we pass over in silence the audacity of those who, not enduring sound doctrine, contend that "without sin and without any sacrifice of the Catholic profession assent and obedience may be refused to those judgments and decrees of the Apostolic See, whose object is declared to concern the Church's general good and her rights and discipline, so only it does not touch the dogmata of faith and morals." But no one can be found not clearly and distinctly to see and understand how grievously this is opposed to the Catholic dogma of the full power given from God by Christ our Lord Himself to the Roman Pontiff of feeding, ruling and guiding the Universal Church.

Amidst, therefore, such great perversity of depraved opinions, we, well remembering our Apostolic Office, and very greatly solicitous for our most holy Religion, for sound doctrine and the salvation of souls which is entrusted to us by God, and (solicitous also) for the welfare of human society itself, have thought it right again to raise up our Apostolic voice. Therefore, by our Apostolic authority, we reprobate, proscribe, and condemn all the singular and evil opinions and doctrines severally mentioned in this letter, and will and command that they be thoroughly held by all children of the Catholic Church as reprobated, proscribed and condemned.

And besides these things, you know very well, Venerable Brethren, that in these times the haters of truth and justice and most bitter enemies of our religion, deceiving the people and maliciously lying, disseminate sundry and other impious doctrines by means of pestilential books, pamphlets and newspapers dispersed over the whole world. Nor are you ignorant also, that in this our age some men are found who, moved and excited by the spirit of Satan, have reached to that degree of impiety as not to shrink from denying our Ruler and Lord Jesus Christ, and from impugning His Divinity with wicked pertinacity. Here, however, we cannot but extol you, venerable brethren, with great and deserved praise, for not having failed to raise with all zeal your episcopal voice against impiety so great.

Therefore, in this our letter, we again most lovingly address you, who, having been called unto a part of our solicitude, are to us, among our grievous distresses, the greatest solace, joy and consolation, because of the admirable religion and piety wherein you excel, and because of that marvellous love, fidelity, and dutifulness, whereby, bound as you are to us, and to this Apostolic See in most harmonious affection, you strive strenuously and sedulously to fulfill your most weighty episcopal ministry. For from your signal pastoral zeal we expect that, taking up the sword of the spirit which is the word of God, and strengthened by the grace of our Lord Jesus Christ, you will, with redoubled care, each day more anxiously provide that the faithful entrusted to your charge "abstain from noxious verbiage, which Jesus Christ does not cultivate because it is not His Father's plantation." Never cease also to inculcate on the said faithful that all true felicity flows abundantly upon man from our august religion and its doctrine and practice; and that happy is the people whose God is their Lord. Teach that "kingdoms rest on the foundation of the Catholic Faith; and that nothing is so deadly, so hastening to a fall, so exposed to all danger, (as that which exists) if, believing this alone to be sufficient for us that we receive free will at our birth, we seek nothing further from the Lord; that is, if forgetting our Creator we abjure his power that we may display our freedom." And again do not fail to teach "that the royal power was given not only for the governance of the world, but most of all for the protection of the Church"; and that there is nothing which can be of greater advantage and glory to Princes and Kings than if, as another most wise and courageous Predecessor of ours, St. Felix, instructed the Emperor Zeno, they "permit the Catholic Church to practice her laws, and allow no one to oppose her liberty. For it is certain that this mode of conduct is beneficial to their interests, viz., that where there is question concerning the causes of God, they study, according to His appointment, to subject the royal will to Christ's Priests, not to raise it above theirs."

But if always, venerable brethren, now most of all amidst such great calamities both of the Church and of civil society, amidst so great a conspiracy against Catholic interests and this Apostolic See, and so great a mass of errors, it is altogether necessary to approach with confidence the throne of grace, that we may obtain mercy and find grace in timely aid. Wherefore, we have thought it well to excite the piety of all the faithful in order that, together with us and you, they may unceasingly pray and beseech the most merciful Father of light and pity with most fervent and humble prayers, and in the fullness of faith flee always to Our Lord Jesus Christ, who redeemed us to God in his blood, and earnestly and constantly supplicate His most sweet Heart, the victim of most burning love toward us, that He would draw all things to Himself by the bonds of His love, and that all men inflamed by His most holy love may walk worthily according to His heart, pleasing God in all things, bearing fruit in every good work. But since without doubt men's prayers are more pleasing to God if they reach Him from minds free from all stain, therefore we have determined to open to Christ's faithful, with Apostolic liberality, the Church's heavenly treasures committed to our charge, in order that the said faithful, being more earnestly enkindled to true piety, and cleansed through the sacrament of Penance from the defilement of their sins, may with greater confidence pour forth their prayers to God, and obtain His mercy and grace.

By these Letters, therefore, in virtue of our Apostolic authority, we concede to all and singular the faithful of the Catholic world, a Plenary Indulgence in the form of Jubilee, during the space of one month only for the whole coming year 1865, and not beyond; to be fixed by you, venerable brethren, and other legitimate Ordinaries of places, in the very same manner and form in which we granted it at the beginning of our supreme Pontificate by our Apostolic Letters in the form of a Brief, dated November 20, 1846, and addressed to all your episcopal Order, beginning, "Arcano Divinae Providentiae consilio," and with all the same faculties which were given by us in those Letters. We will, however, that all things be observed which were prescribed in the aforesaid Letters, and those things be excepted which we there so declared. And we grant this, notwithstanding anything whatever to the contrary, even things which are worthy of individual mention and derogation. In order, however, that all doubt and difficulty be removed, we have commanded a copy of said Letters be sent you.

"Let us implore," Venerable Brethren, "God's mercy from our inmost heart and with our whole mind; because He has Himself added, 'I will not remove my mercy from them.' Let us ask and we shall receive; and if there be delay and slowness in our receiving because we have gravely offended, let us knock, because to him that knocketh it shall be opened, if only the door be knocked by our prayers, groans and tears, in which we must persist and persevere, and if the prayer be unanimous . . . let each man pray to God, not for himself alone, but for all his brethren, as the Lord hath taught us to pray." But in order that God may the more readily assent to the prayers and desires of ourselves, of you and of all the faithful, let us with all confidence employ as our advocate with Him the Immaculate and most holy Virgin Mary, Mother of God, who has slain all heresies throughout the world, and who, the most loving Mother of us all, "is all sweet . . . and full of mercy . . . shows herself to all as easily entreated; shows herself to all as most merciful; pities the necessities of all with a most large affection"; and standing as a Queen at the right hand of her only begotten Son, our Lord Jesus Christ, in gilded clothing, surrounded with variety, can obtain from Him whatever she will. Let us also seek the suffrages of the Most Blessed Peter, Prince of the Apostles, and of Paul, his Fellow-Apostle, and of all the Saints in Heaven, who having now become God's friends, have arrived at the heavenly kingdom, and being crowned bear their palms, and being secure of their own immortality are anxious for our salvation.

Lastly, imploring from our great heart for You from God the abundance of all heavenly gifts, we most lovingly impart the Apostolic Benediction from our inmost heart, a pledge of our signal love towards you, to yourselves, venerable brethren, and to all the clerics and lay faithful committed to your care.

Given at Rome, from St. Peter's, the 8th day of December, in the year 1864, the tenth from the Dogmatic Definition of the Immaculate Conception of the Virgin Mary, Mother of God.

In the nineteenth year of Our Pontificate.

Matthew 23:16–22 "Woe to you, blind guides, who say, 'If any one swears by the 2111
temple, it is nothing; but if any one swears by the gold of the temple, he is bound by his oath.' You blind fools! For which is greater, the gold or the temple that has made the gold sacred? And you say, 'If any one swears by the altar, it is nothing; but if any one swears by the gift that is on the altar, he is bound by his oath.' You blind men! For which is greater, the gift or the altar that makes the gift sacred? So he who swears by the altar, swears by it and by everything on it; and he who swears by the temple, swears by it and by him who dwells in it; and he who swears by heaven, swears by the throne of God and by him who sits upon it. . . ."

(1) **Isaiah 44:9–20** All who make idols are nothing, and the things they delight in 2112
do not profit; their witnesses neither see nor know, that they may be put to shame. Who fashions a god or casts an image, that is profitable for nothing? Behold, all his fellows shall be put to shame, and the craftsmen are but men; let them all assemble, let them stand forth, they shall be terrified, they shall be put to shame together.

The ironsmith fashions it and works it over the coals; he shapes it with hammers, and forges it with his strong arm; he becomes hungry and his strength fails, he drinks no water and is faint. The carpenter stretches a line, he marks it out with a pencil; he fashions it with planes, and marks it with a compass; he shapes it into the figure of a man, with the beauty of a man, to dwell in a house. He cuts down cedars; or he chooses a holm tree or an oak and lets it grow strong among the trees of the forest; he plants a cedar and the rain nourishes it. Then it becomes fuel for a man; he takes a part of it and warms himself, he kindles a fire and bakes bread; also he makes a god and worships it, he makes it a graven image and falls down before it. Half of it he burns in the fire; over the half he eats flesh, he roasts meat and is satisfied; also he warms himself and says, "Aha, I am warm, I have seen the fire!" And the rest of it he makes into a god, his idol; and falls down to it and worships it; he prays to it and says, "Deliver me, for thou art my god!"

They know not, nor do they discern; for he has shut their eyes, so that they cannot see, and their minds, so that they cannot understand. No one considers, nor is there knowledge or discernment to say, "Half of it I burned in the fire, I also baked bread on its coals, I roasted flesh and have eaten; and shall I make the residue of it an abomination? Shall I fall down before a block of wood?" He feeds on ashes; a deluded mind has led him astray, and he cannot deliver himself or say, "Is there not a lie in my right hand?"

2112 (2) **Jeremiah 10:1–16** Hear the word which the Lord speaks to you, O house of Israel. Thus says the Lord:

"Learn not the way of the nations,
　　nor be dismayed at the signs of the heavens
　　because the nations are dismayed at them,
for the customs of the peoples are false.
A tree from the forest is cut down,
　　and worked with an axe by the hands of a craftsman.
Men deck it with silver and gold;
　　they fasten it with hammer and nails
　　so that it cannot move.
Their idols are like scarecrows in a cucumber field,
　　and they cannot speak;
they have to be carried,
　　for they cannot walk.
Be not afraid of them,
　　for they cannot do evil,
　　neither is it in them to do good."

There is none like thee, O Lord;
　　thou art great, and thy name is great in might.
Who would not fear thee, O King of the nations?
　　For this is thy due;
for among all the wise ones of the nations
　　and in all their kingdoms
　　there is none like thee.
They are both stupid and foolish;
　　the instruction of idols is but wood!
Beaten silver is brought from Tarshish,
　　and gold from Uphaz.
They are the work of the craftsman and of the hands of the goldsmith;
　　their clothing is violet and purple;
　　they are all the work of skilled men.
But the Lord is the true God;
　　he is the living God and the everlasting King.
At his wrath the earth quakes,
　　and the nations cannot endure his indignation.

Thus shall you say to them: "The gods who did not make the heavens and the earth shall perish from the earth and from under the heavens."

It is he who made the earth by his power,
　　who established the world by his wisdom,
　　and by his understanding stretched out the heavens.

When he utters his voice there is a tumult of waters in the heavens,
    and he makes the mist rise from the ends of the earth.
He makes lightnings for the rain,
    and he brings forth the wind from his storehouses.
Every man is stupid and without knowledge;
    every goldsmith is put to shame by his idols;
for his images are false,
    and there is no breath in them.
They are worthless, a work of delusion;
    at the time of their punishment they shall perish.
Not like these is he who is the portion of Jacob,
    for he is the one who formed all things,
and Israel is the tribe of his inheritance;
    the Lord of hosts is his name.

(3) **Daniel 14:1–30 (Bel and the Dragon, 1–30: RSV)** When King Astyages 2112
was laid with his fathers, Cyrus the Persian received his kingdom. And Daniel was a companion of the king, and was the most honored of his friends.

Now the Babylonians had an idol called Bel, and every day they spent on it twelve bushels of fine flour and forty sheep and fifty gallons of wine. The king revered it and went every day to worship it. But Daniel worshiped his own God.

And the king said to him, "Why do you not worship Bel?" He answered, "Because I do not revere man-made idols, but the living God, who created heaven and earth and has dominion over all flesh."

The king said to him, "Do you not think that Bel is a living God? Do you not see how much he eats and drinks every day?" Then Daniel laughed, and said, "Do not be deceived, O king; for this is but clay inside and brass outside, and it never ate or drank anything."

Then the king was angry, and he called his priests and said to them, "If you do not tell me who is eating these provisions, you shall die. But if you prove that Bel is eating them, Daniel shall die, because he blasphemed against Bel." And Daniel said to the king, "Let it be done as you have said."

Now there were seventy priests of Bel, besides their wives and children. And the king went with Daniel into the temple of Bel. And the priests of Bel said, "Behold, we are going outside; you yourself, O king, shall set forth the food and mix and place the wine, and shut the door and seal it with your signet. And when you return in the morning, if you do not find that Bel has eaten it all, we will die; or else Daniel will, who is telling lies about us." They were unconcerned, for beneath the table they had made a hidden entrance, through which they used to go in regularly and consume the provisions. When they had gone out, the king set forth the food for Bel. Then Daniel ordered his servants to bring ashes and they sifted them throughout the whole temple in the presence of the king alone. Then they went out, shut the door and sealed it with the king's signet, and departed. In the night the priests came with their wives and children, as they were accustomed to do, and ate and drank everything.

Early in the morning the king rose and came, and Daniel with him. And the king said, "Are the seals unbroken, Daniel?" He answered, "They are unbroken, O king." As soon as the doors were opened, the king looked at the table, and shouted in a loud voice, "You are great, O Bel; and with you there is no deceit, none at all."

Then Daniel laughed, and restrained the king from going in, and said, "Look at the floor, and notice whose footsteps these are." The king said, "I see the footsteps of men and women and children."

Then the king was enraged, and he seized the priests and their wives and children;

and they showed him the secret doors through which they were accustomed to enter and devour what was on the table. Therefore the king put them to death, and gave Bel over to Daniel, who destroyed it and its temple.

There was also a great dragon, which the Babylonians revered. And the king said to Daniel, "You cannot deny that this is a living god; so worship him." Daniel said, "I will worship the Lord my God, for he is the living God. But if you, O king, will give me permission, I will slay the dragon without sword or club." The king said, "I give you permission."

Then Daniel took pitch, fat, and hair, and boiled them together and made cakes, which he fed to the dragon. The dragon ate them, and burst open. And Daniel said, "See what you have been worshiping!"

When the Babylonians heard it, they were very indignant and conspired against the king, saying, "The king has become a Jew; he has destroyed Bel, and slain the dragon, and slaughtered the priests." Going to the king, they said, "Hand Daniel over to us, or else we will kill you and your household." The king saw that they were pressing him hard, and under compulsion he handed Daniel over to them.

2112 (4) **Baruch 6 (The Letter of Jeremiah: RSV)** A copy of a letter which Jeremiah sent to those who were to be taken to Babylon as captives by the king of the Babylonians, to give them the message which God had commanded him.

Because of the sins which you have committed before God, you will be taken to Babylon as captives by Nebuchadnezzar, king of the Babylonians. Therefore when you have come to Babylon you will remain there for many years, for a long time, up to seven generations; after that I will bring you away from there in peace. Now in Babylon you will see gods made of silver and gold and wood, which are carried on men's shoulders and inspire fear in the heathen. So take care not to become at all like the foreigners or to let fear for these gods possess you, when you see the multitude before and behind them worshiping them. But say in your heart, "It is thou, O Lord, whom we must worship." For my angel is with you, and he is watching your lives.

Their tongues are smoothed by the craftsman, and they themselves are overlaid with gold and silver; but they are false and cannot speak. People take gold and make crowns for the heads of their gods, as they would for a girl who loves ornaments; and sometimes the priests secretly take gold and silver from their gods and spend it upon themselves, and even give some of it to the harlots in the brothel. They deck their gods out with garments like men—these gods of silver and gold and wood, which cannot save themselves from rust and corrosion. When they have been dressed in purple robes, their faces are wiped because of the dust from the temple, which is thick upon them. Like a local ruler the god holds a scepter, though unable to destroy any one who offends it. It has a dagger in its right hand, and has an axe; but it cannot save itself from war and robbers. Therefore they evidently are not gods; so do not fear them.

For just as one's dish is useless when it is broken, so are the gods of the heathen, when they have been set up in the temples. Their eyes are full of the dust raised by the feet of those who enter. And just as the gates are shut on every side upon a man who has offended a king, as though he were sentenced to death, so the priests make their temples secure with doors and locks and bars, in order that they may not be plundered by robbers. They light lamps, even more than they light for themselves, though their gods can see none of them. They are just like a beam of the temple, but men say their hearts have melted, when worms from the earth devour them and their robes. They do not notice when their faces have been blackened by the smoke of the temple. Bats, swallows, and birds light on their bodies and heads; and so do cats. From this you will know that they are not gods; so do not fear them.

As for the gold which they wear for beauty—they will not shine unless some one wipes off the rust; for even when they were being cast, they had no feeling. They are bought at any cost, but there is no breath in them. Having no feet, they are carried on men's shoulders, revealing to mankind their worthlessness. And those who serve them are ashamed because through them these gods are made to stand, lest they fall to the ground. If any one sets one of them upright, it cannot move of itself; and if it is tipped over, it cannot straighten itself; but gifts are placed before them just as before the dead. The priests sell the sacrifices that are offered to these gods and use the money; and likewise their wives preserve some with salt, but give none to the poor or helpless. Sacrifices to them may be touched by women in menstruation or at childbirth. Since you know by these things that they are not gods, do not fear them.

For why should they be called gods? Women serve meals for gods of silver and gold and wood; and in their temples the priests sit with their clothes rent, their heads and beards shaved, and their heads uncovered. They howl and shout before their gods as some do at a funeral feast for a man who has died. The priests take some of the clothing of their gods to clothe their wives and children. Whether one does evil to them or good, they will not be able to repay it. They cannot set up a king or depose one. Likewise they are not able to give either wealth or money; if one makes a vow to them and does not keep it, they will not require it. They cannot save a man from death or rescue the weak from the strong. They cannot restore sight to a blind man; they cannot rescue a man who is in distress. They cannot take pity on a widow or do good to an orphan. These things that are made of wood and overlaid with gold and silver are like stones from the mountain, and those who serve them will be put to shame. Why then must any one think that they are gods, or call them gods?

Besides, even the Chaldeans themselves dishonor them; for when they see a dumb man, who cannot speak, they bring him and pray Bel that the man may speak, as though Bel were able to understand. Yet they themselves cannot perceive this and abandon them, for they have no sense. And the women, with cords about them, sit along the passageways, burning bran for incense; and when one of them is led off by one of the passers-by and is lain with, she derides the woman next to her, because she was not as attractive as herself and her cord was not broken. Whatever is done for them is false. Why then must any one think that they are gods, or call them gods?

They are made by carpenters and goldsmiths; they can be nothing but what the craftsmen wish them to be. The men that make them will certainly not live very long themselves; how then can the things that are made by them be gods? They have left only lies and reproach for those who come after. For when war or calamity comes upon them, the priests consult together as to where they can hide themselves and their gods. How then can one fail to see that these are not gods, for they cannot save themselves from war or calamity? Since they are made of wood and overlaid with gold and silver, it will afterward be known that they are false. It will be manifest to all the nations and kings that they are not gods but the work of men's hands, and that there is no work of God in them. Who then can fail to know that they are not gods?

For they cannot set up a king over a country or give rain to men. They cannot judge their own cause or deliver one who is wronged, for they have no power; they are like crows between heaven and earth. When fire breaks out in a temple of wooden gods overlaid with gold or silver, their priests will flee and escape, but the gods will be burnt in two like beams. Besides, they can offer no resistance to a king or any enemies. Why then must any one admit or think that they are gods?

Gods made of wood and overlaid with silver and gold are not able to save themselves from thieves and robbers. Strong men will strip them of their gold and silver and of the robes they wear, and go off with this booty, and they will not be able to help themselves. So it is better to be a king who shows his courage, or a household utensil that serves its owner's need, than to be these false gods; better even the door of a house that protects its contents, than these false gods; better also a wooden pillar in a palace, than these false gods.

For sun and moon and stars, shining and sent forth for service, are obedient. So also the lightning, when it flashes, is widely seen; and the wind likewise blows in every land. When God commands the clouds to go over the whole world, they carry out his command. And the fire sent from above to consume mountains and woods does what it is ordered. But these idols are not to be compared with them in appearance or power. Therefore one must not think that they are gods nor call them gods, for they are not able either to decide a case or to do good to men. Since you know then that they are not gods, do not fear them.

For they can neither curse nor bless kings; they cannot show signs in the heavens and among the nations, or shine like the sun or give light like the moon. The wild beasts are better than they are, for they can flee to cover and help themselves. So we have no evidence whatever that they are gods; therefore do not fear them.

Like a scarecrow in a cucumber bed, that guards nothing, so are their gods of wood, overlaid with gold and silver. In the same way, their gods are like a thorn bush in a garden, on which every bird sits; or like a dead body cast out in the darkness. By the purple and linen that rot upon them you will know that they are not gods; and they will finally themselves be consumed, and be a reproach in the land. Better therefore is a just man who has no idols, for he will be far from reproach.

2112 (5) **Wisdom 13:1–15:19**

For all men who were ignorant of God were foolish by nature;
and they were unable from the good things that are seen to know him
who exists,
nor did they recognize the craftsman while paying heed to his works;
but they supposed that either fire or wind or swift air,
or the circle of the stars, or turbulent water,
or the luminaries of heaven were the gods that rule the world.
If through delight in the beauty of these things men assumed them to
be gods,
let them know how much better than these is their Lord,
for the author of beauty created them.
And if men were amazed at their power and working,
let them perceive from them
how much more powerful is he who formed them.
For from the greatness and beauty of created things
comes a corresponding perception of their Creator.
Yet these men are little to be blamed,
for perhaps they go astray
while seeking God and desiring to find him.
For as they live among his works they keep searching,
and they trust in what they see, because the things that are seen are
beautiful.
Yet again, not even they are to be excused;
for if they had the power to know so much
that they could investigate the world,
how did they fail to find sooner the Lord of these things?

But miserable, with their hopes set on dead things, are the men
who give the name "gods" to the works of men's hands,
gold and silver fashioned with skill,
and likenesses of animals,
or a useless stone, the work of an ancient hand.
A skilled woodcutter may saw down a tree easy to handle
and skilfully strip off all its bark,
and then with pleasing workmanship
make a useful vessel that serves life's needs,
and burn the castoff pieces of his work
to prepare his food, and eat his fill.
But a castoff piece from among them, useful for nothing,
a stick crooked and full of knots,
he takes and carves with care in his leisure,
and shapes it with skill gained in idleness;
he forms it like the image of a man,
or makes it like some worthless animal,
giving it a coat of red paint and coloring its surface red
and covering every blemish in it with paint;
then he makes for it a niche that befits it,
and sets it in the wall, and fastens it there with iron.
So he takes thought for it, that it may not fall,
because he knows that it cannot help itself,
for it is only an image and has need of help.
When he prays about possessions and his marriage and children,
he is not ashamed to address a lifeless thing.
For health he appeals to a thing that is weak;
for life he prays to a thing that is dead;
for aid he entreats a thing that is utterly inexperienced;
for a prosperous journey, a thing that cannot take a step;
for money-making and work and success with his hands
he asks strength of a thing whose hands have no strength.

Again, one preparing to sail and about to voyage over raging waves
calls upon a piece of wood more fragile than the ship which carries him.
For it was desire for gain that planned that vessel,
and wisdom was the craftsman who built it;
but it is thy providence, O Father, that steers its course,
because thou hast given it a path in the sea,
and a safe way through the waves,
showing that thou canst save from every danger,
so that even if a man lacks skill, he may put to sea.
It is thy will that the works of thy wisdom should not be without effect;
therefore men trust their lives even to the smallest piece of wood,
and passing through the billows on a raft they come safely to land.
For even in the beginning, when arrogant giants were perishing,
the hope of the world took refuge on a raft,
and guided by thy hand left to the world the seed of a new generation.
For blessed is the wood by which righteousness comes.

But the idol made with hands is accursed, and so is he who made it;
because he did the work, and the perishable thing was named a god.
For equally hateful to God are the ungodly man and his ungodliness,

for what was done will be punished together with him who did it.
Therefore there will be a visitation also upon the heathen idols,
because, though part of what God created, they became an abomination,
and became traps for the souls of men
and a snare to the feet of the foolish.

For the idea of making idols was the beginning of fornication,
and the invention of them was the corruption of life,
for neither have they existed from the beginning
nor will they exist for ever.
For through the vanity of men they entered the world,
and therefore their speedy end has been planned.
For a father, consumed with grief at an untimely bereavement,
made an image of his child, who had been suddenly taken from him;
and he now honored as a god what was once a dead human being,
and handed on to his dependents secret rites and initiations.
Then the ungodly custom, grown strong with time, was kept as a law,
and at the command of monarchs graven images were worshiped.
When men could not honor monarchs in their presence, since they
lived at a distance,
they imagined their appearance far away,
and made a visible image of the king whom they honored,
so that by their zeal they might flatter the absent one as though
present.
Then the ambition of the craftsman impelled
even those who did not know the king to intensify their worship.
For he, perhaps wishing to please his ruler,
skilfully forced the likeness to take more beautiful form,
and the multitude, attracted by the charm of his work,
now regarded as an object of worship the one whom shortly before
they had honored as a man.
And this became a hidden trap for mankind,
because men, in bondage to misfortune or to royal authority,
bestowed on objects of stone or wood the name that ought not to be
shared.
Afterward it was not enough for them to err about the knowledge of God,
but they live in great strife due to ignorance,
and they call such great evils peace.
For whether they kill children in their initiations, or celebrate secret
mysteries,
or hold frenzied revels with strange customs,
they no longer keep either their lives or their marriages pure,
but they either treacherously kill one another, or grieve one another
by adultery,
and all is a raging riot of blood and murder, theft and deceit,
corruption, faithlessness, tumult, perjury,
confusion over what is good, forgetfulness of favors,
pollution of souls, sex perversion,
disorder in marriage, adultery, and debauchery.
For the worship of idols not to be named
is the beginning and cause and end of every evil.
For their worshipers either rave in exultation, or prophesy lies,

or live unrighteously, or readily commit perjury;
for because they trust in lifeless idols
they swear wicked oaths and expect to suffer no harm.
But just penalties will overtake them on two counts:
because they thought wickedly of God in devoting themselves to idols,
and because in deceit they swore unrighteously through contempt for
holiness.
For it is not the power of the things by which men swear,
but the just penalty for those who sin,
that always pursues the transgression of the unrighteous.

But thou, our God, art kind and true,
patient, and ruling all things in mercy.
For even if we sin we are thine, knowing thy power;
but we will not sin, because we know that we are accounted thine.
For to know thee is complete righteousness,
and to know thy power is the root of immortality.
For neither has the evil intent of human art misled us,
nor the fruitless toil of painters,
a figure stained with varied colors,
whose appearance arouses yearning in fools,
so that they desire the lifeless form of a dead image.
Lovers of evil things and fit for such objects of hope
are those who either make or desire or worship them.

For when a potter kneads the soft earth
and laboriously molds each vessel for our service,
he fashions out of the same clay
both the vessels that serve clean uses
and those for contrary uses, making all in like manner;
but which shall be the use of each of these
the worker in clay decides.
With misspent toil, he forms a futile god from the same clay—
this man who was made of earth a short time before
and after a little while goes to the earth from which he was taken,
when he is required to return the soul that was lent him.
But he is not concerned that he is destined to die
or that his life is brief,
but he competes with workers in gold and silver,
and imitates workers in copper;
and he counts it his glory that he molds counterfeit gods.
His heart is ashes, his hope is cheaper than dirt,
and his life is of less worth than clay,
because he failed to know the one who formed him
and inspired him with an active soul
and breathed into him a living spirit.
But he considered our existence an idle game,
and life a festival held for profit,
for he says one must get money however one can, even by base means.
For this man, more than all others, knows that he sins
when he makes from earthy matter fragile vessels and graven images.

But most foolish, and more miserable than an infant,
are all the enemies who oppressed thy people.
For they thought that all their heathen idols were gods,
though these have neither the use of their eyes to see with,
nor nostrils with which to draw breath,
nor ears with which to hear,
nor fingers to feel with,
and their feet are of no use for walking.
For a man made them,
and one whose spirit is borrowed formed them;
for no man can form a god which is like himself.
He is mortal, and what he makes with lawless hands is dead,
for he is better than the objects he worships,
since he has life, but they never have.

The enemies of thy people worship even the most hateful animals,
which are worse than all others, when judged by their lack of
intelligence;
and even as animals they are not so beautiful in appearance that one
would desire them,
but they have escaped both the praise of God and his blessing.

2113 (1) **Revelation 13–14** And I saw a beast rising out of the sea, with ten horns and seven heads, with ten diadems upon its horns and a blasphemous name upon its heads. And the beast that I saw was like a leopard, its feet were like a bear's, and its mouth was like a lion's mouth. And to it the dragon gave his power and his throne and great authority. One of its heads seemed to have a mortal wound, but its mortal wound was healed, and the whole earth followed the beast with wonder. Men worshiped the dragon, for he had given his authority to the beast, and they worshiped the beast, saying, "Who is like the beast, and who can fight against it?"

And the beast was given a mouth uttering haughty and blasphemous words, and it was allowed to exercise authority for forty-two months; it opened its mouth to utter blasphemies against God, blaspheming his name and his dwelling, that is, those who dwell in heaven. Also it was allowed to make war on the saints and to conquer them. And authority was given it over every tribe and people and tongue and nation, and all who dwell on earth will worship it, every one whose name has not been written before the foundation of the world in the book of life of the Lamb that was slain. If any one has an ear, let him hear:

If any one is to be taken captive,
to captivity he goes;
if any one slays with the sword,
with the sword must he be slain.

Here is a call for the endurance and faith of the saints.

Then I saw another beast which rose out of the earth; it had two horns like a lamb and it spoke like a dragon. It exercises all the authority of the first beast in its presence, and makes the earth and its inhabitants worship the first beast, whose mortal wound was healed. It works great signs, even making fire come down from heaven to earth in the sight of men; and by the signs which it is allowed to work in the presence of the beast, it deceives those who dwell on earth, bidding them make an image for the beast which was wounded by the sword and yet lived; and it was allowed to give breath to the image of the beast so that the image of the beast should even speak, and to cause those who would not worship the image of the beast to be slain. Also it causes all, both small and great, both rich and poor, both free and slave, to be marked on the right hand or the forehead, so that no one can buy or sell unless he has the mark, that is, the name of the beast or the number of its name. This calls for wisdom: let him who has understanding reckon the number of the beast, for it is a human number, its number is six hundred and sixty-six.

Then I looked, and lo, on Mount Zion stood the Lamb, and with him a hundred and forty-four thousand who had his name and his Father's name written on their foreheads. And I heard a voice from heaven like the sound of many waters and like the sound of loud thunder; the voice I heard was like the sound of harpers playing on their harps, and they sing a new song before the throne and before the four living creatures and before the elders. No one could learn that song except the hundred and forty-four thousand who had been redeemed from the earth. It is these who have not defiled themselves with women, for they are chaste; it is these who follow the Lamb wherever he goes; these have been redeemed from mankind as first fruits for God and the Lamb, and in their mouth no lie was found, for they are spotless.

Then I saw another angel flying in midheaven, with an eternal gospel to proclaim to those who dwell on earth, to every nation and tribe and tongue and people; and he said with a loud voice, "Fear God and give him glory, for the hour of his judgment has come; and worship him who made heaven and earth, the sea and the fountains of water."

Another angel, a second, followed, saying, "Fallen, fallen is Babylon the great, she who made all nations drink the wine of her impure passion."

And another angel, a third, followed them, saying with a loud voice, "If any one worships the beast and its image, and receives a mark on his forehead or on his hand, he also shall drink the wine of God's wrath, poured unmixed into the cup of his anger, and he shall be tormented with fire and sulfur in the presence of the holy angels and in the presence of the Lamb. And the smoke of their torment goes up for ever and ever; and they have no rest, day or night, these worshipers of the beast and its image, and whoever receives the mark of its name."

Here is a call for the endurance of the saints, those who keep the commandments of God and the faith of Jesus.

And I heard a voice from heaven saying, "Write this: Blessed are the dead who die in the Lord henceforth." "Blessed indeed," says the Spirit, "that they may rest from their labors, for their deeds follow them!"

Then I looked, and lo, a white cloud, and seated on the cloud one like a son of man, with a golden crown on his head, and a sharp sickle in his hand. And another angel came out of the temple, calling with a loud voice to him who sat upon the cloud, "Put in your sickle, and reap, for the hour to reap has come, for the harvest of the earth is fully ripe." So he who sat upon the cloud swung his sickle on the earth, and the earth was reaped.

And another angel came out of the temple in heaven, and he too had a sharp sickle. Then another angel came out from the altar, the angel who has power over fire, and he called with a loud voice to him who had the sharp sickle, "Put in your sickle, and gather the clusters of the vine of the earth, for its grapes are ripe." So the angel swung his sickle on the earth and gathered the vintage of the earth, and threw it into the great wine press of the wrath of God; and the wine press was trodden outside the city, and blood flowed from the wine press, as high as a horse's bridle, for one thousand six hundred stadia.

(2) **Galatians 5:20** . . . idolatry, sorcery, enmity, strife, jealousy, anger, selfishness, **2113**
dissension, party spirit. . . .

2113 (3) **Ephesians 5:5** Be sure of this, that no fornicator or impure man, or one who is covetous (that is, an idolater), has any inheritance in the kingdom of Christ and of God.

2116 (1) **Deuteronomy 18:10** There shall not be found among you any one who burns his son or his daughter as an offering, any one who practices divination, a soothsayer, or an augur, or a sorcerer. . . .

2116 (2) **Jeremiah 29:8** For thus says the Lord of hosts, the God of Israel: Do not let your prophets and your diviners who are among you deceive you, and do not listen to the dreams which they dream. . . .

2119 (1) **Luke 4:9** And he took him to Jerusalem, and set him on the pinnacle of the temple, and said to him, "If you are the Son of God, throw yourself down from here. . . ."

2119 (2) **1 Corinthians 10:9** We must not put the Lord to the test, as some of them did and were destroyed by serpents. . . .

2119 (3) **Exodus 17:2–7** Therefore the people found fault with Moses, and said, "Give us water to drink." And Moses said to them, "Why do you find fault with me? Why do you put the Lord to the proof?" But the people thirsted there for water, and the people murmured against Moses, and said, "Why did you bring us up out of Egypt, to kill us and our children and our cattle with thirst?" So Moses cried to the Lord, "What shall I do with this people? They are almost ready to stone me." And the Lord said to Moses, "Pass on before the people, taking with you some of the elders of Israel; and take in your hand the rod with which you struck the Nile, and go. Behold, I will stand before you there on the rock at Horeb; and you shall strike the rock, and water shall come out of it, that the people may drink." And Moses did so, in the sight of the elders of Israel. And he called the name of the place Massah and Meribah, because of the faultfinding of the children of Israel, and because they put the Lord to the proof by saying, "Is the Lord among us or not?"

2119 (4) **Psalm 95:9**

. . . when your fathers tested me,
and put me to the proof, though they had seen my work.

2120 (1) **CIC Canon 1367** A person who throws away the consecrated species or who takes them or retains them for a sacrilegious purpose incurs an automatic (*latae sententiae*) excommunication reserved to the Apostolic See; if a cleric, he can be punished with another penalty including dismissal from the clerical state.

2120 (2) **CIC Canon 1376** One who profanes a movable or immovable sacred thing is to be punished with a just penalty.

2121 (1) **Acts 8:9–24** But there was a man named Simon who had previously practiced magic in the city and amazed the nation of Samaria, saying that he himself was somebody great. They all gave heed to him, from the least to the greatest, saying, "This man is that power of God which is called Great." And they gave heed to him, because for a long time he had amazed them with his magic. But when they believed Philip as he preached good news about the kingdom of God and the name of Jesus Christ, they were baptized, both men and women. Even Simon himself believed, and after being baptized he continued with Philip. And seeing signs and great miracles performed, he was amazed.

Now when the apostles at Jerusalem heard that Samaria had received the word of God, they sent to them Peter and John, who came down and prayed for them that they might receive the Holy Spirit; for it had not yet fallen on any of them, but they had only been baptized in the name of the Lord Jesus. Then they laid their hands on them and they received the Holy Spirit. Now when Simon saw that the Spirit was given through the laying on of the apostles' hands, he offered them money, saying, "Give me also this power, that any one on whom I lay my hands may receive the Holy Spirit." But Peter said to him, "Your silver perish with you, because you thought you could obtain the gift of God with money! You have neither part nor lot in this matter, for your heart is not right before God. Repent therefore of this wickedness of yours, and pray to the Lord that, if possible, the intent of your heart may be forgiven you. For I see that you are in the gall of bitterness and in the bond of iniquity." And Simon answered, "Pray for me to the Lord, that nothing of what you have said may come upon me."

(2) **Isaiah 55:1** 2121

"Ho, every one who thirsts,
come to the waters;
and he who has no money,
come, buy and eat!
Come, buy wine and milk
without money and without price. . . ."

(1) **Luke 10:7** And remain in the same house, eating and drinking what they pro- 2122
vide, for the laborer deserves his wages; do not go from house to house.

(2) **1 Corinthians 9:5–18** Do we not have the right to be accompanied by a wife, 2122
as the other apostles and the brothers of the Lord and Cephas? Or is it only Barnabas and I who have no right to refrain from working for a living? Who serves as a soldier at his own expense? Who plants a vineyard without eating any of its fruit? Who tends a flock without getting some of the milk?

Do I say this on human authority? Does not the law say the same? For it is written in the law of Moses, "You shall not muzzle an ox when it is treading out the grain." Is it for oxen that God is concerned? Does he not speak entirely for our sake? It was written for our sake, because the plowman should plow in hope and the thresher thresh in hope of a share in the crop. If we have sown spiritual good among you, is it too much if we reap your material benefits? If others share this rightful claim upon you, do not we still more?

Nevertheless, we have not made use of this right, but we endure anything rather than put an obstacle in the way of the gospel of Christ. Do you not know that those who are employed in the temple service get their food from the temple, and those who serve at the altar share in the sacrificial offerings? In the same way, the Lord commanded that those who proclaim the gospel should get their living by the gospel.

But I have made no use of any of these rights, nor am I writing this to secure any such provision. For I would rather die than have any one deprive me of my ground for boasting. For if I preach the gospel, that gives me no ground for boasting. For necessity is laid upon me. Woe to me if I do not preach the gospel! For if I do this of my own will, I have a reward; but if not of my own will, I am entrusted with a commission. What then is my reward? Just this: that in my preaching I may make the gospel free of charge, not making full use of my right in the gospel.

2122 (3) **1 Timothy 5:17–18** Let the elders who rule well be considered worthy of double honor, especially those who labor in preaching and teaching; for the scripture says, "You shall not muzzle an ox when it is treading out the grain," and, "The laborer deserves his wages."

2125 **Romans 1:18** For the wrath of God is revealed from heaven against all ungodliness and wickedness of men who by their wickedness suppress the truth.

2126 ***Gaudium et spes* 20, 1** Modern atheism often takes on a systematic form also which, in addition to other causes, so insists on man's desire for autonomy as to object to any dependence on God at all. Those who profess this kind of atheism maintain that freedom consists in this, that man is an end to himself, and the sole maker, with supreme control, of his own history *(propriae suae historiae solus artifex et demiurgus).* They claim that this outlook cannot be reconciled with the assertion of a Lord who is author and end of all things, or that at least it makes such an affirmation altogether unnecessary. The sense of power which modern technical progress begets in man may encourage this outlook.

2130 (1) **Numbers 21:4–9** From Mount Hor they set out by the way to the Red Sea, to go around the land of Edom; and the people became impatient on the way. And the people spoke against God and against Moses, "Why have you brought us up out of Egypt to die in the wilderness? For there is no food and no water, and we loathe this worthless food." Then the Lord sent fiery serpents among the people, and they bit the people, so that many people of Israel died. And the people came to Moses, and said, "We have sinned, for we have spoken against the Lord and against you; pray to the Lord, that he take away the serpents from us." So Moses prayed for the people. And the Lord said to Moses, "Make a fiery serpent, and set it on a pole; and every one who is bitten, when he sees it, shall live." So Moses made a bronze serpent, and set it on a pole; and if a serpent bit any man, he would look at the bronze serpent and live.

2130 (2) **Wisdom 16:5–14**

For when the terrible rage of wild beasts came upon thy people
and they were being destroyed by the bites of writhing serpents,
thy wrath did not continue to the end;
they were troubled for a little while as a warning,
and received a token of deliverance to remind them of thy law's command.
For he who turned toward it was saved, not by what he saw,
but by thee, the Savior of all.
And by this also thou didst convince our enemies
that it is thou who deliverest from every evil.
For they were killed by the bites of locusts and flies,
and no healing was found for them,
because they deserved to be punished by such things;
but thy sons were not conquered even by the teeth of venomous serpents,
for thy mercy came to their help and healed them.
To remind them of thy oracles they were bitten,
and then were quickly delivered,
lest they should fall into deep forgetfulness
and become unresponsive to thy kindness.

For neither herb nor poultice cured them,
but it was thy word, O Lord, which heals all men.
For thou hast power over life and death;
thou dost lead men down to the gates of Hades and back again.
A man in his wickedness kills another,
but he cannot bring back the departed spirit,
nor set free the imprisoned soul.

(3) **John 3:14–15** ". . . And as Moses lifted up the serpent in the wilderness, so 2130
must the Son of man be lifted up, that whoever believes in him may have eternal life."

(4) **Exodus 25:10–22** "They shall make an ark of acacia wood; two cubits and a 2130
half shall be its length, a cubit and a half its breadth, and a cubit and a half its height. And you shall overlay it with pure gold, within and without shall you overlay it, and you shall make upon it a molding of gold round about. And you shall cast four rings of gold for it and put them on its four feet, two rings on the one side of it, and two rings on the other side of it. You shall make poles of acacia wood, and overlay them with gold. And you shall put the poles into the rings on the sides of the ark, to carry the ark by them. The poles shall remain in the rings of the ark; they shall not be taken from it. And you shall put into the ark the testimony which I shall give you. Then you shall make a mercy seat of pure gold; two cubits and a half shall be its length, and a cubit and a half its breadth. And you shall make two cherubim of gold; of hammered work shall you make them, on the two ends of the mercy seat. Make one cherub on the one end, and one cherub on the other end; of one piece with the mercy seat shall you make the cherubim on its two ends. The cherubim shall spread out their wings above, overshadowing the mercy seat with their wings, their faces one to another; toward the mercy seat shall the faces of the cherubim be. And you shall put the mercy seat on the top of the ark; and in the ark you shall put the testimony that I shall give you. There I will meet with you, and from above the mercy seat, from between the two cherubim that are upon the ark of the testimony, I will speak with you of all that I will give you in commandment for the people of Israel. . . ."

(5) **1 Kings 6:23–28** In the inner sanctuary he made two cherubim of olivewood, 2130
each ten cubits high. Five cubits was the length of one wing of the cherub, and five cubits the length of the other wing of the cherub; it was ten cubits from the tip of one wing to the tip of the other. The other cherub also measured ten cubits; both cherubim had the same measure and the same form. The height of one cherub was ten cubits, and so was that of the other cherub. He put the cherubim in the innermost part of the house; and the wings of the cherubim were spread out so that a wing of one touched the one wall, and a wing of the other cherub touched the other wall; their other wings touched each other in the middle of the house. And he overlaid the cherubim with gold.

(6) **1 Kings 7:23–26** Then he made the molten sea; it was round, ten cubits from 2130
brim to brim, and five cubits high, and a line of thirty cubits measured its circumference. Under its brim were gourds, for thirty cubits, compassing the sea round about; the gourds were in two rows, cast with it when it was cast. It stood upon twelve oxen, three facing north, three facing west, three facing south, and three facing east; the sea was set upon them, and all their hinder parts were inward. Its thickness was a handbreadth; and its brim was made like the brim of a cup, like the flower of a lily; it held two thousand baths.

2132 (1) **Council of Trent (1563): DS 1821–25** The holy Synod commands all bishops and others who hold the office of teaching and its administration, that in accordance with the usage of the Catholic and apostolic Church, received from primeval times of the Christian religion, and with the consensus of opinion of the holy Fathers and the decrees of sacred Councils, they above all diligently instruct the faithful on the intercession and invocation of the saints, the veneration of relics, and the legitimate use of images, teaching them that the saints, who reign together with Christ, offer up their prayers to God for men; and that it is good and useful to invoke them suppliantly and, in order to obtain favors from God through His Son Jesus Christ our Lord, who alone is our Redeemer and Savior, to have recourse to their prayers, assistance, and support; and that they who deny that those saints who enjoy eternal happiness in heaven are to be invoked, think impiously, or who assert that they do not pray for men, or that our invocation of them, to intercede for each of us individually, is idolatry, or that it is opposed to the word of God, and inconsistent with the honor of the "one mediator of God and men Jesus Christ" [cf. 1 Tim. 2:5], or that it is foolish to pray vocally or mentally to those who reign in heaven.

That the holy bodies of the saints and also of the martyrs and of others living with Christ, who were the living "members of Christ and the temple of the Holy Spirit" [cf. I Cor. 3:16; 6:19; II Cor. 6:16], which are to be awakened by Him to eternal life and to be glorified, are to be venerated by the faithful, through which many benefits are bestowed by God on men, so that those who affirm that veneration and honor are not due to the relics of the saints, or that these and other memorials are honored by the faithful without profit, and that the places dedicated to the memory of the saints for the purpose of obtaining their help are visited in vain, let these be altogether condemned, just as the Church has for a long time condemned and now condemns them again.

Moreover, that the images of Christ, of the Virgin Mother of God, and of the other saints, are to be placed and retained especially in the churches, and that due honor and veneration be extended to them, not that any divinity or virtue is believed to be in them, for which they are to be venerated, or that anything is to be petitioned from them, or that trust is to be placed in images, as at one time was done by the gentiles, who placed their hope in idols [cf. Ps. 134:15 f.], but because the honor which is shown them, is referred to the prototypes which they represent, so that by means of the images, which we kiss and before which we bare the head and prostrate ourselves, we adore Christ, and venerate the saints, whose likeness they bear. This is what was sanctioned by the decrees of the councils, especially that of the second council of Nicea, against the opponents of images.

Indeed let the bishops diligently teach this, that by the accounts of the mysteries of our redemption, portrayed in pictures or in other representations, the people are instructed and confirmed in the articles of faith which should be kept in mind and constantly pondered over; then, too, that from all sacred images great profit is derived not only because the people are reminded of the benefits and gifts, which are bestowed upon them by Christ, but also, because through the saints the miracles of God and salutary examples are set before the eyes of the faithful, so that they may give thanks to God for those things, may fashion their own lives and conduct in imitation of the saints, and be stimulated to adore and love God, and to cultivate piety. But if anyone should teach or maintain anything contrary to these decrees, let him be anathema.

If any abuses shall creep into these holy and salutary observances, the holy Synod earnestly desires that they be entirely abolished, so that no representations of false dogma and those offering occasion of dangerous error to uneducated persons be exhibited. And if at times it happens that the accounts and narratives of the Holy Scripture, when this is of benefit to the uneducated people, are portrayed and exhibited, let the people be instructed that not for that reason is the divinity represented, as if it can be seen with bodily eyes, or expressed in colors and figures. . . .

(2) ***Sacrosanctum concilium* 126** When passing judgment on works of art, local ordinaries should ask the opinion of the diocesan commission on sacred art and—when occasion demands—the opinions of others who are experts, and the commissions mentioned in Articles 44, 45 and 46. **2132**

Ordinaries should ensure that sacred furnishings and works of value are not disposed of or destroyed, for they are ornaments in God's house.

(3) ***Lumen gentium* 67** The sacred synod teaches this Catholic doctrine advisedly and at the same time admonishes all the sons of the Church that the cult, especially the liturgical cult, of the Blessed Virgin, be generously fostered, and that the practices and exercises of devotion towards her, recommended by the teaching authority of the Church in the course of centuries be highly esteemed, and that those decrees, which were given in the early days regarding the cult images of Christ, the Blessed Virgin and the saints, be religiously observed. But it strongly urges theologians and preachers of the word of God to be careful to refrain as much from all false exaggeration as from too summary an attitude in considering the special dignity of the Mother of God. Following the study of Sacred Scripture, the Fathers, the doctors and liturgy of the Church, and under the guidance of the Church's magisterium, let them rightly illustrate the duties and privileges of the Blessed Virgin which always refer to Christ, the source of all truth, sanctity, and devotion. Let them carefully refrain from whatever might by word or deed lead the separated brethren or any others whatsoever into error about the true doctrine of the Church. Let the faithful remember moreover that true devotion consists neither in sterile nor transitory affection, nor in a certain vain credulity, but proceeds from true faith, by which we are led to recognize the excellence of the Mother of God, and we are moved to a filial love towards our mother and to the imitation of her virtues. **2132**

(1) **Zechariah 2:13** Be silent, all flesh, before the Lord; for he has roused himself from his holy dwelling. **2143**

(2) **Psalm 29:2** **2143**

Ascribe to the Lord the glory of his name;
    worship the Lord in holy array.

(3) **Psalm 96:2** **2143**

Sing to the Lord, bless his name;
    tell of his salvation from day to day.

(4) **Psalm 113:1–2** **2143**

Praise the Lord!
Praise, O servants of the Lord,
    praise the name of the Lord!
Blessed be the name of the Lord
    from this time forth and for evermore!

(1) **Matthew 10:32** So every one who acknowledges me before men, I also will acknowledge before my Father who is in heaven. . . . **2145**

(2) **1 Timothy 6:12** Fight the good fight of the faith; take hold of the eternal life to which you were called when you made the good confession in the presence of many witnesses. **2145**

2147 **1 John 1:10** If we say we have not sinned, we make him a liar, and his word is not in us.

2148 **CIC Canon 1369** A person who uses a public show or speech, published writings, or other media of social communication to blaspheme, seriously damage good morals, express wrongs against religion or against the Church or stir up hatred or contempt against religion or the Church is to be punished with a just penalty.

2153 **James 5:12** But above all, my brethren, do not swear, either by heaven or by earth or with any other oath, but let your yes be yes and your no be no, that you may not fall under condemnation.

2154 (1) **2 Corinthians 1:23** But I call God to witness against me—it was to spare you that I refrained from coming to Corinth.

2154 (2) **Galatians 1:20** (In what I am writing to you, before God, I do not lie!)

2158 (1) **Isaiah 43:1**

But now thus says the Lord,
he who created you, O Jacob,
he who formed you, O Israel:
"Fear not, for I have redeemed you;
I have called you by name, you are mine. . . ."

2158 (2) **John 10:3** To him the gatekeeper opens; the sheep hear his voice, and he calls his own sheep by name and leads them out.

2167 (1) **Isaiah 43:1**

But now thus says the Lord,
he who created you, O Jacob,
he who formed you, O Israel:
"Fear not, for I have redeemed you;
I have called you by name, you are mine. . . ."

2167 (2) **Deuteronomy 5:12–15** "'Observe the sabbath day, to keep it holy, as the Lord your God commanded you. Six days you shall labor, and do all your work; but the seventh day is a sabbath to the Lord your God; in it you shall not do any work, you, or your son, or your daughter, or your manservant, or your maidservant, or your ox, or your ass, or any of your cattle, or the sojourner who is within your gates, that your manservant and your maidservant may rest as well as you. You shall remember that you were a servant in the land of Egypt, and the Lord your God brought you out thence with a mighty hand and an outstretched arm; therefore the Lord your God commanded you to keep the sabbath day. . . .'"

2171 **Exodus 31:16** Therefore the people of Israel shall keep the sabbath, observing the sabbath throughout their generations, as a perpetual covenant.

2172 (1) **Exodus 23:12** "Six days you shall do your work, but on the seventh day you shall rest; that your ox and your ass may have rest, and the son of your bondmaid, and the alien, may be refreshed. . . ."

(2) **Nehemiah 13:15–22** In those days I saw in Judah men treading wine presses on the sabbath, and bringing in heaps of grain and loading them on asses; and also wine, grapes, figs, and all kinds of burdens, which they brought into Jerusalem on the sabbath day; and I warned them on the day when they sold food. Men of Tyre also, who lived in the city, brought in fish and all kinds of wares and sold them on the sabbath to the people of Judah, and in Jerusalem. Then I remonstrated with the nobles of Judah and said to them, "What is this evil thing which you are doing, profaning the sabbath day? Did not your fathers act in this way, and did not our God bring all this evil on us and on this city? Yet you bring more wrath upon Israel by profaning the sabbath." 2172

When it began to be dark at the gates of Jerusalem before the sabbath, I commanded that the doors should be shut and gave orders that they should not be opened until after the sabbath. And I set some of my servants over the gates, that no burden might be brought in on the sabbath day. Then the merchants and sellers of all kinds of wares lodged outside Jerusalem once or twice. But I warned them and said to them, "Why do you lodge before the wall? If you do so again I will lay hands on you." From that time on they did not come on the sabbath. And I commanded the Levites that they should purify themselves and come and guard the gates, to keep the sabbath day holy. Remember this also in my favor, O my God, and spare me according to the greatness of thy steadfast love.

(3) **2 Chronicles 36:21** . . . to fulfil the word of the Lord by the mouth of Jeremiah, until the land had enjoyed its sabbaths. All the days that it lay desolate it kept sabbath, to fulfil seventy years. 2172

(1) **Mark 1:21** And they went into Capernaum; and immediately on the sabbath he entered the synagogue and taught. 2173

(2) **John 9:16** Some of the Pharisees said, "This man is not from God, for he does not keep the sabbath." But others said, "How can a man who is a sinner do such signs?" There was a division among them. 2173

(3) **Mark 3:4** And he said to them, "Is it lawful on the sabbath to do good or to do harm, to save life or to kill?" But they were silent. 2173

(4) **Matthew 12:5** Or have you not read in the law how on the sabbath the priests in the temple profane the sabbath, and are guiltless? 2173

(5) **John 7:23** If on the sabbath a man receives circumcision, so that the law of Moses may not be broken, are you angry with me because on the sabbath I made a man's whole body well? 2173

(1) **Matthew 28:1** Now after the sabbath, toward the dawn of the first day of the week, Mary Magdalene and the other Mary went to see the sepulchre. 2174

(2) **Mark 16:2** And very early on the first day of the week they went to the tomb when the sun had risen. 2174

(3) **Luke 24:1** But on the first day of the week, at early dawn, they went to the tomb, taking the spices which they had prepared. 2174

(4) **John 20:1** Now on the first day of the week Mary Magdalene came to the tomb early, while it was still dark, and saw that the stone had been taken away from the tomb. 2174

2174 (5) **Mark 16:1** And when the sabbath was past, Mary Magdalene, and Mary the mother of James, and Salome, bought spices, so that they might go and anoint him.

2174 (6) **Matthew 28:1** Now after the sabbath, toward the dawn of the first day of the week, Mary Magdalene and the other Mary went to see the sepulchre.

2175 **1 Corinthians 10:11** Now these things happened to them as a warning, but they were written down for our instruction, upon whom the end of the ages has come.

2178 (1) **Acts 2:42–46** And they devoted themselves to the apostles' teaching and fellowship, to the breaking of bread and the prayers.

And fear came upon every soul; and many wonders and signs were done through the apostles. And all who believed were together and had all things in common; and they sold their possessions and goods and distributed them to all, as any had need. And day by day, attending the temple together and breaking bread in their homes, they partook of food with glad and generous hearts. . . .

2178 (2) **1 Corinthians 11:17** But in the following instructions I do not commend you, because when you come together it is not for the better but for the worse.

2181 **CIC Canon 1245** With due regard for the right of diocesan bishops which is mentioned in can. 87, for a just reason and in accord with the prescriptions of the diocesan bishop, the pastor in individual cases can dispense from the obligation to observe a feast day or a day of penance; or he can commute it to other pious works; the superior of a religious institute or a society of apostolic life of pontifical right if they are clerical can also do the same for his own subjects and others staying in his house day and night.

2184 ***Gaudium et spes* 67, 3** Since economic activity is, for the most part, the fruit of the collaboration of many men, it is unjust and inhuman to organize and direct it in such a way that some of the workers are exploited. But it frequently happens, even today, that workers are almost enslaved by the work they do. So-called laws of economics are no excuse for this kind of thing. The entire process of productive work, then, must be accommodated to the needs of the human person and the nature of his life, with special attention to domestic life and of mothers of families in particular, taking sex and age always into account. Workers should have the opportunity to develop their talents and their personalities in the very exercise of their work. While devoting their time and energy to the performance of their work with a due sense of responsibility, they should nevertheless be allowed sufficient rest and leisure to cultivate their family, cultural, social and religious life. And they should be given the opportunity to develop those energies and talents, which perhaps are not catered for in their professional work.

2185 **CIC Canon 1247** On Sundays and other holy days of obligation the faithful are bound to participate in the Mass; they are also to abstain from those labors and business concerns which impede the worship to be rendered to God, the joy which is proper to the Lord's Day, or the proper relaxation of mind and body.

2191 ***Sacrosanctum concilium* 106** By a tradition handed down from the apostles, which took its origin from the very day of Christ's resurrection, the Church celebrates the paschal mystery every seventh day, which day is appropriately called the Lord's Day or Sunday. For on this day Christ's faithful are bound to come together into one place.

They should listen to the word of God and take part in the Eucharist, thus calling to mind the passion, resurrection, and glory of the Lord Jesus, and giving thanks to God who "has begotten them again, through the resurrection of Christ from the dead, unto a living hope" (1 Pet. 1:3). The Lord's Day is the original feast day, and it should be proposed to the faithful and taught to them so that it may become in fact a day of joy and of freedom from work. Other celebrations, unless they be truly of the greatest importance, shall not have precedence over Sunday, which is the foundation and kernel of the whole liturgical year.

(1) **Deuteronomy 6:4–5** "Hear, O Israel: The Lord our God is one Lord; and you shall love the Lord your God with all your heart, and with all your soul, and with all your might. . . ." 2196

(2) **Leviticus 19:18** You shall not take vengeance or bear any grudge against the sons of your own people, but you shall love your neighbor as yourself: I am the Lord. 2196

(3) **Matthew 22:34–40** But when the Pharisees heard that he had silenced the Sadducees, they came together. And one of them, a lawyer, asked him a question, to test him. "Teacher, which is the great commandment in the law?" And he said to him, "You shall love the Lord your God with all your heart, and with all your soul, and with all your mind. This is the great and first commandment. And a second is like it, You shall love your neighbor as yourself. On these two commandments depend all the law and the prophets." 2196

(4) **Luke 10:25–28** And behold, a lawyer stood up to put him to the test, saying, "Teacher, what shall I do to inherit eternal life?" He said to him, "What is written in the law? How do you read?" And he answered, "You shall love the Lord your God with all your heart, and with all your soul, and with all your strength, and with all your mind; and your neighbor as yourself." And he said to him, "You have answered right; do this, and you will live." 2196

(5) **Deuteronomy 5:16** "'Honor your father and your mother, as the Lord your God commanded you; that your days may be prolonged, and that it may go well with you, in the land which the Lord your God gives you. . . .'" 2196

(1) ***Lumen gentium* 11** The sacred nature and organic structure of the priestly community is brought into operation through the sacraments and the exercise of virtues. Incorporated into the Church by Baptism, the faithful are appointed by their baptismal character to Christian religious worship; reborn as sons of God, they must profess before men the faith they have received from God through the Church. By the sacrament of Confirmation they are more perfectly bound to the Church and are endowed with the special strength of the Holy Spirit. Hence they are, as true witnesses of Christ, more strictly obliged to spread the faith by word and deed. Taking part in the eucharistic sacrifice, the source and summit of the Christian life, they offer the divine victim to God and themselves along with it. And so it is that, both in the offering and in Holy Communion, each in his own way, though not of course indiscriminately, has his own part to play in the liturgical action. Then, strengthened by the body of Christ in the eucharistic communion, they manifest in a concrete way that unity of the People of God which this holy sacrament aptly signifies and admirably realizes. 2204

Those who approach the sacrament of Penance obtain pardon from God's mercy for the offense committed against him, and are, at the same time, reconciled with the Church which they have wounded by their sins and which by charity, by example and by prayer labors for their conversion. By the sacred anointing of the sick and the prayer of the priests the whole Church commends those who are ill to the suffering and glorified Lord that he may raise them up and save them (cf. Jas. 5:14–16). And indeed she exhorts them to contribute to the good of the People of God by freely uniting themselves to the passion and death of Christ (cf. Rom. 8:17; Col. 1:24; 2 Tim. 2:11–12; 1 Pet. 4:13). Those among the faithful who have received Holy Orders are appointed to nourish the Church with the word and grace of God in the name of Christ. Finally, in virtue of the sacrament of Matrimony by which they signify and share (cf. Eph. 5:32) the mystery of the unity and faithful love between Christ and the Church, Christian married couples help one another to attain holiness in their married life and in the rearing of their children. Hence by reason of their state in life and of their position they have their own gifts in the People of God (cf. 1 Cor. 7:7). From the marriage of Christians there comes the family in which new citizens of human society are born and, by the grace of the Holy Spirit in Baptism, those are made children of God so that the People of God may be perpetuated throughout the centuries. In what might be regarded as the domestic Church, the parents, by word and example, are the first heralds of the faith with regard to their children. They must foster the vocation which is proper to each child, and this with special care if it be to religion.

Strengthened by so many and such great means of salvation, all the faithful, whatever their condition or state—though each in his own way—are called by the Lord to that perfection of sanctity by which the Father himself is perfect.

2204 (2) **Ephesians 5:21–6:4** Be subject to one another out of reverence for Christ. Wives, be subject to your husbands, as to the Lord. For the husband is the head of the wife as Christ is the head of the church, his body, and is himself its Savior. As the church is subject to Christ, so let wives also be subject in everything to their husbands. Husbands, love your wives, as Christ loved the church and gave himself up for her, that he might sanctify her, having cleansed her by the washing of water with the word, that he might present the church to himself in splendor, without spot or wrinkle or any such thing, that she might be holy and without blemish. Even so husbands should love their wives as their own bodies. He who loves his wife loves himself. For no man ever hates his own flesh, but nourishes and cherishes it, as Christ does the church, because we are members of his body. "For this reason a man shall leave his father and mother and be joined to his wife, and the two shall become one flesh." This mystery is a profound one, and I am saying that it refers to Christ and the church; however, let each one of you love his wife as himself, and let the wife see that she respects her husband.

Children, obey your parents in the Lord, for this is right. "Honor your father and mother" (this is the first commandment with a promise), "that it may be well with you and that you may live long on the earth." Fathers, do not provoke your children to anger, but bring them up in the discipline and instruction of the Lord.

2204 (3) **Colossians 3:18–21** Wives, be subject to your husbands, as is fitting in the Lord. Husbands, love your wives, and do not be harsh with them. Children, obey your parents in everything, for this pleases the Lord. Fathers, do not provoke your children, lest they become discouraged.

2204 (4) **1 Peter 3:1–7** Likewise you wives, be submissive to your husbands, so that some, though they do not obey the word, may be won without a word by the behavior of their wives, when they see your reverent and chaste behavior. Let not yours be the outward adorning with braiding of hair, decoration of gold, and wearing of fine clothing, but let it be the hidden person of the heart with the imperishable jewel of a gentle and quiet spirit, which in God's sight is very precious. So once the holy women who hoped in God used to adorn themselves and were submissive to their husbands, as Sarah obeyed Abraham, calling him lord. And you are now her children if you do right and let nothing terrify you.

Likewise you husbands, live considerately with your wives, bestowing honor on the woman as the weaker sex, since you are joint heirs of the grace of life, in order that your prayers may not be hindered.

***Gaudium et spes* 47, 1** The well-being of the individual person and of both human and Christian society is closely bound up with the healthy state of conjugal and family life. Hence Christians today are overjoyed, and so too are all who esteem conjugal and family life highly, to witness the various ways in which progress is being made in fostering those partnerships of love and in encouraging reverence for human life; there is progress too in services available to married people and parents for fulfilling their lofty calling: even greater benefits are to be expected and efforts are being made to bring them about. 2210

***Familiaris consortio* 46** The ideal of mutual support and development between the family and society is often very seriously in conflict with the reality of their separation and even opposition. 2211

In fact, as was repeatedly denounced by the Synod, the situation experienced by many families in various countries is highly problematical, if not entirely negative: institutions and laws unjustly ignore the inviolable rights of the family and of the human person; and society, far from putting itself at the service of the family, attacks it violently in its values and fundamental requirements. Thus the family, which in God's plan is the basic cell of society and a subject of rights and duties before the State or any other community, finds itself the victim of society, of the delays and slowness with which it acts, and even of its blatant injustice.

For this reason, the Church openly and strongly defends the rights of the family against the intolerable usurpations of society and the State. In particular, the Synod Fathers mentioned the following rights of the family:

—the right to exist and progress as a family, that is to say, the right of every human being, even if he or she is poor, to found a family and to have adequate means to support it;

—the right to exercise its responsibility regarding the transmission of life and to educate children;

—the right to the intimacy of conjugal and family life;

—the right to the stability of the bond and of the institution of marriage;

—the right to believe in and profess one's faith and to propagate it;

—the right to bring up children in accordance with the family's own traditions and religious and cultural values, with the necessary instruments, means and institutions;

—the right, especially of the poor and the sick, to obtain physical, social, political and economic security;

—the right to housing suitable for living family life in a proper way;

—the right to expression and to representation, either directly or through associations, before the economic, social and cultural public authorities and lower authorities;

—the right to form associations with other families and institutions, in order to fulfill the family's role suitably and expeditiously;

—the right to protect minors by adequate institutions and legislation from harmful drugs, pornography, alcoholism, etc.;
—the right to wholesome recreation of a kind that also fosters family values;
—the right of the elderly to a worthy life and a worthy death;
—the right to emigrate as a family in search of a better life.

Acceding to the Synod's explicit request, the Holy See will give prompt attention to studying these suggestions in depth and to the preparation of a Charter of Rights of the Family, to be presented to the quarters and authorities concerned.

2214 (1) **Ephesians 3:14** For this reason I bow my knees before the Father. . . .

2214 (2) **Proverbs 1:8**
Hear, my son, your father's instruction,
and reject not your mother's teaching. . . .

2214 (3) **Tobit 4:3–4** So he called him and said, "My son, when I die, bury me, and do not neglect your mother. Honor her all the days of your life; do what is pleasing to her, and do not grieve her. Remember, my son, that she faced many dangers for you while you were yet unborn. When she dies, bury her beside me in the same grave. . . ."

2214 (4) **Exodus 20:12** "Honor your father and your mother, that your days may be long in the land which the Lord your God gives you. . . ."

2217 **Ephesians 6:1** Children, obey your parents in the Lord, for this is right.

2218 **Mark 7:10–12** ". . . For Moses said, 'Honor your father and your mother'; and, 'He who speaks evil of father or mother, let him surely die'; but you say, 'If a man tells his father or his mother, What you would have gained from me is Corban' (that is, given to God)—then you no longer permit him to do anything for his father or mother. . . ."

2221 ***Familiaris consortio* 36** The task of giving education is rooted in the primary vocation of married couples to participate in God's creative activity: by begetting in love and for love a new person who has within himself or herself the vocation to growth and development, parents by that very fact take on the task of helping that person effectively to live a fully human life. As the Second Vatican Council recalled, "since parents have conferred life on their children, they have a most solemn obligation to educate their offspring. Hence, parents must be acknowledged as the first and foremost educators of their children. Their role as educators is so decisive that scarcely anything can compensate for their failure in it. For it devolves on parents to create a family atmosphere so animated with love and reverence for God and others that a well-rounded personal and social development will be fostered among the children. Hence, the family is the first school of those social virtues which every society needs."

The right and duty of parents to give education is *essential*, since it is connected with the transmission of human life; it is *original and primary* with regard to the educational role of others, on account of the uniqueness of the loving relationship between parents and children; and it is *irreplaceable and inalienable*, and therefore incapable of being entirely delegated to others or usurped by others.

In addition to these characteristics, it cannot be forgotten that the most basic element, so basic that it qualifies the educational role of parents, is *parental love*, which finds fulfilment in the task of education as it completes and perfects its service of life:

as well as being a *source*, the parents' love is also the *animating principle* and therefore the *norm* inspiring and guiding all concrete educational activity, enriching it with the values of kindness, constancy, goodness, service, disinterestedness and self-sacrifice that are the most precious fruit of love.

***Lumen gentium* 11:** see 2204 (1). 2226

(1) ***Gaudium et spes* 48, 4** Children as living members of the family contribute in 2227
their own way to the sanctification of their parents. With sentiments of gratitude, affection and trust, they will repay their parents for the benefits given to them and will come to their assistance as devoted children in times of hardship and in the loneliness of old age. Widowhood, accepted courageously as a continuation of the calling to marriage, will be honored by all. Families will generously share their spiritual treasures with other families. The Christian family springs from marriage, which is an image and a sharing in the partnership of love between Christ and the Church; it will show forth to all men Christ's living presence in the world and the authentic nature of the Church by the love and generous fruitfulness of the spouses, by their unity and fidelity, and by the loving way in which all members of the family cooperate with each other.

(2) **Matthew 18:21–22** Then Peter came up and said to him, "Lord, how often 2227
shall my brother sin against me, and I forgive him? As many as seven times?" Jesus said to him, "I do not say to you seven times, but seventy times seven. . . ."

(3) **Luke 17:4** ". . . and if he sins against you seven times in the day, and turns to 2227
you seven times, and says, 'I repent,' you must forgive him."

***Gravissimum educationis* 6** Parents, who have a primary and inalienable duty and 2229
right in regard to the education of their children, should enjoy the fullest liberty in their choice of school. The public authority, therefore, whose duty it is to protect and defend the liberty of the citizens, is bound according to the principles of distributive justice to ensure that the public subsidies to schools are so allocated that parents are truly free to select schools for their children in accordance with their conscience.

But it is the duty of the state to ensure that all its citizens have access to an adequate education and are prepared for the proper exercise of their civic rights and duties. The state itself, therefore, should safeguard the rights of the children to an adequate education in schools. It should be vigilant about the ability of the teachers and the standard of teaching. It should watch over the health of the pupils and in general promote the work of the schools in its entirety. In this, however, the principle of subsidiarity must be borne in mind, and therefore there must be no monopoly of schools which would be prejudicial to the natural rights of the human person and would militate against the progress and extension of education, and the peaceful coexistence of citizens. It would, moreover, be inconsistent with the pluralism which exists today in many societies.

Accordingly the sacred Synod urges the faithful to cooperate readily in the development of suitable methods of education and systems of study and in the training of teachers competent to give a good education to their pupils. They are urged also to further by their efforts, and especially by associations of parents, the entire activity of the schools and in particular the moral education given in them.

Matthew 16:25 For whoever would save his life will lose it, and whoever loses his 2232
life for my sake will find it.

2236 ***Centesimus annus* 25** The events of 1989 are an example of the success of willingness to negotiate and of the Gospel spirit in the face of an adversary determined not to be bound by moral principles. These events are a warning to those who, in the name of political realism, wish to banish law and morality from the political arena. Undoubtedly, the struggle which led to the changes of 1989 called for clarity, moderation, suffering and sacrifice. In a certain sense, it was a struggle born of prayer, and it would have been unthinkable without immense trust in God, the Lord of history, who carries the human heart in his hands. It is by uniting his own sufferings for the sake of truth and freedom to the sufferings of Christ on the Cross that man is able to accomplish the miracle of peace and is in a position to discern the often narrow path between the cowardice which gives in to evil and the violence which, under the illusion of fighting evil, only makes it worse.

Nevertheless, it cannot be forgotten that the manner in which the individual exercises freedom is conditioned in innumerable ways. While these certainly have an influence on freedom, they do not determine it; they make the exercise of freedom more difficult or less difficult, but they cannot destroy it. Not only is it wrong from the ethical point of view to disregard human nature, which is made for freedom, but in practice it is impossible to do so. Where society is so organized as to reduce arbitrarily or even suppress the sphere in which freedom is legitimately exercised, the result is that the life of society becomes progressively disorganized and goes into decline.

Moreover, man, created for freedom, bears within himself the wound of original sin, which constantly draws him towards evil and puts him in need of redemption. Not only is *this doctrine an integral part of Christian revelation;* it also has great hermeneutical value insofar as it helps one to understand human reality. Man tends towards good, but he is also capable of evil. He can transcend his immediate interest and still remain bound to it. The social order will be all the more stable, the more it takes this fact into account and does not place in opposition personal interest and the interests of society as a whole, but rather seeks ways to bring them into fruitful harmony. In fact, where self-interest is violently suppressed, it is replaced by a burdensome system of bureaucratic control which dries up the wellsprings of initiative and creativity. When people think they possess the secret of a perfect social organization which makes evil impossible, they also think that they can use any means, including violence and deceit, in order to bring that organization into being. Politics then becomes a "secular religion" which operates under the illusion of creating paradise in this world. But no political society—which possesses its own autonomy and laws—can ever be confused with the Kingdom of God. The Gospel parable of the weeds among the wheat (cf. Mt 13:24–30; 36–43) teaches that it is for God alone to separate the subjects of the Kingdom from the subjects of the Evil One, and that this judgment will take place at the end of time. By presuming to anticipate judgment here and now, man puts himself in the place of God and sets himself against the patience of God.

Through Christ's sacrifice on the Cross, the victory of the Kingdom of God has been achieved once and for all. Nevertheless, the Christian life involves a struggle against temptation and the forces of evil. Only at the end of history will the Lord return in glory for the final judgment (cf. Mt 25:31) with the establishment of a new heaven and a new earth (cf. 2 Pt 3:13; Rev 21:1); but as long as time lasts the struggle between good and evil continues even in the human heart itself.

What Sacred Scripture teaches us about the prospects of the Kingdom of God is not without consequences for the life of temporal societies, which, as the adjective indicates, belong to the realm of time, with all that this implies of imperfection and impermanence. The Kingdom of God, being *in* the world without being *of* the world, throws light on the order of human society, while the power of grace penetrates that order and gives it life. In this way the requirements of a society worthy of man are better perceived, deviations are corrected, the courage to work for what is good is reinforced. In union with all people of good will, Christians, especially the laity, are called to this task of imbuing human realities with the Gospel.

Romans 13:1–2 Let every person be subject to the governing authorities. For there is no authority except from God, and those that exist have been instituted by God. Therefore he who resists the authorities resists what God has appointed, and those who resist will incur judgment. 2238

(1) ***Centesimus annus* 45** The culture and praxis of totalitarianism also involve a rejection of the Church. The State or the party which claims to be able to lead history towards perfect goodness, and which sets itself above all values, cannot tolerate the affirmation of *an objective criterion of good and evil* beyond the will of those in power, since such a criterion, in given circumstances, could be used to judge their actions. This explains why totalitarianism attempts to destroy the Church, or at least to reduce her to submission, making her an instrument of its own ideological apparatus. 2244

Furthermore, the totalitarian State tends to absorb within itself the nation, society, the family, religious groups and individuals themselves. In defending her own freedom, the Church is also defending the human person, who must obey God rather than men (cf. Acts 5:29), as well as defending the family, the various social organizations and nations—all of which enjoy their own spheres of autonomy and sovereignty.

(2) ***Centesimus annus* 46** The Church values the democratic system inasmuch as it ensures the participation of citizens in making political choices, guarantees to the governed the possibility both of electing and holding accountable those who govern them, and of replacing them through peaceful means when appropriate. Thus she cannot encourage the formation of narrow ruling groups which usurp the power of the State for individual interests or for ideological ends. 2244

Authentic democracy is possible only in a State ruled by law, and on the basis of a correct conception of the human person. It requires that the necessary conditions be present for the advancement both of the individual through education and formation in true ideals, and of the "subjectivity" of society through the creation of structures of participation and shared responsibility. Nowadays there is a tendency to claim that agnosticism and skeptical relativism are the philosophy and the basic attitude which correspond to democratic forms of political life. Those who are convinced that they know the truth and firmly adhere to it are considered unreliable from a democratic point of view, since they do not accept that truth is determined by the majority, or that it is subject to variation according to different political trends. It must be observed in this regard that if there is no ultimate truth to guide and direct political activity, then ideas and convictions can easily be manipulated for reasons of power. As history demonstrates, a democracy without values easily turns into open or thinly disguised totalitarianism.

Nor does the Church close her eyes to the danger of fanaticism or fundamentalism among those who, in the name of an ideology which purports to be scientific or religious, claim the right to impose on others their own concept of what is true and good. *Christian truth* is not of this kind. Since it is not an ideology, the Christian faith does not presume to imprison changing socio-political realities in a rigid schema, and it recognizes that human life is realized in history in conditions that are diverse and imperfect. Furthermore, in constantly reaffirming the transcendent dignity of the person, the Church's method is always that of respect for freedom.

But freedom attains its full development only by accepting the truth. In a world without truth, freedom loses its foundation and man is exposed to the violence of passion and to manipulation, both open and hidden. The Christian upholds freedom and serves it, constantly offering to others the truth which he has known (cf. Jn 8:31–32), in accordance with the missionary nature of his vocation. While paying heed to every fragment of truth which he encounters in the life experience and in the culture of individuals and of nations, he will not fail to affirm in dialogue with others all that his faith and the correct use of reason have enabled him to understand.

2257 **Deuteronomy 5:17** "'You shall not kill. . . .'"

2259 **Genesis 4:8–12** Cain said to Abel his brother, "Let us go out to the field." And when they were in the field, Cain rose up against his brother Abel, and killed him. Then the Lord said to Cain, "Where is Abel your brother?" He said, "I do not know; am I my brother's keeper?" And the Lord said, "What have you done? The voice of your brother's blood is crying to me from the ground. And now you are cursed from the ground, which has opened its mouth to receive your brother's blood from your hand. When you till the ground, it shall no longer yield to you its strength; you shall be a fugitive and a wanderer on the earth."

2260 **Leviticus 17:14** "For the life of every creature is the blood of it; therefore I have said to the people of Israel, You shall not eat the blood of any creature, for the life of every creature is its blood; whoever eats it shall be cut off. . . ."

2262 (1) **Matthew 5:22–39** ". . . But I say to you that every one who is angry with his brother shall be liable to judgment; whoever insults his brother shall be liable to the council, and whoever says, 'You fool!' shall be liable to the hell of fire. So if you are offering your gift at the altar, and there remember that your brother has something against you, leave your gift there before the altar and go; first be reconciled to your brother, and then come and offer your gift. Make friends quickly with your accuser, while you are going with him to court, lest your accuser hand you over to the judge, and the judge to the guard, and you be put in prison; truly, I say to you, you will never get out till you have paid the last penny.

"You have heard that it was said, 'You shall not commit adultery.' But I say to you that every one who looks at a woman lustfully has already committed adultery with her in his heart. If your right eye causes you to sin, pluck it out and throw it away; it is better that you lose one of your members than that your whole body be thrown into hell. And if your right hand causes you to sin, cut it off and throw it away; it is better that you lose one of your members than that your whole body go into hell.

"It was also said, 'Whoever divorces his wife, let him give her a certificate of divorce.' But I say to you that every one who divorces his wife, except on the ground of unchastity, makes her an adulteress; and whoever marries a divorced woman commits adultery.

"Again you have heard that it was said to the men of old, 'You shall not swear falsely, but shall perform to the Lord what you have sworn.' But I say to you, Do not swear at all, either by heaven, for it is the throne of God, or by the earth, for it is his footstool, or by Jerusalem, for it is the city of the great King. And do not swear by your head, for you cannot make one hair white or black. Let what you say be simply 'Yes' or 'No'; anything more than this comes from evil.

"You have heard that it was said, 'An eye for an eye and a tooth for a tooth.' But I say to you, Do not resist one who is evil. But if any one strikes you on the right cheek, turn to him the other also. . . ."

2262 (2) **Matthew 5:44** But I say to you, Love your enemies and pray for those who persecute you. . . .

(3) **Matthew 26:52** Then Jesus said to him, "Put your sword back into its place; 2262
for all who take the sword will perish by the sword. . . ."

Luke 23:40–43 But the other rebuked him, saying, "Do you not fear God, since 2266
you are under the same sentence of condemnation? And we indeed justly; for we are receiving the due reward of our deeds; but this man has done nothing wrong." And he said, "Jesus, remember me when you come into your kingdom." And he said to him, "Truly, I say to you, today you will be with me in Paradise."

(1) **Genesis 4:10** And the Lord said, "What have you done? The voice of your 2268
brother's blood is crying to me from the ground. . . ."

(2) ***Gaudium et spes* 51, 3** God, the Lord of life, has entrusted to men the noble 2268
mission of safeguarding life, and men must carry it out in a manner worthy of themselves. Life must be protected with the utmost care from the moment of conception: abortion and infanticide are abominable crimes. Man's sexuality and the faculty of reproduction wondrously surpass the endowments of lower forms of life; therefore the acts proper to married life are to be ordered according to authentic human dignity and must be honored with the greatest reverence. When it is a question of harmonizing married love with the responsible transmission of life, it is not enough to take only the good intention and the evaluation of motives into account; the objective criteria must be used, criteria drawn from the nature of the human person and human action, criteria which respect the total meaning of mutual self-giving and human procreation in the context of true love; all this is possible only if the virtue of married chastity is seriously practiced. In questions of birth regulation the sons of the Church, faithful to these principles, are forbidden to use methods disapproved of by the teaching authority of the Church in its interpretation of the divine law.

Amos 8:4–10 2269

Hear this, you who trample upon the needy,
    and bring the poor of the land to an end,
saying, "When will the new moon be over,
    that we may sell grain?
And the sabbath,
    that we may offer wheat for sale,
that we may make the ephah small and the shekel great,
    and deal deceitfully with false balances,
that we may buy the poor for silver
    and the needy for a pair of sandals,
    and sell the refuse of the wheat?"

The Lord has sworn by the pride of Jacob:
    "Surely I will never forget any of their deeds.
Shall not the land tremble on this account,
    and every one mourn who dwells in it,
and all of it rise like the Nile,
    and be tossed about and sink again, like the Nile of Egypt?"

"And on that day," says the Lord God,
    "I will make the sun go down at noon,
    and darken the earth in broad daylight.
I will turn your feasts into mourning,
    and all your songs into lamentation;

I will bring sackcloth upon all loins,
and baldness on every head;
I will make it like the mourning for an only son,
and the end of it like a bitter day. . . ."

2270 (1) **Congregation for the Doctrine of the Faith, instruction *Donum vitae* 1, 1**

The human being must be respected — as a person — from the very first instant of his existence.

The implementation of procedures of artificial fertilization has made possible various interventions upon embryos and human fetuses. The aims pursued are of various kinds: diagnostic and therapeutic, scientific and commercial. From all of this, serious problems arise. Can one speak of a right to experimentation upon human embryos for the purpose of scientific research? What norms or laws should be worked out with regard to this matter? The response to these problems presupposes a detailed reflection on the nature and specific identity—the word "status" is used—of the human embryo itself.

At the Second Vatican Council, the Church for her part presented once again to modern man her constant and certain doctrine according to which: "Life once conceived, must be protected with the utmost care; abortion and infanticide are abominable crimes." More recently the *Charter of the Rights of the Family*, published by the Holy See, confirmed that "Human life must be absolutely respected and protected from the moment of conception."

This Congregation is aware of the current debates concerning the beginning of human life, concerning the individuality of the human being and concerning the identity of the human person. The Congregation recalls the teachings found in the Declaration on Procured Abortion: "From the time that the ovum is fertilized, a new life is begun which is neither that of the father nor of the mother: it is rather the life of a new human being with his own growth. It would never be made human if it were not human already. To this perpetual evidence . . . modern genetic science brings valuable confirmation. It has demonstrated that, from the first instant, the program is fixed as to what this living being will be: a man, this individual-man with his characteristic aspects already well determined. Right from fertilization is begun the adventure of human life, and each of its great capacities requires time . . . to find its place and to be in a position to act." This teaching remains valid and is further confirmed, if confirmation were needed, by recent findings of human biological science which recognize that in the zygote resulting from fertilization the biological identity of a new human individual is already constituted.

Certainly no experimental datum can be in itself sufficient to bring us to the recognition of a spiritual soul; nevertheless, the conclusions of science regarding the human embryo provide a valuable indication for discerning by the use of reason a personal presence at the moment of the first appearance of a human life: how could a human individual not be a human person? The Magisterium has not expressly committed itself to an affirmation of a philosophical nature, but it constantly reaffirms the moral condemnation of any kind of procured abortion. This teaching has not been changed and is unchangeable.

Thus the fruit of human generation, from the first moment of its existence, that is to say from the moment the zygote has formed, demands the unconditional respect that is morally due to the human being in his bodily and spiritual totality. The human being is to be respected and treated as a person from the moment of conception; and therefore from that same moment his rights as a person must be recognized, among which in the first place is the inviolable right of every innocent human being to life.

This doctrinal reminder provides the fundamental criterion for the solution of the various problems posed by the development of the biomedical sciences in this field:

since the embryo must be treated as a person, it must also be defended in its integrity, tended and cared for, to the extent possible, in the same way as any other human being as far as medical assistance is concerned.

(2) **Job 10:8–12** 2270

Thy hands fashioned and made me;
 and now thou dost turn about and destroy me.
Remember that thou hast made me of clay;
 and wilt thou turn me to dust again?
Didst thou not pour me out like milk
 and curdle me like cheese?
Thou didst clothe me with skin and flesh,
 and knit me together with bones and sinews.
Thou has granted me life and steadfast love;
 and thy care has preserved my spirit.

(3) **Psalm 22:10–11** 2270

Upon thee was I cast from my birth,
 and since my mother bore me thou hast been my God.
Be not far from me,
 for trouble is near
 and there is none to help.

(1) **Barnabas, *Epistula* 19, 5** Never be in two minds as to whether something is 2271
or is not to be. Never make free with the Name of the Lord. Never do away with an unborn child, or destroy it after its birth. Do not withhold your hand from your son or your daughter, but bring them up in the fear of God from their childhood.

(2) ***Ad Diognetum* 5:1, 4–6** The difference between Christians and the rest of 2271
mankind is not a matter of nationality, or language, or customs. . . . Nevertheless, the organization of their community does exhibit some features that are remarkable, and even surprising. For instance, though they are residents at home in their own countries, their behavior there is more like that of transients; they take their full part as citizens, but they also submit to anything and everything as if they were aliens. For them, any foreign country is a motherland, and any motherland is a foreign country. Like other men, they marry and beget children, though they do not expose their infants.

(3) **Tertullian, *Apologeticus* 9** To refute these points at greater length, I will point 2271
out that you yourselves commit these very crimes—sometimes openly, sometimes secretly—and that, perhaps, is the reason why you have believed them also of us. In Africa, babies used to be sacrificed publicly to Saturn even down to the proconsulate of Tiberius. He impaled the priests themselves on the very trees overshadowing their temple. The crosses were votive offerings to expiate their crimes. As witness of this there is the army of my own country, which performed this task for this very proconsul. Even now this holy crime is continued in secret. Christians are not alone in despising you; no crime is wiped out forever, or else some god is changing his ways. Since Saturn did not spare his own sons, surely he did not insist on sparing the children of others, who, for example, were offered to him by their very own parents. They gladly complied and they fondled their babies so that they would not be crying when they were sacrificed. Yet there is considerable difference between murder and parricide!

Among the Gauls, an older person was sacrificed to Mercury. I leave to their theaters the stories of the Taurians. Look at conditions in that city of the pious race of Aeneas, a city renowned for its religious worship! There is a certain Jupiter whom they bathe in human blood during the games held in his honor. 'But it is the blood of a beast-fighter,' you say. That, I suppose, is something of less value than the blood of a man! Or is it not worse because it is the blood of a bad man? At any rate, it is blood shed in murder. Oh, what a Christian Jupiter! He is his father's only son as far as cruelty goes!

But, with regard to infanticide, since it makes no difference whether it is committed for a religious purpose or according to one's own choosing—although there is a difference between murder and parricide—I will turn to the people. How many, do you suppose, of those here present who stand panting for the blood of Christians—how many, even, of you magistrates who are so righteous and so rigorous against us—want me to touch their consciences for putting their own offspring to death? If there is some distinction in kind between one act of murder and another, it is certainly more cruel to kill by drowning or by exposure to cold, hunger, and the dogs; for an older person would prefer to die by the sword. But, with us, murder is forbidden once for all. We are not permitted to destroy even the fetus in the womb, as long as blood is still being drawn to form a human being. To prevent the birth of a child is a quicker way to murder. It makes no difference whether one destroys a soul already born or interferes with its coming to birth. It is a human being and one who is to be a man, for the whole fruit is already present in the seed.

As for bloody food and such tragic dishes, read—I think it is related by Herodotus, but I am not sure—how, among some tribes, blood was taken from the arms and tasted by both parties in forming a treaty. Something was tasted, too, under Catiline. And they say that it was a custom among certain tribes of Scythians for every deceased member to be eaten by his relatives. But I am going too far afield. Today, right here among you, to mark the devotees of Bellona, a thigh is slashed, the blood is taken in the hand and given them for their benefit. Again, consider those who with greedy thirst, at a show in the arena, take the fresh blood of wicked criminals as it runs down from their throats and carry it off to heal their epilepsy. What about them? And what about those who make a meal on the flesh of wild beasts taken from the arena, who prefer the meat of boar or stag? That boar has licked the blood off him whom he has spattered with blood in the struggle. The stag has rolled in the blood of a gladiator. The very bellies of the bears, still stuffed with undigested human flesh, are the object of their search. Thence does man belch forth flesh that was nourished with human flesh. You who eat these animals, how far removed are you from the banquets of the Christians?

And do those who lust after human flesh, with a beastly passion, commit less grievous crimes because they devour something that is living? Are they less polluted with human blood and less dedicated to lewdness because they lap up that which is to turn into blood? No, they, of course, do not feast on babies, but rather on adults. Let your unnatural ways blush before the Christians. We do not even have the blood of animals at our meals, for these consist of ordinary food. This is why we refrain from eating the meat of any animals which have been strangled or that die of themselves, lest we be in any way contaminated with blood, even if it is hidden in the flesh.

At the trials of Christians you offer them sausages filled with blood. You are convinced, of course, that the very thing with which you try to make them deviate from the right way is unlawful for them. How is it that, when you are confident that they will shudder at the blood of an animal, you believe they will pant eagerly after human blood? Is it, perchance, that *you* have found the latter more to your taste? Human blood, then, and nothing else is certainly the very thing that ought to be employed as the touchstone of Christians, like fire or the incense box. Then they would be proved Christians by their appetite for human blood, just as they are at present by their refusal to offer sacrifice. On the other hand, they would have to be declared non-Christians if they did not taste it, just as if they had offered sacrifice. And, of course, you would have no shortage of human blood provided at the examination and condemnation of prisoners.

Another point—Who are more expert at practicing incest than those whom Jupiter himself has instructed? Ctesias relates that the Persians have intercourse with their own mothers. The Macedonians, too, were suspected of it because, the first time they attended the tragedy of *Oedipus*, they mocked the grief of the incestuous son, saying: 'He lay with his mother!' Well, now! Consider how great chance there is for incestuous unions occasioned by mistaken identity. The promiscuousness of your wanton living affords the opportunity. In the first place, you expose your children to be taken up by some passerby out of the pity of a stranger's heart; or you release them from your authority to be adopted by better parents. Sooner or later, the memory of the alienated family necessarily fades away. As soon as a mistake has occurred, the transmission of the incest goes on, the stock spreading together with its crime. Finally, then, wherever you are, at home, abroad, across the sea, your lust travels as your companion, and its outbursts everywhere—or even some slight indulgence—can easily beget children for you any place at all, though you may not know it. The result is that a brood thus scattered through illicit human intercourse may fall in with its own kindred and in blind ignorance fail to recognize it as begotten of incestuous blood.

As for us, an ever-watchful and steadfast chastity shields us from such an occurrence and, in so far as we refrain from adultery and every excess after marriage, we are safe, too, from the danger of incest. Some are even more secure, since they ward off the entire violence of this error by virginal continence, and as old men are still [as pure as] boys.

If you would realize that these sins exist among yourselves, then you would perceive clearly that they do not exist among Christians. The same eyes would tell you the facts in both cases. But, a two-fold blindness easily imposes itself, so that those who do not see what does exist seem to see what does not. I will point out that this is true in everything. Now I will speak of the more manifest crimes.

CIC Canons 1323–24 2272

Can. 1323—The following are not subject to penalties when they have violated a law or precept:

1° a person who has not yet completed the sixteenth year of age;

2° a person who without any fault was unaware of violating a law or precept; however, inadvertence and error are equivalent to ignorance;

3° a person who acted out of physical force or in virtue of a mere accident which could neither be foreseen nor prevented when foreseen;

4° a person who acted out of grave fear, even if only relatively grave, or out of necessity or out of serious inconvenience unless the act is intrinsically evil or verges on harm to souls;

5° a person who for the sake of legitimate self-defense or defense of another acted against an unjust aggressor with due moderation;

6° a person who lacked the use of reason with due regard for the prescriptions of cann. 1324, §1, n. 2 and 1325;

7° a person who without any fault felt that the circumstances in nn. 4 or 5 were verified.

Can. 1324—§1. One who violates a law or precept is not exempt from a penalty but the penalty set by law or precept must be tempered or a penance substituted in its place if the offense was committed:

1° by a person with only the imperfect use of reason;

2° by a person who lacked the use of reason due to drunkenness or another similar mental disturbance which was culpable;

3° in the serious heat of passion which did not precede and impede all deliberation of mind and consent of will as long as the passion itself had not been voluntarily stirred up or fostered;

4° by a minor who has completed the age of sixteen years;

5° by a person who was forced through grave fear, even if only relatively grave, or through necessity or serious inconvenience, if the offense was intrinsically evil or verged on harm to souls;

6° by a person who for the sake of legitimate self-defense or defense of another acted against an unjust aggressor but without due moderation;

7° against one gravely and unjustly provoking it;

8° by one who erroneously yet culpably thought one of the circumstances in can. 1323, nn. 4 and 5 was verified;

9° by one who without any fault was unaware that a penalty was attached to the law or precept;

10° by one who acted without full imputability provided there was grave imputability.

§2. A judge can act in the same manner if any other circumstance exists which would lessen the seriousness of the offense.

§3. An accused is not bound by an automatic penalty (*latae sententiae*) in the presence of any of the circumstances enumerated in §1.

2275 ***Donum vitae* 1, 3** The Church's Magisterium does not intervene on the basis of a particular competence in the area of the experimental sciences; but having taken account of the data of research and technology, it intends to put forward, by virtue of its evangelical mission and apostolic duty, the moral teaching corresponding to the dignity of the person and to his or her integral vocation. It intends to do so by expounding the criteria or moral judgment as regards the applications of scientific research and technology, especially in relation to human life and its beginnings. These criteria are the respect, defense and promotion of man, his "primary and fundamental right" to life, his dignity as a person who is endowed with a spiritual soul and with moral responsibility and who is called to beatific communion with God.

2285 (1) **1 Corinthians 8:10–13** For if any one sees you, a man of knowledge, at table in an idol's temple, might he not be encouraged, if his conscience is weak, to eat food offered to idols? And so by your knowledge this weak man is destroyed, the brother for whom Christ died. Thus, sinning against your brethren and wounding their conscience when it is weak, you sin against Christ. Therefore, if food is a cause of my brother's falling, I will never eat meat, lest I cause my brother to fall.

2285 (2) **Matthew 7:15** "Beware of false prophets, who come to you in sheep's clothing but inwardly are ravenous wolves. . . ."

2286 (1) **Ephesians 6:4** Fathers, do not provoke your children to anger, but bring them up in the discipline and instruction of the Lord.

(2) **Colossians 3:21** Fathers, do not provoke your children, lest they become discouraged. 2286

Pius XI, encyclical *Casti connubii* (1930): DS 3722 Finally, that pernicious practice should be condemned which is closely related to the natural right of man to enter into matrimony, and also in a real way pertains to the good of the offspring. For there are those who, overly solicitous about the ends of eugenics, not only give certain salutary counsels for more certainly procuring the health and vigor of the future offspring—which certainly is not contrary to right reason—but also place eugenics before every other end of a higher order; and by public authority wish to prohibit from marriage all those from whom, according to the norms and conjectures of their science, they think that a defective and corrupt offspring will be generated because of hereditary transmission, even if these same persons are naturally fitted for entering upon matrimony. Why, they even wish such persons even against their will to be deprived by law of that natural faculty through the operation of physicians; and this they propose not as a severe penalty for a crime committed, to be sought by public authority, nor to ward off future crimes of the guilty, but, contrary to every right and claim, by arrogating this power to the civil magistrates, which they never had and can never have legitimately. 2297

Whoever so act completely forget that the family is more sacred than the state, and that men are generated primarily not for earth and for time, but for heaven and eternity. And, surely, it is not right that men, in other respects capable of matrimony, who according to conjecture, though every care and diligence be applied, will generate only defective offspring, be for this reason burdened with a serious sin if they contract marriage, although sometimes they ought to be dissuaded from matrimony.

Tobit 1:16–18 In the days of Shalmaneser I performed many acts of charity to my brethren. I would give my bread to the hungry and my clothing to the naked; and if I saw any one of my people dead and thrown out behind the wall of Nineveh, I would bury him. And if Sennacherib the king put to death any who came fleeing from Judea, I buried them secretly. For in his anger he put many to death. When the bodies were sought by the king, they were not found. 2300

CIC Canon 1176, §3 The Church earnestly recommends that the pious custom of burying the bodies of the dead be observed; it does not, however, forbid cremation unless it has been chosen for reasons which are contrary to Christian teaching. 2301

(1) **Isaiah 32:17** 2304

And the effect of righteousness will be peace,
and the result of righteousness, quietness and trust for ever.

(2) ***Gaudium et spes* 78, 1–2** Peace is more than the absence of war: it cannot be reduced to the maintenance of a balance of power between opposing forces nor does it arise out of despotic dominion, but it is appropriately called "the effect of righteousness" (Is. 32:17). It is the fruit of that right ordering of things with which the divine founder has invested human society and which must be actualized by man thirsting after an ever more perfect reign of justice. But while the common good of mankind ultimately derives from the eternal law, it depends in the concrete upon circumstances which change as time goes on; consequently, peace will never be achieved once and for all, but must be built up continually. Since, moreover, human nature is weak and wounded by sin, the achievement of peace requires a constant effort to control the passions and unceasing vigilance by lawful authority. 2304

But this is not enough. Peace cannot be obtained on earth unless the welfare of man is safeguarded and people freely and trustingly share with one another the riches of their minds and their talents. A firm determination to respect the dignity of other men and other peoples along with the deliberate practice of fraternal love are absolutely necessary for the achievement of peace. Accordingly, peace is also the fruit of love, for love goes beyond what justice can ensure.

2305 **Colossians 1:20–22** . . . and through him to reconcile to himself all things, whether on earth or in heaven, making peace by the blood of his cross.

And you, who once were estranged and hostile in mind, doing evil deeds, he has now reconciled in his body of flesh by his death, in order to present you holy and blameless and irreproachable before him. . . .

2306 ***Gaudium et spes* 78, 3** Peace on earth, which flows from love of one's neighbor, symbolizes and derives from the peace of Christ who proceeds from God the Father. Christ, the Word made flesh, the prince of peace, reconciled all men to God by the cross, and, restoring the unity of all in one people and one body, he abolished hatred in his own flesh, having been lifted up through his resurrection he poured forth the Spirit of love into the hearts of men. Therefore, all Christians are earnestly to speak the truth in love (cf. Eph. 4:15) and join with all peace-loving men in pleading for peace and trying to bring it about. In the same spirit we cannot but express our admiration for all who forgo the use of violence to vindicate their rights and resort to those other means of defense which are available to weaker parties, provided it can be done without harm to the rights and duties of others and of the community.

2307 ***Gaudium et spes* 81, 3** Therefore, we declare once again: the arms race is one of the greatest curses on the human race and the harm it inflicts on the poor is more than can be endured. And there is every reason to fear that if it continues it will bring forth those lethal disasters which are already in preparation. Warned by the possibility of the catastrophes that man has created, let us profit by the respite we now enjoy, thanks to the divine favor, to take stock of our responsibilities and find ways of resolving controversies in a manner worthy of human beings. Providence urgently demands of us that we free ourselves from the age-old slavery of war. If we refuse to make this effort, there is no knowing where we will be led on the fatal path we have taken.

2310 ***Gaudium et spes* 79, 5** All those who enter the military service in loyalty to their country should look upon themselves as the custodians of the security and freedom of their fellow-countrymen; and when they carry out their duty properly, they are contributing to the maintenance of peace.

2311 ***Gaudium et spes* 79, 3** On the question of warfare, there are various international conventions, signed by many countries, aimed at rendering military action and its consequences less inhuman; they deal with the treatment of wounded and interned prisoners of war and with various kindred questions. These agreements must be honored; indeed public authorities and specialists in these matters must do all in their power to improve these conventions and thus bring about a better and more effective curbing of the savagery of war. Moreover, it seems just that laws should make humane provision for the case of conscientious objectors who refuse to carry arms, provided they accept some other form of community service.

Paul VI, *Populorum progressio* 53 Besides, who does not see that such a fund would make it easier to take measures to prevent certain wasteful expenditures, the result of fear or pride? When so many people are hungry, when so many families suffer from destitution, when so many remain steeped in ignorance, when so many schools, hospitals and homes worthy of the name remain to be built, all public or private squandering of wealth, all expenditure prompted by motives of national or personal ostentation, every exhausting armaments race, becomes an intolerable public scandal. We are conscious of our duty to denounce it. Would that those in authority listened to our words before it is too late! 2315

Isaiah 2:4 2317

He shall judge between the nations,
and shall decide for many peoples;
and they shall beat their swords into plowshares,
and their spears into pruning hooks;
nation shall not lift up sword against nation,
neither shall they learn war any more.

***Gaudium et spes* 49, 2** Married love is uniquely expressed and perfected by the exercise of the acts proper to marriage. Hence the acts in marriage by which the intimate and chaste union of the spouses takes place are noble and honorable; the truly human performance of these acts fosters the self-giving they signify and enriches the spouses in joy and gratitude. Endorsed by mutual fidelity and, above all, consecrated by Christ's sacrament, this love abides faithfully in mind and body in prosperity and adversity and hence excludes both adultery and divorce. The unity of marriage, distinctly recognized by our Lord, is made clear in the equal personal dignity which must be accorded to man and wife in mutual and unreserved affection. Outstanding courage is required for the constant fulfilment of the duties of this Christian calling: spouses, therefore, will need grace for leading a holy life: they will eagerly practice a love that is firm, generous, and prompt to sacrifice and will ask for it in their prayers. 2334

(1) **Genesis 4:1–2** Now Adam knew Eve his wife, and she conceived and bore Cain, saying, "I have gotten a man with the help of the Lord." And again, she bore his brother Abel. Now Abel was a keeper of sheep, and Cain a tiller of the ground. 2335

(2) **Genesis 4:25–26** And Adam knew his wife again, and she bore a son and called his name Seth, for she said, "God has appointed for me another child instead of Abel, for Cain slew him." To Seth also a son was born, and he called his name Enosh. At that time men began to call upon the name of the Lord. 2335

(3) **Genesis 5:1** This is the book of the generations of Adam. When God created man, he made him in the likeness of God. 2335

Matthew 19:6 ". . . So they are no longer two but one flesh. What therefore God has joined together, let not man put asunder." 2336

Matthew 5:37 ". . . Let what you say be simply 'Yes' or 'No'; anything more than this comes from evil. . . ." 2338

Sirach 1:22 2339

Unrighteous anger cannot be justified,
for a man's anger tips the scale to his ruin.

2342 **Titus 2:1–6** But as for you, teach what befits sound doctrine. Bid the older men be temperate, serious, sensible, sound in faith, in love, and in steadfastness. Bid the older women likewise to be reverent in behavior, not to be slanderers or slaves to drink; they are to teach what is good, and so train the young women to love their husbands and children, to be sensible, chaste, domestic, kind, and submissive to their husbands, that the word of God may not be discredited. Likewise urge the younger men to control themselves.

2345 (1) **Galatians 5:22** But the fruit of the Spirit is love, joy, peace, patience, kindness, goodness, faithfulness. . . .

2345 (2) **1 John 3:3** And every one who thus hopes in him purifies himself as he is pure.

2347 **John 15:15** No longer do I call you servants, for the servant does not know what his master is doing; but I have called you friends, for all that I have heard from my Father I have made known to you.

2355 **1 Corinthians 6:15–20** Do you not know that your bodies are members of Christ? Shall I therefore take the members of Christ and make them members of a prostitute? Never! Do you not know that he who joins himself to a prostitute becomes one body with her? For, as it is written, "The two shall become one flesh." But he who is united to the Lord becomes one spirit with him. Shun immorality. Every other sin which a man commits is outside the body; but the immoral man sins against his own body. Do you not know that your body is a temple of the Holy Spirit within you, which you have from God? You are not your own; you were bought with a price. So glorify God in your body.

2357 (1) **Genesis 19:1–29** The two angels came to Sodom in the evening; and Lot was sitting in the gate of Sodom. When Lot saw them, he rose to meet them, and bowed himself with his face to the earth, and said, "My lords, turn aside, I pray you, to your servant's house and spend the night, and wash your feet; then you may rise up early and go on your way." They said, "No; we will spend the night in the street." But he urged them strongly; so they turned aside to him and entered his house; and he made them a feast, and baked unleavened bread, and they ate. But before they lay down, the men of the city, the men of Sodom, both young and old, all the people to the last man, surrounded the house; and they called to Lot, "Where are the men who came to you tonight? Bring them out to us, that we may know them." Lot went out of the door to the men, shut the door after him, and said, "I beg you, my brothers, do not act so wickedly. Behold, I have two daughters who have not known man; let me bring them out to you, and do to them as you please; only do nothing to these men, for they have come under the shelter of my roof." But they said, "Stand back!" And they said, "This fellow came to sojourn, and he would play the judge! Now we will deal worse with you than with them." Then they pressed hard against the man Lot, and drew near to break the door. But the men put forth their hands and brought Lot into the house to them, and shut the door. And they struck with the blindness the men who were at the door of the house, both small and great, so that they wearied themselves groping for the door.

Then the men said to Lot, "Have you any one else here? Sons-in-law, sons, daughters, or any one you have in the city, bring them out of the place; for we are about to destroy this place, because the outcry against its people has become great before the Lord, and the Lord has sent us to destroy it." So Lot went out and said to his sons-in-law, who were to marry his daughters, "Up, get out of this place; for the Lord is about to destroy the city." But he seemed to his sons-in-law to be jesting.

When morning dawned, the angels urged Lot, saying, "Arise, take your wife and your two daughters who are here, lest you be consumed in the punishment of the city." But he lingered; so the men seized him and his wife and his two daughters by the hand, the Lord being merciful to him, and they brought him forth and set him outside the city. And when they had brought them forth, they said, "Flee for your life; do not look back or stop anywhere in the valley; flee to the hills, lest you be consumed." And Lot said to them, "Oh, no, my lords; behold, your servant has found favor in your sight, and you have shown me great kindness in saving my life; but I cannot flee to the hills, lest the disaster overtake me, and I die. Behold, yonder city is near enough to flee to, and it is a little one. Let me escape there—is it not a little one?—and my life will be saved!" He said to him, "Behold, I grant you this favor also, that I will not overthrow the city of which you have spoken. Make haste, escape there; for I can do nothing till you arrive there." Therefore the name of the city was called Zoar. The sun had risen on the earth when Lot came to Zoar.

Then the Lord rained on Sodom and Gomorrah brimstone and fire from the Lord out of heaven; and he overthrew those cities, and all the valley, and all the inhabitants of the cities, and what grew on the ground. But Lot's wife behind him looked back, and she became a pillar of salt. And Abraham went early in the morning to the place where he had stood before the Lord; and he looked down toward Sodom and Gomorrah and toward all the land of the valley, and beheld, and lo, the smoke of the land went up like the smoke of a furnace.

So it was that, when God destroyed the cities of the valley, God remembered Abraham, and sent Lot out of the midst of the overthrow, when he overthrew the cities in which Lot dwelt.

(2) **Romans 1:24–27** Therefore God gave them up in the lusts of their hearts 2357
to impurity, to the dishonoring of their bodies among themselves, because they exchanged the truth about God for a lie and worshiped and served the creature rather than the Creator, who is blessed for ever! Amen.

For this reason God gave them up to dishonorable passions. Their women exchanged natural relations for unnatural, and the men likewise gave up natural relations with women and were consumed with passion for one another, men committing shameless acts with men and receiving in their own persons the due penalty for their error.

(3) **1 Corinthians 6:10** . . . nor thieves, nor the greedy, nor drunkards, nor revilers, 2357
nor robbers will inherit the kingdom of God.

(4) **1 Timothy 1:10** . . . immoral persons, sodomites, kidnapers, liars, perjurers, 2357
and whatever else is contrary to sound doctrine. . . .

(1) **CIC Canon 1056** The essential properties of marriage are unity and indissolu- 2364
bility, which in Christian marriage obtain a special firmness in virtue of the sacrament.

(2) **Matthew 19:1–12** Now when Jesus had finished these sayings, he went away 2364
from Galilee and entered the region of Judea beyond Jordan; and large crowds followed him, and he healed them there.

And Pharisees came up to him and tested him by asking, "Is it lawful to divorce one's wife for any cause?" He answered, "Have you not read that he who made them from the beginning made them male and female, and said, 'For this reason a man shall leave his father and mother and be joined to his wife, and the two shall become one flesh'? So they are no longer two but one flesh. What therefore God has joined together, let not man put asunder." They said to him, "Why then did Moses command one to give a certificate of divorce, and to put her away?" He said to them, "For your hardness of heart Moses allowed you to divorce your wives, but from the beginning it was not so. And I say to you: whoever divorces his wife, except for unchastity, and marries another, commits adultery."

The disciples said to him, "If such is the case of a man with his wife, it is not expedient to marry." But he said to them, "Not all men can receive this saying, but only those to whom it is given. For there are eunuchs who have been so from birth, and there are eunuchs who have been made eunuchs by men, and there are eunuchs who have made themselves eunuchs for the sake of the kingdom of heaven. He who is able to receive this, let him receive it."

2364 (3) **1 Corinthians 7:10–11** To the married I give charge, not I but the Lord, that the wife should not separate from her husband (but if she does, let her remain single or else be reconciled to her husband)—and that the husband should not divorce his wife.

2366 **Pius XI, encyclical *Casti connubii***

To the Venerable Brethren, Patriarchs, Primates, Archbishops, Bishops and other Local Ordinaries enjoying Peace and Communion with the Apostolic See.

Venerable Brethren and Beloved Children, Health and Apostolic Benediction.

How great is the dignity of chaste wedlock, Venerable Brethren, may be judged best from this that Christ Our Lord, Son of the Eternal Father, having assumed the nature of fallen man, not only, with His loving desire of compassing the redemption of our race, ordained it in an especial manner as the principle and foundation of domestic society and therefore of all human intercourse, but also raised it to the rank of a truly and great sacrament of the New Law, restored it to the original purity of its divine institution, and accordingly entrusted all its discipline and care to His spouse the Church.

In order, however, that amongst men of every nation and every age the desired fruits may be obtained from this renewal of matrimony, it is necessary, first of all, that men's minds be illuminated with the true doctrine of Christ regarding it; and secondly, that Christian spouses, the weakness of their wills strengthened by the internal grace of God, shape all their ways of thinking and of acting in conformity with that pure law of Christ so as to obtain true peace and happiness for themselves and for their families.

Yet not only do We, looking with paternal eye on the universal world from this Apostolic See as from a watch-tower, but you, also, Venerable Brethren, see, and seeing deeply grieve with Us that a great number of men, forgetful of that divine work of redemption, either entirely ignore or shamelessly deny the great sanctity of Christian wedlock, or relying on the false principles of a new and utterly perverse morality, too often trample it under foot. And since these most pernicious errors and depraved morals have begun to spread even amongst the faithful and are gradually gaining ground, in Our office as Christ's Vicar upon earth and Supreme Shepherd and Teacher We consider it Our duty to raise Our voice to keep the flock committed to Our care from poisoned pastures and, as far as in Us lies, to preserve it from harm.

We have decided therefore to speak to you, Venerable Brethren, and through you to the whole Church of Christ and indeed to the whole human race, on the nature and dignity of Christian marriage, on the advantages and benefits which accrue from it to the family and to human society itself, on the errors contrary to this most important point of the Gospel teaching, on the vices opposed to conjugal union, and lastly on the principal remedies to be applied. In so doing We follow the footsteps of Our predecessor, Leo XIII, of happy memory, whose Encyclical *Arcanum*, published fifty years ago, We hereby confirm and make Our own, and while We wish to expound more fully certain points called for by the circumstances of our times, nevertheless We declare that, far from being obsolete, it retains its full force at the present day.

And to begin with that same Encyclical, which is wholly concerned in vindicating the divine institution of matrimony, its sacramental dignity, and its perpetual stability, let it be repeated as an immutable and inviolable fundamental doctrine that matrimony was not instituted or restored by man but by God; not by man were the laws made to strengthen and confirm and elevate it but by God, the Author of nature, and by Christ Our Lord by Whom nature was redeemed, and hence these laws cannot be subject to any human decrees or to any contrary pact even of the spouses themselves. This is the doctrine of Holy Scripture; this is the constant tradition of the Universal Church; this the solemn definition of the sacred Council of Trent, which declares and establishes from the words of Holy Writ itself that God is the Author of the perpetual stability of the marriage bond, its unity and its firmness.

Yet although matrimony is of its very nature of divine institution, the human will, too, enters into it and performs a most noble part. For each individual marriage, inasmuch as it is a conjugal union of a particular man and woman, arises only from the free consent of each of the spouses; and this free act of the will, by which each party hands over and accepts those rights proper to the state of marriage, is so necessary to constitute true marriage that it cannot be supplied by any human power. This freedom, however, regards only the question whether the contracting parties really wish to enter upon matrimony or to marry this particular person; but the nature of matrimony is entirely independent of the free will of man, so that if one has once contracted matrimony he is thereby subject to its divinely made laws and its essential properties. For the Angelic Doctor, writing on conjugal honor and on the offspring which is the fruit of marriage, says: "These things are so contained in matrimony by the marriage pact itself that, if anything to the contrary were expressed in the consent which makes the marriage, it would not be a true marriage."

By matrimony, therefore, the souls of the contracting parties are joined and knit together more directly and more intimately than are their bodies, and that not by any passing affection of sense of spirit, but by a deliberate and firm act of the will; and from this union of souls by God's decree, a sacred and inviolable bond arises. Hence the nature of this contract, which is proper and peculiar to it alone, makes it entirely different both from the union of animals entered into by the blind instinct of nature alone in which neither reason nor free will plays a part, and also from the haphazard unions of men, which are far removed from all true and honorable unions of will and enjoy none of the rights of family life.

From this it is clear that legitimately constituted authority has the right and therefore the duty to restrict, to prevent, and to punish those base unions which are opposed to reason and to nature; but since it is a matter which flows from human nature itself, no less certain is the teaching of Our predecessor, Leo XIII of happy memory: "In choosing a state of life there is no doubt but that it is in the power and discretion of each one to prefer one or the other: either to embrace the counsel of virginity given by Jesus Christ, or to bind himself in the bonds of matrimony. To take away from man the natural and primeval right of marriage, to circumscribe in any way the principal ends of marriage laid down in the beginning by God Himself in the words 'Increase and multiply,' is beyond the power of any human law."

Therefore the sacred partnership of true marriage is constituted both by the will of God and the will of man. From God comes the very institution of marriage, the ends for which it was instituted, the laws that govern it, the blessings that flow from it; while man, through generous surrender of his own person made to another for the whole span of life, becomes, with the help and cooperation of God, the author of each particular marriage, with the duties and blessings annexed thereto from divine institution.

I

Now when We come to explain, Venerable Brethren, what are the blessings that God has attached to true matrimony, and how great they are, there occur to Us the words of that illustrious Doctor of the Church whom We commemorated recently in Our Encyclical *Ad salutem* on the occasion of the fifteenth centenary of his death: "These," says St. Augustine, "are all the blessings of matrimony on account of which matrimony itself is a blessing; offspring, conjugal faith and the sacrament." And how under these three heads is contained a splendid summary of the whole doctrine of Christian marriage, the holy Doctor himself expressly declares when he said: "By conjugal faith it is provided that there should be no carnal intercourse outside the marriage bond with another man or woman; with regard to offspring, that children should be begotten of love, tenderly cared for and educated in a religious atmosphere; finally, in its sacramental aspect that the marriage bond should not be broken and that a husband or wife, if separated, should not be joined to another even for the sake of offspring. This we regard as the law of marriage by which the fruitfulness of nature is adorned and the evil of incontinence is restrained."

Thus amongst the blessings of marriage, the child holds the first place. And indeed the Creator of the human race Himself, Who in His goodness wishes to use men as His helpers in the propagation of life, taught this when, instituting marriage in Paradise, He said to our first parents, and through them to all future spouses: "Increase and multiply, and fill the earth." As St. Augustine admirably deduces from the words of the holy Apostle Saint Paul to Timothy when he says: "The Apostle himself is therefore a witness that marriage is for the sake of generation: 'I wish,' he says, 'young girls to marry.' And, as if someone said to him, 'Why?,' he immediately adds: 'To bear children, to be mothers of families.'"

How great a boon of God this is, and how great a blessing of matrimony is clear from a consideration of man's dignity and of his sublime end. For man surpasses all other visible creatures by the superiority of his rational nature alone. Besides, God wishes men to be born not only that they should live and fill the earth, but much more that they may be worshippers of God, that they may know Him and love Him and finally enjoy Him for ever in heaven; and this end, since man is raised by God in a marvellous way to the supernatural order, surpasses all that eye hath seen, and ear heard, and all that hath entered into the heart of man. From which it is easily seen how great a gift of divine goodness and how remarkable a fruit of marriage are children born by the omnipotent power of God through the cooperation of those bound in wedlock.

But Christian parents must also understand that they are destined not only to propagate and preserve the human race on earth, indeed not only to educate any kind of worshippers of the true God, but children who are to become members of the Church of Christ, to raise up fellow-citizens of the Saints, and members of God's household, that the worshippers of God and Our Savior may daily increase.

For although Christian spouses even if sanctified themselves cannot transmit sanctification to their progeny, nay, although the very natural process of generating life has become the way of death by which original sin is passed on to posterity, nevertheless, they share to some extent in the blessings of that primeval marriage of Paradise, since it is theirs to offer their offspring to the Church in order that by this most fruitful Mother of the children of God they may be regenerated through the laver of Baptism unto supernatural justice and finally be made living members of Christ, partakers of immortal life, and heirs of that eternal glory to which we all aspire from our inmost heart.

If a true Christian mother weigh well these things, she will indeed understand with a sense of deep consolation that of her the words of Our Savior were spoken: "A woman . . . when she hath brought forth the child remembereth no more the anguish, for joy that a man is born into the world"; and proving herself superior to all the pains and cares and solicitudes of her maternal office with a more just and holy joy than that of the Roman matron, the mother of the Gracchi, she will rejoice in the Lord crowned as it were with the glory of her offspring. Both husband and wife, however, receiving these children with joy and gratitude from the hand of God, will regard them as a talent committed to their charge by God, not only to be employed for their own advantage or for that of an earthly commonwealth, but to be restored to God with interest on the day of reckoning.

The blessing of offspring, however, is not completed by the mere begetting of them, but something else must be added, namely the proper education of the offspring. For the most wise God would have failed to make sufficient provision for children that had been born, and so for the whole human race, if He had not given to those to whom He had entrusted the power and right to beget them, the power also and the right to educate them. For no one can fail to see that children are incapable of providing wholly for themselves, even in matters pertaining to their natural life, and much less in those pertaining to the supernatural, but require for many years to be helped, instructed, and educated by others. Now it is certain that both by the law of nature and of God this right and duty of educating their offspring belongs in the first place to those who began the work of nature by giving them birth, and they are indeed forbidden to leave unfinished this work and so expose it to certain ruin. But in matrimony provision has been made in the best possible way for this education of children that is so necessary, for, since the parents are bound together by an indissoluble bond, the care and mutual help of each is always at hand.

Since, however, We have spoken fully elsewhere on the Christian education of youth, let Us sum it all up by quoting once more the words of St. Augustine: "As regards the offspring it is provided that they should be begotten lovingly and educated religiously,"—and this is also expressed succinctly in the Code of Canon Law—"The primary end of marriage is the procreation and the education of children."

Nor must We omit to remark, in fine, that since the duty entrusted to parents for the good of their children is of such high dignity and of such great importance, every use of the faculty given by God for the procreation of new life is the right and the privilege of the married state alone, by the law of God and of nature, and must be confined absolutely within the sacred limits of that state.

The second blessing of matrimony which We said was mentioned by St. Augustine, is the blessing of conjugal honor which consists in the mutual fidelity of the spouses in fulfilling the marriage contract, so that what belongs to one of the parties by reason of this contract sanctioned by divine law, may not be denied to him or permitted to any third person; nor may there be conceded to one of the parties anything which, being contrary to the rights and laws of God and entirely opposed to matrimonial faith, can never be conceded.

Wherefore, conjugal faith, or honor, demands in the first place the complete unity of matrimony which the Creator Himself laid down in the beginning when He wished it to be not otherwise than between one man and one woman. And although afterwards this primeval law was relaxed to some extent by God, the Supreme Legislator, there is no doubt that the law of the Gospel fully restored that original and perfect unity, and abrogated all dispensations as the words of Christ and the constant teaching and action of the Church show plainly. With reason, therefore, does the Sacred Council of Trent solemnly declare: "Christ Our Lord very clearly taught that in this bond two persons only are to be united and joined together when He said: 'Therefore they are no longer two, but one flesh.'"

Nor did Christ Our Lord wish only to condemn any form of polygamy or polyandry, as they are called, whether successive or simultaneous, and every other external dishonorable act, but, in order that the sacred bonds of marriage may be guarded absolutely inviolate, He forbade also even wilful thoughts and desires of such like things: "But I say to you, that whosoever shall look on a woman to lust after her hath already committed adultery with her in his heart." Which words of Christ Our Lord cannot be annulled even by the consent of one of the partners of marriage for they express a law of God and of nature which no will of man can break or bend.

Nay, that mutual familiar intercourse between the spouses themselves, if the blessing of conjugal faith is to shine with becoming splendor, must be distinguished by chastity so that husband and wife bear themselves in all things with the law of God and of nature, and endeavor always to follow the will of their most wise and holy Creator with the greatest reverence toward the work of God.

This conjugal faith, however, which is most aptly called by St. Augustine the "faith of chastity" blooms more freely, more beautifully and more nobly, when it is rooted in that more excellent soil, the love of husband and wife which pervades all the duties of married life and holds pride of place in Christian marriage. For matrimonial faith demands that husband and wife be joined in an especially holy and pure love, not as adulterers love each other, but as Christ loved the Church. This precept the Apostle laid down when he said: "Husbands, love your wives as Christ also loved the Church," that Church which of a truth He embraced with a boundless love not for the sake of His own advantage, but seeking only the good of His Spouse. The love, then, of which We are speaking is not that based on the passing lust of the moment nor does it consist in pleasing words only, but in the deep attachment of the heart which is expressed in action, since love is proved by deeds. This outward expression of love in the home demands not only mutual help but must go further; must have as its primary purpose that man and wife help each other day by day in forming and perfecting themselves in the interior life, so that through their partnership in life they may advance ever more and more in virtue, and above all that they may grow in true love toward God and their neighbor, on which indeed "dependeth the whole Law and the Prophets." For all men of every condition, in whatever honorable walk of life they may be, can and ought to imitate that most perfect example of holiness placed before man by God, namely Christ Our Lord, and by God's grace to arrive at the summit of perfection, as is proved by the example set us of many saints.

This mutual molding of husband and wife, this determined effort to perfect each other, can in a very real sense, as the Roman Catechism teaches, be said to be the chief reason and purpose of matrimony, provided matrimony be looked at not in the restricted sense as instituted for the proper conception and education of the child, but more widely as the blending of life as a whole and the mutual interchange and sharing thereof.

By this same love it is necessary that all the other rights and duties of the marriage state be regulated as the words of the Apostle: "Let the husband render the debt to the wife, and the wife also in like manner to the husband," express not only a law of justice but of charity.

Domestic society being confirmed, therefore, by this bond of love, there should flourish in it that "order of love," as St. Augustine calls it. This order includes both the primacy of the husband with regard to the wife and children, the ready subjection of the wife and her willing obedience, which the Apostle commends in these words:

"Let women be subject to their husbands as to the Lord, because the husband is the head of the wife, and Christ is the head of the Church."

This subjection, however, does not deny or take away the liberty which fully belongs to the woman both in view of her dignity as a human person, and in view of her most noble office as wife and mother and companion; nor does it bid her obey her husband's every request if not in harmony with right reason or with the dignity due to wife; nor, in fine, does it imply that the wife should be put on a level with those persons who in law are called minors, to whom it is customary [not] to allow free exercise of their rights on account of their lack of mature judgment, or of their ignorance of human affairs. But it forbids that exaggerated liberty which cares not for the good of the family; it forbids that in this body which is the family, the heart be separated from the head to the great detriment of the whole body and the proximate danger of ruin. For if the man is the head, the woman is the heart, and as he occupies the chief place in ruling, so she may and ought to claim for herself the chief place in love.

Again, this subjection of wife to husband in its degree and manner may vary according to the different conditions of persons, place and time. In fact, if the husband neglect his duty, it falls to the wife to take his place in directing the family. But the structure of the family and its fundamental law, established and confirmed by God, must always and everywhere be maintained intact.

With great wisdom Our predecessor Leo XIII, of happy memory, in the Encyclical on Christian marriage which We have already mentioned, speaking of this order to be maintained between man and wife, teaches: "The man is the ruler of the family, and the head of the woman; but because she is flesh of his flesh and bone of his bone, let her be subject and obedient to the man, not as a servant but as a companion, so that nothing be lacking of honor or of dignity in the obedience which she pays. Let divine charity be the constant guide of their mutual relations, both in him who rules and in her who obeys, since each bears the image, the one of Christ, the other of the Church."

These, then, are the elements which compose the blessing of conjugal faith: unity, chastity, charity, honorable noble obedience, which are at the same time an enumeration of the benefits which are bestowed on husband and wife in their married state, benefits by which the peace, the dignity and the happiness of matrimony are securely preserved and fostered. Wherefore it is not surprising that this conjugal faith has always been counted amongst the most priceless and special blessings of matrimony.

But this accumulation of benefits is completed and, as it were, crowned by that blessing of Christian marriage which in the words of St. Augustine we have called the sacrament, by which is denoted both the indissolubility of the bond and the raising and hallowing of the contract by Christ Himself, whereby He made it an efficacious sign of grace.

In the first place Christ Himself lays stress on the indissolubility and firmness of the marriage bond when He says: "What God hath joined together let no man put asunder," and: "Everyone that putteth away his wife and marrieth another committeth adultery, and he that marrieth her that is put away from her husband committeth adultery."

And St. Augustine clearly places what he calls the blessing of matrimony in this indissolubility when he says: "In the sacrament it is provided that the marriage bond should not be broken, and that a husband or wife, if separated, should not be joined to another even for the sake of offspring."

And this inviolable stability, although not in the same perfect measure in every case, belongs to every true marriage, for the word of the Lord: "What God hath joined together let no man put asunder," must of necessity include all true marriages without exception, since it was spoken of the marriage of our first parents, the prototype of every future marriage. Therefore although before Christ the sublimeness and the severity of the primeval law was so tempered that Moses permitted to the chosen people of God on account of the hardness of their hearts that a bill of divorce might be given in certain circumstances, nevertheless, Christ, by virtue of His supreme legislative power, recalled this concession of greater liberty and restored the primeval law in its integrity by those words which must never be forgotten, "What God hath joined together let no man put asunder." Wherefore, Our predecessor Pius VI of happy memory, writing to the Bishop of Agria, most wisely said: "Hence it is clear that marriage even in the state of nature, and certainly long before it was raised to the dignity of a sacrament, was divinely instituted in such a way that it should carry with it a perpetual and indissoluble bond which cannot therefore be dissolved by any civil law. Therefore although the sacramental element may be absent from a marriage as is the case among unbelievers, still in such a marriage, inasmuch as it is a true marriage there must remain and indeed there does remain that perpetual bond which by divine right is so bound up with matrimony from its first institution that it is not subject to any civil power. And so, whatever marriage is said to be contracted, either it is so contracted that it is really a true marriage, in which case it carries with it that enduring bond which by divine right is inherent in every true marriage; or it is thought to be contracted without that perpetual bond, and in that case there is no marriage, but an illicit union opposed of its very nature to the divine law, which therefore cannot be entered into or maintained."

And if this stability seems to be open to exception, however rare the exception may be, as in the case of certain natural marriages between unbelievers, or amongst Christians in the case of those marriages which though valid have not been consummated, that exception does not depend on the will of men nor on that of any merely human power, but on divine law, of which the only guardian and interpreter is the Church of Christ. However, not even this power can ever affect for any cause whatsoever a Christian marriage which is valid and has been consummated, for as it is plain that here the marriage contract has its full completion, so, by the will of God, there is also the greatest firmness and indissolubility which may not be destroyed by any human authority.

If we wish with all reverence to inquire into the intimate reason of this divine decree, Venerable Brethren, we shall easily see it in the mystical signification of Christian marriage which is fully and perfectly verified in consummated marriage between Christians. For, as the Apostle says in his Epistle to the Ephesians, the marriage of Christians recalls that most perfect union which exists between Christ and the Church: "Sacramentum hoc magnum est, ego autem dico, in Christo et in ecclesia;" which union, as long as Christ shall live and the Church through Him, can never be dissolved by any separation. And this St. Augustine clearly declares in these words: "This is safeguarded in Christ and the Church, which, living with Christ who lives for ever may never be divorced from Him. The observance of this sacrament is such in the City of God . . . that is, in the Church of Christ, that when for the sake of begetting children, women marry or are taken to wife, it is wrong to leave a wife that is sterile in order to take another by whom children may be had. Anyone doing this is guilty of adultery, just as if he married another, guilty not by the law of the day, according to which when one's partner is put away another may be taken, which the Lord allowed in the law of Moses because of the hardness of the hearts of the people of Israel; but by the law of the Gospel."

Indeed, how many and how important are the benefits which flow from the indissolubility of matrimony cannot escape anyone who gives even a brief consideration either to the good of the married parties and the offspring or to the welfare of human society. First of all, both husband and wife possess a positive guarantee of the endurance of this stability which that generous yielding of their persons and the intimate fellowship of their hearts by their nature strongly require, since true love never falls away. Besides, a strong bulwark is set up in defense of a loyal chastity against incitements to infidelity, should any be encountered either from within or from without; any anxious fear lest in adversity or old age the other spouse would prove unfaithful is precluded and in its place there reigns a calm sense of security. Moreover, the dignity of both man and wife is maintained and mutual aid is most satisfactorily assured, while through the indissoluble bond, always enduring, the spouses are warned continuously that not for the sake of perishable things nor that they may serve their passions, but that they may procure one for the other high and lasting good have they entered into the nuptial partnership, to be dissolved only by death. In the training and education of children, which must extend over a period of many years, it plays a great part, since the grave and long enduring burdens of this office are best borne by the united efforts of the parents. Nor do lesser benefits accrue to human society as a whole. For experience has taught that unassailable stability in matrimony is a fruitful source of virtuous life and of habits of integrity. Where this order of things obtains, the happiness and well being of the nation is safely guarded; what the families and individuals are, so also is the State, for a body is determined by its parts. Wherefore, both for the private good of husband, wife and children, as likewise for the public good of human society, they indeed deserve well who strenuously defend the inviolable stability of matrimony.

But considering the benefits of the Sacrament, besides the firmness and indissolubility, there are also much higher emoluments as the word "sacrament" itself very aptly indicates; for to Christians this is not a meaningless and empty name. Christ the Lord, the Institutor and "Perfecter" of the holy sacraments, by raising the matrimony of His faithful to the dignity of a true sacrament of the New Law, made it a sign and source of that peculiar internal grace by which "it perfects natural love, it confirms an indissoluble union, and sanctifies both man and wife."

And since the valid matrimonial consent among the faithful was constituted by Christ as a sign of grace, the sacramental nature is so intimately bound up with Christian wedlock that there can be no true marriage between baptized persons "without it being by that very fact a sacrament."

By the very fact, therefore, that the faithful with sincere mind give such consent, they open up for themselves a treasure of sacramental grace from which they draw supernatural power for the fulfilling of their rights and duties faithfully, holily, perseveringly even unto death. Hence this sacrament not only increases sanctifying grace, the permanent principle of the supernatural life, in those who, as the expression is, place no obstacle *(obex)* in its way, but also adds particular gifts, dispositions, seeds of grace, by elevating and perfecting the natural powers. By these gifts the parties are assisted not only in understanding, but in knowing intimately, in adhering to firmly, in willing effectively, and in successfully putting into practice, those things which pertain to the marriage state, its aims and duties, giving them in fine right to the actual assistance of grace, whensoever they need it for fulfilling the duties of their state.

Nevertheless, since it is a law of divine Providence in the supernatural order that men do not reap the full fruit of the Sacraments which they receive after acquiring the use of reason unless they cooperate with grace, the grace of matrimony will remain for the most part an unused talent hidden in the field unless the parties exercise these supernatural powers and cultivate and develop the seeds of grace they have received. If, however, doing all that lies with their power, they cooperate diligently, they will be able with ease to bear the burdens of their state and to fulfil their duties. By such a sacrament they will be strengthened, sanctified and in a manner consecrated. For, as St. Augustine teaches, just as by Baptism and Holy Orders a man is set aside and assisted either for the duties of Christian life or for the priestly office and is never deprived of their sacramental aid, almost in the same way (although not by a sacramental character), the faithful once joined by marriage ties can never be deprived of the help and the binding force of the sacrament. Indeed, as the Holy Doctor adds, even those who commit adultery carry with them that sacred yoke, although in this case not as a title to the glory of grace but for the ignominy of their guilty action, "as the soul by apostasy, withdrawing as it were from marriage with Christ, even though it may have lost its faith, does not lose the sacrament of Faith which it received at the laver of regeneration."

These parties, let it be noted, not fettered but adorned by the golden bond of the sacrament, not hampered but assisted, should strive with all their might to the end that their wedlock, not only through the power and symbolism of the sacrament, but also through their spirit and manner of life, may be and remain always the living image of that most fruitful union of Christ with the Church, which is to be venerated as the sacred token of most perfect love.

All of these things, Venerable Brethren, you must consider carefully and ponder over with a lively faith if you would see in their true light the extraordinary benefits of matrimony—offspring, conjugal faith, and the sacrament. No one can fail to admire the divine Wisdom, Holiness and Goodness which, while respecting the dignity and happiness of husband and wife, has provided so bountifully for the conservation and propagation of the human race by a single chaste and sacred fellowship of nuptial union.

II

When we consider the great excellence of chaste wedlock, Venerable Brethren, it appears all the more regrettable that particularly in our day we should witness this divine institution often scorned and on every side degraded.

For now, alas, not secretly nor under cover, but openly, with all sense of shame put aside, now by word again by writings, by theatrical productions of every kind, by romantic fiction, by amorous and frivolous novels, by cinematographs portraying in vivid scene, in addresses broadcast by radio telephony, in short by all the inventions of modern science, the sanctity of marriage is trampled upon and derided; divorce, adultery, all the basest vices either are extolled or at least are depicted in such colors as to appear to be free of all reproach and infamy. Books are not lacking which dare to pronounce themselves as scientific but which in truth are merely coated with a veneer of science in order that they may the more easily insinuate their ideas. The doctrines defended in these are offered for sale as the productions of modern genius, of that genius namely, which, anxious only for truth, is considered to have *emancipated* itself from all those old-fashioned and immature opinions of the ancients; and to the number of these antiquated opinions they relegate the traditional doctrine of Christian marriage.

These thoughts are instilled into men of every class, rich and poor, masters and workers, lettered and unlettered, married and single, the godly and godless, old and young, but for these last, as easiest prey, the worst snares are laid.

Not all the sponsors of these new doctrines are carried to the extremes of unbridled lust; there are those who, striving as it were to ride a middle course, believe nevertheless that something should be conceded in our times as regards certain precepts of the divine and natural law. But these likewise, more or less wittingly, are emissaries of the great enemy who is ever seeking to sow cockle among the wheat. We, therefore, whom the Father has appointed over His field, We who are bound by Our most holy office to take care lest the good seed be choked by the weeds, believe it fitting to apply to Ourselves the most grave words of the Holy Ghost with which the Apostle Paul exhorted his beloved Timothy: "Be thou vigilant. . . . Fulfill thy ministry. . . . Preach the word, be instant in season, out of season, reprove, entreat, rebuke in all patience and doctrine."

And since, in order that the deceits of the enemy may be avoided, it is necessary first of all that they be laid bare; since much is to be gained by denouncing these fallacies for the sake of the unwary, even though We prefer not to name these iniquities "as becometh saints," yet for the welfare of souls We cannot remain altogether silent.

To begin at the very source of these evils, their basic principle lies in this, that matrimony is repeatedly declared to be not instituted by the Author of nature nor raised by Christ the Lord to the dignity of a true sacrament, but invented by man. Some confidently assert that they have found no evidence of the existence of matrimony in nature or in her laws, but regard it merely as the means of producing life and of gratifying in one way or another a vehement impulse; on the other hand, others recognize that certain beginnings or, as it were, seeds of true wedlock are found in the nature of man since, unless men were bound together by some form of permanent tie, the dignity of husband and wife or the natural end of propagating and rearing the offspring would not receive satisfactory provision. At the same time they maintain that in all beyond this germinal idea matrimony, through various concurrent causes, is invented solely by the mind of man, established solely by his will.

How grievously all these err and how shamelessly they leave the ways of honesty is already evident from what we have set forth here regarding the origin and nature of wedlock, its purposes and the good inherent in it. The evil of this teaching is plainly seen from the consequences which its advocates deduce from it, namely, that the laws, institutions and customs by which wedlock is governed, since they take their origin solely from the will of man, are subject entirely to him, hence can and must be founded, changed and abrogated according to human caprice and the shifting circumstances of human affairs; that the generative power which is grounded in nature itself is more sacred and has wider range than matrimony—hence it may be exercised both outside as well as within the confines of wedlock, and though the purpose of matrimony be set aside, as though to suggest that the license of a base fornicating woman should enjoy the same rights as the chaste motherhood of a lawfully wedded wife.

Armed with these principles, some men go so far as to concoct new species of unions, suited, as they say, to the present temper of men and the times, which various new forms of matrimony they presume to label "temporary," "experimental," and "companionate." These offer all the indulgence of matrimony and its rights without, however, the indissoluble bond, and without offspring, unless later the parties alter their cohabitation into a matrimony in the full sense of the law.

Indeed there are some who desire and insist that these practices be legitimatized by the law or, at least, excused by their general acceptance among the people. They do not seem even to suspect that these proposals partake of nothing of the modern "culture" in which they glory so much, but are simply hateful abominations which beyond all question reduce our truly cultured nations to the barbarous standards of savage peoples.

And now, Venerable Brethren, we shall explain in detail the evils opposed to each of the benefits of matrimony. First consideration is due to the offspring, which many have the boldness to call the disagreeable burden of matrimony and which they say is to be carefully avoided by married people not through virtuous continence (which Christian law permits in matrimony when both parties consent) but by frustrating the marriage act. Some justify this criminal abuse on the ground that they are weary of children and wish to gratify their desires without their consequent burden. Others say that they cannot on the one hand remain continent nor on the other can they have children because of the difficulties whether on the part of the mother or on the part of family circumstances.

But no reason, however grave, may be put forward by which anything intrinsically against nature may become conformable to nature and morally good. Since, therefore, the conjugal act is destined primarily by nature for the begetting of children, those who in exercising it deliberately frustrate its natural power and purpose sin against nature and commit a deed which is shameful and intrinsically vicious.

Small wonder, therefore, if Holy Writ bears witness that the Divine Majesty regards with greatest detestation this horrible crime and at times has punished it with death. As St. Augustine notes, "Intercourse even with one's legitimate wife is unlawful and wicked where the conception of the offspring is prevented. Onan, the son of Juda, did this and the Lord killed him for it."

Since, therefore, openly departing from the uninterrupted Christian tradition some recently have judged it possible solemnly to declare another doctrine regarding this question, the Catholic Church, to whom God has entrusted the defense of the integrity and purity of morals, standing erect in the midst of the moral ruin which surrounds her, in order that she may preserve the chastity of the nuptial union from being defiled by this foul stain, raises her voice in token of her divine ambassadorship and through Our mouth proclaims anew: any use whatsoever of matrimony exercised in such a way that the act is deliberately frustrated in its natural power to generate life is an offense against the law of God and of nature, and those who indulge in such are branded with the guilt of a grave sin.

We admonish, therefore, priests who hear confessions and others who have the care of souls, in virtue of Our supreme authority and in Our solicitude for the salvation of souls, not to allow the faithful entrusted to them to err regarding this most grave law of God; much more, that they keep themselves immune from such false opinions, in no way conniving in them. If any confessor or pastor of souls, which may God forbid, lead the faithful entrusted to him into these errors or should at least confirm them by approval or by guilty silence, let him be mindful of the fact that he must render a strict account to God, the Supreme Judge, for the betrayal of his sacred trust, and let him take to himself the words of Christ: "They are blind and leaders of the blind: and if the blind lead the blind, both fall into the pit."

As regards the evil use of matrimony, to pass over the arguments which are shameful, not infrequently others that are false and exaggerated are put forward. Holy Mother Church very well understands and clearly appreciates all that is said regarding the health of the mother and the danger to her life. And who would not grieve to think of these things? Who is not filled with the greatest admiration when he sees a mother risking her life with heroic fortitude, that she may preserve the life of the offspring which she has conceived? God alone, all bountiful and all merciful as He is, can reward her for the fulfilment of the office allotted to her by nature, and will assuredly repay her in a measure full to overflowing.

Holy Church knows well that not infrequently one of the parties is sinned against rather than sinning, when for a grave cause he or she reluctantly allows the perversion of the right order. In such a case, there is no sin, provided that, mindful of the law of charity, he or she does not neglect to seek to dissuade and to deter the partner from sin. Nor are those considered as acting against nature who in the married state use their right in the proper manner although on account of natural reasons either of time or of certain defects, new life cannot be brought forth. For in matrimony as well as in the use of the matrimonial rights there are also secondary ends, such as mutual aid, the cultivating of mutual love, and the quieting of concupiscence which husband and wife are not forbidden to consider so long as they are subordinated to the primary end and so long as the intrinsic nature of the act is preserved.

We are deeply touched by the sufferings of those parents who, in extreme want, experience great difficulty in rearing their children.

However, they should take care lest the calamitous state of their external affairs should be the occasion for a much more calamitous error. No difficulty can arise that justifies the putting aside of the law of God which forbids all acts intrinsically evil. There is no possible circumstance in which husband and wife cannot, strengthened by the grace of God, fulfil faithfully their duties and preserve in wedlock their chastity unspotted. This truth of Christian Faith is expressed by the teaching of the Council of Trent. "Let no one be so rash as to assert that which the Fathers of the Council have placed under anathema, namely, that there are precepts of God impossible for the just to observe. God does not ask the impossible, but by His commands, instructs you to do what you are able, to pray for what you are not able that He may help you."

This same doctrine was again solemnly repeated and confirmed by the Church in the condemnation of the Jansenist heresy which dared to utter this blasphemy against the goodness of God: "Some precepts of God are, when one considers the powers which man possesses, impossible of fulfilment even to the just who wish to keep the law and strive to do so; grace is lacking whereby these laws could be fulfilled."

But another very grave crime is to be noted, Venerable Brethren, which regards the taking of the life of the offspring hidden in the mother's womb. Some wish it to be allowed and left to the will of the father or the mother; others say it is unlawful unless there are weighty reasons which they call by the name of medical, social, or eugenic "indication." Because this matter falls under the penal laws of the state by which the destruction of the offspring begotten but unborn is forbidden, these people demand that the "indication," which in one form or another they defend, be recognized as such by the public law and in no way penalized. There are those, moreover, who ask that the public authorities provide aid for these death-dealing operations, a thing, which, sad to say, everyone knows is of very frequent occurrence in some places.

As to the "medical and therapeutic indication" to which, using their own words, we have made reference, Venerable Brethren, however much we may pity the mother whose health and even life is gravely imperiled in the performance of the duty allotted to her by nature, nevertheless what could ever be a sufficient reason for excusing in any way the direct murder of the innocent? This is precisely what we are dealing with here. Whether inflicted upon the mother or upon the child, it is against the precept of God and the law of nature: "Thou shalt not kill:" The life of each is equally sacred, and no one has the power, not even the public authority, to destroy it. It is of no use to appeal to the right of taking away life for here it is a question of the innocent, whereas that right has regard only to the guilty; nor is there here question of defense by bloodshed against an unjust aggressor (for who would call an innocent child an unjust aggressor?); again there is not question here of what is called the "law of extreme necessity" which could even extend to the direct killing of the innocent. Upright and skilful doctors strive most praiseworthily to guard and preserve the lives of both mother and child; on the contrary, those show themselves most unworthy of the noble medical profession who encompass the death of one or the other, through a pretense at practicing medicine or through motives of misguided pity.

All of which agrees with the stern words of the Bishop of Hippo in denouncing those wicked parents who seek to remain childless, and failing in this, are not ashamed to put their offspring to death: "Sometimes this lustful cruelty or cruel lust goes so far as to seek to procure a baneful sterility, and if this fails the fetus conceived in the womb is in one way or another smothered or evacuated, in the desire to destroy the offspring before it has life, or if it already lives in the womb, to kill it before it is born. If both man and woman are party to such practices they are not spouses at all; and if from the first they have carried on thus they have come together not for honest wedlock, but for impure gratification; if both are not party to these deeds, I make bold to say that either the one makes herself a mistress of the husband, or the other simply the paramour of his wife."

What is asserted in favor of the social and eugenic "indication" may and must be accepted, provided lawful and upright methods are employed within the proper limits; but to wish to put forward reasons based upon them for the killing of the innocent is unthinkable and contrary to the divine precept promulgated in the words of the Apostle: Evil is not to be done that good may come of it.

Those who hold the reins of government should not forget that it is the duty of public authority by appropriate laws and sanctions to defend the lives of the innocent, and this all the more so since those whose lives are endangered and assailed cannot defend themselves. Among whom we must mention in the first place infants hidden in the mother's womb. And if the public magistrates not only do not defend them, but by their laws and ordinances betray them to death at the hands of doctors or of others, let them remember that God is the Judge and Avenger of innocent blood which cried from earth to Heaven.

Finally, that pernicious practice must be condemned which closely touches upon the natural right of man to enter matrimony but affects also in a real way the welfare of the offspring. For there are some who, over solicitous for the cause of eugenics, not only give salutary counsel for more certainly procuring the strength and health of the future child—which, indeed, is not contrary to right reason—but put eugenics before aims of a higher order, and by public authority wish to prevent from marrying all those whom, even though naturally fit for marriage, they consider, according to the norms and conjectures of their investigations, would, through hereditary transmission, bring forth defective offspring. And more, they wish to legislate to deprive these of that natural faculty by medical action despite their unwillingness; and this they do not propose as an infliction of grave punishment under the authority of the state for a crime committed, not to prevent future crimes by guilty persons, but against every right and good they wish the civil authority to arrogate to itself a power over a faculty which it never had and can never legitimately possess.

Those who act in this way are at fault in losing sight of the fact that the family is more sacred than the State and that men are begotten not for the earth and for time, but for Heaven and eternity. Although often these individuals are to be dissuaded from entering into matrimony, certainly it is wrong to brand men with the stigma of crime because they contract marriage, on the ground that, despite the fact that they are in every respect capable of matrimony, they will give birth only to defective children, even though they use all care and diligence.

Public magistrates have no direct power over the bodies of their subjects; therefore, where no crime has taken place and there is no cause present for grave punishment, they can never directly harm, or tamper with the integrity of the body, either for the reasons of eugenics or for any other reason. St. Thomas teaches this when inquiring whether human judges for the sake of preventing future evils can inflict punishment, he admits that the power indeed exists as regards certain other forms of evil, but justly and properly denies it as regards the maiming of the body. "No one who is guiltless may be punished by a human tribunal either by flogging to death, or mutilation, or by beating."

Furthermore, Christian doctrine establishes, and the light of human reason makes it most clear, that private individuals have no other power cver the members of their bodies than that which pertains to their natural ends; and they are not free to destroy or mutilate their members, or in any other way render themselves unfit for their natural functions, except when no other provision can be made for the good of the whole body.

We may now consider another class of errors concerning conjugal faith. Every sin committed as regards the offspring becomes in some way a sin against conjugal faith, since both these blessings are essentially connected. However, we must mention briefly the sources of error and vice corresponding to those virtues which are demanded by conjugal faith, namely the chaste honor existing between man and wife, the due subjection of wife to husband, and the true love which binds both parties together.

It follows therefore that they are destroying mutual fidelity, who think that the ideas and morality of our present time concerning a certain harmful and false friendship with a third party can be countenanced, and who teach that a greater freedom of feeling and action in such external relations should be allowed to man and wife, particularly as many (so they consider) are possessed of an inborn sexual tendency which cannot be satisfied within the narrow limits of monogamous marriage. That rigid attitude which condemns all sensual affections and actions with a third party they imagine to be a narrowing of mind and heart, something obsolete, or an abject form of jealousy, and as a result they look upon whatever penal laws are passed by the State for the preserving of conjugal faith as void or to be abolished. Such unworthy and idle opinions are condemned by that noble instinct which is found in every chaste husband and wife, and even by the light of the testimony of nature alone,—a testimony that is sanctioned and confirmed by the command of God: "Whosoever shall look on a woman to lust after her hath already committed adultery with her in his heart." The force of this divine precept can never be weakened by any merely human custom, bad example or pretext of human progress, for just as it is the one and the same "Jesus Christ, yesterday and to-day and the same for ever," so it is the one and the same doctrine of Christ that abides and of which no one jot or tittle shall pass away till all is fulfilled.

The same false teachers who try to dim the luster of conjugal faith and purity do not scruple to do away with the honorable and trusting obedience which the woman owes to the man. Many of them even go further and assert that such a subjection of one party to the other is unworthy of human dignity, that the rights of husband and wife are equal; wherefore, they boldly proclaim the emancipation of women has been or ought to be effected. This emancipation in their ideas must be threefold, in the ruling of the domestic society, in the administration of family affairs and in the rearing of the children. It must be social, economic, physiological:—physiological, that is to say, the woman is to be freed at her own good pleasure from the burdensome duties properly belonging to a wife as companion and mother (We have already said that this is not an emancipation but a crime); social, inasmuch as the wife being freed from the cares of children and family, should, to the neglect of these, be able to follow her own bent and devote herself to business and even public affairs; finally economic, whereby the woman even without the knowledge and against the wish of her husband may be at liberty to conduct and administer her own affairs, giving her attention chiefly to these rather than to children, husband and family.

This, however, is not the true emancipation of woman, nor that rational and exalted liberty which belongs to the noble office of a Christian woman and wife; it is rather the debasing of the womanly character and the dignity of motherhood, and indeed of the whole family, as a result of which the husband suffers the loss of his wife, the children of their mother, and the home and the whole family of an ever watchful guardian. More than this, this false liberty and unnatural equality with the husband is to the detriment of the woman herself, for if the woman descends from her truly regal throne to which she has been raised within the walls of the home by means of the Gospel, she will soon be reduced to the old state of slavery (if not in appearance, certainly in reality) and become as amongst the pagans the mere instrument of man.

This equality of rights which is so much exaggerated and distorted, must indeed be recognized in those rights which belong to the dignity of the human soul and which are proper to the marriage contract and inseparably bound up with wedlock. In such things undoubtedly both parties enjoy the same rights and are bound by the same obligations; in other things there must be a certain inequality and due accommodation, which is demanded by the good of the family and the right ordering and unity and stability of home life.

As, however, the social and economic conditions of the married woman must in some way be altered on account of the changes in social intercourse, it is part of the office of the public authority to adapt the civil rights of the wife to modern needs and requirements, keeping in view what the natural disposition and temperament of the female sex, good morality, and the welfare of the family demands, and provided always that the essential order of the domestic society remain intact, founded as it is on something higher than human authority and wisdom, namely on the authority and wisdom of God, and so not changeable by public laws or at the pleasure of private individuals.

These enemies of marriage go further, however, when they substitute for that true and solid love, which is the basis of conjugal happiness, a certain vague compatibility of temperament. This they call sympathy and assert that, since it is the only bond by which husband and wife are linked together, when it ceases the marriage is completely dissolved. What else is this than to build a house upon sand?—a house that in the words of Christ would forthwith be shaken and collapse, as soon as it was exposed to the waves of adversity "and the winds blew and they beat upon that house. And it fell: and great was the fall thereof." On the other hand, the house built upon a rock, that is to say on mutual conjugal chastity and strengthened by a deliberate and constant union of spirit, will not only never fall away but will never be shaken by adversity.

We have so far, Venerable Brethren, shown the excellency of the first two blessings of Christian wedlock which the modern subverters of society are attacking. And now considering that the third blessing, which is that of the sacrament, far surpasses the other two, we should not be surprised to find that this, because of its outstanding excellence, is much more sharply attacked by the same people. They put forward in the first place that matrimony belongs entirely to the profane and purely civil sphere, that it is not to be committed to the religious society, the Church of Christ, but to civil society alone. They then add that the marriage contract is to be freed from any indissoluble bond, and that separation and divorce are not only to be tolerated but sanctioned by the law; from which it follows finally that, robbed of all its holiness, matrimony should be enumerated amongst the secular and civil institutions. The first point is contained in their contention that the civil act itself should stand for the marriage contract (civil matrimony, as it is called), while the religious act is to be considered a mere addition, or at most a concession to a too superstitious people. Moreover they want it to be no cause for reproach that marriages be contracted by Catholics with non-Catholics without any reference to religion or recourse to the ecclesiastical authorities. The second point which is but a consequence of the first is to be found in their excuse for complete divorce and in their praise and encouragement of those civil laws which favor the loosening of the bond itself. As the salient features of the religious character of all marriage and particularly of the sacramental marriage of Christians have been treated at length and supported by weighty arguments in the encyclical letters of Leo XIII, letters which We have frequently recalled to mind and expressly made our own, We refer you to them, repeating here only a few points.

Even by the light of reason alone and particularly if the ancient records of history are investigated, if the unwavering popular conscience is interrogated and the manners and institutions of all races examined, it is sufficiently obvious that there is a certain sacredness and religious character attaching even to the purely natural union of man and woman, "not something added by chance but innate, not imposed by men but involved in the nature of things," since it has "God for its author and has been even from the beginning a foreshadowing of the Incarnation of the Word of God." This sacredness of marriage which is intimately connected with religion and all that is holy, arises from the divine origin we have just mentioned, from its purpose which is the begetting and education of children for God, and the binding of man and wife to God through Christian love and mutual support; and finally it arises from the very nature of wedlock, whose institution is to be sought for in the farseeing Providence of God, whereby it is the means of transmitting life, thus making the parents the ministers, as it were, of the Divine Omnipotence. To this must be added that new element of dignity which comes from the sacrament, by which the Christian marriage is so ennobled and raised to such a level, that it appeared to the Apostle as a great sacrament, honorable in every way.

This religious character of marriage, its sublime signification of grace and the union between Christ and the Church, evidently requires that those about to marry should show a holy reverence towards it, and zealously endeavor to make their marriage approach as nearly as possible to the archetype of Christ and the Church.

They, therefore, who rashly and heedlessly contract mixed marriages, from which the maternal love and providence of the Church dissuades her children for very sound reasons, fail conspicuously in this respect, sometimes with danger to their eternal salvation. This attitude of the Church to mixed marriages appears in many of her documents, all of which are summed up in the Code of Canon Law: "Everywhere and with the greatest strictness the Church forbids marriages between baptized persons, one of whom is a Catholic and the other a member of a schismatical or heretical sect; and if there is, add to this, the danger of the falling away of the Catholic party and the perversion of the children, such a marriage is forbidden also by the divine law." If the Church occasionally on account of circumstances does not refuse to grant a dispensation from these strict laws (provided that the divine law remains intact and the dangers above mentioned are provided against by suitable safeguards), it is unlikely that the Catholic party will not suffer some detriment from such a marriage.

Whence it comes about not unfrequently, as experience shows, that deplorable defections from religion occur among the offspring, or at least a headlong descent into that religious indifference which is closely allied to impiety. There is this also to be considered that in these mixed marriages it becomes much more difficult to imitate by a lively conformity of spirit the mystery of which We have spoken, namely that close union between Christ and His Church.

Assuredly, also, will there be wanting that close union of spirit which as it is the sign and mark of the Church of Christ, so also should be the sign of Christian wedlock, its glory and adornment. For, where there exists diversity of mind, truth and feeling, the bond of union of mind and heart is wont to be broken, or at least weakened. From this comes the danger lest the love of man and wife grow cold and the peace and happiness of family life, resting as it does on the union of hearts, be destroyed. Many centuries ago indeed, the old Roman law had proclaimed: "Marriages are the union of male and female, a sharing of life and the communication of divine and human rights." But especially, as We have pointed out, Venerable Brethren, the daily increasing facility of divorce is an obstacle to the restoration of marriage to that state of perfection which the divine Redeemer willed it should possess.

The advocates of the neo-paganism of to-day have learned nothing from the sad state of affairs, but instead, day by day, more and more vehemently, they continue by legislation to attack the indissolubility of the marriage bond, proclaiming that the lawfulness of divorce must be recognized, and that the antiquated laws should give place to a new and more humane legislation. Many and varied are the grounds put forward for divorce, some arising from the wickedness and the guilt of the persons concerned, others arising from the circumstances of the case; the former they describe as subjective, the latter as objective; in a word, whatever might make married life hard or unpleasant. They strive to prove their contentions regarding these grounds for the divorce legislation they would bring about, by various arguments. Thus, in the first place, they maintain that it is for the good of either party that the one who is innocent should have the right to separate from the guilty, or that the guilty should be withdrawn from a union which is unpleasing to him and against his will. In the second place, they argue, the good of the child demands this, for either it will be deprived of a proper education or the natural fruits of it, and will too easily be affected by the discords and shortcomings of the parents, and drawn from the path of virtue. And thirdly the common good of society requires that these marriages should be completely dissolved, which are now incapable of producing their natural results, and that legal reparations should be allowed when crimes are to be feared as the result of the common habitation and intercourse of the parties. This last, they say must be admitted to avoid the crimes being committed purposely with a view to obtaining the desired sentence of divorce for which the judge can legally loose the marriage bond, as also to prevent people from coming before the courts when it is obvious from the state of the case that they are lying and perjuring themselves,—all of which brings the court and the lawful authority into contempt. Hence the civil laws, in their opinion, have to be reformed to meet these new requirements, to suit the changes of the times and the changes in men's opinions, civil institutions and customs. Each of these reasons is considered by them as conclusive, so that all taken together offer a clear proof of the necessity of granting divorce in certain cases.

Others, taking a step further, simply state that marriage, being a private contract, is, like other private contracts, to be left to the consent and good pleasure of both parties, and so can be dissolved for any reason whatsoever.

Opposed to all these reckless opinions, Venerable Brethren, stands the unalterable law of God, fully confirmed by Christ, a law that can never be deprived of its force by the decrees of men, the ideas of a people or the will of any legislator: "What God hath joined together, let no man put asunder." And if any man, acting contrary to this law, shall have put asunder, his action is null and void, and the consequence remains, as Christ Himself has explicitly confirmed: "Everyone that putteth away his wife and marrieth another, committeth adultery: and he that marrieth her that is put away from her husband committeth adultery." Moreover, these words refer to every kind of marriage, even that which is natural and legitimate only; for, as has already been observed, that indissolubility by which the loosening of the bond is once and for all removed from the whim of the parties and from every secular power, is a property of every true marriage.

Let that solemn pronouncement of the Council of Trent be recalled to mind in which, under the stigma of anathema, it condemned these errors: "If anyone should say that on account of heresy or the hardships of cohabitation or a deliberate abuse of one party by the other the marriage tie may be loosened, let him be anathema"; and again: "If anyone should say that the Church errs in having taught or in teaching that, according to the teaching of the Gospel and the Apostles, the bond of marriage cannot be loosed because of the sin of adultery of either party; or that neither party, even though he be innocent, having given no cause for the sin of adultery, can contract another marriage during the lifetime of the other; and that he commits adultery who marries another after putting away his adulterous wife, and likewise that she commits adultery who puts away her husband and marries another: let him be anathema."

If therefore the Church has not erred and does not err in teaching this, and consequently it is certain that the bond of marriage cannot be loosed even on account of the sin of adultery, it is evident that all the other weaker excuses that can be, and are usually brought forward, are of no value whatsoever. And the objections brought against the firmness of the marriage bond are easily answered. For, in certain circumstances, imperfect separation of the parties is allowed, the bond not being severed. This separation, which the Church herself permits, and expressly mentions in her Canon Law in those canons which deal with the separation of the parties as to marital relationship and co-habitation, removes all the alleged inconveniences and dangers. It will be for the sacred law and, to some extent, also the civil law, in so far as civil matters are affected, to lay down the grounds, the conditions, the method and precautions to be taken in a case of this kind in order to safeguard the education of the children and the well-being of the family, and to remove all those evils which threaten the married persons, the children and the State. Now all those arguments that are brought forward to prove the indissolubility of the marriage tie, arguments which have already been touched upon, can equally be applied to excluding not only the necessity of divorce, but even the power to grant it; while for all the advantages that can be put forward for the former, there can be adduced as many disadvantages and evils which are a formidable menace to the whole of human society.

To revert again to the expression of Our predecessor, it is hardly necessary to point out what an amount of good is involved in the absolute indissolubility of wedlock and what a train of evils follows upon divorce. Whenever the marriage bond remains intact, then we find marriages contracted with a sense of safety and security, while, when separations are considered and the dangers of divorce are present, the marriage contract itself becomes insecure, or at least gives ground for anxiety and surprises. On the one hand we see a wonderful strengthening of good-will and cooperation in the daily life of husband and wife, while, on the other, both of these are miserably weakened by the presence of a facility for divorce. Here we have at a very opportune moment a source of help by which both parties are enabled to preserve their purity and loyalty; there we find harmful inducements to unfaithfulness. On this side we find the birth of children and their tuition and upbringing effectively promoted, many avenues of discord closed amongst families and relations, and the beginnings of rivalry and jealousy easily suppressed; on that, very great obstacles to the birth and rearing of children and their education, and many occasions of quarrels, and seeds of jealousy sown everywhere. Finally, but especially, the dignity and position of women in civil and domestic society is reinstated by the former; while by the latter it is shamefully lowered and the danger is incurred "of their being considered outcasts, slaves of the lust of men."

To conclude with the important words of Leo XIII, since the destruction of family life "and the loss of national wealth is brought about more by the corruption of morals than by anything else, it is easily seen that divorce, which is born of the perverted morals of a people, and leads, as experiment shows, to vicious habits in public and private life, is particularly opposed to the well-being of the family and of the State. The serious nature of these evils will be the more clearly recognized, when we remember that, once divorce has been allowed, there will be no sufficient means of keeping it in check within any definite bounds. Great is the force of example, greater still that of lust; and with such incitements it cannot but happen that divorce and its consequent setting loose of the passions should spread daily and attack the souls of many like a contagious disease or a river bursting its banks and flooding the land."

Thus, as we read in the same letter, "unless things change, the human family and State have every reason to fear lest they should suffer absolute ruin." All this was written fifty years ago, yet it is confirmed by the daily increasing corruption of morals and the unheard of degradation of the family in those lands where Communism reigns unchecked.

III

Thus far, Venerable Brethren, We have admired with due reverence what the all wise Creator and Redeemer of the human race has ordained with regard to human marriage; at the same time we have expressed Our grief that such a pious ordinance of the divine Goodness should to-day, and on every side, be frustrated and trampled upon by the passions, errors and vices of men.

It is then fitting that, with all fatherly solicitude, We should turn Our mind to seek out suitable remedies whereby those most detestable abuses which We have mentioned, may be removed, and everywhere marriage may again be revealed. To this end, it behooves Us, above all else, to call to mind that firmly established principle, esteemed alike in sound philosophy and sacred theology: namely, that whatever things have deviated from their right order, cannot be brought back to that original state which is in harmony with their nature except by a return to the divine plan which, as the Angelic Doctor teaches, is the exemplar of all right order.

Wherefore, Our predecessor of happy memory, Leo XIII, attacked the doctrine of the naturalists in these words: "It is a divinely appointed law that whatsoever things are constituted by God, the Author of nature, these we find the more useful and salutary, the more they remain in their natural state, unimpaired and unchanged; inasmuch as God, the Creator of all things, intimately knows what is suited to the constitution and the preservation of each, and by his will and mind has so ordained all this that each may duly achieve its purpose. But if the boldness and wickedness of men change and disturb this order of things, so providentially disposed, then, indeed, things so wonderfully ordained, will begin to be injurious, or will cease to be beneficial, either because, in the change, they have lost their power to benefit, or because God Himself is thus pleased to draw down chastisement on the pride and presumption of men."

In order, therefore, to restore due order in this matter of marriage, it is necessary that all should bear in mind what is the divine plan and strive to conform to it.

Wherefore, since the chief obstacle to this study is the power of unbridled lust, which indeed is the most potent cause of sinning against the sacred laws of matrimony, and since man cannot hold in check his passions, unless he first subject himself to God, this must be his primary endeavor, in accordance with the plan divinely ordained. For it is a sacred ordinance that whoever shall have first subjected himself to God will, by the aid of divine grace, be glad to subject to himself his own passions and concupiscence; while he who is a rebel against God will, to his sorrow, experience within himself the violent rebellion of his worst passions.

And how wisely this has been decreed, St Augustine thus shows: "This indeed is fitting, that the lower be subject to the higher, so that he who would have subject to himself whatever is below him, should himself submit to whatever is above him. Acknowledge order, seek peace. Be thou subject to God, and thy flesh subject to thee. What more fitting! What more fair! Thou art subject to the higher and the lower is subject to thee. Do thou serve Him who made thee, so that that which was made for thee may serve thee. For we do not commend this order, namely, 'The flesh to thee and thou to God,' but 'Thou to God, and the flesh to thee.' If, however, thou despisest the subjection of thyself to God, thou shalt never bring about the subjection of the flesh to thyself. If thou dost not obey the Lord, thou shalt be tormented by thy servant." This right ordering on the part of God's wisdom is mentioned by the holy Doctor of the Gentiles, inspired by the Holy Ghost, for in speaking of those ancient philosophers who refused to adore and reverence Him whom they knew to be the Creator of the universe, he says: "Wherefore God gave them up to the desires of their heart, unto uncleanness, to dishonor their own bodies among themselves;" and again: "For this same God delivered them up to shameful affections." And St. James says: "God resisteth the proud and giveth grace to the humble," without which grace, as the same Doctor of the Gentiles reminds us, man cannot subdue the rebellion of his flesh.

Consequently, as the onslaughts of these uncontrolled passions cannot in any way be lessened, unless the spirit first shows a humble compliance of duty and reverence towards its Maker, it is above all and before all needful that those who are joined in the bond of sacred wedlock should be wholly imbued with a profound and genuine sense of duty towards God, which will shape their whole lives, and fill their minds and wills with a very deep reverence for the majesty of God.

Quite fittingly, therefore, and quite in accordance with the defined norm of Christian sentiment, do those pastors of souls act who, to prevent married people from failing in the observance of God's law, urge them to perform their duty and exercise their religion so that they should give themselves to God, continually ask for His divine assistance, frequent the sacraments, and always nourish and preserve a loyal and thoroughly sincere devotion to God.

They are greatly deceived who having underestimated or neglected these means which rise above nature, think that they can induce men by the use and discovery of the natural sciences, such as those of biology, the science of heredity, and the like, to curb their carnal desires. We do not say this in order to belittle those natural means which are not dishonest; for God is the Author of nature as well as of grace, and He has disposed the good things of both orders for the beneficial use of men. The faithful, therefore, can and ought to be assisted also by natural means. But they are mistaken who think that these means are able to establish chastity in the nuptial union, or that they are more effective than supernatural grace.

This conformity of wedlock and moral conduct with the divine laws respective of marriage, without which its effective restoration cannot be brought about, supposes, however, that all can discern readily, with real certainty, and without any accompanying error, what those laws are. But everyone can see to how many fallacies an avenue would be opened up and how many errors would become mixed with the truth, if it were left solely to the light of reason of each to find it out, or if it were to be discovered by the private interpretation of the truth which is revealed. And if this is applicable to many other truths of the moral order, we must all the more pay attention to those things, which appertain to marriage where the inordinate desire for pleasure can attack frail human nature and easily deceive it and lead it astray; this is all the more true of the observance of the divine law, which demands sometimes hard and repeated sacrifices, for which, as experience points out, a weak man can find so many excuses for avoiding the fulfilment of the divine law.

On this account, in order that no falsification or corruption of the divine law but a true genuine knowledge of it may enlighten the minds of men and guide their conduct, it is necessary that a filial and humble obedience towards the Church should be combined with devotedness to God and the desire of submitting to Him. For Christ Himself made the Church the teacher of truth in those things also which concern the right regulation of moral conduct, even though some knowledge of the same is not beyond human reason. For just as God, in the case of the natural truths of religion and morals, added revelation to the light of reason so that what is right and true, "in the present state also of the human race may be known readily with real certainty without any admixture of error," so for the same purpose he has constituted the Church the guardian and the teacher of the whole of the truth concerning religion and moral conduct; to her therefore should the faithful show obedience and subject their minds and hearts so as to be kept unharmed and free from error and moral corruption, and so that they shall not deprive themselves of that assistance given by God with such liberal bounty, they ought to show this due obedience not only when the Church defines something with solemn judgment, but also, in proper proportion, when by the constitutions and decrees of the Holy See, opinions are prescribed and condemned as dangerous or distorted.

Wherefore, let the faithful also be on their guard against the overrated independence of private judgment and that false autonomy of human reason. For it is quite foreign to everyone bearing the name of a Christian to trust his own mental powers with such pride as to agree only with those things which he can examine from their inner nature, and to imagine that the Church, sent by God to teach and guide all nations, is not conversant with present affairs and circumstances; or even that they must obey only in those matters which she has decreed by solemn definition as though her other decisions might be presumed to be false or putting forward insufficient motive for truth and honesty. Quite to the contrary, a characteristic of all true followers of Christ, lettered or unlettered, is to suffer themselves to be guided and led in all things that touch upon faith or morals by the Holy Church of God through its Supreme Pastor the Roman Pontiff, who is himself guided by Jesus Christ Our Lord.

Consequently, since everything must be referred to the law and mind of God, in order to bring about the universal and permanent restoration of marriage, it is indeed of the utmost importance that the faithful should be well instructed concerning matrimony; both by word of mouth and by the written word, not cursorily but often and fully, by means of plain and weighty arguments, so that these truths will strike the intellect and will be deeply engraved on their hearts. Let them realize and diligently reflect upon the great wisdom, kindness and bounty God has shown towards the human race, not only by the institution of marriage, but also, and quite as much, by upholding it with sacred laws; still more, in wonderfully raising it to the dignity of a Sacrament by which such an abundant fountain of graces has been opened to those joined in Christian wedlock, that these may be able to serve the noble purposes of wedlock for their own welfare and for that of their children, of the community and also for that of human relationship.

Certainly, if the latter day subverters of marriage are entirely devoted to misleading the minds of men and corrupting their hearts, to making a mockery of matrimonial purity and extolling the filthiest of vices by means of books and pamphlets and other innumerable methods, much more ought you, Venerable Brethren, whom "the Holy Ghost has placed as bishops, to rule the Church of God, which He hath purchased with His own blood," to give yourselves wholly to this, that through yourselves and through the priests subject to you, and, moreover, through the laity welded together by Catholic Action, so much desired and recommended by Us, into a power of hierarchical apostolate, you may, by every fitting means, oppose error by truth, vice by the excellent dignity of chastity, the slavery of covetousness by the liberty of the sons of God, that disastrous ease in obtaining divorce by an enduring love in the bond of marriage and by the inviolate pledge of fidelity given even to death.

Thus will it come to pass that the faithful will wholeheartedly thank God that they are bound together by His command and led by gentle compulsion to fly as far as possible from every kind of idolatry of the flesh and from the base slavery of the passions. They will, in a great measure, turn and be turned away from these abominable opinions which to the dishonor of man's dignity are now spread about in speech and in writing and collected under the title of "perfect marriage" and which indeed would make that perfect marriage nothing better than "depraved marriage," as it has been rightly and truly called.

Such wholesome instruction and religious training in regard to Christian marriage will be quite different from that exaggerated physiological education by means of which, in these times of ours, some reformers of married life make pretense of helping those joined in wedlock, laying much stress on these physiological matters, in which is learned rather the art of sinning in a subtle way than the virtue of living chastely.

So, Venerable Brethren, we make entirely Our own the words which Our predecessor of happy memory, Leo XIII, in his encyclical letter on Christian marriage addressed to the bishops of the whole world: "Take care not to spare your efforts and authority in bringing about that among the people committed to your guidance that doctrine may be preserved whole and unadulterated which Christ the Lord and the apostles, the interpreters of the divine will, have handed down, and which the Catholic Church herself has religiously preserved, and commanded to be observed by the faithful of every age."

Even the very best instruction given by the Church, however, will not alone suffice to bring about once more conformity of marriage to the law of God; something more is needed in addition to the education of the mind, namely a steadfast determination of the will, on the part of husband and wife, to observe the sacred laws of God and of nature in regard to marriage. In fine, in spite of what others may wish to assert and spread abroad by word of mouth or in writing, let husband and wife resolve: to stand fast to the commandments of God in all things that matrimony demands; always to render to each other the assistance of mutual love; to preserve the honor of chastity; not to lay profane hands on the stable nature of the bond; to use the rights given them by marriage in a way that will be always Christian and sacred, more especially in the first years of wedlock, so that should there be need of continency afterwards, custom will have made it easier for each to preserve it. In order that they may make this firm resolution, keep it and put it into practice, an oft-repeated consideration of their state of life, and a diligent reflection on the sacrament they have received, will be of great assistance to them. Let them constantly keep in mind, that they have been sanctified and strengthened for the duties and for the dignity of their state by a special sacrament, the efficacious power of which, although it does not impress a character, is undying. To this purpose we may ponder over the words full of real comfort of holy Cardinal Robert Bellarmine, who with other well-known theologians with devout conviction thus expresses himself: "The sacrament of matrimony can be regarded in two ways: first, in the making, and then in its permanent state. For it is a sacrament like to that of the Eucharist, which not only when it is being conferred, but also whilst it remains, is a sacrament; for as long as the married parties are alive, so long is their union a sacrament of Christ and the Church."

Yet in order that the grace of this sacrament may produce its full fruit, there is need, as we have already pointed out, of the cooperation of the married parties; which consists in their striving to fulfil their duties to the best of their ability and with unwearied effort. For just as in the natural order men must apply the powers given them by God with their own toil and diligence that these may exercise their full vigor, failing which, no profit is gained, so also men must diligently and unceasingly use the powers given them by the grace which is laid up in the soul by this sacrament. Let not, then, those who are joined in matrimony neglect the grace of the sacrament which is in them; for, in applying themselves to the careful observance, however laborious, of their duties they will find the power of that grace becoming more effectual as time goes on. And if ever they should feel themselves to be overburdened by the hardships of their condition of life, let them not lose courage, but rather let them regard in some measure as addressed to them that which St. Paul the Apostle wrote to his beloved disciple Timothy regarding the sacrament of holy Orders when the disciple was dejected through hardship and insults: "I admonish thee that thou stir up the grace which is in thee by the imposition of my hands. For God hath not given us the spirit of fear; but of power, and of love, and of sobriety."

All these things, however, Venerable Brethren, depend in large measure on the due preparation remote and proximate, of the parties for marriage. For it cannot be denied that the basis of a happy wedlock, and the ruin of an unhappy one, is prepared and set in the souls of boys and girls during the period of childhood and adolescence. There is danger that those who before marriage sought in all things what is theirs, who indulged even their impure desires, will be in the married state what they were before, that they will reap that which they have sown; indeed, within the home there will be sadness, lamentation, mutual contempt, strifes, estrangements, weariness of common life, and, worst of all, such parties will find themselves left alone with their own unconquered passions.

Let then, those who are about to enter on married life, approach that state well disposed and well prepared, so that they will be able, as far as they can, to help each other in sustaining the vicissitudes of life, and yet more in attending to their eternal salvation and in forming the inner man unto the fulness of the age of Christ. It will also help them, if they behave towards their cherished offspring as God wills: that is, that the father be truly a father, and the mother truly a mother; through their devout love and unwearying care, the home, though it suffer the want and hardship of this valley of tears, may become for the children in its own way a foretaste of that paradise of delight in which the Creator placed the first men of the human race. Thus will they be able to bring up their children as perfect men and perfect Christians, they will instill into them a sound understanding of the Catholic Church, and will give them such a disposition and love for their fatherland as duty and gratitude demand.

Consequently, both those who are now thinking of entering upon this sacred married state, as well as those who have the charge of educating Christian youth, should, with due regard to the future, prepare that which is good, obviate that which is bad, and recall those points about which We have already spoken in Our encyclical letter concerning education: "The inclinations of the will, if they are bad, must be repressed from childhood, but such as are good must be fostered, and the mind, particularly of children, should be imbued with doctrines which begin with God, while the heart should be strengthened with the aids of divine grace, in the absence of which, no one can curb evil desires, nor can his discipline and formation be brought to complete perfection by the Church. For Christ has provided her with heavenly doctrines and divine sacraments, that He might make her an effectual teacher of men."

To the proximate preparation of a good married life belongs very specially the care in choosing a partner; on that depends a great deal whether the forthcoming marriage will be happy or not, since one may be to the other either a great help in leading a Christian life, or, a great danger and hindrance. And so that they may not deplore for the rest of their lives the sorrows arising from an indiscreet marriage, those about to enter into wedlock should carefully deliberate in choosing the person with whom henceforward they must live continually: they should, in so deliberating, keep before their minds the thought first of God and of the true religion of Christ, then of themselves, of their partner, of the children to come, as also of human and civil society, for which wedlock is a fountain head. Let them diligently pray for divine help, so that they make their choice in accordance with Christian prudence, not indeed led by the blind and unrestrained impulse of lust, nor by any desire of riches or other base influence, but by a true and noble love and by a sincere affection for the future partner; and then let them strive in their married life for those ends for which the State was constituted by God. Lastly, let them not omit to ask the prudent advice of their parents with regard to the partner, and let them regard this advice in no light manner, in order that by their mature knowledge and experience of human affairs, they may guard against a disastrous choice, and, on the threshold of matrimony, may receive more abundantly the divine blessing of the fourth commandment: "Honor thy father and thy mother (which is the first commandment with a promise) that it may be well with thee and thou mayest be long-lived upon the earth."

Now since it is no rare thing to find that the perfect observance of God's commands and conjugal integrity encounter difficulties by reason of the fact that the man and wife are in straitened circumstances, their necessities must be relieved as far as possible.

And so, in the first place, every effort must be made to bring about that which Our predecessor Leo XIII, of happy memory, has already insisted upon, namely, that in the State such economic and social methods should be adopted as will enable every head of a family to earn as much as, according to his station in life, is necessary for himself, his wife, and for the rearing of his children, for "the laborer is worthy of his hire." To deny this, or to make light of what is equitable, is a grave injustice and is placed among the greatest sins by Holy Writ; nor is it lawful to fix such a scanty wage as will be insufficient for the upkeep of the family in the circumstances in which it is placed.

Care, however, must be taken that the parties themselves, for a considerable time before entering upon married life, should strive to dispose of, or at least to diminish, the material obstacles in their way. The manner in which this may be done effectively and honestly must be pointed out by those who are experienced. Provision must be made also, in the case of those who are not self-supporting, for joint aid by private or public guilds.

When these means which We have pointed out do not fulfil the needs, particularly of a larger or poorer family, Christian charity towards our neighbor absolutely demands that those things which are lacking to the needy should be provided; hence it is incumbent on the rich to help the poor, so that, having an abundance of this world's goods, they may not expend them fruitlessly or completely squander them, but employ them for the support and well-being of those who lack the necessities of life. They who give of their substance to Christ in the person of His poor will receive from the Lord a most bountiful reward when He shall come to judge the world; they who act to the contrary will pay the penalty. Not in vain does the Apostle warn us: "He that hath the substance of this world and shall see his brother in need, and shall shut up his bowels from him: how doth the charity of God abide in him?"

If, however, for this purpose, private resources do not suffice, it is the duty of the public authority to supply for the insufficient forces of individual effort, particularly in a matter which is of such importance to the common weal, touching as it does the maintenance of the family and married people. If families, particularly those in which there are many children, have not suitable dwellings; if the husband cannot find employment and means of livelihood; if the necessities of life cannot be purchased except at exorbitant prices; if even the mother of the family to the great harm of the home, is compelled to go forth and seek a living by her own labor; if she, too, in the ordinary or even extraordinary labors of childbirth, is deprived of proper food, medicine, and the assistance of a skilled physician, it is patent to all to what an extent married people may lose heart, and how home life and the observance of God's commands are rendered difficult for them; indeed it is obvious how great a peril can arise to the public security and to the welfare and very life of civil society itself when such men are reduced to that condition of desperation that, having nothing which they fear to lose, they are emboldened to hope for chance advantage from the upheaval of the state and of established order.

Wherefore, those who have the care of the State and of the public good cannot neglect the needs of married people and their families, without bringing great harm upon the State and on the common welfare. Hence, in making the laws and in disposing of public funds they must do their utmost to relieve the needs of the poor, considering such a task as one of the most important of their administrative duties.

We are sorry to note that not infrequently nowadays it happens that through a certain inversion of the true order of things, ready and bountiful assistance is provided for the unmarried mother and her illegitimate offspring (who, of course must be helped in order to avoid a greater evil) which is denied to legitimate mothers or given sparingly or almost grudgingly.

But not only in regard to temporal goods, Venerable Brethren, is it the concern of the public authority to make proper provision for matrimony and the family, but also in other things which concern the good of souls. Just laws must be made for the protection of chastity, for reciprocal conjugal aid, and for similar purposes, and these must be faithfully enforced, because, as history testifies, the prosperity of the State and the temporal happiness of its citizens cannot remain safe and sound where the foundation on which they are established, which is the moral order, is weakened and where the very fountainhead from which the State draws its life, namely, wedlock and the family, is obstructed by the vices of its citizens.

For the preservation of the moral order neither the laws and sanctions of the temporal power are sufficient, nor is the beauty of virtue and the expounding of its necessity. Religious authority must enter in to enlighten the mind, to direct the will, and to strengthen human frailty by the assistance of divine grace. Such an authority is found nowhere save in the Church instituted by Christ the Lord. Hence We earnestly exhort in the Lord all those who hold the reins of power that they establish and maintain firmly harmony and friendship with this Church of Christ so that through the united activity and energy of both powers the tremendous evils, fruits of those wanton liberties which assail both marriage and the family and are a menace to both Church and State, may be effectively frustrated.

Governments can assist the Church greatly in the execution of its important office, if, in laying down their ordinances, they take account of what is prescribed by divine and ecclesiastical law, and if penalties are fixed for offenders. For as it is, there are those who think that whatever is permitted by the laws of the State, or at least is not punished by them, is allowed also in the moral order, and, because they neither fear God nor see any reason to fear the laws of man, they act even against their conscience, thus often bringing ruin upon themselves and upon many others. There will be no peril to or lessening of the rights and integrity of the State from its association with the Church. Such suspicion and fear is empty and groundless, as Leo XIII has already so clearly set forth: "It is generally agreed," he says, "that the Founder of the Church, Jesus Christ, wished the spiritual power to be distinct from the civil, and each to be free and unhampered in doing its own work, not forgetting, however, that it is expedient to both, and in the interest of everybody, that there be a harmonious relationship. . . . If the civil power combines in a friendly manner with the spiritual power of the Church, it necessarily follows that both parties will greatly benefit. The dignity of the State will be enhanced, and with religion as its guide, there will never be a rule that is not just; while for the Church there will be at hand a safeguard and defense which will operate to the public good of the faithful."

To bring forward a recent and clear example of what is meant, it has happened quite in consonance with right order and entirely according to the law of Christ, that in the solemn Convention happily entered into between the Holy See and the Kingdom of Italy, also in matrimonial affairs a peaceful settlement and friendly cooperation has been obtained, such as befitted the glorious history of the Italian people and its ancient and sacred traditions. These decrees, are to be found in the Lateran Pact: "The Italian State, desirous of restoring to the institution of matrimony, which is the basis of the family, that dignity conformable to the traditions of its people, assigns as civil effects of the sacrament of matrimony all that is attributed to it in Canon Law." To this fundamental norm are added further clauses in the common pact.

This might well be a striking example to all of how, even in this our own day (in which, sad to say, the absolute separation of the civil power from the Church, and indeed from every religion, is so often taught), the one supreme authority can be united and associated with the other without detriment to the rights and supreme power of either thus protecting Christian parents from pernicious evils and menacing ruin.

All these things which, Venerable Brethren, prompted by Our past solicitude We put before you, We wish according to the norm of Christian prudence to be promulgated widely among all Our beloved children committed to your care as members of the great family of Christ, that all may be thoroughly acquainted with sound teaching concerning marriage, so that they may be ever on their guard against the dangers advocated by the teachers of error, and most of all, that "denying ungodliness and worldly desires, they may live soberly and justly, and godly in this world, looking for the blessed hope and coming of the glory of the great God and Our Savior Jesus Christ."

May the Father, "of whom all paternity in heaven and earth is named," Who strengthens the weak and gives courage to the pusillanimous and fainthearted; and Christ Our Lord and Redeemer, "the Institutor and Perfecter of the holy sacraments," Who desired marriage to be and made it the mystical image of His own ineffable union with the Church; and the Holy Ghost, Love of God, the Light of hearts and the Strength of the mind, grant that all will perceive, will admit with a ready will, and by the grace of God will put into practice, what We by this letter have expounded concerning the holy Sacrament of Matrimony, the wonderful law and will of God respecting it, the errors and impending dangers, and the remedies with which they can be counteracted, so that that fruitfulness dedicated to God will flourish again vigorously in Christian wedlock.

We most humbly pour forth Our earnest prayer at the Throne of His Grace, that God, the Author of all graces, the inspirer of all good desires and deeds, may bring this about, and deign to give it bountifully according to the greatness of His liberality and omnipotence, and as a token of the abundant blessing of the same Omnipotent God, We most lovingly grant to you, Venerable Brethren, and to the clergy and people committed to your watchful care, the Apostolic Benediction.

Given at Rome, in Saint Peter's, this 31st day of December, of the year 1930, the ninth of Our Pontificate.

(1) **Ephesians 3:14** For this reason I bow my knees before the Father. . . . 2367

(2) **Matthew 23:9** And call no man your father on earth, for you have one Father, 2367
who is in heaven.

Paul VI, *Humanae vitae* 12 This particular doctrine, often expounded by the Mag- 2369
isterium of the Church, is based on the inseparable connection, established by God, which man on his own initiative may not break, between the unitive significance and the procreative significance which are both inherent to the marriage act.

The reason is that the marriage act, because of its fundamental structure, while it unites husband and wife in the closest intimacy, also brings into operation laws written into the actual nature of man and of woman for the generation of new life. And if each of these essential qualities, the unitive and the procreative, is preserved, the use of marriage fully retains its sense of true mutual love and its ordination to the supreme responsibility of parenthood to which man is called. We believe that our contemporaries are particularly capable of seeing that this teaching is in harmony with human reason.

2370 ***Humanae vitae* 16** However, as We noted earlier (n. 3), some people today raise the objection against this particular doctrine of the Church concerning the moral laws governing marriage, that human intelligence has both the right and the responsibility to control those forces of irrational nature which come within its ambit and to direct them towards ends beneficial to man. Others ask on the same point whether it is not reasonable in so many cases to use artificial birth control if by so doing the harmony and peace of a family are better served and more suitable conditions are provided for the education of children already born. To this question we must give a clear reply. The Church is the first to praise and commend the application of human intelligence to an activity in which a rational creature such as man is so closely associated with his Creator. But she affirms that this must be done within the limits of the order of reality established by God.

If therefore there are reasonable grounds for spacing births, arising from the physical or psychological condition of husband or wife, or from external circumstances, the Church teaches that then married people may take advantage of the natural cycles immanent in the reproductive system and use their marriage at precisely those times that are infertile, and in this way control birth, a way which does not in the least offend the moral principles which we have just explained.

Neither the Church nor her doctrine is inconsistent when she considers it lawful for married people to take advantage of the infertile period but condemns as always unlawful the use of means which directly exclude conception, even when the reasons given for the latter practice are neither trivial nor immoral. In reality, these two cases are completely different. In the former married couples rightly use a facility provided them by nature. In the latter they obstruct the natural development of the generative process. It cannot be denied that in each case married couples, for acceptable reasons, are both perfectly clear in their intention to avoid children and mean to make sure that none will be born. But it is equally true that it is exclusively in the former case that husband and wife are ready to abstain from intercourse during the fertile period as often as for reasonable motives the birth of another child is not desirable. And when the infertile period recurs, they use their married intimacy to express their mutual love and safeguard their fidelity towards one another. In doing this they certainly give proof of a true and authentic love.

2372 (1) ***Humanae vitae* 23** And so We would like to speak to Rulers of Nations, because to them most of all is committed the responsibility of safeguarding the common good, and they can contribute so much to the preservation of morals. Do not ever allow the morals of your Peoples to be undermined. Do not tolerate any legislation which would introduce into the family practices which are opposed to the natural and divine law—for the family is the primary unit in the State. For there are other ways by which a Government can and should solve the population problem—that is to say by enacting laws which will assist families and by educating the people wisely so that the moral law and the freedom of the citizens are both safeguarded.

We are fully aware of the difficulties confronting the public Authorities in this matter, especially in the developing countries. In fact We had in mind the justifiable anxieties which weigh upon them when We published Our Encyclical Letter, *Populorum Progressio*. But now we join Our voice to that of Our Predecessor, John XXIII of venerable memory, and We make Our own his words: 'no statement of the problem and no solution to it is acceptable which does violence to man's essential dignity, and which is based on an utterly materialistic conception of man himself and his life. The only possible solution to this question is one which envisages the social and economic progress both of individuals and of the whole of human society, and which respects and promotes true human values'. No one can, without grave injustice, make divine Providence responsible for what would appear to be the result of misguided governmental policies, of an insufficient sense of social justice, of a selfish accumulation of material goods, and finally of a culpable failure to undertake those initiatives and responsibilities which would raise the standard of living of peoples and their children. If only all governments which were able would do what some are already doing so nobly, and bestir themselves to renew their efforts and their undertakings! There must be no relaxation in the programs of mutual aid between all the branches of the great human family. Here We believe an almost limitless field lies open for the activities of the great international Institutions.

(2) ***Populorum progressio*** **37** It is true that too frequently an accelerated demographic increase adds its own difficulties to the problems of development: the size of the population increases more rapidly than available resources, and things are found to have reached an apparent impasse. From that moment the temptation is great to check the demographic increase by means of radical measures. It is certain that public authorities can intervene, within the limit of their competence, by favoring the availability of appropriate information and by adopting suitable measures, provided that these be in conformity with the moral law and that they respect the rightful freedom of married couples. Where the inalienable right to marriage and procreation is lacking, human dignity has ceased to exist. Finally, it is for the parents to decide, with full knowledge of the matter, on the number of their children, taking into account their responsibilities toward God, themselves, the children they have already brought into the world and the community to which they belong. In all this they must follow the demands of their own conscience enlightened by God's law authentically interpreted, and sustained by confidence in him. 2372

Gaudium et spes **50, 2** Married couples should regard it as their proper mission to transmit human life and to educate their children; they should realize that they are thereby cooperating with the love of God the Creator and are, in a certain sense, its interpreters. This involves the fulfilment of their role with a sense of human and Christian responsibility and the formation of correct judgments through docile respect for God and common reflection and effort; it also involves a consideration of their own good and the good of their children already born or yet to come, an ability to read the signs of the times and of their own situation on the material and spiritual level, and, finally, an estimation of the good of the family, of society, and of the Church. It is the married couple themselves who must in the last analysis arrive at these judgments before God. Married people should realize that in their behavior they may not simply follow their own fancy but must be ruled by conscience—and conscience ought to be conformed to the law of God in the light of the teaching authority of the Church, which is the authentic interpreter of divine law. For the divine law throws light on the meaning of married love, protects it and leads it to truly human fulfilment. Whenever Christian spouses in a spirit of sacrifice and trust in divine providence carry out their duties of procreation with generous human and 2373

Christian responsibility, they glorify the Creator and perfect themselves in Christ. Among the married couples who thus fulfil their God-given mission, special mention should be made of those who after prudent reflection and common decision courageously undertake the proper upbringing of a large number of children.

2380 (1) **Matthew 5:27–28** "You have heard that it was said, 'You shall not commit adultery.' But I say to you that every one who looks at a woman lustfully has already committed adultery with her in his heart. . . ."

2380 (2) **Matthew 5:32** But I say to you that every one who divorces his wife, except on the ground of unchastity, makes her an adulteress; and whoever marries a divorced woman commits adultery.

2380 (3) **Matthew 19:6** ". . . So they are no longer two but one flesh. What therefore God has joined together, let not man put asunder."

2380 (4) **Mark 10:11** And he said to them, "Whoever divorces his wife and marries another, commits adultery against her. . . ."

2380 (5) **1 Corinthians 6:9–10** Do you not know that the unrighteous will not inherit the kingdom of God? Do not be deceived; neither the immoral, nor idolaters, nor adulterers, nor sexual perverts, nor thieves, nor the greedy, nor drunkards, nor revilers, nor robbers will inherit the kingdom of God.

2380 (6) **Hosea 2:7**

". . . She shall pursue her lovers,
but not overtake them;
and she shall seek them,
but shall not find them.
Then she shall say, 'I will go
and return to my first husband,
for it was better with me then than now.' . . ."

2380 (7) **Jeremiah 5:7**

"How can I pardon you?
Your children have forsaken me,
and have sworn by those who are no gods.
When I fed them to the full,
they committed adultery
and trooped to the houses of harlots. . . ."

2380 (8) **Jeremiah 13:27**

". . . I have seen your abominations,
your adulteries and neighings, your lewd harlotries,
on the hills in the field.
Woe to you, O Jerusalem!
How long will it be
before you are made clean?"

2382 (1) **Matthew 5:31–32** "It was also said, 'Whoever divorces his wife, let him give her a certificate of divorce.' But I say to you that every one who divorces his wife, except on the ground of unchastity, makes her an adulteress, and whoever marries a divorced woman commits adultery. . . ."

(2) **Matthew 19:3–9** And Pharisees came up to him and tested him by asking, "Is it lawful to divorce one's wife for any cause?" He answered, "Have you not read that he who made them from the beginning made them male and female, and said, 'For this reason a man shall leave his father and mother and be joined to his wife, and the two shall become one flesh'? So they are no longer two but one flesh. What therefore God has joined together, let not man put asunder." They said to him, "Why then did Moses command one to give a certificate of divorce, and to put her away?" He said to them, "For your hardness of heart Moses allowed you to divorce your wives, but from the beginning it was not so. And I say to you: whoever divorces his wife, except for unchastity, and marries another, commits adultery." 2382

(3) **Mark 10:9** ". . . What therefore God has joined together, let not man put asunder." 2382

(4) **Luke 16:18** "Every one who divorces his wife and marries another commits adultery, and he who marries a woman divorced from her husband commits adultery. . . ." 2382

(5) **1 Corinthians 7:10–11** To the married I give charge, not I but the Lord, that the wife should not separate from her husband (but if she does, let her remain single or else be reconciled to her husband)—and that the husband should not divorce his wife. 2382

(6) **Matthew 19:7–9** They said to him, "Why then did Moses command one to give a certificate of divorce, and to put her away?" He said to them, "For your hardness of heart Moses allowed you to divorce your wives, but from the beginning it was not so. And I say to you: whoever divorces his wife, except for unchastity, and marries another, commits adultery." 2382

CIC Canons 1151–55 2383

Can. 1151—Spouses have the duty and the right to preserve conjugal living unless a legitimate cause excuses them.

Can. 1152—§1. Although it is earnestly recommended that a spouse, moved by Christian charity and a concern for the good of the family, not refuse pardon to an adulterous partner and not break up conjugal life, nevertheless, if the spouse has not expressly or tacitly condoned the misdeed of the other spouse, the former does have the right to sever conjugal living, unless he or she consented to the adultery, gave cause for it, or likewise committed adultery.

§2. Tacit condonation exists if the innocent spouse, after having become aware of the adultery, continued voluntarily to live with the other spouse in marital affection. Tacit condonation is presumed if the innocent spouse continued conjugal living for a period of six months and has not had recourse to ecclesiastical or civil authority.

§3. If the innocent spouse spontaneously severed conjugal living, that spouse within six months is to bring a suit for separation before the competent ecclesiastical authority; this authority, after having investigated all the circumstances, is to decide whether the innocent spouse can be induced to forgive the misdeed and not to prolong the separation permanently.

Can. 1153—§1. If either of the spouses causes serious danger of spirit or body to the other spouse or to the children, or otherwise renders common life too hard, that spouse gives the other a legitimate cause for separating in virtue of a decree of the local ordinary, or even on his or her own authority if there is danger in delay.

§2. In all cases, when the reason for the separation ceases to exist, conjugal living is to be restored unless ecclesiastical authority decides otherwise.

Can. 1154—After the separation of the spouses, suitable provision is to be made for the adequate support and education of the children.

Can. 1155—The innocent spouse can laudably readmit the other spouse to conjugal life, in which case the former renounces the right to separate.

2386 ***Familiaris consortio* 84** Daily experience unfortunately shows that people who have obtained a divorce usually intend to enter into a new union, obviously not with a Catholic religious ceremony. Since this is an evil that, like the others, is affecting more and more Catholics as well, the problem must be faced with resolution and without delay. The Synod Fathers studied it expressly. The Church, which was set up to lead to salvation all people and especially the baptized, cannot abandon to their own devices those who have been previously bound by sacramental marriage and who have attempted a second marriage. The Church will therefore make untiring efforts to put at their disposal her means of salvation.

Pastors must know that, for the sake of truth, they are obliged to exercise careful discernment of situations. There is in fact a difference between those who have sincerely tried to save their first marriage and have been unjustly abandoned, and those who through their own grave fault have destroyed a canonically valid marriage. Finally, there are those who have entered into a second union for the sake of the children's upbringing, and who are sometimes subjectively certain in conscience that their previous and irreparably destroyed marriage had never been valid.

Together with the Synod, I earnestly call upon pastors and the whole community of the faithful to help the divorced, and with solicitous care to make sure that they do not consider themselves as separated from the Church, for as baptized persons they can, and indeed must, share in her life. They should be encouraged to listen to the word of God, to attend the Sacrifice of the Mass, to persevere in prayer, to contribute to works of charity and to community efforts in favor of justice, to bring up their children in the Christian faith, to cultivate the spirit and practice of penance and thus implore, day by day, God's grace. Let the Church pray for them, encourage them and show herself a merciful mother, and thus sustain them in faith and hope.

However, the Church reaffirms her practice, which is based upon Sacred Scripture, of not admitting to Eucharistic Communion divorced persons who have remarried. They are unable to be admitted thereto from the act that their state and condition of life objectively contradict that union of love between Christ and the Church which is signified and effected by the Eucharist. Besides this, there is another special pastoral reason: if these people were admitted to the Eucharist, the faithful would be led into error and confusion regarding the Church's teaching about the indissolubility of marriage.

Reconciliation in the sacrament of Penance, which would open the way to the Eucharist, can only be granted to those who, repenting of having broken the sign of the Covenant and of fidelity to Christ, are sincerely ready to undertake a way of life that is no longer in contradiction to the indissolubility of marriage. This means, in practice, that when, for serious reasons such as for example the children's upbringing, a man and a woman cannot satisfy the obligation to separate, they "take on themselves the duty to live in complete continence, that is, by abstinence from the acts proper to married couples."

Similarly, the respect due to the sacrament of Matrimony, to the couples themselves and their families, and also to the community of the faithful, forbids any pastor, for whatever reason or pretext even of a pastoral nature, to perform ceremonies of any kind for divorced people who remarry. Such ceremonies would give the impression of the celebration of a new sacramentally valid marriage, and would thus lead people into error concerning the indissolubility of a validly contracted marriage.

By acting in this way, the Church professes her own fidelity to Christ and to his truth. At the same time she shows motherly concern for these children of hers, especially those who, through no fault of their own, have been abandoned by their legitimate partner.

With firm confidence she believes that those who have rejected the Lord's command and are still living in this state will be able to obtain from God the grace of conversion and salvation, provided that they have persevered in prayer, penance and charity.

***Gaudium et spes* 47, 2** However, this happy picture of the dignity of these partnerships is not reflected everywhere, but is overshadowed by polygamy, the plague of divorce, so-called free love, and similar blemishes; furthermore, married love is too often dishonored by selfishness, hedonism, and unlawful contraceptive practices. Besides, the economic, social, psychological, and civil climate of today has a severely disturbing effect on family life. There are also the serious and alarming problems arising in many parts of the world as a result of population expansion. On all of these counts an anguish of conscience is being generated. And yet the strength and vigor of the institution of marriage and family shines forth time and again: for despite the hardships flowing from the profoundly changing conditions of society today, the true nature of marriage and of the family is revealed in one way or another. 2387

Leviticus 18:7–20 ". . . You shall not uncover the nakedness of your father, which is the nakedness of your mother; she is your mother, you shall not uncover her nakedness. You shall not uncover the nakedness of your father's wife; it is your father's nakedness. You shall not uncover the nakedness of your sister, the daughter of your father or the daughter of your mother, whether born at home or born abroad. You shall not uncover the nakedness of your son's daughter or of your daughter's daughter, for their nakedness is your own nakedness. You shall not uncover the nakedness of your father's wife's daughter, begotten by your father, since she is your sister. You shall not uncover the nakedness of your father's sister; she is your father's near kinswoman. You shall not uncover the nakedness of your mother's sister, for she is your mother's near kinswoman. You shall not uncover the nakedness of your father's brother, that is, you shall not approach his wife; she is your aunt. You shall not uncover the nakedness of your daughter-in-law; she is your son's wife, you shall not uncover her nakedness. You shall not uncover the nakedness of your brother's wife; she is your brother's nakedness. You shall not uncover the nakedness of a woman and of her daughter, and you shall not take her son's daughter or her daughter's daughter to uncover her nakedness; they are your near kinswomen; it is wickedness. And you shall not take a woman as a rival wife to her sister, uncovering her nakedness while her sister is yet alive. 2388

"You shall not approach a woman to uncover her nakedness while she is in her menstrual uncleanness. And you shall not lie carnally with your neighbor's wife, and defile yourself with her. . . ."

***Familiaris consortio* 81** *De facto free unions.* This means unions without any publicly recognized institutional bond, either civil or religious. This phenomenon, which is becoming ever more frequent, cannot fail to concern pastors of souls, also because it may be based on widely varying factors, the consequences of which may perhaps be containable by suitable action. 2390

Some people consider themselves almost forced into a free union by difficult economic, cultural or religious situations, on the grounds that, if they contracted a regular marriage, they would be exposed to some form of harm, would lose economic advantages, would be discriminated against, etc. In other cases, however, one encounters people who scorn, rebel against or reject society, the institution of the family and the social and political order, or who are solely seeking pleasure. Then there are those who are driven to such situations by extreme ignorance or poverty, sometimes by a conditioning due to situations of real injustice, or by a certain psychological immaturity that makes them uncertain or afraid to enter into a stable and definitive union. In some countries, traditional customs presume that the true and proper marriage will take place only after a period of cohabitation and the birth of the first child.

Each of these elements presents the Church with arduous pastoral problems, by reason of the serious consequences deriving from them, both religious and moral (the loss of the religious sense of marriage seen in the light of the Covenant of God with his people; deprivation of the grace of the sacrament; grave scandal), and also social consequences (the destruction of the concept of the family; the weakening of the sense of fidelity, also towards society; possible psychological damage to the children; the strengthening of selfishness).

The pastors and the ecclesial community should take care to become acquainted with such situations and their actual causes, case by case. They should make tactful and respectful contact with the couples concerned, and enlighten them patiently, correct them charitably and show them the witness of Christian family life, in such a way as to smooth the path for them to regularize their situation. But above all there must be a campaign of prevention, by fostering the sense of fidelity in the whole moral and religious training of the young, instructing them concerning the conditions and structures that favor such fidelity, without which there is no true freedom; they must be helped to reach spiritual maturity and enabled to understand the rich human and supernatural reality of marriage as a sacrament.

The People of God should also make approaches to the public authorities, in order that the latter may resist these tendencies which divide society and are harmful to the dignity, security and welfare of the citizens as individuals, and they must try to ensure that public opinion is not led to undervalue the institutional importance of marriage and the family. And since in many regions young people are unable to get married properly because of extreme poverty deriving from unjust or inadequate social and economic structures, society and the public authorities should favor legitimate marriage by means of a series of social and political actions which will guarantee a family wage, by issuing directives ensuring housing fitting for family life and by creating opportunities for work and life.

2391 *Familiaris consortio* 80 A first example of an irregular situation is provided by what are called "trial marriages", which many people today would like to justify by attributing a certain value to them. But human reason leads one to see that they are unacceptable, by showing the unconvincing nature of carrying out an "experiment" with human beings, whose dignity demands that they should be always and solely the term of a self-giving love without limitations of time or of any other circumstance.

The Church, for her part, cannot admit such a kind of union, for further and original reasons which derive from faith. For, in the first place, the gift of the body in the sexual relationship is a real symbol of the giving of the whole person: such a giving, moreover, in the present state of things cannot take place with full truth without the concourse of the love of charity, given by Christ. In the second place, marriage between two baptized persons is a real symbol of the union of Christ and the Church, which is not a temporary or "trial" union but one which is eternally faithful. Therefore between two baptized persons there can exist only an indissoluble marriage.

Such a situation cannot usually be overcome unless the human person, from childhood, with the help of Christ's grace and without fear, has been trained to dominate concupiscence from the beginning and to establish relationships of genuine love with other people. This cannot be secured without a true education in genuine love and in the right use of sexuality, such as to introduce the human person in every aspect, and therefore the bodily aspect too, into the fullness of the mystery of Christ.

It will be very useful to investigate the causes of this phenomenon, including its psychological and sociological aspect, in order to find the proper remedy.

Genesis 1:26–29 Then God said, "Let us make man in our image, after our likeness; and let them have dominion over the fish of the sea, and over the birds of the air, and over the cattle, and over all the earth, and over every creeping thing that creeps upon the earth." So God created man in his own image, in the image of God he created him; male and female he created them. And God blessed them, and God said to them, "Be fruitful and multiply, and fill the earth and subdue it; and have dominion over the fish of the sea and over the birds of the air and over every living thing that moves upon the earth." And God said, "Behold, I have given you every plant yielding seed which is upon the face of all the earth, and every tree with seed in its fruit; you shall have them for food. . . ." 2402

(1) ***Gaudium et spes* 71, 4** In several economically retarded areas there exist large and sometimes very extensive rural estates which are only slightly cultivated or not cultivated at all for the sake of profit, while the majority of the population have no land or possess only very small holdings and the need to increase agricultural production is pressing and evident to all. Not infrequently those who are hired as laborers or who till a portion of the land as tenants receive a wage or income unworthy of the human being; they are deprived of decent living conditions and are exploited by middlemen. They lack all sense of security and live in such a state of personal dependence that almost all chance of exercising initiative and responsibility is closed to them and they are denied any cultural advancement or participation in social and political life. Reforms are called for in these different situations: incomes must be raised, working conditions improved, security in employment assured, and personal incentives to work encouraged; estates insufficiently cultivated must even be divided up and given to those who will be able to make them productive. In this event the necessary resources and equipment must be supplied, especially educational facilities and proper cooperative organizations. However, when the common good calls for expropriation, compensation must be made and is to be calculated according to equity, with all circumstances taken into account. 2406

(2) ***Sollicitudo rei socialis* 42** Today more than in the past, the Church's social doctrine must be open to an *international outlook*, in line with the Second Vatican Council, the most recent Encyclicals, and particularly in line with the Encyclical which we are commemorating. It will not be superfluous therefore to reexamine and further clarify in this light the characteristic themes and guidelines dealt with by the Magisterium in recent years. 2406

Here I would like to indicate one of them: the *option* or *love of preference* for the poor. This is an option, or a *special form* of primacy in the exercise of Christian charity, to which the whole tradition of the Church bears witness. It affects the life of each Christian inasmuch as he or she seeks to imitate the life of Christ, but it applies equally to our *social responsibilities* and hence to our manner of living, and to the logical decisions to be made concerning the ownership and use of goods.

Today, furthermore, given the worldwide dimension which the social question has assumed, this love of preference for the poor, and the decisions which it inspires in us, cannot but embrace the immense multitudes of the hungry, the needy, the homeless, those without medical care and, above all, those without hope of a better future. It is impossible not to take account of the existence of these realities. To ignore them would mean becoming like the "rich man" who pretended not to know the beggar Lazarus lying at his gate (cf. Lk 16:19–31).

Our *daily life* as well as our decisions in the political and economic fields must be marked by these realities. Likewise the *leaders* of nations and the heads of *international bodies*, while they are obliged always to keep in mind the true human dimension as a priority in their development plans, should not forget to give precedence to the phenomenon of growing poverty. Unfortunately, instead of becoming fewer the poor are becoming more numerous, not only in less developed countries but—and this seems no less scandalous—in the more developed ones too.

It is necessary to state once more the characteristic principle of Christian social doctrine: the goods of this world are *originally meant for all.* The right to private property is *valid and necessary*, but it does not nullify the value of this principle. Private property, in fact, is under a "social mortgage," which means that it has an intrinsically social function, based upon and justified precisely by the principle of the universal destination of goods. Likewise, in this concern for the poor, one must not overlook that *special form of poverty* which consists in being deprived of fundamental human rights, in particular the right to religious freedom and also the right to freedom of economic initiative.

2406 (3) ***Centesimus annus* 40** It is the task of the State to provide for the defense and preservation of common goods such as the natural and human environments, which cannot be safeguarded simply by market forces. Just as in the time of primitive capitalism the State had the duty of defending the basic rights of workers, so now, with the new capitalism, the State and all of society have the duty of *defending those collective goods* which, among others, constitute the essential framework for the legitimate pursuit of personal goals on the part of each individual.

Here we find a new limit on the market: there are collective and qualitative needs which cannot be satisfied by market mechanisms. There are important human needs which escape its logic. There are goods which by their very nature cannot and must not be bought or sold. Certainly the mechanisms of the market offer secure advantages: they help to utilize resources better; they promote the exchange of products; above all they give central place to the person's desires and preferences, which, in a contract, meet the desires and preferences of another person. Nevertheless, these mechanisms carry the risk of an "idolatry" of the market, an idolatry which ignores the existence of goods which by their nature are not and cannot be mere commodities.

2406 (4) ***Centesimus annus* 48** These general observations also apply to the *role of the State in the economic sector.* Economic activity, especially the activity of a market economy, cannot be conducted in an institutional, juridical or political vacuum. On the contrary, it presupposes sure guarantees of individual freedom and private property, as well as a stable currency and efficient public services. Hence the principal task of the State is to guarantee this security, so that those who work and produce can enjoy the fruits of their labors and thus feel encouraged to work efficiently and honestly. The absence of stability, together with the corruption of public officials and the spread of improper sources of growing rich and of easy profits deriving from illegal or purely speculative activities, constitutes one of the chief obstacles to development and to the economic order.

Another task of the State is that of overseeing and directing the exercise of human rights in the economic sector. However, primary responsibility in this area belongs not to the State but to individuals and to the various groups and associations which make up society. The State could not directly ensure the right to work for all its citizens unless it controlled every aspect of economic life and restricted the free initiative of individuals. This does not mean, however, that the State has no competence in this domain, as was claimed by those who argued against any rules in the economic sphere. Rather, the State has a duty to sustain business activities by creating conditions which will ensure job opportunities, by stimulating those activities where they are lacking or by supporting them in moments of crisis.

The State has the further right to intervene when particular monopolies create delays or obstacles to development. In addition to the tasks of harmonizing and guiding development, in exceptional circumstances the State can also exercise a *substitute function*, when social sectors or business systems are too weak or are just getting under way, and are not equal to the task at hand. Such supplementary interventions, which are justified by urgent reasons touching the common good, must be as brief as possible, so as to avoid removing permanently from society and business systems the functions which are properly theirs, and so as to avoid enlarging excessively the sphere of state intervention to the detriment of both economic and civil freedom.

In recent years the range of such intervention has vastly expanded, to the point of creating a new type of state, the so-called "Welfare State." This has happened in some countries in order to respond better to many needs and demands, by remedying forms of poverty and deprivation unworthy of the human person. However, excesses and abuses, especially in recent years, have provoked very harsh criticisms of the Welfare State, dubbed the "Social Assistance State." Malfunctions and defects in the Social Assistance State are the result of an inadequate understanding of the tasks proper to the State. Here again *the principle of subsidiarity* must be respected: a community of a higher order should not interfere in the internal life of a community of a lower order, depriving the latter of its functions, but rather should support it in case of need and help to coordinate its activity with the activities of the rest of society, always with a view to the common good.

By intervening directly and depriving society of its responsibility, the Social Assistance State leads to a loss of human energies and an inordinate increase of public agencies, which are dominated more by bureaucratic ways of thinking than by concern for serving their clients, and which are accompanied by an enormous increase in spending. In fact, it would appear that needs are best understood and satisfied by people who are closest to them and who act as neighbors to those in need. It should be added that certain kinds of demands often call for a response which is not simply material but which is capable of perceiving the deeper human need. One thinks of the condition of refugees, immigrants, the elderly, the sick, and all those in circumstances which call for assistance, such as drug abusers: all these people can be helped effectively only by those who offer them genuine fraternal support, in addition to the necessary care.

***Gaudium et spes* 69, 1** God destined the earth and all it contains for all men and 2408
all peoples so that all created things would be shared fairly by all mankind under the guidance of justice tempered by charity. No matter what the structures of property are in different peoples, according to various and changing circumstances and adapted to their lawful institutions, we must never lose sight of this universal destination of earthly goods. In his use of things man should regard the external goods he legitimately owns not merely as exclusive to himself but common to others also, in the sense that they can benefit others as well as himself. Therefore every man has the

right to possess a sufficient amount of the earth's goods for himself and his family. This has been the opinion of the Fathers and Doctors of the Church, who taught that men are bound to come to the aid of the poor and to do so not merely out of their superfluous goods. When a person is in extreme necessity he has the right to supply himself with what he needs out of the riches of others. Faced with a world today where so many people are suffering from want, the Council asks individuals and governments to remember the saying of the Fathers: "Feed the man dying of hunger, because if you do not feed him you are killing him," and it urges them according to their ability to share and dispose of their goods to help others, above all by giving them aid which will enable them to help and develop themselves.

2409 (1) **Deuteronomy 25:13–16** "You shall not have in your bag two kinds of weights, a large and a small. You shall not have in your house two kinds of measures, a large and a small. A full and just weight you shall have, a full and just measure you shall have; that your days may be prolonged in the land which the Lord your God gives you. For all who do such things, all who act dishonestly, are an abomination to the Lord your God. . . ."

2409 (2) **Deuteronomy 24:14–15** "You shall not oppress a hired servant who is poor and needy, whether he is one of your brethren or one of the sojourners who are in your land within your towns; you shall give him his hire on the day he earns it, before the sun goes down (for he is poor, and sets his heart upon it); lest he cry against you to the Lord, and it be sin in you. . . ."

2409 (3) **James 5:4** Behold, the wages of the laborers who mowed your fields, which you kept back by fraud, cry out; and the cries of the harvesters have reached the ears of the Lord of Hosts.

2409 (4) **Amos 8:4–6**

Hear this, you who trample upon the needy,
  and bring the poor of the land to an end,
saying, "When will the new moon be over,
  that we may sell grain?
And the sabbath,
  that we may offer wheat for sale,
that we may make the ephah small and the shekel great,
  and deal deceitfully with false balances,
that we may buy the poor for silver
  and the needy for a pair of sandals,
  and sell the refuse of the wheat?"

2415 (1) **Genesis 1:28–31** And God blessed them, and God said to them, "Be fruitful and multiply, and fill the earth and subdue it; and have dominion over the fish of the sea and over the birds of the air and over every living thing that moves upon the earth." And God said, "Behold, I have given you every plant yielding seed which is upon the face of all the earth, and every tree with seed in its fruit; you shall have them for food. And to every beast of the earth, and to every bird of the air, and to everything that creeps on the earth, everything that has the breath of life, I have given every green plant for food." And it was so. And God saw everything that he had made, and behold, it was very good. And there was evening and there was morning, a sixth day.

(2) ***Centesimus annus* 37–38** Equally worrying is *the ecological question* which accompanies the problem of consumerism and which is closely connected to it. In his desire to have and to enjoy rather than to be and to grow, man consumes the resources of the earth and his own life in an excessive and disordered way. At the root of the senseless destruction of the natural environment lies an anthropological error, which unfortunately is widespread in our day. Man, who discovers his capacity to transform and in a certain sense create the world through his own work, forgets that this is always based on God's prior and original gift of the things that are. Man thinks that he can make arbitrary use of the earth, subjecting it without restraint to his will, as though it did not have its own requisites and a prior God-given purpose, which man can indeed develop but must not betray. Instead of carrying out his role as a cooperator with God in the work of creation, man sets himself up in the place of God and thus ends up provoking a rebellion on the part of nature, which is more tyrannized than governed by him. 2415

In all this, one notes first the poverty or narrowness of man's outlook, motivated as he is by a desire to possess things rather than to relate them to the truth, and lacking that disinterested, unselfish and aesthetic attitude that is born of wonder in the presence of being and of the beauty which enables one to see in visible things the message of the invisible God who created them. In this regard, humanity today must be conscious of its duties and obligations towards future generations.

In addition to the irrational destruction of the natural environment, we must also mention the more serious destruction of the *human environment*, something which is by no means receiving the attention it deserves. Although people are rightly worried—though much less than they should be—about preserving the natural habitats of the various animal species threatened with extinction, because they realize that each of these species makes its particular contribution to the balance of nature in general, too little effort is made to *safeguard the moral conditions for an authentic "human ecology."* Not only has God given the earth to man, who must use it with respect for the original good purpose for which it was given to him, but man too is God's gift to man. He must therefore respect the natural and moral structure with which he has been endowed. In this context, mention should be made of the serious problems of modern urbanization, of the need for urban planning which is concerned with how people are to live, and of the attention which should be given to a "social ecology" of work.

Man receives from God his essential dignity and with it the capacity to transcend every social order so as to move towards truth and goodness. But he is also conditioned by the social structure in which he lives, by the education he has received and by his environment. These elements can either help or hinder his living in accordance with the truth. The decisions which create a human environment can give rise to specific structures of sin which impede the full realization of those who are in any way oppressed by them. To destroy such structures and replace them with more authentic forms of living in community is a task which demands courage and patience.

(1) **Matthew 6:26** Look at the birds of the air: they neither sow nor reap nor gather into barns, and yet your heavenly Father feeds them. Are you not of more value than they? 2416

(2) **Daniel 3:79–81 (Song of the Three Young Men, 57–59: RSV)** 2416

Bless the Lord, you whales and all creatures that move in the waters,
sing praise to him and highly exalt him for ever.
Bless the Lord, all birds of the air,
sing praise to him and highly exalt him for ever.

Bless the Lord, all beasts and cattle,
sing praise to him and highly exalt him for ever.

2417 (1) **Genesis 2:19–20** So out of the ground the Lord God formed every beast of the field and every bird of the air, and brought them to the man to see what he would call them; and whatever the man called every living creature, that was its name. The man gave names to all cattle, and to the birds of the air, and to every beast of the field; but for the man there was not found a helper fit for him.

2417 (2) **Genesis 9:1–4** And God blessed Noah and his sons, and said to them, "Be fruitful and multiply, and fill the earth. The fear of you and the dread of you shall be upon every beast of the earth, and upon every bird of the air, upon everything that creeps on the ground and all the fish of the sea; into your hand they are delivered. Every moving thing that lives shall be food for you; and as I gave you the green plants, I give you everything. Only you shall not eat flesh with its life, that is, its blood.

2421 ***Centesimus annus* 3:** see 1896 (1).

2422 (1) ***Sollicitudo rei socialis* 1** The social concern of the Church, directed towards an authentic development of man and society which would respect and promote all the dimensions of the human person, has always expressed itself in the most varied ways. In recent years, one of the special means of intervention has been the Magisterium of the Roman Pontiffs which, beginning with the Encyclical *Rerum Novarum* of Leo XIII as a point of reference, has frequently dealt with the question and has sometimes made the dates of publication of the various social documents coincide with the anniversaries of that first document.

The Popes have not failed to throw fresh light by means of those messages upon new aspects of the social doctrine of the Church. As a result, this doctrine, beginning with the outstanding contribution of Leo XIII and enriched by the successive contributions of the Magisterium, has now become an updated doctrinal "corpus." It builds up gradually, as the Church, in the fullness of the word revealed by Christ Jesus and with the assistance of the Holy Spirit (cf. Jn 14:16, 26; 16:13–15), reads events as they unfold in the course of history. She thus seeks to lead people to respond, with the support also of rational reflection and of the human sciences, to their vocation as responsible builders of earthly society.

2422 (2) ***Sollicitudo rei socialis* 41** The Church does not have *technical solutions* to offer for the problem of underdevelopment as such, as Pope Paul VI already affirmed in his Encyclical. For the Church does not propose economic and political systems or programs, nor does she show preference for one or the other, provided that human dignity is properly respected and promoted, and provided she herself is allowed the room she needs to exercise her ministry in the world.

But the Church is an "expert in humanity," and this leads her necessarily to extend her religious mission to the various fields in which men and women expend their efforts in search of the always relative happiness which is possible in this world, in line with their dignity as persons.

Following the example of my predecessors, I must repeat that whatever affects the dignity of individuals and peoples, such as authentic development, cannot be reduced to a "technical" problem. If reduced in this way, development would be emptied of its true content, and this would be an act of *betrayal* of the individuals and peoples whom development is meant to serve.

This is why the Church has *something to say* today, just as twenty years ago, and also in the future, about the nature, conditions, requirements and aims of authentic development, and also about the obstacles which stand in its way. In doing so the Church fulfills her mission to evangelize, for she offers her first contribution to the solution of the urgent problem of development when she proclaims the truth about Christ, about herself and about man, applying this truth to a concrete situation.

As her *instrument* for reaching this goal, the Church uses her *social doctrine.* In today's difficult situation, a *more exact awareness and a wider diffusion* of the "set of principles for reflection, criteria for judgment and directives for action" proposed by the Church's teaching would be of great help in promoting both the correct definition of the problems being faced and the best solution to them.

It will thus be seen at once that the questions facing us are above all moral questions; and that neither the analysis of the problem of development as such nor the means to overcome the present difficulties can ignore this essential dimension.

The Church's social doctrine is *not* a "third way" between *liberal capitalism* and *Marxist collectivism,* nor even a possible alternative to other solutions less radically opposed to one another: rather, it constitutes a *category of its own.* Nor is it an *ideology,* but rather the *accurate formulation* of the results of a careful reflection on the complex realities of human existence, in society and in the international order, in the light of faith and of the Church's tradition. Its main aim is to *interpret* these realities, determining their conformity with or divergence from the lines of the Gospel teaching on man and his vocation, a vocation which is at once earthly and transcendent; its aim is thus *to guide* Christian behavior. It therefore belongs to the field, not of *ideology,* but of *theology* and particularly of moral theology.

The teaching and spreading of her social doctrine are part of the Church's evangelizing mission. And since it is a doctrine aimed at guiding *people's behavior,* it consequently gives rise to a "commitment to justice," according to each individual's role, vocation and circumstances.

The *condemnation* of evils and injustices is also part of that *ministry of evangelization* in the social field which is an aspect of the Church's *prophetic role.* But it should be made clear that *proclamation* is always more important than *condemnation,* and the latter cannot ignore the former, which gives it true solidity and the force of higher motivation.

***Centesimus annus* 24** The second factor in the crisis was certainly the inefficiency 2423
of the economic system, which is not to be considered simply as a technical problem, but rather a consequence of the violation of the human rights to private initiative, to ownership of property and to freedom in the economic sector. To this must be added the cultural and national dimension: it is not possible to understand man on the basis of economics alone, nor to define him simply on the basis of class membership. Man is understood in a more complete way when situated within the sphere of culture through his language, history, and the position he takes towards the fundamental events of life, such as birth, love, work and death. At the heart of every culture lies the attitude man takes to the greatest mystery: the mystery of God. Different cultures are basically different ways of facing the question of the meaning of personal existence. When this question is eliminated, the culture and moral life of nations are corrupted. For this reason the struggle to defend work was spontaneously linked to the struggle for culture and for national rights.

But the true cause of the new developments was the spiritual void brought about by atheism, which deprived the younger generations of a sense of direction and in many cases led them, in the irrepressible search for personal identity and for the meaning of life, to rediscover the religious roots of their national cultures, and to rediscover the person of Christ himself as the existentially adequate response to the desire in every human heart for goodness, truth and life. This search was supported by the witness of those who, in difficult circumstances and under persecution, remained faithful to God. Marxism had promised to uproot the need for God from the human heart, but the results have shown that it is not possible to succeed in this without throwing the heart into turmoil.

2424 (1) ***Gaudium et spes* 63, 3** But the picture is not without its disturbing elements. Many people, especially in economically advanced areas, seem to be dominated by economics; almost all of their personal and social lives are permeated with a kind of economic mentality, and this is true of nations that favor a collective economy as well as of other nations. At the very same time when economic progress (provided it is directed and organized in a reasonable and human way) could do so much to reduce social inequalities, it serves all too often only to aggravate them; in some places it even leads to a decline in the position of the underprivileged and contempt for the poor. In the midst of huge numbers deprived of the absolute necessities of life there are some who live in riches and squander their wealth; and this happens in less developed areas as well. Luxury and misery exist side by side. While a few individuals enjoy an almost unlimited opportunity to choose for themselves, the vast majority have no chance whatever of exercising personal initiative and responsibility, and quite often have to live and work in conditions unworthy of human beings.

2424 (2) ***Laborem exercens* 7** It is precisely these fundamental affirmations about work that always emerged from the wealth of Christian truth, especially from the very message of the "Gospel of work," thus creating the basis for a new way of thinking, judging and acting. In the modern period, from the beginning of the industrial age, the Christian truth about work had to oppose the various trends of *materialistic and economistic* thought.

For certain supporters of such ideas, work was understood and treated as a sort of "merchandise" that the worker—especially the industrial worker—sells to the employer, who at the same time is the possessor of the capital, that is to say, of all the working tools and means that make production possible. This way of looking at work was widespread especially in the first half of the nineteenth century. Since then, explicit expressions of this sort have almost disappeared, and have given way to more human ways of thinking about work and evaluating it. The interaction between the worker and the tools and means of production has given rise to the development of various forms of capitalism—parallel with various forms of collectivism —into which other socioeconomic elements have entered as a consequence of new concrete circumstances, of the activity of worker's associations and public authorities, and of the emergence of large transnational enterprises. Nevertheless, the *danger* of treating work as a special kind of "merchandise," or as an impersonal "force" needed for production (the expression "work force" is, in fact, in common use) *always exists,* especially when the whole way of looking at the question of economics is marked by the premises of materialistic economism.

A systematic opportunity for thinking and evaluating in this way, and in a certain sense a stimulus for doing so, is provided by the quickening process of the development of a onesidedly materialistic civilization, which gives prime importance to the objective dimension of work, while the subjective dimension—everything in direct or indirect relationship with the subject of work—remains on a secondary level. In all cases of this sort, in every social situation of this type, there is a confusion or even a reversal of the order laid down from the beginning by the words of the book of Genesis: Man is treated as an instrument of production, whereas he—he alone, independently of the work he does—ought to be treated as the effective subject of work and its true maker and creator. Precisely this reversal of order, whatever the program or name under which it occurs, should rightly be called "capitalism"—in the sense more fully explained below. Everybody knows that capitalism has a definite historical meaning as a system, an economic and social system, opposed to "socialism" or "communism." But in the light of the analysis of the fundamental reality of the whole economic process—first and foremost of the production structure that work is —it should be recognized that the error of early capitalism can be repeated wherever man is in a way treated on the same level as the whole complex of the material means of production, as an instrument and not in accordance with the true dignity of his work—that is to say, where he is not treated as subject and maker, and for this very reason as the true purpose of the whole process of production.

This explains why the analysis of human work in the light of the words concerning man's "dominion" over the earth goes to the very heart of the ethical and social question. This concept should also find *a central place* in the whole *sphere of social and economic policy*, both within individual countries and in the wider field of international and intercontinental relationships, particularly with reference to the tensions making themselves felt in the world not only between East and West but also between North and South. Both John XXIII in the Encyclical *Mater et magistra* and Paul VI in the Encyclical *Populorum progressio* gave special attention to these dimensions of the modern ethical and social question.

(3) ***Laborem exercens* 20** All these rights, together with the need for the workers 2424
themselves to secure them, give rise to yet another right: *the right of association*, that is to form associations for the purpose of defending the vital interests of those employed in the various professions. These associations are called *labor or trade unions*. The vital interests of the workers are to a certain extent common for all of them; at the same time however each type of work, each profession, has its own specific character which should find a particular reflection in these organizations.

In a sense, unions go back to the medieval guilds of artisans, insofar as those organizations brought together people belonging to the same craft and thus *on the basis of their work*. However, unions differ from the guilds on this essential point: the modern unions grew up from the struggle of the workers—workers in general but especially the industrial workers—to protect their *just rights* vis-a-vis the entrepreneurs and the owners of the means of production. Their task is to defend the existential interests of workers in all sectors in which their rights are concerned. The experience of history teaches that organizations of this type are an indispensable *element of social life*, especially in modern industrialized societies. Obviously, this does not mean that only industrial workers can set up associations of this type. Representatives of every profession can use them to ensure their own rights. Thus there are unions of agricultural workers and of white-collar workers; there are also employers' associations. All, as has been said above, are further divided into groups or subgroups according to particular professional specializations.

Catholic social teaching does not hold that unions are no more than a reflection of the "class" structure of society and that they are a mouthpiece for a class struggle which inevitably governs social life. They are indeed *a mouthpiece for the struggle for social justice*, for the just rights of working people in accordance with their individual professions. However, this struggle should be seen as a normal endeavor "for" the just good: in the present case, for the good which corresponds to the needs and merits of working people associated by profession; but it *is not a struggle "against" others*. Even if in controversial questions the struggle takes on a character of opposition towards others, this is because it aims at the good of social justice, not for the sake of "struggle" or in order to eliminate the opponent. It is characteristic of work that it first and foremost unites people. In this consists its social power: the power to build a community. In the final analysis, both those who work and those who manage the means of production or who own them must in some way be united in this community. *In the light of this fundamental structure* of all work—in the light of the fact that, in the final analysis, labor and capital are indispensable components of the process of production in any social system—it is clear that, even if it is because of their work needs that people unite to secure their rights, their union remains a constructive factor of *social order* and *solidarity*, and it is impossible to ignore it.

Just efforts to secure the rights of workers who are united by the same profession should always take into account the limitations imposed by the general economic situation of the country. Union demands cannot be turned into a kind of *group or class "egoism,"* although they can and should also aim at correcting—with a view to the common good of the whole of society—everything defective in the system of ownership of the means of production or in the way these are managed. Social and socioeconomic life is certainly like a system of "connected vessels," and every social activity directed towards safeguarding the rights of particular groups should adapt itself to this system.

In this sense, union activity undoubtedly enters the field of *politics*, understood as *prudent concern for the common good.* However, the role of unions is not to "play politics" in the sense that the expression is commonly understood today. Unions do not have the character of political parties struggling for power; they should not be subjected to the decision of political parties or have too close links with them. In fact, in such a situation they easily lose contact with their specific role, which is to secure the just rights of workers within the framework of the common good of the whole of society; instead they become *an instrument used for other purposes.*

Speaking of the protection of the just rights of workers according to their individual professions, we must of course always keep in mind that which determines the subjective character of work in each profession, but at the same time, indeed before all else, we must keep in mind that which conditions the specific dignity of the subject of the work. The activity of union organizations opens up many possibilities in this respect, including their *efforts to instruct and educate* the workers and to *foster their self-education.* Praise is due to the work of the schools, what are known as workers' or people's universities and the training programs and courses which have developed and are still developing this field of activity. It is always to be hoped that, thanks to the work of their unions, workers will not only *have* more, but above all *be* more; in other words, that they will realize their humanity more fully in every respect.

One method used by unions in pursuing the just rights of their members is *the strike* or work stoppage, as a kind of ultimatum to the competent bodies, especially the employers. This method is recognized by Catholic social teaching as legitimate in the proper conditions and within just limits. In this connection workers should be assured the *right to strike*, without being subjected to personal penal sanctions for taking part in a strike. While admitting that it is a legitimate means, we must at the same time emphasize that a strike remains, in a sense, an extreme means. *It must not be abused;* it must not be abused especially for "political" purposes. Furthermore it must never be forgotten that, when essential community services are in question, they must in every sense be ensured, if necessary by means of appropriate legislation. Abuse of the strike weapon can lead to the paralysis of the whole of socioeconomic life, and this is contrary to the requirements of the common good of society, which also corresponds to the properly understood nature of work itself.

(4) ***Centesimus annus* 35** Here we find a wide range of *opportunities for commitment and effort* in the name of justice on the part of trade unions and other workers' organizations. These defend workers' rights and protect their interests as persons, while fulfilling a vital cultural role, so as to enable workers to participate more fully and honorably in the life of their nation and to assist them along the path of development. 2424

In this sense, it is right to speak of a struggle against an economic system, if the latter is understood as a method of upholding the absolute predominance of capital, the possession of the means of production and of the land, in contrast to the free and personal nature of human work. In the struggle against such a system, what is being proposed as an alternative is not the socialist system, which in fact turns out to be state capitalism, but rather *a society of free work, of enterprise and of participation*. Such a society is not directed against the market, but demands that the market be appropriately controlled by the forces of society and by the State, so as to guarantee that the basic needs of the whole of society are satisfied.

The Church acknowledges the legitimate *role of profit* as an indication that a business is functioning well. When a firm makes a profit, this means that productive factors have been properly employed and corresponding human needs have been duly satisfied. But profitability is not the only indicator of a firm's condition. It is possible for the financial accounts to be in order, and yet for the people—who make up the firm's most valuable asset—to be humiliated and their dignity offended. Besides being morally inadmissible, this will eventually have negative repercussions on the firm's economic efficiency. In fact, the purpose of a business firm is not simply to make a profit, but is to be found in its very existence as a *community of persons* who in various ways are endeavoring to satisfy their basic needs, and who form a particular group at the service of the whole of society. Profit is a regulator of the life of a business, but it is not the only one; *other human and moral factors* must be considered which, in the long term, are at least equally important for the life of a business.

We have seen that it is unacceptable to say that the defeat of so-called "Real Socialism" leaves capitalism as the only model of economic organization. It is necessary to break down the barriers and monopolies which leave so many countries on the margins of development, and to provide all individuals and nations with the basic conditions which well enable them to share in development. This goal calls for programmed and responsible efforts on the part of the entire international community. Stronger nations must offer weaker ones opportunities for taking their place in international life, and the latter must learn how to use these opportunities by making the necessary efforts and sacrifices and by ensuring political and economic stability, the certainty of better prospects for the future, the improvement of workers' skills, and the training of competent business leaders who are conscious of their responsibilities.

At present, the positive efforts which have been made along these lines are being affected by the still largely unsolved problem of the foreign debt of the poorer countries. The principle that debts must be paid is certainly just. However, it is not right to demand or expect payment when the effect would be the imposition of political choices leading to hunger and despair for entire peoples. It cannot be expected that the debts which have been contracted should be paid at the price of unbearable sacrifices. In such cases it is necessary to find—as in fact is partly happening—ways to lighten, defer or even cancel the debt, compatible with the fundamental right of peoples to subsistence and progress.

(1) ***Centesimus annus* 10** Another important aspect, which has many applications to our own day, is the concept of the relationship between the State and its citizens. *Rerum novarum* criticizes two social and economic systems: socialism and liberalism. The opening section, in which the right to private property is reaffirmed, is devoted 2425

to socialism. Liberalism is not the subject of a special section, but it is worth noting that criticisms of it are raised in the treatment of the duties of the State. The State cannot limit itself to "favoring one portion of the citizens," namely the rich and prosperous, nor can it "neglect the other," which clearly represents the majority of society. Otherwise, there would be a violation of that law of justice which ordains that every person should receive his due. "When there is question of defending the rights of individuals, the defenseless and the poor have a claim to special consideration. The richer class has many ways of shielding itself, and stands less in need of help from the State; whereas the mass of the poor have no resources of their own to fall back on, and must chiefly depend on the assistance of the State. It is for this reason that wage-earners, since they mostly belong to the latter class, should be specially cared for and protected by the government."

These passages are relevant today, especially in the face of the new forms of poverty in the world, and also because they are affirmations which do not depend on a specific notion of the State or on a particular political theory. Leo XIII is repeating an elementary principle of sound political organization, namely, the more that individuals are defenseless within a given society, the more they require the care and concern of others, and in particular the intervention of governmental authority.

In this way what we nowadays call the principle of solidarity, the validity of which both in the internal order of each nation and in the international order I have discussed in the encyclical *Sollicitudo rei socialis*, is clearly seen to be one of the fundamental principles of the Christian view of social and political organization. This principle is frequently stated by Pope Leo XIII, who uses the term "friendship," a concept already found in Greek philosophy. Pope Pius XI refers to it with the equally meaningful term "social charity." Pope Paul VI, expanding the concept to cover the many modern aspects of the social question, speaks of a "civilization of love."

2425 (2) ***Centesimus annus* 13** Continuing our reflections, and referring also to what has been said in the encyclicals *Laborem exercens* and *Sollicitudo rei socialis*, we have to add that the fundamental error of socialism is anthropological in nature. Socialism considers the individual person simply as an element, a molecule within the social organism, so that the good of the individual is completely subordinated to the functioning of the socio-economic mechanism. Socialism likewise maintains that the good of the individual can be realized without reference to his free choice, to the unique and exclusive responsibility which he exercises in the face of good or evil. Man is thus reduced to a series of social relationships, and the concept of the person as the autonomous subject of moral decision disappears, the very subject whose decisions build the social order. From this mistaken conception of the person there arise both a distortion of law, which defines the sphere of the exercise of freedom, and an opposition to private property. A person who is deprived of something he can call "his own," and of the possibility of earning a living through his own initiative, comes to depend on the social machine and on those who control it. This makes it much more difficult for him to recognize his dignity as a person, and hinders progress towards the building up on an authentic human community.

In contrast, from the Christian vision of the human person there necessarily follows a correct picture of society. According to *Rerum novarum* and the whole social doctrine of the Church, the social nature of man is not completely fulfilled in the State, but is realized in various intermediary groups, beginning with the family and including economic, social, political and cultural groups which stem from human nature itself and have their own autonomy, always with a view to the common good. This is what I have called the "subjectivity" of society which, together with the subjectivity of the individual, was cancelled out by "Real Socialism."

If we then inquire as to the source of this mistaken concept of the nature of the person and the "subjectivity" of society, we must reply that its first cause is atheism. It is by responding to the call of God contained in the being of things that man becomes aware of his transcendent dignity. Every individual must give this response, which constitutes the apex of his humanity, and no social mechanism or collective subject can substitute for it. The denial of God deprives the person of his foundation, and consequently leads to a reorganization of the social order without reference to the person's dignity and responsibility.

The atheism of which we are speaking is also closely connected with the rationalism of the Enlightenment, which views human and social reality in a mechanistic way. Thus there is a denial of the supreme insight concerning man's true greatness, his transcendence in respect to earthly realities, the contradiction in his heart between the desire for the fullness of what is good and his own inability to attain it and, above all, the need for salvation which results from this situation.

(3) ***Centesimus annus*** 44 Pope Leo XIII was aware of the need for a sound *theory of* 2425
the State in order to ensure the normal development of man's spiritual and temporal activities, both of which are indispensable. For this reason, in one passage of *Rerum novarum* he presents the organization of society according to the three powers—legislative, executive and judicial—something which at the time represented a novelty in Church teaching. Such an ordering reflects a realistic vision of man's social nature, which calls for legislation capable of protecting the freedom of all. To that end, it is preferable that each power be balanced by other powers and by other spheres of responsibility which keep it within proper bounds. This is the principle of the "rule of law," in which the law is sovereign, and not the arbitrary will of individuals.

In modern times, this concept has been opposed by totalitarianism, which, in its Marxist-Leninist form, maintains that some people, by virtue of a deeper knowledge of the laws of the development of society, or through membership of a particular class or through contact with the deeper sources of the collective consciousness, are exempt from error and can therefore arrogate to themselves the exercise of absolute power. It must be added that totalitarianism arises out of a denial of truth in the objective sense. If there is no transcendent truth, in obedience to which man achieves his full identity, then there is no sure principle for guaranteeing just relations between people. Their self-interest as a class, group or nation would inevitably set them in opposition to one another. If one does not acknowledge transcendent truth, then the force of power takes over, and each person tends to make full use of the means at his disposal in order to impose his own interests or his own opinion, with no regard for the rights of others. People are then respected only to the extent that they can be exploited for selfish ends. Thus, the root of modern totalitarianism is to be found in the denial of the transcendent dignity of the human person who, as the visible image of the invisible God, is therefore by his very nature the subject of rights which no one may violate—no individual, group, class, nation or State. Not even the majority of a social body may violate these rights, by going against the minority, by isolating, oppressing, or exploiting it, or by attempting to annihilate it.

Gaudium et spes 64 Today more than ever before there is an increase in the pro- 2426
duction of agricultural and industrial goods and in the number of services available, and this is as it should be in view of the population expansion and growing human aspirations. Therefore we must encourage technical progress and the spirit of enterprise, we must foster the eagerness for creativity and improvement, and we must promote adaptation of production methods and all serious efforts of people engaged in production—in other words of all elements which contribute to economic progress.

The ultimate and basic purpose of economic production does not consist merely in the increase of goods produced, nor in profit nor prestige; it is directed to the service of man, of man, that is, in his totality, taking into account his material needs and the requirements of his intellectual, moral, spiritual, and religious life; of all men whomsoever and of every group of men of whatever race or from whatever part of the world. Therefore, economic activity is to be carried out in accordance with techniques and methods belonging to the moral order, so that God's design for man may be fulfilled.

2427 (1) **Genesis 1:28** And God blessed them, and God said to them, "Be fruitful and multiply, and fill the earth and subdue it; and have dominion over the fish of the sea and over the birds of the air and over every living thing that moves upon the earth."

2427 (2) ***Gaudium et spes* 34** Individual and collective activity, that monumental effort of man through the centuries to improve the circumstances of the world, presents no problem to believers: considered in itself, it corresponds to the plan of God. Man was created in God's image and was commanded to conquer the earth with all it contains and to rule the world in justice and holiness: he was to acknowledge God as maker of all things and relate himself and the totality of creation to him, so that through the dominion of all things by man the name of God would be majestic in all the earth.

This holds good also for our daily work. When men and women provide for themselves and their families in such a way as to be of service to the community as well, they can rightly look upon their work as a prolongation of the work of the creator, a service to their fellow men, and their personal contribution to the fulfillment in history of the divine plan.

Far from considering the conquests of man's genius and courage as opposed to God's power as if he set himself up as a rival to the creator, Christians ought to be convinced that the achievements of the human race are a sign of God's greatness and the fulfillment of his mysterious design. With an increase in human power comes a broadening of responsibility on the part of individuals and communities: there is no question, then, of the Christian message inhibiting men from building up the world or making them disinterested in the good of their fellows: on the contrary it is an incentive to do these very things.

2427 (3) ***Centesimus annus* 31** Rereading this teaching on the right to property and the common destination of material wealth as it applies to the present time, the question can be raised concerning the origin of the material goods which sustain human life, satisfy people's needs and are an object of their rights.

The original source of all that is good is the very act of God, who created both the earth and man, and who gave the earth to man, so that he might have dominion over it by his work and enjoy its fruits (Gen 1:28). God gave the earth to the whole human race for the sustenance of all its members, without excluding or favoring anyone. This is *the foundation of the universal destination of the earth's goods.* The earth, by reason of its fruitfulness and its capacity to satisfy human needs, is God's first gift for the sustenance of human life. But the earth does not yield its fruits without a particular human response to God's gift, that is to say, without work. It is through work that man, using his intelligence and exercising his freedom, succeeds in dominating the earth and making it a fitting home. In this way, he makes part of the earth his own, precisely the part which he has acquired through work; this is *the origin of individual property*. Obviously, he also has the responsibility not to hinder others from having their own part of God's gift; indeed, he must cooperate with others so that together all can dominate the earth.

In history, these two factors—*work* and *the land*—are to be found at the beginning of every human society. However, they do not always stand in the same relationship to each other. At one time *the natural fruitfulness of the earth* appeared to be, and was in fact, the primary factor of wealth, while work was, as it were, the help and support for this fruitfulness. In our time, *the role of human work* is becoming increasingly important as the productive factor both of nonmaterial and of material wealth. Moreover, it is becoming clearer how a person's work is naturally interrelated with the work of others. More than ever, work is *work with others* and *work for others*: it is a matter of doing something for someone else. Work becomes ever more fruitful and productive to the extent that people become more knowledgeable of the productive potentialities of the earth and more profoundly cognizant of the needs of those for whom their work is done.

(4) **1 Thessalonians 4:11** . . . to aspire to live quietly, to mind your own affairs, **2427**
and to work with your hands, as we charged you. . . .

(5) **Genesis 3:14–19** The Lord God said to the serpent, **2427**

"Because you have done this,
cursed are you above all cattle,
and above all wild animals;
upon your belly you shall go,
and dust you shall eat
all the days of your life.
I will put enmity between you and the woman,
and between your seed and her seed;
he shall bruise your head
and you shall bruise his heel."

To the woman he said,

"I will greatly multiply your pain in childbearing;
in pain you shall bring forth children,
yet your desire shall be for your husband,
and he shall rule over you."

And to Adam he said,

"Because you have listened to the voice of your wife,
and have eaten of the tree
of which I commanded you,
'You shall not eat of it,'
cursed is the ground because of you;
in toil you shall eat of it all the days of your life;
thorns and thistles it shall bring forth to you;
and you shall eat the plants of the field.
In the sweat of your face
you shall eat bread
till you return to the ground,
for out of it you were taken;
you are dust,
and to dust you shall return. . . ."

(6) ***Laborem exercens* 27** There is yet another aspect of human work, an essential **2427**
dimension of it, that is profoundly imbued with the spirituality based on the Gospel. All *work*, whether manual or intellectual, is inevitably linked with *toil*. The book of

Genesis expresses it in a truly penetrating manner: the original *blessing* of work contained in the very mystery of creation and connected with man's elevation as the image of God is contrasted with the *curse* that *sin* brought with it: "Cursed is the ground because of you; in toil you shall eat of it all the days of your life." This toil connected with work marks the way of human life on earth and constitutes *an announcement of death*: "In the sweat of your face you shall eat bread till you return to the ground, for out of it you were taken." Almost as an echo of these words, the author of one of the Wisdom books says: "Then I considered all that my hands had done and the toil I had spent in doing it." There is no one on earth who could not apply these words to himself.

In a sense, the final word of the Gospel on this matter as on others is found in the Paschal Mystery of Jesus Christ. It is here that we must seek an answer to these problems so important for the spirituality of human work. *The Paschal Mystery* contains *the Cross* of Christ and His obedience unto death, which the Apostle contrasts with the disobedience which from the beginning has burdened man's history on earth. It also contains *the elevation* of Christ, who by means of death on a Cross returns to His disciples in *the Resurrection* with the power of the Holy Spirit.

Sweat and toil, which work necessarily involves in the present condition of the human race, present the Christian and everyone who is called to follow Christ with the possibility of sharing lovingly in the work that Christ came to do. This work of salvation came about through suffering and death on a Cross. By enduring the toil of work in union with Christ crucified for us, man in a way collaborates with the Son of God for the redemption of humanity. He shows himself a true disciple of Christ by carrying the cross in his turn every day in the activity that he is called upon to perform.

Christ, "undergoing death itself for all of us sinners, taught us by example that we too must shoulder that cross which the world and the flesh inflict upon those who pursue peace and justice"; but also, at the same time, "appointed Lord *by His Resurrection* and given all authority in heaven and on earth, Christ is now at work in people's hearts through the power of His Spirit. . . . He animates, purifies, and strengthens those noble longings too by which the human family strives to make its life more human and to render the whole earth submissive to this goal."

The Christian finds in human work a small part of the Cross of Christ and accepts it in the same spirit of redemption in which Christ accepted His Cross for us. In work, thanks to the light that penetrates us from the Resurrection of Christ, we always find a *glimmer* of new life, of the *new good*, as if it were an announcement of "the new heavens and the new earth" in which man and the world participate precisely through the toil that goes with work. Through toil—and never without it. On the one hand this confirms the indispensability of the Cross in the spirituality of human work; on the other hand the Cross which this toil constitutes reveals a new good springing from work itself, from work understood in depth and in all its aspects and never apart from work.

Is this *new good*—the fruit of human work—already a small part of that "new earth" where justice dwells? If it is true that the many forms of toil that go with man's work are a small part of the Cross of Christ, what is the relationship of this new good to *the Resurrection of Christ?* The Council seeks to reply to this question also, drawing light from the very sources of the revealed word: "Therefore, while we are warned that it profits a man nothing if he gains the whole world and loses himself" (cf. Lk. 9:25), the expectation of a new earth must not weaken but rather stimulate our concern for cultivating this one. For here grows the body of a new human family, a body which even now is able to give some kind of foreshadowing of the new age. Earthly progress must be carefully distinguished from the growth of Christ's Kingdom. Nevertheless, to the extent that the former can contribute to the better ordering of human society, it is of vital concern to the Kingdom of God.

In these present reflections devoted to human work we have tried to emphasize everything that seemed essential to it, since it is through man's labor that not only "the fruits of our activity" but also "human dignity, brotherhood and freedom" must increase on earth. Let the Christian who listens to the word of the living God, uniting work with prayer, know the place that his work has not only in *earthly progress* but also in *the development of the Kingdom of God,* to which we are all called through the power of the Holy Spirit and through the word of the Gospel.

In concluding these reflections, I gladly impart the Apostolic Blessing to all of you, venerable Brothers and beloved sons and daughters.

I prepared this document for publication on last May 15, on the ninetieth anniversary of the Encyclical *Rerum novarum*, but it is only after my stay in the hospital that I have been able to revise it definitively.

Given at Castel Gandolfo, on the fourteenth day of September, the Feast of the Triumph of the Cross, in the year 1981, the third of the Pontificate.

***Laborem exercens* 6** In order to continue our analysis of work, an analysis linked with 2428
the word of the Bible telling man that he is to subdue the earth, we must concentrate our attention on *work in the subjective sense*, much more than we did on the objective significance, barely touching upon the vast range of problems known intimately and in detail to scholars in various fields and also, according to their specializations, to those who work. If the words of the book of Genesis to which we refer in this analysis of ours speak of work in the objective sense in an indirect way, they also speak only indirectly of the subject of work; but what they say is very eloquent and is full of great significance.

Man has to subdue the earth and dominate it, because as the "image of God" he is a person, that is to say, a subjective being capable of acting in a planned and rational way, capable of deciding about himself, and with a tendency to self-realization. *As a person, man is therefore the subject of work.* As a person he works, he performs various actions belonging to the work process; independently of their objective content, these actions must all serve to realize his humanity, to fulfill the calling to be a person that is his by reason of his very humanity. The principal truths concerning this theme were recently recalled by the Second Vatican Council in the Constitution *Gaudium et spes*, especially in chapter one, which is devoted to man's calling.

And so this "dominion" spoken of in the biblical text being meditated upon here refers not only to the objective dimension of work but at the same time introduces us to an understanding of its subjective dimension. Understood as a process whereby man and the human race subdue the earth, work corresponds to this basic biblical concept only when throughout the process man manifests himself and confirms himself *as the one who "dominates."* This dominion, in a certain sense, refers to the subjective dimension even more than to the objective one: this dimension conditions *the very ethical nature* of work. In fact there is no doubt that human work has an ethical value of its own, which clearly and directly remains linked to the fact that the one who carries it out is a person, a conscious and free subject, that is to say, a subject that decides about himself.

This truth, which in a sense constitutes the fundamental and perennial heart of Christian teaching on human work, has had and continues to have primary significance for the formulation of the important social problems characterizing whole ages.

The ancient world introduced its own typical differentiation of people into classes according to the type of work done. Work which demanded from the worker the exercise of physical strength, the work of muscles and hands, was considered unworthy of free men, and was therefore given to slaves. By broadening certain aspects that already belonged to the Old Testament, Christianity brought about a fundamental change of ideas in this field, taking the whole content of the Gospel message as its point of departure, especially the fact that the one who, while *being God*, became like us in all things devoted most of the years of His life on earth to *manual work* at the carpenter's bench. This circumstance constitutes in itself the most eloquent "Gospel of work," showing that the basis for determining the value of human work is not primarily the kind of work being done but the fact that the one who is doing it is a person. The sources of the dignity of work are to be sought primarily in the subjective dimension, not in the objective one.

Such a concept practically does away with the very basis of the ancient differentiation of people into classes according to the kind of work done. This does not mean that, from the objective point of view, human work cannot and must not be rated and qualified in any way. It only means that the primary basis of the value of work is man himself, who is its subject. This leads immediately to a very important conclusion of an ethical nature: however true it may be that man is destined for work and called to it, in the first place work is "for man" and not man "for work." Through this conclusion one rightly comes to recognize the preeminence of the subjective meaning of work over the objective one. Given this way of understanding things, and presupposing that different sorts of work that people do can have greater or lesser objective value, let us try nevertheless to show that each sort is judged above all by the measure of the dignity of the subject of work, that is to say the person, the individual who carries it out. On the other hand, independently of the work that every man does, and presupposing that this work constitutes a purpose—at times a very demanding one—of his activity, this purpose does not possess a definitive meaning in itself. In fact, in the final analysis it is always man who is the purpose of the work, whatever work it is that is done by man—even if the common scale of values rates it as the merest "service," as the most monotonous, even the most alienating work.

2429 (1) ***Centesimus annus* 32** In our time, in particular, there exists another form of ownership which is becoming no less important than land: *the possession of know-how, technology and skill.* The wealth of the industrialized nations is based much more on this kind of ownership than on natural resources.

Mention has just been made of the fact that *people work with each other*, sharing in a "community of work" which embraces ever widening circles. A person who produces something other than for his own use generally does so in order that others may use it after they have paid a just price, mutually agreed upon through free bargaining. It is precisely the ability to foresee both the needs of others and the combinations of productive factors most adapted to satisfying those needs that constitutes another important source of wealth in modern society. Besides, many goods cannot be adequately produced through the work of an isolated individual; they require the cooperation of many people in working towards a common goal. Organizing such a productive effort, planning its duration in time, making sure that it corresponds in a positive way to the demands which it much satisfy, and taking the necessary risks—all this too is a source of wealth in today's society. In this way, the *role* of disciplined and creative *human work* and, as an essential part of that work, *initiative and entrepreneurial ability* becomes increasingly evident and decisive.

This process, which throws practical light on a truth about the person which Christianity has constantly affirmed, should be viewed carefully and favorably. Indeed, besides the earth, man's principal resource is *man himself*. His intelligence enables him to discover the earth's productive potential and the many different ways in which human needs can be satisfied. It is his disciplined work in close collaboration with others that makes possible the creation of ever more extensive *working communities* which can be relied upon to transform man's natural and human environments. Important virtues are involved in this process, such as diligence, industriousness, prudence in undertaking reasonable risks, reliability and fidelity in interpersonal relationships, as well as courage in carrying out decisions which are difficult and painful but necessary, both for the overall working of a business and in meeting possible setbacks.

The modern *business economy* has positive aspects. Its basis is human freedom exercised in the economic field, just as it is exercised in many other fields. Economic activity is indeed but one sector in a great variety of human activities, and like every other sector, it includes the right to freedom, as well as the duty of making responsible use of freedom. But it is important to note that there are specific differences between the trends of modern society and those of the past, even the recent past. Whereas at one time the decisive factor of production was *the land*, and later capital—understood as a total complex of the instruments of production—today the decisive factor is increasingly *man himself*, that is, his knowledge, especially his scientific knowledge, his capacity for interrelated and compact organization, as well as his ability to perceive the needs of others and to satisfy them.

(2) ***Centesimus annus*** **34** It would appear that, on the level of individual nations and of international relations, *the free market* is the most efficient instrument for utilizing resources and effectively responding to needs. But this is true only for those needs which are "solvent" insofar as they are endowed with purchasing power, and for those resources which are "marketable," insofar as they are capable of obtaining a satisfactory price. But there are many human needs which find no place on the market. It is a strict duty of justice and truth not to allow fundamental human needs to remain unsatisfied, and not to allow those burdened by such needs to perish. It is also necessary to help these needy people to acquire expertise, to enter the circle of exchange, and to develop their skills in order to make the best use of their capacities and resources. Even prior to the logic of a fair exchange of goods and the forms of justice appropriate to it, there exists *something which is due to man because he is man*, by reason of his lofty dignity. Inseparable from that required "something" is the possibility to survive and, at the same time, to make an active contribution to the common good of humanity. 2429

In Third World contexts, certain objectives stated by *Rerum novarum* remain valid, and, in some cases, still constitute a goal yet to be reached, if man's work and his very being are not to be reduced to the level of a mere commodity. These objectives include a sufficient wage for the support of the family, social insurance for old age and unemployment, and adequate protection for the conditions of employment.

Laborem exercens **11** The sketch of the basic problems of work outlined above draws inspiration from the texts at the beginning of the Bible and in a sense forms the very framework of the Church's teaching, which has remained unchanged throughout the centuries within the context of different historical experiences. However, the experiences preceding and following the publication of the Encyclical *Rerum novarum* form a background that endows that teaching with particular expressiveness and the eloquence of living relevance. In this analysis, work is seen as a great reality with a fundamental influence on the shaping in a human way of the world that the Creator has entrusted to man; it is a reality closely linked with man as the subject of work and with man's rational activity. In the normal course of events this reality fills human life and strongly affects its value and meaning. Even when it is accompanied by toil and effort, work is still something good, and so man develops through love for work. This 2430 entirely *positive and creative, educational and meritorious character of man's work* must be the basis for the judgments and decisions being made today in its regard in spheres that include *human rights*, as is evidenced by the international *declarations* on work and the many *labor codes* prepared either by the competent legislative institutions in the various countries or by organizations devoting their social, or scientific and social, activity to the problems of work. One organization fostering such initiatives on the international level is the International Labor Organization, the oldest specialized agency of the United Nations Organization.

In the following part of these considerations I intend to return in greater detail to these important questions, recalling at least the basic elements of the Church's teaching on the matter. I must however first touch on a very important field of questions in which her teaching has taken shape in this latest period, the one marked and in a sense symbolized by the publication of the Encyclical *Rerum novarum*.

Throughout this period, which is by no means yet over, the issue of work has of course been posed on the basis of the great *conflict* that in the age of, and together with, industrial development emerged *between "capital" and "labor*," that is to say between the small but highly influential group of entrepreneurs, owners or holders of the means of production, and the broader multitude of people who lacked these means and who shared in the process of production solely by their labor. The conflict originated in the fact that the workers put their powers at the disposal of the entrepreneurs, and these, following the principle of maximum profit, tried to establish the lowest possible wages for the work done by the employees. In addition there were other elements of exploitation, connected with the lack of safety at work and of safeguards regarding the health and living conditions of the workers and their families.

This conflict, interpreted by some as a socioeconomic *class conflict*, found expression in the *ideological conflict* between liberalism, understood as the ideology of capitalism, and Marxism, understood as the ideology of scientific socialism and communism, which professes to act as the spokesman for the working class and the worldwide proletariat. Thus the real conflict between labor and capital was transformed into *a systematic class struggle*, conducted not only by ideological means but also and chiefly by political means. We are familiar with the history of this conflict and with the demands of both sides. The Marxist program, based on the philosophy of Marx and Engels, sees in class struggle the only way to eliminate class injustices in society and to eliminate the classes themselves. Putting this program into practice presupposes *the collectivization of the means of production* so that, through the transfer of these means from private hands to the collectivity, human labor will be preserved from exploitation.

This is the goal of the struggle carried on by political as well as ideological means. In accordance with the principle of "the dictatorship of the proletariat," the groups that as political parties follow the guidance of Marxist ideology aim, by the use of various kinds of influence, including revolutionary pressure, to win *a monopoly of power in each society*, in order to introduce the collectivist system into it by eliminating private ownership of the means of production. According to the principal ideologists and leaders of this broad international movement, the purpose of this program of action is to achieve the social revolution and to introduce socialism and, finally, the communist system throughout the world.

As we touch on this extremely important field of issues, which constitute not only a theory but a whole fabric of socioeconomic, political, and international life in our age, we cannot *go into the details*, nor is this necessary, for they are known both from the vast literature on the subject and by experience. Instead, we must leave the context of these issues and go back to the fundamental issue of human work, which is the main subject of the considerations in this document. It is clear, indeed, that this issue, which is of such importance for man—it constitutes one of the fundamental dimensions of his earthly existence and of his vocation—can also be explained only by taking into account the full context of the contemporary situation.

***Centesimus annus* 37** Equally worrying is *the ecological question* which accompanies the problem of consumerism and which is closely connected to it. In his desire to have and to enjoy rather than to be and to grow, man consumes the resources of the earth and his own life in an excessive and disordered way. At the root of the senseless destruction of the natural environment lies an anthropological error, which unfortunately is widespread in our day. Man, who discovers his capacity to transform and in a certain sense create the world through his own work, forgets that this is always based on God's prior and original gift of the things that are. Man thinks that he can make arbitrary use of the earth, subjecting it without restraint to his will, as though it did not have its own requisites and a prior God-given purpose, which man can indeed develop but must not betray. Instead of carrying out his role as a cooperator with God in the work of creation, man sets himself up in place of God and thus ends up provoking a rebellion on the part of nature, which is more tyrannized than governed by him. 2432

In all this, one notes first the poverty or narrowness of man's outlook, motivated as he is by a desire to possess things rather than to relate them to the truth, and lacking that disinterested, unselfish and aesthetic attitude that is born of wonder in the presence of being and of the beauty which enables one to see in visible things the message of the invisible God who created them. In this regard, humanity today must be conscious of its duties and obligations towards future generations.

(1) ***Laborem exercens* 19** After outlining the important role that concern for providing employment for all workers plays in safeguarding respect for the inalienable rights of man in view of his work, it is worthwhile taking a closer look at these rights, which in the final analysis are formed within the relationship *between worker and direct employer*. All that has been said above on the subject of the indirect employer is aimed at defining these relationships more exactly, by showing the many forms of conditioning within which these relationships are indirectly formed. This consideration does not however have a purely descriptive purpose; it is not a brief treatise on economics or politics. It is a matter of highlighting the *deontological and moral aspect*. The key problem of social ethics in this case is that of *just remuneration* for work done. In the context of the present there is no more important way for securing a just relationship between the worker and the employer than that constituted by remuneration for work. Whether the work is done in a system of private ownership of the means of production or in a system where ownership has undergone a certain "socialization," the relationship between the employer (first and foremost the direct employer) and the worker is resolved on the basis of the wage, that is, through just remuneration for work done. 2433

It should also be noted that the justice of a socioeconomic system and, in each case, its just functioning, deserve in the final analysis to be evaluated by the way in which man's work is properly remunerated in the system. Here we return once more to the first principle of the whole ethical and social order, namely, *the principle of the common use of goods*. In every system, regardless of the fundamental relationships within it between capital and labor, wages, that is to say *remuneration for work*, are still a *practical means* whereby the vast majority of people can have access to those goods which are intended for common use: both the goods of nature and manufactured goods. Both kinds of goods become accessible to the worker through the wage which he receives as remuneration for his work. Hence, in every case, a just wage is the concrete means of *verifying the justice* of the whole socioeconomic system and, in any case, of checking that it is functioning justly. It is not the only means of checking, but it is a particularly important one and, in a sense, the key means.

This means of checking concerns above all the family. Just remuneration for the work of an adult who is responsible for a family means remuneration which will suffice for establishing and properly maintaining a family and for providing security for its future. Such remuneration can be given either through what is called a *family wage* —that is, a single salary given to the head of the family for his work, sufficient for the needs of the family without the other spouse having to take up gainful employment outside the home—or through *other social measures* such as family allowances or grants to mothers devoting themselves exclusively to their families. These grants should correspond to the actual needs, that is, to the number of dependents for as long as they are not in a position to assume proper responsibility for their own lives.

Experience confirms that there must be a *social reevaluation of the mother's role*, of the toil connected with it, and of the need that children have for care, love and affection in order that they may develop into responsible, morally and religiously mature and psychologically stable persons. It will redound to the credit of society to make it possible for a mother—without inhibiting her freedom, without psychological or practical discrimination, and without penalizing her as compared with other women —to devote herself to taking care of her children and educating them in accordance with their needs, which vary with age. Having to abandon these tasks in order to take up paid work outside the home is wrong from the point of view of the good of society and of the family when it contradicts or hinders these primary goals of the mission of a mother.

In this context it should be emphasized that, on a more general level, the whole labor process must be organized and adapted in such a way as to respect the requirements of the person and his or her forms of life, above all life in the home, taking into account the individual's age and sex. It is a fact that in many societies women work in nearly every sector of life. But it is fitting that they should be able to fulfill their tasks *in accordance with their own nature*, without being discriminated against and without being excluded from jobs for which they are capable, but also without lack of respect for their family aspirations and for their specific role in contributing, together with men, to the good of society. The *true advancement of women* requires that labor should be structured in such a way that women do not have to pay for their advancement by abandoning what is specific to them and at the expense of the family, in which women as mothers have an irreplaceable role.

Besides wages, various *social benefits* intended to ensure the life and health of workers and their families play a part here. The expenses involved in health care, especially in the case of accidents at work, demand that medical assistance should be easily available for workers, and that as far as possible it should be cheap or even free of charge. Another sector regarding benefits is the sector associated with the *right to rest*. In the first place this involves a regular weekly rest comprising at least Sunday, and also a longer period of rest, namely the holiday or vacation taken once a year or possibly in several shorter periods during the year. A third sector concerns the right to a pension and to insurance for old age and in case of accidents at work. Within the sphere of these principal rights, there develops a whole system of particular rights which, together with remuneration for work, determine the correct relationship between worker and employer. Among these rights there should never be overlooked the right to a working environment and to manufacturing processes which are not harmful to the workers' physical health or to their moral integrity.

(2) ***Laborem exercens* 22–23** Recently, national communities and International Organizations have turned their attention to another question connected with work, one full of implications: the question of disabled people. They too are fully human subjects with corresponding innate, sacred and inviolable rights, and, in spite of the limitations and sufferings affecting their bodies and faculties, they point up more clearly the dignity and greatness of man. Since disabled people are subjects with all their rights, they should be helped to participate in the life of society in all its aspects and at all the levels accessible to their capacities. The disabled person is one of us and participates fully in the same humanity that we possess. It would be radically unworthy of man, and a denial of our common humanity, to admit to the life of the community, and thus admit to work, only those who are fully functional. To do so would be to practice *a serious form of discrimination*, that of the strong and healthy against the weak and sick. Work in the objective sense should be subordinated, in this circumstance too, to the dignity of man, to the subject of work and not to economic advantage. 2433

The various bodies involved in the world of labor, both the direct and the indirect employer, should therefore by means of effective and appropriate measures foster the right of disabled people to professional training and work, so that they can be given a productive activity suited to them. Many practical problems arise at this point, as well as legal and economic ones; but the community, that is to say, the public authorities, associations and intermediate groups, business enterprises and the disabled themselves should pool their ideas and resources so as to attain this goal that must not be shirked: *that disabled people may be offered work according to their capabilities*, for this is demanded by their dignity as persons and as subjects of work. Each community will be able to set up suitable structures for finding or creating jobs for such people both in the usual public or private enterprises, by offering them ordinary or suitably adapted jobs, and in what are called "protected" enterprises and surroundings.

Careful attention must be devoted to the physical and psychological working conditions of disabled people—as for all workers—to their just remuneration, to the possibility of their promotion, and to the elimination of various obstacles. Without hiding the fact that this is a complex and difficult task, it is to be hoped that *a correct concept of labor in the subjective sense* will produce a situation which will make it possible for disabled people to feel that they are not cut off from the working world or dependent upon society, but that they are full-scale subjects of work, useful, respected for their human dignity and called to contribute to the progress and welfare of their families and of the community according to their particular capacities.

Finally, we must say at least a few words on the subject of *emigration in search of work*. This is an age-old phenomenon which nevertheless continues to be repeated and is still today very widespread as a result of the complexities of modern life. Man has the right to leave his native land for various motives—and also the right to return—in order to seek better conditions of life in another country. This fact is certainly not without difficulties of various kinds. Above all it generally constitutes a loss for the country which is left behind. It is the departure of a person who is also a member of a great community united by history, tradition and culture; and that person must begin life in the midst of another society united by a different culture and very often by a different language. In this case, it is the loss of *a subject of work*, whose efforts of mind and body could contribute to the common good of his own country, but these efforts, this contribution, are instead offered to another society which in a sense has less right to them than the person's country of origin.

Nevertheless, even if emigration is in some aspects an evil, in certain circumstances it is, as the phrase goes, a necessary evil. Everything should be done—and certainly much is being done to this end—to prevent this material evil from causing greater *moral harm*; indeed every possible effort should be made to ensure that it may bring benefit to the emigrant's personal, family and social life, both for the country to which he goes and the country which he leaves. In this area much depends on just legislation, in particular with regard to the rights of workers. It is obvious that the question of just legislation enters into the context of the present considerations, especially from the point of view of these rights.

The most important thing is that the person working away from his native land, whether as a permanent emigrant or as a seasonal worker, should not be *placed at a disadvantage* in comparison with the other workers in that society in the matter of working rights. Emigration in search of work must in no way become an opportunity for financial or social exploitation. As regards the work relationship, the same criteria should be applied to immigrant workers as to all other workers in the society concerned. The value of work should be measured by the same standard and not according to the difference in nationality, religion or race. For even greater reason the situation of constraint in which the emigrant may find himself should not be exploited. All these circumstances should categorically give way, after special qualifications have of course been taken into consideration, to the fundamental value of work, which is bound up with the dignity of the human person. Once more the fundamental principle must be repeated: the hierarchy of values and the profound meaning of work itself require that capital should be at the service of labor and not labor at the service of capital.

2433 (3) ***Centesimus annus* 48:** see 2406 (4).

2434 (1) **Leviticus 19:13** "You shall not oppress your neighbor or rob him. The wages of a hired servant shall not remain with you all night until the morning. . . ."

2434 (2) **Deuteronomy 24:14–15** "You shall not oppress a hired servant who is poor and needy, whether he is one of your brethren or one of the sojourners who are in your land within your towns; you shall give him his hire on the day he earns it, before the sun goes down (for he is poor, and sets his heart upon it); lest he cry against you to the Lord, and it be sin in you. . . ."

2434 (3) **James 5:4** Behold, the wages of the laborers who mowed your fields, which you kept back by fraud, cry out; and the cries of the harvesters have reached the ears of the Lord of Hosts.

2436 ***Laborem exercens* 18** When we consider the rights of workers in relation to the "indirect employers," that is to say, all the agents at the national and international level that are responsible for the whole orientation of labor policy, we must first direct our attention to *a fundamental issue:* the question of finding work, or, in other words, the issue of *suitable employment for all who are capable of it*. The opposite of a just and right situation in this field is unemployment, that is to say the lack of work for those who are capable of it. It can be a question of general unemployment or of unemployment in certain sectors of work. The role of the agents included under the title of indirect employer is *to act against unemployment*, which in all cases is an evil, and which, when it reaches a certain level, can become a real social disaster. It is particularly painful when it especially affects young people, who after appropriate cultural, technical and professional preparation fail to find work, and see their sincere wish to work and their readiness to take on their own responsibility for the economic and social development of the community sadly frustrated. The obligation to provide unemployment benefits, that is to say, the duty to make suitable grants indispensable for the subsistence of unemployed workers and their families, is a duty springing from the fundamental principle of the moral order in this sphere, namely the principle of the common use of goods or, to put it in another and still simpler way, the right to life and subsistence.

In order to meet the danger of unemployment and to ensure employment for all, the agents defined here as "indirect employer" must make provision for *overall planning* with regard to the different kinds of work by which not only the economic life but also the cultural life of a given society is shaped; they must also give attention to organizing that work in a correct and rational way. In the final analysis this overall concern weighs on the shoulders of the State, but it cannot mean one-sided centralization by the public authorities. Instead, what is in question is a just and rational *coordination*, within the framework of which the *initiative* of individuals, free groups and local work centers and complexes must be *safeguarded*, keeping in mind what has been said above with regard to the subject character of human labor.

The fact of the mutual dependence of societies and States and the need to collaborate in various areas mean that, while preserving the sovereign rights of each society and State in the field of planning and organizing labor in its own society, action in this important area must also be taken in the dimension of *international collaboration* by means of the necessary treaties and agreements. Here too the criterion for these pacts and agreements must more and more be the criterion of human work considered as a fundamental right of all human beings, work which gives similar rights to all those who work, in such a way that the living standard of the workers in the different societies will *less and less show those disturbing differences* which are unjust and are apt to provoke even violent reactions. The International Organizations have an enormous part to play in this area. They must let themselves be guided by an exact diagnosis of the complex situations and of the influence exercised by natural, historical, civil and other such circumstances. They must also be more highly operative with regard to plans for action jointly decided on, that is to say, they must be more effective in carrying them out.

In this direction it is possible to actuate a plan for universal and proportionate progress by all, in accordance with the guidelines of Paul VI's Encyclical *Populorum progressio*. It must be stressed that the constitutive element in this progress and also the most adequate way to verify it in a spirit of justice and peace, which the Church proclaims and for which she does not cease to pray to the Father of all individuals and of all peoples, is the continual reappraisal of man's work, both in the aspect of its objective finality and in the aspect of the dignity of the subject of all work, that is to say, man. The progress in question must be made through man and for man and it must produce its fruit in man. A test of this progress will be the increasingly mature recognition of the purpose of work and increasingly universal respect for the rights inherent in work in conformity with the dignity of man, the subject of work.

Rational planning and the proper organization of human labor in keeping with individual societies and States should also facilitate the discovery of the right proportions between the different kinds of employment: work on the land, in industry, in the various services, white-collar work and scientific or artistic work, in accordance with the capacities of individuals and for the common good of each society and of the whole of mankind. The organization of human life in accordance with the many possibilities of labor should be matched by a suitable *system of instruction* and education, aimed first of all at developing mature human beings, but also aimed at preparing people specifically for assuming to good advantage an appropriate place in the vast and socially differentiated world of work.

As we view the whole human family throughout the world, we cannot fail to be struck by *a disconcerting fact* of immense proportions: the fact that, while conspicuous natural resources remain unused, there are huge numbers of people who are unemployed or under-employed and countless multitudes of people suffering from hunger. This is a fact that without any doubt demonstrates that both within the individual political communities and in their relationships on the continental and world level there is something wrong with the organization of work and employment, precisely at the most critical and socially most important points.

2437 ***Sollicitudo rei socialis* 14** The first *negative observation* to make is the persistence and often widening of the *gap* between the areas of the so-called developed North and the developing South. This geographical terminology is only indicative, since one cannot ignore the fact that the frontiers of wealth and poverty intersect within the societies themselves, whether developed or developing. In fact, just as social inequalities down to the level of poverty exist in rich countries, so, in parallel fashion, in the less developed countries one often sees manifestations of selfishness and a flaunting of wealth which is as disconcerting as it is scandalous.

The abundance of goods and services available in some parts of the world, particularly in the developed North, is matched in the South by an unacceptable delay, and it is precisely in this geopolitical area that the major part of the human race lives.

Looking at all the various sectors—the production and distribution of foodstuffs, hygiene, health and housing, availability of drinking water, working conditions (especially for women), life expectancy and other economic and social indicators—the general picture is a disappointing one, both considered in itself and in relation to the corresponding data of the more developed countries. The word "gap" returns spontaneously to mind.

Perhaps this is not the appropriate word for indicating the true reality, since it could give the impression of a *stationary* phenomenon. This is not the case. The *pace of progress* in the developed and developing countries in recent years has differed, and this serves to widen the distances. Thus the developing countries, especially the poorest of them, find themselves in a situation of very serious delay.

We must also add the *differences of culture* and *value systems* between the various population groups, differences which do not always match the degree of *economic development*, but which help to create distances. These are elements and aspects which render *the social question much more complex*, precisely because this question has assumed a universal dimension.

As we observe the various parts of the world separated by this widening gap, and note that each of these parts seems to follow its own path with its own achievements, we can understand the current usage which speaks of different worlds within our *one world:* the First World, the Second World, the Third World and at times the Fourth World. Such expressions, which obviously do not claim to classify exhaustively all countries, are significant: they are a sign of a widespread sense that the *unity of the world*, that is, *the unity of the human race*, is seriously compromised. Such phraseology, beyond its more or less objective value, undoubtedly conceals a *moral content*, before which the Church, which is a "sacrament or sign and instrument . . . of the unity of the whole human race," cannot remain indifferent.

2438 (1) ***Sollicitudo rei socialis* 17** However much society worldwide shows signs of fragmentation, expressed in the conventional names First, Second, Third and even Fourth World, their *interdependence* remains close. When this interdependence is separated from its ethical requirements, it has *disastrous consequences* for the weakest. Indeed, as a result of a sort of internal dynamic and under the impulse of mechanisms which can only be called perverse, this *interdependence* triggers *negative effects* even in the rich countries. It is precisely within these countries that one encounters, though on a lesser scale, the *more specific manifestations* of underdevelopment. Thus it should be obvious that development either becomes shared in *common* by every part of the world or it undergoes a *process of regression* even in zones marked by constant progress. This tells us a great deal about the nature of *authentic* development: either *all* the nations of the world participate, or it will not be true development.

Among the *specific signs* of underdevelopment which increasingly affect the developed countries also, there are two in particular that reveal a tragic situation. The *first* is the *housing crisis*. During this International Year of the Homeless proclaimed by the United Nations, attention is focused on the millions of human beings lacking adequate housing or with no housing at all, in order to awaken everyone's conscience and to find a solution to this serious problem with its negative consequences for the individual, the family and society.

The lack of housing is being experienced *universally* and is due in large measure to the growing phenomenon of urbanization. Even the most highly developed peoples present the sad spectacle of individuals and families literally struggling to survive, without a *roof* over their heads or with a roof *so inadequate* as to constitute no roof at all.

The lack of housing, an extremely serious problem in itself, should be seen as a sign and summing-up of a whole series of shortcomings: economic, social, cultural or simply human in nature. Given the extent of the problem, we should need little convincing of how far we are from an authentic development of peoples.

(2) ***Sollicitudo rei socialis* 45** None of what has been said can be achieved *without* 2438
the collaboration of all—especially the international community—in the framework of a *solidarity* which includes everyone, beginning with the most neglected. But the developing nations themselves have the duty to practice *solidarity among themselves* and with the neediest countries of the world.

It is desirable, for example, that nations of the *same geographical area* should establish *forms of cooperation* which will make them less dependent on more powerful producers; they should open their frontiers to the products of the area; they should examine how their products might complement one another; they should combine in order to set up those services which each one separately is incapable of providing; they should extend cooperation to the monetary and financial sector.

Interdependence is already a reality in many of these countries. To acknowledge it, in such a way as to make it more operative, represents an alternative to excessive dependence on richer and more powerful nations, as part of the hoped-for development, without opposing anyone, but discovering and making best use of the country's *own potential.* The developing countries belonging to one geographical area, especially those included in the term "South," can and ought to set up *new regional organizations* inspired by criteria of *equality, freedom and participation* in the comity of nations—as is already happening with promising results.

An essential condition for global *solidarity* is autonomy and free self-determination, also within associations such as those indicated. But at the same time solidarity demands a readiness to accept the sacrifices necessary for the good of the whole world community.

(3) ***Centesimus annus* 35:** see 2424 (4). 2438

(1) ***Sollicitudo rei socialis* 16** It should be noted that in spite of the praiseworthy 2440
efforts made in the last two decades by the more developed or developing nations and the international organizations to find a way out of the situation, or at least to remedy some of its symptoms, the conditions have become *notably worse.*

Responsibility for this deterioration is due to various causes. Notable among them are undoubtedly grave instances of omissions on the part of the developing nations themselves, and especially on the part of those holding economic and political power. Nor can we pretend not to see the responsibility of the developed nations, which have not always, at least in due measure, felt the duty to help countries separated from the affluent world to which they themselves belong.

Moreover, one must denounce the existence of economic, financial and social *mechanisms* which, although they are manipulated by people, often function almost automatically, thus accentuating the situation of wealth for some and poverty for the rest. These mechanisms, which are maneuvered directly or indirectly by the more developed countries, by their very functioning favor the interests of the people manipulating them. But in the end they suffocate or condition the economies of the less developed countries. Later on these mechanisms will have to be subjected to a careful analysis under the ethical-moral aspect.

Populorum Progressio already foresaw the possibility that under such systems the wealth of the rich would increase and the poverty of the poor would remain. A proof of this forecast has been the appearance of the so-called Fourth World.

2440 (2) ***Centesimus annus* 26** The events of 1989 took place principally in the countries of Eastern and Central Europe. However, they have world-wide importance because they have positive and negative consequences which concern the whole human family. These consequences are not mechanistic or fatalistic in character, but rather are opportunities for human freedom to cooperate with the merciful plan of God who acts within history.

The first consequence was *an encounter* in some countries *between the Church and the workers' movement*, which came about as a result of an ethical and explicitly Christian reaction against a widespread situation of injustice. For about a century the workers' movement had fallen in part under the dominance of Marxism, in the conviction that the working class, in order to struggle effectively against oppression, had to appropriate its economic and materialistic theories.

In the crisis of Marxism, the natural dictates of the consciences of workers have re-emerged in a demand for justice and a recognition of the dignity of work, in conformity with the social doctrine of the Church. The worker movement is part of a more general movement among workers and other people of good will for the liberation of the human person and for the affirmation of human rights. It is a movement which today has spread to many countries, and which, far from opposing the Catholic Church, looks to her with interest.

The crisis of Marxism does not rid the world of the situations of injustice and oppression which Marxism itself exploited and on which it fed. To those who are searching today for a new and authentic theory and praxis of liberation, the Church offers not only her social doctrine and, in general, her teaching about the human person redeemed in Christ, but also her concrete commitment and material assistance in the struggle against marginalization and suffering.

In the recent past, the sincere desire to be on the side of the oppressed and not to be cut off from the course of history has led many believers to seek in various ways an impossible compromise between Marxism and Christianity. Moving beyond all that was short-lived in these attempts, present circumstances are leading to a reaffirmation of the positive value of an authentic theology of integral human liberation. Considered from this point of view, the events of 1989 are proving to be important also for the countries of the Third World, which are searching for their own path to development, just as they were important for the countries of Central and Eastern Europe.

(1) ***Sollicitudo rei socialis* 32** The obligation to commit oneself to the development of peoples is not just an *individual* duty, and still less an *individualistic* one, as if it were possible to achieve this development through the isolated efforts of each individual. It is an imperative which obliges *each and every* man and woman, as well as societies and nations. In particular, it obliges the Catholic Church and the other Churches and Ecclesial Communities, with which we are completely willing to collaborate in this field. In this sense, just as we Catholics invite our Christian brethren to share in our initiatives, so too we declare that we are ready to collaborate in theirs, and we welcome the invitations presented to us. In this pursuit of integral human development we can also do much with the members of other religions, as in fact is being done in various places. 2441

Collaboration in the development of the whole person and of every human being is in fact a duty *of all towards all*, and must be shared by the four parts of the world: East and West, North and South; or, as we say today, by the different "worlds." If, on the contrary, people try to achieve it in only one part, or in only one world, they do so at the expense of the others; and, precisely because the others are ignored, their own development becomes exaggerated and misdirected.

Peoples or *nations* too have a right to their own full development, which while including—as already said—the economic and social aspects, should also include individual cultural identity and openness to the transcendent. Not even the need for development can be used as an excuse for imposing on others one's own way of life or own religious belief.

(2) ***Centesimus annus* 51** All human activity takes place within a culture and interacts with culture. For an adequate formation of a culture, the involvement of the whole man is required, whereby he exercises his creativity, intelligence, and knowledge of the world and of people. Furthermore, he displays his capacity for self-control, personal sacrifice, solidarity and readiness to promote the common good. Thus the first and most important task is accomplished within man's heart. The way in which he is involved in building his own future depends on the understanding he has of himself and of his own destiny. It is on this level that *the Church's specific and decisive contribution to true culture* is to be found. The Church promotes those aspects of human behavior which favor a true culture of peace, as opposed to models in which the individual is lost in the crowd, in which the role of his initiative and freedom is neglected, and in which his greatness is posited in the arts of conflict and war. The Church renders this service to human society *by preaching the truth about the creation of the world*, which God has placed in human hands so that people make it fruitful and more perfect through their work; and *by preaching the truth about the Redemption*, whereby the Son of God has saved mankind and at the same time has united all people, making them responsible for one another. Sacred Scripture continually speaks to us of an active commitment to our neighbor and demands of us a shared responsibility for all of humanity. 2441

This duty is not limited to one's own family, nation or state, but extends progressively to all mankind, since no one can consider himself extraneous or indifferent to the lot of another member of the human family. No one can say that he is not responsible for the well-being of his brother or sister (cf. Gen 4:9; Lk 10:29–37; Mt 25:31–46). Attentive and pressing concern for one's neighbor in a moment of need—made easier today because of the new means of communication which have brought people closer together—is especially important with regard to the search for ways of resolving international conflicts other than by war. It is not hard to see that the terrifying power of the means of destruction—to which even medium and small-sized countries have access—and the ever closer links between the peoples of the whole world make it very difficult or practically impossible to limit the consequences of a conflict.

2442 ***Sollicitudo rei socialis* 42:** see 2406 (2).

2443 (1) **Matthew 25:31–36** "When the Son of man comes in his glory, and all the angels with him, then he will sit on his glorious throne. Before him will be gathered all the nations, and he will separate them one from another as a shepherd separates the sheep from the goats, and he will place the sheep at his right hand, but the goats at the left. Then the King will say to those at his right hand, 'Come, O blessed of my Father, inherit the kingdom prepared for you from the foundation of the world; for I was hungry and you gave me food, I was thirsty and you gave me drink, I was a stranger and you welcomed me, I was naked and you clothed me, I was sick and you visited me, I was in prison and you came to me.' . . ."

2443 (2) **Luke 4:18**

"The Spirit of the Lord is upon me,
because he has anointed me to preach good news to the poor.
He has sent me to proclaim release to the captives
and recovering of sight to the blind,
to set at liberty those who are oppressed. . . ."

2444 (1) **Luke 6:20–22** And he lifted up his eyes on his disciples, and said:

"Blessed are you poor, for yours is the kingdom of God.

"Blessed are you that hunger now, for you shall be satisfied.

"Blessed are you that weep now, for you shall laugh.

"Blessed are you when men hate you, and when they exclude you and revile you, and cast out your name as evil, on account of the Son of man! . . ."

2444 (2) **Matthew 8:20** And Jesus said to him, "Foxes have holes, and birds of the air have nests; but the Son of man has nowhere to lay his head."

2444 (3) **Mark 12:41–44** And he sat down opposite the treasury, and watched the multitude putting money into the treasury. Many rich people put in large sums. And a poor widow came, and put in two copper coins, which make a penny. And he called his disciples to him, and said to them, "Truly, I say to you, this poor widow has put in more than all those who are contributing to the treasury. For they all contributed out of their abundance; but she out of her poverty has put in everything she had, her whole living."

2444 (4) ***Centesimus annus* 57** As far as the Church is concerned, the social message of the Gospel must not be considered a theory, but above all else a basis and a motivation for action. Inspired by this message, some of the first Christians distributed their goods to the poor, bearing witness to the fact that, despite different social origins, it was possible for people to live together in peace and harmony. Through the power of the Gospel, down the centuries monks tilled the land, men and women religious founded hospitals and shelters for the poor, confraternities as well as individual men and women of all states of life devoted themselves to the needy and to those on the margins of society, convinced as they were that Christ's words "as you did it to one of the least of these my brethren, you did it to me" (Mt 25:40) were not intended to remain a pious wish, but were meant to become a concrete life commitment.

Today more than ever, the Church is aware that her social message will gain credibility more immediately from the *witness of actions* than as a result of its internal logic and consistency. This awareness is also a source of her preferential option for the poor, which is never exclusive or discriminatory towards other groups. This option is not limited to material poverty, since it is well known that there are many other forms of poverty, especially in modern society—not only economic but cultural and spiritual poverty as well. The Church's love for the poor, which is essential for her and a part of her constant tradition, impels her to give attention to a world in which poverty is threatening to assume massive proportions in spite of technological and economic progress. In the countries of the West, different forms of poverty are being experienced by groups which live on the margins of society, by the elderly and the sick, by the victims of consumerism, and even more immediately by so many refugees and migrants. In the developing countries, tragic crises loom on the horizon unless internationally coordinated measures are taken before it is too late.

(1) **Isaiah 58:6–7** 2447

"Is not this the fast that I choose:
to loose the bonds of wickedness,
to undo the thongs of the yoke,
to let the oppressed go free,
and to break every yoke?
Is it not to share your bread with the hungry,
and bring the homeless poor into your house;
when you see the naked, to cover him,
and not to hide yourself from your own flesh? . . ."

(2) **Hebrews 13:3** Remember those who are in prison, as though in prison with them; and those who are ill-treated, since you also are in the body. 2447

(3) **Matthew 25:31–46** "When the Son of man comes in his glory, and all the angels with him, then he will sit on his glorious throne. Before him will be gathered all the nations, and he will separate them one from another as a shepherd separates the sheep from the goats, and he will place the sheep at his right hand, but the goats at the left. Then the King will say to those at his right hand, 'Come, O blessed of my Father, inherit the kingdom prepared for you from the foundation of the world; for I was hungry and you gave me food, I was thirsty and you gave me drink, I was a stranger and you welcomed me, I was naked and you clothed me, I was sick and you visited me, I was in prison and you came to me.' Then the righteous will answer him, 'Lord, when did we see thee hungry and feed thee, or thirsty and give thee drink? And when did we see thee a stranger and welcome thee, or naked and clothe thee? And when did we see thee sick or in prison and visit thee?' And the King will answer them, 'Truly, I say to you, as you did it to one of the least of these my brethren, you did it to me.' Then he will say to those at his left hand, 'Depart from me, you cursed, into the eternal fire prepared for the devil and his angels; for I was hungry and you gave me no food, I was thirsty and you gave me no drink, I was a stranger and you did not welcome me, naked and you did not clothe me, sick and in prison and you did not visit me.' Then they also will answer, 'Lord, when did we see thee hungry or thirsty or a stranger or naked or sick or in prison, and did not minister to thee?' Then he will answer them, 'Truly, I say to you, as you did it not to one of the least of these, you did it not to me.' And they will go away into eternal punishment, but the righteous into eternal life." 2447

(4) **Tobit 4:5–11** "Remember the Lord our God all your days, my son, and refuse to sin or to transgress his commandments. Live uprightly all the days of your life, 2447

and do not walk in the ways of wrongdoing. For if you do what is true, your ways will prosper through your deeds. Give alms from your possessions to all who live uprightly, and do not let your eye begrudge the gift when you make it. Do not turn your face away from any poor man, and the face of God will not be turned away from you. If you have many possessions, make your gift from them in proportion; if few, do not be afraid to give according to the little you have. So you will be laying up a good treasure for yourself against the day of necessity. For charity delivers from death and keeps you from entering the darkness; and for all who practice it charity is an excellent offering in the presence of the Most High. . . ."

2447 (5) **Sirach 17:22**

A man's almsgiving is like a signet with the Lord,
and he will keep a person's kindness like the apple of his eye.

2447 (6) **Matthew 6:2–4** "Thus, when you give alms, sound no trumpet before you, as the hypocrites do in the synagogues and in the streets, that they may be praised by men. Truly, I say to you, they have received their reward. But when you give alms, do not let your left hand know what your right hand is doing, so that your alms may be in secret; and your Father who sees in secret will reward you. . . ."

2447 (7) **1 John 3:17** But if any one has the world's goods and sees his brother in need, yet closes his heart against him, how does God's love abide in him?

2449 **Matthew 25:40** ". . . And the King will answer them, 'Truly, I say to you, as you did it to one of the least of these my brethren, you did it to me.' . . ."

2461 ***Centesimus annus* 29** Finally, development must not be understood solely in economic terms, but in a way that is fully human. It is not only a question of raising all peoples to the level currently enjoyed by the richest countries, but rather of building up a more decent life through united labor, of concretely enhancing every individual's dignity and creativity, as well as his capacity to respond to his personal vocation, and thus to God's call. The apex of development is the exercise of the right and duty to seek God, to know him and to live in accordance with that knowledge. In the totalitarian and authoritarian regimes, the principle that force predominates over reason was carried to the extreme. Man was compelled to submit to a conception of reality imposed on him by coercion, and not reached by virtue of his own reason and the exercise of his own freedom. This principle must be overturned and total recognition must be given to *the rights of the human conscience*, which is bound only to the truth, both natural and revealed. The recognition of these rights represents the primary foundation of every authentically free political order. It is important to reaffirm this latter principle for several reasons:

a) because the old forms of totalitarianism and authoritarianism are not yet completely vanquished; indeed there is a risk that they will regain their strength. This demands renewed efforts of cooperation and solidarity between all countries;

b) because in the developed countries there is sometimes an excessive promotion of purely utilitarian values, with an appeal to the appetites and inclinations towards immediate gratification, making it difficult to recognize and respect the hierarchy of the true values of human existence;

c) because in some countries new forms of religious fundamentalism are emerging which covertly, or even openly, deny to citizens of faiths other than that of the majority the full exercise of their civil and religious rights, preventing them from taking part in the cultural process, and restricting both the Church's right to preach the Gospel and the rights of those who hear this preaching to accept it and to be converted to Christ. No authentic progress is possible without respect for the natural and fundamental right to know the truth and live according to that truth. The exercise and development of this right includes the right to discover and freely to accept Jesus Christ, who is man's true good.

(1) **Luke 17:19–31** And he said to him, "Rise and go your way; your faith has made you well." 2463

Being asked by the Pharisees when the kingdom of God was coming, he answered them, "The kingdom of God is not coming with signs to be observed; nor will they say, 'Lo, here it is!' or 'There!' for behold, the kingdom of God is in the midst of you."

And he said to the disciples, "The days are coming when you will desire to see one of the days of the Son of man, and you will not see it. And they will say to you, 'Lo, there!' or 'Lo, here!' Do not go, do not follow them. For as the lightning flashes and lights up the sky from one side to the other, so will the Son of man be in his day. But first he must suffer many things and be rejected by this generation. As it was in the days of Noah, so will it be in the days of the Son of man. They ate, they drank, they married, they were given in marriage, until the day when Noah entered the ark, and the flood came and destroyed them all. Likewise as it was in the days of Lot—they ate, they drank, they bought, they sold, they planted, they built, but on the day when Lot went out from Sodom fire and sulfur rained from heaven and destroyed them all—so will it be on the day when the Son of man is revealed. On that day, let him who is on the housetop, with his goods in the house, not come down to take them away; and likewise let him who is in the field not turn back. . . ."

(2) **Deuteronomy 5:20** " 'Neither shall you bear false witness against your neighbor. . . .' " 2463

(1) **Proverbs 8:7** 2465

. . . for my mouth will utter truth;
wickedness is an abomination to my lips.

(2) **2 Samuel 7:28** And now, O Lord God, thou art God, and thy words are true, and thou hast promised this good thing to thy servant. . . . 2465

(3) **Psalm 119:142** 2465

Thy righteousness is righteous for ever,
and thy law is true.

(4) **Luke 1:50** 2465

And his mercy is on those who fear him
from generation to generation.

(5) **Psalm 119:30** 2465

I have chosen the way of faithfulness,
I set thy ordinances before me.

(1) **John 14:6** Jesus said to him, "I am the way, and the truth, and the life; no one comes to the Father, but by me. . . ." 2466

(2) **John 17:17** Sanctify them in the truth; thy word is truth. 2466

2472 **Matthew 18:16** But if he does not listen, take one or two others along with you, that every word may be confirmed by the evidence of two or three witnesses.

2476 (1) **Proverbs 19:9**

A false witness will not go unpunished,
and he who utters lies will perish.

2476 (2) **Proverbs 18:5**

It is not good to be partial to a wicked man,
or to deprive a righteous man of justice.

2477 (1) **CIC Canon 220** No one is permitted to damage unlawfully the good reputation which another person enjoys nor to violate the right of another person to protect his or her own privacy.

2477 (2) **Sirach 21:28**

A whisperer defiles his own soul
and is hated in his neighborhood.

2489 (1) **Sirach 27:16**

Whoever betrays secrets destroys confidence,
and he will never find a congenial friend.

2489 (2) **Proverbs 25:9–10**

Argue your case with your neighbor himself,
and do not disclose another's secret;
lest he who hears you bring shame upon you,
and your ill repute have no end.

2494 ***Inter mirifica* 11** A special responsibility for the proper use of the means of social communication rests on journalists, writers, actors, designers, producers, exhibitors, distributors, operators, sellers, critics—all those, in a word, who are involved in the making and transmission of communications in any way whatever. It is clear that a very great responsibility rests on all of these people in today's world: they have power to direct mankind along a good path or an evil path by the information they impart and the pressure they exert.

It will be for them to regulate economic, political and artistic values in a way that will not conflict with the common good. To achieve this result more surely they will do well to form professional organizations capable of imposing on their members—if necessary by a formal pledge to observe a moral code—a respect for the moral law in the problems they encounter and in their activities.

They should always be mindful of the fact that a very large proportion of their readership and audience are young people who are in need of publications and entertainments for wholesome amusement and inspiration. They should ensure that religious features are entrusted to serious and competent persons and are handled with proper respect.

2501 (1) **Wisdom 7:16–17**

For both we and our words are in his hand,
as are all understanding and skill in crafts.
For it is he who gave me unerring knowledge of what exists,
to know the structure of the world and the activity of the elements. . . .

(2) Pius XII, encyclical *Musicae sacrae* (December 25, 1955) 2501

To our Venerable Brethren, the Patriarchs, Primates, Archbishops, Bishops and other Local Ordinaries in peace and communion with the Apostolic See:

Health and Apostolic Benediction.

The subject of sacred music has always been very close to Our heart. Hence it has seemed appropriate to Us in this encyclical letter to give an orderly explanation of the topic and also to answer somewhat more completely several questions which have been raised and discussed during the past decades. We are doing so in order that this noble and distinguished art may contribute more every day to greater splendor in the celebration of divine worship and to the more effective nourishment of spiritual life among the faithful.

At the same time We have desired to grant what many of you, venerable brethren, have requested in your wisdom and also what has been asked by outstanding masters of this liberal art and distinguished students of sacred music at meetings devoted to the subject. The experience of pastoral life and the advances being made in the study of this art have persuaded Us that this step is timely.

We hope, therefore, that what St. Pius X rightly decreed in the document which he accurately called the "legal code of sacred music" may be confirmed and inculcated anew, shown in a new light and strengthened by new proofs. We hope that the noble art of sacred music—adapted to contemporary conditions and in some way enriched—may ever more perfectly accomplish its mission.

I

Music is among the many and great gifts of nature with which God, in Whom is the harmony of the most perfect concord and the most perfect order, has enriched men, whom He has created in His image and likeness. Together with the other liberal arts, music contributes to spiritual joy and the delight of the soul.

On this subject St. Augustine has accurately written: "Music, that is the science or the sense of proper modulation, is likewise given by God's generosity to mortals having rational souls in order to lead them to higher things."

No one, therefore, will be astonished that always and everywhere, even among pagan peoples, sacred song and the art of music have been used to ornament and decorate religious ceremonies. This is proved by many documents, both ancient and new. No one will be astonished that these arts have been used especially for the worship of the true and sovereign God from the earliest times. Miraculously preserved unharmed from the Red Sea by God's power, the people of God sang a song of victory to the Lord, and Miriam, the sister of Moses, their leader, endowed with prophetic inspiration, sang with the people while playing a tambourine.

Later, when the ark of God was taken from the house of Abinadab to the city of David, the king himself and "all Israel played before the Lord on all manner of instruments made of wood, on harps and lutes and timbrels and cornets and cymbals." King David himself established the order of the music and singing used for sacred worship. This order was restored after the people's return from exile and was observed faithfully until the Divine Redeemer's coming.

St. Paul showed us clearly that sacred chant was used and held in honor from the very beginning in the Church founded by the Divine Redeemer when he wrote to the Ephesians: "Be filled with the Spirit, speaking to one another in psalms and hymns and spiritual songs." He indicates that this custom of singing hymns was in force in the assemblies of Christians when he says: "When you come together each of you has a hymn."

Pliny testifies that the same thing held true after apostolic times. He writes that apostates from the Faith said that "this was their greatest fault or error, that they were accustomed to gather before dawn on a certain day and sing a hymn to Christ as if He were God." These words of the Roman proconsul in Bithynia show very clearly that the sound of church singing was not completely silenced even in times of persecution.

Tertullian confirms this when he says that in the assemblies of the Christians "the Scriptures are read, the psalms are sung, sermons are preached."

There are many statements of the fathers and ecclesiastical writers testifying that after freedom and peace had been restored to the Church the psalms and hymns of liturgical worship were in almost daily use. Moreover, new forms of sacred chant were gradually created and new types of songs were invented. These were developed more and more by the choir schools attached to cathedrals and other important churches, especially by the School of Singers in Rome.

According to tradition, Our predecessor of happy memory, St. Gregory the Great, carefully collected and wisely arranged all that had been handed down by the elders and protected the purity and integrity of sacred chant with fitting laws and regulations.

From Rome, the Roman mode of singing gradually spread to other parts of the West. Not only was it enriched by new forms and modes, but a new kind of sacred singing, the religious song, frequently sung in the vernacular, was also brought into use.

The choral chant began to be called "Gregorian" after St. Gregory, the man who revived it. It attained new beauty in almost all parts of Christian Europe after the 8th or 9th century because of its accompaniment by a new musical instrument called the "organ." Little by little, beginning in the 9th century, polyphonic singing was added to this choral chant. The study and use of polyphonic singing were developed more and more during the centuries that followed and were raised to a marvelous perfection under the guidance of magnificent composers during the 15th and 16th centuries.

Since the Church always held this polyphonic chant in the highest esteem, it willingly admitted this type of music even in the Roman basilicas and in pontifical ceremonies in order to increase the glory of the sacred rites. Its power and splendor were increased when the sounds of the organ and other musical instruments were joined with the voices of the singers.

Thus, with the favor and under the auspices of the Church the study of sacred music has gone a long way over the course of the centuries. In this journey, although sometimes slowly and laboriously, it has gradually progressed from the simple and ingenuous Gregorian modes to great and magnificent works of art. To these works not only the human voice, but also the organ and other musical instruments, add dignity, majesty and a prodigious richness.

The progress of this musical art clearly shows how sincerely the Church has desired to render divine worship ever more splendid and more pleasing to the Christian people. It likewise shows why the Church must insist that this art remain within its proper limits and must prevent anything profane and foreign to divine worship from entering into sacred music along with genuine progress, and perverting it.

The Sovereign Pontiffs have always diligently fulfilled their obligation to be vigilant in this matter. The Council of Trent also forbids "those musical works in which something lascivious or impure is mixed with organ music or singing." In addition, not to mention numerous other Sovereign Pontiffs, Our predecessor Benedict XIV of happy memory, in an encyclical letter dated February 19, 1749, which prepared for a Holy Year and was outstanding for its great learning and abundance of proofs, particularly urged Bishops to firmly forbid the illicit and immoderate elements which had arrogantly been inserted into sacred music.

Our predecessors Leo XII, Pius VIII, Gregory XVI, Pius IX, and Leo XIII followed the same line.

Nevertheless it can be rightly said that Our predecessor of immortal memory, St. Pius X, made as it were the highest contribution to the reform and renewal of sacred music when he restated the principles and standards handed down from the elders and wisely brought them together as the conditions of modern times demanded. Finally, like Our immediate predecessor of happy memory, Pius XI, in his Apostolic Constitution *Divini cultus sanctitatem (The Holiness of Divine Worship)*, issued December 20, 1929, We ourself in the encyclical *Mediator Dei (On the Sacred Liturgy)*, issued November 20, 1947, have enriched and confirmed the orders of the older Pontiffs.

II

Certainly no one will be astonished that the Church is so vigilant and careful about sacred music. It is not a case of drawing up laws of aesthetics or technical rules that apply to the subject of music. It is the intention of the Church, however, to protect sacred music against anything that might lessen its dignity, since it is called upon to take part in something as important as divine worship.

On this score sacred music obeys laws and rules which are no different from those prescribed for all religious art and, indeed, for art in general. Now we are aware of the fact that during recent years some artists, gravely offending against Christian piety, have dared to bring into churches works devoid of any religious inspiration and completely at variance with the right rules of art. They try to justify this deplorable conduct by plausible-looking arguments which they claim are based on the nature and character of art itself. They go on to say that artistic inspiration is free and that it is wrong to impose upon it laws and standards extraneous to art, whether they are religious or moral, since such rules seriously hurt the dignity of art and place bonds and shackles on the activity of an inspired artist.

Arguments of this kind raise a question which is certainly difficult and serious, and which affects all art and every artist. It is a question which is not to be answered by an appeal to the principles of art or of aesthetics, but which must be decided in terms of the supreme principle of the final end, which is the inviolate and sacred rule for every man and every human act.

The ordination and direction of man to his ultimate end—which is God—by absolute and necessary law based on the nature and the infinite perfection of God Himself is so solid that not even God could exempt anyone from it. This eternal and unchangeable law commands that man himself and all his actions should manifest and imitate, so far as possible, God's infinite perfection for the praise and glory of the Creator. Since man is born to attain this supreme end, he ought to conform himself and through his actions direct all the powers of his body and his soul, rightly ordered among themselves and duly subjected to the end they are meant to attain, to the divine Model. Therefore even art and works of art must be judged in the light of their conformity and concord with man's last end.

Art certainly must be listed among the noblest manifestations of human genius. Its purpose is to express in human works the infinite divine beauty of which it is, as it were, the reflection. Hence that outworn dictum, "art for art's sake" entirely neglects the end for which every creature is made. Some people wrongly assert that art should be exempted entirely from every rule which does not spring from art itself. Thus this dictum either has no worth at all or is gravely offensive to God Himself, the Creator and Ultimate End.

Since the freedom of the artist is not a blind instinct to act in accordance with his own whim or some desire for novelty, it is in no way restricted or destroyed, but actually ennobled and perfected, when it is made subject to the divine law.

Since this is true of works of art in general, it obviously applies also to religious and sacred art. Actually religious art is even more closely bound to God and the promotion of His praise and glory, because its only purpose is to give the faithful the greatest aid in turning their minds piously to God through the works it directs to their senses of sight and hearing. Consequently the artist who does not profess the truths of the faith or who strays far from God in his attitude or conduct should never turn his hand to religious art. He lacks, as it were, that inward eye with which he might see what God's majesty and His worship demand. Nor can he hope that his works, devoid of religion as they are, will ever really breathe the piety and faith that befit God's temple and His holiness, even though they may show him to be an expert artist who is endowed with visible talent. Thus he cannot hope that his works will be worthy of admission into the sacred buildings of the Church, the guardian and arbiter of religious life.

But the artist who is firm in his faith and leads a life worthy of a Christian, who is motivated by the love of God and reverently uses the powers the Creator has given him, expresses and manifests the truths he holds and the piety he possesses so skillfully, beautifully and pleasingly in colors and lines or sounds and harmonies that this sacred labor of art is an act of worship and religion for him. It also effectively arouses and inspires people to profess the faith and cultivate piety.

The Church has always honored and always will honor this kind of artist. It opens wide the doors of its temples to them because what these people contribute through their art and industry is a welcome and important help to the Church in carrying out its apostolic ministry more effectively.

These laws and standards for religious art apply in a stricter and holier way to sacred music because sacred music enters more intimately into divine worship than many other liberal arts, such as architecture, painting and sculpture. These last serve to prepare a worthy setting for the sacred ceremonies. Sacred music, however, has an important place in the actual performance of the sacred ceremonies and rites themselves. Hence the Church must take the greatest care to prevent whatever might be unbecoming to sacred worship or anything that might distract the faithful in attendance from lifting their minds up to God from entering into sacred music, which is the servant, as it were, of the sacred liturgy.

The dignity and lofty purpose of sacred music consist in the fact that its lovely melodies and splendor beautify and embellish the voices of the priest who offers Mass and of the Christian people who praise the Sovereign God. Its special power and excellence should lift up to God the minds of the faithful who are present. It should make the liturgical prayers of the Christian community more alive and fervent so that everyone can praise and beseech the Triune God more powerfully, more intently and more effectively.

The power of sacred music increases the honor given to God by the Church in union with Christ, its Head. Sacred music likewise helps to increase the fruits which the faithful, moved by the sacred harmonies, derive from the holy liturgy. These fruits, as daily experience and many ancient and modern literary sources show, manifest themselves in a life and conduct worthy of a Christian.

St. Augustine, speaking of chants characterized by "beautiful voice and most apt melody," says: "I feel that our souls are moved to the ardor of piety by the sacred words more piously and powerfully when these words are sung than when they are not sung, and that all the affections of our soul in their variety have modes of their own in song and chant by which they are stirred up by an indescribable and secret sympathy."

It is easy to infer from what has just been said that the dignity and force of sacred music are greater the closer sacred music itself approaches to the supreme act of Christian worship, the Eucharistic sacrifice of the altar. There can be nothing more exalted or sublime than its function of accompanying with beautiful sound the voice of the priest offering up the Divine Victim, answering him joyfully with the people who are present and enhancing the whole liturgical ceremony with its noble art.

To this highest function of sacred music We must add another which closely resembles it, that is its function of accompanying and beautifying other liturgical ceremonies, particularly the recitation of the Divine Office in choir. Thus the highest honor and praise must be given to liturgical music.

We must also hold in honor that music which is not primarily a part of the sacred liturgy, but which by its power and purpose greatly aids religion. This music is therefore rightly called religious music. The Church has possessed such music from the beginning and it has developed happily under the Church's auspices. As experience shows, it can exercise great and salutary force and power on the souls of the faithful, both when it is used in churches during non-liturgical services and ceremonies, or when it is used outside churches at various solemnities and celebrations.

The tunes of these hymns, which are often sung in the language of the people, are memorized with almost no effort or labor. The mind grasps the words and the music. They are frequently repeated and completely understood. Hence even boys and girls, learning these sacred hymns at a tender age, are greatly helped by them to know, appreciate and memorize the truths of the faith. Therefore they also serve as a sort of catechism. These religious hymns bring pure and chaste joy to young people and adults during times of recreation. They give a kind of religious grandeur to their more solemn assemblies and gatherings. They bring pious joy, sweet consolation and spiritual progress to Christian families themselves. Hence these popular religious hymns are of great help to the Catholic apostolate and should be carefully cultivated and promoted.

Therefore when We praised the manifold power and the apostolic effectiveness of sacred music, We spoke of something that can be a source of great joy and solace to all who have in any way dedicated themselves to its study and practice. All who use the art they possess to compose such musical compositions, to teach them or to perform them by singing or using musical instruments, undoubtedly exercise in many and various ways a true and genuine apostolate. They will receive from Christ the Lord the generous rewards and honors of apostles for the work they have done so faithfully.

Consequently they should hold their work in high esteem, not only as artists and teachers of art, but also as ministers of Christ the Lord and as His helpers in the work of the apostolate. They should likewise show in their conduct and their lives the dignity of their calling.

III

Since, as We have just shown, the dignity and effectiveness of sacred music and religious chant are so great, it is very necessary that all of their parts should be diligently and carefully arranged to produce their salutary results in a fitting manner.

First of all the chants and sacred music which are immediately joined with the Church's liturgical worship should be conducive to the lofty end for which they are intended. This music—as our predecessor St. Pius X has already wisely warned us—"must possess proper liturgical qualities, primarily holiness and goodness of form; from which its other note, universality, is derived."

It must be *holy*. It must not allow within itself anything that savors of the profane nor allow any such thing to slip into the melodies in which it is expressed. The Gregorian chant which has been used in the Church over the course of so many centuries, and which may be called, as it were, its patrimony, is gloriously outstanding for this holiness.

This chant, because of the close adaptation of the melody to the sacred text, is not only most intimately conformed to the words, but also in a way interprets their force and efficacy and brings delight to the minds of the hearers. It does this by the use of musical modes that are simple and plain, but which are still composed with such sublime and holy art that they move everyone to sincere admiration and constitute an almost inexhaustible source from which musicians and composers draw new melodies.

It is the duty of all those to whom Christ the Lord has entrusted the task of guarding and dispensing the Church's riches to preserve this precious treasure of Gregorian chant diligently and to impart it generously to the Christian people. Hence what Our predecessors, St. Pius X, who is rightly called the renewer of Gregorian chant, and Pius XI have wisely ordained and taught, We also, in view of the outstanding qualities which genuine Gregorian chant possesses, will and prescribe that this be done. In the performance of the sacred liturgical rites this same Gregorian chant should be most widely used and great care should be taken that it should be performed properly, worthily and reverently. And if, because of recently instituted feast days, new Gregorian melodies must be composed, this should be done by true masters of the art. It should be done in such a way that these new compositions obey the laws proper to genuine Gregorian chant and are in worthy harmony with the older melodies in their virtue and purity.

If these prescriptions are really observed in their entirety, the requirements of the other property of sacred music—that property by virtue of which it should be an example of true art—will be duly satisfied. And if in Catholic churches throughout the entire world Gregorian chant sounds forth without corruption or diminution, the chant itself, like the sacred Roman liturgy, will have a characteristic of universality, so that the faithful, wherever they may be, will hear music that is familiar to them and a part of their own home. In this way they may experience, with much spiritual consolation, the wonderful unity of the Church. This is one of the most important reasons why the Church so greatly desires that the Gregorian chant traditionally associated with the Latin words of the sacred liturgy be used.

We are not unaware that, for serious reasons, some quite definite exceptions have been conceded by the Apostolic See. We do not want these exceptions extended or propagated more widely, nor do We wish to have them transferred to other places without due permission of the Holy See. Furthermore, even where it is licit to use these exemptions, local Ordinaries and the other pastors should take great care that the faithful from their earliest years should learn at least the easier and more frequently used Gregorian melodies, and should know how to employ them in the sacred liturgical rites, so that in this way also the unity and the universality of the Church may shine forth more powerfully every day.

Where, according to old or immemorial custom, some popular hymns are sung in the language of the people after the sacred words of the liturgy have been sung in Latin during the solemn Eucharistic sacrifice, local Ordinaries can allow this to be done, "if, in the light of the circumstances of the locality and the people, they believe that (custom) cannot prudently be removed." The law by which it is forbidden to sing the liturgical words themselves in the language of the people remains in force, according to what has been said.

In order that singers and the Christian people may rightly understand the meaning of the liturgical words joined to the musical melodies, it has pleased Us to make Our own the exhortation made by the Fathers of the Council of Trent. "Pastors and all those who have care of souls," were especially urged that "often, during the celebration of Mass, they or others whom they delegate explain something about what is read in the Mass and, among other things, tell something about the mystery of this most holy sacrifice. This is to be done particularly on Sundays and holy days."

This should be done especially at the time when catechetical instruction is being given to the Christian people. This may be done more easily and readily in this age of ours than was possible in times past, because translations of the liturgical texts into the vernacular tongues and explanations of these texts in books and pamphlets are available. These works, produced in almost every country by learned writers, can effectively help and enlighten the faithful to understand and share in what is said by the sacred ministers in the Latin language.

It is quite obvious that what We have said briefly here about Gregorian chant applies mainly to the Latin Roman Rite of the Church. It can also, however, be applied to a certain extent to the liturgical chants of other rites—either to those of the West, such as the Ambrosian, Gallican or Mozarabic, or to the various eastern rites.

For as all of these display in their liturgical ceremonies and formulas of prayer the marvelous abundance of the Church, they also, in their various liturgical chants, preserve treasures which must be guarded and defended to prevent not only their complete disappearance, but also any loss or distortion.

Among the oldest and most outstanding monuments of sacred music the liturgical chants of the different eastern rites hold a highly important place. Some of the melodies of these chants, modified in accordance with the character of the Latin liturgy, had a great influence on the composition of the musical works of the Western Church itself. It is Our hope that the selection of sacred eastern rite hymns—which the Pontifical Institute of Oriental Studies, with the help of the Pontifical Institute of Sacred Music, is busily working to complete—will achieve good doctrinal and practical results. Thus eastern rite seminarians, well trained in sacred chant, can make a significant contribution to enhancing the beauty of God's house after they have been ordained priests.

It is not Our intention in what We have just said in praise and commendation of the Gregorian chant to exclude sacred polyphonic music from the rites of the Church. If this polyphonic music is endowed with the proper qualities, it can be of great help in increasing the magnificence of divine worship and of moving the faithful to religious dispositions. Everyone certainly knows that many polyphonic compositions, especially those that date from the 16th century, have an artistic purity and richness of melody which render them completely worthy of accompanying and beautifying the Church's sacred rites.

Although over the course of the centuries genuine polyphonic art gradually declined and profane melodies often crept into it, during recent decades the indefatigable labors of experts have brought about a restoration. The works of the old composers have been carefully studied and proposed as models to be imitated and rivalled by modern composers.

So it is that in the basilicas, cathedrals and churches of religious communities these magnificent works of the old masters and the polyphonic compositions of more recent musicians can be performed, contributing greatly to the beauty of the sacred rite. Likewise We know that simpler but genuinely artistic polyphonic compositions are often sung even in smaller churches.

The Church favors all these enterprises. As Our predecessor of immortal memory, St. Pius X, says, the Church "unceasingly encourages and favors the progress of the arts, admitting for religious use all the good and the beautiful that the mind of man has discovered over the course of the centuries, but always respecting the liturgical laws."

These laws warn that great prudence and care should be used in this serious matter in order to keep out of churches polyphonic music which, because of its heavy and bombastic style, might obscure the sacred words of the liturgy by a kind of exaggeration, interfere with the conduct of the liturgical service, or, finally, lower the skill and competence of the singers to the disadvantage of sacred worship.

These norms must be applied to the use of the organ or other musical instruments. Among the musical instruments that have a place in church the organ rightly holds the principal position, since it is especially fitted for the sacred chants and sacred rites. It adds a wonderful splendor and a special magnificence to the ceremonies of the Church. It moves the souls of the faithful by the grandeur and sweetness of its tones. It gives minds an almost heavenly joy and it lifts them up powerfully to God and to higher things.

Besides the organ, other instruments can be called upon to give great help in attaining the lofty purpose of sacred music, so long as they play nothing profane, nothing clamorous or strident and nothing at variance with the sacred services or the dignity of the place. Among these the violin and other musical instruments that use the bow are outstanding because, when they are played by themselves or with other stringed instruments or with the organ, they express the joyous and sad sentiments of the soul with an indescribable power. Moreover, in the encyclical *Mediator Dei*, We Ourselves gave detailed and clear regulations concerning the musical modes that are to be admitted into the worship of the Catholic religion.

"For, if they are not profane or unbecoming to the sacredness of the place and function and do not spring from a desire to achieve extraordinary and unusual effects, then our churches must admit them, since they can contribute in no small way to the splendor of the sacred ceremonies, can lift the mind to higher things, and can foster true devotion of the soul."

It should hardly be necessary to add the warning that, when the means and talent available are unequal to the task, it is better to forego such attempts than to do something which would be unworthy of divine worship and sacred gatherings.

As We have said before, besides those things that are intimately associated with the Church's sacred liturgy, there are also popular religious hymns which derive their origin from the liturgical chant itself. Most of these are written in the language of the people. Since these are closely related to the mentality and temperament of individual national groups, they differ considerably among themselves according to the character of different races and localities.

If hymns of this sort are to bring spiritual fruit and advantage to the Christian people, they must be in full conformity with the doctrine of the Catholic faith. They must also express and explain that doctrine accurately. Likewise they must use plain language and simple melody and must be free from violent and vain excess of words. Despite the fact that they are short and easy, they should manifest a religious dignity and seriousness. When they are fashioned in this way these sacred canticles, born as they are from the most profound depths of the people's soul, deeply move the emotions and spirit and stir up pious sentiments. When they are sung at religious rites by a great crowd of people singing as with one voice, they are powerful in raising the minds of the faithful to higher things.

As we have written above, such hymns cannot be used in Solemn High Masses without the express permission of the Holy See. Nevertheless at Masses that are not sung solemnly these hymns can be a powerful aid in keeping the faithful from attending the Holy Sacrifice like dumb and idle spectators. They can help to make the faithful accompany the sacred services both mentally and vocally and to join their own piety to the prayers of the priest. This happens when these hymns are properly adapted to the individual parts of the Mass, as We rejoice to know is being done in many parts of the Catholic world.

In rites that are not completely liturgical religious hymns of this kind—when, as We have said, they are endowed with the right qualities—can be of great help in the salutary work of attracting the Christian people and enlightening them, in imbuing them with sincere piety and filling them with holy joy. They can produce these effects not only within churches, but outside of them also, especially on the occasion of pious processions and pilgrimages to shrines and at the time of national or international congresses. They can be especially useful, as experience has shown, in the work of instructing boys and girls in Catholic truth, in societies for youth and in meetings of pious associations.

Hence We can do no less than urge you, venerable brethren, to foster and promote diligently popular religious singing of this kind in the dioceses entrusted to you. There is among you no lack of experts in this field to gather hymns of this sort into one collection, where this has not already been done, so that all of the faithful can learn them more easily, memorize them and sing them correctly.

Those in charge of the religious instruction of boys and girls should not neglect the proper use of these effective aids. Those in charge of Catholic youth should make prudent use of them in the highly important work entrusted to them. Thus there will be hope of happily attaining what everyone desires, namely the disappearance of worldly songs which because of the quality of their melodies or the frequently voluptuous and lascivious words that go with them are a danger to Christians, especially the young, and their replacement by songs that give chaste and pure pleasure, that foster and increase faith and piety.

May it thus come about that the Christian people begin even on this earth to sing that song of praise it will sing forever in heaven: "To Him who sits upon the throne, and to the Lamb, blessing and honor and glory and dominion forever and ever."

What we have written thus far applies primarily to those nations where the Catholic religion is already firmly established. In mission lands it will not be possible to accomplish all these things until the number of Christians has grown sufficiently, larger church buildings have been erected, the children of Christians properly attend schools established by the Church and, finally, until there is an adequate number of sacred ministers. Still We urgently exhort apostolic workers who are laboring strenuously in these extensive parts of the Lord's vineyard to pay careful attention to this matter as one of the serious problems of their ministry.

Many of the peoples entrusted to the ministry of the missionaries take great delight in music and beautify the ceremonies dedicated to the worship of idols with religious singing. It is not prudent, then, for the heralds of Christ, the true God, to minimize or neglect entirely this effective help in their apostolate. Hence the preachers of the Gospel in pagan lands should sedulously and willingly promote in the course of their apostolic ministry the love for religious song which is cherished by the men entrusted to their care. In this way these people can have, in contrast to their own religious music which is frequently admired even in cultivated countries, sacred Christian hymns in which the truths of the faith, the life of Christ the Lord and the praises of the Blessed Virgin Mary and the Saints can be sung in a language and in melodies familiar to them.

Missionaries should likewise be mindful of the fact that, from the beginning, when the Catholic Church sent preachers of the Gospel into lands not yet illumined by the light of faith, it took care to bring into those countries, along with the sacred liturgical rites, musical compositions, among which were the Gregorian melodies. It did this so that the people who were to be converted might be more easily led to accept the truths of the Christian religion by the attractiveness of these melodies.

IV

So that the desired effect may be produced by what We have recommended and ordered in this encyclical, following in the footsteps of Our predecessors, you, venerable brethren, must carefully use all the aids offered by the lofty function entrusted to you by Christ the Lord and committed to you by the Church. As experience teaches, these aids are employed to great advantage in many churches throughout the Christian world.

First of all see to it that there is a good school of singers in the cathedral itself, and, as far as possible, in other major churches of your dioceses. This school should serve as an example to others and influence them to carefully develop and perfect sacred chant.

Where it is impossible to have schools of singers or where there are not enough choir boys, it is allowed that "a group of men and women or girls, located in a place outside the sanctuary set apart for the exclusive use of this group, can sing the liturgical texts at Solemn Mass, as long as the men are completely separated from the women and girls and everything unbecoming is avoided. The Ordinary is bound in conscience in this matter."

Great care must be taken that those who are preparing for the reception of sacred orders in your seminaries and in missionary or religious houses of study are properly instructed in the doctrine and use of sacred music and Gregorian chant according to the mind of the Church by teachers who are experts in this field, who esteem the traditional customs and teachings and who are entirely obedient to the precepts and norms of the Holy See.

If, among the students in the seminary or religious house of study, anyone shows remarkable facility in or liking for this art, the authorities of the seminary or house of study should not neglect to inform you about it. Then you may avail yourself of the opportunity to cultivate these gifts further and send him either to the Pontifical Institute of Sacred Music in Rome or to some other institution of learning in which this subject is taught, provided that the student manifests the qualities and virtues upon which one can base a hope that he will become an excellent priest.

In this matter care must also be taken that local Ordinaries and heads of religious communities have someone whose help they can use in this important area which, weighted down as they are by so many occupations, they cannot easily take care of themselves.

It would certainly be best if in diocesan Councils of Christian Art there were someone especially expert in the fields of religious music and chant who could carefully watch over what is being done in the diocese, inform the Ordinary about what has been done and what is going to be done, receive the Ordinary's commands and see that they are obeyed. If in any diocese there is one of these associations, which have been wisely instituted to foster sacred music and have been greatly praised and commended by the Sovereign Pontiffs, the Ordinary in his prudence may employ this association in the task of fulfilling responsibility.

Pious associations of this kind, which have been founded to instruct the people in sacred music or for advanced study in this subject, can contribute greatly by words and example to the advance of sacred music.

Help and promote such associations, venerable brethren, so that they may lead an active life, may employ the best and the most effective teachers, and so that, throughout the entire diocese, they may diligently promote the knowledge, love and use of sacred music and religious harmonies, with due observance of the Church's laws and due obedience to Ourselves.

Moved by paternal solicitude, We have dealt with this matter at some length. We are entirely confident that you, venerable brethren, will diligently apply all of your pastoral solicitude to this sacred subject which contributes so much to the more worthy and magnificent conduct of divine worship.

It is Our hope that whoever in the Church supervises and directs the work of sacred music under your leadership may be influenced by Our encyclical letter to carry on this glorious apostolate with new ardor and new effort, generously, enthusiastically and strenuously.

Hence, We hope that this most noble art, which has been so greatly esteemed throughout the Church's history and which today has been brought to real heights of holiness and beauty, will be developed and continually perfected and that on its own account it will happily work to bring the children of the Church to give due praise, expressed in worthy melodies and sweet harmonies, to the Triune God with stronger faith, more flourishing hope and more ardent charity.

May it produce even outside the walls of churches—in Christian families and gatherings of Christians—what St. Cyprian beautifully spoke of to Donatus, "Let the sober banquet resound with Psalms. And if your memory be good and your voice pleasant, approach this work according to custom. You give more nourishment to those dearest to you if we hear spiritual things and if religious sweetness delights the ears."

In the meantime, buoyed up by the hope of richer and more joyous fruits which We are confident will come from this exhortation of Ours, as a testimony of Our good will and as an omen of heavenly gifts to each one of you, venerable brethren, to the flock entrusted to your care and to those who observe Our wishes and work to promote sacred music, with abundant charity, We impart the Apostolic Benediction.

Given at St. Peter's in Rome, December 25, on the feast of the Nativity of Our Lord Jesus Christ, in the year 1955, the 17th of Our Pontificate.

(3) **Pius XII, allocution of 3 September 1950 to the International Congress of Catholic Artists** 2501

You have undertaken a timely and useful initiative, my dear sons, in proposing and organizing the first international congress of Catholic artists whose distinguished representatives we are happy to greet here.

Much has already been said about art, an inexhaustible topic! Your present activity leads us to draw attention—very briefly—to the role of art in the work of Peace. Pax Romana!

The frenzied activity of a world shaken to its foundations, misunderstandings among men, conflicting interests, the hypersensitivity of narrow views that too easily take offense have, in spite of the multiplication of contacts and of exchanges of goods, accentuated the isolation, enlarged and deepened the moral distance. The very excess of evil has little by little shed a brighter light on the necessity of uniting in a community of action all the dispersed forces of nations and peoples desirous of peace.

The persistent and skilled efforts to foster unity and cooperation among nations did not begin today or yesterday. The present events are not a sign of the futility or uselessness of these efforts, but of their insufficiency and impermanence. And so with a praiseworthy enthusiasm efforts are being made to promote, despite all sorts of difficulties, international political, juridical, economic, and social associations. But it has very quickly become clear that there is a need for something more intimate, more human, and there has been, at least in part, a beginning of common activities in the technical, scientific, and cultural spheres.

In this intellectual order, the association of Catholic artists who are now celebrating their first congress, has a most honorable place. That goes without saying, given the fact that art is, under certain aspects, the most vital and synthetic expression of human thought and feeling. It is also the most universally intelligible since, addressing the senses directly, art transcends the diversity of languages and knows only the extremely suggestive diversity of temperaments and attitudes. Moreover, by its refinement and sensitivity, art, whether heard or seen, penetrates the intelligence and sensibility of the observer or listener to depths that neither the written nor spoken word, with its insufficiently nuanced analytic precision, can ever reach.

For these two reasons, art helps men, notwithstanding all the differences of character, education, or civilization, to know one another, or at least to form some idea of each other and, then, to place their resources in common with a view to mutual enrichment.

There is a necessary first condition for art to be able to produce such a desirable result: the quality of its expression, without which it ceases to be true art. This remark is not superfluous today when too often, in certain schools, a work of art does not suffice of itself to translate the thought, exteriorize the sentiment, reveal the soul of its author. But as soon as it needs to be explained in words, it loses its sign value and only provides the senses with a physical pleasure that remains at that level, or it provides the mind with a subtle and empty game. Another condition for art to be able to accomplish with dignity and fruit its glorious mission of understanding, concord, and peace is that through it the senses, far from weighing down the soul and nailing it to the ground, serve it rather as wings to lift it up, from trivial and passing banalities towards the eternal, towards the true, towards the beautiful, towards the only true good, towards the only center where union is found, where unity is achieved, towards God. Is it not here that the Apostle's splendid manifesto finds its literal application: "Ever since the creation of the world God's invisible nature, namely, his eternal power and deity, has been clearly perceived in the things that have been made" (Rom 1:20).

This is why all the slogans which deprive art of its sublime role profane and sterilize it. "Art for art's sake": as if it could be its own end, condemned to move and languish in the realm of sensible and material things; as if through art man's senses did not obey a higher calling than that of mere perception of material nature, the calling to arouse in the spirit and the soul of man, in virtue of the transparency of that nature, the desire for "things no eye has seen, nor ear heard, nor the heart of man conceived" (1 Cor 2:9).

We will say nothing here of immoral art which works to debase and subjugate the spiritual powers of the soul to carnal passions. Indeed, "art" and "immoral" are two words in blatant contradiction, and your program does not conjoin them. You are to be congratulated for having understood the task incumbent upon you and to have chosen, in the face of a "culture without hope", to consider art as the "source of a new hope". Let the reflection of the divine beauty and light smile upon the earth, upon mankind, and you will have greatly contributed to the work of peace in helping man love "all that is true, all that is pure, just, holy, and worthy of love", and "the God of peace will be with you" (cf. Phil 4:8–9). May the immaculate Virgin, mirror of justice and splendor of God, Queen of peace and, one may well say, Queen of the arts, inspire and assist you; may she bring down upon you, for whom she is the lovingly contemplated ideal, the graces of her Son, as a pledge of which we give to you, to the whole group of Catholic artists, to all those dear to you, our apostolic blessing.

***Sacrosanctum concilium* 122–27** The fine arts are rightly classed among the noblest activities of man's genius; this is especially true of religious art and of its highest manifestation, sacred art. Of their nature the arts are directed toward expressing in some way the infinite beauty of God in works made by human hands. Their dedication to the increase of God's praise and of his glory is more complete, the more exclusively they are devoted to turning men's minds devoutly toward God. **2503**

For that reason holy Mother Church has always been the patron of the fine arts and has ever sought their noble ministry, to the end especially that all things set apart for use in divine worship should be worthy, becoming, and beautiful, signs and symbols of things supernatural. And to this end she has trained artists. In fact the Church has, with good reason, always claimed the right to pass judgment on the arts, deciding which of the works of artists are in accordance with faith, piety, and the laws religiously handed down, and are to be considered suitable for sacred use.

The Church has been particularly careful to see that sacred furnishings should worthily and beautifully serve the dignity of worship. She has admitted changes in material, style, or ornamentation prompted by the progress of technical arts with the passage of time.

Wherefore it has pleased the Fathers to issue the following decrees on these matters:

The Church has not adopted any particular style of art as her own. She has admitted styles from every period, in keeping with the natural characteristics and conditions of peoples and the needs of the various rites. Thus in the course of the centuries she has brought into existence a treasury of art which must be preserved with every care. The art of our own times from every race and country shall also be given free scope in the Church, provided it bring to the task the reverence and honor due to the sacred buildings and rites. Thus it is enabled to join its voice to that wonderful chorus of praise in honor of the Catholic faith sung by great men in past ages.

Ordinaries are to take care that in encouraging and favoring truly sacred art, they should seek for noble beauty rather than sumptuous display. The same principle applies also to sacred vestments and ornaments.

Bishops should be careful to ensure that works of art which are repugnant to faith, morals, and Christian piety, and which offend true religious sense either by depraved forms or through lack of artistic merit or because of mediocrity or pretense, be removed from the house of God and from other sacred places.

And when churches are to be built, let great care be taken that they be suitable for the celebration of liturgical services and for the active participation of the faithful.

The practice of placing sacred images in churches so that they be venerated by the faithful is to be maintained. Nevertheless their number should be moderate and their relative positions should reflect right order. For otherwise the Christian people may find them incongruous and they may foster devotion of doubtful orthodoxy.

When passing judgment on works of art, local ordinaries should ask the opinion of the diocesan commission on sacred art and—when occasion demands—the opinions of others who are experts, and the commissions mentioned in Articles 44, 45 and 46.

Ordinaries should ensure that sacred furnishings and works of value are not disposed of or destroyed, for they are ornaments in God's house.

Bishops, either personally or through suitable priests who are gifted with a knowledge and love of art, should have a special concern for artists, so as to imbue them with the spirit of sacred art and of the sacred liturgy.

It is also desirable that schools or academies of sacred art should be established in those parts of the world where they would be useful for the training of artists.

All artists who, prompted by their talents, desire to serve God's glory in holy Church should ever remember that they are engaged in a kind of holy imitation of God the

Creator: that they are concerned with works destined to be used in Catholic worship, for the edification of the faithful and to foster their piety and religious formation.

2514 **1 John 2:16** For all that is in the world, the lust of the flesh and the lust of the eyes and the pride of life, is not of the Father but is of the world.

2515 (1) **Galatians 5:16** But I say, walk by the Spirit, and do not gratify the desires of the flesh.

2515 (2) **Galatians 5:17** For the desires of the flesh are against the Spirit, and the desires of the Spirit are against the flesh; for these are opposed to each other, to prevent you from doing what you would.

2515 (3) **Galatians 5:24** And those who belong to Christ Jesus have crucified the flesh with its passions and desires.

2515 (4) **Ephesians 2:3** Among these we all once lived in the passions of our flesh, following the desires of body and mind, and so we were by nature children of wrath, like the rest of mankind.

2515 (5) **Genesis 3:11** He said, "Who told you that you were naked? Have you eaten of the tree of which I commanded you not to eat?"

2515 (6) **Council of Trent (1546): DS 1515** If anyone denies that by the grace of our Lord Jesus Christ, which is conferred in baptism, the guilt of original sin is remitted, or even asserts that the whole of that which has the true and proper nature of sin is not taken away, but says that it is only touched in person or is not imputed, let him be anathema.

2516 **Galatians 5:25** If we live by the Spirit, let us also walk by the Spirit.

2518 (1) **1 Timothy 4:3–9** . . . who forbid marriage and enjoin abstinence from foods which God created to be received with thanksgiving by those who believe and know the truth. For everything created by God is good, and nothing is to be rejected if it is received with thanksgiving; for then it is consecrated by the word of God and prayer.

If you put these instructions before the brethren, you will be a good minister of Christ Jesus, nourished on the words of the faith and of the good doctrine which you have followed. Have nothing to do with godless and silly myths. Train yourself in godliness; for while bodily training is of some value, godliness is of value in every way, as it holds promise for the present life and also for the life to come. The saying is sure and worthy of full acceptance.

2518 (2) **2 Timothy 2:22** So shun youthful passions and aim at righteousness, faith, love, and peace, along with those who call upon the Lord from a pure heart.

2518 (3) **1 Thessalonians 4:7** For God has not called us for uncleanness, but in holiness.

2518 (4) **Colossians 3:5** Put to death therefore what is earthly in you: fornication, impurity, passion, evil desire, and covetousness, which is idolatry.

2518 (5) **Ephesians 4:19** . . . they have become callous and have given themselves up to licentiousness, greedy to practice every kind of uncleanness.

(6) **Titus 1:15** To the pure all things are pure, but to the corrupt and unbelieving nothing is pure; their very minds and consciences are corrupted. 2518

(7) **1 Timothy 1:3–4** As I urged you when I was going to Macedonia, remain at Ephesus that you may charge certain persons not to teach any different doctrine, nor to occupy themselves with myths and endless genealogies which promote speculations rather than the divine training that is in faith. . . . 2518

(8) **2 Timothy 2:23–26** Have nothing to do with stupid, senseless controversies; you know that they breed quarrels. And the Lord's servant must not be quarrelsome but kindly to every one, an apt teacher, forbearing, correcting his opponents with gentleness. God may perhaps grant that they will repent and come to know the truth, and they may escape from the snare of the devil, after being captured by him to do his will. 2518

(1) **1 Corinthians 13:12** For now we see in a mirror dimly, but then face to face. Now I know in part; then shall I understand fully, even as I have been fully understood. 2519

(2) **1 John 3:2** Beloved, we are God's children now; it does not yet appear what we shall be, but we know that when he appears we shall be like him, for we shall see him as he is. 2519

(1) **Romans 12:2** Do not be conformed to this world but be transformed by the renewal of your mind, that you may prove what is the will of God, what is good and acceptable and perfect. 2520

(2) **Colossians 1:10** . . . to lead a life worthy of the Lord, fully pleasing to him, bearing fruit in every good work and increasing in the knowledge of God. 2520

(1) **1 John 2:16** For all that is in the world, the lust of the flesh and the lust of the eyes and the pride of life, is not of the Father but is of the world. 2534

(2) **Micah 2:2** 2534

They covet fields, and seize them;
    and houses, and take them away;
they oppress a man and his house,
    a man and his inheritance.

(3) **Wisdom 14:12** 2534

For the idea of making idols was the beginning of fornication,
and the invention of them was the corruption of life. . . .

Sirach 5:8 2536

Do not depend on dishonest wealth,
    for it will not benefit you in the day of calamity.

(1) **2 Samuel 12:1–4** And the Lord sent Nathan to David. He came to him, and said to him, "There were two men in a certain city, the one rich and the other poor. The rich man had very many flocks and herds; but the poor man had nothing but one little ewe lamb, which he had bought. And he brought it up, and it grew up with him and with his children; it used to eat of his morsel, and drink from his cup, and 2538

lie in his bosom, and it was like a daughter to him. Now there came a traveler to the rich man, and he was unwilling to take one of his own flock or herd to prepare for the wayfarer who had come to him, but he took the poor man's lamb, and prepared it for the man who had come to him."

2538 (2) **Genesis 4:3–7** In the course of time Cain brought to the Lord an offering of the fruit of the ground, and Abel brought of the firstlings of his flock and of their fat portions. And the Lord had regard for Abel and his offering, but for Cain and his offering he had no regard. So Cain was very angry, and his countenance fell. The Lord said to Cain, "Why are you angry, and why has your countenance fallen? If you do well, will you not be accepted? And if you do not do well, sin is couching at the door; its desire is for you, but you must master it."

2538 (3) **1 Kings 21:1–29** Now Naboth the Jezreelite had a vineyard in Jezreel, beside the palace of Ahab king of Samaria. And after this Ahab said to Naboth, "Give me your vineyard, that I may have it for a vegetable garden, because it is near my house; and I will give you a better vineyard for it; or, if it seems good to you, I will give you its value in money." But Naboth said to Ahab, "The Lord forbid that I should give you the inheritance of my fathers." And Ahab went into his house vexed and sullen because of what Naboth the Jezreelite had said to him; for he had said, "I will not give you the inheritance of my fathers." And he lay down on his bed, and turned away his face, and would eat no food.

But Jezebel his wife came to him, and said to him, "Why is your spirit so vexed that you eat no food?" And he said to her, "Because I spoke to Naboth the Jezreelite, and said to him, 'Give me your vineyard for money; or else, if it please you, I will give you another vineyard for it'; and he answered, 'I will not give you my vineyard.'" And Jezebel his wife said to him, "Do you now govern Israel? Arise, and eat bread, and let your heart be cheerful; I will give you the vineyard of Naboth the Jezreelite."

So she wrote letters in Ahab's name and sealed them with his seal, and she sent the letters to the elders and the nobles who dwelt with Naboth in his city. And she wrote in the letters, "Proclaim a fast, and set Naboth on high among the people; and set two base fellows opposite him, and let them bring a charge against him, saying, 'You have cursed God and the king.' Then take him out, and stone him to death." And the men of his city, the elders and the nobles who dwelt in his city, did as Jezebel had sent word to them. As it was written in the letters which she had sent to them, they proclaimed a fast, and set Naboth on high among the people. And the two base fellows came in and sat opposite him; and the base fellows brought a charge against Naboth, in the presence of the people, saying, "Naboth cursed God and the king." So they took him outside the city, and stoned him to death with stones. Then they sent to Jezebel, saying, "Naboth has been stoned; he is dead."

As soon as Jezebel heard that Naboth had been stoned and was dead, Jezebel said to Ahab, "Arise, take possession of the vineyard of Naboth the Jezreelite, which he refused to give you for money; for Naboth is not alive, but dead." And as soon as Ahab heard that Naboth was dead, Ahab arose to go down to the vineyard of Naboth the Jezreelite, to take possession of it.

Then the word of the Lord came to Elijah the Tishbite, saying, "Arise, go down to meet Ahab king of Israel, who is in Samaria; behold, he is in the vineyard of Naboth, where he has gone to take possession. And you shall say to him, 'Thus says the Lord, "Have you killed, and also taken possession?"' And you shall say to him, 'Thus says the Lord: "In the place where dogs licked up the blood of Naboth shall dogs lick your own blood."'"

Ahab said to Elijah, "Have you found me, O my enemy?" He answered, "I have found you, because you have sold yourself to do what is evil in the sight of the Lord. Behold, I will bring evil upon you; I will utterly sweep you away, and will cut off from Ahab every male, bond or free, in Israel; and I will make your house like the house of Jeroboam the son of Nebat, and like the house of Baasha the son of Ahijah, for the anger to which you have provoked me, and because you have made Israel to sin. And of Jezebel the Lord also said, 'The dogs shall eat Jezebel within the bounds of Jezreel.' Any one belonging to Ahab who dies in the city the dogs shall eat; and any one of his who dies in the open country the birds of the air shall eat."

(There was none who sold himself to do what was evil in the sight of the Lord like Ahab, whom Jezebel his wife incited. He did very abominably in going after idols, as the Amorites had done, whom the Lord cast out before the people of Israel.)

And when Ahab heard those words, he rent his clothes, and put sackcloth upon his flesh, and fasted and lay in sackcloth, and went about dejectedly. And the word of the Lord came to Elijah the Tishbite, saying, "Have you seen how Ahab has humbled himself before me? Because he has humbled himself before me, I will not bring the evil in his days; but in his son's days I will bring the evil upon his house."

St. Augustine, *De catechizandis rudibus* 4, 8 If, therefore, Christ came chiefly for this reason that man might learn how much God loves him, and might learn this to the end that he might begin to glow with love of Him by whom he was first loved, and so might love his neighbor at the bidding and after the example of Him who made Himself man's neighbor by loving him, when instead of being His neighbor he was wandering far from Him; if, moreover, all divine Scripture that was written before was written to foretell the coming of the Lord, and if whatever has since been committed to writing and established by divine authority tells of Christ and counsels love, then it is evident that on these two commandments of the love of God and the love of our neighbor depend not merely the whole law and the Prophets (which at the time when the Lord uttered these precepts were as yet the only Holy Scripture), but also all the inspired books that have been written at a later period for our welfare and handed down to us. Therefore, in the Old Testament the new is concealed, and in the New the Old is revealed. In keeping with that concealment, carnal men, understanding only carnally, both then were, and now are, made subject to the fear of punishment. But in keeping with this revelation spiritual men, understanding spiritually (both these of former times to whom, when they devoutly knocked, hidden things were revealed, and those of the present time, who do not seek in pride, lest even what is manifest should be hidden from them), are made free by the bestowal of love. Since therefore nothing is more opposed to love than envy, and the mother of envy is pride, the same Lord Jesus Christ, God-Man, is at once a token of divine love towards us and an example among us of man's lowliness, to the end that our swollen conceit, great as it is, may be healed by an even greater antidote. For the misery of man's pride is great, but the commiseration of God's humility is greater. **2539**

With this love, then, set before you as an end to which you may refer all that you say, so give all your instructions that he to whom you speak by hearing may believe, and by believing may hope, and by hoping may love.

(1) **Romans 7:7** What then shall we say? That the law is sin? By no means! Yet, if it had not been for the law, I should not have known sin. I should not have known what it is to covet if the law had not said, "You shall not covet." **2542**

(2) **Romans 7:10** . . . the very commandment which promised life proved to be death to me. **2542**

(1) **Romans 8:14** For all who are led by the Spirit of God are sons of God. **2543**

2543 (2) **Romans 8:27** And he who searches the hearts of men knows what is the mind of the Spirit, because the Spirit intercedes for the saints according to the will of God.

2544 (1) **Mark 8:35** For whoever would save his life will lose it; and whoever loses his life for my sake and the gospel's will save it.

2544 (2) **Luke 21:4** ". . . for they all contributed out of their abundance, but she out of her poverty put in all the living that she had."

2546 (1) **Luke 6:20** And he lifted up his eyes on his disciples, and said:
"Blessed are you poor, for yours is the kingdom of God. . . ."

2546 (2) **2 Corinthians 8:9** For you know the grace of our Lord Jesus Christ, that though he was rich, yet for your sake he became poor, so that by his poverty you might become rich.

2547 **Matthew 6:25–34** "Therefore I tell you, do not be anxious about your life, what you shall eat or what you shall drink, nor about your body, what you shall put on. Is not life more than food, and the body more than clothing? Look at the birds of the air: they neither sow nor reap nor gather into barns, and yet your heavenly Father feeds them. Are you not of more value than they? And which of you by being anxious can add one cubit to his span of life? And why are you anxious about clothing? Consider the lilies of the field, how they grow; they neither toil nor spin; yet I tell you, even Solomon in all his glory was not arrayed like one of these. But if God so clothes the grass of the field, which today is alive and tomorrow is thrown into the oven, will he not much more clothe you, O men of little faith? Therefore do not be anxious, saying, 'What shall we eat?' or 'What shall we drink?' or 'What shall we wear?' For the Gentiles seek all these things; and your heavenly Father knows that you need them all. But seek first his kingdom and his righteousness, and all these things shall be yours as well.

"Therefore do not be anxious about tomorrow, for tomorrow will be anxious for itself. Let the day's own trouble be sufficient for the day. . . ."

2550 (1) **Revelation 22:17** The Spirit and the Bride say, "Come." And let him who hears say, "Come." And let him who is thirsty come, let him who desires take the water of life without price.

2550 (2) **Leviticus 26:12** And I will walk among you, and will be your God, and you shall be my people.

2550 (3) **1 Corinthians 15:28** When all things are subjected to him, then the Son himself will also be subjected to him who put all things under him, that God may be everything to every one.

2557 **John 4:14** ". . . but whoever drinks of the water that I shall give him will never thirst; the water that I shall give him will become in him a spring of water welling up to eternal life."

IV

CHRISTIAN PRAYER

Luke 18:9–14 He also told this parable to some who trusted in themselves that they were righteous and despised others: "Two men went up into the temple to pray, one a Pharisee and the other a tax collector. The Pharisee stood and prayed thus with himself, 'God, I thank thee that I am not like other men, extortioners, unjust, adulterers, or even like this tax collector. I fast twice a week, I give tithes of all that I get.' But the tax collector, standing far off, would not even lift up his eyes to heaven, but beat his breast, saying, 'God, be merciful to me a sinner!' I tell you, this man went down to his house justified rather than the other; for every one who exalts himself will be humbled, but he who humbles himself will be exalted." 2559

St. Augustine, *De diversis quaestionibus octoginta tribus* 64, 4 Nonetheless, one can ask: Why did the Lord request a drink of the Samaritan woman who had come to fill her jar with water, when afterwards he himself was going to say that he could give the gushing of a spiritual fountain to those asking? Well, obviously, the Lord was thirsty for the trust of that woman, because she was a Samaritan, and Samaria usually represents idolatry. For, separated from the Jewish people, they had delivered the dignity of their souls over to the images of dumb animals, i.e., to golden cows. However, our Lord Jesus had come that he might lead the multitude of nations who were serving idols to the protection of Christian faith and uncorrupted religion. "For," he says, "the healthy have no need of a physician—only the ill." Therefore he is thirsty for the trust of those for whom he shed his blood. Consequently Jesus said to the woman: "Woman, give me a drink." 2560

Moreover, to see what our Lord was thirsty for, [note that] after a little while come his disciples, who had gone into the city to buy food, and they say to him: "'Rabbi, eat.' But he said to them: 'I have food to eat of which you have no knowledge.' Therefore his disciples say to one another: 'Has anyone brought him [anything] to eat?' Jesus said to them: 'My food is to do the will of him who has sent me and to complete his work.'" There is here no doubt, is there, that these two things—the will of the Father who has sent him and the work of the Father which Jesus answers that he wants to complete—are nothing other than our conversion from the ruinous error of the world to faith in him? Therefore, Jesus's drink is the same as his food. Accordingly he was thirsty for this in the woman, that he might do in her the Father's will and complete his work.

However, understanding in a carnal manner, she answers: "Since you yourself are a Jew, how do you ask of me a drink, since I am a Samaritan woman? For the Jews have no dealings with Samaritans." Our Lord said to her: "If you knew the gift of God and who it is who says to you: 'Give me a drink,' you rather would have asked of him, and he would have given you living water." [He said this] to show her that he had not asked for the kind of water that she herself had understood, but that he himself was thirsty for her trust and was desirous of giving the Holy Spirit to her in her own thirst, for we correctly understand this living water to be the gift of God, as the Lord himself says: "If you knew the gift of God." Likewise the same evangelist John testifies in another place with these words: "that Jesus was standing and crying out; 'If anyone is thirsty, let him come and drink. He who believes in me, as the Scripture says, out of his belly will flow rivers of living water.'" Jesus speaks altogether consistently when he says: "He who believes in me, out of his belly will flow rivers of living water," because we first believe in order to merit these gifts. Therefore these rivers of living water, which the Lord wanted to give to that woman, are the reward of the trust which he was first thirsting for in her. The evangelist provides the interpretation of this living water when he says: "But he was saying this about the Holy Spirit whom those who would believe in him were going to receive. However, the Spirit had not yet been given, because Jesus had not yet been glorified." Consequently this gift is the Holy Spirit, a gift which he gave to the Church after his glorification, as the Scripture elsewhere says: "Ascending to the heights, he has taken captive captivity, he has given gifts to men."

2561 (1) **John 7:37–39** On the last day of the feast, the great day, Jesus stood up and proclaimed, "If any one thirst, let him come to me and drink. He who believes in me, as the scripture has said, 'Out of his heart shall flow rivers of living water.'" Now this he said about the Spirit, which those who believed in him were to receive; for as yet the Spirit had not been given, because Jesus was not yet glorified.

2561 (2) **John 19:28** After this Jesus, knowing that all was now finished, said (to fulfill the scripture), "I thirst."

2561 (3) **Isaiah 12:3** With joy you will draw water from the wells of salvation.

2561 (4) **Isaiah 51:1**

"Hearken to me, you who pursue deliverance,
    you who seek the Lord;
look to the rock from which you were hewn,
    and to the quarry from which you were digged. . . ."

2561 (5) **Zechariah 12:10** "And I will pour out on the house of David and the inhabitants of Jerusalem a spirit of compassion and supplication, so that, when they look on him whom they have pierced, they shall mourn for him, as one mourns for an only child, and weep bitterly over him, as one weeps over a first-born. . . ."

2561 (6) **Zechariah 13:1** "On that day there shall be a fountain opened for the house of David and the inhabitants of Jerusalem to cleanse them from sin and uncleanness. . . ."

2565 (1) **Romans 6:5** For if we have been united with him in a death like his, we shall certainly be united with him in a resurrection like his.

2565 (2) **Ephesians 3:18–21** . . . may have power to comprehend with all the saints what is the breadth and length and height and depth, and to know the love of Christ which surpasses knowledge, that you may be filled with all the fullness of God.

Now to him who by the power at work within us is able to do far more abundantly than all that we ask or think, to him be glory in the church and in Christ Jesus to all generations, for ever and ever. Amen.

2566 **Acts 17:27** . . . that they should seek God, in the hope that they might feel after him and find him. Yet he is not far from each one of us. . . .

2569 (1) **Genesis 4:4** . . . and Abel brought of the firstlings of his flock and of their fat portions. And the Lord had regard for Abel and his offering. . . .

(2) **Genesis 4:26** To Seth also a son was born, and he called his name Enosh. At 2569
that time men began to call upon the name of the Lord.

(3) **Genesis 5:24** Enoch walked with God; and he was not, for God took him. 2569

Genesis 15:2–3 But Abram said, "O Lord God, what wilt thou give me, for I 2570
continue childless, and the heir of my house is Eliezer of Damascus?" And Abram said, "Behold, thou hast given me no offspring; and a slave born in my house will be my heir."

(1) **Genesis 15:6** And he believed the Lord; and he reckoned it to him as righ- 2571
teousness.

(2) **Genesis 17:1–2** When Abram was ninety-nine years old the Lord appeared to 2571
Abram, and said to him, "I am God Almighty; walk before me, and be blameless. And I will make my covenant between me and you, and will multiply you exceedingly."

(3) **Genesis 18:1–15** And the Lord appeared to him by the oaks of Mamre, as he 2571
sat at the door of his tent in the heat of the day. He lifted up his eyes and looked, and behold, three men stood in front of him. When he saw them, he ran from the tent door to meet them, and bowed himself to the earth, and said, "My lord, if I have found favor in your sight, do not pass by your servant. Let a little water be brought, and wash your feet, and rest yourselves under the tree, while I fetch a morsel of bread, that you may refresh yourselves, and after that you may pass on—since you have come to your servant." So they said, "Do as you have said." And Abraham hastened into the tent to Sarah, and said, "Make ready quickly three measures of fine meal, knead it, and make cakes." And Abraham ran to the herd, and took a calf, tender and good, and gave it to the servant, who hastened to prepare it. Then he took curds, and milk, and the calf which he had prepared, and set it before them; and he stood by them under the tree while they ate.

They said to him, "Where is Sarah your wife?" And he said, "She is in the tent." The Lord said, "I will surely return to you in the spring, and Sarah your wife shall have a son." And Sarah was listening at the tent door behind him. Now Abraham and Sarah were old, advanced in age; it had ceased to be with Sarah after the manner of women. So Sarah laughed to herself, saying, "After I have grown old, and my husband is old, shall I have pleasure?" The Lord said to Abraham, "Why did Sarah laugh, and say, 'Shall I indeed bear a child, now that I am old?' Is anything too hard for the Lord? At the appointed time I will return to you, in the spring, and Sarah shall have a son." But Sarah denied, saying "I did not laugh"; for she was afraid. He said, "No, but you did laugh."

(4) **Luke 1:26–38** In the sixth month the angel Gabriel was sent from God to 2571
a city of Galilee named Nazareth, to a virgin betrothed to a man whose name was Joseph, of the house of David; and the virgin's name was Mary. And he came to her and said, "Hail, O favored one, the Lord is with you!" But she was greatly troubled at the saying, and considered in her mind what sort of greeting this might be. And the angel said to her, "Do not be afraid, Mary, for you have found favor with God. And behold, you will conceive in your womb and bear a son, and you shall call his name Jesus.

He will be great, and will be called the Son of the Most High;
and the Lord God will give to him the throne of his father David,

and he will reign over the house of Jacob for ever;
and of his kingdom there will be no end."

And Mary said to the angel, "How shall this be, since I have no husband?" And the angel said to her,

"The Holy Spirit will come upon you,
and the power of the Most High will overshadow you;
therefore the child to be born will be called holy,
the Son of God.

And behold, your kinswoman Elizabeth in her old age has also conceived a son; and this is the sixth month with her who was called barren. For with God nothing will be impossible." And Mary said, "Behold, I am the handmaid of the Lord; let it be to me according to your word." And the angel departed from her.

2571 (5) **Genesis 18:16–33** Then the men set out from there, and they looked toward Sodom; and Abraham went with them to set them on their way. The Lord said, "Shall I hide from Abraham what I am about to do, seeing that Abraham shall become a great and mighty nation, and all the nations of the earth shall bless themselves by him? No, for I have chosen him, that he may charge his children and his household after him to keep the way of the Lord by doing righteousness and justice; so that the Lord may bring to Abraham what he has promised him." Then the Lord said, "Because the outcry against Sodom and Gomorrah is great and their sin is very grave, I will go down to see whether they have done altogether according to the outcry which has come to me; and if not, I will know."

So the men turned from there, and went toward Sodom; but Abraham still stood before the Lord. Then Abraham drew near, and said, "Wilt thou indeed destroy the righteous with the wicked? Suppose there are fifty righteous within the city; wilt thou then destroy the place and not spare it for the fifty righteous who are in it? Far be it from thee to do such a thing, to slay the righteous with the wicked, so that the righteous fare as the wicked! Far be that from thee! Shall not the Judge of all the earth do right?" And the Lord said, "If I find at Sodom fifty righteous in the city, I will spare the whole place for their sake." Abraham answered, "Behold, I have taken upon myself to speak to the Lord, I who am but dust and ashes. Suppose five of the fifty righteous are lacking? Wilt thou destroy the whole city for lack of five?" And he said, "I will not destroy it if I find forty-five there." Again he spoke to him, and said, "Suppose forty are found there." He answered, "For the sake of forty I will not do it." Then he said, "Oh let not the Lord be angry, and I will speak. Suppose thirty are found there." He answered, "I will not do it, if I find thirty there." He said, "Behold, I have taken upon myself to speak to the Lord. Suppose twenty are found there." He answered, "For the sake of twenty I will not destroy it." Then he said, "Oh let not the Lord be angry, and I will speak again but this once. Suppose ten are found there." He answered, "For the sake of ten I will not destroy it." And the Lord went his way, when he had finished speaking to Abraham; and Abraham returned to his place.

2572 **Romans 4:16–21** That is why it depends on faith, in order that the promise may rest on grace and be guaranteed to all his descendants—not only to the adherents of the law but also to those who share the faith of Abraham, for he is the father of us all, as it is written, "I have made you the father of many nations"—in the presence of the God in whom he believed, who gives life to the dead and calls into existence the things that do not exist. In hope he believed against hope, that he should become the father of many nations; as he had been told, "So shall your descendants be." He did not weaken in faith when he considered his own body, which was as good as dead because he was about a hundred years old, or when he considered the barrenness of Sarah's womb. No distrust made him waver concerning the promise of God, but he grew strong in his faith as he gave glory to God, fully convinced that God was able to do what he had promised.

(1) **Genesis 28:10–22** Jacob left Beersheba, and went toward Haran. And he came 2573
to a certain place, and stayed there that night, because the sun had set. Taking one of the stones of the place, he put it under his head and lay down in that place to sleep. And he dreamed that there was a ladder set up on the earth, and the top of it reached to heaven; and behold, the angels of God were ascending and descending on it! And behold, the Lord stood above it and said, "I am the Lord, the God of Abraham your father and the God of Isaac; the land on which you lie I will give to you and to your descendants; and your descendants shall be like the dust of the earth, and you shall spread abroad to the west and to the east and to the north and to the south; and by you and your descendants shall all the families of the earth bless themselves. Behold, I am with you and will keep you wherever you go, and will bring you back to this land; for I will not leave you until I have done that of which I have spoken to you." Then Jacob awoke from his sleep and said, "Surely the Lord is in this place; and I did not know it." And he was afraid, and said, "How awesome is this place! This is none other than the house of God, and this is the gate of heaven."

So Jacob rose early in the morning, and he took the stone which he had put under his head and set it up for a pillar and poured oil on the top of it. He called the name of that place Bethel; but the name of the city was Luz at the first. Then Jacob made a vow, saying, "If God will be with me, and will keep me in this way that I go, and will give me bread to eat and clothing to wear, so that I come again to my father's house in peace, then the Lord shall be my God, and this stone, which I have set up for a pillar, shall be God's house; and of all that thou givest me I will give the tenth to thee."

(2) **Genesis 32:24–30** And Jacob was left alone; and a man wrestled with him until 2573
the breaking of the day. When the man saw that he did not prevail against Jacob, he touched the hollow of his thigh; and Jacob's thigh was put out of joint as he wrestled with him. Then he said, "Let me go, for the day is breaking." But Jacob said, "I will not let you go, unless you bless me." And he said to him, "What is your name?" And he said, "Jacob." Then he said, "Your name shall no more be called Jacob, but Israel, for you have striven with God and with men, and have prevailed." Then Jacob asked him, "Tell me, I pray, your name." But he said, "Why is it that you ask my name?" And there he blessed him. So Jacob called the name of the place Peniel, saying, "For I have seen God face to face, and yet my life is preserved."

(3) **Luke 18:1–8** And he told them a parable, to the effect that they ought always 2573
to pray and not lose heart. He said, "In a certain city there was a judge who neither feared God nor regarded man; and there was a widow in that city who kept coming to him and saying, 'Vindicate me against my adversary.' For a while he refused; but afterward he said to himself, 'Though I neither fear God nor regard man, yet because this widow bothers me, I will vindicate her, or she will wear me out by her continual coming.'" And the Lord said, "Hear what the unrighteous judge says. And will not God vindicate his elect, who cry to him day and night? Will he delay long over them? I tell you, he will vindicate them speedily. Nevertheless, when the Son of man comes, will he find faith on earth?"

2577 (1) **Exodus 34:6** The Lord passed before him, and proclaimed, "The Lord, the Lord, a God merciful and gracious, slow to anger, and abounding in steadfast love and faithfulness. . . ."

2577 (2) **Exodus 17:8–13** Then came Amalek and fought with Israel at Rephidim. And Moses said to Joshua, "Choose for us men, and go out, fight with Amalek; tomorrow I will stand on the top of the hill with the rod of God in my hand." So Joshua did as Moses told him, and fought with Amalek; and Moses, Aaron, and Hur went up to the top of the hill. Whenever Moses held up his hand, Israel prevailed; and whenever he lowered his hand, Amalek prevailed. But Moses' hands grew weary; so they took a stone and put it under him, and he sat upon it, and Aaron and Hur held up his hands, one on one side, and the other on the other side; so his hands were steady until the going down of the sun. And Joshua mowed down Amalek and his people with the edge of the sword.

2577 (3) **Numbers 12:13–14** And Moses cried to the Lord, "Heal her, O God, I beseech thee." But the Lord said to Moses, "If her father had but spit in her face, should she not be shamed seven days? Let her be shut up outside the camp seven days, and after that she may be brought in again."

2577 (4) **Exodus 32:1–34:9** When the people saw that Moses delayed to come down from the mountain, the people gathered themselves together to Aaron, and said to him, "Up, make us gods, who shall go before us; as for this Moses, the man who brought us up out of the land of Egypt, we do not know what has become of him." And Aaron said to them, "Take off the rings of gold which are in the ears of your wives, your sons, and your daughters, and bring them to me." So all the people took off the rings of gold which were in their ears, and brought them to Aaron. And he received the gold at their hand, and fashioned it with a graving tool, and made a molten calf; and they said, "These are your gods, O Israel, who brought you up out of the land of Egypt!" When Aaron saw this, he built an altar before it; and Aaron made proclamation and said, "Tomorrow shall be a feast to the Lord." And they rose up early on the morrow, and offered burnt offerings and brought peace offerings; and the people sat down to eat and drink, and rose up to play.

And the Lord said to Moses, "Go down; for your people, whom you brought up out of the land of Egypt, have corrupted themselves; they have turned aside quickly out of the way which I commanded them; they have made for themselves a molten calf, and have worshiped it and sacrificed to it, and said, 'These are your gods, O Israel, who brought you up out of the land of Egypt!'" And the Lord said to Moses, "I have seen this people, and behold, it is a stiff-necked people; now therefore let me alone, that my wrath may burn hot against them and I may consume them; but of you I will make a great nation."

But Moses besought the Lord his God, and said, "O Lord, why does thy wrath burn hot against thy people, whom thou hast brought forth out of the land of Egypt with great power and with a mighty hand? Why should the Egyptians say, 'With evil intent did he bring them forth, to slay them in the mountains, and to consume them from the face of the earth'? Turn from thy fierce wrath, and repent of this evil against thy people. Remember Abraham, Isaac, and Israel, thy servants, to whom thou didst swear by thine own self, and didst say to them, 'I will multiply your descendants as the stars of heaven, and all this land that I have promised I will give to your descendants, and they shall inherit it for ever.'" And the Lord repented of the evil which he thought to do to his people.

And Moses turned, and went down from the mountain with the two tables of the testimony in his hands, tables that were written on both sides; on the one side and on the other were they written. And the tables were the work of God, and the writing was the writing of God, graven upon the tables. When Joshua heard the noise of the people as they shouted, he said to Moses, "There is a noise of war in the camp." But he said, "It is not the sound of shouting for victory, or the sound of the cry of defeat, but the sound of singing that I hear." And as soon as he came near the camp and saw the calf and the dancing, Moses' anger burned hot, and he threw the tables out of his hands and broke them at the foot of the mountain. And he took the calf which they had made and burnt it with fire, and ground it to powder, and scattered it upon the water, and made the people of Israel drink it.

And Moses said to Aaron, "What did this people do to you that you have brought a great sin upon them?" And Aaron said, "Let not the anger of my lord burn hot; you know the people, that they are set on evil. For they said to me, 'Make us gods, who shall go before us; as for this Moses, the man who brought us up out of the land of Egypt, we do not know what has become of him.' And I said to them, 'Let any who have gold take it off'; so they gave it to me, and I threw it into the fire, and there came out this calf."

And when Moses saw that the people had broken loose (for Aaron had let them break loose, to their shame among their enemies), then Moses stood in the gate of the camp, and said, "Who is on the Lord's side? Come to me." And all the sons of Levi gathered themselves together to him. And he said to them, "Thus says the Lord God of Israel, 'Put every man his sword on his side, and go to and fro from gate to gate throughout the camp, and slay every man his brother, and every man his companion, and every man his neighbor.'" And the sons of Levi did according to the word of Moses; and there fell of the people that day about three thousand men. And Moses said, "Today you have ordained yourselves for the service of the Lord, each one at the cost of his son and of his brother, that he may bestow a blessing upon you this day."

On the morrow Moses said to the people, "You have sinned a great sin. And now I will go up to the Lord; perhaps I can make atonement for your sin." So Moses returned to the Lord and said, "Alas, this people have sinned a great sin; they have made for themselves gods of gold. But now, if thou wilt forgive their sin—and if not, blot me, I pray thee, out of thy book which thou hast written." But the Lord said to Moses, "Whoever has sinned against me, him will I blot out of my book. But now go, lead the people to the place of which I have spoken to you; behold, my angel shall go before you. Nevertheless, in the day when I visit, I will visit their sin upon them."

And the Lord sent a plague upon the people, because they made the calf which Aaron made.

The Lord said to Moses, "Depart, go up hence, you and the people whom you have brought up out of the land of Egypt, to the land of which I swore to Abraham, Isaac, and Jacob, saying, 'To your descendants I will give it.' And I will send an angel before you, and I will drive out the Canaanites, the Amorites, the Hittites, the Perizzites, the Hivites, and the Jebusites. Go up to a land flowing with milk and honey; but I will not go up among you, lest I consume you in the way, for you are a stiff-necked people."

When the people heard these evil tidings, they mourned; and no man put on his ornaments. For the Lord had said to Moses, "Say to the people of Israel, 'You are a stiff-necked people; if for a single moment I should go up among you, I would consume you. So now put off your ornaments from you, that I may know what to do with you.'" Therefore the people of Israel stripped themselves of their ornaments, from Mount Horeb onward.

Now Moses used to take the tent and pitch it outside the camp, far off from the camp; and he called it the tent of meeting. And every one who sought the Lord would go out to the tent of meeting, which was outside the camp. Whenever Moses went out to the tent, all the people rose up, and every man stood at his tent door, and looked after Moses, until he had gone into the tent. When Moses entered the tent, the pillar of cloud would descend and stand at the door of the tent, and the Lord would speak with Moses. And when all the people saw the pillar of cloud standing at the door of the tent, all the people would rise up and worship, every man at his tent door. Thus the Lord used to speak to Moses face to face, as a man speaks to his friend. When Moses turned again into the camp, his servant Joshua the son of Nun, a young man, did not depart from the tent.

Moses said to the Lord, "See, thou sayest to me, 'Bring up this people'; but thou hast not let me know whom thou wilt send with me. Yet thou hast said, 'I know you by name, and you have also found favor in my sight.' Now therefore, I pray thee, if I have found favor in thy sight, show me now thy ways, that I may know thee and find favor in thy sight. Consider too that this nation is thy people." And he said, "My presence will go with you, and I will give you rest." And he said to him, "If thy presence will not go with me, do not carry us up from here. For how shall it be known that I have found favor in thy sight, I and thy people? Is it not in thy going with us, so that we are distinct, I and thy people, from all other people that are upon the face of the earth?"

And the Lord said to Moses, "This very thing that you have spoken I will do; for you have found favor in my sight, and I know you by name." Moses said, "I pray thee, show me thy glory." And he said, "I will make all my goodness pass before you, and will proclaim before you my name 'The Lord'; and I will be gracious to whom I will be gracious, and will show mercy on whom I will show mercy. But," he said, "you cannot see my face; for man shall not see me and live." And the Lord said, "Behold, there is a place by me where you shall stand upon the rock; and while my glory passes by I will put you in a cleft of the rock, and I will cover you with my hand until I have passed by; then I will take away my hand, and you shall see my back; but my face shall not be seen."

The Lord said to Moses, "Cut two tables of stone like the first; and I will write upon the tables the words that were on the first tables, which you broke. Be ready in the morning, and come up in the morning to Mount Sinai, and present yourself there to me on the top of the mountain. No man shall come up with you, and let no man be seen throughout all the mountain; let no flocks or herds feed before that mountain." So Moses cut two tables of stone like the first; and he rose early in the morning and went up on Mount Sinai, as the Lord had commanded him, and took in his hand two tables of stone. And the Lord descended in the cloud and stood with him there, and proclaimed the name of the Lord. The Lord passed before him, and proclaimed, "The Lord, the Lord, a God merciful and gracious, slow to anger, and abounding in steadfast love and faithfulness, keeping steadfast love for thousands, forgiving iniquity and transgression and sin, but who will by no means clear the guilty, visiting the iniquity of the fathers upon the children and the children's children, to the third and the fourth generation."

And Moses made haste to bow his head toward the earth, and worshiped. And he said, "If now I have found favor in thy sight, O Lord, let the Lord, I pray thee, go in the midst of us, although it is a stiff-necked people; and pardon our iniquity and our sin, and take us for thy inheritance."

1 Samuel 1:9–18 After they had eaten and drunk in Shiloh, Hannah rose. Now 2578
Eli the priest was sitting on the seat beside the doorpost of the temple of the Lord. She was deeply distressed and prayed to the Lord, and wept bitterly. And she vowed a vow and said. "O Lord of hosts, if thou wilt indeed look on the affliction of thy maidservant, and remember me, and not forget thy maidservant, but wilt give to thy maidservant a son, then I will give him to the Lord all the days of his life, and no razor shall touch his head."

As she continued praying before the Lord, Eli observed her mouth. Hannah was speaking in her heart; only her lips moved, and her voice was not heard; therefore Eli took her to be a drunken woman. And Eli said to her, "How long will you be drunken? Put away your wine from you." But Hannah answered, "No, my lord, I am a woman sorely troubled; I have drunk neither wine nor strong drink, but I have been pouring out my soul before the Lord. Do not regard your maidservant as a base woman, for all along I have been speaking out of my great anxiety and vexation." Then Eli answered, "Go in peace, and the God of Israel grant your petition which you have made to him." And she said, "Let your maidservant find favor in your eyes." Then the woman went her way and ate, and her countenance was no longer sad.

2 Samuel 7:18–29 Then King David went in and sat before the Lord, and said, 2579
"Who am I, O Lord God, and what is my house, that thou hast brought me thus far? And yet this was a small thing in thy eyes, O Lord God; thou hast spoken also of thy servant's house for a great while to come, and hast shown me future generations, O Lord God! And what more can David say to thee? For thou knowest thy servant, O Lord God! Because of thy promise, and according to thy own heart, thou hast wrought all this greatness, to make thy servant know it. Therefore thou art great, O Lord God; for there is none like thee, and there is no God besides thee, according to all that we have heard with our ears. What other nation on earth is like thy people Israel, whom God went to redeem to be his people, making himself a name, and doing for them great and terrible things, by driving out before his people a nation and its gods? And thou didst establish for thyself thy people Israel to be thy people forever; and thou, O Lord, didst become their God. And now, O Lord God, confirm for ever the word which thou hast spoken concerning thy servant and concerning his house, and do as thou hast spoken; and thy name will be magnified for ever, saying, 'The Lord of hosts is God over Israel,' and the house of thy servant David will be established before thee. For thou, O Lord of hosts, the God of Israel, hast made this revelation to thy servant, saying, 'I will build you a house'; therefore thy servant has found courage to pray this prayer to thee. And now, O Lord God, thou art God, and thy words are true, and thou hast promised this good thing to thy servant; now therefore may it please thee to bless the house of thy servant, that it may continue for ever before thee; for thou, O Lord God, hast spoken, and with thy blessing shall the house of thy servant be blessed for ever."

1 Kings 8:10–61 And when the priests came out of the holy place, a cloud filled 2580
the house of the Lord, so that the priests could not stand to minister because of the cloud; for the glory of the Lord filled the house of the Lord.

Then Solomon said,

> "The Lord has set the sun in the heavens,
>   but has said that he would dwell in thick darkness.
> I have built thee an exalted house,
>   a place for thee to dwell in for ever."

Then the king faced about, and blessed all the assembly of Israel, while all the assembly of Israel stood. And he said, "Blessed be the Lord, the God of Israel, who with his hand has fulfilled what he promised with his mouth to David my father, saying, 'Since the day that I brought my people Israel out of Egypt, I chose no city in all the tribes of Israel in which to build a house, that my name might be there; but I chose David to be over my people Israel.' Now it was in the heart of David my father to build a house for the name of the Lord, the God of Israel. But the Lord said to David my father, 'Whereas it was in your heart to build a house for my name, you did well that it was in your heart; nevertheless you shall not build the house, but your son who shall be born to you shall build the house for my name.' Now the Lord has fulfilled his promise which he made; for I have risen in the place of David my father, and sit on the throne of Israel, as the Lord promised, and I have built the house for the name of the Lord, the God of Israel. And there I have provided a place for the ark, in which is the covenant of the Lord which he made with our fathers, when he brought them out of the land of Egypt."

Then Solomon stood before the altar of the Lord in the presence of all the assembly of Israel, and spread forth his hands toward heaven; and said, "O Lord, God of Israel, there is no God like thee, in heaven above or on earth beneath, keeping covenant and showing steadfast love to thy servants who walk before thee with all their heart; who hast kept with thy servant David my father what thou didst declare to him; yea, thou didst speak with thy mouth, and with thy hand hast fulfilled it this day. Now therefore, O Lord, God of Israel, keep with thy servant David my father what thou hast promised him, saying, 'There shall never fail you a man before me to sit upon the throne of Israel, if only your sons take heed to their way, to walk before me as you have walked before me.' Now therefore, O God of Israel, let thy word be confirmed, which thou hast spoken to thy servant David my father.

"But will God indeed dwell on the earth? Behold, heaven and the highest heaven cannot contain thee; how much less this house which I have built! Yet have regard to the prayer of thy servant and to his supplication, O Lord my God, hearkening to the cry and to the prayer which thy servant prays before thee this day; that thy eyes may be open night and day toward this house, the place of which thou hast said, 'My name shall be there,' that thou mayest hearken to the prayer which thy servant offers toward this place. And hearken thou to the supplication of thy servant and of thy people Israel, when they pray toward this place; yea, hear thou in heaven thy dwelling place; and when thou hearest, forgive.

"If a man sins against his neighbor and is made to take an oath, and comes and swears his oath before thine altar in this house, then hear thou in heaven, and act, and judge thy servants, condemning the guilty by bringing his conduct upon his own head, and vindicating the righteous by rewarding him according to his righteousness.

"When thy people Israel are defeated before the enemy because they have sinned against thee, if they turn again to thee, and acknowledge thy name, and pray and make supplication to thee in this house; then hear thou in heaven, and forgive the sin of thy people Israel, and bring them again to the land which thou gavest to their fathers.

"When heaven is shut up and there is no rain because they have sinned against thee, if they pray toward this place, and acknowledge thy name, and turn from their sin, when thou dost afflict them, then hear thou in heaven, and forgive the sin of thy servants, thy people Israel, when thou dost teach them the good way in which they should walk; and grant rain upon thy land, which thou hast given to thy people as an inheritance.

"If there is famine in the land, if there is pestilence or blight or mildew or locust or caterpillar; if their enemy besieges them in any of their cities; whatever plague, whatever sickness there is; whatever prayer, whatever supplication is made by any man or by all thy people Israel, each knowing the affliction of his own heart and stretching out his hands toward this house; then hear thou in heaven thy dwelling place, and forgive, and act, and render to each whose heart thou knowest, according to all his ways (for thou, thou only, knowest the hearts of all the children of men); that they may fear thee all the days that they live in the land which thou gavest to our fathers.

"Likewise when a foreigner, who is not of thy people Israel, comes from a far country for thy name's sake (for they shall hear of thy great name, and thy mighty hand, and of thy outstretched arm), when he comes and prays toward this house, hear thou in heaven thy dwelling place, and do according to all for which the foreigner calls to thee; in order that all the peoples of the earth may know thy name and fear thee, as do thy people Israel, and that they may know that this house which I have built is called by thy name.

"If thy people go out to battle against their enemy, by whatever way thou shalt send them, and they pray to the Lord toward the city which thou hast chosen and the house which I have built for thy name, then hear thou in heaven their prayer and their supplication, and maintain their cause.

"If they sin against thee—for there is no man who does not sin—and thou art angry with them, and dost give them to an enemy, so that they are carried away captive to the land of the enemy, far off or near; yet if they lay it to heart in the land to which they have been carried captive, and repent, and make supplication to thee in the land of their captors, saying, 'We have sinned, and have acted perversely and wickedly'; if they repent with all their mind and with all their heart in the land of their enemies, who carried them captive, and pray to thee toward their land, which thou gavest to their fathers, the city which thou hast chosen, and the house which I have built for thy name; then hear thou in heaven thy dwelling place their prayer and their supplication, and maintain their cause and forgive thy people who have sinned against thee, and all their transgressions which they have committed against thee; and grant them compassion in the sight of those who carried them captive, that they may have compassion on them (for they are thy people, and thy heritage, which thou didst bring out of Egypt, from the midst of the iron furnace). Let thy eyes be open to the supplication of thy servant, and to the supplication of thy people Israel, giving ear to them whenever they call to thee. For thou didst separate them from among all the peoples of the earth, to be thy heritage, as thou didst declare through Moses, thy servant, when thou didst bring our fathers out of Egypt, O Lord God."

Now as Solomon finished offering all this prayer and supplication to the Lord, he arose from before the altar of the Lord, where he had knelt with hands outstretched toward heaven; and he stood, and blessed all the assembly of Israel with a loud voice, saying, "Blessed be the Lord who has given rest to his people Israel, according to all that he promised; not one word has failed of all his good promise, which he uttered by Moses his servant. The Lord our God be with us, as he was with our fathers; may he not leave us or forsake us; that he may incline our hearts to him, to walk in all his ways, and to keep his commandments, his statutes, and his ordinances, which he commanded our fathers. Let these words of mine, wherewith I have made supplication before the Lord, be near to the Lord our God day and night, and may he maintain the cause of his servant, and the cause of his people Israel, as each day requires; that all the peoples of the earth may know that the Lord is God; there is no other. Let your heart therefore be wholly true to the Lord our God, walking in his statutes and keeping his commandments, as at this day."

2583 (1) **1 Kings 17:7–24** And after a while the brook dried up, because there was no rain in the land.

Then the word of the Lord came to him, "Arise, go to Zarephath, which belongs to Sidon, and dwell there. Behold, I have commanded a widow there to feed you." So he arose and went to Zarephath; and when he came to the gate of the city, behold, a widow was there gathering sticks; and he called to her and said, "Bring me a little water in a vessel, that I may drink." And as she was going to bring it, he called to her and said, "Bring me a morsel of bread in your hand." And she said, "As the Lord your God lives, I have nothing baked, only a handful of meal in a jar, and a little oil in a cruse; and now, I am gathering a couple of sticks, that I may go in and prepare it for myself and my son, that we may eat it, and die." And Elijah said to her, "Fear not; go and do as you have said; but first make me a little cake of it and bring it to me, and afterward make for yourself and your son. For thus says the Lord the God of Israel, 'The jar of meal shall not be spent, and the cruse of oil shall not fail, until the day that the Lord sends rain upon the earth.'" And she went and did as Elijah said; and she, and he, and her household ate for many days. The jar of meal was not spent, neither did the cruse of oil fail, according to the word of the Lord which he spoke by Elijah.

After this the son of the woman, the mistress of the house, became ill; and his illness was so severe that there was no breath left in him. And she said to Elijah, "What have you against me, O man of God? You have come to me to bring my sin to remembrance, and to cause the death of my son!" And he said to her, "Give me your son." And he took him from her bosom, and carried him up into the upper chamber, where he lodged, and laid him upon his own bed. And he cried to the Lord, "O Lord my God, hast thou brought calamity even upon the widow with whom I sojourn, by slaying her son?" Then he stretched himself upon the child three times, and cried to the Lord, "O Lord my God, let this child's soul come into him again." And the Lord hearkened to the voice of Elijah; and the soul of the child came into him again, and he revived. And Elijah took the child, and brought him down from the upper chamber into the house, and delivered him to his mother; and Elijah said, "See, your son lives." And the woman said to Elijah, "Now I know that you are a man of God, and that the word of the Lord in your mouth is truth."

2583 (2) **1 Kings 19:1–14** Ahab told Jezebel all that Elijah had done, and how he had slain all the prophets with the sword. Then Jezebel sent a messenger to Elijah, saying, "So may the gods do to me, and more also, if I do not make your life as the life of one of them by this time tomorrow." Then he was afraid, and he arose and went for his life, and came to Beersheba, which belongs to Judah, and left his servant there.

But he himself went a day's journey into the wilderness, and came and sat down under a broom tree; and he asked that he might die, saying, "It is enough; now, O Lord, take away my life; for I am no better than my fathers." And he lay down and slept under a broom tree; and behold, an angel touched him, and said to him, "Arise and eat." And he looked, and behold, there was at his head a cake baked on hot stones and a jar of water. And he ate and drank, and lay down again. And the angel of the Lord came again a second time, and touched him, and said, "Arise and eat, else the journey will be too great for you." And he arose, and ate and drank, and went in the strength of that food forty days and forty nights to Horeb the mount of God.

And there he came to a cave, and lodged there; and behold, the word of the Lord came to him, and he said to him, "What are you doing here, Elijah?" He said, "I have been very jealous for the Lord, the God of hosts; for the people of Israel have forsaken thy covenant, thrown down thy altars, and slain thy prophets with the sword; and I, even I only, am left; and they seek my life, to take it away." And he said, "Go forth, and stand upon the mount before the Lord." And behold, the Lord passed by, and a great and strong wind rent the mountains, and broke in pieces the rocks before the Lord, but the Lord was not in the wind; and after the wind an earthquake, but the Lord was not in the earthquake; and after the earthquake a fire, but the Lord was not in the fire; and after the fire a still small voice. And when Elijah heard it, he wrapped his face in his mantle and went out and stood at the entrance of the cave. And behold, there came a voice to him, and said, "What are you doing here, Elijah?" He said, "I have been very jealous for the Lord, the God of hosts; for the people of Israel have forsaken thy covenant, thrown down thy altars, and slain thy prophets with the sword; and I, even I only, am left; and they seek my life, to take it away."

(3) **Exodus 33:19–23** And he said, "I will make all my goodness pass before you, 2583
and will proclaim before you my name 'The Lord'; and I will be gracious to whom I will be gracious, and will show mercy on whom I will show mercy. But," he said, "you cannot see my face; for man shall not see me and live." And the Lord said, "Behold, there is a place by me where you shall stand upon the rock; and while my glory passes by I will put you in a cleft of the rock, and I will cover you with my hand until I have passed by; then I will take away my hand, and you shall see my back; but my face shall not be seen."

(4) **Luke 9:30–35** And behold, two men talked with him, Moses and Elijah, who ap- 2583
peared in glory and spoke of his departure, which he was to accomplish at Jerusalem. Now Peter and those who were with him were heavy with sleep, and when they wakened they saw his glory and the two men who stood with him. And as the men were parting from him, Peter said to Jesus, "Master, it is well that we are here; let us make three booths, one for you and one for Moses and one for Elijah"—not knowing what he said. As he said this, a cloud came and overshadowed them; and they were afraid as they entered the cloud. And a voice came out of the cloud, saying, "This is my Son, my Chosen; listen to him!"

(1) **Amos 7:2** When they had finished eating the grass of the land, I said, 2584
"O Lord God, forgive, I beseech thee!
How can Jacob stand?
He is so small!"

(2) **Amos 7:5** Then I said, 2584
"O Lord God, cease, I beseech thee!
How can Jacob stand?
He is so small!"

(3) **Isaiah 6:5** And I said, "Woe is me! For I am lost; for I am a man of unclean 2584
lips, and I dwell in the midst of a people of unclean lips; for my eyes have seen the King, the Lord of hosts!"

(4) **Isaiah 6:8** And I heard the voice of the Lord saying, "Whom shall I send, and 2584
who will go for us?" Then I said, "Here am I! Send me."

(5) **Isaiah 6:11** Then I said, "How long, O Lord?" And he said: 2584
"Until cities lie waste
without inhabitant,
and houses without men,
and the land is utterly desolate. . . "

2584 (6) **Jeremiah 1:6** Then I said, "Ah, Lord God! Behold, I do not know how to speak, for I am only a youth."

2584 (7) **Jeremiah 15:15–18**

O Lord, thou knowest;
remember me and visit me,
and take vengeance for me on my persecutors.
In thy forbearance take me not away;
know that for thy sake I bear reproach.
Thy words were found, and I ate them,
and thy words became to me a joy
and the delight of my heart;
for I am called by thy name,
O Lord, God of hosts.
I did not sit in the company of merrymakers,
nor did I rejoice;
I sat alone, because thy hand was upon me,
for thou hadst filled me with indignation.
Why is my pain unceasing,
my wound incurable,
refusing to be healed?
Wilt thou be to me like a deceitful brook,
like waters that fail?

2584 (8) **Jeremiah 20:7–18**

O Lord, thou hast deceived me,
and I was deceived;
thou art stronger than I,
and thou hast prevailed.
I have become a laughingstock all the day;
every one mocks me.
For whenever I speak, I cry out,
I shout, "Violence and destruction!"
For the word of the Lord has become for me
a reproach and derision all day long.
If I say, "I will not mention him,
or speak any more in his name,"
there is in my heart as it were a burning fire
shut up in my bones,
and I am weary with holding it in,
and I cannot.
For I hear many whispering.
Terror is on every side!
"Denounce him! Let us denounce him!"
say all my familiar friends,
watching for my fall.
"Perhaps he will be deceived,
then we can overcome him,
and take our revenge on him."
But the Lord is with me as a dread warrior;
therefore my persecutors will stumble,
they will not overcome me.

They will be greatly shamed,
    for they will not succeed.
Their eternal dishonor
    will never be forgotten.
O Lord of hosts, who triest the righteous,
    who seest the heart and the mind,
let me see thy vengeance upon them,
    for to thee have I committed my cause.

Sing to the Lord;
    praise the Lord!
For he has delivered the life of the needy
    from the hand of evildoers.

Cursed be the day
    on which I was born!
The day when my mother bore me,
    let it not be blessed!
Cursed be the man
    who brought the news to my father,
"A son is born to you,"
    making him very glad.
Let that man be like the cities
    which the Lord overthrew without pity;
let him hear a cry in the morning
    and an alarm at noon,
because he did not kill me in the womb;
    so my mother would have been my grave,
    and her womb for ever great.
Why did I come forth from the womb
    to see toil and sorrow,
    and spend my days in shame?

(1) **Ezra 9:6–15** . . . saying: "O my God, I am ashamed and blush to lift my face to 2585
thee, my God, for our iniquities have risen higher than our heads, and our guilt has mounted up to the heavens. From the days of our fathers to this day we have been in great guilt; and for our iniquities we, our kings, and our priests have been given into the hand of the kings of the lands, to the sword, to captivity, to plundering, and to utter shame, as at this day. But now for a brief moment favor has been shown by the Lord our God, to leave us a remnant, and to give us a sure hold within his holy place, that our God may brighten our eyes and grant us a little reviving in our bondage. For we are bondmen; yet our God has not forsaken us in our bondage, but has extended to us his steadfast love before the kings of Persia, to grant us some reviving to set up the house of our God, to repair its ruins, and to give us protection in Judea and Jerusalem.

"And now, O our God, what shall we say after this? For we have forsaken thy commandments, which thou didst command by thy servants the prophets, saying, 'The land which you are entering, to take possession of it, is a land unclean with the pollutions of the peoples of the lands, with their abominations which have filled it from end to end with their uncleanness. Therefore give not your daughters to their sons, neither take their daughters for your sons, and never seek their peace or prosperity, that you may be strong, and eat the good of the land, and leave it for an inheritance to your children for ever.' And after all that has come upon us for our evil deeds and for our great guilt, seeing that thou, our God, hast punished us less than our iniquities deserved and hast given us such a remnant as this, shall we break thy commandments again and inter-marry with the peoples who practice these abominations? Wouldst thou not be angry with us till thou wouldst consume us, so that there should be no remnant, nor any to escape? O Lord the God of Israel, thou art just, for we are left a remnant that has escaped, as at this day. Behold, we are before thee in our guilt, for none can stand before thee because of this."

2585 (2) **Nehemiah 1:4–11** When I heard these words I sat down and wept, and mourned for days; and I continued fasting and praying before the God of heaven. And I said, "O Lord God of heaven, the great and terrible God who keeps covenant and steadfast love with those who love him and keep his commandments; let thy ear be attentive, and thy eyes open, to hear the prayer of thy servant which I now pray before thee day and night for the people of Israel thy servants, confessing the sins of the people of Israel, which we have sinned against thee. Yea, I and my father's house have sinned. We have acted very corruptly against thee, and have not kept the commandments, the statutes, and the ordinances which thou didst command thy servant Moses. Remember the word which thou didst command thy servant Moses, saying, 'If you are unfaithful, I will scatter you among the peoples; but if you return to me and keep my commandments and do them, though your dispersed be under the farthest skies, I will gather them thence and bring them to the place which I have chosen, to make my name dwell there.' They are thy servants and thy people, whom thou hast redeemed by thy great power and by thy strong hand. O Lord, let thy ear be attentive to the prayer of thy servant, and to the prayer of thy servants who delight to fear thy name; and give success to thy servant today, and grant him mercy in the sight of this man."

Now I was cupbearer to the king.

2585 (3) **Jonah 2:3–10**

". . . For thou didst cast me into the deep,
into the heart of the seas,
and the flood was round about me;
all thy waves and thy billows
passed over me.
Then I said, 'I am cast out
from thy presence;
how shall I again look
upon thy holy temple?'
The waters closed in over me,
the deep was round about me;
weeds were wrapped about my head
at the roots of the mountains.
I went down to the land
whose bars closed upon me for ever;
yet thou didst bring up my life from the Pit,
O Lord my God.
When my soul fainted within me,
I remembered the Lord;
and my prayer came to thee,
into thy holy temple.
Those who pay regard to vain idols
forsake their true loyalty.

But I with the voice of thanksgiving
will sacrifice to thee;
what I have vowed I will pay.
Deliverance belongs to the Lord!"
And the Lord spoke to the fish, and it vomited out Jonah upon the dry land.

(4) **Tobit 3:11–16** So she prayed by her window and said, "Blessed art thou, O 2585
Lord my God, and blessed is thy holy and honored name for ever. May all thy works praise thee for ever. And now, O Lord, I have turned my eyes and my face toward thee. Command that I be released from the earth and that I hear reproach no more. Thou knowest, O Lord, that I am innocent of any sin with man, and that I did not stain my name or the name of my father in the land of my captivity. I am my father's only child, and he has no child to be his heir, no near kinsman or kinsman's son for whom I should keep myself as wife. Already seven husbands of mine are dead. Why should I live? But if it be not pleasing to thee to take my life, command that respect be shown to me and pity be taken upon me, and that I hear reproach no more."

The prayer of both was heard in the presence of the glory of the great God.

(5) **Judith 9:2–14** "O Lord God of my father Simeon, to whom thou gavest a sword 2585
to take revenge on the strangers who had loosed the girdle of a virgin to defile her, and uncovered her thigh to put her to shame, and polluted her womb to disgrace her; for thou hast said, 'It shall not be done'—yet they did it. So thou gavest up their rulers to be slain, and their bed, which was ashamed of the deceit they had practiced, to be stained with blood, and thou didst strike down slaves along with princes, and princes on their thrones; and thou gavest their wives for a prey and their daughters to captivity, and all their booty to be divided among thy beloved sons, who were zealous for thee, and abhorred the pollution of their blood, and called on thee for help—O God, my God, hear me also, a widow.

"For thou hast done these things and those that went before and those that followed; thou hast designed the things that are now, and those that are to come. Yea, the things thou didst intend came to pass, and the things thou didst will presented themselves and said, 'Lo, we are here'; for all thy ways are prepared in advance, and thy judgment is with foreknowledge.

"Behold now, the Assyrians are increased in their might; they are exalted, with their horses and riders; they glory in the strength of their foot soldiers; they trust in shield and spear, in bow and sling, and know not that thou art the Lord who crushest wars; the Lord is thy name. Break their strength by thy might, and bring down their power in thy anger; for they intend to defile thy sanctuary, and to pollute the tabernacle where thy glorious name rests, and to cast down the horn of thy altar with the sword. Behold their pride, and send thy wrath upon their heads; give to me, a widow, the strength to do what I plan. By the deceit of my lips strike down the slave with the prince and the prince with his servant; crush their arrogance by the hand of a woman.

"For thy power depends not upon numbers, nor thy might upon men of strength; for thou art God of the lowly, helper of the oppressed, upholder of the weak, protector of the forlorn, savior of those without hope. Hear, O hear me, God of my father, God of the inheritance of Israel, Lord of heaven and earth, Creator of the waters, King of all thy creation, hear my prayer! Make my deceitful words to be their wound and stripe, for they have planned cruel things against thy covenant, and against thy consecrated house, and against the top of Zion, and against the house possessed by thy children. And cause thy whole nation and every tribe to know and understand that thou art God, the God of all power and might, and that there is no other who protects the people of Israel but thou alone!"

2586 **General Instruction of the Liturgy of the Hours 100–109** In the Liturgy of the Hours the prayer of the Church is in large measure in the words of those great hymns composed under the inspiration of the Holy Spirit by sacred writers of the Old Testament. Their origin gives them great power to raise minds to God, to inspire devotion, to evoke gratitude in favorable times and to bring consolation and fortitude in times of trial.

The psalms are, however, only a foreshadowing of the fullness of time that came to be in Christ the Lord, from which the prayer of the Church derives its power. Hence, while the faithful are all agreed on the supreme value to be placed on the psalms, they can sometimes experience difficulty in making these inspired hymns their own prayer.

Yet the Holy Spirit, under whose inspiration the psalms were written, is always present by his grace to those who use them with faith and good will. More, however, is necessary: they must "acquire a richer scriptural formation, especially in regard to the psalms," according to each one's capacity, so that they may understand how, and by what method, they may pray them properly.

The psalms are not readings or prose prayers. They can on occasion be recited as readings, but they are properly called *tehillim* ("songs of praise") in Hebrew and *psalmoi* ("songs to be sung to the lyre") in Greek. In fact, all the psalms have a musical quality which determines the correct way of delivering them. When a psalm is recited and not sung, its delivery must still be governed by its musical character. A psalm presents a text to the minds of the faithful, but it aims rather at moving the hearts of those singing it or listening to it, and also of those accompanying it "on the lyre and harp."

To sing the psalms "with understanding" we must meditate on them verse by verse, our hearts always ready to respond in the way the Holy Spirit desires. The Holy Spirit, as the one who inspired the psalmist, will also be present to those who in faith and love are ready to receive his grace. For this reason the singing of the psalms, though it demands the reverence due to God's majesty, should be the expression of a joyful spirit and a loving heart, in keeping with their character as sacred poetry and inspired song, and above all with the freedom of the children of God.

Often the words of a psalm help us to pray with greater ease and fervor, whether in thanksgiving and joyful praise of God or in prayer for help in the depths of suffering. But difficulties may arise, especially when the psalm is not addressed directly to God. The psalmist is a poet, and he often addresses the people as he recalls Israel's history; sometimes he addresses others, even the brute creation. He even introduces dialogue between God and men, even (as in psalm 2) between God and his enemies. This shows that a psalm is a different kind of prayer from a prayer or collect composed by the Church. Besides, it is in keeping with the poetic and musical character of the psalms that they do not necessarily address God but are sung in God's presence. Saint Benedict warns us: "We must consider what it means to be in the sight of God and his angels, and stand to sing so that our mind may be in harmony with our voice."

In praying the psalms we should open our hearts to the different attitudes they express, varying with the class of writing to which each belongs (psalms of grief, trust, gratitude, etc.), and which Scripture scholars rightly emphasize.

In keeping to the meaning of the words the person who prays the psalms is looking for the human value of the text for the life of faith.

It is clear that each psalm was written in its own individual circumstances, which the titles given at the head of each psalm in the Hebrew psalter are meant to indicate.

But whatever its historical origin each psalm has its own meaning, which we cannot overlook even in our own day. Though the psalms originated very many centuries ago in the East they express accurately the pain and hope, the unhappiness and trust, of people of every age and country, and celebrate especially faith in God, revelation and redemption.

The person who prays the psalms in the Liturgy of the Hours prays not so much in his own person as in the name of the Church, and, in fact, in the person of Christ himself. If one bears this in mind difficulties disappear when one notices in prayer that the feelings of the heart in prayer are different from the emotions expressed in the psalm, for example, when a psalm of joy confronts a person who is sad and overcome with grief, or a psalm of sorrow confronts a person full of joy. This kind of situation is easily avoided in purely private prayer, when it is permissible to choose a psalm matching one's mood. But in the divine Office the public cycle of the psalms is gone through, not as a private exercise but in the name of the Church, even by someone saying an Hour by himself. The person who prays the psalms in the name of the Church can always find a reason for joy or sadness, for the saying of the Apostle applies in this case also: "Rejoice with the joyful and weep with those who weep" (Romans 12:15). In this way human frailty, wounded by self-love, is healed in that degree of love in which the mind and voice of one praying the psalms are in harmony.

The person who prays the psalms in the name of the Church should be aware of their total meaning (*sensus plenus*), especially their messianic meaning, which was the reason for the Church's introduction of the psalter into its prayer. This messianic meaning was fully revealed in the New Testament and indeed was publicly acknowledged by Christ the Lord in person when he said to the apostles: "All that is written about me in the law of Moses and the prophets and the psalms must be fulfilled" (Luke 24:44). The best known example of this messianic meaning is the dialogue in Matthew's gospel on the Messiah as Son of David and David's Lord: there, psalm 110 is interpreted as messianic.

Following this line of thought, the Fathers of the Church saw the whole psalter as a prophecy of Christ and the Church and explained it in this sense; for the same reason the psalms have been chosen for use in the sacred liturgy. Though somewhat tortuous interpretations were at times proposed, yet, in general, the Fathers, and the liturgy itself, could legitimately hear in the singing of the psalms the voice of Christ crying out to the Father, or of the Father conversing with the Son; indeed, they also recognized in the psalms the voice of the Church, the apostles and the martyrs. This method of interpretation also flourished in the middle ages; in many manuscripts of the period the Christological meaning of each psalm is set out at its head. A Christological meaning is by no means confined to the recognized messianic psalms but is given also to many others. Some of these interpretations are doubtless Christological only in an accommodated sense, but they have the traditional approval of the Church.

On feast days especially, the choice of psalms is often based on their Christological meaning, and antiphons taken from these psalms are frequently used to throw light on this meaning.

(1) **Luke 1:49** **2599**

> . . . for he who is mighty has done great things for me,
> and holy is his name.

(2) **Luke 2:19** But Mary kept all these things, pondering them in her heart. **2599**

(3) **Luke 2:51** And he went down with them and came to Nazareth, and was obedient to them; and his mother kept all these things in her heart. **2599**

2600 (1) **Luke 3:21** Now when all the people were baptized, and when Jesus also had been baptized and was praying, the heaven was opened. . . .

2600 (2) **Luke 9:28** Now about eight days after these sayings he took with him Peter and John and James, and went up on the mountain to pray.

2600 (3) **Luke 22:32** ". . . but I have prayed for you that your faith may not fail; and when you have turned again, strengthen your brethren."

2600 (4) **Luke 6:12** In these days he went out to the mountain to pray; and all night he continued in prayer to God.

2600 (5) **Luke 9:18–20** Now it happened that as he was praying alone the disciples were with him, and he asked them, "Who do the people say that I am?" And they answered, "John the Baptist; but others say, Elijah; and others, that one of the old prophets has risen." And he said to them, "But who do you say that I am?" And Peter answered, "The Christ of God."

2600 (6) **Luke 22:41–44** And he withdrew from them about a stone's throw, and knelt down and prayed, "Father, if thou art willing, remove this cup from me; nevertheless not my will, but thine, be done." And there appeared to him an angel from heaven, strengthening him. And being in an agony he prayed more earnestly; and his sweat became like great drops of blood falling down upon the ground.

2602 (1) **Mark 1:35** And in the morning, a great while before day, he rose and went out to a lonely place, and there he prayed.

2602 (2) **Mark 6:46** And after he had taken leave of them, he went up on the mountain to pray.

2602 (3) **Luke 5:16** But he withdrew to the wilderness and prayed.

2602 (4) **Hebrews 2:12** . . . saying,
"I will proclaim thy name to my brethren,
in the midst of the congregation I will praise thee."

2602 (5) **Hebrews 2:15** . . . and deliver all those who through fear of death were subject to lifelong bondage.

2602 (6) **Hebrews 4:15** For we have not a high priest who is unable to sympathize with our weaknesses, but one who in every respect has been tempted as we are, yet without sin.

2603 (1) **Matthew 11:25–27** At that time Jesus declared, "I thank thee, Father, Lord of heaven and earth, that thou hast hidden these things from the wise and understanding and revealed them to babes; yea, Father, for such was thy gracious will. All things have been delivered to me by my Father; and no one knows the Son except the Father, and no one knows the Father except the Son and any one to whom the Son chooses to reveal him. . . ."

(2) **Luke 10:21–23** In that same hour he rejoiced in the Holy Spirit and said, "I thank thee, Father, Lord of heaven and earth, that thou hast hidden these things from the wise and understanding and revealed them to babes; yea, Father, for such was thy gracious will. All things have been delivered to me by my Father; and no one knows who the Son is except the Father, or who the Father is except the Son and any one to whom the Son chooses to reveal him." 2603

Then turning to the disciples he said privately, "Blessed are the eyes which see what you see! . . ."

(3) **Ephesians 1:9** For he has made known to us in all wisdom and insight the mystery of his will, according to his purpose which he set forth in Christ. . . . 2603

(1) **John 11:41–42** So they took away the stone. And Jesus lifted up his eyes and said, "Father, I thank thee that thou hast heard me. I knew that thou hearest me always, but I have said this on account of the people standing by, that they may believe that thou didst send me." 2604

(2) **John 17** When Jesus had spoken these words, he lifted up his eyes to heaven and said, "Father, the hour has come; glorify thy Son that the Son may glorify thee, since thou hast given him power over all flesh, to give eternal life to all whom thou hast given him. And this is eternal life, that they know thee the only true God, and Jesus Christ whom thou hast sent. I glorified thee on earth, having accomplished the work which thou gavest me to do; and now, Father, glorify thou me in thy own presence with the glory which I had with thee before the world was made. 2604

"I have manifested thy name to the men whom thou gavest me out of the world; thine they were, and thou gavest them to me, and they have kept thy word. Now they know that everything that thou hast given me is from thee; for I have given them the words which thou gavest me, and they have received them and know in truth that I came from thee; and they have believed that thou didst send me. I am praying for them; I am not praying for the world but for those whom thou hast given me, for they are thine; all mine are thine, and thine are mine, and I am glorified in them. And now I am no more in the world, but they are in the world, and I am coming to thee. Holy Father, keep them in thy name, which thou hast given me, that they may be one, even as we are one. While I was with them, I kept them in thy name, which thou hast given me; I have guarded them, and none of them is lost but the son of perdition, that the scripture might be fulfilled. But now I am coming to thee; and these things I speak in the world, that they may have my joy fulfilled in themselves. I have given them thy word; and the world has hated them because they are not of the world, even as I am not of the world. I do not pray that thou shouldst take them out of the world, but that thou shouldst keep them from the evil one. They are not of the world, even as I am not of the world. Sanctify them in the truth; thy word is truth. As thou didst send me into the world, so I have sent them into the world. And for their sake I consecrate myself, that they also may be consecrated in truth.

"I do not pray for these only, but also for those who believe in me through their word, that they may all be one; even as thou, Father, art in me, and I in thee, that they also may be in us, so that the world may believe that thou hast sent me. The glory which thou hast given me I have given to them, that they may be one even as we are one, I in them and thou in me, that they may become perfectly one, so that the world may know that thou hast sent me and hast loved them even as thou hast loved me. Father, I desire that they also, whom thou hast given me may be with me where I am, to behold my glory which thou hast given me in thy love for me before the foundation of the world. O righteous Father, the world has not known thee, but

I have known thee; and these know that thou hast sent me. I made known to them thy name, and I will make it known, that the love with which thou hast loved me may be in them, and I in them."

2605 (1) **Psalm 22:2 (22:1: RSV)**
My God, my God, why hast thou forsaken me?
Why art thou so far from helping me, from the words of my groaning?

2605 (2) **Mark 15:37** And Jesus uttered a loud cry, and breathed his last.

2605 (3) **John 19:30b** . . . and he bowed his head and gave up his spirit.

2606 **Acts 13:33** ". . . this he has fulfilled to us their children by raising Jesus; as also it is written in the second psalm,
'Thou art my Son,
today I have begotten thee.' . . ."

2608 (1) **Matthew 5:23–24** So if you are offering your gift at the altar, and there remember that your brother has something against you, leave your gift there before the altar and go; first be reconciled to your brother, and then come and offer your gift.

2608 (2) **Matthew 5:44–45** But I say to you, Love your enemies and pray for those who persecute you, so that you may be sons of your Father who is in heaven; for he makes his sun rise on the evil and on the good, and sends rain on the just and on the unjust.

2608 (3) **Matthew 6:7** "And in praying do not heap up empty phrases as the Gentiles do; for they think that they will be heard for their many words. . . ."

2608 (4) **Matthew 6:14–15** For if you forgive men their trespasses, your heavenly Father also will forgive you; but if you do not forgive men their trespasses, neither will your Father forgive your trespasses.

2608 (5) **Matthew 6:21** For where your treasure is, there will your heart be also.

2608 (6) **Matthew 6:25** "Therefore I tell you, do not be anxious about your life, what you shall eat or what you shall drink, nor about your body, what you shall put on. Is not life more than food, and the body more than clothing? . . ."

2608 (7) **Matthew 6:33** But seek first his kingdom and his righteousness, and all these things shall be yours as well.

2609 (1) **Matthew 7:7–11** "Ask and it will be given you; seek, and you will find; knock, and it will be opened to you. For every one who asks receives, and he who seeks finds, and to him who knocks it will be opened. Or what man of you, if his son asks him for bread, will give him a stone? Or if he asks for a fish, will give him a serpent? If you then, who are evil, know how to give good gifts to your children, how much more will your Father who is in heaven give good things to those who ask him! . . ."

2609 (2) **Matthew 7:13–14** "Enter by the narrow gate; for the gate is wide and the way is easy, that leads to destruction, and those who enter by it are many. For the gate is narrow and the way is hard, that leads to life, and those who find it are few."

(1) **Matthew 21:22** ". . . And whatever you ask in prayer, you will receive, if you have faith." 2610

(2) **Mark 6:6** And he marveled because of their unbelief. 2610
And he went about among the villages teaching.

(3) **Matthew 8:26** And he said to them, "Why are you afraid, O men of little faith?" Then he rose and rebuked the winds and the sea; and there was a great calm. 2610

(4) **Matthew 8:10** When Jesus heard him, he marveled, and said to those who followed him, "Truly, I say to you, not even in Israel have I found such faith. . . ." 2610

(5) **Matthew 15:28** Then Jesus answered her, "O woman, great is your faith! Be it done for you as you desire." And her daughter was healed instantly. 2610

(1) **Matthew 7:21** "Not every one who says to me, 'Lord, Lord,' shall enter the kingdom of heaven, but he who does the will of my Father who is in heaven. . . ." 2611

(2) **Matthew 9:38** ". . . pray therefore the Lord of the harvest to send out laborers into his harvest." 2611

(3) **Luke 10:2** And he said to them, "The harvest is plentiful, but the laborers are few; pray therefore the Lord of the harvest to send out laborers into his harvest. . . ." 2611

(4) **John 4:34** Jesus said to them, "My food is to do the will of him who sent me, and to accomplish his work. . . ." 2611

(1) **Mark 13** And as he came out of the temple, one of his disciples said to him, "Look, Teacher, what wonderful stones and what wonderful buildings!" And Jesus said to him, "Do you see these great buildings? There will not be left here one stone upon another, that will not be thrown down." 2612

And as he sat on the Mount of Olives opposite the temple, Peter and James and John and Andrew asked him privately, "Tell us, when will this be, and what will be the sign when these things are all to be accomplished?" And Jesus began to say to them, "Take heed that no one leads you astray. Many will come in my name, saying, 'I am he!' and they will lead many astray. And when you hear of wars and rumors of wars, do not be alarmed; this must take place, but the end is not yet. For nation will rise against nation, and kingdom against kingdom; there will be earthquakes in various places, there will be famines; this is but the beginning of the birth-pangs.

"But take heed to yourselves; for they will deliver you up to councils; and you will be beaten in synagogues; and you will stand before governors and kings for my sake, to bear testimony before them. And the gospel must first be preached to all nations. And when they bring you to trial and deliver you up, do not be anxious beforehand what you are to say; but say whatever is given you in that hour, for it is not you who speak, but the Holy Spirit. And brother will deliver up brother to death, and the father his child, and children will rise against parents and have them put to death; and you will be hated by all for my name's sake. But he who endures to the end will be saved.

"But when you see the desolating sacrilege set up where it ought not to be (let the reader understand), then let those who are in Judea flee to the mountains; let him who is on the housetop not go down, nor enter his house, to take anything away; and let him who is in the field not turn back to take his mantle. And alas for those who are with child and for those who give suck in those days! Pray that it may not happen in winter. For in those days there will be such tribulation as has not been from the beginning of the creation which God created until now, and never will be. And if the Lord had not shortened the days, no human being would be saved; but for the sake of the elect, whom he chose, he shortened the days. And then if anyone says to you, 'Look, here is the Christ!' or 'Look, there he is!' do not believe it. False Christs and false prophets will arise and show signs and wonders, to lead astray, if possible, the elect. But take heed; I have told you all things beforehand.

"But in those days, after that tribulation, the sun will be darkened, and the moon will not give its light, and the stars will be falling from heaven, and the powers in the heavens will be shaken. And then they will see the Son of man coming in clouds with great power and glory. And then he will send out the angels, and gather his elect from the four winds, from the ends of the earth to the ends of heaven.

"From the fig tree learn its lesson: as soon as its branch becomes tender and puts forth its leaves, you know that summer is near. So also, when you see these things taking place, you know that he is near, at the very gates. Truly, I say to you, this generation will not pass away before all these things take place. Heaven and earth will pass away, but my words will not pass away.

"But of that day or that hour no one knows, not even the angels in heaven, nor the Son, but only the Father. Take heed, watch; for you do not know when the time will come. It is like a man going on a journey, when he leaves home and puts his servants in charge, each with his work, and commands the doorkeeper to be on the watch. Watch therefore—for you do not know when the master of the house will come, in the evening, or at midnight, or at cockcrow, or in the morning—lest he come suddenly and find you asleep. And what I say to you I say to all: Watch."

2612 (2) **Luke 21:34–36** "But take heed to yourselves lest your hearts be weighed down with dissipation and drunkenness and cares of this life, and that day come upon you suddenly like a snare; for it will come upon all who dwell upon the face of the whole earth. But watch at all times, praying that you may have strength to escape all these things that will take place, and to stand before the Son of man."

2612 (3) **Luke 22:40** And when he came to the place he said to them, "Pray that you may not enter into temptation."

2612 (4) **Luke 22:46** . . . and he said to them, "Why do you sleep? Rise and pray that you may not enter into temptation."

2613 (1) **Luke 11:5–13** And he said to them, "Which of you who has a friend will go to him at midnight and say to him, 'Friend, lend me three loaves; for a friend of mine has arrived on a journey, and I have nothing to set before him'; and he will answer from within, 'Do not bother me; the door is now shut, and my children are with me in bed; I cannot get up and give you anything'? I tell you, though he will not get up and give him anything because he is his friend, yet because of his importunity he will rise and give him whatever he needs. And I tell you, Ask, and it will be given you; seek, and you will find; knock, and it will be opened to you. For every one who asks receives, and he who seeks finds, and to him who knocks it will be opened. What father among you, if his son asks for a fish, will instead of a fish give him a serpent; or if he asks for an egg, will give him a scorpion? If you then, who are evil, know how to give good gifts to your children, how much more will the heavenly Father give the Holy Spirit to those who ask him!"

(2) **Luke 18:1–8** And he told them a parable, to the effect that they ought always 2613
to pray and not lose heart. He said, "In a certain city there was a judge who neither feared God nor regarded man; and there was a widow in that city who kept coming to him and saying, 'Vindicate me against my adversary.' For a while he refused; but afterward he said to himself, 'Though I neither fear God nor regard man, yet because this widow bothers me, I will vindicate her, or she will wear me out by her continual coming.'" And the Lord said, "Hear what the unrighteous judge says. And will not God vindicate his elect, who cry to him day and night? Will he delay long over them? I tell you, he will vindicate them speedily. Nevertheless, when the Son of man comes, will he find faith on earth?"

(3) **Luke 18:9–14** He also told this parable to some who trusted in themselves that 2613
they were righteous and despised others: "Two men went up into the temple to pray, one a Pharisee and the other a tax collector. The Pharisee stood and prayed thus with himself, 'God, I thank thee that I am not like other men, extortioners, unjust, adulterers, or even like this tax collector. I fast twice a week, I give tithes of all that I get.' But the tax collector, standing far off, would not even lift up his eyes to heaven, but beat his breast, saying, 'God, be merciful to me a sinner!' I tell you, this man went down to his house justified rather than the other; for every one who exalts himself will be humbled, but he who humbles himself will be exalted."

John 14:13–14 Whatever you ask in my name, I will do it, that the Father may be 2614
glorified in the Son; if you ask anything in my name, I will do it.

(1) **John 14:23–26** Jesus answered him, "If a man loves me, he will keep my word, 2615
and my Father will love him, and we will come to him and make our home with him. He who does not love me does not keep my words; and the word which you hear is not mine but the Father's who sent me.

"These things I have spoken to you, while I am still with you. But the Counselor, the Holy Spirit, whom the Father will send in my name, he will teach you all things, and bring to your remembrance all that I have said to you. . . ."

(2) **John 15:7** If you abide in me, and my words abide in you, ask whatever you 2615
will, and it shall be done for you.

(3) **John 15:16** You did not choose me, but I chose you and appointed you that 2615
you should go and bear fruit and that your fruit should abide; so that whatever you ask the Father in my name, he may give it to you.

(4) **John 16:13–15** When the Spirit of truth comes, he will guide you into all the 2615
truth; for he will not speak on his own authority, but whatever he hears he will speak, and he will declare to you the things that are to come. He will glorify me, for he will take what is mine and declare it to you. All that the Father has is mine; therefore I said that he will take what is mine and declare it to you.

(5) **John 16:23–27** ". . . In that day you will ask nothing of me. Truly, truly, I say 2615
to you, if you ask anything of the Father, he will give it to you in my name. Hitherto you have asked nothing in my name; ask, and you will receive, that your joy may be full.

"I have said this to you in figures; the hour is coming when I shall no longer speak to you in figures but tell you plainly of the Father. In that day you will ask in my name; and I do not say to you that I shall pray the Father for you; for the Father himself loves you, because you have loved me and have believed that I came from the Father. . . ."

2616 (1) **Mark 1:40–41** And a leper came to him beseeching him, and kneeling said to him, "If you will, you can make me clean." Moved with pity, he stretched out his hand and touched him, and said to him, "I will; be clean."

2616 (2) **Mark 5:36** But ignoring what they said, Jesus said to the ruler of the synagogue, "Do not fear, only believe."

2616 (3) **Mark 7:29** And he said to her, "For this saying you may go your way; the demon has left your daughter."

2616 (4) **Luke 23:39–43** One of the criminals who were hanged railed at him, saying, "Are you not the Christ? Save yourself and us!" But the other rebuked him, saying, "Do you not fear God, since you are under the same sentence of condemnation? And we indeed justly; for we are receiving the due reward of our deeds; but this man has done nothing wrong." And he said, "Jesus, remember me when you come into your kingdom." And he said to him, "Truly, I say to you, today you will be with me in Paradise."

2616 (5) **Mark 2:5** And when Jesus saw their faith, he said to the paralytic, "My son, your sins are forgiven."

2616 (6) **Mark 5:28** For she said, "If I touch even his garments, I shall be made well."

2616 (7) **Luke 7:37–38** And behold, a woman of the city, who was a sinner, when she learned that he was at table in the Pharisee's house, brought an alabaster flask of ointment, and standing behind him at his feet, weeping, she began to wet his feet with her tears, and wiped them with the hair of her head, and kissed his feet, and anointed them with the ointment.

2616 (8) **General Instruction of the Liturgy of the Hours 7** There is a special, and very close, bond between Christ and those whom he makes members of his body, the Church, through the sacrament of rebirth. Thus, from the head all the riches that belong to the Son flow throughout the whole body: the fellowship of the Spirit, the truth, the life and the sharing of his divine sonship, manifested in all his prayer when he dwelt among us.

The priesthood of Christ is also shared by the whole body of the Church, so that the baptized are consecrated as a spiritual temple and holy priesthood through the rebirth of baptism and the anointing by the Holy Spirit, and become able to offer the worship of the New Covenant, a worship that derives, not from our own powers but from the merit and gift of Christ.

"God could give no greater gift to mankind than to give them as their head the Word through whom he created all things, and to unite them to him as his members, so that he might be Son of God and Son of man, one God with the Father, one man with men. So, when we speak to God in prayer we do not separate the Son from God, and when the body of the Son prays it does not separate its head from itself, but it is the one savior of his body, our Lord Jesus Christ, the Son of God, who himself prays for us, and prays in us, and is the object of our prayer. He prays for us as our priest, he prays in us as our head, he is the object of our prayer as our God. Let us then hear our voices in his voice, and his voice in ours."

The excellence of Christian prayer lies in this, that it shares in the very love of the only-begotten Son for the Father and in that prayer which the Son put into words in his earthly life and which still continues unceasingly in the name of the whole human race and for its salvation, throughout the universal Church and in all its members.

(1) **Luke 1:38** And Mary said, "Behold, I am the handmaid of the Lord; let it be 2617
to me according to your word." And the angel departed from her.

(2) **Acts 1:14** All these with one accord devoted themselves to prayer, together with 2617
the women and Mary the mother of Jesus, and with his brothers.

(1) **John 2:1–12** On the third day there was a marriage at Cana in Galilee, and the 2618
mother of Jesus was there; Jesus also was invited to the marriage, with his disciples. When the wine gave out, the mother of Jesus said to him, "They have no wine." And Jesus said to her, "O woman, what have you to do with me? My hour has not yet come." His mother said to the servants, "Do whatever he tells you." Now six stone jars were standing there, for the Jewish rites of purification, each holding twenty or thirty gallons. Jesus said to them, "Fill the jars with water." And they filled them up to the brim. He said to them, "Now draw some out, and take it to the steward of the feast." So they took it. When the steward of the feast tasted the water now become wine, and did not know where it came from (though the servants who had drawn the water knew), the steward of the feast called the bridegroom and said to him, "Every man serves the good wine first; and when men have drunk freely, then the poor wine; but you have kept the good wine until now." This, the first of his signs, Jesus did at Cana in Galilee, and manifested his glory; and his disciples believed in him.

After this he went down to Capernaum, with his mother and his brothers and his disciples; and there they stayed for a few days.

(2) **John 19:25–27** So the soldiers did this. But standing by the cross of Jesus were 2618
his mother, and his mother's sister, Mary the wife of Clopas, and Mary Magdalene. When Jesus saw his mother, and the disciple whom he loved standing near, he said to his mother, "Woman, behold, your son!" Then he said to the disciple, "Behold, your mother!" And from that hour the disciple took her to his own home.

Luke 1:46–55 And Mary said, 2619

"My soul magnifies the Lord,
and my spirit rejoices in God my Savior,
for he has regarded the low estate of his handmaiden.
For behold, henceforth all generations will call me blessed;
for he who is mighty has done great things for me,
and holy is his name.
And his mercy is on those who fear him
from generation to generation.
He has shown strength with his arm,
he has scattered the proud in the imagination of their hearts,
he has put down the mighty from their thrones,
and exalted those of low degree;
he has filled the hungry with good things,
and the rich he has sent empty away.
He has helped his servant Israel,
in remembrance of his mercy,
as he spoke to our fathers,
to Abraham and to his posterity for ever."

John 14:26 But the Counselor, the Holy Spirit, whom the Father will send in my 2623
name, he will teach you all things, and bring to your remembrance all that I have said to you.

2625 (1) **Luke 24:27** And beginning with Moses and all the prophets, he interpreted to them in all the scriptures the things concerning himself.

2625 (2) **Luke 24:44** Then he said to them, "These are my words which I spoke to you, while I was still with you, that everything written about me in the law of Moses and the prophets and the psalms must be fulfilled."

2627 (1) **Ephesians 1:3–14** Blessed be the God and Father of our Lord Jesus Christ, who has blessed us in Christ with every spiritual blessing in the heavenly places, even as he chose us in him before the foundation of the world, that we should be holy and blameless before him. He destined us in love to be his sons through Jesus Christ, according to the purpose of his will, to the praise of his glorious grace which he freely bestowed on us in the Beloved. In him we have redemption through his blood, the forgiveness of our trespasses, according to the riches of his grace which he lavished upon us. For he has made known to us in all wisdom and insight the mystery of his will, according to his purpose which he set forth in Christ as a plan for the fulness of time, to unite all things in him, things in heaven and things on earth.

In him you also, who have heard the word of truth, the gospel of your salvation, and have believed in him, were sealed with the promised Holy Spirit, which is the guarantee of our inheritance until we acquire possession of it, to the praise of his glory.

2627 (2) **2 Corinthians 1:3–7** Blessed be the God and Father of our Lord Jesus Christ, the Father of mercies and God of all comfort, who comforts us in all our affliction, so that we may be able to comfort those who are in any affliction, with the comfort with which we ourselves are comforted by God. For as we share abundantly in Christ's sufferings, so through Christ we share abundantly in comfort too. If we are afflicted, it is for your comfort and salvation; and if we are comforted, it is for your comfort, which you experience when you patiently endure the same sufferings that we suffer. Our hope for you is unshaken; for we know that as you share in our sufferings, you will also share in our comfort.

2627 (3) **1 Peter 1:3–9** Blessed be the God and Father of our Lord Jesus Christ! By his great mercy we have been born anew to a living hope through the resurrection of Jesus Christ from the dead, and to an inheritance which is imperishable, undefiled, and unfading, kept in heaven for you, who by God's power are guarded through faith for a salvation ready to be revealed in the last time. In this you rejoice, though now for a little while you may have to suffer various trials, so that the genuineness of your faith, more precious than gold which though perishable is tested by fire, may redound to praise and glory and honor at the revelation of Jesus Christ. Without having seen him you love him; though you do not now see him you believe in him and rejoice with unutterable and exalted joy. As the outcome of your faith you obtain the salvation of your souls.

2627 (4) **2 Corinthians 13:13** All the saints greet you.

2627 (5) **Romans 15:5–6** May the God of steadfastness and encouragement grant you to live in such harmony with one another, in accord with Christ Jesus, that together you may with one voice glorify the God and Father of our Lord Jesus Christ.

2627 (6) **Romans 15:13** May the God of hope fill you with all joy and peace in believing, so that by the power of the Holy Spirit you may abound in hope.

(7) **Ephesians 6:23–24** Peace be to the brethren, and love with faith, from God 2627
the Father and the Lord Jesus Christ. Grace be with all who love our Lord Jesus Christ with love undying.

(1) **Psalm 95:1–6** 2628

O come, let us sing to the Lord;
let us make a joyful noise to the rock of our salvation!
Let us come into his presence with thanksgiving;
let us make a joyful noise to him with songs of praise!
For the Lord is a great God,
and a great King above all gods.
In his hand are the depths of the earth;
the heights of the mountains are his also.
The sea is his, for he made it;
for his hands formed the dry land.

O come, let us worship and bow down,
let us kneel before the Lord, our Maker!

(2) **St. Augustine, *Enarratio in Psalmos* 62, 16** "And in the covering of Thy wings 2628
I will exult." I am cheerful in good works, because over me is the covering of Thy wings. If thou protect me not, forasmuch as I am a chicken, the kite will seize me. For our Lord Himself saith in a certain place to that Jerusalem, a certain city, where He was crucified: "Jerusalem," He saith, "Jerusalem, how often I have willed to gather thy sons, as though a hen her chickens, and thou wouldest not" (Matt. xxiii. 37). Little ones we are: therefore may God protect us under the shadow of His wings. What when we shall have grown greater? A good thing it is for us that even then He should protect us, so that under Him the greater, always we be chickens. For always He is greater, however much we may have grown. Let no one say, let Him protect me while I am a little one: as if sometime he would attain to such magnitude, as should be self-sufficient. Without the protection of God, nought thou art. Always by Him let us desire to be protected: then always in Him we shall have power to be great, if always under Him little we be. "And in the covering of Thy wings I will exult."

(1) **Romans 15:30** I appeal to you, brethren, by our Lord Jesus Christ and by the 2629
love of the Spirit, to strive together with me in your prayers to God on my behalf. . . .

(2) **Colossians 4:12** Epaphras, who is one of yourselves, a servant of Christ Jesus, 2629
greets you, always remembering you earnestly in his prayers, that you may stand mature and fully assured in all the will of God.

1 John 1:7–2:2 . . . but if we walk in the light, as he is in the light, we have fellowship 2631
with one another, and the blood of Jesus his Son cleanses us from all sin. If we say we have no sin, we deceive ourselves, and the truth is not in us. If we confess our sins, he is faithful and just, and will forgive our sins and cleanse us from all unrighteousness. If we say we have not sinned, we make him a liar, and his word is not in us.

My little children, I am writing this to you so that you may not sin; but if any one does sin, we have an advocate with the Father, Jesus Christ the righteous; and he is the expiation for our sins, and not for ours only but also for the sins of the whole world.

2632 (1) **Matthew 6:10**
Thy kingdom come.
Thy will be done,
On earth as it is in heaven.

2632 (2) **Matthew 6:33** But seek first his kingdom and his righteousness, and all these things shall be yours as well.

2632 (3) **Luke 11:2** And he said to them, "When you pray say:
"Father, hallowed be thy name. Thy kingdom come. . . ."

2632 (4) **Luke 11:13** ". . . If you then, who are evil, know how to give good gifts to your children, how much more will the heavenly Father give the Holy Spirit to those who ask him!"

2632 (5) **Acts 6:6** These they set before the apostles, and they prayed and laid their hands upon them.

2632 (6) **Acts 13:3** Then after fasting and praying they laid their hands on them and sent them off.

2632 (7) **Romans 10:1** Brethren, my heart's desire and prayer to God for them is that they may be saved.

2632 (8) **Ephesians 1:16–23** I do not cease to give thanks for you, remembering you in my prayers, that the God of our Lord Jesus Christ, the Father of glory, may give you a spirit of wisdom and of revelation in the knowledge of him, having the eyes of your hearts enlightened, that you may know what is the hope to which he has called you, what are the riches of his glorious inheritance in the saints, and what is the immeasurable greatness of his power in us who believe, according to the working of his great might which he accomplished in Christ when he raised him from the dead and made him sit at his right hand in the heavenly places, far above all rule and authority and power and dominion, and above every name that is named, not only in this age but also in that which is to come; and he has put all things under his feet and has made him the head over all things for the church, which is his body, the fulness of him who fills all in all.

2632 (9) **Philippians 1:9–11** And it is my prayer that your love may abound more and more, with knowledge and all discernment, so that you may approve what is excellent, and may be pure and blameless for the day of Christ, filled with the fruits of righteousness which come through Jesus Christ, to the glory and praise of God.

2632 (10) **Colossians 1:3–6** We always thank God, the Father of our Lord Jesus Christ, when we pray for you, because we have heard of your faith in Christ Jesus and of the love which you have for all the saints, because of the hope laid up for you in heaven. Of this you have heard before in the word of the truth, the gospel which has come to you, as indeed in the whole world it is bearing fruit and growing—so among yourselves, from the day you heard and understood the grace of God in truth. . . .

2632 (11) **Colossians 4:3–4** . . . and pray for us also, that God may open to us a door for the word, to declare the mystery of Christ, on account of which I am in prison, that I may make it clear, as I ought to speak.

(12) **Colossians 4:12** Epaphras, who is one of yourselves, a servant of Christ Jesus, greets you, always remembering you earnestly in his prayers, that you may stand mature and fully assured in all the will of God. 2632

(1) **John 14:13** Whatever you ask in my name, I will do it, that the Father may be glorified in the Son. . . . 2633

(2) **James 1:5–8** If any of you lacks wisdom, let him ask God, who gives to all men generously and without reproaching, and it will be given him. But let him ask in faith, with no doubting, for he who doubts is like a wave of the sea that is driven and tossed by the wind. For that person must not suppose that a double-minded man, unstable in all his ways, will receive anything from the Lord. 2633

(3) **Ephesians 5:20** . . . always and for everything giving thanks in the name of our Lord Jesus Christ to God the Father. 2633

(4) **Philippians 4:6–7** Have no anxiety about anything, but in everything by prayer and supplication with thanksgiving let your requests be made known to God. And the peace of God, which passes all understanding, will keep your hearts and your minds in Christ Jesus. 2633

(5) **Colossians 3:16–17** Let the word of Christ dwell in you richly, teach and admonish one another in all wisdom, and sing psalms and hymns and spiritual songs with thankfulness in your hearts to God. And whatever you do, in word or deed, do everything in the name of the Lord Jesus, giving thanks to God the Father through him. 2633

(6) **1 Thessalonians 5:17–18** . . . pray constantly, give thanks in all circumstances; for this is the will of God in Christ Jesus for you. 2633

(1) **Romans 8:34** . . . who is to condemn? Is it Christ Jesus, who died, yes, who was raised from the dead, who is at the right hand of God, who indeed intercedes for us? 2634

(2) **1 John 2:1** My little children, I am writing this to you so that you may not sin; but if any one does sin, we have an advocate with the Father, Jesus Christ the righteous. . . . 2634

(3) **1 Timothy 2:5–8** For there is one God, and there is one mediator between God and men, the man Christ Jesus, who gave himself as a ransom for all, the testimony to which was borne at the proper time. For this I was appointed a preacher and apostle (I am telling the truth, I am not lying), a teacher of the Gentiles in faith and truth. 2634

I desire then that in every place the men should pray, lifting holy hands without anger or quarreling. . . .

(1) **Acts 7:60** And he knelt down and cried with a loud voice, "Lord, do not hold this sin against them." And when he had said this, he fell asleep. 2635

(2) **Luke 23:28** But Jesus turning to them said, "Daughters of Jerusalem, do not weep for me, but weep for yourselves and for your children. . . ." 2635

(3) **Luke 23:34** And Jesus said, "Father, forgive them; for they know not what they do." And they cast lots to divide his garments. 2635

2636 (1) **Acts 12:5** So Peter was kept in prison; but earnest prayer for him was made to God by the church.

2636 (2) **Acts 20:36** And when he had spoken thus, he knelt down and prayed with them all.

2636 (3) **Acts 21:5** And when our days there were ended, we departed and went on our journey; and they all, with wives and children, brought us on our way till we were outside the city; and kneeling down on the beach we prayed and bade one another farewell.

2636 (4) **2 Corinthians 9:14** . . . while they long for you and pray for you, because of the surpassing grace of God in you.

2636 (5) **Ephesians 6:18–20** Pray at all times in the Spirit, with all prayer and supplication. To that end keep alert with all perseverance, making supplication for all the saints, and also for me, that utterance may be given me in opening my mouth boldly to proclaim the mystery of the gospel, for which I am an ambassador in chains; that I may declare it boldly, as I ought to speak.

2636 (6) **Colossians 4:3–4** . . . and pray for us also, that God may open to us a door for the word, to declare the mystery of Christ, on account of which I am in prison, that I may make it clear, as I ought to speak.

2636 (7) **1 Thessalonians 5:25** Brethren, pray for us.

2636 (8) **2 Thessalonians 1:11** To this end we always pray for you, that our God may make you worthy of his call, and may fulfil every good resolve and work of faith by his power. . . .

2636 (9) **Colossians 1:3** We always thank God, the Father of our Lord Jesus Christ, when we pray for you. . . .

2636 (10) **Philippians 1:3–4** I thank my God in all my remembrance of you, always in every prayer of mine for you all making my prayer with joy. . . .

2636 (11) **Romans 12:14** Bless those who persecute you; bless and do not curse them.

2636 (12) **Romans 10:1** Brethren, my heart's desire and prayer to God for them is that they may be saved.

2639 **Romans 8:16** . . . it is the Spirit himself bearing witness with our spirit that we are children of God. . . .

2641 (1) **Philippians 2:6–11** . . . who, though he was in the form of God, did not count equality with God a thing to be grasped, but emptied himself, taking the form of a servant, being born in the likeness of men. And being found in human form he humbled himself and became obedient unto death, even death on a cross. Therefore God has highly exalted him and bestowed on him the name which is above every name, that at the name of Jesus every knee should bow, in heaven and on earth and under the earth, and every tongue confess that Jesus Christ is Lord, to the glory of God the Father.

(2) **Colossians 1:15–20** He is the image of the invisible God, the first-born of all **2641**
creation; for in him all things were created, in heaven and on earth, visible and invisible, whether thrones or dominions or principalities or authorities—all things were
created through him and for him. He is before all things, and in him all things hold
together. He is the head of the body, the church; he is the beginning, the first-born
from the dead, that in everything he might be preeminent. For in him all the fulness
of God was pleased to dwell, and through him to reconcile to himself all things,
whether on earth or in heaven, making peace by the blood of his cross.

(3) **Ephesians 5:14** Therefore it is said, **2641**
"Awake, O sleeper, and arise from the dead,
and Christ shall give you light."

(4) **1 Timothy 3:16** Great indeed, we confess, is the mystery of our religion: **2641**
He was manifested in the flesh,
vindicated in the Spirit,
seen by angels,
preached among the nations,
believed on in the world,
taken up in glory.

(5) **1 Timothy 6:15–16** . . . and this will be made manifest at the proper time by **2641**
the blessed and only Sovereign, the King of kings and Lord of lords, who alone has
immortality and dwells in unapproachable light, whom no man has ever seen or can
see. To him be honor and eternal dominion. Amen.

(6) **2 Timothy 2:11–13** The saying is sure: **2641**
If we have died with him, we shall also live with him;
if we endure, we shall also reign with him;
if we deny him, he also will deny us;
if we are faithless, he remains faithful—
for he cannot deny himself.

(7) **Ephesians 1:3–14:** see 2627 (1). **2641**

(8) **Romans 16:25–27** Now to him who is able to strengthen you according to my **2641**
gospel and the preaching of Jesus Christ, according to the revelation of the mystery
which was kept secret for long ages but is now disclosed and through the prophetic
writings is made known to all nations, according to the command of the eternal God,
to bring about the obedience of faith—to the only wise God be glory for evermore
through Jesus Christ! Amen.

(9) **Ephesians 3:20–21** Now to him who by the power at work within us is able to **2641**
do far more abundantly than all that we ask or think, to him be glory in the church
and in Christ Jesus to all generations, for ever and ever. Amen.

(10) **Jude 24–25** Now to him who is able to keep you from falling and to present **2641**
you without blemish before the presence of his glory with rejoicing, to the only God,
our Savior through Jesus Christ our Lord, be glory, majesty, dominion, and authority,
before all time and now and for ever. Amen.

2642 (1) **Revelation 4:8–11** And the four living creatures, each of them with six wings, are full of eyes all round and within, and day and night they never cease to sing,

"Holy, holy, holy, is the Lord God Almighty,
who was and is and is to come."

And whenever the living creatures give glory and honor and thanks to him who is seated on the throne, who lives for ever and ever, the twenty-four elders fall down before him who is seated on the throne and worship him who lives for ever and ever; they cast their crowns before the throne, singing,

"Worthy art thou, our Lord and God,
to receive glory and honor and power,
for thou didst create all things,
and by thy will they existed and were created."

2642 (2) **Revelation 5:9–14** . . . and they sang a new song, saying,

"Worthy art thou to take the scroll and to open its seals,
for thou wast slain and by thy blood didst ransom men for God
from every tribe and tongue and people and nation,
and hast made them a kingdom and priests to our God,
and they shall reign on earth."

Then I looked, and I heard around the throne and the living creatures and the elders the voice of many angels, numbering myriads of myriads and thousands of thousands, saying with a loud voice, "Worthy is the Lamb who was slain, to receive power and wealth and wisdom and might and honor and glory and blessing!" And I heard every creature in heaven and on earth and under the earth and in the sea, and all therein, saying, "To him who sits upon the throne and to the Lamb be blessing and honor and glory and might for ever and ever!" And the four living creatures said, "Amen!" and the elders fell down and worshiped.

2642 (3) **Revelation 7:10–12** . . . and crying out with a loud voice, "Salvation belongs to our God who sits upon the throne, and to the Lamb!" And all the angels stood round the throne and round the elders and the four living creatures, and they fell on their faces before the throne and worshiped God, saying, "Amen! Blessing and glory and wisdom and thanksgiving and honor and power and might be to our God for ever and ever! Amen."

2642 (4) **Revelation 18:24**

". . . And in her was found the blood of prophets and of saints,
and of all who have been slain on earth."

2642 (5) **Revelation 19:1–8** After this I heard what seemed to be the loud voice of a great multitude in heaven, crying,

"Hallelujah! Salvation and glory and power belong to our God,
for his judgments are true and just;
he has judged the great harlot who corrupted the earth with her fornication,
and he has avenged on her the blood of his servants."

Once more they cried,

"Hallelujah! The smoke from her goes up for ever and ever."

And the twenty-four elders and the four living creatures fell down and worshiped God who is seated on the throne, saying, "Amen. Hallelujah!" And from the throne came a voice crying,

"Praise our God, all you his servants,
you who fear him, small and great."

Then I heard what seemed to be the voice of a great multitude, like the sound of many waters and like the sound of mighty thunderpeals, crying,

"Hallelujah! For the Lord our God the Almighty reigns.
Let us rejoice and exult and give him the glory,
for the marriage of the Lamb has come,
and his Bride has made herself ready;
it was granted her to be clothed with fine linen, bright and pure"—

for the fine linen is the righteous deeds of the saints.

Malachi 1:11 For from the rising of the sun to its setting my name is great among the nations, and in every place incense is offered to my name, and a pure offering; for my name is great among the nations, says the Lord of hosts. 2643

***Dei Verbum* 8** Thus, the apostolic preaching, which is expressed in a special way in the inspired books, was to be preserved in a continuous line of succession until the end of time. Hence the apostles, in handing on what they themselves had received, warn the faithful to maintain the traditions which they had learned either by word of mouth or by letter (cf. 2 Th. 2:15); and they warn them to fight hard for the faith that had been handed on to them once and for all (cf. Jude 3). What was handed on by the apostles comprises everything that serves to make the People of God live their lives in holiness and increase their faith. In this way the Church, in her doctrine, life and worship, perpetuates and transmits to every generation all that she herself is, all that she believes. 2651

The Tradition that comes from the apostles makes progress in the Church, with the help of the Holy Spirit. There is a growth in insight into the realities and words that are being passed on. This comes about in various ways. It comes through the contemplation and study of believers who ponder these things in their hearts (cf. Lk. 2:19 and 51). It comes from the intimate sense of spiritual realities which they experience. And it comes from the preaching of those who have received, along with their right of succession in the episcopate, the sure charism of truth. Thus, as the centuries go by, the Church is always advancing towards the plenitude of divine truth, until eventually the words of God are fulfilled in her.

The sayings of the Holy Fathers are a witness to the life-giving presence of this Tradition, showing how its riches are poured out in the practice and life of the Church, in her belief and her prayer. By means of the same Tradition the full canon of the sacred books is known to the Church and the holy Scriptures themselves are more thoroughly understood and constantly actualized in the Church. Thus God, who spoke in the past, continues to converse with the spouse of his beloved Son. And the Holy Spirit, through whom the living voice of the Gospel rings out in the Church—and through her in the world—leads believers to the full truth, and makes the Word of Christ dwell in them in all its richness (cf. Col. 3:16).

Guigo the Carthusian, *Scala Claustralium* 2654

I. PROLOGUE

BROTHER GUIGO to his dear brother Gervase: rejoice in the Lord. I owe you a debt of love, brother, because you began to love me first; and since in your previous letter you have invited me to write to you, I feel bound to reply. So I decided to send you my thoughts on the spiritual exercises proper to cloistered monks, so that you who have come to know more about these matters by your experience than I have by theorizing about them may pass judgment on my thoughts and amend them. And it is fitting that I should offer these first results of our work together to you before anyone else, so that you may gather the first fruits of the young tree which by praiseworthy stealth you extracted from the bondage of Pharaoh, where it was tended alone, and set it in its place among the ordered rows, once you had grafted on to the stock like a good nurseryman the branch skillfully cut from the wild olive.

II. THE FOUR RUNGS OF THE LADDER

One day when I was busy working with my hands I began to think about our spiritual work, and all at once four stages in spiritual exercise came into my mind: reading, meditation, prayer and contemplation. These make a ladder for monks by which they are lifted up from earth to heaven. It has few rungs, yet its length is immense and wonderful, for its lower end rests upon the earth, but its top pierces the clouds and touches heavenly secrets. Just as its rungs or degrees have different names and numbers, they differ also in order and quality; and if anyone inquires carefully into their properties and functions, what each one does in relation to us, the differences between them and their order of importance, he will consider whatever trouble and care he may spend on this little and easy in comparison with the help and consolation which he gains.

Reading is the careful study of the Scriptures, concentrating all one's powers on it. Meditation is the busy application of the mind to seek with the help of one's own reason for knowledge of hidden truth. Prayer is the heart's devoted turning to God to drive away evil and obtain what is good. Contemplation is when the mind is in some sort lifted up to God and held above itself, so that it tastes the joys of everlasting sweetness. Now that we have described the four degrees, we must see what their functions are in relation to us.

III. THE FUNCTIONS OF THESE DEGREES

Reading seeks for the sweetness of a blessed life, meditation perceives it, prayer asks for it, contemplation tastes it. Reading, as it were, puts food whole into the mouth, meditation chews it and breaks it up, prayer extracts its flavor, contemplation is the sweetness itself which gladdens and refreshes. Reading works on the outside, meditation on the pith: prayer asks for what we long for, contemplation gives us delight in the sweetness which we have found. To make this clearer, let us take one of many possible examples.

IV. THE FUNCTION OF READING

I hear the words read: 'Blessed are the pure in heart, for they shall see God.' This is a short text of Scripture, but it is of great sweetness, like a grape that is put into the mouth filled with many senses to feed the soul. When the soul has carefully examined it, it says to itself, There may be something good here. I shall return to my heart and try to understand and find this purity, for this is indeed a precious and desirable thing. Those who have it are called blessed. It has for its reward the vision of God which is eternal life, and it is praised in so many places in sacred Scripture. So, wishing to have a fuller understanding of this, the soul begins to bite and chew upon this grape, as though putting it in a wine press, while it stirs up its power of reasoning to ask what this precious purity may be and how it may be had.

V. THE FUNCTION OF MEDITATION

When meditation busily applies itself to this work, it does not remain on the outside, is not detained by unimportant things, climbs higher, goes to the heart of the matter, examines each point thoroughly. It takes careful note that the text does not say: 'Blessed are the pure in body', but 'the pure in heart', for it is not enough to have hands clean from evil deeds, unless our minds are cleansed from impure thoughts. We have the authority of the prophet for this, when he says: 'Who shall climb the mountain of the Lord, and who shall stand in His holy place? He whose hands are guiltless and whose heart is pure.' And meditation perceives how greatly that same prophet seeks for this purity of heart when he prays: 'Create a pure heart in me, God', and in another place: 'If I know that there is wickedness in my heart, the Lord will not hear me.' It thinks what care the saintly man Job took to preserve this purity; when he said: 'I have made a pact with my eyes, so that I would not think about any maid.' See how this holy man guarded himself, who shut his eyes lest he should look upon vain things, lest he should perhaps unguardedly see that which afterward he should long for despite himself.

After meditation has so pondered upon purity of heart, it begins to think of the reward, of how glorious and joyful it would be to see the face of the Lord so greatly longed for, 'fairer than all the sons of men', no longer rejected and wretched, not with that earthly beauty with which His mother clothed Him, but wearing the robe of immortality and crowned with the diadem which His Father bestowed upon Him on the day of His resurrection and glory, the day 'which the Lord has made'. It thinks how this vision will bring it the fullness of which the prophet says: 'I shall be filled when your glory appears.' Do you see how much juice has come from one little grape, how great a fire has been kindled from a spark, how this small piece of metal, 'Blessed are the pure in heart, for they shall see God', has acquired a new dimension by being hammered out on the anvil of meditation? And even more might be drawn from it at the hands of someone truly expert. I feel that 'the well is deep', but I am still an ignorant beginner, and it is only with difficulty that I have found something in which to draw up these few drops. When the soul is set alight by this kindling, and when its flames are fanned by these desires, it receives a first intimation of the sweetness, not yet by tasting but through its sense of smell, when the alabaster box is broken; and from this it deduces how sweet it would be to know by experience the purity that meditation has shown to be so full of joy.

But what is it to do? It is consumed with longing, yet it can find no means of its own to have what it longs for; and the more it searches the more it thirsts. As long as it is meditating, so long is it suffering, because it does not feel that sweetness which, as meditation shows, belongs to purity of heart, but which it does not give. A man will not experience this sweetness while reading or meditating 'unless it happened to be given him from above'. The good and the wicked alike can read and meditate; and even pagan philosophers by the use of reason discovered the highest and truest good. But 'although they knew God, they did not glorify Him as God', and trusting in their own powers they said: 'Let us sing our own praises, our words are our own.' They had not the grace to understand what they had the ability to see. 'They perished in their own ideas', and 'all their wisdom was swallowed up', that wisdom to which the study of human learning had led them, not the Spirit of wisdom who alone grants true wisdom, that sweet-tasting knowledge that rejoices and refreshes the soul in which it dwells with a sweetness beyond telling. Of this wisdom it is said: 'Wisdom will not enter a disaffected soul.' This wisdom comes only from God; and just as the Lord entrusted the office of baptizing to many, but reserved to Himself alone the power and the authority truly to remit sins in baptism, so that John called Him by His office and defined it when he said: 'This is He who baptizes', so we may say of Him: 'This is He who gives the sweetness of wisdom and makes knowledge sweet to the soul.' He gives words to many, but to few that wisdom of the soul which the Lord apportions to whom He pleases and when He pleases.

VI. THE FUNCTION OF PRAYER

So the soul, seeing that it cannot attain by itself to that sweetness of knowing and feeling for which it longs, and that the more 'the heart abases itself', the more 'God is exalted', humbles itself and betakes itself to prayer, saying: Lord, you are not seen except by the pure of heart. I seek by reading and meditating what is true purity of heart and how it may be had, so that with its help I may know you, if only a little. Lord, for long have I meditated in my heart, seeking to see your face. It is the sight of you, Lord, that I have sought; and all the while in my meditation the fire of longing, the desire to know you more fully, has increased. When you break for me the bread of sacred Scripture, you have shown yourself to me in that breaking of bread, and the more I see you, the more I long to see you, no more from without, in the rind of the letter, but within, in the letter's hidden meaning. Nor do I ask this, Lord, because of my own merits, but because of your mercy. I too in my unworthiness confess my sins with the woman who said that 'even the little dogs eat of the fragments that fall from the table of their masters.' So give me, Lord, some pledge of what I hope to inherit, at least one drop of heavenly rain with which to refresh my thirst, for I am on fire with love.

VII. THE EFFECTS OF CONTEMPLATION

So the soul by such burning words inflames its own desire, makes known its state, and by such spells it seeks to call its spouse. But the Lord, whose eyes are upon the just and whose ears can catch not only the words, but the very meaning of their prayers, does not wait until the longing soul has said all its say, but breaks in upon the middle of its prayer, runs to meet it in all haste, sprinkled with sweet heavenly dew, anointed with the most precious perfumes, and He restores the weary soul, He slakes its thirst, He feeds its hunger, He makes the soul forget all earthly things: by making it die to itself He gives it new life in a wonderful way, and by making it drunk He brings it back to its true senses. And just as in the performance of some bodily functions the soul is so conquered by carnal desire that it loses all use of the reason, and man becomes as it were wholly carnal, so on the contrary in this exalted contemplation all carnal motives are so conquered and drawn out of the soul that in no way is the flesh opposed to the spirit, and man becomes, as it were, wholly spiritual.

VIII. THE SIGNS OF THE COMING OF GRACE

But, Lord, how are we to know when you do this, what will be the sign of your coming? Can it be that the heralds and witnesses of this consolation and joy are sighs and tears? If it is so, then the word consolation is being used in a completely new sense, the reverse of its ordinary connotation. What has consolation in common with sighs, joy with tears, if indeed these are to be called tears and not rather an abundance of spiritual dew, poured out from above and overflowing, an outward purification as a sign of inward cleansing. For just as in the baptism of infants by the outward washing, the inward cleansing is typified and shown, here conversely an outward washing proceeds from the inner cleansing. These are blessed tears, by which our inward stains are cleansed, by which the fires of our sins are put out. 'Blessed are they who weep' so, 'for they shall rejoice.' When you weep so, O my soul, recognize your spouse, embrace Him whom you long for, make yourself drunk with this torrent of delight, and suck the honey and milk of consolation from the breast. The wonderful reward and comforts which your spouse has brought and awarded you are sobbings and tears. These tears are the generous draught which He gives you to drink. Let these tears be your bread by day and night, the bread which strengthens the heart of man, sweeter than honey and the honeycomb. O Lord Jesus, if these tears, provoked by thinking of you and longing for you, are so sweet, how sweet will be the joy which we shall have to see you face to face? If it is so sweet to weep for you, how sweet will it be to rejoice in you? But why do we give this public utterance to what should be said in secret? Why do we try to express in everyday language affections that no language can describe? Those who have not known such things do not understand them, for they could learn more clearly of them only from the book of experience where God's grace itself is the teacher. Otherwise it is of no use for the reader to search in earthly books: there is little sweetness in the study of the literal sense, unless there be a commentary, which is found in the heart, to reveal the inward sense.

IX. HOW GRACE IS HIDDEN

O my soul, we have talked like this too long. Yet it would have been good for us to be here, to look with Peter and with John upon the glory of the spouse and to remain awhile with Him, had it been His will that we should make here not two, not three tabernacles, but one in which we might all dwell and be filled with joy. But now, the spouse says, 'Let me go, for now the dawn is coming up', now you have received the light of grace and the visitation which you asked for. So He gives His blessing, and withers the nerve of the thigh, and changes Jacob's name to Israel, and then for a little while He withdraws, this spouse waited for so long, so soon gone again. He goes, it is true, for this visitation ends, and with it the sweetness of contemplation; but yet He stays, for He directs us, He gives us grace, He joins us to Himself.

X. HOW, WHEN GRACE IS HIDDEN FOR A TIME, IT WORKS IN US FOR GOOD

But do not fear, bride of the spouse, do not despair, do not think yourself despised, if for a little while He turns His face away from you. These things all work together for your good, and you profit from His coming and from His withdrawal. He comes to you, and then He goes away again. He comes for your consolation, He goes away to put you on your guard, for fear that too much consolation should puff you up, and that you having the spouse always with you, should begin to despise your brethren, and to attribute this consolation not to His grace but to your natural powers. For this grace the spouse bestows when He pleases and to whom He pleases; it is not possessed as though by lawful title. There is a common saying that too much familiarity breeds contempt. And so He withdraws Himself, so that He is not despised for being too attentive, so that when He is absent He may be desired the more, that being desired He may be sought more eagerly, that having been sought for He may at last be found with greater thankfulness.

Then, too, if we never lacked this consolation, which is a mere shadow and fraction in comparison with the future glory that will be shown in us, we might think that we have here on earth our eternal home, and so we should seek the less for our life in eternity. So, therefore, lest we should consider this present exile our true home, this pledge our whole reward, the spouse comes and withdraws by turn, now bringing us consolation, now exchanging all this for weakness. For a short time He allows us to taste how sweet He is, and before our taste is satisfied He withdraws; and it is in this way, by flying above us with wings outspread, that He encourages us to fly, and says in effect: See now, you have had a little taste of how sweet and delightful I am, but if you wish to have your fill of this sweetness, hasten after me, drawn by my sweet-smelling perfumes, lift up your heart to where I am at the right hand of God the Father. There you will see me not darkly in a mirror but face to face, and 'your heart's joy will be complete and no one shall take this joy away from you.'

XI. HOW MUCH THE SOUL MUST BE ON ITS GUARD AFTER IT HAS BEEN VISITED BY GRACE

But take care, bride of the spouse. When He goes away, He does not go far; and even if you cannot see Him, you are always in His sight. He is full of eyes in front and behind, you cannot hide from Him anywhere, for He surrounds you with those messengers of His, spirits who serve to bring back shrewd reports, to watch how you behave when He is not there, to accuse you to Him if they detect in you any marks of wantonness and vileness. This is a jealous spouse. He will leave you at once and give His favors to others if you play Him false with anyone, trying to please any more than Him. This spouse is fastidious, He is of gentle birth, He is rich, 'He is fairer than all the sons of men,' and so He will not deign to take a bride who is not fair. If He sees in you any blemish, any wrinkle, He will at once turn away from you. He cannot bear uncleanness of any kind. So be chaste, be truly modest and meek, if you wish often to enjoy your spouse's company.

I am afraid that I have talked too long of this to you, but I have been compelled to it by the abundance and the sweetness of my material. I have not deliberately drawn it out, but its very sweetness has drawn it out of me against my will.

XII. RECAPITULATION

Let us now gather together by way of summary what we have already said at length, so that we may have a better view by looking at it altogether. You can see, from what has already been said by way of examples, how these degrees are joined to each other. One precedes another, not only in the order of time but of causality. Reading comes first, and is, as it were, the foundation; it provides the subject matter we must use for meditation. Meditation considers more carefully what is to be sought after; it digs, as it were, for treasure which it finds and reveals, but since it is not in meditation's power to seize upon the treasure, it directs us to prayer. Prayer lifts itself up to God with all its strength, and begs for the treasure it longs for, which is the sweetness of contemplation. Contemplation when it comes rewards the labors of the other three; it inebriates the thirsting soul with the dew of heavenly sweetness. Reading is an exercise of the outward senses; meditation is concerned with the inward understanding; prayer is concerned with desire; contemplation outstrips every faculty. The first degree is proper to beginners, the second to proficients, the third to devotees, the fourth to the blessed.

XIII. HOW THESE DEGREES ARE LINKED ONE TO ANOTHER

At the same time these degrees are so linked together, each one working also for the others, that the first degrees are of little or no use without the last, while the last can never, or hardly ever, be won without the first. For what is the use of spending one's time in continuous reading, turning the pages of the lives and sayings of holy men, unless we can extract nourishment from them by chewing and digesting this food so that its strength can pass into our inmost heart? It is only thus that we can from their example carefully consider our state of soul, and reflect in our own deeds the lives about which we read so eagerly. But how is it possible to think properly, and to avoid meditating upon false and idle topics, overstepping the bounds laid down by our holy fathers, unless we are first directed in these matters by what we read or what we hear? Listening is a kind of reading, and that is why we are accustomed to say that we have read not only those books which we have read to ourselves or aloud to others but those also which our teachers have read to us.

Again, what use is it to anyone if he sees in his meditation what is to be done, unless the help of prayer and the grace of God enable him to achieve it? For 'every gift and every perfect gift is from above, coming down from the Father of lights.' We can do nothing without Him. It is He who achieves our works in us, and yet not entirely without us. 'For we are God's fellow workers', as the apostle says. It is God's will, then, that we pray to Him, His will that when His grace comes and knocks at our door, we should willingly open our hearts to Him and give Him our consent.

It was this consent that He demanded from the Samaritan woman when He said: 'Call your husband.' It was as if He said: 'I want to fill you with grace, and you must exercise your free choice.' He demanded prayer from her: 'If you only knew the gift of God, and who He is who says to you, Give me drink, you would perhaps ask Him for living waters.' When the woman heard this, it was as if the Lord had read it to her, and she meditated on this instruction in her heart, thinking that it would be good and useful for her to have this water. Fired with the desire for it, she had recourse to prayer, saying: 'Lord, give me this water, that I may thirst no more.' You can see that it was because she had heard the Lord's word and then had meditated on it that she was moved to prayer. How could she have pressed her petition, had she not first been fired by meditation? What profit would her meditation have been, if the prayer that followed had not asked for what she had been shown she should desire? From this we learn that if meditation is to be fruitful, it must be followed by devoted prayer, and the sweetness of contemplation may be called the effect of prayer.

XIV. SOME CONCLUSIONS FROM WHAT HAS BEEN SAID

From this we may gather that reading without meditation is sterile, meditation without reading is liable to error, prayer without meditation is lukewarm, meditation without prayer is unfruitful, prayer when it is fervent wins contemplation, but to obtain it without prayer would be rare, even miraculous. However, there is no limit to God's power and His merciful love surpasses all His other works; and sometimes He creates sons for Abraham from the very stones, when He forces the hard-hearted and reluctant to comply of their own free will. He acts like a prodigal father, or as the proverb has it, He gives the ox by the horn, when He enters where He has not been invited, when He dwells in the soul that has not sought Him. Although we are told that this has occasionally happened to St. Paul, for instance, and certain others, we ought not to presume that it will, for this would be like tempting God. Rather we should do our part, which is to read and meditate on the law of God, and pray to Him to help our weakness and to look kindly on our infirmities. He teaches us to do this when He says: 'Ask and you will receive, seek and you will find, knock and the door will be opened to you.' For then 'the kingdom of heaven submits to force, and the forceful take it by storm.'

From these definitions you can see how the various qualities of these degrees are linked one with another, and the effects which each one produces in us. Blessed is the man whose heart is not possessed by any other concern and whose desire is always to keep his feet upon this ladder. He has sold all his possessions, and has bought the field in which lies hid the longed-for treasure. He wants to be free from all else, and to see how sweet the Lord is. The man who has worked in this first degree, who has pondered well in the second, who has known devotion in the third, who has been raised above himself in the fourth, goes from strength to strength by this ascent on which his whole heart was set, until at last he can see the God of gods in Sion. Blessed is the man to whom it is given to remain, if only for a short time, in this highest degree. In truth he can say: 'Now indeed I experience God's grace, now with Peter and John upon the mountain I gaze upon his glory, now with Jacob I delight in the embraces of the lovely Rachel.'

But let such a man beware lest after this contemplation, in which he was lifted up to the very heavens, he plunged violently into the depths, and after such great graces turn again to the sinful pleasures of the world and the delights of the flesh. Since, however, the eye of the human heart has not the power to bear for long the shining of the true light, let the soul descend gently and in due order to one or other of the three degrees by means of which it made its ascent. Let it rest now in one, now in another, as the circumstances of time and place suggest to its free choice, even though, as it seems to me, the soul is the nearer to God the farther it climbs from the first degree. Such, alas, is the frailty and wretchedness of human nature!

In this way, then, we see clearly by reason and the testimony of the Scriptures that the perfection of the blessed life is contained in these four degrees, and that the spiritual man ought to occupy himself in them continually. But is there anyone who holds to this way of life? 'Tell us who he is and we will praise him.' There are many who desire it, but few who achieve it. Would that we were among these few!

XV. FOUR OBSTACLES TO THESE DEGREES

There are commonly four obstacles to these three degrees: unavoidable necessity, the good works of the active life, human frailty, worldly follies. The first can be excused, the second endured, the third invites compassion, the fourth blame. Blame truly, for it would be better for the man who for love of the world turns his back on the goal if he had never known God's grace, rather than, having known it, to retrace his steps. For what excuse will he find for his sin? Will not the Lord justly say to him: 'What more should I have done for you that I have not done? When you did not exist I created you, when you sinned and became the devil's slave I redeemed you, when you were going about with the wicked of this world I called you away. I let you find favor in my sight, I wanted to make my dwelling with you, and you gave me nothing but contempt. It was not my words alone that you repudiated, it was my own self, and instead you turned away in pursuit of your desires.'

But O my God, so good so tender and kind, dear friend, wise counsellor, powerful support, how heartless and how rash is the man who rejects you, who casts from his heart so humble and gentle a guest! What a wretched and ruinous bargain, to accept evil and harmful thoughts in exchange for his creator, so quickly to throw open the inner chamber of the Holy Spirit, that secret place of the heart which so recently echoed with heavenly joys, to unclean thoughts, to turn it into a pig sty. Adulterous desires press in upon the heart where the footprints of the spouse are still plain to be seen. How ill it accords, how unseemly it is, for ears which so recently listened to words which man may not utter, so quickly to attend to idle and slanderous stories, for eyes so newly purified by holy tears to turn their gaze so soon on worldly vanities, for the tongue which has scarcely ended its sweet song of welcome to the spouse, scarcely has made peace between Him and the bride with its burning and pleading eloquence, and has greeted her in the banqueting hall, to revert to foul talk, to scurrility, to lampoons and libels. Never let this happen to us, Lord, and even if we do so fall away through human frailty, never let us despair on that account, but let us hasten back to the merciful healer who lifts up the helpless ones out of the dust, and rescues the poor and wretched from the mire; for He who never desires the death of a sinner will tend us and heal us again and again.

Now it is time for us to end our letter. Let us beseech the Lord together that at this moment He will lighten the load that weighs us down so that we cannot look up to Him in contemplation, and in days to come remove it altogether, leading us through these degrees from strength to strength, until we come to look upon the God of gods in Sion, where His chosen enjoy the sweetness of divine contemplation, not drop by drop, not now and then, but in an unceasing flow of delight which no one shall take away, an unchanging peace, the peace of God.

So, my brother Gervase, if it is ever granted to you from above to climb to the topmost rung of this ladder, when this happiness is yours, remember me and pray for me. So, when the veil between you and God is drawn aside, may I too see Him, 'and may He who listens say to me also: Come.'

2655 **Matthew 6:6** But when you pray, go into your room and shut the door and pray to your Father who is in secret; and your Father who sees in secret will reward you.

2659 (1) **Matthew 6:11** Give us this day our daily bread. . . .

(2) **Matthew 6:34** "Therefore do not be anxious about tomorrow, for tomorrow will be anxious for itself. Let the day's own trouble be sufficient for the day. . . ." **2659**

Luke 13:20–21 And again he said, "To what shall I compare the kingdom of God? It is like leaven which a woman took and hid in three measures of flour, till it was all leavened." **2660**

***Dei Verbum* 10** Sacred Tradition and sacred Scripture make up a single sacred deposit of the Word of God, which is entrusted to the Church. By adhering to it the entire holy people, united to its pastors, remains always faithful to the teaching of the apostles, to the brotherhood, to the breaking of bread and the prayers (cf. Acts 2:42 Greek). So, in maintaining, practicing and professing the faith that has been handed on there should be a remarkable harmony between the bishops and the faithful. **2663**

But the task of giving an authentic interpretation of the Word of God, whether in its written form or in the form of Tradition, has been entrusted to the living teaching office of the Church alone. Its authority in this matter is exercised in the name of Jesus Christ. Yet this Magisterium is not superior to the Word of God, but is its servant. It teaches only what has been handed on to it. At the divine command and with the help of the Holy Spirit, it listens to this devotedly, guards it with dedication and expounds it faithfully. All that it proposes for belief as being divinely revealed is drawn from this single deposit of faith.

It is clear, therefore, that, in the supremely wise arrangement of God, sacred Tradition, sacred Scripture and the Magisterium of the Church are so connected and associated that one of them cannot stand without the others. Working together, each in its own way under the action of the one Holy Spirit, they all contribute effectively to the salvation of souls.

(1) **Exodus 3:14** God said to Moses, "I AM WHO I AM," And he said, "Say this to the people of Israel, 'I AM has sent me to you.'" **2666**

(2) **Exodus 33:19–23** And he said, "I will make all my goodness pass before you, and will proclaim before you my name 'The Lord'; and I will be gracious to whom I will be gracious, and will show mercy on whom I will show mercy. But," he said, "you cannot see my face; for man shall not see me and live." And the Lord said, "Behold, there is a place by me where you shall stand upon the rock; and while my glory passes by I will put you in a cleft of the rock, and I will cover you with my hand until I have passed by; then I will take away my hand, and you shall see my back; but my face shall not be seen." **2666**

(3) **Matthew 1:21** ". . . she will bear a son, and you shall call his name Jesus, for he will save his people from their sins." **2666**

(4) **Romans 10:13** For, "every one who calls upon the name of the Lord will be saved." **2666**

(5) **Acts 2:21** "'. . . And it shall be that whoever calls on the name of the Lord shall be saved.'" **2666**

(6) **Acts 3:15–16** . . . and killed the Author of life, whom God raised from the dead. To this we are witnesses. And his name, by faith in his name, has made this man strong whom you see and know; and the faith which is through Jesus has given the man this perfect health in the presence of you all. **2666**

2666 (7) **Galatians 2:20** I have been crucified with Christ; it is no longer I who live, but Christ who lives in me; and the life I now live in the flesh I live by faith in the Son of God, who loved me and gave himself for me.

2667 (1) **Mark 10:46–52** And they came to Jericho; and as he was leaving Jericho with his disciples and a great multitude, Bertimaeus, a blind beggar, the son of Timaeus, was sitting by the roadside. And when he heard that it was Jesus of Nazareth, he began to cry out and say, "Jesus, Son of David, have mercy on me!" And many rebuked him, telling him to be silent; but he cried out all the more, "Son of David, have mercy on me!" And Jesus stopped and said, "Call him." And they called the blind man, saying to him, "Take heart; rise, he is calling you." And throwing off his mantle he sprang up and came to Jesus. And Jesus said to him, "What do you want me to do for you?" And the blind man said to him, "Master, let me receive my sight." And Jesus said to him, "Go your way; your faith has made you well." And immediately he received his sight and followed him on the way.

2667 (2) **Luke 18:13** But the tax collector, standing far off, would not even lift up his eyes to heaven, but beat his breast, saying, "God, be merciful to me a sinner!"

2668 (1) **Matthew 6:7** "And in praying do not heap up empty phrases as the Gentiles do; for they think that they will be heard for their many words. . . ."

2668 (2) **Luke 8:15** And as for that in the good soil, they are those who, hearing the word, hold it fast in an honest and good heart, and bring forth fruit with patience.

2671 (1) **Luke 11:13** ". . . If you then, who are evil, know how to give good gifts to your children, how much more will the heavenly Father give the Holy Spirit to those who ask him!"

2671 (2) **John 14:17** . . . even the Spirit of truth, whom the world cannot receive, because it neither sees him nor knows him; you know him, for he dwells with you, and will be in you.

2671 (3) **John 15:26** But when the Counselor comes, whom I shall send to you from the Father, even the Spirit of truth, who proceeds from the Father, he will bear witness to me. . . .

2671 (4) **John 16:13** When the Spirit of truth comes, he will guide you into all the truth; for he will not speak on his own authority, but whatever he hears he will speak, and he will declare to you the things that are to come.

2671 (5) ***Roman Missal*, Pentecost, Sequence**

Come, Holy Spirit, come
And from your celestial home
    Shed a ray of light divine!

Come, Father of the poor!
Come, source of all our store!
    Come, within our bosoms shine!

You, of comforters the best;
You, the soul's most welcome guest;
    Sweet refreshment here below;

In our labor, rest most sweet;
Grateful coolness in the heat;
    Solace in the midst of woe.

O most blessed Light divine,
Shine within these hearts of yours,
    And our inmost being fill!

Where you are not, man has naught,
Nothing good in deed or thought,
    Nothing free from taint of ill.

Heal our wounds, our strength renew;
On our dryness pour your dew;
    Wash the stains of guilt away:

Bend the stubborn heart and will;
Melt the frozen, warm the chill;
    Guide the steps that go astray.

On the faithful, who adore
And confess you, evermore
    In your sev'nfold gifts descend;

Give them virtue's sure reward;
Give them your salvation, Lord;
    Give them joys that never end. Amen. Alleluia.

Acts 1:14 All these with one accord devoted themselves to prayer, together with **2673**
the women and Mary the mother of Jesus, and with his brothers.

Luke 1:46–55: see 2619. **2675**

(1) **Luke 1:48** **2676**
. . . for he has regarded the low estate of his handmaiden.
For behold, henceforth all generations will call me blessed. . . .

(2) **Zephaniah 3:17** **2676**
The Lord, your God, is in your midst,
    a warrior who gives victory;
he will rejoice over you with gladness,
    he will renew you in his love;
he will exult over you with loud singing. . . .

(3) **Genesis 12:3** ". . . I will bless those who bless you, and him who curses you I **2676**
will curse; and by you all the families of the earth shall bless themselves."

John 19:27 Then he said to the disciple, "Behold, your mother!" And from that **2677**
hour the disciple took her to his own home.

(1) **John 19:27:** see previous document. **2679**

(2) ***Lumen gentium* 68–69** In the meantime the Mother of Jesus in the glory which **2679**
she possesses in body and soul in heaven is the image and beginning of the Church as it is to be perfected in the world to come. Likewise she shines forth on earth, until the day of the Lord shall come (cf. 2 Pet. 3:10), a sign of certain hope and comfort to the pilgrim People of God.

It gives great joy and comfort to this sacred synod that among the separated brethren too there are those who give due honor to the Mother of Our Lord and Savior, especially among the Easterns, who with devout mind and fervent impulse give honor to the Mother of God, ever virgin. The entire body of the faithful pours forth urgent supplications to the Mother of God and of men that she, who aided the beginnings of the Church by her prayers, may now, exalted as she is above all the angels and saints, intercede before her Son in the fellowship of all the saints, until all families of people, whether they are honored with the title of Christian or whether they still do not know the Savior, may be happily gathered together in peace and harmony into one People of God, for the glory of the Most Holy and Undivided Trinity.

2683 (1) **Hebrews 12:1** Therefore, since we are surrounded by so great a cloud of witnesses, let us also lay aside every weight, and sin which clings so closely, and let us run with perseverance the race that is set before us. . . .

2683 (2) **Matthew 25:21** ". . . His master said to him, 'Well done, good and faithful servant; you have been faithful over a little, I will set you over much; enter into the joy of your master.'. . ."

2684 (1) **2 Kings 2:9** When they had crossed, Elijah said to Elisha, "Ask what I shall do for you, before I am taken from you." And Elisha said, "I pray you, let me inherit a double share of your spirit."

2684 (2) **Luke 1:17**

". . . and he will go before him in the spirit and power of Elijah,
to turn the hearts of the fathers to the children,
and the disobedient to the wisdom of the just,
to make ready for the Lord a people prepared."

2684 (3) ***Perfectae caritatis* 2** The up-to-date renewal of the religious life comprises both a constant return to the sources of the whole of the Christian life and to the primitive inspiration of the institutes, and their adaptation to the changed conditions of our time. This renewal, under the impulse of the Holy Spirit and with the guidance of the Church, must be promoted in accordance with the following principles:

(a) Since the final norm of the religious life is the following of Christ as it is put before us in the Gospel, this must be taken by all institutes as the supreme rule.

(b) It is for the good of the Church that institutes have their own proper characters and functions. Therefore the spirit and aims of each founder should be faithfully accepted and retained, as indeed should each institute's sound traditions, for all of these constitute the patrimony of an institute.

(c) All institutes should share in the life of the Church. They should make their own and should foster to the best of their ability, in a manner consonant with their own natures, its initiatives and undertakings in biblical, liturgical, dogmatic, pastoral, ecumenical, missionary and social matters.

(d) Institutes should see to it that their members have a proper understanding of men, of the conditions of the times and of the needs of the Church, this to the end that, making wise judgments about the contemporary world in the light of faith, and burning with apostolic zeal, they may be able to help men more effectively.

(e) Before all else, religious life is ordered to the following of Christ by its members and to their becoming united with God by the profession of the evangelical counsels. For this reason it must be seriously and carefully considered that even the best-contrived adaptations to the needs of our time will be of no avail unless they are animated by a spiritual renewal, which must always be assigned primary importance even in the active ministry.

Presbyterorum ordinis 4–6 The People of God is formed into one in the first place 2686
by the Word of the living God, which is quite rightly sought from the mouth of priests. For since nobody can be saved who has not first believed, it is the first task of priests as co-workers of the bishops to preach the Gospel of God to all men. In this way they carry out the Lord's command "Go into all the world and preach the Gospel to every creature" (Mk. 16:15) and thus set up and increase the People of God. For by the saving Word of God faith is aroused in the heart of unbelievers and is nourished in the heart of believers. By this faith then the congregation of the faithful begins and grows, according to the saying of the apostle: "Faith comes from what is heard, and what is heard comes by the preaching of Christ" (Rom. 10:17).

Priests then owe it to everybody to share with them the truth of the Gospel in which they rejoice in the Lord. Therefore, whether by their exemplary behavior they lead people to glorify God; or by their preaching proclaim the mystery of Christ to unbelievers; or teach the Christian message or explain the Church's doctrine; or endeavor to treat of contemporary problems in the light of Christ's teaching—in every case their role is to teach not their own wisdom but the Word of God and to issue a pressing invitation to all men to conversion and to holiness. Moreover, the priest's preaching, often very difficult in present-day conditions, if it is to become more effective in moving the minds of his hearers, must expound the Word of God not merely in a general and abstract way but by an application of the eternal truth of the Gospel to the concrete circumstances of life.

Thus the ministry of the Word is exercised in many different ways according to the needs of the hearers and the spiritual gifts of preachers. In non-Christian territories or societies people are led by the proclamation of the Gospel to faith and by the saving sacraments. In the Christian community itself on the other hand, especially for those who seem to have little understanding or belief underlying their practice, the preaching of the Word is required for the sacramental ministry itself, since the sacraments are sacraments of faith, drawing their origin and nourishment from the Word. This is of paramount importance in the case of the liturgy of the Word within the celebration of Mass where there is an inseparable union of the proclamation of the Lord's death and resurrection, the response of its hearers and the offering itself by which Christ confirmed the new covenant in his blood. In this offering the faithful share both by their sacrificial sentiments and by the reception of the sacrament.

God, who alone is the holy one and sanctifier, has willed to take men as allies and helpers to become humble servants in his work of sanctification. The purpose then for which priests are consecrated by God through the ministry of the bishop is that they should be made sharers in a special way in Christ's priesthood and, by carrying out sacred functions, act as his ministers who through his Spirit continually exercises his priestly function for our benefit in the liturgy. By Baptism priests introduce men into the People of God; by the sacrament of Penance they reconcile sinners with God and the Church; by the Anointing of the Sick they relieve those who are ill; and especially by the celebration of Mass they offer Christ's sacrifice sacramentally. But in the celebration of all the sacraments—as St. Ignatius Martyr already asserted in the early Church—priests are hierarchically united with the bishop in various ways and so make him present in a certain sense in individual assemblies of the faithful.

But the other sacraments, and indeed all ecclesiastical ministries and works of the apostolate are bound up with the Eucharist and are directed towards it. For in the most blessed Eucharist is contained the whole spiritual good of the Church, namely Christ himself our Pasch and the living bread which gives life to men through his flesh—that flesh which is given life and gives life through the Holy Spirit. Thus men are invited and led to offer themselves, their works and all creation with Christ. For this reason the Eucharist appears as the source and the summit of all preaching of the Gospel: catechumens are gradually led up to participation in the Eucharist, while the faithful who have already been consecrated in baptism and confirmation are fully incorporated in the Body of Christ by the reception of the Eucharist.

Therefore the eucharistic celebration is the center of the assembly of the faithful over which the priest presides. Hence priests teach the faithful to offer the divine victim to God the Father in the sacrifice of the Mass and with the victim to make an offering of their whole life. In the spirit of Christ the pastor, they instruct them to submit their sins to the Church with a contrite heart in the sacrament of Penance, so that they may be daily more and more converted to the Lord, remembering his words: "Repent, for the kingdom of heaven is at hand" (Mt. 4:17). They teach them to take part in the celebrations of the sacred liturgy in such a way as to achieve sincere prayer in them also. They guide them to the exercise of an ever more perfect spirit of prayer throughout their lives in proportion to each one's graces and needs. They lead all the faithful on to the observance of the duties of their particular state in life, and those who are more advanced to the carrying out of the evangelical counsels in the way suited to their individual cases. Finally they train the faithful so that they will be able to sing in their hearts to the Lord with psalms and hymns and spiritual canticles, giving thanks always for all things in the name of our Lord Jesus Christ to God the Father.

By their fulfilment of the Divine Office priests themselves should extend to the different hours of the day the praise and thanksgiving they offer in the celebration of the Eucharist. By the Office they pray to God in the name of the Church for the whole people entrusted to them and in fact for the whole world.

The house of prayer in which the most holy Eucharist is celebrated and reserved, where the faithful assemble, and where is worshipped the presence of the Son of God our Savior, offered for us on the sacrificial altar for the help and consolation of the faithful—this house ought to be in good taste and a worthy place for prayer and sacred ceremonial. In it pastors and faithful are called upon to respond with grateful hearts to the gifts of him who through his humanity is unceasingly pouring the divine life into the members of his Body. Priests ought to go to the trouble of properly cultivating liturgical knowledge and art so that by means of their liturgical ministry God the Father, Son, and Holy Spirit may be daily more perfectly praised by the Christian communities entrusted to their care.

Priests exercise the function of Christ as Pastor and Head in proportion to their share of authority. In the name of the bishop they gather the family of God as a brotherhood endowed with the spirit of unity and lead it in Christ through the Spirit to God the Father. For the exercise of this ministry, as for the rest of the priests' functions, a spiritual power is given them, a power whose purpose is to build up. And in building up the Church priests ought to treat everybody with the greatest kindness after the model of our Lord. They should act towards people not according to what may please men, but according to the demands of Christian doctrine and life. They should teach them and warn them as their dearest children, according to the words of the apostle: "Be urgent in season and out of season, convince, rebuke, and exhort, be unfailing in patience and in teaching" (2 Tim. 4:2).

For this reason it is the priests' part as instructors of the people in the faith to see to it either personally or through others that each member of the faithful shall be led in the Holy Spirit to the full development of his own vocation in accordance with the

Gospel teaching, and to sincere and active charity and the liberty with which Christ has set us free. Very little good will be achieved by ceremonies however beautiful, or societies however flourishing, if they are not directed towards educating people to reach Christian maturity. To encourage this maturity priests will make their help available to people to enable them to determine the solution to their problems and the will of God in the crises of life, great or small. Christians must also be trained so as not to live only for themselves. Rather, according to the demands of the new law of charity every man as he has received grace ought to minister it one to another, and in this way all should carry out their duties in a Christian way in the community of their fellow men.

Although priests owe service to everybody, the poor and the weaker ones have been committed to their care in a special way. It was with these that the Lord himself associated, and the preaching of the Gospel to them is given as a sign of his messianic mission. Priests will look after young people with special diligence. This applies also to married couples and parents. It is desirable that these should meet in friendly groups to help each other in the task of more easily and more fully living in a Christian way of life that is often difficult. Priests should keep in mind that all religious, men and women, being a particularly eminent group in the Lord's house, are deserving of having special care directed to their spiritual progress for the good of the whole Church. Finally, priests ought to be especially devoted to the sick and the dying, visiting them and comforting them in the Lord.

The pastor's task is not limited to individual care of the faithful. It extends by right also to the formation of a genuine Christian community. But if a community spirit is to be properly cultivated it must embrace not only the local church but the universal Church. A local community ought not merely to promote the care of the faithful within itself, but should be imbued with the missionary spirit and smooth the path to Christ for all men. But it must regard as its special charge those under instruction and the newly converted who are gradually educated in knowing and living the Christian life.

However, no Christian community is built up which does not grow from and hinge on the celebration of the most holy Eucharist. From this all education for community spirit must begin. This eucharistic celebration, to be full and sincere, ought to lead on the one hand to the various works of charity and mutual help, and on the other hand to missionary activity and the various forms of Christian witness.

In addition the ecclesial community exercises a truly motherly function in leading souls to Christ by its charity, its prayer, its example and its penitential works. For it constitutes an effective instrument for showing or smoothing the path towards Christ and his Church for those who have not yet found faith; while also encouraging, supporting and strengthening believers for their spiritual struggles.

In building up a community of Christians, priests can never be the servants of any human ideology or party. Rather their task as heralds of the Gospel and pastors of the Church is the attainment of the spiritual growth of the Body of Christ.

***Catechesi tradendae* 54–55** Another question of method concerns the utilization in catechetical instruction of valid elements in popular piety. I have in mind devotions practiced by the faithful in certain regions with moving fervor and purity of intention, even if the faith underlying them needs to be purified or rectified in many aspects. I have in mind certain easily understood prayers that many simple people are fond of repeating. I have in mind certain acts of piety practiced with a sincere desire to do penance or to please the Lord. Underlying most of these prayers and practices, besides elements that should be discarded, there are other elements which, if they were properly used, could serve very well to help people advance towards knowledge 2688 of the mystery of Christ and of His message: the love and mercy of God, the Incarnation of Christ, His redeeming cross and resurrection, the activity of the Spirit in each Christian and in the Church, the mystery of the hereafter, the evangelical virtues to be practiced, the presence of the Christian in the world, etc. And why should we appeal to non-Christian or even anti-Christian elements refusing to build on elements which, even if they need to be revised or improved, have something Christian at their root?

The final methodological question the importance of which should at least be referred to—one that was debated several times in the synod—is that of memorization. In the beginnings of Christian catechesis, which coincided with a civilization that was mainly oral, recourse was had very freely to memorization. Catechesis has since then known a long tradition of learning the principal truths by memorizing. We are all aware that this method can present certain disadvantages, not the least of which is that it lends itself to insufficient or at times almost non-existent assimilation, reducing all knowledge to formulas that are repeated without being properly understood. These disadvantages and the different characteristics of our own civilization have in some places led to the almost complete suppression—according to some, alas, the definitive suppression—of memorization in catechesis. And yet certain very authoritative voices made themselves heard on the occasion of the fourth general assembly of the synod, calling for the restoration of a judicious balance between reflection and spontaneity, between dialogue and silence, between written work and memory work. Moreover certain cultures still set great value on memorization.

At a time when, in non-religious teaching in certain countries, more and more complaints are being made about the unfortunate consequences of disregarding the human faculty of memory, should we not attempt to put this faculty back into use in an intelligent and even an original way in catechesis, all the more since the celebration or "memorial" of the great events of the history of salvation require a precise knowledge of them? A certain memorization of the words of Jesus, of important Bible passages, of the Ten Commandments, of the formulas of profession of the faith, of the liturgical texts, of the essential prayers, of key doctrinal ideas, etc., far from being opposed to the dignity of young Christians, or constituting an obstacle to personal dialogue with the Lord, is a real need, as the synod fathers forcefully recalled. We must be realists. The blossoms, if we may call them that, of faith and piety do not grow in the desert places of a memory-less catechesis. What is essential is that the texts that are memorized must at the same time be taken in and gradually understood in depth, in order to become a source of Christian life on the personal level and the community level.

The plurality of methods in contemporary catechesis can be a sign of vitality and ingenuity. In any case, the method chosen must ultimately be referred to a law that is fundamental for the whole of the Church's life; the law of fidelity to God and of fidelity to man in a single loving attitude.

2691 (1) **Matthew 6:6** But when you pray, go into your room and shut the door and pray to your Father who is in secret; and your Father who sees in secret will reward you.

2691 (2) ***Perfectae caritatis* 7** There are institutes which are entirely ordered towards contemplation, in such wise that their members give themselves over to God alone in solitude and silence, in constant prayer and willing penance. These will always have an honored place in the mystical Body of Christ, in which "all the members do not have the same function" (Rom. 12:4), no matter how pressing may be the needs of the active ministry. For they offer to God an exceptional sacrifice of praise, they lend luster to God's people with abundant fruits of holiness, they sway them by their example, and they enlarge the Church by their hidden apostolic fruitfulness. They are thus an ornament to the Church and a fount of heavenly graces. However, their way of life should be revised in accordance with the aforesaid principles and criteria of up-to-date renewal, the greatest care being taken to preserve their withdrawal from the world and the exercises which belong to the contemplative life.

(1) **Matthew 11:25–26** At that time Jesus declared, "I thank thee, Father, Lord of heaven and earth, that thou hast hidden these things from the wise and understanding and revealed them to babes; yea, Father, for such was thy gracious will. . . ." 2701

(2) **Mark 14:36** And he said, "Abba, Father, all things are possible to thee; remove this cup from me; yet not what I will, but what thou wilt." 2701

(1) **Mark 4:4–7** And as he sowed, some seed fell along the path, and the birds came and devoured it. Other seed fell on rocky ground, where it had not much soil, and immediately it sprang up, since it had no depth of soil; and when the sun rose it was scorched, and since it had no root it withered away. Other seed fell among thorns and the thorns grew up and choked it, and it yielded no grain. 2707

(2) **Mark 4:15–19** And these are the ones along the path, where the word is sown; when they hear, Satan immediately comes and takes away the word which is sown in them. And these in like manner are the ones sown upon rocky ground, who, when they hear the word, immediately receive it with joy; and they have no root in themselves, but endure for a while; then, when tribulation or persecution arises on account of the word, immediately they fall away. And others are the ones sown among thorns; they are those who hear the word, but the cares of the world, and the delight in riches, and the desire for other things, enter in and choke the word, and it proves unfruitful. 2707

Song of Solomon 3:1–4 2709

Upon my bed by night
  I sought him whom my soul loves;
I sought him, but found him not;
  I called him, but he gave no answer.
"I will rise now and go about the city,
  in the streets and in the squares;
I will seek him whom my soul loves."
  I sought him, but found him not.
The watchmen found me,
  as they went about in the city.
"Have you seen him whom my soul loves?"
Scarcely had I passed them,
  when I found him whom my soul loves.
I held him, and would not let him go
  until I had brought him into my mother's house,
  and into the chamber of her that conceived me.

(1) **Luke 7:36–50** One of the Pharisees asked him to eat with him, and he went into the Pharisee's house, and took his place at table. And behold, a woman of the city, who was a sinner, when she learned that he was at table in the Pharisee's house, brought an alabaster flask of ointment, and standing behind him at his feet, weeping, she began to wet his feet with her tears, and wiped them with the hair of her head, and 2712

kissed his feet, and anointed them with the ointment. Now when the Pharisee who had invited him saw it, he said to himself, "If this man were a prophet, he would have known who and what sort of woman this is who is touching him, for she is a sinner." And Jesus answering said to him, "Simon, I have something to say to you." And he answered, "What is it, Teacher?" "A certain creditor had two debtors; one owed five hundred denarii, and the other fifty. When they could not pay, he forgave them both. Now which of them will love him more?" Simon answered, "The one, I suppose, to whom he forgave more." And he said to him, "You have judged rightly." Then turning toward the woman he said to Simon, "Do you see this woman? I entered your house, you gave me no water for my feet, but she has wet my feet with her tears and wiped them with her hair. You gave me no kiss, but from the time I came in she has not ceased to kiss my feet. You did not anoint my head with oil, but she has anointed my feet with ointment. Therefore I tell you, her sins, which are many, are forgiven, for she loved much; but he who is forgiven little, loves little." And he said to her, "Your sins are forgiven." Then those who were at table with him began to say among themselves, "Who is this, who even forgives sins?" And he said to the woman, "Your faith has saved you; go in peace."

2712 (2) **Luke 19:1–10** He entered Jericho and was passing through. And there was a man named Zacchaeus; he was a chief tax collector, and rich. And he sought to see who Jesus was, but could not, on account of the crowd, because he was small of stature. So he ran on ahead and climbed up into a sycamore tree to see him, for he was to pass that way. And when Jesus came to the place, he looked up and said to him, "Zacchaeus, make haste and come down; for I must stay at your house today." So he made haste and came down, and received him joyfully. And when they saw it they all murmured, "He has gone in to be the guest of a man who is a sinner." And Zacchaeus stood and said to the Lord, "Behold, Lord, the half of my goods I give to the poor; and if I have defrauded any one of anything, I restore it fourfold." And Jesus said to him, "Today salvation has come to this house, since he also is a son of Abraham. For the Son of man came to seek and to save the lost."

2713 **Jeremiah 31:33** But this is the covenant which I will make with the house of Israel after those days, says the Lord: I will put my law within them, and I will write it upon their hearts; and I will be their God, and they shall be my people.

2715 **St. Ignatius of Loyola, *Spiritual Exercises* 104** This is to ask for what I desire. Here it will be to ask for an intimate knowledge of our Lord, who has become man for me, that I may love Him more and follow Him more closely.

2719 **Matthew 26:40** And he came to the disciples and found them sleeping; and he said to Peter, "So, could you not watch with me one hour? . . ."

2728 **Mark 10:22** At that saying his countenance fell, and he went away sorrowful; for he had great possessions.

2729 (1) **Matthew 6:21** For where your treasure is, there will your heart be also.

2729 (2) **Matthew 6:24** "No one can serve two masters; for either he will hate the one and love the other, or he will be devoted to the one and despise the other. You cannot serve God and mammon. . . ."

2731 (1) **Luke 8:6** And some fell on the rock; and as it grew up, it withered away, because it had no moisture.

(2) **Luke 8:13** And the ones on the rock are those who, when they hear the word, 2731
receive it with joy; but these have no root, they believe for a while and in time of temptation fall away.

Romans 5:3–5 More than that, we rejoice in our sufferings, knowing that suffering 2734
produces endurance, and endurance produces character, and character produces hope, and hope does not disappoint us, because God's love has been poured into our hearts through the Holy Spirit which has been given to us.

(1) **Matthew 6:8** Do not be like them, for your Father knows what you need before 2736
you ask him.

(2) **Romans 8:27** And he who searches the hearts of men knows what is the mind 2736
of the Spirit, because the Spirit intercedes for the saints according to the will of God.

(1) **James 4:1–10** What causes wars, and what causes fightings among you? Is it 2737
not your passions that are at war in your members? You desire and do not have; so you kill. And you covet and cannot obtain; so you fight and wage war. You do not have, because you do not ask. You ask and do not receive, because you ask wrongly, to spend it on your passions. Unfaithful creatures! Do you not know that friendship with the world is enmity with God? Therefore whoever wishes to be a friend of the world makes himself an enemy of God. Or do you suppose it is in vain that the scripture says, "He yearns jealously over the spirit which he has made to dwell in us"? But he gives more grace; therefore it says, "God opposes the proud, but gives grace to the humble." Submit yourselves therefore to God. Resist the devil and he will flee from you. Draw near to God and he will draw near to you. Cleanse your hands, you sinners, and purify your hearts, you men of double mind. Be wretched and mourn and weep. Let your laughter be turned to mourning and your joy to dejection. Humble yourselves before the Lord and he will exalt you.

(2) **James 1:5–8** If any of you lacks wisdom, let him ask God, who gives to all 2737
men generously and without reproaching, and it will be given him. But let him ask in faith, with no doubting, for he who doubts is like a wave of the sea that is driven and tossed by the wind. For that person must not suppose that a double-minded man, unstable in all his ways, will receive anything from the Lord.

(3) **James 5:16** Therefore confess your sins to one another, and pray for one an- 2737
other, that you may be healed. The prayer of a righteous man has great power in its effects.

(1) **Romans 10:12–13** For there is no distinction between Jew and Greek; the same 2739
Lord is Lord of all and bestows his riches upon all who call upon him. For, "every one who calls upon the name of the Lord will be saved."

(2) **Romans 8:26–39** Likewise the Spirit helps us in our weakness; for we do not 2739
know how to pray as we ought, but the Spirit himself intercedes for us with sighs too deep for words. And he who searches the hearts of men knows what is the mind of the Spirit, because the Spirit intercedes for the saints according to the will of God.

We know that in everything God works for good with those who love him, who are called according to his purpose. For those whom he foreknew he also predestined to be conformed to the image of his Son, in order that he might be the first-born among many brethren. And those whom he predestined he also called; and those whom he called he also justified; and those whom he justified he also glorified.

What then shall we say to this? If God is for us, who is against us? He who did not spare his own Son but gave him up for us all, will he not also give us all things with him? Who shall bring any charge against God's elect? Is it God who justifies; who is to condemn? Is it Christ Jesus, who died, yes, who was raised from the dead, who is at the right hand of God, who indeed intercedes for us? Who shall separate us from the love of Christ? Shall tribulation, or distress, or persecution, or famine, or nakedness, or peril, or sword? As it is written, "For thy sake we are being killed all the day long; we are regarded as sheep to be slaughtered." No, in all these things we are more than conquerors through him who loved us. For I am sure that neither death, nor life, nor angels, nor principalities, nor things present, nor things to come, nor powers, nor height, nor depth, nor anything else in all creation, will be able to separate us from the love of God in Christ Jesus our Lord.

2741 (1) **Hebrews 5:7** In the days of his flesh, Jesus offered up prayers and supplications, with loud cries and tears, to him who was able to save him from death, and he was heard for his godly fear.

2741 (2) **Hebrews 7:25** Consequently he is able for all time to save those who draw near to God through him, since he always lives to make intercession for them.

2741 (3) **Hebrews 9:24** For Christ has entered, not into a sanctuary made with hands, a copy of the true one, but into heaven itself, now to appear in the presence of God on our behalf.

2743 (1) **Matthew 28:20** ". . . teaching them to observe all that I have commanded you; and lo, I am with you always, to the close of the age."

2743 (2) **Luke 8:24** And they went and woke him, saying, "Master, Master, we are perishing!" And he awoke and rebuked the wind and the raging waves; and they ceased, and there was a calm.

2744 **Galatians 5:16–25** But I say, walk by the Spirit, and do not gratify the desires of the flesh. For the desires of the flesh are against the Spirit, and the desires of the Spirit are against the flesh; for these are opposed to each other, to prevent you from doing what you would. But if you are led by the Spirit you are not under the law. Now the works of the flesh are plain: fornication, impurity, licentiousness, idolatry, sorcery, enmity, strife, jealousy, anger, selfishness, dissension, party spirit, envy, drunkenness, carousing, and the like. I warn you, as I warned you before, that those who do such things shall not inherit the kingdom of God. But the fruit of the Spirit is love, joy, peace, patience, kindness, goodness, faithfulness, gentleness, self-control; against such there is no law. And those who belong to Christ Jesus have crucified the flesh with its passions and desires.

If we live by the Spirit, let us also walk by the Spirit.

2746 **John 17** When Jesus had spoken these words, he lifted up his eyes to heaven and said, "Father, the hour has come; glorify thy Son that the Son may glorify thee, since thou hast given him power over all flesh, to give eternal life to all whom thou hast given him. And this is eternal life, that they know thee the only true God, and Jesus Christ whom thou hast sent. I glorified thee on earth, having accomplished the work which thou gavest me to do; and now, Father, glorify thou me in thy own presence with the glory which I had with thee before the world was made.

"I have manifested thy name to the men whom thou gavest me out of the world; thine they were, and thou gavest them to me, and they have kept thy word. Now they know that everything that thou hast given me is from thee; for I have given them the words which thou gavest me, and they have received them and know in truth that I came from thee; and they have believed that thou didst send me. I am praying for them; I am not praying for the world but for those whom thou hast given me, for they are thine; all mine are thine, and thine are mine, and I am glorified in them. And now I am no more in the world, but they are in the world, and I am coming to thee. Holy Father, keep them in thy name, which thou hast given me, that they may be one, even as we are one. While I was with them, I kept them in thy name, which thou hast given me; I have guarded them, and none of them is lost but the son of perdition, that the scripture might be fulfilled. But now I am coming to thee; and these things I speak in the world, that they may have my joy fulfilled in themselves. I have given them thy word; and the world has hated them because they are not of the world, even as I am not of the world. I do not pray that thou shouldst take them out of the world, but that thou shouldst keep them from the evil one. They are not of the world, even as I am not of the world. Sanctify them in the truth; thy word is truth. As thou didst send me into the world, so I have sent them into the world. And for their sake I consecrate myself, that they also may be consecrated in truth.

"I do not pray for these only, but also for those who believe in me through their word, that they may all be one; even as thou, Father, art in me, and I in thee, that they also may be in us, so that the world may believe that thou hast sent me. The glory which thou hast given me I have given to them, that they may be one even as we are one, I in them and thou in me, that they may become perfectly one, so that the world may know that thou hast sent me and hast loved them even as thou hast loved me. Father, I desire that they also, whom thou hast given me, may be with me where I am, to behold my glory which thou hast given me in thy love for me before the foundation of the world. O righteous Father, the world has not known thee, but I have known thee; and these know that thou has sent me. I made known to them thy name, and I will make it known, that the love with which thou hast loved me may be in them, and I in them."

(1) **John 17:11** And now I am no more in the world, but they are in the world, and I am coming to thee. Holy Father, keep them in thy name, which thou hast given me, that they may be one, even as we are one. **2747**

(2) **John 17:13** But now I am coming to thee; and these things I speak in the world, that they may have my joy fulfilled in themselves. **2747**

(3) **John 17:19** And for their sake I consecrate myself, that they also may be consecrated in truth. **2747**

Ephesians 1:10 . . . as a plan for the fulness of time, to unite all things in him, things in heaven and things on earth. **2748**

(1) **John 17:11:** see 2747 (1). **2749**

(2) **John 17:13:** see 2747 (2) **2749**

(3) **John 17:19:** see 2747 (3). **2749**

(4) **John 17:24** Father, I desire that they also, whom thou hast given me, may be with me where I am, to behold my glory which thou hast given me in thy love for me before the foundation of the world. **2749**

2750 (1) **John 17:6** "I have manifested thy name to the men whom thou gavest me out of the world; thine they were, and thou gavest them to me, and they have kept thy word. . . ."

2750 (2) **John 17:11:** see 2747 (1).

2750 (3) **John 17:12** While I was with them, I kept them in thy name, which thou hast given me; I have guarded them, and none of them is lost but the son of perdition, that the scripture might be fulfilled.

2750 (4) **John 17:26** ". . . I made known to them thy name, and I will make it known, that the love with which thou hast loved me may be in them, and I in them."

2750 (5) **John 17:1** When Jesus had spoken these words, he lifted up his eyes to heaven and said, "Father, the hour has come; glorify thy Son that the Son may glorify thee. . . ."

2750 (6) **John 17:5** . . . and now, Father, glorify thou me in thy own presence with the glory which I had with thee before the world was made.

2750 (7) **John 17:10** . . . all mine are thine, and thine are mine, and I am glorified in them.

2750 (8) **John 17:24** Father, I desire that they also, whom thou hast given me, may be with me where I am, to behold my glory which thou hast given me in thy love for me before the foundation of the world.

2750 (9) **John 17:23–26** ". . . I in them and thou in me, that they may become perfectly one, so that the world may know that thou hast sent me and hast loved them even as thou hast loved me. Father, I desire that they also, whom thou hast given me, may be with me where I am, to behold my glory which thou hast given me in thy love for me before the foundation of the world. O righteous Father, the world has not known thee, but I have known thee; and these know that thou hast sent me. I made known to them thy name, and I will make it known, that the love with which thou hast loved me may be in them, and I in them."

2750 (10) **John 17:2** . . . since thou hast given him power over all flesh, to give eternal life to all whom thou hast given him.

2750 (11) **John 17:4** I glorified thee on earth, having accomplished the work which thou gavest me to do. . . .

2750 (12) **John 17:6:** see 2750 (1)

2750 (13) **John 17:9** I am praying for them; I am not praying for the world but for those whom thou hast given me, for they are thine. . . .

2750 (14) **John 17:11:** see 2747 (1).

2750 (15) **John 17:12:** see 2750 (3)

(16) **John 17:24:** see 2749 (4). 2750

(17) **John 17:15** I do not pray that thou shouldst take them out of the world, but that thou shouldst keep them from the evil one. 2750

(1) **John 17:3** And this is eternal life, that they know thee the only true God, and Jesus Christ whom thou hast sent. 2751

(2) **John 17:6–10** "I have manifested thy name to the men whom thou gavest me out of the world; thine they were, and thou gavest them to me, and they have kept thy word. Now they know that everything that thou hast given me is from thee; for I have given them the words which thou gavest me, and they have received them and know in truth that I came from thee; and they have believed that thou didst send me. I am praying for them; I am not praying for the world but for those whom thou hast given me, for they are thine; all mine are thine, and thine are mine, and I am glorified in them. . . ." 2751

(3) **John 17:25** O righteous Father, the world has not known thee, but I have known thee; and these know that thou hast sent me. 2751

John 17: see 2746. 2758

(1) **Luke 11:2–4** And he said to them, "When you pray, say: 2759
"Father, hallowed be thy name. Thy kingdom come. Give us each day our daily bread; and forgive us our sins, for we ourselves forgive every one who is indebted to us; and lead us not into temptation."

(2) **Matthew 6:9–13** Pray then like this: 2759

Our Father who art in heaven,
Hallowed be thy name.
Thy kingdom come.
Thy will be done,
  On earth as it is in heaven.
Give us this day our daily bread;
And forgive us our debts,
  As we also have forgiven our debtors;
And lead us not into temptation,
  But deliver us from evil.

***Roman Missal* 126** (Embolism after the Lord's Prayer) 2760

Deliver us, Lord, from every evil,
and grant us peace in our day.
In your mercy keep us free from sin
and protect us from all anxiety
as we wait in joyful hope
for the coming of our Savior, Jesus Christ.

For the kingdom, the power, and the glory are yours,
  now and for ever.

Luke 11:9 And I tell you, Ask, and it will be given you; seek, and you will find; knock, and it will be opened to you. 2761

2763 (1) **Luke 24:44** Then he said to them "These are my words which I spoke to you, while I was still with you, that everything written about me in the law of Moses and the prophets and the psalms must be fulfilled."

2763 (2) **Matthew 5–7:** see 1454 (1).

2765 **John 17:7** Now they know that everything that thou hast given me is from thee. . . .

2766 (1) **Matthew 6:7** "And in praying do not heap up empty phrases as the Gentiles do; for they think that they will be heard for their many words. . . ."

2766 (2) **1 Kings 18:26–29** And they took the bull which was given them, and they prepared it, and called on the name of Baal from morning until noon, saying, "O Baal, answer us!" But there was no voice, and no one answered. And they limped about the altar which they had made. And at noon Elijah mocked them, saying, "Cry aloud, for he is a god; either he is musing, or he has gone aside, or he is on a journey, or perhaps he is asleep and must be awakened." And they cried aloud, and cut themselves after their custom with swords and lances, until the blood gushed out upon them. And as midday passed, they raved on until the time of the offering of the oblation, but there was no voice; no one answered, no one heeded.

2767 ***Didache* 8, 3** You should pray in this way [the Lord's prayer] three times a day.

2769 **1 Peter 2:1–10** So put away all malice and all guile and insincerity and envy and all slander. Like newborn babes, long for the pure spiritual milk, that by it you may grow up to salvation; for you have tasted the kindness of the Lord.

Come to him, to that living stone, rejected by men but in God's sight chosen and precious; and like living stones be yourselves built into a spiritual house, to be a holy priesthood, to offer spiritual sacrifices acceptable to God through Jesus Christ. For it stands in scripture:

"Behold, I am laying in Zion a stone, a cornerstone chosen and precious,
and he who believes in him will not be put to shame."

To you therefore who believe, he is precious, but for those who do not believe,

"The very stone which the builders rejected
has become the head of the corner,"

and

"A stone that will make men stumble,
a rock that will make them fall";

for they stumble because they disobey the word, as they were destined to do.

But you are a chosen race, a royal priesthood, a holy nation, God's own people, that you may declare the wonderful deeds of him who called you out of darkness into his marvelous light. Once you were no people but now you are God's people; once you had not received mercy but now you have received mercy.

2772 **Colossians 3:4** When Christ who is our life appears, then you also will appear with him in glory.

2777 **Galatians 4:6** And because you are sons, God has sent the Spirit of his Son into our hearts, crying, "Abba! Father!"

2778 (1) **Ephesians 3:12** . . . in whom we have boldness and confidence of access through our faith in him.

(2) **Hebrews 3:6** . . . but Christ was faithful over God's house as a son. And we are his house if we hold fast our confidence and pride in our hope. 2778

(3) **Hebrews 4:16** Let us then with confidence draw near to the throne of grace, that we may receive mercy and find grace to help in time of need. 2778

(4) **Hebrews 10:19** Therefore, brethren, since we have confidence to enter the sanctuary by the blood of Jesus. . . . 2778

(5) **1 John 2:28** And now, little children, abide in him, so that when he appears we may have confidence and not shrink from him in shame at his coming. 2778

(6) **1 John 3:21** Beloved, if our hearts do not condemn us, we have confidence before God. . . . 2778

(7) **1 John 5:14** And this is the confidence which we have in him, that if we ask anything according to his will he hears us. 2778

(1) **John 1:1** In the beginning was the Word, and the Word was with God, and the Word was God. 2780

(2) **1 John 5:1** Every one who believes that Jesus is the Christ is a child of God, and every one who loves the parent loves the child. 2780

1 John 1:3 . . . that which we have seen and heard we proclaim also to you, so that you may have fellowship with us; and our fellowship is with the Father and with his Son Jesus Christ. 2781

***Gaudium et spes* 22, 1** In reality it is only in the mystery of the Word made flesh that the mystery of man truly becomes clear. For Adam, the first man, was a type of him who was to come, Christ the Lord. Christ the new Adam, in the very revelation of the mystery of the Father and of his love, fully reveals man to himself and brings to light his most high calling. It is no wonder, then, that all the truths mentioned so far should find in him their source and their most perfect embodiment. 2783

Matthew 11:25 At that time Jesus declared, "I thank thee, Father, Lord of heaven and earth, that thou hast hidden these things from the wise and understanding and revealed them to babes. . . ." 2785

(1) **Hosea 2:21–22** 2787

"And in that day, says the Lord,
I will answer the heavens
and they shall answer the earth;
and the earth shall answer the grain, the wine, and the oil,
and they shall answer Jezreel. . . ."

(2) **Hosea 6:1–6** 2787

"Come, let us return to the Lord;
for he has torn, that he may heal us;
he has stricken, and he will bind us up.

After two days he will revive us;
 on the third day he will raise us up,
 that we may live before him.
Let us know, let us press on to know the Lord;
 his going forth is sure as the dawn;
he will come to us as the showers,
 as the spring rains that water the earth."

What shall I do with you, O Ephraim?
 What shall I do with you, O Judah?
Your love is like a morning cloud,
 like the dew that goes early away.
Therefore I have hewn them by the prophets,
 I have slain them by the words of my mouth,
 and my judgment goes forth as the light.
For I desire steadfast love and not sacrifice,
 the knowledge of God, rather than burnt offerings.

2790 (1) **1 John 5:1** Every one who believes that Jesus is the Christ is a child of God, and every one who loves the parent loves the child.

2790 (2) **John 3:5** Jesus answered, "Truly, truly, I say to you, unless one is born of water and the Spirit, he cannot enter the kingdom of God. . . ."

2790 (3) **Ephesians 4:4–6** There is one body and one Spirit, just as you were called to the one hope that belongs to your call, one Lord, one faith, one baptism, one God and Father of us all, who is above all and through all and in all.

2791 (1) ***Unitatis redintegratio* 8** This change of heart and holiness of life, along with public and private prayer for the unity of Christians, should be regarded as the soul of the whole ecumenical movement, and merits the name, "spiritual ecumenism."

It is a recognized custom for Catholics to meet for frequent recourse to that prayer for the unity of the Church with which the Savior himself on the eve of his death so fervently appealed to his Father: "That they may all be one" (Jn. 17:20).

In certain circumstances, such as in prayer services "for unity" and during ecumenical gatherings, it is allowable, indeed desirable that Catholics should join in prayer with their separated brethren. Such prayers in common are certainly a very effective means of petitioning for the grace of unity, and they are a genuine expression of the ties which still bind Catholics to their separated brethren. "For where two or three are gathered together in my name, there am I in the midst of them" (Mt. 18:20).

Yet worship in common (*communicatio in sacris*) is not to be considered as a means to be used indiscriminately for the restoration of unity among Christians. There are two main principles upon which the practice of such common worship depends; first, that of the unity of the Church which ought to be expressed; and second, that of the sharing in the means of grace. The expression of unity very generally forbids common worship. Grace to be obtained sometimes commends it. The concrete course to be adopted, when all the circumstances of time, place and persons have been duly considered, is left to the prudent decision of the local episcopal authority, unless the bishops' conference according to its own statutes, or the Holy See, has determined otherwise.

2791 (2) ***Unitatis redintegratio* 22** By the sacrament of Baptism, whenever it is properly conferred in the way the Lord determined and received with the proper dispositions of soul, man becomes truly incorporated into the crucified and glorified Christ and is reborn to a sharing of the divine life, as the Apostle says: "For you were buried together with him in baptism, and in him also rose again through faith in the working of God who raised him from the dead."

Baptism, therefore, constitutes the sacramental bond of unity existing among all who through it are reborn. But baptism, of itself, is only a beginning, a point of departure, for it is wholly directed toward the acquiring of fullness of life in Christ. Baptism is thus ordained toward a complete profession of faith, a complete incorporation into the system of salvation such as Christ himself willed it to be, and finally, toward a complete integration into eucharistic communion.

Although the ecclesial communities separated from us lack the fullness of unity with us which flows from baptism, and although we believe they have not preserved the proper reality of the eucharistic mystery in its fullness, especially because of the absence of the sacrament of Orders, nevertheless when they commemorate the Lord's death and resurrection in the Holy Supper, they profess that it signifies life in communion with Christ and await his coming in glory. For these reasons, the doctrine about the Lord's Supper, about the other sacraments, worship, and ministry in the Church, should form subjects of dialogue.

(1) **Matthew 5:23–24** So if you are offering your gift at the altar, and there remember that your brother has something against you, leave your gift there before the altar and go; first be reconciled to your brother, and then come and offer your gift. **2792**

(2) **Matthew 6:14–15** ". . . For if you forgive men their trespasses, your heavenly Father also will forgive you; but if you do not forgive men their trespasses, neither will your Father forgive your trespasses." **2792**

***Nostra aetate* 5** We cannot truly pray to God the Father of all if we treat any people in other than brotherly fashion, for all men are created in God's image. Man's relation to God the Father and man's relation to his fellow-men are so dependent on each other that the Scripture says "he who does not love, does not know God" (1 Jn. 4:8). **2793**

There is no basis therefore, either in theory or in practice, for any discrimination between individual and individual, or between people and people arising either from human dignity or from the rights which flow from it.

Therefore, the Church reproves, as foreign to the mind of Christ, any discrimination against people or any harassment of them on the basis of their race, color, condition in life or religion. Accordingly, following the footsteps of the holy apostles Peter and Paul, the sacred Council earnestly begs the Christian faithful to "conduct themselves well among the Gentiles" (1 Pet. 2:12) and if possible, as far as depends on them, to be at peace with all men (cf. Rom. 12:18) and in that way to be true sons of the Father who is in heaven (cf. Mt. 5:45).

(1) **Genesis 3** Now the serpent was more subtle than any other wild creature that the Lord God had made. He said to the woman, "Did God say, 'You shall not eat of any tree of the garden'?" And the woman said to the serpent, "We may eat of the fruit of the trees of the garden; but God said, 'You shall not eat of the fruit of the tree which is in the midst of the garden, neither shall you touch it, lest you die.' " But the serpent said to the woman, "You will not die. For God knows that when you eat of it your eyes will be opened, and you will be like God, knowing good and evil." So when the woman saw that the tree was good for food, and that it was a delight to the eyes, and that the tree was to be desired to make one wise, she took of its fruit and **2795**

ate; and she also gave some to her husband, and he ate. Then the eyes of both were opened, and they knew that they were naked; and they sewed fig leaves together and made themselves aprons.

And they heard the sound of the Lord God walking in the garden in the cool of the day, and the man and his wife hid themselves from the presence of the Lord God among the trees of the garden. But the Lord God called to the man, and said to him, "Where are you?" And he said, "I heard the sound of thee in the garden, and I was afraid, because I was naked; and I hid myself." He said, "Who told you that you were naked? Have you eaten of the tree of which I commanded you not to eat?" The man said, "The woman whom thou gavest to be with me, she gave me fruit of the tree, and I ate." Then the Lord God said to the woman, "What is this that you have done?" The woman said, "The serpent beguiled me, and I ate." The Lord God said to the serpent,

"Because you have done this,
cursed are you above all cattle,
and above all wild animals;
upon your belly you shall go,
and dust you shall eat
all the days of your life.
I will put enmity between you and the woman,
and between your seed and her seed;
he shall bruise your head,
and you shall bruise his heel."

To the woman he said,

"I will greatly multiply your pain in childbearing;
in pain you shall bring forth children,
yet your desire shall be for your husband,
and he shall rule over you."

And to Adam he said,

"Because you have listened to the voice of your wife,
and have eaten of the tree
of which I commanded you,
'You shall not eat of it,'
cursed is the ground because of you;
in toil you shall eat of it all the days of your life;
thorns and thistles it shall bring forth to you;
and you shall eat the plants of the field.
In the sweat of your face
you shall eat bread
till you return to the ground,
for out of it you were taken;
you are dust,
and to dust you shall return."

The man called his wife's name Eve, because she was the mother of all living. And the Lord God made for Adam and for his wife garments of skins, and clothed them.

Then the Lord God said, "Behold, the man has become like one of us, knowing good and evil; and now, lest he put forth his hand and take also of the tree of life, and eat, and live for ever"—therefore the Lord God sent him forth from the garden of Eden, to till the ground from which he was taken. He drove out the man; and at the east of the garden of Eden he placed the cherubim, and a flaming sword which turned every way, to guard the way to the tree of life.

(2) **Isaiah 45:8** 2795

"Shower, O heavens, from above,
and let the skies rain down righteousness;
let the earth open, that salvation may sprout forth,
and let it cause righteousness to spring up also;
I the Lord have created it. . . ."

(3) **Psalm 85:12 (85:11: RSV)** 2795

Faithfulness will spring up from the ground,
and righteousness will look down from the sky.

(1) **Philippians 3:20** But our commonwealth is in heaven, and from it we await a 2796
Savior, the Lord Jesus Christ. . . .

(2) **Hebrews 13:14** For here we have no lasting city, but we seek the city which is 2796
to come.

***Gaudium et spes* 22, 1** In reality it is only in the mystery of the Word made flesh 2799
that the mystery of man truly becomes clear. For Adam, the first man, was a type of him who was to come, Christ the Lord. Christ the new Adam, in the very revelation of the mystery of the Father and of his love, fully reveals man to himself and brings to light his most high calling. It is no wonder, then, that all the truths mentioned so far should find in him their source and their most perfect embodiment.

(1) **Luke 22:14** And when the hour came, he sat at table, and the apostles with 2804
him.

(2) **Luke 12:50** I have a baptism to be baptized with; and how I am constrained 2804
until it is accomplished!

(3) **1 Corinthians 15:28** When all things are subjected to him, then the Son him- 2804
self will also be subjected to him who put all things under him, that God may be everything to every one.

(1) **Psalm 111:9** 2807

He sent redemption to his people;
he has commanded his covenant for ever.
Holy and terrible is his name!

(2) **Luke 1:49** 2807

. . . for he who is mighty has done great things for me,
and holy is his name.

(1) **Psalm 8** 2809

O Lord, our Lord,
how majestic is thy name in all the earth!

Thou whose glory above the heavens is chanted
by the mouth of babes and infants,
thou hast founded a bulwark because of thy foes,
to still the enemy and the avenger.

When I look at thy heavens, the work of thy fingers,
the moon and the stars which thou hast established;
what is man that thou art mindful of him,
and the son of man that thou dost care for him?

Yet thou hast made him little less than God,
and dost crown him with glory and honor.
Thou hast given him dominion over the works of thy hands;
thou hast put all things under his feet,
all sheep and oxen,
and also the beasts of the field,
the birds of the air, and the fish of the sea,
whatever passes along the paths of the sea.

O Lord, our Lord,
how majestic is thy name in all the earth!

2809 (2) **Isaiah 6:3** And one called to another and said:
"Holy, holy, holy is the Lord of hosts;
the whole earth is full of his glory."

2809 (3) **Genesis 1:26** Then God said, "Let us make man in our image, after our likeness; and let them have dominion over the fish of the sea, and over the birds of the air, and over the cattle, and over all the earth, and over every creeping thing that creeps upon the earth."

2810 (1) **Hebrews 6:13** For when God made a promise to Abraham, since he had no one greater by whom to swear, he swore by himself. . . .

2810 (2) **Exodus 3:14** God said to Moses, "I AM WHO I AM." And he said, "Say this to the people of Israel, 'I AM has sent me to you.'"

2810 (3) **Exodus 19:5–6** ". . . Now therefore, if you will obey my voice and keep my covenant, you shall be my own possession among all peoples; for all the earth is mine, and you shall be to me a kingdom of priests and a holy nation. These are the words which you shall speak to the children of Israel."

2811 **Leviticus 19:2** "Say to all the congregation of the people of Israel, You shall be holy; for I the Lord your God am holy. . . ."

2812 (1) **Matthew 1:21** ". . . she will bear a son, and you shall call his name Jesus, for he will save his people from their sins."

2812 (2) **Luke 1:31** And behold, you will conceive in your womb and bear a son and you shall call his name Jesus.

2812 (3) **John 8:28** So Jesus said, "When you have lifted up the Son of man, then you will know that I am he, and that I do nothing on my own authority but speak thus as the Father taught me. . . ."

2812 (4) **John 17:8** . . . for I have given them the words which thou gavest me, and they have received them and know in truth that I came from thee; and they have believed that thou didst send me.

(5) **John 17:17–19** Sanctify them in the truth; thy word is truth. As thou didst send me into the world, so I have sent them into the world. And for their sake I consecrate myself, that they also may be consecrated in truth. 2812

(6) **Ezekiel 20:39** "As for you, O house of Israel, thus says the Lord God: Go serve every one of you his idols, now and hereafter, if you will not listen to me; but my holy name you shall no more profane with your gifts and your idols. . . ." 2812

(7) **Ezekiel 36:20–21** ". . . But when they came to the nations, wherever they came, they profaned my holy name, in that men said of them, 'These are the people of the Lord, and yet they had to go out of his land.' But I had concern for my holy name, which the house of Israel caused to be profaned among the nations to which they came. . . ." 2812

(8) **John 17:6** "I have manifested thy name to the men whom thou gavest me out of the world; thine they were, and thou gavest them to me, and they have kept thy word. . . ." 2812

1 Thessalonians 4:7 For God has not called us for uncleanness, but in holiness. 2813

(1) **Romans 2:24** For, as it is written, "The name of God is blasphemed among the Gentiles because of you." 2814

(2) **Ezekiel 36:20–22** ". . . But when they came to the nations, wherever they came, they profaned my holy name, in that men said of them, 'These are the people of the Lord, and yet they had to go out of his land.' But I had concern for my holy name, which the house of Israel caused to be profaned among the nations to which they came. 2814

"Therefore say to the house of Israel, Thus says the Lord God: It is not for your sake, O house of Israel, that I am about to act, but for the sake of my holy name, which you have profaned among the nations to which you came. . . ."

(1) **John 14:13** Whatever you ask in my name, I will do it, that the Father may be glorified in the Son. . . . 2815

(2) **John 15:16** You did not choose me, but I chose you and appointed you that you should go and bear fruit and that your fruit should abide; so that whatever you ask the Father in my name, he may give it to you. 2815

(3) **John 16:24** Hitherto you have asked nothing in my name; ask, and you shall receive, that your joy may be full. 2815

(4) **John 16:26** In that day you will ask in my name; and I do not say to you that I shall pray the Father for you. . . . 2815

(1) **Hebrews 4:11** Let us therefore strive to enter that rest, that no one fall by the same sort of disobedience. 2817

(2) **Revelation 6:9** When he opened the fifth seal, I saw under the altar the souls of those who had been slain for the word of God and for the witness they had borne. . . . 2817

(3) **Revelation 22:20** He who testifies to these things says, "Surely I am coming soon." Amen. Come, Lord Jesus! 2817

2818 **Titus 2:13** . . . awaiting our blessed hope, the appearing of the glory of our great God and Savior Jesus Christ. . . .

2819 (1) **Galatians 5:16–25** But I say, walk by the Spirit, and do not gratify the desires of the flesh. For the desires of the flesh are against the Spirit, and the desires of the Spirit are against the flesh; for these are opposed to each other, to prevent you from doing what you would. But if you are led by the Spirit you are not under the law. Now the works of the flesh are plain: fornication, impurity, licentiousness, idolatry, sorcery, enmity, strife, jealousy, anger, selfishness, dissension, party spirit, envy, drunkenness, carousing, and the like. I warn you, as I warned you before, that those who do such things shall not inherit the kingdom of God. But the fruit of the Spirit is love, joy, peace, patience, kindness, goodness, faithfulness, gentleness, self-control; against such there is no law. And those who belong to Christ Jesus have crucified the flesh with its passions and desires.

If we live by the Spirit, let us also walk by the Spirit.

2819 (2) **Romans 6:12** Let not sin therefore reign in your mortal bodies, to make you obey their passions.

2820 (1) ***Gaudium et spes* 22** In reality it is only in the mystery of the Word made flesh that the mystery of man truly becomes clear. For Adam, the first man, was a type of him who was to come, Christ the Lord. Christ the new Adam, in the very revelation of the mystery of the Father and of his love, fully reveals man to himself and brings to light his most high calling. It is no wonder, then, that all the truths mentioned so far should find in him their source and their most perfect embodiment.

He who is the "image of the invisible God" (Col. 1:15), is himself the perfect man who has restored in the children of Adam that likeness to God which had been disfigured ever since the first sin. Human nature, by the very fact that it was assumed, not absorbed, in him, has been raised in us also to a dignity beyond compare. For, by his incarnation, he, the son of God, has in a certain way united himself with each man. He worked with human hands, he thought with a human mind. He acted with a human will, and with a human heart he loved. Born of the Virgin Mary, he has truly been made one of us, like to us in all things except sin.

As an innocent lamb he merited life for us by his blood which he freely shed. In him God reconciled us to himself and to one another, freeing us from the bondage of the devil and of sin, so that each one of us could say with the apostle: the Son of God "loved me and gave himself for me" (Gal. 2:20). By suffering for us he not only gave us an example so that we might follow in his footsteps, but he also opened up a way. If we follow this path, life and death are made holy and acquire a new meaning.

Conformed to the image of the Son who is the firstborn of many brothers, the Christian man receives the "first fruits of the Spirit" (Rom. 8:23) by which he is able to fulfil the new law of love. By this Spirit, who is the "pledge of our inheritance" (Eph. 1:14), the whole man is inwardly renewed, right up to the "redemption of the body" (Rom. 8:23). "If the Spirit of him who raised Jesus from the dead dwells in you, he who raised Christ Jesus from the dead will give life to your mortal bodies also through his Spirit who dwells in you" (Rom. 8:11). The Christian is certainly bound both by need and by duty to struggle with evil through many afflictions and to suffer death; but, as one who has been made a partner in the paschal mystery, and as one who has been configured to the death of Christ, he will go forward, strengthened by hope, to the resurrection.

All this holds true not for Christians only but also for all men of good will in whose hearts grace is active invisibly. For since Christ died for all, and since all men are in fact called to one and the same destiny, which is divine, we must hold that the Holy Spirit offers to all the possibility of being made partners, in a way known to God, in the paschal mystery.

Such is the nature and the greatness of the mystery of man as enlightened for the faithful by the Christian revelation. It is therefore through Christ, and in Christ, that light is thrown on the riddle of suffering and death which, apart from his Gospel, overwhelms us. Christ has risen again, destroying death by his death, and has given life abundantly to us so that, becoming sons in the Son, we may cry out in the Spirit: Abba, Father!

(2) ***Gaudium et spes* 32** Just as God did not create men to live as individuals but to come together in the formation of social unity, so he "willed to make men holy and save them, not as individuals without any bond or link between them, but rather to make them into a people who might acknowledge him and serve him in holiness." At the outset of salvation history he chose certain men as members of a given community, not as individuals, and revealed his plan to them, calling them "his people" (Ex. 3:7–12) and making a covenant on Mount Sinai with them. 2820

This communitarian character is perfected and fulfilled in the work of Jesus Christ, for the Word made flesh willed to share in human fellowship. He was present at the wedding feast at Cana, he visited the house of Zacchaeus, he sat down with publicans and sinners. In revealing the Father's love and man's sublime calling he made use of the most ordinary things of social life and illustrated his words with expressions and imagery from everyday life. He sanctified those human ties, above all family ties, which are the basis of social structures. He willingly observed the laws of his country and chose to lead the life of an ordinary craftsman of his time and place.

In his preaching he clearly outlined an obligation on the part of the sons of God to treat each other as brothers. In his prayer he asked that all his followers should be "one." As the redeemer of all mankind he delivered himself even unto death for the sake of all: "Greater love has no man than this, that a man lay down his life for his friends" (Jn. 15:13). His command to the apostles was to preach the Gospel to all peoples in order that the human race would become the family of God, in which love would be the fullness of the law.

As the firstborn of many brethren, and by the gift of his Spirit, he established, after his death and resurrection, a new brotherly communion among all who received him in faith and love; this is the communion of his own body, the Church, in which everyone as members one of the other would render mutual service in the measure of the different gifts bestowed on each.

This solidarity must be constantly increased until that day when it will be brought to fulfilment; on that day mankind, saved by grace, will offer perfect glory to God as the family beloved of God and of Christ their brother.

(3) ***Gaudium et spes* 39** We know neither the moment of the consummation of the earth and of man nor the way the universe will be transformed. The form of this world, distorted by sin, is passing away and we are taught that God is preparing a new dwelling and a new earth in which righteousness dwells, whose happiness will fill and surpass all the desires of peace arising in the hearts of men. Then with death conquered the sons of God will be raised in Christ and what was sown in weakness and dishonor will put on the imperishable: charity and its works will remain and all of creation, which God made for man, will be set free from its bondage to decay. 2820

We have been warned, of course, that it profits man nothing if he gains the whole world and loses or forfeits himself. Far from diminishing our concern to develop this earth, the expectancy of a new earth should spur us on, for it is here that the body of a new human family grows, foreshadowing in some way the age which is to come. That is why, although we must be careful to distinguish earthy progress clearly from the increase of the kingdom of Christ, such progress is of vital concern to the kingdom of God, insofar as it can contribute to the better ordering of human society.

When we have spread on earth the fruits of our nature and our enterprise—human dignity, brotherly communion, and freedom—according to the command of the Lord and in his Spirit, we will find them once again, cleansed this time from the stain of sin, illuminated and transfigured, when Christ presents to his Father an eternal and universal kingdom "of truth and life, a kingdom of holiness and grace, a kingdom of justice, love and peace." Here on earth the kingdom is mysteriously present; when the Lord comes it will enter into its perfection.

2820 (4) ***Gaudium et spes* 45** Whether it aids the world or whether it benefits from it, the Church has but one sole purpose—that the kingdom of God may come and the salvation of the human race may be accomplished. Every benefit the people of God can confer on mankind during its earthly pilgrimage is rooted in the Church's being "the universal sacrament of salvation," at once manifesting and actualizing the mystery of God's love for men.

The Word of God, through whom all things were made, was made flesh, so that as a perfect man he could save all men and sum up all things in himself. The Lord is the goal of human history, the focal point of the desires of history and civilization, the center of mankind, the joy of all hearts, and the fulfilment of all aspirations. It is he whom the Father raised from the dead, exalted and placed at his right hand, constituting him judge of the living and the dead. Animated and drawn together in his Spirit we press onwards on our journey towards the consummation of history which fully corresponds to the plan of his love: "to unite all things in him, things in heaven and things on earth" (Eph. 1:10).

The Lord himself said: "Behold, I am coming soon, bringing my recompense, to repay every one for what he has done. I am the alpha and the omega, the first and the last, the beginning and the end" (Apoc. 22:12–13).

2820 (5) ***Evangelii nuntiandi* 31** In fact, there are close links between evangelization and human advancement, that is development and liberation. There is a connection in the anthropological order because the man who is to be evangelized is not an abstract being but a person subject to social and economic factors. There is also a connection in the theological sphere because the plan of creation cannot be isolated from the plan of redemption which extends to the very practical question of eradicating injustice and establishing justice. There is, finally, a connection in the evangelical order, that is the order of charity: for how can the new law be proclaimed unless it promotes a true practical advancement of man in a spirit of justice and peace? This is what we intended to assert when we pointed out that in the work of evangelization 'we cannot and must not disregard the immense importance of those questions which are so much at issue today: questions concerning justice, liberation, progress and world peace. If we disregard these we are likewise disregarding the teaching of the gospel about the love of our neighbor who is suffering and in want.'

The wise and forceful contribution made in the synod furnished, to our great joy, clear principles from which can be deduced the significance and the full meaning of liberation as Jesus of Nazareth proclaimed it and achieved it and as the church now preaches it.

2821 (1) **John 17:17–20** ". . . Sanctify them in the truth; thy word is truth. As thou didst send me into the world, so I have sent them into the world. And for their sake I consecrate myself, that they also may be consecrated in truth.

"I do not pray for these only, but also for those who believe in me through their word. . . ."

(2) **Matthew 5:13–16** "You are the salt of the earth; but if salt has lost its taste, how 2821
shall its saltness be restored? It is no longer good for anything except to be thrown out and trodden under foot by men.

"You are the light of the world. A city set on a hill cannot be hid. Nor do men light a lamp and put it under a bushel, but on a stand, and it gives light to all in the house. Let your light so shine before men, that they may see your good works and give glory to your Father who is in heaven. . . ."

(3) **Matthew 6:24** "No one can serve two masters; for either he will hate the one 2821
and love the other, or he will be devoted to the one and despise the other. You cannot serve God and mammon. . . ."

(4) **Matthew 7:12–13** ". . . So whatever you wish that men would do to you, do 2821
so to them; for this is the law and the prophets.

"Enter by the narrow gate; for the gate is wide and the way is easy, that leads to destruction, and those who enter by it are many. . . ."

(1) **Matthew 18:14** So it is not the will of my Father who is in heaven that one of 2822
these little ones should perish.

(2) **1 John 3** See what love the Father has given us, that we should be called children 2822
of God; and so we are. The reason why the world does not know us is that it did not know him. Beloved, we are God's children now; it does not yet appear what we shall be, but we know that when he appears we shall be like him, for we shall see him as he is. And every one who thus hopes in him purifies himself as he is pure.

Every one who commits sin is guilty of lawlessness; sin is lawlessness. You know that he appeared to take away sins, and in him there is no sin. No one who abides in him sins; no one who sins has either seen him or known him. Little children, let no one deceive you. He who does right is righteous, as he is righteous. He who commits sin is of the devil; for the devil has sinned from the beginning. The reason the Son of God appeared was to destroy the works of the devil. No one born of God commits sin; for God's nature abides in him, and he cannot sin because he is born of God. By this it may be seen who are the children of God, and who are the children of the devil: whoever does not do right is not of God, nor he who does not love his brother.

For this is the message which you have heard from the beginning, that we should love one another, and not be like Cain who was of the evil one and murdered his brother. And why did he murder him? Because his own deeds were evil and his brother's righteous. Do not wonder, brethren, that the world hates you. We know that we have passed out of death into life, because we love the brethren. He who does not love abides in death. Any one who hates his brother is a murderer, and you know that no murderer has eternal life abiding in him. By this we know love, that he laid down his life for us; and we ought to lay down our lives for the brethren. But if any one has the world's goods and sees his brother in need, yet closes his heart against him, how does God's love abide in him? Little children, let us not love in word or speech but in deed and in truth.

By this we shall know that we are of the truth, and reassure our hearts before him whenever our hearts condemn us; for God is greater than our hearts, and he knows everything. Beloved, if our hearts do not condemn us, we have confidence before

God; and we receive from him whatever we ask, because we keep his commandments and do what pleases him. And this is his commandment, that we should believe in the name of his Son Jesus Christ and love one another, just as he has commanded us. All who keep his commandments abide in him, and he in them. And by this we know that he abides in us, by the Spirit which he has given us.

2822 (3) **1 John 4** Beloved, do not believe every spirit, but test the spirits to see whether they are of God; for many false prophets have gone out into the world. By this you know the Spirit of God: every spirit which confesses that Jesus Christ has come in the flesh is of God, and every spirit which does not confess Jesus is not of God. This is the spirit of antichrist, of which you heard that it was coming, and now it is in the world already. Little children, you are of God, and have overcome them; for he who is in you is greater than he who is in the world. They are of the world, therefore what they say is of the world, and the world listens to them. We are of God. Whoever knows God listens to us, and he who is not of God does not listen to us. By this we know the spirit of truth and the spirit of error.

Beloved, let us love one another; for love is of God, and he who loves is born of God and knows God. He who does not love does not know God; for God is love. In this the love of God was made manifest among us, that God sent his only Son into the world, so that we might live through him. In this is love, not that we loved God but that he loved us and sent his Son to be the expiation for our sins. Beloved, if God so loved us, we also ought to love one another. No man has ever seen God; if we love one another, God abides in us and his love is perfected in us.

By this we know that we abide in him and he in us, because he has given us of his own Spirit. And we have seen and testify that the Father has sent his Son as the Savior of the world. Whoever confesses that Jesus is the Son of God, God abides in him, and he in God. So we know and believe the love God has for us. God is love, and he who abides in love abides in God, and God abides in him. In this is love perfected with us, that we may have confidence for the day of judgment, because as he is so are we in this world. There is no fear in love, but perfect love casts out fear. For fear has to do with punishment, and he who fears is not perfected in love. We love, because he first loved us. If any one says, "I love God," and hates his brother, he is a liar; for he who does not love his brother whom he has seen, cannot love God whom he has not seen. And this commandment we have from him, that he who loves God should love his brother also.

2822 (4) **Luke 10:25–37** And behold, a lawyer stood up to put him to the test, saying, "Teacher, what shall I do to inherit eternal life?" He said to him, "What is written in the law? How do you read?" And he answered, "You shall love the Lord your God with all your heart, and with all your soul, and with all your strength, and with all your mind; and your neighbor as yourself." And he said to him, "You have answered right; do this, and you will live."

But he, desiring to justify himself, said to Jesus, "And who is my neighbor?" Jesus replied, "A man was going down from Jerusalem to Jericho, and he fell among robbers, who stripped him and beat him, and departed, leaving him half dead. Now by chance a priest was going down that road; and when he saw him he passed by on the other side. So likewise a Levite, when he came to the place and saw him, passed by on the other side. But a Samaritan, as he journeyed, came to where he was; and when he saw him, he had compassion, and went to him and bound up his wounds, pouring on oil and wine; then he set him on his own beast and brought him to an inn, and took care of him. And the next day he took out two denarii and gave them to the innkeeper, saying, 'Take care of him; and whatever more you spend, I will repay you when I come back.' Which of these three, do you think, proved neighbor to the man who fell among the robbers?" He said, "The one who showed mercy on him." And Jesus said to him, "Go and do likewise."

(1) **John 4:34** Jesus said to them, "My food is to do the will of him who sent me, and to accomplish his work. . . ." **2824**

(2) **John 5:30** "I can do nothing on my own authority; as I hear, I judge; and my judgment is just, because I seek not my own will but the will of him who sent me. . . ." **2824**

(3) **John 6:38** For I have come down from heaven, not to do my own will, but the will of him who sent me. . . . **2824**

John 8:29 ". . . And he who sent me is with me; he has not left me alone, for I always do what is pleasing to him." **2825**

(1) **Ephesians 5:17** Therefore do not be foolish, but understand what the will of the Lord is. **2826**

(2) **Hebrews 10:36** For you have need of endurance, so that you may do the will of God and receive what is promised. **2826**

(1) **1 John 5:14** And this is the confidence which we have in him, that if we ask anything according to his will he hears us. **2827**

(2) **Luke 1:38** And Mary said, "Behold, I am the handmaid of the Lord; let it be to me according to your word." And the angel departed from her. **2827**

(3) **Luke 1:49** **2827**

. . . for he who is mighty has done great things for me,
and holy is his name.

(1) **Matthew 6:25–34** "Therefore I tell you, do not be anxious about your life, what you shall eat or what you shall drink, nor about your body, what you shall put on. Is not life more than food, and the body more than clothing? Look at the birds of the air: They neither sow nor reap nor gather into barns, and yet your heavenly Father feeds them. Are you not of more value than they? And which of you by being anxious can add one cubit to his span of life? And why are you anxious about clothing? Consider the lilies of the field, how they grow; they neither toil nor spin; yet I tell you, even Solomon in all his glory was not arrayed like one of these. But if God so clothes the grass of the field, which today is alive and tomorrow is thrown into the oven, will he not much more clothe you, O men of little faith? Therefore do not be anxious, saying, 'What shall we eat?' or 'What shall we drink?' or 'What shall we wear?' For the Gentiles seek all these things; and your heavenly Father knows that you need them all. But seek first his kingdom and his righteousness, and all these things shall be yours as well. **2830**

"Therefore do not be anxious about tomorrow, for tomorrow will be anxious for itself. Let the day's own trouble be sufficient for the day. . . ."

(2) **2 Thessalonians 3:6–13** Now we command you, brethren, in the name of our Lord Jesus Christ, that you keep away from any brother who is living in idleness and **2830**

not in accord with the tradition that you received from us. For you yourselves know how you ought to imitate us; we were not idle when we were with you, we did not eat any one's bread without paying, but with toil and labor we worked night and day, that we might not burden any of you. It was not because we have not that right, but to give you in our conduct an example to imitate. For even when we were with you, we gave you this command: If any one will not work, let him not eat. For we hear that some of you are living in idleness, mere busybodies, not doing any work. Now such persons we command and exhort in the Lord Jesus Christ to do their work in quietness and to earn their own living. Brethren, do not be weary in well-doing.

2831 (1) **Luke 16:19–31** "There was a rich man, who was clothed in purple and fine linen and who feasted sumptuously every day. And at his gate lay a poor man named Lazarus, full of sores, who desired to be fed with what fell from the rich man's table; moreover the dogs came and licked his sores. The poor man died and was carried by the angels to Abraham's bosom. The rich man also died and was buried; and in Hades, being in torment, he lifted up his eyes, and saw Abraham far off and Lazarus in his bosom. And he called out, 'Father Abraham, have mercy upon me, and send Lazarus to dip the end of his finger in water and cool my tongue; for I am in anguish in this flame.' But Abraham said, 'Son, remember that you in your lifetime received your good things, and Lazarus in like manner evil things; but now he is comforted here, and you are in anguish. And besides all this, between us and you a great chasm has been fixed, in order that those who would pass from here to you may not be able, and none may cross from there to us.' And he said, 'Then I beg you, father, to send him to my father's house, for I have five brothers, so that he may warn them, lest they also come into this place of torment.' But Abraham said, 'They have Moses and the prophets; let them hear them.' And he said, 'No, father Abraham; but if some one goes to them from the dead, they will repent.' He said to him, 'If they do not hear Moses and the prophets, neither will they be convinced if some one should rise from the dead.'"

2831 (2) **Matthew 25:31–46** "When the Son of man comes in his glory, and all the angels with him, then he will sit on his glorious throne. Before him will be gathered all the nations, and he will separate them one from another as a shepherd separates the sheep from the goats, and he will place the sheep at his right hand, but the goats at the left. Then the King will say to those at his right hand, 'Come, O blessed of my Father, inherit the kingdom prepared for you from the foundation of the world; for I was hungry and you gave me food, I was thirsty and you gave me drink, I was a stranger and you welcomed me, I was naked and you clothed me, I was sick and you visited me, I was in prison and you came to me.' Then the righteous will answer him, 'Lord, when did we see thee hungry and feed thee, or thirsty and give thee drink? And when did we see thee a stranger and welcome thee, or naked and clothe thee? And when did we see thee sick or in prison and visit thee?' And the King will answer them, 'Truly, I say to you, as you did it to one of the least of these my brethren, you did it to me.' Then he will say to those at his left hand, 'Depart from me, you cursed, into the eternal fire prepared for the devil and his angels; for I was hungry and you gave me no food, I was thirsty and you gave me no drink, I was a stranger and you did not welcome me, naked and you did not clothe me, sick and in prison and you did not visit me.' Then they also will answer, 'Lord, when did we see thee hungry or thirsty or a stranger or naked or sick or in prison, and did not minister to thee?' Then he will answer them, 'Truly, I say to you, as you did it not to one of the least of these, you did it not to me.' And they will go away into eternal punishment, but the righteous into eternal life."

Apostolicam actuositatem **5** The work of Christ's redemption concerns essentially 2832
the salvation of men; it takes in also, however, the renewal of the whole temporal order. The mission of the Church, consequently, is not only to bring men the message and grace of Christ but also to permeate and improve the whole range of the temporal. The laity, carrying out this mission of the Church, exercise their apostolate therefore in the world as well as in the Church, in the temporal order as well as in the spiritual. These orders are distinct; they are nevertheless so closely linked that God's plan is, in Christ, to take the whole world up again and make of it a new creation, in an initial way here on earth, in full realization at the end of time. The layman, at one and the same time a believer and a citizen of the world, has only a single conscience, a Christian conscience; it is by this that he must be guided continually in both domains.

2 Corinthians 8:1–15 We want you to know, brethren, about the grace of God 2833
which has been shown in the churches of Macedonia, for in a severe test of affliction, their abundance of joy and their extreme poverty have overflowed in a wealth of liberality on their part. For they gave according to their means, as I can testify, and beyond their means, of their own free will, begging us earnestly for the favor of taking part in the relief of the saints—and this, not as we expected, but first they gave themselves to the Lord and to us by the will of God. Accordingly we have urged Titus that as he had already made a beginning, he should also complete among you this gracious work. Now as you excel in everything—in faith, in utterance, in knowledge, in all earnestness, and in your love for us—see that you excel in this gracious work also.

I say this not as a command, but to prove by the earnestness of others that your love also is genuine. For you know the grace of our Lord Jesus Christ, that though he was rich, yet for your sake he became poor, so that by his poverty you might become rich. And in this matter I give my advice: it is best for you now to complete what a year ago you began not only to do but to desire, so that your readiness in desiring it may be matched by your completing it out of what you have. For if the readiness is there, it is acceptable according to what a man has, not according to what he has not. I do not mean that others should be eased and you burdened, but that as a matter of equality your abundance at the present time should supply their want, so that their abundance may supply your want, that there may be equality. As it is written, "He who gathered much had nothing over, and he who gathered little had no lack."

(1) ***Rule of St. Benedict*** **20** 2834

Reverence at prayer

If we wish to ask a favor of those who hold temporal power, we dare not do so except with humility and respect. It is far more important that we present our pleas to God with the utmost humility and purity of devotion. We realize that we will be heard for our pure and sorrowful hearts, not for the numbers of our spoken words. Our prayer must be heartfelt and to the point. Only a divine inspiration should lengthen it. The prayer of the assembled community should be short. When the superior signals, all rise as one.

(2) ***Rule of St. Benedict*** **48** 2834

Daily manual labor

Idleness is an enemy of the soul. Therefore, the brothers should be occupied according to schedule in either manual labor or holy reading. These may be arranged as follows: from Easter to October, the brothers shall work at manual labor from Prime until the fourth hour. From then until the sixth hour they should read. After dinner they should rest (in bed) in silence. However, should anyone desire to read, he should do so without disturbing his brothers.

None should be chanted at about the middle of the eighth hour. Then everyone shall work as they must until Vespers. If conditions dictate that they labor in the fields (harvesting), they should not be grieved for they are truly monks when they must live by manual labor, as did our fathers and the apostles. Everything should be in moderation, though, for the sake of the timorous.

From October first until Lent, the brothers should read until the end of the second hour. Tierce will then be said, after which they will work at their appointed tasks until None. At the first signal for None all work shall come to an end. Thus all may be ready as the second signal sounds. After eating they shall read or study the psalms.

During Lent the brothers shall devote themselves to reading until the end of the third hour. Then they will work at their assigned tasks until the end of the tenth hour. Also, during this time, each monk shall receive a book from the library, which he should read carefully cover to cover. These books should be handed out at the beginning of Lent.

It is important that one or two seniors be chosen to oversee the reading periods. They will check that no one is slothful, lazy or gossiping, profiting little himself and disturbing others. If such a brother is discovered, he is to be corrected once or twice. If he does not change his ways, he shall be punished by the Rule (to set an example for others). Nor should brothers meet at odd and unsuitable hours.

All shall read on Saturdays except those with specific tasks. If anyone is so slothful that he will not or cannot read or study, he will be assigned work so as not to be idle.

Sick and frail brothers should be given work that will keep them from idleness but not so oppressive that they will feel compelled to leave the monastery. Their frailty is to be considered by the abbot.

2834 (3) **Joseph de Guibert, *The Jesuits* p. 148, note 55** Along the same line is the thought printed in Hevenesi's *Scintillae Ignatianae*, and often reproduced thereafter: "Sic Deo fide, quasi rerum successus omnis a te, nihil a Deo penderet: ita tamen iis operam omnem admove, quasi tu nihil, Deus omnia solus sit facturus." In this precise formula, the thought is nowhere found in Ignatius' writings nor in any contemporary documents; but nevertheless it does correspond to his ideas. See C. A. Kneller, "Ein Wort des hl. Ignatius von Loyola," *ZAM*, III (1929), 253–257. Ribadeneyra reported the thought in a less contorted form, in *SdeSI*, I, 466. [The words which Ribadeneyra used about Ignatius in *De ratione in gubernando*, ch. 6, no. 14 (in *SdeSI*, I, 466; *FN*, III, 631) are these: "In matters which he took up pertaining to the service of our Lord, he made use of all the human means to succeed in them, with a care and efficiency as great as if the success depended on these means; and he confided in God and depended on His providence as greatly as if all the other human means which he was using were of no effect." Cf. also Vachon in *Theology Digest*, X (1962), 45–50.]

2835 **John 6:26–58** Jesus answered them, "Truly, truly, I say to you, you seek me, not because you saw signs, but because you ate your fill of the loaves. Do not labor for the food which perishes but for the food which endures to eternal life, which the Son of man will give to you; for on him has God the Father set his seal." Then they said to him, "What must we do, to be doing the works of God?" Jesus answered them, "This is the work of God, that you believe in him whom he has sent." So they said to him, "Then what sign do you do that we may see, and believe you? What work do you perform? Our fathers ate the manna in the wilderness; as it is written, 'He gave them bread from heaven to eat.'" Jesus then said to them, "Truly, truly, I say to you, it was not Moses who gave you the bread from heaven; my Father gives you the true bread from heaven. For the bread of God is that which comes down from heaven, and gives life to the world." They said to him, "Lord, give us this bread always."

Jesus said to them, "I am the bread of life; he who comes to me shall not hunger, and he who believes in me shall never thirst. But I said to you that you have seen me and yet do not believe. All that the Father gives me will come to me; and him who comes to me I will not cast out. For I have come down from heaven, not to do my own will, but the will of him who sent me; and this is the will of him who sent me, that I should lose nothing of all that he has given me, but raise it up at the last day. For this is the will of my Father, that every one who sees the Son and believes in him should have eternal life; and I will raise him up at the last day."

The Jews then murmured at him, because he said, "I am the bread which came down from heaven." They said, "Is not this Jesus, the son of Joseph, whose father and mother we know? How does he now say, 'I have come down from heaven'?" Jesus answered them, "Do not murmur among yourselves. No one can come to me unless the Father who sent me draws him; and I will raise him up at the last day. It is written in the prophets, 'And they shall all be taught by God.' Every one who has heard and learned from the Father comes to me. Not that any one has seen the Father except him who is from God; he has seen the Father. Truly, truly, I say to you, he who believes has eternal life. I am the bread of life. Your fathers ate the manna in the wilderness, and they died. This is the bread which comes down from heaven, that a man may eat of it and not die. I am the living bread which came down from heaven; if any one eats of this bread, he will live for ever; and the bread which I shall give for the life of the world is my flesh."

The Jews then disputed among themselves, saying, "How can this man give us his flesh to eat?" So Jesus said to them, "Truly, truly, I say to you, unless you eat the flesh of the Son of man and drink his blood, you have no life in you; he who eats my flesh and drinks my blood has eternal life, and I will raise him up at the last day. For my flesh is food indeed, and my blood is drink indeed. He who eats my flesh and drinks my blood abides in me, and I in him. As the living Father sent me, and I live because of the Father, so he who eats me will live because of me. This is the bread which came down from heaven, not such as the fathers ate and died; he who eats this bread will live for ever."

(1) **Matthew 6:34** "Therefore do not be anxious about tomorrow, for tomorrow will be anxious for itself. Let the day's own trouble be sufficient for the day. . . ." 2836

(2) **Exodus 16:19** And Moses said to them, "Let no man leave any of it till the morning." 2836

(3) **Psalm 2:7** 2836

I will tell of the decree of the Lord:
He said to me, "You are my son,
today I have begotten you. . . ."

(1) **Exodus 16:19–21** And Moses said to them, "Let no man leave any of it till the morning." But they did not listen to Moses; some left part of it till the morning, and it bred worms and became foul; and Moses was angry with them. Morning by morning they gathered it, each as much as he could eat; but when the sun grew hot, it melted. 2837

2837 (2) **1 Timothy 6:8** . . . but if we have food and clothing, with these we shall be content.

2837 (3) **John 6:53–56** So Jesus said to them, "Truly, truly, I say to you, unless you eat the flesh of the Son of man and drink his blood, you have no life in you; he who eats my flesh and drinks my blood has eternal life, and I will raise him up at the last day. For my flesh is food indeed, and my blood is drink indeed. He who eats my flesh and drinks my blood abides in me, and I in him. . . ."

2837 (4) **John 6:51** ". . . I am the living bread which came down from heaven; if any one eats of this bread, he will live for ever; and the bread which I shall give for the life of the world is my flesh."

2839 (1) **Luke 15:11–32** And he said, "There was a man who had two sons; and the younger of them said to his father, 'Father, give me the share of property that falls to me.' And he divided his living between them. Not many days later, the younger son gathered all he had and took his journey into a far country, and there he squandered his property in loose living. And when he had spent everything, a great famine arose in that country, and he began to be in want. So he went and joined himself to one of the citizens of that country, who sent him into his fields to feed swine. And he would gladly have fed on the pods that the swine ate; and no one gave him anything. But when he came to himself he said, 'How many of my father's hired servants have bread enough and to spare, but I perish here with hunger! I will arise and go to my father, and I will say to him, "Father, I have sinned against heaven and before you; I am no longer worthy to be called your son; treat me as one of your hired servants."' And he arose and came to his father. But while he was yet at a distance, his father saw him and had compassion, and ran and embraced him and kissed him. And the son said to him, 'Father, I have sinned against heaven and before you; I am no longer worthy to be called your son.' But the father said to his servants, 'Bring quickly the best robe, and put it on him; and put a ring on his hand, and shoes on his feet; and bring the fatted calf and kill it, and let us eat and make merry; for this my son was dead, and is alive again; he was lost, and is found.' And they began to make merry.

"Now his elder son was in the field; and as he came and drew near to the house, he heard music and dancing. And he called one of the servants and asked what this meant. And he said to him, 'Your brother has come, and your father has killed the fatted calf, because he has received him safe and sound.' But he was angry and refused to go in. His father came out and entreated him, but he answered his father, 'Lo, these many years I have served you, and I never disobeyed your command; yet you never gave me a kid, that I might make merry with my friends. But when this son of yours came, who has devoured your living with harlots, you killed for him the fatted calf!' And he said to him, 'Son, you are always with me, and all that is mine is yours. It was fitting to make merry and be glad, for this your brother was dead, and is alive; he was lost, and is found.'"

2839 (2) **Luke 18:13** ". . . But the tax collector, standing far off, would not even lift up his eyes to heaven, but beat his breast, saying, 'God, be merciful to me a sinner!'. . ."

2839 (3) **Matthew 26:28** . . . for this is my blood of the covenant, which is poured out for many for the forgiveness of sins.

2839 (4) **John 20:23** ". . . If you forgive the sins of any, they are forgiven; if you retain the sins of any, they are retained."

1 John 4:20 If any one says, "I love God," and hates his brother, he is a liar; for he who does not love his brother whom he has seen, cannot love God whom he has not seen. 2840

(1) **Matthew 6:14–15** For if you forgive men their trespasses, your heavenly Father also will forgive you; but if you do not forgive men their trespasses, neither will your Father forgive your trespasses. 2841

(2) **Matthew 5:23–24** So if you are offering your gift at the altar, and there remember that your brother has something against you, leave your gift there before the altar and go; first be reconciled to your brother, and then come and offer your gift. 2841

(3) **Mark 11:25** ". . . And whenever you stand praying, forgive, if you have anything against any one; so that your Father also who is in heaven may forgive you your trespasses." 2841

(1) **Galatians 5:25** If we live by the Spirit, let us also walk by the Spirit. Let us have no self-conceit, no provoking of one another, no envy of one another. 2842

(2) **Philippians 2:1** So if there is any encouragement in Christ, any incentive of love, any participation in the Spirit, any affection and sympathy. . . . 2842

(3) **Philippians 2:5** Have this mind among yourselves, which is yours in Christ Jesus. . . . 2842

(1) **John 13:1** Now before the feast of the Passover, when Jesus knew that his hour had come to depart out of this world to the Father, having loved his own who were in the world, he loved them to the end. 2843

(2) **Matthew 18:23–35** "Therefore the kingdom of heaven may be compared to a king who wished to settle accounts with his servants. When he began the reckoning, one was brought to him who owed him ten thousand talents; and as he could not pay, his lord ordered him to be sold, with his wife and children and all that he had, and payment to be made. So the servant fell on his knees, imploring him, 'Lord, have patience with me, and I will pay you everything.' And out of pity for him the lord of that servant released him and forgave him the debt. But that same servant, as he went out, came upon one of his fellow servants who owed him a hundred denarii; and seizing him by the throat he said, 'Pay what you owe.' So his fellow servant fell down and besought him, 'Have patience with me, and I will pay you.' He refused and went and put him in prison until he should pay the debt. When his fellow servants saw what had taken place, they were greatly distressed, and they went and reported to their lord all that had taken place. Then his lord summoned him and said to him, 'You wicked servant! I forgave you all that debt because you besought me; and should not you have had mercy on your fellow servant, as I had mercy on you?' And in anger his lord delivered him to the jailers, till he should pay all his debt. So also my heavenly Father will do to every one of you, if you do not forgive your brother from your heart." 2843

(1) **Matthew 5:43–44** "You have heard that it was said, 'You shall love your neighbor and hate your enemy.' But I say to you, Love your enemies and pray for those who persecute you. . . ." 2844

2844 (2) **2 Corinthians 5:18–21** All this is from God, who through Christ reconciled us to himself and gave us the ministry of reconciliation; that is, in Christ God was reconciling the world to himself, not counting their trespasses against them, and entrusting to us the message of reconciliation. So we are ambassadors for Christ, God making his appeal through us. We beseech you on behalf of Christ, be reconciled to God. For our sake he made him to be sin who knew no sin, so that in him we might become the righteousness of God.

2844 (3) ***Dives in misericordia* 14** Jesus Christ taught that man not only receives and experiences the mercy of God, but that he is also called "to practice mercy" towards others: "Blessed are the merciful, for they shall obtain mercy." The Church sees in these words a call to action, and she tries to practice mercy. All the beatitudes of the Sermon on the Mount indicate the way of conversion and of the reform of life, but the one referring to those who are merciful is particularly eloquent in this regard. Man attains to the merciful love of God, His mercy, to the extent that he himself is interiorly transformed in the spirit of that love towards his neighbor.

This authentically evangelical process is not just a spiritual transformation realized once for all: it is a whole lifestyle, an essential and continuous characteristic of the Christian vocation. It consists in the constant discovery and persevering practice of *love as a unifying and also elevating power* despite all difficulties of a psychological or social nature: it is a question, in fact, of a *merciful love* which, by its essence, is a creative love. In reciprocal relationships between persons merciful love is never a unilateral act or process. Even in the cases in which everything would seem to indicate that only one party is giving and offering, and the other only receiving and taking (for example, in the case of a physician giving treatment, a teacher teaching, parents supporting and bringing up their children, a benefactor helping the needy), in reality the one who gives is always also a beneficiary. In any case, he too can easily find himself in the position of the one who receives, who obtains a benefit, who experiences merciful love; he too can find himself the object of mercy.

In this sense *Christ* crucified is for us the loftiest model, inspiration and encouragement. When we base ourselves on this *disquieting model*, we are able with all humility to show mercy to others, knowing that Christ accepts it as if it were shown to Himself. On the basis of this model, we must also continually purify all our actions and all our intentions in which mercy is understood and practiced in a unilateral way, as a good done to others. An act of merciful love is only really such when we are deeply convinced at the moment that we perform it that we are at the same time receiving mercy from the people who are accepting it from us. If this bilateral and reciprocal quality is absent, our actions are not yet true acts of mercy, nor has there yet been fully completed in us that conversion to which Christ has shown us the way by His words and example, even to the cross, nor are we yet sharing fully in the *magnificent source of merciful love* that has been revealed to us by Him.

Thus, the way which Christ showed to us in the Sermon on the Mount with the beatitude regarding those who are merciful is much richer than what we sometimes find in ordinary human opinions about mercy. These opinions see mercy as a unilateral act or process, presupposing and maintaining a certain distance between the one practicing mercy and the one benefitting from it, between the one who does good and the one who receives it. Hence the attempt to free interpersonal and social relationships from mercy and to base them solely on justice. However, such opinions about mercy fail to see the fundamental link between mercy and justice spoken of by the whole biblical tradition, and above all by the messianic mission of Jesus Christ. *True mercy is, so to speak, the most profound source of justice.* If justice is in itself suitable for "arbitration" between people concerning the reciprocal distribution of objective goods in an equitable manner, love and only love (including that kindly love that we call "mercy") is capable of restoring man to Himself.

Mercy that is truly Christian is also, in a certain sense, *the most perfect incarnation* of "equality" between people, and therefore also the most perfect incarnation of *justice* as well, insofar as justice aims at the same result in its own sphere. However, the equality brought by justice is limited to the realm of objective and extrinsic goods, while love and mercy bring it about that people meet one another in that value which is man himself, with the dignity that is proper to him. At the same time, "equality" of people through "patient and kind" love does not take away differences: the person who gives becomes more generous when he feels at the same time benefitted by the person accepting his gift; and vice versa, the person who accepts the gift with the awareness that, in accepting it, he too is doing good, is in his own way serving the great cause of the dignity of the person; and this contributes to uniting people in a more profound manner.

Thus, mercy becomes an indispensable element for *shaping* mutual relationships between people, in a spirit of deepest respect for what is human, and in a spirit of mutual brotherhood. It is impossible to establish this bond between people, if they wish to regulate their mutual relationships solely according to the measure of justice. In every sphere of interpersonal relationships justice must, *so to speak, be "corrected" to a considerable extent* by that love which, as St. Paul proclaims, "is patient and kind" or, in other words, possesses the characteristics of that *merciful love which* is so much of the essence of the Gospel and Christianity. Let us remember, furthermore, that *merciful love* also means the cordial *tenderness and sensitivity* so eloquently spoken of in the parable of the prodigal son, and also in the parables of the lost sheep and the lost coin. Consequently, merciful love is supremely indispensable between those who are closest to one another: between husbands and wives, between parents and children, between friends; and it is indispensable in education and in pastoral work.

Its sphere of action however, is not limited to this. If Paul VI more than once indicated the "civilization of love" as the goal towards which all efforts in the cultural and social fields as well as in the economic and political fields should tend, it must be added that this good will never be reached if in our thinking and acting concerning the vast and complex spheres of human society we stop at the criterion of "an eye for an eye, a tooth for a tooth" and do not try to transform it in its essence, by complementing it with another spirit. Certainly, the Second Vatican Council also leads us in this direction, when it speaks repeatedly of the need *to make the world more human*, and says that the realization of this task is precisely the mission of the Church in the modern world. Society can become ever more human only if we introduce into the many-sided setting of interpersonal and social relationships, not merely justice, but also that "merciful love" which constitutes the messianic message of the Gospel.

Society can become "ever more human" only when we introduce into all the mutual relationships which form its moral aspect the moment of forgiveness, which is so much of the essence of the Gospel. Forgiveness demonstrates the presence in the world of *the love which is more powerful than sin.* Forgiveness is also the fundamental condition for reconciliation, not only in the relationship of God with man, but also in relationships between people. A world from which forgiveness was eliminated would be nothing but a world of cold and unfeeling justice, in the name of which each person would claim his or her own rights *vis-à-vis* others; the various kinds of selfishness latent in man would transform life and human society into a system of oppression of the weak by the strong, or into an arena of permanent strife between one group and another.

For this reason, the Church must consider it one of her principal duties—at every stage of history and especially in our modern age—*to proclaim and to introduce into life* the mystery of mercy, supremely revealed in Jesus Christ. Not only for the Church herself as the community of believers but also in a certain sense for all humanity, this mystery is the *source* of a life different from the life which can be built by man, who is exposed to the oppressive forces of the threefold concupiscence active within him. It is precisely in the name of this mystery that Christ teaches us to forgive always. How often we repeat the words of the prayer which He Himself has taught us, asking "*forgive us* our trespasses *as we forgive* those who trespass against us," which means those who are guilty of something in our regard! It is indeed difficult to express the profound value of the attitude which these words describe and inculcate. How many things these words say to every individual about others and also about himself! The consciousness of being trespassers against each other goes hand in hand with the call to fraternal solidarity, which St. Paul expressed in his concise exhortation to "forbear one another in love." What a lesson of humility is to be found here with regard to man, with regard both to one's neighbor and to oneself! What a school of good will for daily living, in the various conditions of our existence! If we were to ignore this lesson, what would remain of any "humanist" program of life and education?

Christ emphasizes so insistently the need to forgive others that when Peter asked Him how many times he should forgive his neighbor He answered with the symbolic number of "seventy times seven," meaning that he must be able to forgive everyone every time. It is obvious that such a generous requirement of *forgiveness does not cancel out* the objective *requirements of justice*. Properly understood, justice constitutes, so to speak, the goal of forgiveness. In no passage of the Gospel message does forgiveness, or mercy as its source, mean indulgence towards evil, towards scandals, towards injury or insult. In any case, reparation for evil and scandal, compensation for injury, and satisfaction for insult are conditions for forgiveness.

Thus the fundamental structure of justice always enters into the sphere of mercy. Mercy, however, has the power to confer on justice a new content, which is expressed most simply and fully in forgiveness. Forgiveness, in fact, shows that, over and above the process of "compensation" and "truce" which is specific to justice, love is necessary, so that man may affirm himself as man. Fulfillment of the conditions of justice is especially indispensable in order that love may reveal its own nature. In analyzing the parable of the prodigal son, we have already called attention to the fact that *he who forgives and he who is forgiven* encounter one another at an essential point, namely the dignity or essential value of the person, a point which cannot be lost and the affirmation of which, or its rediscovery, is a source of the greatest joy.

The Church rightly considers it her duty and the purpose of her mission *to guard the authenticity of forgiveness*, both in life and behavior and in educational and pastoral work She protects it simply by guarding its *source*, which is the mystery of the mercy of God Himself as revealed in Jesus Christ.

The basis of the Church's mission, in all the spheres spoken of in the numerous pronouncements of the most recent Council and in the centuries-old experience of the apostolate, is none other than "drawing from the wells of the Savior": that is what provides many guidelines for the mission of the Church in the lives of individual Christians, of individual communities, and also of the whole People of God. This "drawing from the wells of the Savior" can be done only in the spirit of that poverty to which we are called by the words and example of the Lord: "You received without pay, give without pay." Thus, in all the ways of the Church's life and ministry—through the evangelical poverty of her ministers and stewards and of the whole people which bears witness to "the mighty works" of its Loıd—the God who is "rich in mercy" has been made still more clearly manifest.

(1) **Matthew 18:21–22** Then Peter came up and said to him, "Lord, how often shall my brother sin against me, and I forgive him? As many as seven times?" Jesus said to him, "I do not say to you seven times, but seventy times seven. . . ." 2845

(2) **Luke 17:3–4** ". . . Take heed to yourselves; if your brother sins, rebuke him, and if he repents, forgive him; and if he sins against you seven times in the day, and turns to you seven times, and says, 'I repent,' you must forgive him." 2845

(3) **Matthew 5:23–24** So if you are offering your gift at the altar, and there remember that your brother has something against you, leave your gift there before the altar and go; first be reconciled to your brother, and then come and offer your gift. 2845

(4) **1 John 3:19–24** By this we shall know that we are of the truth, and reassure our hearts before him whenever our hearts condemn us; for God is greater than our hearts, and he knows everything. Beloved, if our hearts do not condemn us, we have confidence before God; and we receive from him whatever we ask, because we keep his commandments and do what pleases him. And this is his commandment, that we should believe in the name of his Son Jesus Christ and love one another, just as he has commanded us. All who keep his commandments abide in him, and he in them. And by this we know that he abides in us, by the Spirit which he has given us. 2845

(5) **Matthew 5:24** . . . leave your gift there before the altar and go; first be reconciled to your brother, and then come and offer your gift. 2845

Matthew 26:41 ". . . Watch and pray that you may not enter into temptation; the spirit indeed is willing, but the flesh is weak." 2846

(1) **Luke 8:13–15** And the ones on the rock are those who, when they hear the word, receive it with joy; but these have no root, they believe for a while and in time of temptation fall away. And as for what fell among the thorns, they are those who hear, but as they go on their way, they are choked by the cares and riches and pleasures of life, and their fruit does not mature. And as for that in the good soil, they are those who, hearing the word, hold it fast in an honest and good heart, and bring forth fruit with patience. 2847

(2) **Acts 14:22** . . . strengthening the souls of the disciples, exhorting them to continue in the faith, and saying that through many tribulations we must enter the kingdom of God. 2847

(3) **Romans 5:3–5** More than that, we rejoice in our sufferings, knowing that suffering produces endurance, and endurance produces character, and character produces hope, and hope does not disappoint us, because God's love has been poured into our hearts through the Holy Spirit which has been given to us. 2847

(4) **2 Timothy 3:12** Indeed all who desire to live a godly life in Christ Jesus will be persecuted. . . . 2847

(5) **James 1:14–15** . . . but each person is tempted when he is lured and enticed by his own desire. Then desire when it has conceived gives birth to sin; and sin when it is full-grown brings forth death. 2847

2847 (6) **Genesis 3:6** So when the woman saw that the tree was good for food, and that it was a delight to the eyes, and that the tree was to be desired to make one wise, she took of its fruit and ate; and she also gave some to her husband, and he ate.

2849 (1) **Matthew 4:1–11** Then Jesus was led up by the Spirit into the wilderness to be tempted by the devil. And he fasted forty days and forty nights, and afterward he was hungry. And the tempter came and said to him, "If you are the Son of God, command these stones to become loaves of bread." But he answered, "It is written,

'Man shall not live by bread alone,
but by every word that proceeds from the mouth of God.'"

Then the devil took him to the holy city, and set him on the pinnacle of the temple, and said to him, "If you are the Son of God, throw yourself down; for it is written,

'He will give his angels charge of you,'

and

'On their hands they will bear you up,
lest you strike your foot against a stone.'"

Jesus said to him, "Again it is written, 'You shall not tempt the Lord your God.'" Again, the devil took him to a very high mountain, and showed him all the kingdoms of the world and the glory of them; and he said to him, "All these I will give you, if you will fall down and worship me." Then Jesus said to him, "Begone, Satan! for it is written,

'You shall worship the Lord your God
and him only shall you serve.'"

Then the devil left him, and behold, angels came and ministered to him.

2849 (2) **Matthew 26:36–44** Then Jesus went with them to a place called Gethsemane, and he said to his disciples, "Sit here, while I go yonder and pray." And taking with him Peter and the two sons of Zebedee, he began to be sorrowful and troubled. Then he said to them, "My soul is very sorrowful, even to death; remain here, and watch with me." And going a little farther he fell on his face and prayed. "My Father, if it be possible, let this cup pass from me; nevertheless, not as I will, but as thou wilt." And he came to the disciples and found them sleeping; and he said to Peter, "So, could you not watch with me one hour? Watch and pray that you may not enter into temptation; the spirit indeed is willing, but the flesh is weak." Again, for the second time, he went away and prayed, "My Father, if this cannot pass unless I drink it, thy will be done." And again he came and found them sleeping, for their eyes were heavy. So, leaving them again, he went away and prayed for the third time, saying the same words.

2849 (3) **Mark 13:9** "But take heed to yourselves; for they will deliver you up to councils; and you will be beaten in synagogues; and you will stand before governors and kings for my sake, to bear testimony before them. . . ."

2849 (4) **Mark 13:23** But take heed; I have told you all things beforehand.

2849 (5) **Mark 13:33–37** ". . . Take heed, watch; for you do not know when the time will come. It is like a man going on a journey, when he leaves home and puts his servants in charge, each with his work, and commands the doorkeeper to be on the watch. Watch therefore—for you do not know when the master of the house will come, in the evening, or at midnight, or at cockcrow, or in the morning—lest he come suddenly and find you asleep. And what I say to you I say to all: Watch."

(6) **Mark 14:38** ". . . Watch and pray that you may not enter into temptation; the spirit indeed is willing, but the flesh is weak." **2849**

(7) **Luke 12:35–40** "Let your loins be girded and your lamps burning, and be like men who are waiting for their master to come home from the marriage feast, so that they may open to him at once when he comes and knocks. Blessed are those servants whom the master finds awake when he comes; truly, I say to you, he will gird himself and have them sit at table, and he will come and serve them. If he comes in the second watch, or in the third, and finds them so, blessed are those servants! But know this, that if the householder had known at what hour the thief was coming, he would not have left his house to be broken into. You also must be ready; for the Son of man is coming at an unexpected hour." **2849**

(8) **1 Corinthians 16:13** Be watchful, stand firm in your faith, be courageous, be strong. Let all that you do be done in love. **2849**

(9) **Colossians 4:2** Continue steadfastly in prayer, being watchful in it with thanksgiving. . . . **2849**

(10) **1 Thessalonians 5:6** So then let us not sleep, as others do, but let us keep awake and be sober. **2849**

(11) **1 Peter 5:8** Be sober, be watchful. Your adversary the devil prowls around like a roaring lion, seeking some one to devour. **2849**

Reconciliatio et poenitentia **16:** see 1869. **2850**

Romans 8:31 What then shall we say to this? If God is for us, who is against us? **2852**

(1) **Revelation 1:4** John to the seven churches that are in Asia: **2854**
Grace to you and peace from him who is and who was and who is to come, and from the seven spirits who are before his throne. . . .

(2) **Ephesians 1:10** . . . as a plan for the fulness of time, to unite all things in him, things in heaven and things on earth. **2854**

(1) **Revelation 1:6** . . . and made us a kingdom, priests to his God and Father, to him be glory and dominion for ever and ever. Amen. **2855**

(2) **Revelation 4:11** **2855**
"Worthy art thou, our Lord and God,
to receive glory and honor and power,
for thou didst create all things,
and by thy will they existed and were created."

(3) **Revelation 5:13** And I heard every creature in heaven and on earth and under the earth and in the sea, and all therein, saying, "To him who sits upon the throne and to the Lamb be blessing and honor and glory and might for ever and ever!" **2855**

(4) **Luke 4:5–6** And the devil took him up, and showed him all the kingdoms of the world in a moment of time, and said to him, "To you I will give all this authority and their glory; for it has been delivered to me, and I give it to whom I will. . . ." **2855**

2855 (5) **1 Corinthians 15:24–28** Then comes the end, when he delivers the kingdom to God the Father after destroying every rule and every authority and power. For he must reign until he has put all his enemies under his feet. The last enemy to be destroyed is death. "For God has put all things in subjection under his feet." But when it says, "All things are put in subjection under him," it is plain that he is excepted who put all things under him. When all things are subjected to him, then the Son himself will also be subjected to him who put all things under him, that God may be everything to every one.

2856 **Luke 1:38** And Mary said, "Behold, I am the handmaid of the Lord; let it be to me according to your word." And the angel departed from her.

ACKNOWLEDGMENTS

Ignatius Press gratefully acknowledges permissions granted to reprint excerpts from the following sources:

Ambrose. *The Explanatio Symboli ad Initiandos*: A Work of Saint Ambrose, translated by the late Dom R. H. Connolly. Cambridge: Cambridge University Press, 1952. Reprinted by Kraus Reprint Limited, Nendeln and Liechtenstein, 1967. Reprinted with the permission of Cambridge University Press.

Aristides. *The Apology of Aristides on Behalf of the Christians*. Cambridge: Cambridge University Press, 1893. Reprinted with the permission of Cambridge University Press.

Augustine. *De Libero Arbitrio* (Libri tres), *The Free Choice of the Will* (three books), Latin text translated by Francis E. Tourscher, S.T.M., O.S.A. Philadelphia: The Peter Reilly Company, 1937.

Augustine. *The First Catechetical Instruction*, translated by the Rev. Joseph P. Christopher, Ph.D. In *Ancient Christian Writers*, vol. 2, pages 18–19. New York: Newman Press, 1946. Copyright 1946 by the Rev. Johannes Quasten and the Rev. Joseph C. Plumpe. Excerpts reprinted with the permission of Paulist Press.

Augustine. *Saint Augustine: Eighty-three Different Questions*, translated by David L. Mosher. Washington, D.C.: Catholic University of America Press, 1982. Reprinted with the permission of the Catholic University of America Press, Washington, D.C.

Augustine. *Expositions on the Books of Psalms*. In *A Select Library of the Nicene and Post-Nicene Fathers of the Christian Church*, 1st series, edited by Philip Schaff, D.D., LL.D., vol. 8. Grand Rapids, Michigan: Wm. B. Eerdmans, 1956. Reprinted with permission of Wm. B. Eerdmans Publishing Company.

Augustine. *Saint Augustine on Genesis, Two Books on Genesis against the Manichees and on the Literal Interpretation of Genesis: An Unfinished Book*, translated by Roland J. Teske, S.J. *Against the Manichees*, book 1. The Fathers of the Church, vol. 84. Washington, D.C.: Catholic University of America, 1990. Reprinted with the permission of the Catholic University of America Press, Washington, D.C.

Augustine. *St. Augustin: On the Holy Trinity*. In *A Select Library of the Nicene and Post-Nicene Fathers of the Christian Church*, 2d series, edited by Philip Schaff, D.D., LL.D., vol. 3. Grand Rapids, Michigan: Wm. B. Eerdmans, 1956. Reprinted with permission of Wm. B. Eerdmans Publishing Company.

Barnabas. *Epistle of Barnabas* in Maxwell Staniforth, *Early Christian Writings*. London: Penguin Books, Ltd., 1968. Copyright 1968 by Maxwell Staniforth. Reprinted with the permission of Penguin Books, Ltd.

Clement of Rome. *The Epistles of St. Clement of Rome and St. Ignatius of Antioch*, translated by James A. Kleist. In *Ancient Christian Writers*, vol. 1. Copyright 1946 by the Rev. Johannes Quasten and the Rev. Joseph C. Plumpe. Reprinted with the permission of Paulist Press.

Code of Canon Law, Latin-English Edition. Washington, D.C.: Canon Law Society of America, 1983. Reprinted with the permission of the Canon Law Society of America.

Code of Canons of the Eastern Churches. Latin-English Edition. Washington, D.C.: Canon Law Society of America, 1990. Original Latin text copyright 1990 by the Administration of the Patrimony of the Apostolic See, Vatican City. Reprinted with the permission of the Canon Law Society of America.

Cyprian. *The Unity of the Catholic Church*, translated and edited by Roy J. Deferrari. New York: Fathers of the Church, Inc., 1958. Reprinted with the permission of the Catholic University of America Press, Washington, D.C.

Denzinger-Schönmetzer. *Enchiridion Symbolorum: Definitionum et Declarationum de Rebus Fidei et Morum*. Reprinted with the permission of Verlag Herder, Freiburg im Breisgau, Germany.

Egeria: Diary of a Pilgrimage, translated by George E. Gingras, Ph.D. In *Ancient Christian Writers*, vol. 38, pages 123–25. New York: Newman Press, 1970. Copyright 1970 by Johannes Quasten, Rev. Walter J. Burghardt, S.J., and Thomas Comerford Lawler. Reprinted with the permission of Paulist Press.

Epiphanius. *The Panarion of Epiphanius of Salamis*, translated by Frank Williams, book 1. Leiden: E.J. Brill, 1987. Reprinted with the permission of E.J. Brill, Leiden, The Netherlands.

Epistle to Diognetes in Maxwell Staniforth, *Early Christian Writings*. London: Penguin Books, Ltd., 1968. Copyright 1968 by Maxwell Staniforth. Reprinted with the permission of Penguin Books, Ltd.

Gregory the Great. *Sermons*. In *A Select Library of Nicene and Post-Nicene Fathers of the Christian Church*, 2d series, edited by Philip Schaff, D.D., L.L.D., vol. 12, 1895. Reprinted with permission of Wm. B. Eerdmans Publishing Company.

Guigo the Carthusian (Guigo II). *The Ladder of Monks, A Letter on the Contemplative Life, and Twelve Meditations*. Copyright 1978 by Edmund College and James Walsh. Reprinted with permisssion of Doubleday, a division of Bantam Doubleday Dell Publishing Group, Inc.

Hippolytus. *The Apostolic Tradition of St Hippolytus*. Cambridge: Cambridge University Press, 1934. Reprinted with the permission of Cambridge University Press.

Ignatius of Antioch. *The Epistles of St. Clement of Rome and St. Ignatius of Antioch*, translated by James A. Kleist. In *Ancient Christian Writers*, vol. 1. Copyright 1946 by the Rev. Johannes Quasten and the Rev. Joseph C. Plumpe. Reprinted with the permission of Paulist Press.

Ignatius of Loyola. *Spiritual Exercises of Saint Ignatius Loyola*. Image Books. Garden City, N.Y.: Doubleday and Company, 1964. Reprinted with the permission of Doubleday, a division of Bantam Doubleday Dell Publishing Group, Inc.

John of the Cross. *The Collected Works of St. John of the Cross*. Washington, D.C.: ICS Publications, 1964. Reprinted with the permission of ICS Publications.

John Paul II. Apostolic Exhortation *Catechesi tradendae*, "On Catechesis in Our Time". Boston: St. Paul Books and Media, 1979.

John Paul II. Apostolic Exhortation *Reconciliatio et paenitentia*, "On Reconciliation and Penance in the Mission of the Church Today". Boston: St. Paul Books and Media, 1984.

John Paul II. Apostolic Letter *Mulieris dignitatem*, "On the Dignity and Vocation of Women on the Occasion of the Marian Year". Boston: St. Paul Books and Media, 1988.

John Paul II. Encyclical Letter *Dominum et vivificantem*, "On the Holy Spirit in the Life of the Church and the World". Boston: St. Paul Books and Media, 1986.

John Paul II. Encyclical Letter *Laborem exercens*, "On Human Work". Boston: St. Paul Books and Media, 1981.

John Paul II. Encyclical Letter *Redemptor hominis*. "The Redeemer of Man". Boston: St. Paul Books and Media, 1979.

John Paul II. Encyclical Letter *Sollicitudo rei socialis*, "On Social Concern". Boston: St. Paul Books and Media, 1987.

Justin Martyr. *Saint Justin Martyr: The Second Apology* and *Dialogue with Trypho*, translated by Thomas B. Falls. The Fathers of the Church, vol. 6. New York: Christian Heritage, [1949]. Copyright 1948 by Ludwig Schopp. Reprinted with the permission of the Catholic University of America Press, Washington, D.C.

Leo XIII. Encyclical *Diuturnum illud* (*On the Origin of Civil Power*, June 29, 1881). In *The Papal Encyclicals 1878–1903*, edited by Claudia Carlen, I.H.M. Volume 2 of 5 volumes, 1981; reprint Ann Arbor: Pierian Press, 1990. Copyright by Claudia Carlen. Reprinted with the permission of Claudia Carlen, I.H.M.

Leo XIII. Encyclical *Immortale Dei* (*On the Christian Constitution of States*, November 1, 1885). In *The Papal Encyclicals 1878–1903*, edited by Claudia Carlen, I.H.M. Volume 2 of 5 volumes, 1981; reprint Ann Arbor: Pierian Press, 1990. Copyright by Claudia Carlen. Reprinted with the permission of Claudia Carlen, I.H.M.

Leo XIII. Encyclical *Libertas* (*On the Nature of Human Liberty*, June 20, 1888). In *The Papal Encyclicals 1878–1903*, edited by Claudia Carlen, I.H.M. Volume 2 of 5 volumes, 1981; reprint Ann Arbor: Pierian Press, 1990. Copyright by Claudia Carlen. Reprinted with the permission of Claudia Carlen, I.H.M.

Leo the Great. *Letters and Sermons of Leo the Great*, translated by the Rev. Charles Lett Feltoe, M.A. In *A Select Library of Nicene and Post-Nicene Fathers of the Christian Church*, 2d series, edited by Philip Schaff, D.D., LL.D. and Henry Wace, D.D., vol. 12. Reprinted with permission of Wm. B. Eerdmans Publishing Company.

Origen. *Contra Celsum*, translated by Henry Chadwick. Cambridge: Cambridge University Press, 1953. Reprinted with the permission of Cambridge University Press.

Pastoral Theology of the Anointing of the Sick by Dr. Adolf Knauber, translated by Matthew J. O'Connell. Reprinted with permission of the Liturgical Press, St. John's Abbey, Collegeville, Minnesota.

Pius IX. Encyclical *Quanta cura* (December 8, 1864). In *The Papal Encyclicals 1740–1878*, edited by Claudia Carlen, I.H.M. Volume 1 of 5 volumes, 1981; reprint Ann Arbor: Pierian Press, 1990. Copyright by Claudia Carlen. Reprinted with the permission of Claudia Carlen, I.H.M.

Pius XI. Encyclical *Casti connubii* (*On Christian Marriage*, December 31, 1931). In *The Papal Encyclicals 1903–1939*, edited by Claudia Carlen, I.H.M. Volume 3 of 5 volumes, 1981; reprint Ann Arbor: Pierian Press, 1990. Copyright by Claudia Carlen. Reprinted with the permission of Claudia Carlen, I.H.M.

Pius XI. Encyclical *Divini redemptoris* (*On Atheistic Communism*, March 19, 1937). In *The Papal Encyclicals 1903–1939*, edited by Claudia Carlen, I.H.M. Volume 3 of 5 volumes, 1981; reprint Ann Arbor: Pierian Press, 1990. Copyright by Claudia Carlen. Reprinted with the permission of Claudia Carlen, I.H.M.

Pius XI. Encyclical *Quadragesimo anno* (*On the Reconstruction of the Social Order*, May 15, 1931). In *The Papal Encyclicals 1903–1939*, edited by Claudia Carlen, I.H.M. Volume 3 of 5 volumes, 1981; reprint Ann Arbor: Pierian Press, 1990. Copyright by Claudia Carlen. Reprinted with the permission of Claudia Carlen, I.H.M.

Pius XI. Encyclical *Quas primas* (*On the Feast of Christ the King*, December 11, 1925). In *The Papal Encyclicals 1903–1939*, edited by Claudia Carlen, I.H.M. Volume 3 of 5 volumes, 1981; reprint Ann Arbor: Pierian Press, 1990. Copyright by Claudia Carlen. Reprinted with the permission of Claudia Carlen, I.H.M.

Pius XII. Encyclical *Musicae sacrae* (*On Sacred Music*, December 25, 1955). in *The Papal Encyclicals 1939–1958*, edited by Claudia Carlen, I.H.M. Volume 4 of 5 volumes, 1981; reprint Ann Arbor: Pierian Press, 1990. Copyright by Claudia Carlen. Reprinted with the permission of Claudia Carlen, I.H.M.

Roman Missal. Easter Vigil Prayer after the First Reading, Preface for Feasts of the Apostles, Sequence of Pentecost, General Introduction to the Roman Missal reprinted with permission of the Liturgical Press, St. John's Abbey, Collegeville, Minnesota.

Tertullian. *Apologetical Works and Minucius Felix Octavius*, translated by Rudolph Arbesmann, O.S.A., Sister Emily Joseph Daly, C.S.J., and Edwin A. Quain, S.J. New York: Fathers of the Church, Inc., 1950. Reprinted with the permission of the Catholic University of America Press, Washington, D.C.

Thomas Aquinas. *On the Truth of the Catholic Faith. Summa contra Gentiles*, book 3, Providence, part 1, translated by Vernon J. Bourke. Image Books. New York: Doubleday and Company, 1956. Reprinted with the permission of Doubleday, a division of Bantam Doubleday Dell Publishing Group, Inc.

ACKNOWLEDGMENTS

Thomas Aquinas. *Summa Theologica*. Cambridge: Blackfriars, 1920. Reprinted with the permission of the Prior Provincial of the Order of Preachers, London.

Excerpts from *Vatican Council II: The Conciliar and Post Conciliar Documents, New Revised Edition* edited by Austin Flannery, O.P., copyright 1992, Costello Publishing Company, Inc., Northport, N.Y. are used by permission of the publisher, all rights reserved. No part of these excerpts may be reproduced, stored in a retrieval system, or transmitted in any form or by any means—electronic, mechanical, photo-copying, recording or otherwise, without express permission of Costello Publishing Company.